INTERNATIONAL ORGANIZATION AND GLOBAL GOVERNANCE

Featuring a diverse and impressive array of authors, this volume is the most comprehensive textbook available for all interested in international organization and global governance. Organized around a concern with how the world is and could be governed, the book offers:

- in-depth and accessible coverage of the history and theories of international organization and global governance;
- discussions of the full range of state, intergovernmental, and nonstate actors;
- examinations of key issues in all aspects of contemporary global governance.

The book's 50 chapters are arranged into seven parts and woven together by a comprehensive introduction to the field, separate section introductions designed to guide students and faculty, and helpful pointers to further reading. *International Organization and Global Governance* is a self-contained resource enabling readers to better comprehend the role of myriad actors in the governance of global life as well as to assemble the many pieces of the contemporary global governance puzzle.

Thomas G. Weiss is Presidential Professor of Political Science at The Graduate Center and Director of the Ralph Bunche Institute for International Studies, The City University of New York, and Research Professor at SOAS, University of London.

Rorden Wilkinson is Professor of International Political Economy in the School of Social Sciences, and Research Director of the Brooks World Poverty Institute, at the University of Manchester.

International Organization and Global Governance should have a place on any international relations scholar's shelf. In addition to its sheer comprehensiveness as a reference work, it takes the crucial conceptual leap of focusing not on organizations, institutions, regimes, or any other piece of international order, but instead on the presence or absence of actual governance: the successful exercise of power to achieve outcomes. As one important chapter asks, who are the actual governors of the international system? The answers, with respect to many areas of international life, are surprising.

Anne-Marie Slaughter, Bert G. Kerstetter '66 University Professor of Politics and International Affairs, Princeton University, USA.

It is impossible to understand global governance without recognizing the important roles played by international organizations and non-state actors. This volume brings together cutting edge work by experts in their various fields to synthesize actor based and issue based insights about global governance.

Peter M. Haas, University of Massachusetts Amherst, USA.

A comprehensive survey of the theory and practice of global governance in the modern world. Comprised of outstanding essays by acknowledged experts and filled with important insights, *International Organization and Global Governance* is essential reading for scholars and students as well as practitioners.

David A. Lake, Jerri-Ann and Gary E. Jacobs Professor of Social Sciences and Distinguished Professor of Political Science, University of California, San Diego, USA.

Never before has a book demonstrated so systematically that 'global governance' offers a useful lens to analyze world politics. Extraordinarily comprehensive, it will become a vital reference for academics and practitioners.

Jean-Philippe Thérien, Université de Montréal, Canada.

This volume brings together contributions from an outstanding group of scholars. It is an indispensable guide for understanding the full range of contemporary challenges of global governance and international organizations, from a variety of perspectives.

Keith Krause, Professor, Graduate Institute of International and Development Studies, Geneva, Switzerland.

This very comprehensive collection, which includes contributions from many of the leading figures in the field, is sure to be the principal reference work on international organizations and global governance for many years to come.

John Ravenhill, Australian National University, Australia.

Weiss and Wilkinson have assembled a magnificent set of chapters from leading scholars that simultaneously provides a tour de force of international organizations and a clear guide to conceptualizing and understanding global governance. This persuasive account of the history, power and authority of international organizations should be required reading for all students, professors and practitioners of global governance and international relations.

Catherine Weaver, Associate Professor of Public Affairs,
The University of Texas at Austin, USA.

A tour de force . . . This meticulously conceived textbook on global governance and international organizations with essays by some of the world's finest experts will be a classic for scholars and practitioners from day 1.

Jan Wouters, Jean Monnet Chair EU and Global Governance, Director of the Leuven
Centre for Global Governance Studies, KU Leuven, Belgium.

Extensive and rigorous, Weiss and Wilkinson present in a single volume the history, theory, cross-cutting issues and empirical cases vital to understanding International Organizations. This is a must have for scholars of IOs.

Susan Park, Senior Lecturer in International Relations,
University of Sydney, Australia.

Kofi Annan was right: we are creating a global village. Hence, the need for stronger global village councils becomes more pressing day by day. Despite this, few understand how spectacularly global governance—in all its manifestations—has grown and why it needs to keep growing to keep the world safe. Weiss and Wilkinson have done us a remarkable service by producing this volume now: it provides an indispensable guide to the fastest growing global industry. And it will be read and studied for several decades as the world continues to converge.

Kishore Mahbubani, Dean of the Lee Kuan Yew School of
Public Policy, National University of Singapore.

The fifty chapters in this book, written by scholars from around the world, provide a comprehensive overview of the expanding agenda and participation in global governance. All readers will become aware of how they are involved in global governance, and how they might respond.

Chadwick F. Alger, Mershon Professor of Political Science and Public Policy, Mershon
Center for International Security Studies, Ohio State University, USA.

The reach and scope of this collection renders it invaluable for situating the study of international organizations in the broader field of IR.

Thomas Biersteker, The Graduate Institute, Geneva, Switzerland.

INTERNATIONAL ORGANIZATION AND GLOBAL GOVERNANCE

Edited by
Thomas G. Weiss and
Rorden Wilkinson

 Routledge
Taylor & Francis Group

LONDON AND NEW YORK

First published 2014
by Routledge
2 Park Square, Milton Park, Abingdon, Oxon OX14 4RN

and by Routledge
711 Third Avenue, New York, NY 10017

Routledge is an imprint of the Taylor & Francis Group, an informa business

British Library Cataloguing in Publication Data
A catalogue record for this book is available from the British Library

Library of Congress Cataloging in Publication Data
International organization and global governance/edited by Thomas Weiss and
Rorden Wilkinson.
   pages cm
   Summary: "Featuring a strikingly diverse and impressive team of authors,
   this is the most comprehensive textbook available for courses on international
   organization and global governance. This book covers the history, theories,
   structure, activities and policies of both state-centred institutions, and non-state
   actors in global politics"—Provided by publisher.
   Includes bibliographical references and index.
   1. International organization. 2. International agencies. 3. International relations.
   4. Globalization. I. Weiss, Thomas George. II. Wilkinson, Rorden, 1970–
   JZ5566.I592013
   341.2–dc23
   2013006787

ISBN: 978-0-415-62743-6 (hbk)
ISBN: 978-0-415-62760-3 (pbk)
ISBN: 978-0-203-79597-2 (ebk)

Typeset in Adobe Garamond by
Florence Production Ltd, Stoodleigh, Devon, UK

Contents

ILLUSTRATIONS

Figures

Tables

Boxes

CONTRIBUTORS

Amitav Acharya is the UNESCO Chair in Transnational Challenges and Governance and Professor of International Relations at the School of International Service, American University, Washington, DC.

Michael Barnett is University Professor of International Affairs and Political Science in the Elliott School of International Affairs at George Washington University.

Alex J. Bellamy is Professor of International Security in the Griffith Asia Institute at Griffith University.

Gülay Caglar is Research Fellow in the Division of Gender and Globalization at the Humboldt-University of Berlin, Germany.

Paul Cammack is Professor of Global Political Economy and head of the Department of Asian and International Studies at the City University of Hong Kong.

Jason Charrette is a Doctoral Candidate in the Department of Political Science at the University of Connecticut.

Simon Chesterman is Dean of the Faculty of Law at the National University of Singapore.

Jennifer Clapp is Canada Research Chair in Global Food Security and Sustainability and Professor in the Environment and Resource Studies Department at the University of Waterloo.

Roger A. Coate is Paul D. Coverdell Professor of Public Policy at Georgia College and State University.

Andrew F. Cooper is a Professor in the Balsillie School of International Affairs and the Department of Political Science, and Director of the Centre for Studies on Rapid Global Change, at the University of Waterloo.

Robert W. Cox is Emeritus Professor of Political Science at York University.

Elizabeth R. DeSombre is Camilla Chandler Frost Professor of Environmental Studies at Wellesley College.

Raymond Duvall is Morse-Alumni Professor of Political Science at the University of Minnesota.

David P. Forsythe is Emeritus Charles J. Mach Distinguished Professor in the Department of Political Science at the University of Nebraska-Lincoln.

Richard J. Goldstone is Visiting Professor of Law, University of Virginia Law School.

Leon Gordenker is Emeritus Professor of Politics at Princeton University.

Catia Gregoratti is Senior Lecturer in the Department of Political Science at Lund University.

Rodney Bruce Hall is University Lecturer in International Political Economy in the Department of International Development, and a Governing Body Fellow of St. Cross College, University of Oxford.

Fen Osler Hampson is Distinguished Fellow and Director of Global Security at the Centre for International Governance Innovation and Chancellor's Professor at Carleton University.

Sophie Harman is Senior Lecturer in the School of Politics and International Relations at Queen Mary, University of London.

Nigel Haworth is Professor of Human Resource Development at the University of Auckland.

David Held is Master of University College and Professor of Politics and International Relations, Durham University.

Monica Herz is Associate Professor at the Pontifical Catholic University, Rio de Janeiro.

Bernard Hoekman is Professor and Research Director of Global Economics in the Robert Schuman Centre for Advanced Studies (Global Governance Programme) at the European University Institute.

Peter J. Hoffman is Assistant Professor of International Relations in the Graduate Program in International Affairs at the New School.

Matthew J. Hoffmann is Associate Professor in the Department of Political Science at the University of Toronto.

Steve Hughes is Professor of International Organisations at Newcastle University Business School.

David Hulme is Professor of Development Studies, Head of the Institute for Development Policy and Management, and Executive Director of the Brooks World Poverty Institute at the University of Manchester.

Rob Jenkins is Professor of Political Science at Hunter College and The Graduate Center, The City University of New York.

Christer Jönsson is Professor of Political Science at Lund University and a member of the Royal Swedish Academy of Sciences.

W. Andy Knight is Director of the Institute of International Relations at the University of the West Indies and Professor in the Department of Political Science at the University of Alberta.

Khalid Koser is Deputy Director and Academic Dean at the Geneva Centre for Security Policy.

Charlotte Ku is Professor of Law and Assistant Dean for Graduate and International Legal Studies and Co-Director for the Center on Law and Globalization at the University of Illinois College of Law.

S. Neil MacFarlane is Lester B. Pearson Professor of International Relations and Fellow at St. Anne's College, University of Oxford.

James G. McGann is Assistant Director of the International Relations Program and Director of the Think Tanks and Civil Societies Program at the University of Pennsylvania.

Frank G. Madsen is Researcher in Transnational Crime at the University of Cambridge.

Katherine Marshall is Senior Fellow at the Berkley Center for Religion, Peace, and World Affairs at Georgetown University and Executive Director of the World Faiths Development Dialogue.

Julie Mertus is Professor and Co-Director of the Ethics, Peace and Global Affairs Program in the School of International Service at the American University.

Bessma Momani is Associate Professor at the University of Waterloo Balsillie School of International Affairs and a Senior Fellow at the Center for International Governance Innovation and the Brookings Institution.

Michael Moran is Research Fellow at the Asia-Pacific Centre for Social Investment and Philanthropy at Swinburne University of Technology, Australia.

Craig N. Murphy is M. Margaret Ball Professor of International Relations at Wellesley College, and Professor of Global Governance at the John W. McCormack Graduate School of Global and Policy Studies, University of Massachusetts, Boston.

M. J. Peterson is Professor of Political Science at the University of Massachusetts, Amherst.

Elisabeth Prügl is Professor of International Relations and Deputy Director of the Graduate Institute of International and Development Studies, Geneva.

Mark Raymond is Research Fellow at the Centre for International Governance Innovation.

Peter Romaniuk is Associate Professor of Political Science at John Jay College of Criminal Justice, the City University of New York.

Ben Rosamond is EURECO Professor of Political Science at the University of Copenhagen.

Jan Aart Scholte is Chair of Peace and Development at Gothenburg University and Professor of Politics and International Studies at the University of Warwick.

Susan K. Sell is Professor of Political Science and International Affairs at the George Washington University.

Waheguru Pal Singh Sidhu is Senior Fellow at the Center on International Cooperation at New York University.

Timothy J. Sinclair is Associate Professor of International Political Economy in the Department of Politics and International Studies at the University of Warwick and Professor in the Center for History, Finance and Politics at Kyung Hee University, Korea.

Duncan Snidal is Professor of International Relations and Fellow at Nuffield College, University of Oxford.

Jennifer Sterling-Folker is Professor of International Relations in the Department of Political Science at the University of Connecticut.

Jonathan R. Strand is Associate Professor in the Department of Political Science at the University of Nevada, Las Vegas.

Henning Tamm is a Post Doctoral Prize Research Fellow at St. Hilda's College, University of Oxford.

Ian Taylor is Professor of International Relations and African Politics at the University of St. Andrews.

Ramesh Thakur is Professor of International Relations in the Asia-Pacific College of Diplomacy and Director of the Centre for Nuclear Non-proliferation and Disarmament in the Crawford School at the Australian National University.

Oliver Turner is Hallsworth Fellow in Political Economy at the University of Manchester.

Thomas G. Weiss is Presidential Professor of Political Science at The Graduate Center and Director of the Ralph Bunche Institute for International Studies, The City University of New York, and Research Professor at SOAS, University of London.

Fabrice Weissman is Director of the Centre de Réflexion sur l'Action et les Savoirs Humanitaires at the Médecins Sans Frontières Foundation.

Rorden Wilkinson is Professor of International Political Economy in the School of Social Sciences, and Research Director of the Brooks World Poverty Institute, at the University of Manchester.

Paul D. Williams is Associate Professor in the Elliott School of International Affairs at the George Washington University.

Susanne Zwingel is Associate Professor in the Department of Politics at the State University of New York, Potsdam.

ACKNOWLEDGMENTS

We began thinking about putting this volume together more than a decade ago when we first discussed a book series on global institutions. As the series' tenth anniversary approached, we put together a proposal that contained what we thought a book on international organization and global governance should look like if we were given *carte blanche*. Craig Fowlie and Nicola Parkin at Routledge were enthusiastic about our idea and promptly sent the proposal to ten referees. We were pleasantly surprised when not too long thereafter ten glowing endorsements for the proposal came back. The feedback we received in each of those reviews helped us refine aspects of the proposal and the book that follows. We are grateful to each of those reviewers for their support and constructive criticisms. Craig and Nicola also gave us valuable feedback. A decade of collaborating closely on the Global Institutions Series, among other projects, has been fruitful and rewarding. We value their support and look forward to many more years of working together. We are also grateful to the rest of the editorial and production team at Routledge for their work on this volume.

The book would not have come together without the first-rate support provided by Oliver Turner. A rising academic star in his own right, Oliver helped organize and oversee the delivery of this project from the moment that the chapters started coming in to the correction of the final anomaly in the proverbial last endnote. His industry, willingness, and attention to detail improved immensely the quality of this book, in addition to making our lives and roles as editors easier. We are truly grateful for his efforts. Oliver also provided valuable comments on our own chapter in this volume as well as a related piece entitled "Rethinking Global Governance? Complexity, Authority, Power and Change," published in *International Studies Quarterly* 58, no. 2 (March 2014).

We are also grateful to Erin Hannah, Craig Murphy, and Tim Sinclair, who were also terrific reviewers of our joint scribbling. Erin turned around a draft of our introductory chapter in record time and provided suggestions that improved the text and argument. Craig and Tim did likewise for our *International Studies Quarterly* submission, which also helped shape our thinking for the introductory chapter.

We are grateful to David Hulme at the Brooks World Poverty Institute (BWPI) for enabling us to use BWPI as the institutional base for this project and for the use of the Institute's resources, and to Denise Redston for providing Rorden with invaluable administrative support.

We are also thankful for Martin Burke's assistance when this book was on the drawing board for helping to get us organized and started, as he has done so capably for the last several years for the Global Institutions Series. The fact that 35 of the 62 contributors to this edited collection also have books in our series is a source of pride.

Tom was able to devote so much time to this endeavor because he was on sabbatical leave. He thus would like to acknowledge support from The City University of New York's Graduate Center and several other institutions during this period: the One Earth Future Foundation; the Centre for Global Governance Studies at the University of Leuven; the Kulturwissenschaftliches Kolleg of the University of Konstanz; and the Centre for International Studies and Diplomacy at the School of Oriental and African Studies, the University of London.

T.G.W. and R.W.
New York and Manchester, June 2013

ABBREVIATIONS

ABM	Anti-Ballistic Missile Treaty
ACSRT	African Union's African Center for Study and Research on Terrorism
ACTA	Anti-Counterfeiting Trade Agreement
ADB	Asian Development Bank
AfDB	African Development Bank
AG	Australia Group
AIDS	Acquired Immune Deficiency Syndrome
ALAC	At-Large Advisory Committee
ALBA	Bolivarian Alternative of the Americas
AMIS	Agricultural Market Information System
AMISOM	African Union Mission in Somalia
AoA	Agreement on Agriculture
APEC	Asia Pacific Economic Cooperation
ASEAN	Association of Southeast Asian Nations
ASEM	Asia–Europe Meeting
ASP	Assembly of States Parties
AU	African Union
BASIC	Brazil, South Africa, India, and China
BI	Brookings Institution
BIAC	Business and Industry Advisory Committee
BOAD	West African Development Bank
BoP	base of the pyramid
BPA	Beijing Platform for Action
BPoA	Barbados Programme of Action
BRAC	Bangladesh Rehabilitation Assistance Committee (but superseded by the abbreviation alone)
BRIC	Brazil, Russia, India, China
BRICS	Brazil, Russia, India, China, South Africa
BRICSAM	Brazil, Russia, India, China, South Africa, Mexico
BRIICS	Brazil, Russia, India, Indonesia, China, South Africa
BTWC	Biological and Toxin Weapons Convention
BWC	Biological Weapons Convention
BWI	Bretton Woods institution
CABEI	Central American Bank for Economic Integration
CAN	Andean Community of Nations
CAT	Committee/Convention Against Torture
CBD	Convention on Biological Diversity
CBDR	common but differentiated responsibilities
CDB	Caribbean Development Bank
CEB	Chief Executives Board
CEDAW	Committee/Convention on the Elimination of All Forms of Discrimination Against Women

CEIP	Carnegie Endowment for International Peace
CEMENT	countries of emerging markets excluded from new terminology
CEO	chief executive officer
CERD	Committee/Convention on the Elimination of All Forms of Racial Discrimination
CERDI	Center for Studies and Research on Development at the University of Auvergne
CFA	Comprehensive Framework for Action
CFCs	chlorofluorocarbons
CFS	Committee on World Food Security
CGIAR	Consultative Group on International Agricultural Research
CHR	Commission on Human Rights
CIGI	Centre for International Governance Innovation
CIMMYT	International Maize and Wheat Improvement Center
CIS	Commonwealth of Independent States
CITES	Convention on International Trade in Endangered Species of Fauna and Flora
CIVETS	Colombia, Indonesia, Vietnam, Egypt, Turkey, South Africa
CMS	Convention for the Conservation of Migratory Species
CONGO	Conference of Non-Governmental Organizations in Consultative Relationship with the United Nations
CoP	Conference of the Parties
COP	Communication on Progress
CRC	Committee/Convention on the Rights of the Child
CRPD	Committee/Convention on the Rights of Persons with Disabilities
CRS	Catholic Relief Services
CSC	country-specific configuration
CSCE	Commission on Security and Cooperation in Europe
CSD	Commission on Sustainable Development
CSDMT	Comprehensive Statistical Database of Multilateral Treaties
CSDP	Common Security and Defence Policy
CSI	Container Security Initiative
CSR	corporate social responsibility
CSW	Commission on the Status of Women
CTAG	Counterterrorism Action Group
CTAP	Counterterrorism Action Plan
CTBT	Comprehensive Test Ban Treaty
CTC	Counterterrorism Committee
CTED	Counterterrorism Executive Directorate
CTITF	United Nations Counterterrorism Implementation Taskforce
CVE	countering violent extremism
CWC	Chemical Weapons Convention
DAC	Development Assistance Committee
DAW	Division for the Advancement of Women
DDT	dichlorodiphenyltrichloroethane
DESA	Department of Economic and Social Affairs

DfID	Department for International Development (UK)
DFS	Department of Field Support
DPI	Department of Public Information
DPKO	UN Department of Peacekeeping Operations
DPRK	Democratic People's Republic of Korea
DRC	Democratic Republic of Congo
EAC	East African Cooperation Treaty
EADB	East African Development Bank
EBRD	European Bank for Reconstruction and Development
EC	European Community
ECB	European Central Bank
ECJ	European Court of Justice
ECOMOG	Economic Community of West African States Monitoring Group
ECOSOC	Economic and Social Council
ECOWAS	Economic Community of West African States
ECSC	European Coal and Steel Community
EEA	European Economic Area
EEC	European Economic Community
EFTA	European Free Trade Association
ELCI	Environment Liaison Centre International
EMs	emerging market economies
ENDA	Environnement et Développement du Tiers-Monde
EP	European Parliament
ETUC	European Trade Union Council
EU	European Union
EULEX KOSOVO	European Union Rule of Law Mission in Kosovo
EUPM	European Union Police Mission in Bosnia and Herzegovina
EUPOL COPPS	European Union Police Mission for the Palestinian Territories
Euratom	European Atomic Energy Community
FACI	forensic accounting and corporate investigations
FAO	Food and Agriculture Organization
FATF	Financial Action Task Force
FCL	Flexible Credit Line
FCTC	Framework Convention on Tobacco Control
FDI	foreign direct investment
FES	Friedrich Ebert Stiftung
FIFA	Fédération Internationale de Football Association
FIU	financial intelligence unit
FMCT	Fissile Material Cutoff Treaty
FSAP	Financial Sector Assessment Program
FSB	Financial Stability Board
FSC	Forest Stewardship Council
FTAA	Free Trade Area of the Americas
FYR	Former Yugoslav Republic
G7	Group of Seven
G8	Group of Eight

G20	Group of 20
G77	Group of 77
GAIN	Global Alliance for Improved Nutrition
GATT	General Agreement on Tariffs and Trade
GAVI	Global Alliance for Vaccines and Immunisation
GCIM	Global Commission on International Migration
GCTF	Global Counterterrorism Forum
GDP	gross domestic product
GEF	Global Environment Facility
GEI	Green Economy Initiative
GFATM	Global Fund to Fight AIDS, Tuberculosis and Malaria
GFC	global financial crisis
GHG	greenhouse gas
GOARN	Global Outbreak Alert and Response Network
GPN	global production networks
GRI	Global Reporting Initiative
GUF	Global Union Federation
GVC	global value chain
GWOT	global war on terrorism
HIPC	heavily indebted poor country
HIV	Human Immunodeficiency Virus
HLP	High-level Panel
HLPE	High-level Panel of Experts
HLTF	High-level Task Force on the Food Security Crisis
HRC	Human Rights Council
HST	hegemonic stability theory decapitalise
IAASTD	International Assessment of Agricultural Knowledge, Science and Technology for Development
IAEA	International Atomic Energy Agency
IASC	Inter-Agency Standing Committee
IAVI	International AIDS Vaccine Initiative
IBRD	International Bank for Reconstruction and Development
IBSA	India, Brazil, South Africa
ICANN	Internet Corporation for Assigned Names and Numbers
ICAO	International Civil Aviation Organization
ICC	International Criminal Court
ICCPR	International Covenant on Civil and Political Rights
ICEM	Intergovernmental Committee for European Migration
ICESCR	International Covenant on Economic, Social and Cultural Rights
ICFTU	International Confederation of Free Trade Unions
ICG	International Crisis Group
ICIS	Interpol Criminal Information System
ICISS	International Commission on Intervention and State Sovereignty
ICJ	International Court of Justice
ICM	Intergovernmental Committee for Migration

ICPAT	Intergovernmental Authority on Development's, IGAD, Capacity-building Program Against Terrorism
ICPD	International Conference on Population and Development
ICPO	International Criminal Police Organization
ICRC	International Committee of the Red Cross
ICSID	International Centre for the Settlement of Investment Disputes
ICSU	International Council of Scientific Unions
ICTR	International Criminal Tribunal for Rwanda
ICTSD	International Centre for Trade and Sustainable Development
ICTY	International Criminal Tribunal for the former Yugoslavia
IDA	International Development Association
IDB	Inter-American Development Bank
IDP	internally displaced person
IDRC	International Development Research Centre
IDS	Institute of Development Studies
IEA	International Energy Agency
IFAD	International Fund for Agricultural Development
IFC	International Finance Corporation
IFI	international financial institution
IFOR	Implementation Force in Bosnia
IFPRI	International Food Policy Research Institute
IGBP	International Geosphere–Biosphere Programme
IGO	intergovernmental organization
IIED	International Institute for Environment and Development
IISD	International Institute for Sustainable Development
IISS	International Institute for Strategic Studies
ILO	International Labour Organization
IMF	International Monetary Fund
IMO	International Maritime Organization
INC	Intergovernmental Negotiating Committee
INF	Intermediate Range Nuclear Forces Treaty
INGO	international nongovernmental organization
INTERFET	International Force for East Timor
INTERPOL	International Criminal Police Organization
IO	international organization
IOC	International Oceanographic Commission
IOM	International Organization for Migration
IOSCO	International Organization of Security Commissions
IPCC	Intergovernmental Panel on Climate Change
IPPDDHH	Instituto de Politicas Públicas de Derechos Humanos
IPRs	intellectual property rights
IR	international relations
IRO	International Refugee Organization
IRRI	International Rice Research Institute
ISAF	International Security Assistance Force
ISO	International Organization for Standardization

ITO	International Trade Organization
ITS	international trade secretariats
ITU	International Telecommunication Union
ITUC	International Trade Union Confederation
ITUC-PERC	ITUC-Pan European Regional Council
IUCN	International Union for the Conservation of Nature
JCLEC	Jakarta Centre for Law Enforcement Cooperation
KFOR	Kosovo Force
LDC	least developed country
LED	light-emitting diode
LGBTI	lesbian, gay, bisexual, transgender, and intersex
LLDC	landlocked developing country
LNHO	League of Nations Health Organization
MAD	mutually assured destruction
MAP	mutual assessment process
MARPOL	International Convention for the Prevention of Pollution from Ships
MDB	multilateral development bank
MDG	Millennium Development Goal
MFN	most-favored nation
MIGA	Multilateral Investment Guarantee Agency
MIST	Mexico, Indonesia, South Korea, Turkey
MNC	multinational corporation
MONUC	United Nations Organization Mission in the Democratic Republic of Congo
MONUSCO	United Nations Organization Stabilization Mission in the Democratic Republic of the Congo
MOU	memorandum of understanding
MPRI	Military Professional Resources, Inc.
MSF	Médecins Sans Frontières
MTCR	Missile Technology Control Regime
NAALC	North American Agreement on Labor Cooperation
NAB	New Agreement to Borrow
NAFTA	North American Free Trade Agreement
NAM	Nonaligned Movement
NATO	North Atlantic Treaty Organization
NCUC	Noncommercial Users Constituency
NEPAD	New Economic Partnership for Africa's Development
NHS	National Health Service
NIEO	New International Economic Order
NIIO	New International Information Order
NGF	new global finance
NGLS	Non-Governmental Liaison Service
NGO	nongovernmental organization
NPE	normative power Europe
NPT	Nuclear Non-Proliferation Treaty
NRSRO	nationally recognized statistical rating organizations

NSA	non-state actors
NSG	Nuclear Suppliers Group
NTB	non-tariff barriers
NWFZ	Nuclear Weapon Free Zone
O5	Outreach 5
OAS	Organization of American States
OAU	Organization of African Unity
OCHA	Office for the Coordination of Humanitarian Affairs
ODA	official development assistance
ODI	Overseas Development Institute
OECD	Organisation for Economic Co-operation and Development
OEEC	Organisation for European Economic Co-operation
OHCHR	Office of the High Commissioner for Human Rights
OIC	Organization of the Islamic Conference
OIHP	Office International d'Hygiène Publique
ONUC	United Nations Operation in the Congo
OPCW	Organisation for the Prohibition of Chemical Weapons
OPEC	Organization of the Petroleum Exporting Countries
OSAGI	Office of the Special Adviser on Gender Issues and the Advancement of Women
OSCE	Organization for Security and Co-operation in Europe
P5	permanent five members of the UN Security Council
PA	principal–agent
PAMECA	Police Assistance Mission of the European Community to Albania
PBA	peacebuilding architecture
PBC	Peacebuilding Commission
PBF	Peacebuilding Fund
PBSO	Peacebuilding Support Office
PCL	precautionary credit line
PDP	product development partnership
PEPFAR	President's Emergency Plan for AIDS Relief
PfP	Partnership for Peace
PICMME	Provisional Intergovernmental Committee for the Movement of Migrants from Europe
PIPA	Protect Intellectual Property Act
PMSC	private military and security company
POC	protection of civilians
POPs	persistent organic pollutants
POW	prisoner of war
PPP	purchasing power parity
PRC	People's Republic of China
PREJAL	Promoting Youth Employment in Latin America
PSI	Proliferation Security Initiative
PTA	preferential trade agreement
PTBT	Partial Test Ban Treaty
R&D	research and development

R2P	responsibility to protect
RATS	Regional Antiterrorism Structure of the Shanghai Cooperation Organization
RDB	regional development bank
RFMO	Regional Fisheries Management Organization
S&P	Standard & Poor's
SAARC	South Asian Association for Regional Co-operation
SADC	Southern African Development Community
SAFE	Standards to Secure and Facilitate Global Trade Framework
SALT	Strategic Arms Limitation Talks
SARS	severe acute respiratory syndrome
SCIMF	Sub-Committee on IMF Matters
SCN	UN Standing Committee on Nutrition
SCOPE	Scientific Committee on the Problems of the Environment
SDB	sub-regional development bank
SDG	sustainable development goal
SDR	special drawing rights
SDSN	Sustainable Development Solutions Network
SDT	special and differential treatment
SEARCCT	Southeast Asian Regional Centre for Counterterrorism in Kuala Lumpur
SEATO	Southeast Asia Treaty Organization
SEC	Securities and Exchange Commission
SIDS	small island developing state
SIPRI	Stockholm International Peace Research Institute
SOPA	Stop Online Piracy Act
SORT	Strategic Offensive Reductions Treaty
START	Strategic Arms Reduction Treaty
TEEB	Economics of Ecosystems and Biodiversity
TNC	transnational corporation
TPS	Temporary Protected Status
TRIMs	Agreement on Trade Related Investment Measures
TRIPs	Agreement on Trade Related Aspects of Intellectual Property Rights
TUAC	Trade Union Advisory Committee
TUCA	Trade Union Confederation of the Americas
UCLG	United Cities and Local Governments
UDHR	Universal Declaration of Human Rights
UK	United Kingdom
UN	United Nations
UNAIDS	Joint United Nations Programme on HIV/AIDS
UNAMID	United Nations Hybrid Operation in Darfur
UNAMIR	United Nations Assistance Mission for Rwanda
UNAMSIL	United Nations Mission in Sierra Leone
UNAVEM	United Nations Angola Verification Mission
UNCCD	United Nations Convention to Combat Desertification in Those Countries Experiencing Drought and/or Desertification, Particularly in Africa

UNCCT	United Nations Counterterrorism Centre
UNCED	United Nations Conference on Environment and Development
UNCHE	United Nations Conference on the Human Environment
UNCLOS	United Nations Conference on the Law of the Sea
UNCSD	United Nations Conference on Sustainable Development
UNCTAD	United Nations Conference on Trade and Development
UNDP	United Nations Development Programme
UNEF	United Nations Emergency Force
UNEP	United Nations Environment Programme
UNESCO	United Nations Educational, Scientific and Cultural Organization
UNFCCC	United Nations Framework Convention on Climate Change
UNFICYP	United Nations Peacekeeping Force in Cyprus
UNFPA	United Nations Population Fund
UNGA	United Nations General Assembly
UNHABITAT	United Nations Human Settlements Programme
UNHCR	Office of the United Nations High Commissioner for Refugees
UNHLTF	United Nations High-level Task Force
UNICEF	United Nations International Children's Emergency Fund
UNIDIR	United Nations Institute for Disarmament Research
UNIDO	United Nations Industrial Development Organization
UNIFEM	United Nations Development Fund for Women
UNIFIL	United Nations Interim Force In Lebanon
UNITA	National Union for the Total Independence of Angola
UNITAF	Unified Task Force
UNITAID	Global Fund to Fight AIDS, Tuberculosis and Malaria
UNMA	United Nations Mine Action
UNMIK	United Nations Interim Administration Mission in Kosovo
UNMIL	United Nations Mission in Liberia
UNMIS	United Nations Mission in Sudan
UNMIS(S)	United Nations Mission in South Sudan
UNMOGIP	United Nations Military Observer Group in India and Pakistan
UNOCI	United Nations Mission in Côte d'Ivoire
UNODC	United Nations Office on Drugs and Crime
UNOSOM	United Nations Operations in Somalia
UNPROFOR	United Nations Protection Force
UNRRA	United Nations Relief and Rehabilitation Agency
UNRWA	United Nations Relief and Works Agency for Palestine Refugees
UNSCOB	United Nations Special Committee on the Balkans
UNSCOM	United Nations Special Commission
UNSMS	United Nations Security Management System
UNTAC	United Nations Transitional Authority in Cambodia
UNTAET	United Nations Transitional Administration in East Timor
UNTSO	United Nations Truce Supervision Organization
UNWOMEN	United Nations Women
UNWTO	United Nations World Tourism Organization
UPR	universal periodic review

UPU	Universal Postal Union
US	United States
USAID	United States Agency for International Development
USSR	Union of Soviet Socialist Republics
USTR	United States Trade Representative
VIP	very important person
WAGS	Working Group on Situations
WBG	World Bank Group
WCL	World Confederation of Labour
WCO	World Customs Organization
WEP	Women Empowerment Principles
WEU	Western European Union
WFP	World Food Programme
WFTO	World Fair Trade Organization
WFTU	World Federation of Trade Unions
WGC	Working Group on Communications
WHA	World Health Assembly
WHO	World Health Organization
WIPO	World Intellectual Property Organization
WMDs	weapons of mass destruction
WMO	World Meteorological Organization
WSSD	World Summit on Social Development
WTO	World Trade Organization

PART I
INTRODUCTION

International Organization and Global Governance

What matters and why

Thomas G. Weiss and Rorden Wilkinson

Few things point to the importance of understanding international organization and global governance more than their stark failings. The capacity of global humanitarian instruments to protect the lives of many of the world's "at-risk" populations has repeatedly been called into question, with the all-too-harrowing images of past failures in Rwanda and Somalia still searing our memories, and Syria's and Darfur's suffering continuing as daily media bill-of-fare.[1]

The absence of a robust global regulatory regime governing financial transactions and innovations helped heighten the effects of the 2007–08 global financial and economic crises, plunging western economies into more than half a decade of recession and sparing little of the rest of the world. Just a decade earlier, the Asian Financial Crisis of 1997–98 had also drawn attention to the inadequacies of global financial governance, including to the International Monetary Fund's (IMF) role in exacerbating the crisis.[2]

The global development architecture has presided over the feeblest of reductions in the proportion of the world's population living on less than US$1.25 per day. As David Hulme summarizes, "our world is organized in such a way that around 1.5 to 2.5 billion people (depending on how you define poverty) have little or no access to the most basic needs."[3] And an unprecedented growth in the gap between rich and poor has occurred within and across nations.[4]

Existing intergovernmental mechanisms for dealing with infectious disease have fallen short in dealing with cholera pandemics, HIV/AIDS, Ebola, and dengue fever, among others.[5] Meanwhile, global development programs have been implicated in the stagnation and decline of the health of populations on the periphery of the world economy.[6]

Despite a congested institutional terrain and the appearance of much activity, the pace of climate change, species loss, and desertification continues to call into question intergovernmental mechanisms for dealing with the deteriorating condition of the global environment. And efforts to stem the rate of growth of greenhouse gas (GHG) emissions continue to be frustrated by a lack of political will among the politicians in leading industrialized countries and their newly "emerging" counterparts, as well as among officials from the private sector and indeed citizens everywhere.[7] A well-populated institutional terrain should not hide the fact that we are treading water, or perhaps drifting even farther out to sea and wasting the energy and time necessary to move toward safety.

It is, of course, not just these failings that point to the importance of understanding international organization and global governance. It is the increasingly pluralistic nature of global politics and the change of roles therein. States have experimented with alternative intergovernmental arrangements—such as the current profusion of "groups," with the Group of 7/8 (G7/8) and the Group of 20 (G20) being the most prominent —to coordinate policy in key areas. Regional arrangements continue to drive forward economic integration, and states have taken on the role of managers of global inter-dependence.

A burgeoning nongovernmental sector is engaged in myriad activities ranging from familiar roles in disaster relief and poverty alleviation through to the implementation of micro-credit and micro-finance programs, to shaping global policy frameworks in development and health.[8] Knowledge networks play an important role in policy formulation and dissemination.[9] At the same time, other less salubrious actors have emerged in the governance of global affairs. Private military and security companies (PMSCs) are increasingly prominent in almost all arenas of conflict.[10] Criminal gangs traffic indentured workers, women, and children from the borderlands of the industrialized world to the plantations of the southern US and the sex industries of Western Europe. Terrorist groups and networks have become involved in many countries across the globe, generating and fueling instability and raising questions over the capacity of international mechanisms to control their spread.[11]

Credit rating agencies and multinational corporations are key players in the global economy.[12] Transnational religious movements—some interfaith, many not—have come to be seen as important development actors.[13] And of course it is not just the number of actors involved in the governance of the globe that also requires us to develop a keen sense of the way that the world is organized. We also need to get a better grip on the way that financial markets and the internet, among many other mechanisms, shape life on the planet.

What is striking, however, is that understanding the way that these actors and mechanisms are arranged one to another, the relations of power that underpin such arrangements, and the ideas and ideologies that drive their organizational forms and overall assemblage are not central to the study of international relations (IR). International organization (IO) and global governance are all too often taught as subfields within the wider discipline; they are commonly treated as synonyms for one another; and the relationship between them is seldom fully unpacked. Yet for us they are not merely curious phenomena but rather essential elements of the form and function of world order—and this chapter and the 50 others that follow demonstrate why.

We aim to correct this misrepresentation in the remainder of the chapter and in our further introductions that begin each subsequent part of the book. Certainly, others have written important works that seek to shed light on the global governance puzzle,[14] but none has done so as comprehensively as the chapters that follow. The centrality of questions about how the world is organized and governed—and a better understanding of the role myriad actors play in the governance of global life—offers an intriguing framework for what we believe is the most comprehensive guide yet published to help readers assemble the many pieces of the contemporary global governance puzzle.

This introduction spells out first what matters and why with an overview of the field, and why we as a community of scholars have not really put international organization and global governance together very well to date. After our interpretation of why this book's contents are essential reading, we parse briefly the substance of its seven main parts with more detailed introductions at the beginning of each of the sections of the book that follow.

Bringing international organization and global governance to the fore

International relations—as a field of study and as a real-world pursuit—has always been centrally concerned with questions of international organization and global governance. Indeed, it could be argued that understanding how the world is governed, of which an appreciation of how relations between states are organized is a key part, has always been and remains one of the primary concerns of IR scholars.[15] Yet, the central relationship of IO and global governance to the study and practice of IR is seldom acknowledged or understood. Rather, IO and global governance have tended to be presented as a combination of all or some of the following elements:

- activities by the UN and other major international organizations;
- subsets of the broader field of international relations;
- the preserve of normative and idealistic projects concerned with making the world a better place;
- the low politics of mundane bureaucracies working on more technical economic, environmental, and social issues and not the high politics of security, warfare, and defense; and
- conspiracies about world government.

Yet to present IO and global governance in these terms means misunderstanding that the questions with which they are concerned are actually core endeavors of the major intellectual traditions in IR. A brief *tour d'horizon* illustrates why.

Realism, in both its classical and neorealist variants, has as a constitutive tenet an assumption of how the world is organized. Hans J. Morgenthau was, among other things, concerned with varying forms of global organization—imperialism, world government, alliances, and self-determination; and mechanisms of governance—balances of power, international law, and supranational forms of arms control. Moreover, he examined (but did not necessarily advocate) alternative "future" forms of global governance—world state, world community, and the politics of accommodation.[16] Kenneth Waltz's neorealist formulation posits the international system as comprising a structure and a set of interacting units.[17] As in the classical formulation, there is no central authority that orders the units; instead, their relations vis-à-vis one another are determined by their relative power capabilities. In both these variants, realism has a clear idea of the overall structure of how the world is governed, and the primary task at hand is to deal with the negative effects of this form of organization.

Liberal internationalists and their modern neoliberal institutionalist, neofunctionalist, cosmopolitan, and constructivist counterparts also recognize the pernicious aspects of the way that world politics is organized. However, rather than focusing on the development of self-help manuals designed to bolster state power in the face of changes in relative power capabilities, they emphasize moments of common interest in which cooperation between and among states occurs, and in which such cooperation becomes institutionalized and regularized. These moments of cooperation shape and constrain state behavior via systems of rules, norms, practices, and decision-making procedures that may or may not be guided by progressive ideas and ideologies.[18] The result is a focus on possibility, entertaining questions not only of how the world is governed but also of how it *ought* to be governed.[19]

More critical traditions too have ideas of world order as central tenets in their intellectual cannon. Classical Marxist, and more recent Gramscian and neo-Gramscian, approaches understand transnational and global organization as political responses to the exigencies of the spread of capitalism across the world.[20] The organizing imperative is the facilitation of capitalist expansion. International and transnational organizations and their administrative and legal frameworks are the superstructural manifestations of that imperative.[21] And the core purposes of these manifestations are to mitigate the conflicts that result from industrial expansion;[22] create economic opportunities conducive with further accumulation;[23] and stabilize and perpetuate particular relations of power.[24]

Feminist approaches—liberal and Marxist alike—likewise share a notion of the central organizing tenets of world politics. Here forms of organization, institutionalization, and regularization are shaped by and help perpetuate unequal gender relations between women and men, and girls and boys, irrespective of what might look like progressive policies and elements.[25] A core concern is the reconstitution of existing social institutions that better reflect gender equities.[26]

Postcolonial approaches also have an understanding of how the world is organized. Common among scholars working in this tradition is a concern with historical processes that have ensured that European (including US) imperial orders continue to be the dominant mode in which relations in the periphery are governed in an ostensibly postcolonial order.[27] The key challenge for them is to render instances of dominance and subordination visible and to bring to the fore other forms of social organization in a general movement that Dipesh Chakrabarty terms "provincializing Europe."[28] And an array of other antifoundationalist and poststructural approaches to IR have a concern for the way the world is governed as a central tenet of their intellectual traditions.[29]

Yet for all their (albeit largely unrecognized) centrality to the core intellectual traditions of IR, IO and global governance are hardly unproblematic, nor is the relationship between them uncomplicated. Partly because IO and global governance are often taught as IR subfields rather than as primary concerns in and of themselves, little clarity exists about their core meanings, overlaps, and contradictions. In some instances, IO and global governance are treated synonymously; in others, both relate only to what international organizations "do"; and in others still, such variance exists in what is treated as the intellectual and empirical terrain as to render both of the terms meaningless.

International organization and global governance: one to another

At its most basic, international organization refers to an instance—or, in an historical sense, a moment—of institutionalization in relations among states. Inis Claude's formulation argues that: "International *organization* is a process; international *organizations* are representative aspects of the phase of that process which has been reached at a given time."[30] His and other classic definitions of IO are inexorably bound up with a normative desire to see the organizations that we currently have as moments in a progressive march toward growing global institutionalization. We tend to take IO to refer to formal interstate institutions that are, or which have the potential to be, planetary in reach, such as the United Nations (UN) or World Trade Organization (WTO), though any regional, less formal interstate arrangement can be and often is classified in this way as well. Indeed, analyses of the European Union (EU) are often features of North American classes on international organization; whereas in Europe supranational European institutions and their relationship to the post-war political economy of that continent are commonly viewed as distinct enough to merit separate courses from other international organizations.

Confusing matters further, at least initially for students, is the seeming conflation of the term IO with "institutions" and "regimes." Although they are not one and the same, there is a family relationship here that requires explanation. Strictly speaking, international organizations (as opposed to IO as a process) are formal intergovernmental bureaucracies. They have a legal standing, physical headquarters, executive head, staff, and substantive focus of operations. Hence, the World Intellectual Property Organization—a UN specialized agency—exists to coordinate and entrench in international legal frameworks the protection of intellectual property rights across the globe; it has its headquarters in Geneva; it has 185 member states; and its secretariat is overseen by a director-general. Other organizations might also be considered to be "international" in their focus and remit—such as the World Economic Forum that meets every year in Davos, Switzerland—but are not intergovernmental and are better described as "institutions"—forums, semi-permanent gatherings, or transnational arrangements depending on their specific character—to which we now turn.

An international institution is broader. Whereas international organizations are formalized bureaucracies (and again it is worth bearing in mind that the "s" not only pluralizes the word but refers to specific entities and not a process of institutionalization), international institutions can be both formal and informal instances of regularized interstate behavior. So, while international organizations are also international institutions, a moment of regularized interstate behavior that does not have a legal personality, a headquarters, a secretariat, and an executive head is not. Here we can think of a range of institutions, including, but not limited to, semi-formalized groups of states—the Group of 7/8, Group of 77—and regularized balances of power between states, including the nineteenth century Concert of Europe and the twentieth century Cold War. Thus, international institutions are instances of international organization, but they are not necessarily international organizations. As such, we tend to define them—as Robert Keohane does—as "persistent and connected sets of rules (formal and informal) that prescribe behavioral roles, constrain activity, and shape expectations."[31]

An international regime is slightly different again, although there is a relationship between both international organizations and international institutions, on the one hand, and regimes, on the other hand. Stephen Krasner's formulation remains the most widely accepted definition of an international regime: "Implicit or explicit principles, norms, rules and decision-making procedures around which actors' expectations converge in a given area of international relations."[32] Despite this commonly accepted definition that suggests they are nearly synonyms of international institutions, international regimes are more accurately viewed as the range of activities that are, in part, created by the behavior-shaping effects of international organizations and institutions. What we have in mind here are areas of activity such as the international trade regime. Clearly international trade took place in the absence of global, regional, and national rules, systems of regulation, and organizational structures. What is distinct about the current international trade regime is that its volume, value, and content are shaped by the behavioral rules, practices, norms, and decision-making procedures of the WTO, myriad regional trade arrangements such as the North American Free Trade Agreement, and an even greater number of bilateral agreements, not to mention the combination of national trade policies, the behavioral practices of private firms, and the lobbying efforts (effective or otherwise) of various nongovernmental actors.[33]

A key concern of scholars is to understand how power relationships are embedded in the way that the behavior of states—and their economic and political agents, including firms that may be multinational but which nonetheless emanate from and retain an organic connection to their states of origin—is shaped by international organizations, institutions, and regimes. Work by Robert Cox and Craig Murphy, for instance, has explored the organic connection between dominant states and the creation and evolution of international institutions.[34] Robert Keohane, Robert Wade, and Rorden Wilkinson have examined how the interests of powerful states are embedded in the very design of institutions and the effect that this has on institutional and regime development over time.[35] Catherine Weaver has explored how institutional development can reinforce a form of organization that perpetuates dominant relations of power.[36] Kenneth Abbott and Duncan Snidal's work on principal–agent theory likewise examines how state imperatives are manifest in organizational behavior and the deviations that occur therefrom.[37] Thomas G. Weiss probes the relationship between ideas and the creation and development of international organizations.[38] And Susan Park and Antje Vetterlin examine the role norms play in shaping state behavior and the construction of economic regimes.[39]

Although stellar work continues within the confines of what we might conceive as traditional IO studies, the field requires a specific recognition of greater global complexity and ongoing changes (technological, economic, political, ethical) that demonstrate how the world is governed in a multidimensional fashion. Part of this evolution was foreshadowed by work being carried out under the auspices of international institutions and regimes, but it was the end of the Cold War that brought into full view the range of actors operating across borders—and increasingly globally—that needed explaining. Regimes and institutions provided a partial analytical solution, as did attempts to refresh multilateralism as a specific organizational type.[40] However, it was the emergence of the term "global governance" in the 1990s—with the publication of James Rosenau and Ernst Czempiel's edited volume, the report by the Commission on Global Governance, and the first issue of a new journal[41]—that really captured the post-Cold War *Zeitgeist* and that has enabled us as an intellectual community to grapple more fully with how the world is organized in all of its complexity. Nonetheless, and as we argue below, the analytical utility of the term global governance has not yet been fully realized.

Suffice to say, global governance is different from international organization and related work on international institutions and regimes, The core idea is still one of organization—in the sense of the structure and order of things—but the scale and level are different, as is the understanding of the form of organization. Scale-wise, global governance refers to the totality of the ways, formal and informal, in which the world is governed. The emergence and widespread recognition of transnational issues that circumscribe state capacity along with the proliferation of non-state actors responding to perceived shortfalls in national capabilities and a willingness to address them in the context of a perceived crisis of multilateralism combined to stimulate new thinking. The imperative is to establish the general character of global governance and to identify the dominant actors and mechanisms. Critics have suggested that it is little more than a kitchen-sink approach with an all-too-fuzzy grasp of the way the world works.[42] While seemingly accurate, this characterization misses the importance of struggling to capture more fully the totality of ways in which life on the planet is ordered. It has encouraged investigators to ask questions not only about who and what were involved in governing the world but also about how any particular form of organization came about and the results of its particular mechanisms of control.

It is not just this scale and comprehensive embrace that make global governance distinct, it is also the manner that it encompasses the interactions at all levels of life. What happens in one corner or at any level (local, national, or regional) can have repercussions in all other corners and at all levels. And global governance is not just about relations among and between states—although this remains a crucial aspect of the wider puzzle—it is also about the relationship between global policy-making processes and their implementation in particular localities, the effects of local actions on global life, and the interrelationships that exist between institutions, actors, and mechanisms at every level in between. As James Rosenau noted, inevitably in this mix are countervailing tendencies—what he called "fragmegration" in reference to the centripetal and centrifugal, integration versus fragmentation, tendencies toward lower and higher levels of the contemporary order[43]—but the continued compartmentalization of global social life into easily consumable levels of analysis hinders our understanding of how the world is governed.

Thus, although an obvious relationship exists between IO and global governance—because international organizations are aspects of understanding how the global is currently governed—the terms are not synonymous and certainly not coterminous. Moreover, whereas IO points primarily toward states and emphasizes intergovernmental organizations (IGOs), global governance is far more encompassing. Clearly the UN Security Council is an important actor but so too are multinational corporations, private security firms, transnational criminal networks, private regulators, and nongovernmental organizations (NGOs).

Equally, the range of mechanisms by which governance is exercised dramatically increases in moving from IO to global governance. International governance (by which we mean interstate) is limited to those structures that can be agreed by member states to operate under the auspices of a given organization. International legal frameworks are the most common, occasionally backed up by some kind of enforcement mechanism—as with the WTO's dispute settlement body, the International Criminal Court's pursuit of perpetrators of mass atrocities, or the Security Council's authorization of forcible or non-forcible sanctions. Ad hoc instances of states acting in concert are part of the picture and the bill-of-fare of foreign policy. In the realm of global governance more broadly, however, a range of other mechanisms are perhaps equally influential, of which financial markets are the most prominent. The mechanisms for buying and selling, and the commercial innovations that they drive and encourage, can have dramatic effects, as Jennifer Clapp and Eric Helleiner's work on the financialization of global food markets shows.[44]

Moreover, any emphasis on states alone misses numerous examples of steps in issue-specific global governance—for instance by the International Committee of the Red Cross for the laws of war and humanitarian principles, by the Fédération Internationale de Football Association (or FIFA, its familiar abbreviation) for the world's most popular sport (football/soccer), and by the Internet Corporation for Assigned Names and Numbers (ICANN) for the internet. Increasingly, private-sector standard-setting is becoming a foundation for addressing global food and hunger problems, with representatives of industry, NGOs, and multi-stakeholder coalitions determining policies and compliance as much or more than many governments, while public–private partnerships are being forged between state and non-state actors at all levels.[45]

Less obvious structures of global governance are found not only in the standard-setting activities of IGOs like the International Organization of Standardization but also in the lobbying activities of commercial interests in trying to get particular sizes, shapes, weights, and other standards established as concrete norms.[46] Other sources of governance can be found in fledgling and evolving electronic and social media regimes,[47] and in the activities of the super-rich, not only in their consumption patterns but also in their philanthropic activities.[48]

Similarly, Moody's Investors Service and Standard & Poor's Ratings Group render judgments that are authoritative enough to cause substantial market responses.[49] Private regulatory initiatives govern supply chains across the globe to set environmental, food safety, and social standards to such an extent that private not public standards are the prime determinants of access to most western markets.[50] And even for a security issue like piracy, a hybrid private–public initiative seems at least as likely to help forge agreement on the parameters of addressing that global problem as governments by themselves or shipping and insurance companies on their own.[51]

Thinking differently about global governance

That said, "global governance" is not, as we have noted, an unproblematic label. Many criticisms are exercised because of its apparent catch-all quality as well as by the refusal of proponents who find it useful to confine their intellectual remit to a static and known range. Yet global governance's primary utility lies not in working out theoretical and empirical parameters but rather in reorienting the way that we ask questions about the world around us. More particularly still, we need to ask and answer questions about how the world is governed, ordered, and organized. These questions not only give us an insight into the way, as John Ruggie remarked, the "world hangs together,"[52] but they also have the potential to overcome some of the fragmentation that IR as a scholarly pursuit has suffered over the last three decades.

Increasingly IR consists of a set of separate and discrete intellectual endeavors that make it possible to develop sophisticated frameworks that generate introverted debate among members of a particular theoretical bent rather than more open conversations among wide-ranging scholars to find fertile common ground to be plowed for the field as a whole. The transatlantic divide in international political economy is one example of such a division, and that between positivist and antifoundationalist approaches to world politics is another. Refocusing on questions of how the world is organized or governed—which, as we show at the outset of this chapter, has been a preserve of all of the major theoretical traditions—has the potential to reverse this intellectual fragmentation and reinvigorate the discipline as a whole.

There is, however, a related problem that first needs to be addressed if global governance is to fully realize its potential as a core IR pursuit, which relates to the empirical terrain associated with the term. The paucity of existing IR frameworks to explain adequately changes ushered in by the end of the Cold War and the emergence of a host of new actors on the world stage were key dynamics in the emergence of the term "global governance" and the cottage analytical industry that has grown over the last two decades. One consequence of its use in capturing growing global complexity has been a close association with the term and the specific post-Cold War moment from which it emerged. A related consequence has been a failure by analysts to rescue the term from this narrow historical association and to test its utility as a lens through which to view past and future world orders in addition to better understanding that of today.

If global governance provides a helpful perspective for today, it should also help to understand the relations that were maintained by, and the systems of governance between and among, a variety of actors in historic epochs different from our own: the Greek city states; China and its tributaries; various Indian empires and states and other regimes across the Middle East and Asia; the empires of Rome, Persia, and Egypt, as well as the kingdoms and empires of pre-colonial Africa; the Islamic caliphates and non-Muslim empires; and the European papal and non-papal states and empires. The framework should also shed light on Cold War bipolarity and the post-Cold War's uni- or multi-polar moment. In short, global governance should provide ample insights into the differing forms of overarching world organization that have existed—and which need further investigation to unravel the full range of means by which they were and are held together. Global governance thus should help us understand where we came from and why we have got to where we have, as well as a way to develop strategies for where we should be going. We have attempted to begin this task elsewhere.[53]

The term global governance was and continues to be deployed as a means of capturing the pluralization of the world political stage that has been manifest since the end of the Cold War. Even skeptics would not dispute that large multinational corporations, transnational religious institutions, global NGOs, and credit rating agencies are significant in influencing how the world is governed; they would not argue that financial markets and transnational legal frameworks have little more than a passing effect on how the world "hangs together." What we have come to realize also is that a range of actors operating in concert—international organizations alongside labor groups, NGOs, and global corporations in the UN Global Compact, private sector security and logistic firms in multinational humanitarian operations, and nongovernmental relief agencies working alongside the UN and military forces in complex humanitarian emergencies, to name but a few—also have important effects on the overall shape of how the world is governed. Moreover, we have become increasingly sensitive to the role played by ideas, ideologies, norms, and knowledge in global governance; and we have come to see states as important global governance actors directing, transmitting, receiving, and holding together forms of organization.

Yet few scholarly works have attempted to offer a complete overview of the actors, institutions, and mechanisms that constitute contemporary global governance. We too cannot claim to have captured contemporary global governance in its entirety or to present readers with every conceivable conceptualization of early twenty-first century world order. Our aim, however, has been to make the best attempt yet. The chapters that follow provide a comprehensive overview of the historical foundations of the current order's evolution as well as its key dynamics; the major approaches to the study of international organization and global governance; and the role of states, their coalitions, and intergovernmental institutions as well as important non-state humanitarian, security, and economic actors. We also explore in detail how global governance is manifest in humanitarian, economic, and social arenas. We have sought, at one and the same time, to put an end to the separation and confusion between the way that we conceptualize and study IO and global governance, to examine the role of many major actors, and to explore the differential manifestations of governance in particular fields while not losing sight of the big picture.

About this book

Part II of this book has five chapters that launch this inquiry by "Contextualizing international organization and global governance." We begin with essays that provide the backdrop for reading the rest of the book. Craig N. Murphy (Chapter 1) shows that moves to formalize institutional relations have been much longer lived than many suppose and that these were inevitably tied up with developments in an industrializing and globalizing world economy. Charlotte Ku (Chapter 2) explores a key building block, the development of public international law across the *longue durée*. Michael Barnett and Raymond Duvall (Chapter 3) build upon their own oft-cited edited volume and examine power in the broadest sense and not simply that emanating from a barrel of a gun, while David Held (Chapter 4) turns to the diffusion of authority. Susan K. Sell (Chapter 5) asks the question that few ask (and many forget to answer), namely which agents actually govern the world.

The nine chapters that follow thereafter in Part III deal with "Theories of international organization and global governance." While critics are bound to claim that looking at "isms" is old-fashioned, we strongly believe that readers should understand the dominant or even emerging ways that key schools of thought have tried to make sense of the way the world is governed before attempting their own original syntheses. These essays look at how we have come to understand the way that the world is governed since the beginning of the Westphalian order: "Realism" (Jason Charrette and Jennifer Sterling-Folker, Chapter 6); "Classical liberal internationalism" (Christer Jönsson, Chapter 7); "Neoliberal institutionalism" (David P. Forsythe, Chapter 8); "Rational choice and principal–agent theory" (Henning Tamm and Duncan Snidal, Chapter 9); "Constructivism" (Rodney Bruce Hall, Chapter 10); "Critical theory" (Robert W. Cox, Chapter 11); "Classical Marxism" (Paul Cammack, Chapter 12); and "Feminism" (Susanne Zwingel, Elisabeth Prügl, and Gülay Caglar, Chapter 13). This part closes with an essay on "Post-hegemonic multilateralism" (Amitav Acharya, Chapter 14) that examines how multilateralism can be reformulated and bring the normative project underlying many of the "isms" back to breaking new ground. It is worth pointing out that many of these approaches have been adapted from dominant IR perspectives, while only a few have been more tailored to look specifically at international organization; and it remains the case that we as an intellectual community have yet to develop specific theories of global governance.

Part IV of the book contains seven chapters that summarize "States and international institutions in global governance." As indicated earlier, international organizations have often been seen to be the main pillars undergirding the way the world is governed, and so this part examines some of the main units around which the field has revolved, including of course the role that states and the institutions that they have created play in contemporary global governance: "The UN system" (Leon Gordenker, Chapter 15); "The UN General Assembly" (M. J. Peterson, Chapter 16); "Regional governance" (Monica Herz, Chapter 17); "The European Union" (Ben Rosamund, Chapter 18); "The BRICS in the new global economic geography" (Andrew F. Cooper and Ramesh Thakur, Chapter 19); "The global South" (Ian Taylor, Chapter 20); and "US hegemony" (W. Andy Knight, Chapter 21).

The eight chapters of Part V move beyond state-centrism to cover "Non-state actors in global governance." As indicated, the proliferation of actors and the scope of their activities have been central to explaining the burgeoning field of global governance, and so this part parses many of the key actors: "UN–business partnerships" (Catia Gregoratti, Chapter 22); "Civil society and NGOs" (Jan Aart Scholte, Chapter 23); "Labor" (Nigel Haworth and Steve Hughes, Chapter 24); "Credit rating agencies" (Timothy J. Sinclair, Chapter 25); "Think tanks and global policy networks" (James G. McGann, Chapter 26); "Global philanthropy" (Michael Moran, Chapter 27); "Private military and security companies" (Peter J. Hoffman, Chapter 28); and "Transnational criminal networks" (Frank G. Madsen, Chapter 29). We look at non-state actors, those bodies often added into the mix which is then stirred, because all too often they appear as adjuncts to books that are otherwise really just about IO. Our aim is to take these actors as mainstream components, introducing them before exploring how they contribute to governance across issues.

Part VI contains ten chapters on "Securing the world, governing humanity." One of the main explanations for human efforts to better govern the world has been the need to foster international peace and security, and so the reader encounters four familiar topics: "UN Security Council and peace operations" (Paul D. Williams and Alex J. Bellamy, Chapter 30); "Regional organizations and global security governance" (S. Neil MacFarlane, Chapter 31); "Weapons of mass destruction" (Waheguru Pal Singh Sidhu, Chapter 32); and "From 'global war' to global governance: counterterrorism cooperation in world politics" (Peter Romaniuk, Chapter 33). In most texts these would be the "security" institutions, but here we also explore issues across areas in ways that offer a more complete and complex picture of how the humanitarian world is governed: "Human rights in global governance" (Julie Mertus, Chapter 34); "The pursuit of international justice" (Richard J. Goldstone, Chapter 35); "Humanitarian intervention and R2P" (Simon Chesterman, Chapter 36); "Crisis and humanitarian containment" (Fabrice Weissman, Chapter 37); "Post-conflict peacebuilding" (Rob Jenkins, Chapter 38); and "Human security as a global public good" (Fen Osler Hampson and Mark Raymond, Chapter 39).

The eleven chapters of Part VII, the final part of the book, attempt the impossible task of surveying what passes for "Governing the economic and social world." Whatever we mean by "peace," it certainly entails more than the absence of war and large-scale organized violence, and so the book concludes by examining the various components of a fairer world order, including several pressing issues that many would also characterize as "security" challenges: "Global financial governance" (Bessma Momani, Chapter 40); "Global trade governance (Bernard Hoekman, Chapter 41); "Global development governance" (Katherine Marshall, Chapter 42); "Global environmental governance" (Elizabeth R. DeSombre, Chapter 43); "The regional development banks and global governance" (Jonathan R. Strand, Chapter 44); "Climate change" (Matthew J. Hoffmann, Chapter 45); "Sustainable development" (Roger A. Coate, Chapter 46); "Poverty reduction" (David Hulme and Oliver Turner, Chapter 47); "Food and hunger" (Jennifer Clapp, Chapter 48); "Global health governance" (Sophie Harman, Chapter 49); and "Refugees and migration" (Khalid Koser, Chapter 50).

Conclusion: moving forward

By disaggregating topics in the way that we have and then putting them back together, we can understand the complexity, the range of sources of authority, and the multiple ways that power and authority are exercised. This approach provides building blocks for the way that we need to think about world order today and in the future. What has become clearer and clearer to us is that the field of IR should be widened and deepened. We are proud in these pages to have assembled a strikingly diverse and impressive team of authors whose essays—which we discuss in more detail in separate introductions to the parts that follow—help all of us to continue the unfinished journey toward better understanding global governance. We nonetheless have a long way to go.

Notes

1 Michael N. Barnett and Thomas G. Weiss, *Humanitarianism Contested: Where Angels Fear to Tread* (London: Routledge, 2009).

2 Jonathan Michie and John Grieve Smith, eds., *Global Instability: The Political Economy of World Economic Governance* (London: Routledge, 1999); and Joseph E. Stiglitz, *Globalization and Its Discontents* (New York: Norton and Company, 2002).

3 David Hulme, *Global Poverty: How Global Governance Is Failing the Poor* (London: Routledge, 2010), 1.

4 Erik S. Reinert, *How Rich Countries Got Rich and Why Poor Countries Stay Poor* (London: Public Affairs, 2007).

5 Sophie Harman, *Global Health Governance* (London: Routledge, 2012); Kelley Lee, *The World Health Organization* (London: Routledge, 2009); Ilari Regondi and Alan Whiteside, "Global Development Goals and the International HIV Reponse: A Chance for Renewal," in *The Millennium Development Goals and Beyond: Global Development After 2015*, eds. Rorden Wilkinson and David Hulme (London: Routledge, 2012), 174–191.

6 Jim Yong Kim, Joyce V. Millen, Alec Irwin, and John Gershman, eds., *Dying for Growth: Global Inequality and the Health of the Poor* (Monroe, ME: Common Courage Press, 2000); and James Orbinski, *An Imperfect Offering: Humanitarian Action in the Twenty-First Century* (New York: Random House, 2008).

7 Elizabeth R. DeSombre, *Global Environmental Institutions* (London: Routledge, 2006); Harriet Bulkeley and Peter Newell, *Governing Climate Change* (London: Routledge, 2010); and Peter Newell, *Globalization and the Environment* (Cambridge: Polity Press, 2012).

8 Jonathan A. Fox and L. David Brown, eds., *The Struggle for Accountability: The World Bank, NGOs and Grassroots Movements* (Cambridge, MA: MIT Press, 1998); and Jan Aart Scholte with Albrecht Schnabel, ed., *Civil Society and Global Finance* (London: Routledge, 2002).

9 Diane Stone, "Introduction: Global Knowledge and Advocacy Networks," *Global Networks: A Journal of Transnational Affairs* 2, no. 1 (2002): 1–11.

10 Peter Singer, *Corporate Warriors: the Rise of the Privatized Military Industry* (Ithaca: Cornell University Press, 2003).

11 Peter Romaniuk, *Multilateral Counterterrorism: The Global Politics of Cooperation and Contestation* (New York: Routledge, 2010).

12 Timothy J. Sinclair, "Round up the Usual Suspects: Blame and the Subprime Crisis," *New Political Economy* 15, no. 1 (2010): 91–107.

13 Katherine Marshall, "Governance and Inequality: Reflections on Faith," in *Global Governance, Poverty and Inequality*, eds. Jennifer Clapp and Rorden Wilkinson (London: Routledge, 2010), 295–313.

14 Anthony McGrew and David Held, eds., *Governing Globalization* (Cambridge: Polity Press, 2002); Margaret P. Karns and Karen Mingst, *International Organizations: The Politics and Processes of Global Governance* (Boulder, CO: Lynne Rienner, 2009); and Deborah D. Avant, Martha Finnemore, and Susan Sell, eds., *Who Governs the Globe?* (Cambridge: Cambridge University Press, 2010).

15 Mark Mazower, *Governing the World: The History of an Idea* (New York: Penguin, 2012).

16 Hans J. Morgenthau, *Politics Among Nations: The Struggle for Power and Peace*, 6th edition (New York: McGraw Hill, 1985).

17 Kenneth Waltz, *Theory of International Politics* (New York: Addison-Wesley, 1979).

18 Robert O. Keohane, *After Hegemony: Cooperation and Discord in the World Political Economy* (Princeton: Princeton University Press, 1984).

19 For example, David Held, *Global Covenant: The Social Democratic Alternative to the Washington Consensus* (Cambridge: Polity Press, 2004).

20 Paul Cammack, "The Governance of Global Capitalism: A New Materialist Perspective," in *The Global Governance Reader*, ed. Rorden Wilkinson (London: Routledge, 2005), 156–173.

21 Stephen Gill, "New Constitutionalism, Democratisation and Global Political Economy," *Pacifica Review: Peace, Security & Global Change* 10, no. 1 (1998): 23–38.

22 Craig N. Murphy, *International Organization and Industrial Change: Global Governance since 1850* (Cambridge: Polity Press, 1994), 2.

23 Paul Cammack, "The Mother of All Governments: The World Bank's Matrix for Global Governance," in *Global Governance: Critical Perspectives*, eds. Rorden Wilkinson and Steve Hughes (London: Routledge, 2002), 36–54.

24 Robert W. Cox, *Approaches to World Order* (Cambridge: Cambridge University Press), 99.

25 Shirin Rai and Georgina Waylen, *Global Governance: Feminist Perspectives* (Basingstoke: Palgrave, 2008).

26 Gülay Caglar, Elisabeth Prügl, and Susanne Zwingel, *Feminist Strategies in International Governance* (London: Routledge, 2013).

27 Himadeep Muppidi, "Colonial and Postcolonial Global Governance," in *Power in Global Governance*, eds. Michael Barnett and Raymond Duvall (Cambridge: Cambridge University Press, 2005), 273–293.

28 Dipesh Chakrabarty, *Provincializing Europe: Postcolonial Thought and Historical Difference*, 2nd edition (Princeton: Princeton University Press, 2007).

29 See, for example, Heikki Patomäki, "Problems of Democratising Global Governance: Time, Space and the Emancipatory Process," *European Journal of International Relations* 9, no. 34 (2003): 347–376; and Luigi Pellizzoni, "Governing through Disorder: Neoliberal Environmental Governance and Social Theory," *Global Environmental Change* 21, no. 3 (2011): 795–803.

30 Inis L. Claude, Jr., *Swords into Plowshares*, 3rd edition (New York: Random House, 1964), 4.

31 Robert O. Keohane, "International Institutions: Two Approaches," *International Studies Quarterly* 32, no. 4 (1988): 383.

32 Stephen D. Krasner, "Structural Causes and Regime Consequences: Regimes as Intervening Variables," *International Organization* 36, no. 2 (1982): 185.

33 Erin Norma Hannah, "NGOs and the European Union: Examining the Power of Epistemes in the EC's TRIPS and Access to Medicines Negotiations," *Journal of Civil Society* 7, no. 2 (2011): 179–206.

34 Robert W. Cox, ed., *The New Realism: Perspectives on Multilateralism and World Order* (Basingstoke: Macmillan, 1997); and Craig Murphy, *International Organization and Industrial Change*.

35 Robert O. Keohane, *Power and Governance in a Partially Globalized World* (London: Routledge, 2002); Robert Hunter Wade, "What Strategies Are Viable for Developing Countries Today? The World Trade Organization and the Shrinking of 'Development Space,'" *Review of International Political Economy* 10, no. 4 (2003): 621–644, and Rorden Wilkinson, *The WTO: Crisis and the Governance of Global Trade* (London: Routledge, 2006).

36 Catherine Weaver, *The Hypocrisy Trap: The World Bank and the Poverty of Reform* (Princeton: Princeton University Press, 2008).

37 Kenneth W. Abbott and Duncan Snidal, "Why States Act through Formal International Organizations," *Journal of Conflict Resolution* 42, no. 1 (1998): 3–32. See also Darren Hawkins, David A. Lake, Daniel L. Nielson, and Michael J. Tierney, eds., *Delegation under Agency: States, International Organizations, and Principal–Agent Theory* (Cambridge: Cambridge University Press, 2006).

38 Thomas G. Weiss, *Global Governance: Why? What? Whither?* (Cambridge: Polity Press, 2013); Thomas G. Weiss and Ramesh Thakur, *Global Governance and the UN: An Unfinished Journey* (Bloomington: Indiana University Press, 2010); and Richard Jolly, Louis Emmerij, and Thomas G. Weiss, *UN Ideas That Changed the World* (Bloomington: Indiana University Press, 2009).

39 Susan Park and Antje Vetterlin, eds., *Owning Development: Creating Policy Norms in the IMF and World Bank* (Cambridge: Cambridge University Press, 2010).

40 Yoshikazu Sakamoto, ed., *Global Transformations: Challenges to the State System* (Tokyo: United Nations University Press, 1992); Keith Krause and W. Andy Knight, eds., *State, Society and the UN System: Changing Perspectives on Multilateralism* (Tokyo: United Nations University Press, 1995); Robert W. Cox, ed., *The New Realism: Perspectives on Multilateralism and World Order* (Basingstoke: Macmillan, 1997); Stephen Gill, ed., *Globalization, Democratization and Multilateralism* (London: Macmillan, 1997); Michael G. Schechter, ed., *Future Multilateralism: The Political and Social Framework* (London: Macmillan, 1999) and *Innovation in Multilateralism* (London: Macmillan, 1999).

41 James N. Rosenau and Ernst Czempiel, eds., *Governance without Government: Order and Change in World Politics* (Cambridge: Cambridge University Press, 1992); Commission on Global Governance, *Our Global Neighbourhood* (Oxford: Oxford University Press, 1995); and since 1995 the quarterly *Global Governance: A Review of Multilateralism and International Organizations*.

42 Lawrence Finkelstein, "What Is Global Governance," *Global Governance* 1, no. 3 (1995): 367–372.

43 James N. Rosenau, "Governance in the Twenty-First Century," in *The Global Governance Reader*, ed. Wilkinson, 45–67.

44 Jennifer Clapp and Eric Helleiner, "Troubled Futures? The Global Food Crisis and the Politics of Agricultural Derivatives Regulation," *Review of International Political Economy* 19, no. 1 (2012): 181–207.

45 Benedicte Bull, "The Global Elite, Public–Private Partnerships and Multilateral Governance," in *Global Governance, Poverty and Inequality*, eds. Jennifer Clapp and Rorden Wilkinson (London and New York: Routledge, 2010), 209–234.

46 Craig N. Murphy and JoAnne Yates, *The International Organization for Standardization (ISO): Global Governance through Voluntary Consensus* (London: Routledge, 2009).

47 John Mathiason, *Internet Governance: The New Frontier of Global Institutions* (London: Routledge, 2009).

48 Michael Moran, *Private Foundations and Development Partnerships: American Philanthropy and Global Development Agendas* (London and New York: Routledge 2013).

49 Timothy J. Sinclair, *The New Masters of Capital: American Bond Rating Agencies and the Politics of Creditworthiness* (Ithaca, NY: Cornell University Press, 2005).

50 Axel Marx et al., eds., *Private Standards and Global Governance: Economic, Legal and Political Perspectives* (Cheltenham, UK: Edward Elgar, 2012).

51 Danielle Zach, Conor Seyle, and Jens Vestergaard Madsen, *Glocalizing Governance: The Case of the Contact Group on Piracy off the Coast of Somalia* (Broomfield, CO: OneEarthFuture Foundation, 2013).

52 John Gerard Ruggie, *Constructing the World Polity* (London: Routledge, 1998), 2.

53 Thomas G. Weiss and Rorden Wilkinson, "Rethinking Global Governance? Complexity, Authority, Power and Change," *International Studies Quarterly* 58, no. 2 (2014): forthcoming.

PART II
CONTEXTUALIZING INTERNATIONAL ORGANIZATION AND GLOBAL GOVERNANCE

INTRODUCTION

How to use this book

In designing this book we wanted to bring together as many of the pieces of the global governance puzzle as we could. Our aim was not only to be as comprehensive as possible. We also sought to enable course leaders to design classes around the issues that they wanted to highlight while at the same time providing a one-stop resource for further reading and wider contextualization. So, classes emphasizing the security, economic, social, legal, or other aspects of international organization and global governance are able to cherry-pick chapters from each of the parts of this book while at the same time pointing students to other related and seemingly not so related topics for further investigation. Likewise, more introductory classes might be designed around the empirical aspects of international organization and global governance with a bit of theory added into the mix to help make sense of the material. More advanced classes will inevitably make greater use of the full range of contextualization and theory chapters as well as a broader slew of the empirical contributions.

To guide readers, we have included a handful of "Additional readings" at the end of each chapter, which enable readers to pursue themes developed in each of the chapters to be unpacked at great length in specialized publications. Inevitably we will have omitted aspects and areas of international organization and global governance that readers would have liked to see included. Should this book prove to be successful—which we hope it will—further editions would be a natural outcome; and so we are keen to get readers' feedback generally and more specifically about topics that we ought to consider for subsequent editions.

How to read the chapters in this part of the book

Students are often poorly serviced when it comes to the background of—or what might better be thought of as the "back stories" to—international organization and global governance. All too often accounts of the formation of particular international organizations are prefaced with potted accounts of the end of war and an aspiration to avert the possibility of a slide back into hostilities as the engine for a bout of institution building. Certainly there is merit in these interpretations. Often, however, they do not offer a sufficiently rounded account of the slow and incremental processes that lie behind the emergence of international organizations or of the dramatic accelerators of transformational moments in history.

Part of our willingness to consume easily digestible pieces of history as substitutes for more involved stories results from our natural eagerness to become familiar with a terrain of study as quickly as possible. Part of it results from the limitations of space that any publishing form determines. And part of it is because these stories are not straightforward and their content is often contested—the nuances of which potted introductions find it impossible to convey.

We do not claim to have a monopoly on the sufficiency of the background necessary to understand contemporary global governance or the role of international organizations therein. We have, however, tried to be as extensive in our coverage as our limitations of space allow. And we have done so by bringing together five chapters by some of the academy's leading lights.

We asked authors to write only on those areas in which they are expert, to build upon but also take forward their existing work, and to offer as fulsome an account as they could of one particular aspect of the formation of, and dynamics within, the way the world is currently organized. The chapters are organized so that this part of the book begins with an exploration of the evolution of global governance as a phenomenon before unpacking in further detail some of its constitutive aspects: law, power, authority, and agents. Thus, the chapters focus on driving impulses and "creeping" incremental developments that ushered forth a global institutional complex (Craig N. Murphy, Chapter 1); the evolution of an international legal apparatus as both a necessity for states—and other actors—to manage their relations with one another, as well as a vehicle pressing for change (Charlotte Ku, Chapter 2); the manner in which power is diffused and concentrated among international organizations as core components of contemporary global governance (Michael Barnett and Raymond Duvall, Chapter 3); the forces and tendencies that have led to a diffusion of authority across the globe and the challenges that this has brought (David Held, Chapter 4); and the identity of the governors in this complex, multilayered, multifaceted, and multi-actor system (Susan K. Sell, Chapter 5).

In Chapter 1, Murphy outlines the private, hidden, and seldom acknowledged origins of contemporary global governance beginning in the "inter-imperial world" (the term he uses for the nineteenth century, in which world organization was predicated on managing relations between the colonial powers), where technical standards helped spread industrial capitalism and soothe the tensions that its spread necessarily created. This is a world of "creeping" global governance wherein seemingly inconsequential agreements on such things as common chemical and electrical units paved the way for companies to exploit new markets and for ever greater numbers of new consumers to acquire goods that previously had been unavailable while simultaneously bringing them into an expanding market system. Alongside these technical developments went progressive social agendas driven forward by constellations of civil society actors, interstate conferences on human health, among others, and transnational associations dealing with working conditions and the plight of industrial labor. But he also shows how states were important components of this nascent system. This creeping global governance produced a step-change in world organization under US leadership after World War II, generating, among other things, the UN system; and it has helped create the kind of world economy that we currently have.

Murphy's chapter offers an insight into the incrementalism that lies behind the forms of organization and governance that we have today. Locking in the developments that this incrementalism generated in the form of transnational, international, and global legal frameworks is also a key part of the story. Ku picks up precisely this aspect of the story and explores the evolution of a complex and multifaceted international legal system in Chapter 2. She shows how, since the 1648 Treaty of Westphalia, a body of international agreements, norms and declarations, interstate concordats, and public and private arrangements have all combined to generate an international legal regime that, despite lacking the enforcement capabilities of a domestic legal regime, mediates state behavior, helping promote peace, human rights, and other progressive social agendas. Moreover, the way that international law has evolved has imbued it with a dynamism that enables it to respond to stakeholder needs and continue to, as she puts it, "address the wellbeing and safety of individuals, provide order for the collective political and economic interests of states, and facilitate increased levels of cross-border/transnational activity". Crucially, she shows how the kind of global governance that we had—the strictly interstate system of the post-Westphalian era—has generated forms of international law that have also fundamentally changed that system into the multivariate incarnation we have today.

In tandem, Murphy and Ku show how incremental developments in forms of regulation at multiple levels—movements in which international organizations have played key roles—have been major drivers in establishing today's complex system of global governance. In Chapter 3, Barnett and Duvall add power into this mix by exploring how international organizations can act simultaneously to reinforce existing—that is, status quo—power relations, as well as to diffuse power among a greater range of actors. They explore the means by which institutions enable power to be used and the way these bodies can act as progressive forces mediating the capacity of powerful states and elites. And they lay the ground for the exploration of existing theoretical approaches to IO and global governance discussed in Part III of this book by showing how power is understood by various schools of thought.

Held further develops the back stories to international organization and global governance in his chapter on the diffusion of authority (Chapter 4). His aim is to take in not just international organizations but also a range of transnational and other actors active in shaping the way the world is currently governed. Yet, for all of this diffusion and the positive elements it has brought—particularly in constraining the capacity of states to exercise power in illegitimate ways—his argument, much like Barnett and Duvall's, is that even in a complex multilayered, multi-sector, and multi-actor system of global governance, state sovereignty remains a stumbling block to the realization of many agendas, particularly on climate change.

In Chapter 5, the final one in this part, Sell asks that question that is so often missing from debates about the way the world is organized: who governs? Set against an account of the development of the IO and global governance literatures Sell illuminates those agents able to exercise power across borders, set agendas, influence policy, establish rules, implement programs, and evaluate and adjudicate outcomes. Importantly, she notes, despite the range of agents involved in the governance of world affairs, and the vast capabilities of some, none is able to govern alone. Moreover, the means by which representation, accountability, and legitimacy are attained are far from straightforward.

Where to now?

Each of these chapters is essential reading, helping us get a better grip on the origins of, key aspects within, and principal questions pertaining to contemporary IO and global governance. For extensive investigations into the shape of the current global order, none is dispensable. For time-pressured introductions on IO alone, Ku, and Barnett and Duvall are a must. More wide-ranging classes on global governance should begin with Murphy and take in at least Held and Sell also. Once these have been read, readers should turn to explore the main theoretical traditions in the field that are surveyed in Part III.

The Emergence of Global Governance

Craig N. Murphy

Most things exist long before they are named. So it is with global governance. A century ago, before World War I, the globe was already governed by a thin network of public and private international organizations linking the industrial core countries of the mainly European empires that had so recently succeeded in conquering and divvying up the entire world. The organizations served a small but crucial part of the new imperial economies: their fundamentally new industries—electrical power, pharmaceuticals, and various new consumer products—were the economic engines of the Second Industrial Revolution.

This particular moment in the globalization of industrial capitalism ended with the Great War, the inter-war Depression, and the war's more horrible successor. Yet even throughout that dark 30-year period, activists and statesmen tried to form new international institutions that could rebuild the pre-war global economy on a more secure, more peaceful foundation. The League of Nations failed, but its experiment with enlarging international peace was more successfully replicated in the United Nations (UN), the center of a new global system of public and private organizations that also helped foster a second age of rapid economic transformation—the Automobile and Jet Age of economic growth from the 1940s into the 1970s.

By the mid-1990s, this mid-twentieth century world economy was changing once again, in part because China and the former socialist bloc countries were clamoring for deeper integration into the dominant international economy and in part because this dominant and Western-centered economy had been stagnant for 20 years even while it was being transformed by revolutions in global communications, transportation, and trade—transformations that mid-twentieth century international institutions had fostered, but were unable to control. It was in this context of a global manufacturing economy emerging outside the confines of existing international regulations that the phrase "global governance" was first heard. The phrase referred to something that existed, yet something that needed to be reformed, something that demanded as much creative attention of the world's leaders as their predecessors had devoted to the inter-imperial institutions that they built in the 1880s and 1890s, and to the UN system in the 1940s.

The unsolved problems of global governance that existed when the term was first used are still with us. They define a large part of the field that this volume addresses. A related second large part of the field is connected to what global governance has done so successfully: fostering the internationalization (now, the globalization) of industrial capitalism. This chapter describes the nineteenth century origins of global governance and the later rise of the UN system. It then outlines the more recent crises that led to the development of the term "global governance," identifies the most fruitful ways the term has been used by activists and scholars, and concludes with some questions to keep in mind when studying and reflecting on global governance.

Global governance before the Great War

Looking back to the world before World War I at the time of the Wall Street crash, a young American economist, Robert Brady, wrote about the consequences of the late nineteenth century expansion of Japan, the United States, and at least eight European powers:

> All of these are, of course, matters of common knowledge to any schoolboy. But their significance lies in this—for the first time in many centuries, the known world was politically organized into definite imperial states whose political, military, and naval power depended directly upon their respective industrial resources. The greatest market areas in human history were open for exploitation. Science, invention, and the machine process had made mineral and chemical resources the key to power and placed the wellbeing of the peoples within national[/imperial] borders. In other words, the world was organized on the basis of mass markets, mass production, and mass distribution. In the task of exploiting the resources of national and dependent territories, of refining, transporting, fabricating, and distributing products, machine technology played a dominant role.[1]

The part of the world where the machines were made, where most of the machines lay, and where the overwhelming bulk of the trade in industrial goods took place was held together by the strong but thin threads of international institutions: the score or so public international unions and the hundreds of international nongovernmental organizations created in the last third of the nineteenth century.

The public international unions linked together the communication and transportation systems of separate empires (the International Telegraph Union was established in 1865 and the International Railway Congress Association in 1885). They established necessary industrial standards and inter-imperial rules governing intellectual property (the

International Bureau of Weights and Measure was established in 1875 and the International Bureau for the Protection of Intellectual Property in 1893). They also administered aspects of the inter-imperial monetary system and helped maintain rules of trade (the Latin Monetary Union was established in 1865 and the Brussels Tariff Union in 1890). Of course, the Bank of England and the British government (the putative nineteenth century hegemonic power) played central roles in these aspects of early global governance, too.

In addition, a few international organizations supported large groups within the industrial core of the inter-imperial world that were likely to be harmed by the growing trade in industrial products fostered by the other public international unions. The International Association for Labour Legislation, established in 1889, attempted to end the race to the bottom in wages and labor standards that had begun when low-wage newly industrialized countries entered the inter-imperial trading system, a system of relatively free trade in industrial goods. Today it may seem ironic that the major concern was the relative poverty of workers in places like Norway and Sweden. The International Institute of Agriculture was established in 1905 and aimed to redress the information imbalance between, on the one hand, shippers and agricultural cartels, who had a great deal of knowledge about both agricultural supply and demand, and, on the other hand, small European and American farmers, who had little knowledge of either.

The Labour Association, which began as a cooperative project of labor unions and concerned citizens, is typical of global governance in the inter-imperial world: some of it was done by private international nongovernmental organizations (NGOs). This was especially true when it came to creating essential measurement and interoperability standards for the new industries of the Second Industrial Revolution. Late nineteenth century international conferences of scientists and engineers reached agreement on common chemical and electrical units and measurement systems. Electrical engineers established their major industrial standard setting body, the International Electrotechnical Commission, in 1906. Chemists and chemical engineers created the predecessor of today's International Union of Pure and Applied Chemistry in 1911, institutionalizing a chemical standards regime that they had established in 1892.

NGOs and the international social movements that they helped institutionalize played an additional important role by broadly championing the internationalization of the economy that the public international unions would secure. The Free Trade Movement (which included working class consumers and homemakers throughout the industrialized world as well as the more often remembered manufacturers who benefited from lower tariffs) gave many governments the political will to extend the most-favored nation trading system that was pioneered by Britain and France in 1860. The Red Cross Movement, the International Labor Movement, International Law Movement, and Peace Movement all worked for progressive social measures that directly helped secure the newly internationalized economic order.

They and other international social movement organizations also helped secure the new economy indirectly by promoting "internationalism" in general. In case after case, international NGOs used the political space created by the unions to argue that it was only right for similar forms of international cooperation to be tried in the various social fields, as well.

The UN era

Eminent global historian Akira Iriye writes about how the pre-war experience of the international NGOs began to shape the world that the US government tried to create first through the League of Nations and then through the UN:

> In a book published during the [first] war, Mary Follett, an American political scientist, wrote that "association is the impulse, the core of our being," and since "the creative characteristic of war is doing things together," it was imperative to "begin to do things together in peace" through the efforts of people united not by herd instinct but by group conviction.

Iriye argues that Follett

> may well have had in mind the American Friends Service Committee and other organizations established during the war when she noted, ". . . the modern hero goes out to disarm his enemy through creating a mutual understanding." The American Century was beginning to be defined ... through the spread of NGOs, both domestic and international.[2]

In 1933, Robert Brady wrote that the new associations—whether made up of engineers, workers, or social reformers—all looked forward to a world economy of the greatest possible engineering efficiency: the production of the greatest number of useful goods with the least waste of resources and labor. Such an economy required regulation, *global* regulation, because "*national* regulation is largely, and in some cases, completely ineffective in the modern world."[3]

Yet, ironically, Brady argued, the desire to achieve the greatest possible engineering efficiencies initially only gained ground as part of a struggle to create ever more efficient *national* economies, a struggle initiated by the shortsightedness of the Treaty of Versailles:

> The reparation debts to be paid by Germany to the Allies . . . called for an export value surplus, which Germany could achieve only by underselling its commercial rivals—Britain, France, Italy, and the United States. These countries, the future recipients of the reparations, in order to protect their own disorganized industries and markets, imposed tariff barriers against the flood of cheap German goods. Needless to say, this action necessitated still cheaper production in Germany in order that its goods might climb over the tariff walls. . . . Meanwhile, international competition took the form of concerted national movements to regain markets formerly held and to keep present markets by producing cheaply at home—and, under large-scale industry, that means by realizing the economies of mass production by rigid standardization and simplification. . . . The rapid

> growth of trade associations and industrial mergers in this country [the United States] and the renewal of the cartel movement in Europe, made possible standardization and simplification throughout entire industries.[4]

Long before European butchery resumed in 1939, mixed economies of capitalist enterprises regulated by private associations and the state to achieve engineering efficiencies existed throughout the industrialized world, except in the Soviet Union, where the state attempted to follow a more thoroughgoing form of planning directed toward the same end.

As World War I wound down, the Roosevelt administration remained committed to creating the foundation of world peace on which a *global* system of regulation could ensure the prosperity that could come from production of the greatest number of useful goods with the least waste of resources and labor. The administration's chosen instrument for achieving this end was the wartime alliance, which Roosevelt had named "the United Nations." The allies reconfigured the world organization into the peace-maintaining instrument of the Security Council supplemented by a universal membership General Assembly, which was given light oversight over the central administration (the Secretariat), and a smaller Economic and Social Council with similarly light oversight over a system of relatively autonomous UN specialized agencies, most of which were direct descendants of the public international unions. A few new ones—the International Civil Aviation Organization (ICAO), the International Monetary Fund (IMF), the World Bank, and a stillborn trade agency (the International Trade Organization) that generated the General Agreement on Tariffs and Trade (GATT)—were designed to play critical roles in the new post-war world economy.

The Security Council was a substantial innovation in global governance. Recent research, however, suggests that the UN system has contributed more through peacemaking between adversaries (especially before they engage in all-out war) through peacekeeping and through peacebuilding via the work of the UN development system. Joshua Goldstein's book that documents this impact, *Winning the War on War*, also points to the post-war role of the international peace movement and of its close allies in international peace research. Above the title on the cover of the book's paperback edition, celebrated psychologist Steven Pinker writes, "The greatest untold story of the last two decades."[5] It certainly is, although the story really begins in 1946 when the post-war UN first opened shop.

Beyond contributing to this foundation of peace, the UN system has played roles similar to those that the public international unions played before World War I: supporting the communication and transportation infrastructures that link the world economy, maintaining global rules governing intellectual property, working with the complex system of standard-setting bodies united under ISO (the International Organization for Standardization, established in 1946) to maintain necessary industrial standards and to establish them in the new industries of the post-war Automobile Age and Jet Age, working with key national governments and private international associations to support and regulate the global monetary and financial system, and maintaining the rules for international trade.

When it came to supporting groups that could have been harmed by a growing international industrial economy, the post-war global governance system included fundamentally new activities and practices. Labor was in part protected by standards established by the International Labour Organization (ILO, the successor to the nineteenth century International Association of Labour Legislation), but the more important protections for workers and farmers through the non-communist industrialized world came from formal and informal agreements among Western powers to protect their growing welfare states and the domestic class compromises on which they were based. As the levelheaded international political economist and sometime senior UN official John G. Ruggie has long argued, the post-war international economic order involved the embedding of a system of increasingly free trade in industrialized goods within a larger set of social norms. The GATT actually protected Western and Japanese farmers *from* international *laissez faire* by keeping their products off the negotiating table and by facilitating a host of other domestic social policies throughout the industrialized world.[6]

The other great innovation came in the way the UN system treated the less industrialized peripheries of the pre-war empires, the peoples of what was first known as the "Third World" and now the "global South." People there, just like farmers in the industrialized world, had reason to fear a more deeply integrated but unregulated global capitalist economy. The post-war system did not give the global South the prosperity of the growing industrial economies of the global North or the protections offered to farmers and industrial workers there, far from it. The GATT provided no exception (implicit or explicit) for the agricultural products of the global South and parts of the UN system (especially the IMF and the World Bank) were always ready to oppose new welfare policies in Africa, Asia, Latin America, or the Caribbean. Nevertheless, the UN system *did* provide significant support for decolonization and for a limited form of economic development: something short of catch-up with the industrialized world.

Support for decolonization began as early as 1946 and increased as the former colonial majority of the UN grew. From its beginning the world organization provided technical assistance and humanitarian support that has strengthened state institutions in every part of the developing world. In fact, since the 1970s, the vast majority of the UN system's staff and resources have been devoted to its country offices throughout the developing world; from the point of view of staff time and expenditures, the "UN system" and the "UN development system" are largely coterminous, and both are quite different from the image of the UN that we get by observing the goings on in the multilateral talking shops in New York and Geneva.[7]

Of course, the system's role as an interlocking set of talking shops matters a great deal, and, just as in pre-war public international unions, some of the most important talking has always been done by NGOs, especially social movement organizations pushing for global attention to social and environmental issues. The relatively constant post-war expansion of international human rights law and of the UN system's human rights activities reflects the long-standing process of NGOs using the political space created by organizations that promote the internationalization of the economy to demand international cooperation in other fields as well.

The UN's environmental work differs only slightly. The global environmental harms that have been the focus of the UN's environmental conferences, the UN Environment

Programme, and the environmental assistance provided by the UNDP and the World Bank are all consequences of the type of economy that global governance always fostered.

Late twentieth century crises and "global governance"

The environmental agenda became a permanent part of the UN's work with the 1972 Stockholm Conference on the Human Environment, where governments affirmed 26 principles. Over half were concerned with adding support for national environmental problems to the agenda of the UN development system. Six referred to the degradation of parts of the global commons. Included were specific references to biological diversity ("wildlife" in the outdated and imprecise terms of the day) and the oceans. The remaining items included a "polluter pays" principle and support for more environmental education and research to be undertaken by international organizations.[8] In keeping with this declaration, the main result of the Conference was a UN system committed to aiding developing countries with *all* their environmental problems, and to studying and proposing ways to deal with those *few* environmental problems of a truly global nature. Those problems, especially the consequences of pollution of the atmosphere, along with species depletion and pollution of the oceans, became the first of four long-term crises of international governance.

The second crisis emerged at almost the same time. With their proposals for a New International Economic Order (NIEO), governments of developing countries began demanding that global economic governance be reformed to ensure that their countries actually caught up with the industrialized world. Some governments hoped to achieve this through a kind of general strike of raw materials producers. When Arab oil producers successfully carried out a producers' strike against the United States and some Western European countries as part of Arab strategy in the 1973 war against Israel, many in the North saw that action and the subsequent worldwide recession as causing the end of the long period of post-war growth. While that conclusion may be unfounded, the crisis in North–South relations certainly has continued throughout the decades of relatively slow growth in Western economies that started in the 1970s.

At the beginning of that era, first Great Britain, then the United States, and then many other Western countries turned away from welfare-oriented policies based on constant increases in productivity (ever greater engineering efficiency), to *laissez faire*-oriented policies of limited government and reliance on the market to lower the prices of labor and raw materials. To use the words of Thorstein Veblen, the economist who had inspired the young Robert Brady, governments and business elites stopped relying on the efficiencies provided by "the engineers" to ensure prosperity; they turned instead to "the price system"—in the same way that Veblen described their predecessors as having done after World War I,[9] and with similar results. The fact that the economic policies of the 1980s onward led to greater income inequality and income stagnation for most wage earners in the industrialized world created the third long crisis. Income inequality across countries also increased as lenders (especially the IMF and World Bank) imposed the new Western economic orthodoxy on much of the developing world.

Many early analyses of this economic shift overlooked the degree to which a further internationalization of industrial capitalism underlay the observed crisis—a further internationalization supported by revolutions in communication, transportation, and industrial standards that had been fostered by global governance in the UN era. The latest communication revolution began with the fantastic increase in available bandwidth for intercontinental messages provided by early communication satellites. In the first year that we had such a satellite, 1962, it carried about 400 such messages. Today, every person who reads this book probably uses more intercontinental bandwidth every week; think only of the sources of the internet pages that people typically access, and how frequently they do so. A major source of all that bandwidth is the satellites maintained by Intelsat, a hybrid organization whose original members included both governments and private companies. Similarly, consider the clothes people today typically wear and the objects they have around them; most of these things travel great distances before they get to the people who use them, something that would not have been possible 40 years ago. This is a consequence of the global manufacturing economy, a precondition for which was the tremendous reduction in intercontinental shipping costs that came with containerized shipping, which only took off after the ISO established a shipping container standard in 1968.[10] Of course, a second key element in the making of the contemporary world was China's initially cautious entry into the global economy beginning in 1978, something facilitated by UN technical assistance.[11]

With the fall of the socialist bloc regimes of Eastern Europe a decade later, the UN system faced a fourth crisis: the massive increase in demands for peacemaking and peacekeeping services in conflicts that became resolvable because the sides were no longer supported by competing superpowers (as in Central America and Southern Africa) and those that flared up because the control imposed by the Cold War balance of forces was lifted (as in the Caucasus and the former Yugoslavia).

The end of the Cold War also provided new opportunities for global governance. The promoters of the more integrated global manufacturing economy—especially major companies and the US government—used the opening provided by the evaporation of the major alternative to global capitalism to promote stronger rules for liberalizing international trade and investment (through the World Trade Organization, WTO, and the Agreement on Trade Related Investment Measures, TRIMs) and for increasing the power of owners of patents and copyright (through the Agreement on Trade Related Aspects of Intellectual Property, TRIPs). Of course, the critics of a more powerful, less regulated global capitalism saw in these developments a deepening of the third crisis, the turn away from welfare-oriented economic policies to a kind of liberal fundamentalism that increased inequality. In Ruggie's terms, by the early 1990s, the challenge of embedding global markets in a system of larger social norms became much greater than ever before.

It was in the context of these four crises that an independent commission supported by the UN secretary-general and chaired by Swedish Prime Minister Ingvar Carlsson and former Commonwealth Secretary-General Shridath Ramphal coined the current usage of the term "global governance." The 1995 report of the self-named "Global Governance Commission" proposed reforms in international institutions and some national policies to: address global environmental problems; respond to the demands of developing countries for a more equitable and less hypocritical global economic order; restart a global industrial economy focused on real increases in productivity and strong commitments to sharing the benefits of growth; and strengthen the UN system to deal with all the new demands for its peacekeeping and humanitarian services.[12] In the same year, the Academic Council on the UN System launched a new journal called *Global Governance: A Review of Multilateralism and International Organizations.* In 1999, the fifth year that the phrase was used, Google Scholar reports that there were over 1,000 articles and books published that used it. Twelve years later, there were about ten times that number, about the same number that used "international security," and more than twice the number that refer to "international political economy." The use of "global governance" continues to grow faster than that of either of these other terms.

What the phrase denotes

Obviously, scholars have found "global governance" to be a useful term, but perhaps activists have found it even more useful. If Google Scholar gives us about 10,000 new citations to "global governance" in the last year, Google *per se* gives us 200,000, most of them from advocacy organizations or individuals who want to change some aspect of the way the world is governed. The term is used in a multitude of different, if related, ways across these many thousands of sources. It may be helpful to close this opening chapter to the subject by suggesting that the most fruitful use of the term has been contributing to our understanding of how the world works and what we might do to change that.

In that context, any definition that pulls us toward treating global governance as "all kinds of governance, everywhere" should probably be avoided because such definitions (and they do exist) give us little opportunity to say anything that we could not say just by referring to "governance." "*Global* governance" more reasonably refers to a kind of governance—or at least, to attempts to establish governance—at a particular level.

Miles Kahler has observed that some of the most useful literature on global governance seems to embed within it a preference for "subsidiarity," an idea that collective problems are best solved at the lowest level at which they can be solved. Therefore, the best form of global governance would be limited to collective problems that could not be solved by organizations at any lower level, for example by national governments (individually or in coalition) or by international professional associations and the like.[13] This is a view that Kishore Mahbubani, a founder of one of the first public policy graduate programs that focuses on global governance, expressed when he wrote:

> Mao Zedong was right. We should always focus on the primary, not secondary, contradictions. And right now, our primary global contradiction is painfully obvious: the biggest challenges of governance are global in origin, but all the politics that respond to them are local. There are many wise leaders around the world, but there is not enough global leadership.[14]

Arguably, we can still point to some successful forms of governance at the global level; consider the decreasing frequency and violence of war that Goldstein attributes to the governance provided by the UN and the peace and peace research movements.

Yet, even if we embrace the desirability of subsidiarity, we need to recognize that organizations or coalitions often try to exercise governance at a global level, even if it is unwarranted. The wonderfully contrarian Andrew M. Scott was deeply convinced that all the attempts to increase the world's many channels of communication, lower the costs of travel and transportation, and otherwise facilitate trade and interaction did more harm than good. From Scott's point of view, ICAO, ISO, the WTO, TRIPs, and TRIMs are all global governance, but it is governance that *creates* global problems rather than solves them.[15]

It may be worthwhile remaining agnostic about that point, but there is less reason to be agnostic about Scott's (or Mahbubani's) conclusion that industrial capitalism and the economic globalization fostered by the standards and controls exercised by the governments and organizations promoting an unregulated liberal world economy create global problems that are dealt with by relatively ineffective structures of global governance. The late Susan Strange, one of the founders of the field of International Political Economy and someone suspicious of the notion of global governance, in her last article, "The Westfailure System," pointed to three global problems of this sort, problems about which both Mahbubani and Scott would agree: the limited number of truly global environmental problems created by two centuries of industrial economies in a world in which no one has effective responsibility for maintaining the various global commons; the regular recurrence of international financial crises created by the vested interest of most of the relevant actors in maintaining geographic spaces in which the main rules do not apply; and persistent and sometimes growing inequalities across classes and regions, a problem of capitalism at all levels, but one that becomes increasingly global as economies become more integrated.[16]

Strange relates these three core global problems to another small set of problems that some analysts might want to consider separately: pandemics such as HIV/AIDS (which during Strange's lifetime was the subject of global governance as ineffective as that directed toward climate change), global organized crime and the particular fields in which it tends to operate—drugs, human trafficking, and the arms trade—and the connected problem of internationalized terrorism (made possible by unregulated global finance and the arms trade). Scholars and policy-makers might want to add to this list. For example, in thinking about the sources of the power of global organized crime, the persistence of the unregulated arms trade, and problems created by dictators and warlords, we need to add a global tendency to overvalue the military. Nevertheless, the number of such issues will still be small.

Even when we add all the fields in which there is some kind of global governance that is not needed—such as in encouraging economic globalization, according to people like Andrew Scott—the entire field of "global governance" is not a large one, even if it is one of great significance.

Conclusion

If the approach to global governance suggested here is appealing, it would be worthwhile to ask of anything written on the subject, including each of the chapters in this volume: "Is this a field in which there should be global governance? Is it a field in which problems exist at a global level that cannot be solved at any other level? If not, and if some kind of system of global governance does exist or is being attempted, then why is that the case? Who is being served by this unnecessary global governance, how and why has this happened, and is there anything that can be done about it?" If it is a field in which there should be effective global governance, but none exists, ask, "Why not? Who is being served by this lack of governance, why and how has this happened, and is there anything that can be done about it?"

After all, whether or not global governance, in itself, exists (as this chapter argues that it has for more than a century), the concept of "global governance" exists. And it does so for a particular purpose: to help us think critically about problems that humanity (and even the whole planet) shares that cannot be solved by individuals, families, private organizations, states, or traditional international relations alone.

Additional reading

1. Craig N. Murphy, *International Organization and Industrial Change: Global Governance since 1850* (Cambridge: Polity Press, 1994).
2. Michael Barnett and Raymond Duvall, eds., *Power in Global Governance* (Cambridge: Cambridge University Press, 2005).
3. Jennifer Clapp and Rorden Wilkinson, eds., *Global Governance, Poverty, and Inequality* (Abingdon: Routledge, 2010).
4. Mark Malloch Brown, *The Unfinished Global Revolution: The Pursuit of a New International Politics* (New York: Penguin, 2011).
5. Thomas G. Weiss and Ramesh Thakur, *Global Governance and the United Nations: An Unfinished Journey* (Bloomington: Indiana University Press, 2010).

Notes

1 Robert A. Brady, *Industrial Standardization* (New York: National Industrial Conference Board, 1929), 8.
2 Akira Iriye, "A Century of NGOs," *Diplomatic History* 23, no. 3 (1999): 425–426, quoting Mary Parker Follett, *The New State: Group Organization the Solution of Popular Government* (New York: Longmans, Green), 193–195.
3 Robert A. Brady, *The Rationalization Movement in German Industry: A Study in the Evolution of Economic Planning* (Berkeley: University of California Press, 1933), 395.
4 Brady, *Industrial Standardization*, 14.
5 Steven Pinker, quoted on the cover of Joshua S. Goldstein, *Winning the War on War: The Decline of Armed Conflict Worldwide* (New York: Plume [Penguin], 2012).
6 One of the best assessments of the continuing value of Ruggie's analysis is Andrew T. F. Lang, "Reconstructing Embedded Liberalism: John Gerard Ruggie and Constructivist Approaches to the Study of International Trade," in *Embedding Global Markets: An Enduring Challenge*, ed. John Gerard Ruggie (Aldershot: Ashgate, 2008), 13–45.
7 Two recent empirical studies of these roles are Craig N. Murphy, *The UN Development Programme: A Better Way?* (Cambridge: Cambridge University Press, 2006) and Stephen Browne, *UN Development Programme and System* (Abingdon: Routledge, 2011). Murphy's "Foreword" to Browne's book, xix–xx, provides the data for the assertion about UN system staff and expenditures.

8 "Declaration of the United Nations Conference on the Human Environment," 15 June 1972, http://www.unep.org/Documents.Multilingual/Default.asp?documentid=97&articleid=1503.

9 Thorstein Veblen, *The Engineers and the Price System* (New York: B. W. Huebsch, Inc., 1921).

10 A clear introduction to Intelsat's organizational history and impact is Patricia McCormick, "The Privatization of Intelsat: The Transition of an Intergovernmental Organization to Private Equity Ownership," in *Telecommunications Research Trends*, eds. Hans F. Erlich and Ernst P. Lehrmann (New York: Nova Science Publishers, 2008), 45–74. On containerized shipping, see Marc Levinson, *The Box: How the Shipping Container Made the World Smaller and the World Economy Bigger* (Princeton: Princeton University Press, 2006).

11 Murphy, *The UN Development Programme*, 177–181.

12 Commission on Global Governance, *Our Global Neighborhood* (New York: Oxford University Press, 1995).

13 Miles Kahler, "Global Governance Redefined," in *Challenges of Globalization: Immigration, Social Welfare, Global Governance*, ed. A. C. Sobel (Abingdon: Routledge, 2009), 174–198.

14 Kishore Mahbubani, "The Problem with Presidents," *Newsweek*, 30 August 2010, http://www.thedailybeast.com/newsweek/2010/08/16/mahbubani-the-problem-with-presidents.html.

15 Andrew M. Scott, *The Dynamics of Interdependence* (Chapel Hill: University of North Carolina Press, 1982).

16 Susan Strange, "The Westfailure System," *Review of International Studies* 25, no. 3 (1999): 345–354.

CHAPTER 2

The Evolution of International Law

Charlotte Ku

The international legal system comprises norms, processes, and institutions.[1] The interaction of these elements creates international law's authority, legitimacy, and effectiveness. International law is therefore implemented and given effect less through the threat of sanctions than through the cumulative actions of the system's stakeholders. This self-enforcing characteristic is often regarded as a weakness or flaw in international law as a legal system but in fact it provides international law the opportunity to grow and to develop as it responds to stakeholder needs and desires. The cumulative effect of this process produced revolutionary developments that today address the wellbeing and safety of individuals, provide order for the collective political and economic interests of states, and facilitate increased levels of cross-border/transnational activity. And the process continues. International law now covers environmental protection, family relations, and criminal activities that were little covered or even recognized as subject to international law only decades ago. International law now has a robust operating platform to facilitate the development, implementation, and assessment of international norms. Nevertheless, international law faces the same challenges that all institutions confront in moving toward global governance, including multiple sources of authority, complex interrelated and multi-jurisdictional issues, and short time horizons.

As an institution and factor in international relations, international law predated both international organizations and global governance. As this chapter shows, it has nevertheless played a crucial role in the development of both by facilitating their creation and by drawing on their capacities to meet its own objectives of recognizing individual human dignity and responsibility, of elaborating the scope of state responsibility, and of finding effective pathways to give life to international obligations. Having met these needs, however, international law now struggles in a global political environment where its hold on regulating international behavior and its coherence as a legal system are challenged. International law has not yet conceived or operationalized a framework that effectively harnesses sub-national activities and players. As a result, it has under-recognized and under-used the resulting nuances and opportunities in the implementation of international obligations. International organizations and other institutions or processes of global governance will therefore play increasingly central roles in international law's further development as they provide the venues and tools to assess whether local or private actions meet the object and purpose of international obligations. At the same time, global governance will provide the necessary normative and political input to keep international law dynamic and relevant. The chapter examines this relationship and its implications for the future.

The status of international law today

The process of development, implementation, and evaluation of international law occurs over large numbers of transactions in numerous locations and settings. The volume of activity is impressive, with one study accounting for 82,000 publicized international agreements and as many as 100,000 additional interstate agreements negotiated since the beginning of diplomatic history.[2] These agreements are supplemented by numerous other "atypical" instruments that include multilateral frameworks and general declaratory instruments in treaty form; soft law in non-treaty form, like codes of conduct, guidelines, and statements of principles; memoranda of understanding and other informal implementation instruments; political accords; the implementation activities of nongovernmental organizations; United Nations General Assembly resolutions of a law-making quality; United Nations Security Council resolutions; resolutions of other international organizations with law-making capacity; and declarations of intergovernmental conferences.[3] To this list, we might now add private standards and principles and practices agreed upon by states, international organizations, nongovernmental organizations, and other non-state actors like corporations. To be sure, not all international agreements or actions are of equal importance—for example the significance of the United Nations Charter as compared to the International Convention for the Unification of Methods of Sampling and Analysing Cheeses—or involve the same number of states or parties.[4] The overall volume of activity generated by these treaty and non-treaty forms of international cooperation is nevertheless significant and has contributed to developing the capacity of international law to function.

Law-making is a competitive process in which conflicting values or approaches vie for adoption as a prevailing norm. The competition can be played out in actual state practice that may give rise to customary practice or in negotiations that produce a treaty or some other forms of international agreement. In the case of custom, the formation of a new rule of customary international law requires that "State practice, including that of States whose interests are directly affected, should have been both extensive and virtually uniform . . . and should moreover have occurred in such a way as to show a general recognition that a rule of law or legal obligation is involved."[5] The same criteria apply to any exception to general practice that is claimed. See, for example, the Fisheries Case (United Kingdom v. Norway, 1951), where the International Court of Justice ruled

> that the method of straight baselines [as differing from the general practice of following the contours and indentations of the coastline], established in the Norwegian system, was imposed by the peculiar geography of the Norwegian coast; that even before the dispute arose, this method had been consolidated by a constant and sufficiently long practice, in the face of which the attitude of governments bears witness to the fact that they did not consider it to be contrary to international law.[6]

The opportunity to express consent and to see the obligations incurred by parties is key to the importance of international agreements. Contemporary practice, however, shows that it is less the form of an agreement than the implementation of an obligation and the ability to assess its effect on international behavior that is significant. The 1975 Helsinki Final Act of the Conference on Security and Cooperation in Europe, for example, was a political statement rather than a legal instrument. Nevertheless, the system of follow-up conferences generated by this Act gave effect to international human rights standards and provided the opportunity for political activism and networking by nongovernmental organizations within the Warsaw Pact countries that contributed to the collapse of the Soviet Union and an end to the Cold War.[7] Close attention must therefore now be given to the institutional frameworks—international and domestic, public and private—available to parties to carry out international obligations as well as their capacity to do so. As Rosalyn Higgins describes it, "international law is a continuing process of authoritative decisions."[8] Given this, where and when authoritative decisions can be made and who can make them is important.

Authoritative decision-making

A key milestone in the development of international law is 1648 when the Peace of Westphalia concluded the Thirty Years War. Although the war itself was of greatest immediate significance for Europe, the Peace of Westphalia's global order legacy was even more far-reaching: it provided the foundation for authoritative decision-making in modern international law. It did so by confirming an international order based on a multiplicity of states with responsibilities to each other and to the people and resources they govern. In the more than 350 years since the conclusion of the Peace of Westphalia, both the breadth and depth of those responsibilities and the modes of discharging them have undergone substantial change. Although states remain sovereign within their territories, they have also come to accept levels of scrutiny and intrusion that would have been unthinkable only a few decades ago.[9] More significantly, the legitimacy of domestic actions like decisions to use military force is now increasingly judged based on consistency with international standards, practices, and policies.[10]

Authority today, whether international or domestic, public or private, is no longer a given, but must be earned with an increased emphasis on performance as a basis for legitimacy. Individuals are more vocal about what they like or dislike about governments or other institutions, and they use technology to connect with like-minded individuals to create networks to pursue their agendas.[11] Facilitating the creation of appropriate channels for ongoing validation and assessment of authoritative actions is therefore an important characteristic and function of international law today. As the Westphalian state form was a response to the domestic and political needs of seventeenth century Europe that required a distinct locus of authority, by the late twentieth century states began to respond to complex cross-border issues that involved a range of emerging authorities and governing capacities.[12] State authority remains vital today, but flexibility and agility are now also the hallmarks of statehood operating within a complex govern-ance environment of international organizations and private entities, and multiple authorities are now routinely involved, even within one government, to pursue a policy.

Within each government agency there are multiple levels of clearance and coordin-ation. In the US Department of State alone, for example, an agreement like the Montreal Protocol on Substances that Deplete the Ozone Layer (adopted 1987) had to be cleared by multiple offices, including the regional bureaus, the office handling environmental issues, that handling international organizations, the Legal Adviser's office, and the legislative liaison office to Congress, among others. Where compliance with inter-national obligations requires changes in the laws of the constituent states of the United States or any country with a federal system, the "interagency minuet" is replicated at each level.[13]

What we have seen in the centuries since the 1648 Peace of Westphalia, and particularly for the past 100 years, is a state governance framework—including inter-national law—responding to the adaptations and adjustments made by states to fulfill their new responsibilities to people in their jurisdictions, stewardship of their territory and resources, and multilateral coordination and cooperation. The state may no longer be the only broker of power and interests, but it remains the most widely accepted actor that, since the seventeenth century, has already proven its own capacity to adapt to the changing needs of domestic and international governance. One manifestation of this adaptability is the establishment of international organizations to enhance the capacity of the state to provide for the wellbeing of its citizens and global economic development. The state originally emerged as a dominant governing form following a competitive exercise, war. The state form triumphed because it best served the organizing needs of the time, and it provided the financial and political resources to field the armies needed to protect and to advance elites' interests. Once they were established, state leaders undertook to mutually empower other entities that most closely resembled their own, thereby squeezing out alternative forms of governance over time. International law was used to express and to validate the characteristics of the state—capacity to control people and territory and to carry out international obligations.

In contemporary terms, mutual empowerment of the state took place in the 1950s and 1960s with the increasing intensity of calls for an end to colonialism that came from the concerted efforts of newly independent states. On attaining their own membership of the United Nations, these states worked assiduously through the General Assembly to maintain a focus on the issue of independence, to pressure states into decolonization, and ultimately to vilify and to shun states that failed to conform. The colonial empire chapter of world history came to a dramatic end with the actions taken by the United Nations against South Africa to advance both the causes of human rights and decol-onization. The UN's end of South African control over South West Africa (originally a mandate of the League of Nations) ultimately led to the independence of Namibia in

1988, the ending of apartheid in South Africa, and the election of Nelson Mandela as president of South Africa in 1994.

That a forum like the UN was available to new states to set and pursue this agenda of decolonization shows how the existence of a structure created by states under classical Westphalian international law facilitated the pursuit of a new agenda and substantive norms. International organizations originally were created to help states meet their own objectives, but IOs developed independent capacities of their own—including secretariats and other derivative organizations or emanations. Each such step introduces a new dynamic and potentially a new actor to the international system that can provide new capacity, but may also complicate international relations. Each step may also produce new norms, such as self-government which developed from the independence movements of the 1960s.

That the privilege of self-government came with responsibilities like the responsibility to protect (R2P) populations from mass violence and brutality shows that the development of norms and institutions does not stand still. Once adopted, new norms and practices become part of international law and international relations. And the modes used to achieve this level of acceptance are also strengthened and made available for use on other issues. Working in the UN General Assembly to advance a particular agenda, for example, would be one such pathway. The practice of using the infrastructure, staff, and know-how of international organizations to facilitate treaty-making, and the number of multilateral treaties that have now been concluded under the auspices of IOs, have provided IOs with a stature and possibly even authority that states did not foresee at their founding. Jonathan Charney notes that "[international organizations] contribute to the coordination and facilitation of contemporary international relations on the basis of legal principles."[14] They do so by providing an established venue in which to take decisions that may have legal effect. In so doing, they supplement the traditional modes of international law-making, state practice, and ad hoc bilateral and multilateral negotiations and treaty-making, and provide the secondary rules of recognition that international law is said to lack.[15] The product of these interactions is something Charney dubs "universal" international law.

International law and the global political environment

The enhanced role of individuals and private enterprises, for example, in the international arena has created a post-Westphalian environment where the international level can join directly with the local, private, or individual level without a state or public intermediary.[16] This creates a form of cosmopolitan democracy where individuals may have direct access to international activities and may even be able to assert rights and challenge their own government's actions either in court or through institutions like the World Bank Inspection Panels. For this more active role, individuals have also now acquired direct international responsibility and can be held accountable for mass violations of human rights, as in the case of the indictment of Sudan's president Omar-al-Bashir for crimes against humanity, war crimes, and genocide in Darfur.[17]

On the eve of the new millennium, UN Secretary-General Kofi Annan wrote: "while the post-war multilateral system made it possible for the new globalization to emerge and flourish, globalization, in turn, has progressively rendered its designs antiquated. Simply put, our post-war institutions were built for an inter-*national* world, but we now live in a *global* world."[18] The actors and the relationships that provided the basis for governance for nearly 400 years are changing. In so doing, they have changed the relationships that historically undergirded the making and implementation of international law.

Historically, international law prescribed conduct between states. As such, it reflected the interests and values of the states involved. Obligations were undertaken only through an expression of state consent. Enforcement of the obligations, if necessary, was based on self-help, with reciprocity serving as both carrot and stick. Where disputes occurred, they might be referred for resolution to a fellow sovereign or other mutually acceptable third party like the pope. Failure of a state to perform could trigger some form of retaliation on the part of the allegedly injured state, if it had the capability to do so. As international society and international life have become more complicated, international law is also more complex. Its present scope reflects the reality that states' responsibilities are now more extensive than they were even in the middle of the twentieth century.

Today, states are expected to provide for their people, safeguard their environment, and generally enhance wellbeing through productive interactions within their own societies and transnationally across borders. As governments have become more involved in more aspects of life and responsible for more tasks, the apparatus of government has grown, with an increasing number of cabinet-level ministries and offices reflecting new tasks that citizens expect them to accomplish. In cases like the environment, new tasks may also be created by international obligations like the Montreal Protocol on Substances that Deplete the Ozone Layer. The nature of the issues and the variety of people and institutions that are now affected by and crucial to its effective functioning have profoundly changed international law. It is now a dense system of legal interactions with connections to national and subnational institutions, IOs, and a host of private actors.

José Alvarez notes that "[t]he age of global compacts is not coincidentally the age of IOs."[19] There are now multiple venues for treaty-making that can determine the scope and content of an agreement. State power is also altered in these settings, with smaller states able to wield influence that may be disproportionate to their size.[20] An example is the United Nations Conference on the Law of the Sea, inspired by Malta, with its representative, Arvid Pardo, coining the phrase "common heritage of mankind," that appears in Article 136 of the 1982 United Nations Convention on the Law of the Sea. An equally significant move made in the UN General Assembly by Trinidad and Tobago in 1989 led to efforts in 1990 to establish an International Criminal Court. These efforts culminated in the signing of the Rome Statute of the International Criminal Court in July 1998.[21]

IOs generally provide publicly accessible venues with copious amounts of information available to those interested in initiating a treaty or in participating in the treaty-making process. The 1998 Rome Conference that completed the Statute of the International Criminal Court, for example, recorded participation from representatives of 160 states, 33 international organizations, over 200 nongovernmental organizations, and more than 400 journalists.[22] Contrast this with the 1899 Hague Peace Conference that included 100 delegates from 24 countries, with little press access to the delegates, even though journalists were in attendance and there was great public interest in the Conference proceedings.[23] The existence of IOs can lower the costs of undertaking international treaty-making because the mechanisms, structures, and personnel needed to support such efforts are now permanently available through UN organs and those of the UN specialized agencies, as well as regional organizations. Used over time, these institutions and procedures have become well established and can take actions with international legal effect.

Douglas Johnston's overview of international agreement activity included a group of "atypical instruments" that can also be grouped under the heading of "soft law." The spectrum of arrangements that might fall under a soft law heading is wide and the term has created controversy because it blurs the distinction between binding and non-binding commitment.[24] It includes political instruments like the 1945 Yalta Agreement and the 1975 Final Act of the Conference on Security and Cooperation in Europe, and statements and practices undertaken to supplement or to correct a treaty are another form of soft law. The 1987 Montreal Protocol to the 1985 Vienna Convention for the Protection of the Ozone Layer provided for a non-compliance procedure worked out by a working party and subsequently adopted by a meeting of the parties to the Protocol in 1992. Resolutions, declarations, codes of conduct, and guidelines of IOs, including the World Bank's operational guidelines, are yet another form of soft law, as are world conference declarations, agendas, programs, and platforms for action.[25] Norm-making also occurs through "statements of principle from individuals in a non-governmental capacity, texts prepared by expert groups, the establishment of 'peoples' tribunals, and self-regulating codes of conduct for networks of professional peoples and multinational corporations," such as the MacBride and Sullivan Principles.[26]

A growing body of empirical work shows that such informal mechanisms do influence state behavior.[27] Of further relevance is work showing that norms have influence if the organizational culture at both the national and international level supports them. In this approach, compliance can be achieved regardless of whether the norm is hard or soft as long as there is a culture that encourages adherence to the norm. Jeffrey Legro concluded from a series of case studies that the "organizational culture perspective matched the outcome [or actual behavior] more consistently than predictions from a norm perspective."[28] This finding puts a premium on the widespread acceptance of the processes and venues that international organizations have provided global actors.

Soft law fills a gap when it provides for norm creation and implementation when formal agreements are not possible. An executive might choose to circumvent a disagreement with the state's legislative or judicial branch through soft international law. For example, entering commodity agreements, including those on the marketing of specific products such as breast milk substitutes, provides a way to monitor and regulate domestic behavior of international concern without resorting to a treaty on the subject of milk substitutes.[29] Similarly, soft law is a vehicle to link international law to private entities regulated principally by domestic law, such as individuals and transnational corporations. The codes of practice of corporate social responsibility are an example of how corporations doing business across borders adhere to good labor practices and environmental protection by complying with domestic law in their worldwide operations.[30]

States also adopt soft international law provisions as an interim step in areas where they have not yet produced hard law, albeit without the same obligations for compliance (or penalties and responsibilities for non-compliance). A good example of this is preservation of the world's forests through the Forest Stewardship Council (FSC). Formed in 1993 by loggers, foresters, environmentalists, and sociologists, its purpose is to provide an international forum for dialogue on what constitutes a sustainable forest and to set forth principles and standards to guide "forest management towards sustainable outcomes." FSC standards are now in use in over 57 countries around the world, including the United States.[31] Such soft law provides states great flexibility, as they do not risk creating institutions that turn out to be costly and possibly inappropriate, ineffective, or difficult to adapt or eliminate over time.[32] Soft law institutions and processes can enable states to work on compliance first and to develop an appreciation of the costs and benefits of creating formal mechanisms before entering a formal agreement in the future.[33]

In these ways, the present globalized legal environment provides an opportunity for global actors to draw on the strongest operating capacity, whether that is national or international. International soft law can draw on hard national institutions to strengthen it, and soft private sector practices might harden by virtue of their incorporation into a hard law international instrument like a treaty. The key is that global actors seek to promote orderly and reliable behavior, and that they look to law and legal institutions to help shape those expectations. This has enriched international law's capacity to address global needs, but the resulting complexity in its normative and institutional structure has not yet been fully appreciated, especially by critics of international law, most notably at the national level.

Globalizing international law

Interactions and connections among institutions and structures of global order, including law, have been the focus of this chapter. These interactions developed in response to specific needs and together have generated new capacities that in turn have changed the governance environment by producing new governing institutions, norms, structures, partnerships, and relationships. These have empowered new actors and recognized new values that form the basis of global governance today. They have also created new responsibilities and obligations. The cumulative effects of these interactions have contributed to globalization.

Governance today occurs in a much more open and participatory environment than it did only a few decades ago. The move towards greater openness and participation is occurring at all levels of government, within international institutions, and throughout the private sector in corporate and other non-state entities. There are three key developments: the building of international institutions and structures that may constrain certain state behaviors in the short run, but are likely to contribute to a more stable and secure order in the long run; the reliance on reporting and monitoring procedures as well as follow-up conferences in order to make states and other responsible parties review compliance with their obligations and publicly assess progress toward stated objectives; and the culture of civil society, mass media, and early warning that is becoming more and more effective at putting the spotlight on emerging areas of potential international concern.

From 1648 to 1918, the principal focus of international activity was on the development and strengthening of the state. Global governance in the Westphalian order was one of facilitating the relations among sovereigns and sovereign states. To the extent people benefited from any privileges, for example freedom of religion, it was a by-product of state interest. The privilege won in the 1555 Peace of Augsburg, for example, provided for *cujus ancien ejus religio*, which allowed religious freedom, albeit for the monarch or sovereign and not necessarily for their subjects. In fact, the Latin maxim provided that the people would follow the religion of their ruler.[34] The sovereign would therefore dictate the religion of the realm without consideration as to the wishes or traditions of the people of that realm. Indeed, dissent from the established religion could result in persecutions, including deprivation of property rights, lower status, expulsion, and, on occasion, pogroms or mass killings.

Early treaty-making reflects this focus on the state, with a substantial portion of treaty activity devoted to such state interests as alliances, trade, and the waging of war.[35] These interests created the state values that became the values of global order: autonomy, mutual respect, and non-interference. The Westphalian system focused on a balance of power among the most powerful states in order to maintain order and to preserve peace. When interests fell out of balance, a state could seek to redress that balance by armed conflict. Individual quality of life and livelihood were determined by state authorities. To the extent that the treatment of people was an issue, it was subjected to the domestic values and policies of each individual country and its ruler.

As long as the effects of a state's actions did not spill over into another state, its rulers generally were free to govern within their territory as they deemed appropriate. This changed in the late nineteenth and twentieth centuries as the requirements of industrialization forced states to act effectively across borders and as governments were increasingly expected to respond to and to provide for their citizens. As Louis Henkin observes, in the course of the twentieth century, the international system turned its attention from state values to human values in its diplomatic activity and treaty-making.[36] Traditional state activities continued, of course, but addressing areas of human concern has become an increasingly large portion of state activity.

International organizations were created to enhance the ability of states to pursue their interests and to carry out their functions. Starting with structured, but non-institutionalized meetings, groups of states would gather to address problems of common concern. It seems commonplace today for an IO like the UN to call attention to an area of international concern, but the creation of such a voice independent of states in the early twentieth century was accepted with extreme caution and skepticism. The political environment created by the presence of an IO was something on which other actors like nongovernmental organizations capitalized. IOs provided a readily accessible platform and connection to a worldwide audience to promote their agendas. International law-making and implementation have become more generally accessible and participatory than at any other time since the advent of international political institutions, and the process is ongoing.

Emergence of interstitial norms as a blend of existing and potentially conflicting norms demonstrates the growing complexity of international life and the issues international law addresses. Vaughan Lowe coined the term "interstitial norm" to describe a connective norm that draws together differing norms from hard and soft law as well as domestic and transnational law.[37] The 1997 International Court of Justice ruling in the Gabcikovo case between Hungary and Slovakia illustrates Lowe's point when the two objectives of economic development and environmental protection collided. The outcome was a resort to the principle of sustainable development.[38] However, as Lowe noted, there was not sufficient state practice to support the position that sustainable development had acquired the status of a norm of customary international law. Instead, he found this to be an interstitial principle that established "the relationship between the neighbouring primary norms when they threaten to overlap or conflict with each other."[39] Another example of an interstitial norm is the principle of the responsibility to protect that attempts to balance the norm of nonintervention in the internal affairs of a state with that of the norm to protect the human rights of people.

Characteristic of today's more globalized international law is a less hierarchical law-making and implementation process. Law and regulated behavior can develop through networks and social movements rather than exclusively through institutions or governments. Movements may come and go, but their normative legacies are important, as was the case with the movement to end the use of landmines. Globalized international law functions in an environment that is shaped by ongoing interactions rather than abrupt system-wide changes.[40] These interactions create denser and denser political and normative connections between the local and global, the individual and the institutional, and the national and transnational. As diverse forces that add capacity and depth to international norms, global politics enriches international law. But these forces can also create confusion as to the authority or content of a norm, with negative consequences for global order and governance.

International law is now called upon to address multidimensional, multi-sector, and multi-level issues like sustainable development, environmental protection, and the economic and other wellbeing of individuals. This requires a specialization and focus that have raised questions in the international law community about the ongoing coherence of international law as a legal system. The International Law Commission described the problem as follows:

> The fragmentation of the international social world has attained legal significance especially as it has been accompanied by the emergence of specialized and (relatively) autonomous rules or rule-complexes, legal institutions and spheres of legal practice . . . The result is conflicts between rules or rule systems, deviating institutional practices and, possibly, the loss of an overall perspective on the law.[41]

This fragmentation is further accentuated by the emergence of an increasingly complex global political environment where authoritative international action may come from sub-national or private entities.

Conclusion

Despite the pressures of various needs and competing law-making authorities today, international law remains a separate legal system with its own unique functions and purposes. The challenge is to ensure recognition and understanding of the principles and structure of international law that enable international and transnational relations and interactions even as these principles change and develop. Further, this requires understanding at the domestic level that international norms and practices are part of all legal systems and need to be understood and integrated. The relationship between international, national, and sub-national legal systems is less a hierarchical one than a partnership among systems that connect with each other to give life to global norms and to transform national norms and local practices into global norms. International organizations exist today because of a perceived need to address cross-border issues. States used international law to create them and international organizations, in turn, have increased the capacity of international law to meet its objectives by organizing permanent staffs, creating venues for legal interaction, and for ongoing development. These connections and relationships will deepen as international norm development and implementation connect increasingly with domestic political discourse and norm development. As they do, new capacities are generated, new challenges will emerge, and the evolution of international law within the multifaceted global legal system it helped create will continue.

Additional reading

1. Charlotte Ku, *International Law, International Relations, and Global Governance* (London: Routledge, 2012).
2. José E. Alvarez, *International Organizations as Law-Makers* (New York: Oxford University Press, 2005).
3. Jutta Brunée and Stephen Toope, *Legitimacy and Legality in International Law: An Interactional Account* (Cambridge: Cambridge University Press, 2010).
4. Paul F. Diehl and Charlotte Ku, *The Dynamics of International Law* (Cambridge: Cambridge University Press, 2010).
5. David Held, *Democracy and the Global Order: From the Modern State to Cosmopolitan Governance* (Stanford: Stanford University Press, 1995).
6. Andrew Hurrell, *On Global Order: Power, Values, and the Constitution of International Society* (Oxford: Oxford University Press, 2007).
7. Beth A. Simmons, *Mobilizing for Human Rights: International Law in Domestic Politics* (New York: Cambridge University Press, 2009).

Notes

1 Portions of this essay are adapted from Charlotte Ku, *International Law, International Relations, and Global Governance* (London: Routledge, 2012).
2 Douglas M. Johnston, *Consent and Commitment in the World Community* (Irvington-on-Hudson, NY: Transnational Publishers, Inc., 1997), 8–9.
3 Ibid., 25.

4 Example provided by Lauren Kolb, Research Assistant, Behrend College, Pennsylvania State University, the Comprehensive Statistical Database of Multilateral Treaties (CSDMT) Project, August 2012.

5 ICJ Reports, *North Sea Continental Shelf Cases*, Judgment of 20 February 1969, 75.

6 ICJ Reports, *Fisheries Case (United Kingdom v. Norway)*, Judgment of 18 December 1951, 27.

7 See Daniel Thomas, *The Helsinki Effect: International Norms, Human Rights, and the Demise of Communism* (Princeton: Princeton University Press, 2001).

8 Rosalyn Higgins, "Policy Considerations and International Judicial Process," *International and Comparative Law Quarterly* 17 (1968): 58–59.

9 The US Department of State, for example, listed 50 separate transactions and reports—often book length—completed and submitted to United Nations human rights treaty bodies to fulfill a variety of reporting requirements. See http://www.state.gov/j/drl/hr/treaties. Additional similar reports are required of States Parties to environmental and other treaties.

10 See Charlotte Ku and Harold K. Jacobson, "Conclusion: Toward a Mixed System of Democratic Accountability," in *Democratic Accountability and the Use of Force in International Law*, eds. Charlotte Ku and Harold K. Jacobson (Cambridge: Cambridge University Press, 2002).

11 James N. Rosenau, *Turbulence in World Politics: A Theory of Change and Continuity* (Princeton: Princeton University Press, 1990), 195.

12 Hendrik Spruyt, *The Sovereign State and Its Competitors* (Princeton: Princeton University Press, 1994), 6.

13 Abram Chayes and Antonia Handler Chayes, *The New Sovereignty: Compliance with International Regulatory Agreements* (Cambridge, MA: Harvard University Press, 1995), 5.

14 Jonathan I. Charney, "Universal International Law," *American Journal of International Law* 87 (1993): 529.

15 Charney, "Universal International Law," 547.

16 See David Held, *Democracy and the Global Order: From the Modern State to Cosmopolitan Governance* (Palo Alto: Stanford University Press, 1995).

17 See *The Prosecutor v. Omar Hassan Ahmad Al Bashir*, http://www.icc-cpi.int/menus/icc/situations%20and%20cases/situations/situation%20icc%200205/related%20cases/icc02050109/icc02050109?lan=en-GB).

18 Kofi A. Annan, *We the Peoples: The Role of the United Nations in the 21st Century* (New York: United Nations, 2000), 11.

19 José E. Alvarez, "The New Treaty-Makers," *Boston College of International and Comparative Law Review* 25, no. 2 (2002), 217.

20 Alvarez, "The New Treaty-Makers," 223–232.

21 See Christiane E. Philipp, "The International Criminal Court—A Brief Introduction," in *Max Planck Yearbook of United Nations Law*, vol. 7, eds. A. von Bogdandy and R. Wolfrum (The Netherlands: Koninklijke Brill NV, 2003), 331–339.

22 See Alvarez, "The New Treaty-Makers," 220.

23 Arthur Eyffinger, *The 1899 Hague Peace Conference: The Parliament of Man, the Federation of the World* (The Hague: Kluwer Law International, 1999).

24 Dinah Shelton, "Introduction: Law, Non-Law and the Problem of Soft Law," in *Commitment and Compliance: The Role of Non-Binding Norms in the International Legal System*, ed. Dinah Shelton (Oxford: Oxford University Press, 2000), 8.

25 See Michael G. Schechter, "Conclusions," in *United Nations-Sponsored World Conferences: Focus on Impact and Follow Up*, ed. Michael G. Schechter (Tokyo: United Nations University Press, 2001), 218–222.

26 Christine Chinkin, "Normative Development in the International Legal System," in *Commitment and Compliance: The Role of Non-Binding Norms in the International Legal System*, ed. Dinah Shelton (Oxford: Oxford University Press, 2000), 29.

27 Xinyuan Dai, *International Institutions and National Policies* (Cambridge: Cambridge University Press, 2007).

28 Jeffrey W. Legro, "Which Norms Matter?: Revisiting the 'Failure' of Internationalism," *International Organization* 51, no. 1 (1997): 35.

29 Christine Chinkin, "The Challenge of Soft Law: Development and Change in International Law," *International and Comparative Law Quarterly* 38, no. 4 (1989): 850–866.

30 See Isabella D. Bunn, "Global Advocacy for Corporate Accountability," *American University International Law Review* 19, no. 6 (2004): 1265–1306.

31 See Forest Stewardship Council United States, www.fscus.org.

32 Andrew Guzman, *How International Law Works* (Oxford: Oxford University Press, 2005).

33 See Richard L. Williamson, Jr., "International Regulation of Land Minds," in *Commitment and Compliance: The Role of Non-Binding Norms in the International Legal System*, ed. Dinah Shelton (Oxford: Oxford University Press, 2000), 505–521.

34 See Leo Gross, "The Peace of Westphalia, 1648–1948," *American Journal of International Law* 42 (1948): 22.

35 See CSDMT as cited in Charlotte Ku, "Global Governance and the Changing Face of International Law," 2001 John W. Holmes Memorial Lecture, ACUNS Reports & Papers no. 2 (2001), 4.

36 See Louis Henkin, *International Law: Politics & Values* (Dordrecht: Martinus Nijhoff Publishers, 1995).

37 Vaughan Lowe, "The Politics of Law-Making," in *The Role of Law in International Politics*, ed. Michael Byers (Oxford: Oxford University Press, 2000), 212–221.

38 See International Court of Justice, Judgment of 25 September 1997, Gabcikovo-Nagymaros Project (Hungary/Slovkia), www.icj-cij.org/docket, and Nico Schrijver, *Development without Destruction: The UN and Global Resource Management* (Bloomington and Indianapolis: Indiana University Press, 2010).

39 Lowe, "The Politics of Law-Making," 216.

40 See Margaret E. Keck and Kathryn Sikkink, *Activists Beyond Borders: Advocacy Networks in International Politics* (Ithaca and London: Cornell University Press, 1998), 213.

41 UN Doc. A/CN.4/L/682, 13 April 2006, International Law Commission, "Fragmentation of International Law: Difficulties Arising from the Diversification and Expansion of International Law," Report of the Study Group of the International Law Commission Finalized by Martti Koskenniemi, 10.

CONTENTS

International Organizations and the Diffusion of Power

Michael Barnett and Raymond Duvall

At the risk of simple-mindedness, there are two schools of thought regarding the relationship between international organizations (IOs) and the diffusion of power.[1] One school suggests that IOs are conservative organizations that are designed to freeze existing configurations of power. If they are doing their job, then they are not diffusing power. The other is that IOs are expected to pluralize power. The world is constituted by radical inequalities of power, with some states having an abundance and others a scarcity, and the United Nations and other IOs essential to global governance help to level the playing field by giving an opportunity for the weak to have a voice and neglected issues to be seen. Both camps are right: IOs can be defenders of the powerful and agents of reform. In fact, individual IOs such as the United Nations can function in both capacities. The UN Security Council, for instance, is a bastion of privilege reflecting the distribution of power in the international system seven decades ago, while many of the UN's specialized agencies seat NGOs from the global South and powerful states at the same table.

This chapter offers one way of thinking about how IOs might be simultaneously reform-minded and defenders of the status quo. We begin by briefly discussing several prominent theories of international organizations and their depiction of the role that IO plays in the global order. While several of the best-known theories see IOs as preserving the existing distribution of power and interests, constructivist and critical approaches to IOs offer several reasons why they might also be intended and accidental agents of inclusion and empowerment. Specifically, our discussion of the diffusion of power focuses on how IOs might potentially reshape the social relations that affect the ability of actors to control the conditions of their future. In other words, we want to consider how IOs can further the conditions that allow actors to speak for themselves and to act in ways that further their interests. In what ways might IOs have this kind of impact? In order to provide a partial answer, we observe that the ability of IOs to have this intended effect can be accomplished via two different kinds of power—compulsory and institutional. Compulsory power highlights how IOs can take direct action to alter the conditions of existence for actors, for instance when peacekeeping forces defend the lives of civilians in the Congo. Institutional power emphasizes how IOs can work indirectly to guide action in directions that potentially improve the positions and ability of once marginalized and vulnerable actors; for instance, former UN Secretary-General Boutros Boutros-Ghali's *Agenda for Peace* drastically altered how the international community defined international peace and security and debated the kinds of tools that were needed for the post-Cold War system. These mechanisms of power highlight how IOs might be able to shape the conditions of existence of other actors, not whether that effect of their actions ultimately preserves or diffuses power. To fill in the blanks, we return to theories of IOs for guidance, because different theories make different claims regarding the likelihood of whether IOs will defend or assail the status quo. Our takeaway line is this: modern IOs are often designed by (the most powerful) states to advance their interests, which can have the principal effect of reproducing the existing distribution of power; but they also have certain qualities and characteristics that can lead them to act in ways that improve the capacity of actors to shape the conditions of their fate.

Theories of IOs

The literature on international organizations identifies two primary reasons why states create IOs. The first is to help stabilize an international order and a set of political arrangements. Put more accurately, the most powerful states in the international system have the most say over the design and function of IOs, and, since their primary goal is to preserve power, they are likely to design IOs as instruments of their foreign policy goals, ensuring that they can block action that they perceive to be counter to their interests. In this view most closely associated with realist international relations theory, IOs are accomplices of powerful states and serve an essential function in freezing the existing international order, defending the privileges of the powerful, and making sure that the weak continue to suffer what they must. Specifically, the most powerful states decide which IOs are created, what they are, how they make decisions, and how they operate. In order to ensure their dominance, powerful states constrain IOs in various ways, including making them dependent on states for financing and establishing decision-making procedures that give powerful states preferential treatment. If we want to know what IOs do, we should look to what the most powerful states allow and want them to do.

The second reason, found in institutionalist theories, offers a slightly less severe but nonetheless rather button-down view. These approaches argue that states create institutions to enhance the prospects of cooperation, overcome problems associated with collective choice, and increase individual and collective wellbeing. In other words, states have an interest in creating the conditions for cooperation and mutual welfare gains, and institutions are invaluable in that regard. Institutionalized cooperation is no guarantee that all will benefit equally. In fact, the most powerful states are likely to benefit more than the least powerful, with the important consequence that institutions might well be responsible for widening existing asymmetries of power. For all their disagreements regarding whether IOs matter, realists and institutionalists largely concur that IOs are either conservatives or compassionate conservatives, but in either case they are largely sympathetic to (or captured by) the existing distribution of power. Radical theories of international organizations, including Marxist approaches, also see IOs as defenders of privilege, though in most analyses the real beneficiaries are not states but rather elites or dominant classes at the expense of workers, migrants, peasants; that is, most of the world's population. In general, these approaches give little reason for hope that IOs provide the have-nots of the world with the ability to improve the conditions that shape their lives as they see fit.

Yet there are other schools of thought that can imagine IOs not just as defenders of the *ancien régime* but also as levelers of privilege. Both constructivism and critical theory shift attention away from interests toward culture, norms, ideas, rules, and discourse, demonstrating that the "social" features of life play a primary role in shaping how the world is understood, how actors understand themselves and others, and what sorts of practices and arrangements are considered legitimate. In so doing, they make three valuable moves, which combine to generate a more nuanced understanding of the simultaneously conservative and reformist tendencies of IOs.

First, these theories move us away from actors and toward underlying structures, thus enabling us to better understand how the already existing global culture shapes what IOs are and what they do. In this respect, they are like Marxist theories, but with an important difference: whereas Marxist theories typically reduce the underlying structure to economics and property relations, constructivist and critical theories are more attentive to the different, and not always consistent, presence of a variety of cultures. For instance, important elements of global culture include liberalism, rationality, and technocracy.

Second, the presence of these overlapping and sometimes contradictory cultures will give IOs relative autonomy. In other words, it is not accurate to argue that IOs are merely playthings of states; nor to claim that IOs are free to do as they will. IOs, like most actors, have some relative autonomy. But the fact that they have some relative autonomy does not tell us what they will do with that autonomy. They might use their relative autonomy to act in ways that are consistent with the underlying rules of the game, or they might use their autonomy to challenge those rules.

Third, constructivist and critical approaches to the study of IOs point to two culturally inscribed reasons why they might, however unwittingly, diffuse power. To begin with, IOs seek legitimacy. In many respects, legitimacy is the IO's fuel and currency of power. Because they are viewed as legitimate, member states are willing to support IO activities and rely on the resulting legitimacy to persuade other states and non-state actors to defer to their decisions. In short, IOs will be effective, and others will defer to them, to the extent that they and their decisions are viewed as legitimate. Legitimacy has procedural and substantive dimensions. Procedural legitimacy refers to the process by which decisions are made. Although there are lots of ways to make decisions, in contemporary affairs modern governance is seen as legitimate to the extent that it operates according to basic principles of democracy and rationality. While great powers might establish IOs to reflect their interests, to the extent that international organizations are viewed as their instrument they will suffer a democratic deficit and lose legitimacy in the eyes of many; a consequence of this "unmasking" is that it will become more difficult for powerful states to rule without coercion. IOs, therefore, need to appear to be inclusive rather than exclusive, which often means practicing the principles they preach and operating in subtle ways that level power.

IOs are valued to the extent that they operate with efficiency, impartiality, and objectivity, values that are prized in all modern organizations. Although IOs are often a far cry from the idealized image of a well-oiled machine, they aspire to have various kinds of qualities that are associated with the best features of bureaucracy: control on the basis of expert knowledge; the division of the organization into spheres of competence and specialization; the establishment of procedures that standardize its responses to the environment, and the creation of a decision process that is driven not by politics but rather by the objective application of rules in a fair-minded way. These organizing principles are technical and political. The rise of the bureaucratic ideal in the nineteenth century was seen as a way of removing existing advantages and power because decisions would now be made on rational, objective criteria and not on the basis of who has influence and connections. In general, IOs that tip their hand to the principles of democracy and rationality are less likely to include "who wins and who loses" as defining criteria of their decision-making procedures.

IOs also need substantive legitimacy. That is, their decisions need to be seen as broadly consistent with the values of the community. Substantively many of these values have a decidedly liberal quality, which brings us to a second factor that potentially pluralizes power. The contemporary global order has a liberal character; and IOs are constituted by that order, which contains a paradox that is central to understanding IOs and their relationship to processes of diffusion. The liberal states that shape the existing world order and its defining institutions imprint that order on the identity and interests of existing international organizations. In other words, IOs have a defining liberal quality, and this characteristic is likely to lead them to act in ways that protect and preserve the existing liberal order. Yet some of liberalism's values also provide opportunities to level existing power inequalities.

IOs, in the liberal view, are valued because they help to bring about liberal progress— that is, they nurture development, security, justice, and protect individual autonomy. Liberalism is characterized by a concern with the concentration of power and the need to protect the liberal rights of individuals, and these concerns have translated into a strong preference for institutions that honor the rule of law, democracy, and markets. Accordingly, liberal institutions operate in ways that are intended, at least nominally, to ensure individual freedoms. These virtues are among the reasons why liberals have been the most ardent and long-standing champions of IOs. Importantly, many IOs are established not only to protect the interests of the most powerful states but also to help diffuse values that can constrain their ability to act with arbitrary power. Liberally minded IOs often work to ensure that even small and weak states have their interests represented in international policy discussions (but still acceptable to a liberal world order) and to promote the establishment of markets, democracy and human rights. In general, IOs are often opponents of the *ancien régime*, champions of those whose voices might otherwise not be heard, and promoters of global and domestic institutions that advance equality and inclusion.

In sum, because international organizations are frequently created by powerful states to preserve their interests, the reasonable expectation is that they will serve the status quo and work against any sort of redistribution, diffusion, or pluralization of power. Yet because IOs require legitimacy to be effective, because they are seen as advocates of a liberal world view, and because they are supposed to operate according to rule-governed principles, they also can be expected to work against the status quo and toward the conditions that enable states and non-state actors to have a greater say over their lives. IOs not only demonstrate both tendencies, but individual IOs are often at war within themselves, simultaneously championing and critiquing the existing world order.

Power and IOs

Power is the production, in and through social relations, of effects on actors that shape their capacity to control their fate. This definition is broader than the one favored by international relations theorists: the ability of A to get B to do something it would rather not do. In that standard approach, generally associated with realist international relations theory, power is largely limited to how one state is able to use resources to force another state to do something against its will. But power is not only overt; it can be covert as well.

We exist in social contexts that constrain our ability to influence decisions that matter to us by keeping items off the agenda and even excluding actors from decision-making. Moreover, power not only shapes what we can do but also how we see the world, how we see ourselves, how we define our interests, and what we believe is possible and even qualifies as a problem to be addressed. In other words, power's effects are evident not only in terms of acting but also in terms of constituting, comprehending, and interpreting the world. The world is not a democracy, and even democracies contain features that give advantages to some and disadvantages to others. We inhabit structures, such as capitalism, replete with mechanisms that help to make the rich richer, the poor poorer, and convince the poor that this system of inequality is in their interest. But we also exist in a world in which various kinds of discourse, including racism, civilization, and gender, have lasting effects on the identity, interests, and practices of everyone involved. The standard realist approach articulates only one way to conceptualize how our ability to shape our future is limited; we need to imagine the existence of other kinds of global relations that can be disempowering.

In a previous effort to demonstrate the many ways in which power exists in international affairs, we defined power as premised on two analytical dimensions: the kinds of social relations through which power works (in relations of interaction or in social relations of constitution); and the specificity of social relations through which effects are produced (specific/direct or diffuse/indirect). These distinctions draw our attention to the question of whether power operates through actions (i.e. the ability by some actors to keep issues off the agenda) or structures (i.e. the underlying distribution of wealth that allocates privilege and vulnerability); or whether these effects are easily traceable to an identifiable source (i.e. the person holding the gun) or diffuse and not traceable to an identifiable source (i.e. discourses of civilization that produce the categories of civilized and uncivilized). We used these different analytical dimensions (actions and structure; direct and diffuse) to generate four concepts of power: compulsory, institutional, structural, and productive. These different conceptualizations of power provide different answers to the fundamental question: in what respects are actors able to control their own fate, and how is that ability limited or enhanced through social relations with others?

To explore how IOs diffuse power entails situating IOs in relationship to these different kinds of power, and examining how they might be directly and indirectly implicated in altering the social relations that enhance the ability of actors to control their fate. Simply put, how do IOs enable or constrain the ability of actors to shape the circumstances of their lives? Compulsory, institutional, structural, and productive power point to different mechanisms whereby these effects are accomplished—with the former two pointing to interactions and the latter two to structures. We limit discussion here to compulsory and institutional power, the most important explanatory factors in explaining the diffusion of power.

Compulsory power

This first and most infamous kind of power concerns the conditions that allow one actor to force another actor to do something that the latter does not believe is in its interests; that is, the ability of A to get B to do something that B would not do otherwise. We can see this kind of power when three conditions are met. One, there is *intentionality* on the part of Actor A. What counts is that A wants B to alter its actions in a particular direction. If B alters its actions under the mistaken impression that A wants it to, then that would not count as power because it was not A's intent that B do so. Two, there must be a *conflict* of desires to the extent that B now feels compelled to alter its behavior. A and B want different outcomes, and B loses. Three, A is successful because it has material and ideational *resources* at its disposal that lead B to alter its actions. As theorists of international relations tend to illuminate material and neglect ideational resources, we emphasize that resources can be either material or ideational. Some states are able to "punch above their weight" because they are seen as being principled and virtuous. Scandinavian countries arguably are able to influence global outcomes because they have a perceived quality of character and not because these thinly populated countries are closer to the Arctic and go months without daylight. Nongovernmental organizations use normative resources to compel targeted states to alter their policies through a strategy of "naming and shaming."

IOs exhibit compulsory power if they intend to influence the behavior of another state or non-state actor, if there is a conflict between what the IO wants and what the other actor wants, and if a particular IO's material and ideational resources account for why the targeted actor changed its behavior. This is not an uncommon occurrence. IOs often have interests that are aligned against those of another state or non-state actor, and they often attempt to deploy material and ideational resources to compel a target actor to change its ways.

Although IOs might not have the same recourse to material resources as states, they are not without these methods of persuasion. International financial institutions such as the World Bank and the International Monetary Fund are able to use their capital to force borrowing states to adopt "best practices," slash budgets, and redirect economic resources. The Office of the UN High Commissioner for Refugees (UNHCR) can shape the life-chances of refugees and other displaced peoples by giving them strong incentives to return home by decreasing their rations. Peacekeeping troops, at times, use force to deter would-be violators of the ceasefire and protect civilians from gangs and thugs. Yet when IOs do exercise compulsory power, it is often through symbolic and normative resources rather than material ones. Because of its administrative and bureaucratic role, UNHCR has the power to determine who gets legal protection as a refugee and who does not. The International Criminal Court has the power to indict government officials, but because this capacity is not backed by any real enforcement mechanisms, the primary effect is to create global *personas non grata*.

Institutional power

Institutional power highlights how actors are able to guide, steer, and constrain the actions and circumstances of others through the rules that exist in structural positional differences in formal and informal institutions. Institutional power differs from compulsory power in various ways, but two are most important for this discussion. Whereas compulsory power entails the direct control of one actor over the conditions and actions of another, institutional power reflects indirect control. Specifically, the conceptual focus is on the formal and informal institutions that mediate between A and B. Working through the rules and procedures that define those institutions, A can guide, steer, and constrain the actions (or non-actions) and conditions of existence of others. Institutions are nothing if not bundles of rules that specify who is admitted to the club, who can talk, whose voice carries weight and counts, and what can be discussed and when. While often the rules were originally formulated by those with the most power, few institutions remain the instrument of a single actor or coalition. It is certainly possible that a dominant actor maintains total control over an institution. If so, then it is arguably best to conceptualize that institution as possessed by the actor, and with its compulsory power. But rarely is the institution completely dominated by one actor. Instead, most institutions have some independence from even the most specific resource-laden actors; rules that can take on a life of their own; and even their own independent personality and existence to the point of frustrating their original creators.

Second, institutional power also highlights the sometimes hidden power at work even without an obvious struggle between two actors. Compulsory power looks for a chain of events like: "Do it!" "No." "If you don't, we will deny you what you need." "OK." But institutional power acknowledges the existence of power even when there is no observable action. Rules, in other words, can create the proverbial dogs that do not bark. Rules for determining what is on the agenda, for example, mean that some topics are never discussed. There are lots of international crises, but the great powers determine which ones are discussed by the Security Council. Rules also determine who gets to discuss an issue. Only states can be members of the UN. Other international organizations, though, have been more welcoming of NGOs, and these venues have enabled disadvantaged populations to ensure that the issues they care about—including human rights—are discussed. There are rules to determine when votes are cast and whose vote counts. There are voting procedures, including weighted voting and the existence of veto power reserved for special states. This institutional context, moreover, lingers into the future, thus constraining action in ways that might not have been intended but nevertheless limit choice and shape action. Accordingly, even those institutions that are established for the ostensible purpose of producing cooperation create winners and losers and even stack the deck so that some actors win all the time.

IOs often exhibit this form of power, possessing the formal and informal capacity to determine the agenda at forums, meetings, and conferences. This capacity gives them a substantial role in determining what is and is not discussed. The Secretary-General frequently structures the options for particular peacekeeping operations and therefore establishes the parameters of Security Council deliberations. The Secretary-General's decision to make humanitarian intervention a defining theme of his 1999 address to the General Assembly had a decisive impact on all subsequent discussions, and arguably helped to pave the way for the Responsibility to Protect. European Union officials are renowned for possessing this sort of influence. UNHCR and World Bank officials are directly involved in drawing up the agenda for meetings. In this significant way, IO staff can help to orient discussions and actions in some directions and away from others.

Although IOs might use material resources to have these kinds of effects, it is their position as authorities and use of symbolic resources such as frames that give them the ability to steer action in some directions and away from others. As Barnett and Finnemore have argued, IOs are both of authority and in authority.[2] In addition to authority delegated from states, IOs have authority because they embody rational-legal principles that modern societies value and that are identified with liberal values viewed as legitimate and "progressive." There are many different kinds of authority in social relations, and many organizations are viewed as authorities because they are seen as experts of their domain. One important reason why states create bureaucracies is that states want important social tasks to be executed by individuals with detailed, specialized knowledge. Derived from training or experience, such knowledge persuades us to confer on experts, and the bureaucracies that house them, the power to make judgments and solve problems. Deployment of specialized knowledge is central to the very rational-legal authority which constitutes bureaucracy in the first place since what makes such authority rational is, at least in part, the use of socially recognized relevant knowledge to carry out tasks.

Expertise thus makes IOs authoritative and also shapes their behavior. Just as these organizations authorized by a moral principle must serve that principle and make their actions consistent to remain legitimate and authoritative, so too IOs with authorized expertise must serve that specialized knowledge and ensure that their actions are consistent with it. The IMF cannot propose policies beyond those supported by the economic knowledge it deploys. Professional training, norms, and occupational cultures strongly shape the way that experts view the world. They influence what problems are visible to staff and what range of solutions are entertained. Expert authority also creates the appearance of depoliticization. By emphasizing the "objective" nature of their knowledge, international organizations are able to present themselves as technocrats whose advice is unaffected by partisan squabbles. The greater the appearance of depoliticization, the greater the power of the expertise.

IOs, like all other actors using rhetoric to shape the behavior of others, can and do use a variety of techniques for this purpose. They may "frame" issues in particular ways, so that desired choices seem particularly compelling or so that the sanctions and penalties associated with particular policies are excessively high. They may manipulate emotions of decision-makers and publics, creating empathy for landmine victims, refugees, and genocide survivors. They may use information strategically, gathering some kinds of information but not others. They may manipulate audiences strategically, inviting or including only some participants in their bureaucratic process—for instance, bankers not peasants sit at diplomatic high tables.

IOs also guide behavior through classificatory practices. An elementary feature of bureaucracies is that they classify and organize information and knowledge. This classification process is a form of power because it constitutes a way of "making, ordering, and knowing social worlds" by "mov[ing] persons among social categories or by inventing and applying such categories."[3] The ability to classify objects, to shift their very definition and identity, is one of the bureaucracy's greatest sources of power. This power is frequently treated by the objects of that power as accomplished through caprice and without regard to their circumstances, but it is legitimated and justified by bureaucrats with reference to any rules and regulations. The IMF has a particular way of categorizing economies and determining whether they are on the "right track," defined in terms of their capital accounts, balance of payments, budget deficits, and reserves. To be categorized as not "on track" can have detrimental consequences for external financing at reasonable rates, access to IMF funds, and conditionality. The world is filled with individuals who have either been forced or chosen to flee their homes, and the UNHCR imposes upon them a classification scheme that distinguishes between refugees, migrants, and internally displaced peoples. Similarly, classification of a conflict as a "civil war" or "genocide" triggers one set of responses by international actors rather than another.

Not only do IOs help identify problems, they also help solve them by crafting particular solutions and persuading others to accept them. Identifying a particular solution from a range of options is consequential and an important exercise of power. The next logical step is to identify a set of actors that should take responsibility for implementing the solution. Authorities, including IOs, once again step into the breach as they are viewed as qualified to manage these solutions to already identified problems.

Diffusing power

We have argued that IOs can be seen as relatively autonomous actors that can directly and indirectly shape the conditions of existence for other actors, and that exhibit these effects through compulsory or institutional power. Moreover, because of their organizational characteristics (both internally and in their relationship to states), they are more likely to exhibit institutional than compulsory power. These claims, though, say nothing about the substance of their actions, that is, whether they preserve the existing distribution of power or attempt to diffuse the underlying conditions that enable actors to determine their fates. The earlier discussion of theories of IOs can help address this issue. To repeat, realist, institutionalist, and Marxist theories assume that IOs will act in ways that are intended to preserve the existing distribution of privileges. Realists see IOs as playthings of states and Marxists as instruments of capitalism; and even institutionalists, who grant that IO staff have some relative autonomy and discretion, are limited in their ability or desire to effect real change.

Critical and constructivist theories acknowledge that IOs are defenders of the status quo, but they also provide theoretical and conceptual grounds for observing real independence and the attempt to provide greater equality of opportunities for other actors. This is not just because these theories are better able to imagine IOs as relatively independent actors, but also because they recognize that IOs are actors that are potentially constituted by broader global cultural forces, such as liberalism and rationalism, and by the desire to be seen as legitimate by states and non-state actors. IOs constituted by global liberalism are defenders of an international order that contains the ingredients for the diffusion of power. Most IOs express a strong commitment to the existing liberal international order and the desire to spread, defend, and protect liberalism's values. They are committed to the existing order, whose values include equality, liberty, and autonomy. These are values that create a strong cultural disposition for institutions of the rule of law, democracy, and markets. Such institutions are interested in preserving the existing order but whose individualism nevertheless is designed (at least rhetorically) to ensure that basic political rights are observed; and the commitment to rights has the potential of creating the conditions for individuals to, at least, have some measure of self-determination.

IOs are not just shaped by the liberal world order but also by a commitment to basic principles of rationality. IOs are constituted by rules, which are designed to: standardize the world and the IO's response to it; ensure a continuity and consistency in action; divide the organization into areas of competence and specialization to improve the efficiency and predictability of action; and minimize the costs of action and maximize the benefits. The rules associated with rationality are intended to be objective. Unlike the rules of non-rational organizations (such as pre-modern bureaucracies), the rules are supposed to treat everyone equally because all humans are juridically equal. IOs, like all modern bureaucracies, are not supposed to have one set of rules for the powerful and another set of rules for the powerless. Fair is fair. Of course, gaps exist between theory and reality, but the theory can have a disciplinary effect. These rules also are intended to remove the politics from decision-making. Rather than make decisions based on who is likely to win and who is likely to lose, rules are applied on the basis of technical criteria. Although such depoliticization does not automatically mean that the powerless will always be heard, or be heard in the same way as the powerful, at least it gives them a fighting chance. Because liberalism and rationality, in short, are supposed to dilute power and politics, they potentially help diffuse power. To the extent that IO staff see these values as their own, they might act accordingly.

Even if all IO staff are not liberal bureaucrats, the desire for legitimacy is likely to encourage them to at least play the role. The ability of IOs to survive and be effective is dependent on their legitimacy. In the modern international order, their legitimacy is dependent on their being seen as acting on behalf of the international community, which, in turn, gives them an incentive to operate according to rules that can be traced to principles and not politics. These rules are not only substantive but also procedural. IOs are supposed to be moving toward an inclusive decision-making process (not that they always do), making decisions on the basis of objective knowledge and expertise, and orienting themselves toward values that favor all rather than some.

Conclusion

This chapter has briefly explored how compulsory and institutional power illuminate the relationship between IOs and the diffusion of power. We repeat three earlier items. IOs are two-faced: they can either preserve or diffuse power, altering the underlying social relations that limit or enhance the ability of actors to control the circumstances of their lives. They also are relatively autonomous actors. Lastly, they can be linked to the diffusion and preservation of power in and through their position in existing structures, but they also can be linked to these effects through their actions.

The world cultural values of democracy and technocracy can help diffuse power, but we want to close with a word of warning: these values can operate at cross-purposes. A classic dilemma of modern liberal governance is the presumed trade-off between democracy and technocracy. In democracy (or the rule of the people), there is deference to respect the "general will," the "majority," and the "will of the people" on various grounds, including autonomy, liberty, and the belief that the people know best. In technocracy (or the rule of experts), there is deference to those who have specific knowledge. The immediate implication is that the rule of experts can be anti-democratic. Experts are not expected to always respect the preferences of the people but instead are supposed to use their presumably objective judgment. In these and other instances, outsiders feel justified in ignoring or dismissing the stated needs of the "people." For instance, peacebuilders often argue that they cannot practice the democracy that they preach because war-torn societies do not have the institutions to enable them to debate and aggregate preferences and because listening to the "people" might mean privileging the powerful and thus reproducing existing societal inequalities. This suggests the possibility that moral progress might depend not on the revolutionary character of the "people" but rather on the role of morally minded elite. Regardless of whether one thinks that elitism has its positive qualities, it is indisputably anti-democratic. In the race between technocracy and democracy, arguably technocracy seems to be winning. If so, IOs might be diffusing and conserving power—for themselves.

Additional reading

1. Michael Barnett and Raymond Duvall, eds., *Power in Global Governance* (Cambridge and New York: Cambridge University Press, 2004).
2. Michael Barnett and Martha Finnemore, *Rules for the World: International Organizations in World Politics* (Ithaca: Cornell University Press, 2004).
3. Iver Neumann and Ole Jacob Sending, *Governing the Global Polity: Practice, Mentality, and Rationality* (Ann Arbor: University of Michigan Press, 2010).
4. Thomas G. Weiss and Ramesh Thakur, *Global Governance and the UN: An Unfinished Journey* (Bloomington: Indiana University Press, 2010).

Notes

1   This chapter relies heavily on previous work on power: Michael Barnett and Raymond Duvall, "Power in International Politics," *International Organization* 59, no. 1 (2005): 39–75; and Michael Barnett and Martha Finnemore, "The Power of Liberal International Organizations," in *Power in Global Governance*, eds. Michael Barnett and Raymond Duvall (Cambridge and New York: Cambridge University Press, 2004), 161–184.

2   Michael Barnett and Martha Finnemore, *Rules for the World: International Organizations in World Politics* (Ithaca: Cornell University Press, 2004).

3   Don Handelman, "Comment," *Current Anthropology* 36, no. 2 (1995): 280–281.

CONTENTS

The Diffusion of Authority

David Held

This chapter examines the impact of the growth of multilateral and transnational govern-ance on sovereignty and the diffusion of political authority.[1] It begins by exploring the legacy of World War II and the building of the UN system. The rise of intergovern-mentalism and transnational governance arrangements are examined, followed by an assessment of some of the leading changes in the post-war global politics landscape. These issues are explored in greater depth across two cases: security and the environment. The chapter concludes by drawing together the threads of the discussion.

World War II and the building of the UN system

World War II created conflict and violence on a scale that had never been witnessed before, and was an experience that drastically reshaped the global order. As Hobsbawm put it, World War II was a "global human catastrophe."[2] The scale of the war effort, of destruction and of human suffering, was historically unprecedented. As war embraced Europe and East Asia, military hostilities raged across almost every single continent and ocean, excepting Latin America and southern Africa. Few of those states not engaged directly or indirectly in military combat could effectively remain neutral, since supplying the war effort of both the Axis (German, Italy, and Japan) and the Allied powers (United States, Britain, and France) required extensive sourcing. As McNeill notes, "transnational organization for war . . . achieved a fuller and far more effective expression during the Second World War than ever before."[3] But one of the most profound consequences of the war was the resultant transformation in the structure of world power. The year 1945 marked the end of Europe's global hegemony and confirmed the US and the Soviet

Union as global superpowers. This structural transformation heralded dramatic consequences for the pattern of post-war global political and security relations.

Against this backdrop, the UN's mandate could not be clearer. Article 1 explicitly states that the purpose of the UN is to "maintain international peace and security, and to that end: to take effective collective measures for the prevention and removal of threats to the peace."[4] Moreover, Article 1 goes on to stress that peace would be sought and protected through principles of international law. It concludes with the position that the UN is to be "a centre for harmonizing the actions of nations in the attainment of these common ends." This is particularly important for the purposes of this chapter since it speaks to the deliberate, facilitated interdependence that was sought by the UN. Where preceding efforts failed (e.g. the League of Nations), the UN aimed for inclusive buy-in from world powers in order to maintain global peace and security. Through centralized coordination and cooperation the UN created mechanisms that established mutual accountability between states, governed by growing and increasingly entrenched principles of international law. Moreover, the focus on principles of international law emphasized the significance of the formal institutionalization of such prevention and mitigation mechanisms. By facilitating integration in this way the UN sought to replace the tendency toward unilateral military action with collective action that could still preserve central aspects of state sovereignty. The UN Charter enshrined state sovereignty, but it also planted the seeds of qualification and conditionality; seeds that have grown in certain respects over the last 60 years such that sovereignty is increasingly understood as legitimate, or rightful, authority; an authority that is qualified by human rights and humanitarian principles, as well as both recognized and regulated by the international community.

The titanic struggles of World Wars I and II led to a growing acknowledgment that the nature and process of global governance (the manner in which global actors, ranging from states to multinational corporations and civil society organizations, cooperate formally and informally on global collective action problems) would have to change if the most extreme forms of violence against humanity were to be outlawed, and the growing interconnectedness and interdependence of nations recognized. Slowly, the subject, scope, and very sources of the Westphalian conception of international regulation, particularly its conception of international law, were all called into question.[5] The image of international regulation projected by the UN Charter (and related documents) was one of "states still jealously 'sovereign'," but now linked together in a "myriad of relations"; under pressure to resolve disagreements by peaceful means and according to legal criteria; subject in principle to tight restrictions on the resort to force; and constrained to observe "certain standards" with regard to the treatment of all persons in their territory, including their own citizens.[6] Of course, how restrictive the provisions of the Charter have been to states, and to what extent they have been actually operationalized, are important issues.

The rise of intergovernmentalism and transnationalism

It is, of course, commonplace to criticize the UN for the many ways it and the nations that created it have fallen short of its ideals. Yet it would be utterly mistaken to underestimate the successes wrought by the UN system overall and the geopolitical stability that followed its foundation. The decades that followed World War II were marked by peace between the great powers, although there were many proxy wars fought out in the global South. This relative stability created the conditions for what now can be recognized as the almost unprecedented period of prosperity that characterized the 1950s onward.[7] The UN is central to this story, although it is by no means the only important institutional innovation of the post-war settlement. A year prior to the founding of the UN, the Bretton Woods organizations were established in an effort to foster economic cooperation and a prosperous global economy: the International Monetary Fund (IMF) and the World Bank (previously the International Bank for Reconstruction and Development). The former focused on exchange rate stability and balance of payments assistance, the latter on long-term economic development. A sister institution, the General Agreement on Tariffs and Trade (GATT), which would later develop into the World Trade Organization (WTO), committed countries to open their borders to foreign trade. All of these institutions lay at the heart of what we now call post-war "economic globalization"—the growing enmeshment of economies across the world through trade, finance, and foreign direct investment and a slew of policies that facilitate economic interdependence. While the economic record of the post-war years varies by country, many experienced significant economic growth and living standards rose rapidly across large parts of the world. It was not just the West that was redefined by these developments; a global division of labor emerged which linked economic flows across large swathes of the world. In the wake of these changes, the world began to shift—slowly at first, but later more rapidly—from a bipolar toward a multipolar structure. By the late 1980s a variety of East Asian countries were beginning to grow at an unprecedented speed, and by the late 1990s countries such as China, India, and Brazil had gained significant economic momentum, a process that continues to this day.

The geopolitical stability engendered throughout the post-war years was a precondition for economic globalization, which subsequently transformed the way business and commerce were organized. Markets that were first and foremost domestic networks increasingly took on global dimensions. National economies became heavily enmeshed in the global system of production and exchange. Multinational corporations, many of which came to enjoy turnovers that dwarfed the gross domestic product (GDP) of even medium-sized nations, expanded across the globe. Financial markets exploded into a world of 24 hour trading, aided by competition between states eager to attract increasingly mobile capital flows. Economic globalization, with all its benefits and costs, winners and losers, came to embrace all regions and continents, and global interdependence deepened to a hitherto unknown degree.[8]

Meanwhile, international cooperation proceeded at an impressive pace. Whereas once participation in the multilateral order was sporadic and tenuous, it became both more entrenched and regularized. The most obvious illustration of this is the rapid emergence of diverse multilateral organizations and transnational agencies. New forms of multilateral and global politics became established, involving states, intergovernmental organizations (IGOs), international nongovernmental organizations (INGOs), and a wide variety of pressure groups. The numbers of active IGOs and INGOs increased exponentially. There was substantial growth in the number of international treaties in force, as well as the number of international regimes, formal and informal, altering the political and legal context in which states operated. To this dense web of mechanisms of coordination and collaboration can be added the routine meetings and activities of the key international policy-making bodies, including not only the UN and Bretton Woods organizations, but also the G-groups (the Group of 5, Group of 7, Group of 20, among others). Whereas in the middle of the nineteenth century there were just one or two interstate conferences or congresses per annum, the numbers increased to the many thousands each year.[9] Accordingly, states became enmeshed in an array of global governance systems and arrangements.

At the same time, new kinds of institutional arrangements have emerged alongside formal intergovernmental bodies. Networks of ostensibly "domestic" government officials now link with their peers across borders.[10] Different kinds of actors, public and private, form partnerships with each other to tackle issues of mutual concern. And purely private actors have created an array of their own governance institutions, ranging from voluntary regulations to private arbitral tribunals.[11] In some ways these new institutions reveal the adaptability and flexibility of global governance. But they also face, as the sections below show, significant limitations.

As forums for collaboration and engagement multiplied, they facilitated direct links between world powers, regardless of how explosive the rhetoric between them sometimes became, and opened the door for peripheral states to participate in the global order. Significantly, however, these institutions also embedded in their infrastructures and modus operandi the privileged positions of the 1945 victors. This was, arguably, a compromise needed to give incentives for great powers to participate in the new multilateral order.

The changed landscape of global politics

A number of trends can be identified within the changed landscape of world politics. First, there has been a general trend of integration between national and international political arenas.[12] The relationship between national governments and international bodies is not unilinear, but rather overlapping and reflexive to pressures coming from all sides (domestic constituencies, IGOs, global civil society, and so on). The two distinct spheres of traditional politics—national and international—have merged in some key respects. From global trade rules to intellectual property rights, from the global financial crisis to climate change, issues are posed for all levels of politics. A significant variety of institutional arrangements have been created in response to this trend, and this has included substantial innovation and change resulting in diverse forms of multi-actor, multi-sector, and multi-level governance.

However, the integration of national and international politics has also had an impact on our understanding of politics. The manner in which politics is conceived in the contemporary world can no longer be focused only on realist state-centric modes of analysis. While this shift in perception has had its critics, the realities of politics today give little support for seeing the nature and form of global governance through the lens of the unitary state acting alone, despite the resilience of great power politics. The greatest issues now confronting the world are not delineated and distributed neatly along national boundaries, and neither is the debate on how to solve them. The diffusion and growth of transborder governance arrangements reflect this integration of politics in significant ways. Any other starting point simplifies the character of the form and nature of global politics and masks the nature of political relationships in the contemporary world.

A second trend that can be observed since 1945 is the emergence of powerful non-state actors in the development of transborder governance. Non-state actors such as INGOs, multinational corporations (MNCs), and even individuals have always been active agents in political debate, but the manner in which they influence international politics has changed in significant ways. While these actors had varying degrees of influence in international politics in earlier periods, their impact came largely through lobbying their national governments. In this mode of political influence, non-state actors aggregate and articulate domestic interests to the state, shaping the preferences of a state, which in turn determine the state's behavior in international politics.

Although the direct relationship between non-state actors and the state remains an important link for political participation, non-state actors now also influence international politics more directly.[13] Through direct lobbying of global governance bodies, non-state actors shape political debate internationally, in turn impacting upon the behavior of states from above and below. The process which led to the Ottawa Treaty (concerning the ban of landmines) is perhaps the most prominent example of non-state actors participating in security governance with marked success.[14] This trend in general is strongest, however, in environmental governance, where INGOs have become such important actors that their influence has been called "functionally equivalent to diplomats" since they perform "many of the same functions as state delegates," such as interest aggregation and articulation, negotiation, and submitting policy recommendations.[15] The emergence of non-state actors certainly creates a more complex governance system than one comprised of traditional principal–agent relationships between states and purely intergovernmental organizations. This can pose potential problems of governance fragmentation, but it also broadens the platform for political deliberation and debate.[16]

Third, there has been a shift in how regulation and governance are enforced. The diverse forms of global governance produce equally diverse regulation that is intended to shape the behavior of states. This requires, first and foremost, the participation of states in regulatory structures, but it also requires that states comply with the result of negotiations even if it is against their own self-interest. Traditionally, compliance in international agreements is linked to the possibility of punitive measures (i.e. sanctions) that penalize violators in order to ensure appropriate conduct. Increasingly, however, trends can be detected that ensure that rules are enforced through alternative means such as voluntary-based arrangements and initiatives, as well as international standards that are adhered to by actors because of their reputational and coordinative effects.[17] Norm diffusion and capacity building can be an even more powerful tool for behavioral change than punitive measures.[18] This approach seeks to do more than just punish violators by building the capacity and incentives for actors to comply with established international standards. Institutions such as the UN Global Compact and the International Network for Environmental Compliance and Enforcement are good examples of the voluntary and informal regulation that is growing in global governance bodies.[19] These innovations in compliance schemes are positive steps in developing more effective governance; they indicate a range of productive experiments in new methods of creating rules and systems of enforcement which a diversity of public and private actors can both engage with and uphold. Self-evidently, however, they are not sufficient in and of themselves to solve the problem of compliance and enforcement as a spiral of global "bads," from global financial market instability to climate change, continues to form.

Fourth, overlapping with the trends mentioned above, there has been a proliferation of new types of global governance institutions in the post-war era, and especially since the end of the Cold War.[20] These are not multilateral, state-to-state institutions, but instead combine various actors under varying degrees of institutionalization. In some areas of global governance these kinds of institutions rank among the most important. The case of global finance stands out in this regard (e.g. the Basel Committee on Banking Supervision, the Financial Stability Forum),[21] but other examples include global health governance (e.g. the Global Fund, the GAVI alliance, and polio eradication efforts)[22] and standard setting.[23]

In aggregate, these new institutions have contributed to the growing polycentricism observed in many areas of global governance. A polycentric approach can have advantages and disadvantages. On the one hand, it can mean that more issues are addressed in meaningful ways—through specialized bodies qualified to regulate and govern a specific issue area. On the other hand, it can exacerbate institutional fragmentation. More importantly, in many areas of global governance it is by no means clear that institutional innovation alone is sufficient to fill the governance gap created by new global challenges such as global economic imbalances and climate change. At best these new institutional forms represent a partial solution.[24]

The complex architecture of global governance

The contemporary global governance system has features of both complexity and polycentricity. It can be usefully characterized as a multilayered, multi-sectoral, and multi-actor system in which institutions and politics matter in important ways to the determination of global policy outcomes; that is, to who gets what, when, and why.

Global governance is multilayered insofar as the making and implementation of global policies can involve a process of political cooperation and coordination between suprastate, national, transnational, and often substate agencies. Humanitarian relief operations, for example, often require the coordinated efforts of global, regional, national, and local agencies. In this respect, global governance is not so much hierarchical (command and control from the top) as horizontal: a process which involves coordination and cooperation between agencies across various levels, from the local to the global. However, the configuration of power and politics differs from sector to sector and from issue to issue, such that policy outcomes are not readily controlled by the same groups; interests and influence may vary from issue to issue. For instance, in the December 2012 climate negotiations in Qatar poor nations formed a strong lobbying coalition to establish the prospect, in principle, of rich nations having to compensate poorer nations for material losses resulting from climate change. In the Doha trade round, coordinated developing country action by the Group of 77 (G77) has essentially blocked progress in the negotiations by insisting that the trade-distorting effects of industrialized agriculture subsidies be addressed at least along with issues like services and further tariff reductions. Outcomes can be contingent, in other words, on bargaining, coalition politics, consensus, and compromise, rather than on deference to hegemonic power, significant though this may be.[25] The politics of global governance is, thus, significantly differentiated: the politics of global trade regulation is quite, for instance, distinct from the politics of climate or peacekeeping. Rather than being monolithic or unitary the system is best understood as sectoral or segmented.

Finally, many of the agencies of, and participants in, the global governance complex are no longer simply public bodies. There is considerable involvement of representatives from transnational civil society, from Greenpeace to Oxfam and an array of NGOs; of the corporate sector, from Monsanto to British Petroleum and trade or industrial associations; and of mixed public–private organizations such as the International Organization of Security Commissions (IOSCO). In addition to being multilayered and multisectoral, global governance is a multi-actor complex in which diverse agencies participate in the formulation and conduct of global public policy.

A polycentric conception of global governance does not imply that all states or agencies have an equal voice or input into—let alone an equal influence over—its agenda or programs. On the contrary, there is a recognition that the system is institutionally biased or distorted in favor of powerful states and vested interests: it is not by chance that in recent years the promotion of the global market has taken priority over tackling poverty, reducing inequality, and achieving the Millennium Development Goals more broadly. Yet the very nature of economic globalization is such that in weaving, however unevenly, thickening webs of worldwide interconnectedness, hierarchical and hegemonic forms of governance become more costly and demanding to pursue and less effective and legitimate. A notion of shared or common global problems ensures that multilateralism can work to moderate (though not to eliminate) power asymmetries.[26] Even the most powerful recognize that without, at least, the formal participation and tacit agreement of the weak or marginalized, effective and especially legitimate solutions to global problems—whether terrorism or money laundering, which directly impinge on their own welfare—would be impracticable. In these new circumstances of "complex interdependence," in which the returns to hierarchy are outweighed generally by the benefits of multilateral cooperation, traditional "hard" power instruments—military force or economic coercion—have a more circumscribed influence. This too creates new political opportunities for private actors and the forces of transnational civil society, which can mobilize considerable "soft power" resources in the pursuit of diverse objectives.[27]

Sovereignty and the limits to the diffusion of authority

To further understand the impact of intergovernmentalism and transnational governance on sovereignty and political authority, it is important to reflect more closely on how, and to what extent, the former reshapes the latter. In this regard, it is possible to formulate a hypothesis that illuminates the willingness of states to share and diffuse their authority to other agencies in the global governance complex. It could be put thus: when international and transnational agencies pursue policy agendas that are congruent with state interests, states are more likely to comply with policy outcomes and regulatory standards. When this is not the case, however, and states are confronted with policy outcomes and standards contrary to their interests, principles of sovereignty are typically evoked as a means to trump the agenda of global collaboration and coordination. Moreover, this will more commonly occur among those states able to challenge and ignore international and transnational pressures and forces. Take the areas of security and environment as examples.

Security

At the core of the post-war multilateral security order sits the UN Security Council and various disarmament treaties. These are two domains where problems of great power politics and the forces of growing multipolarity meet with complex ramifications. Both domains fundamentally reflect the post-war balance of power, which is simultaneously a source of their historical effectiveness and an impediment to addressing emergent security challenges. The need to foster great power inclusion in the UN system at the end of World War II led to the arrangement whereby permanent positions on the Security Council—and a veto—were granted to China, France, the Soviet Union (now Russia), the UK, and the US (the P-5). This system has remained intact across socio-economic and political transformations in the global order and now inhibits progress on some of the most pressing security concerns.

The historical use of the Security Council veto illustrates how the five permanent members have operated to protect and further their interests over time. The US has consistently exercised its veto on questions pertaining to Israel, and, more recently, Russia and China have invoked theirs against Security Council resolutions concerning the Syrian state's violent attacks on its civilians, the Sudanese government's brutality in Darfur, and in other similar cases. Attempts at reforming the Security Council veto have failed to date, with the result that the threats facing the world, especially with the rise of intrastate conflict, are infrequently and ineffectively addressed by the very institution responsible for maintaining global peace and security. Dominant interests have, in short, continued to trump the reform of security arrangements and multilateral approaches to security challenges.

Similar problems of institutional intransigence and increasing multipolarity are found in the disarmament regimes and concomitant efforts made to contain and reduce the most deadly weapons ever created. The Nuclear Non-Proliferation Treaty (NPT) is the primary mechanism intended to prevent the spread and use of nuclear weapons; the three principle goals of the NPT are non-proliferation, disarmament, and the management of pacific nuclear capacities. While it can be argued that the NPT and related bilateral agreements (such as the Strategic Arms Limitation Talks and Strategic Arms Reduction Treaties between Russia and the US) have been successful in helping to prevent the use of nuclear weapons, weaknesses in the regime are apparent when one considers the path that North Korea has taken to develop nuclear weapons: by developing the capacity allowed under Article IV, then by withdrawing from the treaty as allowed by Article X. Similar concerns now exist over Iran's nuclear program, with widespread speculation over its ambitions to develop weapons grade enrichment. India, Pakistan, and Israel simply never joined the treaty, exempting themselves from its requirements. These examples notwithstanding, "horizontal" proliferation has been largely avoided (e.g. in South Africa, South America, and East Asia). The same cannot be said, however, about "vertical" proliferation and disarmament—evidenced by the vast nuclear stockpiles that were developed by the Soviet Union/Russia and the US in the post-war years. Continued bilateral agreements between these two countries have been celebrated as successes, yet they have not amounted to actual disarmament by any significant measure. The vested interests of these states, and the structural protections they enjoy in the NPT and UN systems, have allowed them to sustain arsenals capable of global destruction should they ever be operationalized. While the staggered and incremental successes of great power negotiation are important steps, they fall far short of a robust and effective multilateral system capable of eliminating nuclear threats.

Additionally, harder and more complex problems have emerged in the global security arena. A primary example of this can be seen in the contemporary terrorism threat faced by the world community. Terrorism itself is not a new threat but in many ways it has changed, as have the strategies employed to mitigate it. It is a threat that requires effective coordination at the global level engaging multi-level partners, including states, regional bodies, and financial organizations, to name a few.

While multilateral efforts to deal with terrorism have been multifaceted, they have been limited in effect. Perhaps the greatest success has occurred in the tracking and freezing of terrorists' finances though bodies such as the Financial Action Task Force (FATF), and the Basel Committee on Banking Supervision.[28] Having said this, the UN Global Counter-Terrorism Strategy has two different bureaucracies: a Counter-Terrorism Committee, which exists within the Security Council, and the "Ad Hoc Sixth Committee," which operates within the General Assembly to focus on legal issues. Although the UN has been able to agree to some specific conventions aimed at particular aspects of terrorism, it still cannot agree on a basic definition of terrorism itself. This lack of basic agreement highlights just how challenging it has been for the multilateral order to form and implement coordinated global responses to terrorist threats.

In the absence of a robust global anti-terror regime, dominant states—primarily the US—have filled the void with national strategies and policies. In this arena, President Obama has drastically accelerated the use of armed unmanned aerial vehicles (i.e. drones) as a favored tool in US anti-terror strategy. With active drone operations in Afghanistan, Iraq, Pakistan, Yemen, and Somalia, Obama has instituted a policy that is increasingly calling into question the efficacy of international law and emerging security principles. US drone strikes have recently drawn sharp criticism from both the international community,[29] as well as from national leaders—for example from Pakistan.[30] Yet, despite this criticism the US shows no sign of changing its course. Given the power of the US in the international system, Obama's unilateral abrogation of international law undermines the potential for and effectiveness of a rule-based multilateral system. This trend risks deepening the institutional stagnation currently found in global security governance because it subverts effective transborder cooperation on pressing security issues.

Environment

Although the environment was not a significant policy concern when the post-war institutions were established in the 1940s, it has emerged as one of the most developed areas of global politics. Today there are over 200 multilateral environmental agreements and scores of specialized international organizations covering issues ranging from transboundary air pollution, to desertification, biodiversity, and the ozone layer.[31] There are also several intergovernmental bodies that act as focal points for the broader environmental regime, namely the United Nations Environment Programme (UNEP—an international organization), the Commission on Sustainable Development (a UN-based intergovernmental forum), and the Global Environment Facility (GEF—a World Bank-housed specialized fund for environmental projects).

Despite this plethora of institutions, global environmental governance remains fragmented, disjointed and, ultimately, weak. Successful environmental regimes—such as the one limiting ozone-depleting substances—are rare. In turn, failures—deforestation, biodiversity, fisheries, and climate change—are all too common. In response, a wide array of new forms of global governance has emerged, and private firms and civil society groups have played a leading, even dominant role in creating and sustaining these initiatives. Yet despite this intense activity, stalemate all too often pervades environmental politics. Climate change politics is indicative.

Climate change provides perhaps the starkest example of how new levels of interdependence and the interplay between leading and emerging powers can overwhelm the capacity of existing institutions to resolve global collective action problems. Climate change is a quintessentially global issue, as greenhouse gas emissions anywhere have impacts everywhere. Furthermore, the impacts are large. The 2006 Stern Report estimated, among other things, that climate change could reduce global GDP by up to 20 percent compared to what it otherwise would be. We are thus all deeply affected by the carbon usage of all other inhabitants of the planet—a remarkable degree of interconnectedness and interdependence.

Equally troubling, the costs of mitigating climate change, though much smaller than the costs of allowing it to occur, are substantial, and have decisive distributional impacts for countries, industries, firms, and individuals. Rich countries have created the majority of carbon in the atmosphere, and continue to have significantly higher per capita emissions rates than emerging economies, especially in North America, Australia, and the Persian Gulf. However, the majority of future emissions will come from the developing world, meaning that the participation of countries like China, India, and Brazil is required for any effort to mitigate climate change to succeed. In sum, climate change has created perhaps unprecedented levels of interdependence even as the power to stop it diffuses to a range of different actors.

Cooperation, then, is necessary, but in short supply. Since the 1992 Rio Summit almost every country in the world has met annually to discuss how to mitigate and adapt to climate change. The objective has been to create a global treaty specifying binding emissions reductions, along the lines of the successful ozone regime. Two decades of negotiations have yielded exactly one treaty requiring reductions in greenhouses gases (GHGs), the 1997 Kyoto Protocol that committed rich nations to a tiny 5 percent average reduction in emissions below 1990 levels by 2012. Even this weak target proved unacceptable to the United States, which refused to implement the treaty. Indeed, it proved even too ambitious for many signatories, such as Canada, which are on track to violate their commitments (and will face no penalty for doing so). Developing countries, which will produce the lion's share of future emissions, accepted no commitments at all under Kyoto. The Protocol was meant, of course, as a building block toward future commitments. A similar incremental approach had, after all, succeeded within the ozone regime. As the fateful 2009 Copenhagen summit demonstrated, where world leaders were unable (or unwilling) to produce an agreement on climate change, no global deal is likely any time soon.

Instead, the world has turned to a more piecemeal approach. Keohane and Victor describe a "regime complex" for climate change that includes the United Nations Framework Convention on Climate Change but also an array of other intergovernmental bodies like the G20 and the international financial institutions.[32] Unable to reach an agreement on a global treaty in the UN process, states will increasingly turn to other, more fragmented forums.

Domestic policy plays a large role. Individual governmental commitments to reduce emissions, like those implemented by the European Union or various US states, seek to make a major contribution to resolving the problem. Some of these measures are quite significant. In the United States, for example, one study has estimated that the commitments of 17 states and 684 cities (representing 53 percent of the US population and 43 percent of its emissions) could stabilize the nation's emissions at 2010 levels by 2020.[33] Other types of policies, such as China's ambitious energy intensity targets, also have important effects. Yet, unlike many areas of environmental politics (forestry, fishing, and biodiversity), climate change is an "all or nothing" collective action problem. Here it is the case that the altruistic initiatives of some actors will matter little unless all the major emitters control their greenhouse gases. The fragmented, domestic, and transnational climate initiatives thus face the enormous challenge of reaching a scale where they can have a meaningful impact.[34] As the December 2012 meeting in Qatar highlighted, we are a long way from this position. Runaway climate change remains the prospect unless the US, China, and India, among other major emitters, become genuine partners in a new climate regime.

Conclusion

The proliferation of intergovernmentalism and transnational governance mechanisms in the post-war period is a striking trend. While the complex global governance system has characteristics of a multilayered, multi-sector, and multi-actor system, the question remains how far political authority has been diffused, in practice, throughout the global order. The global political agenda is increasingly shaped by a diversity of voices and agents, but sovereignty remains a powerful obstacle to the development and execution of policy in areas sensitive to the interests of leading states. Breakthroughs in post-war nuclear disarmament, along with new binding commitments from the major emitters of GHGs, still seems some distance from the world envisaged by many of the architects of the post-war multilateral order and of the complex transnational institutions that now struggle to govern it.

Additional reading

1. Thomas Hale, David Held, and Kevin Young, *Gridlock: Why Global Cooperation Is Failing When We Need It Most* (Cambridge: Polity Press, 2013).
2. Thomas G. Weiss and Ramesh Thakur, *Global Governance and the UN: An Unfinished Journey* (Bloomington: Indiana University Press, 2010).
3. David Held and Thomas Hale, ed., *Handbook of Transnational Governance* (Cambridge: Polity Press, 2011).
4. Anne-Marie Slaughter, *A New World Order* (Princeton: Princeton University Press, 2004).
5. David Held and Kevin Young, "Crisis in Parallel Worlds: The Governance of Global Risks in Finance, Security and the Environment," in *The Deepening Crisis: Governance Challenges after Neoliberalism*, eds. Craig Calhoun and Georgi Derluguian (New York: New York University Press, 2011).

Notes

1 Many of the themes of this article are explored at greater length in Thomas Hale, David Held, and Kevin Young, *Gridlock: Why Global Cooperation Is Failing When We Need It Most* (Cambridge: Polity Press, 2013). I am indebted to my coauthors of this book for the many discussions we had about these issues.
2 Eric Hobsbawm, *Age of Extremes: The Short Twentieth Century 1914–1991* (London: Michael Joseph, 1994), 52.
3 William McNeill, *The Pursuit of Power* (Oxford: Blackwell, 1982), 356.
4 UN Charter, Chapter I, Article 1.
5 Hedley Bull, *The Anarchical Society* (London: Macmillan, 1977), 6; David Held, *Democracy in the Global Order* (Cambridge: Policy Press, 1995), 4.
6 Antonio Cassese, "Violence, War and the Rule of Law in the International Community," in *Political Theory Today*, ed. David Held (Cambridge: Polity Press, 1991): 255–275.
7 Hale, Held, and Young, *Gridlock*.
8 David Held et al., *Global Transformations: Politics, Economics and Culture* (Cambridge: Polity Press, 1999).
9 Union of International Associations, *Yearbook of International Organizations* (Leiden: Brill, 2012).
10 Robert Keohane and Joseph Nye, *Power and Interdependence: World Politics in Transition* (Boston, MA: Little Brown, 1977); Anne-Marie Slaughter, *A New World Order* (Princeton: Princeton University Press, 2004).
11 Tim Büthe, "Private Regulation in the Global Economy: A (P)Review," *Business and Politics* 12, no. 3 (2010): 1–38.
12 Helen Milner, *Interests, Institutions and Information* (Princeton: Princeton University Press, 1997); Slaughter, *A New World Order*.
13 Peter M. Haas, "Policy Responses to Stratospheric Ozone Depletion," *Global Environmental Change* 1, no. 3 (1991): 224–234; and Margaret Keck and Kathryn Sikkink, *Activists Beyond Borders* (Ithaca: Cornell University Press, 1998).
14 David Held and Kevin Young, "Crisis in Parallel Worlds: The Governance of Global Risks in Finance, Security, and the Environment," in *The Deepening Crisis: Governance Challenges after Neoliberalism*, eds. Craig Calhoun and Georgi Derluguian (New York: New York University Press, 2011): 19–42.
15 David Held and Thomas Hale, eds., *Handbook of Transnational Governance* (Cambridge: Polity Press, 2011); and Michelle Betsill and Elisabeth Corell, eds., *NGO Diplomacy: The*

Influence of Nongovernmental Organization in International Environmental Negotiations (Cambridge, MA: MIT Press, 2008).

16 Thomas Risse-Kappen, *Bringing Transnational Relations Back In: Non-State Actors, Domestic Structures and International Institutions* (Cambridge: Cambridge University Press, 1995).

17 Dieter Kerwer, "Rules That Many Use: Standards and Global Regulation," *Governance* 18, no. 4 (2005): 611–632.

18 Abram Chayes and Antonia H. Chayes, *The New Sovereignty: Compliance with International Regulatory Agreements* (Cambridge, MA: Harvard University, 1995).

19 Held and Hale, *Handbook of Transnational Governance.*

20 Ibid.

21 Held and Young, "Crisis in Parallel Worlds."

22 Johanna Hanefield, "The Global Fund to Fight AIDS, Malaria, and Tuberculosis," in *Handbook of Transnational Governance,* eds. Held and Hale, 161–165; Mathias Koenig-Archibugi, "Global Polio Eradication Initiative," in *Handbook of Transnational Governance,* eds. Held and Hale, 166–175.

23 Tim Büthe, *The New Global Rulers: The Privatization of Regulation in the World Economy* (Princeton: Princeton University Press, 2011).

24 Thomas Hale and David Held, "Gridlock and Innovation in Global Governance: The Partial Transnational Solution," *Global Policy* 3, no. 2 (2012): 169–181.

25 Robert Keohane, "Governance in a Partially Globalized World," *American Political Science Review* 95, no. 1 (2001): 1–13.

26 John Ikenberry, *After Victory* (Princeton: Princeton University Press, 2001).

27 Thomas Risse, "Let's Argue: Communicative Action in World Politics," *International Organization* 54, no. 1 (2000): 1–39.

28 John Taylor, *Global Financial Warriors: The Untold Story of International Finance in the Post-9/11 World* (London: Norton, 2007); and Elini Tsingou, "Global Financial Governance and the Developing Anti-Money Laundering Regime: What Lessons for International Political Economy?," *International Politics* 47, no. 6 (2010): 617–637.

29 Owen Bowcott, "Drone Strikes Threaten 50 Years of International Law, Says UN Rapporteur," *Guardian,* 21 June 2012, http://www.guardian.co.uk/world/2012/jun/21/drone-strikes-international-law-un?newsfeed=true.

30 Qasim Nauman, "Pakistan Condemns US Drone Strikes," *Reuters,* 4 June 2012, http://www.reuters.com/article/2012/06/04/us-pakistan-usa-drones-idUSBRE8530MS20120604.

31 Held et al., *Global Transformations.*

32 Robert Keohane and David G. Victor, "The Regime Complex for Climate Change," Discussion Paper 2010–33, Harvard Project on International Climate Change Agreements (Cambridge, MA: Harvard University, 2010); and Thomas Hale, "A Climate Coalition of the Willing," *Washington Quarterly* (2011): 89–101.

33 Nicholas Lutsey and Daniel Sperling, "America's Bottom-up Climate Change Mitigation Policy," *Energy Policy* 36, no. 2 (2008): 673–685.

34 Bruce Au et al., *Beyond a Global Deal: A UN+ Approach to Climate Governance* (Berlin: Global Governance 2020, 2011).

Who Governs the Globe?

Susan K. Sell

Scholars of international politics have long been interested in global governance. It is easy to think of global problems that overwhelm the capacities of individual states to solve them. Climate change, nuclear proliferation, financial crises, disease and hunger come readily to mind. Many scholars conceive of the international system as a system of sovereign states that answer to no higher authority. States differ in their resources and capacities; they may be equally sovereign but are not equally capable of tackling global problems. Beyond trying to understand global governance, scholars seek to devise strategies for addressing global problems and imagine possibilities for an alternative future.

At the same time analysts have observed increasing stalemate in multilateral governance organizations such as the World Trade Organization (WTO), the World Intellectual Property Organization (WIPO), and the Kyoto Protocol of the United Nations Framework Convention on Climate Change. Multilateral interstate treaty-making seems to be on the decline, with bilateral, regional, and plurilateral initiatives gaining ground. Some scholars have suggested that international law has stagnated and others point out that traditional interstate multilateral governance plays a much smaller role than one might expect. Recent scholarship in political science, sociology, and law is addressing this arc of change and exploring alternative forms and processes of global governance.[1]

The proliferation of new actors and new forms and processes of global governance raises important questions. Who are the global governors? What do they do? Why does anyone defer to them? What are the relationships between various governors? Since no governor governs alone, relationships between them will have an impact on processes and outcomes. What are the relationships between the governors and the governed?

In a world lacking a global *demos*, to whom exactly are governors accountable? Whom do they represent? On what basis can one evaluate their legitimacy?

This chapter tackles precisely these questions. It proceeds in four sections. First, the chapter offers a brief overview of the development of global governance literature. Second, the chapter examines the actors, their activities, their bases of authority, and their relationships with each other. Section three addresses the relationships between the governors and the governed and some of the relevant challenges for accountability, representation, and legitimacy. The chapter concludes with suggestions for further research and development of the ideas presented.

History and development

During the Cold War American neorealist Kenneth Waltz argued that the world was anarchic, and that the distribution of capabilities across states was the most analytically fruitful way to think about the international system.[2] Anarchy simply meant the absence of world government. This perspective has remained influential, and has informed mainstream American scholarship on international cooperation. Studies of the problem of cooperation under anarchy have informed much of the contemporary scholarship on global governance. With anarchy as the central trope, scholars of international politics have explored the concept of governance without government.[3]

In the 1980s international relations scholars focused on international regimes, "principles, norms, rules and decision-making procedures around which actor expectations converge in a given issue area."[4] Stephen Krasner's volume on regimes featured analytic variety, with realists, constructivists, and functionalists weighing in on the sources and contours of international cooperation.[5] Realists focused on power, constructivists on ideas and identity, and functionalists on institutions. However, Robert Keohane's rationalist functionalism, that global needs gave rise to governance arrangements, came to dominate the literature on cooperation and international institutions. Keohane argued that, despite anarchy, states cooperated because institutions provided them with benefits. International institutions reduced transaction costs, provided information, and, if well designed, discouraged cheating and free-riding. Thereafter, the literature on institutions, international regimes, and international organizations dominated mainstream American scholarship on international cooperation. Interstate dynamics, treaty-making and international law occupied much of the analytic terrain in studies of global governance.

Produced during an era of the perceived hegemonic decline of the United States in the 1980s, Keohane's analysis foregrounded stability as the chief normative value. The question was how the United States could maintain its "benign" hegemony while losing power relative to other states. Many related analyses were statist and functionalist. They focused on structures or forms of cooperation and downplayed both the contestation and the politics animating international relationships. They exhibited a static conservative bias intended to preserve a particular US-led international order. Susan Strange offered a trenchant critique of this approach, pointing out its inherent normative bias, its preoccupation with stasis, and the limits of its state-centric paradigm.[6]

Subsequent development of this strand of theorizing addressed questions of institutional design, such as membership and decision-rules.[7] Ample scholarship on global governance has focused on the forms or structures of governance. This literature focused on intergovernmental interactions and technocratic, managerial, approaches to global governance. Yet just because some problems were global, this did not mean that global governance arrangements would arise. This line of work implicitly assumed that international cooperation and global governance were inherently good. Cooperation was good; more cooperation was better. Governance was good; more governance was better. Even analysts of sub-state actors coordinating across borders emphasized a benign, managerial style of governance. As Ronen Palan argues:

> The results are theories of form without substance. Regime theories are theories about coordination problems that states are facing with no particular reasons or cause for coordination besides some vague notion that those states that join regimes have a reason for doing so. Regime theory supposedly tells us about the impact of coordination, but has little to say about the substance of the regime as such.[8]

Not only did this rationalist functionalist approach say little about substance, it provided little insight into whose needs were being met by governance arrangements. International politics is largely about who gets what, who benefits, how costs and benefits are distributed, who pays adjustment costs, and contestation over all of these. By downplaying these central issues the functionalist approach failed to address some of the more fraught elements of international politics.

Four important developments in the 1980s and 1990s prompted new thinking about international cooperation and led scholars to question this mainstream approach. First, the rapid pace of economic globalization more tightly connected people across space and time. This triggered shifts in thinking from the local and national scales to the global scale. Second, economic privatization and deregulation increased the social power of private actors, especially globally engaged multinational enterprises and titans of global finance. Third, the development of new information and communication technologies radically compressed space and time, and provided both new opportunities for, and constraints on, conflict and cooperation. Fourth, the end of the Cold War ushered in a period of renewed commitment to and optimism about international cooperation. In response to these developments scholars such as James Rosenau and Philip Cerny explored analytic territory that sought to better capture these momentous changes.[9]

Rosenau and Cerny highlighted the ways in which globalization strained state capacity. They revealed the poor fit between a system of territorially based sovereign states and rapid processes of globalization that both overwhelmed and undermined that system. Newly connected networks of actors both disaggregated and transcended the state. Rosenau highlighted turbulence in world politics coupled with an increasingly skilled global citizenry. Cerny and Rosenau emphasized the bigger role that private actors were playing. Cerny argued that states were re-purposing themselves to compete in global markets and globalization had produced the "competition state" that undermined domestic welfare bargains.

Many scholars focus on international organizations, treaties, and international law, yet these governance foundations are based upon thin state consent. For instance, international treaties only require that states agree to them: "international law is agnostic on how this agreement was reached (process), who participated in its establishment (actors), what form it takes (instrument) and what is actually agreed on (substance)."[10] Multilateral treaty-making in international organizations features high transaction costs and "once concluded is hard to adapt to changing circumstances."[11] Miles Kahler and David Lake have found that this traditional supranational governance structure "plays a less central role than many believe or expect."[12] Joost Pauwelyn, Ramses Wessel, and Jan Wouters have noted the increasing stagnation of international law and the simultaneous emergence of new actors, new outputs, and new processes that have led to a much broader range of governance practices.

Many global governors operate in the space between thin state consent and "thick stakeholder" consensus. Sovereign states are just one constituency. Stakeholders include the rule-makers, the governors, and the rule-takers, the governed. More informal processes, non-state actors, and networks that strive for more robust, or thick, stakeholder consensus are edging out the traditional state-centric modes of global governance. Globalization has strained more traditional governance mechanisms. As Pauwelyn, Wessel, and Wouters point out:

> The state remains a pivotal entity of interest aggregation, legitimation and control. Yet it is supplemented, assisted, corrected and continuously challenged by a variety of other actors be they regulators, national and international agencies, city mayors, businesses or NGOs who can make cooperation not only more legitimate but also more effective.[13]

Hybrid coalitions and networks of state and non-state actors have emerged as prominent sources of global governance and regulatory change.

Governors and their authority

In the 1990s analysts such as Claire Cutler, Virginia Haufler, Tony Porter, Thomas Biersteker, Rodney Hall, Margaret Keck, and Kathryn Sikkink established the prominence of a variety of non-state actors in global governance.[14] They highlighted the proliferation of potential governors, ranging from business firms, social movements, and NGOs. Scholars began to look more deeply into *who* governs the globe and began to analyze the agency of global governors. "Global governors are authorities who exercise power across borders for purposes of affecting policy. Governors thus create issues, set agendas, establish and implement rules or programs, and evaluate and/or adjudicate outcomes."[15] Global governors can be NGOs, civil society campaigns, experts, intergovernmental organizations, states, regulators, judges, lobbyists, business firms, and hybrid networks blending multiple types of actors.

Global governors engage in numerous tasks, including: agenda setting, negotiation, decision-making, implementation, monitoring, and enforcement. Global governors' activities vary depending on what resources they bring to bear. For example, at the agenda-setting stage NGOs, transnational advocacy networks, and experts may play prominent roles. They work to engage decision-makers by defining and framing issues, and advocating for particular approaches to the problem at hand. For example, environmental scientists have played a significant role in defining climate change. Transnational advocacy networks championed the ban on landmines. Hybrid networks of NGOs, experts, and states pressed for access to generic antiretroviral medicines to address the HIV/AIDS pandemic.

Governors play different roles: they may act as "lobbyists, acting as interest groups; partners, providing expertise or participat[ing] in common projects; adversaries, blaming and shaming governmental authorities; and functional substitutes for states, performing regulatory functions."[16] Clifford Bob offers an adversarial example in the role of the National Rifle Association mobilizing to oppose UN efforts to regulate the small arms trade; the result has been stalemate, or, as Bob puts it, "zombie policy."[17]

Different types of global governors' roles vary according to policy stages and issue areas. For traditional interstate multilateral negotiations states may want to include experts or firms for advice, but states are less likely to invite transnational advocacy networks to participate in negotiations. Alexander Cooley and James Ron have analyzed the substantial role that non-state actors such as accounting firms and humanitarian aid organizations play in policy implementation in economic reform and relief work.[18] Jonsson and Tallberg have found that states are less likely to include transnational actors in decision-making and enforcement.[19] Overall, existing work in this area tells us that transnational advocacy networks are less likely to be included in finance and security policy, yet are more likely to be included in human rights, environment, and development issues.

Global governors' bases of authority, the ability to induce deference in others, are varied and are not mutually exclusive.[20] Authority may be institutional. A global governor's authority may derive from her position in an organizational structure, such as a multinational corporation or an international organization. Such a global governor is both empowered and constrained by the institution's rules and mandates. Authority can be delegated; states often delegate authority to international organizations or firms. Some global governors are recognized for their expertise in complex or technical areas. Environmental scientists, economists, and development professionals are examples of governors whose authority is a product of their education and training. Principle-based authority derives from service to some widely accepted principles, morals, or values. These principles may be either religious or secular and may include commitments to peace, human rights, a nuclear-free world, ending global hunger or ending gender-based violence. Global governors frequently promote principles such as liberty, dignity, security, and prosperity. Amnesty International's commitment to human rights and Greenpeace's promotion of environmental preservation are examples of principled authority. Finally, capacity-based authority arises from perceived competence. This is related to expert authority, but tilts toward a known track record for problem solving. This may be more about experience or performing an action effectively rather than professional training, education, or epistemic certification.

In global governance, no governor governs alone. Foregrounding agency and its authoritative bases offers insights into relationships among the governors themselves and the presence or lack of synergistic partnerships. Highlighting agency and relationships allows us to analyze synergies and conflicts across competencies. For example, governors face dilemmas when their delegated authority is in tension with their expertise.

The economists at the International Monetary Fund (IMF) are experts in financial stability, not poverty reduction; yet the IMF has been charged with addressing the Millennium Development Goals. Such mismatches can result in poor performance and reduced authority over time.

Kenneth Abbott and Duncan Snidal identified multiple combinations of types of governors in their "governance triangle" to capture interactions and partnerships between the three points of the triangle: NGOs, firms, and states.[21] Distilling potential global governors into three types, they map out a variety of governance arrangements into seven zones defined by the relative participation of combinations of governors. For example, one zone captures governance by states alone, a second by NGOs alone, and a third by firms alone. The other four represent various mixtures, such as NGOs partnering with firms; NGOs partnering with states; states partnering with firms; and a relatively balanced blend of all three types of governors participating in governance (e.g. the International Labour Organization). Whether or not these partnerships will be synergistic and constructive depends, in part, on how well their respective competencies complement each other and whether or not they compete or conflict with one another.

Governors' relationships between each other and to their institutional environment can shape outcomes. Alexander Cooley and James Ron have demonstrated that at the implementation stage of governance these factors can cause suboptimal outcomes.[22] In their cases—accounting consultancies for market reforms in Eastern Europe and humanitarian aid provision in Rwanda—would-be governors compete in bidding on short-term contracts. This competitive bidding with short time-horizons ensures that implementation and/or delivery of services will be suboptimal because providers are motivated to secure the next contract. To do so they will be particularly motivated to secure a positive report, which can exacerbate tensions between the purported mission and the wishes of the recipients. For instance, while the mission may be to implement thorough economic liberalization, the local government may wish to drag its heels. Therefore the local government will be disposed to produce the most positive report for the provider that gives it the most latitude in implementation. The provider then may be inclined to exaggerate progress in order to secure the next contract.

While acting in an institutional environment, global governors may exercise considerable agency. At times they can bypass established institutions to achieve desired governance outcomes. As Jakobi suggests:

> Actors on the periphery of a field are more likely to innovate given that they are less bound to the fields [sic] dominant logic of action. . . . Central actors usually have more resources and contacts to help innovate. . . . [But marginal actors] can overcome barriers through inter organizational networking and through networking with higher status organizations, groups and individuals.[23]

Actors at the periphery of powerful institutions have been able to use their networking and technological skills to alter governance outcomes. One important example comes from the regulatory field of intellectual property. The United States Trade

Representative's Office (USTR) and global business firms have driven the movement toward higher international standards of property protection and enforcement. The tight relationship between USTR and private global firms largely has kept civil society actors, consumers, and transnational advocacy networks out of the policy-making process. In 2006 the United States pressed for an Anti-Counterfeiting Trade Agreement (ACTA), with Japan and the European Union, as a plurilateral treaty to adopt and promote protection and enforcement standards well above and beyond the WTO standards. The official negotiations began in 2008; they were secret and not transparent. Only global business firms were consulted and kept abreast of developments. Transnational advocacy networks, civil society actors, and consumers learned of the substance of the negotiations only through leaked documents, and only after much of the process had taken place. On 4 October 2011 the United States and seven other countries signed ACTA. The European Union signed in 2012.

Meanwhile, in the United States two domestic laws aimed at foreign websites that hosted copyright-infringing material were moving through Congress. In the fall of 2011, the two bills were Protect Intellectual Property Act (PIPA) in the Senate, and Stop Online Piracy Act (SOPA) in the House of Representatives. If passed, the bills would block US Internet users from accessing foreign websites such as Pirate Bay and would block US Internet users' payments through services, such as PayPal, to foreign sites hosting copyright infringing content. Given their deep entrenchment in USTR and generosity toward members of Congress, rights holders, representing the motion picture and sound recording industries, fully expected to secure support for the legislation. As powerful political players they had grown accustomed to getting what they wanted.

However, this time a transnational hybrid coalition of outsiders and Internet users exercised agency by mobilizing protest against SOPA and PIPA. They deployed their considerable technical skills to scale up protest and got millions of users to participate in protesting the proposed bills. Internet activism has lowered the costs of collective action. Using a combination of blogs, denial of service attacks, electronic petitions, and website postings informing users of the dangers of SOPA and PIPA, this coalition mobilized millions of people to try to "kill the bills." They organized a coordinated web blackout. On 18 January 2012, more than 15,000 websites went dark for 24 hours, including Wikipedia, Mozilla, and Reddit, to protest against the legislation and underscore the consequences if the bills were passed. Throughout the day an increasing number of Members of Congress renounced their support of the bills, and by 20 January the bills were dead.

This hybrid transnational coalition of hackers, Internet users, consumers, and anticensorship groups won an unexpected victory over rights holders. Inspired by the successful anti-SOPA/PIPA campaign in the United States, hundreds of thousands of Europeans took to the streets to protest the Anti-Counterfeiting Trade Agreement that the EU had negotiated and signed. The transnational coalition of Internet users now mobilized to kill ACTA, and in February 2012 Bulgaria, the Czech Republic, Germany, Cyprus, Latvia, Romania, Estonia, Austria, the Netherlands, and Slovakia suspended ACTA ratification. On 4 July 2012, the Members of the European Parliament voted 478 against and 39 in favor of ACTA (165 abstained), and ACTA's future looks bleak. The scale shifting that the Internet facilitated between transnational, international, plurilateral, and domestic scales, and the offline mobilization of anti-ACTA forces halted the policy trajectory of locking in higher standards that rights holders had considered to be a sure thing. With low barriers to entry, and a nimble and fluid digital network, these global governors successfully challenged those governors who had been more deeply entrenched in core institutions in this policy area.

Governors and the governed: accountability and legitimacy

The previous section examined governors' diverse bases of authority to understand why the governed defer to the governor and to answer the question: "Why are they in charge?" However, exploring relationships between the governors and the *governed* raises important normative issues. Global governors must be attentive to their audiences and constituents. They must manage and adapt to constant change. As Jakobi points out, "although power is important, it also involves partnerships, cooperation and coalitions, material and discursive interventions. Institutional change is a social enterprise, and any activity of an institutional entrepreneur or political leader is targeted to a reaction of others."[24]

Global governance raises particular challenges for accountability, representation and legitimacy. Richard Mulgan offers this definition of accountability:

> Accountability, the obligation to be called "to account," is a method of keeping the public informed and powerful in check. It implies a world which is at once complex, where experts are needed to perform specialized tasks, but still fundamentally democratic in aspiration, in that members of the public assert their right to question the experts and exercise ultimate control over them.[25]

The inherent tension between independence of action required for governors to be effective in governance tasks, and the accountability required to limit their power poses another set of dilemmas. By what metric should global governors be held to account? What mechanisms can enhance accountability? To whom should governors be accountable? Inspired by democratic theory, many commentators suggest that transparency and participation can facilitate accountability. In response to complaints about non-transparency, both the WTO and WIPO have begun to post many more reports and documents on their websites and to make them available with far less delay than in the past. Yet transparency is not enough. In response to pressure for broader stakeholder participation, a number of international organizations have opened up their processes to transnational advocacy groups and civil society actors. Exceptions to this include the IMF, and to some degree the WTO. The extent to which stakeholder participation shapes policy is an empirical question that an exclusive focus on formal institutional design can obscure.

Using participation as a yardstick raises additional questions about representation. Since we have no global democracy, how do we determine who should be represented?

Jens Bartelson points out that "there is no *demos* at the global level that could endow global political authorities with the kind of legitimacy that supposedly derives from popular consent."[26] The fragile nexus between the authority of those who make law and the question of who is subject to law "certainly does not vanish in the context of transnational governance regimes."[27]

Scholars have suggested a number of ways to address the unwieldiness of representing the whole world. One approach is to include, or represent the interests of, those who would be most affected by the decision or policy. Who should be at the table when decisions are made, the regulators, the regulated, or both? This is even more contested at a global level than it is in domestic democratic politics. Those who have a bigger stake should have a bigger voice. However, in the case of the IMF, who has the bigger stake? Should it be the donors or the citizens who will experience structural adjustment first hand? Furthermore, it is often not immediately obvious who will, in fact, be affected. For instance, at the time of the WTO negotiations on an Agreement on Trade Related Aspects of Intellectual Property (TRIPs) no one foresaw how much the Agreement would affect the millions of sub-Saharan African and Thai and Brazilian HIV/AIDS patients who needed access to generic antiretroviral medicines. As such, defining the "all affected" political community is hardly a straightforward exercise. Relevant political communities are not static.

In response to these problems some scholars have offered an alternative "discursive representation" approach to democracy. Rather than worrying about *numbers* of citizens represented, "all the relevant political discourses ought to get represented, regardless of how many people subscribe to each."[28] However, this approach begs the question of who gets to identify and present "all the relevant political discourses." Whose expertise and whose empathy would determine this? Who is the expert? In the case of intellectual property protection, what range of discourses would be provided? Would trade, investment, and rights holders' interests be represented? Or would public health, open science, education, and agriculture also be included? Would this devolve into a kind of tyranny of expertise or a contest over moral righteousness and more far-flung representation? Advocating discursive representation hardly dodges the political contestation at the heart of global governance.

Legitimacy is a social relationship; to be legitimate is to be "*socially recognized as rightful*"[29] by those over whom global governors claim authority. This immediately raises thorny normative issues. As Regine Kreide asks, "What normative demands must transnational governance comply with? And when is transnational governance legitimate?"[30] One prominent approach to thinking about legitimacy and supranational governance comes from the European Union literature; Fritz Scharpf, for instance, has focused on "input" and "output" legitimacy.[31] Briefly, input legitimacy refers to participation and representation in the process of defining policy goals, and output legitimacy refers to the translation of these goals into policy. While complications of participation and representation were discussed above, output legitimacy raises a different set of challenges.

Many scholars have tried to derive checklists of criteria for legitimacy that are informed by democratic theory and then applied to the global level. Yet critics point out that *ex ante* checklists tend to be ahistorical and inattentive to social context. For instance, a legitimate participation norm did not always include women; and one should expect legitimacy to vary according to cultural and social context. Daniel Mugge argues that "assessments of legitimacy have to focus on the actual workings of institutions, not on formal flows of authority, information and accountability."[32] This concern with substance over form underscores the fact that legitimacy is not static; it involves continual interaction between governors and the governed. As Steven Bernstein points out, "what constitutes legitimacy results from an interaction of the community of actors affected by the regulatory institution, i.e. the public who grant legitimacy, with broader institutionalized norms—or social structure—that prevail in the relevant issue area."[33]

In developing a more dynamic way of thinking about legitimacy Calliess and Zumbasen argue that it is implausible to separate "the sphere where official author-ities decide over law or non-law from the societal sphere in which the relevant actors recognize legal norms, by the authority these norms exercise over their lives or actions."[34] Authority, procedure, and substance map onto "actors," "processes," and "outputs" as well as to the benchmark of thick consensus.[35] Pauwelyn and his colleagues endorse procedural integrity rooted in checks and balances that examine the following three elements: "(i) the source, respectability of the norm-creating body, (ii) transparency, openness and neutrality in the norm's procedural elaboration and (iii) the substantive quality, consistency and overall acceptance (consensus) of the norm."[36] Calliess and Zumbasen propose a "rough consensus and running code" approach to governance. The "rough consensus" applies to the front end of the policy process and would feature "*ex ante* controls (such as setting a clear mandate or benchmark against which actors can be held accountable; guidelines; appointments; or rules on conflicts of interest) and *ex post* controls (such as re-adjustment of guidelines; financial accountability or complaint mechanisms)."[37]

Thus legitimacy might better be conceptualized as an ongoing *process* of legitimation. As a process, one important criterion for legitimacy would be the extent to which policy, or output, is open to contestation.[38] This is an important criterion that could address the flexibility and responsiveness that global governors and the governed need to have. Many issues in global governance, such as intellectual property, finance, and the environment exhibit a huge discrepancy between the narrow representation and technical focus of global governors and the huge societal footprint of these policy areas.[39] Finding ways to recognize and institutionalize the ongoing processes of legitimation and interaction of governance policies with communities "on the ground" is a worthwhile goal. This might help to allow for adjustments when communities whose interests were never considered when devising the policy are suddenly deeply affected. For instance, intellectual property rules came to sharply affect HIV/AIDS patients in the developing world. Global governance processes must try to address such unintended consequences in a systematic way.

Notions of legitimacy are bound to change as the governed experience the big societal footprint in unexpected or unintended ways. This evolving process requires an explicitly normative statement of the social purpose of the policy. Focusing on institutional legitimacy alone is insufficient; analysts must squarely face the question of substantive legitimacy. This brings us back to Susan Strange's emphasis on winners and losers in governance contests. What substantive benefits do we want to achieve and for whom? And how shall we do it? Distributional consequences lie at the heart of contestation over global governance and cannot be ignored.

Conclusion

This chapter has presented an account of how the literature on global governance has evolved. Global governance is a dynamic interactive process. Focusing on agency and the bases of global governors' authority allows us to better understand what global governors do. Focusing on relationships between global governors that have to work together can reveal sources of dysfunctional outcomes and constructive collaboration. Further research is needed to develop a more precise account of the conditions that lend themselves to better and worse outcomes. Highlighting relationships between the governors and the governed directs our attention to crucial considerations of accountability, representation, and legitimacy. Scholars who dodge explicitly normative issues about substance run the risk of "uncritically adopting dominant notions of the 'public good' that policy should provide."[40]

Looking ahead, one of the trickiest analytic issues is to clearly define the boundaries of global governance. How do we know governance when we see it? Having opened up the analysis to focus on a much larger range of global governors, who is and who is not a global governor? Issues of scope and boundaries will benefit from more empirical research and further conceptual development.

Additional reading

1. Deborah Avant, Martha Finnemore, and Susan K. Sell, eds., *Who Governs the Globe?* (Cambridge: Cambridge University Press, 2010).
2. Gralf-Peter Calliess and Peer Zumbasen, *Rough Consensus and Running Code: A Theory of Transnational Private Law* (Oxford: Hart Publishing, 2012).
3. Christer Jönsson and Jonas Tallberg, eds., *Transnational Actors in Global Governance: Patterns, Explanations, and Implications* (New York: Palgrave Macmillan, 2010).
4. Jonathan Koppell, *World Rule: Accountability, Legitimacy, and the Design of Global Governance* (Chicago: University of Chicago Press, 2010).
5. Joost Pauwelyn, Ramsel Wessel, and Jan Wouters, "The Stagnation of International Law," Working Paper No. 97, Leuven Centre for Global Governance Studies (October 2012): 1–40.

Notes

1 Gralf-Peter Calliess and Peer Zumbasen, *Rough Consensus and Running Code: A Theory of Transnational Private Law* (Oxford: Hart Publishing, 2012); Christer Jönsson and Jonas Tallberg, eds., *Transnational Actors in Global Governance: Patterns, Explanations, and Implications* (New York: Palgave Macmillan, 2010); Anja Jakobi, "Leadership in World Society: Power and Change from the Perspective of Sociological Institutionalism," *Peace Research Institute Frankfurt, Working Paper No. 10*, December 2011; Walter Mattli and Ngaire Woods, eds., *The Politics of Global Regulation* (Princeton: Princeton University Press, 2009); Deborah Avant, Martha Finnemore, and Susan K. Sell, eds., *Who Governs the Globe?* (Cambridge: Cambridge University Press, 2010).
2 Kenneth Waltz, *Theory of International Politics* (Reading, MA.: Addison Wesley, 1979).
3 James Rosenau and Ernst-Otto Czempiel, eds., *Governance Without Government: Order and Change in World Politics* (New York: Cambridge University Press, 1992).

4 Stephen D. Krasner, "Structural Causes and Regime Consequences: Regimes as Intervening Variables," *International Organization* 36, no. 2 (1982): 185.

5 Stephen Krasner, ed., *International Regimes* (Ithaca: Cornell University Press, 1983).

6 Susan Strange, "Cave! Hic Dragones: A Critique of Regime Analysis," *International Organization* 36, no. 2 (1982): 479–498.

7 Barbara Koremenos, Charles Lipson, and Duncan Snidal, eds., *The Rational Design of International Institutions* (Cambridge: Cambridge University Press, 2004).

8 Ronen Palan, "Cave! Alius Draco: There Was a Sixth Dragon!," http://www.e-ir.info/2012/09/21/cave-alius-draco-there-was-a-sixth-dragon/.

9 Philip Cerny, "Neomedievalism, Civil War and the New Security Dilemma: Globalization as Durable Disorder," *Civil Wars* 1, no. 1 (1998): 36–64; Philip Cerny, "Globalization and the Changing Logic of Collective Action," *International Organization* 49, no. 4 (1995): 595–625; James Rosenau, *Turbulence in World Politics: A Theory of Change and Continuity* (Princeton: Princeton University Press, 1990).

10 Joost Pauwelyn, "Informal International Lawmaking: Framing the Concept," in *Informal International Lawmaking*, eds. Joost Pauwelyn, Ramses A. Wessel, and Jan Wooters (Oxford: Oxford University Press, 2012): 20.

11 Ibid., 26.

12 Miles Kahler and David Lake, "Economic Integration and Global Governance: Why so Little Supranationalism?" in *Politics of Regulation*, eds. Mattli and Woods, 274.

13 Joost Pauwelyn, "An Introduction to Informal International Lawmaking," in *Informal International Lawmaking*, eds. Pauwelyn, Wessel, and Wooters, 11.

14 A. Claire Cutler, Virginia Haufler, Tony Porter, eds., *Private Authority and International Affairs* (Albany: State University of New York Press, 1999); Thomas Biersteker and Rodney Hall, eds., *The Emergence of Private Authority in Global Governance* (Cambridge: Cambridge University Press, 2002); Margaret Keck and Kathryn Sikkink, *Activists Beyond Borders: Advocacy Networks in International Politics* (Ithaca: Cornell University Press, 1998).

15 Avant, Finnemore, and Sell, eds., *Who Governs the Globe?*, 2.

16 Christer Jönsson, "Capturing the Transnational: A Conceptual History," in *Transnational Actors*, eds. Jönsson and Tallberg, 36.

17 Clifford Bob, "Packing Heat: Pro-Gun Groups and the Governance of Small Arms," in *Who Governs the Globe?*, eds. Avant, Finnemore, and Sell, 183–201.

18 Alexander Cooley and James Ron, "The NGO Scramble: Organizational Insecurity and the Political Economy of Transnational Action," *International Security* 27, no. 1 (2002): 5–39; Alexander Cooley, "Outsourcing Authority: How Project Contracts Transform Global Governance Networks," in *Who Governs the Globe?*, eds. Avant, Finnemore, and Sell, 238–265.

19 Jönsson and Tallberg, "Transnational Access: Findings and Future Research," in *Transnational Actors*, eds. Jönsson and Tallberg, 237–246.

20 Avant, Finnemore, and Sell, eds., *Who Governs the Globe?*, 9. This discussion of authority is based on Avant, Finnemore and Sell, *Who Governs the Globe?*, 9–14.

21 Kenneth Abbott and Duncan Snidal, "The Governance Triangle: Regulatory Standards Institutions and the Shadow of the State," in *The Politics of Global Regulation*, eds. Walter Mattli and Ngaire Woods (Princeton: Princeton University Press, 2009): 50.

22 Cooley and Ron, "NGO Scramble," 5–39.

23 Jakobi, "Leadership in World Society," 7.

24 Ibid., 8.

25 Richard Mulgan, *Holding Power to Account: Accountability in Modern Democracies* (New York: Palgrave, 2003): 1, quoted in *Informal International Lawmaking*, eds. Pauwelyn, Wessel, and Wooters, 20 note 95.

26 Jens Bartelson, "Beyond Democratic Legitimacy: Global Governance and the Promotion of Liberty," in *Transnational Actors*, eds. Jönsson and Tallberg, 226.

27 Calliess and Zumbasen, *Rough Consensus*, 125.

28 Sofia Naastrom, "Democracy Counts: Problems of Equality in Transnational Advocacy," in *Transnational Actors*, eds. Jönsson and Tallberg, 210.

29 Bartelson, "Beyond Democratic Legitimacy," 219, emphasis in original.

30 Regine Kreide, "The Ambivalence of Juridification. On Legitimate Governance in the International Context," *Global Justice: Theory, Practice and Rhetoric* 2 (2009): 19.

31 Fritz Scharpf, *Governing in Europe: Effective and Democratic?* (Oxford: Oxford University Press, 1999).

32 Daniel Mugge, "Limits of Legitimacy and the Primacy of Politics in Financial Governance," *Review of International Political Economy* 18, no. 1 (2011): 54.

33 Steven Bernstein, "Legitimacy in Intergovernmental and Non-State Global Governance," *Review of International Political Economy* 18, no. 1 (2011): 19.

34 Calliess and Zumbansen, *Rough Consensus*, 129.

35 *Informal International Lawmaking*, eds. Pauwelyn, Wessel, and Wooters, 34.

36 Ibid., 33.

37 Ibid., 25.

38 Bartelson, "Beyond Democratic Legitimacy," 220.

39 Mugge, "Limits of Legitimacy," 68.

40 Ibid., 68.

PART III
THEORIES OF INTERNATIONAL ORGANIZATION AND GLOBAL GOVERNANCE

INTRODUCTION

Much of the way that we think theoretically about international organization and global governance is derived from broader approaches to the study of international relations (IR). This is perhaps unsurprising—as we outline in the introduction to this volume—given that all of the major theoretical traditions in IR have a concern with understanding the way that the world is governed and organized as a central feature of their respective approaches. This is both a reason why we, as a scholarly community, have seldom ventured beyond our comfortable intellectual silos to explain forms of world organization past and present and why, in turn, we have so few approaches specifically tailored to deal with global governance rather than relations between states *per se*.

In the nine chapters that follow in this part, some of the world's leading authorities set out the major theoretical approaches to international organization and global governance. In each case we asked authors to refrain from merely describing the general tenets of an approach but instead to tailor their accounts to specifically engage with international organization and global governance. Thus, this next part of the book comprises one of the very few dedicated realist views of international organization and global governance, a compelling piece by Jason Charrette and Jennifer Sterling-Folker (Chapter 6); a meticulous full-length treatment of classical liberal internationalism by Christer Jönsson (Chapter 7); an incisive account of one of the most influential approaches in the field— neoliberal institutionalism—by David P. Forsythe (Chapter 8); a *tour de force* of rational approaches to IO and global governance and principal–agent theory by Henning Tamm and Duncan Snidal (Chapter 9); a first-rate synopsis of the current favorite of the field— constructivism—by Rodney Bruce Hall (Chapter 10); the most significant challenge to mainstream thinking on international organization and global governance by its leading proponent, critical theory by Robert W. Cox (Chapter 11); a stellar account of classical Marxism by one of the clearest contemporary thinkers, Paul Cammack (Chapter 12); the power and compunction of feminism by three of the best scholars working in the field today, Susanne Zwingel, Elisabeth Prügl, and Gülay Caglar (Chapter 13); and a visionary account of an alternative form of global organization by Amitav Acharya (Chapter 14).

None of these approaches is dispensable in pursuit of a clear view of paradigmatic thinking in the field. The dominant approaches fall in the first five chapters in this part of the book (Chapters 6–10); while the more critical heterodox perspectives comprise the four that follow (Chapters 11–14). A different way of distinguishing between them would be, on the one hand, to conceive of Chapters 6–10 as dealing with frameworks designed to understand international organization and global governance as it exists (and what might be termed "status quo observing"); and, on the other hand, Chapters 11–14 as seeking to change the forms of international organization and global governance that we currently have (which could be referred to as "status quo transforming").

Introductory classes on international organization would most likely take in Chapters 6 ("Realism"), 7 ("Classical liberal internationalism"), 12 ("Classical Marxism"), and 13 ("Feminism"). The focus here would be on understanding core pillars of the discipline's intellectual cannon, taking in two chapters each on status quo observing and status quo transforming approaches. More advanced courses of study would supplement these with further investigations into liberal approaches ("Neoliberal institutionalism," Chapter 8), the rational methodology that underpins much contemporary mainstream research ("Rational choice and principal–agent theory," Chapter 9), "Constructivism" (Chapter 10), the rebuke of orthodoxy by critical theory (Chapter 11), and alternative ways of thinking about world order (in the form of "Post-hegemonic multilateralism," in Chapter 14).

In order to facilitate moving into this part, we next offer synopses of the chapters. We spend comparatively longer introducing readers to the content of these chapters than we do in the introductory sections for subsequent parts of the book because of the difficulty that some readers have in grasping theory, as well as because we firmly believe that a solid theoretical foundation is an essential component of understanding contemporary international organization and global governance.

Theories of international organization and global governance: chapter synopses

In Chapter 6, Jason Charrette and Jennifer Sterling-Folker show how, contrary to popular conceptions, international organization is a central concern of realist thought. They detail how the distribution of relative power capabilities in the international system and the forms of order that result therefrom shape the kind of global governance we have. In this account—unlike in most caricatures of realism—they show how this basic starting point for IR actually accounts for the multiplicity of actors in the current system, the relatively prolonged periods of peace and international cooperation that are associated with that system, and the kind of global governance that is contingent on state power and US power in particular. Charrette and Sterling-Folker's contribution goes a long way to addressing some of the misconceptions made of and about realism in relation to international organization and global governance. The manner in which realism views moments of relative peace and cooperation nonetheless suggests that stability is a precarious phenomenon, with shifts in relative power distributions having historically generated painful and violent upheavals.

In contrast, classical liberal internationalism focuses very much on the art of the possible, rather than the pessimism of the inevitable. In Chapter 7, Christer Jönsson explores the foundations of classical liberal internationalism, whose importance for international organization and global governance should not be underestimated. Although unfairly pilloried for being out of touch with "reality" by a new generation of realist scholars after World War II, classical liberal internationalism—in all of its variants—was clear about how the world ought to be organized. Unfettered commerce and the right of all peoples to self-determination were broad organizing principles that were thought to be the appropriate foundations upon which a more just form of world order would exist. Early liberal thinking did not, however, focus on the construction of grand international organizations, but instead sought to generate a more peaceful world order organically through the extension of peaceful ties among peoples. It was only with the onset of a more interventionist form of liberal internationalism that top-down initiatives were proposed and advocated to assist in the creation of a more just world order. In their classical formulation, however, these ideas were not always devoid of hierarchical understandings of race and "civilization"—as Article 22 of the Covenant of the League of Nations amply demonstrates.

Jönsson offers a masterly overview of the many varieties of classical liberal internationalism that serves as an important resource for understanding why liberal ideas and ideologies continue to have a purchase in debate about IO and global governance. Yet, as he illustrates, in its classic form liberalism was severely damaged by the horrors of World War II. In Chapter 8, David P. Forsythe picks up the baton from Jönsson and explores the form in which liberalism was resurrected and in which it has come to be applied to IO and global governance—neoliberal institutionalism. Forsythe guides readers through the main tenets of the approach, continually contrasting it with neo-realism—the modern-day, rationalist variant of classic realism. He not only unpacks the nuances of each approach but also demonstrates their utility. Part of his comparative method leads Forsythe to apply neoliberalism and neorealism to various cases, thereby showing how each aids our understanding. He compares and contrasts, for instance, neorealist and neoliberal accounts of the foreign policies of the John F. Kennedy and George W. Bush administrations, the international refugee regime, and the European Union.

Classical realism and liberal internationalism both draw their analytical purchase from philosophical understandings of human nature—for realists humans are inherently untrustworthy, whereas for liberals humanity has the capacity to exist in a harmonious and cooperative state. What "revolutionized" the study of international relations in the 1950s and 1960s was the shift away from these more abstract assertions about human nature as the bases of these approaches toward a more "scientific" foundation. Drawing heavily from work in economics that assumed the preferences of each actor could be determined and the behavior they engaged in predicted, IR scholars began to develop analyses of state behavior drawn from understandings of what might be "rational" as a course of action in a given situation and what a set of national preferences might look like. While the normative character of realism and liberalism did not change—they still assumed the worst (realism) or hoped for the best (liberalism)—the means by which analyses were conducted changed dramatically. And this change has had a profound impact on the way we think about IO and global governance.

In Chapter 9, Henning Tamm and Duncan Snidal explore the rational foundations of much recent work on international organization. They explore the way that scholars have sought to answer questions such as "Why do states create and work with international organizations?" by drawing on understandings of the preferences and foreign policy objectives that states have. In so doing, they also unpack simple and more complex variants of "principal–agent" (PA) theory as an approach for understanding why states operate in the way that they do. This form of analysis starts from the assumption that in particular instances "principals"—not only states but also non-state actors, voters, agencies, and the like—delegate responsibilities for certain tasks to various "agents"— which again range from international, transnational, national, to local agencies, among others. Here, not only is the nature of the relationship between principals and agents able to be better understood, attention can be directed at instances when problems arise, in which agents lose an element of control in the fulfillment of task, where chains of delegation become too extended and unstable, as well as about the value and social purpose of a principal–agent relationship. As they note, while PA theory has most often been applied to the relationship between states and international organizations as their agents, it has explanatory purchase for myriad principal–agent relationships among the full range of global governance actors.

Chapter 10 switches the focus away from the rational bases of much mainstream thinking to the explanatory power of an approach—constructivism—that sees knowledge about the world as socially constructed. In this chapter, Rodney Bruce Hall unpacks constructivist approaches to IO and global governance by first detailing its intellectual roots in Grotian thinking about the study of world politics and then moving towards a more Weberian account. He then unpacks the core components of constructivism as an approach, contrasting it with realism and neoliberal institutionalism as a means of highlighting points of departure and areas of commonality. Thereafter, Hall illustrates how constructivism has not only helped plow new intellectual furrows but also (re-)energized existing research programs in the area. With regard to the latter he places particular emphasis on constructivism's contributions to regime theory and multi-lateralism (and in particular in taking it beyond a mere numerical understanding of a form of international organization). In the latter sections of the chapter, Hall illustrates how constructivism has helped us develop an understanding of the autonomy of international organizations and the role of private authority before surveying current debates and research in the field.

Chapter 11 moves away from mainstream thinking about international organization and global governance—what might be considered the "cannon"—towards more heterodox thinking. In the first of the four chapters that comprise this section, Robert W. Cox offers a synopsis of his major contribution to the study of world politics, critical theory. With characteristic clarity and insight, Cox offers a perspective that views processes of international organization and formations of global governance over time. This perspective, which he terms "critical theory," differs from mainstream approaches to international organization and global governance—which he terms "problem solving" approaches—in that it stands back from the existing order and asks how it came about. But his focus is not just on understanding; it is also concerned with bringing about change. To do this Cox focuses on "inside" aspects of how we have come to the forms of order that we currently have—the "thought, reasoning and emotion that 'makes' history"—so that they can be understood and changed in a way that overcomes instances of dominance and subordination as well as averting crises more effectively, such as climate change. Cox's approach is thus a holistic view of the evolution of international organization and formations of global governance rather than one that is focused on specific aspects or events related to individual international organizations (albeit that these are not unimportant).

In Chapter 12, Paul Cammack offers a clear and concise account of the explanatory power of classical Marxism as it relates to international organization and global governance. Cammack endeavors to show how a classical Marxist approach makes sense of global governance, and global economic governance in particular, through its capacity to identify a logic and a project at its heart. Thus, global governance is best understood as a transnational and global means of facilitating the spread of capitalism worldwide through a focus on trade and competitiveness and as a means of bringing about the creation of a global proletariat. Cammack's account reflects a concern with the evolution of capitalism and the centrality of the mode of production as a driving force of world history, and understands international organization, international organizations, and formations of global governance in that context.

Like Cox and Cammack, the authors of Chapter 13—Susanne Zwingel, Elisabeth Prügl, and Gülay Caglar—also focus on advancing a means of understanding designed to bring about change. In their case, the social inequalities that provide the normative impulse to seek change go beyond market-based forms of governance; they are concerned with correcting gender inequalities in modes of governing that both give rise to and reproduce inequalities between women and men, girls and boys.

Zwingel, Prügl, and Caglar show how feminist approaches have contributed to debates about IO and global governance by rendering visible the way that aspects of these forms of organization have supported and helped constitute and reconstitute forms of gender discrimination and the subordination and suppression of women. They show how feminists have sought to intervene in these forms and processes of governance to destabilize existing relationships and reconfigure ways that promote gender equality and correct engrained biases. Zwingel, Prügl, and Caglar also reflect on current debates in feminist thinking as well as outline some of the innovations feminists have developed to overcome, among other things, the essentialization of women as a "problem," and to more effectively bring about change.

Part III comes to a close with a contribution from Amitav Acharya (Chapter 14). His task is to show how an existing form of international organization—multilateralism —could be re-crafted in a way that moves beyond embedded inequalities of power. His purpose is to identify how an alternative form of multilateralism can be established that coordinates relations among states and other actors at the global and regional levels on the basis of principles that are not dominated by a single power or group of powers. He contrasts this "post-hegemonic multilateralism" with existing forms of multilateralism that are too closely associated with US forms of IO established after World War II. Acharya explores the possible triggers that might lead to a reconfiguration of multilateralism, what current shifts in the global distribution of power might generate it, the norms and principles that might underpin such an organizational realignment, the role of regions and regionalisms, and what multilateralism might look like beyond US power.

Where to now?

We have purposely spent time guiding readers through the chapters in this section as theory is often the most challenging component of any class. In pointing not only to how these chapters might be read, but the order in which they could be consulted, what they contain, and how this helps us understand IO and global governance, we aim to provide a secure foundation upon which readers can embark on their more empirical investigations of world order in the chapters that follow.

Realism

Jason Charrette and Jennifer Sterling-Folker

In reviewing the literature on international organization (IO) and global governance, one gets the impression that realism contributes very little to the topic. Many of its critics treat realism as a nemesis to be defeated before analysis can even proceed, rather than as an approach with something important to say in its own right about these subjects. Yet realists have always contributed to discussions of IO and global governance. How realism defines these terms may be part of the reason it is often given short shrift. From a realist perspective, the term IO is a reference to the Westphalian system comprised of sovereign states.[1] As the phrase inter-national (meaning "between" or "among" national units) suggests, states do not exist in a vacuum but interact in predictable ways that generate patterns of order and disorder in world politics.

Central to these patterns has been the relative power of states. This is because in an anarchic environment in which there is no world government to impose order and stability, states engage in self-help behavior to ensure their own survival. Anarchy heightens the stakes of state interaction so that competing interests have the potential to escalate into military conflict. This is why states are concerned with relative power, as power capabilities become the central means within anarchy of obtaining self-interests and defending against other states. In such an environment, relative power—or the distribution of capabilities—determines outcomes. Periods of relative peace or violence are traceable to the interactions of the relatively more powerful states in the system. From a realist perspective, then, the term IO is a reference to the specific patterns of order that can arise from great power self-interests and interaction.[2]

While never fully divorced from patterns of disorder, periods of relatively greater order, organization, and management have existed since Westphalia. Realism explains this by focusing on the interactions and efforts of relatively powerful states. Patterns of order are not beyond the authority or control of powerful states, nor do these patterns displace the significance of relative power to global affairs or states as its constitutive unit. Patterns of IO are instead *contingent* on the interests of powerful states. Hence if there appear to be patterns of authority, control, and legitimacy in contemporary world politics—global governance in common parlance—it is because of the relative power and ongoing interactions among powerful states.

Realist insistence that states and power remain fundamental to the subject of IO and global governance is an important contribution to our understanding of order, organization, and management in world affairs. Realist claims are also essential for understanding the arguments and concerns of many other approaches to IO and global governance, which often juxtapose themselves to realist explanations. The next section of this chapter reviews the historical development of IO from a realist perspective, with a focus on the implications of polarity and hegemonic stability for contemporary world order. We then discuss a number of current debates among realists involving balancing and power transitions that involve the future of contemporary IO. Because these debates reflect realism's ongoing skepticism about some of the bolder claims in the IO and global governance literature about the future, we then consider how realism addresses key criticisms and emerging issues. In so doing, we argue that the ethical concerns evoked by realism's ongoing pessimism serve as an important check against an undue optimism that masks deep inequalities and exploitations. In this respect, realism provides not only a compelling explanation for IO and global governance, but also a basis from which to consider the normative biases of many other perspectives.

IO from a realist perspective

Because states are suspicious of one another's intentions in an anarchic environment, relative harmony among powerful states has been historically rare. Cooperation does occur but it has usually been when a collection of states have faced a common threat and have pooled their relative power to defend against it. These dynamics account for the coalitions against Napoleon in the early nineteenth century, as well as opposing alliances during World Wars I and II. Such cooperation can be difficult to achieve, however, as states are just as suspicious of the intentions of potential alliance partners, and these suspicions reassert themselves after the common enemy has been vanquished. And because continued cooperation is difficult to maintain, security alliances are an unstable form of cooperation, as the Westphalian historical record demonstrates.

The contemporary international system is remarkable for the extensiveness of cooperation that exists, as well as for the relatively lengthy period of peace among the great powers. While interstate violence and warfare continue to be endemic to many parts of the globe, their centrality to great power politics declined in the latter half of the twentieth century. A variety of analytical perspectives have tried to explain why contemporary international relations (IR) appears to be qualitatively different from the past. Many of these theories highlight the fundamental role of democracy, economic interdependence, and international organizations (whether intergovernmental, IGOs, or nongovernmental, NGOs) as the progenitors of international peace and cooperation.[3] The term global governance is often preferred because global politics is seen as the sum of all global actors and their interests and their practices, not just state interests, as the term IO implies. Thus, global governance is sometimes defined as the management of this decentralized web of interdependent transnational actors through public–private partnerships, network entanglements, and institutions that enable increasing cooperation despite the anarchic environment.[4] From a realist perspective, however, the term global governance misdirects attention from deeper structures of power that shape patterns of global management by implying that these activities occur independently of states.

In contrast, realism insists that states remain the primary actors in international affairs; it is suspicious of claims about international institutional causality; and it argues that global governance is a phenomenon contingent on power politics. The disagreement between realism and other perspectives is not "over the existence of institutions or the fact that they are found where cooperation is high," as Robert Jervis points out, "but over the claim that they are more than instruments of statecraft and have an independent impact, 'a life of their own.'"[5] To account for the extensiveness of cooperation today, realists argue that while an anarchic, self-help environment makes suspicion endemic and hence a severe inhibitor to cooperation, these dynamics may be overcome on an ongoing—albeit impermanent—basis if particular circumstances related to relative power occur. Beyond security alliances there are two other circumstances in which more extensive forms of cooperation, organization, and order may be achieved. Both involve the presence of exceptionally powerful states whose interactions shape global interactions in ways that conform to their own interests and values.

The first circumstance involves the concept of polarity, which is the relative distribution of capabilities in the international system during particular time periods. Realists argue that distributional changes affect system stability by producing different patterns of behavior and hence the probability and scale of international violence.[6] Distributional changes also have consequences for international order and management, which Randall Schweller and David Priess review in terms of the polarity–IO relationship.[7] A multipolar system, which consists of many great powers, can produce two different forms of IO and global governance. If some states are "revisionist," they will be dissatisfied with existing arrangements and seek to dominate the system. This makes other states wary of the existing balance of power so they prefer a freer hand to react to changes in relative power differentials. The resulting international management will be shallow, temporary, and spontaneous, as managing the global space through formal institutions takes a back seat to the needs of survival. Examples of this form of management include Europe during the Napoleonic era and interstate relations prior to World War I. Conversely, in a multipolar system with no revisionist states and in which defensive weaponry has the advantage, more formal, permanent, and negotiated modes of organization among the great powers are likely. States can afford to be relatively less worried about survival and more concerned with peacefully solving differences. An example of this system is the Concert of Europe after Napoleon's defeat in the early nineteenth century.

In a system with two great powers—referred to as bipolarity—organization will be a by-product of relations between the two superpowers. The example of this type of IO is the American and Soviet spheres of influence during the Cold War. According to Kenneth Waltz, the two states learned "to behave as sensible duopolists" by "moderating the intensity of their competition and cooperating at times to mutual advantage while continuing to eye each other warily."[8] The resulting pattern of bipolar systemic organization had two characteristics according to Schweller and Priess. First, there were explicit and implicit arrangements, of an informal, spontaneous nature, between the two superpowers to respect each other's spheres of influence and avoid unnecessary conflict. Second, within each sphere of influence, behavior conformed to the organization found in unipolarity (or one great power), with each superpower either imposing or negotiating an order within its sphere of influence.

Unipolarity is pertinent for understanding contemporary international order, given that the US became the sole superpower after the Cold War. In a unipolar system, the most powerful state attempts to establish rules that benefit itself, but its internal characteristics shape the organizational choices it pursues. If it is a non-liberal state, it uses domination alone to establish and enforce the rules of the game in its favor. This is referred to as "imperial" rule, with historical examples ranging from Rome to the Soviet Empire. If it is a liberal state, it will rely on a combination of domination and the creation of a constitutional order that rests on the consent of other states. In this circumstance, unipolarity can result in a negotiated form of IO. Although the resulting system reflects that pole's preferences, it also provides other goods that make its rule attractive to weaker states. Schweller and Priess argue that such a superpower is the "ideal" realist state in that it "understands the limits of coercive power and so promotes legitimacy and emulation of its values while tolerating pluralism and diversity."[9]

The second circumstance in which more extensive forms of organization and management can occur in anarchy involves hegemonic stability. In this situation, a predominant state, or hegemon, uses its greater capabilities to shape international politics for the promotion of more order, stability, and cooperative behavior within the system. Both polarity and hegemony are based on the distribution of capabilities but, as Elke Krahmann notes, "unipolarity does not necessarily entail hegemony; nor can hegemony only be found in unipolar structures."[10] Thus not all unipoles or great powers are hegemons, and most scholars identify just three periods of hegemonic stability: the Netherlands in the seventeenth century, the British in the late nineteenth century, and the Americans after World War II. What distinguishes hegemony is the great power's desire to promote international trade and investment with other states, which can only be done effectively by encouraging regularized, cooperative relationships.[11]

While the hegemon's goal in encouraging international economic organization is to benefit itself economically and militarily, its promotion of greater stability can also benefit other participating states. This does not mean that coercion is absent from how these hegemonic "goods" are spread among participants, but it is the combination of a single state's relatively greater capability *and* the existence of collective self-interests in economic exchange that differentiates hegemony from imperialism and unipolarity. In a period of hegemonic stability "the distribution of power among states is the primary determinant of the character of the international economic system" and it explains "patterns of economic relations among the advanced capitalist countries."[12] It also accounts for the relatively greater cooperation and order we see in contemporary world affairs.

Most of the IGOs that serve as the backbone for contemporary international cooperation can be traced to American hegemony in the immediate aftermath of World War II. The United States emerged from that conflict as the most powerful state in the international system, and its reliance on formal institutions and international law is a distinguishing feature of its hegemony. The United States promoted the creation of the UN as an umbrella organization for treaty-based cooperation in a variety of global concerns and issue areas. It also oversaw the creation of the International Monetary Fund

(IMF), the World Bank, and the informal General Agreement on Tariffs and Trade (GATT), with the express goal of encouraging cooperative economic exchange. In so doing, the United States rewarded cooperation, punished defectors, and served as a guarantor for the international economic system it shared with its allies. Its presence, combined with the common threat posed by the Soviet Union, was also an inducement to avoid warfare among the states within its alliance system. Hence the term *Pax Americana* is often used to indicate the post-World War II period of American hegemonic stability.

While there are clear differences between a hegemonic stability and polarity perspective, both assume that contemporary world order can be traced to and remains contingent upon the current distribution of capabilities. That distribution involves the relatively greater power of the United States and its continued willingness to support an extensively formal and legalized cooperative world order in order to obtain its own economic and military interests. This means that if US relative power were to change, then so too would existing patterns of organization and management. In other words, if contemporary world order is sustained through a particular distribution of power, there are significant implications for IO when that distribution changes. Because realists are pessimistic that US primacy can be maintained in the face of rising powers and increased economic and military competition, they are also skeptical about the preservation of the current liberal international order. This has led to debate among realists over whether the United States is in decline and what that would mean for world affairs.

Current debates

There are a variety of reasons why powerful states cannot count on a lasting favorable distribution of capabilities. One reason is that anarchy induces a competitive drive among states to balance unchecked power as a potential threat to their survival.[13] States try to increase their own military capability (internal balancing) or ally with other states to benefit from their pooled military capability (external balancing). Unipolarity is expected to be short lived in such a context, since states face a security risk from the unipole's potential military aggression and are therefore more likely to balance against it—especially if the threat is existential. As a result, realists anticipate that a challenger or group of challengers faced with the presence of a single great power and dissatisfied with its international order will eventually balance against it. Such moments of power transition are often fraught with interstate violence and, at the very least, the system will revert to multipolarity, which is associated with higher levels of warfare among the great powers. This is why realists are concerned with the rise of China as a potential challenger to US dominance. Historical patterns indicate an increased risk for interstate violence in moments of power transition, and it is unclear what sort of IO and patterns of global governance would evolve from an international system dominated by China.

A second reason why particular distributions of capability do not last relates to technological advances that may contribute to the rapid rise of its potential challengers, particularly in strategic planning and warfare.[14] Rapid shifts in technology can make weapons systems obsolete almost overnight and, in an environment where other states have an incentive to compete to acquire more power, the maintenance of relative power is precarious. Even in economic affairs, a hegemonic state cannot expect to dominate the global market indefinitely. The very states that benefit from its international order will also innovate and may eventually prove to be its greatest economic challengers.

A third reason why relative power does not last is because hegemony comes at a high price. To ward off potential challengers to its world order, the hegemon must constantly stay economically and militarily ahead. However, the maintenance of its order inflicts an inescapable and eventually fatal "economic drain" on the hegemon.[15] Since its own economy is critical to the health of the global economy, the hegemon must remain open to commerce and trade—even if it hurts its own people. It must also commit itself (at the very least) to pay for the defense of far-flung allies who are a part of its system—even when its own country is not directly threatened. It might even need to share its military technology with other allies, allowing those states to erode its own military advantage. Put simply, the greater a state's reach and influence, the more territory and core interests it is forced to defend. Eventually, the hegemon will suffer "imperial overstretch" and decline, ending the world order that was dependent on it. Whatever order might replace it will be contingent on an entirely new distribution of capabilities, with no guarantee that a hegemon (as opposed to an imperial unipole) will emerge to encourage and support a system of economic exchange.

If we consider US pre-eminence and decline from either a unipolar or hegemonic perspective, then, pessimism about the preservation of contemporary world order is warranted. However, not everyone believes the United States is destined to decline, and some realists argue that the United States is categorically different from previous hegemons.[16] For example, rather than exhaust its own resources to maintain its global order, Michael Mastanduno argues that the United States is a "system-maker and privilege-taker," because it pays a lot to maintain its world order but also gets a disproportionate share of the benefits.[17] Moreover, as the most powerful state, the United States sets the international rules for finance and security, thus allowing it to enable some foreign policies while constraining others. Despite potential challenges to its dominance from global financial crises, recessions, and alternative currencies, the US dollar remains the top international currency, and it can slant the rules of international trade in its favor, including using access to its huge consumer market as both a carrot and a stick.[18]

Other scholars, such as Stephen Brooks, William Wohlforth, Barry Posen, and Paul Kennedy, have argued that US military capabilities are without peer.[19] The material gap between the United States and all other countries is so large that the traditional systemic boundaries no longer apply. Similarly, American military capabilities can weaken an adversary's economic and military capabilities as soon as the United States perceives it to be a potential threat. What is more, it has attained this capability without breaking the bank, spending only 4.8 percent of its GDP on military expenditures, so that, as Paul Kennedy has observed, "being Number One at great cost is one thing; being the world's single superpower on the cheap is astonishing."[20]

Of course, even if the United States is not in decline, its own behavior may provoke balancing against it. Not surprisingly, "the sole remaining great power has behaved as unchecked powers have usually done. In the absence of counterweights, a country's internal impulses prevail, whether fueled by liberal or by other urges."[21] Thus one of the key debates within realism about the future of IO concerns how we are to see balancing against the United States as a result of its own behavior. US unilateralism in its invasion of Iraq and the Global War on Terror is often cited as confirmation of the existential danger of a unipole aspiring to global hegemony, leading Waltz (among others) to argue that, "even if a dominant power behaves with moderation, restraint, and forbearance, weaker states will worry about its future behavior."[22]

Yet other realists disagree that we should expect to see balancing behavior, because "the stronger the leading state and the more entrenched its dominance, the more unlikely and thus less constraining are counterbalancing dynamics."[23] That is, if a hegemon becomes too powerful, the cost of both external and internal balancing against it grows enormously. And if Posen is correct that both the immensity and projection capabilities of US military power can diffuse challenges before they even occur, then states would have considerable difficulty creating an alliance against the United States. What, after all, is to stop it from picking off potential balancers one by one in the formative stage of any grand balancing coalition?

Additionally, Schweller argues that the costs of internally balancing against a country as powerful as the United States make it difficult for foreign leaders to convince an often fragmented domestic constituency to undertake the burden.[24] Few states are single-minded enough to pursue such a strategy, and if given a choice many smaller states will bandwagon with the United States, rather than challenge it. Finally, some scholars, such as G. John Ikenberry and Stephen Walt, have argued that a benign foreign policy will mitigate the imperative to balance the United States.[25] They argue that as long as it pursues liberal hegemonic rather than imperial policies to support the liberal international order, there should be no reason for other states to challenge that order. In other words, if the unipole remains reasonable and respectfully distant in its policies, its order can be maintained. As these arguments indicate, balance of power politics remains central to international order, even in an international order dominated by a liberal hegemon.

Key criticisms and emerging issues

Realism is concerned with the effect of relative power on contemporary world order. Because states are the central actors in world affairs, it is the distribution of capabilities among them that sets the stage for patterns of global authority, control, and legitimacy. States should not be analyzed as first among equals in relation to non-state actors (NSAs), such as IGOs, NGOs, transnational corporations, activists, or transnational civil society. No realist scholar would deny that these actors exist, are currently engaged in governance of some sort, or can make a difference to the quality of some people's daily lives. However, their existence does not grant them status as a primary driver of world order. Rather, this web of formal and informal actors, institutions, and arrangements is contingent on the authority and legitimacy of the state. Far from displacing the pre-eminence of states, there is considerable evidence that non-state actor activities actually reinforce it.[26]

NSAs are important not because they are independent of states but because they allow states to more efficiently achieve their state interests and so are useful to powerful states. Institutions and NSAs "enable great powers to rule others and to manage regional and world affairs more effectively and efficiently than would be possible in their absence," while international law "direct(s) great power behavior in accordance with the established rules of the game."[27] States can, if they wish, halt increasing governance regardless of how binding or permanent it may seem given that global governance is an inherently contingent condition. Even the strongest institutions for governing a global space—such as the economic and political institutions of the Soviet Union—can be fractured once they no longer serve a state's interests, and dense, entrenched networks of capital and trade can be insufficient for preventing management collapse.[28]

Realism's critics often suggest that it fails to read contemporary international order correctly. They argue that it *a priori* privileges the state, misses the importance of NSAs, fails to recognize the social construction of IR because of its rationalist assumptions, and its fatalistic tendencies counsel conservative foreign policies that reinforce power politics and hence its own explanations for world affairs. The result is a widespread accusation that it is realism's hold on policy-maker imaginations, not power politics itself, which stands in the way of achieving greater progress in world affairs.[29] Certainly its assumptions can lead realism to make predictions that appear to be wrong, although this is an issue for other IR theories as well. Its analyses can also have significant blind spots regarding the actual processes that comprise the daily activities of global management. And because realism suggests that activism separated from the distribution of capabilities will be ineffective, its underlying fatalism raises serious ethical questions about whether it is suggesting resignation to the oppression and exploitation associated with all power politics. In a liberal world order, realism appears to be out of step with the ideals and aspirations of the majority of its participants.

It is at this juncture, however, that realism makes one of its most important contributions to the discussion of contemporary IO and global governance. Realism's pessimistic reading of the contemporary world order is shaped by its understanding of human history, in which patterns of competition and violence have continually reflected the unfortunate truism that "might makes right." Powerful entities throughout history have always determined what was politically, economically, socially, and ethically acceptable. In so doing, they shaped the boundaries of thought and behavior for the actors and individuals that existed under their exigencies.[30] This is just as true for the contemporary world order, in which "right" is derived from the "might" of the powerful states in the system, among whom a set of Western ideals (involving the desirability of democracy, capitalism, and state sovereignty) shape what international order should look like. The have-nots are well aware that power determines outcomes in this system and that they are not necessarily beneficiaries of it. Yet much of the IO and global governance literature would have one believe that relative power is superfluous because there is an obvious "rightness" to the liberal world order that is globally recognized and shared.

Realism serves as an important corrective for this contemporary tendency to equate liberal ideals, global reach, and normative desirability without also acknowledging the relative power (both among and of states) that necessarily and coercively supports this equation. As Martin Griffiths has observed, "realists in the US are at the forefront of contemporary debates about the future of US foreign policy," because they recognize the "close nexus between political and economic stability at the global level" and "between power, authority and legitimacy."[31] International organization is dependent upon and a reflection of the interests and preferences of the most powerful states in the system. We should not be surprised, then, to discover that the world order they have created supports their continued dominance over others. Hence realism draws attention to the error of what Duncan Bell (drawing on the work of C. A. J. Coady) calls "the moralism of imposition," in which we "seek to impose values (even if we think they are universally applicable in principle) on other people and communities" without also recognizing that doing so "almost always requires the use of coercion, disrespect or force."[32]

Conclusion

Despite the contemporary rhetoric about global governance, we do not live in a brave new world in which old ways of thinking and behaving have become irrelevant. We live in a world that continues to be dominated, for better or worse, by the preferences, values, and goals of relatively powerful states. While contemporary world order is characterized by relatively more extensive cooperation, management, and NSA involvement, using the term global governance to describe this order is highly problematic. The term suggests that management occurs independently of its deep structural foundations, instead of as a contingent pattern arising from great power interactions. Hence the term IO is still a more appropriate signifier for world order. Other analytical perspectives prefer the term global governance because they divorce the study of systemic organization and governance from these overt and implicit power structures. In doing so, they unnecessarily disconnect the study of world order from the study of IR more broadly. The consequence of so doing is an ever-present risk of getting lost in the novelty of a particular international moment and reading its durability with undue sanguinity.

This is hardly a new phenomenon. Remarking about the typical pre-World War I London inhabitant, who could engage in international commerce at home using cutting edge communications technology, John Maynard Keynes noted that such an individual "regarded this state of affairs as normal, certain, and permanent, except in the direction of further improvement, and any deviation from it as aberrant, scandalous, and avoidable."[33] With little modification, such a statement could describe many contemporary explanations for IO and global governance. Alternatively, the enduring contribution of the realist tradition is both to contextualize the current management of the international environment within the larger sweep of history and to provide a check on the blind optimism that assumes the hegemony of liberal ideas and institutions is natural and inevitable. Realism provides a critical voice to the larger debate about IO and global governance by drawing attention to power politics—reminding the discipline that, despite the fluidity of international politics, some things never change.

Additional reading

1. Michael E. Brown et al., eds., *Primacy and Its Discontents: American Power and International Stability* (Cambridge, MA: MIT Press 2008).
2. Robert Gilpin, "A Realist Perspective on International Governance," *Governing Globalization: Power, Authority and Global Governance*, eds. Anthony McGrew and David Held (Oxford: Polity, 2002): 237–248.

3. Jennifer Sterling-Folker, "Realist Global Governance: Revisiting *Cave! Hic Dragones* and Beyond," in *Contending Perspectives on Global Governance: Coherence, Contestation, and World Order*, eds. Matthew Hoffmann and Alice Ba (London: Routledge, 2005).

Notes

1 Westphalia refers to the treaties ending Europe's 30 Years War, which are considered important markers in the transition from Feudalism to a world of sovereign states.

2 See Robert Gilpin, *War and Change in World Politics* (New York: Cambridge University Press, 1981); Randall L. Schweller and David Priess, "A Tale of Two Realisms: Expanding the Institutions Debate," *Mershon International Studies Review* 41, no. 1 (1997): 1–32; Kenneth Waltz, *Theory of International Politics*, (New York: McGraw-Hill, 1979).

3 For example, Helen V. Milner and Andrew Moravcsik, eds., *Power, Interdependence, and Nonstate Actors in World Affairs* (Princeton: Princeton University Press, 2009); Bruce Russett and John Oneal, *Triangulating Peace: Democracy, Interdependence, and International Organizations* (New York: W. W. Norton & Company, 2001).

4 James N. Rosenau and Ernst Czempiel, eds., *Governance without Government: Order and Change in World Politics* (Cambridge: Cambridge University Press, 1992); Jim Whitman, ed., *Global Governance* (Basingstoke: Palgrave Macmillan, 2009).

5 Robert Jervis, "Realism, NeoLiberalism, and Cooperation," *International Security* 24, no. 1 (1999): 54; See also John J. Mearsheimer, "The False Promise of International Institutions," *International Security* 19, no. 3 (1994/95): 5–49; Charles L Glaser, "Realists as Optimists: Cooperation as Self-Help," *International Security* 19, no. 3 (1994/95): 50–90.

6 See, for example, Paul Kennedy, *The Rise and Fall of the Great Powers: Economic Change and Military Conflict from 1500 to 2000* (New York: Vintage Books, 1987); John J. Mearsheimer, "Back to the Future: Instability in Europe After the Cold War," *International Security* 15, no. 1 (1990): 5–56.

7 The following discussion is drawn from Schweller and Priess, "A Tale of Two Realisms," 18–21, Gilpin, *War and Change*, ch. 2; and Waltz, *Theory of International Politics*, ch. 9.

8 Waltz, *Theory of International Politics*, 203.

9 Schweller and Priess, "A Tale of Two Realisms," 18.

10 Elke Krahmann, "American Hegemony or Global Governance? Competing Visions of International Security," *International Studies Review* 7, no. 4 (2005): 533.

11 Variants of hegemonic stability theory can be found in realism, liberalism, and world system theory, for example Christopher Chase-Dunn et al., "The Forum: Hegemony and Social Change," *Mershon International Studies Review* 38, no. 2 (1994): 361–376; David Lake, "Leadership, Hegemony, and the International Economy: Naked Emperor or Tattered Monarch with Potential?," *International Studies Quarterly* 37, no. 4 (1993): 459–489; David Wilkinson, "Unipolarity without Hegemony," *International Studies Review* 1, no. 2 (1999): 141–172.

12 Michael C. Webb and Stephen D. Krasner, "Hegemonic Stability Theory: An Empirical Assessment," *Review of International Studies* 15, no. 2 (1989): 183.

13 See Christopher Layne, "The Unipolar Illusion Revisited," *International Security* 31, no. 2 (2006): 7–41; Jack S. Levy and William R. Thompson, "Hegemonic Threats and Great-Power Balancing in Europe, 1945–1999," *Security Studies* 14, no. 1 (2005): 29–30; John J. Mearsheimer, *The Tragedy of Great Power Politics* (New York: W. W. Norton, 2001), 139, 156–157; Robert Pape, "Soft Balancing against the United States," *International Security* 30, no. 1 (2005): 7–45; Stephen Walt, *Taming American Power: The Global Response to US Primacy* (New York: Norton, 2005), 132; Waltz, *Theory of International Politics*, 118–127, 168–172; Kenneth Waltz, "Structural Realism after the Cold War," *International Security* 25, no. 1 (2000): 27–30.

14 Dima P. Adamsky, "Through the Looking Glass: The Soviet Military-Technical Revolution and the American Revolution in Military Affairs," *Journal of Strategic Studies* 31, no. 2 (2008): 257–294; Michael C. Horowitz, *The Diffusion of Military Power: Causes and Consequences for International Politics* (Princeton: Princeton University Press, 2010); Joao Resende-Santos, *Neorealism, States, and the Modern Mass Army* (Cambridge: Cambridge University Press, 2007).

15 Gilpin, *War and Change*, 156–157, 175–185; Kennedy, *The Rise and Fall*, xvi; Charles P. Kindleberger, "Dominance and Leadership in the International Economy: Exploitation, Public Goods, and Free Riders," *International Studies Quarterly* 25, no. 2 (1981): 246–248; Lake, "Leadership, Hegemony," 462–463, 469–483.

16 See Ewan Harrison, "The Contradictions of Unipolarity," in *Rethinking Realism in International Relations: Between Tradition and Innovation*, eds. Annette Freyberg-Inan, Ewan Harrison, and Patrick James (Baltimore, MD: Johns Hopkins University Press, 2009); Krahmann, "American Hegemony"; Christopher Layne, "The Waning of US Hegemony—Myth or Reality? A Review Essay," *International Security* 34, no. 1 (2009): 147–172; and Steven Lamy, Robert English, and Steve Smith, eds., "Hegemony and Its Discontents: A Symposium: Introduction," *International Studies Review* 7, no. 4 (2005): 525–529.

17 Michael Mastanduno, "System Maker and Privilege Taker: US Power and the International Political Economy," *World Politics* 61, no. 1 (2009): 121–154.

18 Benjamin J. Cohen, "The International Monetary System: Diffusion and Ambiguity," *International Affairs* 84, no. 3 (2008): 455–470; Daniel W. Drezner, "Bad Debts: Assessing China's Financial Influence in Great Power Politics," *International Security* 34, no. 2 (2009): 7–45; Carla Norrlof, *America's Global Advantage* (Cambridge, MA: Cambridge University Press, 2009), ch. 4; Susan Strange, "The Persistent Myth of Lost Hegemony," *International Organization* 41, no. 4 (1987): 551–574 .

19 Stephen Brooks and William Wohlforth, *World Out of Balance* (Princeton: Princeton University Press, 2008); Paul Kennedy, "The Greatest Superpower Ever," *New Perspectives Quarterly* 19, no. 2 (2002): 8–18; Barry Posen, "Command of the Commons: The Military Foundations of US Hegemony," *International Security* 28, no. 1 (2003): 5–46.

20 The World Bank, *World Development Indicators* (Washington, DC: The World Bank, 2012), 310; Kennedy, "The Greatest Superpower," 13.

21 Waltz, "Structural Realism," 24.

22 Waltz, "Structural Realism," 27–28. See also Christopher Layne, "The War of Terrorism and the Balance of Power," in *Balance of Power: Theory and Practice in the 21st Century*, eds. T. V. Paul, James J Wirtz, and Michel Ofrtmann (Stanford: Stanford University Press, 2004); and Pape, "Soft Balancing."

23 Brooks and Wohlforth, *World Out of Balance*, 23.

24 Randall L. Schweller, *Unanswered Threats: Political Constraints on the Balance of Power* (Princeton: Princeton University Press, 2006).

25 G. John Ikenberry, *Liberal Leviathan: The Origins, Crisis, and Transformation of the American World Order* (Princeton: Princeton University Press, 2011); Walt, *Taming American Power*, 119–120.

26 Kim D. Reimann, "A View from the Top: International Politics, Norms and the Worldwide Growth of NGOs," *International Studies Quarterly* 50, no. 1 (2006): 45–67; Anna Stavrianakis, "Missing the Target: NGOs, Global Civil Society and the Arms Trade," *Journal of International Relations and Development* 15, no. 2 (2011): 224–249; and Randall W. Stone, *Controlling Institutions: International Organizations and the Global Economy* (Cambridge: Cambridge University Press, 2011).

27 Schweller and Priess, "Tale of Two Realisms," 3–4.

28 Jervis, "Realism, Neoliberalism, and Cooperation," 56–7; Jeffry Frieden, *Global Capitalism: Its Fall and Rise in the Twentieth Century* (New York: W. W. Norton & Company, 2006).

29 For example, Beverly Crawford, "Toward a Theory of Progress in International Relations," in *Progress in Postwar International Relations*, eds. Emanuel Adler and Beverly Crawford (New York: Columbia University Press, 1991): 440–444.

30 Iver B. Neumann and Ole Jacob Sending, *Governing the Global Polity* (Ann Arbor: University of Michigan Press, 2010); Christian Reus-Smit, *The Moral Purpose of the State: Culture, Social Identity, and Institutional Rationality in International Relations* (Princeton: Princeton University Press, 1999).

31 Martin Griffiths, *Rethinking International Relations Theory* (Basingstoke: Palgrave Macmillan, 2011).

32 Duncan Bell, "Political Realism and the Limits of Ethics," in *Ethics and World Politics*, ed. Duncan Bell (Oxford: Oxford University Press, 2010), 100.

33 John Maynard Keynes, *Economic Consequences of the Peace* (New York: Harcourt, Brace & Howe, 1919), 6.

Classical Liberal Internationalism

Christer Jönsson

As none of the three terms in the title of this chapter is self-explanatory or uncontroversial each warrants some clarification. *Internationalism* has been described succinctly as "the ideology of international bonding" or "the idea that we both are and should be part of a broader community than that of the nation or the state." As such, it has a range of overlapping meanings, all revolving around attempts to regulate political life at the global level in the pursuit of peace. Internationalism can be seen as the opposite of nationalism, which emphasizes national interests and values in opposition to internationalist ideas and programs that are perceived to threaten national independence. Both ideologies have rational as well as emotional qualities. Internationalism should also be distinguished from cosmopolitanism. Whereas cosmopolitanism envisages a universalistic community, internationalism takes the existing division into particularistic communities as its point of departure. Internationalists, in other words, do not share the cosmopolitan vision of transcending the state but take the division into states as a given and look for ways of aligning conflicting interests.[1]

The label *liberal* indicates one distinct variety of internationalist thought that may be distinguished from conservative and socialist internationalism. In contrast to its conservative counterpart, which views balance of power as the principal way of restraining states, liberal internationalism is more optimistic about the prospects for interstate cooperation. And against the socialist vision of the withering away of states and an ensuing classless world society, liberal internationalism posits a zone of peace and cooperation among liberal states. Another, partly overlapping typology contrasts liberal internationalism with hegemonic internationalism—the belief that the only possible and desirable way of integrating the world is on asymmetrical, unequal terms—and with radical or revolutionary internationalism.[2]

This chapter deals with *classical* liberal internationalism. It is a tradition of thought with roots in the Enlightenment. Where the classical era ends and neoliberalism takes over is debatable. For the purpose of this chapter, the border is arbitrarily drawn at World War II. The war entailed a crisis for liberal internationalism. Criticized as idealistic, naïve, and utopian, it was overtaken by realism as the prevailing paradigm. The post-war re-establishment of liberal internationalism is treated in Chapter 8, which explores neoliberal institutionalism. It should be noted that whereas the classical tradition was primarily a prescriptive and prospective ideology with minimal empirical claims, neoliberalism offers an analytical framework for the study of historical processes rather than a remote ideal.[3]

A caveat seems called for at the outset: When we attach the label "liberal internationalism," especially with the epithet "classical," to a number of early thinkers from the eighteenth to the twentieth century, we apply a terminology of later origin. "Many thinkers are retrospectively categorized as liberal internationalists despite the fact that they would neither recognize nor identify with the term."[4]

This chapter first outlines some of the basic values and tenets associated with liberal internationalism, then gives a brief account of the evolution of the tradition, pointing to some of its most prominent exponents. The section thereafter identifies and discusses recurrent tensions and controversies within liberalism related to international relations. The concluding remarks dwell on the legacy of classical liberal internationalism and its relevance to contemporary realities.

Basic tenets of liberal internationalism

In Michael Doyle's oft-quoted words, "there is no canonical description of liberalism," only something resembling "a family portrait of principles and institutions" associated with liberal states.[5] If liberalism in general defies precise definition, liberal internationalism appears even more ambiguous. "Few political notions are at once so normative and so equivocal as liberal internationalism."[6] Yet there is a fair degree of agreement on identifying a cluster of values characterizing liberalism as a political ideology and their application to international affairs.

The most fundamental value shared by all liberals concerns individual *freedom*. Commitment to this principle entails challenging vested interests and arbitrary authority while defending human rights and promoting popularly based institutions. Power is considered legitimate only if it is based on popular consent and respects basic freedoms. Liberalism rests on confidence in the rational and moral qualities of human beings. The emphasis on the liberty and welfare of individuals over and above social structures sets liberalism apart from socialism. Another core element of liberalism is a belief in progress. Classical liberalism is thus an ideology of reform, reflecting confidence in the corrigibility and improvability of all political arrangements. Malfunctioning behavior is viewed as a product of counterproductive institutions and practices that can be remedied by reforming the system that produces it. This emphasis on progressive change sets liberalism apart from conservatism.[7]

How, then, do these core values translate into the international arena? First, it should be noted that the international dimension is not an afterthought or a later derivative, but has always been an integral part of liberal thinking. The growth of international interaction and cooperation is seen as a central element in the realization of greater human freedom. The belief in progress applies to the international arena as well. Liberal internationalism envisages a gradual transformation of international relations, which helps promote human freedom by establishing conditions of peace, prosperity and justice.[8] Thus, "liberal accounts of international politics were characteristically those of a process, not what we have today, but what we may have later if we keep to a certain course."[9] Like all liberals, internationalists celebrate the possibility of deliberate reforms, but their expectations go beyond the domestic sphere to include international relations. While not teleological, liberal internationalism offers a broad vision of an open, rule-based system where states have overcome constraints and are prepared to cooperate and pursue collective action.[10]

Other themes characteristic of classical liberal internationalism include free trade, national self-determination, nonintervention in the internal affairs of other states, and strengthened international law. Free trade is seen to generate peace and prosperity by binding people together in material interdependencies that would raise the costs of war and create an international division of labour. The belief that national self-determination promotes peace is a variant of democratic liberalism. It draws on an assumed similarity of relationships between states and international order, on the one hand, and individuals and domestic order, on the other, as does the principle of nonintervention. In the same way that morally autonomous citizens hold rights to liberty, states that represent them democratically have the right to be free from foreign intervention. Similarly, the progress of international law is measured by its increasing similarity to domestic law.

As pointed out by several observers, the classical liberal vision of international reform is built to a considerable degree on a domestic analogy: the same general principles that had led to the transformation of political life domestically were seen to apply externally as well. Stanley Hoffmann argues that "the international dimension of liberalism was little more than the projection of domestic liberalism on a world scale."[11] Critics claim that early liberals overlooked the differences between domestic and international politics. However, more nuanced accounts posit that the liberal vision did not rest on a naïve analogy but reflected "the view that the anarchic system of sovereign states can and ought to be *domesticated* in a way that resembles, however imperfectly, the liberal vision of political society within the state."[12]

Classical liberal internationalism is best characterized as an ideology, that is, a system of political thought arising out of, and reflecting, the economic, political, and cultural experience of particular social groups. As such, it is geared toward political action in a political realm where it has to struggle with the world views of other social groups. Historically bound, ideologies are constantly changing. To account for liberal internationalism as an ideology therefore requires "an engagement with its conditions of emergence and an historical account of its struggle with internal and external competitors."[13]

The origins and evolution of liberal internationalism

Liberalism originated in Europe around the turn of the seventeenth and eighteenth century, a tumultuous period in European history. The feudal system had fallen; the political control of papal Christendom was broken; the Renaissance had renewed interest in the republican and cultural traditions of antiquity; a system ordered on sovereign states was emerging; and the Enlightenment introduced ideas about reforming society, using reason rather than tradition, and advancing knowledge through science. It was during this era of change that liberalism emerged to become the dominant theory of modernity. Domestically, the feudal legacy of ruling aristocracies and autocratic rule became targets of liberal criticism; internationally, the prevalence of violence and hypocrisy in a system dominated by balance-of-power thinking came under attack.

The earliest liberal intellectuals sought to use an empiricist methodology developed in the natural sciences to determine a political theory that would organize and defend the aspirations of the emergent middle class for a defense of private property, a rationalized system of laws, and a voice in law-making while still providing a basis for moral and ethical life consistent with deep-seated Christian values and beliefs.[14]

John Locke's seventeenth century philosophy laid the foundation of modern liberal individualism. He believed in human rationality, which was ultimately to be embodied in government by consent and the protection of private property. Arguing that the duty of the state was to uphold the "life, liberty and property" of its citizens, Locke drew a moral parallel between external aggression and domestic oppression. Aggressive war was seen to violate the *raison d'être* of society, thus being inconceivable as a delegated power of legitimate government.[15]

Early liberal internationalists tended to believe, with Adam Smith, in the unhampered pursuit of economic interests. Government intervention needed to be minimized in order to allow the private sector to flourish. If trade and manufacture were to be conducted freely throughout the world, a pattern of cooperation and peaceful competition would ensue. In his "Plan for an Universal and Perpetual Peace," written in 1786–89 as part of his *Principles of International Law*, the British utilitarian Jeremy Bentham argued that free trade would bring the greatest economic benefits to the greatest number of people at the same time as trade relations would discourage war. Similar ideas of "commercial pacifism" based on *laissez faire* principles were developed by later British liberal thinkers, such as James Mill, John Stuart Mill, and Richard Cobden.

The role of republican governments based on liberal principles in developing peaceful international relations was highlighted by Immanuel Kant in his influential book *Perpetual Peace* (*Zum ewigen Frieden*), written in 1795. In this he envisioned the widening acceptance of three "definitive articles" of peace. The first requires that state constitutions be republican. In contrast to the aggressive interests of absolutist monarchies, republics are not inclined to go to war because this requires the consent of the citizens, who are reluctant to accept the costs in lives and financial resources. According to Kant's second definitive article, liberal republics will progressively establish peace among themselves by means of a pacific federation (*foedus pacificum*). As more and more republics join, an expanding "zone of peace" is created. Even if Kant does not elaborate on the organizational embodiment of this pacific union, it is clearly more than a single peace treaty but less than a world state. It is not seen to acquire any power or authority over and above each autonomous state. The third definitive article outlines the idea of a cosmopolitan law "limited to conditions of universal hospitality" as a complement to the pacific union. Cosmopolitan law would guarantee access to foreigners and the flow of goods and ideas across national borders.[16]

Even if Kant himself would hardly have recognized the concept of "liberalism," his philosophy has inspired subsequent generations of liberal internationalists to the present era. For instance, contemporary theories of "democratic peace" and "cosmopolitan democracy" draw on Kant's idea of a republican zone of peace.[17] The popularity of his writings, in combination with their complexity and ambiguity, has entailed differing interpretations. By some he has been interpreted as an idealist; by others as a revolutionary. "These readings hover between two distinct forms of expectation: either they emphasize the moral aspect of the Kantian idea of peace, and end up interpreting it as a *promise*; or they emphasize the natural necessity of this idea and the inevitability of its realization, and end up interpreting it as a *prognosis*."[18]

The nineteenth century is generally considered the golden age of liberalism, especially in Britain. While beginning as an expression of middle-class industrial interests, English liberalism developed into a national political movement. It was now that a number of thinkers, such as John Stuart Mill, Richard Cobden, and Herbert Spencer, combined different liberal internationalist strands into a credo that free trade would produce international prosperity, peace, and cooperation; a vital private sector constituted the engine of progress; and this vitality depended on the freedom provided by democratic or republican government.[19]

Nineteenth century industrialism produced a new setting "in which the implementation of ideas of equal rights and opportunities became more feasible, but only if the state were accorded a more positive role than in classical liberal theory."[20] Although much of the liberal agenda had been achieved in the advanced capitalist states, the envisaged domestic and international effects had disappointingly not appeared. In addition, liberalism now had to take up the struggle with another radical ideology, socialism. A downturn in the world economy in combination with *fin de siècle* fatalism and pessimism precipitated a crisis of liberalism around the turn of the century. The outbreak of World War I delivered a severe blow to liberal internationalism and is sometimes conceived as the end of the liberal century that had begun in 1815.[21]

The "new liberalism" that gradually emerged promoted a greater role for the state. Earlier versions had paid more attention to what states should refrain from doing than what they could positively do. Among new liberals the emphasis moved from "negative" to "positive" liberty, from "freedom from" government interference to "freedom to" enjoy work and social improvements. This entailed calls for appropriate institutional responses domestically as well as internationally, not only to problems of law and order but also to those of economic and social welfare. Increasingly suspicious of private exchanges domestically, the new liberals came to doubt their efficacy in the management of international relations. The emerging "welfare internationalism" demanded government engagement in regulating international intercourse.[22]

Two prominent exponents of the new liberal internationalism were Norman Angell and J. A. Hobson. Angell is best known for his argument concerning the futility of war. In *The Great Illusion*, published in 1912, he argued that modern production, transportation, and communication technologies had made national economies so interdependent that war would be disruptive to all. In his treatment, not only free trade but also the international networks of financial elites contributed to these interdependencies. Angell also believed that extensive education was necessary to overcome public ignorance and "the crowd mind," which tended to encourage war. Angell was awarded the Nobel Peace Prize in 1933.

While Hobson is usually associated with his work on imperialism, his prolific writings dealt with a number of issues that modified early liberal internationalism. Proceeding from an analogy of society to an organism, Hobson criticized the individualism of nineteenth century liberalism. Applying the organic analogy to international relations, he envisaged expanding cooperation within an emerging world society made up not only of interacting states but also of networks of individuals and groups. Hobson suggested that the international realm was an integral part of social life, with people living in "concentric circles of association." In the same way that he argued for more interventionist government domestically, he saw the need for international control and organization—both intergovernmental and nongovernmental—to regulate and mitigate the excesses of the world market. His ideal was a loose international federation with associated functional organizations. He can be seen as a precursor of, and formed a theoretical basis for, David Mitrany's functional approach to international integration. Hobson, in short, played an important role in the transformation from nineteenth century to twentieth century liberal internationalism.[23]

Early twentieth century internationalism reflected the transition domestically from old liberalism to the doctrine of the welfare state. This entailed a drift toward institutional arguments. Plans for, and the eventual performance of, the League of Nations provided foci of attention and contention. Whereas nineteenth century liberals saw the internal reform of states inexorably leading to external reform, most twentieth century liberals argued that external reform was integral to, or a precondition for, domestic reform. They also imagined reform, not in terms of limitations on government, but as positive engagement in international policies encouraging wealth creation and social stability. Mitrany's functionalism, for example, focused on economic and social welfare issues that were increasingly becoming issues for government policy, arguing that the national basis was inadequate. His criticism of the limits of the League is telling: "It is no use putting a policeman at the street corner to keep the traffic in order and to watch for burglars if at the same time the water and food supply for that street is being cut off."[24]

At the end of World War I Woodrow Wilson's vision of a liberal world order became a controversial component of world politics. This was a "one-world" vision of an orderly international community of states interacting in a system of laws and international organization. Following Kant, Wilson believed that peace could be established only by a compact among inherently peaceful democracies. "Wilson had fought his war to make the world safe *for* democracy; he created his League to make the world safe *by* democracy." National self-determination, in Wilson's view, was an essential corollary of democracy. "Just as the people had a right to govern themselves within the national system, so the nations had the right to govern themselves within the global system."[25]

Taken together, the Wilsonian vision of liberal internationalism was both breathtakingly ambitious and surprisingly limited. It sought to transform the old global system based on the balance of power, spheres of influence, military rivalry, and alliances into a unified liberal international order based on nation-states and the rule of law. Power and security competition would be decomposed and replaced by a community of nations. But Wilsonian liberal internationalism did not involve the construction of deeply transformative legally binding political institutions. Liberal international order was to be constructed around the "soft law" of public opinion and moral suasion.[26]

During the interwar era liberal internationalism became the target of much criticism, most famously in E. H. Carr's *The Twenty Years' Crisis*. Characterizing liberal internationalism as based on idealist or even "utopian" myths of a "harmony of interests" among states, Carr laid the foundation of realism as an alternative perspective on international relations. The pejorative labels of "idealists" or "utopians" have had a lasting impact. Carr's critique is echoed, for instance, by Stanley Hoffman, who speaks of liberal internationalism's "fallacy of believing that all good things can come together." Yet recent scholarship has demonstrated that Carr painted too simplistic a picture and created a straw man out of the diverse views held by liberal internationalists. And Woodrow Wilson's Fourteen Points, which came to be seen as "something approaching an idealist Magna Carta" in the interwar period, have provided the foundation of efforts to resuscitate "neo-idealism" after the end of the Cold War.[27]

In sum, it was only in the twentieth century that international organization entered the liberal internationalist agenda in earnest. Before then, either free trade or an expanding network of liberal republics was seen as producing future prosperity and peace. As the nineteenth century drew to an end, the "domestic analogy" took on another meaning, as the proactive welfare state came to serve as a model for intensified collaboration internationally.

Tensions and controversies in liberal internationalism

We need to be reminded that "liberalism did not just enter this world as a benevolent rational force which gradually conquered ground by the authority of example, but rather as a sectarian political position which had to fight its way to the top and adjusted its goals and means to the given circumstances."[28] As the brief account of the evolution of liberal internationalism indicates, this struggle was not only with contending ideologies but included internal disagreements. One may speak of "contending liberalisms."[29] In the following some of the most prominent tensions and controversies within liberal internationalism will be identified.

At a general level, liberalism encompasses two different perspectives on human nature: one proceeding from human selfishness, defining interests in material terms, and believing that human greed may produce general benefits; the other promoting the moral aptitude, self-fulfillment, and civic virtues of human beings and emphasizing rights and duties.[30] Another recurrent general tension is that between experience and expectation. Liberal internationalism is a container of past experience as well as expectations for the future.[31] A more tangible division concerns the importance accorded to economic and political factors. The question of whether economic or political driving forces will produce international improvement and reforms has divided liberals throughout history. Moreover, within each faction there have been contentious issues.

Economic issues

One of the first liberal debates concerned the relationship between freedom and property. Whereas individual liberty and the right to private property were fundaments in early liberal thinking, the question was whether all citizens should have a voice in government or whether popular rule should be restricted to the propertied. The defense of property rights was central in the early *laissez faire* formulations of liberal internationalism. The role of the state was to be constrained to enforcing a limited set of laws, adjudicating disputes, and defending property and individual rights. State intervention in the domestic economy as well as in international economic transactions was seen as detrimental. Unconstrained activity by the private sector would contribute to a steady improvement of the material and moral condition of all people. This "liberalism of privilege" demoted or shunned the doctrine of equal rights.[32]

Although *laissez faire* liberalism continued to hold sway throughout the nineteenth century, a number of later liberal thinkers questioned the classical idea of the independence of the economy from political pressure or social concern. They had less confidence in the progressive potential of the private sector, arguing that previous liberal thought had neglected powerful political interests of industrial and financial elites. Capitalism was not necessarily a force for peace, but could be an incitement to war because of the influence of sectional interests.[33] The re-evaluation of economic actors entailed a more favorable view of the state as a vehicle for the redistribution of wealth and power and guarantor of liberal values, not only at home but abroad as well. Several liberals advocated foreign intervention for liberal ends. As early as 1849 John Stuart Mill declared that every liberal government "has a right to assist struggling liberalism, by mediation, by money, or by arms, wherever it can prudently do so; as every despotic government, when its aid is needed or asked for, never scruples to aid despotic governments."[34]

Political issues

If classical liberal internationalism harbors certain economic divergences against the backdrop of a general belief in the beneficial effects of a free private sector, there is a greater amount of contentious political issues. The common denominator is the conviction that liberal states constitute the foundation of a peaceful and prosperous world. This, however, does not exclude significant disagreements.

Related to the *laissez faire* problematic is the contrast between "negative" and "positive" freedom. Whereas the early English tradition equated liberalism with freedom from control by the state, the "new liberals" in the 1880s advanced a positive ideal of freedom as "the liberation of the powers of all men equally for contributions to a common good" and "the maximum of power for all members of human society to make the best of themselves."[35] This debate recurs as differing views of the international role of the state. Early liberals were critical of the traditional practices of power politics, mistrusted foreign policy elites, diplomats and the military, and wanted to minimize government intervention not only within but also beyond national borders. The more "positive" conceptions of self-actualization and social welfare entailed a more active role for the state in the international arena as well. Thus, the divisive issue of intervention for "positive" freedom meant that liberal internationalism might encompass a wide span from what we today label isolationism to moral crusades.[36]

Retrospective analyses have raised the question whether classical liberal internationalism was genuinely inclusive and *international*. Postcolonialist scholars, in particular, have portrayed liberalism as Eurocentric, paternalist, and imperialist, insofar as it regarded Western values as universally applicable and served as a justification of Western superiority. They point out that the nineteenth century witnessed the triumph of Western liberalism at the very time that British imperialism expanded. Among liberal internationalists there were, in fact, different views concerning the "civilizing mission" of liberal states. For instance, Mill believed in hierarchical relations between civilized and barbarian peoples, arguing for colonial government intervention. By contrast, Kant's principle of nonintervention, his expectation that republican constitutions would emerge through internal political processes rather than outside interference, and his emphasis on consent as the basis of republican constitutions precluded imperialist policies. Hobson, for his part, argued that a "civilizing mission" was necessary but only under the tutelage of an independent international organization.[37]

Classical liberal internationalism also exhibits a tension between *moral* and *institutional* arguments.[38] Moral arguments point to a new international consciousness as the agent of a positive transformation of international relations. The conscience of civilized humankind was to safeguard the internationalist goals of order and progress. In the words of L. T. Hobhouse: "Moral rights and duties are founded on relations between man and man, and therefore applicable to all humanity. To deny this applicability is merely to throw back civilized ethics to the savage state."[39] According to institutional arguments, international progress cannot be left to ethics alone, but requires institutional mechanisms. The aim is then to devise political institutions that can induce people to act in morally defensible ways. World War II tipped the balance in favor of institutional arguments. Humanitarian ethics had proved inadequate to avert warfare, and an international organization to promote peace and prevent the recurrence of war, a league of nations, became a cornerstone of liberal internationalism.

Another unresolved question concerns whether the sovereign state facilitates or impedes the overarching goal of individual freedom. On the one hand, the political and legal framework of sovereignty permits freedom from the coercion of others; on the other hand, it allows the state to impose arbitrary and oppressive ends on individual citizens. Kant, for instance, was ambiguous on this issue, at times considering state sovereignty as a *sine qua non* condition of freedom, on other occasions viewing sovereignty as a threat to freedom.[40] The classical liberal internationalist solution, or vision, is that "the *external* sovereignty of states will be exercised with more restraint—and anarchy will thereby be mitigated—when *internal* sovereignty is located in the people."[41]

Nineteenth century *nationalism* confronted liberals with a new quandary. Eighteenth century liberals viewed the relationship of state and society in rational terms—as a set of mutual obligations or a social contract. Nationalism drew on emotional bonds of allegiance, loyalty, and passion. The predominant liberal position was to embrace the principle of national self-determination, which was seen as an external extension of the principle of consent, a corollary of liberal self-government. Yet this entailed an incongruity, insofar as liberalism had originally been an appeal to reason. Nationalism had more to do with emotion and a common national will. By overrunning the restraints on power and creating new sources of intense conflict between states, nationalism threatened both the liberal program at home and the vision of international order and peace.[42]

Another question concerns the interstate/transnational dimension: would national reforms establishing liberal states in and by themselves establish the desired world order, or is the formation of a transnational society, linking people across borders beyond government control, an additional precondition? Free commerce, cultural interaction, and the formation of a world public opinion were part of the classical liberal internationalist vision. Most liberals would include both national and transnational processes in their perspectives, but with varying emphasis. Some, such as Kant and Woodrow Wilson, believed in a world order created mainly by self-determining states, whereas Mitrany's functionalism saw the world of states as a constraint and envisaged transnational associations of legitimacy transforming human attachment to particular states.[43]

The location of rules and authority—how the envisaged liberal order is to be governed—is another unresolved and contested question. At issue is essentially to what extent the liberal order entails legal-political restrictions on state sovereignty. As we have seen, there have been different ideas about the need for an international organization, and those who have advocated one have not concurred on its scope and mandate. By the same token, the "rule of law" has been a significant part of the liberal vision of a peaceful world, but there has been no consensus as to the proper role of international law. Some have advocated "soft law," that is, rules and norms enforced through moral suasion and world public opinion; others have called for articulated sets of rules that prescribe and proscribe state action. The variety of liberal institutional and legal proposals have one thing in common: they have been "attempts to align an unwillingness to give up on the nation-state with a desire for peace."[44]

In sum, whereas liberal internationalists have shared a belief in international progress defined as movement toward increasing levels of harmonious cooperation between states, they have had varying views on how to achieve these goals. The "domestic analogy" pervades this debate, as "the competing liberal instruments with which to pursue individual freedom within the state have been directed outward as mechanisms for domesticating the international realm."[45] Modes of governance within and between states are interlinked in the liberal internationalist conception.

Conclusion

The evolution of liberal internationalism in its first centuries reveals a set of recurring themes and unresolved issues. In the period covered here liberal internationalism is best characterized as an ideology, pointing to a more peaceful and harmonious international order. Based on a belief in progress, it adapted continually to new circumstances. Both world wars represented serious disappointments and exposed liberal internationalism to charges of idealism. And the liberal vision of an improved international order did indeed remain a remote ideal for centuries.

Although there were earlier international developments in directions desired and proposed by liberals, it was only after the end of World War II—with the removal of a vast number of barriers to trade, successive waves of democratization, and the proliferation of international organizations—that significant parts of the classical ideals became reality. This meant that liberal internationalism changed character from a prospective ideology to an analytical framework challenging realism, and substituted the prefix "neo" for the epithet "classical." Yet classical liberal internationalism bequeaths a legacy of themes and issues that each new generation will relate to and recognize.

Additional reading

1. Hans Reiss, ed., *Kant: Political Writings* (Cambridge: Cambridge University Press, 1990).
2. Carsten Holbraad, *Internationalism and Nationalism in European Political Thought* (Basingstoke: Palgrave Macmillan, 2003).
3. Mark W. Zacher and Richard A. Matthew, "Liberal International Theory: Common Threads, Divergent Strands," in *Controversies in International Relations Theory*, ed. Charles W. Kegley, Jr. (New York: St. Martin's Press, 1995).
4. Michael Pugh, *Liberal Internationalism: The Interwar Movement for Peace in Britain* (Basingstoke: Palgrave Macmillan, 2012).

Notes

1 For definitions of internationalism, see Carsten Holbraad, *Internationalism and Nationalism in European Political Thought* (Basingstoke: Palgrave Macmillan, 2003), 1–2; Fred Halliday, "Three Concepts of Internationalism," *International Affairs* 64, no. 2 (1988): 187–198, 187; Anthony F. Lang, Jr., "Internationalism," in *International Encyclopedia of the Social Sciences*, Vol. 4, ed. William A. Darity, Jr. (Detroit: Macmillan Reference USA, 2008), 102–103; Jens Bartelson, *Visions of World Community* (Cambridge: Cambridge University Press, 2009), 1–3.
2 Cf. Holbraad, *Internationalism and Nationalism*, 7–10; Halliday, "Three Concepts of Internationalism," 192–197.
3 Cf. Duncan Bell, "Liberal Internationalism," in *Encyclopedia of Governance*, ed. Mark Bevir (Thousand Oaks, CA: Sage, 2006), 525.
4 Antonio Franceschet, "The Ethical Foundations of Liberal Internationalism," *International Journal* 54, no. 3 (1999): 468. The first recorded use of the word "internationalism" in English dates from 1851. Casper Sylvest, "Continuity and Change in British Liberal Internationalism, *c.* 1900–1930," *Review of International Studies* 31, no. 2 (2005): 263–283, 265. Halliday ("Three Concepts of Internationalism," 189) claims that the first use of the term came as late as 1877.
5 Michael W. Doyle, "Liberalism and World Politics," *American Political Science Review* 80, no. 4 (1986): 1152; also in Michael W. Doyle, *Ways of War and Peace* (New York: W. W. Norton, 1997), 206–207.
6 Jamie Munn, "Review of Antonio Franceschet, *Kant and Liberal Internationalism*," *Canadian Journal of Political Science* 37, no. 4 (2004): 1063.
7 Cf. Doyle, *Ways of War and Peace*, 207; Antonio Franceschet, "Sovereignty and Freedom: Immanuel Kant's Liberal Internationalist 'Legacy,'" *Review of International Studies* 27, no. 2 (2001): 213; Franceschet, "The Ethical Foundations," 471; Stanley Hoffmann, "The Crisis of Liberal Internationalism," *Foreign Policy* 98 (1995): 160; James L. Richardson, "Contending Liberalisms: Past and Present," *European Journal of International Relations* 3, no. 1 (1997): 8; David Long, "Conclusion: Inter-War Idealism, Liberal Internationalism, and Contemporary International Theory," in *Thinkers of the Twenty Years' Crisis*, eds. David Long and Peter Wilson (Oxford: Clarendon Press, 1995), 313.

8 Holbraad, *Internationalism and Nationalism*, 39; Hoffmann, "The Crisis of Liberal Internationalism," 160; Mark W. Zacher and Richard A. Matthew, "Liberal International Theory: Common Threads, Divergent Strands," in *Controversies in International Relations Theory*, ed. Charles W. Kegley, Jr. (New York: St. Martin's Press, 1995), 109–110.

9 Gal Gerson, "Review of Casper Sylvester, British Liberal Internationalism, 1880–1950: Making Progress?," *Victorian Studies* 53, no. 3 (2011): 541.

10 Jens Bartelson, "The Trial of Judgment: A Note on Kant and the Paradoxes of Internationalism," *International Studies Quarterly* 39, no. 2 (1995): 259; John Ikenberry, "Liberal Internationalism 3.0: America and the Dilemmas of Liberal World Order," *Perspectives on Politics* 7, no. 1 (2009): 72.

11 Hoffmann, "The Crisis of Liberal Internationalism," 160.

12 Franceschet, "Sovereignty and Freedom," 211 (emphasis in original); cf. Chiara Bottici, "The Domestic Analogy and the Kantian Project of *Perpetual Peace*," *Journal of Political Philosophy* 11, no. 4 (2003): 392–410.

13 Beate Jahn, "Liberal Internationalism: From Ideology to Empirical Theory—and Back Again," *International Theory* 1, no. 3 (2009): 436.

14 Zacher and Matthew, "Liberal International Theory," 111.

15 Jahn, "Liberal Internationalism," 424; Lee Ward, "Locke on the Moral Basis of International Relations," *American Journal of Political Science* 50, no. 3 (2006): 702.

16 See, e.g., Doyle, *Ways of War and Peace*, 253–258.

17 Cf. Antonio Franceschet, "Popular Sovereignty or Cosmopolitan Democracy? Liberalism, Kant and International Reform," *European Journal of International Relations* 6, no. 2 (2000): 277–302.

18 Bartelson, "The Trial of Judgment," 263.

19 George H. Sabine, *A History of Political Theory*, 3rd edition (London: George G. Harrap & Co., 1963), 703; Zacher and Matthew, "Liberal International Theory," 114.

20 Richardson, "Contending Liberalisms," 13.

21 See, e.g., Long, "Conclusion: Inter-War Idealism," 314–316.

22 Hidemi Suganami, *The Domestic Analogy and World Order Proposals* (Cambridge: Cambridge University Press, 1989), 108; cf. Cornelia Navari, *Internationalism and the State in the Twentieth Century* (London: Routledge, 2000), 231.

23 On Angell, see J. D. B. Miller, "Norman Angell and Rationality in International Relations," in *Thinkers of the Twenty Years' Crisis*, eds. Long and Wilson; cf. Zacher and Matthew, "Liberal International Theory," 114–115. On Hobson, see David Long, *Towards a New Liberal Internationalism: The International Theory of J.A. Hobson* (Cambridge: Cambridge University Press, 1996); David Long, "J.A. Hobson and Economic Internationalism," in *Thinkers of the Twenty Years' Crisis*, eds. Long and Wilson.

24 See Sylvest, "Continuity and Change in British Liberal Internationalism"; Navari, *Internationalism and the State*, 248; Suganami, *The Domestic Analogy*, 106–107 (including Mitrany quotation).

25 Inis L. Claude, Jr., *Swords into Plowshares*, 3rd edition (New York: Random House, 1964), 47.

26 Ikenberry, "Liberal Internationalism 3.0," 75.

27 E. H. Carr, *The Twenty Years' Crisis* (London: Macmillan, 1939). Cf. Hoffmann, "The Crisis of Liberal Internationalism," 167; Franceschet, "The Ethical Foundations," 464, 466; Franceschet, "Sovereignty and Freedom," 211; Peter Wilson, "Introduction: *The Twenty Years' Crisis* and the Category of 'Idealism' in International Relations," in *Thinkers of the Twenty Years' Crisis*, eds. Long and Wilson, 14; Charles W. Kegley, Jr. "The Neoidealist Moment in International Studies? Realist Myths and the New International Realities," *International Studies Quarterly* 37, no. 2 (1993): 131–146.

28 Jahn, "Liberal Internationalism," 429.

29 Richardson, "Contending Liberalisms," 8.

30 Hoffmann, "The Crisis of Liberal Internationalism," 174.
31 Bartelson, "The Trial of Judgment," 256.
32 Richardson, "Contending Liberalisms," 9, 13.
33 Cf. Zacher and Matthew, "Liberal International Theory," 112; Long, *Towards a New Liberal Internationalism*, 184–185.
34 As quoted in Holbraad, *Internationalism and Nationalism*, 41.
35 T. H. Green, as quoted in Richardson, "Contending Liberalisms," 11–12.
36 Hoffmann, "The Crisis of Liberal Internationalism," 162.
37 Cf., e.g., Martin Hall and John M. Hobson, "Liberal International Theory: Eurocentric but Not Always Imperialist?," *International Theory* 2, no. 2 (2010): 210–245; Beate Jahn, "Kant, Mill, and Illiberal Legacies in International Affairs," *International Organization* 59, no. 1 (2005): 177–207.
38 Sylvest, "Continuity and Change in British Liberal Internationalism."
39 As quoted in ibid., 272.
40 Franceschet, "The Ethical Foundations," 473; Franceschet, "Sovereignty and Freedom," 218.
41 Franceschet, "Popular Sovereignty or Cosmopolitan Democracy?," 284 (emphasis in original).
42 Hoffmann, "The Crisis of Liberal Internationalism," 162–164.
43 Cf. Franceschet, "Sovereignty and Freedom," 213; Franceschet, "The Ethical Foundations," 477.
44 Ikenberry, "Liberal Internationalism 3.0," 72–73; Lang, "Internationalism," 102.
45 Franceschet, "The Ethical Foundations," 468.

CONTENTS

Neoliberal Institutionalism

David P. Forsythe

Neoliberal institutionalism is one of several major approaches to understanding world affairs. The dominant approach has been some version of realism, and currently neorealism and neoliberalism are usually pictured as offering contrasting conclusions about the nature of the world and what policies should be fashioned for it. Other major approaches include constructivism, neo-conservatism ("the neo-cons"), and neo-Marxism. All address the absence of world government. Of all these theories, neoliberalism pays particular attention to global governance.

This chapter begins with the core of neoliberal thought by contrasting it with neorealism as well as with some reference to other schools of thought. Readers would do well to recall that several book length treatments exist on IR theories; what follows can only cover a few essential points. The chapter then suggests that most situations manifest both neoliberal and neorealist elements, just as most states manifest both neoliberal and neorealist policies depending on shifting factors. It continues by elaborating these fundamental points with two additional illustrations. The conclusion argues that both neoliberal and neorealist perspectives can be valid, depending on situations, issues, and policies. Macro-theories like neoliberalism may help orient students and policy-makers in considering a range of views about world affairs and global governance; but the devil, as always, resides in the details, and a more eclectic approach to theory (i.e. moving beyond any one macro-theory) is necessary for full understanding.

Neoliberalism in context

There are many different approaches, emphases, or schools of thought applied to understanding world affairs. This is true for IR in general and global governance in particular. For example, two books on the subject of understanding IR each note ten approaches, albeit that they are not exactly the same ten.[1] Two leading scholars in the field each discuss three main approaches to understanding, but they differ on some points of analysis.[2] Among these approaches, some form of realism has been the dominant approach. It is a school of thought, theory, or philosophical position, depending on which analyst one reads. For this writer and many others, the key common factor in various realist approaches is seeing the world as a struggle for power among self interested states, with a pervasive pessimism about the status of, and prospects for, the human condition—whether because of the inherent dark side of human nature, the anarchic structure of international relations, or other factors.[3]

Appropriately, a leading textbook on US foreign policy notes pessimism as one of the defining features of realism.[4] Characteristically, such a leading practitioner of realism as Henry Kissinger was known for his minimalist goals in foreign policy and his acceptance of avoiding disaster—such as a nuclear war—as a sufficiently moral justification for the policy of détente with the Soviet Union. For him, trying to improve human rights inside the Soviet Union, much less trying to totally defeat that adversary, was a bridge too far—an idealistic and unwise crusade that endangered more essential and achievable goals. For him, trying to block the spread of neo-Marxist views in Salvador Allende's Chile and other countries of the Western Hemisphere justified support for the brutal dictator Augusto Pinochet, whose regime killed and tortured thousands of suspected "subversives." Realists mostly consider the various versions of liberalism to be idealism, as did Kissinger. Characteristically he wrote, "in the world of diplomacy, a loaded gun is often more potent than a legal brief."[5]

A second major approach has been some form of liberalism. As often noted, a basic feature of liberal theory as opposed to realist theory is optimism about the prospects for, and impact of, international cooperation and progress. In all versions of liberalism, whether because of such matters as democracy (republican liberalism) or free trade (economic liberalism), persons are not inherently condemned by either human nature or the structure of international relations to a life that tends to be nasty, brutish, and short. In the liberal view, whether focusing on the management of violence, reduction of poverty, or just the human capacity to rationally learn from past mistakes, progress is possible. In this view, one can aspire to more than simply avoiding disaster or making slightly tolerable gains in a fundamentally bad situation; one can make substantial improvements in the global condition. It is for this reason that Kissinger did not consider Ronald Reagan a realist, because Reagan was optimistic about such matters of ridding the world of nuclear weapons and greatly expanding the number of democracies—subjects on which Kissinger was deeply pessimistic. He wrote, "Reagan had been elected . . . to reaffirm the traditional verities of American exceptionalism,"[6] with its belief in the American capacity to remake the world for the better.

Neoliberal institutionalism, or neoliberalism for short, focuses on the supposedly important role, and beneficial impact, of international institutions. This has obvious relevance for the subject of global governance because the latter overlaps considerably with the former. That is, global governance consists, among other things, of the sum of different international institutions whose reason for being is the management of transnational problems in a peaceful, humane, and sometimes legal way. In a classic treatment, Bruce Russett and John O'Neal argue that when states join international organizations, commit to regulated free trade, and maintain a democratic polity, world peace is enhanced.[7] In this sense any regularized set of expectations or behavior is an institution.[8] International law is an institution. The United Nations is an institution, albeit also a formal intergovernmental organization. An international regime is an institution, but one taking the form of principles, rules, and organizations (in the plural) for the management of an issue area and around which actor expectations converge.[9] A regime may entail one or more formal organizations but is broader than such. The international refugee regime is broader than the Office of the UN High Commissioner for Refugees (UNHCR), as discussed below.

Neorealists—or "structural realists," in Kenneth Waltz's formulation—focus on the harsh effects of the absence of a global government backed by effective force.[10] They share certain assumptions with neoliberals like Robert Keohane and his scholarly disciples,[11] most especially that the territorial state is the most important actor in world affairs, because of either material power or political psychology—such as popular identification with and loyalty to the state. Both schools of thought also assume that the state, as represented by its government, is a rational actor that will try to pursue positives and avoid negatives. Thus both schools see states as rationally doing a cost–benefit calculation about how to adjust national policies to changing international situations.

In general, all varieties of realists believe that the state will prioritize national independence, coercive or hard power, and flexibility in policy-making rather than rigid commitment to legal rules. Realists mostly believe in the continuing relevance of war and other forms of military intervention. Thus, in the language of the "English school," realists see national decision-makers as rationally pursuing a pluralist world order based on "sovereign" states which are strong in terms of independent legal authority and hard power. It follows in the realist view that states will keep international institutions relatively weak and insignificant. The realist scholar John Mearsheimer has, for instance, written about "the false promise" of international institutions.[12]

Neoliberals believe that international institutions are more important than realists think. Particularly under conditions of globalization, when international interconnectedness has become a potent form of interdependence, and thus when mutual dependence among states is highly sensitive and important, international institutions become more important and significant. Neoliberals generally believe in the declining utility of military force under conditions of increased interdependence—including mutually assured destruction (MAD) from a war between great powers. In the neoliberal view, states rationally delegate significant authority and capability to organs and officials of international institutions to reduce transaction costs and other negatives in a pluralist world order. In this view, the principals (states) will delegate to their agents (international organizations based on international law) in important ways. Hence neoliberals believe states will rationally, if gradually, move to a world order characterized by more transnational solidarity and less national separateness. They see the ongoing proliferation of international organizations—both intergovernmental and nongovernmental—as indicative of continuing and important trends in an era of globalization. Neoliberals see growing influence in world affairs from the sum total of all these non-state actors.

Realists tend to emphasize traditional security issues such as protecting the homeland from external attack. This emphasis presumably leads to the clear conclusion that the rational state trusts no one but itself and its allied states when it comes to defense of vital national interests. They allow for multilateral arrangements such as the North Atlantic Treaty Organization (NATO). But there they see little independent power for the organization as such and even less independent authority and capability for NATO officials. Rather, they see a continuation of state power wrapped in multilateral trappings, and in the case of NATO they often see decisive hegemonic power for the United States. Realists note that most Americans could not name the secretary-general of NATO in any given year. The central elements of US security do not depend on the decisions by NATO's most senior official.

Neoliberals, by contrast, tend to emphasize economic issues such as regulated free trade as well as development and finance. Keohane's seminal writings are mostly about international political economy, which he has acknowledged as limited.[13] Neoliberals point to international institutions such as the European Union, World Trade Organization (WTO), International Monetary Fund, and World Bank as examples of not only the results of economic interdependence but also powerful international organizations with independent and influential officials. Neoliberals see these organizations, and their rules, as capable of getting states to change how they think about themselves and their interests.

Here it is useful to bring into the discussion the main points of constructivism, which is a pre-theory philosophy about ontology—the nature of being.[14] It can feed into either realism or liberalism. It is an approach that above all stresses two factors: ideas in comparison to material conditions, and especially ideas about identity and reputation. As for the first factor, a constructivist would note that while Switzerland has much less hard power than the United States, the small neutral nation, whose primary contribution to history is sometimes said to be the invention of the cuckoo clock, does not fear invasion and occupation by the United States. Hence, as argued by Alexander Wendt and others, anarchy is what one makes of it. Ideas about peaceful friendship negate any importance about the absence of a world government that might protect weaker parties.[15] In the Swiss–US relationship, the imbalance in hard power is irrelevant. Moreover, to continue with the same example, if both Switzerland and the United States identify themselves as friendly, Western, democratic, and capitalist partners, there is no reason to count either guns or sticks of butter. The two states exhibit much cooperation and some conflict on transnational matters, but relations remain within peaceful, legal, and respectful parameters.

Constructivists make the point that states, or more precisely the individuals who speak for the state, have multiple identities. Some policy-makers may desire to be known for, or in other words to have a reputation for, moral or responsible or legal or dependable foreign policy behavior. They do not wish to be known for attacking other democratic, capitalist, and friendly states. It follows that such an identity might lead to giving great attention to international institutions reflecting the common norms of democracy, free trade, non-aggression, and so forth. And one might say, for example, that China's membership in the UN, WTO, and other international organizations has caused it over time to see itself less as a revolutionary actor and more as status quo actor that has been incorporated into the existing world order.[16] In this view, China seeks influence within the state system and not to overthrow it. It is in this sense that international institutions are said to affect the identities and interests of states, which is both a neoliberal and constructivist interpretation. Constructivists delve deeper into the ideas, especially about identity and reputation, that create international institutions and sometimes make them influential.

Two examples from US foreign policy

Two historical examples help make the points set out above. It is a principle of international law that military force is most legal when used in self-defense, clearly so if an armed attack has already occurred. President John F. Kennedy during the 1962 Cuban missile crisis, when advised to employ a military strike on Cuba to destroy Soviet missiles, remarked that he did not want to go down in history as another Tojo—referring to the Japanese leader who authorized the 1941 first strike on Pearl Harbor. So clearly Kennedy's concern for image, reputation, and identity affected his policy-making. He undoubtedly had not read a textbook on international law, although he did consult with lawyers. Rather his concern for his standing in history, and other reputational or image factors, was one of the influences that resulted in a decision (no first strike on Cuba) that was consistent with an important international institution—the international law concerning use of force.

In contrast, after 9/11, in the George W. Bush administration, a core of high officials were dominant who strongly identified as US patriots and who saw reference to international law as a type of "lawfare" in which reference to most international institutions represented a devious attempt to restrain the virtuous United States.[17] In such an inner core of officials, for whom nothing was more important than preventing further attacks on the United States, one found little serious attention to traditional understandings of international law or to critical comments by UN or other foreign officials about, for example, abuse of suspected enemy prisoners.

In both 1962 and 2001, concerns about national security were filtered by ideas about identities and about reputations. This is a point stressed by constructivists. Kennedy was sensitive to building support for his policies not only at home but also in the Western Hemisphere and beyond. In addition to concern about his own historical legacy, he was sensitive to international reputation for other, quite practical reasons. He rejected advice to base his policies on the Monroe Doctrine, because that would create the image of continued US domination of the region and be quite unappealing to other states in the region whose support Kennedy desired.

By contrast, Bush's key decision-makers, such as Vice-President Richard Cheney and Secretary of Defense Donald Rumsfeld, were overwhelmingly focused on preventing any further attacks on the homeland and cared not what UN officials might say or what damage might be done to the international legal framework protecting the rights of detainees. They were not at all sensitive to the "reputational costs" associated with torture and cruelty toward prisoners then being implemented by both the military and the Central Intelligence Agency. A similar attitude characterized the absence of any damage from reputational costs about invading Iraq in 2003.

In both 1962 and after 9/11, one can explain a great deal about resulting decisions by looking closely at officials' core identities or self-image, and whether or not they were sensitive to international reputational factors. The more one identifies as a unilateral ultra-nationalist, the more one is likely to endorse a realist or neo-conservative orientation.[18] The more one identifies as a nationalist who also lives in a global society, the more one is likely to address security issues within the neoliberal framework—entailing considerable attention to international institutions.

In both of these historical cases hard power was relevant. Materialism mattered. Whether the United States had the capability to launch a military strike on Cuba (or exchange missile strikes with the Soviet Union, for that matter) was relevant. Likewise, whether the United States had the hard power to strike at the Taliban and Al-Qaeda in southwest Asia was relevant. But constructivists argue that a fuller understanding of policies adopted in both cases requires a detailed awareness of ideas and not just military arsenals. They also argue that identity and reputation, in global context, matter. Some neoliberals also emphasize the role of international institutions in constructing identity and arriving at definitions of the national interest.

Constructivists and neoliberals often emphasize the international social structure: fundamental ideas such as non-aggression, human rights, peaceful relations, and state sovereignty but only as conditioned by international norms, and so on. The international social structure—viz. a dominant set of ideas—overlaps with international institutions. But there is also a traditional national social structure: dominant ideas such as the sovereign right to choose national policies, national security as decided by elected leaders, various forms of national exceptionalism, and so forth. An important question is whether, in any given situation, a national social structure is at variance with the international social structure. It is in the interplay of these two sets of ideas—the first stressing international institutions and the second usually stressing national prerogatives—that one finds the complex and elusive keys to an otherwise superficial understanding of foreign policy.

Neoliberalism argues that, once created, international institutions can affect national identities as well as definitions and choices about national interests. It is, arguably, a chicken-and-egg process. Once states created the United Nations, the activities and policy positions of the UN secretary-general, or other independent agency heads, may have some impact on national decision-making. Or, the decisions taken by member states in a UN body may affect subsequent national deliberations. Or, a ratified treaty may be championed by a faction within a national legislature. The actual impact or influence from an international institution may be indirect and highly complex.

For example, Washington's abuse of suspected enemy prisoners after 9/11 took place in spite of the fact that the United States had ratified in the 1950s the four 1949 Geneva Conventions, including the third Convention on prisoner protections. By 2004 there was strong concern in the Congress about the Bush policy of prisoner abuse, especially after emergence of pictures of abuse at the Abu Ghraib prison in Iraq carried out during 2003. Led by Republican Senator John McCain, who had been badly abused in North Vietnam during the late 1960s when his Navy fighter jet was shot down, a group of members of Congress were mostly successful in helping to bring about a change in US military policy concerning detention and interrogation. One argument was clearly about identity—namely that Americans were too good a people to engage in such abuse. Another argument was that it was not in the national interest to engage in such abuse—either because prisoner information was suspect, or because our security personnel could be so abused in the future, or because the main result was producing more "terrorists." For present purposes, the point is that all these arguments used the international institution of international law, and more precisely the provisions of both the 1949 Geneva Conventions for war victims and the UN Convention against Torture, as a central reference.[19]

The effect of international law, and the actors related to it such as by UN or Red Cross officials, can be sometimes intertwined with national officials and domestic arguments. The congressional push back against Bush policies of abuse toward enemy prisoners was based partly on concern for American reputation and US military honor, as well as protection of various US interests in the future. However, it was also partially based on respect for international law as duly consented to, and the support that has been built up for international organizations over time. When some Republican members of Congress spoke of new pressures on the International Committee of the Red Cross (ICRC)—the "guardian" of the 1949 Geneva Conventions, which had openly criticized some aspects of US detention policy at the Guantánamo naval base—Secretary of State Condoleeza Rice warned her Republican colleagues about tearing down an organization that had been established under American leadership and was in the US national interest.

In the summer of 2006 the US Supreme Court decided that part of the 1949 Geneva Conventions pertained to all prisoners held at the US prison at Guantánamo. Before that time various legal arguments had been circulating in Washington. After the Hamdan judgment, it was clear that international institutions like the 1949 Geneva Conventions, and the ICRC, which carries out prison visits related to that law, had enhanced status. In 2006 the principal "decider" was the US Supreme Court, but what was adjudicated, in part, was international law. Harold Koh, State Department legal adviser in the first Obama administration, had previously written that much US law was actually trans-national law, with international and domestic norms and processes effectively integrated into one legal stream.[20] All this made it difficult to separate out, and analyze precisely, the importance of international institutions. This is also to say that it was difficult to judge precisely the validity of neoliberal interpretations (or realist ones, for that matter).

Clearly, in this case and others, international institutions were involved in, and had some impact on, public policy. International law on prisoner affairs took on increased importance over time, and for a variety of reasons the Bush administration's policy shifted from widespread to less abuse, both by the military and by the Central Intelligence Agency. International institutions were not the only factors at play, but they were influential. The Bush administration's policy shifted from either aggressive realism or strong neo-conservatism, to something more moderate—with international institutions having a central, but not simple, role in developments.[21]

It is all too evident that, even during one era, some issues or cases in international relations validate a realist interpretation whereas other issues or cases validate a neoliberal conclusion. It was certainly possible for the very same government to manifest realist or neoliberal thinking over time. The George W. Bush administration invaded Iraq in 2003 without UN Security Council approval or much support from major powers (aside from the United Kingdom), but in 2006 it decided to allow the council to request the International Criminal Court (ICC) to consider the question of atrocities in Sudan (Darfur in particular). The eventual request asked the office of the ICC Prosecutor for further investigation and possible arrest warrants. The invasion of Iraq is mostly cited as an example of a unilateral security operation that was either realist or neo-conservative in nature. It is often said to have been an exercise in power superiority regardless of international institutions, perhaps also on the basis of a special role in the world for the United States that was not subject to the normal international rules of restraint. At the same time, Washington turned back to the United Nations to approve post-war operations. Likewise, it is often said that the follow-on Obama administration manifested much more concern for international institutions and did not engage in military intervention in Libya in 2012 until it was authorized by the Security Council. That said, the Obama foreign policy team also engaged in unilateral intervention in Pakistani jurisdiction repeatedly, not only to kill Osama bin Laden but also to conduct drone strikes of suspected enemy combatants.

So it would seem that both of these administrations had their neorealist or neoliberal moments. Depending on which policy was being addressed, it was possible to arrive at either realist or neoliberal conclusions about any US administration—with other summary labels sometimes thrown in the mix, such as neo-conservatism.

The following examples expand on the basic points made thus far. They all demonstrate the complex analysis involved in trying to apply the prism of neoliberalism, or other approaches for that matter, to IO and global governance. An eclectic, as opposed to pure, application across theories is clearly the most useful approach.

Two additional illustrations

The previous examples, drawn from the high politics of security and the domestic politics of the United States, indicated how difficult it is to use neoliberalism or any other IR theory to explain a discrete event. The same conclusion results from looking at two other issues, the refugee regime and the Eurozone.

Leading states in world affairs had been concerned with various types of refugees since the end of World War I. After World War II states built on precedent and over time created the international regime for refugees and persons in refugee-like situations. There is a core treaty: the 1951 UN Convention on Refugees. There is a core international organization: the Office of the UN High Commissioner for Refugees. There are various supplemental rules established by either the UN General Assembly, the UNHCR Executive Committee, or numerous other UN bodies. There are many non-governmental organizations (NGOs) that have been contracted by the UNHCR to run the refugee camps and provide the food, clothing, shelter, and the health care necessary for those in need. The original focus on those fleeing across an international boundary because of "a well founded fear of persecution" was expanded, at least sometimes, to include others in situations of distress and whose relations with their government had broken down—such as internally displaced persons (IDPs) who have not crossed a border, and/or war refugees fleeing not individual persecution but larger political unrest.[22]

From a realist perspective, one can note that states created and maintained this regime, even if officials from public and private international organizations played a role. It was Western, including NATO, states that created the regime in the first place, defining international refugees in such a way as to focus on individuals fleeing European communism. The Soviet Union and its communist allies did not join the regime. Later, when the regime found itself dealing with very large numbers of persons uprooted and in distress in the developing world, it was Western states that pushed the UNHCR into emphasizing socio-economic assistance and at times repatriation, rather than asylum and resettlement in Western countries. The top positions in the UNHCR have always been held by persons acceptable to Western countries, the latter being the major donors to the UNHCR voluntary budget. The UNHCR has no guaranteed funds of any importance and of course no means of taxation. The UNHCR can offer its opinion as to who might qualify for refugee status according to international law, and thus who is supposed to be granted temporary asylum in a host country—and hence not to be returned to a situation of persecution or danger. Yet, it is states that make the final decision and that control who is granted asylum. So a realist might argue that states and state power are the key factors in the international regime, and their calculations are based on narrow, self-serving interests. If powerful Western states want to keep refugees and those in a refugee-like situation "over there" and away from Western borders, that is how the regime functions. And if a powerful Western state like the United States wants to block the flow of numerous Cuban or Haitian asylum seekers into the country, that is what will transpire and the UNHCR is powerless to prevent it.[23] One of the more visible high commissioners, Sadako Ogata, wrote: "The international response to humanitarian crisis situations is largely determined by the degree of strategic interests held by the major states."[24]

At the same time, from a neoliberal perspective, the UNHCR and its partners have exercised some influence as independent actors, being "agents" that the "principals" have to deal with. Influence is not always a one-way street flowing from states downward to IGOs and NGOs. According to various scholars, one can find decisions emanating from the UNHCR of some importance "even in the absence of state pressures."[25] The agency, running relief convoys into Bosnia in the early 1990s, negotiated various arrangements with the fighting parties. Likewise, the agency, running various relief camps in the wake of the Rwandan genocide of 1994, negotiated various arrangements with what was then Zaire (now the Democratic Republic of Congo, DRC). In that case High Commissioner Ogata addressed the Security Council and pressed governments for more support, acting independently, albeit often unsuccessfully. Still, when it came to managing the transnational problems of uprooted persons, it is clear that international institutions are an important part of the response. Rather than address each crisis of uprooted persons *de novo*, it is obviously advantageous for states to create norms, organizations, and processes for coping across time and space.

Moreover, with the Refugee Convention sometimes adjudicated in national courts, refugee legal norms have taken on an independent existence of their own. There is a transnational law of refugee affairs, with the treaty being interpreted by various courts without regard necessarily to the preferences of those making political calculations. Sometimes UNHCR legal definitions and interpretations have been codified via national courts. That said, whether the 1951 Refugee Convention and 1967 Protocol changed the identity of ratifying states—causing them to adopt the image of refugee protectors—is dubious, certain academic claims notwithstanding.[26] Nevertheless, neoliberals—with some reason—can point to contemporary refugee affairs as showing how states have come to share the political and legal stage with international institutions of some importance.

After World War II, the United States used the Marshall Plan to make available massive aid to Europe for reconstruction on the condition that recipient countries pool resources and coordinate rebuilding. Many Europeans themselves were greatly in favor of regional planning, not just for economic reasons but also in pursuit of peace. In particular, a merger of important economic sectors in France and Germany would make war between the two very difficult, if not impossible. Thus was born the European Economic Community (EEC), which in a hugely complicated process had by 2012 morphed into the European Union (EU), comprising—at the time of writing—27 countries across both Eastern and Western Europe, 17 of which in 2002 adopted a common currency, the Euro.

At first glance it would appear that the EU provides very strong evidence of trends highlighted by neoliberalism. Some observers see the EU as a quasi-state, given the economic power and independence of this international institution; and it certainly has more supranational characteristics than any other intergovernmental organization. The European Commission, while called a collective executive, is a rule-making body. It is supplemented by the European Court of Justice (ECJ), an international court with supranational authority. As in the Commission, ECJ justices are not state representatives but sit in their independent, personal capacity. There is no doubt that EU law has a binding quality and in many cases is held to be superior to national law. It is adjudicated in national courts as well as the ECJ. In the Eurozone, the European Central Bank (ECB) has the authority to take decisions, many of which are crucial determinants of state policy. By 2012, statements and decisions taken independently by the Italian head of the ECB caused stock markets to rise and fall, not only in Europe but worldwide.

At second glance, however, states and their independent power have not been eviscerated, or their narrow nationalism totally weakened. First, decisions about EU membership and participation in the Eurozone remain with states. Second, while 17 states have opted for the Euro, they have not agreed on a common fiscal or taxation policy, or many other aspects of economic union. Much debate in 2012 centered on whether Greece would decide to leave the Eurozone rather than try to meet conditions that had been required for bailout loans. Much debate also occurred over whether Germany in particular would continue to adopt policies assisting Greece and other debt-ridden partners, at considerable cost to German citizens. Hence many decisions within the EU and especially within the Eurozone remain essentially state decisions, and often a narrow or local conception of vital interests is at work. There is a push back against EU law in many member states, and thus attempts to reassert the primacy of national law over regional international law. Indeed, "Euro skeptics" are realists who thought the EU and especially the Eurozone were overly idealistic attempts at regional governance that were bound to fail. These realists argue that European identity is weak, traditional nationalism strong, and the various EU institutions a matter of overreach.

In the past, various crises within the EEC and EU were managed by decisions to pursue further integration. In order to block "spillback" and a reduction of European economic integration, state members have decided on a further pooling of resources and centralized decision-making. It remains to be seen whether the Euro crisis of 2011–12 will be managed by a repetition of this pattern—for example through more integrated financial planning and taxation policy to avoid a repetition of the debt crisis and undermining of confidence in the Euro. Yet there has been much criticism of centralized authority and power "in Brussels," because the EU commissioners and judges on the ECJ are not directly elected. The EU Assembly is relatively weak, and there is little genuine link between grassroots opinion in the 27 EU states and key decisions taken by unelected officials of the EU. Debates about the EU "democracy deficit" make further integration difficult without even more restructuring of core EU institutions.

It remains to be seen whether the EU turns out to be the best example to date of growing authority and power for international institutions, as neoliberals predict, or whether the EU and especially its Eurozone represent another "bridge too far" in which international hopes exceed practical realities, as realists expect. Can this economic aspect of European regional governance ultimately work, and how, or will it collapse under the pressure of disparate national values and interests?

Conclusion

In 2011 four scholars published an article in the *International Studies Quarterly* showing that while professors teach the macro-theories of international relations such as some version of realism, liberalism, constructivism, and Marxism, most researchers and analysts do not frame their work according to any of those theories.[27] This chapter has indicated some of the reasons why that perspective makes sense.

Neoliberal institutionalism is useful to alert observers and policy-makers to certain trends and expectations in world affairs. A theory can be used as a benchmark or point of reference. But when one examines the details of a given issue, situation, or policy, one usually finds elements of the explanatory capability of more than one theory. This is also the conclusion of such other scholars as Stephen Walt and Jack Snyder. Whether one looks at the international refugee regime, the EU and Eurozone, the foreign policies of John F. Kennedy, George W. Bush or Barack Obama, or congressional debates about detention and interrogation of terror suspects after 9/11, one finds for each subject matter both neorealist *and* neoliberal dimensions. Sometimes there are also constructivist and neo-conservative elements that can provide useful insights as well.

A final example would seem to illustrate current and future trends. If we take the case of nuclear weapons proliferation and Iran, we find that states like Israel and the United States view the situation with much concern and have taken policy and military stances that reflect perceived self-interests. The possibility of a unilateral military strike is much discussed, as Israel in particular seems to think that an Iran with nuclear weapons would be a major threat to its vital interests. Yet these and other states are influenced to a considerable degree by the independent role of the International Atomic Energy Agency (IAEA). Its inspection reports on Iran—and whether those reports reflect adequate access to suspected Iranian weapons development sites—have been important factors in the evolution of policies, debates, and events. Clearly states continue to be major players and manifest much hard power put at the service of traditional security interests. Neorealism emphasizes this reality. But also clearly, the IAEA, as a non-state actor functioning under the non-proliferation regime as established under international law, is also a significant player in events. Neoliberals emphasize this reality.

In sum, international institutions are a growing and sometimes essential component of contemporary global governance. But these institutions do not usually eliminate the role of states and many of their traditional views and approaches. Sometimes the institutions mostly reflect the power and narrow interests of states—concerns that are usually emphasized in traditional approaches to IR like neorealism. International institutions sometimes generate an independent, important, and beneficial impact on world affairs, as noted by neoliberalism, but sometimes not. Usually one has to delve into the specifics of a given subject without a predetermined preference for any one approach in order to fully understand the case. Or, one needs to be alert to multiple approaches in order not to arrive at predetermined—and probably quite slanted—conclusions.

Additional reading

1. Emanuel Adler, "Constructivism and International Relations," in *Handbook of International Relations*, ed. Walter Carlsnaes et al. (London: Sage, 2002), 95–118.
2. Michael Barnett and Martha Finnemore, *Rules for the World: International Organizations in Global Politics* (Ithaca: Cornell University Press, 2004).
3. Daniel Maliniak et al., "International Relations in the Academy," *International Studies Quarterly* 55, no. 2 (2011): 437–464.
4. Robert O. Keohane, ed., *Neorealism and Its Critics* (New York: Columbia University Press, 1986).
5. Stephen Krasner, ed., *International Regimes* (Ithaca: Cornell University Press, 1983).
7. Bruce Russett and John Oneal, *Triangulating Peace: Democracy, Interdependence, and International Organization* (New York: Norton, 2001).
6. Jack Snyder, "One World, Rival Theories," *Foreign Policy* 145 (2004): 53–62.
7. Stephen M. Walt, "One World: Many Theories," *Foreign Policy* 110 (1998): 29–46.

Notes

1 Jennifer Sterling-Folker, ed., *Making Sense of International Relations Theory* (Boulder: Lynne Reinner, 2006); Scott Burchill et al., *Theories of International Relations* (Basingstoke: Palgrave, 2005).
2 Stephen M. Walt, "One World: Many Theories," *Foreign Policy* 110 (1998): 29–46; Jack Snyder, "One World, Rival Theories," *Foreign Policy* 145 (2004): 53–62.
3 Snyder in "One World" contests the idea that realism is pessimistic, but his is a minority position.
4 Steven W. Hook, *U.S. Foreign Policy: The Paradox of World Power*, 2nd edition (Washington, DC: CQ Press, 2008), 68.
5 Henry Kissinger, *Diplomacy* (New York: Simon and Schuster, 1994), 809.
6 Ibid., 763. For Kissinger there are only two foreign policy traditions, realism and idealism. To him, Reagan would be in the second school.
7 Bruce Russett and John O'Neal, *Triangulating Peace: Democracy, Interdependence, and International Organization* (New York: Norton, 2001).
8 There are also negative or highly problematic international institutions such as human trafficking. See, for example, Jorge Heine and Ramesh Thakur, eds., *The Dark Side of Globalization* (Tokyo: UNU Press, 2011).

9　The classic definition and explanation remains that by Stephen Krasner, ed., *International Regimes* (Ithaca: Cornell University Press, 1983), reflecting a special issue of the journal *International Organization*.

10　The seminal work is Kenneth N. Waltz, *Theory of International Relations* (New York: Random House, 1979).

11　From a virtual library of publications, see Robert O. Keohane, ed., *Neorealism and Its Critics* (New York: Columbia University Press, 1986); and Keohane, *After Hegemony: Cooperation and Discord in the World Political Economy* (Princeton: Princeton University Press, 1984).

12　John Mearsheimer, "The False Promise of International Institutions," *International Security* 19, no. 3 (1994–1995): 5–49.

13　See the introduction to his revised work, *After Hegemony*, 2005.

14　The present author believes Walt, "One World: Many Theories," and also Snyder, "One World, Rival Theories," misunderstand constructivism. Snyder seems especially off the mark, as he equates constructivism with idealism and presents one of its practitioners as Osama bin Laden.

15　The key work, despite its heavy reading, is Alexander Wendt, *The Social Theory of International Politics* (Cambridge: Cambridge University Press, 1999). For a useful conception of constructivism, see also Emanuel Adler, "Constructivism and International Relations," in *Handbook of International Relations*, ed. Walter Carlsnaes (London: Sage, 2002).

16　See further G. John Ikenberry, *Liberal Leviathan: The Origin, Crisis, and Transformation of the American World Order* (Princeton: Princeton University Press, 2012). See also the other publications by this author, who discusses foreign policy and international relations with a healthy dose of neoliberalism. See also Ann Kent, *Beyond Compliance: China, International Organizations and Global Security* (Palo Alto: Stanford University Press, 2007).

17　See especially Jack Goldsmith, *The Terror Presidency: Law and Judgment inside the Bush Administration* (New York: Norton, 2007). Goldsmith was an official in the Justice Department with inside access to views and documents. No great champion of international law, he nevertheless understood the dangers to circumventing international institutions.

18　There is no agreement on the definition or practitioners of neo-conservatism. For a summary of the literature, see David P. Forsythe, *The Politics of Prisoner Abuse: The United States and Enemy Prisoners after 9/11* (Cambridge: Cambridge University Press, 2011), 32 and passim. If the first President Bush was mostly a realist in the tradition of Nixon and Kissinger, George W. Bush was mostly different in his views and policies. This is why Brent Scowcroft and James Baker, officials for the first President Bush, were openly critical of the second President Bush. Baker's defense of realism and his strong critique of the second President Bush's foreign policy record can be found at http://thecable.foreignpolicy.com/posts/2012/08/09/jim_baker_realists_have_been_successful_stewards_of_foreign_policy#.UCUJoD_v7sA.email. George W. Bush was certainly not a neoliberal most of the time. So in regard to US foreign policy and its views of world affairs, there are three major traditions: realism, liberalism, and something else which has recently been called neo-conservatism. Snyder, "One World, Rival Theories," and some others consider it a blend of realism (emphasis on unilateral force) with liberalism (e.g. push for democracy). Whereas George W. Bush saw the United States as having Providence's blessing to force democracy on Iraq, realists like Scowcroft and Baker were deeply skeptical about such views. Rightly or wrongly this third tradition has been called neo-conservatism. It might be similar to (Andrew) Jacksonian nativism. See further Walter Russell Mead, *Special Providence: American Foreign Policy and How It Changed the World* (New York: Knopf, 2001).

19　See further the excellent study by Beth A. Simmons, *Mobilizing for Human Rights: International Law in Domestic Politics* (Cambridge: Cambridge University Press, 2009).

20　Harold H. Koh, "Transnational Legal Process," *Nebraska Law Review* 75 (1996): 181–207.

21　Forsythe, *Politics of Prisoner Abuse*.

22 For an overview, see Gil Loescher, *The UNHCR and World Politics: A Perilous Path* (Oxford: Oxford University Press, 2001); also Guy Goodwin-Gill, *The Refugee in International Law* (Oxford: Clarendon Press, 1996).

23 For a critique of how states restrict the application of supposedly universal human rights provisions and protections, see Mark Gibney, *International Human Rights Law: Returning to Universal Principles* (Lanham: Rowman & Littlefield, 2008). States create laws and regimes; then, when and if they find the norms inconvenient, various non-state actors seek to hold their feet to the fire.

24 Sadako Ogata, *The Turbulent Decade: Confronting the Refugee Crises of the 1990s* (New York: W. W. Norton, 2005), 318.

25 Michael Barnett and Martha Finnemore, *Rules for the World: International Organizations in Global Politics* (Ithaca: Cornell University Press, 2004), 74.

26 See further Emma Haddad, *The Refugee in International Society: Between Sovereigns* (Cambridge: Cambridge University Press, 2008), 119 and passim.

27 Daniel Maliniak et al., "International Relations in the Academy," *International Studies Quarterly* 55, no. 2 (2011): 437–464.

Rational Choice and Principal–Agent Theory

Henning Tamm and Duncan Snidal

Rational choice is one of the main approaches to the study of international relations, as well as to more specific topics such as international organizations (IOs) and global governance. It has long underpinned realist theories of peace and war, but its central role has become more explicit with the development of nuclear deterrence theory, and with expected utility and bargaining models of war. Rational choice has also played a central role in international political economy and, more recently, in theories of international cooperation and in explanations of the importance and design features of international institutions. Even constructivist approaches, which are usually taken as a critique of rationalist approaches, often invoke rationality and strategic action as part of their own explanation of behavior. In short, rational choice lies at the heart of many explanations of international politics and, perhaps more than any other approach, provides a connected way to think about questions of international organization and global governance.[1]

This chapter examines the use of rational choice approaches to study international organization and global governance with special attention to principal–agent (PA) models. PA models investigate the circumstances under which states delegate problems to IOs. For example, the International Atomic Energy Agency conducts nuclear inspections, the World Bank supports economic development, and the World Health Organization monitors global health. PA theory addresses both why states delegate such tasks to IOs and the problems inherent in that delegation. Increasingly, it looks at IOs as proactive agents shaping the terms of relations among states, between IOs and states, and between IOs and civil society. However, PA analysis is only beginning to develop its potential in this regard and can benefit by drawing on discussions from within and outside rational choice.

This chapter begins with a discussion of rational choice and its application to international politics, including through its use of models. The central part of the chapter looks at applications of PA models to state–IO relations, which is one of the most important recent applications of rational choice to IR. We begin with a simple example of states using an IO to distribute development aid, examine the advantages and pitfalls of their doing so, and consider extensions of the model to situations involving multiple principals and/or agents and chains of delegation. Then we canvass several leading applications of PA analysis to IOs and recent uses of PA to understand global governance more generally. Here we criticize the failure of the literature (with notable exceptions) to fully address the agency of IOs and other non-state actors. The final part of the chapter considers further limitations of the PA approach, which also hold the key to understanding its future extensions. These include ways to put IOs more at the center of the analysis and to bring in transnational relations, including non-state actors and their implications for global governance. This critical examination also shows how rational choice in general, and PA models in particular, provides a valuable framework for understanding international relations that can be adapted to the many different circumstances of international politics.

Rational choice in international relations

Rational choice theory assumes that, given their beliefs about how the world works and their ability to affect it, actors choose their actions in order to best attain their goals. Actors can be any agents which make choices that matter—including states, IOs, NGOs, business firms, and individuals. Their goals need not be material and can include aesthetic and moral objectives such as preserving cultural heritages and promoting human rights; their goals also do not need to be selfish or self-interested but can include helping others, such as through development aid. This makes rational choice a very flexible framework for explaining deliberate choices of various actors; it can also be adapted to more normative questions regarding how actors *should* behave in different circumstances.

The full power of rational choice theory for international relations is unleashed when it moves beyond explaining individual choice in isolation to understanding situations where multiple actors make choices that matter. This is the realm of strategic interaction (and game theory), where achieving the best outcome depends on finding the right combination of individual choices. If we want global aviation to be safe, for example, pilots and ground controllers must all speak the same language. If we want to gain the benefits of open international trade, states must refrain from imposing unilateral tariffs. Such choices become complicated when circumstances involve a mix of conflicting and coinciding consideration: No one wants airplanes to crash but Lufthansa pilots prefer to communicate in German and Air France pilots prefer French; every state wants other states to lower tariffs but each would prefer to keep their own tariffs in place. To understand and resolve such tensions, we need to consider both individual and collective interests.

A particular advantage of rational choice is that many of its central arguments have been expressed very precisely in terms of models, sometimes in mathematical form, which makes it particularly amenable to exploring further theoretical implications of the argument. Because these models are fairly abstract, they are not tied to particular substantive questions and so can be transferred across different substantive topics without great difficulty. Thus, even though much rational choice was developed initially in economics—although not entirely, since some important analyses have been prompted by international relations problems such as nuclear deterrence—its arguments have been widely transferred to international relations. However, the abstractness of rational choice means that its models must be supplemented by substantive analysis to apply them to any specific problem. Finally, the advantage of models rests partly in their (relative) simplicity and clarity but there are significant trade-offs in using such simple devices to study the enormous complexity of real-world problems.

The PA model we discuss below is a prime example of a simple model that helps explain seemingly diverse problems. It was originally developed to examine economic problems such as how a business firm might ensure that its employees work hard, then was adapted by students of American politics to understand how Congressmen can control regulatory agencies, and then was adapted by international relations scholars to consider how states might use international organizations.[2] Each application requires careful attention to the particular substantive problems—management—employee relations are different from Congress—regulatory agency relations, which are different from state—IO relations—but the PA model can be applied across these seemingly different contexts to obtain important implications. However, it is important not to force the analysis onto a problem it does not fit properly and not to overlook key elements of the problem that the model does not emphasize. We illustrate these issues below with respect to the advantages and limitations of PA analysis of IOs.

While most rational choice theory in international relations has focused on states as actors, the theory has been increasingly applied to non-state actors, including not only IOs but also nongovernmental organizations, firms, and terrorist groups. The inclusion of terrorist groups is an instructive reminder that rational action is not necessarily desirable from all perspectives and that cooperation benefiting one group may harm another group. Of course, in many cases the interests of actors are not diametrically opposed—PA models look at situations in which the principal and agent are able to work together, although imperfectly.

The logic of principal—agent theory

PA theory is based on the idea that a principal delegates authority to an agent to perform tasks on its behalf.[3] The specific terms of this relationship are defined by a contract, which in practice may be either a formal or an informal agreement. One central question that PA models address is how the principal can best design this contract to maximize its benefits and minimize the costs of delegation. Here, we use the example of international aid to illustrate the basic logic of PA theory.

Consider a scenario in which a wealthy state wants to provide development assistance to poorer countries. Although it could do so directly, it may have several good reasons to delegate this task to an IO. First, an IO specialized in development aid (such as a multilateral development bank, MDB) will have specific expertise and organizational capacity to manage the complex issues involved in delivering aid effectively. Thus PA relations are often central to obtaining the benefits of specialization through a division of labor. Second, the state may want to convince others that it will not use aid as a foreign policy tool. Recipient countries may be concerned that donors will use aid for diplomatic leverage; public opinion polls in wealthy countries also suggest that voters favor need-based over strategic allocation of aid. By delegating this task to an MDB, which is generally considered more independent of direct state interference than are individual states' aid agencies, the state can commit to need-based policies. Finally, the donor state may prefer to work through an IO to avoid political responsibility if projects do not work, to make it easier to avoid long-run commitments or even to obscure its current involvement in the activity. Regardless of its motives, by acting though an IO, the state becomes a principal and the IO becomes its agent.

Delegation, however, also involves costs. The obvious cost is paying the agent for its services, but that is presumably offset by the benefits of the intended project. More significant but less obvious forms of *agency costs* arise because of two factors that make PA analysis vital for understanding delegation. One is that the agent's preferences may at least partly differ from those of its principal and therefore the agent may act opportunistically in pursuit of its own goals instead of the principal's goals. The other is that the agent may have information that is unavailable to the principal (hidden information) or its actions may not be fully observable by the principal (hidden action). The conjunction of these considerations creates costs for the principal because they potentially allow an agent to pursue its own interests unless it is somehow constrained or incentivized to do what the principal wants. If the principal can perfectly observe the agent, then the former can control the latter perfectly by creating the right incentives or constraints. If hidden information or hidden action pertains, then agency problems arise.

Thus if the principal is not able to monitor every single step the agent takes, the latter can engage in its own preferred behavior rather than do what is desired by its principal. Such *agency slack* is sometimes further divided into *shirking* (minimizing the effort it exerts on behalf of the principal) and *slippage* (actively pursuing its own interests, which differ from or even conflict with the principal's). In our scenario, the wealthy state will therefore seek to minimize agency slack by offering the MDB a contract that rewards good performance but also includes control mechanisms such as monitoring and reporting requirements that trigger penalties if slack is detected. Unfortunately, oversight procedures themselves create costs (e.g. of monitoring and reporting) that reduce the principal's gains from the division of labor. Moreover, there is the problem of incomplete contracting: It is typically impossible to design a contract that covers all potential sources of agency slack. In sum, the wealthy state faces an unavoidable trade-off. Given its roots in rational choice, the logic of PA theory suggests that the wealthy state will only choose delegation to a MDB if the expected overall benefits are greater than the overall costs.

Two special cases of agency problems are adverse selection and moral hazard. *Adverse selection* occurs if an agent can misrepresent its abilities and preferences in order to ensure being engaged by a principal. For instance, some IOs may wish to use donor money to expand their bureaucracy or pursue other projects, whereas the donor state wants to minimize bureaucratic costs so that more money goes to its desired programs. Of course, the MDB will claim its priorities are the same as the principal's, which will therefore need to screen potential agents to be sure it selects an IO that will serve its needs. But gathering information for effective screening is costly, and screening will not always be effective; the principal may only realize after the fact (if ever) that its wishes were not being fulfilled.

Moral hazard emerges when an agent is able to take risks whose costs will fall on the principal if the risky policy fails and things go badly. For example, the International Monetary Fund is often seen as contributing to moral hazard through its willingness to bail out countries that experience balance-of-payments problems—which encourages countries to behave in ways that cause such problems in the first place.[4]

Our scenario of a single state and a single IO is useful for thinking through the basics of PA models, but it does not adequately capture the complexities of international relations. Consider a more realistic scenario where several wealthy states want to provide aid through an MDB. For simplicity, we first assume that the MDB will have separate contracts with each state but that they all relate to the same MDB policy (action). If these multiple principals all have the same preferences, they face the same problems that we have already described in the earlier scenario. If their preferences diverge, however, the model will predict greater potential MDB autonomy (and thus greater room for agency slack), as the agent will now play different principals off against each other. In contrast, if a single wealthy state faces multiple MDBs, agency slack will decrease, as the MDB would fear that its slack could lead the state principal to switch to another MDB agent. Moreover, in this setting the state might engage several MDBs each in charge of different development projects and then use their comparative performance as a measure of agency slack. Finally, if there were multiple states and multiple MDBs, these effects would cancel each other out so that we should expect a medium level of slack. Figure 9.1 summarizes these arguments.[5]

Some PA models incorporate further empirical complexities by disaggregating both principals and agents, and by studying chains of delegation. In the case of our basic scenario, one could disaggregate the wealthy state into voters (as principals) and the government (as agent), and then extend the chain of delegation with the government/state as principal to the MDB agent, followed by the MDB (as principal) to a recipient

	Single principal	Multiple principals
Single agent	Medium	High
Multiple agents	Low	Medium

Figure 9.1 Possibilities for agency slack

developing country bureaucracy (as agent).[6] The model would now include three distinct PA relationships—voters to government; government to MDB; and MDB to recipient country. These conceptual maneuvers, which we discuss further in the next section, raise the question of how much real-world complexity a good model should incorporate.

We conclude this section by highlighting two potentially problematic aspects of PA theory. First, agency problems hinge on the assumption that agents' preferences diverge from principals' preferences. If this is not the case, the models lose their power. Second, PA models focus largely on how principals can avoid agency slack; at least in their formal variants, it is the principal who acts first by offering a contract, typically on a "take-it-or-leave-it" basis. This is somewhat ironic insofar as cooperation theorists have argued that introducing PA theory to IR enables them to study IO—rather than state—agency. We address these aspects in greater detail in the following sections on applications and critiques of PA models in the literature on international organization and global governance.

Principal–agent models of international organization and global governance

Here we begin with examples of PA analysis applied to international as well as supranational organizations and outline key complicating features that occur with delegation in the international context. Second, we consider why most PA models in IR concentrate on the principal rather than the agent—which is peculiar if we wish to focus on IOs—and we present efforts to alleviate this bias. Third, we review the growing literature on transnational relations that applies insights from PA theory to both states and non-state actors, thus shedding new light on global governance structures.

Given that institutionalist scholars brought PA theory to IR, it is not surprising that the first sustained applications were to the European Union (EU), where states had delegated more authority than to any other international institution. Researchers thus began to ask whether the EU's supranational organizations—such as the European Commission, the European Parliament, or the European Court of Justice (ECJ)—would undermine the authority of its member states. In response, Mark Pollack drew on PA theory to show how these states were able to maintain control in varying degrees.[7] The ECJ has provided one of the most important cases of how delegation creates autonomous power and, along with the experiences of other international courts, has also led to one of the main critiques of PA models, which we address in the next section.[8]

In another important early contribution, Daniel Nielson and Michael Tierney use PA theory as an extension of neoliberal institutionalism in explaining how the World Bank long exerted significant autonomy in its operations but then suddenly adjusted its behavior under pressure from member governments. They highlight three complicating features of PA relationships in the context of IOs. First, states often act as a "collective principal," designing a common contract for an agent; they first need to solve collective-action problems amongst themselves before interacting with that agent. Second, IOs sometimes face multiple principals from the same state— e.g. when the legislature and the executive have separate "contracts" with the agent. Third, as suggested in the previous section, delegation chains are often long.

These early studies culminated in the edited volume *Delegation and Agency in International Organizations*, which shows the wide applicability of PA analysis to international organizations across such diverse areas as development, finance, health, justice, security, and trade. The contributors to this volume point out specific benefits of international delegation that result from the fact that it often involves collective principals. For instance, delegating to an agent may facilitate collective decision-making or help resolve disputes between principals because the agent can serve as an agenda setter or arbitrator. Nonetheless, the last chapter comes to the conclusion that "PA theory applies equally well to international delegations as it does to domestic delegations. Delegation 'under anarchy' appears to be pretty much the same as delegation in other political forums."[9] This overlooks what is possibly the greatest promise of PA theory, however, which is to show not just how states control IOs but how IOs can gain and exercise autonomy precisely because control mechanisms are not as strong under anarchy, while the need for global governance is ever growing.

Delegation and Agency in International Organizations is representative of the broader literature on PA models of IOs in focusing on the principal rather than on the agent, and emphasizes two related issues: why states delegate to IOs and how they control IOs after delegating authority. These are essentially questions about institutional choice and design.[10] Drawing on the Americanist literature, Pollack discusses methodological reasons for not studying actual agent behavior in greater detail. Because agents can rationally anticipate the reactions of their principals, they are expected to adjust their behavior in order to avoid costly sanctions; in the presence of control mechanisms, it is thus impossible to ascertain whether or not agents actually have opportunistic preferences. Moreover, the very idea of hidden action implies that it is difficult to measure agency slack directly.

There are ways of addressing these problems, however. Pollack suggests that careful analysis of open conflicts between principals and agents can be revealing even if these episodes are not necessarily representative.[11] Furthermore, several chapters in *Delegation and Agency in International Organizations* actually address the principal bias of PA models. In particular, Hawkins and Jacoby discuss how agents may be able to influence contract design at the selection stage; they may also be able to reinterpret their mandates afterwards.[12] We return to questions of agent preferences and behavior in the next section.

In the literature discussed so far, the agents are organizations created by states and tightly constrained by them. There is, however, also an emerging literature that uses PA theory to model transnational relations between states, on the one hand, and international nongovernmental organizations (INGOs), rebel groups, and terrorists, on the other. This literature both pushes the boundaries of PA theory and raises interesting questions about global governance. In a study of transnationalism, for example, Alexander Cooley and James Ron model a delegation chain that involves governments as donors, INGOs as contractors, and local actors as recipients. Their main insight is that INGOs operate in a context of organizational insecurity characterized by PA problems which creates "imperatives that promote self-interested action, inter-INGO competition, and poor project implementation."[13] Thus even actors, such as INGOs, which are typically motivated by "good" normative agendas may be compelled to act opportunistically to ensure organizational survival.

Turning to less savory agendas, Idean Salehyan examines state support to foreign rebel groups as a PA relationship. Like Daniel Byman and Sarah Kreps in their analysis of state-sponsored terrorism, Salehyan highlights the benefit of plausible deniability —hence evading international condemnation—when delegating violent attacks to third party actors.[14] While Salehyan and his colleagues discuss the "resources-versus-autonomy dilemma" that rebel groups face in this context, Lucy Hovil and Eric Werker go one step further: they suggest that some rebel groups use excessive violence against civilians, even to the extent of undermining their own long-term objectives, in order to send a credible signal to their foreign patrons that they remain committed to destabilizing the target state.[15]

This research on rebel and terrorist groups suggests interesting new approaches for studying the "dark side" of global governance; it challenges scholars to analyze delegation in a context of political violence and demonstrates the strategic dimensions of transnational relations, where the strategies of the agents need to be addressed more centrally.

Going beyond principal–agent models? Critiques, extensions, and alternatives

In this section, we briefly address four critiques of PA applications in international relations. The first two find fault with some of its assumptions, the third proposes an alternative to delegation, and the fourth simply comes to different conclusions regarding states' ability to control IOs. Rather than view these only as weaknesses of PA analysis, however, we argue that part of the value of the model is that it opens up these critical lines of inquiry as well.

Even before PA theory took off in IR, Michael Barnett and Martha Finnemore criticized its assumptions and offered a constructivist explanation for agency slack—or, in their terminology, pathologies—of IOs. Drawing on sociological institutionalism, they conceived of IOs as bureaucracies that embody rational-legal authority, which gives them legitimacy and power independent of the states that created them. It is this authority, rather than the lack of control mechanisms, that enables IOs to act autonomously. At the same time, however, their internal bureaucratic culture can breed pathologies— dysfunctional behavior that is neither in the member states' nor necessarily in the IO's own interest.[16] Moreover, the two authors rightly argue that there "are good reasons to assume that organizations care about their resource base and turf, but there is no reason to presume that such matters exhaust or even dominate their interests."[17] It is important to add that IO culture need not be dysfunctional and may include promoting collective values which states espouse but are themselves unable to practice. Good examples include the role of the WTO secretariat in promoting the free trade agenda or of the Intergovernmental Panel on Climate Change in pressing the climate change agenda despite the reluctance of state parties. Whatever the mix, IO goals need to be addressed more explicitly whenever delegation leaves significant room for agency slack. In order to theorize more specific agent preferences, however, scholars will have to bring in substantive considerations from outside of PA theory.[18]

Karen Alter also criticizes the assumptions of PA models, but in the more limited context of delegation to international courts. Building on Giandomenico Majone's work on fiduciary relations, Alter argues that international courts need to be seen as "trustees" and that principal–trustee relations are fundamentally different from those between principals and agents. In the former case, delegation aims to improve the legitimacy of decision-making by harnessing the authority of the trustee. Principals deliberately give up large parts of control, for the very authority of trustees hinges on their independence.[19] Other scholars disagree, arguing that PA theory can capture the fact that different tasks require different degrees of agent discretion. Pollack, for instance, argues that a complete and irrevocable transfer of authority is unlikely in international relations and that it is more useful to study the far-reaching independence of international courts in the context of a continuum of discretion.[20]

Rather than criticizing how PA theory models delegation, Kenneth Abbott and his colleagues propose an alternative mode of governance—orchestration—that has so far not received the same amount of attention. Orchestration involves enlisting and supporting intermediary actors to address target actors in the pursuit of governance goals. These intermediaries can include INGOs, business organizations, public–private partnerships, transgovernmental networks, and even other IOs. The targets can be states themselves or private actors, such as firms, which IOs have not traditionally been allowed to govern. Orchestration models thus address the complexities and reach of global governance.

We can distinguish orchestration from other governance modes and compare it to PA analysis by reference to two dimensions: direct and indirect; hard and soft (see Figure 9.2). In both delegation and orchestration, the governing actor works through a third party to achieve its goals; the difference is that in the first case formal authority is transferred and can be rescinded, whereas there are no formal (hard) means of control in the second case.[21] Orchestration can be seen as showing the limits of PA theory: when goals are correlated and the third party's cooperation is voluntary, orchestrator–intermediary–target (O–I–T) models may have greater purchase than PA models. It can alternatively be seen as adapting and extending PA theory—thinking of states as principals to IOs and IOs as orchestrators of non-state intermediaries suggests a governance chain that involves both delegation and orchestration.

The fourth and last critical reaction is based on conclusions from positive theory but focuses largely on normative concerns. Roland Vaubel argues that the delegation chain from voters to an IO typically involves three intermediate bodies—national parliaments, national governments, and international supervisory boards or courts—and thus four distinct PA relationships. Furthermore, interest groups exert pressure at each node. In contrast to much of the literature in IR that primarily highlights how principals can maintain control over agents, Vaubel suggests that the ultimate principals in this chain of delegation, voters, have very little control over the ultimate agents, IOs. In the international context, information costs and weak or distorted incentives mean that PA problems cannot be overcome.[22] This raises the issue of the democratic deficit: if IOs cannot be held accountable by the voters of democratic states, should we want more delegation in world politics? Can additional mechanisms be established to prevent abuses of power? Such questions have led to important debates across the positive–normative theory divide.[23]

	Direct	Indirect
Hard	Hierarchy	Delegation
Soft	Collaboration	Orchestration

Figure 9.2 Modes of governance

Conclusion

Rational choice is a very flexible and versatile approach for studying international politics; PA theory illustrates its particular importance for understanding international organizations and governance. Early work in PA analysis emphasized the role of states, individually and collectively, as the principal in designing and controlling the IO as its agent. While this had the virtue of treating IOs as partially autonomous actors which had to be controlled, it did not treat IOs as full actors or capture their ability to shape relations with states and other actors. Various critiques have picked up on these and other limitations to suggest further directions that PA analysis must pursue to address the emerging questions surrounding global governance. Our view is that rational choice approaches and PA models are an essential component of any comprehensive understanding of global governance but are insufficient by themselves. One of the virtues of rational choice and PA analysis is that they can be connected to alternative explanations in a complementary way that broadens our understanding of international organization and global governance.

Additional reading

1. Duncan Snidal, "Rational Choice and International Relations," in *Handbook of International Relations*, ed. Walter Carlsnaes, Thomas Risse, and Beth A. Simmons (Los Angeles: Sage Publications, 2013), 85–111.
2. Curtis A. Bradley and Judith G. Kelley, "The Concept of International Delegation," *Law and Contemporary Problems* 71, no. 1 (2008): 1–36.
3. Daniel Byman and Sarah E. Kreps, "Agents of Destruction? Applying Principal–Agent Analysis to State-Sponsored Terrorism," *International Studies Perspectives* 11, no. 1 (2010): 1–18.
4. Darren G. Hawkins, David A. Lake, Daniel L. Nielson, and Michael J. Tierney, eds., *Delegation and Agency in International Organizations* (Cambridge: Cambridge University Press, 2006).
5. Mark A. Pollack, *The Engines of European Integration: Delegation, Agency, and Agenda Setting in the EU* (Oxford: Oxford University Press, 2003).

Notes

1 For more detailed discussion of the use of rational choice in international relations, see Duncan Snidal, "Rational Choice and International Relations," in *Handbook of International Relations*, eds. Walter Carlsnaes, Thomas Risse and Beth A. Simmons (Los Angeles: Sage Publications, 2013), 85–111; and Andrew H. Kydd, "Methodological Individualism and Rational Choice," in *The Oxford Handbook of International Relations*, eds. Christian Reus-Smit and Duncan Snidal (Oxford: Oxford University Press, 2008), 425–443.

2 On the origins of PA theory in economics, see Kathleen M. Eisenhardt, "Agency Theory: An Assessment and Review," *Academy of Management Review* 14, no. 1 (1989): 57–74. For reviews of PA models in political science, see Gary J. Miller, "The Political Evolution of Principal–Agent Models," *Annual Review of Political Science* 8 (2005): 203–225; and J. Bendor, A. Glazer, and T. Hammond, "Theories of Delegation," *Annual Review of Political Science* 4 (2001): 235–269.

3 For a more elaborate discussion of the PA model in the international context, see Darren G. Hawkins, David A. Lake, Daniel L. Nielson, and Michael J. Tierney, "Delegation under Anarchy: States, International Organizations, and Principal–Agent Theory," in *Delegation and Agency in International Organizations*, eds. Hawkins et al. (Cambridge: Cambridge University Press, 2006), which we discuss and draw upon further below. For a still broader concept of delegation with particular application to international law, see Curtis A. Bradley and Judith G. Kelley, "The Concept of International Delegation," *Law and Contemporary Problems* 71, no. 1 (2008): 1–36.

4 See J. Lawrence Broz and Michael Brewster Hawes, "US Domestic Politics and International Monetary Fund Policy," in *Delegation and Agency in International Organizations*, eds. Hawkins et al., 77–106.

5 Figure 9.1 extends arguments regarding the number of available agents developed in Darren G. Hawkins and Wade Jacoby, "How Agents Matter," in *Delegation and Agency in International Organizations*, eds. Hawkins et al., 203–205.

6 On disaggregating states into voters and governments, see Helen V. Milner, "Why Multilateralism? Foreign Aid and Domestic Principal-Agent Problems," in *Delegation and Agency in International Organizations*, eds. Hawkins et al., 107–139. On recipient bureaucracies as agents in a delegation chain, see Alexander Cooley and James Ron, "The NGO Scramble: Organizational Insecurity and the Political Economy of Transnational Action," *International Security* 27, no. 1 (2002): 14–24.

7 See Mark A. Pollack, "Delegation, Agency, and Agenda Setting in the European Community," *International Organization* 51, no. 1 (1997): 99–134; and Mark A. Pollack, *The Engines of European Integration: Delegation, Agency, and Agenda Setting in the EU* (Oxford: Oxford University Press, 2003).

8 See Anne-Marie Burley and Walter Mattli, "Europe before the Court: A Political Theory of Integration," *International Organization* 47, no. 1 (1993): 41–76; and Geoffrey Garrett and Barry R. Weingast, "Ideas, Interests and Institutions: Constructing the European Community's Internal Market," in *Ideas and Foreign Policy: Beliefs, Institutions, and Political Change*, eds. Judith Goldstein and Robert O. Keohane (Ithaca: Cornell University Press, 1993), 173–206.

9 David A. Lake and Mathew D. McCubbins, "The Logic of Delegation to International Organizations," in *Delegation and Agency in International Organizations*, eds. Hawkins et al., 344.

10 See Barbara Koremenos, Charles Lipson, and Duncan Snidal, "The Rational Design of International Institutions," *International Organization* 55, no. 4 (2001): 761–799.

11 See Pollack, *The Engines of European Integration*, 69.

12 See Hawkins and Jacoby, "How Agents Matter," 212.

13 Cooley and Ron, "The NGO Scramble," 14.

14 See Idean Salehyan, "The Delegation of War to Rebel Organizations," *Journal of Conflict Resolution* 54, no. 3 (2010): 503; Daniel Byman and Sarah E. Kreps, "Agents of Destruction? Applying Principal–Agent Analysis to State-Sponsored Terrorism," *International Studies Perspectives* 11, no. 1 (2010): 6.

15 Idean Salehyan, Kristian Skrede Gleditsch, and David E. Cunningham, "Explaining External Support for Insurgent Groups," *International Organization* 65, no. 4 (2011): 717; Lucy Hovil and Eric Werker, "Portrait of a Failed Rebellion: An Account of Rational, Sub-Optimal Violence in Western Uganda," *Rationality and Society* 17, no. 1 (2005): 7–8.

16 See Michael N. Barnett and Martha Finnemore, "The Politics, Power, and Pathologies of International Organizations," *International Organization* 53, no. 4 (1999): 699–732. For a critical appraisal of these arguments from a rational choice scholar, see Mark A. Pollack, "Principal–Agent Analysis and International Delegation: Red Herrings, Theoretical Clarifications, and Empirical Disputes," *Bruges Political Research Papers* no. 2 (2007): 15–21.

17 Barnett and Finnemore, "The Politics, Power, and Pathologies," 706.

18 See Erica R. Gould, "Delegating IMF Conditionality: Understanding Variations in Control and Conformity," in *Delegation and Agency in International Organizations*, eds. Hawkins et al., 308. For an interesting way of theorizing agent preferences based on staffing rules, see Andrew P. Cortell and Susan Peterson, "Dutiful Agents, Rogue Actors, or Both? Staffing, Voting Rules, and Slack in the WHO and WTO," in *Delegation and Agency in International Organizations*, eds. Hawkins et al., 258–262.

19 See Karen J. Alter, "Agents or Trustees? International Courts in their Political Context," *European Journal of International Relations* 14, no. 1 (2008): 33–63; Giandomenico Majone, "Two Logics of Delegation: Agency and Fiduciary Relations in EU Governance," *European Union Politics* 2, no. 1 (2001): 103–122.

20 See Pollack, "Principal–Agent Analysis," 9–12.

21 See Kenneth W. Abbott and Duncan Snidal, "International Regulation without International Government: Improving IO Performance through Orchestration" *Review of International Organizations* 5, no. 3 (2010): 315–344; and Kenneth W. Abbott, Philipp Genschel, Duncan Snidal, and Bernhard Zangl, "Orchestration: Global Governance through Intermediaries," presented at the International Studies Association, Montreal, March 2011.

22 See Roland Vaubel, "Principal–Agent Problems in International Organizations," *Review of International Organizations* 1, no. 2 (2006): 125–138. On delegation within IOs, see also Manfred Elsig, "Principal–Agent Theory and the World Trade Organization: Complex Agency and 'Missing Delegation,'" *European Journal of International Relations* 17, no. 3 (2010): 495–517.

23 See Ruth W. Grant and Robert O. Keohane, "Accountability and Abuses in World Politics," *American Political Science Review* 99, no. 1 (2005): 29–43; Hans Agné, "The Myth of International Delegation: Limits to and Suggestions for Democratic Theory in the Context of the European Union," *Government and Opposition* 42, no. 1 (2007): 18–45.

Constructivism

Rodney Bruce Hall

This chapter explores the contribution of constructivist thought to the study of inter-national organization and global governance. It begins with a brief history and development of constructivism as an intellectual approach. It then parses current debates in the field and surveys the key criticisms that have been leveled at constructivist thinking. The chapter then concludes with a discussion of future directions for constructivist analyses of international organization and global governance.

History and development

The earliest manifestations of constructivism in the study of international organization and global governance arose with the application of the Grotian tradition to the study of world politics, largely with English School scholars such as Hedley Bull, whose classic *The Anarchical Society*[1] strongly demurred from the questions of neorealists, namely, how is cooperation possible under the conditions of international anarchy? The Grotian tradition takes its name from Hugo Grotius (1583–1645) and his pre-Westphalia text *The Law of War and Peace*, published in 1625 during the Thirty Years War. International order, in this tradition, is rule based, supplemented by Roman *ius gentium* and existing treaty law.

Like the Grotian tradition, Bull's work begins with the assumption of the notion of an international society of states. Natural law provides a basis for attempts to formulate rules to limit violence between members of international society, but war is not utterly proscribed, consistent with Thomist conceptions of "just war." Many of the principles upheld by this view of international order and organization stem from analogies with private contracts from Roman law (e.g. *pactus sunt servanda*, the notion that treaties shall be observed, irrespective of *clausula rebus sic stantibus*, the notion that it is illicit to invalidate contracts without fundamental change in material conditions of contracting parties).

Structural realists infer the absence of a normative structure in international politics from the absence of a central authority. Anarchy is, in their view, the overwhelming international organizing principle and is largely understood negatively. They miss the Grotian and constructivist insight that social interaction is rule governed. Grotian approaches are norm based and rule based. International politics is not an anarchy or war of all against all, but it is more like a game with rules. Norms and rules guide behavior. Conventions are the political organizing principle of international organization, and conventions are constituted by constitutive rules, regulative rules, rights, and other structural features of the international order. Constitutive rules are needed to understand what is going on in the game, and to understand the rules required to constitute the activity of international politics and organization. They take the form X counts as Y in context Z. Regulative rules regulate behavior once this has been constituted by constitutive rules. They prescribe and proscribe behavior in international politics and organization, and they take the form of X in context Z, or not of Y in context Z.

Unlike structural realists, or economic neoliberals, Grotians and constructivists do not seek "general laws" governing the processes of international organization and global governance. They approach the study of world order by studying processes of change in the human social conventions that constitute international organization and global governance. Conventions change, thus constructivists study changes in the norms, principles, rules, and institutions of international organization and global governance both synchronically and diachronically. This approach also allows us to make historical comparisons of the processes, conventions, and institutions of various international systems.

Conventions are norms that foster and give rise to games of coordination. In game theoretic terms, structural realists and neoliberal institutionalists argue that all actors try to coordinate their action and settle on an equilibrium point where there are pareto-optimal solutions to a game of coordination. The problem in the real world, however, is that it is often unclear upon which of the pareto-optimal solutions available actors should converge. In actual processes of global governance, few simple games of coordination actually arise. There are two criteria for a simple coordination game: interests are not mixed (there are no incentives to defect) and there are at least two equilibrium points available to constitute a solution. In such simple games of coordination we do not need norms to help us find a rational solution. Interests alone can govern play. But in mixed motive games, with asymmetric payoff structures, we often need recourse to norms and rules to explain how coordination is achieved. Norms select relevant factors from social situations and thus simplify choices. Norms are reasons for action—not causes of action. Thus we cannot generate a simple Humean causal account of how norms function in helping to coordinate cooperation among actors with competing interests. Much of this discussion is developed in Friedrich Kratochwil's 1989 classic treatment.[2]

Norms arise out of interaction and can become institutionalized as rules. In the formulation of Max Weber, a present norm of behavior can become a future rule for behavior. Moreover, norms cannot be subsumed under the notion of interests but have their own functions. Conventions, in this context, serve as coordination norms. If one breaks a norm or rule, a course of action will be required. The violator can either explain her behavior, or apologize for violating the norm or rule with assurances the behavior will not be repeated, or she can pretend there never was a norm, though this course is possible only with tacit norms that result from implicit expectations of behavior rather than explicit prescriptions for behavior. Thus we see the need for explicit rules. If our interaction partners are disappointed by our behavior, we can argue on the merits of a specific instance, and still sustain social interaction, if we have violated an explicit norm or rule. This is not the case if we violate a tacit norm that we subsequently fail to acknowledge. Denial of a tacit norm or rule is socially destructive. We cannot so easily bind conflict with an apology or explanation. The immediate escalation of a conflict in such circumstances is likely. Thus, for constructivists, game theoretic analytical approaches are too restrictive, and resulting research agendas are exercises in thematic reduction rather than analytical abstraction.

Moreover, conventions and norms of coordination are self-enforcing. We cannot take a purely behavioral approach to the study of international organization and global governance in which norms and conventions are a prevalent feature as coordinating devices. We cannot set aside norms or regularities of behavior and "observe" them. Importantly, norms are counterfactually valid. Rules and norms are not consistent with the epistemology of logical positivism. In the natural sciences, if we observe an empirical counterfactual to a general proposition, we have invalidated that proposition, and it becomes a failed theory. For example, in the laboratory, should a scientist observe a single instance where heat transfers from a cooler to a warmer body, the Second Law of Thermodynamics clearly would have been invalidated. The social sciences are different. If we observe a single counterfactual where a norm or rule is violated, we cannot infer the norm or rule is invalid. For example, that in a particular instance we observe someone committing a murder does not invalidate a general societal injunction against killing.

In constructivist thought, norms and rules are conceptualized as constraints. If we do not observe constrained behavior in a particular instance, we cannot infer that rules and norms are not in place. We thus can understand power as a social relationship rather than the more primitive conception of power as a resource, as power can be embedded in social understandings and practices.

Constructivist contributions to regime theory

The earliest influential constructivist work on international organization and global governance probably came with John Gerard Ruggie's contribution to the special issue of *International Organization* that introduced regime theory in the literature. Stephen Krasner, the editor of that special issue, as well as other rationalist scholars contributing, tended to view international regimes as intervening variables between causes and outcomes in international organization. For rationalist scholars, regimes and international organizations are constructed as a consequence of the demand for them by states in accordance with the useful functions that they can perform.[3]

Ruggie began a move away from this neoliberal functionalist theory of regimes, articulated purely in neoliberal (cost/benefit) terms. He spoke in a Grotian/constructivist vocabulary and emphasized the role of international regimes in the institutionalization of new norms. He countered the consensus definition of regimes purely in terms of descriptive elements but asserted that we can recognize regimes by their "generative grammar," or the underlying principles of order and meaning that shape the manner of their formation and transformation. He proposed that we examine deviations from regime norms not just in neoliberal terms but in the context of an inter-subjective framework of meaning, suggesting that transformations of regimes may be concrete institutional manifestations of the internationalization of political authority.[4]

In this context, Ruggie criticized the structural realists, for whom elements of international authority are predicated on underlying capabilities of actors. Hegemonic Stability Theory (HST), for example, builds upon this assumption, and argues that highly capable hegemons are required to create and maintain regimes in accordance with their own purposes, and allow them to decay when they lack the power to enforce their will upon them. Ruggie argued that such a framework is inadequate for understanding international economic regimes because it fails to encompass observable phenomenological dimensions of economic regimes. He developed three theoretical arguments to help formulate a corrective. First, he argued that this emphasis on power ignores the dimension of social purpose. We cannot discover the generative grammar of regime formation or the structure of internationalization of political authority with an excessive emphasis on power because, he argued, political authority represents a fusion of power with legitimate social purpose. Power may predict the form of international order, but not the content. To discern the content, we must look at how power and legitimate social purpose become fused to project political authority in the international system, or else we cannot say anything about the content of international economic orders and regimes that serve them. This perspective led Ruggie to characterize the post-war international economic order by the term "embedded liberalism." A liberal social purpose was embedded in post-war international economic regimes by powerful actors, which was legitimated by generating wealth for all participants as well as establishing a compromise permitting social protections.

Second, he argued that *de facto* discrimination and preferences were observed empirically in the post-war regime, and that explanations of these observations are required to understand the relationship between economic regimes and actual developments in the international political economy. However, the domain of international regimes concerns interstate relations and relations between states and markets, not pure market relations. Ruggie thus argued that regimes provide a permissive environment for certain kinds of transactions informed by prevailing notions of legitimate social purpose that upholds the regimes. Regimes are neither irrelevant nor determinative in structuring transactional outcomes.

Third, Ruggie indicated that HST postulates a single source of regime change (maintenance or decline of economic hegemonic power) and only two possible directions of regime change (openness or closure). But this perspective assumes that power and social purpose co-vary. If they do not, even in the absence of a hegemon, a congruence of social purpose among leading economic powers can result in regime maintenance. Ruggie argued that this would be a case of "norm-governed change rather than norm-transforming change." For example, the 1971 collapse of Bretton Woods monetary arrangements did not result in a reversion to pre-war mercantilist practice. Ruggie's constructivist formulation of international regimes provided a useful corrective to purely power-based or interest-based formulations. His work teaches us that international economic regimes do not determine outcomes, but they do play a mediating role.

Ruggie subsequently teamed up with Kratochwil to offer another major constructivist contribution to the literature on international regimes in the form of a thoroughgoing critique of regimes theory as overly rationalist and positivist.[5] They argued that the concept of international regimes was created to fill a void in the study of international governance left by rational choice theoretic assumptions. Regime theory as initially formulated constituted a theoretical claim by rational choice theory that both conflict and cooperation can be explained by a single, logical apparatus. Yet Ruggie and Kratochwil identified a major problem with this claim, pointing out that the ontology of regime theory rests upon the inter-subjectivity of social meanings, while the epistemology employed to study regimes comes from logical positivism. The latter posits a radical separation of subject and object in generating a "causal" explanation. Yet, as already noted, norms are reasons for actions and not causes of actions. Further, unlike general propositions of a causal nature, norms are counterfactually valid. Positivism really cannot contend with the inter-subjective nature of the manner in which norms are employed to coordinate outcomes.

Ruggie and Kratochwil argued that in regime theory epistemology fundamentally contradicts ontology. Thus, theorists make the incorrect assumption that every behavior communicates a meaning. However, often social actors communicate one thing and behave differently. In the real world, actors often violate norms, which requires an explanation of why they are violating norms. They do not intend to communicate anything in the act of doing so. They often intend to communicate the opposite of what their behavior implies. Then, having offered an explanation of the violation, their partners will assess the adequacy of the explanation, and "adjudicate" against an accumulating body of similar decisions. Functioning like "case law" in civil jurisprudence, often the violator is forgiven if the explanation is "accepted." Importantly, then, they remind us that norms are a medium through which state action is interpreted. Violation of regime norms must be interpreted in light of mitigating claims and circumstances.

They argue that there are consequences of the inter-subjective basis of international regimes, which expose actor behaviors and expectations. Thus, they help to create stable expectations. Ruggie and Kratochwil are in agreement then with neoliberal institutionalists. Regimes provide legitimation, as regime norms and rules prescribe some behaviors and proscribe others. Ian Hurd has recently elaborated on the legitimation function of regime norms in debates regarding UN Security Council reform.[6] Finally regimes provide an epistemic function, as they assist in the creation of consensual knowledge as the basis for negotiation and bargaining, as Peter Haas illustrated so effectively in his work describing the implementation of the Mediterranean Action Plan to mitigate pollution in the Mediterranean basin.[7]

Constructivism and multilateralism

Ruggie is also the essential constructivist contributor to the literature on multilateralism, which emerged in the early 1990s with the demise of the Soviet Union and the bipolar distribution of global power that has since characterized the post-Cold War era. It was an important moment for IR theory. The demise of the bipolar international system was not predicted by structural realist theory. In chapters of Kenneth Waltz's book that are seldom read as often and thoroughly as they once were, he argued that bipolar distributions of power are the most stable of all possible outcomes.[8] Realist theory predicts that if bipolarity ended, it is external competition that should have led to the demise of one or the other of the actors. There is no mechanism in structural realism for explaining changes in the structure of the international system resulting from *domestic* causes—as was the case with the Soviet Union. Whatever the causes, there is little question that multilateral norms and institutions helped stabilize international consequences, leading scholars to subject multilateralism to intensive study.

While hopes for a multilateral order were revived by the end of the Cold War, there was little reference to the term "multilateralism" in the literature on international organization in 1992 when Ruggie was writing.[9] He noted that Robert Keohane's somewhat spare definition, namely "the practice of coordinating national policies in groups of three or more states,"[10] is purely nominal and misses the qualitative dimension of the phenomena that make "multilateral action" distinct.[11] Ruggie argued that it is the kind of relations that matter. The concepts of international regimes or international organizations do not capture what makes multilateral action distinct. For example, "multilateral trade" refers to trade organized on the basis of certain principles of state conduct, e.g. non-discrimination. Thus, the purposes of the basis on which multilateral forms organize and order relations among states are what make multilateral institutions distinctive. He argued that multilateralism is a generic institutional form of modern international life that has long been present. Typically in his writing, Ruggie provides us with a reminder of the importance of social purposes of governance arrangements. In this context, he argues that the post-World War II explosion of multilateral arrangements were the result less of US *hegemony* than the fact that it was an explicitly *US* hegemony. Thus, it was no accident that the General Agreement on Tariffs and Trade, the International Monetary Fund (IMF), and the World Bank are multilateral institutions designed to serve particularly liberal social and economic purposes. International arrangements of multilateral form have adaptive and reproductive capacities that other forms lack. This observation helps explain the role of multilateral institutions in stabilizing subsequent international transformation.

Current debates

From this first generation of pioneering constructivist scholars of international organization, international regimes, and multilateralism—especially Kratochwil and Ruggie—a second generation emerged and moved the debate toward such topics as pathologies in international organizations, a constructivist theory of international organizations as bureaucracies, and the emergence of private authorities. These scholars moved the discussion away from the more restricted realm of public international governance (international organization) to private international governance.

A constructivist theory of IOs, their autonomy, and consequences

Michael Barnett and Martha Finnemore have generated a powerful constructivist theory of international organization with a seminal book developing IOs as bureaucracies, with specific focus on why things go wrong.[12] Contrary to structural realists, who view IOs as epiphenomenal, and neoliberals, who view IO creation and maintenance as governed by an economistic and functional consequences of state demand for their services, Barnett and Finnemore develop an understanding of the autonomy of IOs. Building on Weber's analysis of bureaucracy, they argue that IOs are powerful actors, but that the same characteristics of bureaucracy that generate this power can also make them prone to dysfunctional behavior. They argue that IOs are powerful because, like all bureaucracies, they make rules and, in so doing, create social knowledge that they can deploy to define shared international tasks, create new categories of social actors, and transform definitions of interests. However, as bureaucracies constructed and acting impersonally, they also can pursue their rule-based agendas and procedures to extremes, even at the expense of primary missions. Their constructivist approach expands the research agenda in international organization beyond the conditions of IO creation and maintenance, to the consequences of global bureaucratization and the effects of IOs as autonomous actors in world politics.

Barnett and Finnemore argue that IOs acquire this autonomy from state agendas and action via bureaucratization. Bureaucracy is a distinctive social form of authority that was well studied by Weber. International and domestic bureaucracies alike exercise social power as a result of their expertise and through their ability to make impersonal rules. As a consequence, IOs not only regulate but also constitute and construct the social world. Four aspects of IO behavior are important in this light: autonomy, power, dysfunction, and change.

IOs win autonomy through being authorities in their own right. Here authority is defined as the ability of one actor to use institutional and discursive resources to induce deference from others. In contrast to realism and neoliberalism, IOs and not just states are authorities because they act to promote socially valued goals by means that are mostly rational, technocratic, impartial, and non-violent, and because IOs appear legitimate and disinterested relative to states. Also in contrast to realism and neoliberalism, Barnett and Finnemore argue that IOs matter and are responsible for independent effects. Moreover, some IOs have material resources to wield influence. Some influence outcomes by manipulating information to change incentives. They can use their authority to orient action and create social reality; they have epistemic functions and can transform information into shared knowledge; they use knowledge and exercise power to regulate the social world and thereby change incentives and help create social reality; and they help determine the kind of world that is to be governed. In one effective example, Barnett and Finnemore argue that the United Nations determines "*not only who is in violation of human rights, but what human rights are.*"[13]

Barnett and Finnemore argue that IOs' authority stems from three sources. First, they possess delegated authority. IOs are authoritative because they represent the collective will of their members. They have to be autonomous to fulfill their tasks. States create IOs to sort out problems. At some level, being autonomous is their mandate and IOs represent themselves as acting on behalf of principles agreed upon by members.

Second, they possess moral authority because IOs serve and protect widely shared principles; and they have charters that represent the international community of states. Third, IOs possess expert or specialized knowledge central to legal-rational authority. There is a moral dimension to these claims as well. It is technical knowledge that might benefit society. It creates the appearance of being apolitical.

Barnett and Finnemore illustrate, in three well-researched empirical chapters that make for sobering reading, how the rule-following, procedure-following character of IOs as bureaucracies can have pathological, and even devastating effects, generating outcomes that are wildly at variance with their core missions. They have taught us a great deal about sources of IO power, authority, and autonomy; and they have also taught us not to uncritically celebrate the existence of such organizations but to examine their results. What Churchill once referred to as "the dead hand of bureaucracy" can have, in the most functionally useful and internationally inclusive and progressive institutions, utterly appalling consequences.

Constructivist analyses of private authority and global governance

With the rise in the literature on globalization in the 1990s, constructivist and sociological analyses of global governance focused on phenomena integral to these approaches, namely the question of the legitimacy emerging from global practices and the nature of authority in relationship to raw power. Also of consequence were the private actors that were increasingly present in the globalized marketplace and in other areas central to the practice of global governance. While not himself overtly constructivist in orientation, James Rosenau pointed out as early as 1992 that global governance was not to be confused with government. Rather, governance "is thus a system of rule that is as dependent on intersubjective meanings as on formally sanctioned constitutions and charters."[14] Claire Cutler, Virginia Haufler, and Tony Porter edited a ground-breaking collection of essays on the question of private authority in the international political economy, in which they introduced the concept and identified the phenomena of "private international regimes" in the global economic realm.[15]

Thomas Biersteker and I assembled another collection of scholars interested in the emergence and nature of private authority—in the Weberian sociological tradition, authority is legitimated by power. The phenomenon was observed not only in globalized markets but in such other realms as environmental regulations, in which private actors such as NGOs have been influential, security areas such as religious terrorism, private security firms, and transnational organized crime along with its networks (e.g. mercenaries and mafias). We were careful to analyze the conditions under which these private actors can contribute to authoritative governance structures, or, in the cases of mercenaries and mafias, to analyze the sources of legitimacy they can enjoy with locals in the regions in which they operate.[16]

What emerged from the studies was a taxonomy of private authority in global governance that is by no means exhaustive of the forms of private authority. This taxonomy structured the book under three major categories of private authority: "market authority," "moral authority," and "illicit authority." Market authority results essentially from a move from politically based decision-making to market-based decision-making. It is a consequence of the sovereign state's complicity in transferring various forms of sovereign or political perquisites to fundamentally private actors. Contributors to this 2002 volume widely debated the notion of market authority, and the state's complicity in it. Louis Pauly's contribution somewhat prophetically, in light of the regulatory initiatives in the wake of the 2008–09 financial and economic crisis, argued that the state can, and will in an emergency, assume sovereign authority that it once delegated to market actors.[17]

Biersteker and I argued that private actors attain "moral authority" by advancing successfully three claims about their status as private authorities. If they have the capacity to provide expertise, they can enjoy the authority of authorship. If they successfully claim the status of being non-statist or non-self-interested actors whose conduct is dominated by neutrality, they can enjoy the authority of the referee. If they successfully advance a claim to represent a socially progressive or morally transcendent position, they can enjoy normative moral authority. These are the bases of the authority for NGOs as private actors contributing to authoritative governance outcomes, often in the company of states and IOs. Non-corporate NGO regulatory authority is one governance result (whereas corporate NGOs and firms form Cutler et al.'s private international regimes). Transnational religious organizations also draw from one or more of these forms of moral authority.

Finally, we argued that some private actors whose activities are proscribed by international law (mercenaries and mafias, among others) nonetheless can enjoy substantial normative legitimacy among populations subject to their activities—thus, they can have "illicit authority." These actors often penetrate weak states and provide public goods (security, welfare, even education) underprovided by the state, and they often function as a surrogate for the state by establishing a monopoly over the use of armed force. All of these forms of private authority are, however, reversible, as Pauly warned, and we were anxious to provide an extended discussion of the conditions under which each form of private authority discussed might be reversed and reclaimed by public authorities.

Key criticisms and emerging issues

Key criticisms regarding the legitimacy and democratic standing of the notion of a global civil society have emerged and generated useful debates about whether or not private actors of global governance help create a global public domain for transnational democratic debate. Other useful debates attend the social mechanisms of norm diffusion. A constructivist analysis of global financial governance has surfaced among emerging issues in the literature. Three topics in particular are prominent: global civil society and democratic deficits; norm diffusion; and global financial architecture.

Global civil society and democratic deficits

Ruggie began a useful debate about whether the emerging authority of private actors helps reconstitute a global public domain for contestation with public actors.[18] His arguments have drawn strong criticisms from scholars arguing from a Foucauldian perspective of governmentality,[19] and from a neo-Hegelian perspective.[20] However, if we settle for a lower standard of legitimacy and relinquish a teleological understanding of global civil society as something that will progressively bring about democracy at the global level, perhaps we can at least appreciate it as a zone for the contestation of ideas, norms, and power. This is what Ruggie has argued with his notion of a "global public domain" that he asserts is being constructed by the proliferation of global civil society organizations and their deliberatory participation in global public policy processes. For him, the global public domain comprises "the arena in which expectations regarding legitimate social purposes, including the respective roles of different social sectors and actors, are articulated, contested and take shape as social facts."[21] In this formulation, it is no longer the case that, to the extent that global civil society organizations yield influence, it is directed towards, channeled through, and implemented by states. Ruggie argues that civil society actors have helped make possible genuinely political activity at the global level apart from the state system.

In this context, Jens Steffek and Maria Paola Ferretti argue that, through the deliberative model (vs. a representative model) of democracy, public participation through the inclusion of global civil society organizations can lead to new democratizing functions within the global governance arena, correcting the purported democratic deficit.[22] It acts as a "connective tissue" between citizens and international institutions by ensuring input from and accountability towards citizens. It thus represents a "semantic shift" away from "representative democracy toward decentralized and participatory governance." They argue that civil society organizations can fulfill these functions by enhancing the democratic accountability of intergovernmental organizations and regimes; and by increasing the epistemic quality of rules and decisions. Finally, Steffek and Feretti argue that participation by global civil society, despite its obvious limitations, may facilitate a positive democratic impact simply because more actors participate and thereby pluralize perspectives.

Norm diffusion

The literature on norm diffusion has also generated useful debates. Its purpose is to define the social mechanisms by which norms are diffused to more general acceptance in global civil society once instigated by norm entrepreneurs. Many of the earlier contributions to this literature posited the triumph of a moral cosmopolitanism, whereby norms that are being propagated by transnational agents[23] are "cosmopolitan" or "universal"[24] by virtue of their persuasion and pressure. A social movement perspective on norm diffusion emphasizes naming and shaming and the implementation of sanctions, suggesting that norm-takers ultimately bow to persuasion and pressure from comparatively morally gifted norm-makers.[25] Conversion of the recalcitrant to cosmopolitan norms is the goal in the cosmopolitan view of norm diffusion and contestation of these norms is illegitimate.

A different perspective is provided by Amitav Acharya, who challenges moral cosmopolitanism and instead proposes norm localization (or "constitutive localization") and norm subsidiarity to highlight the role of local actors in the processes of norm diffusion. For him, "localization" is the active construction (through discourse, framing, grafting, and cultural selection) of emerging universal ideas by local actors, which results in the latter's developing significant congruence with local beliefs and practices. Norm subsidiarity occurs when local actors create rules with a view to preserve their autonomy from dominance, neglect, violation, or abuse by more powerful central actors."[26] This process usually comes about when local actors resent the excessive dominance of central actors or authorities, especially when the latter are deemed to be inadequately representative of, indifferent to, or even subversive of local ideas, interests and identities. Acharya's work provides a constructivist explanation of processes of norm diffusion that ascribe some agency to local (often developing world) actors whose local cultures and beliefs cannot implement "cosmopolitan" norms without some, and often significant, local adaptations.

Global financial governance

A constructivist literature is emerging on topics at the intersection of global governance and international political economy. Jeffrey Chwieroth has undertaken a constructivist analysis of the role of ideas in generating the policies of the IMF.[27] Doris Fuchs has provided a constructivist account of the power of transnational corporate actors.[28] Paul Haslam[29] as well as Matthias Hofferberth and colleagues[30] have explored corporate social responsibility networks as constructivist regimes.

Among recent monographs, Rawi Abdelal has written an exceptional constructivist account of the construction of Europe's liberal capital mobility regime.[31] Jacqueline Best has generated a compelling constructivist account of the collapse of the Bretton Woods gold–dollar parity exchange rate system.[32] Timothy J. Sinclair's transition from Gramscian analysis to constructivism was made manifest by his examination of the role of credit rating agencies in global financial governance.[33] Benjamin Cohen's book on the "geography of money" set in motion much of this activity, relying on the role of inter-subjective social understandings about what constitutes money.[34] Nicholas Veron, Matthieu Autret, and Alfred Galichon have provided a startling constructivist account of the role of modern accounting practices in gaming corporate balance sheets.[35]

I recently put forward an account, drawing on the institutional philosophy of John Searle and on the pioneering work by Cohen on money, of central banking as global governance. If money is not a "thing" or a commodity but a social relationship—a promise from the central bank—there are consequences for a system of fiat monies for the governance of global finance.[36]

Conclusion

Constructivist analysis of international organization and global governance has to date enriched this sub-discipline by emphasizing the importance of inter-subjectively shared social understandings in political communication and action, and the importance of the fusion of power and social purpose in the analyses of international institutions, both public, such as the Bretton Woods institutions, and private, such as the contribution of civil society organizations in generating a global public domain for transnational discursive debate. Strong constructivist analysis might be expected of the possible processes through which the world could extract itself from the ongoing global financial and economic crisis. As such, constructivists could examine how public and private actors with varying social purposes could contest the future of the international financial architecture, global regulatory domains, and troubled supranational institutions in Europe, as well as a supranational currency that is itself a social construct.

Additional reading

1. Emanuel Adler and Steven Bernstein, "Knowledge in Power: The Epistemic Construction of Global Governance," in *Power in Global Governance*, eds. Michael Barnett and Raymond Duvall (Cambridge: Cambridge University Press, 2005): 294–318.
2. Jeffrey M. Chwieroth, *Capital Ideas: The IMF and the Rise of Financial Liberalization* (Princeton: Princeton University Press, 2010).
3. Jeffrey M. Chwieroth and Timothy J. Sinclair, "How You Stand Depends on How We See: International Capital Mobility as Social Fact," *Review of International Political Economy* (forthcoming 2013).
4. Anna Leander, "The Power to Construct International Security: On the Significance of Private Military Companies," *Millennium: Journal of International Studies* 33, no. 3 (2005): 803–825.
5. Brent J. Steele and Jacque L. Amoureux, "NGOs and Monitoring Genocide: The Benefits and Limits to Human Rights Panopticism," *Millennium: Journal of International Studies* 34, no. 2 (2005): 403–432.

Notes

1 Hedley Bull, *The Anarchical Society* (New York: Columbia University Press, 1977).
2 Friedrich V. Kratochwil, *Rules, Norms, and Decisions: On the Conditions of Practical and Legal Reasoning in International Relations and Domestic Affairs* (Cambridge: Cambridge University Press, 1989), 69–94.
3 Robert O. Keohane, "The Demand for International Regimes," *International Organization* 36, no. 2 (1982): 185–205.
4 John Gerard Ruggie, "International Regimes, Transactions and Change: Embedded Liberalism in the Postwar Economic Order," *International Organization* 36, no. 2 (1982): 378–415.
5 Friedrich Kratochwil and John Gerard Ruggie, "International Organization: A State of the Art on an Art of the State," *International Organization* 40 (1986): 753–775.
6 Ian Hurd, "Myths of Membership: The Politics of Legitimation in UN Security Council Reform," *Global Governance* 14 (2008): 199–217.
7 Peter M. Haas, "Do Regimes Matter? Epistemic Communities and Mediterranean Pollution Control," *International Organization* 43 (1989): 377–404.
8 Kenneth Waltz, *Theory of International Politics* (New York: McGraw Hill, 1979).
9 John Gerard Ruggie, "Multilateralism: The Anatomy of an Institution," *International Organization* 46, no. 3 (1992): 561–598.
10 Robert O. Keohane, "Multilateralism: An Agenda for Research," *International Journal* 45, no. 4 (1990): 731–764.
11 See also Rorden Wilkinson, *Multilateralism and the World Trade Organisation: The Architecture and Extension of International Trade Regulation* (London: Routledge, 2000).
12 Michael Barnett and Martha Finnemore, *Rules for the World: International Organizations in Global Politics* (Ithaca: Cornell University Press, 2004).
13 Ibid., 7.
14 James N. Rosenau, "Governance, Order and Change in World Politics," in *Governance Without Government: Order and Change in World Politics*, eds. James N. Rosenau and Ernst O. Czempiel (Cambridge: Cambridge University Press, 1992): 1–30.
15 A. Claire Cutler, Virginia Haufler, and Tony Porter, *Private Authority and International Affairs* (Albany: SUNY Press, 1999).
16 Rodney Bruce Hall and Thomas J. Biersteker, eds., *The Emergence of Private Authority in Global Governance* (Cambridge: Cambridge University Press, 2002).

17 Louis W. Pauly, "Global Finance, Political Authority, and the Problem of Legitimation," in *The Emergence of Private Authority in Global Governance*, eds. Hall and Biersteker.

18 John Gerard Ruggie, "Reconstituting the Global Public Domain—Issues, Actors, and Practices," *European Journal of International Relations* 10, no. 4 (2004): 499–531.

19 Jens Bartleson, "Making Sense of Global Civil Society," *European Journal of International Relations* 12, no. 3 (2006): 371–395.

20 Ronnie D. Lipschutz, "Power, Politics and Civil Society," *Millennium: Journal of International Studies* 33, no. 2 (2005): 747–769.

21 Ruggie, "Reconstituting the Global Public Domain," 504.

22 Jens Steffek and Maria Paola Ferretti, "Accountability or 'Good Decisions'? The Competing Goals of Civil Society Participation in International Governance," *Global Society* 23, no. 1 (2009): 37–57.

23 See, for example, Margaret Keck and Kathryn Sikkink, *Activists Beyond Borders: Advocacy Networks in International Politics* (Ithaca: Cornell University Press, 1998).

24 See, for example, Richard Price, "Reversing the Gun Sights: Transnational Civil Society Targets Land Mines," *International Organization* 52, no. 3 (1998): 613–644.

25 See, for example, Thomas Risse, Stephen C. Ropp, and Kathryn Sikkink, *The Power of Human Rights: International Norms and Domestic Change* (Cambridge: Cambridge University Press, 1999).

26 Amitav Acharya, "How Ideas Spread: Whose Norms Matter? Norm Localization and Institutional Change in Asian Regionalism," *International Organization* 58, no. 2 (2004): 239–275.

27 Jeffery M. Chwieroth, "Testing and Measuring the Role of Ideas: The Case of Neoliberalism in the International Monetary Fund," *International Studies Quarterly* 51, no. 1 (2007): 5–30.

28 Doris Fuchs, "Commanding Heights? The Strength and Fragility of Business Power in Global Politics," *Millennium: Journal of International Studies* 33, no. 3 (2005): 771–801.

29 Paul Alexander Haslam, "Is Corporate Social Responsibility a Constructivist Regime? Evidence from Latin America," *Global Society* 21, no. 2 (April 2007): 269–296.

30 Matthias Hofferberth et al., "Multinational Enterprises as 'Social Actors'—Constructivist Explanations for Corporate Social Responsibility," *Global Society* 25, no. 2 (2011): 205–226.

31 Rawi Abdelal, *Capital Rules: The Construction of Global Finance* (Cambridge, MA: Harvard University Press, 2007).

32 Jacqueline Best, *The Limits of Transparency: Ambiguity and the History of International Finance* (Ithaca: Cornell University Press, 2005).

33 Timothy J. Sinclair, *The New Masters of Capital: American Bond Rating Agencies and the Politics of Creditworthiness* (Ithaca and London: Cornell University Press, 2005).

34 Benjamin Cohen, *The Geography of Money* (Ithaca: Cornell University Press, 1998).

35 Nicholas Veron, Matthieu Autret, and Alfred Galichon, *Smoke & Mirrors, Inc.: Accounting for Capitalism*, translated by Goerge Holoch (Ithaca and London: Cornell University Press, 2006).

36 Rodney Bruce Hall, *Central Banking as Global Governance: Constructing Financial Credibility* (Cambridge: Cambridge University Press, 2008).

Critical Theory

Robert W. Cox

The states of the world have created international organization as a means of dealing with common problems through negotiation. Global governance would be the result of this process as it develops into a regular method of reaching consensus. Critical theory is concerned with understanding and influencing how this process works. When we speak of "process," we are thinking about something which evolves over time. So, critical theory is a way of thinking about development and change over time.

One perspective on the world about us is to think of how states, institutions, people, and other forces are interacting in the same time, how they influence each other directly. This is a synchronic perspective, or simultaneous interactions. Critical theory is not unconcerned about this perspective but is most of all concerned with change over time and with the choices we may have to make about the kind of future we may have. Critical theory is about the making of history.

The British historian and philosopher R. G. Collingwood wrote about the "inside" and the "outside" of history.[1] The "inside" is the story of the motivations, intentions, and reactions of the historical actors. The "outside" is all that can be observed—material resources and constraints and recordable events. Critical theory is concerned with understanding the "inside"—the thought, reasoning, and emotions that "make" history.

What follows here discusses the distinction between problem solving and critical theory—the synchronic and diachronic perspectives; the nature of time and of how people of different civilizations have understood time in historical change; distinguishing eras of creativity and decline; dominance and subordination among civilizations; and the problem of world order in the present world.

The term "critical theory" is used here in a generic sense independently of any particular meaning that has been given it in the work of others.[2] To be critical is to examine something carefully so as to become aware of any flaws or weaknesses. Theory is a systematic approach to understanding and explanation. Criticism, of its nature, should seek to improve upon what is criticized; so critical theory does not stop with the negative part of criticism but extends to envisage transformation of existing reality. It is reformist or revolutionary in essence.

Theory is always *for* someone and *for* some purpose.[3] All theories have a perspective. Perspectives derive from a position in time and space, specifically social and political time and space. The world is seen from a standpoint which can be defined in terms of nation or social class, of dominance or subordination, of rising or declining power, of a sense of immobility or of present crisis, of past expectations, and of hopes and expectations for the future. Of course, sophisticated theory is never just the expression of standpoint or perspective. The more sophisticated a theory is, the more it reflects upon and transcends its own perspective; but the initial perspective is always contained within a theory and is relevant to its explication. There is, accordingly, no such thing as theory in itself, divorced from a standpoint in time and space. When any theory so represents itself, it should be examined as ideology so as to lay bare its concealed perspective.

Problem-solving theory and critical theory

Broadly speaking, there are two purposes that define different kinds of theory. One purpose is to make a simple, direct response to the pressure of events: to be a guide to help solve the problems presented in the realities immediately confronted. This purpose leads to the development of *problem-solving theory*. The other purpose is more reflective upon the process of theorizing itself, namely, to search for a theoretical perspective that would comprehend how the present world has come about and what forces are at work transforming it. This is the purpose of *critical theory*.

Problem-solving theory takes the world as it finds it, with the prevailing social and power relationships and the institutions into which they are organized, as the given framework for analysis. The general aim of problem solving is to make these relationships work smoothly by dealing effectively with particular sources of trouble. Since the general pattern of institutions and relationships is not called into question, particular problems can be considered in relation to the specific areas of activity in which they arise. Problem-solving theories are thus fragmented in dealing with a multiplicity of spheres of action, each of which assumes a certain stability in the other spheres (which enables these other spheres of activity in practice to be ignored) when confronting a problem in the particular sphere concerned. The strength of the problem-solving approach lies in its ability to fix limits or parameters to a problem area and to reduce the statement of a particular problem to a limited number of variables which are amenable to relatively close and precise examination or measurement. The *ceteris paribus* assumption, upon which such theorizing is based, makes it possible to arrive at statements of conclusions or regularities which may appear to have general applicability but which imply, of course, the continuing existence of the institutional and relationship parameters assumed or taken for granted in the problem-solving approach.

Critical theory is critical in the sense that it stands apart from the prevailing order of the world and asks how that order came about. Unlike problem-solving theory, critical theory does not take institutions and social power relations for granted but calls them into question by concerning itself with their origins and how and whether they may be in the process of changing. It is directed towards an appraisal of the very framework for action which problem-solving theory accepts as its parameters. Critical theory is directed to the social and political complex as a whole rather than to its separate parts.

As a matter of practice, critical theory, like problem-solving theory, takes as its starting point some aspect or particular sphere of human activity. But whereas the problem-solving approach leads to further analytical subdivision and limitation of the issue to be dealt with, the critical approach leads towards the construction of a larger picture of the whole of which the initially contemplated part is just one component, and seeks to understand the processes of change in which both parts and whole are involved. Problem-solving theory, for example, is applicable to evaluating the various policies and practices of states with regard to specific international organizations as to whether these policies and practices strengthen or weaken cooperation. Critical theory is concerned with the development of international organization as a whole and the opportunities and obstacles to its further development.

Critical theory is theory of history in the sense of being concerned not just with the past but with a continuing process of historical change. Problem-solving theory is non-historical (or ahistorical), since it, in effect, posits a continuing present the permanence of the institutions and power relations which constitute its parameters. The strength of the one is the weakness of the other. Because it deals with a changing reality, critical theory must continually adjust its concepts to the changing object it seeks to understand and explain.[4] These concepts and the accompanying methods of inquiry seem to lack the precision that can be achieved by problem-solving theory, which posits a fixed order as a point of reference. This relative strength of problem-solving theory, however, rests upon a false premise, since the social and political order is not fixed but (at least in a long-range perspective) is changing. Moreover, the assumption of fixity is not merely a convenience of method, but is also an ideological bias. Problem-solving theories can be represented, in the broader perspective of critical theory, as serving particular national, sectional, or class interests which are comfortable within the given order. Indeed, the purpose served by problem-solving theory is conservative, since it aims to solve the problems arising in various parts of a complex whole in order to smooth the functioning of the whole.

Critical theory is, of course, not unconcerned with the problems of the real world. Its aims are just as practical as those of problem-solving theory, but it approaches practice from a perspective which transcends that of the existing order, which problem-solving theory takes as its basis. Critical theory allows for a normative choice in favor of (or against) a social and political order different from the prevailing order, but it limits the choice to alternative orders which are feasible transformations of the existing world. Critical theory must reject improbable alternatives just as it rejects the permanency of the existing order. In this way critical theory can be a guide to strategic action for bringing about an alternative order, whereas problem-solving theory is a guide to tactical actions which, intended or unintended, sustain the existing order.

The perspectives of different historical periods favor one or the other kind of theory. Periods of apparent stability or fixity in power relations favor the problem-solving approach. The Cold War was one such period. In international relations, it fostered a concentration upon the problems of how to manage an apparently enduring relationship between two superpowers. A condition of uncertainty in power relations beckons to critical theory as people seek to understand the opportunities and risks of change.

Time and change in history

Thinking about the nature of time is an essential step in contemplating historical change and the goal of creating a desirable future. The *Annales* group of French historians, chief among them Fernand Braudel, have distinguished three different categories of time. The time they are thinking of is not the movement of hands on a clock but rather experienced time, the time of living and acting (or of failing to act). The first kind of experienced time is the time in which events happen, in which they are recorded, which the *Annales* writers call *événementiel* (events time). More complex is the convergence of forces that shape and limit what *can* happen. This, the *Annales* writers call the *conjuncture.* The third kind is long-term time in which society evolves in all its interrelated aspects, change in populations, in economic structures, in political structures, and in ways of thinking. This they call the *longue durée.* In all three cases time is seen as lived experience, how people experience either historical change or stasis.

Beyond the experience of lived time is the way of conceiving the future. People in different civilizations and in different eras have thought about the nature of movement into the future in one of two ways. The most natural way has been to think of change in the human condition by analogy with the change in nature as a cyclical process like that of the seasons: spring, summer, autumn, winter, and then a new spring, etc. This has been a natural way of conceiving change not only for primitive peoples who have lived close to nature but also for people in evolved civilizations who knew their own history as a heroic beginning, leading to a period of relative prosperity, to be followed by a phase of decadent decline, ultimately saved by a stimulus probably from the periphery of their civilization or from a hitherto marginal group which proved to be capable of launching a creative revival. This cyclical pattern of understanding historical time has been characteristic not only of primitive peoples but also of all the major civilizations, with one exception.

The exception has been Western civilization, which has had the peculiarity of conceiving historical time as a continuing progressive development into the future with an imagined apotheosis. We can trace the origins of this way of thinking about the future to the birth of monotheistic religion. The primitive religion everywhere, and evolved religions in most parts of Asia, saw spirituality in the many different manifestations of nature, as a multiplicity of gods, and required man to live in harmony with nature. Monotheism posited one all-powerful God, with a capital G, who was separate from and supreme over man and nature. Nature appeared to be God's gift to be exploited by man.

The origins of monotheism may be traced to the Middle East in the Axial age. It may have been derived from the centralized power of the ancient hydraulic empires, where everything appeared to flow from a single central source. Egypt in the age of the pyramids conveyed the idea of an all-powerful centre. Everything was subordinate to and directed by the emperor and his agents. This experience of the all-powerful in everyday life could be easily transferred to the idea of one all-powerful God. People who lived close to nature could not, however, so easily abandon the sense of spirituality of nature in its manifold forms. The worship of saints in medieval Christianity preserved that polytheistic element of primitive religion within the formal monotheism of their faith. St. Francis of Assisi represented that loosening in the rigidity of monotheistic doctrine. With Calvinism, however, in its simplified purity, monotheism achieved a total break with nature.

Unilinear progressive theories of history came to elaborate the monotheistic vision. The earliest version was put forward by the twelfth century Calabrian monk Joachim of Floris, who introduced a three-stage conception of historical development which was built upon the doctrine of the Trinity. History, for him, was Christian history. There was no other. He divided history into three periods: first, the reign of the Father, the rule of the unincarnate God, an authoritarian pre-Christian era; second, the reign of the Son or the Christian era, in which political institutions were necessary to constrain people's behavior in conformity with the revelations of Christianity; and third, the reign of the Holy Spirit, which Joachim imagined as a communitarian future in which harmony would prevail naturally without the need for political constraints.

This triadic form, entrenched in Western consciousness, was, perhaps unconsciously, taken over in a secular form by Hegel in his three-stage version of history as progressing from the rule of one (monarchy), through the rule of several (aristocracy), to culminate in the rule of all under the law (the republic). Marx, in his turn, presented yet another secularized version of the triadic progression. His vision was of an historical movement beginning with the primitive social exchange economy, followed by its displacement by the development of capitalism, which would then in time collapse from its own contradictions, leading, as the third and final phase, to the coming of the communist society, not so different in conception from the communitarian society that Joachim of Floris had forecast.

The Western sense of a unilinear history was confirmed in the popular imagination by economic expansion. Britain's economy was expanded by trade; and trade, as the saying went, "followed the flag"; in other words, trade and military/naval power were interrelated and mutually supporting. Other Western nations, Germany and France, followed in Britain's wake. All together they expanded European power into Asia and Africa. Meanwhile, the United States was following the British example, initially in Latin America, and ultimately during the twentieth century, following the Cold War and the collapse of the Soviet Union, becoming the single dominant world power, the global hegemon.

During the nineteenth century, the idea of Progress, with a capital P, became prominent in popular culture. It conveyed the sense that European economic growth and imperial expansion were both inevitable and beneficent. The word "progress" had become less current in political discourse by the early years of the twenty-first century. It had been substantially displaced by the new word "globalization," which, without actually putting it in these words, implied the global extension of the American way in which the world was becoming organized.

Eastern civilizations never embraced the European idea of Progress, which in its practical meaning put them in an inferior position. Now they are resistant to the idea of an unregulated "globalization," which can seem to them to be just a new ideology of imperialism.

Building global governance involves understanding how people in the different civilizations that coexist in the world today may understand time, in the sense of historical evolution, differently. Effective global governance requires that each party is able to understand the thought processes of the others; and differences in the way people understand the nature of historical time are fundamental in this respect.

Creativity and decline

Thinking in the time dimension—the diachronic—leads us to consider whether society, civilization, or culture is in a period of a creative movement, or whether it seems to be stalled or in a phase of decline. Production in the arts and technology and innovations in social organization are indicative of creativity. These are all activities that take time to develop. The space dimension—the synchronic—focuses on things as they are, on their interrelationships, and particularly on the means of controlling activity. At the present time finance, which functions synchronically, dominates and controls production. One can speak of the financialization of society, meaning the dominance of the synchronic over the diachronic. Finance operates at electronic speed. The development of production in its manifold spheres, in goods and services, in invention and innovation, and in artistic and cultural creativity, is slow and painstaking.

The struggle between the synchronic and the diachronic—put in abstract terms—is perhaps the underlying issue of our time. It will determine whether people will be able to muster the stimulus for a new creative forward movement or whether a blockage of the creative potential in society, manifested most likely by prolonged financial crisis, will forestall that possibility. The issue is being fought out in Europe at the present time between the concept of financial Europe and social Europe at the level of the European Union. In the world as a whole, it is a question of whether the consequences of the global financial crisis of 2008 and its sequel will obstruct the reform of prevailing social structures and so prevent the emergence of new forms of social, economic, and political organization.

The doubt that hangs over this confrontation is whether the protest movements that challenge the "inevitability" of "globalization" will have sufficient creativity to generate both the bonds of solidarity and the innovation of institutions and practices that could become the harbinger of an alternative society. There is much pessimism about this. This is the predicament of the Left in the Western world. The will to resist may be there, but is the vision of a really creative alternative still missing? And if present, who has the capacity to communicate it?

Whether or not societies possess the creativity to reinvent themselves is a question that has to be asked in eras when the "inevitable" seems to overwhelm any possibility for fundamental change. Those in authority will close the discussion by saying, with Mrs. Thatcher, "There is no alternative." Yet at other times it seemed that people were more inspired to change.

This is not a matter peculiar to our present world. Studies of the Roman imperial period have reflected upon this question of the innate creative capacity of a civilization. The Canadian historian Charles Cochrane saw the question as a matter of the balance between what, in the classical terminology, was known as virtue and fortune, *virtù* and *fortuna*, two words that have become transformed and trivialized in meaning from their Latin origins.[5] In a more modern idiom, we could render these ideas as creative collective energy, for the first, and the objective limits of the possible, for the second.

Cochrane saw the failure of the classical world in its final stage as a waning of confidence in the creative capacity of politics when confronted with the despair engendered by sheer degradation of the material conditions of existence. The balance in the classical mind had shifted from virtue to fortune, in other words from creativity to fate.

A millennium later, Machiavelli made a similar analysis of his own society: too corrupt to restore from within itself the spirit of civic capability, or *virtù*. He looked to a prince who would be capable of arousing once again the civic spirit that in earlier times had sustained a Republic.[6] Four centuries later, Antonio Gramsci looked to the Party, as a modern prince, to perform the same function. What is common is the awareness of a moral and intellectual failure and a search for a means of moral and intellectual regeneration.[7]

This problem of creativity is not a peculiarity of Western civilizations. The fourteenth century North African Islamic diplomat and historian Ibn Khaldun confronted the same predicament. Though by all accounts a devout Muslim, he wrote history with an accent of historical materialism. He was attentive, in the first place, to the geographical and ecological constraints upon human action. He was, however, primarily concerned with the presence or absence of the quality he called *'asabiya*, the sense of solidarity through which people, in the course of their history, became capable of founding and sustaining a state.[8] The state will make possible the enjoyment of sedentary, urban civilization; but urban life and the affluence it generates prove to be corrupting and ultimately erode the spirit of solidarity which created it.

The traditional Chinese conception of history is of a fundamental rhythm of the universe alternating between *yin*, a quiescent phase of unity and harmony, and *yang*, a phase of activity, conflict, and fragmentation. History, in both Chinese and Ibn Khaldun's conceptions, is cyclical rather than progressive and unilinear.

Virtù and *'asabiya* are words that apply to something missing, something required to trigger a response to a failure of culture or civilization. They give a diagnosis, not a prescription for recovery. What would it take to generate a sufficient collective response? Where would the necessary stimulus come from?

Ibn Khaldun, Machiavelli, and others have taught us where to look: first to an analysis of the material conditions of existence and the mental and institutional structures that delineate the conditions of civilization; and then at the marginal and marginalized social forces from which contestation and innovation may come.

Those marginal forces today, as in earlier times, are both internal and external and they are contradictory. They include: those groups of people who are being adversely affected by the dominant trend of globalization; the mass migrations that are mixing traditions of civilization at the most popular level; and transformations taking place in contiguous civilizations. A primary example at the present time is the conflict within Islam between modernizers who seek to adapt Islam to modern material and social practices and reactionary obscurantists like the Taliban and al-Qaeda. The challenge is to distill some coherence and common purpose out of these contradictory elements—and this challenge is directed in the first instance to marginal intellectuals, to those who work outside the mainstream. It is from that quarter, uncompromised as it is by the weight of presently dominant thought and practice, that a new vision of a possible future may come.

Dominance and subordination

A common purpose in the world today would be to resolve the problems of coexistence of contiguous civilizations. In this regard it will be necessary to deal with a lot of historical baggage in the conflicts among cultures and civilizations. Edward Said characterized the Western approach to the study of Eastern civilizations as "orientalism."[9] "Orientalism," for him, was a form of knowledge through which Eastern civilizations were seen as subordinate to the West. Western scholarship, assuming a position of universal objectivity, has defined the characteristics of dominated civilizations and has had the power to transmit to the dominated this knowledge about themselves. The elites of the dominated could thus become absorbed into an alien universalism. Kinhide Mushakoji has used the term "occultation" to describe the manner in which the thought processes of one civilization have been displaced by those of another dominant one. Yet the thought processes of the dominated civilization are not totally suppressed but remain latent, ready to be aroused by some crisis.[10]

Antonio Gramsci's concept of "passive revolution" has some relevance here.[11] Gramsci took the term from Vincenzo Cuocuo, the historian of Naples under Napoleonic rule, for whom passive revolution was the introduction of ideas from an alien society which were embraced by a local elite though they did not resonate with the common people. The result was a situation Gramsci called revolution/restoration, in which the newly adopted ideas and modes of behavior were never securely entrenched since they never penetrated thoroughly to the mass of the people. One might draw a parallel with British intellectual and institutional influence in India, seemingly secure in the Nehru era but subsequently contested and displaced from its dominant position in society by the Hindu nationalists when they gained power.

Oswald Spengler put forward an interesting concept that suggests how an impetus from one civilization penetrating into another can partially transform that other civilization but be constrained by the persisting structures of the penetrated civilization. Borrowing a term from mineralogy, he called the process "pseudomorphosis."[12] He applied it to the formation of the European Middle Ages from the time of Augustus to the tenth century. A nascent Arabian spiritual energy became configured by a fixed and persistent Greco-Roman political form. Spengler discerned a similar phenomenon in the way Westernization imported into Russia by Peter the Great framed and shackled the Russian spirit. The tragedy of the Russian pseudomorphosis, in Spengler's analysis, has been the continuing dominance of Western imported thought over a suppressed and barely articulate Russian spirit. By analogy, the more recent "market reformers" coming on the heels of the collapse of the Soviet Union were but an extension of the Western-inspired Communist managers, themselves natural successors to Peter the Great's modernization. In the post-Communist débacle, opposition to the Westernizing advocates of "shock therapy" has revived an anti-Western *narodnik* sentiment. One literary instance is in a revived interest in the work of Nicholas Berdyaev.[13] Those with a longer historical perspective could trace the phenomenon of an alien culture overlaying the Russian spirit back to the Varangians!

All of these concepts—orientalism, occultation, passive revolution, and pseudomorphosis—evoke the phenomenon of the dominance of one civilization over another but also of the latency of the dominated culture and the potential for reaffirmation of its authenticity. A most important object of inquiry is thus to trace the evidence of linguistic and conceptual superposition, and to identify the kinds of crisis likely to precipitate a rejection of the superimposed discourse by subordinate groups.

The channels of international organization and global governance allow for a continuing dialogue of civilizations through which the creativity or decline of different civilizations becomes apparent and issues of dominance and subordination may be confronted. These channels exist to provide a means for the world to adjust to changes in the power structure of world order.

The problem of world order

The central problem for critical thinking in the world today is to understand the dynamics of world order and to give guidance towards achieving a harmonious development of world politics. On one side, for the moment the apparently dominant side, are the theorists of globalization who envisage American-style capitalism absorbing the rest of the world into a single global political economy that would bring about a comprehensive global political organization, and social and intellectual habits and practices that would be consistent with that dominant politico-economic structure.

On the other side is the political and intellectual rejection of that view of the future. One can look back a century earlier to the geopolitical vision of Halford Mackinder. He envisaged a "Heartland" or "World Island," a unified force of Eurasia as the dominant central world power. Another century before Mackinder, the American naval historian Alfred Thayer Mahan envisaged the strategy for American dominance as encirclement by sea power of the rest of the world. These two geopolitical constellations are now taking shape. The American "empire" is one. Eurasia is the other.

Russia feels the threat of encirclement by the US presence or influence in Georgia, Ukraine, and American penetration into the Central Asian republics. China, the greatest and growing Eurasian power, shares the concern about encirclement, specifically US influence in Taiwan and its military presence in Japan and South Korea. The American challenge of encirclement of Eurasia is countered by the coming together of the Eurasian powers. The Shanghai Cooperation Organization, a body which has been given very little attention in the Western media, has as its members China, Russia, and the Central Asian republics. It foreshadows the prospect of Eurasian geopolitical consolidation.

The first side has the advantage of momentum. The United States has built up an imperial constellation of power. Major American allies have become so aligned with the United States as for all practical purposes to abandon their real independence from US policy in world affairs. Zbigniew Brzezinski, a realist strategic thinker and American policy advisor, in an historical analogy, referred to them as America's *vassals*.[14]

The United States leads something that might be called an empire but is different from what the word "empire" has represented in the past. States retain a formal independence but are bound into the agglomeration of American power by complex bonds of dependency. Yet at the same time, America's power has been sundered into a dualism at the top. Since the American débacle in Vietnam, the US army ceased to be a draft of citizens called up for exceptional military duty; it became a disciplined professional body separate and distinct from a permissively self-indulgent society.[15] The Pentagon, though formally under the command of the president of the United States, has developed as an autonomous force in the formation and application of foreign policy.[16]

This became apparent with the election of Barack Obama as president in 2008. The enthusiasm of popular mobilization for change that marked his election campaign settled months later into resignation that all was still the same. There were evident limits to the power of the president in his conduct of world affairs and those limits were fixed by what former President Eisenhower, in his valedictory warning to the American people, called the military-industrial complex.

The Pentagon, the directing centre of that complex, remained supreme in determining the strategy of American world leadership. It has divided the world into its regional spheres of control, each under the supervision of a proconsul: the Pacific Command, headquartered in Pearl Harbor, Hawaii, covering the Pacific ocean and all of East Asia; the European Command, headquartered in Stuttgart, Germany, which covered all of Europe and most of Africa and part of the Middle East, including Israel (it also had the command of all NATO forces); the Central Command, headquartered in Tampa, Florida, which covered the remainder of the Middle East, including the Persian Gulf, Central Asia, and the Horn of Africa; and, finally, the Southern Command, located in Miami, Florida, which covered Central and South America and the Caribbean. The proconsuls charged with these commands had resources vastly greater than those possessed by other government agencies, notably the State Department.[17]

There are two directions in which the forces, political, military, economic, and social, alive in the world today could move in shaping world order for the coming years. One is that the decline of American power, which is manifest in relation to a group of major countries of growing weight in world affairs, could lead to a plural world with several centers of world power engaged in a continuous negotiation for a constantly adjustable *modus vivendi*. This would depend very largely on American acceptance of a new role as one among several major powers.

One common threat to all the major powers would hang over this process of negotiation and adjustment of power relations. The problem of global warming and the fragility of the biosphere would put pressure on all of them, particularly if civil society had aroused public awareness, to subordinate particular interests to the common interest of saving life on the planet.

The other direction in which the world seems to be heading is towards a catastrophic confrontation of America with Eurasia. The trigger may well be the determination of Israeli leadership to strike Iran and the reluctance or political weakness of the US leadership to prevent it. Unfortunately, this direction is the more likely, absent the arousal of public protest on a world scale.

The first scenario, a movement towards a plural world with the United States playing a role in company with other world powers, would make it possible to subordinate particular national interests to the common interest of the survival of the planet. The second would subordinate the global interest to the clash of a global cleavage.

Conclusion

Critical theory is rooted in the movement of history. It is a method both for understanding history, especially contemporary history, by seeking to know the interaction of forces unobstructed by any ideological gloss, and for thinking how the future course of events might be influenced so as to yield the optimum result for mankind. Thus as critical theory foresees a coming collapse of the biosphere unless immediate and continuing steps are taken to curb the noxious effects produced by human activities in our present way of doing things, it must give both a warning and a guideline for a different way of doing things that would be consistent with bringing the biosphere back into a tolerable equilibrium. The possibility of approaching general agreement among the world powers on how to stop the destruction of the biosphere is, however, negated by the build-up of global military confrontation. Critical theory can lay bare the political choices the great powers have to make towards saving the biosphere. It is a question of priorities: survival of life on the planet vs. "full spectrum dominance" and catastrophic confrontation.

International organization and the procedures of global governance would maintain the existence of a plural world in which the major powers together with the lesser powers would negotiate and seek consensus on global problems. The impetus of "globalization" towards the effective integration of an American-led "empire" would bypass the existing structures of international organization and global governance or else it would subvert them to its own purposes. A catastrophic confrontation of the American "empire" with Eurasia would utterly destroy the remnants of international organization and global governance.

Additional reading

1. Robin George Collingwood, *The Idea of History* (Oxford: Oxford University Press, 1956).
2. Charles Norris Cochrane, *Christianity and Classical Culture: A Study of Thought and Action from Augustus to Augustine* (London: Oxford University Press, 1944).
3. Niccolo Machiavelli, *The Prince*, eds. Quentin Skinner and Russell Price (Cambridge: Cambridge University Press, 1988).
4. Nikolai Berdyaev, *The Russian Idea* (London: Geoffrey Bles, 1947).
5. Andrew Bacevich, *American Empire* (Cambridge, MA: Harvard University Press, 2002).
6. Robert Cox, "Social Forces, States and World Orders: Beyond International Relations Theory," in *Millennium: Journal of International Studies* 10, no. 2 (1981): 126–155.

Notes

1 Robin George Collingwood, *The Idea of History* (Oxford: Oxford University Press, 1956).
2 For example, the term "critical theory" has been associated with Max Horkheimer and others of the Frankfurt School.
3 This sentence is a quote from Robert W. Cox, "Social Forces, States and World Orders: Beyond International Relations Theory," *Millennium: Journal of International Studies* 10, no. 2 (1981): 126–155.

4 Edward Palmer Thompson argues that historical concepts must often "display extreme elasticity and allow for great irregularity." His treatment of historical logic develops this point in his essay "The Poverty of Theory," in *The Poverty of Theory and Other Essays*, ed. Edward Palmer Thompson (London: Merlin Press, 1978), esp. 231–242.

5 Charles Norris Cochrane, *Christianity and Classical Culture: A Study of Thought and Action from Augustus to Augustine* (London: Oxford University Press, 1944), esp. 157–161.

6 Niccolo Machiavelli, *The Prince*, eds. Quentin Skinner and Russell Price (Cambridge: Cambridge University Press, 1988); also Federigo Chabod, *Machiavelli and the Renaissance* (London: Bowes and Bowes, 1958).

7 Antonio Gramsci, *Selections from the Prison Notebooks of Antonio Gramsci*, eds. Quintin Hoare and Geoffrey Nowell Smith (New York: International Publishers, 1971), esp. 123–205.

8 Ibn Khaldun, *The Muqaddimah*, translated by Franz Rosenthal (Princeton: Princeton University Press, 1967). See also Robert W. Cox, "Towards a Post-Hegemonic Conceptualization of World Order: Reflections on the Relevancy of Ibn Khaldun," in *Governance Without Government: Order and Change in World Politics*, eds. James Rosenau and Ernst-Otto Czemliel (Cambridge: Cambridge University Press, 1992).

9 Edward Said, *Orientalism* (New York: Vintage Books, 1979).

10 Kinhide Mushakoji, "Multilateralism in a Multicultural World: Notes for a Theory of Occultation," in *The New Realism: Perspectives on Multilateralism and World Order*, ed. Robert W. Cox (London: Macmillan for the United Nations University, 1996).

11 Gramsci, *Selections from the Prison Notebooks*, 105–120.

12 "In a rock stratum are embedded crystals of a mineral. Clefts and cracks occur, water filters in, and the crystals are gradually washed out so that in due course only their hollow mould remains. Then come volcanic outbursts which explode the mountain; molten masses pour in, stiffen, and crystallize in their turn. But these are not free to do so in their own special forms. They must fill up the spaces that they find available. Thus there arise distorted forms, crystals whose inner structure distorts their external shape, stones of one kind presenting the appearance of stones of another kind. The mineralogists call this phenomenon *Pseudomorphosis*. By the term 'historical pseudomorphosis' I propose to designate those cases in which an older alien Culture lies so massively over the land that a young Culture born in this land, cannot get its breath and fails not only to achieve pure and specific expression forms, but even fully to develop its own self-consciousness. All that wells up from the depths of the young soul is cast in the old moulds, young feelings stiffen in senile works, and instead of rearing up in its own creative power, it can only hate the distant power with a hate that grows to be enormous." See Oswald Spengler, *The Decline of the West*, Vol. II (New York: Knopf, 1939), 189.

13 Nikolai Berdyaev, *The Russian Idea* (London: Geoffrey Bles, 1947).

14 Zbigniew Brzezinski, *The Grand Chessboard* (New York: Basic Books, 1998), 40, states that the three grand imperatives of imperial policy, expressed in deliberately archaic terminology, are "to prevent collusion and maintain security dependence among the vassals, to keep the tributaries pliant and protected, and to keep the barbarians from coming together."

15 Andrew Bacevich, *American Empire* (Cambridge, MA: Harvard University Press, 2002), 168, writes: "Vietnam had created a gulf separating the armed services from American society as a whole."

16 Andrew Bacevich, in *American Empire: The Realities and Consequences of U.S. Diplomacy* (Cambridge, MA: Harvard University Press, 2002), gives a description of the emergence of the Pentagon's autonomy in foreign policy. See esp. 215–223.

17 Bacevich, *American Empire*, 178, writes: "Those resources included not just military assets— carrier battle groups or fighter squadrons—but executive jets, instantly available secure communications, retinues of attentive aides, and lavish budgets for discretionary spending that no mere ambassador could even dream of."

CONTENTS

Classical Marxism

Paul Cammack

This chapter makes the argument— perhaps surprising at first sight—that the best insights into the contemporary governance of the global economy are found in the writings of Karl Marx and Friedrich Engels from the 1840s. This, I suggest, is because the world that they envisaged—one in which capitalism is globally dominant—is only now becoming a reality; and because their unique focus on the orientation of governments and international organizations towards competitiveness in the world market captures the most powerful dynamic shaping global politics today.

My starting point is a passage from the 1848 *Manifesto of the Communist Party* that is widely cited as an early description of "globalization":

> The bourgeoisie has through its exploitation of the world market given a cosmopolitan character to production and consumption in every country. To the great chagrin of Reactionists, it has drawn from under the feet of industry the national ground on which it stood. All old-established national industries have been destroyed or are daily being destroyed. They are dislodged by new industries, whose introduction becomes a life and death question for all civilized nations, by industries that no longer work up indigenous raw material, but raw material drawn from the remotest zones; industries whose products are consumed, not only at home, but in every quarter of the globe. In place of the old wants, satisfied by the production of the country, we find new wants, requiring for their satisfaction the products of distant lands and climes. In place of the old local and national seclusion and self-sufficiency, we have intercourse in every direction, universal interdependence of nations. And as in material, so also in intellectual production. The intellectual creations of individual nations become common property. National one-sidedness and narrow-mindedness become more and more impossible, and from the numerous national and local literatures there arises a world literature. The bourgeoisie, by the rapid improvement of all instruments of production, by the immensely facilitated

means of communication, draws all, even the most barbarian, nations into civilization. The cheap prices of commodities are the heavy artillery with which it batters down all Chinese walls, with which it forces the barbarians' intensely obstinate hatred of foreigners to capitulate. It compels all nations, on pain of extinction, to adopt the bourgeois mode of production; it compels them to introduce what it calls civilization into their midst, i.e. to become bourgeois themselves. In one word, it creates a world after its own image.[1]

This remarkable passage, written in Manchester and London when Marx and Engels were in their twenties and when the developments they described were in their earliest stages, addresses topics that were scarcely in evidence at the time, but that figure prominently in global politics today—the emergence of a global culture, the "interdependence of nations," the global reach of markets and supply chains, and above all the establishment of capitalism and the intensification of competition on a genuinely global scale. This chapter reconstructs the theory of world history that underpins it, and shows how it provides an understanding and a critique of contemporary global politics and governance. As it addresses the original Marxist approach to world history, it takes no account of later work in the Marxist tradition. I have kept the use of Marxist terminology to a minimum, but there is no escaping the fact that a willingness to engage with the conceptual framework developed by Marx and Engels is essential if their approach is to be understood.

The chapter begins by outlining the method of *historical materialism*, which distinguishes classical Marxism from constructivism, liberalism, and realism. It shows how Marx and Engels employed it in practice to identify the specific forces driving change in world history. Put simply, they thought that the advent of modern industry changed the world, both because it created a society of two classes, bourgeoisie and proletariat, with opposed interests, and because it obliged all countries, as they were drawn into the world market, to pursue industrialization themselves. Foreign trade was important because it was the main mechanism through which local industry was forced to modernize and compete, but reforms to establish the power of capital over labor and to create a modern working class were just as significant. In the contemporary world, the pressure to be competitive in the global market has become universal. The chapter then turns directly to contemporary global governance and argues that the international organizations involved in global *economic* governance—the Bretton Woods institutions and others—are primarily involved in promoting the spread of capitalism, or global competitiveness. In line with the classical Marxist perspective, they are as interested in the creation of a modern working class as they are in the promotion of trade and global markets. The conclusion pinpoints the distinctiveness and particular strength of the classical Marxist approach.

Historical materialism

The approach that is the focus here was developed by Marx and Engels over two decades or so from the early to mid-1840s. The first full version came not in the *Manifesto of the Communist Party*, but in the *Critique of the German Ideology*, composed in 1845–46;

the underlying materialist theory of history was summarized in the Preface and developed further in the Introduction to the *Contribution to the Critique of Political Economy* [1857–58], and further related material is scattered through Marx's voluminous notebooks from the same years, eventually published as the *Foundations of the Critique of Political Economy* or *Grundrisse* (1973), and in the first volume of *Capital* [1867]. Its intended structure (never realized in full) is set out in Marx's statement at the beginning of the Preface: "I examine the system of bourgeois economy in the following order: *capital, landed property, wage-labour; the state, foreign trade, world market.*"[2] Underpinning this was what Marx described as the "guiding principle" of his studies: "In the social production of their existence men inevitably enter into definite relations, which are independent of their will, namely relations of production appropriate to a given stage in the development of their material forces of production."[3] The lines immediately following state the implications for institutions and ideas:

> The totality of these relations of production constitutes the economic structure of society, the real foundation, on which arises a legal and political superstructure and to which correspond definite forms of consciousness. The mode of production of material life conditions the general process of social, political and intellectual life. It is not the consciousness of men that determines their existence, but their social existence that determines their consciousness.

The "real foundation" of society, then, is the set of social relations arising from the way in which the material necessities of life are produced. This approach is *materialist*, in its insistence on the centrality of the "mode of production of material life"; this differentiates it from the constructivist approach and its starting point in "changing human conventions," as a classical Marxist would seek to relate such changes to prior changes in underlying material circumstances. At the same time, it does not derive institutional change mechanically from the "economic structure of society." As Marx and Engels note, observation "must in each separate instance bring out empirically, and without any mystification or speculation, the connection of the social and political structure with production,"[4] not least because in a society of classes in continuous struggle with each other, outcomes are always uncertain. Institutions and ideas, as Marx and Engels strikingly put it, themselves have "no history, no development," because "men, developing their material production and their material intercourse, alter, along with this, their real existence, their thinking and the products of their thinking,"[5] but they still matter, as class conflict is the driving force in history, and these are the "ideological forms in which men become conscious of this conflict and fight it out."[6]

All this must be borne in mind when assessing the account that Marx and Engels give of the process of *historical* change, and the roles played in it by the state, foreign trade, and the world market. In the Preface, the macro-historical claim is made that successive "epochs marking progress in the economic development of society" come about as the material productive forces of one epoch come into conflict with the existing social structure, or the *relations* of production, giving rise to an era of social revolution, and "sooner or later to the transformation of the whole [legal and political] superstructure."[7]

They concluded that the polarization of conflict in the "modern bourgeois mode of production" between the minority bourgeoisie and the majority proletariat would create the conditions for the overthrow of capitalism and the institution of a communist society in which private property was abolished—but also that this would only happen, if at all, after the bourgeois social order had developed "all the productive forces for which it [was] sufficient."[8] The significance of this is that even if this is taken as an unqualified prediction (it certainly should not be), it is still too early to say whether it is right or wrong, and speculative even to try. In order to grasp the relevance of classical Marxism today, we do better to focus on what Marx and Engels had to say about the development of capitalism, or the modern bourgeois mode of production, as it was coming into being when they wrote, and is continuing and reaching maturity only in the present day. Their thoughts about an eventual global revolution continue to command attention, but they remain unproven either way.

The state, foreign trade, and the world market

In the opening pages of the *German Ideology*, Marx and Engels move briskly from the statement that what individuals are "coincides with their production, both with what they produce and with how they produce," to the implications for the "relations of different nations among themselves." These, they suggest, "depend upon the extent to which each has developed its productive forces, the division of labor and internal intercourse," adding that "not only the relation of one nation to others, but also *the whole internal structure of the nation itself* depends on the stage of development reached by its production and its internal and external intercourse" (emphasis mine). A little later on they insist that "the history of humanity must always be studied and treated in relation to the history of industry and exchange."[9] On this basis they offer a quite distinctive model of long-term social change, and one that distinguishes them clearly from realism, with its emphasis upon the centrality of survival, the need for a primary focus on self-reliance in a world of anarchy, and the resulting dynamics revolving around the balance of power. For Marx and Engels, "world history" begins only with the advent of large-scale industry and is played out *from the start* not in a realm of anarchy but in the (evolving) "world market." "Big industry" (machinofacture) and foreign trade are the production and exchange (structural and spatial) mechanisms that promote the co-constitution of the world market and the global proletariat once world history proper begins. In this approach there is no gulf between international and domestic politics—both derive their logic from the character of large-scale industry, and particularly from the changes it brings about between capitalist and workers, and the implications this has for the domestic and international role of the state.

The development of large-scale industry is so significant because the constant revolution in labor productivity ("the rapid improvement of all instruments of production," as the *Manifesto* put it) that it entails transforms relations between labor and capital, and with it the world market. Marx and Engels were impressed with the scale of the changes in both output and productivity that the industrial revolution made possible, with the consequence that producers relying on more labor-intensive forms of production simply could not compete. For this reason, they argued that it was only in the world market dominated by modern industrial production that the "inner laws of capital"—the inescapability of competition, and the need to invest constantly in the production process—were truly revealed.[10] The immense revolution in productivity brought about by the ever-increasing application of capital to the production process far outstripped the capacity of protection to offset it.

There are two equally important points here. First, the laws of capital, captured in shorthand in the idea of free competition, do not operate as laws until the world market is fully constituted. Second, the constitution of the world market is a question not only of the expansion of domestic and international trade (or "intercourse" in the terminology of Marx and Engels), but also of the transformation of social relations, and the creation of "free labor," or proletarianization. It is this focus on the creation of a global proletariat, as well as on the expansion of trade, that distinguishes the Marxist approach from the liberal perspective, which tends to focus exclusively on the benefits of trade, or exchange. And whereas liberals see everyone as benefiting from the expansion of markets and trade, Marx and Engels see it as a process that robs the majority, who become propertyless workers, of autonomy, dignity, and control over their lives.

Thus Marx and Engels note as an "empirical fact" that "separate individuals have, with the broadening of their activity into world-historical activity, become more and more enslaved under a power alien to them . . . a power which has become more and more enormous and, in the last instance, turns out to be the world market."[11] At the same time, they argue that it is only when proletarianization does become *universal* that the discipline that subjects the "mass of propertyless workers" to the sway of capital and gives them a common interest can truly operate. The creation of a proletariat on a global scale is therefore a consequence of the creation of a world market—it "presupposes the world market through competition."[12] As noted at the outset, it was a process that was only beginning to get under way when Marx and Engels wrote. It is because global competitiveness is such a feature of the contemporary world that these ideas are so relevant today. The distinctiveness of the Marxist approach is that this is identified as the central unifying theme in world history, in contrast perhaps to ideas, in the case of constructivism, cooperation in pursuit of human freedom, in the case of liberalism, and the eternal pursuit of survival in an anarchic global system, in the case of realism. "World history did not always exist," Marx notes at one point: "history as world history is a result."[13] It was a result, that is, of the advent of "big industry," and, as Marx would later define it, the "real subsumption of labour to capital," or the reliance on "relative surplus value" as the principal source of accumulation.[14] In other words, it was a result of the revolution involved in bringing workers together in large factories under the direct control of capital, in new forms of industry in which the scale of production and profitability was transformed by investment in the production process and greatly increased productivity. Again, as foreign direct investment and domestic industrialization in what was once called the developing world have spread these forms of production much more widely around the world, these ideas become more universally relevant than ever before.

In this context, finally, the state plays a crucial role in promoting these developments. But neither the individual, nor the state, nor the "system of states" is the starting point. The starting point is the world market. As big industry develops, states find themselves compelled, "on pain of extinction," as the *Manifesto* puts it, "to adopt the bourgeois mode of production." Crucially, again, this is not simply a matter of moving from protectionism to free trade, but rather of developing for themselves large-scale industry and its necessary corollary—a propertyless proletariat available for and subject to exploitation by capital. Hence, as argued in a passage from the *German Ideology*, preceding the more frequently quoted statement in the *Manifesto* by two years, the advent of big industry

> soon compelled every country that wished to retain its historical role to protect its manufactures by renewed customs regulations (the old duties were no longer any good against big industry) and soon after to introduce big industry under protective duties. Big industry universalized competition in spite of these protective measures (*it is practical free trade; the protective duty is only a palliative, a measure of defense within free trade*), established means of communication and the modern world market, subordinated trade to itself, transformed all capital into industrial capital, and thus produced the rapid circulation (development of the financial system) and the centralization of capital. By universal competition it forced all individuals to strain their energy to the utmost. It destroyed as far as possible ideology, religion, morality, etc. and, where it could not do this, made them into a palpable lie. It produced world history for the first time, insofar as it made all civilized nations and every individual member of them dependent for the satisfaction of their wants on the whole world, thus destroying the former natural exclusiveness of separate nations (emphasis mine).[15]

What are the implications for the state? As Peter Burnham argues, in a pioneering contemporary account of the significance of the world market, the state is to be understood in class terms, as "a form of the class relation which constitutes global capitalist society," or, as he puts it in a complementary account of "globalization," a political "node" or "moment" in the global flow of capital.[16] The following sections explore the implications of this approach for contemporary "global governance," and assess critically the potential of the classical Marxist account as an alternative to constructivist, liberal, and realist approaches.

World history and global governance

If we consider the two dimensions that Marx and Engels identified in the "world market"—the growth of exchange between nations, and the process of proletarianization, it is apparent both that a dramatic transformation of the world market is under way, and that it is at a relatively early stage. Richard Freeman, estimating that the global supply of labor doubled in the early 1990s, from under 1.5 billion to close on 3 billion workers, comments that "almost at once . . . China, India, and the former Soviet bloc joined the global economy, and the entire world came together into a single economic world based on capitalism and markets."[17] But this did not in itself constitute a process of proletarianization—rather, it marked its *initiation*. Defining informal employment as comprising "workers in small enterprises of fewer than five workers, self-employed own account workers, unpaid family helpers and workers with no proper contract in the formal sector" (a definition that admittedly will include some measure of engagement with modern industry), the International Labour Organization (ILO) estimates that informal employment still accounts for "over 40 per cent of non-agricultural employment in two-thirds of the countries for which data is available."[18]

On trade, although a dramatic shift is under way, the process is similarly incipient. The share of world merchandise exports originating in the advanced economies remained fairly constant (with a slight tendency to rise) between 1950 and 1990, but it fell sharply from 69 percent to 52 percent between 1990 and 2011.[19] On current trends, this is only the beginning of a far more dramatic shift. Buiter and Rahbari report that world trade in goods and services was 39 percent of world GDP in 1990, and rose to 61 percent by 2010 as new producers entered the world market; and they estimate that by 2030 it will stand at 76 percent.[20] They summarize as follows the historical transformation now in prospect:

> What is new, at least since the industrial revolution of the late eighteenth century, is the prominence of today's emerging market economies (EMs) in world trade. Emerging Asia is set to overtake Western Europe to become the world's largest trading region by 2015. We expect China, already the world's largest exporter in 2010, to be the world's largest trading nation by 2015, overtaking the US. We expect Emerging Asia to become the largest region by trade in 2025, even though its share of world trade was only about half the level of Western Europe—the largest trading region today—in 2010. And India, currently not even on the list of the 10 largest nations by trade, will overtake the US and Germany to become the world's second largest country by trade in 2050 ... EMs will rise in significance as both exporters and importers. Thus, intra-EM trade, which rose from only 6 percent of world trade in 2000 to 15 percent in 2010, is set to account for 27 percent of world trade in 2030 and 38 percent in 2050.[21]

Among other things, this scenario gives substance to the suggestion that the "bourgeois mode of production" is as yet far from exhausting its potential to develop the productive forces. The complex conjuncture of the last quarter of the twentieth century has given rise to a new phase in the development of capitalism, in which the completion of the world market theorized by the youthful Marx and Engels finally comes into prospect. The dawning of the age of global competitiveness puts it onto the agenda of all governments, and all international organizations concerned with the governance of global capitalism. World history, then, has reached a point at which the classical Marxist analysis outlined above can provide both an understanding and a critique of *contemporary* global governance.

Governing the global economy with the completion of the world market

In classical Marxism, ruling institutions and ideas are conditioned but not mechanically determined by material circumstances (in this case, the state of development of the global economy, and the social relations of production within it). If the approach is to have any credibility, it should be possible to "bring out empirically, and without any mystification or speculation, the connection of the social and political structure with production."[22] In other words, we should be able to explain the actions and arguments of international organizations concerned with the governance of the global economy and their evolution in terms of the relationship between states, foreign trade, and the world market. The classical Marxist approach would be validated further if their policy advice revolved around the expansion of trade *and* the transformation of social relations of production, and further still if they echoed and endorsed the specific logic identified by Marx and Engels, aimed at the pursuit of greater productivity and global competitiveness. If these conditions were met, it would then also be possible to subject global economic governance to a Marxist *critique*, or in other words to unmask any ideological claims to support "human development," or "poverty alleviation" and suchlike, and reveal it as oriented towards the "completion of the world market," and thereby representing specific global capitalist interests. It would remain to be seen whether adherents of alternative analytical frameworks could offer a better account of the observed character and logic of global economic governance.

In fact all the international organizations concerned with the governance of the global economy or regions within it do consistently argue for the development of capitalism on a genuinely global scale, and within that broad perspective for the maximum development of trade and for proletarianization on a universal scale (the latter in terms of support for competitive labor markets, the promotion of foreign direct investment, the pursuit of greater productivity, and the alignment of policy in all areas—from internal and international migration and social protection, to the education of girls and employment of women—to the logic of competitiveness). One finds this approach wherever one looks, in increasingly explicit and detailed manifestos published from the early 1990s on—whether in the sequential "global capitalist manifesto" built up in successive World Bank *World Development Reports* throughout the 1990s, and the Bank's subsequent celebration of education for girls as "smart economics," in the UN-backed *Our Global Neighbourhood* (1995), a liberal manifesto which welcomed the return of the former Soviet bloc on the grounds that it would "increase competition on the world market," or in the celebration by the OECD—often derided as a "rich countries' club"—of the "prospect of a genuinely global economy" in the late 1990s.[23]

Recognizing that "developments in the global economy can lead to social unrest and protectionist pressures, especially when they coincide with the high and persistent unemployment seen in many OECD countries over the last two decades," the OECD drew the conclusion that the politics of competitiveness should prevail: "The response from OECD governments should be to improve the flexibility of labor and product markets, foster life-long learning and reform social policies in order to improve the capacity of individuals and firms to adjust and innovate, and maximize the benefits of globalization."[24] The same document foresaw with equanimity the prospect that by 2020 the OECD share of world trade could fall (from 67 percent in 1995) to as little as 49 percent in 2020, while its share of world GDP might fall (from 61 percent in the same year) to as little as 38 percent. In short, not only did the international organizations consistently welcome the advent of a genuinely global economy once it emerged as a real possibility in the 1990s, but they explicitly promoted policies that would intensify competitive pressures across the global economy as a whole.[25]

In the first decade of the twenty-first century annual series such as the OECD's *Going for Growth* and the World Bank's *Doing Business* series made the case for the reform of product and labor markets and the regulatory structures surrounding business, as these organizations situated themselves, in the words of OECD Director-General Angel Gurría, as "strategic partners in the political economy of reform," stressing the need for "country ownership" of policy initiatives, but striving at the same time to promote reforms that could contribute simultaneously to both *national* and *global* competitiveness.[26] The abiding commitment to driving forward competitiveness in the global economy even in circumstances of deep economic crisis that enveloped the advanced capitalist economies towards the end of that decade is reflected in the OECD's insistence, in the 2012 issue of *Going for Growth*, that a moment of crisis is particularly propitious for the pursuit of structural reform. Reviewing its recommendations over five years for the OECD countries in this context, it observed that "relaxing anti-competitive product market regulations and reforming social benefit systems are fairly common recommendations for raising productivity and labor utilization, respectively," while for the BRIICS (Brazil, Russia, India, Indonesia, China, South Africa), with whom they had systematically engaged over the period, "a number of recommendations are intended to address the major challenge of labor informality. These include increasing the coverage of social protection systems or containing labor costs and relaxing overly strict job protection for formal workers."[27]

The substantive theme of shaping the reform of social protection in order to align it with the promotion of global productivity and competitiveness was shared not only with the World Bank and the Asian Development Bank, but also with the ILO, whose call for "a fair and inclusive globalization" endorsed "as core social protection floor objectives the need to promote productive economic activity and entrepreneurship, with sustainable enterprises and access to decent employment opportunities," on the grounds that properly calibrated social protection floors "are not only affordable but can, in the long run, pay for themselves by enhancing the productiveness of the labor force, the resilience of society and the stability of the political process."[28]

None of this is to say that the international organizations that dominate in the governance of the global economy and the ideas they disseminate play a fundamental causal role. Nor is it to suggest that the conversion of the vast informal sector around the world into a modern proletariat is an imminent prospect. But we can say that their activity and discourse reflect and are conditioned by the "given stage in the development of the material forces of production;" and that their thinking and the products of their thinking adapt in accordance with changes in "material production and material intercourse" in the world market. First, they intervene crucially in the global class conflict between capital and labor, as the principal collective producers of an ideology that seeks to shape policy and behavior in accordance with the logic of the world market, or capitalist competition on a global scale. Second, they do this in particular not only by promoting free trade, but also by advocating strategies that bring workers more directly under the sway of capital. Third, they do so from the perspective of global capital (that is, through the continuous development of the means of production and of proletarianization on a global scale, and the enforcement of competition between capitals in domestic and global arenas alike), with no regard for the fortunes either of existing firms, domestic or transnational, or of particular countries, whatever their past or current standing in the global capitalist economy. In other words, they do stand for the development of capital*ism* on the widest possible scale, looking, as Marx and Engels did to a future world in which capital is universally dominant over a fully developed global proletariat. They stand, in other words, for global capital yet to be. Classical Marxism not only enables us to recognize this, but also provides the critique by showing that this is a strategy of capital, not one of human development or emancipation.

Conclusion

The classical Marxist approach reviewed here does not address every aspect of global governance. But its focus on the governance of industry and exchange on a global scale is increasingly powerful as the logic of global competitiveness becomes increasingly influential in shaping aspects of global governance across a wide range of domestic social and political issues. The classical Marxist perspective identifies a "grand strategy" or project for command and control at the heart of the institutional system of global authority, centered precisely on the dissemination of the forms of competitiveness that enhance the power of global capital to discipline global labor; its shows how regional and local (national) systems intersect, in particular by unveiling the logic of country ownership and partnership in the political economy of reform; it identifies the crucial role of international organizations in developing the ideas and discourses that establish, maintain, and perpetuate the hegemony of global capital (and primarily global capital yet to be), this being the only means, in the long run, by which local capital can sustain hegemony over local labor; it illuminates the *structural* power of capital at the heart of the system, and depicts states as driven to embrace its logic in a world market increasingly characterized by a politics of global competitiveness; and it does so by insisting, in this case against the competing liberal point of view, that "It is not individuals who are set free by free competition; it is, rather, capital which is set free."[29]

Additional reading

1. Alexander Anievas, ed., *Marxism and World Politics: Contesting Global Capitalism* (Abingdon: Routledge, 2010).
2. Werner Bonefeld, "The Spectre of Globalization: On the Form and Content of the World Market," in *The Politics of Change: Globalization, Ideology and Critique*, eds. Werner Bonefeld and Kosmas Psychopedis (Basingstoke: Palgrave, 2000).
3. Peter Burnham, "Open Marxism and Vulgar International Political Economy," *Review of International Political Economy* 1, no. 2 (1994): 221–231.
4. Karl Marx, *A Contribution to the Critique of Political Economy*, edited and introduced by Maurice Dobb (London: Lawrence & Wishart, 1970).
5. Karl Marx and Friedrich Engels, *Critique of the German Ideology* (Moscow: Progress Publishers, 1968; online: Marx/Engels Internet Archive, 2000).
6. Mark Rupert and Hazel Smith, eds., *Historical Materialism and Globalization* (London: Routledge, 2002).

Notes

1   Karl Marx and Friedrich Engels, *Manifesto of the Communist Party* [1848], in Karl Marx, *Political Writings, Volume 1: The Revolutions of 1848*, ed. David Fernbach (London: Penguin Books/New Left Review, 1973), 71.
2   Karl Marx, Preface [1859], in Karl Marx, *A Contribution to the Critique of Political Economy*, ed. and introduced by Maurice Dobb (London: Lawrence & Wishart, 1970), 19. From this point I use short forms in the text for these titles in this paragraph, and the publication date of the edition cited, not the date of composition. But the sequence and timing of composition—a little over two decades in the middle of the nineteenth century—should be borne in mind throughout.

3 Ibid., 20.

4 Karl Marx and Friedrich Engels, *Critique of the German Ideology* [1845–46] (Moscow: Progress Publishers, 1968; Online version: Marx/Engels Internet Archive, 2000), Part A, 5. Pagination is taken from the PDF download at www.marxists.org.

5 Ibid., 6.

6 Marx and Engels, Preface, 21.

7 Ibid.

8 Ibid.

9 Marx and Engels, *German Ideology*, Part A, 3, 8.

10 Karl Marx, *Grundrisse: Introduction to the Critique of Political Economy* [1857–58] (Harmondsworth: Penguin, 1973), 650.

11 Marx and Engels, *German Ideology*, Part A, 10.

12 Ibid., 11.

13 Karl Marx, Introduction [1857], in Karl Marx, *Critique of Political Economy*, 215.

14 Karl Marx, *Results of the Immediate Process of Production* [1863–66?], in Marx, *Capital*, Appendix 1, 948–1084.

15 Marx and Engels, *German Ideology*, Part C, 7. It follows that "Smithian" and "Listian" approaches are not opposites, but variations on a theme.

16 Peter Burnham, "Open Marxism and Vulgar International Political Economy," *Review of International Political Economy* 1, no. 2 (1994): 229; and "Marx, International Political Economy and Globalisation," *Capital & Class* 75 (2001): 107–108.

17 Richard B. Freeman, "The New Global Labor Market," *Focus* (University of Wisconsin-Madison Institute for Research on Poverty) 26, no. 1 (2008): 1.

18 ILO, *World of Work Report 2012: Better Jobs for a Better Economy* (Geneva: ILO, 2012), 6–8 and Figure 1.5 (9). For a fuller analysis see ILO, *Decent Work and the Informal Economy*, Report VI, International Labour Conference, 90th Session, 2002.

19 UN data, international merchandise trade, various years, http://unstats.un.org/unsd/databases.htm.

20 Willem Buiter and Ebrahim Rahbari, *Trade Transformed: The Emerging New Corridors of Trade Power*, Citi GPS: Global Perspectives and Solutions, October 2011, 8–9.

21 Ibid., 7. Similar projections are common among international and regional organizations. See, for example, World Bank, *Multipolarity: The New Global Economy* (Washington: World Bank, 2011); Asian Development Bank, *Asia 2050: Realizing the Asian Century* (Manila: ADB, 2011).

22 Marx and Engels, *German Ideology*, Part A, 4.

23 See Paul Cammack, "Attacking the Poor," *New Left Review*, Second Series, 13, January–February 2002, 125–134; World Bank, "Gender Equality as Smart Economics: A World Bank Group Gender Action Plan (Fiscal Years 2007–2010)," World Bank, September 2006; Commission on Global Governance, *Our Global Neighbourhood* (Oxford and New York: Oxford University Press, 1995), 23–24; Makoto Taniguchi and John West, "On the Threshold of a Global Economy," *OECD Observer*, 207, 1997, 6, 7.

24 Taniguchi and West, "On the Threshold of a Global Economy," *OECDObserver*, 207, 1997, 6.

25 Paul Cammack, "The Politics of Global Competitiveness," *Papers in the Politics of Global Competitiveness*, No. 1, Institute for Global Studies, Manchester Metropolitan University, e-space Open Access Repository, 2006.

26 Paul Cammack, "Poverty Reduction and Universal Competitiveness," *Labour, Capital and Society*, 42, no. 1–2 (2009): 45–46.

27 OECD, *Going for Growth: Economic Policy Reforms 2012* (Paris: OECD, 2012), 23–24.

28 ILO, *Social Protection Floor: For a Fair and Inclusive Globalization* (Geneva: ILO, 2011), xxiv–xxv. On the World Bank and the ADB, see Paul Cammack, "Risk, Social Protection and the World Market," *Journal of Contemporary Asia* 42, no. 3 (2012): 359–377.

29 Marx, *Grundrisse*, 650.

Feminism

Susanne Zwingel, Elisabeth Prügl, and Gülay Caglar

Feminism is a political movement for change, and feminist theories are theories of change. Accordingly, feminist engagements with international organizations and global governance center on efforts to combat gender discrimination, fight various forms of subordination and oppression of women, and problematize entrenched heteronormativity —i.e. the tendency to treat the male–female binary as a natural given. Both feminist activism and feminist theory are thus inherently political. Aware of the deep gender biases in scholarship carrying the mantle of objectivity, feminist researchers recognize that all knowledge is interested and strive for a "dynamic objectivity" that makes knowledge interests explicit.[1]

Gender is a central (and perhaps the central) analytical concept for feminist scholars. The concept is complex, capturing multiple facets of social reality. It designates individual identity as much as social relations, and functions as a structuring principle of discourse. Thus, at the individual level feminist scholars have explored the construction of gendered selves in processes of socialization; at the level of social relations they have analyzed gender divisions of labor and the gendered structures of institutions; and with regard to discourses they have probed the deployment of gender binaries as a way of distributing value. These different uses of gender share an important theoretical commitment: In all instances gender is treated as a social construction. That is, gender is a product of processes of socialization, structured agency, performances, and discursive practices. It is mobile and malleable, but the continuation of gender as a structuring relation requires considerable effort.

This is because gender politics is power politics. Through their politics and writing feminists seek to destabilize existing arrangements, challenging existing orthodoxies and habits, and running into opposition from those benefiting from current arrangements. Multiple facets of power thus emerge as a central preoccupation of feminist activists and theorists. How can and do feminists influence agendas? How can and do they counter backlashes, resistances, and mechanisms of power that deflect and co-opt their agendas?

What is the power of international norms to impact gender relations worldwide? How does discursive power operate in the governance of gender?

This chapter surveys a range of approaches that feminists have put forward in order to explain why and how international organizations and processes of global governance contribute to constructing and re-constructing gender relations globally. It begins with an historical overview of feminist efforts to create an agenda for gender equality and for gender mainstreaming, together with the challenges that these efforts have encountered. It then reviews new approaches and current issues in international feminist scholarship. Three particularly compelling areas are research that probes the continuous translation of international gender norms within and beyond global governance structures, that analyzes the disciplinary and governmental character of international discourses in a Foucauldian sense, and that challenges the hegemonic focus on gender as locked into a heteronormative logic. The last field includes a renewed emphasis on studying masculinities in particular as related to security governance, the political recognition of the intersectional character of women's identities, and the articulation of claims on behalf of lesbian, gay, bisexual, transsexual, and intersex (LGBTI) persons. Reflecting the ways that feminist theory and practice are intertwined, the narrative combines a review of theoretical approaches with a recounting of experiences of feminist engagements with international organizations and global governance.

History

The discourse on global governance within International Relations (IR) can be seen as a reaction to the rather rigid assumption of state-centeredness and an international system built on relative state power. Initially informed by high expectations in regard to the new forms of "governance without government," global governance literature of the last decades has explored the functions of international, regional, and multi-level governance institutions as well as the crucial role of the reconfigured state in the regulation of an increasingly globalized world. Feminists have intervened both in the scholarly debate on and the real-life formations of global governance. In a nutshell, feminist emphasis in this context has been on making mechanisms of global governance inclusive, in particular in terms of the traditionally ignored relevance of gender in international politics, and on critically examining the conditions as well as obstacles for meaningful inclusion of gendered interests. This focus has to be understood as part of the broader feminist endeavor of exposing the absence of female bodies and interests in international politics and debunking a supposedly disembodied discourse as derived from male-only human experience.

Feminists have conceptualized global governance not as benevolent, but as a set of configurations of hegemonic power next to the state in which struggles against patriarchal social structures may make a difference. Since state bureaucracies and formal political institutions are typically themselves entrenched in patriarchal norms, gender equality advocates have a long tradition of ambivalence towards the state and of organizing outside of formal institutions. On the global level, women's organizations have created transnational networks in order to make collective claims for gender equality toward the international community of states. However, such feminist voices have typically not been embraced in all their transformative potential; more often, they have been exploited to achieve other ends, or were converted from an emancipatory vision into management tools added to (and buried in) bureaucratic processes. Hence, feminist literature has focused on the tension between the inclusion of gender awareness into global governance structures on the one hand and the preservation of core feminist goals on the other. Increasingly, it also reflects on what exactly the "gender awareness" in global governance actually entails: while it originally meant to bring women into the picture and elevate them from subordinate positions, exclusions based on gender have a much broader scope, including for example the marginalization of gender identities produced by heteronormativity (see section below on new approaches and issues).

We see three broad developments of feminist interventions in global governance: First, in virtually all global policy fields, gender equality advocates both from the nongovernmental sector and from within global governance bureaucracies have engaged in agenda setting, that is in making gender a relevant dimension of global politics. In some areas, such claims faced only modest resistance. For example, women's work became understood as a crucial part of development in the 1970s, and the notion that population policies should be connected to the education of women and measures to increase their reproductive health has gained attention since the 1980s. Other areas such as security policies or macro-economic and finance policies have proven to be more resistant. Interestingly, the recognition of gender as an important dimension for managing security through Security Council Resolution 1325 and subsequent resolutions has been successful within a hyper-masculinized context. This is less true for macro-economic and finance policies, where the androcentric underpinnings of "expertise" are not questioned and gender equality is understood as a tool to maximize performance, not as a goal *per se*. Thus, while gender now plays a role on diverse global agendas, gender awareness is not necessarily considered at the heart of each policy issue.[2]

Second, it has become clear that despite the difficulties of agenda *setting*, agenda *keeping* is the real challenge for feminist advocates. They have to ensure that gender equality is kept alive as an important organizational vision and that it is being consistently translated into specific policies and programs. Globally agreed-upon language on gender equality does not automatically gain traction. Within historically patriarchal institutions, documents representing gender equality success turn easily into paper tigers, unless their legitimacy and recognition are actually produced through sustained activism, as in the case of the Convention on the Elimination of Discrimination Against Women (CEDAW). Likewise, rhetorical feminist victories cannot be taken for granted and may come under severe attack if the general political climate becomes less favorable, as was the case of the 1995 Beijing Platform for Action (BPA) in the post-9/11 period. Further, the organizational realization of cases of successful agenda setting often turns out to be disappointingly superficial. The strategy of gender mainstreaming, maybe the most widely implemented element of the ambitious BPA, has often been converted into a management tool, to the extent that its original radical intent of creating gender-equal policy processes *and* outcomes "evaporated."[3] Feminist literature has identified a number of factors that influence the degree of meaningful inclusion of gender equality claims, among them the nature of the policy field, the solidification or flexibility of the organizational structure, and, maybe most importantly, the critical feedback loop between institutional "insiders" and autonomous "outsider" perspectives. The lack of such outsider feedback, often reinforced by a construction of superior gender expertise of insiders, almost inevitably leads to co-optation of gender equality goals. This risk has strengthened gender activism that rejects global governance institutions as a meaningful site for intervention altogether.[4]

Third, we have thus far only sketchy knowledge about the connection between gendering global governance mechanisms and the state of gender relations worldwide. Two bodies of literature have started to close this gap. On the one hand empiricist literature that measures the status of gender relations cross-nationally and correlates these with state commitments to global standards; depending on the indicators and global standards used, the conclusions as to the real-life impact of instruments of global governance are more or less optimistic.[5] On the other hand, literature on norm translation conceptualizes norm creation and realization as complex processes between variously contextualized agencies that produce a myriad of interpretations of global gender norms. We discuss the latter approach in more detail below.

New approaches and current issues

The focus on transformative inclusiveness in the feminist literature on international organizations and global governance has produced three particularly salient current debates. The first focuses on the translation of gender norms; it expands on the boundaries of global governance structures and draws connections between global and manifold contextualized gender norms through the analysis of translating agency. The second debate is on the transformation of gender equality norms from marginalized claims into governance tools produced and applied by resourceful bureaucracies; this transformation raises new issues of power, exclusion, emancipation, and discipline. The third debate reflects on the scope of meaning of "gendering global governance." Expanding on the notion of women as marginalized subjects, this debate focuses on masculinities as the other, typically more privileged pole within the heterosexual male–female dichotomy, on the intersectional identities of women in all their diversity, and on modes of non-discriminatory inclusion of all identities that have been marginalized by heteronormative standards.

Norm translation

Feminist literature on the translation of gender norms is embedded in the general concern of IR scholarship with the power of norms, and, at the same time, an attempt to overcome some shortcomings of this approach. If the first step of norm-related literature was to argue for the global relevance of norms and ideas vis-à-vis interests and material power, and the second to analyze institutions and actors that engaged in diffusing these norms, then the third step is to question the assumption that global norms originate from institutions of global governance and then radiate (more or less successfully) into other contexts. Rather, the notion of norm translation conceives of norms as generated in *various* sites and explores ways in which connecting agency translates norms from one context into another. This translation process is multi-directional and it is not value neutral, but informed by various ways of engagement that range from support to partial or entire rejection of the norms in question. Norm translation literature has a strong focus on gender norms, partly because ideas on appropriate gender orders are ubiquitously (and not just internationally) produced and thus processes of norm translation are often highly contested.

Norm translation literature takes a transnational rather than a global-centrist perspective. This entails a re-conception of the global, national, and local and their relationship to each other in such a way that connectivity and mutual constitutiveness are stressed over hierarchy, separation, and qualitative difference. Accordingly, all contexts are viewed as locales that produce their own idiosyncratic norms and practices, and are influenced by phenomena beyond their demarcation.[6] Literature on transnational feminism has focused on the manifold forms of contextualized women's activism as well as the border-crossing connections between them.[7] It has also produced insightful re-readings of the actors relevant for gender norm translation. Thus, international institutions are far from representing a consistent set of gender equality ideas if women's human rights standards are contrasted with the promotion of free trade and structural adjustment programs implemented by international finance institutions; states differ widely not only in their levels of factual sovereignty, but also in respect to national gender orders that may perpetuate notions of hierarchy or equality or both simultaneously; and NGOs may be weak, altruistic actors putting pressure on states in the name of globally agreed-upon gender norms, but they may as well be resourceful, interest driven, and voicing opposition to global norms.[8]

Within this reconstructed global landscape norm translation literature has identified two broad movements of "traveling" gender norms. The first movement is toward and within global governance institutions; a number of studies have analyzed activism that aims at influencing such institutions and activists' use of global spaces to create transnational links and strategies of action.[9] While an earlier focus of this literature was on the dimension of agenda setting, it has more recently shed light on the dynamics of continuous contestations of norms after they are placed on the international agenda;[10] in other words, this literature has taught us to understand "global gender norms" as a principally unfinished discourse rather than a fixed set of ideas to be domestically implemented. The second direction of norm translation is toward and within domestic contexts. The literature tracing such processes looks into agency that uses international gender norms to influence domestic gender regimes; it thoroughly analyzes both actor constellations and context characteristics as these shape strategies and outcomes of norm translation processes. Levitt and Merry have coined the term "vernacularization" for the process of making international gender norms understandable and acceptable in other than global contexts.[11] Translation processes are not necessarily flows of mutual enforcement; they could as well be shaped by disconnect, for example when women's activists openly reject global gender norms in a domestic context where this adds legitimacy to their claims.[12] Taken together, norm translation literature conceptually stretches IR theorizing on global governance dynamics beyond the international and sheds light on the modes of connection between various contexts.

Gender politics as governmentality

A burgeoning literature in the field of feminist IR analyzes gender politics in global governance through the lens of discourse theory as well as governmentality studies.

This Foucauldian perspective has profound implications for the analysis of gender politics in global governance; it implies a shift in the focus of attention: Feminist analyses on agenda setting have provided valuable insights on institutional opportunities as well as barriers; they have illustrated how feminist actors seize political opportunities and which institutional obstacles they face within male-dominated organizations and environments in the international arena.[13] Thus, they conceptualize power in global governance as something that limits agency: the focus is on identifying the gendered power asymmetries that work against the meaningful inclusion of gender issues in international policies and programs. In contrast, studies inspired by Foucauldian theorizing highlight the productive character of power. Feminist scholars drawing on Foucault are interested in the ways power effects are produced through discourses, practices, and knowledge systems. These discourses, practices, and knowledge systems shape actors' identities, constitute them as subjects, and, thus, enable a certain kind of agency. This understanding of power is akin to what Steven Lukes calls the third dimension of power, which is "the power to shape, influence or determine others' beliefs and desires, thereby securing their compliance."[14]

Feminist scholars draw in diverse ways on Foucauldian thought; some employ a discourse analytical approach, others use the concept of governmentality. Discourse analysis puts the emphasis on the production of meaning. Feminist studies that employ a discourse analytical approach probe how both subjects and objects of knowledge come into existence through discourse.[15] They focus on the norms and rules which facilitate a certain set of statements and practices (but not others), and which thereby demarcate what is meaningful within a particular historical and socio-political context. As a consequence, they do not regard an object of political intervention (such as gendered violence or economic development) as exogenously given but rather as discursively constructed.[16] Studies drawing on Foucault sketch the multiple ways in which a policy issue becomes relevant, which gendered meanings are assigned to it, and how it is made governable. Megan MacKenzie, for instance, examines "development policies as a source of regulation and discipline"[17] and illustrates how empowerment initiatives in the disarmament, demobilization, and reintegration process in Sierra Leone prescribe appropriate gender roles. One telling example is the design of micro-credit programs as a tool to make female ex-combatants fit into the role of supportive wives within the nuclear family rather than to facilitate their economic independence.

Another concept which feminist scholars increasingly draw on is that of governmentality. These studies probe how gendered subjectivities are spawned and what role state institutions play in this process. Feminist scholars drawing on the governmentality framework agree with Michel Foucault's critique of the conventional conceptualization of the state as a monolithic entity that possesses all power and that exerts this power over its population. Instead, state power is regarded as diverse and diffuse. These studies refer to the term "government" as denoting the "conduct of conduct." In other words, government is "any more or less calculated and rational activity, undertaken by a multiplicity of authorities and agencies, employing a variety of techniques and forms of knowledge, that seeks to shape conduct by working through the desires, aspirations, interests and beliefs of various actors."[18] Thus, governmentality is a (neoliberal) technology of power as it induces free subjects to control their behavior and optimize their actions through techniques of observation, calculation, and administration. The concept of governmentality has been taken up by feminist IR scholars and has mostly been applied to analyze the strategy of gender mainstreaming in international organizations. Gender mainstreaming is an interesting example insofar as it comprises disciplinary practices of benchmarking, monitoring, and evaluation. These studies theorize gender mainstreaming as a technology of government, through which gendered identities are shaped and gender relations are governed.[19] Lynne Phillips, for instance, shows for the case of the United Nations Food and Agriculture Organization how gender mainstreaming activities seek to put the responsibility of food security on rural women by shaping their subjectivities as active and knowledgeable agents in regard to food and by creating the image of the "new rural woman."[20] In this way regulatory practices of gender mainstreaming are infused with specific ways of knowing about gender roles. New subjectivities are produced on the basis of the idea that "women feed the world" while stereotypes about gender roles remain intact.

In a nutshell, feminist studies referring to a Foucauldian framework conceptualize gender politics in international governance as discursively constructed and/or as a technique of government that reproduces and reinforces traditional gender roles. Thus, they shift the focus of attention away from androcentric power asymmetries toward the productive dimension of power inherent in gender politics themselves.

Masculinities, intersectionality, and justice for LGBTI persons

Feminist strategies to make global governance structures more inclusive have long placed the rights and empowerment of women at the center of attention. This focus on women has become a target of critique: for making women into the problem, for obscuring multiple and intersecting structures of inequality, and for hiding the role of men in the continuation of women's subordination. Partially in response to this critique, feminists and gender experts in the 1980s shifted the focus from women to gender, replacing the Women-in-Development approach with the Gender-in-Development approach, and in the 1990s introduced gender mainstreaming in order to address the way in which gender is embedded in all policies and programs. The express intent of these shifts was to make visible relationships of power between women and men and to meet these power relationships head on. In addition, feminist scholarship and politics in international governance have developed a much broader understanding of gender that includes a problematization of men and masculinities; bringing into view intersecting status positions and diversity among women; and making visible heteronormative foundations of international governance structures as well as LGBTI identities and claims for inclusion.

Gender theory puts in the center of analysis not only women, but also the structured relationship between women and men and the relational construction of *masculinity*. Theorists of masculinity have followed feminist theorists in emphasizing that characteristics associated with men are an outcome of cultural and historical practices. Accordingly, masculinities vary depending on cultural and institutional contexts. However, theorists of masculinity also have emphasized that these identities are always constructed in relation to femininity, and typically in a way that subordinates femininities to masculinity. Furthermore, multiple masculinities coexist, with one type of masculinity emerging as hegemonic. The problem of patriarchy is thus reformulated as a problem of hegemonic masculinity.[21]

The notion of hegemonic masculinity has been deployed most productively in the area of security governance, an area dominated by men and masculine cultures. Feminist academics have long unveiled the privileging of masculine values and practices and the parallel denigration of femininity in foreign policy and security establishments, militaries, and peacekeeping operations. They have argued that this produces a variety of dysfunctional outcomes, from sex trafficking by peacekeepers and sexual violence in wartime to the systematic exclusion of women from processes of post-war reconstruction. While a number of Security Council resolutions in the new millennium have formulated an agenda on "women, peace, and security," they have largely failed to problematize structures of gender subordination and associated militarist masculinities. The promise of a gender approach that does not reduce gender to women and problematizes gendered power relations thus remains to be realized in the area of security governance, and continues to form the basis of critical feminist strategizing and theorizing.[22]

Another reaction to the "woman-centeredness" of international gender politics has been the claim to understand women as shaped by diverse social dimensions beyond gender. Critiques from Third World women in the 1980s began to question whether women across the globe really have common interests. At the UN women's conferences this became visible in arguments over the question of whether racism in South Africa and the Israeli–Palestinian conflict were feminist issues. While feminists from the North considered government discussions of these matters a distraction from the "real" issue, i.e. gender inequality, self-identified Third World feminists regarded these topics as a matter of life and death and a crucial part of their politics. They questioned whether Western feminists spoke for the world's women. This type of argument received an academic formulation in Chandra Mohanty's trenchant critique of Western feminist scholarship as colonial, exercising power by producing the "Third World Woman" as a singular and monolithic subject.[23] Today feminists have embraced the understanding that feminist politics must recognize the "intersectionality" of status positions, i.e. they must recognize that women are very differently located depending on their place in the international system, their race, class, and other markers of difference. In some international organizations, such as the European Union, this new approach has led to a shift from gender mainstreaming to "diversity mainstreaming" and the effort to treat markers of difference simultaneously. While feminists value this recognition of the complexity of the politics of difference on the one hand, they also have been weary of tendencies to set gender equal to other status positions, thereby obscuring the profoundly constitutive character of gender for the formation of core identities and the relational logic of gender producing structural subordination.

One particular dimension that plays into intersectional forms of marginalization is that of gender identity beyond the heteronormative frame in the form of heterosexual desire and the unambiguous construction of a male–female binary. LGBTI activists have long drawn attention to the discriminatory consequences of heteronormativity, and they increasingly frame it as a concern of global justice. Whether such activism falls under the umbrella of feminist politics is contested; yet the theoretical suggestion that both sex and gender, bodies and identities are a matter of social construction lends itself to understanding the problematique of sexual identity as linked with processes of gendering. If academics argue about the matter, the Vatican and the American religious right seem to have made the connection. In various UN forums and in alliance with fundamentalists of various religious shades they have fiercely contested using the term "gender," considering it a Trojan horse that makes it possible to claim rights for LGBTI persons and thus undermine what they consider the "natural family."[24]

Indeed, the matter of LGBTI rights is one of the most contested in current human rights politics. It has received some support from international courts, in particular the European Court of Human Rights, but finds considerable opposition in more political forums, such as the Human Rights Council. This is not surprising since homosexuality continues to be prohibited in more than one-third of countries globally, and in seven countries it is punishable by death.[25] Because it makes visible the link between compulsory heterosexuality and gender subordination, the claim of LGBTI activists for human rights has been particularly threatening to reactionary patriarchal ideologies that construe women's secondary status as a natural outcome of a god-given, reproductive imperative.

Conclusion

The encounter of feminist activists with international organizations and global governance constitutes a particular kind of power politics, one in which the state is not the main actor and nongovernmental actors seek to win international organizations and governance structures for their emancipatory agendas. Through their engagement with international organizations feminists seek to change gendered power relations. Their focus is on gender as a socio-political construct and as an organizer of international policies and discourses. International norms in a broad range of issue areas typically have been silent on gender and in claiming gender neutrality often have inadvertently reproduced gendered power relations. From a feminist perspective, international governance in this way perpetuates masculine rule, and such masculine hegemony deserves to be attacked.

Successful feminist agenda setting in some issue areas has begun to shake masculine hegemony through the creation of international law, such as CEDAW, and through organizational strategies such as gender mainstreaming. In other words, feminist politics has activated the power of norms to influence international agendas and governments worldwide. In these efforts, international feminist politics, like all politics that attacks fundamental commitments of individuals and institutions, encounters resistance that provides a challenge for what we have called "agenda keeping." Feminist agendas are being co-opted for various purposes and translated into multiple contexts. While feminist discourses thus have come to pervade the antechambers of power, they sometimes have become distant from the feminist critiques that spawned their formulation.

Processes of co-optation join the logic of governmentality to generate a new type of power politics as feminism has become a part of international government in this way. A narrow focus on women has functioned to obscure the diversity of experiences of women differently located, and it has cemented a binary between women and men. The LGBTI challenge has made visible the exclusionary effects of such politics and shown the shortcomings of feminist governmentality. Feminist ambiguity towards engaging with nation-states thus is replicated in engagements with international organizations.

Feminist research of international organizations and global governance has as its object the power politics enacted in these structures. It seeks to comprehend the way in which international feminist commitments can generate change, the mechanisms of power that obstruct such change, and the disciplining and exclusions that are generated as feminists engage with international power structures. Feminist researchers share with movement activists an interest in emancipatory knowledge, seeking to overcome the seemingly endless continuation of gender subordination globally.

Additional reading

1. Gülay Caglar, Elisabeth Prügl, and Susanne Zwingel, eds., *Feminist Strategies in International Governance* (London: Routledge, 2013).
2. Devaki Jain, *Women, Development, and the UN: A Sixty-Year Quest for Equality and Justice* (Bloomington: Indiana University Press, 2005).
3. Annica Kronsell and Erika Svedberg, eds., *Making Gender, Making War: Violence, Military and Peacekeeping Practices* (New York: Routledge, 2012).
4. Shirin M. Rai and Georgina Waylen, eds., *Global Governance: Feminist Perspectives* (Basingstoke and New York: Palgrave Macmillan, 2008).
5. Laura Shepherd, ed., *Gender Matters in Global Politics: A Feminist Introduction to International Relations* (London, New York: Routledge, 2010).

Notes

1 Sandra Harding, *The Science Question in Feminism* (Ithaca: Cornell University Press, 1986).
2 Arvonne S. Fraser and Irene Tinker, eds., *Developing Power: How Women Transformed International Development* (New York: The Feminist Press, 2004); Jutta Joachim, *Agenda Setting, the UN and NGOs: Gender Violence and Reproductive Rights* (Washington, DC: Georgetown University Press, 2007); Carol Cohn, "Mainstreaming Gender in UN Security Policy: A Path to Political Transformation," in *Global Governance: Feminist Perspectives*, eds. Shirin M. Rai and Georgina Waylen (New York: Palgrave Macmillan, 2008), 185–206; Shahra Razavi, "Governing the Economy for Gender Equality? Challenges of Regulation," in *Feminist Strategies in International Governance*, eds. Gülay Caglar, Elisabeth Prügl, and Susanne Zwingel (London: Routledge, 2013), 217–232.
3 Jacqui True, "Mainstreaming Gender in International Institutions," in *Gender Matters in Global Politics: A Feminist Introduction to International Relations*, ed. Laura. J. Sheperd (London and New York: Routledge, 2010), 189–203; Caroline Moser, "Has Gender Mainstreaming Failed? A Comment on International Development Agency Experiences in the South," *International Feminist Journal of Politics* 7, no. 4 (December 2005): 576–590.
4 Catherine Eschle and Bice Maiguashca, *Making Feminist Sense of the Global Justice Movement* (Lanham: Rowman & Littlefield, 2010).
5 For an optimistic assessment, see Mark M. Gray, Miki Caul Kittilson, and Wayne Sandholtz, "Women and Globalization: A Study of 180 Countries, 1975–2000," *International Organization* 60, no. 2 (2006): 293–333; for a pessimistic one, see Emilie Hafner-Burton, Kiyoteru Tsutsui, and John W. Meyer, "International Human Rights Law and the Politics of Legitimation: Repressive States and Human Rights Treaties", *International Sociology* 23, no. 1 (2008): 115–141.
6 Doreen Massey, *For Space* (London: Sage, 2005); Ulf Hannerz, *Transnational Connections: Culture, Peoples, Places* (New York: Routledge, 1996); Sally Engle Merry, "Constructing a

Global Law—Violence Against Women and the Human Rights System," *Law and Social Inquiry* 28, no. 4 (2003): 941–977.

7 Inderpal Grewal and Caren Kaplan, eds., *Scattered Hegemonies: Postmodernity and Transnational Feminist Practices* (Minneapolis: University of Minnesota Press, 1994); Amrita Basu, ed., *The Challenge of Local Feminisms: Women's Movements in Global Perspective* (Boulder: Westview Press, 1995).

8 Uché U. Ewelukwa, "Centuries of Globalization; Centuries of Exclusion: African Women, Human Rights, and the 'New' International Trade Regime," *Berkeley Journal of Gender, Law and Justice* 20 (2005): 75–149; Lynn Savery, *Engendering the State: The International Diffusion of Women's Human Rights* (New York: Routledge, 2007); Kim D. Reiman, "A View from the Top: International Politics, Norms, and the Worldwide Growth of NGOs," *International Studies Quarterly* 50, no. 1 (2006): 45–67.

9 Devaki Jain, *Women, Development, and the UN: A Sixty-Year Quest for Equality and Justice* (Bloomington: Indiana University Press, 2005); Valentine M. Moghadam, *Globalizing Women: Transnational Feminist Networks* (Baltimore: Johns Hopkins University Press, 2005).

10 Mona Lena Krook and Jacqui True, "Rethinking the Life Cycles of International Norms: The United Nations and the Global Promotion of Gender Equality," in *European Journal of International Relations* 18, no. 1 (2012): 103–127.

11 Peggy Levitt and Sally Merry, "Vernacularization on the Ground: Local Uses of Global Women's Rights in Peru, China, India and the United States," *Global Networks* 9, no. 4 (2009): 441–461.

12 Rebecca Foley, "Muslim Women's Challenge to Islamic Law: The Case of Malaysia," *International Feminist Journal of Politics* 6, no. 1 (2004): 53–84.

13 E.g. Joachim, *Agenda Setting*; Robert O'Brien, Anne Marie Goetz, Jan Aart Scholte, and Marc Williams, *Contesting Global Governance* (Cambridge: Cambridge University Press, 2000); Anne Winslow, ed., *Women, Politics, and the United Nations* (Westport: Greenwood Publishing Group, 1995); Nüket Kardam, *Bringing Women In: Women's Issues in International Development Programs* (Boulder, London: Lynne Rienner, 1991).

14 Steven Lukes, "Power and the Battle of Hearts and Minds: On the Bluntness of Soft Power," in *Power in World Politics*, eds. Felix Berenskoetter and M.J. Williams (London and New York: Routledge, 2007), 90; cf. Jane Parpart, "Gender, Power and Governance in a Globalizing World," *Development Research Series*, Working Paper no. 126 (Aalborg: Research Center on Development and International Relations, 2004).

15 Discourse, in a Foucauldian sense, is a set of statements and practices that produce both the subjects and objects of knowledge. See Michel Foucault, "Truth and Power," in *Power/Knowledge. Michel Foucault: Selected Interviews and Other Writings 1972–1977*, ed. Colin Gordon (New York: Pantheon Books, 1980), 117.

16 See, for example, Laura J. Shepherd, "Loud Voices Behind the Wall: Gender Violence and the Violent Reproduction of the International," *Millennium: Journal of International Studies* 34, no. 2 (2006): 377–401; Gülay Caglar, "Gender Knowledge and Economic Knowledge in the World Bank and UNDP: Multiple Meanings of Gender Budgeting," in *Gender Knowledge and Knowledge Networks in International Political Economy*, eds. Christoph Scherrer and Brigitte Young (Baden-Baden: Nomos, 2010), 55–74.

17 Megan MacKenzie, "Empowerment Boom or Bust? Assessing Women's Post-Conflict Empowerment Initiatives," *Cambridge Review of International Affairs* 22, no. 2 (2009), 201.

18 Mitchel Dean, *Governmentality: Power and Rule in Modern Society*, 2nd edition (London, Thousand Oaks and New Delhi: Sage Publications, 2010), 18.

19 For example Lynne Phillips, "Gender Mainstreaming: The Global Governance of Women?," *Canadian Journal of Development Studies* 26, no. 1 (2005), 651–663; Magdalena Bexell, "Global Governance, Gains and Gender," *International Feminist Journal of Politics* 14, no. 3 (2012): 389–407; Audrey Reeves, "Feminist Knowledge and Emerging Governmentality in UN Peacekeeping: Patterns of Co-optation and Empowerment," *International Feminist*

Journal of Politics 14, no. 3 (2012): 348–369; Elisabeth Prügl, "Diversity Management and Gender Mainstreaming as Technologies of Government," *Politics and Gender* 7, no. 1 (2011): 71–89.

20 Lynne Phillips, "Gender Mainstreaming: The Global Governance of Women?," 656ff.

21 R. W. Connell and James W. Messerschmidt,, "Hegemonic Masculinity: Rethinking the Concept," *Gender and Society* 19, no. 6 (2005): 829–859.

22 Maria Eriksson Baaz and Maria Stern, "Why Do Soldiers Rape? Masculinity, Violence, and Sexuality in the Armed Forces in the Congo (DRC)," *International Studies Quarterly* 53, no. 2 (2009): 495–518; Christine Bell and Catherine O'Rourke, "Peace Agreements or Pieces of Paper? The Impact of UNSC Resolution 1325 on Peace Processes and Their Agreements," *International Comparative Law Quarterly* 59 (October 2010): 941–980; Cohn, "Mainstreaming Gender in UN Security Policy," 185–206; Reeves, "Feminist Knowledge," 1–22.

23 Chandra Talpade Mohanty, "Under Western Eyes: Feminist Scholarship and Colonial Discourse," *Feminist Review* 30 (Autumn 1988): 61–88.

24 Doris E. Buss, "Finding the Homosexual in Women's Rights: The Christian Right in International Politics," *International Feminist Journal of Politics* 6, no. 2 (2004), 257–284.

25 Joke Swiebel and Dennis van der Veur, "Hate Crimes Against Lesbian, Gay, Bisexual and Transgender Persons and the Policy Response of International Governmental Organisations," *Netherlands Quarterly of Human Rights* 27, no. 4 (2009): 485–524. Homosexuality draws the death penalty in Iran, Mauritania, Saudi Arabia, Sudan, Yemen, and in some parts of Nigeria and Somalia. Ibid., 513.

Post-Hegemonic Multilateralism

Amitav Acharya

It is fashionable in academic and policy debates to ask, does multilateralism have a future? A more appropriate question is which multilateralism has a future? There is little question that, barring a global cataclysm, some form of multilateralism will remain as a building block of global order. But the traditional conceptualization of multilateralism is under challenge. That version was too beholden to the state, American power, Western leadership, and the global level of interactions. What is coming in its place is as yet indeterminate, but I propose one possible direction, post-hegemonic multilateralism.

This chapter begins by examining the dominant version in the post-World War II period, which I call "hegemonic multilateralism." It continues by analyzing three principal challenges: civil society, emerging powers, and regionalism. Despite their limitations, they could redefine the residual elements of the multilateral order developed under American hegemony. While some liberal protagonists hope and foresee that the old multilateralism might outlive US power, I argue that the challenges are strong enough to make the prospects for change greater than commonly thought. Moreover, these challenges could also form the basis for a new "post-hegemonic multilateralism."

Some basics

I use the term post-hegemonic multilateralism to refer broadly to formal and informal interactions among states and other actors, at global and regional levels, on the basis of common principles and institutions that are not dominated by a single power or group of powers. Instead, leadership is diffuse and shared among actors that are not bound into a hierarchical relationship linked to differential material capabilities. This concept differs not only from the classic hegemonic stability theory, but also from its more refined siblings, including: the notion of multilateralism as a unique product of post-war American hegemony: the neoliberal institutionalist claim that institutions originally created by the hegemon would continue after hegemony; and the idea of a constitutional order under which a hegemon creates and controls legally defined hierarchical institutions to trade its benevolent self-restraint for the deference and compliance of the lesser actors.

The concept also takes us beyond the past debate between liberals and critical theorists on the future of multilateralism. Liberals, led by Robert Keohane, believed that multilateral regimes created by the United States as the hegemonic power could survive its decline on the strength of common interests and such continuing benefits as providing information, lowering transactions costs, preventing cheating, and reducing overall uncertainty.[1] The critical perspectives group led by Robert Cox argued that institutions that promote the values and purpose of the capitalist world order could be seriously challenged for their deeply anti-egalitarian, coercive, and exploitative roles, whether the hegemon itself declines or not.

In some respects, post-hegemonic multilateralism is similar to Cox's notion of a "counter-hegemonic" bloc, which is "anchored in a broader diffusion of power, in which a large number of collective forces, including states, achieve some agreement upon universal principles of an alternative order without dominance."[2] But unlike Cox, who uses "post-hegemonic" and "counter-hegemonic" interchangeably, I define the former as a distinctive and broader category. The idea of a counter-hegemonic bloc stresses resistance from social movements. Despite admitting a role for states, Cox nonetheless argued that a "reinvigorated civil society" could genuinely reconstruct a world order because "very little can be accomplished towards fundamental change through the state system as it now exists."[3] But resistance to hegemony and its key organizing principles can also come from other states (especially emerging powers and regions) and non-state actors—including extremist groups.[4]

There is no necessary correlation between hegemonic decline and post-hegemonic multilateralism. One should not assume that the former will automatically trigger greater resistance to its rules and institutions. A declining hegemon may soften resistance by embracing multilateralism as a legitimizing device. Post-hegemonic multilateralism may emerge even when the hegemon remains physically dominant and committed to peaceful and cooperative conduct and hence does not provoke much resistance. Other forces come into play here, with or without hegemonic decline, including the rise of transnational issues, non-state actors, and new regional and non-Western centers of influence. These forces will severely challenge and subvert the purpose and governance structure of the hegemonic multilateralism more than the key texts of hegemonic multilateralism suggest.

While agreeing that one should not underestimate the continued authority and adaptability of existing state-led institutions to changing circumstances that call for a more socially inclusive and democratic multilateralism,[5] multilateralism could be more fundamentally challenged and reinvented "after hegemony" and "without victory" if weaker or newly empowered actors disagree with the supposed material and normative benefits of an existing framework relative to the costs imposed and the vulnerabilities induced. Even the "stickiness" of institutions resulting from their socializing functions, stressed by constructivists, may not spare them from a fundamental restructuring over the long term if these new forces challenge old norms and socialization frameworks associated with hegemonic multilateralism.

What are the catalysts of post-hegemonic multilateralism? Most analysts would quickly point to the changes in the international distribution of power, as found in the discourse on "rising" or "emerging" powers. But to conceive it simply as a function of a "power shift" is misleading because it also entails a fundamental reshaping of ideational forces and modes and networks of socialization, especially those at the regional levels. Post-hegemonic multilateralism can be rooted in the changing aspirations for autonomy and identity, a central political norm of regional forms of multilateralism in the developing world, as well as political changes in the domestic sphere of the actors, such as nationalism and democratization. Other important factors that could move a group of states to question their continued acquiescence with a hegemonic framework include the need to respond to such transnational challenges as climate change or labor migration. Some such problems are often induced or aggravated by the hegemon's ideological (i.e. neoliberal) paradigm. As a result, a variety of actors may be moved towards a new sense of multilateral purpose and identity even under the material conditions of continued hegemony. They may be prompted to redefine and broaden their multilateral space beyond what was permitted under a framework of hegemonic multilateralism.

Hegemonic multilateralism

John Ruggie's influential 1993 edited volume *Multilateralism Matters* embodies the traditional or hegemonic concept of multilateralism, which was dominant during the Cold War and in the immediate post-Cold War period. Here, he defines multilateralism as "coordinating relations among three or more states in accordance with certain principles,"[6] and thus claims to improve upon a prior "nominal" definition by Keohane, for whom multilateralism was simply "the practice of coordinating national policies in groups of three or more states."[7] Multilateralism is not just a matter of numbers; Ruggie specifies the qualitative and normative aspects of multilateralism, the latter embodying certain principles, such as indivisibility, non-discrimination, and diffuse reciprocity. Compared to Keohane's functional definition, Ruggie's is a constructivist formulation before constructivism became widespread.

Ruggie's other, more important claim had less to do with the creation than with the creator. While multilateralism was not necessarily a post-war American invention, "Looking more closely at the post-World War II situation . . . it was less the fact of American *hegemony* that accounts for the explosion of multilateral arrangements than of *American* hegemony."[8] Ruggie contrasted the post-war, American-inspired and American-led multilateralism with the New Economic Order of Nazi Germany.[9] That order functioned as a sphere of influence, lacking in openness and equal access, even though Germany often imported more from its partners than it exported to them. True multilateralism must be non-discriminatory, as enshrined in the General Agreement on Tariff and Trade's (later World Trade Organization's) "most favored nation" principle.

Curiously, Ruggie does not cite the example of Japan's Greater East Asia Co-Prosperity Sphere, although it too exhibited sphere-of-influence qualities, albeit that it was presented as a collective arrangement among three or more states.

In this explication of multilateralism, the state is the primary actor. The place and role of civil society or non-state actors, which would present a powerful challenge to the dominant post-war conceptualization of multilateralism led by Keohane and Ruggie, are discussed below. But the close association between multilateralism and American hegemony remained less challenged, even by those who questioned the statist concept of multilateralism and proposed civil society multilateralism as a "counterhegemonic" solution. This leads to the question that is central to this chapter: could multilateralism be conceivable and viable without US sponsorship and leadership?

Part of the answer to this question lies in *Multilateralism Matters'* take on regionalism. For Ruggie multilateralism is not an exclusively global phenomenon. Regional organizations can be multilateral because they too may abide by the principles of indivisibility and diffuse reciprocity. This helpfully challenged a view which tends to view regionalism and multilateralism (or universalism) as mutually competitive and exclusive.[10] It is revealing that *Multilateralism Matters* contained three chapters on Europe—the North Atlantic Treaty Organization (NATO), the European Community, and the Conference and later Organization for Security and Co-operation in Europe—as examples of such region-specific multilateralism but left out all other parts of the world. Moreover, this omission did not merit an explanation except for the Asia-Pacific. Here Ruggie contrasted Europe's growing turn to multilateralism, including the adaptation of NATO "to the new European geopolitical realities," rather than to a "return to a system of competitive bilateral alliances" with the Asia-Pacific region's lack of multilateralism. "In the Asia-Pacific, there had been no NATO, no European Union, no 'Helsinki-like process' through which to begin the minimal task of mutual confidence building."[11] Yet there was no explanation of why this was the case.

Why was there no multilateralism in the Asia-Pacific? If one accepts that the United States intrinsically favored a multilateral approach, why did it not encourage an Asia-Pacific version of NATO? Surely, the absence of a US interest in creating a NATO in Asia would challenge the close association between multilateralism and US hegemony that *Multilateralism Matters* posited. One answer to this puzzle could be that the power asymmetries between the United States and its putative multilateral partners were so large that a multilateral approach would have amounted to free-riding on the part of the allies without significantly adding to the US strategic capacity to meet the Soviet and Chinese threats.[12] Challenging this, Christopher Hemmer and Peter Katzenstein offer a constructivist explanation, focusing less on the "power gap" and more on identity dissonance. Genuine multilateralism requires a measure of collective identification among partners. While post-war US strategic planners identified with their European partners, who "could be trusted with the additional power a multilateral institution would give them," they "did not believe that the Southeast Asian states could be trusted with the increased influence a multilateral institution would offer, nor was there any sense that these states deserved such a multilateral structure."[13] Yet evidence suggests that while both views have some merit, a third view that deserves attention is that the United States under the Eisenhower administration wanted, but could not get, a viable multilateral security framework because of normative opposition from a group of nationalist leaders in Asia, who saw an unequal alliance with the US as an unacceptable form of neocolonial dominance.[14]

In *After Victory*, John Ikenberry offered a powerful supplement to the idea of hegemonic multilateralism. While he agreed that multilateralism went hand in hand with American hegemony, which described how the United States had pursued multilateralism as the new global hegemon, Ikenberry explained why it pursued multilateralism. Through multilateral institutions a hegemon can exercise strategic self-restraint by institutionally self-binding itself in return for loyalty and compliance from weaker and subordinate actors. In such a constitutional order, "power is tamed by making it less consequential."[15] Why does the hegemon resort to institution-binding? The short answer is "to get the willing participation of and compliance of other states." Because it "has an interest in conserving its power,"[16] by offering "to limit its own autonomy and ability to exercise power arbitrarily," the leading state gains recognition and legitimacy.[17] Multilateralism is thus the key to the hegemon's ability to gain trust, respect, and legitimacy for its preponderant power.

Despite this concession to legitimation, *After Victory*'s focus was still overwhelmingly on hegemonic power and initiative. It is the victorious hegemon that crafts the institutional framework and bargaining process through which it can self-bind. The weaker states merely "accept the deal,"[18] mainly to mitigate their fear of domination or abandonment.[19] They do receive credible commitments from the hegemon to refrain from exploitation and domination,[20] but does the shadow of coercion disappear in the event of non-compliance with the hegemon's wishes? Ignored in this hegemonic universe are possibilities that institutions created by hegemonic power, even if they are not primarily motivated by a desire to secure its objectives through non-coercive means (or "strategic restraint"), might not still be viewed as legitimate or benign by the weaker states because they fundamentally represent an unequal relationship and a form of dominance. For every NATO, there are two examples of hegemonic illegitimacy: the so-called multilateral security systems proposed initiated by the United States in the Third World, such as the Southeast Asia Treaty Organization and the Central Treaty Organization, the rejection of which was part of the basis of the Nonaligned Movement.

Hence, other possibilities for multilateralism suggest themselves. One such form is "extrication" as opposed to "binding." Weaker states may develop institutions to keep out all great powers, including the hegemon, whose power and purpose, even with the offer of self-binding multilateralism, they normatively reject. Many Asian nationalist leaders, indeed leaders from the Third World, rejected US security and economic multilateralism during the Cold War because it conflicted with the normative aspirations for autonomy and equality. Another possibility is that multilateralism might emerge not only "after victory" but also "after defeat." Even if its global hegemony continues, a hegemon may sometimes be "defeated" or seriously exhausted in limited wars (Vietnam in the past, possibly Afghanistan today), thereby compromising the credibility of its strategic commitment. Such situations may provide opportunities and incentives for institution-building, especially for local actors. A regional grouping of small and weak states, the Association of Southeast Asian Nations (ASEAN), did this after the Vietnam War, although it was also inspired by the normative quest for regional autonomy.

Indigenously developed regional norms may not only frustrate any form of multi-lateralism proposed by outside powers. Because of distinctive local conditions, material and normative, weaker states may develop alternative institutions to a globally hegemonic order that are more suited to their own specific goals and identities. Such institutions may exclude stronger powers, especially if the objective is management of internal security or development (such as the doctrine of "comprehensive security" in Asia). They may also socialize stronger powers on their own terms and on the basis of locally developed norms, as opposed to principles and modalities laid down by the hegemon. One finds examples in Latin America's success in securing an end to the Monroe Doctrine in the early twentieth century, ASEAN's Zone of Peace, Freedom and Neutrality during the Cold War. Materially stronger powers, unable to secure local legitimacy for institutions proposed by themselves, may well accept institutional designs that are proposed and developed by weaker states and which constrain their behavior. It is impossible to understand the origin and growth of multilateral institutions in Asia today—especially ASEAN and its Regional Forum and the East Asia Summit—without taking into consideration such possibilities for post-hegemonic multilateralism.

Multilateralism: old and "new"

The first major challenge to the hegemonic conceptualization of multilateralism came in the post-Cold War period and was especially catalyzed by the concept of "new multilateralism," which evolved through the work of Robert Cox and *Multilateralism and the United Nations System*.[21] The "new multilateralism" made a number of claims: new multilateralism differs from existing notions of multilateralism in three different respects. The first is that it is an evolving, rather than a finished product. Second, it is a bottom-up, rather than state-centric phenomenon as the role of states has to be seen in conjunction with that of social forces, especially civil society groups. The third aspect is its "post-hegemonic organizing," which "acknowledges the differences in assumptions about the social world and attempts to find common ground for cooperation. In the place of universalistic principles of neoclassical economics, one is aware of alternative methods of social organizing and cultural diversity."[22]

The hallmark of this concept was not just embracing a more broad and dynamic scope of multilateralism but also the focus of the idea on protest and resistance—as noted earlier, "counter-hegemonic" seems more appropriate than "post-hegemonic" or "new." But "new multilateralism" did suffer from its own uncertainties and controversies, some of which are associated with the concept of a global civil society,[23] the main platform for resistance to the hegemonic world order. Given the diversity of its constituents in terms of locations, issues, strategies of mobilization, and normative orientations, it is difficult to convince skeptics why global civil society is any more coherent and meaningful than such terms as "international system" or "international community" that underpin traditional multilateralism. Transnational civil society, which suggests civil society activism across borders but not necessarily on a global scale, may be more apt. But even here controversies persist over "who elected the NGOs" or the legitimacy of social movements "to substitute for the state."[24] Moreover, given that its leadership and discursive agenda were centered in the West, new multilateralism was especially susceptible to a "moral cosmopolitanism" bias, which privileged the role of Western transnational moral agents at the expense of non-Western regional or local actors. For example, the dominant explanation of transnational human rights advocacy, the "boomerang" model, privileged the role of transnational actors and "paid far less attention to the local embodiments of human rights norms in the developing world."[25] Although in it local groups initiate "the process, their location, obscure language, and marginality have limited scholarly inquiry."[26] Yet the agency of local civil society groups is critical: "Transnational NGOs and networks can monitor, inform, and advocate all they want, but without serious investments of time and effort by local human rights champions, nothing much will change on the ground."[27]

The new multilateralism concept was overshadowed by two developments in global affairs. First, it remained, at least for a while, more of an aspiration than a reality because of the sudden appearance of the unipolar moment, and its most extreme manifestation —the unilateralism of George. W. Bush's foreign and security policy leading to the invasion of Iraq. This led to considerable soul searching and concern about the future of multilateralism as a whole, whether old or "new."[28] Although the Bush challenge to multilateralism would be explained by some liberals as the result of a short-term hijacking by a small power elite, the neo-cons, rather than as a fundamental deviation from the American commitment to multilateralism, the Iraq invasion raised the question whether there was anything really natural or structural about the association of American power and purpose with multilateralism. Indeed, some would question whether power (hence the traditional concept of hegemony) matters as much in multilateralism as had been claimed by previous scholars: "whilst today many observers suggest that pre-eminent US power is enabling—or perhaps motivating—the country to ignore or undermine [multilateral] institutions, in the past theorists of international relations argued on the contrary that *declining* power resulted in declining support for multilateral institutions and regimes."[29] This supported a fundamental element of new multilateralism, but it did render it more aspirational than might have been the case.

Second, the new multilateralism highlighted the role of social movements but was less cognizant of the role of emerging powers in resisting and reshaping hegemonic multilateralism. This is presumably because in the 1990s the BRICs were not yet recognized (Goldman-Sachs coined the term in 2001 to designate Brazil, Russia, India, and China) and the G20 was only finance ministers and not the more prominent platform it has been since 2008.

Multilateralism and the emerging powers: much ado about something

The concept of emerging powers gained currency following the BRICS (which has included South Africa since 2010), the G20, and other clubs such as IBSA (India, Brazil, and South Africa), BRICSAM (Brazil, Russia, India, China, South Africa, Mexico). But there is little question that the emerging powers and their clubs constitute the second major challenge to hegemonic multilateralism and necessitate a re-conceptualization of multilateralism generally. Here, the task is to figure out who count as the principal actors in global multilateralism and also what to consider as issue areas.

Yet, this task is far from complete or uncontroversial. The term "emerging powers" is hardly coherent or uncontested. The G20 has emerged as the key site for attempts to redefine and re-legitimize multilateralism today with a focus on economics and finance. But questions cloud the legitimacy of the G20 itself. Its membership criteria remain shrouded in controversy, including the overrepresentation of Europe and absence of such important players in the developing world as Egypt and Nigeria. This is especially important if the G20 is to go beyond its initial role in stabilizing the world financial system, where it has proven its worth, and take on a political and security role, as some proponents advocate.

As the most visible institution featuring the emerging powers, the G20 is supposed to represent, as Andrew Cooper put it, "universalistic values"—i.e. values "favoring equity and justice for the less powerful and seeking curtailment of unilateral or plurilateral or coalitional activity by the most powerful."[30] Yet, it is not clear whether the G20 really embodies these new principles that could form the basis for a post-hegemonic multilateralism. Many of the emerging power members of the G20, including China and India, remain beholden to Westphalian principles of sovereignty and resistant to emerging principles such as the responsibility to protect, and stand accused of resource mercantilism (especially China).

A novelty of the G20 is that its membership is supposed to bridge the traditional North–South divide. Yet is the G20 representative of the developing world or reflective of a new fault-line between the "poor South" and the "power South?" Unless and until these issues are addressed, the potential of the emerging powers in general and the G20 in particular as the catalyst for a post-hegemonic multilateralism will remain unfulfilled.

Yet, while the influence of the emerging powers may have been exaggerated, they do challenge the existing multilateral framework that has underpinned the post-war order. It is inconceivable that their demands would not lead to some institutional reform and leadership change in existing multilateralism. The early literature on multilateralism paid more attention to the role of institutions as the arbiter of the legitimacy of state action than to the legitimacy of the institutions themselves. The debate over the Iraq war was not about the legitimacy of existing multilateralism but of action by the United States without multilateralism—the UN failed to authorize the use of force.[31] But the emerging powers discourse highlights the issue of legitimacy within the existing multilateral structure. Here, the issue hinges on improving the representation and decision-making authority of the emerging powers through reform of the Security Council or additional changes to the voting structures of the Washington-based financial institutions. As such, the emerging powers phenomenon challenges not only American but Western dominance over the traditional post-war multilateralism.

Regionalism as the foundation

A third challenge to the dominant post-war conceptualization of multilateralism is an old if changing phenomenon: the relationship between regionalism and multilateralism. If multilateralism is a matter of both interactions and principles, whose interactions and principles might they be? As noted, the literature on multilateralism no longer views it as antithetical to regionalism but complementary. At least some forms of regional interactions can be multilateral if they embrace certain principles. But need they exclusively be American-led global and European-based regional interactions and principles?

The key principle of multilateralism is inclusiveness. If so, then privileging NATO and the European Union and neglecting regional multilateralism in other parts of the world, a hallmark of hegemonic multilateralism, makes little sense. First, was or is NATO a truly multilateral organization? It is based on the principle of collective defense (security against an outside threat) rather than collective security (security against an inside threat), a fact that earlier writers on collective security had correctly recognized, but which Ruggie and others in the post-Cold War had conveniently ignored.[32] One of the foremost writers on collective security, Inis Claude reminds us that "the label has frequently been attached to NATO and other alliances, despite the fact that collective security was originally proposed as a substitute for the alliance system, a way of managing international relations that was deemed incompatible with, antithetical to, and infinitely more promising than the old system that featured competitive alliances."[33] While NATO operates on the basis of indivisibility, that principle is applied only to its members. Despite its post-Cold War expansion of membership and roles, it is not an inclusive enough grouping to qualify the true meaning of multilateralism, even for the whole of the European region. On the contrary, the continued existence and expansion of NATO might have undermined other, more inclusive security frameworks such as the Organization for Security and Co-operation in Europe (OSCE).

At the same time, a host of regional organizations have been more inclusive and non-discriminatory. With limited exceptions, they have been fairly inclusive—the Organization of American States for Cuba, the Organization for African Unity for South Africa under apartheid, and the Arab League for Israel inclusive. In Asia, cited by Ruggie as an antithesis of multilateralism in the Cold War, they would include ASEAN (since 1967) and "ASEAN-led" regional institutions, which emerged after the end of the Cold War. Asia also defied Ruggie's prognosis in *Multilateralism Matters*, with the creation in 1994 of the ASEAN Regional Forum, which had been widely called a multilateral institution from its inception.[34] Its underlying security formula and that of many other regional groups (including the OSCE) is common or cooperative security—different from collective security or collective defense because it does not rely on "security against" an adversary but "security with." As such, common or cooperative security frameworks do not rely on deterrence or military force, but on confidence-building measures, which can be military, political-diplomatic, and normative.

This leads to another question: is multilateralism compatible with norms and principles other than liberal ones, such as diffuse reciprocity and indivisibility (in the sense of collective security)? What about principles such as nonintervention, equality of states, and more recently human security, which militate against the organization of multilateralism on the basis of hierarchy and hegemony? Regional organizations in the Americas, Africa, Asia, and the Middle East have pursued inclusiveness and championed other principles such as anti-colonialism, anti-racism, and the norms of nonintervention and equality of states.[35] Liberal theorists often assume a close nexus between multilateralism and liberal democracy, hence multilateralism is seen as a distinctive aspect of the leadership of liberal world powers. Yet this linkage is questionable as we have seen security communities emerging out of interactions among non-democratic states.[36] We have seen that some democratic states can be anti-multilateral, while authoritarian regimes can be pro-multilateral (e.g. Singapore for the global trade regime and UN). This redefinition of multilateralism has been more commonplace in the literature on regionalism, especially what has become known as "new regionalism," where there is a greater recognition of the diversity of actors, principles, and modalities, thereby redressing some of the Euro-centrism of previous literature.[37]

To be sure, not all forms of regionalism are post-hegemonic. Some regionalisms may emerge within the sphere of influence of a regionally dominant power. In fact, such regional orders had once been advocated by Winston Churchill, Walter Lipmann, and George Liska, among others. Today, regionalism in West Africa, Southern Africa, the Russian near abroad, South Asia, and the Persian Gulf are dominated by regional powers. But this type of regional order may be the very opposite of the principles of genuine multilateralism. By contrast Asian regional institutions anchored in ASEAN are more in tune with post-hegemonic regionalism.

A role for regionalism and regions is integral to post-hegemonic multilateralism. While regionalism by itself is not sufficient to fulfill the demand and necessity for multi-lateralism, it can play an important bridging role between the emerging powers and the multilateral requirements of global governance. Many global issues have strong regional roots. Yet not all aspiring global powers that want to reinvent the existing multilateral system globally are capable of exercising regional leadership. While some emerging powers like Japan after World War II, or Indonesia in ASEAN, take an accommodationist and communitarian approach towards their neighbors, others are known for pursuing a domineering attitude. Still others fall somewhere in between. Many emerging powers are embroiled in conflicts within their own neighborhoods, which undercuts their regional legitimacy. Without regional legitimation, emerging powers may get bogged down in their own neighborhood's problems and thus undermine their capacity for global leadership. However, regional legitimation and effective regional leadership may not only free them from such neighborhood security dilemmas but also help them prepare better for a global governance role.

Conclusion: multilateralism and the invisible imperium

While the three challenges to hegemonic multilateralism emerged at the height of US global primacy, we now should reconsider the future of multilateralism in the post-unipolar era. As in the past, liberals contest the extent and implications of the changes occurring today. Some dismiss the view that the United States is a declining power and argue, as Keohane does, that "Among democracies in the world today, only the United States has the material capacity and political unity to exercise consistent global leadership."[38] Yet what may be declining is not necessarily US power but its status, legitimacy, and influence, which were also ingredients of hegemonic multilateralism. These are much more difficult to monopolize in a world of growing diversity of regions, non-state actors, and emerging powers. Others argue that the waning of US hegemony, if true at all, is not the end of the existing multilateral order because the rules and institutions established have staying power, and even the capacity to co-opt the emerging powers. Thus, Ikenberry argues that the "liberal hegemonic order" (which he also calls by other names, including "American-led liberal world order" and "American-led liberal hegemony,"[39] but which I would call American World Order) was built with "the acquiescence and support of other states"[40] but is now facing a "crisis of authority." It will endure because no alternatives—or serious prospect for transformation—have emerged. On the contrary, "the rise of non-Western powers and the growth of economic and security interdependence are creating new constituencies and pressures for liberal international order."[41]

This selective but hopeful account of the American world order sidesteps major controversies that predate the challenges acknowledged by Ikenberry, including the unipolar moment.[42] The claim that "The British and American-led liberal orders have been built in critical respects around consent"[43] vastly underplays the ever-present hand of violence and coercion in both the hegemonies, including colonialism and Cold War era interventions. The controversies are not just recent but have routinely been present, from within and outside that order, especially in the global North–South divide during the Cold War. Moreover, there are more challenges than the three that Ikenberry identifies. For example, the shifting sources of violence—the privatization of war and the rise of informal violence (i.e. the war on terror) were preceded by other redefinitions of security, including the call for human security, not a US invention that frontally challenges the "national security" paradigm developed under US hegemony.[44]

Indeed, the three principal ingredients of post-hegemonic multilateralism have not had an easy relationship with the American World Order. The United States was either opposed to or selective in its support for the forces behind them—civil society, regional order, and some if not all of the emerging powers. The relationship between the US-led multilateralism, especially economic multilateralism and global civil society, has been hostile. The United States has also been selective in its enthusiasm for regional multilateralism: supportive in Europe but not Asia. For emerging powers, it has encouraged India's emergence while resisting China's. The United States opposes the introduction of values other than its own as the basis for refining old and creating new multilateral institutions. The decline of the US hegemony could mean redefinition of existing multilateral institutions, encouragement of new forms of multilateralism, including regional multilateralism, and new coalitions of transnational and local actors. It will accentuate the three challenges to hegemonic multilateralism discussed above. While each of the three has limitations, although none of these challenges could individually suffice to unseat hegemonic multilateralism, together they could facilitate the transition to a post-hegemonic multilateralism.

Additional reading

1. Amitav Acharya, "Norm Subsidiarity and Regional Orders: Sovereignty, Regionalism and Rule Making in the Third World," *International Studies Quarterly* 55 (2011): 95–123.
2. Amitav Acharya and Barry Buzan, eds., *Non-Western International Relations Theory: Reflections on and Beyond Asia* (Oxford and New York: Routledge, 2010).
3. Mohammed Ayoob, *The Third World Security Predicament: State Making, Regional Conflict, and the International System* (Boulder: Lynne Rienner, 1995).

Notes

1 Robert O. Keohane, *After Hegemony: Cooperation and Discord in the World Political Economy* (Princeton: Princeton University Press, 1984).

2 Robert W. Cox, "Multilateralism and World Order," *Review of International Studies* 18, no. 2 (1992): 180.

3 Robert W. Cox, "Civil Society at the Turn of the Millennium: Prospects for an Alternative World Order," *Review of International Studies* 25, no. 1 (1999): 27–28.

4 Amitav Acharya, "State Sovereignty after 9/11: Disorganised Hypocrisy?," *Political Studies* 55, no. 2 (2007): 274–296; and "The Emerging Regional Architecture of World Politics," *World Politics* 59, no. 4 (2007): 629–652.

5 G. John Ikenberry, *After Victory: Institutions, Strategic Restraint, and the Rebuilding of Order after Major Wars* (Princeton: Princeton University Press, 2000); and *Liberal Leviathan: The Origins, Crisis, and Transformation of the American World Order* (Princeton: Princeton University Press, 2011).

6 John G. Ruggie, "Multilateralism: The Anatomy of an Institution," in *Multilateralism Matters: The Theory and Praxis of an Institutional Form*, ed. John G. Ruggie (New York: Columbia University Press, 1993), 8.

7 Ibid., 6.

8 Ibid., 8 (emphasis original).

9 Ibid., 9.

10 Francis Wilcox, "Regionalism and the United Nations," *International Organization* 19, no. 3 (1965): 789–811. This tendency is more common now from such economists as Jagdish Bhagwati, "Regionalism versus Multilateralism," *World Economy* 15, no. 5 (1992): 535–556.

11 Ruggie, "Multilateralism," 3, 4.

12 Donald Crone, "Does Hegemony Matter? The Reorganization of the Pacific Political Economy," *World Politics* 45, no. 4 (1993): 501–525.

13 Christopher Hemmer and Peter J. Katzenstein, "Why Is There No NATO in Asia? Collective Identity, Regionalism, and the Origins of Multilateralism," *International Organization* 56, no. 3 (2002): 588.

14 Amitav Acharya, *Whose Ideas Matter: Agency and Power in Asian Regionalism* (Ithaca: Cornell University Press, 2009).

15 Ikenberry, *After Victory*, 29.

16 Ibid., 53.

17 Ibid., 51.

18 Ibid., 56.

19 Ibid., 51.

20 Ibid., 53.

21 Cox, "Multilateralism and World Order"; Robert W. Cox, ed., *The New Realism: Perspectives on Multilateralism and World Order* (New York: St. Martin's Press, 1997); Michael G. Schechter, ed., *Future Multilateralism: The Political and Social Framework* (Bassingstoke: Palgrave Macmillan, 1999).

22 Robert O'Brien et al., *Contesting Global Governance: Multilateral Economic Institutions and Global Social Movements* (Cambridge: Cambridge University Press, 2000).

23 Ronnie D. Lipschutz, "Power, Politics and the Global Civil Society," *Millennium* 33, no. 3 (2005): 747–769.

24 O'Brien et al., *Contesting Global Governance*.

25 James Ron, "Legitimate or Alien? Human Rights Organizations in the Developing World," paper circulated at the Workshops on Religion and Human Rights Pragmatism: Promoting Rights across Cultures, Columbia University, New York, 24 September 2011.

26 Ibid.

27   Ibid.

28   See, for example, Edward Newman, Ramesh Thakur, and John Tirman, eds., *Multilateralism under Challenge: Power, International Order, and Structural Change* (Tokyo: United Nations University Press, 2006).

29   Newman, Thakur, Tirman, "Introduction," *Multilateralism under Challenge*, 8.

30   Andrew F. Cooper, "Labels Matter: Interpreting Rising States through Acronyms," in *Rising States, Rising Institutions*, eds. Alan S. Alexandroff and Andrew F. Cooper (Waterloo, Ontario: The Center for International Governance Innovation, 2010), 71.

31   Acharya, "State Sovereignty after 9/11."

32   In his debate with institutionalists, John J. Mearsheimer dismissed references to NATO to defend institutionalist theory. See "A Realist Reply," *International Security* 20, no. 1 (1995): 82–93.

33   Inis L. Claude, "Collective Security after the Cold War," in *Collective Security in Europe and Asia*, ed. Gary L. Guertner (Carlisle Barracks, PA: Strategic Studies Institute, US Army War College, 1992), 8. See also Arnold Wolfers, "Collective Defense versus Collective Security," in *Discord and Collaboration*, ed. Arnold Wolfers (Baltimore: Johns Hopkins University Press 1962), 181–204.

34   Amitav Acharya, "Multilateralism: Is There an Asia-Pacific Way?," *NBR Analysis* 8, no. 2 (Seattle, WA: National Bureau of Asian Research, 1997); Desmond Ball and Amitav Acharya, eds., *The Next Stage: Preventive Diplomacy and Security Cooperation in the Asia-Pacific Region* (Canberra: Strategic and Defence Studies Centre, Australian National University, 1999).

35   Amitav Acharya and Alastair Iain Johnston, "Comparing Regional Institutions: An Introduction," in *Crafting Cooperation: Regional International Institutions in Comparative Perspective*, eds. Amitav Acharya and Alastair Iain Johnston (Cambridge: Cambridge University Press, 2007).

36   Amitav Acharya, *Constructing a Security Community in Southeast Asia: ASEAN and the Problem of Regional Order*, 2nd edition (London and New York: Routledge, 2009).

37   Björn Hettne, András Inotai, and Osvaldo Sunkel, *Globalism and the New Regionalism* (Basingstoke: Palgrave Macmillan, 1999).

38   Robert O. Keohane, "Hegemony and After," *Foreign Affairs* (July–August 2012): 5.

39   Ikenberry, *Liberal Leviathan*, xi, xii, 224.

40   Ibid., 224.

41   Ibid., 6.

42   Ibid., xiii. For a recent view, see David Deudney and G. John Ikenberry, *Democratic Internationalism: An American Grand Strategy for a Post-Exceptionalist Era* (New York: Council on Foreign Relations, 2012).

43   Ibid., 15.

44   Amitav Acharya, "Human Security: East Versus West," *International Journal* LVI, no. 3 (2001): 442–460.

PART IV
STATES AND INTERNATIONAL INSTITUTIONS IN GLOBAL GOVERNANCE

INTRODUCTION

Part IV comprises seven chapters designed to introduce readers to the role of "States and international institutions in global governance." State-sponsored intergovernmental organizations have traditionally been the main pillars underpinning the way that the world is governed, so this part of the book examines the main intergovernmental aspects of international organization as well as the key powers that underpin these formations. As elsewhere, readers should not be surprised to see the prominent role that states and the institutions that they have created play in contemporary global governance. Yet relatively few works take states and state power seriously in international organization and global governance. As the chapters that comprise this part of the book illustrate, states and their intergovernmental creations are and remain the central components of the contemporary global governance puzzle.

In the seven chapters that follow, we bring together contributions from leading experts on the key statist aspects of global governance. As elsewhere in the book, we have designed this section to lend itself to use in a variety of courses. The section is organized from the largest global intergovernmental organization, through regional associations and broad "groups" of states, to the globe's most powerful singular actor—the United States. All classes on international organization and global governance should take in Leon Gordenker's chapter on "The UN system" (Chapter 15)—the most obvious and largest intergovernmental aspect of contemporary global governance. This would most likely be supplemented by Monica Herz's chapter on "Regional governance" (Chapter 17), Andrew F. Cooper and Ramesh Thakur's chapter on "The BRICS in the new global economic geography" (Chapter 19), and W. Andy Knight's on "US hegemony" (Chapter 21). More extensive investigations into the intergovernmental aspects of global governance might also then supplement the chapters by M. J. Peterson ("The UN General Assembly," Chapter 16), Ben Rosamond ("The European Union," Chapter 18), and Ian Taylor ("The global South," Chapter 20). These chapters provide important pieces in the global governance puzzle and are first-stop contributions to better understanding how the world is organized.

States and international institutions in global governance: chapter synopses

Leon Gordenker, one of the founders of UN studies in the United States and whose own contributions to understanding the world organization are widely acknowledged, begins this part of the book in Chapter 15 with an incisive investigation into the "UN system." Drawing on his own lifetime of research and analysis, Gordenker frames the so-called system as a "clan," thereby indicating the relevance for the Hatfield and McCoy clashes to explain a dysfunctional family of intergovernmental bodies that is anything except what the appellation "system" connotes.

The closest but inadequate approximation that we have to a world parliament is one of the UN organization's six principal organs, and in "The UN General Assembly" M. J. Peterson brings to bear her career-long interest in this body. In Chapter 16 she teases out a series of lessons about the difficulties of having a conversation among 193 member states as well as the benefits of attempting such a dialogue. A talk-shop it is, but the alternative to "jaw-jaw," as Winston Churchill noted, is "war-war."

Chapter 17 probes the nature and varieties of "Regional governance." Monica Herz explores the nuts and bolts of a phenomenon that has become an important building block for global governance, particularly in its economic variant. She contrasts the idea of regional governance with actual practice, which has returned in the last two decades to the forefront of scholarly inquiry following the previous preoccupation with globalization. One of the future challenges will be to find a balance between globalization, driven by the private sector and transnational corporations, and the forms of regionalism, driven by governments.

The regional experiment that has advanced furthest—administratively, economically, legally, and politically—is "The European Union," which is the subject of Ben Rosamond's synthesis of the continent's experience with integration since World War II. While earlier chapters were quick to indicate that the United Nations is not a world government, Chapter 18 examines the intergovernmental organization that has to date the most supranational features. The award of the 2012 Nobel Peace Prize suggests that, in spite of the ups and downs with the Euro and the possibility that members may—forcibly or otherwise—leave the currency or the union, there is much to learn from the European experiment that provides numerous insights into multi-level governance.

Andrew F. Cooper and Ramesh Thakur's focus in Chapter 19 is on "The BRICS in the new global economic geography." One of the key insights from global governance is the critical importance of informal arrangements and multilateralisms of various stripes that complement more formal institutions. This transformation of the map of global governance is especially marked by a new constellation of informal groupings of states without fixed physical sites and with an emphasis on intimate intergovernmental interactions. Cooper and Thakur focus on various "clubs" that pool like-minded countries, from the emerging economies in the global South to the gathering of the world's most powerful economies in the Group of 20 (G20). They focus particularly on the importance of the BRICs (Brazil, Russia, India, and China) and more recently the BRICS (with the addition of South Africa), an unusual grouping in light of the diversity and spread of continents, political systems, values, and economic models.

Ian Taylor's exploration of "The global South" in Chapter 20 follows nicely, shedding light on the longer-standing history of developing countries in pooling their efforts to level the actual and symbolic playing field of world politics. Among other things, Taylor probes the impact on world politics of both the Nonaligned Movement and the Group of 77 developing countries in changing the political and economic agendas of what is usually dubbed the "North–South dialogue," but which often appears to be a conversation among deaf diplomats. Given the diversity of postcolonial countries, Taylor ends with a plea to rethink the idea of the global South in global governance.

This part of the book ends with the proverbial elephant in the room, US power. W. Andy Knight's overview of "US hegemony" in Chapter 21 probes the role of the United States which, since 1945 at least, has been the driver of constructing a liberal international order held in place by the institutions that we currently have. Drawing on the history of what he sees as earlier hegemons (the United Provinces in the seventeenth century and the United Kingdom in the nineteenth and twentieth centuries), Knight examines the substantial body of theory and counter-theory along with the recent historical record regarding the pluses and minuses of American power, both hard and soft, and its meaning for contemporary global governance.

Where to now?

As readers quickly see, each of these chapters brings together major pieces of the global governance puzzle. It is overlaying the insights of subsequent parts of this book on the insights gleaned herein that enables a better appreciation of the depth, breadth, and diversity of IO and global governance in their contemporary manifestations.

The UN System

Leon Gordenker

In the halls of the United Nations, the standard diplomatic language implies the existence of a United Nations system. A search of the official records of the UN disclosed in early 2012 more than 30,000 listings of the phrase. It suggests a deliberately created harmonious operator based on unity of purpose, process, action, and result. Further scrutiny discloses that this phrase covers the existence and activity of more than 30 formal international organizations. Aside from the United Nations itself, altogether they budget expenditures for 2011 of some $6.9 billion[1] and directly employ several tens of thousands of personnel, yet the history and work of this institutional complex suggests that the UN system is at best a rather fuzzy metaphor, or perhaps only a euphemism for a "non-system,"[2] rather than an accurate description.

A better term might be "UN clan." Its member agencies have identical or similar genes, concerns covering all or much of the world and its people; connections to the central UN organization; founding and participation by governments; and capacity for growth of scope and functions. Some entities that have functions related to the clan are offspring of parents or guests in the circle. As usual in clan and family histories, the UN system includes triumphs, dysfunction, explicit and implicit rules; ability to reproduce; protection of territory; and mutations leading to adaptations to new circumstances.

What follows sketches the emergence, process, activity, and inherent difficulties of the so-called UN system.[3] So complex has that clan become that full exploration requires many volumes. Rather, this overview will survey the tangle of sustained activity that in some manner seeks to deal with global problems and difficulties.

Genealogy and heritage

Direct ancestors of the UN system began to appear in the nineteenth century.[4] Then the entire world began to use such new technology as steamships, railroads, mail services, and the telegraph. To handle the traffic and to coordinate national postal services and the telegraph, some governments organized international agencies to set legal standards. Evolved through many decades, the Universal Postal Union (UPU) and the International Telecommunication Union (ITU) now are part of the UN system. Other multilateral treaties, rather than institutions, represented national commitments to join in, for example, controlling ship-borne epidemics, suppressing trade in narcotics, and prohibiting traffic in humans.

While governments coped with such social issues, their militaries embraced new, ever-deadlier, technology. Its use in the first global war reduced any presumed difference between military and civil targets. It generally rattled society and opened the way to novel international relationships. This was most clearly displayed in the League of Nations.[5] Of vast ambition in the shadow of failed prescriptions to prevent warfare, the League was put together at the end of World War I amidst the usual political fumbling and human need after military action.

The architecture of the League of Nations in 1919 set some patterns that still apply in the UN institutions. The League was founded by states that claimed sovereignty. It was no world government. Its basic intention was rather—as with earlier international institutions—to discover and promote common interests. Its central purpose was avoiding war. Around that, national governments could cooperatively design policies that they would carry out. They pledged to apply international law and to augment it by practice and by recommending law-making treaties for ratification by members.

The League, however, had little to do with individual persons, could not levy taxes, and had no military force. It promoted global governance by identifying common problems and searching for solutions by both formal legal arrangements and accepted national practices. This is far from the top-down application of authoritative rules by a world government. It relies primarily on respecting international law and on specific recommendations on which members agree.

The initial enthusiasm for the League was short lived. As its prestige was fractured in the 1930s by national decisions that led to a war of unparalleled destruction, the League lost any effect on international politics. Despite some lasting accomplishment, it was treated as a failure by the governments that, in hope, had founded it.

Early in World War II, the eventual victors began thinking about the post-war world. Addressing the US Congress in January 1941, President Roosevelt set out broad aims for the future—freedom of speech, from want, of religion, and from fear.[6] Known as the "Four Freedoms," these maxims defined a wide scope for post-war cooperation. Institutionalizing these aims relied silently, but in fact, on the structural design and experience of the League of Nations, its progeny, and ancestors. The ambitions, however, went far beyond any earlier attempt to promote and organize peaceful, cooperative international relations. The eventual victors were using the title "United Nations" in 1942, and announcing their intentions long before the outcome of the war was certain.[7]

Institutional construction

With the end of World War II, new international institutions were constructed at an unprecedented rate. By the time that the San Francisco Conference of 1945 approved the UN Charter that created the central organization of the UN system,[8] plans had been made and some executed for the new agencies.[9] Even before military operations had stilled, a short-lived international organization, the now largely forgotten UN Relief and Rehabilitation Agency (UNRRA), had stretched precedent to bring supplies, shelter, and technical advice to liberated territories.[10]

This spurt of construction could be explained in several overlapping ways. To begin with, because the UN alliance had defeated Germany, Japan, and lesser allies, it could both dictate the peace and convincingly plan for the post-war world. This was a moment to shape the future, to approve far-reaching global goals and to produce means to reach them. Unlike the earlier, diplomatic dances to ensure the future, for example after Napoleonic wars, or even the Versailles Conference that constructed the League of Nations, the victors had experienced multilateral military cooperation on a global scale. They could use that in constructing a new world from the ashes of the old. Moreover, there was every reason to think that such an edifice would be popular. And it could include those global institutions that had survived the war. Several factors merit further discussion: US leadership; the theory of functionalism; and policy processes.

US leadership

As in 1919, the United States government took the lead in building that new world. This time, however, the planning showed special sensitivity to American domestic politics. Much was done to avert the political divisions that led the United States to abandon the League of Nations before it was fully organized. President Franklin Roosevelt and his envoys used diplomatic skills to get backing from the UN allies, especially Great Britain, in blueprinting what would get universal accord, notably that of the US Senate. At the same time, his prestige supported the argument that international cooperation was indispensable in maintaining peace. Furthermore, Roosevelt's leadership during the Great Depression of the 1930s and the onset of war powerfully argued for the use of government in building strong economic and social programs.

Yet that did not mean that American-tinted ideas envisaged, any more than those suggested in other states, that a world government was being born. Rather, the doctrine, accepted for centuries, that sovereign states made their decisions without outside interference would be an enduring pillar of any new international community. This was embodied in the UN Charter, the constitutional document of the new organization.

Functionalism

If some momentum propelling the post-war institutional construction rested on the hopes of the Four Freedoms speech, other impulses came from experience. These impulses had most relevance to the Specialized Agencies (discussed shortly) and are conceptualized in functionalist theory.[11] Its claim holds that the experts who deal with practical international issues, such as wartime merchant shipping, regulation of labor conditions in mines or medical protocols to limit epidemics, must and can leap over international boundaries to succeed. Short-term politics could be bypassed to favor long-term evolution.

The experts, it was said, had done so during World War I. They did so in World War II in more complex supply problems. UNRRA, too, provided an example. Comparable examples were provided by the International Labour Organization (ILO) and some programs of the League of Nations. Moreover, relief undertaken by private transnational bodies—what the UN Charter calls nongovernmental organizations (NGOs)—had a similar character. All succeeded, it was argued, because they had common aims, technology, and practice, not political whims. Their practices, it was asserted, would eventually spill over from their successes into yet others. That general acceptance would broaden out and reduce international conflict. In short, technologists could build patterns of cooperation that elude the political leaders and generalist diplomats.

However much functionalist notions may have affected planning the augmented Specialized Agency ranks, they did not convince critics of what governments then accepted. The most negative criticism came from realists, who dismissed this line as neglecting the role of power in politics. The Specialized Agencies, they held, signified mostly the power of the United States. After all, it was argued, no government would agree to change its ways, to hand over resources or reduce its influence if that would strengthen its competitors. Moreover, national interests so vary that even weak common denominators could seldom emerge from parliamentary-like debates among instructed delegates. The voting formulas in most of the Specialized Agencies ensured that majorities would only hide the competing interests. Therefore, what was adopted would merely save face and not signify dependable commitment. In short, this line rejects the usefulness of searching for general interests of states. Promoting national interest, however that was defined, was the supreme goal.

Another line of negative criticism came not from the defenders of the state but from its skeptics. These critics argued that the issues assigned to the UN system were too complicated, important, and urgent to be submitted to processes that had already proved lacking. Real governing was what was needed, not this feeble mirroring of fuzzy images. The world needed a global government with a democratic constitution and strength enough to enforce its writ and to cope with the danger of the new nuclear weapons.[12] This government should be organized at once. Some of its advocates nevertheless saw the UN system as a way station. Along the way, the United Nations could be strengthened.

The San Francisco Conference of 1945 took little notice of theoretical criticism. It was busy with approving the Charter, the central constitutional instrument and model for what became the UN system. The world organization fitted nicely with the general aims of the Four Freedoms and the words of the preamble of the Charter: the UN system would "employ international machinery for the promotion of economic and social advancement of all peoples." That would help, as the UN Charter put it, to create "conditions of stability and wellbeing which are necessary for peace and friendly relations among nations" [Art. 55]. It presumed that the members would be "peace-loving states" [Art. 3–4] that pledged to "fulfill in good faith" their obligations [Art. 2.2]. The model of sovereign states was guaranteed by a prohibition of UN action on matters "which are essentially within the domestic jurisdiction of states" [Art. 2.7].

That "international machinery"—the Specialized Agencies spelled out in Figure 15.1—would operate within a legal framework that respects their autonomy. Their relationship to the UN rests on negotiated agreements that always include reporting to the Economic and Social Council (ECOSOC). Their responses to be endorsed by the General Assembly are recommendations, not mandates. That applies, too, to the instruction of ECOSOC to promote coordination of the reporting agencies. The clear intention was governance to cope cooperatively with common problems, not mandating what states and their subjects did.

Name; Founding Date; Location

Food and Agriculture Organization of the United Nations (FAO); 1945; Rome

International Atomic Energy Agency (IAEA); 1957; Vienna

International Civil Aviation Organization (ICAO); 1947; Montreal

International Fund for Agricultural Development (IFAD); 1977; Rome

International Labour Organization (ILO); 1919; Geneva

International Maritime Organization (IMO); 1958; London

International Monetary Fund (IMF); 1945; Washington

International Telecommunication Union (ITU); 1865; Geneva

United Nations Educational, Scientific and Cultural Organization (UNESCO); 1946; Paris

United Nations Industrial Development Organization (UNIDO); 1986; Vienna

Universal Postal Union (UPU); 1875; Berne

World Health Organization (WHO); 1948; Geneva

World Intellectual Property Organization (WIPO); 1970; Geneva

World Meteorological Organization (WMO); 1950; Geneva

World Bank Group; 1945; Washington

    Comprises five agencies:

    International Bank for Reconstruction andDevelopment (IBRD)

    International Development Association (IDA)

    International Finance Corporation (IFC)

    Multilateral Investment Guarantee Agency (MIGA)

    International Centre for the Settlement of Investment Disputes (ICSID)

Figure 15.1 UN specialized agencies

Source: UN Chief Executive Board [http://www.unsceb.org/directory].

Policy processes

To obtain consent for policy recommendations directed to governments, a process was required. Like the League of Nations, the clan employs rich diplomatic experience. Official representatives of governments, usually professional diplomats or specialists in international relations, come together to seek solutions to common problems. In principle, diplomats follow instructions of their governments in participating in international organs. They try to find and decide on cooperative responses to issues that both elements of the system and their governments identify.

Multinational decisional organs were institutionalized in the UN system. All members would participate in periodic, usually annual, meetings to give overall approval to policy recommendations. Between meetings, the League had vested all supervisory and decisional activity in a council in which leading "national powers" were permanent members. To help in housekeeping and in providing advice to facilitate the decisional process, the League had created the first international secretariat headed by an independent secretary-general. He and his staff were barred from accepting any direction from governments. It became the template for an international civil service. The UN Charter followed the same pattern but gave his office the added prestige of a principal organ. That and explicit access to issues of war and peace broadened his political reach and capacity for leadership of the Secretariat.

The UN employs specialized architecture for work between General Assembly sessions where last-word decisions are made by majority voting. Always prepared to meet, a 15-member Security Council, including five permanent, veto-wielding states, deals with issues of peace and security. Two other specialized councils work between General Assembly sessions, one on economic and social issues and the other, now defunct, on colonial issues. The non-members of the councils are chosen there by majority vote.

Both the League's Covenant and the UN's Charter, the constitutional instruments of the organizations, were accepted as binding law by the members. The international organizations were thus empowered to recommend and help with the creation of additional services and organizations. The structures associated with the UN were multiplied mostly along architectural lines that diverged little from known forms. These include hints of organizational hierarchy that resembles that of clans or traditional families, more than governments.

Central as the General Assembly is, it nevertheless produces persuasion, not orders, in the form of resolutions. While these are not binding, they are approved by majority votes. The underlying political logic relies on member governments to make their own choices, developed in their own national ministries, as to how they will carry out the policies urged in the UN system. In actuality, such policies are not self-executing and require national programming. Moreover, as the UN itself does, the clan participants rely on financial contributions from members and make up their own budgets.[13] In short, the member governments retain the ultimate discretionary policy-making and administrative power.

The quasi-parliamentary style from which formal decisions emerge in the UN system in practice cannot ensure that recommendations, however informed by expert knowledge, will have a uniform outcome. The membership of some clan agencies exceeds the 193 of the UN. Not all governments—perhaps in fact a minority—have capacities effectively to act on, or even fully consider, agendas that range from suppression of swamp fever to the allocation of frequencies for electronic communications; from the protection of historic monuments to efficient collection of weather data; from planting genetically engineered seeds to preserving biodiversity; from intellectual property law to population control; and enough more to suggest that practically all of earthly life is included. Nor is every member government equally engaged in the goals of these organizations, in which they usually have equal votes.[14] Furthermore, the organizational agendas tend to grow with globalization and with changing technology.

The effect of such national constraints on the UN system tends to vary according to the specific subject matter of its agencies. The ultimate goal of maintaining international peace and security, including the possible use of force, connects directly to classical diplomacy. It linked rulers and now governments directly with each other by diplomats stationed on each other's territories. In current practice, the instructions to diplomats come from the ministry of foreign affairs, which in the traditional ranking is the senior department of government. Thus communications among governments were directed exclusively there. This remained the model, usually but not exclusively, followed by the League of Nations. That meant that recommendations on handling technical problems in, say, promoting international commerce went first to the foreign ministry of member governments, where priority went to national security. They were then referred by it to the financing or trade ministry for action or recommendation.

In the UN system, routine contacts between organizations and governments are usually determined by subject matter. This echoes a central notion of the functionalist doctrine. For instance, the WHO stays in touch with the health ministries of its members, the ILO with labor ministries of its members. In all-member assemblies, analogous to the UN General Assembly, the relevant minister usually in person attends part or all of sessions and speaks for the government. At the UN headquarters in New York, member states maintain permanent missions with an ambassador in charge, often aided by specialists. Many also maintain representation in Geneva and Vienna, where several important agencies have headquarters. The missions there, especially of the larger, richer countries, usually include experts familiar with specialized issues. In Washington, the World Bank Group and the International Monetary Fund provide for continuous attendance of financial experts representing member governments. Moreover, some of the clan agencies routinely station representatives in the national capitals.

Policies, words, and deeds

However expert the national spokespersons in UN meetings may be, their work involves many controversial choices defined by a political process. For instance, in the International Telecommunication Union negotiations take place on the allocation of wave bands for electronic communication—the artery system of the Internet and the mobile telephone. The results affect every part of the world and all of its population, and need execution by all governments.

Typically, agreements in the UN clan on policies that governments are *obliged* to carry out are formulated as international legal conventions. These law-making treaties, or agreements with similar intentions, rely on the proposition that governments will act according to what they have agreed. The long history of such legal obligations on technical issues supports the expectation that most will be reasonably respected and carried out by member governments in actions that they design.

Many other decisions only recommend practices and policies for governments. They are expected to consider these recommendations, adapt them, and follow them. But they are not legally obliged to do so. Yet the legal status is hardly the point. Rather, such recommendations reflect the majority opinion and in many cases are highly informed by experts. States thus can benefit from following them or assume the costs of failing to do so. A veteran diplomat points out that "international negotiations and decision-making cannot be separated from national policy-making on issues coming up in international fora."[15] This section discusses briefly several topics necessary to understand that statement: international secretariats; operational agencies; emergencies; and peacekeeping.

International secretariats

The rather modest functions of the independent staff of the League of Nations has evolved in the UN system to indispensable partnership in the policy process. They of course organize meetings and perform house-keeping services. Of more political significance, the ubiquitous secretariats increasingly have grown into a source of leadership and open communication channels among experts and governments. Each of the system secretariats has a chief officer and a staff that delivers expert advice, studies of issues on the agenda, and a ready memory of earlier difficulties, decisions, and outcomes. Their outputs include vast collections of statistics and original analyses as well as routine official records. In a sense, the international civil servants form "a second" UN, parallel to that of national representatives.[16]

Some of the chief officers of the UN system secretariats, originally seen as mere helpers of the national diplomats, soon found ways to offer impartial leadership on organizational policies and outputs. Beyond providing grease for the organizational wheels, they could offer ideas and knowledge, based on the institutional memories, past practices, and new approaches. As the UN agendas expanded, some of them even originated policies applied by many member governments.[17]

Operational agencies

With its emphasis on standard setting, research, and national execution of recommendations, the original design of the Specialized Agencies offered little capacity for concrete assistance and emergency help to governments. From their beginning, however, the IMF and the World Bank provided direct assistance to some governments on economic and development issues. And even before they began to function, UNRRA had provided a suggestive model for true international assistance to displaced persons and many countries damaged during World War II. This model led to another line of expansion, parallel to and sometimes overlapping with the Specialized Agencies.

This was accomplished in the General Assembly. At first, the new agencies responded, as UNRRA had, mainly to emergency needs. Then followed long-term services to governments for the economic and social development sketched in the Charter. This line was eventually expanded as broadly as the protection of the world environment.

Over decades, the General Assembly thus created new and path-breaking agencies based on its decisions, rather than following the pattern of the multilateral conventions of the Specialized Agencies. Like the latter, they also report through ECOSOC. They are financed mainly by voluntary contributions by governments willing to commit themselves to cooperation and grants from private sources. They conduct their affairs in accordance with decisions made by their own councils of governmental representatives.

Emergencies

"Surviving the war was one thing," observed historian Tony Judt, "surviving the peace was another."[18] Hunger, disease, and displacement, beyond the scope of UNRRA, which itself was on the way out, grew even while the United Nations began to work. Driven by human misery, governments used the new global organization to create the UN International Children's Emergency Fund (UNICEF) and the agency from which the UN High Commissioner for Refugees (UNHCR) evolved. In 1946, these fixtures in the current UN system at first had only short-term mandates to deal with what mistakenly were seen as temporary needs. By now they link with permanent organizations with global agendas, such as protection of the world environment, industrial development, and most recently the needs and potentials of women.[19]

The UN system now has a long list of emergency functions, ranging from rapid responses organized by the UN Secretariat to disasters, such as earthquakes and tsunamis, to provision of food to displaced persons. Massive food supplies for emergencies are handled by the World Food Programme (WFP), one of the giants of the system. Some of the Specialized Agencies, such as WHO and ILO, also provide mainly useful counsel. UNHCR now tries to protect and help internally displaced persons—well beyond the originally closely defined status of refugees. UNICEF emphasizes technical advice that reaches for long-term development to benefit mothers and children.

Responding to the growth of the UN membership list and the rapidly accruing theoretical understanding of economic and social development,[20] the clan was further built up via the General Assembly. Some of these put together programs—all of them approved by the host governments—that require international civil servants as well as local employees and private contractors. Others use occasional visiting missions or a resident adviser or two to keep in touch with programs on the ground. In particular, UN Development Programme (UNDP) offices in most of the more than 177 states and territories where it operates serve as coordinators of UN efforts and as what resembles a specialized diplomatic service.

UN peacekeeping

The notion that "politics" and peace maintenance could in fact be confined to the Security Council long ago disappeared. Its silent refutation came with a long list of humanitarian emergencies to which UN clan organizations responded. Practically every peacekeeping venture mandated by the Security Council took place adjacent to large forced migrations, hunger, disease, and social collapse. Beyond relief, demands for reconstruction followed.

Two of UN clan agencies, UNHCR and WFP, recently have been especially visible in such UN operations in Bosnia-Herzegovina, Sierra Leone, Côte d'Ivoire, Sudan, and

Somalia. While UNHCR organized camps and tried to protect the rights of people displaced by fighting, WFP provided great parts of the emergency food relief. Their originally modest mandates have turned into involvement with the threatened lives of millions of people. Moreover, parts of the UN system offered specialist help that engages NGO personnel. Altogether the wide mobilization of the UN clan represents widespread direct contact with the consequences of violations by governments of human rights and their undertakings intended to control the use of violence.

Interlocking agendas and coordination

The names themselves of the clan agencies suggest overlaps and complexities. From the beginning, the Charter provided for "consultation with and recommendations" for coordination with the other system members. In addition, the Charter opened a rapidly widening door to participation by NGOs in both policy decisions and field. Furthermore, as the agencies evolved separate organizational cultures, the participating governments sought reduction of the resulting complexity at both national and international levels.

For some of the UN system's agencies, the word "coordination" summoned up visions of ignorant meddlers pushing microphones and cameras into their realms. For others, it means combining talents to achieve better results. It may also offer a channel by which some help can be made available for UN peace-maintaining tasks. Perhaps for all, it signified yet more meetings and documents. For none, it meant hierarchical commands from somewhere on high.

Consequently, a main instrument of coordination—the UN Chief Executives Board (CEB) that is spelled out in Figure 15.2—came into being through effort by the secretary-general and his secretariat. It brings together the most senior officials of the UN system with the UN secretary-general as the presiding officer. His staff organizes the now routine gatherings. Gradually, once-reluctant agencies such as the World Bank, IMF, and WFP discovered utility in the consultations, thus recognizing "that the UN has legitimacy that can help those organizations."[21]

From its beginning under the signally bureaucratic title of Administrative Committee on Coordination, the CEB has served to dispense information, to voice suggestions, and to bargain about who does what and how. Moreover, its stock-taking functions encouraged the penetration of such central themes as protection of human rights into agency programs. It helped to inject expert arguments into unprecedented global conferences, such as on the status of women and the protection of the global environment.[22] These included increasingly large NGO participation. It served Secretary-General Kofi Annan as an instrument for simulating the system to fulfill the Millennium Development Goals (MDGs), which set quantitative and time-bound goals and thus accountability for much that the clan does.

The CEB became something more than a gathering of feudal dukes, as some early observers had it, but something less than a producer of blueprints. It owes much to the convictions and energy of international civil servants. Yet the governments that legitimize and finance the system usually have the last word. Furthermore, if NGOs could provide something resembling a voice of "the public," the CEB offers no direct access.

United Nations (chair)

Food and Agriculture Organization of the United Nations (FAO)

International Atomic Energy Agency (IAEA)

International Civil Aviation Organization (ICAO)

International Fund for Agricultural Development (IFAD)

International Labour Organization (ILO)

International Monetary Fund (IMF)

International Telecommunication Union (ITU)

UN International Children's Emergency Fund (UNICEF)

UN Conference on Trade and Development (UNCTAD)

UN Development Programme (UNDP)

UN Environment Programme (UNEP)

UN High Commissioner for Refugees (UNHCR)

UN Educational, Scientific and Cultural Organization (UNESCO)

UN Habitat (UNHABITAT)

UN Office on Drugs and Crime (UNODC)

UN Population Fund (UNFPA)

UN Industrial Development Organization (UNIDO)

UN Relief and Works Agency for Palestine Refugees (UNRWA)

UN World Food Programme (WFP)

UN Women (UNWOMEN)

UN World Tourism Organization (UNWTO)

Universal Postal Union (UPU)

World Bank Group (WBG) [5 agencies]

World Health Organization (WHO)

World Intellectual Property Organization (WIPO)

World Maritime Organization (WMO)

World Trade Organization (WTO)

Figure 15.2 UN Chief Executives Board membership

Source: http://www.unsceb.org/members.

At the field level, NGO personnel may provide indispensable aid in coordinating clan activity. NGOs frequently provide essential services that mesh with the detailed programs that national and international officials work up for carrying out system decisions. As subcontractors in arrangements made by UN clan agencies and governments, NGO personnel operate at ground level. Where either long-term development programs created in the system or emergency help are offered, a UNDP office may labor to ensure coherence in the work of the involved agencies and NGOs. Given the innate centrifugal tendencies of the autonomous participants, success is anything but guaranteed but is increasingly reported.[23]

Conclusion

The UN system can be characterized as demand driven but always far short of supply of goods and services. In safeguarding conventional state autonomy, it offers many openings for persuasion but few for compulsion. Built around decentralized management, successful operations require coordination from the policy level to the specified consumer.

The history of the clan suggests a primacy of procedures and seemingly parliamentary decisions. These involve a torrent of rhetoric, a mountain of reports and contradictory agendas handled by a variety of participants in a non-stop whirl of meetings. Overwhelming or not, they reflect the underlying global needs and adaptations in trying to meet them. Simplistic claims that the UN system has been imposed on the world are belied by changes in the agendas and programs accepted by members. Granted that not all governments carry out what they have agreed to in one or another international gathering. Nevertheless, the UN clan enables governance in a world that could not get it without organized cooperation of national governments. Furthermore, the organizational layering increasingly connects to classical diplomatic concerns with use of force. Linking the UN clan to peacekeeping missions helps with humanitarian needs and the reconstruction of fractured societies. Beyond that, with its goals of protection of human rights and of development, the clan and its collaborating NGOs reflect the groping towards promoting the conditions of peace.

However deep the hopes, they clearly are far from fulfilled. Official reports of the agencies and academic research acknowledge less than full accomplishment. Although some governments rail against bureaucracy, complexity, costs, and content, none have entirely turned away. Yet they have declined fully to reform the system. Nevertheless, one UN secretary-general after another has offered reform plans and pressed hard for their adoption.[24] The last of these major efforts, made by Kofi Annan, also got agreement on the MDGs. Beside them, UNDP's *Human Development Report* clarifies the effects of uneven national social and political backgrounds. It was clear by 2012 that the MDGs would not be reached. But progress, mixed in terms of location and depth, has been made.

The UN system obviously is constrained by the inherent complexities of its aims. By now, enough has no doubt been learned to exclude ignorance as an excuse for ignoring goals. Each member can add constraints. These include undermining the independence of the international civil services. Others often emerge from national politics, including ideological refusal to carry out particular policies, objections voiced in election campaigns, inability to supply financing, inadequate infrastructures and limitations on speech and enterprise. Thus, while collectively they support augmented global governance, each protects far-reaching autonomy.

Additional reading

1. Kofi Annan, *Renewing the United Nations: A Programme for Reform* (New York: UN, 1997).
2. Mark Malloch Brown, *The Unfinished Global Revolution* (New York: Penguin Press, 2011).
3. Jeffrey A. Meyer and Mark G. Califano, *The Oil-for-Food Scandal and the Threat to the U.N.* (New York: Public Affairs, 2006).
4. Thomas G. Weiss, David P. Forsythe, Roger A. Coate, and Kelly-Kate Pease, *The United Nations and Changing World Politics*, 7th edition (Boulder: Westview Press, 2013).

Notes

1 Calculated from UN General Assembly, *Budgetary and Financial Situation of the Organizations of the United Nations System*, Report of the Secretary-General (General Assembly document A/65/187), 3 August 2010.

2 Jacques Fomerand and Dennis Dijkzeul, "Coordinating Economic and Social Affairs," in *Oxford Handbook on the United Nations*, eds. Thomas G. Weiss and Sam Daws (Oxford: Oxford University Press, 2007), 561.

3 The term "UN system" after this is used interchangeably with "UN clan."

4 For an analytic account, see Craig N. Murphy, *International Organization and Industrial Change: Global Governance Since 1850* (New York: Oxford University Press, 1994).

5 For a detailed history, see F.P. Walters, *A History of the League of Nations*, 2 vols. (London: Oxford University Press, 1952).

6 Address to US Congress, 6 January 1941. For full text, see http://docs.fdrlibrary.marist.edu/od4freed.html

7 At the beginning of 1942 the 26 governments then allied as the United Nations issued a declaration that they intended to construct a post-war organization. Other governments later adhered to the declaration.

8 For details, see Ruth B. Russell, *A History of the United Nations Charter* (Washington, DC: Brookings Institution, 1958); Robert Hildebrand, *Dumbarton Oaks: The Origins of the United Nations and the Search for Postwar Security* (Chapel Hill: University of North Carolina Press, 1990); and Stephen L. Schlesinger, *Act of Creation: The Founding of the United Nations* (Boulder: Westview Press, 2003).

9 Georg Schild, *Bretton Woods and Dumbarton Oaks* (New York: St. Martin's Press, 1995).

10 George Woodbridge, *UNRRA: The History of the United Nations Relief and Rehabilitation Administration* (New York: Columbia University Press, 1950), offers details. Negative experiences are related in William I. Hitchcock, *Liberation: The Bitter Road to Freedom, Europe 1944–1945* (London: Faber and Faber, 2009), Part III. See also Thomas G. Weiss, "Renewing Washington's Multilateral Leadership," *Global Governance* 18, no. 3 (2012): 253–266, for the assertion that UNRRA still provides a model for international leadership.

11 A wartime tract published in Great Britain expertly set out a theoretical basis: reissued as David Mitrany, *A Working Peace System* (Chicago: Quadrangle Books, 1955).

12 For an argument that this approach still has relevance, see Thomas G. Weiss, "What Happened to the Idea of World Government," in *Thinking about Global Governance: Why People and Ideas Matter*, ed. Thomas G. Weiss (London: Routledge, 2011), 66–86.

13 In recent years private donors (mostly American) have made substantial contributions to the program budgets of some clan agencies.

14 Voting in the World Bank Group and the IMF reflects the size of contributions made by members.

15 Johan Kaufmann, ed., *Effective Negotiation: Case Studies in Conference Diplomacy* (Dordrecht, Martinus Nijhoff Publishers, 1989), 173.

16 A concept developed by Inis L. Claude, *Swords into Plowshares: The Problems and Prospects of International Organization* (New York: Random House, 1956).

17 For further discussion, see Leon Gordenker, *The UN Secretary-General and Secretariat*, 2nd edition (London and New York: Routledge, 2010), which includes bibliography. Thomas G. Weiss, Tatiana Carayannis, Louis Emmerij, and Richard Jolly, eds., *UN Voices: The Struggle for Development and Social Justice* (Bloomington: Indiana University Press, 2005). Chapters 9–10 offer insights of some direct participants in sustaining the international civil service.

18 Tony Judt, *Postwar: A History of Europe Since 1945* (London: Vintage Books, 2010), 21.

19 Articles 1.3 and 55 of the UN Charter set non-discrimination by sex as specific aims.

20 The vital role of secretariat thinkers, hitherto little documented, is given personal dimensions in Weiss et al., *UN Voices*, Part Two.

21 Interview with John Ruggie, scholar and erstwhile senior UN official, in Weiss et al., *UN Voices*, 367.

22 See Michael G. Schechter, *United Nations Conferences* (New York: Routledge, 2005), and Michael G. Schechter, ed., *United Nations-Sponsored World Conferences* (Tokyo: United Nations University, 2001).

23 For revealing observations of UNDP's history and process, see Craig N. Murphy, *The United Nations Development Programme: A Better Way?* (Cambridge: Cambridge University Press, 2006).

24 For overview, see Thomas G. Weiss, *What's Wrong with the United Nations and How to Fix It* (Cambridge, MA: Polity Press, 2008).

Contents

The UN General Assembly

M. J. Peterson

In 1945 the UN was firmly anchored in the world of intergovernmental relations. Though the Preamble to the UN Charter begins with a ringing affirmation that "We the Peoples of the United Nations" are determined to create a better world, it ends with a shift of the active role to "our respective Governments" which agree to the Charter and establish the United Nations. While most of the Charter's substantive and organizational provisions make sense only in an international system where autonomous states are the primary actors, it also includes intimations of a world in which states coexist with webs of transnational activity by individuals, groups, firms, and private organizations. Article 41 suggests that suspension or reduction of economic transactions, travel to or from, and communications to or from a state threatening international peace will help curb aggression; Article 71 creates the possibility of direct consultations between the UN Economic and Social Council and "non-governmental organizations which are concerned with matters within its competence"; and Article 87 establishes direct contact between the Trusteeship Council and the inhabitants of a Trust Territory as part of the scheme for UN supervision of state administration.

These intimations have expanded over the years into a much broader array of contacts between various parts of the UN system and non-state actors, but the General Assembly remains insulated. Increased contacts with non-state actors occur in subsidiary bodies or at special "high-level meetings" on particular topics, but the plenary and main committee meetings remain firmly in an intergovernmental world. This persistence of an intergovernmental shape explains why proposals to transform the United Nations into some type of world government include either replacing the General Assembly with a unicameral world legislature of popularly elected representatives or using it as one house—an "Assembly of States"—flanked by an elected "Assembly of Peoples" in a bicameral world legislature.

This chapter contains four sections and a conclusion. The first briefly examines how international relations theory has viewed the General Assembly, and the second outlines its institutional design and evolution. The third examines its role and impact within the current UN structure, and the fourth takes up ongoing debate about how the General Assembly might fit into efforts to make the United Nations more relevant to contemporary global governance.

International relations theory

The General Assembly has attracted relatively little theoretical discussion because few outside its halls regard it as having significant effects on world politics. Realists, particularly neorealists concerned primarily with the distribution of capability among states, regard it as irrelevant. In the visions of the post-World War II functionalists, in which international cooperation would take hold first in technical areas and then spread out eventually to political questions, other intergovernmental bodies were more important. Similarly, world federalists looked past the existing General Assembly in anticipation of a future world legislature.

Nor has the General Assembly figured prominently in the work of later generations of theorists. Neoliberal institutionalist and rationalist work, including the stream of principal–agent analysis that emerged in the 1990s, focuses mainly on the intergovernmental organizations managing particular international regimes. As a general forum with an annual agenda of some 200 items, the assembly is involved too infrequently in the functioning of any particular international regime to appear significant. Though constructivists and feminists are more attuned to Inis Claude's argument that UN bodies provide major forums for collective affirmation of shared aspirations or collective endorsement or condemnation of particular states' positions or actions,[1] they pay only scattered attention to the General Assembly. While it might figure in analysis of how new problems are identified and get on to the international agenda, interest quickly shifts to whatever intergovernmental or private bodies become most closely engaged with addressing the issue.

Most current studies of the General Assembly are not concerned with its functioning. Rather, they use the formal votes to develop metrics for assessing the degree of political affinity among pairs of states or tracking the cohesion of coalitions of states.[2]

History and development

The hybrid of traditional diplomatic practices and parliamentary procedure already tried out in earlier ad hoc conferences like the 1899 and 1907 Hague Conferences on the laws of warfare and the nineteenth century "public international unions" addressing technical matters before World War I was extended into the economic and military domains by the League of Nations Assembly between 1930 and 1939. In 1946 the UN General Assembly took up where the League Assembly left off, and the hybrid was so familiar that it inspired discussions of "parliamentary diplomacy" or "conference diplomacy" as a distinct form of interstate negotiation.[3] Yet it was not unique to the General Assembly; ad hoc conferences organized under UN or other auspices often used it more effectively.

The traditional diplomatic side of General Assembly procedures manifests in its composition and distribution of votes. The individuals participating in meetings are delegates chosen by the governments of their states; the principle of sovereign equality asserted in diplomatic practice is evident in the rule that each national delegation has one vote. Yet in a major departure from traditional diplomatic practice, which operated by unanimity, Article 18 of the UN Charter specifies that a simple majority of "those present and voting" is needed on most questions and a two-thirds majority on those defined as "important questions." This combination of one-state-one-vote and majoritarian decision establishes the General Assembly as the "egalitarian" balancer of the explicit acknowledgment of great power importance in rules about membership and veto rights in the Security Council. However, this was and remains an egalitarianism of states, not an egalitarianism of peoples; the boundaries of states do not partition the global population into equal sized groupings.

Even in 1946 when representatives of the 51 original UN member states met in London for its first session, it was clear that the General Assembly would have to divide up the work if it were to get through its agenda, which combined addressing major global issues while attending to the various matters of UN organization, budget, and staffing. The dynamics created by many members and many issues brought the parliamentary aspects of assembly procedure to the fore. Like national legislatures, the General Assembly works mainly through committees and has rules of procedure designed to balance individual rights of expression with methods for moving the work along.[4] Individual members or groups of members have the right to introduce proposals, counterproposals, and amendments to proposals. Debate time in both committees and the plenary is allocated among members according to common rules. Members can use a full range of procedural motions, including closing debate, suspending or adjourning a meeting, and changing the order of voting on proposals. Yet in some important respects, General Assembly practice continues diplomatic traditions. One significant remnant is allocation of speaking time in the order in which delegations sign up on the speakers' list. This generally limits delegates' ability to respond directly to different viewpoints, and has inspired some efforts to develop other discussion formats. As an unnamed delegate commented, "[I]t is simply a fact of UN life that with such a large number of member states it is difficult to balance inclusiveness on the one hand and frank and interactive discussions on the other."[5]

Historical accident now coalesced into well-established practice accounts for another reversion. Beyond common opposition to the World War II Axis, political alignments among UN member states were unclear in 1944–47. This encouraged allocating committee leadership positions and seats on any assembly subsidiary bodies that would not include all member states among geographically based regional groups. Though stable voting coalitions did appear shortly afterward—first the Cold War divisions into East and West (later supplemented by the Nonaligned) and then the division into South and North based on level of economic development—they never displaced the regional groupings as the device for allocating seats. The Cold War-induced division of Europe into Eastern and Western groups meant that the regional groups seemed to match up adequately enough with the coalitional divides to serve for allocating seats. As UN membership expanded from 51 to 193 states, the General Assembly did as well and most of its limited membership subsidiary bodies doubled from approximately 20 seats to 45 so that sub-regional groupings could be accommodated within each regional group's allocation of seats. Such a size makes them negotiating and deliberation forums, not compact executive committees managing some cooperative activity.

Delegates themselves shifted the balance between the diplomatic and the parliamentary. After a few years of acting out the Cold War stalemate through highly formalized use of the parliamentary procedures, member governments converged on using the General Assembly in a different way in the mid-1960s. For different reasons, both the Soviet bloc—interested in getting out of isolation—and the Nonaligned Movement (NAM)—needing to maintain a sprawling coalition of developing countries—converged on substituting consensus-seeking. This preference has persisted and become stronger over time.

Second, the General Assembly moved from attempting detailed negotiation and considering rival draft resolutions in the formal meetings to negotiating most of the details in various subcommittees, working groups, "friends of the chair," and other informal gatherings. Most formal plenary and main committee meetings became occasions for putting governments' views on the record and adopting the sole draft resolution put forward. General Assembly work is thus a confusing mix of a visible formal "tip of the iceberg" and a much larger submerged set of informal negotiations. The intertwining is best presented visually, as in Figure 16.1.

The informal negotiations can end in consensus or in continued disagreement. When they end in consensus on a particular draft, that text is adopted as a resolution without a vote; the assembly president reads the number and name of the draft and indicates that since there is no objection the draft is adopted. In the 1950s 20–30 percent of resolutions were adopted by consensus; 50–60 percent by the mid-1980s; and around 75 percent since the early 1990s.[6] The likelihood of reaching consensus depends on the type of issue, as can be seen from Table 16.1, which summarizes proceedings in the six main committees during the 64th session.[7] The current division is: First Committee, Disarmament; Second Committee, Economic; Third Committee, Social, Humanitarian, and Cultural; Fourth Committee, Political and Decolonization; Fifth Committee, Administrative and Budgetary; and Sixth Committee, Legal.

The main committees specialize by type of issue, and whether a main committee refers a draft to the plenary by consensus or by vote foreshadows what happens there. Issues not referred to a main committee are a mix of very hot political items and very routine matters, which explains why the level of contention in the plenary ranks well below that in the First (Disarmament) and Fourth (Political and Decolonization) Committees. The Fifth Committee has long addressed the strong divergence between numbers of votes and level of assessed contributions by favoring consensus whenever possible; the lawyers working on refinement of international law in the Sixth Committee also prefer getting to consensus before referring a project to the plenary. Resolutions condemning human rights abuses in particular countries inspire most of the Third Committee contention.

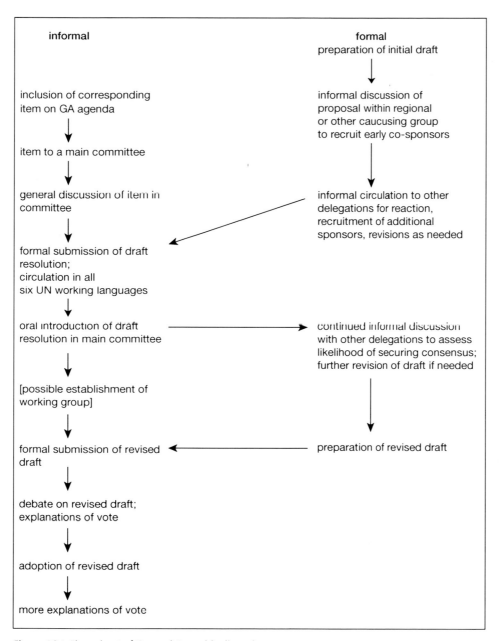

Figure 16.1 Flow chart of General Assembly discussions

When informal negotiations end in continued disagreement, supporters of the various proposals on the table need to decide whether to hold off and continue negotiating next year or to present their preferred draft for a vote. Moving to a vote occurs when any member state wants its own or others' individual views placed on the record; a large supporting coalition wants to adopt a particular text now rather than continue negotiating; or an overwhelmingly large coalition wants to isolate opponents.

Table 16.1 Proportion of draft resolutions recommended by a split vote, 2009

	%
Discussed in plenary only	14.1
First Committee	40.0
Second Committee	10.3
Third Committee	29.1
Fourth Committee	65.4
Fifth Committee	4.3
Sixth Committee	0.0

While delegates on the floor and journalists in the gallery understand the maneuvers, they can be perplexing to the general public. Early in the General Assembly's history abstaining in a vote became almost as strong a negative signal as voting against rather than the middle ground suggested by the ordinary use of the word, and large coalitions of states seek to keep adherents from abstaining as well as from voting against. There are two situations in which this ambiguity is reduced. Whenever the total of "no" votes and abstentions rises above one-third of the membership (65 of 193 members), the resolution's weak support makes it a poor platform for advancing some proposition by expressing it modestly now and then negotiating incrementally stronger statements in future resolutions. Members with reputations for typically abstaining or voting no on particular issues can express different attitudes towards particular resolutions by shifting from one to the other.

With isolated opponents, conclusions to be drawn from how they vote depend on their attitudes towards abstaining. Initially the United States was like most members in preferring to avoid deep isolation by abstaining rather than voting "no." By the early 1970s a stream of elite opinion believing that it was better to vote against unacceptable texts became more influential.[8] This confrontational approach resonated particularly strongly in the administrations of Ronald Reagan and George W. Bush but has influenced others as well. However, the United States is not the only member willing to cast the only "no" vote; in recent sessions others, including India, Turkey, and Zimbabwe, have cast lone "no" votes.

The General Assembly shifted other procedures to handle the increasing time pressure created by going from a body composed of 51 delegations adopting 113 resolutions on about that many agenda items in 1946 to a body of 192 delegations addressing 174 agenda items and adopting 288 resolutions plus 73 decisions in 2011 in three main ways. First, it does most of its deliberative work in the six main committees, which are committees of the whole membership specializing in particular types of issue. This permits the larger national delegations to assign personnel according to their individual areas of expertise, while straining the ability of smaller delegations to keep up with everything. The General Assembly began with six main committees, added a seventh in 1956, but returned to six in 1993 as workloads on different types of issues changed. Specialization has been taken further over the years through ample use of the assembly's authority to create additional subsidiary bodies; the result has been a vast array of standing and ad hoc committees and commissions dealing with particular matters, each of which reports to a main committee.

The second way of dealing with the pressures has involved carving out more meeting time. The shift to informal negotiations means that more work is done outside official meetings. The General Assembly has also raised the level of activity occurring during its 13-week primary session between September and late December. In the 1970s it returned to an expectation, lost in early sessions, that meetings start promptly. It also began holding more simultaneous meetings of main committees, though this was limited by availability of meeting spaces and the needs of smaller delegations. While the tiniest delegations, numbering four or fewer, cannot hope to cover all simultaneous meetings, the smaller delegations of 10–15 have exerted pressure to keep the schedule manageable for them.

The UN Charter also allows for convening Special Sessions, and Resolution 377(V) established a procedure for short-notice Emergency Special Sessions. Such sessions were more common in the past, but no new ones have been convened since 2005. Except for occasional continuations of the 10th Special Session on Palestine, the assembly has shifted to "high-level meetings." These typically coincide with the approximately two weeks of plenary general debate in mid- to late September that start a regular session to take advantage of the presence of heads of state, heads of government, and foreign ministers. Since 2003 the assembly has also accelerated its proceedings in the fall by electing officers and main committee chairs at a short organizational meeting the preceding June.

Third, the General Assembly has adopted some agenda-pruning measures, including the grouping of related items and staggering consideration of some long-standing issues by addressing them every other or every third year. However, such pruning is limited by members' desires to address certain issues every year and a reluctance among developing countries to settle priorities within their now lengthy agenda.[9]

Any stable coalition of member states holding two-thirds of the votes can control the General Assembly and use it to shape global discourse and influence the course of particular conflicts by supporting or condemning participants. Two such coalitions have existed in the assembly's history: the US-led coalition from 1947 through 1960, and the Third World coalition prevailing since 1967. The transition between them was generated primarily by decolonization. The US-led coalition did not experience a dramatic falling out; it was gradually superseded as the newly independent states joining the UN in the 1960s swelled the ranks of the NAM (focused originally on political issues) and the Group of 77 (focused on economic issues) that constituted the "South." The Soviet bloc was able to escape isolation in the General Assembly by siding with the NAM and G77 against the West. However, the revolutionary optimism of the 1970s was replaced by a loss of confidence in the 1980s as its economy stagnated and the Soviet Union found itself as mired in unsuccessful military ventures abroad as the US had been in the early 1970s. After the Soviet bloc collapsed, the South–North divide remained as the primary cleavage among UN members.

Even before the Third World coalition acquired the two-thirds majority to control the General Assembly, the Cold War had affected the relative positions of the Security Council and the General Assembly. In the original Charter design, the Security Council was the central body for coordinating responses to threats to peace, and the General Assembly was the central forum for developing broad rules for the conduct of world politics. However, the Cold War meant stalemate in the Security Council. While the

US-led coalition pioneered using the General Assembly to provide a UN mandate for member action in a crisis with Resolution 377 (V), "Uniting for Peace," in 1950, the Soviets were equally willing to use the assembly in 1956 when British and French vetoes would have stymied Security Council action in the Suez crisis. Yet, as East and West generally preferred, the Security Council remained the primary authorizer of peacekeeping operations. Continuing disagreement among the five permanent members (P-5)—which became even more complex when the People's Republic of China replaced the Republic of China in 1971—limited Security Council approval to neutral truce-observation and mediation missions.

The end of the Cold War did not affect Third World control of the General Assembly but changed dynamics in the Security Council. The unanimity with which Saddam Hussein's invasion of Kuwait was condemned and joint action to force Iraqi withdrawal endorsed in 1990 began an era when the leading powers were readier to use the Security Council as a forum for agreeing on how to deal with crises and inspired much optimistic and commentary on how collective security might be revived or the UN move from peacekeeping to peace-enforcement. Even as events of the mid- and late 1990s eroded the post-Kuwait euphoria, the P-5 did not invoke the assembly when they could not agree. They either settled on doing nothing or some bypassed the UN altogether, a choice that has intensified developing countries' insistence that the General Assembly become more prominent.

Though New York is the site of many public demonstrations on issues being considered by the General Assembly and some of its subsidiary bodies engage in considerable interaction with nongovernmental organizations (NGOs), global advocacy coalitions, business firms, and economic interest groups, the General Assembly's plenary and main committees remain firmly intergovernmental. Member states are allowed to send delegations consisting of up to five representatives and any number of "experts" and "advisers" to sessions, and some use those expert and adviser slots to include persons drawn from outside government. A few have appointed politicians, officials from outside the diplomatic service, or other prominent persons, but the typical delegate is a career diplomat most of whose career is spent representing the country at some UN body.

Current debates

Improving General Assembly procedures has been a long-standing concern, with the current discussion of "revitalization" well into its second decade. The current Ad Hoc Working Group on Revitalization is the fifth in a series of committees charged with identifying improvements in procedures and working methods that stretch back to the early 1950s. Most of the current proposals for improving the General Assembly are familiar: reduce the agenda by focusing on fewer issues, adopt fewer resolutions, and reduce the verbiage of those it does adopt. Most of the new ideas, such as providing the assembly president with a more adequate support staff, organizing debate in different formats to permit more interactive exchanges, or finding ways to help the smallest delegations cope with the press of meetings, are useful but do not address the main institutional problems.

Many developing countries share a broad desire to see the General Assembly become more prominent, particularly vis-à-vis the Security Council. In their eyes, this reform would be a return to the original design of the Charter establishing the General Assembly as the primary global deliberative body, while the Security Council handles a defined set of security issues. The NAM and G77 routinely claim that because the General Assembly is the most inclusive intergovernmental forum with the broadest agenda it is the proper place to determine the basic terms of global order. A few developing country diplomats have gone further and argued that General Assembly resolutions adopted under the current one-state-one-vote should be regarded as legally binding.[10] However, there is much opposition to this idea and little consensus about the assembly's role. Proposals for increasing the role of the "G193" in global governance abound, but many of them involve creating new global bodies—a Global Economic Coordination Council or an Economic Security Council—rather than using the General Assembly.[11]

The General Assembly's regular sessions are now overshadowed by global conferences and summits. Its efforts to develop commentary on the global financial crisis in 2008–09 were complicated not only by serious substantive disagreements among governments but also by strong reactions against the assembly president's efforts to steer the discussions himself through a special global summit (which had to be delayed several months and in the end attracted few heads of state or government) and circulating his own proposal to create eight new global bodies to deal with economic and financial issues.[12] In the end the General Assembly settled on establishing an ad hoc open-ended working group to continue discussion of the broad policy directions suggested by the June 2009 Conference on the World Financial and Economic Crisis and Its Impact on Development, which stopped well short of proposing any new governance structures. Nor was the assembly, which took on acting as the preparatory committee able to produce a preliminary conference document for the June 2012 Rio+20 conference. This was left to the Brazilian government as conference chair.[13] On both occasions, the assembly performed its traditional function of revealing the state of intergovernmental thinking, but the result was mainly information about the size and intensity of remaining disagreements.

Other developments in the UN's organizational structure indicate the continuing strength of South–North differences. The UN Human Rights Council, established in 2006 to make a new start on human rights issues, has become more similar to the supplanted Commission on Human Rights than its supporters hoped. The member states are chosen by the General Assembly based on a division of seats among regional groups, and the groups have short-circuited hopes that these would become competitive elections allowing exclusion of representatives from the world's most repressive governments by putting forward only as many candidates as the group is allocated seats. The 2010 creation of UN Women, which consolidated UN activity on the position of women in society by replacing four smaller agencies, revealed the ongoing tensions between control of votes and possession of resources. Developing countries, which do not like "the discretionary use of non-core money," pressed to constrain industrial donor country influence over the agency by limiting Western states to less than 20 percent of the seats on the governing board.[14] After long negotiations, the General Assembly approved a two-sided structure. "Normative support functions" are coordinated through the existing 45-member UN Commission on Women, a subsidiary body of the Economic and Social

Council with all seats allocated by regional group, while "operations" are supervised by an Executive Board of 41 members, with 35 seats divided among the regional groups and the last 6 given to 4 industrial and 2 developing "contributing countries."[15]

Key criticisms and emerging issues

Though diplomats instructed to reach agreement regard attaining consensus as success, outside observers regard the General Assembly's high proportion of resolutions adopted by consensus as a sign of failure. They see the 75 percent consensus rate as produced by texts expressing the lowest common denominator by avoiding contentious questions or incorporating weak or ambiguous wording, and the long string of such resolutions issued year after year as weakening rather than enhancing the assembly's reputation and prominence. Agreeing to define assembly resolutions as legally binding commitments might encourage sharper discussions and adoption of resolutions accepted by a large majority. Yet, in the political conditions prevailing today a string of such votes along the coalitional lines described above would harden divisions, increase industrial state tendencies to cooperate elsewhere, and implementation would not follow. Some analysts have sought to overcome the problem by proposing that any power to adopt binding resolutions be linked to adoption of a weighted voting system in which UN membership, share of world population, and share of UN assessment would be combined to give member states differing numbers of votes.[16]

In any event, agreement to accept General Assembly resolutions as binding would only occur as part of a more general move toward world government. Since the present trajectory of world politics is towards global governance, the key issue for the assembly today is defining a role that makes sense in that context.[17] In many respects the UN Charter anticipated many features of contemporary global governance. The General Assembly was defined as intergovernmental and situated as a deliberative forum overlaying a system of more specialized entities that would provide governments with expert assistance in addressing problems of common concern. Article 10 gives it a broad remit to "discuss any questions or any matters within the scope of the present Charter or relating to the powers and functions of any organs provided for in the present Charter." Articles 11 and 12 define its relation with the Security Council as one where the General Assembly takes up broad principles while the council deals with particular disputes and situations. Articles 13 and 55–58 define a similar relationship with the rest of the UN system. Article 13 authorizes the General Assembly to "initiate studies and make recommendations" for "promoting international cooperation" in political, economic, social, cultural, education, and health and for "assisting in the realization of human rights and fundamental freedoms for all." Articles 55–58 indicate that the actual cooperation will be pursued through the specialized agencies and other bodies. Though the Charter's authors underestimated the extent to which various groups of states would engage in cooperative activities outside the UN system, it does foreshadow the broad outlines of contemporary global governance.

It is more difficult to discern what was expected of the General Assembly; the early references to "town meeting of the world" or "parliament of man" were clearly flights of fancy. Charter Articles 10, 13, and 15 suggest four roles the assembly could fill if member governments and their delegations break the habits of decades and seriously rethink its work. First, the general debate and the high-level meetings could function even more effectively as sounding boards where governments try out new ideas and listen to responses. These responses might not come immediately, but having some years pass between initial mention of some idea and its adoption by governments or UN agencies is entirely consistent with earlier experience. Second, the General Assembly could continue using its convening power to channel the work of hammering out agreements on new issues into appropriately structured bodies able to devote the time needed to assess the situation and, when warranted, produce agreements that contain more than the lowest common denominator existing at the start of discussions. Third, it could shift more of its attention to reviewing the results and impacts of global governance efforts. Though each distinct agency or network is already monitoring action and outcomes, their horizon tends to be limited to their areas of immediate concern. The General Assembly could take up monitoring the cross-cutting implications of cooperation in particular areas for efforts in others. This monitoring function would need to be broader than assessing UN system efforts to provide "global public goods," popular as that notion is among those seeking to energize the UN system. Delivering public goods is only one aspect of governance; much more of it involves providing the common normative and operational frameworks within which actors of various types pursue their activity. Fourth, it would continue to be the supervisor and structure of the UN system of organizations. On occasion, as with revision of the staff discipline system in 2007, the General Assembly can make significant improvements.

Conclusion

The political context for redefining the General Assembly's role is not promising. The South–North division remains the primary cleavage among the UN's 193 members, but the NAM and the G77, which together function as the global South, do not appear of one mind about how to use control of the assembly. Though the industrial countries of the North are the primary targets, NAM and G77 rhetoric is sometimes directed against the G20 as a whole and the most powerful of the "emerging countries" in particular. The G20's claim that its members account for 85 percent of the world economy, 80 percent of world trade, and 70 percent of world population are countered with insistence that countries of the global South include the largest share of world population, generate most world income, rule most world territory, encompass greater diversity of peoples, have the greatest number of consumers, and are where most global economic growth is occurring.[18]

Maintaining those claims, and with them NAM and G77 influence more generally, depends on keeping the major emerging countries—particularly Brazil, China, India, and South Africa—within the coalition of developing countries. Without them, the rest of the global South lacks sufficient capacity and politico-economic importance to have significant weight in the emerging network structure of global governance. For their part, Chinese leaders say they will not join the industrial countries' Organisation for Economic Co-operation and Development (OECD) or abandon the global South. Yet there is some sentiment among others for separation. The G77 expelled Mexico and South Korea after they joined the OECD, and at least one diplomat from a G77 country has been quoted as saying that countries participating in the G20 should also be excluded.[19] Much of the General Assembly's future depends on whether other developing countries decide to accept that the G20 will be a major venue for discussion of global economic issues and maintain ties with its emerging country members or to follow the lead of others—most notably Bolivia, Cuba, Ecuador, Nicaragua, and Venezuela—in confronting the whole G20.

The General Assembly began as and remains an intergovernmental body designed for broad deliberation rather than close management of operational activities. As long as independent states remain the key political units and governments continue to possess the largest measure of administrative and enforcement capacity, that design is appropriate. The task facing reformers is finding ways to better structure the activities of that intergovernmental forum for a world of global governance. Governments and their delegates should acknowledge that the General Assembly is ill adapted to settling the precise terms of global governance and shift it towards a position as global assessor of whether new concerns require attention and how well global governance in its various parts is working overall.

Additional reading

1. The UN General Assembly's website provides the official record of its work, and is available in all six official languages. For the English version, see http://www.un.org/en/ga/.
2. M. J. Peterson, *The UN General Assembly* (London: Routledge, 2006).
3. *Annual Review of United Nations Affairs*, published by Oxford University Press.
4. Several institutes and think tanks provide commentary about the General Assembly and its proceedings: the Council on Foreign Relations (New York) (www.cfr.org), which presents a range of US views; Foreign Policy Magazine (www.foreignpolicy.com); the European Council on Foreign Relations (www.ecfr.eu), an EU-sponsored think tank.
5. Sources of proposals for improving the UN include the Center for UN Reform Education (www.centerforunreform.org), which covers developments in the General Assembly from vantage points sympathetic with developing countries; the Committee for a Democratic UN (Germany) (www.uno-komitee.de/en/index.php); and the South Centre, the G77's think tank (www.southcentre.org).

Notes

1 Inis L. Claude, Jr., "Collective Legitimization as a Function of the United Nations," *International Organization* 20, no. 3 (1966): 367–379.
2 Such as Kisuke Iida, "Third World Solidarity: The G77 in the United Nations General Assembly," *International Organization* 42, no 2. (1988): 375–395; S.Y. Kim and Bruce Russett, "The New Politics of Voting Alignments in the United Nations General Assembly," *International Organization* 50, no. 4 (1996): 629–643; Axel Dreher and Jan-Egbert Sturm, "Do the IMF and World Bank Influence Voting in the UN General Assembly?," *Public Choice* 151, no. 1–2 (2012): 363–397.
3 Philip Jessup, "Parliamentary Diplomacy," Hague Academy of International Law *Recueil des cours* 89 (1956): 181–320; and John G. Hadwin and Johan Kaufman, *How United Nations Decisions are Made* (Leiden: Sijthoff, 1961).

4 General Assembly Rules of Procedure. UN Doc. A/520/Rev.17 (April 2008), http://www.un. org/en/ga/about/ropga.

5 Quoted in Lydia Swart, "Revitalization of the Work of the General Assembly," in *Managing Change at the United Nations*, ed. Estelle Perry (New York: Center for UN Reform, 2008), 21–34. Available from the Center on UN Reform, www.centerforunreform.org/.

6 M. J. Peterson, *The UN General Assembly* (London: Routledge, 2006), 75–77; later sessions calculated from list of resolutions available at http://www.un.org/en/ga/[session number]/ resolutions.shtml.

7 John R. Mathiason, "The General Assembly: Addressing Global Problems, Incrementally," in *Annual Review of United Nations Affairs 2009/2010*, Vol. 1, eds. Joachim Müller and Karl P. Sauvant (New York: Oxford University Press, 2011), 4.

8 Expressed most forcefully in Daniel P. Moynihan, "The United States in Opposition," *Commentary* (March 1975): 31–42; and Daniel P. Moynihan and Suzanne Weaver, *A Dangerous Place* (Boston: Little, Brown, 1978).

9 Lydia Swart, "The Future of the G77," in Lydia Swart and Jakob Lund, *The Group of 77: Perspectives on Its Role in the United Nations General Assembly* (New York: Center for UN Reform, 2011), chapter 7.

10 Such as Miguel D'Escoto Brockmann of Nicaragua in his opening speech as president of the 63rd session, 16 September 2008, UN Doc. A/63/PV.1.

11 *Report of the Commission of Experts of the President of the United Nations General Assembly on Reforms of the International Monetary and Financial System* (Stiglitz Commission) 21 September 2009, http://www.un.org/ga/econcrisissummit/docs/FinalReport_CoE.pdf; José Antonio Ocampo, "The United Nations and Global Finance," *Annual Review of United Nations Affairs 2008–2009* 1: xliv–xlv.

12 General Assembly Resolution 63/305, 31 July 2009. The distance between the assembly president's ideas and what the members adopted can be judged by comparing the conference outcome document, given in the Annex to General Assembly Resolution 63/303 of 9 July 2009, with a president's draft dated 18 May 2009, available at http://www.un.org/ga/ president/63/interactive/financialcrisis/outcomedoc.pdf

13 Transition noted in "Rio+20: 'Encouraging Progress' Made on Outcome Document," UN News Centre, 16 June 2012, http://www.un.org/apps/news/story.asp?NewsID=42255&Cr =sustainable%20development&Cr1=.

14 Jakob Lund, "The G77's Limited Role in the Third Committee," in *The Group of 77: Perspectives on its Role in the UN General Assembly*, eds. Lydia Swart and Jakob Lund (New York: Center for UN Reform Education, 2011), 113.

15 General Assembly Resolution 64/289, 14 September 2009, paras. 57 and 60. This is a long resolution titled Systemwide Coherence that also deals with several other matters.

16 Such as Richard Hudson, *The World Needs a Way to Make up Its Mind: The Case for the Binding Triad* (New York: Center for War/Peace Studies, 1981); or Joseph Schwartzberg, *Revitalizing the United Nations: Reform through Weighted Voting* (New York and The Hague: Institute for Global Policy, World Federalist Movement, 2005), Appendix A, 60–63.

17 Wolfgang Reineke and Francis Deng, *Critical Choices, the United Nations, Networks, and the Future of Global Governance* (Ottawa: International Development Research Centre, 2000), explores some possibilities.

18 G20 description on Australian Government's G20 information page at http://www.dfat. gov.au/trade/g20/index.html#representation; G77 claims in remarks of Argentine foreign minister, while chairing the September 2011 meeting of G77 Foreign Ministers in New York, quoted in Swart, "The Future of the G77," 154, note 182.

19 Quoted in Swart, "The Future of the G77," 154.

Regional Governance

Monica Herz

The concept of governance became part of our vocabulary in the 1990s, in the context of the need to capture conceptually an international reality composed of "systems of rule at all levels of human activity" that are ultimately interlinked in relationships of interdependence.[1] We have been engaged in a conversation on political rule and the concept of governance that allows scholars and political actors to pay due attention to the significance of rules that are produced in social spheres beyond (though not in spite of) the state and in the absence of an overarching political authority. The disaggregation of the loci of governance, a dispersion of sites of authority,[2] can be detected, and the wider concept of governance allows for a theoretical and political debate on the process.

Complex interactions at different institutional levels lead to the production of norms, public policy, and dispute-settlement mechanisms. The administration of social life takes place in the context of disaggregated loci of governance, involving states and other actors as collective interests are pursued. In Ulrich Beck's terms, "debounded" risks,[3] such as terrorism, financial crises, transnational crime, infectious diseases, environmental degradation, human rights abuses, and humanitarian crises, which are not contained by national boundaries are to be dealt with on different levels or within different social spheres. In other words, globalization generates a drive to manage risks on a scale wider than the boundaries of the national state; and in this context, regions acquire a new significance. The idea of region was marginalized from the academic debate on governance during the second half of the twentieth century as globalization and global issues drove the search for answers and concepts, but it has been revived during the last 20 years as geography and territory become a reference for the debate on all levels of governance.

This chapter looks into the idea and practice of regional governance during the last 20 years, presenting a contribution for the debate on the role and specificity of this form of governance in the context of the wider discussion of global governance mechanisms.

It begins with definitions and discusses the "idea" itself, and then contrasts this with the actual practice of regional governance.

Key definitions

Regions can be defined in a non-political manner if we depart from one or several criteria such as the level of commerce or geographical design. But here we shall be working with human choices. The political process that leads to the creation of institutions that play a role in governance is the focus of this analysis, thus political processes and social actors invent the regions that become relevant for global governance. Regions are social spaces. They are part of the interactions that generate governance, not solely the stage where this process takes place.[4] The term "region," in fact, originates from the idea of rule, as in *regere*, command, and we shall be looking into regions as the locus for the production of norms, public policy, and dispute mechanisms as a result of the choices by governing elites in the countries that form the region. Thus the definition of regions, although having a geographic reference, is politically contested; and we acknowledge that regions can be the basis for the economic and social interaction, environmental processes, or the construction of identity.[5] But here we shall limit the analysis to geographic regional institutions for governance.

The peculiarity of regional governance is its attachment to a geographic space beyond the nation-state, in contrast with regions as geographic spaces within national states. Regions in the sense used here are areas of the world formed by a number of countries that are economically and politically interdependent and are defined politically by the actors involved in building regional institutions. But we should remember that, initially and more generally, to think in terms of regions implies a specific cut of space, a cognitive move initially made by geographers in the nineteenth century, first by Carl Ritter and through the search for elements of categorization such as climate or water boundaries.

The distinction between regionalization and regionalism should be remembered, as the objective here is to focus on the production of rules. On the one hand, "regionalization" refers to the intensification of economic and social interactions in one region. The deepening of transnational production networks, the growing share of intraregional trade and investment flows, cultural manifestations, and human mobility forge this tendency. Wider interdependence and the emergence of regional actors are part of this process as well. A concentration of activity at the regional level occurs,[6] and as a result regional awareness or identity may develop.[7]

"Regionalism," on the other hand, can be defined as state-led political projects to promote intergovernmental collaboration within the region. It may involve the generation of regional identities and building regional political communities.[8] The phenomenon is today widespread, present throughout the global system. Both spatially and functionally, it is a major part of international relations—and, as we see, both in theory and practice.

Finally, regional governance is a wider process involving state and non-state actors and several locations for authority. It is relevant to the organization of political reality, as indicated by the role the concept has played in the establishment of institutions, discourse, and practice. It is also relevant to the organization of knowledge, as seen in the manner the pertinent literature tackles crucial questions regarding politics, conflict, and cooperation. International cooperation in such different spheres as economic policy coordination, peace processes, peace operations, combating terrorism and transnational crime, building trust, arms control, and disarmament has taken place regionally.

This chapter explores regional governance mechanisms and the functions that they perform. As governance can be generated by an array of actors, including nongovernmental organizations (NGOs), transnational social movements, networks, coalitions, and epistemic communities, intergovernmental regional organizations provide the focus of the analysis as they often are the hub of regional interactions leading to the generation of rules. The next section looks at the development of the idea of regional governance in the 1990s as a prelude to the actual practice of regional organizations in the following section.

The idea of regional governance

The idea of regional governance emerges as one of the crucial concepts devised for an understanding of the complexity of rules in the post-Cold War era. It stems, on the one hand, from the debate about global governance presented throughout this volume and, on the other hand, from diverse perspectives on regionalism and regionalization. This encounter has led to a substantial amount of scholarly literature on the subject.[9]

The space of governance has become more diverse and fragmented, which demands new concepts; and the focus on regional governance is part of a wider debate about rules: who governs what or from what social base? States, sub-national governmental institutions, international organizations, nongovernmental forms of association on different levels are of course part of this story. The idea of regional governance emerges from this broader debate.

Regional integration projects initiated in the 1950s and 1960s were an innovation that put regions in the spotlight. Trade and monetary integration attracted the attention of economists as free trade areas, custom unions, common external tariffs, common markets, and the free movement of factors of production in general were considered. This debate[10] seemed marginal to the understanding of the international system in its bipolar Cold War version even though questions relevant today, such as the proposition by neofunctionalist authors that spillover effects from one sphere of interaction[11] to another could take place, were put forward. By the end of the 1980s, analyses of regional integration processes involved the debate between intergovernmentalists and supranationalists on the role and format of regional institutions and their relations with the changing nature of sovereignty. But only as the multidimensional regionalism of the 1990s emerged, involving economic, cultural, military, political, and social forms of interaction, would the debate on regional integration become part of the broader discussion about regional governance. Regional organizations acquired various new functions, and projects and institutions for cooperation in economic, cultural, military, and other social spheres became interconnected. Regional integration processes solely focused on economic interaction incorporated new tasks and became a basis for cooperation in other social spheres. Moreover, new actors became involved in these regional experiences, demanding a broader concept for the understanding of the process.

As the European Community (and later the European Union, EU) became more integrated in the 1990s, the concept of multi-level governance became prominent in the debates about this regional experience, vying for academic attention with older concepts such as federalism and liberal institutionalism. It was possible to focus on the EU as a political system rather than a process of integration[12] and deal with multiple actors, processes, jurisdictions, and layers of government in place. The dispersion of authoritative decision-making was conceptualized by several authors in this manner and was internalized by political discourse within what became the EU. Thus, this concept allows for an understanding of regional governance as one institutional level in a web of complex governance mechanisms.

Regional governance employs different institutional designs that incorporate states and non-state actors as well. The concept of multi-level or multilayered governance allows us to depict the involvement of states, nongovernmental and informal networks, and activities among academics, researchers, and journalists all taking part in the production of governance.

In order to understand the idea of regional governance, it is crucial to look into the relation between this idea and three other processes taking place in the international system: the changing nature of sovereignty, globalization, and the challenges to nationally based representative democracy.

Regional governance has been conceptualized in close connection with the discussion about the erosion of the concept of sovereignty. The changing nature of sovereignty and regional governance are intertwined, as governing mechanisms are produced in a social sphere beyond the boundaries of the state, and regional governing mechanisms deal with the debounded issues of a globalized world mentioned earlier. State sovereignty may thus be limited by the need to comply with rules produced regionally. At the same time, cooperative decision-making on a regional basis can be seen as a way to strengthen the sovereignty of territorial states. The concept of meta-governance allows us to understand how, in spite of the emergence of rules on a regional basis, the state retains the ultimate decision-making capacity associated with sovereignty.[13] In fact, regional governance often involves the participation of national agencies in practices of regulation,[14] and the concept of regional governance becomes relevant to understand the changing nature of states in the context of global governance. The architecture of states changes as they interact with governing mechanisms emerging at all levels, including the regional. As regional norms are agreed, states adapt to this new reality by creating new agencies, new coalitions, new forms of intervention, and new discourses. At the same time, states need to interact with regional policy networks building coalitions on the regional level necessary to put forward and implement ruling mechanisms. New forms of dialogue and negotiations take place that demand new narratives and institutional designs. Thus "re-spatialization"[15] of the state takes place, involving the redefinition of the locus of state power, actors exercising state power, and normative-ideological justifications for state power.[16]

The relation between regionalization, regionalism or regional governance, and globalization has been hotly debated. Globalization is a concept that allows us to concentrate on the compression of time and on social processes that transcend space, taking into account the relevance of new actors and de-territorialized networks.[17] Neoliberal market-oriented policies since the 1980s have been associated with the intensification of globalization. This phenomenon, whether traced back to the sixteenth century European explorers or to the intensification of the transnationalization of production, investment, and commerce since the 1980s, generates the demand for new rules. Regional governance is one possible answer to such a growing demand. Moreover, regional governance acquired prominence with liberal globalization that produced porous regions in contrast to earlier regional integration schemes of the 1960s and 1970s. The earlier efforts were geared towards building trade blocks based on protectionist policies and areas of production integration that were more competitive internationally and faced unequal relations produced by different rhythms of development. Economic regions open to the world economy but more able to compete are created in the context of the "new regionalism"[18] associated with globalization. Regionalism thought of in terms of social processes that involve civil society and transnational companies, associated with the globalization of commerce, financial transactions, production and technology,[19] is often referred to as new regionalism. In this sense regionalism and regionalization can be understood as one feature of the neoliberal multilateral order.[20]

Regional institutions can be a reaction to or compensation for the market forces of globalization. For the countries in the global South, they may appear to be a way to promote national interests in a world increasingly dominated by the industrialized countries of the North. Several authors view the new role acquired by regional groupings in the global South specifically after the end of the Cold War as a positive sign of regional autonomy, facing up to the specificity of the conflicts in these areas.[21]

As is the case with other forms of governance that do not respect the boundaries of the state, a democratic deficit emerges. Modern representative democratic government is based on the idea that a national community is affected by decisions made by a governing body that represents its voice. In a globalized world where decisions are made on many different levels a democratic deficit emerges.[22] Thus, one is generated when decisions are made on a level that is either regional or international. International and regional organizations have had great difficulty in tackling this issue. The concepts of representation and of debate and negotiation within a political community, on which modern democracy is based, have been finding a torturous way into international and regional organizations, in spite of the generation of mechanisms to bring in nongovernmental organizations and the creation of regional parliaments. Democratic governance,[23] in contrast to democratic government, refers to the institutionalization of spaces for the expression of voices in a context where the agency of the state is not the sole focus, where there is no single player with the capacity to make decisions. Thus the debate on regional governance should also incorporate questions on how democratic governance can be built on this level, and an interesting path lies ahead for research on this subject. The technical functions of international and regional organizations, often portrayed as neutral, further increase the problem. Thus the rise of the unelected[24] in particular raises questions on accountability and the decision-making processes prescribed by representative democracy.

This chapter has not reviewed the literature on regional governance but major theoretical perspectives should be highlighted. The debate on regional governance has been pursued mainly by such liberal institutionalist and constructivist authors as Andrew Hurrell, Ramesh Thakur, Björn Hettne, and Amitav Acharya. Rationalist institutionalists stress the role of regional institutions' diminishing transaction costs, generating transparency and trust, thus increasing the incentives for cooperation. Constructivists, in contrast, look into the historical process of social interactions, mentioned earlier, that change ideas, identities, interests, and preferences and that allow for creating regional governance mechanisms. This perspective takes into account processes of socialization by which norms and values are diffused. In contrast, realism focuses on the distribution of power within a region, on the role of hegemons, and the incorporation of regional power politics into a broader international strategy. These contributions, which can be found in the analysis of specific regions, may prove relevant for an understanding of the relations of power that help shape regional governance. In fact, the tendency in the literature about regional governance is to allow these different perspectives to exist side by side and to inform one another. However, the focus on state interests and the production of more complex political and social processes remains central.

The practice of regional governance

Regionalization processes have generated diverse forms of regional governance mechanisms involving states, non-state actors, and intergovernmental organizations. Using the principle of subsidiarity—working at the lowest level to achieve results— regional actors perceive that some issues can be better managed at the regional rather than the global level, either because the region is more homogeneous or because there is awareness of collective problems or even regional identity, or because it seems more efficient to manage a specific issue, such as migration in Europe or transnational crime in Latin America. Thus for certain issues it may become easier to mobilize resources or agree on a common agenda.

Regional governance is uneven throughout the international system. The levels of institutionalization, of involvement of public and private actors, or of areas of focus and institutional design vary immensely. The contrast is striking, for instance, between Europe—where institutions are highly complex, well funded, and robust—and the Asia-Pacific region—where regional governance is a more recent phenomena.[25] Some institutional settings were initially geared towards one sphere of interaction, moving in a latter period to other spheres of interactions such as the Association of Southeast Asian Nations (ASEAN), which was created in 1967 for a security agenda and then was geared towards emerging forms of regional economic governance in Asia.[26]

Regional governance is intertwined with other forms of governance and, as Peter Katzenstein reminds us, regional institutions were a central part of US strategy in the context of the Cold War, most clearly expressed in the regional alliances generated, such as the North Atlantic Treaty Organization (NATO) and Southeast Asia Treaty Organization (SEATO).[27] The decline of the rivalry between the great powers diminished their perceived interests in different regions; and strategic competition in distant regions in many cases was considered less important.[28] The door was opened for greater and more autonomous interactions within the regional sphere as regional dynamics were no longer solely determined by global dynamics. Moreover, the process of decolonization, which began in the late 1940s and accelerated to the 1960s, laid the basis for regionalization, having created specific dynamics in the international relations of the newly independent countries of Africa, Asia, and the Middle East. This process continued with the end of the Soviet empire and the territorial changes in Asia and Eastern Europe that followed.[29]

The relationship between regional and global governance also acquires meaning when we look at the historical relations between the United Nations and regional organizations. Regions were specifically mentioned in Chapter VIII of the Charter, and cooperation between the UN and regional organizations became part of the debate on the reform of the UN system after the end of the Cold War.[30] The UN secretary-general convened high-level meetings with regional organizations involved in security operations, which produced a framework for cooperation between regional organizations and the UN.[31] In fact, if we look back in time, Article 21 of the Covenant of the League of Nations mentions regional arrangements in deference to the Monroe Doctrine. Moreover, regions have been a reference for the forms of representation within the UN system, and for the five regional economic and social commissions working mainly on development.[32]

It is also relevant to note that regional governance mechanisms do not have an impact restricted to the specific geographic area that they represent. Practices and discourses developed in one region may have an impact in other regions or in the system as a whole. For instance, the European example was considered a point of departure (and sometimes even a "model") for other experiments with regional economic integration; similarly, in considering how to deploy military force or build democratic institutions, NATO or the Organization for Security and Co-operation in Europe (OSCE) serves as a reference. The involvement of regional institutions in out-of-area operations, such as NATO in Afghanistan and Libya, or the EU in the Congo, has also facilitated such a trend.[33]

Regional organizations are central to regional governance and may perform a centripetal role, bringing together private and public actors to focus on one specific issue. A very large number of regional integration agreements, for example, have been generated, and the World Trade Organization (WTO) registers more than 500,[34] many with histories stemming back to the regional integration projects of the 1950s and 1960s. The second phase of regionalism, associated with the idea of new regionalism discussed earlier, began in the 1980s when the EU was re-energized, moving towards monetary union and a single market with more openness towards world markets, but also by multidimensional experiences in which regional organizations expanded their areas of activities.

Other regions followed the European experience, such as the Economic Community of West African States (ECOWAS) or the Common Market of the South (Mercosur), that were a forum and an actor in different spheres, including economic integration, security cooperation, functional coordination, and technical assistance. Table 17.1 lists the most important such organizations.

The process of socialization of regional institutions, which has been taking place since the 1990s, is the most obvious expression of the link between global and regional governance but also of the example effect mentioned earlier. Regional organizations incorporate the discourse and practice that have become legitimate and has legitimized their role in an increasingly homogeneous manner. States, the UN system, and regional organizations are part of this social process where power relations, the success and failure of previous experiences, and the internalization of rules and concepts permit the socialization

Table 17.1 Regional organizations with multiple dimensions

Europe and North America	Americas	Africa	Asia-Pacific and Middle East	Non-territorial definition
NATO	Andean Community	African Union	Arab League	Commonwealth
OSCE	Central American Common Market	South African Customs Union	Gulf Cooperation Council	Organisation of Islamic Conference
EU	Southern Cone Common Market	Communauté Economique de l'Afrique de l'Ouest	Collective Security Treaty Organization	Community of Portuguese Speaking Nations
CSCE	Bolivarian Alliance for the Peoples of Our America	Communauté Economique et Monétaire d'Afrique Centrale	Economic Cooperation—Iran, Turkey, Pakistan	Organisation Internacionale de la Francophonie
EEA	Union of South American Nations	Community of Sahelian Saharan States	Commonwealth of Independent States	
	North American Free Trade Agreement	Common Market for East and Southern Africa	Association of Southeast Asian Nations	
	Organization of East Caribbean States	Economic Community of West African States	Asia Pacific Economic Cooperation	
		East African Community	Mekong Ganga Cooperation	
		Economic Community of Central African States	Indian Ocean Rim Association for Regional Cooperation	
		Southern African Development Coordination Conference	Shanghai Cooperation Organisation	
		Union Economique et Monétaire de l'Ouest African	Security Cooperation Organisation	
		West African Economic and Monetary Union	South Asian Association for Regional Cooperation	
			South Asian Free Trade Agreement	

of regional institutions. Thus, multidimensional regional organizations often perform similar tasks in the economic and political spheres.

Democratic governance is considered today a central link between domestic and international governance, and regional organizations have since the 1990s been moving towards a common agenda and institutional design for the promotion of democratic governance. They have created normative devices, established conditions for participation in their activities and decision-making, formulated assistance programs, and provided a model for the development of representative democracy. The human rights and humanitarian crisis management agendas are linked to the broader democratic governance agenda. Regional organizations also created an apparatus to deal with this area. Table 17.2 lists the range of such measures in several regional organizations.

Regional institutions are involved in promoting development and the coordination of economic policies and in fostering greater regional economic integration. The post-World War II order incorporated a role for regional organizations in the sphere of development promotion and this experience became intertwined with regional integration processes. The role of regional governance mechanisms within the sphere of global economic competition, including the need for mobility of factors of production, acted as an incentive for a host of development promotion initiatives. In the Asia-Pacific region in particular, the 1997–98 financial crisis generated a strong incentive for economic governance on a regional level.

The administration of international security increasingly reflects a preoccupation of regional organizations with security in their region. The negotiation of territorial disputes, an end to intra-state conflicts, and the creation of security regimes increasingly take place within regional organizations. Moreover, regional leaders play a major role in bearing the costs of these processes and shaping their outcomes. Obviously, this is not a single model or homogeneous pattern; in some regions institutions are very developed, and in others ad hoc measures are more common. Some issues, such as territorial disputes, are more prone to regional administration, while others, such as the proliferation of weapons of mass destruction, tend to be dealt with in global forums. Nevertheless, a widespread trend towards the regional administration of issues within the security sphere can be observed. The United States and other major powers have provided incentives and support to foster the acceleration of this tendency.

After the initial optimism regarding the new role of the United Nations in the post-Cold War period, the notion of a "new international order" faded; thus, the discourse on the regionalization of security acquired increasing prominence. There were clear indications that the UN would not be able to deal with its new tasks. Financial limitations, political deadlock, and the problems of coordination between different agencies became evident. The Rwanda tragedy turned this reality into a media event. One of the responses to the crisis of UN overstretch, presented by both practitioners and specialists,[35] was sharing responsibilities and tasks with regional organizations or ad hoc coalitions. NATO, the Organization of American States (OAS), the OSCE, and others offered themselves as mechanisms for security administration in this context, as they redefined their role and identities in the new international environment. The 1990 intervention by ECOWAS in Liberia marked the beginning of greater participation by regional agencies in fostering international peace and security. The coordination between regional organizations and the UN became especially evident and acute as international

Table 17.2 Regional organizations for human rights and humanitarian action

International organization	Human rights/humanitarian institutions	Documents and conventions
African Union	African Court on Human and Peoples' Rights Peace and Security Council	
ECOWAS	Department of Humanitarian and Social Affairs Office of the Commissioner of Political Affairs, Peace and Security	
ASEAN	ASEAN Intergovernmental Commission on Human Rights	
South Asian Association for Regional Cooperation	Technical committees on gender inequalities and reduction of poverty	
OSCE	Office for Democratic Institutions and Human Rights	
Organisation for the Islamic Conference		Cairo Declaration on Human Rights in Islam
Organisation Internationale de la Francophonie	Réseaux Institutionelles de la Francophonie	
European Union	European Instrument for Democracy and Human Rights (European Commission) EU Special Representative for Human Rights (European Commission) The Commission's European Community Humanitarian Office (European Commission) Monitoring and Information Centre (European Commission) Committee on Civil Liberties, Justice and Home Affairs (European Parliament) Subcommittee on Human Rights (European Parliament) Human Rights Unit (European Parliament) EU Agency for Fundamental Rights (Council of European Union)	
Commonwealth of Independent States		Convention on Human Rights
Arab League	Civil Emergency Planning	
OAS	Inter-American Court of Human Rights Inter-American Commission on Human Rights Inter-American Program on the Promotion of Women's Human Rights and Gender Equity and Equality Inter-American Commission of Women Inter-American Children's Institute Inter-American Program and Protection of the Human Rights of Migrants, Including Migrant Workers and their Families Inter-American Program of Judicial Facilitators	
Mercosur	Instituto de Politicas Públicas de Derecho Humanos (IPPDDHH) Reunión de Atlas Autobridades enel Área de Derechos Humanos	
CAN	Programa de Trabajo para la Difusion y Ejecucion de la Carta Andina para la Promocion y Protección de los Derechos Humanos	Declaración del Consejo Presidencial Andino sobre Democracia e Integración Declaración de Machu Picchu sobre la Democracia, los Derechos de los Pueblos Indigenas y la Lucha Contra la Pobreza

Table 17.3 Contributions of regional organizations to peace operations, 2011*

Multilateral Operations 2011	
Multilateral Operations	Country
North Atlantic Treaty Organization	
International Security Assistance Force	Afghanistan
Kosovo Force	Kosovo
Training Mission in Iraq	Iraq
European Union	
EUFOR ALTHEA	Bosnia
EU Mission to Provide Advice and Assistance for Security Sector Reform in Congo	Congo
European Union Border Assistance Mission Rafah	Palestine
European Union Monitoring Mission	Georgia
European Union Police Mission	Afghanistan
European Union Police Mission for the Palestinian Territories (EUPOL COPPS)	Palestine
European Union Police Mission in Bosnia and Herzegovina (EUPM)	Bosnia
European Union Rule of Law Mission in Kosovo (EULEX KOSOVO)	Kosovo
Police Assistance Mission of the European Community to Albania (PAMECA)	Albania
Organization for Security and Co-operation in Europe	
Mission to Kosovo	Kosovo
Mission to Moldova	Moldova
Mission to Serbia	Serbia
Presence in Albania	Albania
Spillover Monitor Mission to Skopje	Macedonia
Organization of American States	
Mission to Support the Peace Process in Colombia	Colombia
Ad hoc	
Operation Licorne	Ivory Coast
Regional Assistance Mission to Solomon Islands	Solomon
Timor Leste Defense	Timor Leste
African Union	
Mission in Somalia	Somalia
Operation in Darfur UNAMID	Sudan
Commonwealth	
Joint Control Commission for Georgian–Ossetian Conflict Resolution	Georgia

Note: * Stockholm International Peace Research Institute, *SIPRI Map of Multilateral Peace Operation Deployments*, http://books.sipri.org/files/misc/SIPRIPKOMAP0911.pdf.

involvement in the conflict in Bosnia grew. *The Agenda for Peace*, written by Boutros Boutros-Ghali at the outset of his tenure as UN secretary-general, promoted the activities of regional agencies; and the 2000 Brahimi Report sought to regulate the relationship between the UN and these regional actors.[36] Thus, regional organization became increasingly relevant for the administration of international security, allowing for a new vocabulary to emerge, such as regionalization of security and subcontracting.[37]

The concern with state failure became the focus. The need to provide assistance to strengthen state institutions has been a common theme in different strands of the academic and policy literatures since the 1990s following the "failure" of the Somali state. Violence, refugees, and economic disruption that follow state failure acquire a regional dimension as they inevitably move across borders. In this context, regional actors tend to be willing to engage in action in support of internal and international governance. Countries such as Brazil and Nigeria and organizations such as the African Union (AU) are considered important allies in dealing with institutional crises, internal conflicts, and humanitarian crisis.

Finally, after the attacks on the United States in September 2001, the fight against terrorism has become an organizing device in the international arena; and thus, the role that regional mechanisms play in strengthening governance acquired new meaning and intensity. Regional organizations have been portrayed as complementary to global organizations, concerts of great powers, or the states in fighting terrorism and state failure.

The contribution of regional organizations to peace operations has increased dramatically and is a useful indication of their participation in global governance.[38] They contribute troops for the maintenance of international peace and security, help build or rebuild state institutions, and are involved actively in conflict management. Table 17.3 highlights the contributions of regional organizations to peace operations in 2011.

Conclusion

This chapter has presented the idea and practices of regional governance, highlighting the relations between these mechanisms and global processes in a context of the fragmentation of authority and the diversifications of forms of governance. The historical processes that led to the current debate about regional governance were analyzed with a special focus on the end of the bipolar system. The dynamics that take place in different regions generate a very diverse range of experiences, and none more so than the role of previous integration processes and of globalization. Moreover, the level of institutionalization, areas of cooperation, and strength of actors vary in each region. Though acknowledging diversity, this chapter spells out the role played by multidimensional organizations since the 1990s in the sphere of economic cooperation, political change, and security.

Regional mechanisms are part of more universal processes led by the most powerful in the international system and have adapted to the demands posed by a global debate on debounded threats and challenges. They can only be understood in the context of these wider processes. In fact, as we have seen, peace operations or human rights mechanisms are created throughout the globe within regional organizations, and the same could be said of the fight against terrorism, transnational crime, or environmental degradation. The focus on regions as relevant political spaces has produced distinct political choices, which requires more research as the pursuit of past policy options continuously generates new rules, identities, and regions.

Additional reading

1. Mary Farrell, Björn Hetne, and Luk Van Langenhove, eds., *Global Politics of Regionalism* (London: Pluto Press, 2005).
2. Andrew F. Cooper, Christopher W. Hughes, and Philippe de Lombaerde, *Regionalisation and Global Governance* (London: Routledge, 2008).
3. Ian Bache and Matthew V. Flinders, eds., *Multi-level Governance* (Oxford: Oxford University Press, 2004).
4. Barry Buzan and Ole Waever, *Regions and Powers: The Structure of International Security* (Cambridge: Cambridge University Press, 2004).

Notes

1 James N. Rosenau, "Governance in the Twenty-First Century," *Global Governance* 1, no. 1 (1995): 13; Thomas G. Weiss, "Governance, Good Governance and Global Governance," *Third World Quarterly* 21, no. 5 (2000): 795–814.
2 James N. Rosenau, *Distant Proximities: Dynamics beyond Globalization* (Princeton: Princeton University Press, 2003).
3 Ulrich Beck, *World Risk Society* (Cambridge: Polity Press, 1999).
4 Rogério Haesbaert, *Regional-Global: Dilemas da Região e da Regionalização na Geografia Contemporânea* (Rio de Janeiro, Brazil: Bertrand Brasil, 2010), 114.
5 Haesbaert, *Regional-Global*, 238.
6 Louise Fawcett, "Regionalism from an Historical Perspective," in *Global Politics of Regionalism*, eds. Mary Farrell, Björn Hetne, and Luk Van Langenhove (London: Pluto Press, 2005), 25.
7 Andrew Hurrell, "The Regional Dimension in International Relations Theory," in *Global Politics of Regionalism*, eds. Farrell, Hetne, and Van Langenhove, 38–53.
8 Fawcett, "Regionalism from an Historical Perspective," 21–37.
9 See Andrew F. Cooper, Christopher W. Hughes, and Philippe de Lombaerde, *Regionalisation and Global Governance* (London: Routledge, 2008); Farrell, Hettne, and Van Langenhove, *Global Politics of Regionalism*; and a special issue of the *Australian Journal of International Affairs* 63, no. 3 (2009).
10 Ernst B. Haas and Philippe Schiter, "Economics and Differential Patterns of Integration Projections about Unity in Latin America," *International Organization* 18, no. 4 (1964): 259–299.
11 Ernst B. Haas, *The Uniting of Europe Political, Social and Economic Forces, 1950–1957* (Stanford: Stanford University Press, 1958).
12 Gary Marks, "Structural Policy and Multi-Level Governance," in *The State of the European Community, Vol 2: The Maastricht Debates and Beyond*, eds. Alan W. Carfuny and Glenda G. Rosenthal (London: Longman, 1993).
13 Bob Jessop, "Multi-Level Governance and Multi-Level Metagovernance," in *Multi-Level Governance*, eds. Ian Bache and Matthew Flinders (Oxford: Oxford University Press, 2004), 49–74.
14 Kanishka Jayasuriya, "Regulatory Regionalism in the Asia Pacific Region," *Australian Journal of International Affairs* 63, no. 3 (2009): 335–347.

15 I refer to the reconstruction of the relation between social relations and space central to the debate on globalization in social theory. Relations between space and social interaction have been at the center of Anthony Giddens' analysis of social relations. Particularly relevant here is his focus on relations that are not face to face but emerge in the context of social systems. The stretching of social relations from face-to-face interaction to other spaces allows for rules and resources to be reproduced as part of social integration. As Giddens says, "space is not an empty dimension along which social groupings become structured, but has to be considered in terms of its involvement in the constitution of systems of interaction." Anthony Giddens, *The Constitution of Society* (Cambridge, Cambridge University Press 1984), 368.

16 Shahar Hameiri, "Beyond Methodological Nationalism, but Where to for the Study of Regional Governance?," *Australian Journal of International Affairs* 63, no. 3 (2009): 439.

17 Jan Aart Sholte, *Globalization: A Critical Introduction* (New York: St. Martin's Press, 2000).

18 Literature on the subject includes Björn Hettne, Andras Inotai, and Osvaldo Sunkel, eds., *The New Regionalism Series*, Vol. I–V (London: Macmillan, 1999–2001); Finn Laursen, ed., *Comparative Regional Integration: Theoretical Perspectives* (Aldershot: Ashgate, 2003).

19 For an analysis of new regionalism, see Björn Hettne and Fredrik Söderbaum, "The New Regionalism Approach," *Politeia* 17, no. 3 (1998): 6–21.

20 James Mittelman and Richard Falk, "Global Hegemony and Regionalism," in *Regionalism in the Post-Cold War World*, ed. Stephen C. Calleya (Aldershot: Ashgate, 2000), 3.

21 Amitav Acharya, "The Periphery as the Core: The Third World and Security Studies," in *Critical Security Studies*, eds. Keith Krause and Michael C. Williams (Minneapolis: University of Minnesota Press, 1997), 299–327.

22 David Held, *Democracy and the Global Order: From the Modern State to Cosmopolitan Governance* (Stanford: Stanford University Press, 1995).

23 Amit Ron, "Modes of Democratic Governance," in *Oxford Handbook of Governance*, ed. David L. Faur (Oxford: Oxford University Press, 2012), 472–484.

24 Frank Vilbert, *The Rise of the Unelected: Democracy and the New Separation of Powers* (Cambridge: Cambridge University Press, 2007).

25 Yasumasa Komori, "Regional Governance in East Asia and the Asia Pacific," *East Asia* 26, no. 4 (2009): 321–341.

26 Heribert Dieter, "Changing Patterns of Regional Governance: From Security to Political Economy?," *The Pacific Review* 22, no. 1 (2009): 73–90.

27 Peter Katzenstein, *A World of Regions: Asia and Europe in the American Imperium* (Ithaca: Cornell University Press, 2005).

28 Barry Buzan and Ole Waever, *Regions and Powers: The Structure of International Security* (Cambridge: Cambridge University Press, 2004), 10.

29 Ibid., 15–16.

30 See, for example, Michael Pugh and Waheguru Pal Singh Sidhu, *The United Nations and Regional Security: Europe and Beyond* (Boulder: Lynne Rienner, 2003).

31 Ramesh Thakur and Luk Van Langenhove, "Enhancing Global Governance through Regional Integration," in *Regionalisation and Global Governance*, eds. Andrew F. Cooper, Christopher W. Hughes, and Philippe de Lombaerde (London: Routledge, 2008).

32 Yves Berthelot, ed., *Unity and Diversity in Development Ideas: Perspectives from the UN Regional Commissions* (Indianapolis: Indiana University Press, 2004).

33 Fawcett, "Regionalism from an Historical Perspective," 25.

34 See World Trade Organization's *Regional Trade Agreements*, www.wto.org/english/tratop_e/region_e/region_e.htm.

35 Thomas G. Weiss, ed., *Beyond UN Sub-Contracting: Task-Sharing with Regional Security Arrangements and Service-Providing NGOs* (London: Macmillan, 1998); and Pugh and Sidhu, eds., *The United Nations and Regional Security*.

36 Boutrous Boutrous-Gali, *An Agenda for Peace: Preventive Diplomacy, Peacemaking and Peacekeeping* (A/47/277 – S/24111), June 1992, http://www.unrol.org/files/A_47_277.pdf; Lakhdar Brahimi, *Report of the Panel on United Nations Peace Operations* (A/55/305 – S/2000/809), 2000, http://www.un.org/peace/reports/peace_operations/docs/full_report.htm.
37 Pugh and Sidhu, *The United Nations and Regional Security.*
38 For regional organizations and peace operations, see Alex Bellamy and Paul D. Williams, "Who's Keeping the Peace? Regionalization and Contemporary Peace Operations," *International Security* 29, no. 4 (2005): 157–195.

The European Union

Ben Rosamond

The European Union (EU) is both a regime of regional governance and an actor within the global governance system. This relatively simple observation needs to be fleshed out to consider the relationship between these two roles. Is the EU's primary purpose to insulate its member states from global pressures while protecting and advancing a distinctive European model of society and political economy? Alternatively, does it function as a kind of cipher through which European societies are globalized? Questions like this are not easily answered. They are the sources of considerable debate within International Relations and the more specialized subfield of EU Studies, with discussion tending to cluster around two distinct understandings of the interplay between the nature of the union's internal governance and its status as an actor within the global system.

The first position maintains that the EU's primary rationale is to transplant global governance norms into the European context. This line of argument tends to associate European integration with the "constitutionalization" of neoliberal global governance norms.[1] The second position treats the EU as an important managerial intermediary between global processes and European societies. The EU thus "manages" globalization and seeks to fashion a distinctive European approach to political economy and to protect certain types of institutions and values. In this second version, the EU is also an actor seeking to use its "normative power" to propagate its norms globally and/or its "market" power to fashion the global regulatory order in ways that suit its interests.[2] What the EU does matters because membership involves a significant delegation of powers from the national governments to the European level. Since member states have voluntarily ceded parts of their sovereignty to European institutions, it is important to ask why and with what purpose.

This chapter concentrates on the relationship between the EU's own character as a regime of European economic governance on the one hand and its participation in global governance. It begins with an overview of the structures and then summarizes the development of the EU from its origins in the 1950s, noting the significance of two features: its distinctive institutional design and its status as a "market order." It is suggested that these two features are important to the constitution of the EU as an actor in the politics of global governance. The chapter then considers interest-driven and "normative power" accounts of the EU's external behavior before considering some examples of the way in which it seeks to influence outcomes in global economic governance and how these relate back to its internal characteristics. The chapter closes with a few concluding comments about the sustainability of the EU.

A complex institution

Needless to say, there is—within these discussions—a temptation to "essentialize" the EU: to insist, in other words, that it must conform to one or other of these ideal typical positions. But two features of the EU need to be taken into account in this context: its longevity and its complexity. The union's longevity—its direct ancestor the European Coal and Steel Community (ECSC) was created by the Treaty of Paris in 1951—means that its character may have shifted and indeed drifted over time. Nothing illustrates this point more vividly than the controversy surrounding the award of the Nobel Peace Prize to the EU in 2012. Critics of the award were puzzled as to how an organization responsible for the imposition of harsh austerity budgeting on one of its member states (Greece) could be given an award designed to recognize the promotion of "fraternity between nations." The most typical counter-argument stated that the prize was recognition of a *historic* achievement: the role of European integration in securing over six decades of peace in Europe.

Also, by the standards of most other international organizations and forms of regional cooperation, the EU is institutionally complex. It has intergovernmental and supranational institutions. The Commission is a supranational bureaucratic body that is formally responsible for the initiation of legislation. The Commission's proposals must be compliant with the treaties and it must be able to show that EU-level action is justified. Intergovernmental interests are represented by the Council of Ministers (often known simply as the Council). A Council meeting consists of government ministers from the member states with responsibility for the policy area under discussion. The Council's primary task is to legislate the proposals forwarded to it by the Commission. EU legislation takes two primary forms. Regulations are directly and immediately applicable in national law, whereas Directives have to be legislated into national law by national parliaments. The implementation of Directives is normally allowed to take account of specific national circumstances and administrative arrangements. When first created in the 1950s, the European Parliament (EP) consisted of delegates from national parliaments and was merely consulted for an opinion on legislative proposals.

Since 1979 the EP has been directly elected and since the 1980s it has gradually acquired more powers, including powers of legislative co-decision with the Council. The EP formally approves the appointment of the Commission and has oversight of the EU budget. The Commission's agenda-setting monopoly has been progressively challenged since the 1970s by the evolution of the European Council: the regular summit meetings of member-state heads of government. The EU oversees a large body of supranational law that is supreme over any conflicting legislation in the member states.

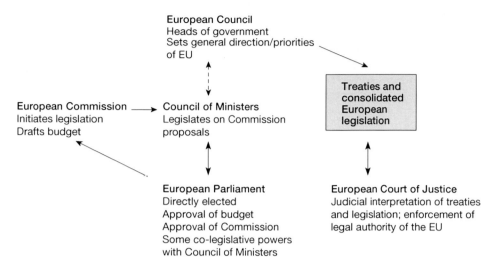

Figure 18.1 The institutions of the European Union

The European Court of Justice is charged with interpreting EU law, and its jurisprudence has been very significant to advancing integration and establishing the authority of the European legal order over national systems. The institutions of the EU are illustrated in Figure 18.1.

The EU has competence over a large number of policy areas, primarily relating to economic governance. The Commission is currently organized into 33 Directorates General, each charged with a particular policy domain. However, the degree to which any given policy area is Europeanized varies, and each policy domain has its own distinct trajectory as well as its own institutional logic.

The evolution of the EU

The EU's growth and development are perhaps most easily understood by looking through two prisms: treaties and institutional design; and the internal market.

Treaties and institutional design

The EU's origins lie in the dilemmas confronting European states in the aftermath of World War II. The ECSC sought to integrate the coal and steel sectors of its six founding member states (Belgium, France, the Federal Republic of Germany, Italy, Luxembourg, and the Netherlands) under the auspices of a common high authority. The foundation of the ECSC was notable for a number of reasons. First, although a limited project of sectoral integration, it was explicitly designed to solve Europe's major security dilemma: the historic enmity between France and Germany. As the ECSC's primary proponent, French foreign minister Robert Schuman, put it: "The solidarity in production thus established will make it plain that any war between France and Germany becomes not merely unthinkable, but materially impossible."[3] Thus the second feature of lasting interest was the method selected to resolve the European security dilemma. The integration of economies, starting with the strategically important coal and steel sectors, would be used to create radical and lasting economic interdependence between the participating countries.

Following a clear commercial liberal logic, deep economic interdependence would significantly reduce (to the point of eradication) the probability of violent conflict between member states. Their economies would be bound together in welfare-enhancing ways that would make it irrational to defect from the arrangement. Interdependence would be further underscored by the institutionalization of the new regime. So the third feature of the ECSC that generates lasting interest is its institutional design. The most striking feature of this design was the creation of the High Authority, a supranational bureaucratic body charged with the strategic oversight, management of the integration process, and the initiation of relevant legislative measures in accordance with the treaty. The supranationalism of the High Authority (which later became the Commission) was offset by an intergovernmental institution (the Council of Ministers), but the ECSC Treaty set in place the principle of policy initiation as the responsibility of a European-level bureaucratic actor. Indeed the Treaty of Paris laid down the basic institutional pattern (described above and illustrated in Figure 18.1) that has survived into the modern incarnation of the EU.

As suggested earlier, the EU is unusually institutionalized by the standards of conventional international organizations. Moreover, the EU's institutional design— inherited from decisions taken in the 1950s—contains a much greater degree of supranationality than that of any other regional integration project. This observation confirms something of quite significant theoretical importance: institutional designs can be "sticky" over time and can remain intact despite the solution of the original dilemmas which prompted policy-makers to create them in the first place. The communities of the 1950s were institutional solutions created by politicians living under the shadow of the unprecedented violence of two world wars, both fought to a large extent in the European "theatre." That context and those imperatives changed, but the institutional framework and the core policy methodology (supranational initiative–intergovernmental legislation–supranational judicial oversight) remained intact. This issue also relates to a controversial analytical puzzle: is the EU comparable to other regional organizations, or rather is it a unique case without historical precedent or contemporary parallel? There is a sizable and still-growing academic literature on this problem, but it is also an inter-national policy issue: to what degree does the EU provide a template for other regional organizations to emulate? Is there a "European model" of regionalism? And if so what does that model consist of beyond a basic institutional design? This question matters in the context of debates about global governance.

The subsequent evolution of the EU was first defined by the signing by the original "Six" of the Treaties of Rome in 1957, which created the European Atomic Energy Community (Euratom) and, most importantly, the European Economic Community (EEC). The three communities (thereafter "The European Communities," EC) were fused into a common institutional framework by the Merger Treaty of 1965). The main treaty changes in the EU's history are illustrated in Table 18.1. On the face of it, this history of treaty reform suggests that the EU has become more deeply integrated over time (for example from single market to monetary union), that policy competence in an increasing number of domains has moved from national to (at least partially) supranational level, and that integration has moved decisively beyond the sphere of the economy (most notably the incursion of the EU into matters of policing and internal security and foreign security). While this "bird's-eye view" account is undoubtedly correct, it masks the extent to which ratification of new treaties has become highly contentious. Most recently, the attempt to create a so-called "constitutional treaty" had to be abandoned after the proposal was defeated in ratification referendums in France and the Netherlands in 2005. The first evidence of domestic discontent with the direction of the EU came with the surprise rejection of the Maastricht Treaty on European Union by the Danish electorate in June 1992.

This tendency has been thought of in terms of a breakdown of a 40-year "permissive consensus" in which domestic publics had tolerated the advance of integration as orchestrated by their governing elites. Debate exists about why that "permissive con-

Table 18.1 Evolution of the treaties of the EU*

Date of signing	Treaty	Purpose
1951	Treaty of Paris	Establishment of the European Coal and Steel Community.
1957	Treaties of Rome	Establishment of the European Economic Community and the European Atomic Energy Community
1965	Merger Treaty	Fusion of the three existing communities into a single set of institutions.
1986	Single European Act	Specification of a timetable for completion of the common market. Move to qualified majority voting in matters relating to the internal market. Expansion of powers of the European Parliament.
1992	Maastricht Treaty on European Union	Formal creation of the EU. Creation of the category of European citizenship. Specification of institutional format, process, and conditions for the creation of monetary union. Creation of the Common Foreign and Security Policy. Creation of EU competence in "Justice and Home Affairs." Introduction of the co-decision procedure, giving the European Parliament powers of co-legislation with the Council in some areas.
1997	Treaty of Amsterdam	Increased use of co-decision. Incorporation of the Schengen Agreement into the Treaties. Pre-enlargement institutional reforms.
2001	Treaty of Nice	Institutional reforms, including changes to the composition of the Commission and recalibration of voting weights in the Council.
2007 (not in force until 2009)	Treaty of Lisbon	Creation of permanent Council Presidency and a New High Representative for Foreign Affairs. Creation of European External Action Service. New powers to the European Parliament. Changes in voting procedures in the Council. Introduction of the "citizens' initiative." Legally binding "Charter of Fundamental Rights."

Note: * The treaties are consolidated into the Treaty on European Union and the Treaty on the Functioning of the European Union.

sensus" has eroded. One line of argument links the advance of integration into areas where core sovereignty concerns are raised (control of monetary policy, border management and policing, foreign policy) to the absence of EU-level mechanisms to allow proper democratic oversight. This is part and parcel of what is often called the "democratic deficit," a problem that has become amplified in public consciousness across Europe over the past two decades. The management of these ratification dilemmas has led to one important consequence: the proliferation of derogations and opt-outs negotiated by and granted to some member states (for example the Danish and British opt-outs from monetary union). This in turn leads to a much more flexible, variegated, and differentiated picture of integration than might be apparent at first sight.[4] This is important for debates about the relationship between European and global governance and the possible status of the former as a model for the latter.

The significance of the internal market

The 1957 EEC Treaty committed the member states not only to the elimination of internal customs duties, but also to the establishment of a customs union (which would levy a common external tariff on imports to the community) and to the abolition of obstacles to the free movement of goods, persons, services, and capital. In other words, from its inception the EU was a market-making project. Indeed, for some scholars this is the EU's central defining feature. It is seen from this perspective as an organization tasked with the creation, maintenance, and regulation of a liberal market order.[5] Of course, 17 of the current member states have moved well beyond the common market stage of integration by engaging in a monetary union and the creation of a single currency. EU membership is meant to imply willingness to adopt the Euro, but member-state economies need to be performing suitably in terms of a series of "convergence criteria" covering budget deficits, accumulated national debt, and exchange rate stability before transition to the single currency can be sanctioned. These performance parameters are not required for membership of the EU, which means that the union consists of three groups: countries that have dissolved their national currencies, those which are committed to do so, but are not yet ready, and those which have either negotiated opt-outs from monetary union (Denmark and the UK) or found ways to stay out (Sweden).

In addition, the EU has significant and growing policy competences in two other areas: justice and home affairs, and foreign and security policy. A major part of the latter is the Common Security and Defence Policy (CSDP), which allows for the EU to operate as an entity in military operations, notably in the realms of humanitarian assistance, peacekeeping, and crisis management. The emergence of this policy competence, while still limited, challenges the post-war division of labor between the EU (charged with economic integration) and the likes of NATO and the Western European Union (WEU), which organized and delivered European security through military means. Whether the EU *should* have extended its reach in this way is a significant political question for some member states, and for some close observers of the EU there are strong technical and normative grounds for the EU not extending beyond the delivery and regulation of the single market.[6]

The EU's foundational commitment to its own internal market has a number of important ancillary implications. These are not usually present in regional organizations,

Table 18.2 European Union enlargements

Date	New member states
1951	Belgium, France, (Federal Republic of) Germany, Italy, Luxembourg, Netherlands (6 member states in total)
1973	Denmark, Ireland, United Kingdom (9)
1981	Greece (10)
1986	Portugal, Spain (12)
1995	Austria, Finland, Sweden (15)
2004	Cyprus, Czech Republic, Estonia, Hungary, Latvia, Lithuania, Malta, Poland, Slovakia, Slovenia (25)
2007	Bulgaria, Romania (27)
2013	Croatia* (28)
	Official candidates: Iceland (applied for membership in 2009), FYR Macedonia (2004), Montenegro (2004), Serbia (2009), Turkey (1987)

Note: *Croatia is scheduled to join the EU on 1 July 2013, assuming ratification of the Accession Treaty by all other member states.

which typically exist to deliver a less intense form of integration (recall that most regional organizations operate with nothing more that the *aspiration* to create a free trade area). First, the quest for a common market requires a significant transfer of regulatory authority from the national to the European level. This is needed to secure the approximation of relevant laws and standards across the member states. While this has been made somewhat simpler following the acceptance of the mutual recognition principle (the idea that a product or service cannot be excluded from the territory of another state even if the technical or quality specifications differ between originating and receiving countries) over the past three decades, that simplicity has been offset by two facets of European integration: the enlargement to include significantly more member states (the "Six" have become 27, soon to be 28—a summary of EU enlargements is in Table 18.2) and the expansion of EU policy competence over time. The thousands of legislative acts and European Court of Justice judgments that constitute the *acquis communautaire* run to 35 chapters, covering—mostly—matters pertaining to the regulation of the single market. Adoption of the *acquis* is a basic requirement for new prospective member states.

The second implication of the commitment to the single market is that it spawns a need for common policies. A single market cannot operate without an active competition policy (the regulation of mergers, acquisitions, cartels, market dominance, and state aid to industry) and this has become one of the most important EU policy regimes. Likewise, the development of a common external tariff and a collective commercial (trade) policy is needed to guarantee that no single member state can acquire competitive advantage by applying differential tariffs to imports from outside the EU at the national border. The single market, even if considered straightforwardly as a set of measures to reduce barriers to factor movement, brings a number of policy domains into the purview of the EU: the regulation of banking and financial services, environmental policy, and company law, to take but three prominent examples.

This leads to a third outgrowth of the single market, which relates specifically to the free movement of persons. Labor mobility implies the freedom of a citizen of one member state to work and live in another. This brings with it a range of additional issues that would need to be resolved for the single market to function properly: rights of access to social security and healthcare, the right of residence, the capacity of mobile workers to access banking and credit facilities, and voting rights. The 1992 Treaty on European Union's creation of the category of EU citizen showed the extent to which the requirement of a transnationally mobile workforce "spilled over" into something rather deeper (and somewhat beyond the scope of what was functionally necessarily from the point of view of economic imperatives). In addition, the incorporation of the Schengen Agreement (allowing border-free movement within the area defined by participating states) into the treaties in 1997 amounted to the moment when the free movement of persons within (large parts of) the EU was legally guaranteed.

The fourth concern is whether the commitment to complete the single market carries with it an imperative to integrate more extensively and more deeply. Scholars of the early communities together with economic theorists of the time held that this was an inherent dynamic of the integration process.[7] For example, creating conditions for free factor movement would create significant pressures for supranational involvement in social policy. A single market might be made more efficient by the adoption of a single currency to enhance transparency and reduce transaction costs in the process of cross-border economic exchange. Indeed, in the history of the EU one tactic (used principally by the Commission) has been to initiate deliberation on deeper integration when progress on a more modest set of integration commitments has stalled. This might explain why the Commission began work on monetary union in the early 1960s, despite there being no mention of it in the EEC Treaty. In the present period a similar dynamic may be at play in moves towards the creation of a fiscal union as a way to solve deep dilemmas associated with monetary union, dilemmas that became apparently intractable after 2010 in the context of the sovereign debt crisis in the Eurozone.

The fifth and final implication of the internal market is external, and vital for broader questions of global economic governance. Because the EU is a customs union, it operates with a single voice within the WTO. This places the EU as a major force within global trade politics, but it is also important to note that the EU is one of the world's primary regulators and a major site of regulatory innovation. According to the *Economist*, it "is becoming the world's regulatory capital."[8] For example, external producers seeking access to the internal market—the largest "economy" in the world by GDP and one of the largest by population (a little over half a billion)—must conform to EU product standards. And some producers have actively chosen to adopt EU standards rather than those of other major regulatory powers, most notably the US.[9] This is an example of how the internal market is generative of the EU's "market power" and of how the single market is "nested" within the global economy. Indeed, former EU Trade Commissioner Peter Mandelson was keen to make the point that European power more generally was enhanced by the EU's successes in the global spread of its regulatory norms and standards (and the principles that sit beneath these).

The EU and global governance

It has been suggested already that the EU is a significant player in global governance almost by default. As a trade bloc with a common external tariff it operates formally as a collective unitary actor in international trade negotiations. Moreover, its single market means that the EU is one of the most significant suppliers of regulatory standards in the global economy. The global domains of trade and regulation are the most obvious venues for the "externalization" of EU policy competence. But they are also interesting for two other reasons. First of all, we might ask about the extent to which the EU actively pursues discernible (European) interests in the global governance arena. Second, we might wonder whether the EU works on behalf of a specific set of values. Needless to say, these two questions correspond to quite different readings of the EU as an actor within global governance. These in turn tend to map onto respectively rationalist and constructivist understandings of world politics. A variety of rationalist understandings of the EU as an actor are possible, but all would expect the EU's preferences as a regulator or as a trade negotiator to reflect certain underlying interests that would be traceable back to the "domestic" context of intra-European integration (and in turn to, *inter alia,* the interests of particular member states, or organized interests, or particular supranational institutions). The constructivist position would expect the EU's actions in global politics to be driven by certain ideas and for its actions to seek to set certain normative standards in world politics. The recent debate about whether the EU is a "normative power"[10] is, in many ways, the key intellectual space for discussion between these two characterizations.

Advocates of the "normative power Europe" (NPE) position hold that the EU's external behavior is founded upon a set of core values that are inscribed into the treaties. The EU's actions should be interpreted in terms of setting standards for what is "normal" in world politics, where that "normality" is the effective spread of the EU's core norms globally. Ian Manners identifies the EU's nine core norms as "sustainable peace," "social freedom," "consensual democracy," "associative human rights," "supranational rule of law," "inclusive equality," "social solidarity," "sustainable development," and "good governance." This suggests that the EU's "foreign policy" (broadly defined) might be a very distinctive presence and a quite important component in the politics of global governance. Manners, for example, argues that the EU has been a major force in struggles to spread global human rights norms such as the abolition of the death penalty—a position which marks it out very clearly from a major normative rival in the democratic world, the US.[11]

The most developed critiques of the NPE position fall into three types. The first simply maintains that it is mistaken to see the EU's behavior as value driven. The EU is seen as an interest-driven actor like any other, its normative language seen as little more than rhetorical cover for behavior that is strategically motivated and inconsistent in application. A second position does not necessarily dispute that the EU seeks to propagate and spread its norms. Rather the objection is that it—through policy frameworks such as the European Neighbourhood Policy—actually promotes these norms coercively and without allowing any form of dialogue between its norms and the norms of others. A third position is yet more sympathetic to the basic claims that external behavior is internally constituted by core values and that external action is "normative" in character. But it suggests that the standard NPE account overemphasizes a set of positive civic liberal values while neglecting the importance of economic liberalism as also (and perhaps predominantly) constitutive of the EU and its behavior.[12]

The NPE account of Europe's role in global governance is a normative position in itself. In other words, those using the term are not only analyzing what the EU is, but also saying something about what they think the EU *should be*. The NPE position dovetails quite precisely with the self-image of the EU that is found in, for example, the Commission's communicative discourse, where the term has been adopted to describe the EU's comparative advantage as the source of important values. The idea of spreading Europe's core values has been a part of the treaties since Amsterdam (1997) and the European Security Strategy is explicit in articulating that external military deployments in the name of the EU should operate on behalf of key values that closely resemble the list assembled by Manners: "The best protection for our security is a world of well-governed democratic states. Spreading good governance, supporting social and political reform, dealing with corruption and abuse of power, establishing the rule of law and protecting human rights are the best means of strengthening the international order."[13]

A few examples of the EU's engagement in global economic governance illustrate the complexities that are raised in the course of any attempt to ascertain the essence of the EU's external behavior. The fact that the picture is complex should not surprise regular students of European integration, for whom the question of what (if anything) the EU is remains an ongoing puzzle. Since the onset of debates around the concept of globalization in the mid-1990s two basic positions about the EU have taken shape in the literature (and have been, at the same time, reflected in policy discourse). For some the EU is nothing less than an incarnation of neoliberal globalization: an institutional device for the accelerated globalization of European societies. For others the EU is a vital buffer between the ravages of a global market order and European societies and a vital and successful "manager" of globalization.[14]

Of course, it may be that the EU's relationship to globalization is differentiated—between policy domains or over time. Some scholars draw attention to a neoliberal "drift" in certain areas of economic policy such as the EU's competition regime or company law and corporate governance, not to mention trade policy.[15] This might emerge from a dynamic internal to the EU whereby market liberal principles have become progressively "constitutionalized" at the supranational level, leaving market-correcting policies underdeveloped and largely confined to the national level,[16] but it may also reflect the continued ascendancy of neoliberal ideas within policy circles more generally.[17]

This movement has been discernible in an apparent doctrinal shift in EU trade policy over the course of the first decade and a half of this century. Between 2001 and 2006, under then Commissioner for Trade Pascal Lamy, EU trade policy seemed to be governed by a doctrine of so-called "managed globalization," which Sophie Meunier describes as "a broad and encompassing doctrine that subordinated trade policy to a variety of trade and non-trade objectives such as multilateralism, social justice and sustainable development."[18] For some the importance of this position was that it constituted a clear rival stance to the trade doctrine of the US. While the EU sought to use the WTO to regulate and manage globalization, the approach of the US in contrast was to involve itself in an increasing number of free areas as a means to the end of accelerating market liberalization.[19] While the doctrinal positions of the EU and the US may have converged over the past half-decade, the difference that became apparent in the mid-1990s is of particular interest to students of global governance. It raises the question of what the ends of global governance are: market liberalization (the assumption being that the progressive removal of barriers to factor movement on a global scale will be welfare enhancing for all) or the use of market liberalization as a tool to service a broader set of social, political, security, and perhaps environmental ends.

By focusing on doctrines and their meaning, we focus on the role of ideas in global governance and the role of actors such as the EU as carriers of those ideas. The EU is complex in this regard because it seems to express at least three types of liberalism in its external actions. We have noted two of these already. The first is economic liberalism, which suggests an approach to governance that prioritizes the making and maintenance of a market order. The second is the package of positive civic liberal principles associated with human rights, the rule of law, and the propagation of political rights through the spread of democracy. The third is bound up with what is arguably the EU's greatest achievement: the delivery of a pacific international system in line with the precepts of liberal international theory.[20]

That said, there may be other reasons for diverging approaches to global economic governance among different actors. One theme that has become popular in the literature on the global politics of regulation notes the EU's affiliation with the "precautionary principle" when assessing public policy risks.[21] The idea is embedded within the treaties (Article 191 of the Treaty on the Functioning of the European Union) and presupposes a cautious approach to the management of risk, particularly in relation to matters of public health and the environment when scientific assessment of those risks is not definitive. This is often contrasted with a more relaxed attitude toward scientific certainty in the US. Perhaps the most famous application of the precautionary principle occurred in 1999 when the EU moved to ban the import of American beef injected with growth hormones that were thought to be potentially carcinogenic. The EU ban was quickly ruled in breach of WTO rules, and some suggest that the invocation of ideas such as the precautionary principle can be used as a cover for old-fashioned protectionist policies.[22] Nevertheless, the very idea of the precautionary principle as a policy tool suggests that approaches to global economic governance may not simply be about the application of different ideas and interests, but also about divergence between different policy cultures. And while it may be true that there is actually significant sectoral and national variation within European policy cultures,[23] the fact that there is an EU approach written into the treaty provides evidence of at least the potential importance of the EU as an actor in global governance.

None of this is to suggest that interests are unimportant. Mitchell Smith argues that two important overlapping determinants of the EU's involvement in global regulatory politics are: (1) the Commission's rational strategy of seeking to ensure that the EU's market rules become the global rules; and (2) efforts by European firms to ensure that they are not put at a competitive disadvantage by regulations formulated in Brussels.[24] This does not mean that the EU ends up delivering and defending "lowest common denominator" regulation—far from it. Take environmental policy, where the EU is well known as an advocate of high regulatory standards and tough emissions targets in the global politics of climate change. How a multi-country entity where member states have quite distinct approaches to environmental regulation became a global leader on climate change is an interesting puzzle. The original EEC Treaty did not mention environmental policy. The Communities did not possess environmental policy competence until the ratification of the Single European Act in the mid-1980s. Yet the Commission, using arguments about the utility of environmental policy for market completion, was able to establish a supranational regime of environmental rule-making in the early 1970s.[25] Powerful environmental lobbies in EU member states ensured the upload of stringent environmental regulation to the EU level. The constructivist argument at this point would be to suggest that the EU's external behavior in global environmental governance reflects the externalization of a set of principles that have been settled within the European context. The rationalist alternative is to suggest that, once settled, these environmental standards need to be advocated globally by the EU in order to prevent a loss of competitiveness for European business.[26] Again, it is worth noting that the determination of how the EU acts globally and the preferences it expresses cannot be separated from the internal politics of European integration, which in turn incorporates domestic political processes in the member states.

Environmental policy is a domain in which the EU has been reasonably successful at externalizing its internal standards. This is in part because of the existence of clear supranational environmental policy competence. As suggested above, market-correcting social policy is less Europeanized, but even where there exist EU-level standards their export into the relevant international regimes is much more problematic. A good example is core labor standards, where the EU has no obvious competence to act authoritatively in relevant international fora such as the International Labour Organization (ILO). This is not to say that the EU does not pursue this agenda, but it is instead worked into trade and development policies, where the EU's competence to act is more clear cut.[27]

Conclusion

This chapter began with the observation that the EU operates both as an actor in the global system and as a system of regional governance. The latter is clearly constitutive of the former, but as the foregoing has shown the question of how internal governance influences external behavior is not straightforwardly answered. Moreover, this is not simply an analytical question, but also a normative one. The factor that most obviously supplies the EU with global agency is its status as a market order. Whether the EU operates as a "manager" of globalization that subordinates the market to other priorities or as a force of economic liberalization driven by the logic of the market alone is an empirical question; in the wake of the financial crisis that morphed into a sovereign debt crisis in the Eurozone in 2009–10 it is also an intensely political question.

It is often said that the EU suffers from a legitimacy crisis or a democratic deficit. There is something to be said for this claim. Eurobarometer polls show that trust in the EU and its institutions is falling,[28] while there is no obvious space for European-level debate and contestation around the appropriate solutions to the crisis or indeed about the principles upon which those solutions might be premised. Instead, conflicts within tend to take a centre–periphery form, with either a politics of resentment developing between northern and southern Eurozone countries, or more inclusive integrative solutions such as fiscal union being stymied by reluctant states such as the United Kingdom. These tensions do not necessarily mean that the EU will collapse. What is rather more likely is a scenario where integration is more differentiated, and a more differentiated future is one where the EU's voice in global governance debates may be somewhat less coherent.

Additional reading

1. Michelle Cini and Nieves Pérez-Solórzano Borragán, eds., *European Union Politics*, 4th edition (Oxford: Oxford University Press, 2013).
2. Chad Damro, "Market Power Europe," *Journal of European Public Policy* 19, no. 5, 682–699.
3. Wade Jacoby and Sophie Meunier, eds., *Europe and the Management of Globalization* (London: Routledge, 2010).
4. Knud Erik Jørgensen, Mark A. Pollack, and Ben Rosamond, eds., *Handbook of European Union Politics* (London: Sage, 2007).
5. Ian Manners, "Normative Power Europe: A Contradiction in Terms?," *Journal of Common Market Studies* 40, no. 2 (2002): 235–258.

Notes

1 See, for example, Stephen Gill, "A Neo-Gramscian Approach to European Integration," in *A Ruined Fortress? Neoliberal Hegemony and Transformation in Europe*, eds. Alain Cafruny and Magnus Ryner (Lanham, MD: Rowman & Littlefield, 2003), 47–70.

2 Wade Jacoby and Sophie Meunier, "Europe and the Management of Globalization," *Journal of European Public Policy* 17, no. 3 (2010): 299–317; Ian Manners, "Normative Power Europe: A Contradiction in Terms?," *Journal of Common Market Studies* 40, no. 2 (2002): 235–258; Chad Damro, "Market Power Europe," *Journal of European Public Policy* 19, no. 5 (2012): 682–699.

3 Robert Schuman, "The Schuman Declaration – 9 May 1950," http://europa.eu/about-eu/basic-information/symbols/europe-day/schuman-declaration/index_en.htm.

4 See Alex Warleigh, *Flexible Integration: Which Model for the European Union* (Sheffield: Sheffield Academic Press, 2002); Rebecca Adler-Nissen, *Opting Out of the European Union: Diplomacy, Sovereignty and European Integration* (Cambridge: Cambridge University Press, 2013).

5 Giandomenico Majone, *Dilemmas of European Integration: The Ambiguities and Pitfalls of Integration by Stealth* (Oxford: Oxford University Press, 2005).

6 For example, David Cameron, "EU Speech at Bloomberg," 23 January 2013, http://www.number10.gov.uk/news/eu-speech-at-bloomberg; Giandomenico Majone, *Europe as the Would-be Superpower: The EU at Fifty* (Cambridge: Cambridge University Press, 2009).

7 Ernst B. Haas, *The Uniting of Europe: Political, Social and Economic Forces, 1950–1957* (Stanford: Stanford University Press, 1958); Leon N. Lindberg, *The Political Dynamics of European Economic Integration* (Stanford: Stanford University Press, 1963); Bela Balassa, *The Theory of Economic Integration* (Homewood, IL: Richard D. Irwin Inc., 1961).

8 "Charlemagne: Brussels Rules OK," *Economist*, 20 September 2007.

9 Mark Schapiro, *Exposed: The Toxic Chemistry of Everyday Products and What's at Stake for American Power* (White River Junction, VT: Chelsea Green Publishing, 2009).

10 Manners, "Normative Power Europe"; Ian Manners, "The Normative Ethics of the European Union," *International Affairs* 84, no. 1 (2008): 45–60.

11 Manners, "Normative Power Europe," 245–252.

12 See Richard Youngs, "Normative Dynamics and Strategic Interests in the EU's External Identity," *Journal of Common Market Studies* 42, no. 2 (2004): 415–435; Thomas Diez, "Constructing the Self and Changing Others: Reconsidering 'Normative Power Europe,'" *Millennium: Journal of International Studies* 33, no. 3 (2005): 613–636; and Owen Parker and Ben Rosamond, "Normative Power Europe Meets Economic Liberalism: Complicating Cosmopolitanism Inside/Outside the EU," *Cooperation and Conflict* (forthcoming 2013); Ben Rosamond, "Three Ways of Speaking Europe to the World: Markets, Peace, Cosmopolitan Duty and the EU's Normative Power', *British Journal of Politics and International Relations* (forthcoming 2013).

13 European Security Strategy, *A Secure Europe in a Better World*, 12 December 2003, http://www.consilium.europa.eu/uedocs/cmsUpload/78367.pdf.

14 Jacoby and Meunier, "Europe and the Management of Globalization"; Nicolas Jabko, "The Hidden Face of the Euro," *Journal of European Public Policy* 17, no. 3 (2010): 318–334.

15 Hubert Buch-Hansen and Angela Wigger, "Revisiting 50 Years of Market-Making: The Neoliberal Transformation of EC Competition Policy," *Review of International Political Economy* 17, no. 1 (2010), 20–44; Laura Horn, *Regulating Corporate Governance in the EU: Towards a Marketization of Corporate Control* (Basingstoke: Palgrave Macmillan, 2011); Gabriel Siles-Brügge, "Resisting Protectionism After the Crisis: Strategic Economic Discourse and the EU–Korea Free Trade Agreement," *New Political Economy* 16, no. 5 (2011): 627–653.

16 Fritz Scharpf, "The European Social Model," *Journal of Common Market Studies* 40, no. 4 (2002): 645–670.

17 Colin Crouch, *The Strange Non-Death of Neoliberalism* (Cambridge: Polity Press, 2011); Mark Blyth, *Austerity: The History of a Dangerous Idea* (New York: Oxford University Press, 2013).

18 Sophie Meunier, "Managing Globalization? The EU in International Trade Negotiations," *Journal of Common Market Studies* 45, no. 4 (2007): 906.

19 Alberta Sbragia, "The EU, the US, and Trade Policy: Competitive Interdependence in the Management of Globalization," *Journal of European Public Policy* 17, no. 3 (2010): 368–382.

20 Rosamond, "Three Ways of Speaking."

21 Jale Tosun, *Risk Regulation in Europe: Assessing the Application of the Precautionary Principle* (New York: Springer, 2013); David Vogel, "The Hare and the Tortoise Revisited: The New Politics of Consumer and Environmental Protection in Europe," *British Journal of Political Science* 33, no. 4 (2003): 557–580.

22 Giandomenico Majone, "What Price Safety? The Precautionary Principle and Its Policy Implications," *Journal of Common Market Studies* 40, no. 1 (2002): 89–109.

23 Alasdair R. Young, "Confounding Conventional Wisdom: Political Not Principled Differences in the Transatlantic Regulatory Relationship," *British Journal of Politics and International Relations* 11, no. 4 (2009): 666–689.

24 Mitchell P. Smith, "Single Market, Global Competition: Regulating the European Market in a Global Economy," *Journal of European Public Policy* 17, no. 7 (2010): 936–953.

25 Christoph Knill and Duncan Liefferink, "The Establishment of EU Environmental Policy," in *Environmental Policy in the EU: Actors, Institutions and Processes*, 3rd edition, eds. Andrew Jordan and Camilla Adelle (London: Routledge, 2013), 13–31.

26 R. Daniel Kelemen, "Globalizing European Union Environmental Policy," *Journal of European Public Policy* 17, no. 3 (2010): 335–349.

27 Jan Orbie and Olufemi Babarinde, "The Social Dimension of Globalization and EU Development Policy: Promoting Core Labour Standards and Corporate Social Responsibility," *Journal of European Integration* 30, no. 3 (2008): 459–477.

28 See European Commission, *Standard Eurobarometer 75*, http://ec.europa.eu/public_opinion/archives/eb/eb75/eb75_en.htm.

The BRICS in the New Global Economic Geography

Andrew F. Cooper and Ramesh Thakur

The architecture of global governance is made up of intergovernmental global and regional organizations as the inner core of formal multilateral machinery; informal but functionally specific and single-problem oriented institutions such as the Proliferation Security Initiative; and a "soft" layer of informal, general-purpose institutions such as the myriad of "G" groups which "serve as consensus incubators and direction-setters, not direct action decision-makers."[1] They can range from G zero—a world in which no country exercises hegemonic power or influence—to G1, a unipolar world. In recent times there has been much talk of a possible G2, meaning the United States and China, and some talk of a possible G3 (with either the European Union, EU, or India being the third member).

The global shift in economic power is filtered though the dual trends of multipolarity and a deepening systemic interdependence among states.[2] The pivotal institutional manifestation of this transformation is the emergence of a new constellation of smaller informal groupings without fixed physical sites and with a focus on intergovernmental interaction.[3] Amidst the plethora of informal groupings, the initial BRIC (Brazil, Russia, India, and China) and then the BRICS (with the addition of South Africa in 2011) stand out for being important, intriguing and yet also of uncertain unity, coherence, and staying power. The group is important because it brings together the big emerging markets whose economic growth will outstrip and indeed anchor the rest of the world. That tremendous promise has already given them considerable clout individually and collectively. It is intriguing because of the diversity and spread of continents, political systems and values, and economic models that they span between them. Yet it attracts skepticism also precisely because the diversity hides the reality of a lack of unifying values, principles, goals, and even interests. Shared frustration with the architecture and management of the existing international financial and political order does not in and by itself translate into joint initiatives and leadership to replace it with a new and improved order.

All three propositions were on display in 2012. The world's premier informal economic grouping today is the G20.[4] During the G20 summit in Los Cabos, Mexico, in June, the BRICS leaders held consultations on the sidelines to announce increased contributions to the International Monetary Fund (IMF) in order to strengthen its currency stabilization role.[5] It was a significant moment in cementing the shift in international economic relationships, with the BRICS being the world's dominant creditors and Europe and the United States the leading new debtors. To reflect this change, the BRICS have been calling for increased voice and vote on issues of global finance. Yet, even with the reforms of 2008 and 2010 the advanced economies retain a 55.3 percent voting share in the IMF, with EU countries by themselves accounting for 29.4 percent.[6] There is today a spectacular but unsustainable disconnect between the highly indebted but politically dominant industrialized economies and, following that, between the distribution of decision-making authority in the existing international financial institutions (IFIs) and the realignment of economic power equations in the real world. Or, to put it another way, in the emerging new global balance of power, the old global political imbalances need to be readjusted to the new global economic imbalances. The disconnect persists because of the absence of the necessary cohesion among the BRICS, but may disappear in time when they realize and act on the conviction that it is in their best joint interests to restructure formal multilateral machinery to bring political clout into line with the new economic geography.

This chapter begins by describing the BRIC(S) amid the constellation of the various "Gs" in global governance, with particular focus on the G20. It then reviews the emergence of the BRICs in the circumstances after the end of the Cold War. There follows a discussion of the catalytic effect of the outreach effort by the G8 on the sense of solidarity and common interests among the major developing countries, before situating the BRICS in its conceptual and comparative settings as an informal G of the big emerging markets spread across four continents. The final section reviews the challenges of, as well as for, the BRICS.

A world of "Gs"

The BRIC(S) model, developed by Goldman Sachs a decade ago, has attracted considerable attention and now serves as the key tag of the major emerging countries.[7] The projections of the future size of their economies paired with the, then stellar, reputation of the large investment bank changed the popular image of those countries and started scholarly debate on the accuracy and applicability of the model.

The rise of BRICS is inextricably linked to the G7/8 as the rival grouping of establishment powers and reflects the massive gaps in post-1945, post-1975, and even post-1989 systems of governance. Frustrated by the ineffectual performance of the UN system as the core of formal multilateral governance, powerful states increasingly worked around rather than through formal multilateral institutions in their own pre-eminent informal G8 grouping (Canada, France, Germany, Italy, Japan, Russia, the United Kingdom, and the United States). The BRICS emerged with the lack of capacity of the G8 countries to govern the international system effectively or legitimately. If multilateralism is to remain viable, international organizations and the values of multilateralism embedded in them must be reconstituted in order to address contemporary challenges effectively, and in line with twenty-first century principles of legitimate governance.[8]

In many ways the G20 filled these governance gaps and represents the best crossover point between legitimacy, effectiveness, and efficiency. The G20 grouping of the world's systemically most important finance ministers and central bankers was brought into being as a result of the Asian financial crisis of the late 1990s. It was transformed into a grouping of the heads of government of the world's top countries in order to deal with the global financial crisis of 2008–09. Its very composition in turn positions it to be the potential forum of choice for addressing a range of additional pressing global problems. Because the G20 collects all the systemically important countries into one grouping, it has considerable political clout to enhance its effectiveness. Because it spans both the global North and South, it has a far better representational legitimacy than the G8 as the grouping of industrialized countries. But because the G20 is not a formally mandated organization it cannot match the UN's unique legitimacy and must still seek ratification of its informal collective agreements from the multilateral machinery. And because it embraces both North and South, it lacks the cohesiveness of perspectives, values, and interests of either. Which is why, like the G8, the BRICS in turn is a complement to, rather than a substitute for, either the universal UN and IFI entities or the more compact G20. Interestingly, in 2012 Russia's president Vladimir Putin chose to miss the G8 summit in the United States in May (the first absence of a Russian president from a G8 summit),[9] but attended the G20 summit in Mexico in June.

At the same time, though, the existence of the BRICS demonstrates the degree of fragmentation and competition in the global system. The meaning of this separation remains unclear. The BRICS can be taken to be part of a hedging approach that allows its members some flexibility. It can also be analyzed as a lobby group that attempts to leverage the weight of the "rising" big powers (China, India, and Brazil) through collective action. It can finally be interpreted as a revisionist challenge to the global order.

An overview of the BRICS in the post-Cold War architecture

Emerging markets have shifted from the margins to the center of global economic action. On the eve of the first BRIC summit in Yekaterinburg, Russia in 2009, Brazil's president noted that the four countries, with only 15 percent of world GDP, account for 65 percent of world growth.[10] China's ambassador to India similarly noted on the eve of the fourth summit in New Delhi that the BRICS "account for 42 percent of the global population, make up 18 percent of the world GDP and 15 percent of the world total trade volume. Their contribution to the world economic growth rate has exceeded 50 percent."[11] Brazil's president Dilma Rousseff added that intra-BRICS trade had climbed from $27bn in 2002 to $212bn in 2010.[12] The ambition is to double the volume to $500bn by 2015. On current projections, in 2025 the G8—the world's eight biggest economies—will most likely be the US, China, India, Japan, Germany, the United Kingdom, France, and Russia.[13] The BRICS should match the original G7's share of global output around 2040. Their growing economic self-confidence finds expression increasingly in political assertiveness as well, and there is no hiding the declaratory message of global transition that underlies the group's policy priorities. Brazilian president Lula da Silva, host of the April 2010 summit, declared grandly that "A new global economic geography has been born."[14]

Although generic in some respects, the BRICS are different from other countries from the global South, with each being either too big or uncomfortable with its immediate neighborhood. All have demonstrated an impressive global reach in terms of their diplomatic profile. The stretch of China's international influence has been well documented.[15] For example, Beijing's concerted charm offensive toward Africa has been conducted not only bilaterally but also multilaterally through the convening of the impressive Forum on China–Africa Cooperation in November 2006.[16] Opening the 2012 meeting, President Hu Jintao announced $20bn in loans to African countries over the next three years, "cementing an alliance that appears increasingly hostile to the west."[17] Similarly, New Delhi hosted its first India–Africa Summit in April 2008. India has become a hub of diplomatic interaction—network as well as club diplomacy—as old and new friends alike vie for attention and deals. Brazil under President Lula launched a number of high-profile diplomatic initiatives, from leadership on the G20 developing countries via the World Trade Organization (WTO), to the proposal for a global fund against hunger and a push on biofuel diplomacy using its sugar-cane-based ethanol production. South Africa shares an innovative partnership with India and Brazil—the India–Brazil–South Africa (IBSA) Dialogue Forum—as well as playing a strong role in the G77, the African Union (AU), and the New Economic Partnership for Africa's Development (NEPAD).

Focusing attention on the four big original BRICs as the dynamic global motors of growth has enormous appeal. On the basis of GDP/PPP (purchasing power parity) China, India, Russia, and Brazil are all in the top 10, followed closely by Mexico, Indonesia, and South Africa in the top 25. On the surface, it seems that their ever deeper engagement and presence in the global economy are fairly recent. However, a longer historical perspective reveals that China's economic success has its roots in the adoption of agricultural reforms in the mid-1970s, supplemented in the 1990s with large increases of foreign direct investment (FDI) in manufacturing. The average growth rate in China since the late 1970s stands at about 9 percent. In India, major policy reforms begun in the late 1980s triggered higher growth. After the period of "Hindu growth," India has experienced a sustained high average GDP growth of 5.8 percent over the past 20 years. Significantly, the developmental paths have been quite different. Growth in India has been led by the indigenous services sector rather than exports of manufactures financed by FDI inflows as in China.

Brazil also enjoyed strong growth of approximately 7 percent annually from 1940 until the debt crises of the 1980s. Strong growth returned in the mid-1990s but was halted by the end of the decade with yet another currency crisis. Economic growth in Brazil remained until recently on the lower side and was quite uneven and volatile, with export growth concentrated in agriculture and natural resources.

South Africa is substantially out of line with the other BRICS in population, economy, size, and growth rate. These are offset, however, by its resource endowments, infrastructure, and corporate and financial footprints into the rest of Africa,[18] which explain why it retains a pivotal status as a diplomatic actor and a regional economic powerhouse. In the post-apartheid period, a gradual recovery has been possible because of extensive structural reforms and closer links to global markets.

The galvanizing effect of the O5/Heiligendamm process

The economic and social transformation in the BRICS countries, combined with their diplomatic and political rise, underpinned the shift in the global balance of power and triggered changes in the global order, especially the system of international financial governance. The G8 performed its coordinating role in a dualistic fashion,[19] with a keen eye on both the one big G8 table and the individual domestic tables back at home. In managing the affairs of the rising powers, however, the G8 has little credibility. It could not simply dictate to others; it had to engage with the "upstarts" in the system.

Attempts to reform the G8 from the inside were directed through the so-called Heiligendamm or Outreach 5 (O5) process between 2005 and 2009, through which different members of the G8 took the lead in reaching out to the Big Five emerging markets and regional hubs of Brazil, China, India, Mexico, and South Africa. One unanticipated effect of this was the consolidation of a small group of big countries from the global South into new habits of working together. At the Evian Summit in 2003, France chose to showcase members of the Big Five along with those from other G20 potential members, including Mexico and Saudi Arabia. At Gleneagles in 2005, the United Kingdom invited the same core countries (albeit without Middle East representation) to discuss climate change. A similar framework was used in key ancillary bodies, most notably the G7 forum of finance ministers. Chinese and Indian finance ministers attended the two 2005 meetings in St. Petersburg and London. So entrenched had this hub approach become that the exclusion of the O5 became a focus for reproach. French president Jacques Chirac publicly rebuked the United States for not being more inclusive of these regional hubs at the 2004 Sea Island Summit: "We cannot discuss major economic issues nowadays without discussing these issues with China, with India, Brazil, South Africa."[20]

The functional range of every Big Five member on the diplomatic axis is far greater than that of other G20 developing country members. Confirmation of this elevated status accorded to the BRICS came in the rotation of the presidency of G20 Finance: India in 2002, China in 2005, South Africa in 2007, and Brazil in 2008, amid the central moment of the financial crisis. By the 2007 Heiligendamm summit, it was clear that major international challenges could not be addressed without ongoing cooperation of the large countries of the global South. The formalization of the Heiligendamm process tried to accomplish this goal, if within clear boundaries.

In initiating the Heiligendamm process, Chancellor Angela Merkel made it quite clear that "We don't want to turn the G8 into a G13." Rather, she explained to her parliament, "without the emerging economies, progress on issues such as climate change, the world trade round and intellectual property rights is unimaginable."[21] Even so, the idea of establishing a dialogue between the G8 and the O5, and of creating a secretariat within the Organisation for Economic Co-operation and Development (which caused some important developing countries some discomfort, as they view the OECD as itself an elitist Western club) to manage the developing contacts between the G8–O5, suggested that the G8 was already reinventing itself "as a vehicle for informal problem-solving between the most powerful countries of today and tomorrow."[22] In addition to increased legitimacy of the G8, the informal dialogue was intended to create trust, bring more understanding of common responsibilities on global issues, and explore avenues for stalled negotiations in other international forums, especially the Doha Round. The basic structure relied on a steering committee and four working groups (co-chaired by G8 and O5 countries) on investment, energy, development, and innovation—topics of most interest to the G8. Migration and governance, preferred topics of the O5, were excluded.

However, several mishaps at the launch of the Heiligendamm process as well as the general approach to it as "outreach" did not contribute positively to the process. The most infamous incident was the release of the communiqué that announced the establishment of the Heiligendamm process without any input from the O5 and before the emerging powers actually joined the G8 meetings.[23] Indian prime minister Manmohan Singh's remark—"We have come here not as petitioners but as partners in an equitable, just and fair management of the global community of nations, which we accept as reality in the globalized world"[24]—was seconded by a hopeful statement from China that the G8 Outreach would not be used as "a means of exerting pressure on developing countries."[25]

Although all the O5 countries became engaged in the process, this incremental approach was unlikely to have resulted in wider reform without a global shock such as the financial crisis. Traditionally focused on the formal, more inclusive structures (such as the United Nations), China never actively sought full membership in the G8. If comfortable with the language of dialogue, cooperation, and partnership, it had serious reservations about a tight embrace, potential attempts at "socialization" by the Western powers, and the possibility of pressures on domestic policies, to which Beijing is very sensitive.[26] For India and Brazil, G8 enlargement was seen as a "consolation" prize and a stepping stone toward UN Security Council permanent membership. Brazil, China, and India have a strong self-image rooted in the developing world, expect more recognition of their growing role in the world, regard themselves as entitled to equal status in the G8, question the current global governance architecture, and push for comprehensive reforms.

South Africa strongly supported the Heiligendamm process as a structured opportunity for expanding the Africa–G8 dialogue. But Pretoria's role as the representative of the "African cause" or "continental voice" on the international stage is somewhat awkward, with internal hesitation and African reservations. Another challenge for South Africa is "the interplay of three factors: costs, capacity, and global constraints." These are factors that no developing country, and no African country in particular, can ignore.[27]

The BRICS in conceptual and comparative context

A decade ago the standard terminology for representing the group of rising countries was the Big Emerging Markets or Big Ten.[28] A wider array of labels has emerged since for portraying rising powers. At one end of the spectrum, the cluster can be sharply compressed. The term "Chindia" is popular as a means to differentiate the super-sized character of China and India. At the other end, an element of diffuseness is added in constellations such as CIVETS (Colombia, Indonesia, Vietnam, Egypt, Turkey, South Africa), MIST (Mexico, Indonesia, South Korea, Turkey), and the Next 11 (Bangladesh, Egypt, Indonesia, Iran, Mexico, Nigeria, Pakistan, the Philippines, Turkey, South Korea, Vietnam). An alternative way of slicing groups of countries—conceptually and theoretically more coherent and of greater policy utility—is to classify them as "pivot states," those with profitable relationships with multiple other countries, and "shadow states," those unable to break free of the gravitational pull of a single powerful state, such as Mexico and Ukraine vis-à-vis the United States and Russia respectively.[29]

What these conceptualizations lack is the same degree of balance between economic clout and geopolitical agency built into the Big Emerging Market model. The criterion for assessing the status of these countries is in terms of material/commercial strength. Capabilities involving diplomatic will and skill are completely neglected. GDP is showcased, but diplomatic leverage is not.[30]

If facing competition from a number of other acronyms—above all IBSA and BASIC (Brazil, South Africa, India, and China)[31]—BRICS has established a dominant position both conceptually and in terms of comparative perspective. BRICS is a rare, if not unique, phenomenon: a diplomatic grouping that follows an acronym coined by a private sector analyst. It is not the product of diplomatic negotiations based on shared political values or common economic interests. From a turn of phrase by Jim O'Neill of Goldman Sachs in 2001, a grouping was born in 2009.

Not surprisingly, therefore, BRICS has its flaws. Conceptually, the portrayal of the BRICS as similar entities distorts the verisimilitude of these countries.[32] No distinction is made between the state–corporate relationships in the five countries. Nor is any reference made to the problem of systemic corruption. At odds with the optimism of the Goldman Sachs appraisal is the placement of the BRICS on Transparency International's corruption index, with Brazil, China, and India sharing the lowly position of 72nd, and Russia way down at 143rd.

To be sure, Goldman Sachs did have concerns with some aspects of the development in the original BRIC countries, for example problems related to tertiary education, the need for reforms in key sectors such as power and telecoms, the lack of an independent judiciary and property rights, infrastructural bottlenecks, and red tape.[33] But even with these types of obstacles, Goldman Sachs continued to be bullish about the BRICs. As the global financial crisis deepened in 2008, the prediction was made that the BRICs would be able to lever this situation into catching up with the traditional pacesetters among the G8 industrialized countries at an even faster rate.[34] This miscalculation has eroded some of the aura of Goldman Sachs' predictive qualifications. It had over-hyped the impression that the BRICs would remain completely "decoupled" from weak Western economics.

Signs appeared that the concept of BRICs was being reconfigured as a grouping prior to the financial crisis. In October 2007 the foreign ministers of Russia, China, and India met in Harbin, China. In May 2008 all four BRICs foreign ministers met for a day in Yekaterinburg. The global financial crisis shifted the balance more dramatically between the old establishment and the "rising" states. The first official BRIC summit was held in Yekaterinburg (June 2009), with subsequent meetings in Brasilia (April 2010), Hainan (April 2011), and New Delhi (March 2012). In a further sign of expansion, South Africa was formally added to the BRICS at the Hainan and New Delhi summits.

If the objective is to conceive which of the contenders will be among the cluster of the emerging powers, the BRICS label holds some clear conceptual strengths. The biggest common interest of the BRICS is in global economic governance. A former Chilean ambassador to India, Jorge Heine, and his Indian diplomatic colleague have noted that New Delhi "developed a new sheen as the capital of the global south" and that Brazil and India, with "common global aspirations and a common agenda on many multilateral issues, have together taken on the role of leading the New South—that is, the post-Cold War developing world."[35]

BRICS is a useful grouping for members to share and learn from one another's development experiences. They come to the global governance table with a mutually reinforcing sense of historical grievances and claims to represent the interests of all developing countries.[36] They share a neo-Westphalian commitment to state sovereignty and nonintervention. They profess a shared vision of inclusive global growth and the rapid socio-economic transformation of their own nations in which no village is left behind. Their resource endowments show many complementarities. They proclaim the need for a rules-based, stable, and predictable world order that respects the diversity of political systems and stages of development. Politically, the Delhi Declaration signals a growing self-consciousness among the five BRICS that they have global weight and mean to begin using it. The statements on Syria and Iran mark out a clear "product differentiation" from the dominant trans-Atlantic policy on contemporary global controversies. To be sure, in the crucial vote on a draft Security Council resolution on Syria in July 2012, reflecting its identity as an open economy and a plural democracy,[37] India sided with the West, while China and Russia cast a double veto. Yet, "One of the *advantages* of the BRICS process is that it remains a loose association of states with somewhat disparate interests, so no effort is made to force a common position when the BRICS states cannot agree on one. But these states have also found a way to disagree on some key issues . . . without torpedoing the entire enterprise."[38]

The increasingly confident BRICS resent calls for "responsible" stakeholder policies as efforts to subjugate their world views to the global North's priorities (as a responsible actor, you will do what we say). Instead they generally take an instrumental approach to international governance. For example, China and Russia are instinctively suspicious of the very notion of global governance as a self-serving Western concept, preferring informal gatherings of big powers and regional institutions to formal multilateral machinery.[39]

The global financial crisis, as President Lula bluntly put it, "was created by white men with blue eyes."[40] In comparison to most Western economies responsible for the crisis, the BRICS had exemplary budgetary and fiscal performances. They blamed the European and US central banks for "aggressive policy actions" to stabilize their domestic economies that had spilled over into emerging market economies by generating "excessive liquidity" and fostered "excessive capital flows and commodity prices."[41] Deliciously turning the tables, they called for the advanced economies "to adopt responsible macro-economic and financial policies, avoid creating excessive global liquidity and undertake structural reforms to lift growth that create jobs."[42]

BRICS offers both China and Russia a forum for creating a buffer zone between themselves and the West and drawing influential nonaligned countries into their orbit.[43] Thus with respect to the extra-UN sanctions imposed on Iran by the West, the day before the fourth BRICS summit in New Delhi, India's Commerce and Industry Minister Anand Sharma noted pointedly that "We respect UN resolutions" and China's Trade Minister insisted that Beijing was "not obliged to follow any domestic laws and rules of any particular country."[44] The summit communiqué also signaled opposition to the US and European efforts to isolate Syria and Iran as preludes to regime change or war. It emphasized the importance of peaceful transition and diplomatic dialogue in "a Syrian-led inclusive process" that respects its independence, territorial integrity, and sovereignty.[45] "The situation concerning Iran cannot be allowed to escalate into conflict," the five leaders added.[46]

Nonetheless some caution is warranted about the robustness of these contours of transition in the international hierarchy. One explanation of the trajectory of the BRICS points to a comprehensive process of realignment of power, with a new alternative concert of oppositional/adversarial states taking shape. Equally, however, there are strong counter-forces to reconfigured interstate polarization and "overt balancing."[47] The most serious drag on the prospects of the BRICS being a major force in global governance is not resistance by the old order but serious differences of values and interests among the group's members that leave them open to the dismissive comment of being "bricks in search of cement."[48]

In all of them, domestic priorities and problems trump club solidarity. All are still at early stages of development. The April 2010 Brasilia summit was shortened into a one-day event when President Hu Jintao went home early to deal with a major earthquake that killed over 600 people in western China. In June, another BRIC summit around the Toronto G20 was canceled when President Lula stayed home because of the massive floods in northeast Brazil.[49]

The BRICS are riven with rivalries over borders, resources, and status. With long and not always settled borders, India and Russia have problems with China. China's highly competitive exports inflict material harm on Brazil. In an environment of growing energy and food demand, China's and India's anxiety about rising energy prices must be set against Russia being a beneficiary, while Brazil is both a cause and beneficiary of rising food prices. India is vulnerable to internal and exogenous shocks, while South Africa's place at the table may make political sense but is economically less defensible. Two of the five are authoritarian states, although all the three democracies have a tradition of reticence in global democracy-promotion efforts. They are divided on reform of the UN Security Council, with China's interest lying more in a bipolar than a genuinely multipolar global order, and on the global economic effects of China's currency value.

Moreover, in 2012 Brazil and India seemed to be stuttering economically,[50] which would undercut the very basis of their recently added global clout. In part this may be because they share cultural and political traits with each other that set them apart from the largely command-and-control Chinese economic model.[51] Casual about meeting deadlines, prone to make promises that cannot be fulfilled, with citizens demanding high levels of income support despite economies that cannot support a welfare state, both have shown symptoms of public corruption and excessive government spending that sets off hyperinflation, crowds out private investment, and ends the cycle of economic boom. In 2012 there were several warning signs that India's economic miracle story was stalling badly, with a massive power outage in July being widely interpreted as a metaphor for the country's growing misfortunes.[52] Meanwhile China too has lost some luster owing to a string of assertive actions around its neighborhood, slowing rates of growth, and worries that its construction industry is about to take a major tumble.

Each of the BRICS retains deep and specific ties with the pivotal Northern countries in the general context of complex interdependence vis-à-vis the global economy. All five have a greater stake in bilateral relations with the United States for reasons of market power, investments, and high technology. Realist scholars also signal the prospect of an alternative alignment with the US-led North if one of the BRICS rises faster and in a more antagonistic manner than the others. John Mearsheimer points in particular to "China's Unpeaceful Rise" as a catalyst for this type of balancing response.[53]

Nor do the BRICS always act as a concerted bloc within other institutional settings. Schirm's analysis, for instance, highlights the presence of mixed coalitions within G20, where ad hoc groupings reflect a variety of arrangements comprising both developed and developing countries, and where like-minded groupings such as the established G8 and the BRICS co-mingle on a variety of issue areas.[54] This in turn illustrates that cohesiveness among the BRICS has not congealed to the point where the diplomatic grouping acts as a bloc across an array of institutional settings. This was highlighted in 2012 when the BRICS failed to mount a united campaign for either the Nigerian or the Colombian candidate against the ultimately successful US nominee for president of the World Bank.[55] The net result is that groupings like the BRICS cannot as yet fill the leadership void left by the West with the nearly defunct status and authority of the G7/8. Although many countries are strong enough to veto Western action, "none has the political and economic muscle to remake the status quo."[56]

Conclusion

The BRICS are a reflection of the widening multipolar structure of the international system and thus a challenge to the old establishment. The existence of the BRICS is a function of the renewed prominence of informal multilateralism or plurilateralism, as well as the newfound agency and enhanced capacity of these countries in international politics. The consolidation of these countries into such groupings has placed them in a strategic position within the wider governance architecture where, at summit-level institutions, emphasis is placed on South–South solidarity.

The challenge for the BRICS is in working from economic reality to a tighter sense of normative and ideational identity amongst the grouping's membership. It is easy and tempting to dismiss the BRICS as "more a way station than a summit"[57] because of the lack of commonality, existing tensions and squabbles, and potential serious conflicts that divide more than unite them. Yet the grouping has tried to put pressure on the West to facilitate and accommodate and not block the rise of the emerging economies.[58] In comparison to the first three summits, the 2012 one in New Delhi could mark a watershed. The grouping advanced from a mere talk-shop opportunity to sketching the outlines of an alternative configuration of global governance. For the first time, the sense of frustrated entitlement found expression in some concrete ideas on how to break through the frozen configuration of global privilege and power. The BRICS have put down markers that they intend to use their demographic and economic clout to challenge and change the way that the world is governed through formal multilateral machinery and informal groupings. One critical test of whether BRICS can make the transition from a critic of the Western-led system of global economic governance to a leader-cum-manager of an alternative system of, by, and for developing countries will be whether the idea of a BRICS development bank (or a South–South development fund), floated for study at the New Delhi summit, is successfully implemented.

Additional reading

1. Alan Alexandroff and Andrew F. Cooper, eds., *Rising States, Rising Institutions: Challenges for Global Governance* (Washington, DC: Brookings Institution Press, 2010).
2. Leslie E. Armijo, "The BRICs Countries (Brazil, Russia, India, and China) as Analytical Category: Mirage or Insight?," *Asian Perspective* 31, no. 4 (2007): 7–42.
3. Andrew F. Cooper and Ramesh Thakur, *The Group of Twenty (G20)* (London: Routledge, 2013).
4. Pepe Escobar, "A History of the World, BRIC by BRIC," *Asia Times*, 28 April 2012, http://www.atimes.com/atimes/Global_Economy/ND28Dj04.html.
5. Marina Larionova and John Kirton, eds., *Stability, Security and Prosperity: BRICS New Delhi Summit 2012* (London: Newsdesk Communications for the BRICS Research Group, 2012).
6. Ruchir Sharma, *Breakout Nations: In Pursuit of the Next Economic Miracles* (New York: W. W. Norton, 2012).

Notes

1 Remarks by Richard Stanley at the UN General Assembly President's Thematic Debate on the United Nations in Global Governance, New York, 28 June 2011. Ramesh Thakur's notes from the event.
2 Bates Gill, "Going South: Capitalist Crisis, Systemic Crisis, Civilizational Crisis," *Third World Quarterly* 31, no. 2 (2010): 169–184; Giovanni Grevi, *The Interpolar World: A New Scenario* (European Union Institute for Security Studies Occasional Paper No. 79, 2009).
3 Risto Pentilla, *Multilateralism Light: The Rise of Informal International Governance* (London: Centre for European Reform, 2009).
4 Andrew F. Cooper and Ramesh Thakur, *The Group of Twenty (G20)* (London: Routledge, 2013).
5 Martin Gilman, "Much Ado about Little News: BRIC Money for the IMF?," *East Asia Forum*, 18 July 2012, http://www.eastasiaforum.org/2012/07/18/much-ado-about-little-news-bric-money-for-the-imf/.
6 IMF, "Illustration of Proposed Quota and Voting Shares," http://www.imf.org/external/np/sec/pr/2010/pdfs/pr10418_table.pdf.

7   Dominic Wilson and Roopa Purushothaman, "Dreaming with BRICs: The Path to 2050," Global Economics Paper no. 99 (New York: Goldman Sachs, October 2003), http://dspace. cigilibrary.org/jspui/bitstream/123456789/17375/1/Global%20Economics%20Paper%20No %2099%20Dreaming%20with%20BRICs%20The%20Path%20to%202050.pdf?1. See the creation of the BRIC acronym in Jim O'Neill, "The World Needs Better Economic BRICs," Global Economics Paper no. 66 (New York: Goldman Sachs, October 2001).

8   Alan Alexandroff and Andrew F. Cooper, eds., *Rising States, Rising Institutions: Challenges for Global Governance* (Washington, DC: Brookings, 2010).

9   Vladimir Radyuhin, "From Russia, No Love," *Hindu* (Chennai), 18 May 2012.

10 Lula da Silva, "At Yekaterinburg, the BRICs Come of Age," *Hindu*, 16 June 2009. See also Ira Iosebashvili, "BRIC Leaders Search for Greater Influence," *St. Petersburg Times*, 19 June 2009.

11 Zhang Yan, "Powering the World," *Indian Express* (Delhi), 28 March 2012.

12 Dilma Rousseff, "We're All in It Together," *Times of India*, 29 March 2012.

13 US National Intelligence Council, *Global Trends 2025: A Transformed World* (Washington, DC: US Government Printing Office, November 2008), 7.

14 Quoted in Pepe Escobar, "The BRIC Post-Washington Consensus," *Asia Times*, 17 April 2010. See also Andrew F. Cooper, "Consolidated Institutional Cooperation and/or Competitive Fragmentation in the Aftermath of the Financial Crisis," *Whitehead Journal of Diplomacy and International Relations* XIII, no. 2 (2011): 19–31.

15 See Gregory Chin and Ramesh Thakur, "Will China Change the Rules of Global Order?," *Washington Quarterly* 33, no. 4 (2010): 119–138; Andrew F. Cooper, Timothy M. Shaw, and Gregory Chin, "Emerging Powers and Africa: Implications for/from Global Governance?," *Politikon: South African Journal of Political Studies* 36, no. 1 (2008): 27–44.

16 See Ian Taylor, *The Forum on China–Africa Cooperation (FOCAC)* (London: Routledge, 2012).

17 David Smith, "China Offers $20bn of Loans to African nations," *Guardian* (London), 19 July 2012.

18 Andrew England, "Politics Starts to Unsettle Investors," *Financial Times*, 4 November 2011.

19 Robert D. Putnam, "Diplomacy and Domestic Politics: The Logic of Two-Level Games," *International Organization* 48, no. 3 (1988): 427–460.

20 G8, "Press Briefing by French President Jacques Chirac," 9 June 2004, Sea Island, www.g8. utoronto.ca/summit/2004seaisland/chirac040609.html.

21 Quoted in Hugh Williamson, "Great Powers Present and Future Try to Keep It Casual," *Financial Times*, 4 June 2007.

22 Ibid.

23 Hugh Williamson, "Emerging Powers Flex Muscles to Push for More Power in the G8," *Financial Times*, 4 July 2007.

24 Quoted in Praful Bidwai, "India's Clumsy Balancing Act," *Asia Times*, 26 June 2007.

25 Tiankai Cui in F. Chen, "G8 Not Platform for Exerting Pressure," Beijing, 4 June 2007, http://www.gov.cn/misc/2007-06/04/content_636224.htm.

26 M. Nalapat, "G8 Must Make Way for New System," *China Daily*, 7 July 2010.

27 Brendan Vickers, "South Africa: Global Reformism, Global Apartheid and the Heiligendamm Process," in *Emerging Powers in Global Governance: Lessons from the Heiligendamm Process*, eds. Andrew F. Cooper and Agata Antkiewicz (Waterloo: Wilfrid Laurier University Press, 2008), 187.

28 Jeffrey Garten, *The Big Ten: The Big Emerging Markets and How They Will Change Our Lives* (New York: Basic Books, 1997).

29 Ian Bremmer, "Which Countries Will Rise to the Top in a Leaderless World?," *Harvard Business Review*, 30 May 2012, http://blogs.hbr.org/cs/2012/05/which_countries_will_rise_to_t.html.

30 Denise Gregory and Paulo Roberto de Almeida, "Brazil and the G8 Heiligendamm Process," in *Emerging Powers in Global Governance*, eds. Cooper and Antkiewicz, 137–162.

31 On a less serious note, there is also CEMENT—countries of emerging markets excluded from new terminology.

32 Leslie E. Armijo, "The BRICs Countries (Brazil, Russia, India, and China) as Analytical Category: Mirage or Insight?," *Asian Perspective* 31, no. 4 (2007): 7–42.

33 Goldman Sachs, *BRICs & Beyond* (New York, November 2007), http://www.goldmansachs.com/our-thinking/archive/archive-pds/brics-book/brics-full-book.pdf

34 Guy Faulconbridge, "Brics Helped by Western Finance Crisis, Goldman," Reuters, 8 June 2008.

35 Jorge Heine and R. Viswanathan, "The Other BRIC in Latin America: India," *Americas Quarterly* (2011), http://www.americasquarterly.org/node/2422.

36 The claims to developing country representation are widely contested within their own respective regions: Marco Antonio Vieira and Chris Alden, "India, Brazil and South Africa (IBSA): South–South Cooperation and the Paradox of Regional Leadership," *Global Governance* 17, no. 4 (2011): 507–528.

37 See William H. Avery, *China's Nightmare, America's Dream: India as the Next Global Power* (New Delhi: Amaryllis, 2012).

38 Nikolas Gvosdev, "The Realist Prism: What the US Can Learn from the BRICS," *World Politics Review*, 22 June 2012 (emphasis added).

39 Charles Grant, *Russia, China and Global Governance* (London: Centre for European Reform, 2012).

40 Quoted in Paul Gillespie, "Brics Highlight Skewed Nature of Global Power," *Irish Times*, 31 March 2012.

41 "BRICS Summit—Delhi Declaration" (New Delhi: Ministry of External Relations, Government of India, 29 March 2012), para. 5.

42 Ibid., para. 6.

43 Seth Mandel and Christina Lin, "NATO's New Neighbors," *National Review Online*, 17 May 2012, http://www.nationalreview.com/node/299791; Richard Weitz, "Russia's Asia Play Mustn't Be Ignored," *The Diplomat*, 17 May 2102, http://the-diplomat.tumblr.com/post/23238257235/russias-asia-play-mustnt-be-ignored.

44 "China Leads, BRICS Backs Iran," *Times of India*, 29 March 2012, http://timesofindia.indiatimes.com/business/india-business/China-leads-BRICS-backs-Iran/articleshow/12449551.cms. On the relationship between China and India with the UN more generally, see Andrew F. Cooper and Thomas Fues, "Do the Asian Drivers Pull Their Diplomatic Weight? China, India and the United Nations," *World Development* 36, no. 2 (2008): 293–307.

45 "BRICS Summit—Delhi Declaration," para. 21

46 Ibid., para. 22.

47 Andrew Hurrell, "Hegemony, Liberalism and Global Order: What Space for Would-Be Great Powers?," *International Affairs* 82, no. 1 (2006): 1–19.

48 Gillespie, "Brics Highlight Skewed Nature of Global Power."

49 Guy Faulconbridge, "BRIC Calls off Meeting at G20 as Lula Stays Home," Reuters, 26 June 2010, http://in.reuters.com/article/2010/06/27/idINIndia-49680920100627.

50 See Ruchir Sharma, "Bearish on Brazil," *Foreign Affairs* 91, no. 3 (May/June 2012): 80–87.

51 Ruchir Sharma, *Breakout Nations: In Pursuit of the Next Economic Miracles* (New York: W. W. Norton, 2012).

52 Ramesh Thakur, "Dark Times for 'Shining' India," *Ottawa Citizen*, 2 August 2012.

53 John J. Mearsheimer, "China's Unpeaceful Rise" *Current History* (April 2006): 160–162.

54 A. Stefan Schirm, "Global Politics Are Domestic Politics: How Societal Interests and Ideas Shape Ad Hoc Groupings in the G20 Which Supersede International Alliances," paper prepared for the International Studies Association Convention in Montreal, Canada, 16–19 March 2011.

55 Ramesh Thakur, "Wealth and Power Trump Good Governance," *Australian*, 18 April 2012.
56 Ian Bremmer, *Every Nation for Itself: Winners and Losers in a GZero World* (New York: Penguin, 2012), 10.
57 Sanjaya Baru, "BRICS in Search of Cement," *Business Standard* (Delhi), 18 April 2011.
58 See Alice Amsden, *The Rise of "The Rest": Challenges to the West from Late-Industrializing Economies* (New York: Oxford University Press, 2003).

CONTENTS

The Global South

Ian Taylor

In normal usage, the terms "South" and "global South"—alongside "Third World," "developing world," and, less frequently but more accurately "Majority World"—refer to those countries in an uneven process of development and industrialization. These countries are primarily the ex-colonial states of Africa, Asia, and Latin America; and the very notion of *a* or *the* South implies a commonality of material and ideational interests. This may, to a greater or lesser extent, have been the case in the immediate postcolonial moment, but it has progressively become ever more problematic. The more recent addition of "global" is intended to suggest the worldwide geographical dimensions of these countries. In today's world, it is debatable whether or not the global South actually exists.

A coherent Southern bloc has long been an aspiration of various elites located in the postcolonial world. Yet, the capacity for a coherent bloc to emerge has been at variance with economic and political developments across the developing world. This chapter examines some of the attempts to institutionalize the South—and thus lend it a degree of coherence as an entity—through the creation of various organizations. In so doing, it explores the involvement of developing countries in global governance. Attempts by the developing world to formulate institutions to express a notional Southern position have been undermined by both the diversity of elite interests in postcolonial states as well as robust responses by industrialized countries to undermine and sabotage such efforts. This has taken place at a variety of levels, but the end result has been a progressive weakening of any putative voice from the global South. When talking of "the South," does it actually exist?

The idea of the South

The idea of the South itself is derivative of Third Worldism, which has been described as "the universal institutionalization of national sovereignty as the representation of independence of decolonized peoples, political confrontation with European racism, and a movement of quasi-nationalist elites whose legitimacy depended on negotiating their economic and political dependence."[1] The notion of a commonality of interests that all ex-colonial states possessed was the driving force behind such expressions. This sense of community was grasped by emerging elites as one way through which newfound economic and political freedoms could be guaranteed and protected in the context of the Cold War, into which a whole swathe of "new" countries were inserted.

Yet the elite classes who attained power once the colonial flags were lowered had no intention of surrendering their newfound political power and the advantages that it conferred. At once, then, Third Worldism—which has been the ideational underpinning supposedly uniting a variegated global South—was Janus faced. It sought to legitimize extant elites as representing the "poor and dispossessed" of the postcolonial world when objectively the exact opposite often occurred. Another aim was to have as much maneuverability as possible within the world order for personal aggrandizement and regime stabilization. In other words, the South has always been a domestic and externally oriented project and in so being has always been an elite political expression. The heyday of the South was really at an historic juncture when the newly independent countries were flexing their muscles, and a heady optimism existed about the maneuverability of the developing world vis-à-vis the North. It was a moment when the institutionalization of the South emerged and when the South momentarily appeared coherent.

Bandung

The Asian African Conference in Bandung, Indonesia—convened between 18 and 24 April 1955—may be seen as the watershed moment when newly emerging postcolonial elites expressed the idea that they shared interests. The concept of an Asian–African conference had first been suggested at a meeting of the prime ministers of Burma, Ceylon, India, Indonesia, and Pakistan in Colombo, Ceylon, in April 1953. Representatives from 29 countries attended the conference, at a time when the United Nations had only 59 member states. It was at Bandung that many provisional contacts between various newly emerging elites from the postcolonial world were made. Bandung has since been described as "a celebration of the wave of independence that had swept across Asia and was then cresting in Africa."[2]

The motives for convening such a conference varied widely among participants, as did their economic and political orientations. Nonetheless, Bandung saw the adoption of a number of resolutions that have been described as "an augur of a future protest against the subordinating stays of the developing countries in the international system,"[3] and which established a set of normative values which aimed at a more equitable world order. Such expressions from elite voices in the notional South found their institutional manifestation in two important organizations that have historically been the main loci of the South in international affairs: the Nonaligned Movement (NAM) and the United Nations Conference on Trade and Development (UNCTAD), and more particularly the Group of 77 (G77) within it. By looking at the histories of these two organizations, the development of the South as an idea and its effective defeat by the assertive dominance of the West can be traced and delineated.

NAM

Bandung was followed by the Belgrade Conference of 1961, where the NAM was officially launched. A declaration containing the common views of delegates on international problems was issued that was in line with the general Bandung position, and an agreement on the summits being triennial was reached. The NAM was established as a loose multilateral project with very little formal organization, which resulted in "conference diplomacy [becoming] a specific characteristic of nonalignment."[4] By confirming the "Spirit of Bandung" in 1961, the NAM also adopted a posture that rejected the bilateral impulses that dominated the world through the system of Cold War alliances. For instance, newly independent states could not be admitted to the United Nations unless Moscow and Washington agreed, which was never. Yet what was perhaps the most important outcome from Belgrade, which has continued to the contemporary period, was the general establishment of behavioral norms for state activity. Although they have certainly been compromised over time, it is important to remember that when they were first expressed such normative expressions were "innovative, even revolutionary and consciously rejected big power domination of the global order."[5]

By so doing, the NAM committed itself to a project that privileged the role of the United Nations as the proper forum for interstate activity. The "Lusaka Declaration" of 1970 explicitly promoted the United Nations to the position and aimed to strengthen the body "so that it will be a more effective obstacle against all forms of aggressive action and the threat to use force against the freedom, independence, sovereignty and territorial integrity of any country."[6] Such calls, while rhetorical to be sure, did express a desire by a large number of states to operate in a world less beholden to the superpowers and other major players. At the same time, the NAM's focus began to shift from relations with the superpowers and East–West confrontation towards development issues involving questions regarding North and South. Indeed, this focus on constructing a normative order to resolve the developmental contradictions produced by global capitalism henceforth began to preoccupy the lion's share of summit activity—in itself a reflection of changes in the international system, stimulated by the heady growth in the South's representation at multilateral fora such as the United Nations.

The NAM, alongside UNCTAD, as discussed below, became in the 1970s an important platform in the South's efforts to put forward the New International Economic Order (NIEO). The document consisted of proposals put forward by some developing countries to improve the terms of trade for postcolonial states, increase aid, and reduce the tariff barriers that their exports attracted in industrial markets. In essence, it was a call for a restructured global economy that would help facilitate development in the South. These attempts came to a head at the Sixth Special Session of the United Nations in 1974, where, under the NAM's then leader, Algerian president Honari Boumedienne, the South deployed NAM and G77 texts in successfully pushing for a comprehensive normative declaration detailing the aspirations of the developing world's elites. Craig Murphy writes:

[F]or the first time the General Assembly approved a massive resolution covering all of the economic issues the Third World had raised since the Second World War.

> The resolution touched on sovereignty over natural resources, improving terms of trade through international regulation of trade based on equitable treatment, reforming the global monetary system to include an aid component, expanding concessionary multilateral aid, providing debt relief, controlling TNCs [transnational corporations], promoting international support for industrialization, and reforming the United Nations system to give Third World governments greater control over international economic decisions.[7]

Much of this rhetoric was derivative of leading Southern elites' perceptions of their own domestic interests within the context of the breakdown of the Bretton Woods system and the maneuverings of the Organization of the Petroleum Exporting Countries (OPEC). It is important here to assert that the more economically advanced developing countries led the way. Already, there had been a tacit recognition that the South was a divided entity, with the nomenclature "Least developed country (LDC)" being introduced at the United Nations in November 1971. LDCs were those states that, according to the UN, exhibited the lowest indicators in terms of socio-economic development. While commonsensical, what the LDC appellation officially admitted—arguably for the first time—was that the South was not monolithic.

Negotiations regarding the future architecture to replace existing forms of international organization seemed logical to many Southern elites. In short, "they took the opportunities offered by the evolving politics of international economic relations to create leadership roles for themselves," thereby bolstering their own standing at the domestic level.[8] This was important as "their position as the ruling class at the periphery remain[ed] tenuous, hence, the imperative of external association and support"—and public posturing on the international stage.[9]

The NAM platform

Until the Jakarta Summit in 1992, the NAM position was fairly consistent, centering around territorial integrity, resistance to "imperialism," and a rejection of hierarchies of power and privilege in the international system. The essential aims were crystallized in the Lusaka Declaration of 1970, which stated that the NAM was committed to

> The pursuit of world peace and strengthening the role of nonaligned countries within the United Nations so that it will be a more effective obstacle against all forms of aggressive action ... opposition to great power military alliances and pacts ... the universality of and strengthening of the efficacy of the United Nations; and the struggle for economic independence and mutual co-operation on a basis of equality and mutual benefits.[10]

Paradoxically, though the Lusaka Declaration came as the push for liberation in southern Africa was reaching a climax, and as the calls for an NIEO were to focus the minds of the elites in both North and South, Lusaka was also a watershed in the sense that membership of the NAM had by this point become predominantly African; and as membership of the body expanded, the principles upon which the organization were founded and its political orientation became more dependent on the view and needs of poverty-stricken African, particularly Francophone, states. Many of these were by no means nonaligned, being firmly within the French and hence Western capitalist camp. Nevertheless, the ongoing process of decolonization and global politics that resulted from the Cold War meant that by the mid-1970s the NAM was ostensibly "socialist" in orientation. This was probably the case by the 1976 Colombo summit, and most certainly by the 1979 Havana summit.

The reassertion of Northern politico-economic dominance over the South came at a historical juncture when financial indebtedness was acting to drastically undermine—if not emasculate—sovereignty and maneuverability in developing countries. At the same time, leadership factions within the South were increasingly drawn into the ongoing neoliberal processes of restructuring, and their specific class interests tended to be different from those of their own constituencies, who were suffering from the liberalization programs restructuring entailed. Indeed, the call for liberalization—dressed up as it was in the rhetoric of economic "realities"—gave space for conservative elements within the ruling elites of the South who had always been reluctant to commit themselves to a concrete plan of action vis-à-vis the NIEO. Their seizing upon the globalization discourse to help explain away unpopular policies (which concomitantly reified the positions of certain externally oriented class factions within the domestic polity) reflected not only a minimal commitment to any major restructuring of the global economy (except where it benefited Southern elites); it also mirrored the tensions and contradictions inherent within an organization such as the NAM, whose membership was so disparate. As Walden Bello succinctly put it:

> The ambivalence of the NIEO program as expressed by NAM reflect[ed] the fact that despite rhetorical unity, the alliance that advanced this program was an uneasy one, composed of conservative, radical, and liberal states with divergent objectives. For status quo states like Mexico, world economic reform along NIEO lines was seen as a means to alleviate pressures for much-needed internal economic reforms and thus solidify the position of the ruling elites. Also, waving the NIEO flag was a perfect ideological weapon to blunt criticism from forces for change within the country.[11]

Furthermore, abandonment of such confrontational posturing as the NIEO served the interests not only of specific class factions throughout the South but also the specific foreign policies of NAM states. For example, towards the end of the 1980s the elites within Yugoslavia became aware of the pressing need to tie the country's economic future to the ongoing European integration project, particularly in the light of the decline of the rest of the socialist world. Thus, at the ninth summit in Belgrade in 1989, Yugoslavia "pleaded for the modernization of the Movement [thus] discarding the NAM's attitude of assertiveness vis-à-vis the two power blocs. Instead, the NAM [adopted] a more tolerant and flexible position with emphasis on co-operation and dialogue."[12] Such a position was not simply a reflection of Yugoslavia's needs and wants; it also reflected a playing out of the increasing integration of the world's markets and the desire by local Southern-based elites to benefit from this process wherever possible.

Combative posturing against the structural inequalities of the capitalist system was seen to be of little use in facing up to globalization, particularly when—as has been pointed out—many of the elites in the South subscribed to the hegemonic project of neoliberalism. Even those that did not fully accede to this "New World Order" were painfully aware of the ongoing marginalization that much of the South was enduring and, in the words of the then Indonesian ambassador to South Africa, were "willing to undertake whatever was necessary to ensure that [they] could engage the rest of the international community in dialogue."[13] Yet the international community clearly set much of the agenda in the new North–South dialogue. While the NAM adopted what can be seen as a "trade unionist" approach to the world economy, discussion of the structural inequalities that underpinned the global capitalist system were quietly shelved. Meanwhile, rhetoric concerning "economic realities," appeals to "universal standards," and claims regarding the "de-ideologization" of global politics became the norm.

UNCTAD

UNCTAD was formed in 1964 to "create a forum in which the more prosperous member countries [of the United Nations] would come under pressure to agree to measures benefiting the less-developed countries." More specifically, its formation was "a deliberate effort to use international bureaucracy and conference diplomacy to alter current norms affecting trade and development."[14] UNCTAD's founding reflected the growth in membership of the UN of newly independent states from European colonial empires. A large number of the elites of these new entities keenly felt the iniquity of a world order into which they had emerged, an order informed by the ideologies of the North, and which the new states had had no hand in crafting.

The caucus within UNCTAD of the global South (groups from Africa, Asia, and Latin America) was dubbed the "Group of 77," which took its name from the original number of countries that gathered in preparation for the 1964 "conference"; and while UNCTAD has become an organization, the "C" in its acronym still stands for "Conference." As the membership subsequently increased (132 at present), the number in the abbreviation remained unchanged at G77; and the group remained and became a permanent feature of negotiations, in UNCTAD and elsewhere.

As an organization UNCTAD had a mandate to perform a variety of purposes. Perhaps most important was the policy formulation aspect of the body, designed to create general and explicit prescriptions associated with trade and development. Such a process was guided by the research work conducted by the staff of the UNCTAD secretariat in consultation with experts engaged by the organization. This process was then followed by, at times, painstaking negotiations with the UNCTAD membership. This was dependent upon consensus and invariably strengthened the hand of the developed world. If and when a decision was reached, UNCTAD took on an observational role to monitor compliance while technical cooperation and assistance sought to enable member countries to follow the prescriptions agreed upon by the body. That much of this process resulted in a skewed scenario in favor of the ongoing order reflected the organizational bias inherent in UNCTAD's constitutional principles, as well as the negative perceptions the developed world possessed towards the organization. Historically UNCTAD was

> The first real confrontation of North and South, symbolic of the new, fundamental structure of international politics, in which the problems of relations of industrialized rich and agricultural poor had replaced the problem of relations between western capitalist and eastern Communist. It was an occasion to redress the injustices perpetrated under colonial regimes . . . UNCTAD would begin to apply in practice what Western political theory had taught since the time of Plato, that no political community could be stable if it contained extremes of rich and poor.[15]

For its part, the West was highly ambivalent towards UNCTAD's establishment, preferring to rely upon the General Agreement on Tariffs and Trade (GATT) to regulate global trading relations. Such a preference suited the West's own interests, and the developed world's reluctance to discuss substantial issues vis-à-vis development (which threatened to open up all manner of questions regarding the global trading architecture, unequal terms of trade, and so on) was manifest in the demand to allow decisions made by UNCTAD to be reached by consensus.[16] Such a "procedure of conciliation" meant that the terms of the debate and the maneuverability of UNCTAD were constrained from the beginning, with the developed world granted effective influence in line with their material power (thus perpetuating their global dominance over the South), but out of all proportion to their numerical strength. Such structural power enabled the North to "generally confine their role [in UNCTAD] to opposing any proposals for change," while ostensible "positive proposals" of their own were invariably "of a cosmetic nature designed to conceal their underlying resistance to change."[17]

This is not to say that UNCTAD was a doomed body from the start. Indeed, during calls for a NIEO, UNCTAD had some limited success, notably with the formulation of the Generalized System of Preferences and the Integrated Program for Commodities. Yet much of the success of such formulations was curtailed by the North's unwillingness to fully implement the agreements such that "it had become obvious by the late 1970s that the high expectations held in some quarters for progress towards a new order were being frustrated." This was symbolized by the breakdown of the Paris Conference on International Economic Cooperation in June 1977 and the failures of UNCTAD IV, V, and VI (May 1976, June 1979, and June 1983, respectively).[18] Furthermore, the inflexibility of the North vis-à-vis the developing world began to harden as the neoliberal counterrevolution gained momentum under Reagan and Thatcher. This was perhaps most graphically illustrated by Reagan's response to the Brandt Commission's proposals for a meeting to overcome the deadlock in global negotiations over questions concerning trade and development. Reagan only agreed to attend provided that Cuba was excluded; the meeting was to avoid substantive issues; and it did not release any form of final communiqué!

The reassertion by the North over the South

This attitude towards the South was compounded by Washington's behavior at the actual summit in Cancún when Reagan used the meeting as an "opportunity to lecture Third World leaders on Reaganomics and offer American technical assistance to Third World governments that wanted to emulate his domestic policies . . . Afterwards, the U.S. simply refused to engage in global negotiations, forcing the North–South dialogue to a stall."[19] Such actions were applauded by Margaret Thatcher, who suggested that one of the "valuable" outcomes of Cancún had been that it "was the last of such gatherings." Henceforth, "the intractable problems of Third World poverty, hunger, and debt would not be solved by misdirected international intervention, but rather by liberating enterprise, promoting trade—and defeating socialism in all its forms."[20]

Throughout the 1980s, Washington (and London) actively pressured the South into accepting neoliberal macro-economic reform. As such, the focal point for conversations about global economic governance moved to those international financial institutions where the North was preponderant.

In addition, the ability to withstand the liberalizing thrust promoted by the North was further weakened by the Uruguay Round of GATT negotiations, which not only sought to lock in the developing world to the increasingly globalized world economy, but also made UNCTAD's role as a discussion forum—attempting to arrive at consensus on trade issues—somewhat redundant. This was particularly so as the World Trade Organization (WTO)—the successor to the GATT created in 1995—took on a more substantive and enforcement-oriented role. In short, the previous tendency of UNCTAD to base its assumptions around the regulation of the global economy as a means to promote development was dramatically undercut.

It was in this context that the state elites and UNCTAD staff sought to repackage the organization. While the logic of neoliberalism was broadly accepted, the negative effects of a liberalized world were equally becoming obvious. The acceptance of the new normative order was exemplified by the abandonment of any confrontational posturing. Instead, the rhetoric spoke of the need to "overcome confrontation and to foster a climate of genuine cooperation and solidarity." As Hoogvelt put it post-UNCTAD VIII (Cartagena, 1992):

> Whereas up until that time [Cartagena] UNCTAD had been a platform where developing countries demanded adjustment of the international . . . system to their developmental needs, it now expressed the belief that adoption of [neoliberal] laws and related efforts in . . . GATT would facilitate technology transfers to developing countries. The structural power of transnational capital has not just formed the policy agenda of *deregulation*, it is also responsible for the drive to *privatisation* of the state sector in all countries of the world.[21]

Acceptance of hegemonic discourse while attempting to ameliorate the worst aspects of the established order became the tactic for much of the global South. This was a remarkable sea-change in UNCTAD's normative posture, for "until [Cartagena] UNCTAD could be viewed as a counter-hegemonic organization resisting the dominance of the Bretton Woods institutions. The restructuring of the organization [gave] it a less confrontational role in the North–South dialogue."[22]

Explaining the demise of the South

The reassertion of the North over the South came within a context where high debt levels and economic stagnation in most of the postcolonial world acted to drastically undermine the South's maneuverability. Since formal independence, the South has—because of its dependent relationship on the North—continually borrowed from the North to nurture their economies. With the recycling of petro-dollars in the 1970s and 1980s making borrowing an easy option, most of the South indulged in massive borrowing with their external debt expanding at a very rapid—and unsustainable—rate. The recklessly adventurous lending practices of the North's bankers contributed to this process. The massive debts created immense problems for the South by creating a vicious Catch-22 situation, whereby funds to finance development were diverted to pay off debt, thereby diminishing future growth that could have repaid the debt. In addition, the necessity to secure foreign currencies to service debt led to a quick depreciation of many Southern currencies and hyperinflation.

Paradoxically, high oil prices, which had initially stimulated the lending/borrowing spree, exacerbated the problem, particularly for oil-importing countries. At the same time, the call for liberalization—dressed up as it was in the rhetoric of economic "realities"—gave space for conservative elements within the ruling elites of the South, who had always been reluctant to concretely commit themselves to the NIEO, to assume control. Their seizing upon the growing globalization discourse to help explain away unpopular policies to cope with debt crises reflected a long-standing minimal commitment to any major restructuring of the global economy—except when it benefited Southern elites. It was in this context that those within Southern-dominated bodies such as UNCTAD and NAM sought to repackage their organizations. An acceptance of the normative principles of neoliberalism came to define principles upon which both NAM and UNCTAD operate and which characterize other political expressions of the global South.

The BRICS and the global South

Both UNCTAD and the NAM have continued their broad trajectories, but concern has increasingly been expressed that the historic bargain by the global South to drop its confrontational posture in return for benefiting from globalization has been largely a one-sided affair. As the economic power of emerging economies has accelerated in the last ten years, initiatives such as the BRICS might be seen as concrete manifestations of this new line. In May 2008, Russia hosted the first formal Brazil, Russia, India, and China (BRIC) summit in Yekaterinburg, and in December 2010, South Africa was formally invited to join what then became the BRICS group of large emerging economies.

Prior to South Africa's membership invitation, the BRIC members were, according to the IMF, projected to account for around 60 percent of global growth by 2014. The BRIC acronym was originally coined in 2001 by Jim O'Neill, chief economist for Goldman Sachs, when the global investment banking and securities firm advanced the argument that these emerging economies were likely to surpass the traditional economic powerhouses of the global economy by 2040. According to the report prepared by Goldman Sachs, "in less than 40 years" the states dubbed the BRICs were expected to surpass the G6, making up the world's main "engine of new demand growth and spending power," thereby "offset[ting] the impact of graying populations and slower growth in the advanced economies."[23] The Goldman Sachs report saw the four initial BRIC states as prospective "engines of growth," arguing that stable and cumulative growth in Brazil and India alongside the sheer size of China and Russia's economies would fundamentally change the global economy and, by implication, the global balance of power away from the West. Though methodologically the concept has some severe flaws (such as extrapolating growth rates along a straight and progressively increasing line) and was not based on sound research, the concept caught on rapidly and has entered the global lexicon.

The BRICS' relevance for any discussion of the global South is that for the first time in years it appears that leading nations among developing countries are forcing themselves onto the global stage over issues pertaining to global governance. At one level this radically destabilizes the very notion of the South because of the economic power of some of them. Of course, there can be little doubt that China has indeed grown spectacularly since the inception of its modernization policies and that the other BRICS have steadily—if more gradually—expanded their economies. Revealingly, if purchasing power parity (PPP) measures of gross domestic product (GDP) are used, Beijing's economy is already three-quarters the size of that of the United States, while Brazil, Russia, and India have economies of similar size to Japan, Germany, Britain, France, and Italy.

The BRICS already have a bigger share of world trade than the United States, but what the BRICS term really captures revolves around both anxieties and expectations within international politics regarding how these rapidly emerging economies from the notional "developing world" will interact with the established powers, possibly stimulating a fundamental shift of influence away from the Western world. Yet, such concerns reflect a realist understanding of the world and do not properly investigate the actual claims of these new voices from the global South.

While the global South has accepted a less overly hostile attitude to various international financial institutions and dominant global players, and it has actively facilitated forums where business can be involved in economic matters, the reform of various facets of the world economy has also been put on the agenda. In this post-hegemonic world order, the WTO is seen as having strengthened the rules-based trading system, furthered liberalization, and opened up opportunities for sustainable development and growth. Confrontation with the North has given way to "dialogue."

Yet this reality in itself raises important issues about the very existence of the global South. In the immediate postcolonial period, it was perhaps permissible to assert that the newly independent states possessed a notional set of common interests: guarding their newfound sovereignty, the promotion of development, the aspiration to be taken seriously by the major powers, and the need to address the structures into which they found their economic systems inserted. Yet as the years progressed, and as greater and greater differences in both economic and political profiles emerged and became solidified, the coherence of the term diminished. What really does China have in common with Chad or Colombia, or Brazil with Burundi or Barbados? Even within continents the interests of a relatively developed export-based economy such as South Africa's have very little—if anything—in common with Rwanda's or Togo's. These sorts of problems are typified and made clearer if and when the BRICS nations try to position themselves as representatives of the global South. And in a context where the more developed members are vitally interested in maintaining the global status quo—albeit under slightly more favorable conditions—what is left on the agenda when we talk about the South? As it was always an elite-led project, the vagaries of elites and their changeable interests have necessarily doomed the Southern project in terms of its conceptual clarity. The term is still used as shorthand, vaguely indicating that these are not countries of the West. This is probably as much as we can assert when we talk of the global South today.

Conclusion

It is apparent that with the acceptance of the norms of trade liberalization goes recognition of the uneven process of globalization. This has translated itself into a position that has called for a lessening of the worst aspects of this process.[24] This position, as exemplified by the BRICS but also redolent of UNCTAD and NAM positions, has largely taken on board the "realities" of globalization and the ongoing world order, although adopting a more holistic and questioning approach, raising issues of particular concern to the developing world and to the key emerging powers specifically. This is where the institutionalization of the idea of the global South now finds itself.

It is this urgency to expose the hypocrisy of the North in its calculated push for free trade in the South—whilst keeping various of its own markets closed to Southern competition—that impels elements in the South to engage with initiatives rather than confront them. Many Southern elites now accept the call for neoliberal restructuring, but it is more problematic to turn this rhetoric around and urge the North to engage in supposed real free trade rather than the "actually existing free trade." The urge for a critical engagement with the North tends to be characterized as "partnership," which attempts to deal with both the positive and negative aspects of the ongoing globalizing process. Such "pragmatic" policies dominate the agendas of the BRICS, for example.

However, the viability of these positions remains open-ended. Is it actually possible to deregulate markets and roll back the state, allowing a free rein for international capital, and at the same time promote equity and mutual development in both North and global South? Those advocating such a turn need to answer a most fundamental problem: Is it intrinsic to the capitalist system that the generation of wealth is predicated upon poverty-producing principles? And, must there always be a dominant and a dominated sector in society—in international terms, a North and a South? Indeed can this turn actually be seen to exemplify how hegemonic neoliberal ideas have become, with key elites in the South—through such projects as the BRICS—clamoring to sign up to economic prescriptions that have actually helped to immiserate the developing world? As has been shown, institutional expressions of the South progressively converged with the prescriptions of the capitalist heartland and the environment today is very different from the perceived potentialities that the era of the NIEO opened up. Combined with the wide—and ever-growing—divergences in both economic and political terms that now characterize the postcolonial world, the very idea of the South in terms of global governance needs serious rethinking.

Additional reading

1. Jacqueline Braveboy-Wagner, *Institutions of the Global South* (London: Routledge, 2009).
2. Ian Taylor and Karen Smith, *The UN Conference on Trade and Development* (London: Routledge, 2007).
3. Anthony Payne, *The Global Politics of Unequal Development* (London: Palgrave, 2005).
4. Peter Willetts, *The Nonaligned Movement* (London: Verso, 1978).
5. Rorden Wilkinson and James Scott, "Developing Country Participation in the GATT: A Reassessment," *World Trade Review* 7, no. 3 (2008): 473–510.

Notes

1 Rajeev Patel and Phillip McMichael, "Third Worldism and the Lineages of Global Fascism: The Regrouping of the Global South in the Neoliberal Era," *Third World Quarterly* 25, no. 1 (2004): 241.
2 Robert Mortimer, *The Third World Coalition in International Politics* (Boulder: Westview Press, 1984), 9.
3 Ibid.
4 Graham Evans and Jeffrey Newnham, *Dictionary of World Politics: A Reference Guide to Concepts, Ideas and Institutions* (Hemel Hempstead: Harvester Wheatsheaf, 1992), 224.
5 Phillip Nel, "In Defence of Multilateralism: The Movement of the Non-Aligned Countries in the Current Global Order," paper presented at a DFA/FGD workshop on "South Africa and the Non-Aligned Movement in an Era of Globalisation," Pretoria, 25–30 April 1998, 5.
6 Peter Willetts, *The Nonaligned Movement* (London: Verso, 1978), 31.
7 Craig Murphy, *International Organization and Industrial Change: Global Governance since 1850* (Cambridge: Polity Press, 1994), 114.
8 Ibid., 115.
9 Timothy Shaw, "The Non-Aligned Movement and the New International Division of Labour in Onwuka," in *Africa in World Politics*, eds. Ralph Onwuka and Timothy Shaw (Basingstoke: Macmillan, 1989), 6.
10 Cited in Willetts, *The Nonaligned Movement*, 31.
11 Walden Bello, *Brave New Third World: Strategies for Survival in the Global Economy* (London: Earthscan, 1990), 45.
12 J. J. G. Syatauw, "The Non-Aligned Movement at the Cross-roads: The Jakarta Summit Adapting to the Post-Cold War Era," *Asian Yearbook of International Affairs* 3 (1993): 129.
13 Nana Sutresna, "Speech of H.E. Mr Nana S. Sutresna at a Conference on 'South Africa and the Non-Aligned Movement' in Johannesburg on 10 June 1998," *Indonesia in Perspective* 9 (1998): 4.
14 Joseph Nye, "UNCTAD: Poor Man's Pressure Group," in *The Anatomy of Influence: Decision-making in International Organizations*, eds. Robert Cox and Harold Jacobson (New Haven: Yale University Press, 1973), 334.

15 Charles Robertson, "The Creation of UNCTAD," in *International Organization: World Politics*, ed. Robert Cox (London: Macmillan, 1969), 258.

16 Mortimer, *Third World Coalition*, 17.

17 Robert Ramsay, "UNCTAD's Failure: The Rich Get Richer," *International Organization* 38, no. 2 (1984): 388–389.

18 Samuel Asante, "The Role of the Organisation of African Unity in Promoting Peace, Development and Regional Security in Africa," in *Africa: Perspectives on Peace and Development*, ed. Emmanuel Hansen (London: Zed Books, 1987), 132.

19 Enrico Augelli and Craig Murphy, *America's Quest for Supremacy and the Third World: A Gramscian Analysis* (London: Pinter Publishers, 1988), 189.

20 Margaret Thatcher, *The Downing Street Years* (London: HarperCollins, 1993), 170.

21 Ankie Hoogvelt, *Globalization and the Postcolonial World: The New Political Economy of Development* (Baltimore: Johns Hopkins University Press, 1997), 137.

22 Marc Williams, *International Economic Organisations and the Third World* (Hemel Hempstead: Harvester Wheatsheaf, 1994), 179.

23 Dominic Wilson and Roopa Purushothaman, "Dreaming with BRICs: The Path to 2050," Global Economics Paper no. 99 (New York: Goldman Sachs, 1 October 2003), 2.

24 Thandika Mkandawire and Charles Soludo, *Our Continent, Our Future: African Perspectives on Structural Adjustment* (Trenton, NJ: Africa World Press, 1999).

CONTENTS

US Hegemony

W. Andy Knight

Since the early 1970s several scholars and observers of international relations have argued that the United States has lost its hegemonic position in the world or is experiencing a decline in dominance. The late Susan Strange used to chide US academics, in particular, for perpetuating this "myth of America's lost hegemony." She was particularly critical of those who not only "unquestionably accepted" the proposition of American hegemonic decline but also took it upon themselves to spread that myth in such a way that it gained credence outside the United States.[1]

Despite challenges to its hegemonic status, the United States continues to be a global hegemon. However, we need to be cognizant of the very real challenges to US hegemony and of the need to understand it in the context of the *longue durée*. Contrary to what Francis Fukuyama would have us believe, history did not come to an end with the advent of the universalization of Western liberal democracy once the Cold War thawed.[2] In fact, during the immediate post-Cold War era, although many states embraced the Western style of liberal democracy and capitalism, we did not witness a true universalization of Western liberal democracy as a "final" form of government. China and Russia may have embraced capitalism and global markets, but neither of them is "liberal" or fully "capitalist." It is important therefore to question any thesis that posits the continual superiority and progressiveness of the West and the perpetual subordination and backwardness of the Rest. Similarly, it is imperative to take seriously the critiques of those who question the notion that US hegemony is here to stay.[3] At the same time, this chapter heeds Strange's caution not to accept blindly the view that the United States has lost its hegemonic status, that its hegemony is waning, or that a fundamental rupture has occurred in the systems of global governance the US put into place after World War II.

This chapter is divided into four parts. First, the concept of hegemony is explained and a distinction is drawn between hegemony and dominance. Second, a brief historical overview of US hegemony and dominance is provided. Third, some of the challenges to this hegemony are outlined, which have been used by observers to indicate a waning of American power. A brief conclusion follows.

Conceptualizing hegemony

Before we can determine whether or not US hegemony is waning or has been lost—and what the impact of this might be on international organization and global governance—it is important to distinguish between hegemony and dominance. The simplistic view of hegemony postulates that hegemons are pre-eminent powers with material and coercive ability to control the weak. Donald Puchala notes that much of the literature on world order treats hegemony as "the institutionalization of privilege, consequent inequality in the distribution of various values, and the injustices inherent in inequality." In other words, hegemony is generally seen as "a condition in human relations to be resented, rejected, and removed."[4] Immanuel Wallerstein's take on hegemony attaches similar malevolent qualities to the term. Wallerstein defines hegemony as "that situation in which the ongoing rivalry between so-called 'great powers' is so unbalanced that one power is truly primus inter pares; that is, one power can largely impose its rules and its wishes (at the very least by effective veto power) in the economic, political, military, diplomatic and even cultural arenas."[5]

This malevolent interpretation of hegemony rightly evokes resistant/"anti-hegemonic" reaction, or what Robert Cox calls "counter-hegemony."[6] Randolph Persaud explains that counter-hegemony ought to be "seen as dialectically constitutive of the conditions of hegemonic practices on a global scale."[7] This means that whenever there is hegemony, one should expect a counter-hegemonic reaction to it. But Puchala's conception of hegemony is a bit more nuanced than those that equate it with state "dominance" and "preponderance of power." When applied to international relations, a hegemon "arises when a single state attains preponderant power and elects to use its power to manage the international system." Thus, the power of the hegemon can be used in both malevolent and benevolent ways. Such a position is in conformity with hegemonic stability theory that suggests that the hegemon is a dominant power with the ability to shape norms, rules, and institutions of the international system and is expected to enforce the rules it has established by rewarding compliant states while punishing the recalcitrant.

Ian Clark notes that the term hegemon is always associated with "a concentration of power." But he also acknowledges that the concept of hegemony is much richer than that of primacy or dominance. Whereas primacy focuses on "the accretion of material power," hegemony "most readily achieves its distinctive identity when it is associated with legitimacy," respect for the leader, and voluntary or non-coercive acquiescence on the part of those being led.[8] Cox, building on the work of Italian social theorist Antonio Gramsci, drills even deeper to gain a better understanding of the concept of "hegemony." For him, the term refers to "a structure of values and understandings about the nature of order that permeates a whole system of states and non-state entities."[9] In a world order in which a hegemon is present, the values and understandings would be relatively stable and ostensibly unquestioned. In other words, the order created by the hegemon would be considered by most actors in the system as "the natural order."

The structure of values and understandings is always underpinned by a structure of material power in a system where the hegemon is present. That material power is what infuses the hegemon with characteristics of dominance and preponderance. But, as Cox points out, dominance is not sufficient for hegemony to be exhibited. "Hegemony derives from the ways of doing and thinking of the dominant social strata of the dominant state or states insofar as these ways of doing and thinking have acquired the acquiescence of the dominant social strata of other states."[10] Put another way, it is those social practices embedded in institutional arrangements and regimes, and the ideologies that underpin, explain, and legitimize them that, in fact, lay the foundation of any hegemonic order.[11]

Great powers "get their way most effectively by securing voluntary or even unthinking cooperation from others." Thus, a hegemon does not have to rely on costly coercion to get what it wants.[12] It can utilize "soft power" to induce cooperation.[13] Intellectual and moral leadership, framed by ideational terms of reference, is what separates hegemony from dominance. For that kind of leadership to develop in a world order setting there has to be a convergence of interests and attitudes, especially among international elites, and the ideational elements associated with the hegemon must become embedded in the institutions of global governance.[14]

Thus, to fully come to grips with US hegemony, we must understand the extent to which the US has used its materially dominant position in the international hierarchy of states to: take on the management of the international system; create institutions, regimes, and rules that lend order and predictability to the system; promote and embed within those institutions, regimes, and rules certain ideas and ideologies that favor American self-interests and purposes; induce voluntary compliance and concurrence from the international elite class; and absorb or co-opt emerging counter-hegemonic ideas and forces that have the potential to challenge the US hegemonic position.

The primary challenge for the sustainability of any hegemon, including the US, is to somehow combine both hard and soft power in such a way that induces consensus around the principles, norms, and rules that structure the institutional governance of the international system while at the same time protecting that governance apparatus by "the amor of coercion."[15] This is not an easy task, particularly if the hegemon is so predominant that its structural power (military, economic, scientific, and technological) subsumes most challenges to its global role. The US, in fact, was derisively labeled a "hyperpower" immediately following the end of the Cold War precisely because American structural power could not be matched by any other power within the international system.[16] With Washington's greatest challenger, the erstwhile Soviet Union, unraveling as a result of foreign policy over-extension (e.g. the quagmire in Afghanistan) and internal leadership crises, the US was the sole superpower by 1989. Since that time, no challenger has been able to match the preponderance of the US or effectively counter its hegemony.[17]

A brief history of US hegemony and dominance

Achieving global hegemonic status is rare and transient. According to Wallerstein, hegemonic power was exercised only three times in the modern world system: by the

United Provinces[18] in the mid-seventeenth century; Great Britain in the nineteenth century; and the United States from around 1945. In each case, the hegemon achieved its pre-eminent position not only because it was dominant but also because it was able to operate more efficiently than other powers in the international system in at least three economic areas—agro-industrial production, commerce, and finance.[19] Each successive hegemon's competitive edge in efficiency was so great that enterprises based in the hegemonic power could outbid those located elsewhere in the world. The political and cultural influences of each of these hegemonic powers were so pervasive that they were considered more than simply coercive powers. They were able to combine material and military advantages with intellectual and moral leadership to steer the international system in a particular direction.

US hegemony

The transition from the United Provinces' hegemony to British hegemony was a relatively long and drawn-out one that took about 150 years to complete. The transition from British to US hegemony took half as long,[20] in large part because of the strategy adopted by Britain as its hegemony waned. From the late 1870s until 1940, Britain acquiesced to the United States, as the latter began to establish and assert its own sphere of interest in the Americas. Instead of treating the rise of the US in a hostile manner, Britain considered American interests as complementary with its own. For its part, the United States was not yet willing to take on the full mantle of global leadership but seemed content to allow Britain to continue to rule its vast colonial Empire.

Britain ceded priority to the US in certain areas of its sphere of influence (e.g. in South America and the Caribbean)—thus acquiescing to the 1823 Munroe Doctrine[21]—and basically took a cooperative approach with the United States in managing and maintaining the international order. But, as the US gradually assumed the mantle of global leadership from Britain, it initially acted more as a dominant power than a hegemon. For instance, in 1846–48 the US took California, Arizona, and New Mexico from Mexico in the Mexican-American war; in 1888 the US intervened militarily in a civil war in Haiti; in 1895–96 Washington intervened in a boundary dispute between Venezuela and British Guyana; between 1898 and 1932, the US militarily intervened 34 times in nine Central American and Caribbean countries; in 1899, the US occupied Cuba to protect American interests there during the Cuban independence revolution; and in 1903, after seizing Puerto Rico during the Spanish-American War, the United States declared sovereignty over the Panama Canal.[22] These were actions of a dominant power, not necessarily those of a hegemon.

World War I (1914–18) proved beyond the shadow of a doubt that the United States was more than a hemispheric power and that it had the ability to emerge as the new global hegemon.[23] By this time, America enjoyed naval parity with Britain and was the world's leading credit nation and industrial power. Clearly, on several fronts, the United States was indeed a dominant force to be reckoned with. But it began to use its material clout to press for the creation of international institutions of governance.

On 8 January 1918, before the US Congress, President Woodrow Wilson used Washington's rising dominance to argue in one of his Fourteen Points for the creation of "a general association of nations formed on the basis of covenants designed to create mutual guarantees of the political independence and territorial integrity of States, large and small equally."[24] This articulation of a new type of standing international organization dedicated to fostering international cooperation and providing security and enduring peace for all of its members came at a propitious time. Europe was exhausted by the four years of World War I and wanted to avoid the devastation of another systemic conflagration. The League of Nations was created from Wilson's vision. He used his influence to ensure that the Covenant of the League would be attached to the Treaty of Versailles, which ended the war. Wilson drafted that Covenant with two other elites, Georges Clemenceau of France and David Lloyd George of Britain. Despite popular support in America for this new organization, the US Congress failed to ratify the Treaty and the Covenant, fearing that the League would be an expensive organization that would reduce the US' ability to defend its own interest. The US never did join the League, and some analysts argue that its absence doomed that organization to failure. Whether or not that argument holds, the League's collective security apparatus was considerably weakened because of the absence of the emerging hegemon from its membership.

Immediately after World War I, the US seemed unwilling to take on the global hegemonic role. In fact, America resorted to isolationism as the global economic problems caused by World War I led to the collapse of the international financial system by 1931.[25] With the adoption of appeasement strategies by Britain and the absence of US hegemonic leadership on the world stage, both Germany and Japan began to exhibit counter-hegemonic tendencies as the world spiraled into another systemic war.[26] At this point, the US shifted its stance from one of neutrality to one which strengthened its alliance with Britain in order to beat back the counter-hegemonic challenges from Germany and Japan during World War II (1939–45). By the time the US joined the war effort in 1941, after its territory in Pearl Harbor was attacked by the Japanese, it was more prepared to assume the hegemonic role. But it initially did so in collaboration with Britain.

The United States joined Britain in drafting the Atlantic Charter in 1941, which laid out plans for reconstructing the international economic order when the war was over. The Atlantic Charter was a pivotal statement of US policy which hinted at the dismantling of all protected spheres of interest, including the British Empire, and the reconstruction of world order under American leadership. The Charter, negotiated in August 1941 by UK prime minister Winston Churchill and US president Franklin Roosevelt, reflected Washington's and, even more, Roosevelt's idealistic vision of establishing an international organization to serve as arbiter of disputes and a mechanism for protecting the peace. It paved the way for the "Declaration of the United Nations," signed on 1 January 1942 in San Francisco by 26 governments that pledged to continue their fight against the Axis Powers. In San Francisco, on 25 April 1945, two weeks before Roosevelt's death, 50 countries met at the United Nations Conference on International Organization to draft the United Nations Charter. The UN system was initiated with the signing of the Charter (26 June 1945) by those 50 states.[27]

The shift from *pax Britannica* to *pax Americana* was one in which the United States, as emergent hegemon, pushed for as full and complete a liberalization of international economic relations as possible, whilst the outgoing hegemon preferred a transition period of protectionism that would allow it to relinquish gradually its sphere of influence while retaining its imperial preference system and control over large parts of its colonial empire. But the United States, through bilateral and multilateral negotiations, induced Britain to support its aim of recreating an open multilateral trading economy. The United States took the lead in bringing together 730 delegates from 44 allied countries to Mount Washington Hotel in Bretton Woods, New Hampshire, to deliberate and eventually sign the agreements that brought into effect a novel system of rules, institutions, and procedures to regulate the international monetary system.[28] The Bretton Woods agreements represented an unprecedented experiment in international rule-making and institution building for a post-war monetary and financial system that would be led by the US. That system included the International Monetary Fund (IMF), and the International Bank for Reconstruction and Development (IBRD, or the World Bank), and was intended to lay the foundations for the negotiation at a later date of the International Trade Organization (ITO). The US Congress did not support the ITO, but in its place was established a negotiating forum, the General Agreement on Tariffs and Trade (GATT). "The Anglo-American agreements established sophisticated rules that would attempt to reconcile openness and trade expansion with the commitments of national governments to full employment and economic stabilization." This blend of *laissez faire* and interventionist policies was the result of the compromise that the emerging hegemon would reach with the waning hegemon.[29]

Thus, it would seem that US elites recognized limits of coercion and chose to build the American post-war agenda around principles of multilateralism, discourse, and compromise. In so doing, they hoped to lend legitimacy to the post-war order they were constructing. Part of gaining that legitimacy was the approach the US took in addressing the devastation in Europe caused by World War II. In 1947, a reconstruction plan to provide economic and technical assistance to the war-torn countries in Europe was devised by US State Department officials William Clayton and George Kennan. The Organisation for European Economic Co-operation (OEEC) was established to help administer the Marshall Plan. As it turned out, the Plan was used not only to rebuild war-torn European economies but also to expand US trade and economic activity and, at the same time, prevent any more European countries from being absorbed into the Soviet sphere of influence.[30]

The US approach to hegemony after World War II was one that mixed its obvious hard military power with soft power and the principles of multilateralism, discourse, and compromise in creating norms and institutions to steer the international system in a direction of its choosing. But it should be noted that the United States did so in collaboration with Britain and a concert of powers because it had to be mindful of internal political divisions over its hegemonic role, as well as the need to deal with counter-hegemonic challenges.

Challenges to US hegemony

Anglo-American collaboration in the creation of institutions of the post-war world order evolved into collaboration between the US and those European and other states not yet drawn into the Soviet Union's vortex. As noted earlier, at the global level, counter-hegemony can be viewed as dialectically constitutive of the conditions of hegemonic practice. One can see counter-hegemonic reactions to the US preponderance almost immediately after World War II ended.

Chandra Muzaffar has argued, quite convincingly, that US hegemony was never really global or total.[31] Despite the fact that America exhibited a concentration of overwhelming military power, political power, economic power, scientific and technological power, and information and cultural power in the post-World War II period, there were at least five major challenges that checked US hegemony.

First, Moscow posed a stiff challenge to US hegemony almost immediately after World War II. Although both the United States and the Soviet Union were allies during the war, the ideological differences between the capitalist and communist powers were too massive to overcome. The resultant Cold War (roughly 1945 to 1991) was characterized by bipolarity and a precarious balance of power. US president Harry Truman devised the Truman Doctrine in 1947 as a means of containing communist advances. Germany was divided into the German Federal Republic (West Germany) and the German Democratic Republic (East Germany) and the US established a military alliance—the North Atlantic Treaty Organization (NATO)—to protect Western Europe from a possible Soviet security threat. The Soviets countered by creating the Warsaw Pact to protect their European satellites from a possible US threat. What resulted was a bitter ideological confrontation between the two nuclear-armed superpowers that was played out by proxies in different parts of the globe and within the UN Security Council. This Cold War climate of mutually assured destruction (MAD) placed a check on US hegemony. But in 1991, when the Soviet Union imploded, this challenge to US hegemony subsided. Russia was brought into the G7 consortium and the world capitalist system during the post-Cold War era and is no longer a significant counter-hegemonic threat.

Second, in 1949 the US-backed Kuomintang regime in Beijing was overthrown by Mao Tse-Tung in a popular revolution. Although China was a US ally during World War II, it chose under Mao to embrace the communist ideology, and it posed a challenge to US hegemony by rejecting liberal capitalism. North Korea also posed a similar challenge when it separated from South Korea as a result of the Korean War (1950–53) and embraced communism. Vietnam, which suffered huge casualties during its war with the United States, also rejected liberal capitalism. Cuba, in the American backyard, chose to align itself ideologically with the Soviets. These developments countered US global hegemony and its attempt to spread liberal capitalist ideology. But in recent years China has more or less been co-opted into embracing capitalism to save its socialist revolution and has been gradually reversing Mao's heavy emphasis on Marxism and self-reliance by joining the Western-controlled international financial institutions. Indeed, beginning in the 1980s, Washington "in effect became China's patron in encouraging more and more substantial participation by the PRC in the global capitalist system."[32] Vietnam has also embraced Western capitalism, and the communist counter-hegemonic threats from North Korea and Cuba are really insignificant.

The third development which stymied the United States in its quest for global and total hegemony occurred during the 1950s and 1960s: the significant growth of nationalism in territories controlled by colonial powers. During the process of decolonization, some African, Asian, and Caribbean states decided to align themselves with Washington, and others with Moscow, but a large number preferred to stake out an independent path that would put them in neither the US nor the Soviet ambit. Beginning with the 1955 summit in Bandung, Indonesia, many of these states formed the Nonaligned Movement (NAM). The NAM began, and continues, to use the UN General Assembly as a forum to resist Westernization and particularly Americanization. These nonaligned countries adopted resolutions in the General Assembly for the establishment of a New International Economic Order (NIEO), and in the UN Educational, Social and Cultural Organization to establish a New International Information Order (NIIO) as a counter to US-dominated liberal capitalism and media. For a moment, aided by the high prices of oil, the so-called Third World was a counterbalance to US hegemony, but by the early 1980s the coalition of what became known as the "global South" lost steam, and resistance to US hegemony was weakened. Nothing much became of the NIEO or the NIIO, and the United States was able to co-opt many elites from what became known as the global South.

The fourth challenge to American hegemony comes from its own imperial over-stretch.[33] Today, the United States maintains a network of almost 750 military bases and other installations in more than 130 countries. Since the early 1990s, the United States has been involved in a number of wars that have drained its resources (e.g. the 1990 war with Iraq; the fiasco in Somalia; the invasion and occupation of Iraq after the 9/11 terrorist attacks; the ongoing military expedition in Afghanistan; and the so-called "global war on terror").[34] In each case, the financial and personnel costs have "sapped the strength of the US economy" and challenged US hegemony.[35] Military over-extension could become the Achilles heel of US hegemony, as it was in the hegemonies of both the United Provinces and Britain.

The fifth challenge to US hegemony comes from the rise of competing states and blocs. The advent of the European Union (EU) and the economic integration of countries in Europe posed a challenge of sorts to US economic, if not military, hegemony. For instance, the adoption of the Euro by 17 members of the EU has provided competition for the US dollar. The US trade deficit with Europe further contributed to weakening the dollar. The rise of China as an economic power and the fact that Chinese manufacturing companies are out-producing US companies is another reason for concern. China is expected to surpass the US as the world's largest manufacturer by 2020[36] and is predicted to become the world's largest economy in dollar-based GDP by 2041, according to Goldman Sachs, in spite of the fact that its growth has slowed in recent years. The BRICS (Brazil, Russia, India, China, and South Africa) are also expected to out-produce the United States, the United Kingdom, France, Germany, Japan, and Italy combined by 2039.[37] In Latin America, a number of states have joined together to resist US hegemonic pressure. The Bolivarian Alternative of the Americas (ALBA), the brainchild of the Venezuelan president Chavez, was established in 2004 to counter the hegemonic idea of a Free Trade Area of the Americas (FTAA), which would have perpetuated US hegemony over Latin America. However, there are major questions about the ability of any of these rising powers to convert their increasingly material power into "a distinctive, acceptable, form of order." Ian Clark points out, for instance, that "China faces a complex array of severe domestic problems that will dominate its policy priorities for many decades to come."[38] The question becomes: Can any one of the BRICS develop an institution of hegemony that would inspire widespread international consent?

Conclusion

As noted earlier, hegemony is both rare and transient. There have been only three true hegemonic powers in our modern world—the United Provinces, Britain, and the United States. The third maintains its hegemonic position despite several counter-hegemonic challenges. But is it likely, as Earl Fry predicted, that by 2040 the United States will no longer be a global hegemon. Some have argued that its hegemony was always overstated. Indeed, we may be moving towards a post-hegemonic world in which there will be no single overarching dominant power.[39]

The era of *pax Americana* that was ushered in after World War II placed the United States in the unenviable position of being the world's policeman and bearing the brunt of the economic costs of establishing norms and regional and multilateral institutions to sustain its global hegemonic position.[40] Being a global hegemon meant that the United States was pivotal to the construction of the post-War World II order and that it had the military and economic might to support that order. But it did so in collaboration with the waning hegemon and with a concert of states, in particular the members of the Atlantic Alliance. Since the end of the Cold War, the United States has indeed been the foremost superpower in history—the most powerful state in history[41]—and briefly experienced a "unipolar moment."[42] During the immediate post-Cold War era, many historians and political scientists were forced to acknowledge that Henry Luce was right when he forecasted in *Life* magazine, published on 17 February 1941, that the twentieth century would be known as the "American Century."

Despite the recent challenges to its hegemonic position posed by the rising states of China, India, Brazil, South Africa, and a resurgent Russia, the US continues to maintain a hegemonic position in the globe. But as Henry Kissinger warned after the first Gulf War, America's pre-eminence cannot last. While the US is still pre-eminent with respect to military might, it does not have the economic resources to truly dominate the globe any longer.[43] Evidence of this fact reared its head after the first Gulf War when it was revealed that the war was financed to the tune of $37 billion by Arab states and $17 billion by Germany and Japan. As the *Economist* puts it, the US "knows that it no longer has the economic clout to run a hegemony."[44]

That said, as outlined above, hegemony is about more than military or economic dominance. Hegemony is sustained by intellectual and moral leadership at the international level—something the Barack Obama administration seems to be aiming to provide—and the ability to co-opt and absorb counter-hegemonic forces. It is also sustained if the hegemon is able to induce voluntary and sometimes unthinking cooperation from its followers. Joseph Nye uses the term "soft power" to encapsulate the notion that a hegemon can get what it wants "through attraction rather than coercion or payments." For him, soft power "arises from the attractiveness of a country's culture, political ideals, and policies." Nye continues: "When you can get others to admire your ideals and to want what you want, you do not have to spend as much on sticks and carrots to move them in your direction. Seduction is always more effective than coercion, and many values like democracy, human rights and individual opportunities are deeply seductive."[45] It is in the pervasiveness of American culture and the use of its soft power that we see continuing signs of US hegemony. But it has extended well beyond its cultural influences. The United States will remain hegemonic as long as its ideas are embedded in the countless regimes (principles, norms, rules, and decision-making processes) that operate in various corners of the globe, and in the current generation of institutions of global governance.

Major questions that remain at this critical historical juncture are: Has the United States created a post-hegemonic world "that can no longer be dominated by any single state or its cultural fruits?"[46] Are we moving towards a multipolar system in which the United States will simply be *primus inter pares*? While it is a mistake to prophesize the imminent decline of US hegemony, "it would be just as erroneous to engage in American triumphalism."[47]

Additional reading

1. Robert Cox, "Gramsci, Hegemony and International Relations: An Essay in Method," *Millennium: Journal of International Studies* 1, no. 2 (1983): 162–175.
2. Paul Kennedy, *The Rise and Fall of the Great Powers* (New York: Random House, 1987).
3. Joseph S. Nye, Jr., *Soft Power: The Means to Success in World Politics* (New York: Public Affairs, 2004).
4. Randolph B. Persaud, *Counter-Hegemony and Foreign Policy: The Dialectics of Marginalized and Global Forces in Jamaica* (Albany: State University of New York Press, 2001).

Notes

1 Susan Strange, "The Persistent Myth of Lost Hegemony," *International Organization* 41, no. 4 (1987): 552.
2 Francis Fukuyama, *The End of History and the Last Man* (New York: Free Press, 1992).
3 See, for example, Earl H. Fry, "The Decline of the American Superpower," *The Forum* 5, no. 2 (2007), http://www.degruyter.com/view/j/for.2007.5.2_20120105083452/for.2007.5.2/for.2007.5.2.1153/for.2007.5.2.1153.xml.
4 Donald J. Puchala, "World Hegemony and the United Nations," *International Studies Review* 7, no. 4 (2005): 571. Subsequent quotes from 572.
5 Immanuel Wallerstein, *The Politics of the World Economy: The States, the Movements and the Civilizations* (Cambridge: Cambridge University Press, 1984), 3.
6 Robert W. Cox, "Gramsci, Hegemony and International Relations: An Essay in Method," *Millennium* 12, no. 2 (1983), 162–175.
7 Randolph B. Persaud, *Counter-Hegemony and Foreign Policy: The Dialectics of Marginalized and Global Forces in Jamaica* (Albany: State University of New York Press, 2001), 69.
8 See Ian Clark, "China and the United States: A Succession of Hegemonies?," *International Affairs* 87, no. 1 (2011): 1424.
9 Robert W. Cox with Timothy J. Sinclair, *Approaches to World Order* (Cambridge: Cambridge University Press, 1996), 151.
10 Cox, *Approaches to World Order*, 151.

11 See John Gerard Ruggie, "International Regimes, Transactions, and Change: Embedded Liberalism in the Postwar Economic Order," *International Organization* 36, no. 2 (Spring 1982): 379–415.

12 David P. Forsythe, "The U.S. and Trans-Atlantic Relations: On the Difference between Dominance and Hegemony," DIIS Working Paper no. 2005/16: 4.

13 Joseph S. Nye, Jr., *Soft Power: The Means to Success in World Politics* (New York: Public Affairs, 2004).

14 On these points, see Mark Rupert, *Producing Hegemony: The Politics of Mass Production and American Global Power* (Cambridge: Cambridge University Press, 1995): 43–56.

15 William I. Robinson, *Promoting Polyarchy: Globalization, US Intervention, and Hegemony* (Cambridge: Cambridge University Press, 1996): 22.

16 *The New York Times*, "To Paris, the U.S. Looks like a 'Hyperpower,'" 5 February 1999, http://www.nytimes.com/1999/02/05/news/05iht-france.t_0.html.

17 See Peter Van Ness, "Hegemony, Not Anarchy: Why China and Japan Are Not Balancing US Unipolar Power," *International Relations of the Asia-Pacific* 2, no. 1 (2002): 132–134.

18 The United Provinces is another name for the Federated Dutch Republic (or the Netherlands) that emerged as a unified entity in 1581. From 1618 to 1648 the United Provinces exhibited qualities of a hegemonic power and is considered by world system theorist Immanuel Wallerstein as the first global hegemonic state. See Peter J. Taylor, "Ten Years That Shook the World? The United Provinces as First Hegemonic State," *Sociological Perspectives* 37, no. 1 (1994): 25–46.

19 Immanuel Wallerstein, "The Three Instances of Hegemony in the History of the Capitalist World-Economy," in *Current Issues and Research in Macrosociology: International Studies in Sociology and Social Anthropology* 37, ed. Gerhard Lenski (Leiden: E.J. Brill, 1984), 103.

20 Giovanni Arrighi, Po-Keung Hui, Krishnendu Ray, and Thomas Ehrlich Reifer, "Geopolitics and High Finance," in *Chaos and Governance in the Modern World System*, eds. Giovanni Arrighi and Beverly J. Silver (Minneapolis: University of Minnesota Press, 1999), 64.

21 In 1823 US President James Munroe laid claim to regional leadership in Latin America and the Caribbean by asserting, in an address to the US Congress, that any attempt by the European powers to expand their influence in the Western Hemisphere would be considered a threat to American interests and to its peace and security. See George C. Herring, *From Colony to Superpower: U.S. Foreign Relations Since 1776* (Oxford: Oxford University Press, 2008): 153–155.

22 Peadar Kirby, *Introduction to Latin America: Twenty-First Century Challenges* (London: Sage Publications Ltd., 2003): 96–97.

23 Peter J. Hugill, "The American Challenge to British Hegemony," *Geographical Review* 99, no. 3 (July 2009): 408.

24 For Wilson's "Fourteen Points," see http://wwi.lib.byu.edu/index.php/President_Wilson's_Fourteen_Points.

25 Charles P. Kindleberger, *The World in Depression, 1929–1939*, revised edition (Berkeley and Los Angeles: University of California Press, 1986).

26 Andrew Gamble, "Hegemony and Decline: Britain and the United States," in *Two Hegemonies: Britain 1846–1914 and the United States 1941–2001*, eds. Patrick Karl O'Brien and Armand Clesse (Aldershot: Ashgate, 2002), 127–140.

27 Poland, which was not present at the founding, later signed the Charter to become one of the original 51 member states of this organization.

28 Armand Van Dormael, *Bretton Woods: Birth of a Monetary System* (London: Palgrave Macmillan, 1978).

29 G. John Ikenberry, "The Political Origins of Bretton Woods," in *A Retrospective on the Bretton Woods System*, eds. Michael D. Bordo and Barry Eichengreen (Chicago: University of Chicago Press), 179.

30 See M. J. Hogan, *The Marshall Plan: America, Britain and the Reconstruction of Western Europe, 1947–1952* (Cambridge: Cambridge University Press, 1987).

31 Chandra Muzaffer, "The Decline of US Helmed Global Hegemony: The Emergence of a More Equitable Pattern of International Relations," *World Public Forum* "Dialogue of Civilizations" (4 October 2012), http://wpfdc.org/politics/999-the-decline-of-us-helmed-global-hegemony-the-emergence-of-a-more-equitable-pattern-of-international-relations.

32 Van Ness, "Hegemony, Not Anarchy," 139–140.

33 See Paul Kennedy, *The Rise and Fall of the Great Powers* (New York: Random House, 1987).

34 See Muzaffer, "Decline of US Helmed Global Hegemony."

35 Fry, "The Decline of the American Superpower," 17.

36 *Financial Times*, "US to Lose Role as World's Top Manufacturer by 2020," 24 May 2007, http://www.ft.com/cms/s/0/25c8a88e-0958-11dc-a349-000b5df10621.html#axzz2JwGhjYkU.

37 Dominic Wilson and Roopa Purushothaman, "Dreaming with the BRICs: The Path to 2050," Global Economics Paper no. 99 (New York: Goldman Sachs, October 2003).

38 Clark, "China and the United States," 28.

39 Fry, "The Decline of the American Superpower," 1–22.

40 *Independent*, "The Perils of Pax Americana," 6 February 1991.

41 On this point, see Bruce Russett, "America's Continuing Strengths," *International Organization* 39, no. 2 (1985): 213–214.

42 Charles Krauthammer, "The Unipolar Moment," *Foreign Affairs* 70, no. 1 (1991): 23–33.

43 *The Times*, "America Cannot Police the World Forever," 12 March 1991.

44 *The Economist*, "The World Order Changeth," 22 June 1991.

45 Nye, *Soft Power*, x.

46 John Agnew, *Hegemony: The New Shape of Global Power* (Philadelphia, PA: Temple University Press, 2005), viii.

47 Paul MacDonald, "Rebalancing American Foreign Policy," *Daedalus* 138, no. 2 (2009): 124.

PART V
NON-STATE ACTORS IN GLOBAL GOVERNANCE

INTRODUCTION

The proliferation of actors and the scope of their activities have been central to the burgeoning field of global governance. This part of the book introduces readers to the most significant non-state actors that make the study of global governance more interesting and inevitably more unwieldy than focusing simply on IO.

The eight chapters contained in Part V of the book move well beyond state-centrism to address the major aspects of the pluralism that is a feature of the way that the world is currently governed. As with each of the parts in this book, the chapters are arranged to cover as much ground as possible while allowing classes to choose contributions that best suit their purposes. The chapters are arranged so that they flow from those that deal with formalized relations between non-state actors and intergovernmental organizations through to the darker and more subversive end of the global governance spectrum. Taking in the full run of chapters would give readers the best insights into this arena of global governance. That said, introductory courses may wish to emphasize Jan Aart Scholte's chapter on "Civil society and NGOs" (Chapter 23) and Michael Moran's on "Global philanthropy" (Chapter 27). Classes seeking to investigate civil society groups in more depth may then explore James G. McGann's chapter on "Think tanks and global policy networks" (Chapter 26). Relations between corporate actors—including multinational firms—and the United Nations are explored by Catia Gregoratti in her chapter on "UN–business partnerships" (Chapter 22). Non-state economic actors are also the core focus on Timothy J. Sinclair's chapter on "Credit rating agencies" (Chapter 25) and Nigel Haworth and Steve Hughes' on "Labor" (Chapter 24). The security aspects of non-state actors are explored in chapters by Peter J. Hoffman on "Private military and security companies" (Chapter 28) and Frank G. Madsen on "Transnational criminal networks" (Chapter 29). Together these chapters add further color to the emerging mosaic of contemporary global governance.

Non-state actors in global governance: chapter synopses

This part begins in Chapter 22 with "UN–business partnerships," Catia Gregoratti's synthesis of the for-profit part of the global governance puzzle and its formalized relations with the world organization. Gregoratti explains the impact on world politics of a number of phenomena, including transnational corporations, public–private partnerships, and corporate social responsibility. Crucial for this book is her discussion of the UN's Global Compact that has functioned since the 2000 Millennium Summit. She does not focus exclusively on formal intergovernmental organizations because "partnership" is not merely a buzzword but a reality of today's global governance. The United Nations simply had to stop being an intergovernmental club, set aside past prejudices against international civil society and business, and recognize the changing nature of world politics.

The expansive and oftentimes unmanageable topic of "Civil society and NGOs" is masterfully parsed by Jan Aart Scholte in Chapter 23. Scholte opens readers' eyes to the fact that a prominent explanation for the move from international organization to global governance is the growth in the numbers, scope, and impact of civil society and non-governmental organizations. He outlines many of the strengths of involving different voices and energies in global governance, but he also does not shy away from presenting their obvious shortcomings, including their questionable legitimacy.

In Chapter 24, Nigel Haworth and Steve Hughes explore the role of organized labor in global governance. They seek to highlight the ups and downs of labor's capacity to defend its interests and shape a measure of the way the world is organized. Integral to their analysis is a prominent international institution—both a physical structure and a web of conventions, practices, and guidelines—the International Labour Organization (ILO). Yet, the ILO's importance lies in more than just its record in keeping working conditions and worker rights in the global spotlight. It is an unusual—indeed, perhaps unique—institution that has from its very inception (in 1919) embodied a three-pronged partnership among labor, business, and government. For many this tripartite structure lends the ILO great strength, while for others it weakens labor's global capacity to defend itself. What is clear, however, is that this form of partnership was decades ahead of its time and has now found expression in institutions such as the UN Global Compact.

Timothy J. Sinclair's exposition of the role of "Credit rating agencies" in Chapter 25 gives a dramatic insight into the hidden power exercised by those financial bodies. Moody's Investors Service and Standard & Poor's Ratings Group render judgments that are authoritative enough to cause substantial global market responses. Hence, the role of these private agencies is essential in order to understand the nature of order, stability, and predictability in the world economy. Moreover, the spread globally of an essentially US practice has become the general one in all developed country markets and increasingly in emerging ones as well. Recurrent episodes of ratings failure and criticism of these agencies suggest the limits of non-state forms of global governance as well as the need for government regulation.

The adage that "knowledge is power" takes on a new flavor in Chapter 26—"Think tanks and global policy networks." James G. McGann paints a portrait of worldwide efforts to influence elite opinion and actions through research. In a complex, interdependent, and information-rich world, governments and a variety of policy- and decision-makers confront the common challenge of bringing expert knowledge to bear. He describes yet another manifestation of globalization, here the race to produce applicable knowledge. The growth of public policy research organizations, or "think tanks," over the last few decades has been nothing less than explosive—not only have their numbers increased, but the scope and impact of their work have also expanded dramatically at the national, regional, and global levels.

In Chapter 27, Michael Moran examines the importance of "Global philanthropy" in contemporary global governance. The weight and visibility of the Bill and Melinda Gates Foundation—unparalleled in modern private global governance—is the most recent installment of the use of private monies to finance public goods. Moran shows how private fortunes have been invested in projects ranging from the Green Revolution to IR scholarship and human rights. While criticisms abound—a reflection of its salience—global philanthropy should be placed in context. Comparatively marginal in relation to other non-state actors, nonetheless its unique attributes—an endowment and associated financial agency as well as a close association with actors from across sectors— at important junctures has helped develop the institutional architecture of global governance.

A growing part of the privatization puzzle consists of "Private military and security companies" (PMSCs), which became (in)famous especially with their expanded and visible presence in the twenty-first century's wars in Afghanistan and Iraq. In Chapter 28, Peter J. Hoffman investigates why governments as well as intergovernmental and nongovernmental organizations find paying contractors for protection to be not only a cost-effective but also a palatable approach to improving security. Hoffman points out the long history of mercenaries as a feature of world politics. However, what is relevant for both IO and global governance is that PMSCs confound conventional state-centric readings of world politics. They suggest not only that non-state actors are influential, but also that the high politics of security can be outsourced.

Chapter 29 explores another dark side of globalization, namely "Transnational criminal networks." In this chapter Frank G. Madsen evaluates the far-flung and intricate worldwide criminal networks that exist and benefit from modern technologies and pathologies. He also spells out those forms of intergovernmental cooperation, ranging from INTERPOL to financial tracking by banks, that endeavor to improve global criminal governance. In short, in many substantive areas of global problem solving, but especially in criminology, understanding global crime governance requires comprehending the operation of criminal networks and of the networks created by governments to neutralize them. Drawing on illustrations ranging from human trafficking to drugs, Madsen views criminal networks as consisting of several sub-networks, which makes the network concept even more concrete for viewing the range of actors and issues detailed elsewhere in this volume.

Where to from here?

This overview of non-state actors is essential not peripheral. All too often they are adjuncts in texts that are otherwise really just about international organization. What each of these chapters illustrates clearly is how these actors play a key role on the global governance stage. They are serious and substantial components of contemporary world order, not merely a little extra spice to mix into the usual IO casserole.

UN–Business Partnerships

Catia Gregoratti

For UN Secretary-General Ban Ki-moon, creating a secure, sustainable, and more equitable future is underpinned by two enablers: partnerships and a stronger United Nations.[1] This chapter delves more deeply into the former, particularly the collaborative relations that the UN continues to forge with the private sector, or what are commonly known as UN–business partnerships. The buzzword "partnership" has permeated the vocabulary of international organizations for over two decades, re-emerging, more forcefully than ever, in conjunction with Rio+20. *The Future We Want*—the outcome document of Rio+20—not only recognizes that the active participation of the private sector can contribute to sustainable development but also calls for continuing and strengthening existing partnerships and creating new ones. The dominant meaning of a partnership continues to signify a beneficial process, namely the formation of coalitions of public and private actors leading to the realization of universal goals. Yet, a partnership is not only a ubiquitous buzzword invoked by global leaders, it is also a concrete social practice through which development acquires particular meanings, and is realized, showcased, and resisted.

While the literature on partnerships is proliferating,[2] what is known about the way partnerships are changing the UN remains very limited.[3] This chapter starts by addressing the question as to why UN–business partnerships have emerged in global governance and takes stock of the reconfiguration of the institutional architecture in which private authorities[4] closely associated with the market, such as multinational corporations and corporate foundations, are assuming a key role. In the second section, the chapter briefly introduces the partnership universe and illustrates more concretely how the practice of partnering plays out across three UN entities at the forefront of poverty reduction efforts—the United Nations Children's Fund (UNICEF), UN Women, and

International Labour Organization (ILO). It draws attention to both the plurality of agents that constitute partnerships, and the ways they seek to lift out of poverty and protect the rights of children, women and workers in the developing world through philanthropic efforts, the mobilization of business competencies, and the uptake of voluntary principles of conduct. In the third section, the chapter moves beyond the pluralist and "win–win" rhetoric that support the practice of partnering. It does so by scrutinizing the power relations at work in the politics of partnering and their limits as development strategies. The conclusion summarizes the main arguments and explores some of the contemporary tensions in the politics of UN–business partnerships.

A changing United Nations: anchoring UN–business partnerships

Historical narratives on the rapprochement between market authorities and the United Nations share a common juncture, namely the late 1980s. As Craig Murphy notes, throughout much of its history the UN maintained an arm's-length relationship with the private sector.[5] Particularly within the United Nations Development Programme (UNDP) and the United Nations Environment Programme (UNEP), partnerships with the private sector and the promotion of private sector-led development began to be viewed as integral means to fulfill core development functions during this decade. Successive global summits such as the 1992 Rio Earth Summit, the 2001 Monterrey Conference on Financing for Development, and the 2002 Johannesburg World Summit on Sustainable Development, as well as the establishment of partnership initiatives such as the UN Global Compact and Type II partnerships under the auspices of the Commission for Sustainable Development, have been identified as key events that opened the doors to the private sector and facilitated the diffusion of the partnership agenda within the multilateral system. Partnerships now enjoy the endorsement and support of the majority of member states. The early skepticism of the Group of 77 (G77) and China towards a policy agenda that was conceived as friendly to the economic interests of the US, Japan, and Europe has been supplanted by a recognition that "effective partnerships between the UN and the private sector can make an important contribution to . . . achieving internationally agreed development goals including the Millennium Development Goals."[6]

Explanations as to why such a transformation has taken place are not immediately obvious. Some authors point to the wide structural changes set in motion by neoliberal globalization, which put a stress on states and interstate authorities to provide and regulate in a context of increased economic interdependence.[7] Dominant discourses, closely associated with the post-Washington Consensus, have professed public–private coalitions and networks as the solution to the "democratic deficits of global governance and the trans-boundary problems that intergovernmental agencies could no longer tackle alone."[8] For their part, multinational corporations have been quick to reap the opportunity to partner with a moral authority—particularly the UN—to regain legitimacy in the face of growing criticisms against corporate irresponsibility, and, in no small part, to weaken the case for corporate regulation.[9] Partnering, however, is not solely a defensive strategy; it is also a proactive display of corporate social responsibility (CSR). Leadership is also central to understanding why UN–business partnerships have become so popular. Like Kofi Annan, UN Secretary-General Ban Ki-moon has demonstrated an equally unwavering commitment to the partnership agenda. Other commentators have also pointed to the UN's deteriorating finances and declining levels of multilateral overseas development assistance, which coincided with the reactivation of philanthropic sentiments in the 1990s.[10] Indeed, as a financing strategy, partnerships have been considered "the most significant funding trend in the recent past."[11]

Independently of the explanation one privileges, UN–business partnerships have refashioned not only ideas of how development should be achieved and who should deliver it but also the institutional architecture of the UN itself. As Martens suggests, "virtually all UN specialized agencies and subsidiary bodies have significantly increased their engagement with multi-stakeholder partnerships, in particular the World Bank, FAO, UNESCO, WHO, UNIDO, UNDP, UNICEF, UNCTAD and UNEP."[12] Efforts to communicate what types of UN–business partnerships exist and what they achieve have been scaled up at multiple levels. Virtually all agencies, funds, and programs recount their engagements with the private sector through their respective websites and annual reports. In addition, since 2009, the UN portal business.un.org functions as a database for best practices in UN–business partnerships across the entire UN family. It also serves as a means for the UN to attract new private partners and funds, and showcases successes. The portal, and its transparency-enhancing qualities, received praise in the 2011 resolution *Towards Global Partnerships*. In conjunction with making the partnership universe visible, member states' calls for deepening and scaling up the impact, transparency, accountability, and sustainability resulted in the 2009 release of the revised *Guidelines on Cooperation between the United Nations and the Business Sector*.

Efforts have also been directed towards the coordination of partnerships. Platforms such as the Business Focal Point Newsletter and the Annual UN System Private Sector Focal Points Meeting have emerged, and new initiatives are planned for the immediate future. For example, of relevance here is Ban Ki-moon's pledge, upon member states' request, to create a new partnership facility "to harness the full power of transformative partnership across the range of UN activities," and to appoint a Senior Advisor to streamline system-wide partnership efforts.[13] At the Rio+20 Corporate Sustainability Forum, some of the key high-level objectives of the UN Partnerships Services (formerly UN Partnership Facility) were unveiled, which include: (1) creating shared value; (2) building partnering capacity; and (3) strengthening coherence and integrity.[14]

UN–business partnerships for children, women, and workers

The universe of UN–business partnerships is vast and expanding. Within it virtually every global development issue is seemingly addressed. In mid-2012, the business.un.org database counted over 1,500 partnerships and partnership opportunities, to which one could add the 349 partnerships listed by the UN Commission on Sustainable Development. It is populated by large and institutionalized multi-stakeholder partnerships such as the UN Global Compact, the Global Alliance for Vaccine and Immunization, and the Global Fund for AIDS, Malaria and Tuberculosis as well as temporary bound, goal-oriented partnerships, involving fewer actors. Often, partnerships are functionally classified. The UN's own classification includes advocacy, business opportunities in less developed countries, development of standards and principles of conduct, project funding, and the provision of services and goods. As heuristic tools, typologies offer some insights into the different goals a partnership sets to achieve. However, it is nearly impossible to position them neatly into functional categories or single-issue areas. Functions and development issues may overlap and even shift as a result of the flexibility of partnerships or the mobilizing strategies of those excluded or outright opposed to the self-defined purposes of a partnership.

Existing studies on UN–business partnerships have tended to privilege macro-level overviews, or focus on the largest and most institutionalized partnerships. This chapter takes a slightly different turn. In an attempt to identify emerging trends and tensions in the politics of partnering for development, it examines more closely the expanding partnership universe and looks at the UN–business partnerships brokered by UNICEF, UN Women, and the ILO (see Table 22.1). All the three entities are at the forefront of global development efforts. Furthermore, as their respective mandates focus on vulnerable human subjects—children, women and workers—they open up a field of inquiries centered on the relationships between those in a position of power within the global political economy and those who have not reaped the benefits of corporate globalization.

Table 22.1 presents an overview of the partnerships that seek to improve the livelihood of children, women, and workers in developing countries in order for the reader to acquire a degree of familiarity with initiatives that UN agencies, programs, and funds denote as UN–business partnerships. However, some small but important caveats need to be added. UNICEF's collaborations with the private sector have a much longer history and are much more institutionalized than those of the ILO or UN Women. By 2008, a survey counted 628 collaborations between UNICEF and its country offices and companies from across the globe.[15] As such, Table 22.1 includes only the partnerships that UNICEF itself presents as international and national best practices. The remainder of this chapter explores who takes part in UN–business partnerships for development, and the most recurrent ways in which public–private development interventions are performed.

Who is in the business of partnering?

The actors comprising UN–business partnerships for development, commonly known as stakeholders, are: UN bureaucrats, Northern and Southern corporations, corporate foundations not limited to just the "usual suspects" (e.g. the Bill and Melinda Gates or Clinton foundations), subsidiaries of Northern corporations, governmental donors, celebrities, consultants, nongovernmental organizations (NGOs), employer organizations, trade unions, and smaller enterprises (e.g. bottlers, textile and clothing suppliers), as well as children, women, and workers, who are predominantly, but not always, on the receiving end of partnerships' development efforts. This nebulous assemblage of stakeholders is often viewed as reflecting the increased pluralization, if not democratization, of global governance. The principle and practice of stakeholding are thought to have created more

Table 22.1 International and national UN–business partnerships within UNICEF, UN Women, and the ILO: 2000–present

UNICEF*	• Children Rights and Business Principles (2012) • Tefal funds nutrition program in Madagascar (2010) • Telenor Group partnership to improve services of health mediators in Serbia (2008) • Veolia Environmental foundation mobilizes in the event of humanitarian crisis (2008) • P&G Pampers funds UNICEF's Maternal and Neonatal Tetanus Elimination Program (2006) • FC Barcelona funds and promotes awareness around HIV/AIDS (2006) • Gucci funds projects for children affected by HIV/AIDS in sub-Saharan Africa (2005) • ING funds projects in support of education (2005) • Audi China funds project "Audi Driving Dreams" (2005) • Clairefontain funds "Back to School Programme" (2005) • Montblanc funds projects in support of children's education (2004) • The US Fund hosts the UNICEF "Snowflake Ball" (2004) • H&M funds projects on HIV/AIDS prevention, combating child labour, education and healthcare for children (2004) • Diners Club Greece raises funds for UNICEF through Diners Club–UNICEF card (2003) • Esselunga Italy funds UNICEF's health and education projects (2001) • IKEA Foundation funds projects focused on a child's right to a secure and healthy life (2000)
UN Women (formerly UNIFEM)	• The Coca-Cola Company partnership to accelerate women's economic empowerment (2011) • Kumtor partnership "Rural Development Project in Kyrgyzstan" (2010) • OMEGA and Nicole Kidman fundraise to rebuild Haiti (2010) • Avon and the Avon Foundation fund UN Trust Fund to End Violence Against Women (2008) • Tag Heur and Uma Thurman fund UN Trust Fund to End Violence Against Women (2007) • Johnson & Johnson funds UN Trust Fund to End Violence against Women (2005) • Macy's partnership "Rwanda Path to Peace" (2002) • Cisco Network Academy Programme (2001)
ILO	• MasterCard foundation funds "Work4Youth" (2011) • Chocolate and cocoa industry fund partnership to combat child labor in West Africa (2011) • ILO and BP partnership to promote employability in West Papua (2011) • Jacobs Foundation funds evaluation of the impact of youth employment initiatives (2010) • Better Work (2007) • Human resources, telecommunication, and financial industries' support for "Promoting Youth Employment in Latin America (PREJAL)" (2004) • Volkswagen Group partnership "Better Health and Safety for Suppliers" (2004)

Note: *The table draws on the business.un.org website, as well as the press releases and webpages of UNICEF, UN Women and the ILO.

opportunities for those affected by, causing, or having a stake in the issue at hand to have a voice in its resolution.[16]

Moving from the aggregate level to the particular cases, UN–business partnerships remain dominated by Northern corporations and corporate foundations, which have at their disposal larger corporate social responsibility arms and financial endowments. In particular, North American and European corporations and foundations in the financial, telecommunication, retail, and extractive industries figure centrally in the partnerships brokered by UNICEF, UN Women and the ILO (see Table 22.1). Fundraising partnerships, however, are gradually beginning to reflect a global geo-economic re-ordering by attracting donations from corporations and foundations headquartered—and including Northern subsidiaries located—in China, Brazil, South Africa, and India. Smaller donations of this kind do not often figure as partnership champions or best practices; they are recorded in the latest financial reports of UN Women and UNICEF but their specific purposes are left undefined.

Northern and Southern corporations as well as smaller enterprises are also called upon to enroll in partnerships that promote principles of conduct in support of children, women and workers' rights (see Table 22.2). At the time of writing, of the 456 signatories to the Women Empowerment Principles (WEP) only 30 percent are businesses domiciled in non-OECD countries. In an effort to globalize the Children Rights and Business Principles, UNICEF, the UN Global Compact, and Save the Children have organized launch events in the capital cities of Panama, India, Ghana, Colombia, Malaysia, and Kenya. Thus far, however, many of these events have been mainly dialogues among international bureaucrats, NGOs, experts, and Northern and Southern corporate social responsibility champions. At the other end of the spectrum, there are principles of conduct whose signatories are solely Western corporations. Within the ILO Better Work Programme, the signatories to the Buyer Principles are 25 of the most powerful European and American retailers and apparel brands. Together with Better Work country programs, corporate participants enlist Southern suppliers and workers in national labor law and core international labor standards training and compliance schemes in seven developing countries.

"Where are the 99 percent?" asked a reflexive UN partnership broker in an anonymous interview with the author. Indeed, such questions seem to have eluded the practice of partnering. The majority of partnerships for children, women and workers surveyed in Table 22.1 predominantly couch their self-defined beneficiaries as recipients of external interventions, and rarely as participants who can question policy designs, objectives, and outcomes. Such considerations have received relatively more prominence in partnerships setting principles of conduct, which are increasingly underpinned, albeit unevenly, by multi-stakeholder consultations, leadership groups, and, in some cases, monitoring. In the consultations leading up to the release of the Children Rights and Business Rights Principles, children themselves were asked for inputs; whereas in the WEP women's rights organizations—the South African initiative New Faces New Voices and the NGO Women's Environment and Development Organization—have been invited to take part in a Leadership Group heavily dominated by business representatives. A noteworthy case within the repertoire of partnerships is the ILO Better Work Programme. The ILO's unique tripartite structure—comprising governments, employer organizations, and worker representatives—has ensured the institutionalization of

Table 22.2 Principles of conduct

Children's Rights and Business Principles	Women Empowerment Principles	ILO Better Work Buyer Principles
• Principle 1: Meet their responsibility to respect children's rights and commit to supporting the human rights of children	• Principle 1: Establish high-level corporate leadership for gender equality	• Principle 1: Participate consistently in the Buyers' Forum
• Principle 2: Contribute to the elimination of child labor, including in all business activities and business relationships	• Principle 2: Treat all women and men fairly at work—respect and support human rights and non-discrimination	• Principle 2: Actively work toward strategic monitoring
• Principle 3: Provide decent work for young workers, parents, and caregivers	• Principle 3: Ensure the health, safety, and wellbeing of all women and men workers	• Principle 3: Actively encourage engagement by suppliers and agents (where applicable) in Better Work Programmes, including cost sharing for enterprise-level advisory services and training
• Principle 4: Ensure the protection and safety of children in all business activities and facilities	• Principle 4: Promote education, training, and professional development for women	• Principle 4: Focus on improvement processes
• Principle 5: Ensure that products and services are safe, and seek to support children's rights through them	• Principle 5: Implement enterprise development, supply chain, and marketing practices that empower women	**Core Labor Standards**
• Principle 6: Use marketing and advertising that respect and support children's rights	• Principle 6: Promote equality through community initiatives and advocacy	• Freedom of association and right to collective bargaining
• Principle 7: Respect and support children's rights in relation to the environment and to land acquisition and use	• Principle 7: Measure and publicly report on progress to achieve gender equality	• The elimination of all forms of forced or compulsory labor
• Principle 8: Respect and support children's rights in security arrangements		• The effective abolition of child labor
• Principle 9: Help protect children affected by emergencies		• The elimination of discrimination in respect of employment and occupation
• Principle 10: Reinforce community and government efforts to protect and fulfill children's rights		

Note: The table draws on the website of UNICEF CSR (http://www.unicef.org/csr/), the WEP (http://www.weprinciples.org/), and the ILO Better Work Programme (http://www.betterwork.org).

channels for workers' representations at factory level, and trade union representation within the ILO Better Work's Project Advisory Committees at country level as well as within the Global Advisory Committee.

Delivering development

How do partnerships enhance the livelihood of children, women and workers in developing countries? The widest number of partnerships—as opposed to the partnerships that attract most corporate participants—reported by the UNICEF, UN Women, and ILO falls within the category of corporate giving in support of development projects or UN Trust Funds (see Table 22.1). The magnitude of corporate giving varies from the US$200 million donated to UNICEF by the IKEA Foundation over the course of ten years, to one-off donations such as the US$50,000 contribution from the Swiss luxury watchmaker OMEGA in support of UN Women's livelihood and protection program in the aftermath of Haiti's earthquake. Financial contributions translate into diverse material gifts, such as shelters, schools, telephones, and vaccines; or immaterial gifts, such as the shaping of "to-be-developed" subjects through schooling, education, and training programs. For example, the IKEA Foundation and UNICEF partnership is an umbrella partnership that comprises in-kind donations (e.g. tables, bedding, covers, and duvets) in complex emergencies but also an extensive number of philanthropic and cause-related marketing commitments to promote children's protection, survival, and education. Likewise, in 2010, OMEGA's funding was employed to build shelters and to train local organizations involved in the delivery of outreach services to women and girls experiencing gender-based violence.

While the aforementioned partnerships provide specifically defined goods and services during complex emergencies or when developing countries are not able or willing to deliver, particularly among the partnerships for women and workers' rights, one also finds partnerships that seek to provide development not through charitable or emergency aid but through commercial means. These partnerships include both funding disbursed by businesses in support of market-based development programs and partnerships that seek to align core business competencies (e.g. sourcing, investment, sales) with development needs. In 2010, as part of its corporate social responsibility program, Kumtor Operating Company—a controversial gold mining company in Kyrgyzstan—provided funding for UN Women to disburse small grants for local projects aiming to enhance the economic opportunities and economic security of rural populations and vulnerable Kyrgyz women.

In market-development partnerships, as the Director of a UN Department stated in an interview with the author, "Partnerships are not just about donating money!" In recent years, corporations have begun to partner with UN agencies, programs and funds to engage in commercial activities or to mobilize particular market expertise. Within the "Rwanda Path to Peace" partnership with UN Women and Fair Winds Trading, the retailer Macy's sources and sells handcrafted baskets made by Rwandan weavers. In other cases, corporations act—to borrow an expression coined by Michael Lipsky— as street-level bureaucrats. Within such partnerships, corporate knowledge, personnel and expertise are employed on the ground to achieve the partnership's policy objectives. For example, as part of the ILO's publicly funded partnership "Promoting Youth

Employment in Latin America (PREJAL)," the human resources giant Adecco organized and imparted workshops in Argentina, Peru, and Colombia advising youth on interview techniques, CV preparation and job matching. These partnerships lend support to, and are often seen as an expression of, a "win–win" development discourse of business working for the poor.[17]

Unlike fundraising or market-based partnerships, partnerships that promote principles of conduct (see Table 22.2) seek to bring about policy changes in the everyday operations of a company. Signing up to principles of conduct does not, however, preclude engagement in other types of partnerships, which is, at times, explicitly encouraged. By committing to voluntary principles of conduct, a business signatory is normally expected to learn the norms through multi-stakeholder forums and webinars, take active steps to ensure that company policies are aligned with the principles, and report on progress. This is the basic self-regulatory route of the WEP, which was chiefly inspired by one of its progenitors—the UN Global Compact. The Children's Rights and Business Principles follow a similar model but, in line with UN Guiding Principles on Business and Human Rights, they also recommend that companies provide for remediation where children's rights have been adversely impacted. In contrast, with more robust tools and localized services to monitor, assess, and report on labor standards compliance in suppliers' factories, the ILO Better Work Programme and its Buyer Principles leave less room to the self-regulatory discretion of buyers and suppliers. Notwithstanding their procedural differences, what unites these types of partnerships is the functional framing of human rights as something for which there is a business case. Across all three partnerships, one finds abundant references to how "what is good for children is good for business," that "[gender] equality means business," or that compliance with labor standards in global supply chains is both an important part of a pro-poor development strategy and a source of competitive advantage.

The politics and political economy of UN–business partnerships

In this last section, the chapter problematizes the politics and political economy of partnerships, shedding light on the power relations at work in UN–business partnerships and their limits as equitable development strategies. Even if the practice of stakeholding is often hailed as normatively desirable, the emergent nebulous configuration of stakeholders who work towards the articulation of a kinder capitalism is not a flat and level playing field. It reflects North–South imbalances as well as asymmetrical relations of power among those who have a formal stake in defining what counts as a contribution to development and those who do not have a voice in the process, or are not recognized as stakeholders (e.g. home-based workers, non-unionized workers). Echoing the early warnings of the Alliance for a Corporate-Free UN, recent critiques on UN–business partnerships view them as an expression of the corporate takeover of the UN, which is increasingly shrinking the space for the voices of the people.[18] Earlier in the chapter, it was pointed out that some partnerships, particularly those concerned with setting standards of conduct, are becoming more inclusive, and globalized. Yet even in partnerships, such as the WEP or the ILO Better Work Programme, that strive to encompass larger numbers of stakeholders—often only loosely connected to the poor —relations of power, gender, race, and class continue to determine the meaning of development, the means to achieve it and the successes that are identified.

Are partnerships win–win solutions that work for businesses and the poor? Partnerships that mobilize funds or core business competencies might indeed provide some much-needed facilities and social services to some. However, they are often criticized for being temporary, selective, and for bypassing governments, thus standing in stark contrast to a long-term social rights agenda centered on social protection and the right to a voice.[19] Notwithstanding the lack of independent assessments, in some cases partnerships are not able to deliver their set objectives. For example, the evaluation of the ILO's Youth Employment Partnership in Latin America finds that "the project capacity to generate a real chance to find a decent and productive employment seems to be still weak for most young recipients."[20] But even when positive impacts are identified, they hinge on a contested line between the benefits that accrue to the corporation and the opportunities opened for some children, women and workers. In the case of Macy's, the corporate partner claims to perform a gendered and pro-poor development intervention by sourcing and selling Rwandan baskets; here a profitable market relation is also conceived as a development relation. Some recalcitrant NGOs claim that market-based partnerships of this kind serve narrow business interests without tackling the structural roots at the basis of multiple crises and inequalities.[21]

Do partnerships setting standards and principles of conduct fare better? Like more traditional philanthropic partnerships or the newer market-based partnerships the scorecard is rather mixed. On the one hand, principles of conduct have enabled companies to gain exposure and engage in learning and dialogue on human rights and development; on the other, the means through which such rights are realized are often found to be very weak, and at worst toothless. Critics point out that businesses interpret the principles quite loosely; they can pick and choose which principles they wish to apply, how, and what progress to report on. Furthermore, partnerships such as the WEP or the Children Rights and Business Principles do not stipulate provisions for the independent monitoring of corporate commitments, action, or lack thereof. More robust systems of labor compliance assessment, auditing, and computerized reporting are found in the ILO Better Work Programme, but even these systems of social auditing are no panacea. Ngai-Li Sum's study of Wal-Mart—an active participant in ILO Better Work and signatory of the Buyer Principles—finds "that more effort goes into preparing reports, auditing factories, obtaining certificates, ensuring orders and keeping jobs than actual advancement of labor rights protection."[22]

A final, but still pertinent, criticism relates not so much to the power relations within partnerships, their procedural limits and their impacts, but to what partnerships overshadow. Partnerships cloak how UN corporate partners undermine the promotion of equitable development by subverting regulations or lobbying for neoliberal policies. The decade-long partnership between the giant retailer IKEA and UNICEF India is a case in point, but by no means the only one. While the partnership promotional material turns our gaze to the children rescued in India, it tells us little about how IKEA's corporate structure enables the company to minimize taxation, or how the same company has successfully lobbied the Indian government for the relaxation of foreign direct investment in retail, with possibly devastating consequences for millions of small shop-owners and poorer consumers. To the extent that partnerships do not confront how the rights and power of corporations are implicated in reproducing inequalities and injustices and have kept the tensions between the commercial and the CSR logic "off limits,"[23] there are grounds to reflect on whether UN–business partnerships might be considered little more than a sideshow[24] within the contemporary global political economy.

Conclusion

This chapter sheds light on how UN–business partnerships are becoming increasingly embedded in the multilateral system. Far from being an exceptional practice, partnerships are unanimously endorsed by states and supported at the highest levels of leadership, their successes and development aspirations are made increasingly visible, and they are slowly moving towards higher levels of coordination. The chapter has looked more closely at the partnerships brokered by three UN entities at the forefront of poverty reduction efforts—UNICEF, UN Women, and the ILO. It illustrates how dominant players in partnerships are powerful Western multinational corporations and foundations who, in conjunction with other stakeholders, deliver development by mobilizing resources, deploying core business competencies, or through voluntary principles of conduct. Yet, it suggests that there are reasons to be cautious about the rhetoric and promises of partnerships, as they fail to effectively democratize global governance or act as the silver bullet for the everyday plights of exploited children, women, and workers.

What's next for UN–business partnerships? On the one hand they can be better managed, as the proposed UN Partnership Services suggest, but such a proposal has not placated the demands of those who seek stronger instruments for corporate regulation. A rejuvenated coalition of Northern and Southern NGOs and grassroots organizations has requested the UN not to engage in any further partnerships, review the existing ones, and establish a legally binding framework that can hold corporations accountable.[25] As the UN has also become an interlocutor for social forces linked to struggles for social justice, UN–business partnerships are likely to remain at the centre of an agonistic politics in search of development interventions and forms of regulation that benefit and empower "we the people."

Additional reading

1. Benedicte Bull and Desmond McNeill, *Development Issues in Global Governance: Public–Private Partnerships and Market Multilateralism* (Abingdon: Routledge, 2007).
2. Magdalena Bexell and Ulrika Mörth, eds., *Democracy and Public Private Partnerships in Global Governance* (London: Palgrave Macmillan, 2010).
3. Marco Schäferhoff, Sabine Campe, and Christopher Kaan, "Transnational Public–Private Partnerships in International Relations: Making Sense of Concepts, Research Frameworks, and Results," *International Studies Review* 11, no. 3 (2009): 451–474.
4. Peter Utting and Ann Zammit, "United Nations–Business Partnerships: Good Intentions, Contradictory Agendas," *Journal of Business Ethics* 90, Supplement 1 (2009): 39–56.
5. Christer Jönsson, "The John Holmes Memorial Lecture: International Organizations at the Moving Public–Private Borderline," *Global Governance* 19, no. 1 (2013): 1–18.

Notes

1 Ki-moon Ban, *Remarks to the General Assembly on his Five-Year Action Agenda: "The Future We Want,"* speech delivered at the UN General Assembly, 25 January 2012, http://www.un.org/apps/news/infocus/sgspeeches/search_full.asp?statID=1437.

2 Tanja A. Börzel and Thomas Risse, "Effective and Legitimate Tools of Transnational Governance?," *Complex Sovereignty: On the Reconstitution of Political Authority in the 21st Century*, eds. Edgar Grande and Louis W. Pauly (Toronto: University of Toronto Press, 2005), 195–216; Benedicte Bull and Desmond McNeill, *Development Issues in Global Governance: Public–Private Partnerships and Market Multilateralism* (Abingdon: Routledge, 2007); Marco Schäferhoff, Sabine Campe, and Christopher Kaan, "Transnational Public–Private Partnerships in International Relations: Making Sense of Concepts, Research Frameworks, and Results," *International Studies Review* 11, no. 3 (2009): 451–474; and Bexell Magdalena and Ulrika Mörth, eds., *Democracy and Public Private Partnerships in Global Governance* (London: Palgrave Macmillan, 2010).

3 Morten Bøås and Desmond McNeill, *Multilateral Institutions: A Critical Introduction* (London: Pluto Press, 2003), 146–148.

4 Claire Cutler, Virginia Haufler, and Tony Porter, eds., *Private Authority and International Affairs* (New York: Suny Press, 1999); Bruce Hall and Thomas J. Biersteker, eds., *The Emergence of Private Authority in Global Governance* (Cambridge: Cambridge University Press, 2002); Tony Porter and Karsten Ronit, eds., *The Challenges of Global Business Authority – Democratic Renewal, Stalement or Decay?* (New York: SUNY Press, 2010).

5 Craig Murphy, "Private Sector," in *The Oxford Handbook of the United Nations*, eds. Thomas Weiss and Daws Sam (Oxford: Oxford University Press, 2008), 264.

6 G77 and China, *Statement on Behalf of the Group of 77 and China on Agenda Item 61 "Towards Global Partnerships,"* New York, 8 November 2007, http://www.g77.org/statement/getstatement.php?id=071108.

7 Peter Utting and Ann Zammit, "United Nations–Business Partnerships: Good Intentions, Contradictory Agendas," *Journal of Business Ethics* 90, Supplement 1 (2009): 39–56.

8 Wolfgang Reinicke and Francis Deng, *Critical Choices: The United Nations, Networks and the Future of Global Governance* (Ottawa: International Development Research Centre, 2000).

9 Newell Peter, "CSR and the Limit of Capital," *Development and Change* 39, no. 6 (2008): 1063–1078.

10 Bull and McNeill, *Development Issues in Global Governance*.

11 UN General Assembly, "Analysis of the Funding of Operational Activities for Development of the United Nations System for 2009 – Report of the Secretary-General," 66th Session, Item 25 (a), 6 May 2011, paragraphs 21 and 26.

12 Jens Martens, "Multistakeholder Partnerships – Future Models of Multilateralism?," *Dialogue on Globalization*, Occasional Paper no. 29 (2007): 20.

13 Ki-moon Ban, Remarks to the General Assembly on his Five-Year Action Agenda: "The Future We Want."

14 UN Global Compact Lead, *UN Business Partnership Services: Accelerating and Scaling Transformational Impact*, http://www.unglobalcompact.org/issues/Business_Partnerships/tools_publications.html.

15 UN ECOSOC, "Mapping UNICEF partnerships and collaborative relations," UNICEF Executive Board Annual Session, 8–10 June 2009, http://www.unicef.org/about/execboard/files/09-11-mapping-ODS-English.pdf.

16 Karin Bäckstrand, "Democratizing Global Environmental Governance? Stakeholder Democracy after the World Summit on Sustainable Development," *European Journal of International Relations* 12, no. 4 (2006): 467–498.

17 Commission on the Private Sector and Development, *Unleashing Entrepreneurship – Making Business Work for the Poor* (New York: UNDP, 2004).

18 Friends of the Earth, *Reclaim the UN from Corporate Capture*, http://www.foei.org/en/resources/publications/pdfs/2012/reclaim-the-un-from-corporate-capture.

19 Utting and Zammit, "United Nations–Business Partnerships," 51.

20 Youth Employment Inventory, *Promoting Young Employment in Latin America (PREJAL)*, http://www.youth-employment-inventory.org/inventory/view/448/.

21 Friends of the Earth, *Reclaim the UN from Corporate Capture*.

22 Ngai-Ling Sum, "Walt-Martization and CSRization in Developing Countries," in *Corporate Social Responsibility and Regulatory Governance: Towards Inclusive Development?*, eds. Peter Utting and José Carlos Marquez (Basingstoke: Palgrave, 2010), 64.

23 Peter Utting, "The Struggle for Corporate Accountability," *Development and Change* 39, no. 6 (2008): 959–975.

24 Jem Bendell, "Turning Point. What If We Are Failing? Towards a Post-Crisis Compact for Systemic Change," *Journal of Corporate Citizenship* 38 (2010): 26–31.

25 Friends of the Earth, Corporate Europe Observatory, La Via Campesina, Jubilee South America, Peace and Justice in Latin America, SERPAJ-AL, Polaris Institute, the Council of Canadians, the Transnational Institute, Third World Network, World March of Women, *Ending Corporate Capture of the United Nations*, Joint Civil Society Statement, http://www.foei.org/en/get-involved/take-action/pdfs/statement-un-corpcap-en/view.

Civil Society and NGOs

Jan Aart Scholte

A prominent development in the move over recent decades from "international organization" to "global governance" has been the growing involvement of nongovernmental organizations (NGOs) and civil society actors more generally. Civil society participation goes back to the earliest days of global regulation; however, the scale and intensity of contemporary interactions are in a different league. As of 2011 some 3,500 NGOs have consultative status with the United Nations Economic and Social Council (UN-ECOSOC).[1] Since the 1990s hundreds of civil society associations attend the Annual Meetings of the International Monetary Fund (IMF) and the World Bank, as well as Ministerial Conferences of the World Trade Organization (WTO). Summits of the Group of 8 (G8) and the Group of 20 (G20) can attract thousands of street protesters. Questions of global governance have also figured prominently in the World Social Forum movement since 2001. In some cases, such as the Forestry Stewardship Council (FSC) and the World Fair Trade Organization (WFTO), NGOs themselves are making and implementing the rules of global governance.

As global institutions have gained more importance in regulating contemporary society, civil society associations have, not surprisingly, turned more attention to these regimes. Modern political theory has generally conceived of civil society as a counterpart of the state.[2] However, these state-centric conceptions must now be adjusted to reflect altered circumstances where civil society actors also substantially engage with global regulatory processes, sometimes bypassing national governments altogether.

This chapter examines forms, consequences, and challenges of civil society involvement in contemporary global governance. The first section considers definitions of civil society. The second maps the various involvements of civil society actors in global regulatory processes. The third section assesses the substantive impacts of civil society interventions in global governance—that is, how NGOs and other civil society groups affect institutional developments, agendas, decisions, discourses, and deeper structures of global governance. The fourth section considers the relationship between civil society and legitimacy in global governance. The conclusion includes several suggestions for future enhancement of civil society engagement of global-scale regulation.

Space constraints prevent an elaboration about how the various explanatory theories of world politics depict the role of civil society in global governance. Suffice to note that realist, liberal, constructivist, Marxist, poststructuralist, postcolonialist, feminist, and other theories interpret the relationship of civil society to global governance in highly divergent ways. Moreover, a study of civil society and global governance could combine inspirations from several theories to form its own synthesis. The selection of a theoretical framework is a matter for each researcher and tends to involve political as much as intellectual choices.

What is civil society?

Like any key analytical concept, "civil society" is open to multiple and often conflicting interpretations. These debates begin with the very definition of the term. What sorts of activities and circumstances does "civil society" cover?

Many researchers as well as practitioners of global governance treat civil society as synonymous with NGOs. From this perspective civil society is a collection of formally structured, legally registered, and professionally staffed organizations outside official and commercial sectors that undertake a variety of advocacy and service delivery operations. This is the civil society of Amnesty International, Friends of the Earth, Global Policy Forum, International Rescue Committee, Oxfam, Tax Justice Network, Women's Environment and Development Organization, and so on.

Yet the equation of civil society with NGOs can be overly narrow. Such a conception tends to ignore many informal and grassroots engagements of global governance.[3] These might occur, for example, through Facebook groups, paramilitary cells, and spontaneous street demonstrations. In addition, conceptions of NGOs often overlook the activities of social movements such as faith groups, labor unions, nationalist fronts, and peasant mobilizations. Discussions of NGOs also generally neglect the important role in contemporary global governance of business lobbies such as chambers of commerce, employer federations, and industry associations. Foundations and research institutes arguably occupy the civil society field as well. Thus, while NGOs are certainly part of civil society, the net can be cast more widely in order to encompass a fuller scope of nonofficial voices and influences in global regulatory processes.

That said, in another sense the equation of civil society with NGOs can be overly broad, particularly when the range of activities in question is extended to include service delivery. Many NGOs are today involved in global governance as implementers of projects under contract with bodies such as multilateral development banks and the UN Refugee Agency. Yet "civil society" has traditionally been about overtly political concerns, such as relations between authorities and subjects, the dynamics of obtaining and exercising social power, and processes of constructing and embedding norms and rules. Of course, the provision of services such as humanitarian relief, health care, schooling, and policing has political dimensions. However, service delivery by NGOs is often mainly assessed for its efficiency and effectiveness as outsourced policy execution, without explicit attention to the politics of these activities. In such cases treating civil society as synonymous with NGOs can have a depoliticizing effect that underplays the workings of power in global governance.[4]

In order both to widen and to narrow the field relative to NGOs, civil society might be conceptualized as "a political space where associations of citizens seek, from outside political parties, to shape societal rules." Such a definition restores the centrality of politics to civil society. Moreover, reference to a "space" treats civil society less as an organization and more as an arena where people congregate to deliberate, strategize, and mobilize. Reference to "associations" indicates that civil society involves group activities, whether through formal bodies or informal networks. Reference to "citizens" signifies that people enter civil society to exercise their rights and fulfill their obligations as members of a political community. The exclusion of political parties is specified in order to underline that civil society operations do not normally aspire to occupy positions of official authority. However, civil society activities do aim "to shape societal rules": that is, to influence the principles, norms, laws, and standards that govern the collective life of human beings.

Note also what this conception of civil society does not imply. It does not say that civil society is always wholly and neatly distinguishable from commercial, official, and political party activities: in practice these sectors can partly overlap. In addition, this conception does not restrict civil society to a Western-liberal-modern cultural frame: one can also find civil society among clans, religious revivalists, and movements of indigenous peoples.[5] Nor does the phrase "civil society" imply anything about ideological outlook: these groups can pursue mainstream, reactionary, reformist, or transformational visions. Civil society is not necessarily "civil" either: this space can be as crowded with arrogance, fraud, greed, and violence as any other realm of society.[6] The mafia and the Ku Klux Klan also inhabit civil society. Nor is civil society necessarily a level playing field: both the overall arena and many individual associations are marked by hierarchies of age, class, gender, geography, race, sexual orientation, and other inequalities.[7]

Civil society—with its various promises as well as perils—has become increasingly relevant to global governance as more and more societal rules in contemporary history emanate from institutions and processes of worldwide, trans-planetary proportions. For several hundred years prior to the middle of the twentieth century, societal regulation was achieved almost exclusively through states. Hence at this earlier time civil society engaged almost exclusively with individual national-territorial governments, and political theorists related civil society wholly and solely to the state. Yet today, when much governance comes from global quarters, considerable civil society activities are now understandably directed at sites such as the UN system, the G8/20, the Asia–Europe Meeting (ASEM), institutions of private global governance like the Internet Corporation for Assigned Names and Numbers (ICANN), and multi-stakeholder forums like the Global Fund to Fight AIDS, Tuberculosis and Malaria (GFATM). So a twenty-first century textbook on global governance definitely wants a chapter on civil society.

Civil society involvements in global governance

NGOs, social movements, business forums, research institutes, and other civil society associations engage with global governance in many ways, both direct and indirect. Modes of direct participation include accreditation, membership of government delegations, policy consultations, seats on official committees and boards, evaluation exercises, and actual global regulation itself. With indirect engagement civil society groups seek to shape global governance institutions via other sites such as governments, political parties, and the mass media. In other cases civil society associations involve themselves in global governance by openly resisting it through street demonstrations and other defiance.

Direct participation

Direct participation by civil society actors in global governance processes dates back to the early "international organizations."[8] For example, employer federations and trade unions have worked alongside governments in the International Labour Organization (ILO) since its beginnings in 1920. The Conference of Non-Governmental Organizations in Consultative Relationship with the United Nations (CONGO) was set up in 1948. Some 250 NGOs assembled around the Stockholm Conference on the Human Environment in 1972.[9]

However, the main growth of civil society participation in global governance has occurred since 1990. This period has seen most major public global regulatory bodies establish offices for liaison with civil society groups. The World Bank has the largest such provision, with some 120 civil society specialists.[10] Several private global governance bodies such as ICANN have also created civil society liaison bureaus within their organization. In addition, most multilateral development banks and various UN agencies have in the past two decades articulated official guidelines for their staff's relations with civil society organizations.

One formalized way that civil society associations can be involved in global governance is through accreditation. In this case a global regulatory institution accords approved citizen groups official recognition and related possibilities to observe and intervene in policy processes. The most elaborate civil society accreditation scheme exists in respect of the United Nations. NGOs apply and if accepted obtain different degrees of access to UN buildings and deliberations, depending on whether they hold "general consultative status," "special consultative status," or "roster status".[11]

In other cases civil society associations can apply for short-term accreditation with a global governance body in order to attend a particular meeting. An accreditation badge gives approved civil society actors entry into official meeting areas and in some instances also a right to speak in the proceedings. The UN operates such arrangements in respect of global gatherings such as the annual Conference of the Parties (CoP) on climate change and other summits on food, health, population, social development, and further issues. Likewise the IMF and the World Bank have civil society accreditation schemes for their Annual and Spring Meetings, while the WTO permits vetted civil society groups entry to its Ministerial Conferences. Hundreds of civil society associations typically obtain accreditation for such global governance events.

Sometimes certain civil society actors are invited to be members of government delegations to global governance meetings. In these situations civil society activists have a formally equivalent status with government officials. For example, a number of small island states have invited NGO advisers onto their official teams in global conferences on ecological matters. Officers from business associations and development NGOs have regularly joined the delegations of some governments to WTO meetings.

Much additional civil society participation in global governance occurs through ongoing policy consultations in between the big conferences. For this purpose the UN maintains a Department of Public Information (DPI) and a Non-Governmental Liaison Service (NGLS). Since the 1990s the so-called Arria Formula has opened space for civil society associations to brief members of the UN Security Council, particularly on issues of human rights and humanitarian intervention.[12] Among specialized agencies the UN Environment Programme (UNEP) has convened a Global Civil Society Forum, and the UN Development Programme (UNDP) has had a Civil Society Advisory Committee since 2000. The World Bank consults civil society groups on the design and implementation of most of its projects and programs. IMF teams normally meet with some local civil society groups during their country visits to advise governments on macro-economic policy. Since 1998 the WTO has accepted some submissions from civil society groups in its dispute settlement process. The Organisation for Economic Co-operation and Development (OECD) maintains regular consultations, *inter alia*, through its Business and Industry Advisory Committee (BIAC) and Trade Union Advisory Committee (TUAC). ICANN does the same through its At-Large Advisory Committee (ALAC) and Noncommercial Users Constituency (NCUC). Since 1965 the Commonwealth Foundation has assembled civil society groups, while the Commonwealth Secretariat next door has focused on the member governments. The GFATM engages local civil society for its country activities and also holds a biennial Partnership Forum with civil society actors from around the world. The Organization of the Islamic Conference (OIC) has also recently begun informal interactions with NGOs. Through these numerous formalized and ad hoc practices consultation with civil society has become a norm of contemporary global governance.[13]

To be sure, global governance consultations of civil society have not always reached desired levels of quality. Indeed, the preparation, execution, and follow-up of these dialogues have often been wanting. For example, "consultation" of civil society frequently occurs late in the policy-making process, after important decisions have already been taken. In addition, global governance officials can undermine consultations with negative attitudes of arrogance, inflexibility, reluctance, and secrecy. For their part, civil society associations can neglect opportunities to engage global governance and/or can bring to the table inaccurate information and underdeveloped analysis. The quality of global governance engagement of civil society has also suffered, both democratically and practically, when the consultations disproportionately involve associations from elite quarters, marginalizing disadvantaged geographical and social circles.

Beyond consultation, in certain cases civil society associations have obtained formal representation at the decision table in global governance. In addition to the already mentioned ILO tripartism, the International Organization for Standardization (ISO) involves trade associations, professional societies, and universities in its technical committees. Civil society actors have also held several seats on the board and committees of

ICANN and on the global board and the country coordinating mechanisms of the GFATM.[14] The bureau of the International Assessment of Agricultural Knowledge, Science and Technology for Development (IAASTD), started in 2002, has involved 22 civil society representatives along with 30 governments.[15] The Global Reporting Initiative (GRI) is one of several schemes for corporate social responsibility (CSR) that involve business, labor, and NGOs along with government. To be sure, civil society membership of official boards and committees remains far from the norm in contemporary global governance; nevertheless, the spread since the late 1990s of so-called "multi-stakeholder" arrangements is striking.

Civil society associations also participate in global governance through performance evaluations. For example, think tanks have conducted commissioned official policy reviews for ICANN, and NGOs have contributed to investigations by the IMF's Independent Evaluation Office. Civil society groups have also brought various cases to the World Bank's Inspection Panel since its creation in 1994. In addition, civil society organizations are continually publishing their own (often critical) assessments of global governance institutions and policies, thereby serving an important external monitoring function and contributing to public awareness and debate.

Finally, among modes of direct participation in global governance, certain civil society bodies act as regulatory bodies. In these cases it is the civil society associations themselves who do the formulation and administration of global rules, without direct involvement by official actors. For example, the FSC regime for sustainable forestry involves collaboration between business, environmental, indigenous, and labor groups. The WFTO framework of fair trade standards assembles consumer and producer associations. Other examples of global governance by civil society organizations include the Marine Stewardship Council (providing sustainability standards in fisheries) and the Workers Rights Consortium (suggesting labor codes in the sourcing of university and college apparel).

Indirect involvements

In countless other instances civil society associations pursue involvement in global governance indirectly, through third parties. For example, business forums, trade unions, and NGOs commonly bring their concerns about global governance to member states, in hopes of influencing the positions that governments take in global institutions. In this vein civil society groups have engaged foreign ministries regarding the UN, finance ministries regarding the IMF, trade ministries regarding the WTO, and so on. Indeed, some governments actively solicit civil society inputs before attending major global conferences. Sometimes states (especially the major states) are targeted on global governance matters not only by civil society associations from their own country, but also by transnational organizations. Thus, for instance, Global Unions and Oxfam International maintain offices in Washington, DC, in order to engage US government departments as well as the Bretton Woods institutions.

In other cases civil society groups take questions of global governance to the legislative branch of government, e.g. the French National Assembly, Japanese Diet, and US Congress. Civil society groups in these situations seek to shape parliamentary debates on global governance and/or to engage parliamentary committees that scrutinize government policy on global governance. Occasionally, as in Malawi, civil society associations have sponsored workshops and other activities to raise the capacities of national parliamentarians to address issues of global regulation. In respect of the European Union (EU), civil society associations have also gone to a regional parliament on global governance matters, particularly in the area of trade, where the EU is a member of the WTO in its own right.

More generally, too, regional institutions can be indirect channels to global governance for civil society. The European Commission continually addresses global issues, and civil society groups have engaged with, for example, its Sub-Committee on IMF Matters (SCIMF). In Latin America Mercosur (Common Market of the South) has an Economic and Social Consultation Forum where civil society representatives *inter alia* discuss global issues. Similarly, civil society has been involved with the Southern African Development Community (SADC) on global governance questions such as debt, HIV/AIDS, and trade.

Engagement with substate authorities, as well, can be a mode of indirect civil society involvement in global governance. For example, ecology campaigners urged hundreds of "greening cities" in the US to back the Kyoto Protocol on climate change when the Bush Administration refused to ratify this global instrument. Other civil society groups have engaged global organizations of cities, including United Cities and Local Governments (UCLG) and Metropolis, which in turn relate to intergovernmental institutions through agencies like the Commonwealth Local Government Forum and the UN Global Cities Compact.

Multiple nonofficial channels for indirect civil society engagement of global governance are also available. Outside government, citizen associations can take concerns about global institutions to political parties, the mass media, companies, online social networks, and other deliberative spaces such as the World Economic Forum and the World Social Forum. NGOs have sometimes also called on celebrities to publicize global issues, as when Bob Geldof and Bono amplified civil society demands for debt relief vis-à-vis global financial institutions.

Resistance

In addition to the direct participation and indirect pressures reviewed above, civil society actors have also related to global governance by refusing it. Rejectionist groups decline overtures to interact with global institutions. Alternatively these challengers so disrupt the exchanges that officials do not invite them again.

Resistance movements have on various occasions taken to the streets to protest against what they regard as harmful, undemocratic, and unjust global governance arrangements. In the so-called "Battle of Seattle" in 1999, street demonstrations severely disrupted a Ministerial Conference of the WTO. G8/G20 summits and IMF/World Bank meetings have also regularly drawn mass protests.

In another resistance tactic, NGO-inspired boycotts of several major multinational companies have promoted the growth of CSR as an informal global governance of production and investment. Street theatre, videos, and monuments are other mediums through which civil society groups have expressed renunciation of some or all global governance.

In multiple ways, then, civil society engagement of global governance has become widespread since the 1990s. This is not to suggest that business forums, NGOs, and social movements are displacing states in global governance. However, understandings of contemporary politics which restrict civil society to the domestic sphere are clearly obsolete.

Civil society impacts on global governance

Yet does all the civil society activity just surveyed in respect of global governance actually matter? This section explores various possible effects of citizen activism on concrete situations of global regulation. The record shows many correlations between circumstances in civil society on the one hand and developments in global governance on the other. The following paragraphs identify five general dimensions of possible civil society impact on global governance, namely, in relation to institutions, agendas, decisions, discourses, and deeper structures.

Of course it is one thing to observe a concurrence of phenomena and quite another to establish a causal connection between them. How can one demonstrate that civil society specifically affected a given situation of global governance? Different theories and methodologies yield different interpretations of whether, in what ways, and how far civil society has influenced a particular scenario of global regulation. Moreover, it is generally difficult to disentangle the influence of civil society from other forces (states, capitalism, etc.) that might shape the course of global governance. Greater exploration of these theoretical and methodological issues lies beyond the scope of the present chapter, but it is important to underline here that "proving" civil society impacts on global governance is anything but straightforward.

Regarding the first of the five dimensions of impact named above, civil society can shape the institutional evolution of global regulation. Citizen associations have often advocated for the establishment, reform, and/or dissolution of one or the other global governance agency. For example, numerous internationalist groups urged the creation of first the League of Nations and later the United Nations. Some 200 NGOs were present at the San Francisco Conference that founded the UN in 1945, 42 of them as consultants to the US government delegation.[16] Proposals to launch the Uruguay Round negotiations that spawned the WTO emanated initially from the World Economic Forum, a high-profile business association. A major civil society campaign in the 1990s propelled the establishment of the International Criminal Court (ICC). Civil society groups have also figured prominently in drives for various institutional reforms of global governance, such as the establishment of a Human Rights Council in the UN, reallocations of quotas at the IMF, and the inclusion of a vote for Affected Communities on the board of the GFATM. True, rejectionist voices in civil society have not succeeded · in their aims to close certain or all global governance agencies. However, these movements have severely disrupted some official proceedings, such as the WTO Ministerial in Seattle. Moreover, the challenge of strong radical opposition has perhaps made global governance bodies more amenable to institutional reform.

A second general area where civil society can impact on global governance is the agenda. In other words, citizen activism can influence what issues are considered in global regulatory processes and with what relative priorities. Indeed, civil society associations have highlighted a number of global problems that might otherwise have received (considerably) less attention. The many examples include AIDS, arms control, corruption, debt, democracy, disability, ecological degradation, gender, human rights, humanitarian intervention, indigenous peoples, labor standards, land grabs, poverty, and the use of non-Western scripts on the Internet. It seems unlikely that—without civil society pressure—global governance would have addressed such questions, or at any rate given them as much prominence.

In addition to institutional evolution and agenda formation, civil society pressure can be linked to a host of policy decisions taken in global governance. For instance, the WTO move in 2003 to relax intellectual property provisions on essential medicines followed a concerted NGO campaign. Persistent civil society mobilization likewise fed into the reduction and cancellation of many debts of low-income countries in the 1990s and 2000s, as well as the adoption by various European governments of a financial transactions tax in 2012. Civil society associations have arguably also contributed to ratifications of global human rights instruments, initiatives to undertake humanitarian intervention, adjustments to many World Bank projects, and countless other policy decisions in global governance.

In a fourth dimension of impact, civil society involvement can go beyond individual decisions to shape the discourses of global governance. By "discourse" is meant here the overarching concepts, language, and analytical framings that are employed in policy discussions. Civil society associations have arguably furthered innovations in the core vocabulary of global governance by promoting notions such as "fair trade," "human security," "sustainable development," and "global public goods." More generally, civil society critiques have encouraged a shift in discourses of global economic governance from a *laissez faire* neoliberalism that prevailed in the late twentieth century to greater rhetoric of socially and environmentally oriented markets in the early twenty-first century.

Fifth and finally, civil society impacts can reach still deeper to influence the underlying social structures—the primary patterns—of global governance. To give one example, by circumventing states to engage directly with global regulatory institutions civil society associations have promoted a shift in the overall mode of governance from statism (where societal rules emanate more or less entirely from the state) to polycentrism (where governance transpires through multi-actor networks). In addition, civil society involvement in global governance has, by mobilizing multiple types of political community besides nations (e.g. solidarity on lines of caste, class, faith, gender, race, sexual orientation, etc.), encouraged a shift in the primary structure of identity in world politics from nation-centrism to greater pluralism. Also, inasmuch as citizen activism on global governance has enlarged political space for indigenous peoples and religious revivalists, civil society has facilitated challenges to the predominant modern-rationalist knowledge structure in today's world.

Considering in sum these five types of impact—on institutional evolution, agenda formation, policy decision, discourse construction, and deeper structure—is civil society a force of continuity or change in global governance? Moreover, to the extent that civil society brings changes to global governance, do these alterations have more of an incremental reformist character or more of a systemic revolutionary quality? In Gramscian terms, is civil society on the whole a hegemonic force that reinforces and legitimates established interests in global governance; or does civil society play a counter-hegemonic role of subversion and transformation?

Clear and definitive answers to these questions are not available. The picture is messy partly because evidence from civil society involvement in global governance often points in several directions. In addition, different theories emphasize different kinds of evidence and/or interpret the same data in highly different ways. Cumulative experience certainly suggests that civil society has an impact in contemporary global governance, but the precise significance is and will remain debated.

Civil society and legitimacy in global governance

In addition to the substantive impacts considered above, it is important also to assess the normative consequences that civil society might have in terms of the legitimacy of global regulation. Legitimacy refers to a condition where people consent to being governed by one or the other authority. With legitimacy political subjects accord a given regime the right to rule. Without legitimacy a governance apparatus collapses—or survives only through trickery, coercion, and/or violence towards its subjects.

Shortfalls in legitimacy are a major problem for contemporary global governance. Challenges such as climate change, financial instability, and humanitarian crises demand enlarged and strengthened global regulation. However, on the whole citizens have not ascribed legitimacy to global governance in the way that people have generally accepted the authority of (most) national and local governments. As a result, global institutions have struggled to acquire the necessary mandates and resources to deliver effective global public policy.

Many commentators hope that civil society might help to fill this legitimacy gap and thereby promote more effective responses to urgent global problems.[17] As an arena of public deliberation and mobilization, civil society offers major possibilities to link citizens with global issues, global organizations, and global rules. Indeed, at a time when global political parties, global parliaments, and global plebiscites seem remote prospects, civil society arguably provides some of the greatest available potential for a democratization of global governance.[18]

Certainly many civil society associations have highlighted democratic frailties that afflict most existing global governance, and have urged corrective action. NGOs and social movements have also furthered democratic global governance when they provide channels of voice and influence for affected people, including in particular constituencies (for example, indigenous peoples and sexual minorities) that tend otherwise to be silenced in global politics. Civil society groups have often worked to make global governance more transparent and more consultative vis-à-vis implicated publics. Many civil society organizations have in addition promoted learning and debate about global issues and their regulation, so that people can undertake more informed and empowered actions in respect of global governance. Civil society actors have moreover often served as watchdogs who scrutinize global governance in the public interest. Advocacy groups have also regularly demanded redress for harmed people when global regulatory agencies have caused damage. And numerous civil society initiatives have urged, on social-democratic lines, a progressive redistribution of world resources, so as to create a more level playing field in global politics.

That said, the relationship between civil society and democracy in global governance is not unconditionally positive. For one thing, civil society could do much more to advance democracy in global regulation. So far the scale of these democratizing activities has remained quite modest, especially relative to the need. Moreover, civil society interventions in global governance have to date disproportionately favored already privileged circles of society, such as the global North, urban professional classes, and white men. Also, civil society contains some decidedly undemocratic elements such as secretive clubs of corporate capital and terrorist cells. Even "progressive" civil society groups often show shortfalls of democratic accountability in their own practices.[19] Hence civil society involvement in global governance does not automatically generate greater democratic legitimacy: this outcome has to be deliberately and concertedly nurtured.

Democracy is not the only basis for legitimate governance, of course. Civil society activism can also bolster public support for global governance by lending it moral force. In this vein, citizen group initiatives have prodded global regulatory agencies to promote just ends like decolonization, gender equality, human rights, poverty eradication, fair trade, anti-corruption, peace, and ecological integrity. True, civil society also comprises "uncivil" groups of fundamentalists, militarists, racists, and ultra-nationalists; so its interventions in global governance do not always and inherently bolster moral legitimacy. However, civil society pressures have often helped to persuade global regulatory authorities to champion just causes, and this has raised the moral standing of global governance in the public eye.

On other occasions civil society has enhanced the legitimacy of global governance by improving its technical performance. In this case people consent to rule by global authorities because the institutions deliver desired operational outcomes, e.g. a working Internet, food security, disease control, solvent banks, etc. Civil society can contribute to this operational aspect of legitimacy by providing global governance institutions with valuable information, insights, methods, and advice. In addition, civil society associations can, with challenges to established policies, provoke a global governance agency to sharpen its thinking and improve its instruments. Moreover, sometimes subcontracted NGOs can execute global governance policies more effectively than official bureaucracies Needless to say, when civil society inputs undermine performance—e.g. with faulty information or flawed execution—they sooner contribute to a delegitimation of global governance.

Thus the record of civil society consequences for the legitimacy of global governance is mixed. On the one hand, considerable evidence suggests that civil society can be a major source of democracy, moral force, and expertise for global regulation. On the other hand, civil society also includes unaccountable, morally dubious, and incompetent elements. Moreover, many critical theorists worry that much civil society involvement can (however well-meaning the intentions) serve to legitimate global governance arrangements that in practice undermine human dignity and a good society.

Conclusion

This chapter has considered the place of civil society in contemporary global governance. The discussion has identified multifarious involvements by NGOs, social movements, and other citizen groups in global regulation. As seen throughout the chapter, assessments of these activities are much contested: definitions, explanations, evidence, and evaluations go in many directions.

Quite undeniable, however, is that civil society has acquired considerable presence in contemporary global governance. This involvement looks likely to increase still further in the future. Such greater engagement can be welcomed in principle, given that civil society offers some of the best possibilities currently available to connect global regulation with affected people on the ground.

Yet, as repeatedly seen in this chapter, civil society practices vis-à-vis global governance have not always lived up to optimistic expectations. Significant upgrades are required if civil society relations with global regulation are more fully to realize their potential contributions in the future. Five broad suggestions can be briefly mentioned in closing here. First, both sides—civil society as well as global governance—could raise their capacities for meaningful interaction, with greater mutual comprehension, improved institutional arrangements, etc. Second, better coordination of campaigns could allow civil society groups to increase their impact, as witnessed in the wide-ranging networks that pursued debt relief and the prohibition of landmines. Third, all parties to civil society relations with global governance institutions could make deliberate and sustained efforts to increase voice and influence for geographically and socially marginalized groups, who have so far had limited opportunities for participation. Fourth, civil society associations could more strenuously resist co-optation and reinforce their role as critical watchdogs of global governance. Finally, civil society interlocutors with global governance could turn the searching spotlight also onto themselves, with more rigorous attention to their own accountabilities. In the words of one human rights activist, "When you point a finger, you need to do it with a clean hand."[20]

Additional reading

1. John Gaventa and Rajesh Tandon, eds., *Citizen Engagements in a Globalising World* (London: Zed Books, 2010).
2. Christer Jönsson and Jonas Tallberg, eds., *Transnational Actors in Global Governance* (Basingstoke: Palgrave, 2010).
3. Mary Kaldor, *Global Civil Society: An Answer to War* (Cambridge: Polity Press, 2003).
4. Margaret E. Keck and Kathryn Sikkink, *Activists Beyond Borders: Advocacy Networks in International Politics* (Ithaca: Cornell University Press, 1998).
5. Robert J. O'Brien et al., *Contesting Global Governance: Multilateral Economic Institutions and Global Social Movements* (Cambridge: Cambridge University Press, 2000).
6. Jan Aart Scholte, ed., *Building Global Democracy? Civil Society and Accountable Global Governance* (Cambridge: Cambridge University Press, 2011).
7. James W. St. G. Walker and Andrew S. Thompson, eds., *Critical Mass: The Emergence of Global Civil Society* (Waterloo: Wilfred Laurier University Press, 2008).
8. Peter Willetts, *Non-Governmental Organizations in World Politics: The Construction of Global Governance* (Abingdon: Routledge, 2011).

Notes

1 United Nations Economic and Social Council, "List of Non-Governmental Organizations in Consultative Status with the Economic and Social Council as of 1 September 2011," http://csonet.org/content/documents/E2011INF4.pdf.

2 Jean Cohen and Andrew Arato, *Civil Society and Political Theory* (Cambridge, MA: MIT Press, 1992).

3 Donatella Della Porta et al., *Globalization from Below* (Minneapolis: University of Minnesota Press, 2006).

4 William Fisher, "Doing Good? The Politics and Antipolitics of NGO Practices," *Annual Review of Anthropology* 26 (1997): 439–464.

5 Chris Hann and Elizabeth Dunn, eds., *Civil Society: Challenging Western Models* (London: Routledge, 1996).

6 Petr Kopecký and Cas Mudde, eds., *Uncivil Society?* (London: Routledge, 2002).

7 Jan Aart Scholte, "A More Inclusive Global Governance? The IMF and Civil Society in Africa," *Global Governance* 18, no. 2 (April–June 2012): 185–206.

8 Steve Charnovitz, "Two Centuries of Participation: NGOs and International Governance," *Michigan Journal of International Law* 18, no. 2 (1997): 183–286.

9 Carolyn Stephenson, "Women's International Nongovernmental Organizations at the United Nations," in *Women, Politics, and the United Nations*, ed. Anne Winslow (Westport, CT: Greenwood, 1995), 139.

10 World Bank, "World Bank Staff Working with Civil Society," http://web.worldbank.org/WBSITE/EXTERNAL/TOPICS/CSO/0,,contentMDK:20093777~menuPK:225317~pagePK:220503~piPK:220476~theSitePK:228717,00.html.

11 Kerstin Martens, "Civil Society and Accountability of the United Nations," in *Building Global Democracy? Civil Society and Accountable Global Governance*, ed. Jan Aart Scholte (Cambridge: Cambridge University Press, 2011).

12 "Arria and Other Special Meetings between NGOs and Security Council Members," www.globalpolicy.org/security/mtgsetc/brieindx.htm.

13 Scholte, *Building Global Democracy*.

14 Garrett Brown, "Multisectoralism, Participation, and Stakeholder Effectiveness: Increasing the Role of Nonstate Actors in the Global Fund to Fight AIDS, Tuberculosis and Malaria," *Global Governance* 15, no. 2 (April–June 2009): 169–178.

15 Ian Scoones, "The Politics of Global Assessments: The Case of the International Assessment of Agricultural Knowledge, Science and Technology for Development (IAASTD)," *Journal of Peasant Studies* 36, no. 3 (2009): 547–571.

16 Bill Seary, "The Early History: From the Congress of Vienna to the San Francisco Conference," in *"The Conscience of the World." The Influence of Non-Governmental Organisations in the UN System*, ed. Peter Willetts (London: Hurst, 1996), 25.

17 Jan Aart Scholte, "Civil Society and the Legitimation of Global Governance," *Journal of Civil Society* 3, no. 3 (December 2007): 305–326.

18 Jan Aart Scholte, "Civil Society and Democratically Accountable Global Governance," *Government and Opposition* 39, no. 2 (2004): 211–233.

19 Lisa Jordan and Peter van Tuijll, eds., *NGO Accountability* (London: Earthscan, 2006).

20 Perry Arituwa, Uganda Joint Christian Council, cited in Jan Aart Scholte, *Democratizing the Global Economy: The Role of Civil Society* (Coventry: Centre for the Study of Globalisation and Regionalisation, 2004), 95.

Labor

Nigel Haworth and Steve Hughes

Labor's world has been subject to constant upheaval since the Industrial Revolution. As mass labor forces were created in capitalist economies, and as labor forces politicized and mobilized, periods of political accommodation, particularly between the 1930s and 1970s, seemed to provide a degree of political stability and legitimacy for labor and its organizations. But, even then, the emergent labor movements of the developing world faced the upheavals of colonization and postcolonial development. Since the 1970s, labor has confronted the twin challenges of globalization and neoliberalism, which have substantially undermined established political accommodations, whilst introducing new challenges as a result of integrated global production systems. In the early twenty-first century, the institutional and political challenges confronting labor are as grave as at any other time in modern history. Nevertheless, labor activism, coupled with political concerns at national and international levels, has placed issues such as the promotion and regulation of labor standards at the heart of contemporary global governance and in the forefront of debate around the social costs of globalization. Labor standards are an important issue in the agendas of international organizations, and in the boardrooms of global companies. As a result, public opinion and interest mobilization around labor standards have become critical considerations in global governance arrangements.[1]

This chapter assesses the contemporary challenges facing labor and its status in global governance. It begins by providing a context for contemporary labor. It then analyzes briefly the modes and practices of global governance as they engage with labor before addressing the institutional and political approaches adopted by labor in the modern period. Finally, it asks whether the continuing defense of labor's interests requires a major institutional and political reorientation.

We should be clear what we mean by labor in this chapter. Much of its focus will be on the activities of labor in the formal sector, that is, waged labor in "modern" sector employment. However, in terms of political and institutional challenges, and in terms of global governance arrangements, it is no longer possible, if indeed it ever was, to establish a clear dividing line between formally employed labor, and the many and complex forms of "informal" and rural labor practices that exist. The erosion of barriers between these different categories is an important and underdeveloped aspect of the account that follows. We also note that in the International Labour Organization (ILO) and in other international agencies, these categories are being eroded by growing international interest in labor standards for informal and peasant workers. The adoption by the ILO in 2011 of Convention 189 on Domestic Workers illustrates this well.

Labor's context

The transcendent processes that define modern labor are globalization in its many forms, and the post-1970s power of neoliberalism and its global vehicle, the Washington Consensus. We must be brief in our discussion of these phenomena, but, in our view, their impact cannot be underestimated. A third, lesser context is that engendered by the global financial crisis (GFC) of 2008. We argue "lesser" because the GFC is, we suggest, a product of globalization and neoliberalism.

Globalization, understood broadly as systemic global economic integration, often beyond formal political control by national governments, has had four major impacts on labor, which we might order as, first, the "Great Doubling;" second, the emergence of globally integrated production systems; third, the emergence of complex regional geo-political and trade relations; fourth, expansion and reconfiguration of labor migration.

The Great Doubling refers to the period in the 1990s when, with the entry of China, Russia, and the ex-Soviet bloc into the global market, the global workforce available to the market grew from 1.5 to 3 billion.[2] Simultaneously, the global capital to labor ratio nearly halved. As a consequence, developed economies feared the "hollowing out" of their productive sectors, where work might be undertaken more cheaply using these new supplies of cheaper labor. Such fears either could drive a high road model of high-quality, niche production (for example the Mittelstand model of small and medium-sized companies in Germany, often cited as key to explaining Germany's contemporary economic success), or could result in a competitive drive downwards based on competitive wage cost reductions (the feared "race to the bottom"). For our purposes, the Great Doubling signals an increase of power for the employer and investor as capital mobility allows the integration of new workforces into global production. That increase in power is reflected in the difficulty created for trade unions to organize in this new global environment.

The second relevant characteristic of globalization is the emergence of global production systems. Four main streams of global production thinking have been identified.[3] Initially, there developed the idea of the "commodity chain," defined as the network of labor and production processes giving rise to a finished commodity. Subsequently, the "global commodity chain" emerged as a more developed concept, focusing on inter-firm networks and the organization of global production and on production upgrading. Thereafter, the idea of the "global value chain" (GVC) emerged as a third tradition, emphasizing the creation and appropriation of value, the structure and role of governance within global production systems, and, again, system upgrading.[4]

Finally, the idea of "global production networks" (GPN) emphasizes the entirety of network relationships (that is, beyond the linear relationships argued to be key to GVC analysis) and focuses on the full range of networking relationships between actors in the network, rather than on narrower inter-firm governance arrangements.

For labor, such production systems involve systemic integration into the production process, across time, space, and technical functions, under the governance of large, internationally based companies. Global production systems are, in many ways, the embodiment of globalization, able, for example, to link seamlessly the peasant primary producer in a developing economy with the affluent consumer of a sophisticated, transformed commodity in the developed world. Power within such production systems often lies in the governance process, in which the voice of labor is not guaranteed, and work may sometimes be low paid, sweated, and hazardous. There is, in relation to such systems, discussion of "social upgrading," that is, the incorporation of labor standards into these networks at the behest of the buyers and consumers, or their incorporation as a result of supplier strategy, or of government intervention. These standards are most frequently the core labor standards defined by the ILO, reflecting the role and status of the ILO in labor standards setting.

Third, as globalization has developed since the 1970s, there has been a commensurate development of supranational regional arrangements, designed at once to manage and benefit from global economic integration. They tend to differ from the pre-existing forms of regionalism such as the European Union, founded on a broad commitment to economic, political, and social integration. In contrast, modern regional arrangements tend to be narrower, trade and investment-driven agreements, in which the interests of investors and exporters are paramount, and in which the voice of labor is again muted. Interestingly, such arrangements have adopted, on the whole, orthodox economic explanations for free trade and free movement of capital, yet eschew the logical commitment to the promotion of free movement of labor. Indeed, where labor is addressed at all, it is usually in one of several marginalizing fashions—labor understood as skilled, mobile, and highly desirable, for example, or as a politico-social problem that cannot be ignored formally, but is in practice, for example ill-monitored and poorly implemented "Labor Clauses" attached to trade agreements.[5] Yet, despite this marginalization, there is pressure on supranational regional or international arrangements as a result, for example, of the political and organizational pressures imposed by migrant labor, or global skills shortages, or pressure from the developed economies and their consumers for the implementation of labor standards in developing countries, as was seen in the "Social Clause" debate in the World Trade Organization (WTO) in the 1990s.

Fourth, the issue of labor and migration has gained momentum. We have already alluded to the inconsistency in an economic orthodoxy that in general favors free trade and the free movement of capital, yet either ignores, or deliberately excludes, the free movement of labor across national borders. The orthodoxy accepts that labor migration, although perhaps a desirable principle, is politically unachievable. In practice, labor migration is emerging as a matter of major political and policy importance in several ways. First, global skill shortages have been identified by many economies for at least a generation, leading to advanced economies seeking to absorb high-skilled labor from relatively low-pay nations. Qualification recognition and portability have become a key issue in the movement of skilled labor, as has the rise of international education provision. Second, demographics—especially ageing populations—have raised the specter of policy shifts in favor of larger-scale labor migration. For example, we note the tense debate in Japan about the future domestic workforce, the needs of which are unlikely to be met from traditional sources. Third, control of mass migration, be it across the US–Mexico border, across the Mediterranean from North Africa to the EU, or Southeast Asian boat people into Australia, raises policing and human rights issues. Global economic integration inevitably drives increased migration pressures.

The second major process is neoliberalism. In its myriad guises, at international and national levels, neoliberal thinking has promoted a package of economic settings —for example individualism, economic liberalization, privatization, corporatization, the "small state," reduced welfare provision, a single metric focus on inflation, free trade, and investment flows—which dominated policy-making from the 1970s to the early 2000s. Neoliberalism, in principle, does not favor minimum standards or platforms of labor standards, for it prefers wages and conditions to be settled on market terms, that is, by agreement between the employer and the individual employee. Ideologically, neoliberalism also rejects pluralist notions of social partnership. In particular, it rejects corporatist arrangements and the status accorded to organized labor (that is, trade unions) in such arrangements.

This thinking on minimum standards and trade unions was "globalized" in the Washington Consensus that promoted a global neoliberal approach to economic development and which became a generation of policy-makers' blueprint for labor markets. It particularly delegitimized collective employee voice at all levels—workplace and national policy-making included—resulting in that voice being excluded from supranational trade and investment and other international framework setting arrangements. Only after the GFC in 2008 did unemployment and political stability issues reverse that trend a little.

Globalization and neoliberalism—as a mechanism for greater global integration, especially across the financial sector, and as a purveyor of "light" or minimal regulation, respectively—came together in the 2008 GFC, a global crisis preceded by a series of more localized crises, such as the Asian Crisis of the late 1990s. The consequences of the crisis for labor were immediate and sustained. Depression led to rapidly increasing unemployment levels internationally, often compounded by immediate pressure on welfare provision. Moreover, medium-term economic policy responses to the crisis frequently reinforced downward pressure on wages and welfare provision, whilst the specter of "jobless growth" began to haunt policy-makers. It was in this context that finance ministers and central bank governors from the dominant 20 economies (meeting together as the G20) turned to the ILO for input into pro-growth policies in which employment creation played a significant role.

Summarizing the global context in which labor must act, it has been defined by major global integration, often beyond the control of nation-states and their legislations, a policy framework generally inimical to labor as an organized presence, and a series of economic crises, culminating in the 2008 GFC, in which increased unemployment and reduced welfare provision have usually been immediate consequences. It has been in general a bleak generation for labor, in which increased standards of living for many workers in rapidly developing economies are the one great positive.

Labor: modes of global governance

Labor and governance engage at multiple levels—workplace, sector, nation, region, globe. Here we focus primarily on the global aspects of labor and governance. In particular, whilst the national level of governance—the way in which labor movements are formed and organized, and the way in which they act within national industrial relations systems—is important, we will not address it in detail. However, as is clear from the previous discussion, how labor is represented, and the extent to which it is empowered and given voice at national level, is in part an effect of supranational pressures, be they the impacts of, for example, integration into global production systems, of the GFC, or of the Washington Consensus. National industrial relations systems are inevitably subject to external intervention and consequent adaptation.

Here we focus on the firm level (especially in terms of global production systems, corporate social responsibility, and labor standards); the supranational regional level (contrasting the EU with the North American Free Trade Agreement, NAFTA, and Asia Pacific Economic Cooperation, APEC); the global level, focusing on the ILO, particularly since the GFC of 2008. The interrelated nature of these different levels of analysis underpins our understanding of the global governance of labor standards. The regulation of these standards both crosses and integrates the different levels of analysis in the universal recognition of core labor standards established by the ILO, such as freedom from forced and child labor, freedom from discrimination in the workplace and the right to join a union and bargain collectively. Adherence to these standards is promoted primarily on the basis of moral suasion, dialogue, and cooperation rather than by hard, legal regulation. It is a system of governance informed by ethical voluntarism, with institutions at each level playing a role in promoting and monitoring adherence to core labor standards.

The firm

At firm level there are three primary initiatives in operation around labor-related standards—codes of practice, such as the 2000 UN Global Compact, the introduction of corporate social responsibility (CSR) measures by both domestic and international companies, and the "social upgrading" of global production systems. Framework agreements—agreements struck by international unions with international companies—are discussed below in relation to Global Unions.

The Global Compact is a UN initiative and is designed to align businesses with ten universally accepted principles in the areas of human rights, labor, environment, and anti-corruption. In terms of labor, the principles are, first, that businesses should uphold the freedom of association and the effective recognition of the right to collective bargaining; second, there should be the elimination of all forms of forced and compulsory labor; third, the effective abolition of child labor should be prioritized; fourth, the elimination of discrimination in respect of employment and occupation.

These are the core labor standards of the ILO, brought into the Global Compact as essential principles of good business practice. The Global Compact is a voluntary arrangement, governed by a board of business, labor, and civil society representatives, appointed by the UN secretary-general in their personal capacity. The purpose of the compact is to mainstream these ten principles, including core labor standards, across global business.[6]

While the impact of the Global Compact is questioned, the signal to business from the UN has been that, when it comes to appropriate labor market behavior, the standards expected are those laid down by the ILO. The corporate signatories to the Global Compact may be "delisted" for not abiding by the annual requirement of Communication on Progress (COP), a report made public to stakeholders detailing progress in implementing the Global Compact's ten principles. By 2010, 1,693 signatories had been delisted as stakeholders and pressure groups keep a watchful eye on those who view Compact membership more as a marketing exercise than a commitment to its principles.

Modern CSR measures by companies have developed since the 1960s. Their current form proposes a positive view of CSR, in which value is added to company performance as a result of the internal (for example workforce buy-in, productivity improvements) and external (for example customer recognition and loyalty) impacts of responsible company practice in environmental, social, labor, human rights, and other dimensions. The contemporary view supersedes the earlier, somewhat defensive view, which suggested that CSR was primarily a risk assessment and avoidance measure, predicated on the identification and avoidance of company practices with adverse public and market consequences. From the perspective of labor, a standard CSR approach has been for companies to commit unilaterally to the ILO's core labor standards across their operation and on into their subcontracting activities. Internal and external monitoring often follows, with large companies establishing a CSR team within the company, and external agencies, such as the Fair Labor Association, conducting audits of labor practices. The debate about the impact of such measures is fierce. Companies point to changed practices and behaviors. Opponents argue that CSR is adopted insofar as it helps the value-add, but no further, or that it is a sham. Other opponents take a quite different line, arguing that it is not the responsibility of the company to second-guess the market by introducing non-commercial criteria into business decision-making.

In terms of global production systems, there exists a burgeoning discussion of "social upgrading," that is, the incorporation of labor standards into the operation at the behest of the buyers and consumers, or their incorporation as a result of supplier strategy, or of government intervention. These standards are most frequently the core labor standards defined by the ILO, reflecting the role and status of the ILO in labor standards setting.

The debate around social upgrading has a number of dimensions. First, there are important strategic dimensions of these chains in relation to social upgrading. Traditionally, network strategies might be placed on a continuum between "low road" strategies, in which the advantages offered by global production arrangements derive from access to pools of cheap labor, and "high road" strategies, in which skill and quality outputs combine to produce higher value outputs. Social upgrading might traditionally be expected in high road approaches, but not in low road. However, there is also evidence that some sectors traditionally associated with low road approaches, e.g. apparel, are also being required to upgrade on both social and environmental fronts, with the drive to social upgrading coming from the buyers in the chain or network, or from consumers.

Second, there is an interesting discussion of "learning" in these chains. Learning, and the transfer of knowledge, within chains is argued to be uneven and an effect primarily of the different governance arrangements that exist. However, it is agreed that different types of learning and transfer take place, particularly in terms of product, functional, and process arrangements. Recently, it has been argued that transfers and learning associated with both environmental and social upgrading have been under-theorized and the focus of growing empirical study.[7]

Third, there is the "pull–push" mechanism that promotes social upgrading in these networks. Producer firms may adopt improved labor standards as a means to achieve improved deals with buyers and to command associated rents. Equally, buyers, with an eye on consumer expectations, may require social upgrading as a component of a contract. Another aspect of the "push" component is the role of national governments, which are likely to be working with the ILO and other international agencies, and therefore may favor a national "upgrading" of labor standards as part of a broader development strategy.

Supranational regional arrangements

We now turn to the supranational regional dimension of labor and governance. We illustrate this with three contrasting regional arrangements—the EU's "social dialogue" model, NAFTA's "Labor Clause" model, and APEC's refusal to address labor issues in any serious fashion.

One of the defining characteristics of the EU is social dialogue—that is, meetings between the social partners—employers (private and public) and employees, with or without the participation of member state or EU representatives. Social dialogue was reasserted at the 2000 Lisbon summit as one of the fundamental pillars of the "European Social Model," which combines good economic performance and high skills with a high level of social protection. It is in this social dialogue that trade union representation and power within the EU are protected and displayed.

The origins of social dialogue are rooted in European social and political traditions, which gave rise in 1991 to a Social Protocol, created by the social partners, which was eventually adopted at the EU's 1991 Maastricht summit. The social partners therefore were instrumental in defining the emerging EU industrial relations system. When the Social Protocol was adopted as an annex to the Maastricht Treaty of February 1992, the social partnership model became a central theme of the social dimension of European integration and social dialogue increased in importance thereafter. The result was a powerful role for the European Trade Union Council (ETUC) across the EU decision-making process. The social dialogue approach is unique, and provides the most comprehensive engagement by labor in supranational regional arrangements, although the future of that engagement has been brought into question as EU member states seek to overcome the impacts of the GFC.

The case of the North American Agreement on Labor Cooperation (NAALC), a "side agreement" of NAFTA (a trade and investment agreement between Canada, the United States, and Mexico effective from 1 January 1994) presents an example of an intermediate labor standards governance regime. The expressed intention of the side agreement was to allow any failure to sustain appropriate labor standards as an effect of trade and investment arrangements under NAFTA to be subject to investigation and, where proven, sanctions. The efficacy of the side agreement approach has been much questioned. In particular, unions have pointed to a consistent unwillingness to take cases of poor labor standards beyond bureaucratic discussions. Unions believe that the side agreement is cosmetic, rather than a fully supported and implemented arrangement. Canadian unions have pointed to US Democratic presidential candidates who have recognized this weakness and have called for binding obligations on labor (and environmental) standards, drawn into the heart of the NAFTA process, rather than abandoned on its margins. Versions of side agreements or similar "distanced" arrangements are common in contemporary trade and investment deals. All suffer the same criticism, that is, they are secondary to the main issues of trade and investment, lack teeth, and provide limited support for strong labor standards.

APEC is an example of a trade and investment arrangement that has long avoided active engagement with labor standards issues. Founded in the late 1980s, APEC became a powerful trans-Pacific force for free trade and investment. It cast itself as the vanguard of the WTO, pressing for ever deeper and wider trade and investment liberalization. Although it also developed a modest development agenda, member state politics resulted in a deliberate marginalization of labor as an interest group (except, rarely, when individual members chose to include trade union members in delegations) and avoided assiduously any of the Social Clause discussions that took place in the WTO. This contrasted strongly with the powerful business lobby in APEC, which is given high status and privileged access to the top of the APEC process. Only after the 2008 GFC was there some relaxation of this position, at the instigation of China, but APEC remains a major regional trade and investment arrangement without formal labor representation and with an aversion to labor-related matters.

The attitude of APEC to labor-related issues also raises an important question about "who" is responsible for labor standards. The default position, illustrated by APEC, is that labor standards are either a domestic matter, to be regulated at the level of the nation-state, or a matter for specialist agencies such as the ILO. In other words, there remains a strong belief in agencies such as APEC that global action on labor standards is "someone else's problem."

The ILO

The ILO is at the center of contemporary global labor governance, as has been the case since 1919. The ILO is the institutional core and epistemic community at the heart of the International Labor Standards Regime. Its tripartite model of convention and recommendation creation, established on the principle of dialogue, cooperation, and equal voting between government, employer, and labor representatives to the ILO, remains the most powerful institutional location for labor's global voice.

However, the ILO entered the 1990s in search of a response to both globalization and neoliberal policy setting, both of which raised challenges to the ILO's traditional standard-setting model. In particular, neoliberal policy hegemony in the 1980s challenged the tripartite model upon which the ILO was formed in 1919. Trade union density was declining in many economies as free-market policies rejected corporatist arrangements and frequently marginalized union voice. The relevance of the ILO was being questioned, as was its very survival.

Director-General Francis Blanchard recognized the new challenges facing the ILO in the 1980s. His response was to encourage proactive engagement with the Bretton Woods institutions in search of a niche for the ILO in a "structurally adjusted" global economy. Blanchard's initiatives were carried forward by his successors. Michel Hansenne, director-general between 1989 and 1999, significantly reformed the mission of the ILO. The 1998 ILO Declaration on Fundamental Principles and Rights at Work centered ILO activities on a much-contested definition of "core" labor standards, which were to be a fundamental dimension of a "fair" globalization, providing better targeted, more effective labor standards.

Hansenne's successor, Juan Somavía, continued the redirection of the ILO in response to globalization and its impacts. In particular, he addressed three issues: globalization; the engagement with other international organizations, especially the WTO, the World Bank, and the IMF; and the ILO's message and organizing principles. The 2008 "Declaration on Social Justice for a Fair Globalization" brought together ILO thinking on globalization, in turn based on a 2004 ILO report—"A Fair Globalization: Creating Opportunities for All." Renewed efforts to work with other international agencies were supported strongly. The Decent Work agenda became the organizing principle for the ILO, captured in the ILO's four strategic objectives:

1. Creating jobs—an economy that generates opportunities for investment, entrepreneurship, skills development, job creation and sustainable livelihoods.

2. Guaranteeing rights at work—to obtain recognition and respect for the rights of workers. All workers, and in particular disadvantaged or poor workers, need representation, participation, and laws that work for their interests.

3. Extending social protection—to promote both inclusion and productivity by ensuring that women and men enjoy working conditions that are safe, allow adequate free time and rest, take into account family and social values, provide for adequate compensation in case of lost or reduced income and permit access to adequate healthcare.

4. Promoting social dialogue—involving strong and independent workers' and employers' organizations is central to increasing productivity, avoiding disputes at work, and building cohesive societies.

The comprehensive reform of the ILO under Hansenne and Somavía has gone some way towards a successful repositioning of the ILO in a globalized world. This is particularly evident in the high-profile activities undertaken by the ILO around the G20 as a result of the GFC. Hence, labor's global presence remains strong in the ILO and in areas of activity in which it plays an important role. However, stresses remain within the ILO, as was seen in employer attempts in 2012 to undermine some important procedures and institutions (such as the Committee of Experts). Moreover, threatening both EU and ILO traditions of social dialogue, social partnership has been shown to be fragile in EU economies seeking a way through the GFC (especially in the case of Greece). Hence, whilst the ILO remains a vital global institution for labor, its status and influence are not assured, requiring labor to consider complementary institutional and organizational measures.

Labor's institutions

The challenges created for labor by the global environment are reflected also in the changing institutional configuration of the global labor movement. Once again, we do not address the changing conditions and structures of domestic labor movements in any detail, whilst recognizing that such movements are important constituent elements of international labor organizations, and also recognizing that there are synergies between the international and the domestic. Here, we concentrate on three levels of labor organization—supranational regional arrangements, the central global organization (the International Trade Union Confederation, ITUC), and the Global Unions network, including the Global Union Federations.

Supranational regional organizations

A variety of supranational regional labor institutions exist. *Primus inter pares* in terms of power and status is the ETUC, a union presence in the EU defined by the social dialogue mechanisms discussed above. However, there are other supranational regional institutions, primarily linked to the ITUC. These include, for example the ITUC-Africa, the Trade Union Confederation of the Americas (TUCA), and the ITUC-Pan European Regional Council (ITUC-PERC). We discuss these in relation to the ITUC.

The contrast between the organizational presence of labor in the EU and in NAFTA is telling. In the EU, the ETUC is a social partner, recognized by the European Union, by the Council of Europe, and by the European Free Trade Association (EFTA) as the representative trade union organization in the EU. As such, it is consulted consistently on key aspects of European integration. It has a status guaranteed by treaty and an ability to represent trade union issues at all levels of discussion. This is in contrast to the operation of the NAALC. The operating principles of the NAALC are intergovernmental, with national administration offices established in government departments in the three member countries. Complaints relating to labor standards (described as "Public Communications") are initially dealt with in a bureaucratic process, which may lead to Ministerial Consultations, an evaluation by an expert committee, and, finally, independent arbitration. Progress beyond the first stage is rare. Hence, in the EU, trade unions are in principle fully consulted about the design and implementation of policy, and in its subsequent monitoring and evaluation, under the NAALC, labor's voice is reduced to that of one actor amongst others operating in a predetermined intergovernmental arrangement. Needless to say, NAFTA-based unions are both critical of, and cynical about, the impact of the NAALC.

Even in the EU, however, the challenge to social dialogue raised by post-GFC policy developments in members such as Greece suggests that the institutionally privileged status of the ETUC is not a guarantee of power or influence. In terms of presence and influence, supranational regional labor representation is at best a mixed success.

The ITUC

The ITUC was formed in Vienna in 2006, following the merger of the International Confederation of Free Trade Unions (ICFTU) and the World Confederation of Labour

(WCL). Its emergence as the single dominant global trade union organization also reflected the demise of the Eastern bloc-backed World Federation of Trade Unions (WFTU) in the late 1980s and 1990s. The ITUC currently claims a membership of 175 million in 308 affiliates in 153 countries. The ITUC is a major international agency, particularly active in the ILO, but also a frequent attendee of meetings involving the range of UN and other agencies. It enjoys considerable global status as the legitimate voice of labor on issues that consider work and workers—from traditional labor standards issues to contemporary questions such as climate change and human rights. However, presence and size do not ensure influence and power, and question marks remain over the impact of ITUC's voice in international discussions.

Many saw the creation of the ITUC as a great success in comparison with the Cold War clashes that gave rise to the division between the ICFTU and the WFTU, in particular. However, the ITUC has not avoided significant criticism from within labor, primarily in relation to its stance on globalization and neoliberal policies. Critics argue that the ITUC has tempered its political stance on globalization and neoliberalism in order to be accepted as a legitimate body by other international agencies. A key element of this critique is that the ITUC responds mainly to the views of developed world unions, and that the needs of the developing "South" are marginalized. Contemporary "social movement" analysis is frequently invoked as the antidote to a developed world hegemony. The critics argue for a far more political and radical global organization, often believing that the origins of the ITUC will not allow it to become such a force.

Supporters of the ITUC reject the criticism. *Inter alia*, they point to the progress made in creating a single global union body, and in gaining access for labor in global governance arrangements. They argue that the ITUC must be a pluralist agency in that it represents many strands of union thinking, politically, spatially, and experientially. They reject an adventurism which suggests that there are gains to be made by radicalizing the ITUC and taking it out of the global governance networks in which it operates.

A balanced judgment suggests that the ITUC represents a significant step forward by labor in global governance, yet its impact and status cannot yet be established. In particular, its capacity to influence the direction of globalization, and the outcomes of the GFC, to the sustained advantage of workers remains unclear.

Global Unions

Global Unions is a network including the ITUC, the Trade Union Advisory Committee to the OECD (TUAC), and what were for many years known as the International Trade Secretariats (ITS), which remain global sectoral union bodies (for example for engineers, the public sector, education, and so on). The ITS tradition reaches back to the late nineteenth century. The ITS transformed themselves into Global Union Federations (GUFs) in the 1990s.

GUFs are in general seen as successful. Because they are sectorally focused and have a long history of effective international reach, they have grown since the 1990s, especially as the Cold War ended and new membership bases opened up. Growth has also exacerbated a traditional resource constraint, as many affiliates are not resource rich. Some GUFs also have a tradition of greater radicalism and have been the source of creative thinking about global trade union activities. Their members may also belong to the

ITUC, yet, through GUF campaigns, express difference from ITUC positions. Equally, however, GUFs are expected to deliver benefits to members, often in the form of campaigns, solidarity actions, and the promotion of "framework agreements," which are agreements to abide by agreed labor standards, struck across an international company by its management and the relevant GUF. Framework agreements are in many ways the leitmotif of the GUFs.

Labor has a significant institutional presence in global governance. Its institutions draw on experience that reaches back to the late nineteenth century, and take advantage, where possible, of tripartite traditions (as, for example, in the EU and ILO). Labor's global institutions have undergone significant change over the last generation, driven by a combination of factors—the end of the Cold War, globalization, the GFC, and a pressing need to have labor's voice "at the top table" of global governance. Yet the power of that voice remains uncertain, for the role of labor as a social partner in globalization is still to be confirmed, and remains under attack from neoliberalism. And while that uncertainty remains, it also creates an opportunity for traditions within labor to argue for a far more radical stance against capitalism in its modern form, a perennial debate—but one given new vitality by the GFC and pressures from the global South.

Conclusion

The pressing concern for labor is the grounding of its voice in global governance. There is a strong comparison to be made with the epoch which saw the creation of the ILO and the first international legitimation of that voice in 1919. Then, the threat of Bolshevism, coupled with the rise since the nineteenth century of worker militancy, helped to establish the tripartite model of the ILO. The ILO's tripartism was also a reflection of concerns about protectionism in the global trading system. In sum, there were pressing reasons to create a role and voice for labor in the global governance arrangements of the day. Until the GFC, such arguments had lost much of their force. Neoliberalism had sought to destroy unions. Globalization was apace, with little interest in hearing the voice of labor. The reform of the ILO under Hansenne and Somavía was a direct consequence of that marginalization of labor. The GFC has partly halted the marginalization, at least in global governance terms, as fears about political instability and jobless growth have grown. Still, the evidence for cases such as Greece suggests that when hard decisions must be made the voice of labor is marginalized from formal decision-making and must make itself heard on the streets.

Labor's institutions comprehend these pressures and have reformed themselves. However, they also face challenges, not only from marginalization, but also from more radical internal traditions. They are forced to steer a nuanced and at times contradictory course as they seek, on the one hand, to represent labor in the upper reaches of global governance, and, on the other, meet the aspiration of a widely differentiated membership. It is an unenviable task.

In rising to this task, labor's response has long been multilayered and multifaceted. From official structures such as the ITUC to loose coalitions of industry or company-focused shop steward committees, labor has sought to represent its interests, frame its goals and influence policy-making internationally. The multilayered analysis we have provided in this chapter underlines the complexity of global governance, the diffuse articulation of institutional power, and the role of labor standards in frameworking debate around a social dimension to globalization.

The emergence of a multi-actor system with power exercised at different levels has been one of the enduring legacies of post-war economic planning. Our understanding of this system is challenged by the diversity of the institutional and political actors that govern it and the complexity of policy responses it represents. However, the problem for labor has often been framed in terms of local labor versus global capital, the globalization of production and the localization of the wage bargain. International activity has, in these terms, been no more than an addendum to a tradition that emphasizes nationally based accounts of labor rights. The establishment of a set of core labor standards that are deemed universal across national boundaries has provided an organizing platform on which labor is able to mobilize beyond national regimes of labor regulation and into the system of global governance.

Within and across our different levels of analysis, labor has sought to reframe the rules and norms of an international regime to reflect its interests. This reframing has taken different forms with different outcomes, depending on the level of governance and the nature of institutional and political power. Nonetheless, the ability of labor to articulate its voice within the institutions of global governance has been instrumental in developing different frameworks in the regulation of labor standards. While the recognition of core labor standards is at the heart of these activities, the willingness and ability of governmental, labor, and private actors to accommodate their interests within the institutions of global governance provide the political and social wherewithal for regulatory action elsewhere.

Additional reading

1. ILO, *World of Work Report 2012* (Geneva: ILO, 2012).
2. Raphael Kaplinsky, *The Role of Standards in Global Value Chains* (Washington, DC: World Bank, 2010), http://elibrary.worldbank.org/content/workingpaper/10.1596/1813-9450-5396.
3. Stephen Hughes and Nigel Haworth, *The International Labour Organization: Coming in from the Cold* (London: Routledge, 2010).
4. Ronaldo Munck, "Globalization and the Labour Movement: Challenges and Responses," *Global Labour Journal* 1, no. 2 (2010): 218–232.
5. Rob Lambert and Eddie Webster, "Southern Unionism and the New Labour Internationalism," in *Place, Space and the New Labour Internationalisms*, eds. Peter Waterman and Jane Wills (Oxford: Blackwell), 33–57.

Notes

1 Nigel Haworth and Stephen Hughes, "International Political Economy and Industrial Relations," *British Journal of Industrial Relations* 41, no. 4 (2003): 665–682. See also Nigel Haworth and Stephen Hughes, "Internationalisation, International Relations and Industrial Relations," *Journal of Industrial Relations* 42, no. 2 (2000): 195–213.
2 Richard Freeman, "The Great Doubling: The Challenge of the New Global Labor Market," 2006, http://emlab.berkeley.edu/users/webfac/eichengreen/e183_sp07/great_doub.pdf.

3   Leonhard Plank, Cornelia Staritz, and Karin Lukas, *Labour Rights in Global Production Networks* (Vienna: Kammer für Arbeiter und Angestellte für Wien, 2009), 14–15.

4   Gary Gereffi, John Humphrey, and Timothy Sturgeon, "The Governance of Global Value Chains," *Review of International Political Economy* 12, no. 1 (2005): 78–104.

5   Nigel Haworth, Stephen Hughes, and Rorden Wilkinson, "The International Labor Standards Regime: A Case Study in Global Regulation," *Environment and Planning A* 37, no. 12 (2005): 1939–1953. See also Nigel Haworth and Stephen Hughes, "From Marrakesh to Doha and Beyond: The Tortuous Progress of the Contemporary Trade and Labor Standards Debate," in *The Politics of International Trade*, eds. Dominic Kelly and Wyn Grant (London: Palgrave, 2004).

6   A. Rasche and D. Gilbert, "Institutionalizing Global Governance: The Role of the United Nations Global Compact," *Business Ethics: A European Review* 21, no. 1 (2012): 100–114.

7   Stephanie Barrientos, "Contract Labor: The 'Achilles Heel' of Corporate Codes in Commercial Value Chains," *Development and Change* 39, no. 6 (2008): 977–990.

Credit Rating Agencies

Timothy J. Sinclair

Credit rating agencies are among the most puzzling institutions of our times. Formerly largely unknown, the raters have become a focus of political and media attention since the Asian financial crisis of 1997–98, as people have repeatedly questioned the accuracy and timeliness of their ratings with successive episodes of rating "failure." The global financial crisis that started in 2007 has greatly heightened these concerns, while the European sovereign debt crisis that started in 2010 has demonstrated the continuing importance of the agencies despite persistent concerns about their competence.[1]

Moody's Investors Service and Standard & Poor's (S&P), both headquartered in New York City, are the two most important agencies. They are blamed for inflating the ratings of exotic financial products such as subprime securities before 2007. Many of these financial instruments were dramatically downgraded by the agencies in 2008 as their problems emerged. Although criticized for accuracy, the views of the agencies were closely followed again as governments in southern Europe increasingly found themselves in financial trouble as the consequences of the global financial crisis affected their income (reducing their tax take) and expenditure (by greatly increasing expenditure for bank bailouts).

Few have linked the increasing importance of the agencies to the problem of global governance.[2] Although the Commission on Global Governance created by the UN secretary-general in 1992 endorsed a central role for private and market agents of governance in its vision of managing world affairs, the broader implications of the growing role of rating agencies are more significant.

This chapter argues that these agencies have become increasingly important non-state actors with the shift from a world of international organization to a more complex world of global governance. Rating agencies have acquired greater salience because they fit with the predominantly managerial objectives of global governance institutions. The rating agencies are private and turn such political problems as funding a bridge's construction into supposedly technical issues. This transformation reduces the scope for political debate. But recurrent episodes of rating failure and the associated criticism of the agencies highlight the fragility of non-state forms of global governance.

This chapter begins with a discussion of the history and growth of these agencies, which is followed by competing perspectives on them. Thereafter, it explores the current debate about the efficacy and challenges facing the agencies linked to the global financial crisis. The chapter closes with a brief conclusion.

History

Credit rating is a process of determining the probability of default by a borrower or potential borrower. Increasingly, we all have a credit rating and these assessments of our ability to repay our debts are used by credit card companies when we apply for a new credit card, and by mortgage lenders when we want to buy a house. Corporations and governments also have credit ratings. It is these wholesale credit rating agencies that are my focus in this chapter.

Rating agencies emerged after the Civil War in the United States.[3] Between 1865 and 1914 American financial markets experienced an explosion of private information provision in the absence of good, reliable, publicly gathered statistics. The transition between issuing collections of information and actually making judgments about the creditworthiness of debtors occurred after the 1907 financial crisis and before the end of World War I. The 1907 crisis demonstrated the volatility of finance. Rating looked useful in such an uncertain world. By the mid-1920s, all of the US municipal bond market was rated by Moody's. The growth of the bond rating industry subsequently occurred in a number of phases. Up to the 1930s, and the separation of the banking and securities businesses in the United States with the 1933 passage of the Glass–Steagall Act, bond rating was a fledgling activity. Rating entered a period of rapid growth and consolidation with this separation and institutionalization of the securities business after 1929, and rating became a standard requirement to sell any debt issue in the United States after many state governments incorporated rating standards into their prudential rules for investments by pension funds. Securities, like bank loans, are debts, but, unlike bank loans, securities such as bonds can be traded in the market. The price they trade at is affected by the rate of inflation and a judgment about the creditworthiness of the corporation or government that issued them. A series of defaults by major sovereign borrowers, including Germany, made the bond business largely a US one from the 1930s to the 1980s, dominated by American blue chip industrial firms and municipalities.[4] The third period of rating development began in the 1980s, as a market in junk or low-rated bonds developed. This market—a feature of the newly released energies of financial speculation—saw many new entrants participate in the capital markets.

Moody's and S&P are headquartered in the lower Manhattan financial district of New York City and dominate the market in ratings. Moody's was sold in 1998 as a separate corporation by Dun and Bradstreet, the information concern, which had owned it since 1962, while S&P remains a subsidiary of McGraw-Hill, which bought S&P in 1966. Both agencies have numerous branches in the United States, other developed countries, and several emerging markets. S&P is famous for the S&P 500, the benchmark US stock

Table 25.1 Credit rating scales

Moody's Investors Service	Standard & Poor's
Aaa	AAA
Aa	AA
A	A
Baa	BBB
Ba	BB
B	B
Caa	CCC
Ca	CC
C	C
N/A	D

index listing around $1 trillion in assets. Other agencies include Fitch Ratings and the Dominion Bond Rating Service. All the agencies use rating symbols like those listed in Table 25.1 to indicate the relative creditworthiness of bond issues and issuers. Aaa or AAA is the best, with the lowest probability of default or failure to repay by the issuer or borrower. Just as people with better credit pay lower interest rates on their credit card borrowings, borrowers such as governments and corporations pay lower interest on AAA bonds than, say, BB ones. Governments tend to get very upset when their credit-worthiness is downgraded by the agencies.[5]

In the late 1960s and early 1970s, rating agencies began to charge fees to bond issuers to pay for ratings. Both firms have fee incomes of several hundred million dollars a year. Rating agency outputs comprise an important part of the infrastructure of capital markets. They are key benchmarks in the marketplace, which form the basis for subsequent decision-making by participants. In this sense, rating agencies are important not so much for any specific rating they produce, but for the fact that they are a part of the internal organization of the market itself. So, we find that traders may refer to a company as an "AA company," or some other rating category, as if this were a fact, an agreed and uncontroversial way of describing and distinguishing companies, munici-palities, or countries.

Rating agencies operate in a specific context. The New Global Finance (NGF) is a social structure in which rating agencies and other reputational intermediaries assume a new importance. Bank lending is familiar to us. Banks traditionally acted as financial intermediaries, bringing together borrowers and lenders of funds. They borrowed money, in the form of deposits, and lent money at their own risk to borrowers. However, in recent years disintermediation has occurred on both sides of the balance sheet. Depositors have found more attractive things to do with their money at the same time as borrowers have increasingly borrowed from non-bank sources. The reasons for this development seem to lie in the heightened competitive pressures generated by globalization, and the high overhead costs of the bank intermediation infrastructure.

Disintermediation is at the center of the NGF. This process is changing what banks are, and creating what economists call an "information problem" for suppliers and users of funds. In a bank-intermediated environment, lenders depend on the prudential behavior of banks, which are regulated and required to maintain a certain level of reserves. Traditionally, banks lend money, assuming the risk of lending themselves. But this business model is less competitive today as cheaper alternatives exist. Borrowers such as corporations and governments have increasingly sought funds in the capital markets, where costs do not include the cost of running a bank and its infrastructure, and the bad loans the bank has made in the past. In a disintermediated financial environment like the bond market those with funds must make their own judgments about the likelihood of repayment by borrowers they contemplate lending money to—no bank is there to assume this risk for them. Given the high costs of gathering suitable information with which to make an assessment by individual investors, it is no surprise that institutions have developed to solve the information problem in capital markets by providing centralized judgments on creditworthiness.

Before the mid-1990s, most European and Asian companies relied on their market reputations alone to secure market financing for securities. But this situation changed when the pressure of globalization led to the desire to tap the deep American financial markets and to a greater appetite for higher returns (and thus risk). In these circumstances, the informality of old boys' networks was no longer defendable to shareholders or relevant to pension funds halfway around the world. What was an essentially American approach to market organization and judgment has become the global norm in the developed world, and, increasingly, in emerging markets as well.

The growth of rating has a number of central features. Globalization is the most obvious characteristic. As noted, cheaper, more efficient capital markets now challenge the commercial positions of banks everywhere. The New York-based rating agencies have grown rapidly to meet demand for their services in newly disintermediated capital markets. Second, innovation in financial instruments is a major feature. Derivatives and structured financings, amongst other things, place a lot of stress on the existing analytical systems and outputs of the agencies, which are developing new rating scales and expertise in order to meet these changes. The demand for timely information is greater than ever. Third, competition in the rating industry has started to accelerate, for the first time in decades. The basis for this competition lies in niche specialization (for example Fitch Ratings in municipals and financial institutions) and in the "better treatment" of issuers by smaller firms. The global rating agencies, especially Moody's, are sometimes characterized as high-handed, or in other ways deficient, in surveys of both issuers and investors.

Over the one hundred years or so of their existence rating agencies have become more important in the world of global finance as the bond markets have grown in importance. This in itself has made them increasingly significant non-state actors in the system of global governance, which is very much organized around market principles and the value of market-based actors like the agencies. This is in contrast to the state-centric system of international organization which was characteristic of the world order prior to the 1990s. Unlike the International Monetary Fund, the judgments of the agencies have tended to be seen as non-political, enhancing their effectiveness. The growth in the global governance significance of the agencies is matched by increasing recognition in official agencies, development banks, and governments, including the US government, that the agencies are at times useful promoters of market norms as their reach grows around the world.

Current debates

We can identify three competing ways of thinking about these agencies. Two emerge from business schools and law, while the third reflects thinking in the social sciences more broadly. The first is the rationalist approach, which means that what rating agencies do is seen as serving a "function" in the economic system. In this view, rating agencies solve a problem in markets that develops when banks no longer sit at the centre of the borrowing process. Rating agencies serve as what Peter Gourevitch calls "reputational intermediaries," like accountants, analysts, and lawyers, who are "essential to the functioning of the system," monitoring managers through a "constant flow of short-term snapshots."[6] Another way to think about this function is to suggest that rating agencies establish psychological "rules of thumb" that make market decisions less costly for participants.[7] As banks have changed their nature, becoming a less significant part of the governance of markets, the rating agencies have become more significant. Looking at the process of capital market growth around the world, the developing role of the handful of rating agencies seems strategic in character.

The second approach, the regulatory license view, sees whatever power the agencies have in the capital markets as a reflection of delegation from government.[8] Because governments, especially Washington, have used ratings as a way of promoting prudential requirements for pension funds, and have designated specific agencies as suitable for this purpose, whatever power the agencies have is simply a reflection of the power of government, not what the agencies have to offer themselves. This is a much more limited conception of the global governance potential of the credit rating agencies, which views them merely as a reflection of delegated power from sovereign states.

The third approach is the social foundations approach, which has much in common with constructivist ways of thinking about international organization and global governance. Proponents see that purely functional explanations for the existence of rating agencies are deceptive. Attempts to verify or refute the idea that rating agencies must exist because they serve a purpose have proven inconclusive. Rating agencies have to be considered important actors because people view them as important, and act on the basis of that understanding in markets, even if it proves impossible for analysts to actually isolate the specific benefits that agencies generate for these market actors. Investors often mimic other investors, "ignoring substantive private information."[9] The fact that people may collectively view rating agencies as important—irrespective of what "function" the agencies are thought to serve in the scholarly literature—means that markets and debt issuers have strong incentives to act as if participants in the markets take the rating agencies seriously. In the social foundations view, the significance of rating cannot be estimated like a mountain or national population, as a "brute" fact which is true (or not) irrespective of shared beliefs about its existence, nor is the meaning of rating determined by the "subjective" facts of individual perception.[10] What is central to the status and consequentiality of rating agencies is what people believe about the agencies, and then act on collectively—even if those beliefs are clearly false. Indeed, the beliefs may be quite strange to the observer, but if people use them as a guide to action (or inaction) they are significant.

Dismissing collective beliefs misses the fact that actors must take account of the existence of social facts in considering their own action. Reflection about the nature and direction of social facts is characteristic of financial markets on a day-to-day basis. Whether rating agencies actually add new information to the process does not negate their significance, understood in these terms. This third approach to understanding the agencies suggests that the source of their power as agents of global governance is not just their immediate coercive effect on the cost of borrowing money, but their broader impact on the ideas and confidence in the markets, institutions, and governments.

Key criticisms and emerging issues

Recurrent episodes of rating failure and the associated criticism of the agencies highlight the fragility of non-state forms of global governance. The subprime crisis that began in 2007 caused dismay and panic throughout governing circles in developed countries as efforts to reignite confidence in the financial markets failed. The crisis revolved around mortgage lending for housing purchases by buyers with weaker than "prime" personal credit ratings. The financial markets developed a series of exotic financial instruments associated with these housing loans to allow lenders to reduce their balance sheet risk. Other institutions traded in these derivatives to make money. Given that the subprime securities market was worth only $0.7 trillion in mid-2007, out of total global capital markets of $175 trillion, the impact of subprime assets was out of all proportion to its actual weight in the financial system.[11]

The subprime crisis is not a direct consequence of subprime mortgage delinquencies. The paralysis that came over global finance in 2007–09 is a consequence of the nature of markets themselves, rather than the logical result of relatively minor problems with lending to the working poor. But this analysis of the subprime crisis is difficult to incorporate in a rationalist view, in which events have material causes. In a rationalist world, panics, crises, and collapses have to be explained as a result of specific failures rather than understood as a consequence of the social interactions in markets.

Since the 1930s, financial crises have almost always been accompanied by public controversy over who was at fault. Before then, governments were not generally held responsible for economic conditions, but since the 1930s the public has expected governments to manage the financial system. Inevitably, efforts to defuse or redirect blame develop. During the Asian financial crisis (1997–98), corruption in Asian governments and amongst their business leaders was held responsible, even though just a few years before "Asian values" were supposedly responsible for the unprecedented growth in the region. During the Enron scandal of 2001–02 auditors were blamed for not revealing the financial chicanery of the corporation. The subprime crisis was no different, with rating agencies, mortgage lenders, "greedy" bankers, and "weak" regulators all subject to very strong attacks for not doing their jobs.

The rating agencies have been subject to unprecedented criticism and investigation. Congressional committees, the Securities and Exchange Commission (SEC), the European Parliament and Commission, and the Committee of European Securities Regulators have all conducted investigations. The crisis over subprime ratings was the biggest threat to date for these agencies in a century of activity. This effort to blame the agencies is curious given that the rating agency business is now open to greater competition since passage of the Credit Rating Agency Reform Act by the US Congress in 2006. It suggests that the movement from regulation to self-regulation—from "police patrol" to "fire alarm" approaches—has not eliminated the role of the state. Governments are still expected by their citizens to deal with market failure, and when necessary act as lenders of last resort, and governments know it. What we see is a serious disciplining of the agencies by a regulatory state, intent on improving their performance.[12] Although this is a US debate in the first instance, it has global consequences because the internationally respected agencies are US based. It shows how concerns about regulation in a specific domestic context can have transnational implications.

The activities of rating agencies have been largely free of regulation until recently. Starting in the 1930s, the ratings produced by the agencies in the United States have been incorporated into prudential regulation of pension funds so as to provide a benchmark for their investment. This required pension funds to invest their resources in those bonds rated "investment grade" and avoid lower-rated, "speculative grade" bonds. Regulation of the agencies themselves only started in 1975 with the SEC's Net Capital Rule. This gave a discount or "haircut" to issuers whose bonds are rated by "Nationally Recognized Statistical Rating Organizations" (NRSRO). No criteria were established for NRSROs at the time, and this standing was determined by the SEC informally. NRSRO designation acted as a barrier to entry until the Rating Agency Reform Act of 2006, passed in the wake of the Enron scandal, created criteria and a recognized path to NRSRO recognition.

The impulse is to regulate the agencies by creating a framework of regulative rules that are "heavier" or "harder" or somehow more "serious." The impulse to regulate is derived from a failure to understand what it is the rating agencies did that was actually in error, and a failure to accept the social nature of finance and the circumstances that brought the crisis into being in the first place. The prevailing understanding behind the impulse to punish and regulate seems to be that the people involved were doing things wrong. It is as if the mechanic fixing your car has downloaded the wrong software updates to the car's computers. But this mechanical analogy will not do for global finance. Finance is not a natural phenomenon. While financial markets may display regularities in normal times, these regularities are not law-like because change is an ever-present feature of all social mechanisms.

John Searle made a useful distinction between regulative rules that "regulate antecedently or independently existing forms of behavior" and more architectural forms of rule.[13] The latter, or "constitutive rules, do not merely regulate, they create or define new forms of behavior." He goes on to suggest that chess and football are only possible with rules. The rules make the game. The point here is that the public and elite panic has focused on regulative rules (or the lack of them) and those who allegedly broke them. But this is not the problem with rating agencies or what has brought about the global financial crisis. The problem is that deep, constitutive rules have been damaged by the panic, and thus why the crisis was so challenging to the powers that be.

In the case of the rating agencies, regulative issues are insubstantial and no more than a useful rhetorical device to address poor forecasting. What are important and little commented upon are the constitutive issues. The major problem arose in the early 1980s with the rise of structured finance. Structured finance is important because it has been the principal means through which financial innovation has made illiquid debts like credit card receivables, car loans and mortgages into tradable, liquid securities. In a context of low interest rates and the hunt for yield, structured finance grew into around 40 percent of total global debt securities of around $30 trillion in 2007.

When people think of financial innovation, they inevitably think of computers and highly educated "rocket scientists" developing quantitative techniques for managing risk. But that is not at the heart of this matter. Lawyers are the key to the problem. The real essence of structured finance is to be found in the legal rights to revenues organized in the contracts and trusts which underpin the securities. This documentation can run into thousands of pages. These legal underpinnings give different rights to different tranches of a security. Some, such as the AAA tranche, have the right to be paid first, while others have to wait in line. This is how a mass of not very creditworthy subprime mortgages could produce some AAA bonds. These investors had first right to revenue and the expectation was that even if some subprime mortgage holders defaulted as expected, enough would pay so that those with the highly rated securities would be paid in full. Unfortunately, when expectations are upset and people are full of uncertainty, as in 2007–09, this model does not work. When recession is added to the mix, the result is a wholesale write-down of the global market in securities.

As disastrous as this situation was, the rating agencies' real failure was something else, namely their own move into the markets. For decades Moody's and Standard & Poor's had played the role of a judge or referee, standing back from the action and making calls as necessary. They were valued for this role, which allowed them to build up reputational assets. Structured finance is only possible with the active involvement of the rating agencies in designing the financial instruments. The agencies and their ratings actually created the distinct tranches or levels of specific structured finance issues. Some of these tranches were rated AAA. Others were rated lower. Because of the complexity of the legal documentation and protection necessary for these tranches, the raters did not stand back as neutral judges as they normally do. In structured finance, the raters acted more like consultants, helping to construct the securities themselves, indicating how they would rate them if they were organized in ways that offered specific legal protection to investors.

In addition to these concerns, two major sets of issues dominate discussions about the rating agencies in the wake of the ongoing global financial crisis. The first relates to the competence of the agencies and the effectiveness of their work. The second set relates to broader, structural issues. Critics have frequently attacked the timeliness of rating downgrades, suggesting that the agencies do not use appropriate methods and fail to ask the sort of forensic questions needed to properly investigate a company. Concerns about staffing, training, and resourcing are associated with these problems. Recently and increasingly stridently, critics have attacked what are perceived to be broader, structural problems in how the agencies do business. These problems, suggest the critics, create poor incentives and undermine the quality of the work the agencies undertake.

The first of these broader structural issues is the legacy of weak competition between rating agencies as a result of the introduction of the NRSRO designation. Although several new agencies were designated NRSRO after passage of the Rating Agency Reform Act, many critics would like NRSRO status to be abolished, removing any reference to ratings in law. The view here is that weak competition has led to poor analysis, as the rating agencies have had few incentives to reinvest in their product. In this view, the revenues flowing to rating agencies are rents from a government-generated oligopoly.

Concerns about how the agencies are funded became widespread with the onset of the subprime crisis. The idea was that the "issuer pays." Although this worked for 40 years, the scandal resulted from the conflict of interest because the agencies have incentives to make their ratings less critical than they would if they were paid by investors, the ultimate users of ratings. Like NRSRO status, many critics called for an end to the issuer-pays model of rating agency funding.

A vigorous—if often poorly informed—debate about the merits of regulating rating agencies has taken place since the onset of the crisis in spring 2007. Behind the rhetoric, it is very clear that both American SEC and European Commission officials are reluctant to regulate either the analytics of the rating process itself or the business models of the major rating agencies (the issuer-pays model). In amendments to NRSRO rules announced in February 2009, the SEC enhanced required data disclosures on performance statistics and methodology, and prohibited credit analysts from fee setting and negotiation or from receiving gifts from those they rate.[14] How ratings are made and who pays for them are materially unaffected by these changes. This is also the case with the Dodd–Frank Act, 2010, which mandated further SEC reporting. The Dodd–Frank Act was the major US legislative response to the global financial crisis that started in 2007, and was led by Representative Barney Frank and Senator Chris Dodd.

Much the same can be said for European efforts. Hampered by the reality that Moody's and S&P are both headquartered in the United States, for many years rating agencies were little more than "recognized" in European states by local regulators who were free-riders on American regulatory efforts. With the Enron crisis, which led to the bankruptcy of the Texas-based energy trading firm, concerns about rating agencies grew and the International Organization of Securities Commissions (IOSCO) code of conduct was increasingly referred to in Europe as a useful form of self-regulation. With the onset of the global financial crisis European Commission officials have sought to regulate the agencies in Europe, with proposed new laws passed by the European Parliament for referral to the Council of Ministers.[15] This legislation, which is premised on local enforcement, creates a registration process like the NRSRO system, and addresses the limited issues of transparency, disclosure, and process.[16] But it does not change rating analytics or challenge the issuer-pays model of the rating business.

Despite the worst financial crisis since the 1930s and the identification of a suitable culprit in the rating agencies, the proposed regulation would be so insubstantial as to do little to alter the rating system that has been in place in the United States since 1909 and in Europe since the 1980s. Part of this can be put down perhaps to a lack of confidence on the part of regulators and politicians in the efficacy of traditional solutions to market failure. It may also recognize the palpable weakness of ostensibly heavily regulated institutions such as banks and an understanding that the financial system is, despite the rating crisis, likely to continue to move in a more market- and rating-dependent direction in future. Indeed, the rating agencies have been major beneficiaries of the US bailout program, reporting substantial returns during the crisis.[17]

The global financial crisis is a crisis at the constitutive level. It reflects a deep loss of confidence in the basic infrastructure of the capital markets. This loss of confidence is a social rather than a technical process, and tinkering with regulative rules, while tempting and politically distracting, will not address the heart of the matter. Like the

Great Depression, it seems likely that the damage done to the social relationships which underpin global finance, such as the reputational assets of the rating agencies and the trust financiers have in each other, may take many long years to rebuild and could be wiped out again by renewed crisis, perhaps stemming from sovereign debt default. It is tempting in these circumstances to prescribe a simple fix, but institutions develop over time and do not heal instantly. Encouraging institutional diversity and restraining hubris about alleged cures is advisable. For the rating agencies, attending to the relationships and the expectations that built their reputations in the first place is their best course of action. The extent of substantial change is likely to be limited. Thus, seeing the rating agencies as the brave new way forward for a market-centric form of global governance is risky, to say the least. The global financial crisis has not been kind to anyone, but it has highlighted the necessary and vital role of government in times of upheaval.

Conclusion

Ratings have become increasingly central to the regulatory system of modern capitalism and therefore to governments. Getting credit ratings "right" therefore seems vitally important to many observers. But in pursuing improvement in the rating system we need to appreciate the challenges and limits to rating. The increasingly volatile nature of markets has created a crisis in relations between the agencies and governments, which increasingly seek to monitor their performance and stimulate reform in their procedures. Given the inherent challenges in rating it must seem paradoxical that rating is growing in importance as an approach to information problems in a variety of contexts outside the financial markets. This form of governance is increasingly important in health, education, and many other commercial activities.

Credit rating agencies serve a useful purpose on most accounts in an increasingly capital market-based financial system. This form of market institutionalization is growing around the world, displacing traditional bank lending. The agencies have a good track record rating corporations and governments over extended periods of time. But the current reliance on credit rating agencies is problematic. The agencies serve narrow interests; and in times of crisis, such interests can make crises worse as they seek to exit a country or a company because of a rating downgrade. This "procyclical" quality of the agencies makes them troubling as sources of global governance. Yes, in the good times the agencies may appear to offer a neat market-based way of managing future risks. But when things go bad, as they always do eventually, are rating agencies equipped with the sort of wider responsibility and systemic regard we expect of the institutions of global governance?

Additional reading

1. Timothy J. Sinclair, *The New Masters of Capital: American Bond Rating Agencies and the Politics of Creditworthiness* (Ithaca: Cornell University Press, 2005).
2. Andrew Fight, *The Ratings Game* (New York and London: Wiley, 2000).
3. Andreas Kruck, *Private Ratings, Public Regulations: Credit Rating Agencies and Global Financial Governance* (Basingstoke: Palgrave Macmillan, 2011).

4. Herwig Langohr and Patricia Langohr, *The Rating Agencies and Their Credit Ratings: What They Are, How They Work and Why They Are Relevant* (New York and London: Wiley, 2009).
5. Frank Partnoy, "The Siskel and Ebert of Financial Markets? Two Thumbs Down for the Credit Rating Agencies," *Washington University Law Quarterly* 77, no. 3 (1999): 619–719.
6. Lena Rethel and Timothy J. Sinclair, *The Problem with Banks* (London: Zed Books, 2012).

Notes

1 Daniel Inman, "Spain Downgrade Hits Asian Shares," *Wall Street Journal*, 11 October 2012.
2 Timothy J. Sinclair, *Global Governance* (Cambridge: Polity Press, 2012), 23–24.
3 This history is based on Timothy J. Sinclair, *The New Masters of Capital: American Bond Rating Agencies and the Politics of Creditworthiness* (Ithaca: Cornell University Press, 2005).
4 Alvin Toffler, *Powershift: Knowledge, Wealth, and Violence at the Edge of the 21st Century* (New York: Bantam, 1990), 43–57.
5 Reuters, "Argentina Slams Credit Agencies for 'Terrorist' Reports," 16 October 2012, http://uk.reuters.com/article/2012/10/16/uk-argentina-ratings-minister-idUKBRE89F10 B20121016.
6 Peter Gourevitch, "Collective Action Problems in Monitoring Managers: The Enron Case as a Systemic Problem," *Economic Sociology—European Electronic Newsletter* 3, no. 3 (2002): 1 and 11.
7 Jeffrey Heisler, "Recent Research in Behavioral Finance," *Financial Markets, Institutions and Instruments* 3, no. 5 (1994): 78.
8 Frank Partnoy "The Siskel and Ebert of Financial Markets? Two Thumbs Down for the Credit Rating Agencies," *Washington University Law Quarterly* 77, no. 3 (1999): 619–719.
9 David S. Scharfstein and Jeremy C. Stein, "Herd Behavior and Investment," *American Economic Review* 80, no. 3 (1990): 465.
10 John Gerard Ruggie, *Constructing the World Polity: Essays on International Institutionalization* (New York: Routledge, 1998), 12–13.
11 Bank of England, *Financial Stability Report* (London, April 2008), 20.
12 Michael Moran, *The British Regulatory State: High Modernism and Hyper-Innovation* (Oxford: Oxford University Press, 2003), 1–11.
13 John R. Searle, *Speech Acts: An Essay in the Philosophy of Language* (Cambridge: Cambridge University Press, 1969), 33.
14 Securities and Exchange Commission, "17 CFR Parts 240, 243, and 249b Re-Proposed Rules for Nationally Recognized Statistical Rating Organizations; Amendments to Rules for Nationally Recognized Statistical Rating Organizations; Final Rule and Proposed Rule," *Federal Register* 74, no. 25 (9 February 2009): 6456–6484.
15 Commission of the European Communities, "Proposal for a Regulation of the European Parliament and of the Council on Credit Rating Agencies" (Brussels, 11 November 2008); European Parliament, Committee on Economic and Monetary Affairs, "Draft Report on the Proposal for a Regulation of the European Parliament and of the Council on Credit Rating Agencies" (Strasbourg, 13 January 2009).
16 Oliver Kessler, "Towards an Economic Sociology of the Subprime Crisis?," *Economic Sociology: The European Electronic Newsletter* 10, no. 2 (2009): 11.
17 Serena Ng and Liz Rappaport, "Raters See Windfall in Bailout Program," *Wall Street Journal*, 20 March 2009: A1.

Think Tanks and Global Policy Networks

James G. McGann

In an age when the power of a computer chip doubles at least every 18 months, when the average young adult is training for jobs that do not yet exist, and when flying halfway around the world requires less than a day, the resulting surge of new information often raises more questions than it answers. In this increasingly complex, independent, and information-rich world, governments and individual policy-makers face the common problem of bringing expert knowledge to bear in governmental decision-making. In response, although initially behind the wave of globalization, growth of public policy research organizations, or "think tanks," over the last few decades has been nothing less than explosive. Not only have these organizations increased in number, but the scope and impact of their work has also expanded dramatically at the national, regional, and global level. Twenty years ago, when the first global meeting of think tanks in Barcelona, Spain, was organized, many colleagues suggested that the term "think tank" did not travel well across borders. Today, the term is an accepted transnational concept.[1]

This chapter discusses the dramatic growth of think tanks over the last two decades and their increasing influence in global governance. Think tanks have grown not only in numbers but in diversity, with a correspondingly diverse array of definitions and opinions in the literature. However, as think tanks have developed, so too has analysis and understanding of not only their current influence, but also their future potential. Problems facing the world are increasingly complex and spread across borders, and just as it is now more difficult for one state to solve problems on its own, so too think tanks are finding that they must expand globally to further not only their own research and development but their credibility as well. As think tanks expand, they can use their knowledge to assist policy-makers and other actors who are immersed in the day-to-day affairs of governing and have less time for analysis. The progress made by think tanks around the world, as well as the challenges they face and criticisms that have been leveled at them also are discussed in greater detail.

Think tanks: a short history

Think tanks are research, analysis, and engagement institutions that generate policy advice on domestic and international issues, enabling policy-makers to make informed decisions and bridge the gap between the government and the public at large. In simpler terms, think tanks serve as "go-to" institutions when experts on particular topics are needed to provide analysis or commentary on the breaking news of the day. While these organizations are classified in one of the following categories—for-profit, autonomous and independent, quasi-independent, university affiliated, political party affiliated, quasi-governmental, or governmental—a finer line gets drawn when separating internationally oriented think tanks with a domestic focus from those that are truly global or trans-national. Being a global think tank requires many of the same features as multinational corporations, including established operational centers in two or more continents that are linked by a shared mission, programs and operations including field offices with local staff and scholars, product offerings to a global audience, and a variety of international funding sources.

International does not necessarily mean global. Many think tanks conduct research on international issues, but they are not global think tanks. To be a global institution, a think tank must operate on two or more continents and have networked global operations. Some think tanks are regional or merely transnational, meaning they operate in two or more states. When we use these parameters, there are just a dozen or so think tanks that are global and a slightly larger number that are transnational. But the numbers are growing—think tanks have finally gone global. If we count both global and transnational organizations, there are now approximately 60 think tanks that have cross-border operations.

One of the most successful think tanks to employ a truly global strategy is the International Crisis Group (ICG). The ICG has field offices around the world, staff representing 49 nationalities and 47 languages, and 50 percent of its funding coming from governments of 22 different countries. The ICG, however, is not alone in its endeavor. The Carnegie Endowment for International Peace (CEIP) has set goals and has already come a long way in terms of global operations with the opening of its fifth office in Brussels. Think tanks can go global in other ways. The Brookings Institution (BI) and RAND have operational centers outside the United States and have expanded their brands globally through the Internet, collaborative projects, and scholar exchanges. BI has made a big investment in its website since 2006, also adding select content in Arabic, Chinese, and Spanish. The impact is clear. Today, about one-third of the visitors to BI's site are from outside of the United States.

A third approach is the franchise model, where a think tank will transfer its name, strategy, structure, and philosophy to groups operating in other countries. The German political foundations have created what can be described as political party think tank franchises around the globe. Think tanks around the world are clearly globalizing, multiplying, and increasing in importance. There are currently 6,480 think tanks in the world, 57 percent of which are based in North America and Western Europe. But, this scene is dramatically changing year by year. The greatest surge in the number of think tanks being established is taking place in Asia, Africa, and the Middle East. It is important to note that while there has been significant growth in these regions, the institutional capacity, civil societies, and sources of funding remain weak and underdeveloped.

Primary reasons for the dramatic growth of think tanks around the world are democratization, globalization, and modernization. Democratization inspires demands for analysis and information independent of government influence. It also allows for a more open debate about government decision-making, which is an environment in which think tanks thrive. In addition, think tanks can no longer be armchair analysts sitting in Brussels, Paris, or Washington; they must be in country and on the ground covering events if they want to have credibility and influence on the major issues of the day. The growth of international actors and the pressures of globalization have led many think tanks to expand their operations on a global scale. Both the ICG and the CEIP cite the end of the Cold War and the emergence of United States supremacy as inspiration for going global. Others, such as Brookings and the German Marshall Fund, use modernization and advances in technology/communications to pragmatically globalize for added convenience.

The impact of this shift is still slowly being revealed among governments and the policy community, but there is undoubtedly a large potential for positive global policy impact. Global think tanks have the opportunity to provide a constructive forum for the exchange of information between key stakeholders, or a "neutral space" for debate. In a globalizing, fast-paced, information-rich world, think tanks can also provide important field research and efficient, quality responses to time-sensitive foreign policy problems. The CEIP attempts to fill this role by having offices in Moscow, Beirut, Beijing, and Brussels, each specializing in regionally important security issues. Additionally, when think tanks become global and form networks, it is more likely that they will pool their efforts and aggregate resources to accomplish these goals. Some issues, like carbon emissions, health care, and financial systems, are inherently global because they require cross-national coordination and may only take second place to domestic issues and agendas within any individual country.

Think tanks are not necessarily passive research organizations. Some have taken quite an active role when it comes to lobbying for or articulating and implementing policy in distinct areas. They are contractors, trainers, and media outlets. The International Peace Institute, for example, trains military and civilian professionals in peacekeeping strategies. Brookings' Internally Displaced Persons project, operating under the auspices of the United Nations (UN) in partnership with the London School of Economics, seeks to help populations uprooted by violent conflict and civil unrest. These examples stand in sharp contrast to the days when think tank scholars would sit in their "universities without students" and come up with great ideas, and policy-makers would beat a path to their door to seek their advice. Although there are different varieties of think tanks, their importance cannot be understated. In US foreign policy in particular, the ideas coming out of think tanks have reshaped conventional wisdom and changed the direction of strategic issues.[2]

With such a broad range of functions, the global think tank of tomorrow will continue to gain in importance. But for continued growth of this sector around the world, some key obstacles need to be overcome. First, the lack of research institutions in developing countries needs to be addressed. Building up research institutions in those areas is actually an explicit goal of BI's Africa Growth Initiative, which seeks to partner with many different African think tanks and organizations to address that very issue. Global think tanks and policy networks will all increase in utility when expansion is encouraged, a framework for knowledge transfer is provided, and independent and effective management is cultivated in these areas. There are governments that try to create what are known as "phantom think tanks," designed to appear nongovernmental when they are in fact arms of the government that are used to oppose legitimate civil society organizations. Funding also tends to exert direct or indirect influence over the research agenda of think tanks if they fail to put the policies and procedures in place to safeguard the integrity and independence of the organizations. To be truly independent, policy organizations need to have a wide variety and large number of donors so they are not beholden to government or narrow special interests.

Ultimately, global think tanks and policy networks will be crucial in helping policy-makers manage the "Four Mores" on a global scale: more issues, more actors, more competition, and more conflict. To do this, they need to master the "Four Rs": rigor, relevance, reliability, and reach (national, regional, and global). All think tanks face the need to balance academic quality research with information that is understandable and accessible to policy-makers and the public. This becomes even more critical on a larger scale. The surge and spread of global think tanks is exactly that attempt to keep up with globalization and distill avalanches of information down to manageable and understandable analyses. As different countries continue to form more global networks and closer relationships with each other, the think tanks of the future that manage to address obstacles inherent in expansion will continue to grow in both numbers and influence. They are also ideally suited to help us respond to a new trend that I would describe as policy tsunamis (economic, political, social, and health crises). These are issues and events that will appear in one region and then sweep rapidly across the globe with increasing intensity and devastating impact. The economic crisis of 2008, the Arab Spring, and SARS are examples of this new phenomenon. A global network of think tanks could track issues and events and try to understand them before they reach the crisis stage. This is the challenge we face to harness the vast reservoir of knowledge, information, and associational energy that exist in public policy research organizations in every region of the world for public good.

Past, current, and future challenges

Although both global think tanks and global policy networks have the potential to be effective agents for social change, they are faced with a series of internal and external challenges. They are plagued by inadequate funding and the need for sponsorship.

These organizations find it extremely difficult to raise funds for independent policy research, and donors often find it difficult to continue to sponsor an operation that does not produce immediate, quantifiable results. Attracting donors who do not have an immediate or direct interest in a project also proves difficult.[3] Even if funding is secured, these think tanks face the additional challenges of finding a niche in the "global marketplace of ideas" and translating the ability to gather information or consult on policy into the ability to affect or implement policy change. Once these institutions have distilled valuable ideas from the plethora of available information, they must work to get government actors and those in positions of official authority to utilize these ideas and produce results. Creating objectives and defining an agenda can be a potential complication for both think tanks and policy networks; protraction and a subsequent loss of focus are potential issues that inevitably arise due to the considerable start-up costs and the time required to produce and promote viable and visible results.[4]

Global think tanks in particular face distinctive challenges apart from funding and policy change issues. They must overcome the substantial hurdle of finding a balance between communication competencies and research competencies. Although the greatest surge in the number of think tanks being established is taking place in Asia, Africa, and Latin America, these regions face a specific set of challenges. There is a particularly acute lack of resources in developing nations, and not focusing enough on research could undermine think tank missions in such countries. Furthermore, although committing significant resources to research is important, it is also important that these institutions work to increase their visibility. Without a certain amount of legitimacy, credibility and influence is lost. Finally, it is important for global think tanks to identify competitors and avoid being insubstantial. For example, protestors often have the same mission as think tanks.[5]

Policy networks face additional unique challenges because they function in the absence of an established bureaucracy and a rigid hierarchy. Among these challenges are a lack of consensus resulting from poor communication, a poorly developed organizational structure and leadership, difficulties recruiting and retaining members, and questionable legitimacy.[6] In terms of modes of operation, policy networks often lack the intellectual and scholarly resources that many global think tanks have. Instead, they work to influence policy by attracting media attention, political patronage, and government support and resources. Furthermore, consistent commitment, especially investment in strengthening management capacity, as well as sustained monitoring from all participating members within a network, are all critical to remaining effective.

Their evolutionary nature as well as their flexible structure creates a further sense of malleability and fluidity, allowing for the entry of new players and the exit of old ones as the issues and agendas change with time.[7] Networks can be organized as "open assemblies"[8] where admission for prospective membership is quite easy to obtain, or as networks that admit members according to given criteria. Both policy networks and think tanks have significant independence and autonomy from government influence and are free to pursue their own agendas and dictate their own policy goals. However, policy networks can also arise in a different temporal context than global think tanks, taking the form of temporary "issue networks" in order to influence a very specific policy issue.

While think tanks are concerned with bringing knowledge to bear on public policy-making, policy networks are organized to mobilize stakeholders on a specific policy issue in an effort to influence the policy process and achieve policy results that are in the interests of its stakeholders. These results, however, in addition to the network as a whole, are highly contingent on the continued existence of trust amongst the network members, the level of transparency, and equitable power symmetries amongst the network members.[9] Since a defining aspect of a policy network is its adaptability and open structure, establishing and maintaining high levels of sustainable trust as new links are added and old ones are removed can be difficult.

Power asymmetries are yet another critical issue confronting policy networks, especially those that are unable to gain access to financial or other resources and are thus disadvantaged within the partnership process. Moreover, the volatility of policy networks necessitates careful and constant management and much attention in order to maintain and promote their effectiveness. Policy networks tend to be fluid by nature because they are often defined by the policy issue they coalesce around. So unless the issue is an enduring one, the network tends to dissipate after the policy objective is achieved.

Perhaps the most difficult challenges faced by both global think tanks and policy networks are producing results and measuring their impact in the public sphere. Although think tanks and policy networks certainly have political and social influence, they operate externally from existing power structures. As a result, their impact is difficult to infer. Furthermore, because policy networks and think tanks that have expanded their global functions are still in the primary phase of their development, it is very hard to measure their effectiveness and judge their influence, or lack thereof, in the policy-making process.

Implications for global public policy

What do these challenges and opportunities facing global think tanks and structurally independent public policy networks mean for the creation of truly global public policy? Global public policy essentially means public policy that incorporates opinions and analysis from actors across multiple geographical and functional orientations, draws on evidence from the locations in which policy is implemented, and provides solutions that are appropriate for the society and political structure of distinct and disparate locations. The policy problems that must absolutely be addressed in this global way include global warming and carbon emissions concerns, natural disasters recovery, health crisis responses, response to global terrorist units and threats, and now the organization of financial policy and regulatory architecture. In this sense, these problems and issues are simply so large and complex, so global in scale, that one state simply cannot hope to resolve them by itself.

A further complication arises from the fact that many issues have unique and specific effects on individual areas and regions. This fact often means that regionally tailored solutions are the ones with the highest possibility of succeeding, rather than a generalized and uniform policy that attempts to lump everything together. Subsequently, ideas and perspectives that are intricately familiar with the various processes and unique aspects of each particular area and region must be incorporated into potential solutions for these global issues. Naturally, this is a challenge that no institution, entity, or state could possibly resolve alone.

The best way to understand this phenomenon is through brief descriptions of various global think tanks that are particularly successful in utilizing the various opportunities in order to influence global policy. The underlying fact that can be extrapolated from these studies is that there is no absolute, uniform method of going global and achieving success globally. Each of the following global think tanks approaches and engages each opportunity differently, often reacting and adapting to the specific regional, cultural, or societal aspects in its particular locations. Just as there are a diverse number of global think tanks, so too are there numerous means of going global.

Arguably, the best and most powerful opportunity that is available to think tanks and policy networks in order to affect or to influence global policy is to provide important field research and up-to-the-minute information to policy-makers on critical issues or on geographically and socio-economically disparate populations. Subsequently, these organizations should focus on increasing the efficacy of response to time-sensitive policy issues. For example, the ICG was established in 1995 and is based in Brussels; it reports on conflict hot spots and proposes preventative and remedial policy solutions. It has a flexible focus that responds to the scope of current global crises. It produces *CrisisWatch*, a bulletin distributed to all interested parties, and provides up-to-the minute information on various global conflicts. Its 135 staff members on five continents provide field-based analysis, policy prescriptions, and reports that are directed at governments and inter-governmental bodies like the UN, European Union, and World Bank. ICG's sophisticated ability to gather and disseminate information, combined with a focus on high-level advocacy, provides a model for other think tanks that aim to become key players in culling and analyzing information on time-sensitive issues for global policy-makers.

Global think tanks also provide important avenues and entry-points into authoritarian countries. The Brookings Institution, for example, has established global centers in Beijing and Doha, and is especially focused on creating dialogue forums. Brookings has entered into funding or research partnerships with government agencies in both areas, signaling the institution's ability to create relationships with governments in countries where think tanks have little or no independence. Brookings' partnerships abroad help demonstrate to these countries that think tanks can provide high quality advice and act as an important bridge between governments and the public. Brookings' work is of particular importance in that it can create a better environment in which native think tanks can function; the relationships that Brookings and other institutions foster can convince policy-makers of the usefulness and importance of think tanks, thereby facilitating a more widespread acceptance of a functioning civil society governed by authoritarian regimes. These organizations can mobilize and aggregate knowledge and funding resources on global policy issues that span the jurisdiction of national governments. This is critical since there is now a growing number of policy issues that require a global response but which are often sidelined by domestic issues that dominate national policy agendas.

The Friedrich Neimann Institut für die Freiheit is a German foundation and think tank with numerous offices internationally that conduct project work and gather information on democratic transitions. This institution has an ideologically liberal leaning, and its work provides an important model for a means of bridging the space between democracy and autocracy through the provision of basic services, technical training, education, and policy design advisory. As an independent organization providing essential benefits to the local population through its project work, this global think tank perhaps avoids being pegged by the "Western imperialist" label that an international organization or government agency might receive and achieves great success in its project implementation processes. In this sense, global think tanks can function as a barometer of challenges and prospects of the least developed countries. Undertakings carried out by think tanks, by being more "unofficial," can also be more flexible and work in areas where more formal national presences are impossible. As Richard N. Haass notes, the Carnegie Endowment's work in the 1980s brought leading South African citizens together, gatherings which "helped establish the first dialogue and built understanding on South Africa's future during a delicate political transition."[10]

Carbon emissions and energy security are another area in which global think tanks can become heavily involved and assume a position of importance in affecting global policy. For example, the International Institute for Strategic Studies (IISS) is structurally independent and autonomous; IISS is a limited company in the UK and a registered charity. It has global centers in Singapore and the US. It conducts policy-oriented research and promotes dialogue on peace and security policy through an international member network. IISS performs academic research as well as a convening and dialogue-facilitating function in order to promote the provision of solutions to global security problems. IISS is notable for the expansion of its focus on traditional security and defense issues to include new issues of global importance. IISS's Transatlantic Dialogue on Climate Change and Security is a model for the way established networks can utilize their discipline-based membership toward finding solutions to global issues in new discipline areas, such as climate change. Since energy security in particular is a complex process that varies widely from area to area and often requires specific solutions for each region, IISS's structure is at least partially responsible for its success. The IISS is a prime example of how influential and successful a think tank can be if it incorporates a multitude of perspectives and knowledge sets.

Health issues are another area in which global think tanks can become heavily involved, often as a powerful voice of advocacy. The Global Alliance on Vaccination and Immunization (GAVI) is a health-based global public policy network. It was used as a model for the establishment of other health-related global public policy networks such as the Global Fund to Fight Against AIDS, Tuberculosis and Malaria, and the Global Alliance for Improved Nutrition (GAIN).[11] Likewise, the Heritage Foundation is an independent and autonomous foundation that was originally established in 1973 as an educational institute. Its conservative-leaning research agenda includes a focus on healthcare policy. Heritage is an example of a traditional think tank that includes health issues as part of its research and advocacy-based agenda, in contrast to the GAVI model of network establishment for the primary purpose of bringing stakeholders together to address health issues.

Global think tanks can also exert influence over financial architecture and the reform of international organizations. The Center for Financial Studies is a German think tank with a global network of researchers and members. As one of the only global think tanks with a focus on financial innovation and financial regulatory policy, it performs a much-needed research and dialogue function in the area of global finance. In the area of international organization, the Center on International Cooperation is a public policy research institution affiliated with New York University that focuses on enhancing international responses to humanitarian crises and global security threats. The CIC specifically targets multilateral organizations and focuses on UN reform in order to improve post-conflict peacebuilding processes and the functioning of global peacekeeping operations. Conversely, the Friedrich Ebert Stiftung (FES) is quasi-governmental but calls itself a private foundation. Its research priorities include globalization processes, public sector reform, the European Union, democratic development and civic society, social politics in Germany and Europe, international politics, conflict management, and UN reform. The reform focus is only one part of FES's many capabilities. It has over 85 offices worldwide and conducts projects with partners in over 100 countries. FES's global reach contributes to the strength of its advocacy activities.

By providing a constructive forum for the exchange of information and negotiations between key stakeholders, think tanks can create a "neutral space."[12] As independent, non-partisan organizations, think tanks provide a "neutral space" for public policy discussion by organizing seminars, workshops, and conferences where research findings are presented to the wider community and where key experts discuss current policy issues. For example, the Aspen Institute is an independent, non-partisan institute that believes the development of good leadership values and open-minded dialogue will lead to better policy decisions. Aspen is governed by a large board of trustees consisting of 69 members. Its mission is to "foster values-based leadership, encouraging individuals to reflect on the ideals and ideas that define a good society, and to provide a neutral and balanced venue for discussing and acting on critical issues." The Aspen Seminar, the main executive seminar promoting choices for a good society, is the Institute's main method of providing a "neutral space" for public policy discussion. The promotion of dialogue is obviously important as it can lead to greater policy innovation; it also creates an opportunity for policy-makers to intermingle with these institutions, thereby increasing the chances that the civil society sector can become involved in the overall policy-making process.

Networks and think tanks have several unique qualities and functions that distinguish them from other civil society organizations and entities. Networks have "boundary transcending" qualities that allow them to act as mediators.[13] In this sense, they can articulate policy to the policy-makers and the public. Networks can place issues of global importance on the agenda and demand accountability from formal government structures. Global policy networks facilitate the transfer and use of knowledge in the public sphere, preventing a monopoly of information on policy on the part of the government. As discussed earlier, think tanks can do so as well, but the inherent nature of networks, specifically their ability to incorporate an extremely wide array of perspectives, voices, and actors, strongly lends itself to this function. Conversely, a very specialized function that think tanks can perform at the global level is the translation of international governance codes and laws for domestic applicability (World Bank, World Trade Organization, etc.).[14] In other words, these organizations can interpret, analyze, and then adapt the various details of the international codes and laws to fit the specific contexts in which they must operate at the national or legal level.

Criticisms of think tanks

As think tanks and their influence have expanded globally, there has been increased examination of their effectiveness and impact. Perhaps the most difficult aspect of a think tank is measuring its impact in the world and determining how effective think tanks truly are. The most recent decades have seen a dramatic rise in policy paralysis at the government level, and a criticism has developed which maintains that think tanks have become part of the problem instead of the solution, that decreasing general operating support, the rise of specialized think tanks, project-specific funding, and a narrowing set of policy options have led think tanks to support the status quo and not challenge conventional wisdom by providing alternative policy proposals.

One illustration is the policy gridlock that has increasingly gripped Washington. As the number of think tanks has expanded, the American think tank domain in particular has developed increasing levels of politicization. Robert K. Landers believes that the influence of politics on the think tank domain has led to a new breed of think tank, unabashedly partisan and ideological, with an emphasis on "spinning" information instead of producing original research or mediating discussion and debate. Several scholars have asked if the think tank model is broken, maintaining that the value of academic freedom is disappearing at all levels of the organizational structure of think tanks. It remains to be seen, however, if such politicization has created overly partisan organizations and denatured the traditional institutional form of a think tank so much that academic integrity is compromised. There is much variety in the think tank sphere, with several prominent institutions focusing substantial resources on moderating debate and promoting detailed analysis of issues. One such example is the Woodrow Wilson Center in Washington, where scholars research topics of national importance and engage in global outreach through public meetings and events, all with an aim of increasing bipartisan cooperation.

The key question is, "What works?" The complexity of international issues, their overlapping nature, and the turmoil of the arena in which they surface make theorizing more challenging, as there are many points of view and interests to be reconciled, shifting politics, and uncertainties about the efficacies of different policy alternatives. Think tanks have the potential to help policy-makers and the public meet those challenges because of their unique role in the policy-making process and their capacity to engage in interdisciplinary, policy-oriented research. Politicization and gridlock are serious issues in governmental institutions both in Europe and the United States, but think tanks can be outside of these issues and work to move policy-making forward. They can indeed be part of the solution.

Conclusion

Democratization, globalization, and modernization have led to a concern with global governance; so too have these forces contributed to the dramatic growth of think tanks as non-state actors playing an increasingly influential role in international affairs.

Think tanks bridge the gap between academics and policy-makers, generating policy advice and developing new ideas for governance. They illustrate the influence and potential of non-state actors in global governance, along with such challenges inherent in global expansion as adapting to different national and cultural contexts.

They demonstrate that in an increasingly connected world states cannot solve problems alone and should call upon a wide variety of sources for research, analysis, and counsel. A disease, natural disaster, or conflict can easily spill over borders and require various groups to come together to deal with it. In the same way, think tanks and policy networks are going global. To be considered a leading institution, think tanks can no longer only have offices in Washington or Brussels but must increasingly move to put experts on the ground in various regions and build their global presence. Think tanks operating in certain contexts may benefit from a legitimacy that a government lacks; indeed, they often are considered more reliable sources for information and analysis. This is largely because of their perceived independence. Independence is both crucial to a think tank's legitimacy and difficult to maintain, as it is directly connected to funding, both how much is received and from which sources. Sustainable funding permitting autonomous operations is a serious challenge, particularly in developing nations, where opportunities for funding are less available and more likely to come from less diversified sources.

As think tanks proliferate and increase in strength and influence on the world stage, a key challenge is to measure their effectiveness and impact. As political gridlock deepens, some scholars have called into question the effectiveness of think tanks, stating that they are part of the problem because many organizations are moving away from analysis and towards "spinning" information to lobby for their own interests and the interests of their donors. This result reflects the increasing number of think tanks and policy networks that are moving away from the traditional passive image towards active lobbying for or articulation and implementation of policy.

This chapter has demonstrated how think tanks have played a valuable role in helping to address issues as disparate as democratic transitions, environmental collapses, global health, and financial issues. With no decrease in sight of issues, actors, competition, and conflict, global think tanks and policy networks will be increasingly relevant to helping policy-makers manage a changing world often with a surfeit of information. As an unusual type of non-state actor, their comparative advantage lies in moderating debate, generating advice, and influencing policy-makers. In short, they have a specific, significant, and positive role to play in global knowledge governance. Their reservoir of knowledge, information, and networked energy could, if harnessed properly, have a significant effect on the public good.

Additional reading

1. Ann Florini, "Is Global Civil Society a Good Thing?," *New Perspectives Quarterly* 21, no. 2 (March 2004): 72–76.
2. Richard Haass and James G. McGann, "The Role of Think Tanks in US Foreign Policy," *US Foreign Policy Agenda* 7, no. 3 (November 2002), http://guangzhou.usembassy-china.org.cn/uploads/images/QHgRpr9Ar-KtqbselUI05Q/ijpe1102.pdf <http://guangzhou.usembassy-china.org.cn/uploads/images/QHgRpr9Ar-KtqbselUI05Q/ijpe1102.pdf>.
3. Eric Johnson and James G. McGann, *Comparative Think Tanks, Politics, and Public Policy* (Cheltenham: Edward Elgar, 2005).

4. James G. McGann, *Think Tanks and Policy Advice in the US: Academics, Advisors, and Advocates* (London: Routledge, 2007).

5. Kerstin Martens, "Mission Impossible? Defining Nongovernmental Organizations," *Voluntas: International Journal of Voluntary and Nonprofit Organizations* 13, no. 2 (September 2002): 271–285.

Notes

1 Richard N. Haass, "Think Tanks and the Transnationalization of Foreign Policy," in "The Role of Think Tanks in U.S. Foreign Policy," A Journal of the US Department of State, *U.S. Foreign Policy Agenda* 7, no. 3 (November 2002): 5–8.

2 Ronald D. Asmus, quoted in Richard N. Haass and James G. McGann, "The Role of Think Tanks in US Foreign Policy," *U.S. Foreign Policy Agenda* 7, no. 3 (November 2002), http://www.scribd.com/doc/3210628/the-role-of-think-tank-in-us-foreign-policy.

3 Diana Stone, "Knowledge Networks and Global Policy," paper presented to the CEEISA/ISA conference, Central European University in Budapest, Hungary, 28 June 2003, http://www2.warwick.ac.uk/fac/soc/csgr/research/keytopic/other/RIS_Network.pdf/. For funding opportunities, see Julie Kosterlitz, "Going Global," *National Journal* (29 September 2007): 67; Jan Martin Witte, Wolfgang H. Reinicke, and Thorsten Benner, "Global Public Policy Networks: Lessons Learned and Challenges Ahead," *Brookings Review* 21 (2003): 18–21.

4 Raymond J. Struyk, "Management of Transnational Think Tank Networks," *International Journal of Politics, Culture, and Society* 15, no. 4 (2002): 625–638.

5 James G. McGann, "The Global Go-To Think Tanks: What Works Where?," Overseas Development Institute (ODI), 10 March 2009.

6 For an excellent analysis of legitimacy and funding challenges for policy networks, see Struyk, "Management of Transnational Think Tank Networks." For a discussion about establishing leadership and legitimacy, see Stella Theodoulous, *Policy and Politics in Six Nations: A Comparative Perspective on Policy Making* (New Delhi: Pearson, 2007).

7 Charlotte Streck, *The Role of Global Public Policy Networks in Supporting Institutions: Implications for Sustainable Development*, Institute for International and European Environmental Policy, http://www.agro-montpellier.fr/sustra/research_themes/global_governance/papers/Charlotte_Streck.pdf.

8 Struyk, "Management of Transnational Think Tank Networks," 627.

9 Streck, *The Role of Global Public Policy Networks.*

10 Richard N. Haass, "Think Tanks and the Transnationalization of Foreign Policy."

11 Diana Stone, "Transfer Agents and Global Networks in the 'Transnationalization' of Policy," *Journal of European Public Policy* 11, no. 3 (2004): 560.

12 David M. Malone and Heiko Nitzschke, "Think Tanks and the United Nations," *Magazine for Development and Cooperation* (January 2004).

13 Stone, "Knowledge Networks and Global Policy," 13.

14 Diana Stone, "Think Tanks and Policy Advice in Countries in Transition," discussion paper for the How to Strengthen Policy-Oriented Research and Training in Viet Nam, Asian Development Bank Institute Symposium, 31 August 2005, http://www.adbi.org/files/2005.09.dp36.think.tanks.jfppt.pdf.

CONTENTS

Global Philanthropy

Michael Moran

The Rockefeller Foundation, established a century ago, was one of the earliest modern non-state actors to exert its influence on the institutional structures that emerged in the early to mid-twentieth century to govern international development. Its material resources and deep and extensive networks into domestic and international politics, among other factors, made it one of the most formidable players in the development of the nascent international aid architecture. While there are now some 76,000 grant-making founda-tions registered in the United States, an expanding sector in Europe, and embryonic but growing development in East Asia, the number of foundations with substantive international activities is comparatively small. They remain dwarfed in numbers by transnational corporations, international nongovernmental organizations (INGOs), and the resources of official development assistance agencies and international organizations. Still, actors such as the Bill and Melinda Gates Foundation (hereafter the Gates Founda-tion), as with the Rockefeller and the Ford Foundations before it, while lacking formal authority (and legitimacy), can command enormous influence by virtue of their material resources and role in nurturing, developing, structuring, and shaping international public policy networks. At the same time, new types of philanthropic actors, for example the Acumen Fund, are emerging, bringing with them a distinctive focus on cultivating social enterprise.

There has been a perceptible shift in the global governance of development—or what has been described as the "philanthro-capitalist" turn. Controversially this has led to creeping marketization of philanthropy but it also reveals tensions that have long accompanied "big" philanthropy: the power of the wealthy to shape public policy; concerns regarding the accountability and legitimacy of private actors; and the type of development interventions favored by foundations, which, according to some critics, have tended toward the top-down and technical (and more recently the market oriented) at the expense of the social and the political. These tensions have resurfaced in recent years,

BOX 27.1 WHAT ARE PRIVATE FOUNDATIONS?

Private foundations are the most common institutional manifestations of philanthropy and remain the principal philanthropic actors within global governance. While the term varies across different regions, a private foundation is defined by five features: (1) nonprofit and nongovernmental status; (2) tax exemption; (3) a board of trustees/directors; (4) an endowment and/or fund capitalized by a single individual, institution, or family; and (5) distribution of funds, principally through grants, for charitable, educational, or religious purposes.[1] In the US they are registered as tax-exempt organizations under 501(c)(3) of the tax code and precluded by the Internal Revenue Service from directly operating programs or undertaking service delivery. Instead they act as *intermediaries* between their funders (individual and/or institutional) and recipients (usually but not exclusively nonprofits and state agencies) in an attempt to obtain charitable goals as set down in the trust deed.

How much do they give?

Despite an increasingly high profile, giving by foundations both from the US and Europe remains primarily domestically focused. The numbers, however, are not small and are growing. In 2008 US foundation giving reached $7bn, before contracting to $6.7bn in 2009 with the onset of the recession, which led to a 4 percent reduction in international giving. Although if Gates was removed from the data set giving would have contracted by 9 percent, international giving has nonetheless increased from less than 15 percent of total grant dollars in 2002 to 22 percent in 2006, before reaching 24.4 percent in 2009.[2]

with the ever-present Gates Foundation extending its webs of influence and the so-called "new philanthropy" altering the dynamics of the international development landscape.

This chapter begins by charting the activities of foundations in the interwar era through to the present via an examination of areas in which private foundations have been most active. The subsequent section examines key criticisms and controversies before the chapter moves to providing a brief overview of emerging issues and future trends in global philanthropy.

Private foundations: from international organization to global governance

Foundations surfaced in the late nineteenth and early twentieth centuries during what was known in the United States as the "Progressive Era," and were by and large a product of the country's rapid industrialization and emergence as a center of production, consumption, and population growth. The American tradition was driven by wealthy businessmen, known popularly as the "Robber Barons," who were encouraged by Scottish-born industrialist Andrew Carnegie to distinguish their giving from charity. They argued that conventional charity was ameliorative, while philanthropy should tackle the root causes of deprivation. This was premised on a belief that scientific reason would fuel progress, and rationality became "the guiding principle for grant-making once new foundations were chartered."[3] The term *scientific philanthropy* was coined to describe this philosophy, which fused with a range of concurrent ideas, including the liberal internationalism espoused by President Woodrow Wilson, the positivism of the Progressive Era, established American Protestant and Calvinist beliefs, and the associated emphasis on self-help and self-reliance.

Notwithstanding the domestic orientation of many foundations, they emerged as some of the most important international actors of this period. Indeed prior to the emergence of official development assistance as a mainstream function of foreign policy of the industrialized states and the establishment of the major international organizations, foundations were some of the most well-resourced and influential actors in international affairs. This was particularly pronounced in the first decades of the twentieth century, in which the United States exhibited an isolationist approach to foreign policy.

Public health was the first area in which foundations became significant players internationally. The focus on health can be traced to the early programs of the Rockefeller Foundation that had three major components. First, the Foundation played a significant role in the development of *medical education and physician training*. Its programs began in the United States with, among other things, the creation of medical schools, including the fledging Johns Hopkins University, which was used as a laboratory for "transforming medicine through a closer association with science."[4] In 1914 the focus was extended to China, with the founding of the China Medical Board and the Peking University Medical College, the objective of which was to extend Western-style medical education and disseminate Western approaches to public health into the developing world.

Second, the Rockefeller Foundation sought to combat *communicable diseases*, "single-handedly creat[ing] American tropical medicine research"[5] by confronting three diseases in consecutive order: hookworm, yellow fever, and malaria. The hookworm program began first and grew out of the work of the Rockefeller Sanitary Commission in the United States, and was initially extended to Mexico. The Foundation then instigated a yellow fever campaign that expanded the Foundation's reach into South America and then Africa, ending in the development of a vaccine. Finally attention was turned to malaria and to the eventual eradication of the disease in many regions of the world.

Third, the foundation played a seminal role in the early expansion of the international health architecture, providing substantial financial and in-kind support for the League of Nations Health Organization (LNHO) and backing for its successor, the World Health Organization (WHO). The foundation contributed almost half the LNHO's fiscal needs, while also giving technical assistance and making "its own staff available for special purposes."[6] While not a model of success due to its short-lived mandate, Rockefeller's support for a nascent international institution—the LNHO—played a vital role in linking weak domestic health systems with rapidly improving international standards.[7]

Similar approaches were replicated in agriculture in perhaps the most celebrated (and controversial) foundation-initiated project, the "Green Revolution." Like public health this also began as an intervention in the nearest and strategically significant southern neighbor, Mexico, and in a context of strained interstate relations between the two countries. Acting at the request of the US government, concerned that shortfalls in staple crops were causing food shortages, which was in turn leading to political and social instability, the Rockefeller Foundation, in direct partnership with the Mexican government, instigated a program to develop high yield varieties. The objective was to replicate the advances that had occurred in industrialized states in staple crops, notably wheat, by using a combination of inorganic pesticides, fertilizers, and selective plant breeding to increase yields per hectare. To achieve this goal Rockefeller created the Office of Special Studies within the Mexican Ministry of Agriculture; established experimental stations across the country; and trained agricultural scientists, with a series of scholarships, training facilities, and international exchanges to transfer Western scientific knowledge to newly industrializing Mexico.

The program was perceived by its supporters to be a success. Mexico went from being a net importer of wheat in the early 1940s to a net exporter within less than a generation, despite a dramatic increase in population.[8] Efforts were made to replicate the program in other national contexts, including Colombia, Chile, India, and the Philippines, in partnership with the Ford Foundation. In 1960, Rockefeller and Ford collaborated with the Filipino government to establish the International Rice

BOX 27.2 FOUNDATIONS AND INTERNATIONAL RELATIONS THEORY

Foundations not only played a role in international relations, they have also played a part in the development of international relations theory, providing significant individual and institutional support to scholars and fostering research communities. The Ford Foundation, for example, is acknowledged as one of the chief protagonists in the shift toward behavioralism in American political science that began in the 1950s. While this did not initially emerge as the dominant mode of inquiry in IR, it had later ramifications with the drift of rationalism and public choice into American IR. In contrast, the Rockefeller Foundation, under the leadership of Kenneth Thompson, a classical realist scholar and student of Hans Morgenthau, took a different tack, favoring realism and "theory" over the new empirics. To this end the Rockefeller Foundation in 1954 organized the apparently shambolic but nonetheless influential Conference on International Politics. In attendance were luminaries including Hans Morgenthau, Reinhold Niebuhr, Paul H. Nitze, Walter Lippman, and Arnold Wolfers; a young Kenneth Waltz was note taker. While the conference did not achieve its ambitious aims, Guilhot credits Thompson as central in establishing his mentor Morgenthau as a key figure in the emerging field as well as in IR's (and realism's) ascendency in the post-war era as a discipline distinct from the more empiricist political science.[9] On the other side of the Atlantic, Rockefeller also funded the British Committee on International Relations, whose members included, among others, Herbert Butterfield, Martin Wight, and Hedley Bull, laying the basis for the English School of IR.

Research Institute. The chief objective was to apply rapidly evolving gene technologies to the Asian region,[10] which was expected to reach a state of food crisis by the mid-1960s, with widespread famine predicted should productivity not improve. The broader intervention was therefore framed as an "emergency" and was extended to the Indian subcontinent, which had experienced famine with increasing frequency, to the point that some commentators now, somewhat ominously, saw it as a "natural" product of "population pressure."[11] The early successes in Mexico were repeated and, at least in aggregate terms, the project's extension to Asia succeeded in dramatically lifting food production, although this was not evenly spread.

Although technical, the programs nonetheless required significant inter-agency coordination and were as much a suite of agricultural development policies as an apolitical project designed to enhance agricultural productivity. After developing these *national* programs, concurrently with the project's spread into Asia, Rockefeller and Ford *internationalized* the Green Revolution and, in partnership with governmental and intergovernmental bodies, established the Centro Internacional de Mejoramiento de Maíz y Trigo, and the umbrella Consultative Group on International Agricultural Research, which formed the backbone of a global network of agricultural research institutes. This international architecture remains operational today and continues to be the primary institutional hub for agricultural research across the global South, a lasting legacy of foundation activity.

Foundations in global governance: advocacy networks and public–private partnerships

Congressional scrutiny, shifting granting priorities, and global recession had an adverse impact on endowments and led foundations to enter a period of relative caution in their international activities in the 1970s. The international system was also radically changed. New state, intergovernmental, and non-state actors, for example the United States Agency for International Development (USAID), the international finance institutions such as the World Bank, and development NGOs, had emerged as important players and the relative importance of the major foundations waned. Additionally international philanthropy remained a comparatively small component of the otherwise rapidly growing development finance mix. For instance, in 1982, international grants comprised less than 5 percent of all US foundation grants, with international philanthropy dominated by Rockefeller and Ford, whose grants between 1975 and 1995 comprised almost half of all grants given by the largest 50 foundations.[12] Nonetheless, with the rise of new foundations in the 1990s from the burgeoning technology and finance industries, the sector began to diversify.

With the Green Revolution under way and supported by the Consultative Group on International Agricultural Research network, the Ford Foundation moved away from agriculture. Building on earlier support for the civil rights and new social movements of 1960s America, which had attracted some controversy from conservatives as well as the Ford family, in the 1970s the Foundation shifted its focus to civil society development and democratization abroad, a process which began with funding of human rights organizations in Latin America. After employees in its social science program identified threats to academic freedom from authoritarian regimes, they managed, despite resistance from USAID and some internal wrangling, to engender a shift toward funding "activist human rights groups" and dissidents.[13]

This acted as a catalyst for the dissemination of human rights norms throughout Latin America and by the 1980s the Foundation's influence extended across the whole gamut of transnational human rights networks: from anti-apartheid to women's rights. Ultimately Ford became "the principal funder of almost all major human-rights" NGOs, including Helsinki Watch, the forerunner to Human Rights Watch.[14] The Foundation was therefore integral in financing what Margaret Keck and Kathryn Sikkink would later term "transnational advocacy networks"—intrinsically economical, albeit powerful, modes of political advocacy, but nonetheless modes of actions in which the primary non-state actors—international and domestic NGOs and social movements—are often dependent on external funding. Foundations, particularly MacArthur and Ford, performed an integral pecuniary function in this respect.

While the Rockefeller Foundation's priorities also became increasingly diverse, perhaps its most important contribution to global governance occurred in the 1990s, with Rockefeller acting as a catalyst for the development of global health partnerships. Specifically it became one of the central players behind product development partnerships (PDPs) for tackling neglected and communicable diseases that disproportionately impact poor communities in the global South. From the 1970s onwards Rockefeller remained one of the few funders of basic research into such diseases, as rich country governments as well as the transnational pharmaceutical companies that had become integral players in the political economy of drug development shifted funding toward diseases of lifestyle, such as diabetes and cancer, predominantly affecting the rich world. By the late 1980s the dearth of funding for tropical diseases such as malaria through to neglected diseases such as dengue fever was at crisis level. In response Rockefeller, along with a range of other players in the emerging global health community—who coalesced around a range of NGOs and international organizations, including the WHO, the World Bank, Médecins Sans Frontières, the International Federation of Pharmaceutical Manufacturers and Associations, as well various European and North American official development assistance agencies—determined that new institutional and policy responses were required to tackle the crisis and both stimulate research and development (R&D) into these diseases as well as develop financing mechanisms to ensure their distribution to those in need.

Work toward this was facilitated by a number of critical meetings at Rockefeller's Bellagio Center in Northern Italy, as well as in New York, during which the Foundation and its partners focused on tackling the lack of support for an HIV/AIDS vaccine.[15] What emerged was the International AIDS Vaccine Initiative, which became one of the first PDPs to bring together public, civic, and private actors in a partnership to incentivize pro-poor product development. Between 1994 and 2000 the Foundation provided seed funding and in-kind support to incubate a further four global health partnerships, including the Global Alliance for TB Drug Development (TB Alliance), the International Partnership for Microbicides, the Pediatric Dengue Vaccine Initiative, and the Centre for the Management of Intellectual Property in Health R&D, as well as lent its support to the Global Call to Stop Cervical Cancer. While the success of PDPs has been mixed, they nonetheless played a role in reshaping global governance and show how foundations can act as important players in influencing policy outcomes.

Yet, while Rockefeller punched above its weight, as it no longer commanded the resources of earlier epochs, the most influential philanthropic actor in contemporary global health is, without doubt, the Gates Foundation—a private actor whose material influence remains unparalleled in global governance. The emergence of the Gates Foundation has been as rapid as it has been transformational, but its rise also coincided with global health partnerships, to which it quickly attached itself in the early 2000s. Following the lead of its intellectual and institutional antecedent, the Rockefeller Foundation, Gates became the major funder of almost all PDPs.

Nonetheless, the grants with perhaps the most far-reaching implications for global health governance have been the Foundation's $750m to launch the GAVI Alliance in 2000 and an equal commitment in 2002 for the Global Fund to Fight AIDS, Tuberculosis and Malaria (hereafter the Global Fund). GAVI is a health partnership that brings together the major bilateral donors, recipient countries, the WHO, the World Bank, UNICEF, the pharmaceutical industry, and Gates, in a multi-sectoral partnership to finance and facilitate vaccine coverage—for example diphtheria, hepatitis B, and yellow fever, etc.—to the poorest regions of the globe. It was established as a response to the diminishing effectiveness of earlier multilateral initiatives and the abrupt arrival of Gates funds. The Global Fund brings together these same actors with a focus on extending prevention and treatment for the big three communicable diseases: AIDS, tuberculosis, and malaria. Since they were established the two partnerships have emerged as critical players in the governance of global health, and along with the Gates Foundation are part of the informal grouping, the Health 8, in which they, along with the health-related international organizations (World Bank, WHO, UNAIDS, etc.), meet to lobby for, and coordinate, global health aid.

There are three noteworthy features of these funds that illustrate the behaviors of foundations as transnational actors as well as wider shifts within global governance. First, while they retain the trappings of conventional international organizations, including a large staff, secretariat, and regionally based offices, they are not considered institutions, but public–private partnerships that sit outside intergovernmental structures and, although intertwined, outside the UN system. This organizational structure has been adopted to differentiate them from existing UN bodies seen as bound by bureaucratic inertia and institutional inefficiencies. Second, in contrast to most international organizations, with a few notable exceptions, such as the International Labour Organization, they operate a hybrid-governance framework that vests significant decision-making power in private actors, most notably the Gates Foundation, which alone has a renewable seat alongside traditional international organizations such as the WHO, as well as on advisory committees. Third, there is a strong emphasis on emulating private sector approaches and, according to GAVI's mission, acting as a "businesslike partnership for health aid." These three attributes are innately connected to the Foundation's initial provision of philanthropic risk capital that seeded the partnership, with its continuing support reaffirmed in mid-2011 when the Gates Foundation committed another $1bn, bringing its total commitment to $2.5bn to the GAVI and $1.4bn to the Global Fund.

Controversies and criticisms

Despite its benevolent meaning—from the Greek "love of humankind"—philanthropy is not without controversy. In the field of international relations in particular, philanthropy has been the subject of periodic scrutiny that spikes during periods in which foundation influence is seen as significant, or indeed excessive. The main critiques can usefully be discussed under three headings: Northern dominance; legitimacy and accountability; and technical and market orientation.

"Billanthropy," soft power, and Northern influence

Philanthropy is an act that virtually everyone participates in, whether it takes the form of volunteering or cash donations to charitable causes. Yet few have the resources to influence public policy, let alone international public policy. Unsurprisingly, then, perhaps the most frequent and enduring criticism pertains to the perception that philanthropy accords some institutions—and individuals—undue and sometimes unchecked power.

Recently these concerns have been underlined by the growth of "Billanthropy" or "philanthro-capitalism" and the rise of a generation of often highly engaged billionaire philanthropists who have scaled up their philanthropic activities. Examples range from financier George Soros' extensive network of civil society-building organizations through the Open Society Institutes to the influence that Bill, Melinda, Bill Sr., and Warren Buffett exert through the comparatively lean governing board that comprises the Gates Foundation. While few question the humanitarian intention behind these efforts, there is concern among some commentators that big philanthropy can accord a select group agenda-setting power in international public policy that is at worst inconsistent with democratic values or at best contra to participative policy processes.[16]

These are not new arguments. Taking a cue from the work of Antonio Gramsci, scholars have long linked this exercise of elite power with the consolidation of hegemony. Interventions, such as the Green Revolution were, for example, viewed by critics within the context of the Cold War, with some seeing foundations as acting as a surrogate or proxy for the US government. They argued that a loose, although at times strained, interest-alliance emerged in which foundations played a role in limiting the attractiveness of collectivist ideas.[17] These interventions, it is asserted, assisted in shoring up capitalism as well extending US "soft power" and nurturing a favorable image for the ascendant hegemon.

More recent, albeit more muted, criticisms have focused on foundations' role in the continuing dominance of the health architecture by the global North. Recently, for example, the Gates Foundation's grant-making practices have been scrutinized. McCoy et al. have identified an apparent bias to North American and European-based research institutes, international organizations and INGOs, as well as increasingly Northern-based and dominated public–private partnerships.[18] Whether intended or not—indeed grant-making may reproduce geographies of wealth and the location of development institutions and the scientific research infrastructure in the global North—grant-making patterns of foundations do appear to exhibit an intrinsic bias for actors who share foundations' geographic origin as well as their interests and preferences.

Legitimacy and accountability

Underlying these concerns is another common criticism, namely that foundations suffer from a legitimacy deficit and lack adequate accountability. As with other private actors, foundations lack the claim to legitimacy that democratic states derive from electoral processes as well as the periodic accountability of the ballot box. International organizations, also the subject of anxiety associated with a perceived democratic deficit, nonetheless derive some forms of legitimacy from a type of "popular sovereignty" delegated to them by member states and are, in theory, accountable to their members through voting mechanisms and budgetary allocations. Even firms are accountable to their stockholders when public-listed and also subject to the discipline of market forces, which acts as a constraint on their behavior, as well as remaining targets for public scrutiny when they partake in activities seen to exert influence on international public policy. These act as an, albeit imperfect and limited, check on their power. INGOs are also occasionally seen as lacking legitimacy but remain accountable to their donors (including individuals, foundations, and states) and can derive legitimacy from their loose association with social movements and civil society when they are community driven, grassroots, and participative.

The perceived legitimacy deficit of foundations is compounded by the existence of a perpetual endowment—or with a limited-life foundation a defined but generally very large pool of capital—that relieves foundations of the financial pressures that affect and check other actors in global governance. Moreover, philanthropists almost always acquire a tax benefit from their donations, which means that their capital is in effect public monies as it is forgone taxation. Therefore foundations have an obligation for both accountable and transparent use of funds.

Technical and market-oriented interventions

Another criticism that is often leveled at foundations pertains to their approach to development activities, which are seen by some critics to be overly technical in focus, top-down in orientation, and, increasingly, market oriented. The technical focus is generally portrayed as a legacy of philanthropy's emergence in the Progressive Era when confidence in the ability for science to resolve complex social problems was at a high point. Despite foundations gradually moving toward more participatory approaches in line with broader trends in development assistance, the tradition has remained fairly resilient. The public–private partnerships referenced above are a case in point. They operate as what are known in development policy-making circles as *vertical funds*, with a focus on attainment of narrow sectoral goals. Health partnerships, for instance, are often disease-specific, highly targeted funding mechanisms, with tightly measurable objectives. This contrasts with *horizontal* health financing, in which aid is channeled directly through primary-care systems. Critics assert that global health partnerships do not always focus sufficiently on strengthening health systems or on building local capacity. These criticisms are extended to other like modalities, for example in agriculture, which are also seen to be overly technical and to be operating in a relative social and political vacuum.

More pointed criticism concerns two levels of the increasing market orientation of the major foundation-financed projects with relevance for global governance.[19] At the

BOX 27.3 THE NEW GLOBAL PHILANTHROPY

Recent times have seen a perceptible marketization and internationalization of philanthropy. New organizational types, modes of, and vehicles for philanthropy, as well as new philanthropists, from celebrities such as U2's Bono through to former politicians such as Bill Clinton, have emerged as key actors in development finance. These changes have affected the major foundations, which have, to varying degrees, both adapted to and at times driven these sectoral shifts. Nonetheless, the most significant developments are occurring among hybrid entities, primarily with linkages to the technology sector in California's Silicon Valley and, to a lesser extent, global finance.

New organizational types

New funders have emerged that are perceived to be more reflexive actors defined by an emphasis on technology, flexibility, entrepreneurialism, and the flat organizational structures that define managerialism.[20] Often they select former private sector employees over nonprofit managers in leadership roles (not just as trustees); have a heavy focus on evaluation, particularly quantitative-based metrics, such as social return on investment; deploy alternative investment strategies, that utilize the endowment corpus for debt and equity investments, and are high engagement, preferring deep and augmented, rather than shallow and passive, interaction with grantees (or so-called "investees"). Foundations, for example the Skoll Foundation, funded by former eBay CEO Jeff Skoll, and venture philanthropy funds, such as the Acumen Fund, are exemplars of this organizational type.

What they fund

These organizations channel resources toward developing social entrepreneurship and functional forms, such as social enterprise; extending the sectoral blending that characterizes more traditional partnerships, while blurring the increasingly fuzzy lines between nonprofit and for-profit models. Early examples include microfinance schemes, originally developed by Muhammad Yunus, which extend financial services, principally credit, to individuals and firms that struggle accessing capital. Although an established poverty reduction tool, supported by traditional foundations such as Ford, which was an early backer of Yunus, foundations and philanthropists increasingly invest in large microfinance funds, which mediate capital from rich world investors to developing world borrowers. At the other end of the scale are peer-to-peer lending organizations, for example Kiva.org, which facilitates direct small-scale lending between individuals, usually in the rich world, to other individuals, usually in the developing world.

Other examples include the proliferation of activity at the base of the pyramid (BoP) by social venture funds. Although heavily contested, the BoP concept posits that there is a largely untapped market among the world's 2.5 billion poorest people who subsist on less than $2 a day and are overlooked by mainstream firms. Instead of tackling poverty

continued

through, for example, providing cash grants for the construction of a water well, social venture funds, such as the Acumen Fund or Root Capital, finance businesses that provide essential products and services—housing, clean water, health care, etc.—to the poor. Essentially these funds, often seeded with philanthropic capital by the major foundations, invest in organizations in which the risk is perceived as too high and the return too low by traditional bank lenders. This is part of a broader shift from the provision of grants with no expected return, to the use of debt and equity investments, in which return is generally below that which would normally be expected or market related, but in which investors receive a compensatory social return. This is known as impact investing and is emerging as a popular mechanism for philanthropy among both individual and institutional philanthropists.

organizational level, the private sector disposition of funders is said to extend across to the institutional culture of organs established by foundations. From this perspective, a results orientation, a focus on performance measurement, and a businesslike disposition are seen as a donor-driven process. At the broader structural or system level this is seen as advancing an, albeit moderated, form of neoliberal global governance. Evidence can be found in the prevalence of market mechanisms for financing public goods such as vaccines through, for example, the GAVI Alliance or emulating private sector practices for product development in PDPs.

Are these criticisms warranted?

Despite well-founded concerns, there is a tendency in some accounts to overstate foundation power. First, foundations as actors in global governance are characterized by clear structural limitations that are often overlooked. Grant-makers are legally precluded from delivering programs, which renders foundations unusually—almost uniquely—dependent on other actors as they must "work through third parties . . . through grant-making," acting as "facilitators rather than operators."[21] Consequently, despite foundations remaining, in theory at least, one of the most flexible organizational forms in contemporary global governance, they are constrained by their principal function as grant-makers, which often act as largely passive principals, within networked-type arrangements. Foundations are therefore highly dependent on other actors to attain their goals, which constrains and limits their influence, sometimes to the provision of funds.

Second, as with other aspects of global governance, relational and structural imbalances are pervasive, and certain actors, for example foundations, without doubt retain a privileged position within decision-making processes. Nonetheless, collaborative governance arrangements, for example partnerships, are also sites of diffuse power in which influence is dispersed. Moreover, foundations are often dependent on the intelligence and field knowledge of partner entities for new ideas, projects, and field knowledge. Therefore because of a combination of limits on staff, the need to be across diverse areas of technical specialization, and the need for innovative ideas, foundations are arguably as dependent on demand-side actors as demand-side actors are on foundation resources.

Third, obvious questions remain for the accountability and legitimacy of states and international organizations.[22] Moreover, while foundations lack the input or procedural legitimacy of public actors for the reasons sketched above, that deficiency may arguably be offset through output legitimacy or their efficacy in problem resolution.[23] Indeed, concerns regarding the criticisms of foundations sometimes seem inflated, particularly if contrasted with other private actors, as foundations are subject to the same domestic regulatory, legal, and governance requirements as INGOs, as well as extra-territorial legislation that keeps a check on their actions.

Conclusion

Private foundations have historically played a significant, if often obscure, part in world politics. While comparatively marginal in relation to many other non-state actors, they have deployed their unique attributes—an endowment and associated financial agency, as well a close association with actors from across sectors—to exercise influence at important junctures in the development of the institutional architecture. Such influence has been especially obvious during the interwar and early post-war eras, as well as from the 1990s in the period of accelerated globalization. Not surprisingly, perceived influence has led in turn to upsurges in scrutiny, which can be observed in the literature on the "big" foundations, which during the middle decades of the twentieth century attained almost state-like status in international politics. The Gates Foundation, similarly state-like in its scale and influence in global health governance, as well as the growth in philanthropy among private actors and individuals more broadly, has renewed interest in evaluating the mechanics of foundation power. Despite the financial crisis and its impact on endowments, the growth of philanthropy, and in particular that with a global orientation, shows no sign of diminishing. The so-called new philanthropy at present remains somewhat peripheral but points to new directions in philanthropic practice that are also likely to have significant, although as yet difficult to predict, ramifications for the future of global governance.

Additional reading

1. Michael Moran, *Private Foundations and Development Partnerships: American Philanthropy and Global Development Agendas* (London: Routledge, 2014).
2. Lael Brainard and Derek Chollet, eds., *Global Development 2.0: Can Philanthropists, the Public, and the Poor Make Poverty History?* (Washington, DC: Brookings Institution Press, 2008).
3. Michael Edwards, *Small Change: Why Business Won't Save the World* (San Francisco: Berrett-Koehler Publishers, 2010).
4. Peter Frumkin, *Strategic Giving: The Art and Science of Philanthropy* (Chicago: University of Chicago Press, 2006).
5. Nicolas Guilhot, ed., *The Invention of International Relations Theory: Realism, the Rockefeller Foundation, and the 1954 Conference on Theory* (New York: Columbia University Press, 2011).
6. Inderjeet Parmar, *Foundations of the American Century: Ford, Carnegie, and Rockefeller Foundations in the Rise of American Power* (New York: Columbia University Press, 2012).

Notes

1 Foundation Center, "Foundations Today," http://foundationcenter.org/getstarted/tutorials/ft_tutorial/what.html.

2 Foundation Center, *International Grantmaking Update: A Snapshot of US Foundation Trends* (New York: Foundation Center, 2010), 2.

3 Barbara Howe, "The Emergence of Scientific Philanthropy, 1900–1920: Origins, Issues and Outcomes," in *Philanthropy and Cultural Imperialism: The Foundations at Home and Abroad*, ed. Robert Arnove (Boston: G. K. Hall & Co., 1980), 33.

4 Ann Westmore and David Penington, "Courting the Rockefeller Foundation and Other Attempts to Integrate Clinical Teaching, Medical Practice, and Research in Melbourne," *Health and History* 11, no. 2 (2009): 63.

5 Peter J. Hotez, "Vaccines as Instruments of Foreign Policy," *Science and Society* 2, no. 10 (2001): 862.

6 Kelly Loughlin and Virginia Berridge, *Historical Dimensions of Global Health Governance* (Geneva: World Health Organization, 2002).

7 Paul Weindling, "Philanthropy and World Health: The Rockefeller Foundation and the League of Nations Health Organisation," *Minerva* 35, no. 3 (1997): 269–281.

8 Kenneth W. Thompson, "The Green Revolution: Leadership and Partnership in Agriculture," *Review of Politics* 34, no. 2 (1972): 174–189.

9 Nicolas Guilhot, "Introduction: One Discipline, Many Histories," in *The Invention of International Relations Theory: Realism, the Rockefeller Foundation, and the 1954 Conference on Theory*, ed. Nicolas Guilhot (New York: Columbia University Press, 2011), 15.

10 Norman E. Borlaug, "Sixty-Two Years of Fighting Hunger: Personal Recollections," *Euphytica* 157, no. 3 (2007): 292.

11 Eric B. Ross, *The Malthus Factor: Poverty, Politics and Population in Capitalist Development* (London: Zed Books, 1998), 150.

12 Robert W. Herdt, "People, Institutions, and Technology: A Personal View of the Role of Foundations in International Agricultural Research and Development 1960–2010," *Food Policy* 37 no. 2 (2012): 185.

13 Margaret Keck and Kathryn Sikkink, *Activists Beyond Borders: Advocacy Networks in International Politics* (Ithaca: Cornell University Press, 1998), 101.

14 William Korey, *Taking on the World's Repressive Regimes: The Ford Foundation's International Human Rights Policies and Practices* (New York: Palgrave Macmillan, 2007), ix, 93.

15 Michael Moran, "Philanthropic Foundations and Global Health Partnership Formation: The Rockefeller Foundation and IAVI," in *Health for Some: The Political Economy of Global Health Governance*, eds. Sandra J MacLean et al. (New York: Palgrave Macmillan, 2009).

16 Michael Edwards, *Just Another Emperor? The Myths and Realities of Philanthrocapitalism* (London: Demos/The Young Foundation, 2008).

17 Ross, *The Malthus Factor*.

18 David McCoy et al., "The Bill & Melinda Gates Foundation's Grant-Making Programme for Global Health," *The Lancet* 373, no. 9675 (2009): 1645–1653.

19 Linsey McGoey, "Philanthrocapitalism and Its Critics," *Poetics* 40, no. 2 (2012): 185–189.

20 Raj M. Desai and Homi Kharas, "The California Consensus: Can Private Aid End Global Poverty?," *Survival* 50, no. 4 (2008): 155–168.

21 Helmut K. Anheier and Siobhan Daly, eds., *The Politics of Foundations: A Comparative Analysis* (London: Routledge, 2006), 160.

22 Simon Rushton and Owain Williams, "Private Actors in Global Health," in *Partnerships and Foundations in Global Health Governance*, eds. S. Rushton and O. Williams (New York: Palgrave Macmillan, 2011), 19.

23 Michael Moran and Michael Stevenson, "Illumination and Innovation: What Philanthropic Foundations Bring to Global Governance," *Global Society* 27 (forthcoming 2013).

CHAPTER 28

Private Military and Security Companies

Peter J. Hoffman

CONTENTS

Private military and security companies (PMSCs) and contractors raise quintessential issues of global governance and have relevance for international organization. There is a chicken-and-egg type relationship between governance and force; force can be a cornerstone of governance to coerce obedience from those who resist it, and governance can structure the conditions under which force is deployed. In regards to PMSCs this means they can enforce legitimate standards of global governance but are also constrained by them. Consequently, an analysis of PMSCs illuminates authority and power in global governance and, where formalized into rules, in international organization.

PMSCs are confounding to conventional state-based international politics because they suggest not only that non-state actors are influential, but also that the roots of world order may be grounded in economics and that security can be outsourced. This chapter unpacks this particular form of market-based violence. First, it examines the configuration of economic, military, and political factors that explain the genesis and evolution of PMSCs. Second, it surveys the contemporary characteristics of the private military and security sector, including examples of major companies and the range of customers. Third, it reviews relevant core principles and regulatory schema that shape usage of PMSCs and the behavior of armed contractors. Lastly, it considers the pre-eminent issues that inform or should inform pivotal debates regarding PMSCs.

From mercenaries to military and security contractors

Private military and security contractors are the most recent iteration of market-based force, and while they possess unique features that distinguish them from other forms of this phenomenon, their origins should be situated with reference to mercenaries.

Although most military organizations were oriented toward, if not intrinsically connected to political authorities, mercenaries were not. Indeed, the very term "mercenary" comes from the Latin *mercenarius*, which is rooted in the word *merces*, or "pays wages," and highlights the prominence of their economic agendas. The lack of political encumbrance allowed these armed actors to sell their skills on the open market, and this position inspired the language associated with independent contractors under modern capitalism; these "lances" were "free" to work for whomever, hence the term "freelancer."

Mercenaries arose as a result of both military needs and economic logic. First, mercenaries provided crucial capabilities. Producing effective military power is not simply a matter of collective will or organization, but a synergy of manpower, technology, and strategy. Mercenaries furnished the skilled and experienced military labor that has often been in high demand by those who seek to deploy coercion. Second, from an economic point of view, hiring mercenaries was a means of acquiring military power without the costly and time-consuming practice of building and maintaining standing forces. In other words, mercenaries were ready-made forces that could be swiftly deployed and then, after military objectives were achieved, dismissed so as to no longer drain financial resources. Accordingly, there are numerous instances of mercenaries from antiquity to the modern period.

However, starting in the seventeenth century mercenaries began to be displaced as a consequence of the ascendance of the state as the supreme source of political governance (i.e. sovereignty) and its role in organizing warfare. States sought a monopoly on the use of force not only to defend against and dispatch opponents but also because supplying security was a primary means of generating revenues (i.e. taxes). Initially states did not eradicate mercenarism but rather harnessed it to state interests; mercenaries continued to operate but only at the behest of states.[1] For instance, in the fourteen and fifteenth centuries "military companies" (or mercenary armies) were commonly employed by Italian city-states. Additionally, there were also "mercantile companies," large commercial enterprises that were authorized by a state to facilitate trade and colonialism, and these entities often contained a military component. Though mercenaries remained a fixture of warfare into the eighteenth century, their usage declined appreciably throughout the nineteenth century, when during the Napoleonic Wars (1803–15) the model of national armies demonstrated that armed forces composed of citizens and motivated solely by politics could be capable military actors.

In comparison with mercenaries, the benefits of national military forces were seen as threefold.[2] First, they fought for less money, which was economically advantageous for states. Second, they were more disciplined in refraining from plunder, which was important to states seeking to expand political popularity in conquered areas. Third, they were seen as more dependable because they were far less likely to switch sides purely for economic gain. Therefore, during the remainder of the nineteenth century and into the twentieth, the use of mercenaries dwindled greatly as most states made the transition to citizen-based armies. Furthermore, the concern that mercenaries operating from within a state might entangle that state in foreign wars also prompted prohibiting the practice. Although mercenarism persisted into the twentieth century, the practice was of minor importance and essentially only by individuals.

In the 1990s a new form of for-profit armed actor came to the fore, private military and security companies. Although rudiments of this sector originated long before the Cold War ended—defense industries providing arms and maintenance; guards for hire

—it was not until after this period that PMSCs coalesced and materialized as significant stand-alone purveyors of force. The expansion of PMSCs was propelled by factors of supply (providers) and demand (consumers).[3]

On the demand side, states and businesses sought to hire PMSCs for three reasons. First, access to quality military and security personnel had been inhibited by state control, particularly in the context of Cold War rivalries, and this fueled a need for skilled military labor and special proficiencies. Weaker states desired more sophisticated military assets than they themselves produced and businesses sought protection in operating in hostile environments. Moreover, the speed of PMSC deployments is much faster. Second, a belief in the efficiency of the market to allocate resources opened the floodgates for the private sector to provide military and security services. The neoliberal school of thought popularized in the 1980s spread widely in the 1990s and called for a reduced role for governments and greater privatization of a variety of public goods, including war-making and protection. Third, during the 1990s it had become apparent that states were sensitive to, if not outright exhausted by, the political, military, and economic costs associated with the use of force. The "body bag" factor—the political fallout for governments of soldiers killed in missions they authorized, such as in the United States following the grisly 1993 "Black Hawk Down" debacle in Somalia where the bodies of American servicemen were dragged through the streets of Mogadishu—created political momentum to decrease the exposure of national military forces to the dangers of using force that was not paramount to national security interests. Moreover, given that PMSCs are not government employees, their operations and personnel are not subject to legal restrictions or oversight and usually do not receive the level of scrutiny that soldiers do, thus enabling states to pursue their interests under the political radar and even officially deny responsibility.

With respect to the supply side, corporations and contractors that produce violence also sought to open the marketplace for force. This is usually ascribed to purely a profit motive, as force is a lucrative, non-substitutable commodity. But more than that, for those who have military training but lack other marketable skills, military and security contracting may be the optimal, if not only viable, source of income—this was a position many former soldiers found themselves in during the early 1990s when following the Cold War many militaries downsized their forces. In fact, armed contractors may earn $500–$1,500 a day. The economic benefits and "soldiers of fortune" narrative receive the most attention but contractors also may have ideological grounds for selling their wares. Contractors may sympathize or identify with the ideas of the party that hires them. In short, PMSCs fight not just for pay; they also fight for politics.

In considering the organizational and functional elements of PMSCs, in many ways they resemble the military and mercantile companies of the medieval and early modern periods more than the individual and bands of mercenaries that endured into the twentieth century, because these new entities are organized as formal corporations—they have or seek legal standing as legitimate businesses. Furthermore, while some PMSCs are like their predecessors in being directly involved in the production of violence, others play a more indirect role by facilitating and enabling.

The label "PMSC" has been applied to various firms with a wide assortment of services; three basic types can be seen. First, military and security forces require considerable infrastructure and mission support activities to carry out their operations and this type of PMSC furnishes these vital underpinnings—as Napoleon noted in his early campaigns, "an army travels on its stomach." The work of PMSCs that offer support and supply logistics includes serving meals, doing laundry, providing transportation, building bases, and engineering. A good example of this sort of PMSC is the engineering firm KBR, Inc. (formerly known as Kellogg Brown & Root), which was once a subsidiary of the oil services behemoth Halliburton. At present KBR, through its work in building bases, is one of the top contractors for the US Army and Department of Defense.

Second, the intricacies of modern warfare and contemporary dangers have spurred interest in receiving guidance from professionals on the best means to conduct military operations and to manage security. Consulting PMSCs provide training and advice to militaries, businesses, and intergovernmental and nongovernmental organizations, as well as offer command and control services. Less skilled and experienced military forces in particular may require instruction, if not real-time mentoring, in strategy and tactics. Typifying this type of PMSC is Military Professional Resources, Inc. (MPRI), which offers tactical services and boasts, "We've got more generals per square foot here than in the Pentagon."

Third, "trigger-pullers" are by far the most controversial type of PMSCs and are the main focus of concern about the phenomenon. However, some armed contractors, it should be noted, concentrate on combat and specifically offensive actions (i.e. *private military companies*), whereas others are devoted exclusively to defensive tasks and the provision of safety (i.e. *private security companies*), though this is a blurry line. An illustration of force providing PMSCs is the British firm Aegis Defence Services. This company played a major role in United States involvement in Iraq; protecting US Army Corps of Engineers as well as coordinating movements of all armed contractors hired by the US government.

Most analyses of PMSCs revolve around what these companies do, but it should not be overlooked that, like other global corporations, they are influenced by economic globalization, and this impacts what labor they employ. Contractors vary not only by function but also according to training and nationality; three categories can be seen. Those contractors from industrialized countries are usually considered the best, as they tend to be experienced veterans from top militaries, primarily American and British. While these contractors have valuable specialized skills (such as counterinsurgency) and advanced high-tech equipment, they are frequently the most expensive. Local contractors, by contrast, are prized for their ability to blend into their operating environs as well as for their contacts, and their lesser training may make them a cheaper alternative. However, some PMSCs have reservations about hiring locals because their loyalty to their communities may render them unreliable security providers to foreign elements. Lastly, there are "third country nationals," that are neither from wealthy countries nor local. This hodge-podge of armed contractors tends to come from one of three sorts of countries: those that downsized their military forces due to the end of the Cold War (e.g. Belarus); those that disbanded oppressive forces (such as South Africa); or those that simply have international experience in peacekeeping or other exchanges (for instance Fiji). "Third country nationals" often have more training than locals and are less expensive than "First World" contractors.

PMSCs are routinely painted with a broad brush that invariably invokes the specter of mercenaries. Critics lament that PMSCs are illegal, violate human rights, and profiteer.

However, such a one-dimensional portrayal of avaricious "hired guns" neglects the wider political, security, and economic context that gave birth to PMSCs and which sustains the sector. PMSCs may recall mercenaries but their identity as formal corporations, their evolving status under international law (see below), and the variety and complexity of the tasks associated with modern battlefields that they have taken up distinguish them.

The private military and security sector in the world today

Since the private military and security sector surfaced in high-profile activities in the 1990s it has skyrocketed and is now present in a multitude of contemporary armed conflicts and precarious areas, from post-Hurricane Katrina New Orleans to Pakistan. The growth of this industry is remarkable: Estimates gauge that it earned $55.6bn in 1990 and around $100bn in 2003.[4] By 2007 it had reached $138.6bn and by 2009 was to climb to $152.5bn; with an annual growth rate of 7.4 percent, it is projected to reach $218.4bn by 2014.[5] In addition to a burgeoning of revenues, there are a mounting number of people working in this field. In 2011, there were between 19.5 and 25.5 million personnel around the world in the private military and security sector, which represents a doubling or tripling over the last 10–20 years.[6]

PMSCs can be seen in many recent and current wars and zones of instability, particularly those where the West, and specifically the United States, has an interest, principally the global war on terrorism (GWOT). Several illustrations from the past decade are telltale in revealing the prevalence of armed contractors. The template for significant PMSC involvement is the case of Afghanistan since 2001. Following the terrorist attacks of 9/11, the US sought to overthrow the Taliban regime that harbored the al-Qaeda militants that perpetrated the strike. The United States intervened with a rather modest number of troops and successfully ousted the Taliban by the end of 2001. However, by 2006 the Taliban had reconstituted its forces and yet the United States had become impatient with this drain on resources. Starting in 2007, more Western troops were deployed but this was a stopgap measure and in 2011 United States forces began to be withdrawn. Over this same period, the number of PMSCs on the ground started to grow.[7] In 2007, there were 4,000 working for the United States; in 2009, 12,000; and in 2011, 19,000. This leaves out PMSCs that were employed by others, but if they are added to the tally, there are roughly 70,000. Thus, Afghanistan showcases not only an increase in PMSCs but also the notable proliferation of the PMSC footprint relative to that of formal armed forces of states.

The war that was initiated in Iraq in 2003 exhibits similar dynamics, although at the outset the US military deployed a much larger number of troops and this force grew in 2007 as part of the so-called surge strategy. But since that peak, the United States completed a withdrawal of all its combat forces as of the end of 2011. In contrast to Afghanistan, the number of PMSCs employed by the United States rose and fell along with the American presence, but while the US military has officially exited Iraq, at least 5,500 armed contractors remain to protect US State Department activities. Furthermore, like Afghanistan, the overall number of PMSCs in Iraq is large, around 30,000, and growing.[8] Hence, PMSCs began as a complement to US forces but now have taken their place.

Another area of conflict, Somalia—somewhat connected to the GWOT and a failed state for at least 20 years—typifies a scenario for the ballooning involvement of PMSCs. The lack of governance in much of the country has spawned an opportunity for pirates to use it as a base for preying on shipping in the Gulf of Aden, a critical bottleneck in world trade. Few states are willing to commit the military resources necessary to truly address the situation despite the escalation of piracy in recent years. Consequently, there has been a marked expansion in private maritime security, which is viewed as less expensive than tackling governance in Somalia, changing shipping routes, higher insurance premiums, or paying ransoms. Overall, in places that lack order but are not at the top of the military agendas of any large military powers, PMSCs are expanding into such vacuums.

While a vast majority of the consumers of private military and security services are governments and businesses, the sector has its eye on expanding its customer base by seeking to work for intergovernmental (IGOs) and nongovernmental organizations (NGOs). Such arrangements will not yield contracts of a magnitude comparable to those with states and other corporations, but they would improve the reputation of PMSCs. Some argue that the approach and capabilities of PMSCs enable a quicker response than international bureaucracies and that they are adept at providing peacekeeping or protecting humanitarian operations in places lacking order. Therefore, many PMSCs have increasingly developed and sold packages of services designed to suit the particular needs of this clientele.[9] For example, the Paramount Group specializes in services for what it terms the "peacekeeping industry" that enable developing countries to meet United Nations (UN) requirements in equipment, training, and logistics. In fact, the UN has been hiring PMSCs since the early 1990s, and in the last few years usage has been soaring—there has been a 250 percent increase in the value of contracts between the UN and PMSCs over the period 2006–11.[10] While a handful of humanitarian nongovernmental organizations, such as Médecins Sans Frontières and Save the Children, have made strong and public efforts in refusing to work with PMSCs, virtually all other agencies have "hardened" themselves by employing armed contractors at least once.[11]

There are far too many PMSCs in the world today to list them all and they often operate out of the spotlight, though those actively involved in prominent armed hostilities clearly stand out. The first to be the focus of much attention was Executive Outcomes, a South African-based firm that used surprisingly small contingents in routing guerilla groups in Angola and Sierra Leone during the mid-1990s. These operations set a precedent for large-scale privatization of military and security affairs and ignited a boom in hiring PMSCs.

However, by far the most notorious PMSC is the company formerly known as Blackwater, which in 2009 changed its name to Xe Services LLC and in 2011 changed it to Academi. This company prided itself on taking on the most hazardous operations and providing the most professional, robust forces. However, several incidents in Iraq soured perceptions of Blackwater, especially those that resulted in civilian casualties with no legal accountability for its personnel. In a similar fashion, DynCorp has garnered attention for episodes of corruption and its lack of liability. For instance, the company was implicated in a sex trafficking scandal in Bosnia in the late 1990s while working for the UN and yet DynCorp has remained a staple tool of US foreign policy, as evidenced by its role providing surveillance in Colombia as part of the drug war and guards for President Karzai in Afghanistan.

Yet, the single largest firm in the sector and the second largest private employer in the world, G4S, which presently has approximately 625,000 employees and annual revenues over $25bn, is mostly ignored. This company has provided a variety of security services to the British government, among other clients, including protection at the 2012 Summer Olympics in London. G4S's subsidiary ArmorGroup has been hired by the UN in Afghanistan but has been criticized for essentially subcontracting its work to local warlords, though the company continues to receive contracts from many governments and businesses.

Two other illustrations substantiate how PMSCs can be largely unknown because they do not undertake offensive combat operations and work for IGOs and NGOs. In the middle of the 1990s Defense Systems Limited was hired to guard the facilities of the International Committee of the Red Cross (ICRC) in the eastern part of the Democratic Republic of the Congo while it was engaged in humanitarian relief. At roughly the same time but in the northern part of country, the World Wildlife Fund considered hiring Saracen to stop poaching in Garamba National Park, although ultimately no contract was signed.

Lastly, like any other modern industry, PMSCs have formed trade associations to publicize their prowess, court opportunities, and build legitimacy. Examples include the US-based International Stability Operations Association, the British Association of Private Security Companies, and the Private Security Company Association of Iraq. At present the sector is thriving because the norm of armed contractor usage has been well established, with states, businesses, IGOs, and NGOs readily employing them and PMSC interest groups striving to further embed this practice.

Global governance and PMSCs

To those who champion and those who reject PMSCs, the key issue hinges on governance. Supporters look at legal and ethical parameters for realizing contracts and tackling malfeasance. Opponents have traditionally searched for legislative tools to ban the practice outright, but in recent years some from this perspective have instead turned to mechanisms for regulating the sector. For the most part PMSCs inhabit a netherworld of legality; currently there are essentially no binding international agreements that directly address the legal status of private military and security contractors, and therefore much of the jurisprudence applied to them is by way of extrapolation and interpretation. The three main controversies regarding private military and security contractors are, first, are they in effect soldiers—i.e. legal combatants representing a state—and thus entitled to the protections afforded to formal armed forces? Second, if armed contractors are lawful combatants, what activities are they permitted to engage in (conduct)? Third, what mechanisms are in place to ensure they are accountable for illegal activities?

Eight major normative frameworks and legal instruments guide or influence the global governance of PMSCs.[12] The first is The Hague Convention V, Articles 4 and 6 (1907). The first widely recognized international treaty with direct implications for for-pay militarized forces is built on the principle of neutrality. Although this treaty does not use the term mercenaries, let alone PMSCs, it effectively prohibits the recruitment of mercenaries in states that are neutral. However, it does not prevent individuals from crossing borders to become mercenaries.

The second is Geneva Convention III, Article 4 (1949). The four Geneva Conventions of 1949 do not readily discuss either the conduct or place of private military and security contractors under international humanitarian law. Indeed, PMSCs would seem to fall in the gaps—Geneva I and II refer to the formal combatants of states, meaning soldiers and sailors. Geneva IV addresses civilians, but private military and security contractors would not qualify because they are armed and join in hostilities. Geneva III, however, refers to the treatment of the captured and detained in conflict, including the conditions under which they are officially "prisoners of war" (POWs). But according to the criteria enumerated, such as being directly under the command of soldiers or wearing uniforms, PMSCs are likely not covered. Paragraph 4 refers to "supply contractors," which may pertain to support or consulting PMSCs but clearly not those who use force. Overall, the Geneva Conventions do not criminalize armed contractors, but they do not explicitly grant them the privileges of lawful combatants.

The third consequential framework is Additional Protocol I to the Geneva Conventions, Article 47 (1977). An upsurge in non-state actors engaging in armed conflicts in the post-World War II period inspired a reformulation of and additions to the laws of war, including a provision that defines and bans mercenaries, and this is often invoked in regards to PMSCs. Article 47 signals that it is fundamentally illegal to fight for pay and results in forfeiting the protections granted under international humanitarian law. In other words, captured mercenaries are to be treated as criminals, not defeated soldiers. But the criteria for this category are extensive—recruited abroad; directly involved in hostilities; motivation is compensation beyond what other combatants receive; neither a national or resident of territory party to conflict; not acting on official duty from a state—and few armed contractors would seem to meet all of these. Moreover, it would be difficult to verify given that there is little formal documentation of PMSCs. Thus, although this agreement delineates mercenaries it has limited applicability in clarifying the status of PMSCs.

The fourth salient structure is the Organization of African Unity Convention for the Elimination of Mercenarism (1977). The use of mercenaries in support of colonial regimes and to undermine independent nationalist governments in Africa during the Cold War prompted the Organization of African Unity to criminalize the practice. This treaty bears much resemblance to Additional Protocol I to the Geneva Conventions, but it goes further in that it also considers states that enable or allow mercenaries to operate from their territory as liable.

The fifth is the United Nations' International Conventions Against the Recruitment, Use, Financing and Training of Mercenaries (1989). This agreement simplifies the definition of mercenary to the "desire for private gain" and broadens the scope of activities that are illegal to encompass recruiting, using, financing, and training. Furthermore, this convention does not merely urge states to take measures to prevent mercenarism but requires them to do so. But it also somewhat softens treatment of captured mercenaries as it calls for allowing the ICRC to be in touch with and monitor the treatment of guilty parties.

The sixth standard-setting agreement is the Montreux Document (2008). The steady increase in PMSC usage sparked the Swiss government and the ICRC to devise regulations for the sector. After soliciting views from states, scholars, IGOs, NGOs, and PMSCs, the Montreux Document on the Pertinent International Legal Obligations and Good Practices for States Related to Operations of Private Military and Security Companies during Armed Conflicts was signed by "contracting states" (which hire armed contractors), "home states" (where PMSCs are based), and "territorial states" (where they operate). The agreement essentially distills the Geneva Conventions, the ICRC Study on Customary International Humanitarian Law, the UN Basic Principles on the Use of Force and Firearms by Law Enforcement Officials, the UN Code of Conduct for Law Enforcement Officials, and a variety of national regulatory frameworks.

The Montreux Document deems that armed contractors are "civilians" unless they are incorporated into military forces, in which case they are to be treated as soldiers, and if they directly participate in conflicts they are to be considered combatants. This means that PMSCs do not qualify for the protections granted civilians and lawfully can be attacked. Additionally, the document sets out "good practices," which involve a licensing system to strengthen control and oversight as well as a tracking system of PMSCs to encourage the contracting state to only hire those that respect human rights and international law. However, this agreement is not legally binding; it is merely designed to clarify the rights and responsibilities associated with PMSC use. Although there is a statement within it that contends this initiative is not intended to legitimize PMSCs or otherwise take a position on the issue, this agreement does seem to imply an imprimatur of legality. In sum, the Montreux Document fundamentally identifies a way for armed contractors and their users to heed international standards—that is to say, it is a vehicle for demarcating the status of PMSCs under international humanitarian law.

The seventh normative and legal framework is the International Code of Conduct for Private Security Providers (2010). Whereas the Montreux Document called on states to uphold their responsibilities under international humanitarian law, there remained a lack of clear and formal commitment by PMSCs themselves to comply. To address this shortcoming the Swiss Department of Foreign Affairs, along with the Geneva Centre for the Democratic Control of Armed Forces and the Geneva Academy of International Humanitarian Law and Human Rights, and in conjunction with members of the PMSC industry, developed the International Code of Conduct for Private Security Providers. This agreement requires signatories to respect human rights and to adhere to humanitarian legal obligations in their operations with regards to their clients and the populations in the areas where they work, as well as their own personnel. Provisions cover rules for the use of force; standards for recruiting, vetting, and training personnel; and procedures for reporting violations (field auditing and a method for filing complaints). Moreover, should companies commit human rights abuses, under the Code those that hire the offending company could fire them on the grounds of breach of contract. However, this agreement is somewhat limited in terms of its applicability and enforcement as it only governs companies that formally sign on, not the smaller local security providers that have also come to play more pronounced roles in armed conflicts.

The eighth and most recent framework can be discerned in a set of United Nations documents that establish and clarify the legality of PMSCs and address UN usage: the UN Draft Convention on Private Military and Security Companies (2011) and policies and guidelines found in the 2012 manuals of the UN Security Management System. The spread of PMSC utilization coupled with a belief in the inadequacy or inapplicability of legislation proscribing mercenaries initiated concern among many member states of the United Nations and staff of the international organization. Since 1987 the UN had appointed a special rapporteur to examine issues relating to mercenaries, but by 1997 this office recognized that laws against mercenarism did not strictly cover PMSCs. In 2005 the Special Rapporteur was succeeded by a new entity, the Working Group on the use of mercenaries as a means of violating human rights and impeding the exercise of the right of people to self-determination, which was tasked with the same responsibilities and which was intended to develop new principles to coax PMSCs to respect human rights.

A 2010 report by the UN Working Group on mercenaries served as the basis for a new treaty proposed in 2011 that demands states take responsibility for PMSCs in their jurisdiction; international and national laws hold armed contractors accountable; restrictions on the use of force to protect state sovereignty and civilian populations; prohibitions on PMSCs undertaking combat, police, or intelligence work; and constraints on arms intended to prevent illegal trafficking. It also requires vetting personnel and training them in human rights and international humanitarian law; proper identification that distinguishes them from civilians; methods for reporting incidents, field audits and complaint procedures; and means for prosecution when laws are broken. This list of principles embodies current norms of on the use of PMSCs. Most importantly, this treaty would not criminalize armed contractors, but instead regulate them.

The latest rules issued by the UN Security Management System (UNSMS) in November 2012 exemplify this development. At an elementary level, these statements from the UNSMS could be characterized as capstones of the normative and legal shifts toward normalizing PMSC usage by the organization in that they bring together and elaborate upon previous international agreements. the instructions and directives they lay our set forth the conditions under which PMSCs may be used: when security measures by host states, other member states or UN Security and Safety Services are inadequate or inappropriate; the Under Secretary-General for Safety and Security has approved a request based on a thorough security risk assessment; the company and its personnel have been screened; the company's "use of force" policy is as, or more, restrictive than the UN's own "use of force" policy; the company has signed and is in compliance with the International Code of Conduct for Private Security Providers; the company is licensed in its home state as well as the state where it operates as per the Montreaux Document; and the company has registered with the UN Procurement Division. Therefore, the UN has not only played a part in sanctioning PMSC usage, the organization has itself become a user.

What is clear is that although the beliefs and bans regarding mercenaries provide some direction for interpreting ideas about private military and security companies, PMSCs represent a different form of market-based force where the norms and laws are still unfolding. At present, practice seems to have tilted toward considering PMSCs as combatants that can legally be attacked and, if they accompany soldiers, may be granted POW status. However, this has not been set under international humanitarian law. Overall, the growing use of, and dependence on, PMSCs by states and businesses is likely to sap the political will to outlaw armed contractors outright despite the protests of some human rights groups. The proposal for a new convention unambiguously on PMSCs demonstrates just how far the norm of usage has come—while there are still stalwart opponents of any sort of marketization of force, the goalposts of the debate have moved such that international deliberations are no longer centered on whether such actors are legal or legitimate, but rather how to best influence their conduct.

Conclusion

The use of force in international affairs is customarily riddled with a dilemma of means and ends—is violence a solution or does it merely metastasize the problem?—and the uncertain nature of and tensions surrounding PMSCs add new twists to recent debates. Are armed contractors innately dangerous and inherently illegitimate? Are they the next logical and justifiable step in a globalizing world? Are they an imperfect actor reflecting an imperfect world?

The answers to these questions are still open and changing, but four aspects are worth consideration in deliberating the costs and benefits of PMSCs. The first concerns the growth of the sector and the decline of the state's monopoly on the use of force. PMSCs have grown not only in size and scope but also in terms of the roles they play relative to national armed forces. Although some contend that state control over violence may never have been an unadulterated monopoly, it is clear that by the twentieth century governments were the only major players in the international use of force. However, in the past 20 years armed contractors have fundamentally challenged this as power and authority over violence have shifted thereby presenting the prospect that force is governed by "contract culture." PMSCs started by supplementing national armed forces, but now they are in a position to entirely supersede them.

The second issue regards legality and legitimacy. Whether PMSCs are legal increasingly seems moot, but that does not mean that law does not or should not play a role. The lines of authority for using PMSCs and acceptable modes of conduct need to be drawn more clearly to ensure accountability, particularly should inappropriate behavior result. The political blowback from usage is also a factor as many people in places where PMSCs operate are resentful, sometimes to the point of exacerbating armed conflicts. There must be consequences for wrongdoing or there is no legitimacy to the use of PMSCs. Additionally, labor relations are of concern as the treatment of contractors by companies can potentially also undermine the propriety of PMSCs and the actors that hire them.

The third matter of interest is based on economics and efficiency. Supporters claim that the market allocates military and security resources more cost effectively, but the empirical answer is not readily apparent when considering other economic facets such as the loss of investment when personnel trained by states move to the private sector or the expenditures in renting forces rather than owning them. Moreover, the criticism that what may begin as an issue of efficiency becomes a form of extortion or exploitation, as dependency on armed contractors may be the outcome of outsourcing and PMSCs have no incentive to attend to the source of threats, must be addressed.

The fourth and final bone of contention relates to the notion of sacrifice and world order. Part of the popularity of PMSCs with government is the avoidance of the "body bag" factor, but severing the sense of sacrifice associated with participating in armed conflicts subverts the conversation about the human toll of war. Historically, states and societies bargained: states respected the rights of citizens in exchange for societies providing resources to states, including manpower for military service. Contracting undercuts this arrangement; states do not draw on their citizenry to fight and thus may not be beholden to them to ensure rights. Furthermore, without directly experiencing loss from war, citizens may not concern themselves with where states are making war. In a world where PMSCs alone bear the burden of sacrifice debates on the justness of force and the price of order are obscured.

In thinking and talking about PMSCs and the ubiquitous need for security, there is no panacea—sometimes force is required and no other actor is available—but we are better off in being candid about what drives the phenomenon, how it interacts with the nature of governance, and what is at stake.

Additional reading

1. Deborah D. Avant, *The Market for Force: The Consequences of Privatizing Security* (Cambridge: Cambridge University Press, 2005).
2. Simon Chesterman and Chia Lehnardt, eds., *From Mercenaries to Market: The Rise and Regulation of Private Military Companies* (Oxford: Oxford University Press, 2007).
3. Emanuela-Chiara Gillard, "Business Goes to War: Private Military/Security Companies and International Humanitarian Law," *International Review of the Red Cross* 88, no. 863 (September 2006): 525–572.
4. International Stability Operations Association, http://www.stability-operations.org/.
5. Elke Krahmann, *States, Citizens, and the Privatization of Security* (Cambridge: Cambridge University Press, 2010).
6. Malcolm Hugh Patterson, *Privatizing Peace: A Corporate Adjunct to United Nations Peacekeeping and Humanitarian Operations* (New York: Palgrave Macmillan, 2009).
7. Anna Leander, *Eroding State Authority? Private Military Companies and the Legitimate Use of Force* (Fome: Centro Militare di Studi Strategiei, 2006).

Notes

1 Sarah Percy, *Mercenaries: The History of a Norm in International Relations* (Cambridge: Cambridge University Press, 2007), 90–91.
2 Deborah Avant, "From Mercenary to Citizen Armies: Explaining Change in the Practice of War," *International Organization* 54, no. 1 (2000): 41–72.
3 Peter W. Singer, *Corporate Warriors: The Rise of the Privatized Military Industry* (Ithaca: Cornell University Press, 2003), 49–72; David Shearer, *Private Armies and Military Intervention*, Adelphi Paper 316 (Oxford: Oxford University Press, 1998).
4 Cited in Alex Vines, "Mercenaries and the Privatization of Security in Africa in the 1990s," in *The Privatization of Security in Africa*, eds. Greg Mills and John Stremlau (Johannesburg: South African Institute for International Affairs Press, 1997), 47; Peter W. Singer, "Peacekeepers, Inc.," *Policy Review* 119 (June 2003): 60.
5 The Freedonia Group, *World Security Services: Industry Study with Forecasts for 2012 & 2017*, Brochure of Report No. 2395 (September 2008); Freedonia, *World Security Services: Industry Study with Forecasts for 2014 & 2019*, Brochure of Report No. 2711 (March 2011).
6 Nicolas Florquin, "A Booming Business: Private Security and Small Arms," in *Small Arms Survey 2011: States of Security* (Cambridge: Cambridge University Press, 2011), 101.
7 Moshe Schwartz, *The Department of Defense's Use of Private Security Contractors in Afghanistan and Iraq: Background, Analysis, and Options for Congress*, Congressional Research Service (13 May 2011), 3 and 9.
8 Ibid., 3.
9 Malcolm Hugh Patterson, *Privatizing Peace: A Corporate Adjunct to United Nations Peacekeeping and Humanitarian Operations* (New York: Palgrave Macmillan, 2009), 73.
10 Lou Pingeot, *Dangerous Partnership: Private Military & Security Companies and the UN* (New York: Global Policy Forum, July 2012), 47.
11 Abby Stoddard, Adele Harmer, and Victoria DiDomenico, *Providing Aid in Insecure Environments: Trends in Violence against Aid Workers and the Operational Response—2009 Update*, HPG Briefing Paper 34 (April 2009), 8.
12 There are also national regulations and bans on mercenaries—for instance the US Neutrality Act (1797), the UK's Foreign Enlistment Act (1870), and South Africa's Foreign Military Assistance Act (1998)—but the multinational properties of PMSCs and nebulous pertinence and antiquated character of these laws usually hampers them from playing a role in regards to armed contractors.

Transnational Criminal Networks

Frank G. Madsen

Spurred on and empowered by globalization, transnational crime has developed from an issue with relevance for national or, at most, regional criminal law to a priority for states and international organizations. For example, President William J. Clinton addressed transnational organized crime as a threat to the United States in 1995, as did Secretary of State Hillary Clinton in February 2012. In many disciplines, but especially in criminology and international relations, it has become a necessity to understand global crime governance—in other words, the operation of criminal networks and of the networks created to neutralize them.

This chapter provides the theoretical and practical background to evaluate the importance of criminal networks in international relations. It begins by outlining the structure and operation of contemporary governance mechanisms before examining the nature of theoretical, criminal, and institutional theories to understand the phenomenon.

International vs. transnational perspectives

The international illicit traffics in organs for transplantation, narcotics drugs, and prostitutes have in common that they are caused by denied demand, and that the various traffics are made possible by the constitution of networks. Likewise, the corresponding interdiction efforts reflect the use of networks of diplomats, prosecutors, and law enforcement personnel. Thus, cocaine trafficking from the farmer in Columbia to the user in a Western country is made possible by several sub-networks of finance and corruption. Two related but distinct crimes, however, rely very heavily on the operation of networks, human trafficking and the illicit traffic in organs for transplantation; both are exemplified in case studies in this chapter.

Economic globalization, new communication technology, and new transportation technology led, over the last quarter of the twentieth century, to a paradigm shift in organized crime, but which has not changed fundamentally. It still consists of the satisfaction of denied demand but has adopted the networked business models of transnational enterprises. Criminal enterprises now concentrate on production in low-risk and commerce in high-income areas, strategic alliances, subcontracting, and joint ventures.[1] Drug trafficking perhaps is an obvious illustration. From the point of view of international relations and public policy, the most distressing aspect of organized crime is the creation of states that are controlled by criminal groups, working in layered and intersecting networks.

Moisés Naím uses the term "mafia states" for such states with three characteristics: that the national interest and the interests of organized crime are inextricably intertwined; that the conceptual divide between state and non-state actors is blurred; and that their behavior is difficult to predict.[2] These render them dangerous actors in the international environment. As an example, among others, he points to Bulgaria, where from 2000 to 2005 a total of 155 execution-style murders—reportedly at $20,000 a hit—were committed. The victims were individuals with links to the business world, but also a former prime minister and a number of high-ranking government officials.[3] In 2005, the Commission of the European Union (EU) expressed its serious concern that the existence of organized crime and corruption might delay or invalidate the country's application. Nevertheless, Bulgaria became a member of the EU on 1 January 2007.

Likewise, the rapid expansion of crime networks in the former Soviet Union led to, or was partially responsible for, a somewhat distorted transition from a communist to a market regime. Thus, in 1993, the so-called Mafiya, which consisted of 3,000–4,000 gangs with a total membership of some 100,000 individuals, controlled 40 percent of the turnover in goods and services. With *perestroika* at the end of the Cold War, the accumulated funds of both criminal gangs and corrupt party officials were channeled into the stock exchange, joint ventures, and banks; and modern Russian organized crime was born. The organized crime figures, however, could not and would not abide by the rules governing the stock exchange and prudent banking, with the inevitable result that the business and banking world became unstable and domestic and foreign investors grew concerned. An essay in *Foreign Affairs* almost prophetically predicted that such a state of affairs (unchecked economic chaos and gang violence) "could foster the rise of a hostile, totalitarian power on the Eurasian continent, instead of the prosperous partner the West requires for a stable 21st century world."[4]

This chapter deals almost exclusively with transnational as opposed to international crime. Although the use of these terms is fluid, there is nevertheless a tendency to speak of "international" crimes when one refers to war crimes, crimes against humanity, genocide, torture, aggression, and some parts of international terrorism. These crimes are, according to Antonio Cassese, characterized by the cumulative presence of four elements; violation of international customary rules (including treaties that explicitly refer to customary law as their basis); such rules are intended to protect values considered important by the whole international community; there is universal interest in their prosecution; and, if such crimes are committed by state officials *de jure* or *de facto*, the latter cannot invoke state immunity.[5]

Other crimes are most often referred to as "transnational." They are explicitly excluded from international crimes by Cassese, namely, piracy, illicit traffic in narcotics, unlawful arms trade, smuggling of nuclear and other dangerous material, money laundering, slave trade, and traffic in women. These crimes are not considered international crimes because their international interdiction is treaty based and not based on customary international law; they are perpetrated by private individuals or organizations; they are committed against states rather than by states; and finally, if committed by state officials, these are acting in their own personal interest rather than on behalf of the state.

Transnational crime interdiction is obviously part of international law, since such cooperation mostly is treaty based (for example the 2000 United Nations Convention Against Transnational Organized Crime) and treaties are protected under international law, in particular by the 1969 Vienna Convention of the Law of Treaties. They are not international crimes for the reasons outlined above. Yet global crime governance does encompass both transnational and international crime.

The remainder of this chapter introduces three worlds. The first consists of a brief, critical examination of the concept of theoretical networks or the world of imaging; this section aims to highlight how scholars model the criminal world by using network theory and suggest that more emphasis should be placed on the observation of flows rather than on operators and human interaction. The second part discusses criminal networks, or the world of fluxes in persons and goods. A final section examines interdiction networks, the world of information and trust that explains the way that judicial and enforcement authorities have formed themselves into networks as part of international crime governance, as well as the role played by more informal networks in crime interdiction.[6]

Theoretical networks: the world of imaging

Although network theory as an explanatory and illustrative model has gained importance with the progress of computing studies, in particular with the invention of the printed circuit board, the origin of the concept is far from recent. Networks and networking are as old as organized society—inspired in particular by observations of spinning and weaving—and network theory can conveniently be dated from the beginning of the nineteenth century, with Saint-Simonianism.

In 1813 the French social philosopher Count Henri de Saint-Simon developed "organism-network theory" based on his observation of the human organism in his 15-year-long dissection studies. His pupils, known as the Saint-Simonians, developed the ultimate visible network in France, the railway system, and consecutively the communication network, as the telegraph lines more often than not followed the railway network. This, in turn, led to the use of the concept in modern communication theory; in particular, the circulation aspect, referred to above, is exemplified in the printed circuit boards of computers.

In its simplest formulation, one might define a network as a series of nodes that are connected. In considering social relations and, in particular, relations in a criminal network, the definition proposed by Daniel Parrochia is perhaps more adequate, namely that a network is a coherent and ordered distribution in space of a plurality of relations.[7] Several characteristics of criminal networks need, however, to be emphasized. Criminal networks are ordered, self-repairing, and examples of self-organized criticality. Criminal networks are ordered or coherent, where coherent can be taken to mean that the members of the network must be in agreement about the scope and purpose of the network; in a criminal network this accord bears on a desirable or profitable state of affairs in the future.

Perhaps the most crucial characteristic of such networks is that they are self-repairing or, to use another term, resilient. This resilience is due not only to redundancy but also to the ease of actor replacement. Low entrance requirements in educational and capital investment are paired with the absence of opportunities in the communities from which such actors are recruited. In fact, the number of possible recruits in such places as Somalia and Mexico are almost legion.[8]

Criminal networks are also self-organized critical systems. For instance, the abundance of possible neural pathways from a given point to another given point was developed by the US military to ensure information and communications survival after a hostile, military attack on the United States and led to the development of the Internet. A similar description applies to criminal networks, their national and international modes of cooperation, the functioning of money laundering structures, and the operation of terrorist networks. Criminal networks are critical systems because of the tension between the elements in the system itself, between the system and similar systems, and between the system and its legal and socio-political environment. This intrinsic state of affairs is exacerbated by the lack of an external conflict resolution mechanism. Since the illegal character of the activity makes it impossible for participants to address themselves to courts or tribunals for arbitration, differences between participants or between networks are therefore settled with the use of violence, which increases the lack of stability. Nevertheless, the magnitude of the disturbance will be absorbed by the self-repairing property, which characterizes such systems, as one participant is replaced by another and as a new balance is struck between networks. One might say that as good business sense demands that solutions are found, solutions are, indeed, found.

These three crucial characteristics—ordering, self-repairing, and self-organizing criticality—make it necessary to consider what, in the network, we are observing. Since all the criminals can be readily replaced (albeit gradually), and since the merchandise can also gradually be changed (e.g. from drugs to human beings) while the network remains intact, one might ask if it would not be more useful to concentrate the analysis on the flux rather than on the operators of the flux. As the surrounding socio-political and, indeed, business, climate changes, the network must change. In the example, after a period, both all individuals and the nature of the merchandise have changed. In other words, everything has changed; indeed, for everything to remain the same, everything must change. This was the subject of Tomasi di Lampedusa's justly famous 1958 novel *The Leopard*.

Some scholars have claimed that both a premise and a consequence of criminal networks are the existence and generation of intra-network trust, which is discussed below.

Criminal networks: the world of fluxes

Network and network theory were introduced to the study of organized crime in the 1990s, in particular by the scholars Phil Williams and Malcolm Sparrow.[9] This particular use of network theory reflects dissatisfaction with the previously predominant theory of organized crime as hierarchical structures and with the extended use of network theory into various academic disciplines, and especially social network analysis in the social sciences.

To achieve explanatory value in the study of transnational organized crime, network theory can usefully be modeled either as a metaphorical or mathematical model. Criminologists, who most eagerly proselytized the introduction of network theory, have mostly been of the former kind, to such an extent that the concept of network has been stretched so far as to be practically meaningless. This chapter suggests that network theory retains an important explanatory function in the study of transnational organized crime but not in its present garb. Rather, it suggests that study of and return to the Saint-Simonian origins of the concept of networks and a concentration on circulation will revitalize the use of the concept: A network is the theatre of circulation.[10] When studying a network, one might concentrate one's attention on the nodes, as, indeed, is most often done. Nodes are obviously important in a network; knowledge is concentrated in the nodes, and individuals in the nodes act as brokers between sub-networks. The purpose of a network, however, is circulation, namely of information, merchandise, or funds. Therefore, a thorough understanding of the workings of a network must, by necessity, concentrate on the circulatory aspect, rather than on the persons involved.

The development of theory should have a practical application for transnational criminal arrests and prosecutions. A close perusal of the case studies elaborated by two of the major scholars of criminal networks, Phil Williams and Carlo Morselli, shows, however, that their more than a dozen cases have all been successfully investigated by the use of well-known techniques: the infiltration of informants into the networks and the use of physical and electronic surveillance.[11] Network theory provides an understanding of how such networks may operate, but it does not—at least not yet—assist much in the actual dismantling of criminal networks.

Existing criminal networks are protean and hence hard to define; they take on many forms and change as circumstances demand; considering their gestation and volatility, they are probably better viewed as emergent complex systems rather than as resulting from linear developments from explicitly identifiable premises.

The preceding discussion should have illustrated the neglect of the nature of ties between nodes. They may be based on one of four classifications, some of which overlap: blood ties; generational ties (same background and cultural references); ties based on neighborhood and past participation in associations; and ethnic ties. It is not ethnicity as an abstraction that binds the members together but rather the consequences of ethnicity: shared values, language, immigrant philosophy of "us and them," and trust. The most important of such ties are language, which in many instances makes investigative techniques, for example infiltration and electronic surveillance, less efficient, and trust; operating under uncertainty members of the network can, nevertheless, have *a priori* expectations as to the behavior of other members of the same network, in particular as regards information flows to the outside world.

Criminal network theory can be illustrated well with the example of human trafficking. Although victims of human trafficking are commonly referred to as "neo-slaves" and trafficking as "neo-slavery," these terms are unsatisfactory from a methodological point of view. In the so-called "African" slave trade, the relationship between slave catcher, slave trafficker, and slave exploiter ceased on each step of the transaction. Once the catcher obtained his premium from the trafficker, his interest in the slave no longer existed. Likewise, when the trafficker sold the slave to the exploiter, his interest was discontinued. In other words, one is faced with a network configuration where individual networks only meet in the nodes. By contrast, the rupture of relationship on each step of the transaction in many cases does not seem to obtain in the case of human trafficking, where the catcher (in this case more likely the "persuader") may very likely also be responsible for the transportation, and likewise will retain interest in the trafficking victim—in a perverse renaissance of the concept of indenture—until full payment has been obtained from the latter.

Thus, several cases publicized over the last couple of years have revealed the ruthlessness and extent of human trafficking networks. Box 29.1 outlines a case study from Argentina. Unfortunately, the case is not atypical, and numerous similar cases could have been detailed from countries as widespread as Spain (Nicaraguan victims) and Sweden (Romanian typically 18-year-old women). A major recent case illustrates the network aspects of this crime and its disregard for borders. The so-called Operation Pakoul (a traditional Afghan hat) in early 2012 disclosed a network with main nodes in Greece, France, Belgium, and the United Kingdom, which over the preceding ten months had trafficked 5,000 individuals to Europe via Greece.

In fact, the United Nations Office on Drugs and Crime (UNODC) in 2011 identified victims from at least 127 countries. In a study at found that application of the 2000 United Nations Protocol to Prevent, Suppress and Punish Trafficking in Persons, Especially Women and Children, Supplementing the United Nations Convention Against Transnational Organized Crime—although widely accepted—was far from uniform and very inefficient.[12] The organization therefore launched a centralized database on human trafficking, which is discussed later.

A related crime, child pornography, fully relies on the use of networks for the procurement of children, the accumulation of lurid photos, and their dissemination. Since approximately 2005 the age of the children posing has decreased and what used to be an unsavory cottage industry has now developed into international trade, directed by organized crime mostly from Eastern Europe.[13] Furthermore, this particular crime constitutes an important example of a network using a network. While producers and users are linked in one criminal network, they rely more and more on a second, criminal cyber network for exchange of and commerce in child pornography. An example is provided by an operation run by the Italian authorities in early 2012. This led to arrests in 28 countries of ring leaders and to the identification of 700 individuals selling, buying, and exchanging child pornography and videos of child abuse.

Similarly, the application of network theory might be instructive in the area of illicit traffic in organs. Box 29.2 illustrates a case in which such traffic—as is most often the case—is organized by a person who, as broker, sits in a node, from where he or she interacts

BOX 29.1 HUMAN TRAFFICKING

In 2010, a report from the NGO "The House of Encounter" in Argentina was based on information from women who had successfully escaped from the guardians or who had been set free by the police:

- Over 18 months (mid-2009 to end 2010), 700 women from different countries trafficked into the sex trade after having "disappeared—kidnapped by prostitution rings."

- Nationality: 70 percent Argentinean; the rest from Paraguay, the Dominican Republic, Peru, Bolivia, and Brazil.

- Age: the requirement for very young persons in the sex trade is increasing. The kidnapped girls are from 8 to 16 years of age.

- Gender: also young boys and male adolescents are now being kidnapped for the sex trade.

- Young women are lured into the possession of the captors by promises of employment as carers for children or the elderly.

- Break-in: rape, physical and psychological torture.

- Frequency of forced services: up to once every 20 minutes.

- International criminal network: believed to include organized crime in Mexico, Russia, and China.

with networks of surgeons, operating theatre nurses, patients, donors, and transportation agents. In fact, without playing any direct role in the perpetration of the act, the organizer, or information broker, is crucial for completion by ensuring that surgeon, nurses, donor, and patient come together in the right place at the right time, and for brokering the financial arrangements. Again, examples could have been selected from numerous regions worldwide. Indeed, the importance of the broker cannot be overestimated; and Carlo Morselli noted that criminal networks are shaped around the coordinating capacity of brokers in the network.[14] In other words, the coordinating function is typically located in the nodes that connect several networks, in the intersections.

BOX 29.2 ILLICIT TRADE IN ORGANS

In April 2010, Israel indicted five of its citizens, including a retired general, with operating an organ trafficking network. They offered $100,000 per kidney, but at least in two cases did not pay the "donors."

Donors were flown from Israel to other countries, where the organs were excised and implanted.

Networks and social capital

Social capital has been intensely studied over the last decade or more.[15] In the present context, the most pertinent concept is trust. One might think, and some scholars have proposed, that trust is the foundation on which criminal networks are built and concurrently an effect generated by cooperation within the network.

The area of trust inside criminal networks is understudied, but Klaus von Lampe and Per Ole Johansen have extensively researched the subject. They found that trust might be an important issue inside criminal networks but was variegated. Not even an outright act of "treason," the highest possible level of negative trust, necessarily led to a total disruption of relationships within the networks or to punitive measures.[16] This otherwise essential research suffers, however, from the weakness that it is based on a specific type of criminality, revenue evasion, which may not be typical for "crime" in a broader sense and, especially in the very highly taxed northern European countries, may not be the subject of opprobrium. Many if not most people would not consider the sale of non-taxed alcohol in Norway and of non-taxed tobacco product in Germany as crimes. Indeed, many might well benefit from buying tax-free alcohol and cigarettes. It is far from certain that relationships within and reactions to events inside or outside the criminal network will be comparable to a similar network engaged in "real" crime, where disclosure entails lengthy custodial sentences, sometimes and somewhere even capital punishment, and forfeiture of all assets. Von Lampe and Johansen are correct, however, in pointing out that the individuals making up criminal networks are not necessarily the most trustworthy and that, as a result, distrust and treason must be expected to some degree.

Having considered the theoretical foundations of network theory for criminal networks and the networks themselves, the following section considers global crime governance, or interdiction networks.

Interdiction networks: the world of information and trust

The transnational criminal world now consists of dynamic, self-repairing networks, the nodes of which are occupied by actors, in particular brokers, while the fluxes consist of goods, services, and monetary instruments. Interdiction efforts, public and private, have spun a somewhat less dynamic, but close-fitting network around the globe, known as the global crime governance network. The meshes are finer in such areas as money laundering and terrorism, and coarser in such others as human trafficking. The global crime governance network at present represents a complex interplay of interests, including different actors, policies, and processes. Nevertheless, underlying all general and topical areas is information and trust; trust occupies the nodes, and information travels along the many connections. Indeed, without trust, the flows of information would soon cease because law enforcement and, more generally, judicial cooperation between countries on all levels are based on goodwill and therefore trust. Setting out from the premise that it takes a network to defeat a network, first law enforcement and somewhat later prosecutorial authorities forged cooperative networks. The latter offer the advantage that they allow a quicker, informal way of cooperation when compared with the formalized procedures for treating foreign authorities through the ministries of foreign affairs and through the use of Letters Rogatory.

A Letter Rogatory is a demand for judicial assistance issued by a court in one country and transmitted to a court in another. The Letters Rogatory process ensures legal control, but suffers from a reputation for tardiness, because the request must be transmitted from court to Ministry of Justice and from Ministry of Justice to Ministry of Foreign Affairs in one country and then, in the other, to Ministry of Foreign Affairs and from there to Ministry of Justice and finally to requested court. The answer from the requested court must then travel by the same route back to the requesting court.

The interdiction network consists of international and intergovernmental organizations, transnational extensions of states' executive functions, and private or quasi-private initiatives. The result has been the establishment of another, formal interdiction network of treaties and memoranda of understanding between states, and between states and international and intergovernmental organizations. The sum of these treaties and memoranda is important, but the network consisting of extradition treaties is more impressive. In fact, it can be considered one of the finest-meshed networks, that often, but not always, is also one of the most efficient.

The UNODC in Vienna, Austria, is an overarching think tank in the interdiction network, a repository for related statistics, and an active generator of international law. As noted above, the UNODC launched the first global database of human trafficking cases, which demonstrates the use of networks against networks. The database provides immediate, public access to officially documented instances of this crime, and it aims to assist judges, prosecutors, policy-makers, media researchers, and other interested parties by making available details of real cases. At its launch, more than 150 selected cases from over 30 countries and two regional courts were uploaded, including details on victims' and perpetrators' nationalities, trafficking routes, verdicts, and other information related to prosecuted cases from across the world.

While Interpol—or more correctly the International Criminal Police Organization (ICPO)—in Lyon, France, has both educational and think tank functions, from the inception of the organization in 1923, its main task remains operational, namely the exchange of actionable data on criminal activity via the Interpol Criminal Information System (ICIS—created in 1998). An important milestone in the organization's history was reached in 2005, when Interpol issued the first Interpol–United Nations Special Notices for individuals subject to UN sanctions, based on determination by the United Nations Security Council.

The Organisation for Economic Co-operation and Development (OECD) is another vital link in the network, in particular its anti-corruption efforts as witnessed by its Convention on Combating Bribery of Foreign Public Officials in International Business Transactions. After entering into force in 1999 it has been adopted by all 34 member states and five non-member states (Argentina, Brazil, Bulgaria, Russia, and South Africa).

The G7 of leading economic powers (or G8 with Russia) has played a decisive steering role in global crime governance; in its summit declarations it lays down moral and intellectual pointers, and binds summit countries to honor its obligations vis-à-vis international organizations engaged in crime governance. For instance, in 1998 at the G8 Summit meeting in Birmingham, UK, the summit countries noted that globalization had "been accompanied by a dramatic increase in transnational crime" and constituted a global threat "which can undermine the democratic and economic basis of societies."[17] The G20 has continued this trend, but concentrates more on the financial aspects of crime; in particular, corruption has been the subject of G20 declarations (2010 Seoul and 2011 Cannes summits).[18]

Likewise, a number of national enforcement, criminal intelligence, and judicial entities have formed more formal international cooperative organizations to increase the flow of information. Various financial intelligence units (FIUs) in 1997 created the Egmont Group and exchange information through a secure website. Some scholars would postulate a clear democratic deficit with regard to the operation of such networks. Ironically, the anti-money laundering network is extremely developed, allegedly investigating the proceeds of crime, but in reality more likely concentrated on revenue violations. Similar structures, apart from Interpol, do not exist for crimes such as commercial sexual exploitation of children or, indeed, counterfeiting of pharmaceuticals. Counterfeit and substandard anti-malarial drugs alone are responsible for some 200,000 deaths a year.[19]

Finally, a number of countries have created a network of so-called liaison officers (criminal police officers) stationed in countries worldwide. The network is more or less extensive depending on each country, the most active of which are the United States, Germany, and France. A liaison officer maintains good relations between his or her home country's law enforcement and that of the host country. But these officials also play an active and important role in ongoing investigations by obtaining direct access to investigators in both countries and thus to information that is not, or not yet, available via the usual communication systems, for example Interpol. Box 29.3 provides a partial overview of the overseas stations of US law enforcement.

Groups of private citizens also engage in and surface as interdiction networks. An example is the courageous and efficient Libera Terra (Free Land) movement in Sicily, which has successfully faced down local organized crime by refusing payment of protection money (the so-called *pizzo*), by administering assets seized from the Mafia, and by reallocating long-term "Mafia employees" to legal employment. The basic node content in this network is trust, as only cohesion of the network nodes prevents any opposed, typically violent, reaction.[20]

An overlooked transnational interdiction network is referred to as "forensic accounting and corporate investigations" (FACI). The development of this network was a consequence of the major role played by transnational enterprises in globalization:

BOX 29.3 US LAW ENFORCEMENT OFFICES ABROAD[21]

- Drug Enforcement Administration: 85 foreign offices
- Federal Bureau of Investigation: 76 foreign offices
- Secret Service: 20 foreign offices
- Bureau of Alcohol, Tobacco, Firearms and Explosives: 10 foreign offices
- US Immigration and Customs Enforcement: 47 foreign offices

"The growth of transnationals in virtually every sector of modern economies, especially since the 1970s, has added a completely new dimension to global specialization and exchange."[22] Entities within one transnational enterprise, and often enterprises among themselves, are characterized by their ability to share knowledge, resources, and responsibilities.

The propagation of, in particular US, transnational enterprises across the planet led to the concurrent dissemination of FACI. In order to appreciate their financial status, transnational enterprises had to streamline the record-keeping of their domestic as well as non-domestic branches by imposing uniform accounting regulations throughout each individual transnational enterprise and by establishing worldwide auditing functions consisting of teams who inspect and audit each branch office in an unending cycle according to the centrally determined accounting and auditing guidelines. Commonly accepted, understandable, and transparent accounting and auditing rules were slowly established worldwide. These rules were backed by quasi-uniform training of personnel and their professionalization—for example through specialized associations such as the American Society for Industrial Security. Likewise, and based on the central corporate authority, internal corporate investigations imposed, step by step, US concepts of corporate governance that have become widespread—for instance in matters as disparate as the prevention of corruption of foreign officials and of sexual harassment. The influence of transnational enterprises and the dissemination of FACI led over the last three decades to changes in corporate culture and altered rules, regulations, and laws—a quasi-legislative process referred to by Gunther Teubner as "Global Law."[23]

Anne-Marie Slaughter argues that problems of democratic accountability could be overcome by ensuring that such international cooperation through networks was the prerogative of "politically accountable government officials" rather than a "hodgepodge" of "experts, enthusiasts, international bureaucrats, and transnational businesspeople."[24] She sees the modern world very much as a network one—for instance, the European Union is a network of networks. She may be correct but transferring network governance patterns from cooperation in agricultural to criminal matters requires considerable analytical caution. Clearly, today's interconnected world requires new means of governance, including for criminal law. Nevertheless, information being exchanged through such networks as one FIU to another is often about persons and actions that are vaguely "suspect" rather than the subject of or linked to a definable criminal investigation. Such inquiries presumably would not even pass the probable cause test in front of a judge. It may be that this kind of exchange is valid in maintaining the security of the citizen, but as long as these initiatives are not parts of a global rule of law system with appropriate, non-executive overview, the concern of misuse remains.

Conclusion

The notion of networks is widespread in contemporary social science, ranging from criminology to international relations, from anthropology to public administration. Both criminal networks and the concomitant creation of judicial and enforcement networks are properly seen as part of a more generalized use of networks in global governance. This chapter, however, pointed also to the concern that the development of government networks might be outside of democratic and judicial control, in particular in the area of criminal law.

However, networks undoubtedly will continue to develop, as they have characteristics that render them "unstoppable"—to use a term from a recent work on leaderless organizations.[25] In fact, Ori Brafman and Rod Beckstrom stipulate a number of characteristics of leaderless organizations, which they term "starfish." When attacked, a decentralized organization tends to become even more open and decentralized because it is a neural network. Moreover, intelligence is spread throughout the system and is not centralized, which explains resilience. As noted, leaderless systems can easily mutate, and mutate incredibly quickly. These observations echo those of Moisés Naím: "Networks behave like mercury. Once one tries to grab it, it slips through one's fingers, forming many smaller droplets." His conclusion about enforcement follows: often "government interference is nothing more than another cost of doing business, and as often it just serves as a price-boasting intervention."[26] A discouraging, but accurate observation that echoes Anja Jakobi: "the rise of global crime governance does not necessarily imply that crime has decreased."[27]

This chapter has reviewed the use of network theory as an explanatory and illustrative lens through which to analyze international and transnational organized crime and the relevance for contemporary global governance. Seeing criminal networks as consisting of several sub-networks makes the concept even more effective in viewing the range of actors and issues that are detailed throughout this volume. Municipal and international law by necessity describes transnational organized crime in terms of human beings and their acts. This chapter also has suggested that the network concept has been applied too generically and imprecisely, and that a concentration on variations within the networks could revitalize its analytical usefulness.

Additional reading

1. Anja P. Jakobi, *Common Goods or Evils? The Formation of Global Crime Governance* (Oxford: Oxford University Press, forthcoming 2013).
2. Vincent Lemieux, *Criminal Networks* (Ottawa: RCMP, March 2003).
3. Carlo Morselli, *Inside Criminal Networks* (New York: Springer, 2009).
4. Anne-Marie Slaughter, *A New World Order* (Princeton and Oxford: Princeton University Press, 2004).
5. Malcolm K. Sparrow, "Network Analysis and Criminal Intelligence," *Social Networks* 13 (1991): 251–274.
6. Phil Williams, "Transnational Criminal Networks," in *Networks and Netwars: The Future of Terror, Crime, and Militancy,* eds. John Arquilla and David Ronfeld (Santa Monica, CA: RAND, 2001), 61–98.
7. Interpol, http://www.interpol.int.

Notes

1 Manuel Castells, *End of Millennium*, 2nd edition (Oxford: Blackwell, 2000), 171.
2 Moisés Naím, "Mafia States: Organized Crime Takes Office," *Foreign Affairs* 91, no. 3 (2012): 100–111.

3 Nicholas Watt, "Corruption Still Dogs Bulgaria on Eve of Ruling on Membership," *Guardian* (15 May 2006).

4 Stephen Handelman, "The Russian 'Mafiya,'" *Foreign Affairs* 73, no. 2 (1994): 83–96.

5 Antonio Cassese, *International Criminal Law*, 2nd edition (Oxford: Oxford University Press, 2008), 11.

6 I thank Professor Arthur Gibson, Department of Pure Mathematics and Mathematical Statistics, Centre for Mathematical Sciences, University of Cambridge, for advice regarding graph theory and for having read a first draft of the chapter.

7 Daniel Parrochia, "La Rationalité réticulaire," in *Penser les Réseaux*, ed. Daniel Parrochia (Seyssel, France: Editions Champs Vallon, 2001), 13.

8 Phil Williams, "Transnational Criminal Networks," in *Networks and Netwars: The Future of Terror, Crime, and Militancy*, eds. John Arquilla and David Ronfeld (Santa Monica, CA: RAND, 2001), 72; Frank G. Madsen, "International Narcotics Law Enforcement: A Study in Irrationality," *Journal of International Affairs* 66, no. 1 (2012): 123–144.

9 Phil Williams, "The Nature of Drug Trafficking Networks," *Current History* 97, no. 618 (1998): 154–159; and see, in particular, Williams, "Transnational Criminal Networks."

10 Parrochia, "La Rationalité réticulaire," 17.

11 Williams, "Transitional Criminal Networks," 84–90; and Carlo Morselli, *Inside Criminal Networks* (New York: Springer, 2009), chapters 2–8.

12 UNODC, *Trafficking in Persons: Global Patterns* with Appendices (Vienna: UNODC, April 2006). See also Commission on Crime Prevention and Criminal Justice, *Report on the Twentieth Session (3 December 2010 and 11–15 April 2011)* (E/CN.15/2011/21) (New York: United Nations, 2011).

13 Max Taylor and Ethel Quayle, *Child Pornography: An Internet Crime* (Hove, UK, and New York: Brunner-Routledge, 2003), 42–45. *Puppet on a String: The Urgent Need to Set Children Free from Sexual Exploitation* (Barkingside, Ilford, UK: Barnardo's, 2011), 12.

14 Morselli, *Inside Criminal Networks*, 117.

15 See Dario Castiglione, Jan W. van Deth, and Guglielmo Wolleb, eds., *The Handbook of Social Capital* (Oxford: Oxford University Press, 2008).

16 Klaus von Lampe and Per Ole Johansen, "Criminal Networks and Trust," *Global Crime* 6, no. 2 (2004): 159–184.

17 G8 Birmingham Summit, "Drugs and International Crime," 16 May 1998, art. 1.

18 The G20 Seoul summit created an anti-corruption workgroup that wrote the "G20 Anti-Corruption Action Plan," see Annex III to *G20 Seoul Framework for Strong, Sustainable and Balanced Growth*.

19 Gaurvika M. L. Nayyar, Joel G. Breman, Paul N. Newton, and James Herrington, "Poor-Quality Antimalarial Drugs in Southeast Asia and Sub-Saharan Africa," *The Lancet Infectious Diseases Journal* 12, no. 6 (June 2012): 488–496. The article notes that 30 percent of drugs purchased at random in Southeast Asia failed testing of their pharmaceutical ingredient. The same number for sub-Saharan Africa is 35 percent. WHO reports that 655,000 individuals are killed by malaria every year, of which 200,000 deaths are ascribable to substandard and counterfeit production of anti-malarial medication.

20 Joshua Hammer, "In Sicily, Defying the Mafia," *Smithsonian Magazine* (October 2010).

21 The website for each individual administration has been consulted, although the Central Intelligence Agency has not been included along with a number of minor administrations with only a couple of overseas postings, such as US Postal Inspection Service and New York Police Department.

22 Milivoye Panić, *Globalization and National Economic Welfare* (Basingstoke: Palgrave Macmillan, 2003), 5. See also xxi and chapter 6 *in toto*, 148–176.

23 Gunther Teubner, ed., *Global Law without a State* (Aldershot: Dartmouth Publishing, 1997), 87. See also Thomas Mathiesen, "Lex Vigilatoria: Global Control without a State?" in

Surveillance and Governance: Crime Control and Beyond, ed. Mathieu Deflem (Bingley, UK: Emerald, 2008), 101–127.

24 Anne-Marie Slaughter, *A New World Order* (Princeton and Oxford: Princeton University Press, 2004), 262.

25 Ori Brafman and Rod A. Beckstrom, *The Starfish and the Spider: The Unstoppable Power of Leaderless Organizations* (New York: Portfolio, 2006).

26 Moisés Naím, *Illicit* (New York: Doubleday, 2005).

27 Anja P. Jakobi, *Common Goods or Evils? The Formation of Global Crime Governance* (Oxford: Oxford University Press, forthcoming 2013), chapter 1.

PART VI
SECURING THE WORLD,
GOVERNING HUMANITY

INTRODUCTION

Part VI of this book contains ten chapters on "Securing the world, governing humanity." One of the main explanations for human efforts to better govern the world has been the need to foster international peace and security. Wars have typically led to experiments with different generations of international organization—the Congress of Vienna after the Napoleonic wars; the League of Nations after World War I; and the United Nations after World War II.

We have arranged this part of the book to flow from the global governance of conflict prevention through to the reconstruction of war-torn societies and the human aspects of global security governance. This is by no means an order of importance, merely a way of organizing reading around topics that are familiar. All courses on international organization and global governance could, for instance, use Paul D. Williams and Alex J. Bellamy's chapter on "The UN Security Council and peace operations" (Chapter 30)—the most familiar and high-profile aspect of global security governance. "Regional organizations and global security governance"—as S. Neil McFarlane shows in Chapter 31—are also an increasingly salient part of the story, which advanced or specialist classes on global security would also likely take in. Thereafter, Part VI offers readers a suite of chapters dealing with specific issues—"Weapons of mass destruction" (Waheguru Pal Singh Sidhu, Chapter 32), "From 'global war' to global governance: counterterrorism cooperation in world politics " (Peter Romaniuk, Chapter 33), "Human rights in global governance" (Julie Mertus, Chapter 34), "The pursuit of international justice" (Richard J. Goldstone, Chapter 35), "Humanitarian intervention and R2P" (Simon Chesterman, Chapter 36), "Crisis and humanitarian containment" (Fabrice Weissman, Chapter 37) "Post-conflict peacebuilding" (Rob Jenkins, Chapter 38), and "Human security as a global public good" (Fen Hampson and Mark Raymond, Chapter 39)—that can be explored as courses of study and interest allow. They nonetheless cover a large part of the global security governance gambit, the content of which represents a considerable resource.

Securing the world, governing humanity: chapter synopses

Various forms of military force are often the products of decisions made by, and provide the background for, the "UN Security Council and peace operations." One of six UN "principal organs," the council is the only part of the world organization's machinery that makes "decisions" that are binding on member states rather than "recommendations" that states can even more easily ignore. In Chapter 30, Paul D. Williams and Alex J. Bellamy provide an historical overview and analysis of the development of traditional UN peacekeeping in addition to scrutinizing the contemporary debates related to the relationship between the UN and regional arrangements, questions about who provides UN peacekeepers, and controversial issues related to the use of military firepower. UN peace operations have always been a testimony of adaptation and learning, seeing what works in practice not in theory.

In Chapter 31 S. Neil MacFarlane explores "Regional organizations and global security governance" as essential building blocks for global security governance. While regional economic cooperation has long been the subject of scholarly theorizing and analysis, MacFarlane demonstrates the extent to which regional security organizations are a growing reality that requires more understanding if we are to improve global security governance. While always seen as potential partners for the universal United Nations in Chapter VIII of the UN Charter, regional organizations have assumed an unprecedented role in peace operations since the end of the Cold War. Both the UN's overstretch and their comparative advantages made regional organizations far more central to international conflict management and resolution. In particular, the fabric of global security governance has many regional strands, but the diversity in capabilities means that many regions actually have no real organization to help improve security while others are well heeled. Experience suggests a substantial potential for a division of labor between the UN and regional organizations in global security governance, but that potential is far from being realized.

In Chapter 32 Waheguru Pal Singh Sidhu explores "Weapons of mass destruction" (WMDs) by parsing the nuclear, chemical, and biological threats whose proliferation constitutes a major challenge to contemporary global security governance. Sidhu spells out the existing regimes that govern each of the WMDs. He argues that they should not be lumped together but unpacked to understand how far we have come and how far we have to go for each. The task has taken on increased urgency lest they fall into the hands of "rogue" states and non-state actors. Sidhu indicates the hypocrisy of the Security Council's permanent five members pointing fingers at various states that possess or are trying to procure WMDs but without taking significant steps to move forward in global governance by reducing their own obscenely large arsenals of all types.

Peter Romaniuk deals with counterterrorism in Chapter 33—"From 'global war' to global governance: counterterrorism cooperation in world politics"—a topic that seems omnipresent since 9/11 and also since the label is increasingly used as a convenient moniker to describe any dissident that is fighting an entrenched regime. Romaniuk spells out growing but fledgling intergovernmental efforts to improve the prospects for minimizing the damage from terrorism, if not halt every instance. He demonstrates the utility of using global governance as a concept in interpreting counterterrorism cooperation over time because capturing "process" and "activities" among a range of state and non-state actors is the essence of exercising authority and influence in various forms to fight this plague. There are multiple routes to effective action, including the flexible use by states of UN machinery.

In most texts the previous topics would clearly be among "security" institutions. But contemporary notions of the topic require a broader discussion. Thus, we asked a distinguished team to explore issues that provide a more complete and complex depiction of how important components underlying international peace and security, namely human rights and humanitarian affairs, are governed.

In Chapter 34, Julie Mertus addresses "Human rights in global governance." Perhaps the most subversive and revolutionary element contained in the UN Charter—Eleanor Roosevelt used the image of a "grapevine" to indicate that human rights would take on a life of their own—Mertus unpacks how both public international law and an increasing number of organizations of all stripes are working in the vineyard. The emphasis is on intergovernmental machinery, but nongovernmental organizations are a key part of her tale as well.

In Chapter 35, Richard J. Goldstone examines "The pursuit of international justice." Tracing the advance of international criminal justice from the carnage of Solferino and the founding of the International Committee of the Red Cross, through the Nuremberg trials to today's frequent media reports on the prosecution of war criminals, Goldstone demonstrates how much these developments are indicators of advances in global governance. Of particular interest was the institutionalization of international criminal justice through the courts that were established in the last decade of the twentieth century—namely, the two United Nations ad hoc tribunals for the former Yugoslavia and for Rwanda, the various hybrid or mixed tribunals, and the International Criminal Court.

No topic has moved more quickly in the international normative arena than the "responsibility to protect" (R2P), and few people are better placed than Simon Chesterman to analyze that advance. In Chapter 36—"Humanitarian intervention and R2P"—he details the history of the contested moniker "humanitarian intervention" and its replacement by the more palatable, at least to many, norm of "R2P." The international rules governing the use of force and the attempts—largely unsuccessful—to fit humanitarian intervention into those rules are examined. So too are the moral, legal, political, and military challenges that come to the fore in discussing post-Cold War applications of the use of military force for human protection purposes, from northern Iraq to Libya.

Chapter 37 addresses the fallout from such interventions and the politicization of life-saving succor for war victims. Fabrice Weissman's "Crisis and humanitarian containment" reflects his views as a field practitioner whose analytical skills have been honed within one of the more reflective NGOs, Médecins Sans Frontières. The politicized arena for contemporary humanitarian action involves considerable material and symbolic stakes. Coming to the rescue is not necessarily on the side of the angels in today's fraught world of international organization and global governance. Tough decisions and countless political transactions are the daily bill-of-fare, but they often are concealed by legal and moral rhetoric. Distinguishing between "new" (politicized engagement) and "autonomous" humanitarianism, Weissman indicates the costs and benefits of decisions by aid agencies to align themselves with international military forces and to participate in humanitarian and peacebuilding efforts determined by donor priorities. He makes a plea for future global humanitarian governance to return to the tradition of impartial relief; and he questions the wisdom of aid agencies that have solidified an alliance with liberal democracies and the UN based on neutralizing and punishing war criminals as well as establishing a liberal peace in dysfunctional societies torn apart by "new wars."

Picking up the pieces after wars is not new, but the number of civil wars beginning in the late 1980s and their devastation led to a dramatic expansion of such efforts. Theorizing about the challenges ensued, as did the establishment of new UN "architecture" devoted specifically to such efforts—the Peacebuilding Commission, the Peacebuilding Support Office, and the Peacebuilding Fund. In Chapter 38 Rob Jenkins traces the evolution of the idea of "Post-conflict peacebuilding" and the real-world environment in which it takes place, and pays attention to the relationship between them. He also examines why peacebuilding has been contested over time, especially because of interference in domestic affairs. Adaptation is part of the story of both international organization and global governance. Like "peacekeeping," which does not figure in the Charter but is generally considered a creative UN invention, so too has "peacebuilding" become a major task, although without figuring in the UN's constitution.

Chapter 39 concludes Part VI of the book. Fen Hampson and Mark Raymond survey "Human security as a global public good." The move from the international security specialist's obsession with bombs, bullets, and other hardware to a concern with the welfare and empowerment of individuals as the ultimate way to measure security is a conceptual and operational leap for students of IO and global governance. Perhaps the biggest challenge for governing the world is the lack of global public goods, and Hampson and Raymond's approach is ambitious: the provision and protection of basic human liberties, certain key political and civil rights, and basic standards of equity and social justice for all peoples regardless of their ethnic or national origins, socio-economic status, religious creed, or political persuasion. Admitting that all are underprovided, they argue for a portfolio diversification to the provision of global public goods related to human security. Different combinations of actors and institutions and networks are required to maximize the comparative advantages of each.

Where to from here?

This part of the book provides an extensive overview of efforts to attenuate insecurities and the forces behind them. Together these chapters fill in a large part of the global governance puzzle. Once they have been consulted, their wisdom needs to be overlaid with an understanding of how the world is governed in the economic and social world, and how institutions and mechanisms have evolved to address global environmental degradation—issues to which the final part of the book (Part VII) turns.

UN Security Council and Peace Operations

Paul D. Williams and Alex J. Bellamy

The UN Security Council has never possessed a monopoly on either the authorization or conduct of peace operations. But the Council has become the predominant source of authority for legitimizing such operations and the UN's "blue helmets" have conducted more than any other entity—67 missions as of September 2012. By mid-2012, the UN was fielding approximately 100,000 uniformed personnel in its peace operations (i.e. soldiers, police officers, and security experts) at a cost of about US$7bn a year.

Particularly since the end of the Cold War, the Security Council has authorized and conducted increasing numbers of peace operations. It has also tended to give them broader mandates, sometimes encompassing everything from assisting the implementation of peace agreements, establishing the rule of law, protecting civilians, disarming and reintegrating combatants, supporting electoral processes, reforming security sectors, and facilitating humanitarian assistance. A major reason why these mandates broadened was because they were often conducted in the complex theaters of intra-state armed conflicts and because the Security Council displayed an unprecedented level of interest in the internal governance structures of the host state. Not surprisingly, as these operations have increased in number and scope, so too did the number of peacekeepers required and the bill to support them.

Although UN peace operations have received their fair share of criticisms, overall they have had positive effects on many of the world's conflict zones. As one analyst put it, "The answer to the question of whether peacekeeping works is a clear and resounding yes."[1] Some have credited peace operations with helping to lower the number of armed conflicts from the global peak in the early 1990s.[2] Others have noted that peace operations significantly reduce the likelihood of wars reigniting after peace agreements have been concluded. Specifically, where UN peacekeepers are deployed, the likelihood of war reigniting fell by at least 75–85 percent compared to cases where no peacekeepers were deployed.[3] Peace operations have also significantly increased the probability that genocide and mass killing can be slowed or stopped.[4] It is also thought that peace operations can make a positive contribution to building stable, democratic peace in the medium and long term. This is important because while enforcement operations can stop violence they cannot sow the seeds of long-term peace. On the other hand, consent-based operations may struggle to stop violence but are quite effective in helping belligerents build long-term, democratic peace when they choose to put down their arms.[5] If deployed effectively, therefore, enforcement operations can lay the foundations for a subsequent consensual peace operation which can make a significant contribution to building long-term, stable peace.

This chapter provides an historical overview and analysis of the development of peace operations as well as three key contemporary debates related to the relationship between the UN and regional arrangements, questions about participation in peace operations and who provides UN peacekeepers, and issues related to the use of military force.

History and development

Peace operations can be said to involve the expeditionary use of uniformed personnel (police and/or military) with a mandate from an international institution or at the invitation of all parties to a peace agreement to: assist in the prevention of armed conflict by supporting a peace process; serve as an instrument to observe or assist in the implementation of ceasefires or peace agreements; or enforce ceasefires, peace agreements, or the will of the Security Council in order to build stable peace. Although this definition encompasses a wide range of operations—approximately 200 missions since the end of World War II—it does not include the UN's political missions, of which there are currently about a dozen, usually run by the UN's Department of Political Affairs.

In theoretical terms, the story of the Security Council and its relationship to peace operations is best captured through a constructivist lens because the UN Charter did not define or even contain the term "peacekeeping." As a result, the world organization and its member states have developed and legitimized certain norms and practices related to peace operations over time. In short, peace operations are what international society, and particularly the Security Council, make them.

Since the creation of the UN in 1945, the universe of peace operations can be divided into three broad types, depending on the source of authority that established the mission and the type of actor that conducted it. First, there are UN-led operations. These "blue helmet" missions are authorized under Chapters VI and VII of the Charter but are also commanded and conducted by the UN. Second, there are UN-authorized operations. These missions are authorized by the UN with reference to Chapters VI, VII or VIII of the charter, but the command and control of mechanisms are delegated to other actors, such as coalitions of states or other international organizations such as the European Union and African Union. Finally, there are non-UN operations. These missions perform the tasks associated with peace operations but do so without a mandate from the Security Council and are conducted by non-UN actors. Some examples of these

Table 30.1 Peace operations: a typology with examples

Actor	UN operations	UN-authorized operations	Non-UN operations
UN blue helmets	UNEF, UNFICYP, UNOSOM, UNMIL, MONUC, etc.	N/A	N/A
Other international organizations	N/A	• NATO (KFOR) in Kosovo (1999–) • ECOWAS in Côte d'Ivoire (2003–04) • EU in Bosnia (2004–)	• ECOWAS in Liberia (1990–97)[†] • NATO in Kosovo (1999)[††] • SADC in Lesotho (1998)
Coalition of the willing	N/A	• UNITAF in Somalia (1992–93)[††] • INTERFET in East Timor (1999) • ISAF in Afghanistan (2002–)	• Helpem Fren in Solomon Islands (2003–)[†]
Individual government	N/A	No examples	• UK in Sierra Leone (2000)[†] • South Africa in Burundi (2001–03)[†]

Notes: [†] Missions subsequently welcomed by the UN Security Council in either a resolution or presidential statement. [††] Missions conducted without host government consent.

different types of peace operations are displayed in Table 30.1. The rest of this chapter focuses on the first category of UN-led, "blue helmet" peace operations.

The history of peacekeeping is a prime example of constructivism in action—i.e. the rules have been made up as the UN went along. The vision of the UN as the "world's policeman" was severely circumscribed by the Cold War and the organization became more of an instrument of crisis management than an institution concerned with policing international law. Employed first as an ad hoc tool in response to individual crises, peacekeeping became one of the UN's principal instruments for crisis management. Indeed, this has been a constant theme whereby the key characteristics of peacekeeping have evolved in line with the political circumstances in which peacekeepers found themselves.

In 1947 the General Assembly dispatched an observation mission (UNSCOB) in response to a complaint from the Greek government that its Yugoslav neighbor was actively assisting Communist rebels engaged in a civil war against the government. The following year, the Security Council began its engagement in two of the world's most pressing crises, the Israeli–Palestinian conflict and the struggle over Kashmir. In the Middle East, the UN's Ralph Bunche secured a ceasefire agreement that would be overseen by a UN Truce Supervision Organization (UNTSO). UNTSO played an important role in helping to constitute peacekeeping as a distinct practice in international security. A similar model was pursued in Kashmir, where the Council authorized the creation of a mission (UNMOGIP) to observe a ceasefire and write periodic reports. In the space of a few months in 1948, the Security Council had begun to carve out a role for itself in the promotion of international peace and security and to lay the foundations of modern peace operations.

These ad hoc missions began to be seen as an opportunity for the UN to play a coherent role in what was called "preventive diplomacy"—a concept articulated by Secretary-General Dag Hammarskjöld, although his predecessor as secretary-general, Trygve Lie (1946–52), laid the groundwork. Hammarskjöld described "preventive diplomacy" as the "main field of useful activity of the UN in its efforts to prevent conflicts or to solve conflicts." He saw the UN's primary role as intervening in crises to prevent the escalation of local conflicts into regional or global wars.[6] However, it was the need to develop operational guidelines for the UN's first self-styled peacekeeping operation, UNEF I—deployed to the Sinai to help defuse the Suez Crisis of 1956—and not conceptual thinking about the UN's role that prompted the organization to further refine its thinking on peacekeeping.

What became the core principles of consent, impartiality, and minimum use of force were first developed in response to the Suez crisis and were framed by the twin goals of developing a proposal that could make a positive difference whilst being acceptable to member states. At the time, there was little recognition outside the UN Secretariat that important precedents were being established. Nonetheless, the UN went on to conduct several more similar operations before the end of the Cold War. It is important, however, not to fall into the trap of thinking that Cold War peacekeeping was exclusively concerned with ceasefire monitoring and supervision. During this period, the UN also undertook peace enforcement action in the Congo (ONUC), and embarked on complex missions in the Congo and Dutch West New Guinea (West Irian) that had comprehensive mandates for, among other things, helping to build state institutions and promote human rights.

The UN's operation in the Congo (ONUC, 1960–64) was a larger, more complex, costly, and multifaceted operation than anything the organization had attempted previously. Although it accomplished much of its mandate, ONUC proved highly controversial, divided the Security Council, and helped create a financial crisis for UN peace operations. At its height, almost 20,000 troops were deployed alongside a significant civilian component, and the mission was mandated to fulfill a number of different roles. ONUC was mandated to maintain law and order during the Congo's turbulent decolonization after Belgian rule. However, the rapid disintegration of the security situation forced ONUC away from Hammarskjöld's vision of preventive diplomacy (as reflected in the UNEF I mission) towards peace enforcement to help defend the Congo's territorial integrity. The political fallout from ONUC had a profoundly negative effect on UN peace operations. In the 23 years that followed ONUC, the UN conducted only five new missions, four of which were continuations of previous UN engagements in the Middle East and Kashmir, while the fifth, UNFICYP in Cyprus, was aided by a unique set of circumstances that saw Britain keen to divest itself of its colonial responsibilities there.

As the Cold War wound down between 1988 and 1993, peace operations underwent a transformation driven by a combination of demand-side factors (notably the resolution of Cold War proxy conflicts which generated requests for UN support) and supply-side factors which made it easier for the Council to reach a consensus and take a proactive stance. The key aspects were:

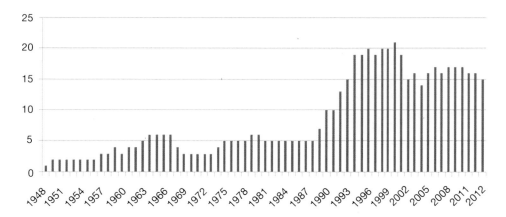

Figure 30.1 Number of ongoing UN-led peacekeeping operations, 1948–2012

- a *quantitative transformation* which saw the number of UN-led peacekeeping operations grow rapidly, such that in a five-year period the UN launched more peace operations than it had in its previous 40 (see Figure 30.1);

- a *normative transformation* catalyzed by a growing belief among some member states that peacekeepers should be at the forefront of defending and extending liberal values; and

- a *qualitative transformation* which led to peacekeepers being asked to deliver humanitarian aid, protect vulnerable populations, deter violations of Security Council mandates, oversee elections, and assist in the building of state institutions.

In short, not only did the Council authorize more peacekeeping missions, they were much larger and more expensive than anything the UN had attempted before, with the important exception of ONUC.

Problems emerged, however, as it became clear—just as it had during the ONUC mission in the 1960s—that the principles and guidelines for peacekeeping were not suited to the operational demands of large and complex missions deployed in situations of ongoing violence. In September 1992, UNAVEM II was unable to prevent the slide back into civil war in Angola or to protect civilians as approximately 300,000 people died when violence resumed. A little over a year later, in October 1993, US attempts to arrest the Somali warlord Mohamed Farah Aidid resulted in the notorious "Black Hawk Down" incident and the eventual withdrawal of UNOSOM II. Then in April 1994 the Arusha peace process in Rwanda collapsed as Hutu militia and coup plotters unleashed genocide on the country that the UN mission (UNAMIR) was unable to prevent or stop and which killed an estimated 800,000 people. In July 1995, around 8,000 men and boys were taken from the UN-protected "safe area" of Srebrenica in Bosnia and killed by Bosnian Serb forces.

Both the traditional approach to UN peacekeeping and the resources made available by member states proved badly insufficient to accomplish the increasingly ambitious mandates handed down by the Security Council. In environments where peace and ceasefire agreements were often precarious, peacekeepers were repeatedly confronted with an awful dilemma: soldier on with the limited resources, authority, and political support offered by international society, or advocate withdrawal. Although the UN received much of the blame for what happened—some of it rightly so—it is important to note the crucial roles played by its member states. It was member states, not the UN Secretariat, which crafted the mandates and determined resources for these four operations. Moreover, the bungled operation in Mogadishu in October 1993 that marked the beginning of the end for UNOSOM II was conducted by US soldiers (not UN peacekeepers); the UN Department of Peacekeeping Operations (DPKO) had warned the Security Council that without adequate resources the so-called "safe areas" in Bosnia would be vulnerable to attack; and the decision to stand aside during Rwanda's genocide in 1994 was taken against the advice of the UN's force commander on the ground.

These catastrophes prompted many states to reassess the value of peace operations and how they would contribute to them. Some senior UN officials also questioned whether the organization should go "back to basics" and focus only on conducting operations in benign conditions and with the consent of the host parties.[7] The number of UN peacekeepers deployed around the world fell dramatically as member states expressed a preference for working through regional organizations and alliances, such as ECOWAS and NATO, and the Security Council became reluctant to create new missions. A period of introspection occurred at the UN which resulted in some important reforms, not least those outlined in four important reports examining various aspects of UN peace operations: the inquiries into the failings at Srebrenica (1999) and Rwanda (1999), the "Brahimi Report" on UN peace operations (2000), and the report on the failure of the UN sanctions regime against UNITA rebels in Angola (2000).

One of the most significant was the 2000 report of the UN Secretary-General's Panel on United Nations Peace Operations. The so-called Brahimi Report, named after its chair, the troubleshooter Lakhdar Brahimi, called for steps to be taken to ensure that peacekeeping operations have the resources, training, and operational guidance needed to complete their work, that missions be deployed rapidly, and that peacekeepers are capable of operating effectively. The phrase "robust peacekeeping" was coined to refer to the idea that, at a minimum, UN peacekeepers should be able to defend themselves, other members of the mission and associated international staff, and protect civilian populations within the area of operations. To achieve this, peacekeepers should be presumed to have permission to use force in defense of the mission's mandate at the operational and tactical levels, while maintaining the consent of the major parties at the strategic level. The report thus ushered in a decade-long process of reform at the United Nations, which has fundamentally changed the way in which peacekeeping is managed.

The world organization also made major strides in terms of professionalizing its operations. Professionalization here refers to the development of a cadre of competent bureaucrats, relevant doctrine, guidelines and procedures for peacekeeping, and the capacity to engage in systematic reflection on the UN's failures and successes.[8] Institutionally, key developments were the establishment of DPKO in early 1992, its gradual strengthening and then its separation from the provision of peacekeeing logistics by the establishment of the Department of Field Support (DFS) in 2007. Among other things, the UN has developed operational guidelines for peacekeeping, basic requirements for national contingents, a stronger system for logistics support, and improved support for training. The DPKO has also become much more cautious in its advice to the Security

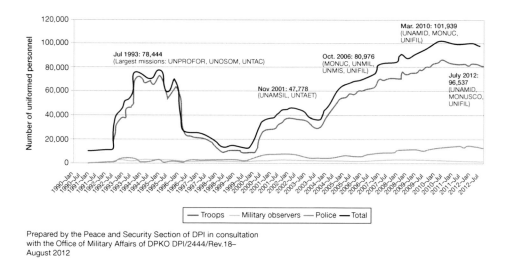

Figure 30.2 Number of uniformed personnel in UN-led peacekeeping operations

Council in relation to what can be achieved through peacekeeping. As a result, an informal division of labor has begun to emerge, with peacekeeping activities being conducted by the UN and regional arrangements or ad hoc coalitions of the willing taking primary responsibility for higher intensity military operations. Often, these two types of operation have worked in unison, whether sequentially (for example in East Timor, where the UN deployed after the conditions had been created by an Australian-led intervention force, INTERFET) or simultaneously (for example the 2003 French-led intervention in eastern DRC conducted alongside the UN mission, MONUC).

In the first decade of the twenty-first century there were significant changes in how the Security Council carried out its peacekeeping business. At the strategic level, the real politics of decision-making concerning peace operations takes place in informal settings. Informal interaction between Council members—whether in the form of external retreats, corridor discussions, seminars, or informal meetings—now occurs very regularly, making it easier for the Council to find consensus on most peacekeeping mandates and to consult on its periodic reviews of ongoing operations. To deal with the increasing complexities of peace operations and the demand for specialized knowledge and expertise, the Security Council has established various mechanisms to support its decision-making. For instance, the Council utilizes Groups of Friends, "Arria formula" meetings, sanctions committees, monitoring groups, and panels of experts, as well as the Council making fact-finding visits outside of New York. The Military Staff Committee has also, from time to time, provided the Security Council with military advice on peacekeeping issues. The Council also now has a dedicated Working Group on Peacekeeping Operations, which is supposed to act as a forum for private expert debate among Council members.

The growing sophistication and professionalism of UN peacekeeping facilitated a partial return of confidence in the 2000s. Rising demand for peacekeepers saw the United Nations operate at a historically unprecedented tempo, with increases in the number and size of missions as well as in the scope and complexity of their mandates. Among other things, peace operations are now regularly mandated to protect civilians, assist in the rebuilding of state institutions, assist in the re-establishment of the rule of law, assist or supervise elections, provide assistance to refugees and internally displaced persons, monitor borders and compliance with embargoes and sanctions regimes, assist with disarming, demobilizing and reintegrating militia members, assist security sector reform, protect VIPs, promote human rights, protect and empower women, and support the provision of humanitarian assistance—all of which extends well beyond the original remit of peacekeeping. Faced with big and complicated new missions, notably in the Sudans —UNAMID in Darfur and UNMIS(S) in Sudan/South Sudan—advances in the conceptual development of UN peacekeeping and its management structures have helped to avoid a repeat of the calamities of the 1990s. That said, significant challenges remain and we examine some of these in the following section.

Current debates, key criticisms, and emerging issues

This section analyses three key debates that have prompted new thinking and practices as well as criticism of UN peacekeeping. They relate to participation, regionalization, and the use of military force.

Participation

One major current debate revolves around the question of troop-contributing countries.[9] Today, the task of providing UN peacekeepers continues to be met in a highly unequal manner, with well over two-thirds of all UN uniformed personnel coming from just 20 or so countries. Among the top ten contributors of uniformed personnel to UN missions during the 2000s were four South Asian states (Pakistan, Bangladesh, India, and Nepal), three African states (Nigeria, Ghana, and Kenya), and one each from the Middle East (Jordan), South America (Uruguay), and the former Soviet Union (Ukraine).[10] Over the same time period, the world's most stable and prosperous governments in the Western world—which also possessed most of the world's high-tech military capabilities —significantly reduced the numbers of troops they contributed to UN-led peace operations.[11] By early 2011, this had created a disquieting situation acknowledged by UN Secretary-General Ban Ki-moon: "Securing the required resources and troops [for UN peacekeeping] has consumed much of my energy. I have been begging leaders to make resources available to us."[12]

The other dimension of this debate was whether countries should provide their peace-keepers to the United Nations or deploy them under other international organizations or coalitions of states. While the 2000s saw a significant increase in the overall number of peacekeepers deployed by various coalitions of states and international organizations— including the UN, NATO, the European Union, and the African Union—the range of alternative institutional vehicles for conducting peacekeeping operations meant the UN has had to compete for personnel. The UN's principal competitors are NATO, the European Union, Western-led coalitions of the willing, and, to a lesser extent, the African Union.

It was in this context that the DPKO and DFS launched their "New Horizon" initiative, which in 2009 called for "an expanded base of troop- and police-contributing countries . . . to enhance collective burden-sharing and to meet future requirements."[13] The following year, the General Assembly's Special Committee on Peacekeeping Operations (C34) also emphasized the need to "expand the available pool of capabilities" for UN peacekeeping. To achieve this goal, the Committee called upon the UN Secretariat to analyze "the willingness and readiness" of contributing countries and "to develop outreach strategies" in order to strengthen contacts and longer-term relationships with current or potential contributing countries, encourage further contributions from existing contributors, and provide practical support to emerging contributors.[14]

Expanding the pool of available capabilities for UN-led operations involves four main tasks: (1) persuading more countries to become major contributors of UN peacekeepers, namely, being able to provide sustained contributions of, say, two or more battalions of troops/police; (2) persuading Western (and other) states with relevant capabilities—such as the European Union's battle groups—to deploy them in order to fulfill specialist UN peacekeeping functions; (3) persuading current major contributors to sustain or expand their contributions while also improving the performance capabilities of their deployed forces; and (4) persuading some contributors to purchase or develop relevant specialist/niche capabilities which they either do not currently possess or do not have in surplus, and to contribute them to UN peacekeeping operations. Each of these areas presents its own challenges, not least as states tend to privilege their own perceived strategic interests and more states come to view UN peacekeeping as one among many forms of crisis management.

Regionalization

In debates about peace operations, regionalization is commonly understood in two senses. Empirically, regionalization is often used as a label to describe the increased level of activities undertaken by regional organizations with regard to conflict management in general and peace operations in particular. Normatively, regionalization refers to the idea that each region of the world "should be responsible for its own peacemaking and peacekeeping, with some financial and technical support from the West but few, if any, military or police contingents from outside the region."[15] With the high demand for peacekeepers and the UN's capacity to deliver straining, some policy-makers and analysts see regionalization as a potential solution.

As a descriptive label for the contemporary peacekeeping landscape, however, "regionalization" is rather misleading in several respects. First, regional organizations are not the only important actors in relation to peace operations: the UN, coalitions, and individual states, as well as private contractors, all play significant roles. Second, regionalization has occurred unevenly around the globe. While some parts of the world have regional organizations that are willing and able to conduct peace operations, others have the will but lack the relevant capabilities, some dislike the idea of conducting military operations but are keen to undertake political and observer missions, still other regional organizations have no desire to engage in collective peace operations of any sort, and some parts of the world have no significant regional arrangements that deal with conflict management issues at all. Third, not all regional arrangements have confined their activities to their own region. Some (Western) regional organizations, NATO and the European Union, for instance, have operated well beyond their own neighborhood.

The starting point for understanding the challenge of regionalization is two fundamental characteristics of the UN system. The first is that Chapter VIII of the UN Charter encourages "regional arrangements" to be proactive in peacefully resolving conflicts that occur within their neighborhood. The Charter thus created a system flexible enough not to grant the Security Council a monopoly of authority on issues of international peace and security. The second fundamental characteristic is the UN's lack of standing armed forces, which has meant that it must sometimes delegate other actors to undertake peace operations, especially those involving large-scale enforcement activities. The growing number of regional arrangements that have taken an explicit interest in conflict management has thus provided the UN with an expanding set of options.

Despite these caveats, the normative debate about the place of regional organizations in peace operations and their relationship to the UN remains on the agenda. This old debate has become more prominent since the end of the 1990s after NATO's intervention in Kosovo/Yugoslavia in 1999. As then UN Secretary-General Kofi Annan put it in 2002, "multilateral institutions and regional security organizations have never been more important than today."[16] By 2009, for the first time ever, the Security Council authorized the use of the UN's assessed peacekeeping budget to pay for the logistical support for a peace operation conducted by a regional organization, the African Union Mission in Somalia (AMISOM).

The contemporary challenge is thus for the UN to find an appropriate working relationship with those regional organizations that are in the business of conducting peace operations. So far, the key practical debates have played out with a focus on Africa, where since 2005 the UN has embarked upon a major capacity-building program to enhance the ability of Africa's regional organizations to conduct peace operations. So have a variety of bilateral (primarily Western) donors and the European Union. This project has made considerable progress, but the African Union is still a long way from being able to train, deploy, and manage its own large peacekeeping operations.

The use of military force

There have been at least three major strands to debates about the use of military force in UN peace operations—debates which stretch back to ONUC in the 1960s. The first relates to humanitarian military intervention; the second to "robust" peacekeeping that emerged with the Brahimi Report; and the third to the emergence of the protection of civilians (POC) as a mandated goal.

The most controversial issue has been the question of when it is legitimate for the UN to conduct humanitarian military intervention. The Security Council has authorized its peacekeepers to use force on numerous occasions notably in Somalia, Haiti, and Bosnia in the 1990s and in the 2000s, where it has frequently authorized the use of "all necessary means" to protect civilians in DRC, Sudan, and Côte d'Ivoire, among others. Nonetheless, its authorizations have traditionally reflected the consent of *de jure* state authorities. To date, outside the context of interstate aggression, the Council has done so only once—when in March 2011 Resolution 1973 authorized the use of force to protect civilians against the wishes of the Libyan authorities. One of the principal lessons from the peacekeeping disasters of the 1990s was that a clear line should be drawn between peacekeeping and peace enforcement, and that situations requiring the use of force to achieve strategic goals (such as creating a safe environment, or disarming belligerents) were not right for UN peacekeeping. In such situations, the DPKO typically advised that the Security Council should consider deploying a multinational force capable of high intensity operations.

The second set of issues relating to the use of military force stems from the notion of "robust" operations developed by the Brahimi Report. "Robustness" referred to the idea that peacekeepers might use tactical force in order to defend themselves or other UN personnel, defend the mandate from spoilers and not cede the initiative to them, and protect civilians. Although the concept won widespread support from some, especially Western member states, which argued that robust peacekeeping had largely succeeded in East Timor (1999 and 2006), Sierra Leone (after the 2000 British intervention), and eastern DRC in 2003, many traditional peacekeeping nations expressed concerns about its potential impact on consent and impartiality. In practice, too, the concept has been difficult to operationalize in environments where peacekeeping forces lack the resources to be credibly robust, where operations depend on local and national consent, and where building sustainable peace demands political solutions. As a result of these, and other, challenges, the DPKO has become more reticent about employing the term.

There has been much greater support for the idea that UN peacekeepers should use force to protect civilians, not least because the moral imperative is clear and the application narrow. The Security Council has, at times, been especially enthusiastic. In 1999 Resolution 1265 expressed the Council's "willingness" to consider "appropriate measures" in response "to situations of armed conflict where civilians are being targeted or where humanitarian assistance to civilians is being deliberately obstructed," and to explore how peacekeeping mandates might be reframed to afford better protection to endangered civilians. The Brahimi Report argued that peacekeepers who witness violence against civilians should "be presumed to be authorized to stop it, within their means." Starting in 1999 with the UN Mission in Sierra Leone (UNAMSIL), the Security Council has regularly invoked Chapter VII of the Charter to create civilian protection mandates, albeit while inserting some important geographical, temporal, and capabilities-based caveats. Gradually the Council has become more relaxed about imposing them. For example, it granted the UN Mission in Côte d'Ivoire (UNOCI) a broad mandate to use "all necessary means" to "protect civilians" in 2011 (Resolution 1975). But this too has raised some fundamental questions about the UN's notion of impartiality as well as creating operational headaches for peacekeepers tasked with implementing such mandates in the field.

However, moves towards "robust" peacekeeping and the protection of civilians have undoubtedly improved the effectiveness and professionalism of UN peacekeeping operations and prevented a repeat of past calamities. But these advances have come at a cost. First, the use of force remains controversial. Second, the demands of robustness, protection, and expanded mandates have led to rising costs for equipment and numbers of required peacekeepers (see Figure 30.3). Indeed, adjusted for inflation, approximately 63 percent of all UN peacekeeping costs incurred since 1948 were spent between 2004 and 2012. However, questions remain about whether UN peace operations have the resources they need to use force effectively. For example, the capacity of UN peacekeepers to collect intelligence information is widely deemed essential for the effective employment of force, but the UN's peacekeepers have traditionally been denied access to

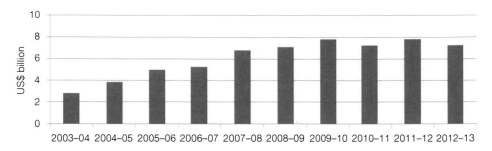

Figure 30.3 Approved UN peacekeeping budgets (fiscal years 1 July–30 June 2003–13)

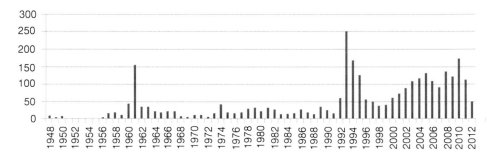

Figure 30.4 Fatalities in UN-led peacekeeping operations (up to 31 August 2012—58 for year 2012)

intelligence-gathering equipment. Debates are currently ongoing about how UN peacekeepers can utilize modern monitoring and surveillance technologies to overcome some of these problems at a reasonable cost.[17] Third, a more proactive approach to the use of force has led to increasing casualties among UN peacekeepers. As of August 2012, the number of UN peacekeeper fatalities since 1948 stood at 3,025. Figure 30.4 demonstrates that there are annual peaks and troughs but that since 2004 the average annual casualty rate has sat consistently above the normal average. Fourth, debate persists over whether the UN is structurally well suited to using military force. There is clearly a consensus that it is not well suited to high intensity combat missions, but in some tactical situations UN peacekeepers have occasionally used force effectively against non-state actors who threaten civilians.

Conclusion

UN peacekeeping is an example of constructivism in action—what started out as a series of ad hoc practices have over time developed their own operating guidelines, standard procedures, professional standards, and methods of evaluation. Peacekeeping institutions, doctrine, and methods have all come *after* peacekeeping practice. As a result, both the history of UN peacekeeping and its current operations are made up of field experiments and lesson learning. Throughout its history the key lessons have focused not just on what might work in theory but what works within the political and material limits set by international society. Sometimes, as in the early 1990s and more recently with the emerging protection of civilians agenda, the Security Council has played a proactive role in driving peacekeeping forward and expanding its scope and mandates. In both cases, the UN Secretariat was left with the challenge of achieving complex mandates with limited resources. That UN peacekeeping has generally avoided the calamities of the mid-1990s is testament to the growing professionalization of the UN and its peacekeepers. Of course, serious questions remain about how the UN will find the necessary resources, how it will relate to emerging regional organizations, and how it will employ force in effective and sustainable ways. But this is how it has always been: UN peacekeeping is, and will remain, a work in progress.

Additional reading

1. Alex J. Bellamy and Paul D. Williams, *Understanding Peacekeeping*, 2nd edition (Cambridge: Polity Press, 2010).
2. Center on International Cooperation, *Annual Review of Global Peace Operations* (Boulder: Lynne Rienner, annual 2006–2012).
3. Virginia Page Fortna, *Does Peacekeeping Work? Shaping Belligerents' Choices after Civil War* (Princeton: Princeton University Press, 2008).
4. Michael W. Doyle and Nicholas Sambanis, *Making War and Building Peace: United Nations Peace Operations* (Princeton: Princeton University Press, 2006).
5. William J. Durch, ed., *Twenty-First Century Peace Operations* (Washington, DC: United States Institute of Peace Press, 2006).

Notes

1 Virginia Page Fortna, *Does Peacekeeping Work? Shaping Belligerents' Choices after Civil War* (Princeton: Princeton University Press, 2008), 173.
2 For example Andrew Mack, *Global Political Violence: Explaining the Post Cold War Decline* (New York: International Peace Academy, 2007).
3 Fortna, *Does Peacekeeping Work?*, 171.
4 Matthew Krain, "International Intervention and the Severity of Genocides and Politicides," *International Studies Quarterly* 49, no. 2 (2005): 363–387. See also Taylor Seybolt, *Humanitarian Military Intervention* (Oxford: Oxford University Press for SIPRI, 2007).
5 Michael W. Doyle and Nicholas Sambanis, "International Peacebuilding: A Theoretical and Quantitative Analysis," *American Political Science Review* 94, no. 4 (2000), 795. See also Michael W. Doyle and Nicholas Sambanis, *Making War and Building Peace: United Nations Peace Operations* (Princeton: Princeton University Press, 2006).
6 Brian Urquhart, *Hammarskjöld: A Life in War and Peace* (New York: Croom Helm, 1972), 265. See also Bertrand G. Ramcharan, *Preventive Diplomacy at the UN* (Bloomington: Indiana University Press, 2008).
7 Shashi Tharoor, "Should UN Peacekeeping Go 'Back to Basics,'" *Survival* 37, no. 4 (1995): 52–64.
8 Thorsten Benner, Stephan Mergenthaler, and Philipp Rotmann, *The New World of UN Peace Operations* (Oxford: Oxford University Press, 2011).
9 This section draws from Alex J. Bellamy and Paul D. Williams, eds., *Providing Peacekeepers: The Politics, Challenges, and Future of United Nations Peacekeeping Contributions* (Oxford: Oxford University Press, 2013).

10   Based on data provided by the UN Department of Peacekeeping Operations at http://www.
     un.org/en/peacekeeping/contributors/. This ranking was calculated by taking the number of
     uniformed personnel contributed by a state to UN-led peacekeeping operations during each
     month of December for the years 2000 through 2010. Points were awarded to each contributor
     in the top ten for each year (i.e. 10 for 1st place, 9 for 2nd place, etc.). The combined total
     of these scores were then ranked to produce the top ten contributor states.

11   Alex J. Bellamy and Paul D. Williams, "The West and Contemporary Peace Operations,"
     Journal of Peace Research 46, no. 1 (2009): 39–57.

12   Ban Ki-moon, Cyril Foster Lecture, University of Oxford, 2 February 2011, www.un.org/
     News/Press/docs/2011/sgsm13385.doc.htm.

13   United Nations, *A New Partnership Agenda: Charting a New Horizon for UN Peacekeeping*
     (New York: UN DPKO/DFS, July 2009), vi.

14   UN General Assembly, *Report of the Special Committee on Peacekeeping Operations 2010
     Substantive Session (22 February–19 March 2010)*, General Assembly Official Records 64th
     Session, Supplement No. 19 (A/64/19, 2010), para. 75.

15   Marrack Goulding, *Peacemonger* (London: John Murray, 2002), 217.

16   Kofi Annan, "Regional Security Organizations Never More Important Than Today," UN
     document SG/SM/8543, 9 December 2002.

17   Walter K. Dorn, *Keeping Watch: Monitoring Technology and Innovation in UN Peace Operations*
     (Tokyo: UN University Press, 2011).

CHAPTER 31

Regional Organizations and Global Security Governance

S. Neil MacFarlane

CONTENTS

The end of the Cold War brought considerable enthusiasm concerning the potential role of regional organizations in generating peace and security in a very promising, but very uncertain, post-Cold War landscape. As Secretary-General Boutros Boutros-Ghali declared in 1992, "In this new era of opportunity, regional arrangements or agencies can render great service if their activities are undertaken in a manner consistent with the Purposes and Principles of the Charter, and if their relationship with the United Nations, and particularly the Security Council, is governed by Chapter VIII."[1] This enthusiasm reflected several factors,[2] but one was a widespread view in the global South that postcolonial states ought to·be allowed to resolve their own problems without interference from the major powers. It followed that regions should take the lead in managing regional security.

From the perspective of the Euro-Atlantic states, the end of bipolar competition in the Third World removed the structural interest in direct engagement in regional disputes. The major Western states were looking forward to a peace dividend. The United Nations was in serious financial difficulty, not least because of the unwillingness of the US Congress reliably to fund contributions to the organization. Operational burden-shifting was attractive. If things did not go well, blame could be shifted too.

There were other reasons for enthusiasm. In principle, actors closer to a regional security problem had a stronger interest in resolving it, since it was likely to affect them more directly. Regional actors were arguably more familiar with the factors resulting in regional armed conflicts. Their knowledge advantage presumably favored more nuanced and sensitive approaches to conflict resolution and management. Regional leaders were more closely acquainted with each other, enhancing predictability and, possibly, trust. Regional bureaucracies were accustomed to dealing with each other. These personal and bureaucratic connections could facilitate mediation. Arguably, decisions taken by regional multilateral organizations would enjoy greater legitimacy than decisions taken by outsiders.

In short, there was a substantial case for empowering regional organizations to address security matters within their geographical area. In the post-Cold War era, this approach has been amply explored, with substantial encouragement from the United Nations.[3] Regional organizations have been engaged as mediators and facilitators, peacekeepers, confidence builders, peace enforcers, and guarantors of settlements. They have adopted and implemented preventive development programs and have been heavily involved in reconstruction and institution building. In other words, they have together constituted a central pillar in international efforts to achieve peace and security since 1991.

This case was not uncontested. Critics suggested that although regional actors might have a greater interest in engagement in local conflict, the interests of neighboring countries might conflict. Their particular interests in the outcome of a regional dispute might outweigh their collective interest in conflict resolution and stability. Likewise, although regional actors might be more familiar with the intricacies of a regional dispute, that was no guarantee of impartiality or legitimacy. In addition, many regional organizations lacked both the capacity and the experience for effective intervention in regional disputes.[4]

This chapter examines the contribution of regional organizations to global security governance since the end of the Cold War.[5] Is there regionalization of security governance? If so, how should one view the relationship between growing regional activity and the role of the United Nations and its Security Council as the locus of global security governance? The chapter begins with conceptual, legal, and historical background to the issue. It continues with an overview of regional organizations' engagement with peace operations and broader governance of security in the 20 years since the end of the Cold War. This is followed by consideration of the interface between regional and global security governance.

Concepts and definitions

This chapter revolves around two concepts: security and regional organization. Concerning the former, there is a broad consensus on the core meaning of security: the absence of threats to core values. However, that definition raises more questions than it answers. Whose security are we talking about—individual human beings, minority groups, states, regions, the international system, the global community? What threats are we talking about—military, criminal, terrorist, cultural, economic, ecological? Where do security threats come from—other states, individuals, non-state political, economic, or religious actors, or from the natural environment?

The degree of contestation and lack of consensus is evident, for example, in the evolution of the notion of human security, which questions both the traditional privileging of the state and the conventional focus on military threats in security studies.[6] While recognizing the importance of the wider conversation, this chapter focuses on threats associated with the existence, or the threat, of organized violence within or between states. Managing, if not eliminating, these threats has been a core function of the United Nations since its establishment in 1945.

Regions are geographically limited spaces linked by notions of shared history, culture, custom, or threat. Regional organizations are groups of states that purport to share common objectives regarding their area.[7] They may cover the entire expanse of a region, for example the Organization of African Unity (OAU, later the African Union, AU) or sub-regional parts of that space, for example the Association of Southeast Asian Nations (ASEAN). They may be inclusive of all states within a space, for example, the Organization for Security and Co-operation in Europe (OSCE) or they may not, for example the North Atlantic Treaty Organization (NATO). Regional organizations may be institutionalized or not; for example, the Conference on Security and Cooperation in Europe was not a formal organization until it was transformed into the OSCE in 1993. They may be permanent or they may be ad hoc and focused on a particular challenge, for example the Contadora Group during Central America's wars of the 1980s.

Their objectives may include peace and security, but that is not a necessary attribute. The European Economic Community (EEC) passed its first 35 years or so without acknowledging any direct security role. In other cases, security was, and is, the reason that they exist—e.g. the OSCE. Organizations without a security role in their initial mandate may adopt such a role over time. Some regional organizations continue to have no explicit security role, but their activities may overlap with a broad security agenda, for example the Council of Europe, whose basic purposes comprise the protection and promotion of human rights and the rule of law.

Early history

Regional organizations engaging in security matters predate the end of the Cold War. Coming together to address a shared threat or to mitigate insecurity has been a common practice throughout international history, classical Greece's alliance against the Persians being an early case in point. The League of Nations Covenant made provision for contribution by "regional arrangements" to international peace. The UN Charter devoted an entire chapter to the "regional arrangements and agencies." Chapter VIII was an attempt not only to legitimate regional arrangements but also to define their relationship to UN security governance. Article 52 notes that members of regional arrangements should seek pacific resolution of disputes before referring them to the Security Council. Article 53 makes provision for the council to use regional arrangements in enforcement actions, while prohibiting enforcement action by regional actors without Security Council authorization. Article 54 obliges regional agencies and arrangements to inform the council of activities that are related to international peace and security.[8]

The Cold War period witnessed four relevant developments. One, and specific to Europe, was development of regional agencies to foster reconstruction and regional economic integration (the OEEC, the ECSC, the EEC). A second was the emergence of regional organizations outside Europe that were linked to decolonization. The third was the creation of numerous Western-sponsored treaty organizations to assist in containment (the Baghdad Pact and the Central Treaty Organization, NATO, and the Southeast Asian Treaty Organization). The communist countries engaged in similar institution building, for example the Warsaw Treaty Organization. These organizations, by and large, had little to do with the promotion of international peace and security, except through their deterrence and collective defense functions. A fourth was the creation of regional and sub-regional organizations for specific (hegemonic) purposes by major regional powers (the Organization of American States—OAS—as successor to the Pan-American Union, and the Southern African Development and Coordination Conference).

The Cold War alliances outside Europe amounted to very little. In Europe, however, NATO and the Warsaw Pact became significant security adversaries. NATO emerged as the multilateral military arm of Western defense and deterrence strategy in Europe. The Warsaw Pact was an instrument of the Soviet Union in the effort to coordinate Soviet and allied military posture vis-à-vis NATO, and also as a means to implement and to legitimize Soviet efforts to maintain control over its satellite states, as in Hungary and Czechoslovakia.

Peace or other military operations by regional organizations during the Cold War were extremely rare. They include the Warsaw Pact interventions just mentioned, the role of the OAS in the Dominican Republic in 1965–66, and an abortive operation by the OAU in Chad's civil war in 1980.

The post-Cold War era

There has clearly been a step-change in the role of regional organizations in security governance after the Cold War. It is useful to analyze this expansion in terms of organizational mandates and of operations.

Organizational mandates

One element of this transformation was organizational, the expansion of institutional mandates by existing regional organizations, for example the transformation of the European Community into the European Union in 1992. The EU embraced a foreign and security policy.[9] This complex process culminated in the acceptance of a mandate for humanitarian and peacekeeping operations and combat tasks associated with crisis management (the Petersberg tasks), elaboration of a European Security Strategy, agreement on the formation of rapid deployment forces, and the creation of EU foreign and security policy institutions.

The 2003 EU Security Strategy acknowledged that, as an "inevitable" global power, the security role was not limited to the territory of its members but extended to the European neighborhood and beyond.[10] Although the EU's original focus was regional, it broadened its notion of security responsibility to the world as a whole, reflecting its aspiration (or at least the aspiration of some of its member states) to become a great power in its own right.

A second example would be the CSCE. The conference was initially a mechanism to manage security (and in particular "soft security") in Cold War Europe. When the Soviet Union collapsed, the question of how to approach its successor states and those of the former Yugoslavia arose. The CSCE took an inclusive approach, sooner or later admitting all the new successor states in Europe, with the exception of Kosovo and the various breakaway sub-states in the former Soviet republics). In addition, it established itself as a formal international organization with a focus on softer security issues. Responding to the evolving conceptualization and practicalities of security, the organization adopted a Human Dimension that focused on the rights of individuals within member states.

The end of the Cold War also posed challenges for NATO. Founded as a defensive alliance, the original mandate did not envisage peacekeeping and peacebuilding. Its operational responsibilities extended to the NATO Treaty Area, but no further.[11] In 1990–91, the threat NATO was designed to deter or to resist evaporated. Its major members took the view that its substantial institutional capacity could be adjusted to address security challenges in the post-Cold War era. NATO readjusted its strategic concept to emphasize the organization's role in confidence building, conflict prevention, crisis management, as well as humanitarian and disaster response. It loosened the alliance's area of operations to allow engagement out of area.[12] It created institutions for dialogue and cooperation with former communist states in order to forge a single cooperative security space across Europe and then embraced enlargement.[13] By 2012 NATO had grown from 16 to 28 states, taking in all of the members of the defunct Warsaw Pact, the Baltic Republics, Slovenia, Croatia, and Albania.

The NATO commitment to crisis management in the European area as a whole implied a willingness to act outside the traditional alliance's area of operations. The "war on terror" expanded NATO threat assessment beyond the European arena. Africa witnessed analogous expansion of mandates. The OAU was founded in 1964 with a multidimensional mandate, including an underspecified security function. The organization had little presence or effect during the Cold War in addressing regional security issues. The end of the Cold War coincided with an increase in civil violence in the region. One consequence was the transition of the OAU into the AU. At its first assembly in 2002, it adopted a protocol establishing a Peace and Security Council whose objectives comprised conflict prevention, management, and resolution. The functions included peacemaking, peace support operations, intervention, peacebuilding, humanitarian action, and disaster assistance. The protocol envisaged the creation of an African Standby Force and a Military Staff Committee.[14] At the sub-regional level, both the Southern African Development Community (SADC) and the Economic Community of West African States (ECOWAS) adopted mandates to produce and maintain peace and security in their sub-regions, and created security organs.[15]

In a limited number of cases new regional organizations were established. One was the Commonwealth of Independent States (CIS), formed by the majority of the Soviet Union's successor states to maintain functional and political integration after the Soviet collapse.[16] The original CIS agreement envisaged close military integration (joint command structures, a general staff, and a headquarters). Some members supplemented the CIS agreement with a Treaty on Collective Security in May 1992. Signatories accepted the obligation to eschew the use of force between states within the treaty and to assist any treaty member attacked by another state. The treaty acknowledged the primacy of the UN Charter in security matters, referring to the right of individual and collective self-defense under Article 51.[17] Both the Collective Security Treaty (implicitly) and the CIS Charter include provisions for peace operations within the membership space.

Implementation

What have these institutions done to implement their new mandates? NATO has developed extensive programs for training both members and partners in peace and disaster operations, through the Partnership for Peace (PfP). More significantly, it led an intervention in Bosnia in 1995 under a Security Council mandate that ended the civil war. It then maintained the peace for nearly a decade before withdrawing. In Kosovo in 1999, NATO attacked Serbia without a UN mandate (China and Russia would have vetoed) and forced its military to withdraw from the region, but NATO then cooperated with the UN to stabilize the internal situation to allow reconstruction and state building. Ten years later, most NATO members recognized the independence of Kosovo. Recalling discussion of NATO's "going global," in 2003—operating under a UN mandate—NATO took on the leadership of the International Security Assistance Force in Afghanistan (ISAF), which was tasked to stabilize the country and to control the threat from terrorism. It will withdraw from the role in 2014.

The EU has been involved in all dimensions of international response to conflict. Non-military security responses include conflict prevention (e.g. Macedonia), humanitarian action (the Balkans and the Caucasus), mediation (the presidency's mediation of a ceasefire agreement between Russia and Georgia in 2008), ceasefire monitoring (in Georgia since 2008) and post-conflict reconstruction, state capacity building, rule-of-law (Kosovo and Georgia), and policing (Bosnia and Macedonia).

Outside the European area, the EU has repeatedly launched missions into conflicts or potential conflicts in Africa (including Chad, the Democratic Republic of Congo, Niger, Chad, Southern Sudan, Somalia, and Guinea-Bissau). The EU has also provided policing and other assistance in Palestine. In general, the organization has taken targeted niche roles with small numbers of personnel involved.[18] However, out-of-area, it has taken on targeted stabilization missions involving combat forces, as, for example, in the case of Operation Artemis in Ituri in the DRC in 2003. Overall, the European Union has embarked on more than 25, and has completed more than 10, missions.

In the meantime, the OSCE has provided considerable assistance on soft security issues. One dimension has been observing and certifying elections by the Office for Democratic Institutions and Human Rights. Another is the deployment of "missions of long-term duration" in transitional states to monitor and report on potential conflicts, to assist in the stabilization of ceasefires, and to promote human rights. A subsidiary unit of the OSCE—the High Commissioner for National Minorities—has mounted an extensive confidential program to monitor potential minority conflicts and to suggest policy changes that might mitigate the potential for violence.

In Africa, ECOWAS, SADC, and the AU operationalized their changes of mandate in peace operations within their regions and sub-regions, including in Liberia, Sierra de d'Ivoire Leone, Guinea-Bissau, the Ivory Coast, Lesotho, the Democratic Republic of Congo, Burundi, Sudan, and Somalia. At the time of writing, a further operation involving regional organizations took place in Mali in conjunction with a French military intervention. In a number of instances, sub-regional organization acted prior to authorization from the Security Council under Chapter VIII of the Charter.

In the former Soviet Union, the CIS mounted a peacekeeping operation in Georgia (concerning the conflict in Abkhazia) and peace enforcement in Tajikistan. In the first instance, a CIS contingent interposed itself between Georgian government and Abkhaz secessionist forces, policing a demilitarized zone and controlling heavy weapons cantonments. In Tajikistan, the Russian army and border forces stationed in the country supported the incumbent government against a challenge from a democratic and Islamist opposition. In both instances, engagement of Russian forces preceded authorization by the Commonwealth of Independent States, with UN approval coming considerably later still.

In short, there has been a large change in security governance in the international system since the end of the Cold War. Where regional actors (organizations, ad hoc coalitions) were rarely active during the Cold War, there is now a multitude of security-related initiatives at this level. The growing operational role of regional organizations both within their regions and (in the case of the EU and NATO) outside their regions produced a substantial "force multiplier," physically in terms of boots on the ground for peacekeeping and peace enforcement, and, metaphorically, through conflict prevention, mediation, peacekeeping, peace enforcement, and post-conflict peacebuilding and state building.

It is also noteworthy in a discussion of regional contribution to global security governance that most of the organizations discussed above have embraced to varying degrees the UN's global principles of human rights, democracy, and the rule of law, and the responsibility to protect as normative underpinnings of their activities. In other words, not only are they lined up with the UN on the need to contribute to the production of peace and security, but they share many aspects of the broadening of the concepts of security and threat characteristic of the UN's discourse on the management of international security.

Diversity in capacity, performance, and discourse

The general observations above conceal a huge amount of diversity in the capabilities and competence of regional organizations to contribute to global security governance. First, the coverage of regional organizations is not universal. Some regions (e.g. Europe) are heavily institutionalized. Others either lack institutionalized regional organizations completely (e.g. Northeast Asia) or, where such institutions exist, they face strong normative and political constraints on multilateral efforts to address threats to peace and security. For example, in South Asia, while there is a shell of regional cooperation (South Asian Association for Regional Co-operation, or SAARC), the shell is empty in terms of security cooperation and management. That reflects a fundamental bipolarity in the region between India and Pakistan, and the concerns of smaller states that regional initiatives would be dominated by their more powerful neighbors. The lack of any significant conflict management response to the civil war in Sri Lanka is a blatant illustration of the absence of regional capacity or will. SAARC has also been passive during periodic exacerbation of Indo-Pakistani relations. The relationship is managed, or mismanaged, bilaterally.

The Association of Southeast Asian Nations (ASEAN) has adopted a very cautious approach to security issues. The prevailing security norms are non-interference in internal affairs and the resolution of interstate disputes by peaceful means. The consequences are evident in the minimal role of the association in efforts to resolve the dispute in East Timor in 1999, and also in the absence of any regional response to widespread unrest with significant humanitarian consequences in Indonesia at the end of the 1990s; the conflicts in Aceh and Western New Guinea; endemic insurgency in the Philippines; chronic human rights abuse and low-level conflict in Myanmar; and potential conflict with China in the South China Sea. Instead, where security issues are engaged, the focus is on informal consultation and mediation (the "ASEAN Way"). Such responses are useful and important, but they highlight the limits for a global security safety net of relying on regional solutions to regional problems in this region, particularly where such solutions might involve engagement in the internal affairs of member states. The result for Asia as a whole is a deficit in regional security multilateralism. This contrasts sharply with, say, Europe, where there is arguably a surplus. Most other regions fall between the two.

In the Middle East, there is no evidence of serious willingness on the part of regional states to engage directly and proactively in the management of security issues. There is no region-wide organization. The Arab League, by definition, excludes the most capable military actor in the region, Israel. Sub-regional organizations such as the Gulf Co-operation Council also exclude key players (notably Iran). The region's states have long been divided by significantly different understandings of legitimacy and community. These differences have probably been exacerbated by the Arab Spring. The net effect is that the region needs bailing out by larger non-regional organizations. An example would be the Arab League's request for a UN response to the meltdown in Libya in 2011. The Security Council subcontracted to a NATO-led coalition of the willing. However, extra-regional bailouts are uncertain. When a civil war broke out in Syria in 2011–12, there was no multilateral response. The contrast between the two cases displays a significant problem. In Libya, the Security Council could achieve consensus. In Syria, it could not. The legitimizing effect of regional endorsement was necessary but insufficient and overpowered by disagreement among the council's permanent members.

Even where there may be the will to engage in the regional management of security issues, there is a wide variation in the capacity to do so. The EU has growing capacity for conflict management. The OSCE, with a smaller brief, draws on the substantial resources of member states for soft security missions. NATO has the largest and best-established multilateral peace enforcement capacity. In contrast, in Africa the funding base is substantially lower, and the experience of national military forces in regional multilateral operations also is substantially lower. In Latin America, experience of UN operations is far more developed than is that of regional multilateral response. The same is true in much of Asia.

In other words, if there is a regionalization of peacekeeping, it is uneven and incomplete. The regional embrace of the emerging UN normative framework on security governance is also uneven. As seen earlier, it appears that the normative embrace of wider conceptions of security, including human rights, democratization, and the rule of law, was spreading. That spread suggests a wider embrace of the responsibility of outsiders to engage in the domestic jurisdiction of states where those states' practices are inconsistent with the preferred normative agenda.

However, regional discourses around this matter fall into at least two categories. One is acceptance of sovereignty as responsibility, and the attenuation of sovereignty where a state is perceived not to be fulfilling its responsibility (e.g. EU and AU). A second is a focus on sovereignty and nonintervention (e.g. ASEAN and CIS), Others fall in the middle, where discursively there is an embrace of international standards but practice suggests a lingering attachment to traditional sovereignty and nonintervention norms. Where there are no organizations actively engaged in regional security (e.g. North East and South Asia), largely because of reluctance to engage in the internal affairs of member states, the issue does not even arise. In short, there is significant variation in the extent to which purportedly universal norms are accepted in principle or pursued in practice.

Normative variability points to a third issue: response to local threats to peace and security is highly politicized. The Syrian example suggests that the UN's capacity to manage international security is highly affected by political conflict. So too is the capacity of regional organizations. The ASEAN normative lowest common denominator mentioned above is a product of political and cultural cleavages. The impotence of regional multilateralism in South Asia reflects the mutual suspicion of India and Pakistan, in addition to the concerns of smaller states in the region with regard to Indian primacy. In West Africa, the regional security role of ECOWAS was hampered by differences of view between Francophone and Anglophone members regarding the conflicts in which ECOWAS engaged and, to a lesser extent, the concerns of smaller states regarding the regional asymmetry of military and economic power favoring Nigeria.[19] In effect, ECOMOG actions in the region involved engagement by a subset of like-minded members operating under a regional multilateral umbrella, while other members (e.g. Burkina Faso and Côte d'Ivoire) materially supported the opposing side.

Similarly, the CIS served as a cover for Russian unilateralism in Georgia. Although the CIS mandated the 1993–2008 peace operation there, the forces were purely Russian and the deployment served to draw Georgia back into Russian-dominated multilateral structures. It also impeded Georgia's adoption of a Western foreign policy orientation.

As in the UN Security Council, political differences in regional organizations can prevent regional responses to crises within regional boundaries. The most obvious recent case is the lack of any significant CIS response to the Russian invasion of Georgia in 2008. This act of aggression was committed by the regional hegemon. The other CIS members were unwilling to condemn a clear violation of their own Charter. They were also unwilling to support the Russian decision to dismember Georgia. The result was silence.

The ability of regional organizations to contribute to global security governance is strongly affected by the degree of normative consensus among member states and also the degree to which they see common purpose in the multilateral management of regional security. In this sense, the unevenness is not only inter-regional but also intra-regional. The CIS is a good example. In the Southern Caucasus, the CIS deployed to keep the peace on the *de facto* boundary between Georgia and Abkhazia, and to create the peace in Tajikistan. It did not do so in South Ossetia, where Russia deployed a peacekeeping force without multilateral authorization. In Moldova also, Russia deployed on a bilateral basis without authorization from the regional organization. In Azerbaijan's Nagorno-Karabakh, Russia mediated a ceasefire, but no peacekeeping force was deployed. The dominant factor in these cases appears to be Russia's perception of its own interest. There are also many threats to peace and security in Africa where regional or sub-regional organizations have not engaged.

The problem of politicization is linked to the matter of authority and legitimacy. The UN Charter is fairly clear on this point. Article 24 indicates that the Security Council has primary responsibility for international peace and security. This is elaborated in Chapter VII, Articles 39–42. Chapter VIII suggests that regional arrangements should address security threats within their spaces (Article 52.2) but that they should seek authorization from the Security Council to do so (Article 53.1).

The Charter establishes the *locus* of authority in law. However, this does not resolve issues of legitimacy in practice. What happens when the Security Council finds it impossible to agree on a Chapter VII response? It is a stretch to suggest that non-response is legitimate when peace is threatened and innocents are dying, as in Syria. What happens if the Security Council mandates a UN-based action, but the response fails to ameliorate the situation to which it is responding (for example the UNAMSIL in Sierra Leone prior to British unilateral intervention or UNAMIR observing Rwanda's genocide)?

In considering the responsibility to protect, the International Commission on Intervention and State Sovereignty suggested that "right" authority lay in the first instance with the Security Council. In conditions where the council failed to act, then regional multilateral response might be justifiable on grounds that action through formal multilateral organizations or informal coalitions of the willing conferred a degree of legitimacy. It concluded by noting that in circumstances where there was no multilateral response it was a real question whether the "greater harm" in the event of unauthorized action was the erosion of Security Council authority through acting without approval, or the damage to that order resulting from mass slaughter while the Security Council ducked. The 2005 World Summit decision that makes Security Council authorization a *sine qua non* for R2P only has exacerbated the problem.

In practice, in some instances regional arrangements or informal coalitions have sought and obtained the authorization of the Security Council under Chapter VII or VIII prior to intervention (NATO's Implementation Force (IFOR) in Bosnia, ISAF in Afghanistan). Some have sought, but have been refused, authorization (the American-led coalition in Iraq in 2003). Some have sought authorization, but after the fact (the CIS in Georgia and Tajikistan, and ECOWAS in Liberia and Sierra Leone). Some, finally, have neither sought nor obtained UN authorization (e.g. SADC in Lesotho). Cases in the latter two categories often reflect the use of the regional multilateral brand by a regionally dominant state. In such cases, the authorizing function of the United Nations is in some doubt. By extension, the contribution of regional arrangements to global security governance needs further interrogation.

Conclusion

Mention of the UN's authorizing function raises the larger question of the relationship between regional organizations and the UN in global security governance, and of possible global–regional synergies. The pluralistic character of the international system intrinsically limits the global governance of security. As discussed, the Charter provides an authoritative definition of the relations between the UN and regional arrangements in security, focusing on notification and authorization. There are numerous instances in which regional organs have failed to notify or seek authorization in their forceful responses to what they deem to be regional threats to peace and security.

Practice also suggests that there is potential for fruitful division of tasks on the basis of comparative advantage between regional organizations and the world organization. The Yugoslav experience involved NATO heavy lifting in enforcement and deterrence and substantial UN engagement in civilian stabilization and reconstruction. The EU has provided critical force in specific situations in Africa where UN peacekeepers could not address a particular threat, as in Ituri.

In addition, regional organizations can legitimize UN action as in Libya, where the Arab League request for action was useful in overcoming objections from some Security Council members about the impact on nonintervention norms of coming to the rescue of civilians.

The two decades since the end of the Cold War have witnessed a sea-change in the engagement of regional organizations in global security governance. This has involved the retooling of alliance systems to address general regional and global security interests, and the acceptance of stronger security mandates by regional multilateral organizations.

This evolution is, however, far from complete. Some regions do not have organizations that engage in efforts to enhance security. Some do not embrace the potential derogation of sovereignty associated with robust international response to internal crises. In practice, regional engagement in local peace and security issues has been uneven; in some areas, it has been absent, in others it has been substantial. In the latter cases, some has been consistent with global norms, and some not. In some cases, regional multilateralism provides a cover for the preferences of regionally dominant powers. Regional organizations vary significantly in their capacity to produce security, whether or not that is their intention, and in the extent to which their versions of security conform to UN norms.

Recent experience suggests a substantial potential for division of labor between the UN and regional organizations in global security governance. This involves not only the multiplication of assets available for response to threats to international peace and security, but also a contribution to the legitimacy of international peace operations. At the same time, cooperation between regional organizations and the UN involves substantial coordination problems. They have different norms, interests, and institutional cultures; they compete for roles, credit, and resources. Moreover, engagement by regional organizations in security issues raises substantial and unresolved issues about authority and legitimacy. To what extent do these organizations accept the primacy of the Security Council in the context of Chapter VIII? If they do not, what should be the global perspective on their independent activities? The risk is that the relationship may not evolve towards effective subsidiarity but fragmentation of global governance.

Additional reading

1. Emmanuel Adler and Michael Barnett, eds., *Security Communities* (Cambridge: Cambridge University Press, 1998).
2. Alex J. Bellamy and Paul D. Williams, "Who's Keeping the Peace? Regionalization and Contemporary Peace Operations," *International Security* 29, no. 4 (2005): 157–195.
3. Shaun Breslin and Stuart Croft, eds., *Comparative Regional Security Governance* (London: Routledge, 2012).
4. T. V. Paul, ed., *Regional Transformation in International Relations* (Cambridge: Cambridge University Press, 2012).
5. Thomas G. Weiss, ed., *Beyond UN Subcontracting: Task-Sharing with Regional Security Arrangements and Service-Providing NGOs* (Basingstoke: Macmillan, 1998).

Notes

1 Boutros Boutros-Ghali, *An Agenda for Peace*, A47/277 – S24111 (New York: United Nations, 1992), para. 63.
2 For a more detailed discussion, see S. Neil MacFarlane and Thomas G. Weiss, "Regional Organizations and Regional Security," *Security Studies* 2, no. 1 (1992): 6–7.
3 Boutros-Ghali, in *An Agenda for Peace*, devotes a full chapter (para. 60–65) to the role of regional organizations in building global peace. See also the General Assembly's *2005 World Summit Outcome*, A/Res/60/1 (24 October 2005), para. 93.
4 MacFarlane and Weiss, "Regional Organizations and Regional Security," *passim*. See also *A More Secure World: Our Shared Responsibility. Report of the High-Level Panel on Threats, Challenges, and Change* (A/59/565, 2 December 2004), 60, para. 220, http://www.un.org/secureworld/report.pdf.
5 The regional organizational element is only one part of a larger set of regional actions that includes ad hoc coalitions of regional actors, or single states within a region. These fall outside the focus of this analysis.
6 S. Neil MacFarlane and Yuen Foong Khong, *The UN and Human Security: A Critical History* (Bloomington: Indiana University Press, 2006).
7 This analysis takes a broad view of regional organizations, following the UN Charter. See United Nations, *Charter of the United Nations* (San Francisco: UN, 1945), art. 52. The UN's flexible approach follows that of the League of Nations Covenant, which speaks of "regional arrangements." See League of Nations, *Covenant of the League of Nations* (League of Nations, 1919), http://avalon.law.yale.edu/20th_century/leagcov.asp.
8 Article 51's reference to collective self-defense has also been seen to legitimize regional security arrangements.
9 See Title I (Common Provisions), Article B, and Title V (Provisions on a Common Foreign and Security Policy) of *The Maastricht Treaty: Treaty on European Union* (7 February 1992), http://www.eurotreaties.com/maastrichteu.pdf.
10 EU, *A Secure Europe in a Better World: European Security Strategy* (12 December 2003), http://www.consilium.europa.eu/uedocs/cmsUpload/78367.pdf.
11 See *The Washington Treaty* (Washington, DC, 4 April 1949), http://www.nato.int/cps/en/natolive/official_texts_17120.htm.
12 See "The Alliance's New Strategic Concept" (7–8 November 1991), http://www.nato.int/cps/en/natolive/official_texts_23847.htm.
13 "Study on NATO Enlargement" (3 September 1995), http://www.nato.int/cps/en/natolive/official_texts_24733.htm.

14 "Protocol Relating to the Establishment of the Peace and Security Council of the African Union" (Durban, 9 July 2002), http://www.au.int/en/sites/default/files/Protocol_peace_and_security.pdf.

15 See, in respect of ECOWAS, the revised treaty of 1993, which permits conflict prevention, peacekeeping, and peacebuilding; and *The Protocol Relating to the Mechanism for Conflict Prevention, Management, Resolution, Peacekeeping and Security* (10 December 1999), which replaced the Protocol on Mutual Defence Assistance of 1981. See http://www.comm.ecowas.int/sec/index.php?id=ap101299&lang=en. In respect of the SADC, see *The Treaty of the Southern African Development Community* (17 August 1992), art. 10A, http://www.sadc.int/documents-publications/show/865.

16 For the text of the agreement, see http://cis.minsk.by/reestr/ru/index.html#reestr/view/text?doc=1. In January 1993, the original agreement was supplemented by a CIS Charter. See http://cis.minsk.by/reestr/ru/index.html#reestr/view/text?doc=187.

17 For the treaty text, see: http://www.dkb.gov.ru/start/index_aengl.htm.

18 European Council, *Peace Operations* (October 2012), http://consilium.europa.eu/eeas/security-defence/eu-operations?lang=en.

19 See Linus Malu, "Background Note on ECOWAS," World Bank Headline Seminar on the Global and Regional Dimensions of Conflict and Peacebuilding (Addis Ababa, 10–12 October 2009), 1–2.

Weapons of Mass Destruction

Waheguru Pal Singh Sidhu

The term weapons of mass destruction (WMDs) was, ironically, defined by the Report of the United Nations General Assembly's Commission on Conventional Armaments in 1948 as

> atomic explosive weapons, radioactive material weapons, lethal chemical or biological weapons, and any weapons developed in the future which have characteristics comparable in destructive effect to those of the atomic bomb or other weapons mentioned above.[1]

In doing so the commission made two clear distinctions: first between conventional arms on the one hand and WMDs on the other; and, second, between atomic (nuclear), chemical, and biological weapons. The commission's definition also tacitly set apart atomic weapons as *primus inter pares* among WMDs and underlined a central role for the United Nations in managing them. Although traditional literature on the subject tends to club nuclear weapons, along with biological and chemical weapons, into a convenient but specious category of WMDs, this chapter will deliberately focus on these weapons separately for a number of reasons, which are explained in the first section.

This chapter begins with a brief historical overview of the evolution and development of the various international institutions and regimes to deal with nuclear, chemical, and biological weapons. It then looks at the role of informal and ad hoc arrangements and their relationship to the formal treaty-based institutions. The following sections identify the challenges ahead; examine the current debates as they relate to nuclear, chemical, and biological weapons and the related international organizations; and explore the prospects of the regimes in addressing them.

Differences among WMDs

Biological, chemical, and nuclear weapons do not belong to the same conceptual category. The lethality of chemical weapons is not significantly different from that of conventional explosives and a variety of masks, suits, and procedures, albeit cumbersome, can be used to protect against the effects of chemical weapons. Similarly, a variety of prophylactic measures exist to mitigate the effects of some biological attacks. In addition, victims of some chemical and biological attacks can be treated. In contrast, apart from some deep underground concrete bunkers, there are no effective preventive or protective measures that can alleviate a nuclear attack and as of now there is no known treatment for the effects of nuclear radiation. So horrific are the effects of a nuclear blast that experts opine that in any nuclear exchange the survivors will envy the dead.[2]

Despite their cataclysmic nature, nuclear weapons are not forbidden by international law (as is the case with biological and chemical weapons). Indeed, during the Cold War they emerged as the ultimate currency of power and the basis for world order, evident in the fact that all the five permanent UN Security Council members (P-5) possess nuclear weapons. Even in the post-Cold War period, the possession of and protection by nuclear weapons remain the ultimate guarantor of security, evident from the continued dependence on nuclear weapons by states already possessing them and the acquisition of these weapons by new states.[3]

In contrast neither chemical nor biological weapons are regarded as either significant symbols of power or underpin international security in the same way as nuclear weapons. Given the fact that chemical weapons are relatively easier and cheaper to make, they are sometimes disparagingly referred to as the "poor man's nuclear weapons." Although some states have sought to equate chemical weapons to nuclear weapons, this has not been universally accepted; nuclear weapons remain unique. This is evident from the fact that while all the P-5 countries continue to resist calls for nuclear disarmament they have either already given up their chemical weapons or are in the process of dismantling them. This is also the case with biological weapons.

Despite these fundamental differences in the characteristics, nature, concepts, and relative value of nuclear, chemical, and biological weapons, the various arrangements designed to deal with them are built around three key international treaties and share three common objectives.[4] The separate regimes seek in the first instance to collectively get rid of all WMDs. Second, the regimes also aim to prevent proliferation—both vertical (the qualitative and quantitative enhancement of these weapons among present possessors) and horizontal (the qualitative and quantitative spread of these weapons to new states)— of all WMDs. Finally, to varying degrees the regimes also endeavor to unfetter, if not encourage, the use of nuclear, chemical, and biological technology for peaceful uses. More recently the WMD regimes have also sought to prevent these weapons being acquired or used by non-state actors.

Historical overview

Chemical and biological weapons, which have been around for centuries, predate nuclear weapons, which only made their appearance in 1945. Consequently, serious multilateral efforts to deal with chemical weapons date back to at least the nineteenth century.[5] Similar efforts for biological weapons date back to the 1925 Geneva Protocol for the Prohibition of the Use of Asphyxiating, Poisonous or Other Gases, and Bacteriological Methods of Warfare, which focused on chemical and biological weapons.[6] It was only around 1970 that multilateral attempts to manage biological and chemical weapons diverged. In contrast, efforts to address the multifaceted threats posed by nuclear weapons began in earnest only in 1946. Ironically despite a latter start the present set of institutions to deal with nuclear weapons have actually preceded those for biological and chemical weapons.

The nuclear weapon regime

Disarmament of nuclear weapons was the subject of the very first General Assembly resolution in January 1946 and called

> (b) for the elimination from national armaments of atomic weapons and all other major weapons adaptable to mass destruction;
> (c) for effective safeguards by way of inspection and other means to protect complying States against the hazard of violations and evasions.[7]

The fact that this resolution was passed a mere five months after the first and only use of nuclear weapons, by the United States on Hiroshima and Nagasaki, indicated the expectations that these weapons needed to be dealt with on a global, multilateral scale by the brand new United Nations.

On 14 June 1946, at the inaugural meeting of the United Nations Atomic Energy Commission (created by the General Assembly's first resolution), the United States, which was still the world's only nuclear weapon state, presented the Baruch Plan[8] to the United Nations. In effect, the plan called for international ownership and control of all production of uranium-235 and plutonium, the ending of all nuclear weapons programs, opening the way for destroying all existing nuclear weapons and thus leading to their complete elimination. The Soviet Union, which had still not built its own nuclear weapon, did not accept this proposal. On 19 June 1946 the Soviet Union presented a plan of its own, named after Andrei Gromyko, who would later become the Soviet foreign minister. The Gromyko Plan[9] proposed the reverse of the American approach: disarm first (within three months) according to the terms of an international convention prohibiting nuclear weapons, and then set up an international system of supervision. The United States rejected the Gromyko Plan and conducted two nuclear tests in July 1946—the first tests since the bombing of Nagasaki on 9 August 1945. Following the first nuclear test by the Soviet Union on 29 August 1949 any hopes that these early efforts to eliminate nuclear weapons would succeed vanished.[10] Indeed, the UN Atomic Energy Commission itself was dissolved in January 1952.

By 1964 three other countries—Great Britain, France, and China—had also conducted nuclear tests. With five states possessing nuclear weapons and the prospect of at least a dozen other countries joining the club, the emphasis of the two superpowers shifted from futile disarmament efforts to trying to prevent further proliferation of these weapons. The result was the 1968 Nuclear Non-Proliferation Treaty (NPT), which sought to prevent further proliferation while also giving the existing possessors the status of nuclear weapon states.[11] The NPT entered into force in March 1970.

The near-universal NPT, with 190 members (only Israel, India, and Pakistan remain non-signatories), also had provisions related to the peaceful uses of nuclear energy and nuclear disarmament, which along with non-proliferation make up the "three pillars" of the Treaty. Peaceful uses was first proposed in US President Dwight Eisenhower's famous *Atoms for Peace*[12] address to the General Assembly on 8 December 1953, which led to the establishment of the International Atomic Energy Agency (IAEA) in Vienna in 1957—over a decade before the NPT was opened for signature.

Consequently, the NPT neither specifies detailed provisions for verification of compliance nor does it set up an inspectorate or verification organization. Instead, it relies on the IAEA to work out the scope, frequency, intrusiveness, and procedures of inspections with member states and also carries them out. Thus, the IAEA has the objective of both promoting peaceful uses of nuclear energy and preventing the proliferation of nuclear weapons; a challenging task, given that the wherewithal for peaceful uses can easily be converted to produce nuclear weapons.

Although the NPT is the lynchpin of the non-proliferation regime, the regime itself is much broader and is considered to comprise of the following elements: the 1963 Partial Test Ban Treaty (PTBT) and the 1996 Comprehensive Test Ban Treaty (CTBT), both of which sought to prevent nuclear proliferation by banning nuclear tests; the proposed Fissile Material Cutoff Treaty (FMCT), which seeks to ban the production of fissile material; bilateral negotiations and agreements to limit nuclear arsenals, particularly of the US and the Soviet Union/Russian Federation, such as Strategic Arms Limitation (SALT) I and II, the Anti-Ballistic Missile (ABM) Treaty, Strategic Arms Reduction Talks (START) I, II, and III, the Intermediate Range Nuclear Forces Treaty (INF), and the Strategic Offensive Reductions Treaty (SORT); ensuring compliance of the NPT provisions through the safeguards of the IAEA; and Nuclear Weapon Free Zones (NWFZs).

In addition to these multilateral institutions, individual states (notably the United States) and groups of like-minded countries (mostly Western industrialized states) have also established national instruments and/or collective plurilateral export control and other arrangements against countries suspected of nuclear weapons proliferation. Perhaps the most prominent national instrument is the 1978 Nuclear Non-proliferation Act passed by the United States Congress. Similarly, the Nuclear Suppliers Group (NSG), the Zangger Committee, and the Missile Technology Control Regime (MTCR) sought to prevent nuclear weapon proliferation by restricting export of nuclear and missile technology.[13] Most of these were prompted by the 1974 Indian nuclear test. While these arrangements have contributed somewhat to slowing down if not curbing proliferation, the ad hoc, exclusive and non-transparent nature of these regimes has laid them open to accusation of being technology-denial regimes, preventing countries from developing peaceful uses of nuclear energy.

The biological weapons regime

The 1925 Geneva Protocol was the first serious international effort to ban the use of biological weapons and drew on the horrendous experience of World War I. However, the Geneva Protocol had two major weaknesses: first, it banned the use of these weapons only during war but did not ban their development, production, or possession; second, some countries that joined the protocol reserved the right to retaliate if they were attacked with biological weapons.[14] Consequently, despite the protocol several countries built biological weapons, particularly during the Cold War. Among them the Soviet Union and the United States had the biggest programs.

International efforts to rid the world of these deadly weapons finally gained momentum in the late 1960s, and the unilateral decision by US President Richard Nixon in 1969 to dismantle its biological weapons program provided a much-needed fillip. These efforts culminated in the Convention on the Prohibition of the Development, Production and Stockpiling of Bacteriological and Toxin Weapons and on their Destruction, or simply the Biological Weapons Convention (BWC), which opened for signature on 10 April 1972.[15] The BWC was the first multilateral disarmament treaty to ban the development, production, stockpiling, acquisition, retention, or transfer of an entire category of weapons. Unlike the NPT the BWC does not recognize any weapon possessors. The BWC does not explicitly prohibit the use of biological weapons; the assumption is that if possession itself is banned, then their use is not possible. The BWC entered into force in March 1975—five years after the NPT. Presently there are 166 states parties to the Convention, including all the five NPT nuclear weapon states who are also the Security Council's permanent members. However, some states with potential biological weapons capability have either not signed the convention (such as Israel) or have signed but not ratified it (such as Egypt and Syria). In addition, some states (such as Russia and Iraq) were discovered to had undeclared biological weapons programs despite being signatories, and it is suspected that some other members might also have clandestine weapons programs.

The BWC also suffers from several other drawbacks: unlike the NPT, which has the IAEA, the convention has no organization or implementing body. Consequently, there is no systematic monitoring of implementation or treaty compliance and there is no mechanism for investigating alleged violations. Indeed, the lack of a verification mechanism, akin to that provided by the IAEA, is, perhaps, the biggest weakness of the BWC. Although parties to the BWC have met regularly at five-yearly intervals to review the operation of the BWC and also between some of these review conferences to strengthen the effectiveness and improve the implementation of the Convention, they have not been able to resolve the vexing issue of how to verify treaty compliance and investigate alleged violations. Nonetheless, the BWC has established a norm against these weapons and has also used confidence-building measures to increase confidence and transparency among its members.

Like the NPT, the formal BWC is supported by the informal forum called the Australia Group (AG), "which, through the harmonisation of export controls, seeks to ensure that exports do not contribute to the development of chemical or biological weapons."[16] The AG, with a majority of Western industrialized countries as members, are all also members of the BWC and "serve to support the objectives of the BWC by enhancing the effectiveness of national export licensing measures."[17] However, as with the NSG, the MTCR, and the Zangger Group, the AG's rules are not legally binding. Finally, the absence of key BWC signatories with significant biological capabilities from the Group, such as India, has led to charges that the AG is merely a technology-denial cartel.

The chemical weapon regime

The extensive and indiscriminate use of chemical weapons during World War I, which reportedly caused 100,000 deaths, was the primary impetus that led to the 1925 Geneva Protocol.[18] However, as noted earlier, the protocol did not prevent the use of these weapons: Italy employed chemical weapons against Abyssinia/Ethiopia in 1935–36 and Japan followed suit in China in 1937–38. Nazi Germany extensively used chemical weapons in its concentration camps and gas chambers. During the Cold War at least 25 countries were suspected of having chemical weapons programs, including the United States and the Soviet Union, which had the largest stockpiles. In addition, in the 1980s Iraq used chemical weapons not only against Iran but also against its own population.

Against this backdrop the 1975 BWC paved the way for a similar convention related to chemical weapons. Article IX of the BWC noted that each signatory

> affirms the recognised objective of effective prohibition of Chemical Weapons and, to this end, undertakes to continue negotiations in good faith with a view to reaching early agreement on effective measures for the prohibition of their development, production and stockpiling and for their destruction.[19]

Despite this affirmation multilateral negotiations remained tortuously slow until the mid-1980s. The revelations of a chemical attack on civilians in northern Iraq in March 1988, followed by the 1990 bilateral agreement on chemical weapons between the United States and the Soviet Union, under which the two countries agreed not to produce chemical weapons, to reduce their stocks to 20 percent, and to begin destruction in 1992, provided the much-needed fillip. Although the US–Soviet treaty never entered into force, the Chemical Weapons Convention (CWC) was finally concluded by January 1993 and entered into force in April 1997—nearly a century after the 1899 Hague Convention first sought to ban the use of chemical weapons.

Although the CWC was the last multilateral instrument established to deal with WMDs, it has three unique characteristics when compared to the NPT and the BWC. First, it aims to eliminate an entire category of weapons of mass destruction under strict international verification. This is distinct from both the NPT (which is relatively very weak on the elimination aspect) and the BWC (which lacks an international verification mechanism). The CWC categorically prohibits the development, production, stockpiling, transfer, and use of chemical weapons. It even prohibits any military preparations for the use of chemical weapons as well as the use of riot control agents as a method of warfare. Second, the CWC is comprehensive—the text itself is some 50 pages in length, and the annexes on verification and confidentiality bring the total to nearly 200, making it the longest WMD-related treaty; non-discriminatory—it does not recognize any state as a legitimate possessor; and, with 188 signatories, including the P-5 and every country with significant chemical industries, it is truly multilateral. Finally, the CWC also established a dedicated international organization to ensure the implementation of its provisions, including verification: the Organisation for the Prohibition of Chemical Weapons (OPCW).

There are four distinct pillars of the CWC: disarmament—the destruction and elimination of chemical weapons stockpiles and their associated production facilities; non-proliferation—ensuring that toxic chemicals and their precursors are developed, produced, transferred, or used only for peaceful purposes; protection and assistance—providing assistance through the OPCW in case of chemical weapon use or threat of use against a signatory; and facilitating international cooperation in the peaceful application of chemistry.

Seven countries declared possessing chemical weapons when they signed the CWC, including the US and Russia—the two biggest possessors. As per their agreements, all the declared chemical weapon stocks (about 71,000 metric tons) should have been destroyed by 2012. However, only 75 percent of all stocks had been verifiably destroyed by then. Even if all the current declared stockpiles are destroyed the world will not be rid of chemical weapons; six countries with suspected chemical weapons or chemical weapons capabilities have either not signed the CWC, including Egypt, North Korea, and Syria or, as in the case of Israel and Myanmar, have signed but not ratified the CWC and remain outside its ambit.

As in the case of the BWC, the AG is the ad hoc plurilateral forum that seeks to support the non-proliferation pillar of the CWC. In fact the AG was established in response to the 1984 UN findings of chemical weapons use by Iraq and that at least some of the precursor chemicals and materials for Baghdad's weapons had been sourced through legitimate trade channels.[20] However, the exclusive and non-binding nature of the AG makes its impact limited.

Current challenges

All the regimes designed to deal with nuclear, chemical, and biological weapons either individually or collectively face three sets of challenges. The first is posed by states within the existing regimes. Here states that either withdraw from the regime and build weapons or violate the regime through clandestine weapons programs pose as much of a challenge as states that, on the one hand, are dragging their feet over disarming their existing arsenals and, on the other, are also seeking to improve the quality of weapons. In the nuclear realm, for instance, much attention has been devoted to Iran and North Korea, but not as much effort has been devoted to the huge arsenals and the modernization plans of the five nuclear weapons states within the NPT.

The second set of challenges comes from states without the existing regimes. In the nuclear arena it includes India, Israel, and Pakistan, which have not signed the NPT, but also states like the China, DPRK, Egypt, Iran, Israel, and the United States, which have still to ratify the CTBT. This is also the case with the CWC and the BWC, which are still missing key countries with weapons capabilities (and, possibly, stocks) as members. There are a variety of reasons why some states either never joined the treaties, or having signed them did not ratify them, or having joined decided to opt out. These reasons could vary from domestic political, technological, or economic factors, to regional security concerns, to prestige and the desire to have a greater say in global governance.

The third and, perhaps, most formidable challenge comes from non-state actors, including but not limited to terrorist groups. All three WMD-related regimes were conceived and designed to deal with state-based nuclear, chemical, and biological weapons, and therefore stipulate obligations for state parties and not non-state entities or individuals. Thus, at best, they address the threat from non-state actors only indirectly. According to Security Council Resolution 1540 of 28 April 2004, a non-state actor is defined as an "individual or entity, not acting under the lawful authority of any State in conducting activities which come within the scope of this resolution."[21] This would include the quest of transnational or sub-national fundamentalist or cult groups, such as Aum Shinrikyo and al-Qaeda, to develop WMDs, as well as the antics of scientists and entities, such as A. Q. Khan, to hawk their materials and expertise. The Khan episode in particular indicates a triple proliferation threat. First, there is a real concern about the ability of a weak state like Pakistan to manage and control its nuclear establishment and scientists and, as a corollary, its nuclear weapons. Second, it also highlights the possibility that states seeking nuclear weapons now have access to another unchecked network for acquiring nuclear weapons technology. Third, there is also the serious possibility that armed transnational non-state actors seeking nuclear weapons (such as al-Qaeda) might also receive the necessary know-how and expertise from the elaborate Khan network.[22]

In addition, each of the WMD regimes described above faces unique challenges to them. For instance, the NPT has been more successful in preventing new states from acquiring nuclear weapons than it has been in either slowing down or disarming states that already possess nuclear weapons.[23] In contrast, the CWC/OPCW, which has been the most successful WMD disarmament arrangement until now, faces the challenge of transitioning to strengthening its non-proliferation capabilities; keeping up with the rapidly evolving science and technology; and preserving and strengthening the norm against chemical weapons. For the BWC there are two critical challenges: first, given the rapidly growing biotech capabilities, technological advances (such as synthetic biology), shrinking costs, and widely expanding interest, participation, availability, and access, there is a concern that the assessment and management of these risks is lagging far behind. The five-yearly review conferences and even the inter-sessional meetings might not be frequent enough to keep pace with the evolving threats. Second, in the absence of a dedicated organization to undertake compliance verification, will the present "network approach" be adequate to ensure compliance?

The way forward

These challenges from states not parties as well as non-state actors to the WMD regimes, coupled with the rapid diffusion of the technology to make these weapons, have led the international community of states to follow at least three different approaches to address them.

First, there is the traditional multilateral institutional approach anchored in negotiated treaty-based regimes, such as the NPT, the BWC, and the CWC. All these treaties were concluded after a protracted negotiating process. In the case of the CWC, for instance, the idea was first proposed in 1899 but reached fruition only in the late 1990s. Given the complexity of negotiating treaties, such treaties are also not amenable to amendments and cannot be easily altered to adjust to new realities. They are invariably strong in setting norms and principles and in international law, but they tend to be relatively weak on enforcement. For instance, the NPT is as incapable of dissuading states from exercising the right to withdraw under Article X as it is of enforcing nuclear disarmament under Article VI.[24] If the treaty-based regime is ineffective in holding member states to their commitments, it is even weaker in its efforts to deal with both non-member states as well as non-state actors. Despite these drawbacks the post-Cold War period was regarded as one of opportunity to strengthen the treaty-based regime. However, in the period of transition to a multipolar world this optimism was dashed. For instance, while the CTBT, the latest attempt to address nuclear weapons, was successfully negotiated in 1996, it has still not entered into force and is unlikely to do so in the foreseeable future. A similar fate is likely for the proposed FMCT.

Second, partly on account of these inherent weaknesses in the treaty-based regimes, in the post-Cold War world the international community embarked on a series of non-treaty-based multilateral approaches, such as the various declarations and resolutions of the General Assembly. This, of course, was not the first time that such an approach was followed: in the 1960s the Assembly passed several resolutions supporting the NPT and, after further revision—concerning mainly the preamble and Articles IV and V— it commended the draft text of the NPT, which is annexed to Resolution 2373 (XXII). Similarly, it was the General Assembly that resurrected the CTBT (after it had been blocked at the Conference on Disarmament in Geneva) by adopting a resolution (A/RES/50/245) on 10 September 1996. In April 2005 the assembly also adopted the International Convention for the Suppression of Acts of Nuclear Terrorism, which addresses non-state actors.

In contrast, the Security Council, which had been in a debilitating paralysis during the Cold War, also became active on the issue of WMD proliferation. The first indication of this was the various resolutions related to Iraq's invasion of Kuwait, which also established the UN Special Commission (UNSCOM) to disarm Iraq's nuclear, biological, and chemical programs. Another significant step was the Security Council Presidential Statement of 31 January 1992, which stressed that "proliferation of all weapons of mass destruction constitutes a threat to international peace and security" and, with specific reference to nuclear weapons, noted "the decision of many countries to adhere to the [NPT] and emphasize the integral role in the implementation of that Treaty." Ironically, this statement also highlighted the failure of the NPT nuclear states (the Security Council's five permanent members) to keep their commitments to the NPT. Subsequently, the council passed several other resolutions related to state actors.[25] In addition, it also passed several resolutions related to non-state actors, including 1373 (2001), 1540 (2004), 1673 (2006), 1810 (2008), 1977 (2011), and 2055 (2012).

The latter sets of resolutions are particularly innovative for two reasons: they seek to deal with non-state actors, and they aim to provide stopgap arrangements to plug existing loopholes in the present treaty-based regime. Security Council Resolution 1540 in particular is far reaching because it calls on all UN member states to "adopt and enforce appropriate effective laws which prohibit any non-State actor to manufacture, acquire, possess, develop, transport, transfer or use nuclear, chemical or biological weapons and their means of delivery," as well as to "take and enforce effective measures to establish domestic controls to prevent the proliferation of nuclear, chemical, or biological weapons and their means of delivery." While the resolution has been generally welcomed given that present treaty-based regimes do not address this aspect of proliferation, there is concern that this approach of using the Security Council to legislate, if exercised often enough, would circumvent the negotiated approach to developing treaty-based regimes.

Third, of even greater concern to some members of the international community, there are a set of ad hoc, non-institutional, non-conventional approaches led by individual states or a group of states to address the immediate challenges of non-proliferation. These include the so-called preventive war against Iraq's nuclear, chemical, and biological weapons in 2003, which was probably the first and perhaps last non-proliferation war, although Iran might emerge as another potential future target; the US-led Proliferation Security Initiative (PSI); the so-called 3+3 negotiations with Iran; the six-party talks to address the DPRK's nuclear ambitions; and the Indo-US civilian nuclear initiative, as well as India's efforts to join the AG, the MTCR, the NSG, and the Wassenaar Group. These arrangements tend to be stronger on the enforcement dimension but are relatively weak in both international law as well as establishing norms and principles. Indeed, all of these initiatives are discriminatory and, predictably, do not enjoy universal adherence. Although the states behind these initiatives—primarily the NPT nuclear weapons states—have attempted to seek greater legitimacy for their actions by having these initiatives endorsed by the Security Council, there is concern that these initiatives might deal a fatal blow to the already weakened treaty-based non-proliferation regime. Nonetheless, given the inability of the existing formal regime to address many of the proliferation challenges of today, these ad hoc initiatives are likely to flourish.

Finally, among ad hoc approaches are several independent commissions and non-governmental initiatives that also endeavor to eliminate WMDs. Prominent among these are the International Commission on Nuclear Non-proliferation and Disarmament; the Weapons of Mass Destruction Commission; Global Zero; and the series of op-eds written by four former US Secretaries of State.[26] However, unlike the International Commission on Intervention and State Sovereignty, which formulated the "Responsibility to Protect," none of the efforts related to nuclear weapons or WMDs in general has had a similar impact on fundamentally altering the normative and policy agenda.

Conclusion

It is evident that liberal institutionalists would prefer strengthening the multilateral treaty-based institutions to address the WMD challenges rather than opt for ad hoc and military options. In contrast, realists would be inclined towards the ad hoc and unilateral or "coalition of the willing" approaches, including the use of force, to ensure the security of the state vis-à-vis other states as well as non-state actors. However, it is equally clear that ad hoc approaches alone are unlikely to be considered legitimate or likely to be effective either in the short or the long term unless they are linked to the treaty-based regime. Similarly, treaty-based regimes by themselves, despite their solid legal and legitimate credentials, are unlikely to be effective in their objectives unless they are non-discriminatory and universal as well as having a strong verification and enforcement mechanism. In short, realists and liberal institutionalists should seek to bridge their differences and find a middle ground. The CWC is, perhaps, the model treaty that builds on this middle ground. Is a similar compromise possible in the case of nuclear and biological weapons?

Additional reading

1. Melissa Gillis, *Disarmament: A Basic Guide*, 3rd edition (New York: United Nations, 2012).
2. Weapons of Mass Destruction Commission, *Weapons of Terror: Freeing the World of Nuclear, Biological and Chemical Arms* (Stockholm: EO Grafiska, 2006).
3. M. Bothe et al., eds., *The New Chemical Weapons Convention: Implementation and Prospects* (Leiden: Brill, 1998).
4. Laura H. Kahn, "The Biological Weapons Convention: Proceeding without a Verification Protocol," *The Bulletin of Atomic Scientists*, http://www.thebulletin.org/web-edition/columnists/laura-h-kahn/the-biological-weapons-convention-proceeding-without-verification.
5. Piers Millett, ed., *Improving Implementation of the Biological Weapons Convention: The 2007–2010 Intersessional Process* (Geneva: UNIDIR, 2011).
6. Waheguru Pal Singh Sidhu, "The Nuclear Disarmament and Non-Proliferation Regime," in *Security Studies: An Introduction*, 2nd edition, ed. Paul D. Williams (New York: Routledge, 2013), 409–424.
7. The Arms Control Association website (http://www.armscontrol.org/) is an authoritative source for the basic facts of the various WMD regimes as well as the ongoing current challenges, debates, and responses.

Notes

1 See Commission for Conventional Armaments, *Resolution Adopted by the Commission at Its Thirteenth Meeting*, 12 August 1948.
2 See, for instance, S. Glasstone and P. J. Dolan, *The Effects of Nuclear Weapons*, 3rd edition (Washington, DC: US Government Printing Office, 1977); Jonathan Schell, *The Fate of the Earth* (New York: Alfred A. Knopf, 1982); and Melissa Gillis, *Disarmament: A Basic Guide*, 3rd edition (New York: United Nations, 2012), 17.
3 Waheguru Pal Singh Sidhu, "The Nuclear Disarmament and Non-proliferation Regime," in *Security Studies: An Introduction*, ed. Paul D. Williams, 2nd edition (New York: Routledge, 2013), 410.
4 These are, in chronological order, the 1968 Nuclear Non-proliferation Treaty (NPT), the 1972 Biological Weapons Convention (BWC) or Biological and Toxin Weapons Convention (BTWC), and the 1992 Chemical Weapons Convention (CWC).
5 The 1899 Hague Convention was the first serious attempt to prevent the use of chemical weapons and called on signatories to "abstain from the use of projectiles the object of which is the diffusion of asphyxiating or deleterious gases." See http://avalon.law.yale.edu/19th_century/dec99-02.asp.
6 The text of the Geneva Protocol is available at: http://www.un.org/disarmament/WMD/Bio/1925GenevaProtocol.shtml.
7 UNGA Resolution 1 (I), Seventeenth Plenary Meeting, 24 January 1946.
8 See AtomicArhive.com, http://www.atomicarchive.com/Docs/Deterrence/BaruchPlan.shtml.

9 See Randy Rydell, "Going for Baruch: The Nuclear Plan that Refused to Go Away," *Arms Control Today*, June 2006, http://www.armscontrol.org/act/2006_06/LookingbackBaruch.

10 CTBTO, http://www.ctbto.org/the-treaty/history-1945-1993/1945-54-early-efforts-to-restrain-nuclear-testing/.

11 Jozef Goldblat, *Nuclear Non-Proliferation: A Guide to the Debate* (Stockholm: SIPRI, 1985); and Gillis, *Disarmament: A Basic Guide*, 31–37.

12 The original speech can be seen at: http://www.world-nuclear-university.org/about.aspx?id=8674&terms=atoms%20for%20peace.

13 For the NSG, see http://www.nuclearsuppliersgroup.org/Leng/default.htm; for the Zangger Committee, see http://www.zanggercommittee.org/Seiten/default.aspx; and for the MTCR, see http://www.mtcr.info/english/index.html. In addition, see the Arms Control Association fact sheets on the Nuclear Suppliers Group (NSG) at a glance at: http://www.armscontrol.org/factsheets/NSG; and on the Missile Technology Control Regime at a glance at: http://www.armscontrol.org/factsheets/mtcr. See also Waheguru Pal Singh Sidhu, "Looking Back: The Missile Technology Control Regime," *Arms Control Today*, April 2007.

14 Gillis, *Disarmament: A Basic Guide*, 43.

15 For details of the BWC, see http://www.unog.ch/bwc and the unofficial http://www.opbw.org/. In addition, see the Arms Control Association fact sheet on the Biological Weapons Conventional at a glance at: http://www.armscontrol.org/factsheets/bwc.

16 See http://www.australiagroup.net/en/index.html.

17 See the Australia Group, http://www.australiagroup.net/en/bwc.html.

18 Gillis, *Disarmament: A Basic Guide*, 39.

19 See http://www.opcw.org/chemical-weapons-convention/about-the-convention/genesis-and-historical-development/; and Julian Perry Robinson, "The Negotiations on the Chemical Weapons Convention: An Historical Overview," in *The New Chemical Weapons Convention: Implementation and Prospects*, eds. M. Bothe et al. (Leiden: Brill, 1998), 17–36.

20 See the Origins of the Australia Group at: http://www.australiagroup.net/en/origins.html.

21 See Security Council resolution S/RES/1540 (2004), 28 April 2004, which specifically seeks to address "the threat of terrorism and the risk that non-State actors . . . may acquire, develop, traffic in or use nuclear, chemical and biological weapons and their means of delivery."

22 Sidhu, "The Nuclear Disarmament and Non-proliferation Regime," 417–418.

23 See, for instance, Waheguru Pal Singh Sidhu, "Overview: Challenges and Prospects of Monitoring," in *The 2010 NPT Action Plan Monitoring Report* (Geneva: Reaching Critical Will, 2012), 3–9.

24 Article X of the NPT gives each signatory the "right to withdraw from the Treaty if it decides that extraordinary events . . . have jeopardised the supreme interests of its country," while Article VI calls on members to "pursue negotiations in good faith on effective measures relating to the cessation of the nuclear arms race at an early date and to nuclear disarmament."

25 These include UN Security Council resolutions 1172 (1998), 1696 (2006), 1718 (2006), 1737 (2006), 1747 (2007), 1803 (2008), 1835 (2008), 1887 (2009), 1929 (2010), 1984 (2011), and 2049 (2012). Although not all of them dealt with chemical and biological weapons, they were about WMDs.

26 For the Report of the International Commission on Nuclear Non-proliferation and Disarmament titled *Eliminating Nuclear Threats: A Practical Agenda for Global Policymakers*, see http://icnnd.org/Reference/reports/ent/default.htm; the report of the Weapons of Mass Destruction Commission is titled *Weapons of Terror: Freeing the World of Nuclear, Biological and Chemical Arms*; for details of Global Zero, see http://www.globalzero.org/; and former US secretaries of state Henry Kissinger, Sam Nunn, Bill Perry, and George Shultz penned their vision in four prominent *Wall Street Journal* op-eds—"A World Free of Nuclear Weapons" (4 January 2007), "Towards a Nuclear Free World" (15 January 2008), "How to Protect Our Nuclear Deterrent" (19 January 2010), and "Deterrence in the Age of Nuclear Proliferation" (7 March 2011).

From "Global War" to Global Governance

Counterterrorism cooperation in world politics

Peter Romaniuk

In her speech at the launch of the Global Counterterrorism Forum (GCTF) in New York in September 2011, US Secretary of State Hillary Clinton was quick to praise international efforts to prevent and suppress terrorism. She noted the strength of bilateral partnerships among states and the impacts of regional organizations in building counterterrorism capacity and expertise. She underscored the importance of the "international policy and legal framework" developed through the United Nations, in particular the General Assembly's "Global Counterterrorism Strategy" (2006) (hereafter, "the Strategy"). "But," she continued, "as important as all of these elements are, all of us have been convinced that a crucial piece of the puzzle against terrorism is missing." Designed to fill gaps in the contemporary architecture for counterterrorism cooperation, the new Forum would provide its 30 members and their partners with a "dedicated global venue to regularly convene key counterterrorism policy makers and practitioners from around the world. We need a place where we can identify essential priorities, devise solutions, and chart a path to implementation of best practices."[1]

Three days earlier, a few blocks away, more than 500 participants—including representatives from all UN member states, a wide range of international and regional organizations, as well as civil society and the media—had joined the UN Secretary-General's Symposium on International Counterterrorism Cooperation. Here, too, the role of the UN and the Strategy were affirmed. Here, too, the importance of multiple levels of cooperation was acknowledged. And here, too, a new multilateral mechanism was announced.[2] The UN Counterterrorism Centre (UNCCT), which is housed in the office of the UN Counterterrorism Implementation Taskforce (CTITF) within the Secretariat's Department of Political Affairs, was launched with funding from the Kingdom of Saudi Arabia ($10 million over three years), with the goals of aiding implementation of the Strategy, fostering international cooperation, and building states' capacity to counter terrorism.[3]

"Governance" refers to the, "sum of the many ways individuals and institutions, public and private, manage their common affairs. It is a continuing process through which conflicting or diverse interests may be accommodated and cooperative action may be taken."[4] It is a deliberately broad concept that "encompasses the activities of governments, but . . . also includes the many other channels through which 'commands' flow in the form of goals framed, directives issued, and policies pursued."[5] In this regard, "global governance"—a concept initiated in the post-Cold War period—is generally understood to subsume the study of formal international organizations, which has been a fixture of post-World War II international relations. In a volume on global governance and international organizations today, the record of counterterrorism cooperation ought to stand out as unique: more or less, it has gone from "woah" to "go" in the space of little more than a decade. That is, for most of the last century, counterterrorism did not lend itself to global governance.

The reasons for this were straightforward: states disagreed about the legitimacy of non-state actors using violence for political purposes and about how to respond. While states concluded 12 international legal instruments against terrorism, and despite an increase in cooperation after the end of the Cold War, multilateralism remained the "mood music" to counterterrorism until 2001.[6] The record changed quickly after the 9/11 terrorist attacks in the United States. Those and subsequent attacks across the globe have elicited a burst of multilateral activity rare in its scope, reach, and intensity. Despite the contentious pronouncement by the United States of a "global war on terror," counterterrorism cooperation has followed an unmistakable trajectory and recent developments point to an ongoing demand for it. At the same time, there remain significant gaps in the multilateral response and, most notably, a consensus definition of terrorism remains elusive.

This chapter demonstrates the utility of "global governance" as a concept in interpreting counterterrorism cooperation over time, as it covers "process" and "activities" among a range of state and non-state actors that exercise authority and influence in various forms. The first two sections summarize counterterrorism cooperation before and after 9/11, showing how multilateral activity in this field has come to manifest this definition of global governance. The third section reflects the experience of counterterrorism cooperation over time, suggesting that it yields generalizable lessons about how states use international organizations and about how global governance works in practice. That is, forms of counterterrorism cooperation after 9/11 illustrate the diversity of global governance but bring to light its fundamentally competitive nature as states use international organizations (IOs) to advance and protect their interests, and influence others. In concluding, I underscore that, just as an understanding of global governance is necessary to interpret counterterrorism cooperation, the achievements and challenges of multilateral counterterrorism today contribute much to our knowledge of IOs and global governance.

Before 9/11: barriers to global governance

The record of counterterrorism cooperation in the twentieth century illustrates well the barriers to global governance (most notably conflicting interests, per the definition above). While states' interests occasionally aligned, yielding episodic examples of cooperation, the form and substance of those interactions reflected a fundamental political cleavage among them. As such, the engagement of IOs was relatively limited (especially when compared to the post-9/11 period) and it is perhaps a stretch to talk about global governance in any robust form in this period. Still, these developments set the stage for what was to follow, when the barriers to cooperation were confronted with renewed purpose.

The deepest origins of global governance on counterterrorism lie in the 1890s, when police officials in Europe convened a series of conferences to discuss the anarchist threat that took the lives of several heads of state. In 1904 these meetings brought to fruition the first international counterterrorism instrument of the modern era, when 10 states signed an anti-anarchist protocol. However, despite the effort to institutionalize cooperative mechanisms at the operational level, anarchist terrorism could not sustain states' attention as the world moved towards war.[7] A second attempt to advance counterterrorism cooperation was made in the interwar years, through the International Association of Penal Law and then the League of Nations. The latter eventually concluded the "Convention for the Prevention and Punishment of Terrorism" in 1937. That convention is unique in that it defined terrorism as "criminal acts directed against a state and intended or calculated to create a state of terror in the minds of particular persons, or a group of persons, or in the public." Despite the apparent circularity of this definition (i.e. it defines "terrorism" by referring to "state of terror") the League's achievement in this regard is unique. As I describe below, the increase in counterterrorism cooperation after 9/11 has not included consensus on how to define "terrorism." Still, the League's members were perhaps only moderately impressed with this achievement, as the Convention attracted 24 signatories and only one ratification, and never entered into force. Terrorism again fell off the international agenda in the march to war.

Without more, one might have assumed that the creation of the United Nations in 1945, in the aftermath of such a bloody conflict, might give rise to a demand for cooperation to suppress the use of violence. Within a few decades of its founding, however, the UN came to be Balkanized on this issue. On one side was the group of Third World states who sought to preserve the legitimacy of "national liberation movements," while labeling others as "state terrorists." This coalition brought together the postcolonial states of the Nonaligned Movement as well as the Soviet Union, who perceived that their interests would be served by opposing the West and supporting regimes and armed groups that might take the side of communism in the Cold War. On the other side was the West, which rejected the notion that violence by non-state actors should be accommodated in these circumstances. The sharp end of this disagreement was the politics of the Middle East. In his 1974 speech to the UN General Assembly, Chairman of the Palestinian Liberation Organization Yasser Arafat proclaimed that "The justice of the cause determines the right to struggle."[8] Such a subjective view on the legitimacy of violence is often summarized in the cliché "one man's terrorist is another man's freedom fighter." And so it was in the UN throughout the 1970s and into the 1980s, especially in General Assembly fora, where a work stream on terrorism produced nothing but repetition and was unable to advance a comprehensive response to terrorism.

What are the possibilities for global governance under conditions of such fundamental political disagreement? Interestingly, states found a way to work around their disagreement and identify convergent interests. Over this period, we see the emergence of a "piecemeal" approach to counterterrorism through IOs. Between 1963 and 1999, 12 international legal instruments emerged, each with a specific topical focus, including in the domains of aviation security, maritime security, the protection of diplomats, nuclear security, and terrorist financing. In other words, even if states disagreed about who should be called a "terrorist," and whether non-state violence could be justified under certain conditions, they appeared to agree that certain acts should be discouraged. True, the conventions often included language to provide exceptions in some circumstances, thereby permitting the forms of violence that they otherwise sought to eradicate. In addition, ratification rates remained modest in some instances. But this body of international law reflects the UN's principal contribution to global governance on counterterrorism prior to 9/11.

As states grew frustrated with the relative stalemate at the UN, they shopped for other fora in which they could advance their counterterrorism objectives. This "spillover effect" meant that specialist organizations (such as the International Civil Aviation Organization, ICAO, International Maritime Organization. IMO, and the International Atomic Energy Agency, IAEA) began to discuss counterterrorism. Similarly, over time a range of regional organizations (including the Arab League, the Organization of American States, OAS, the Council of Europe and the European Commission) elaborated counterterrorism measures, as did limited-membership bodies such as the North Atlantic Treaty Organization (NATO) and the Group of Seven states (G7). So, even under the shadow of political dissension, global governance began to emerge, ever so slightly. In this regard, the post-Cold War record of the Security Council is worth noting. For example, over the course of the 1990s the Council imposed sanctions against Libya, Sudan, and the Taliban for terrorism-related reasons. Among these, the financial sanctions, travel ban, and arms embargo imposed on the Taliban would attain a much higher profile after 9/11. Further, in Resolution 1269 (19 October 1999) the Security Council came as close as was possible to a general statement on terrorism. Sponsored by the Russians, the resolution condemned terrorism in general terms and called on states to take a range of counterterrorism measures and to become parties to the conventions.

In sum, prior to 2011, global governance on counterterrorism was constrained. Politics precluded a comprehensive response through IOs. But in the interstices of these disagreements, cooperation emerged. Not only did this period lay the groundwork for the post-9/11 response, but it illustrated the political barriers that would need to be overcome if counterterrorism cooperation were to advance in more than a piecemeal fashion.

Post-9/11: experiments in global governance

In his televised address on the evening of 9/11, US president George W. Bush stated: "America and our friends and allies join with all those who want peace and security in the world and we stand together to win the war against terrorism."[9] Today, the Bush Administration is more likely to be remembered for its willingness to act unilaterally, or to fashion small "coalitions of the willing," where deemed necessary in pursuing its "global war on terror." But things did not start that way and, indeed, the record suggests that the US has consistently viewed multilateralism as an important, if imperfect, tool of counterterrorism. In turn, US leadership has received a mixed reception from other states: consensus has been more forthcoming since 9/11, but the politics of counterterrorism has evolved—not disappeared. In addition, rather than resisting action through IOs, dissenters have offered competing visions of multilateral counterterrorism. The result is a remarkable volume of cooperative activity, wherein patterns of global governance are a product of both integrative and distributive bargaining.

Within two weeks of the 9/11 attacks, global governance on counterterrorism was broadened and deepened in a previously unimaginable fashion. On 28 September 2001, the Security Council approved Resolution 1373. Passed under Chapter VII of the UN Charter, it requires states to implement a wide range of counterterrorism measures in such areas as financial regulation, migration and customs control, and arms transfers. The resolution calls for bilateral, regional, and international cooperation on law enforcement, extradition, administrative and judicial matters, and as regards exchange of information relating to terrorism. Drafted and introduced by the US—but attracting unanimous support—1373 effectively consolidated and extended preexisting UN measures (e.g. as drawn from the conventions) and made them mandatory. Moreover, the resolution created a mechanism—in the form of a subsidiary organ of the Council, the "Counterterrorism Committee" (CTC)—to oversee its implementation. While subsidiary organs had been established to monitor the implementation of the Council's sanctions regimes in the 1990s, the CTC had a higher profile, and, by May 2003, all member states had submitted to it at least one implementation report, as required under the resolution. To advance its work, experts were seconded to the CTC. In addition to reviewing and responding to the volumes of member state reports, they began identifying "best practices" to implement 1373, while also reaching out to regional, sub-regional, and specialist organizations (more than 65 of whom met in New York in March 2003). Global governance on counterterrorism, it seemed, had finally arrived, and in a big way.

While the initial record of the CTC was promising, its role was unsustainable. In retrospect, it was remarkably ambitious to think that a subsidiary organ of the Council, supported by a small staff of experts, could fulfill the functions delegated to it. Importantly, between 2001 and 2003 the consensus of the immediate post-9/11 period somewhat dissipated, correlative with the politicization of the Council's role in the lead-up to the Bush administration's decision to go to war in Iraq. The CTC's role in monitoring implementation of 1373 was soon viewed by many to be too intrusive, leading to the claims that the Council was acting as a global legislature. Further complicating the Council's role, the sanctions that had been in place on the Taliban since 1999—

which had been expanded to include al-Qaeda and others—became a lightning rod for controversy. After 9/11, the list of targets subject to the range of embargoes grew rapidly. This soon raised concerns about due process and clashed with privacy laws in several jurisdictions. European states, in particular, faced legal challenges in domestic courts from their own citizens, who argued that their assets had been frozen without an opportunity to be heard or to appeal the decision.

Even as the optimism attached to the Security Council's response to 9/11 began to wane, global governance on counterterrorism continued to thicken. As in the pre-9/11 period, we can observe a kind of "spillover effect" here, with specialist and regional organizations pursuing counterterrorism-related measures in new and innovative ways. For example, it was only after 9/11 that the IMO advanced a new regime on ship and port security, and that the ICAO developed new rules on travel document security, incorporating biometric data and computer chips in international standards for passports. Similarly, it was only after 9/11 that Interpol developed a database on lost and stolen passports, and that the world's leading anti-money laundering body (the Financial Action Task Force, FATF) extended its mandate to countering terrorist financing, elaborating new rules and procedures. Indeed, if acronyms are a proxy for the vitality of multilateralism, then global governance positively flourished in this period as we were introduced to the CTAG (the G8's Counterterrorism Action Group), the CTAP process (APEC's Counterterrorism Action Plan), the ACSRT (the African Union's African Center for Study and Research on Terrorism), the ICPAT (the Inter-governmental Authority on Development's, IGAD, Capacity-building Program Against Terrorism), and RATS (the Regional Antiterrorism Structure of the Shanghai Cooperation Organization), as well as SEARCCT (the Southeast Asian Regional Centre for Counterterrorism in Kuala Lumpur) and JCLEC (the Jakarta Centre for Law Enforcement Cooperation, in Semarang), among many others (and these all outside of the UN system). Of course, there is much variation in the scope and impact of such initiatives, but their volume alone is striking. Within a few years, reticence towards cooperation had been overcome, replaced by a crowded field.

The leadership role of the Security Council on counterterrorism has been substantially reestablished over time. The CTC was reviewed and a proposal for "revitalization" emerged in 2004. As part of that, the CTC experts were replaced by the "Counterterrorism Executive Directorate" (CTED), established as a special political mission. Subsequent resolutions have expanded the mandate of the CTC and CTED and, under executive director Mike Smith (appointed in 2007), CTED has carved out a productive role facilitating their implementation. In practice, this means identifying "best practices" (drawn from a wide range of IOs active in the functional domains covered by the CTC's mandates), disseminating them (through workshops, meetings, and outreach), and monitoring their implementation.[10] Regarding the latter, CTED participates in country visits, to observe first hand member states' response to the Council's resolutions. CTED is joined in these visits by other Council organs, such as the committee overseeing the sanctions on the Taliban and al-Qaeda, and the "1540 Committee" (i.e. the committee established to oversee the implementation of Resolution 1540 (2004) on the proliferation of nuclear, chemical, or biological weapons to non-state actors), as well as other UN agencies. This process is surely what scholars intended to capture when they coined the term "global governance."

But the picture is broader still as, amid its travails, the Council has had to share the limelight on counterterrorism. The General Assembly, so often a forum for dissension on this issue, contributed its most important statement in 2006, in the form of the Strategy. Beginning soon after 9/11, then secretary-general Kofi Annan commissioned a series of working groups, panels, meetings, and reports, yielding enough consensus to enable the passage of the Strategy. It comprises four pillars. Two of these (preventing and combating terrorism, and building state capacity to counter terrorism) are essentially repetitive of Council resolutions. But the other two pillars, which refer to "conditions conducive to terrorism" and the importance of human rights while countering terrorism, cover issues that were somewhat elided in the Council's response and had proved controversial. Their inclusion in the Strategy broadened the scope of the UN's response and is generally considered to have enhanced the legitimacy of the world body as a counterterrorism actor. Reflecting consensus, too, a further five legal instruments relating to terrorism have been concluded since 9/11, effectively extending the "piecemeal approach." Still, there remain familiar constraints upon the Assembly as a forum for advancing global governance on counterterrorism. For example, efforts in the Sixth Committee (Legal) to negotiate a Comprehensive Convention on International Terrorism remain stalled, as ever, on the question of a definition.

A related dilemma concerns the implementation of the Strategy. Put simply, its pillars that overlap with Council mandates (and on which CTED and others are active) have advanced further than the others. This reflects the challenges faced by the CTITF, which was initially established in 2005 with the specific mandate of coordinating UN entities working on different aspects of counterterrorism. With more than 30 such entities and observers around the table that task has proven difficult.[11] The CTITF initiated a series of thematic working groups as a means of enhancing coordination, an approach that showed some promise and generated a series of reports that again reflected the breadth of multilateral action on counterterrorism. Some members of the Task Force include counterterrorism among their core mission. For example, the UN Office on Drugs and Crime (UNODC) maintains a Terrorism Prevention Branch that has a long-standing program to assist states in implementing the international conventions. But other members of the Task Force are wary about framing their work (on development, human rights, education, etc.) in terms of "counterterrorism" and have remained reticent to engage. CTITF has since been tasked with an oversight role in coordinating strategy implementation. In response, the Task Force has endeavored to pursue some programmatic activities alongside its core coordination function. In practice it has mastered neither. To be sure, its efforts have been hampered by the absence of a permanent head of the office, a position that has remained unfilled for more than two years as of the time of writing. But the fact that the UN's response has evolved in this way—varied levels of engagement across multiple agencies without strong coordination—has led many observers to argue for a rationalization of the UN's counterterrorism role, consolidating the comparative advantages that the world's most inclusive IO offers in this field.[12]

It is perhaps this urge that informs the recent formation of the GCTF and UNCCT, noted at the beginning of the chapter. As Secretary of State Clinton remarked, GCTF members view the Forum as being complementary to the existing multilateral framework but perceive a gap in terms of broad-based, operational-level cooperation. A similar point can be made about the UNCCT. The revealed preference of Saudi Arabia, it seems, is to advance the Strategy, linking cooperation and capacity building more directly to it. In both cases, states identified shortcomings in the emerging system of global governance on counterterrorism. And in both cases, their response was to seek more, not less, multilateralism. This is telling and provides a sharp contrast with the pre-9/11 period.

In short, multilateral counterterrorism since 9/11 has seen a period in which global governance has expanded in this field in a unique fashion. Some astute observers, writing soon after 9/11 and the passage of Resolution 1373 (2001), foresaw this trend and noted that such an uptake would provide something of a test, or natural experiment, for theories and concepts that aim to describe and explain cooperation.[13] They were right: Multilateral counterterrorism is indeed a laboratory for global governance. Before concluding, we should consider the results.

Counterterrorism's lessons for global governance

If counterterrorism cooperation has been an experiment, what are the results and what do they mean for our understanding of global governance? Two points stand out in this regard. The first concerns the *forms* that counterterrorism cooperation has taken. This discussion illustrates the willingness of states to use the UN in creative ways. The assertive role of the Security Council in passing Resolution 1373 and related resolutions, and in empowering the CTC, CTED, and other subsidiary organs with a robust monitoring function, provides evidence. Such innovation is even more striking outside of the UN. Two US-led examples come to mind. Beginning in 2002, the US Customs and Border Protection Agency launched the "Container Security Initiative" (CSI). It sought bilateral arrangements with foreign ports, in order to station US officials abroad to undertake risk analyses and, in some cases, inspections of US-bound cargo. But what began as reciprocal bilateralism now covers almost 60 of the world's biggest ports and has gained some measure of endorsement from the World Customs Organization (through its 2005 "Standards to Secure and Facilitate Global Trade (SAFE) Framework"), the European Union, and G8. Similarly, from 2003, the United States has coordinated the "Proliferation Security Initiative" (PSI), under which states sign on to a "Statement of Interdiction Principles," committing them to counter WMD proliferation by sea and air, including an agreement to consider requests by other signatories to board and search ships registered in their jurisdiction. States also participate in joint exercises, meetings, workshops, and gaming. PSI was initially met with consternation by some states, who were concerned about the implications for sovereignty of interdiction agreements in the maritime domain. But more than 90 states have now signed on.

In these ways, counterterrorism cooperation reminds us that there are multiple routes to multilateralism and global governance. Indeed, counterterrorism is one area in which the trend to increasing diversity in forms of multilateralism can be observed.[14] Amid the cluster of cooperative activity, we can identify formal and informal transgovernmental networks (particularly favored by law enforcement and intelligence officials), as well as epistemic communities both inside and outside of government. Regarding the latter, numerous NGO and civil society groups have been active in documenting abuses of human rights and civil liberties, criticizing state practices and IOs alike.[15]

While it is premature to claim the existence of a "counterterrorism regime" *per se*,[16] we can observe the formation of relatively coherent regimes in some issue areas. Measures taken to counter terrorist financing are apt to be depicted in this way.[17] Elsewhere, I have argued that multilateral counterterrorism in the post-9/11 period can be understood using the concept of "regime complexes," as it has yielded "an array of partially over-lapping and nonhierarchical institutions governing a particular issue area . . . [and] marked by the existence of several legal agreements that are created and maintained in distinct fora with participation of different sets of actors."[18] The implementation guide to Resolution 1373, prepared by CTED, can be offered as evidence for this, drawing as it does upon norm-building and rule-making activities of multiple specialist IOs and regional bodies.[19] Further, there has been some effort to rethink inherited concepts in light of the recent record of counterterrorism cooperation. For example, Ramesh Thakur and Thomas Weiss venture the argument that, in the area of counterterrorism, the UN can be said to have a "policy."[20] That is, beyond articulating norms, the world body has a program of action in place to respond to the problem of terrorism. The argument is compelling and again suggests an empirical innovation in global governance that ought to be reflected in our conceptual understanding of it. For present purposes, it suffices to note that "global governance" is a broad and permissive concept; counterterrorism cooperation illustrates this *par excellence*.

A final point concerns the *drivers* of global governance. What has motivated states to seek international cooperation on counterterrorism in the unprecedented way that I have described here? What accounts for the volume of cooperative activity on terrorism, and its scope, reach, and intensity since 9/11? The record of cooperation attests to an uncommon amount of consensus, and it is difficult to imagine that global governance would be as vibrant as it is without convergent interests at some level. Further evidence is at hand. For example, global-level initiatives (such as those advanced through the Security Council and General Assembly, as well as specialist organizations like the IMO, ICAO, FATF, and WCO) have been accompanied by a burst of rule-making among regional organizations, wherein the latter often explicitly endorse the former. The GCTF, too, shows how multilateralism can serve collective interests. The Forum is structured around a series of working groups. The topical focus of these is telling, as there are groups addressing criminal justice and rule-of-law approaches to counter-terrorism, as well as terrorism prevention, i.e. measures to counter the narrative of terrorists, abbreviated to "CVE" (countering violent extremism) in the contemporary parlance. These are relatively new tools and tactics of counterterrorism, having been developed and deployed at the domestic level within the last half-decade or so. The fact that the Forum should be engaged on such topics suggests a measure of agreement among states as how to respond to evolving threats. The initial round of working group discussions and related events even hints at a willingness to share experiences and learn about how these innovative approaches should be utilized. In this way, cooperation is truly functional to states.

Impressive though this is, such integrative outcomes on counterterrorism cooperation yield to distributive bargaining with predictable frequency. Exhibit A in this regard is the ongoing inability of UN member states to fashion a Comprehensive Convention on International Terrorism entailing, as that would, agreement on a definition of terrorism under international law. For this reason, students of counterterrorism cooperation should recall recent work on the role of power in global governance, such as reflected in Michael Barnett and Raymond Duvall's claim that "Global governance involves formal and informal institutional contexts that dispose that action in directions that advantage some while disadvantaging others."[21] As in world politics generally, there are relative "winners" and "losers" in multilateral counterterrorism. The former are those powerful states that have been able to set the agenda and launder their preferences through IOs, which now establish and enforce standards for counterterrorism policy across states. The latter are those less powerful states for whom terrorism may not even rank as a priority but who have been increasingly called to account on this issue by IOs and others.

To be sure, the dynamics of these interactions can be subtle, and multilateralism provides opportunities to resist the powerful. For example, efforts to reform the Security Council's al-Qaeda–Taliban sanctions reflect the influence of European states in correcting the prevailing, US-led approach to listing targets. Similarly, the General Assembly's Strategy—which, recall, broadened the UN's counterterrorism agenda to include "conditions conducive to terrorism" and human rights—can be interpreted as a corrective to the assertiveness of the Security Council after 9/11. Moreover, the sheer volume of engagement among IOs and regional bodies suggests a strategy of forum shopping among states, in an effort to craft a normative environment more favorable to them. Beyond forum shopping, as the GCTF and UNCCT attest, states are clearly still prepared to create new fora where they see it in their interests to do so. That they continue to define those interests in terms of multilateralism tells us much about how global governance works: state and non-state actors often compete to shape the processes and activities that define it, aiming to influence the form and substance of their relations. States, big and small, seek the best deal they can get out of multilateral counterterrorism.

Conclusion

The presence of a chapter on counterterrorism in a volume about international organization and global governance is a sign of the times. Prior to 9/11, this topic would not have warranted such attention. But today, counterterrorism cooperation furnishes lessons for scholars and students of IOs and global governance. The forms of multilateralism are diversifying over time, informed by the vagaries of consensus and competition among states, which seek to shape global governance to advance and defend their interests. While US determination to pursue a "global war on terror" may have given rise to concerns about a "crisis of multilateralism,"[22] such concerns are misplaced. Rather, global governance has evolved, and quickly, in this domain. Having come this far, it is apt to ask whether such efforts can be sustained. In turn, this query should prompt additional questions about the proportionality and effectiveness of multilateral counterterrorism in responding to the threats that we face. How much global governance on counterterrorism is the right amount, and in what form? To what extent does multilateral counterterrorism "work"? In the world of counterterrorism, these are difficult questions to address. But if counterterrorism cooperation has been under-studied to date,[23] the next generation of researchers would be well advised to focus their energies in this direction.

Additional reading

1. Peter Romaniuk, *Multilateral Counterterrorism: The Global Politics of Cooperation and Contestation* (London: Routledge, 2010).
2. Naureen Chowdhury Fink, *Meeting the Challenge: A Guide to United Nations Counterterrorism Activities* (New York: International Peace Institute, 2012), http://www.ipacademy.org/publication/policy-papers/detail/363-meeting-the-challenge-a-guide-to-united-nations-counterterrorism-activities.html.
3. James Cockayne, Alistair Millar, David Cortright, and Peter Romaniuk, *Reshaping United Nations Counterterrorism Efforts: Blue-Sky Thinking for Global Counterterrorism Cooperation 10 Years After 9/11* (New York: Center on Global Counterterrorism Cooperation, 2012), http://www.globalct.org/publications/reshaping-united-nations-counterterrorism-efforts/.
4. Barak Mendelsohn, *Combating Jihadism: American Hegemony and Interstate Cooperation in the War on Terrorism* (Chicago: University of Chicago Press, 2009).
5. Bibi van Ginkel, *The Practice of the United Nations in Combating Terrorism from 1946 to 2008: Questions of Legality and Legitimacy* (Antwerp: Intersentia, 2010).

Notes

1 Hillary Rodham Clinton, "Remarks at the Launch of the Global Counterterrorism Forum," New York, 22 September 2011, http://www.state.gov/secretary/rm/2011/09/173768.htm. The Global Counterterrorism Strategy is annexed to A/RES/60/288 (6 September 2006).
2 UN Counterterrorism Implementation Taskforce, "Secretary-General's Symposium on International Counterterrorism Cooperation: Chairman's Summary," 19 September 2011, http://www.un.org/en/terrorism/ctitf/pdfs/chairman_summary_sg_symposium.pdf.
3 See http://www.un.org/en/terrorism/ctitf/uncct/index.shtml; and "Second meeting of the United Nations Counter-Terrorism Centre Advisory Board," Jeddah (3 June 2012), http://www.un.org/en/terrorism/ctitf/pdfs/advisory2012.pdf.
4 Commission on Global Governance, *Our Global Neighborhood: Report of the Commission on Global Governance* (Oxford: Oxford University Press, 1995), 2.
5 James N. Rosenau, "Governance in the Twenty-First Century," *Global Governance* 1, no. 1 (1995): 14.
6 Paul R. Pillar, *Terrorism and US Foreign Policy* (Washington, DC: Brookings Institution Press, 2003). The international instruments on terrorism are available at: www.un.org/en/terrorism/instruments.shtml.
7 Richard Bach Jensen, "The International Campaign Against Anarchist Terrorism, 1880–1930s," *Terrorism and Political Violence* 21, no. 1 (2009): 89–109.
8 Address by Yasser Arafat to the General Assembly of the United Nations, 13 November 1974.
9 The transcript of President Bush's remarks is available at: http://www.nytimes.com/2001/09/12/us/a-day-of-terror-bush-s-remarks-to-the-nation-on-the-terrorist-attacks.html.
10 In particular, readers should note the implementation guides to Resolutions 1373 and 1624 (2005), the global surveys of their implementation, and the reports on CTED activities and achievements, all available at: http://www.un.org/en/sc/ctc/resources/index.html.
11 An overview of CTITF entities is provided in Naureen Chowdhury Fink, *Meeting the Challenge: A Guide to United Nations Counterterrorism Activities* (New York: International Peace Institute, 2012), available at: http://www.ipacademy.org/publication/policy-papers/detail/363-meeting-the-challenge-a-guide-to-united-nations-counterterrorism-activities.html.

12 James Cockayne, Alistair Millar, David Cortright, and Peter Romaniuk, *Reshaping United Nations Counterterrorism Efforts: Blue-Sky Thinking for Global Counterterrorism Cooperation 10 Years after 9/11* (New York: Center on Global Counterterrorism Cooperation, 2012), available at: http://www.globalct.org/publications/reshaping-united-nations-counterterrorism-efforts/.

13 Robert O. Keohane, "The Globalization of Informal Violence, Theories of World Politics and the 'Liberalism of Fear,'" *Dialogue IO* 1, no. 1 (2002): 36; and Kendall W. Stiles, "The Power of Procedure and the Procedures of the Powerful: Anti-Terror Law in the United Nations," *Journal of Peace Research* 43, no. 1 (2006): 38.

14 Shepard Forman and Derk Segaar, "New Coalitions for Global Governance: The Changing Dynamics of Multilateralism," *Global Governance* 12, no. 2 (2006): 205–225.

15 Among other examples, the Charity and Security Network monitors the impact of counter-terrorist financing measures on NGOs and other non-profit organizations: www.charityandsecurity.org.

16 That is, it cannot be said that there is a single regime that covers the breadth of counter-terrorism measures. Here, "regime" is understood in line with Stephen Krasner's definition: "Implicit or explicit principles, norms, rules and decision-making procedures around which actors' expectations converge in a given area of international relations." Stephen D. Krasner, "Structural Causes and Regime Consequences: Regimes as Intervening Variables," in *International Regimes*, ed. Stephen D. Krasner (Ithaca: Cornell University Press, 1983), 2.

17 Thomas J. Biersteker, Sue E. Eckert, and Peter Romaniuk, "International Initiatives to Combat the Financing of Terrorism," in *Countering the Financing of Global Terrorism*, eds. Thomas J. Biersteker and Sue E. Eckert (New York and London: Routledge, 2007), 234–259.

18 Peter Romaniuk, *Multilateral Counterterrorism: The Global Politics of Cooperation and Contestation* (London: Routledge, 2010); Kal Raustiala and David Victor, "The Regime Complex for Plant Genetic Resources," *International Organization* 58, no. 2 (2004): 279.

19 Available at: http://www.un.org/en/sc/ctc/resources/index.html.

20 Ramesh Thakur and Thomas G. Weiss, "United Nations 'Policy': An Argument with Three Illustrations," *International Studies Perspectives* 10, no. 1 (2009): 18–35.

21 Michael Barnett and Raymond Duvall, "Power in Global Governance," in *Power in Global Governance*, eds. Michael Barnett and Raymond Duvall (Cambridge: Cambridge University Press, 2005), 17.

22 Edward Newman, *A Crisis of Global Institutions? Multilateralism and International Security* (London: Routledge, 2007), ch. 7.

23 Ronald D. Crelinsten, "Counter-terrorism as Global Governance: A Research Inventory," in *Mapping Terrorism Research: State of the Art, Gaps and Future Direction*, ed. Magnus Ranstorp (London: Routledge, 2007), ch. 10.

Human Rights in Global Governance

Julie Mertus

States are like people. It takes time for them to mature and develop into fully functioning actors. Young states resemble children. No two are alike, but they share the same developmental phases, beginning at birth. Some babies wait until the planned moment arises and, after one last "push," they let out a tiny yelp to announce their entry to the world (e.g. the "velvet divorce" between the Czech Republic and Slovakia). Others are impatient. As soon as they see some light, they come barreling into the world, kicking and screaming (arguably, e.g., East Timor).[1] And then there are those states (e.g. Kosovo), where the cry for independence has been, over time, both a quiet rumble and a fervent demand.[2] In each of these cases, midwives and doctors are on call to ensure that extra care will be available when the birthing process gets rough. During state formation, various state and non-state actors perform this role, helping the newly created state grow and develop in accordance with its own felt national needs.[3]

Building on the discussion of the scope of international organizations, of supportive philosophies, politics and religions, and theories grounded in realism and constructivism, this chapter examines the legal and institutional framework of the international human rights regime. It then takes a closer look at three interrelated disputes that challenge human rights advocates today: the politicization of human rights—whether states are manipulating human rights claims to serve political purposes; non-state actor accountability—whether non-state actors, including the United Nations, can be held responsible for human rights protection and promotion; and the desired focus of "human rights" and whether a switch to "human security" or "humane governance" is desirable. It concludes with questions for further research.

Background

The most dominant and important elements of the politics of human rights in today's world could usefully be framed in terms of what actually does not exist, namely the International Bill of Rights. The main components consist of three documents that do exist: the Universal Declaration of Human Rights (UDHR), a non-binding declaration, and two "harder" legal documents, the International Covenant on Civil and Political Rights (ICCPR) and the International Covenant on Economic, Social and Cultural Rights (ICESCR).

There is a clear difference between the legal weight of each of these instruments and the support and recognition that states grant them, a difference stemming from the division of these rights during the Cold War. The United States was automatically associated with "civil rights." The Soviet bloc, on the other hand, claimed adherence to "economic rights." The job of standard setting (identification of a right, its limits, and promises) under these fundamental covenants was completed by the time the Cold War drew to a close. Energized by the 1993 UN World Conference on Human Rights in Vienna, human rights advocates turned their attention from standard setting to implementation.

Institutional developments

The growth in institutionalization of concerns with human rights is one way to gauge the crucial growth in the regime governing this fundamental concern. This section reviews this institutionalization in terms of the United Nations proper, treaties, other inter-governmental bodies part of the UN system, and nongovernmental organizations (NGOs).

United Nations

The United Nations has undergone a remarkable transformation in recent years. Throughout the Cold War, UN human rights bodies involved themselves largely in human rights standard setting.[4] This increase in activity was in stark contrast to their initial reluctance to act on behalf of human rights. Indeed, for the first two and a half decades of its existence, the leading UN human rights body, the Commission on Human Rights, restrictively interpreted its own mandate to "promote" human rights as something confined as "promoting only," and less than "protecting" human rights.

During these early years, the UN "saw itself as a benevolent *promoter* of human rights, at a safe distance from where the real responsibilities for human rights *protecting* and *guaranteeing* lied [sic], namely the state."[5] The UN could not conceive of itself as committing human rights violations as it was far from operational in any actions aside from monitoring and bureaucratic policy-making. All this changed, however, in the post-Cold War era as the UN became markedly more engaged in humanitarian operations.[6] Brought to the fore was the UN's proximity to, and indeed responsibility for, human rights violations.[7]

What was the best way to hold the UN accountable for human rights violations? Human rights advocates, UN staff, and states all seemed to agree that the UN needed a central point for human rights information and enforcement. This was the task of the Commission on Human Rights (CHR), but its credibility plummeted as the states with the worst human rights records were often elected to leadership positions. Indeed, one of the best means to prevent criticism was to be elected to the Commission. For instance, among the CHR's 53 elected members in 2005 was Sudan while it was pursuing slow-motion genocide in Darfur, and Zimbabwe while it was bulldozing the houses of 700,000 opposition supporters and rounding up journalists and other critics. That China and Cuba played customarily prominent roles and that Libya was a former chair of the CHR added to the litany of embarrassments.

The possibility existed for individual complaints under the CHR's mandate, but it chose only those states and issues with which it had long-standing conflict. A Dutch human rights scholar and advocate, Morten Kjaerum, found its reports to have been "highly biased, with groups of countries defending themselves against supposedly unfriendly attacks from other groups."[8]

One of the few decisions that resulted from the September 2005 World Summit on the occasion of the UN's 60th anniversary was to replace the CHR with an altered body with a similar abbreviation, the Human Rights Council (HRC). Having been established in 1946 by ECOSOC, the Commission on Human Rights held its final session in Geneva in March 2006 and was abolished the following June.[9] While earlier proposals sought to create a principal organ—an institution at the same level as the Security Council, the Economic and Social Council, or General Assembly—the intergovernmental decision was to create a replacement with some important additions. This gave the Council more of a direct line of communication with the UN Central Office for Human Rights Protection and Promotion. The second institutional improvement was the creation of a strict "universal periodic review" (UPR) process that would apply to all states, with the state members of the Human Rights Council "volunteering" to be in the first cohort.

The Working Group on Communications (WGC) is perhaps the most significant change. Every three years, WGC is chosen by the Human Rights Council Advisory Committee from among its members. A total of four independent experts is selected to be geographically representative, it meets twice a year for a period of five working days to assess the admissibility and the merits of communication, including whether the communication, alone or in combination with other communications, appears to reveal a consistent pattern of gross and reliably attested violations of human rights and fundamental freedoms. All admissible communications and recommendations thereon are transmitted to the Working Group on Situations (WAGS, or "Working Group"), which analyzes the information and reports findings to the Human Rights Council directly. In this manner, the establishment of the WGC allows the UN to more accurately determine what violations are being committed and what actions to undertake in response.

Because the authority of the Human Rights Council derives from the UN Charter, the Council, and its subsidiary bodies, are known as "charter-based institutions." In contrast, the committees that draw their authority from UN treaties are known as "treaty-based institutions."

Treaties

Since the adoption of the Universal Declaration of Human Rights in 1948, all UN member states have ratified at least one core international human rights treaty, and 80 percent have ratified four or more. The most recent treaty addresses people with disabilities. There are currently ten human rights treaty bodies, which are committees of independent experts. Nine of these treaty bodies monitor implementation of the core international human rights treaties, while the tenth treaty body, the Subcommittee on Prevention of Torture, established under the Optional Protocol to the Convention against Torture, monitors places of detention in states that are parties to the Optional Protocol.

Among the various treaty bodies associated with the United Nations other than the ICCPR and ICESCR are the Committee on the Rights of the Child (CRC), the Committee on the Elimination of All Forms of Discrimination Against Women (CEDAW), the Committee on the Elimination of All Forms of Racial Discrimination (CERD), the Committee Against Torture (CAT), and the Committee on the Rights of Persons with Disabilities (CRPD). Each of these bodies works independently from the UN, in that states party to the UN are not automatically held under treaty, yet the committees and the UN as a whole are still linked through reporting and oversight.

Several of these instruments have been under scrutiny for various reasons. The CRC, for example, has not been ratified by the United States, and so it has been criticized for a perceived legitimacy crisis. Additionally, the CAT has been criticized for its vague use of language that has often been warped by state interpretation. Indeed, even when Israel's highest court stated in 1999 that certain actions its government employees had undertaken were illegal under the CAT, it left open the option for the state's legislature to legalize such acts in the future.[10]

Other UN institutions

Many other organizations within the UN system are also directly or indirectly involved in the promotion and protection of human rights. In both normative and operational activities, they interact with the main UN human rights bodies. While space does not permit a detailed examination, the following would be on that list:

- United Nations High Commissioner for Refugees (UNHCR)
- Office for the Coordination of Humanitarian Affairs (OCHA)
- Inter-Agency Internal Displacement Division
- International Labour Organization (ILO)
- World Health Organization (WHO)
- United Nations Educational, Scientific and Cultural Organization (UNESCO)
- Joint United Nations Programme on HIV/AIDS (UNAIDS)
- Inter-Agency Standing Committee (IASC)
- Department of Economic and Social Affairs (DESA)
- Commission on the Status of Women (CSW)
- Office of the Special Adviser on Gender Issues and the Advancement of Women (OSAGI)

- Division for the Advancement of Women (DAW)
- United Nations Population Fund (UNFPA)
- United Nations Children's Fund (UNICEF)
- United Nations Development Fund for Women (UNIFEM)
- United Nations Development Programme (UNDP)
- Food and Agriculture Organization of the United Nations (FAO)
- United Nations Human Settlements Programme (UNHABITAT)
- United Nations Mine Action (UNMA)

Many of these organizations interact, for example, with certain treaty body committees specific to their particular areas of interest and specific expertise. UNICEF is often affiliated with the CRC, while CSW and OSAGI often communicate with the CEDAW. Each particular organization adds to the overall UN capacity, allowing the world organization to address issues that that the treaty bodies have been unable to handle.

The role of nongovernmental voices

Global governance raises questions not only about "who" should be involved in international decision-making, but also about "how" and "where" the decisions are to be made.[11] That decisions are often made outside the regular democratic structures of the state troubles many scholars. They worry that, despite its many foibles, a properly functioning democratic state has the advantage of being kept in check by an inquisitive public. When decisions are made by international bodies (such as the World Bank or the United Nations Human Rights Council) without serious discussion and input at the domestic level and imposed on states, concerns about legitimacy and accountability, invoking familiar democratic deficit critiques, become critical.

Nongovernmental organizations, both international ones like Amnesty International and Human Rights Watch, as well as national ones, are essential components of global human rights governance. Some treaties explicitly provide for NGOs to review state reports and they are granted permission to respond with their own "alternative report" or "shadow report." Shadow reports serve several purposes: educating the general public on particular human rights issues; naming and shaming state and non-state actors in their response to human rights abuses; monitoring actions taken by states and/or government organizations to honor commitments made in national, regional, and international conferences and meetings; and creating and applying "follow up" procedures to address actions taken by state and non-state entities.

A significant development is the growth of national human rights institutions.[12] Another hybrid of contemporary global governance, they are state-based but nominally (and sometimes even more) independent organizations whose potential stems from their role as transmission belts for international human rights law. The transmission belt from global to local is important because the domestic arena is ultimately where human rights are protected. While these agents of international law within states have been criticized as shields for state sovereignty, they also reflect the seeming compunction to appear to be satisfying the growing demand for human rights.[13]

Current debates

Three controversies dominate current debates about international human rights: politicization, the accountability of non-state actors, and human security.

Politicization

In the US, foreign aid has long been tied to political goals and justified in terms of national interests. The Cold War had been driven by sectarian violence, pitting self-proclaimed freedom-loving groups against one other. Once the Cold War ended, being a human rights supporter suddenly became popular throughout the world. In his second inaugural address, in January 2005, US president George W. Bush declared that

> it is the policy of the United States to seek and support the growth of democratic movements and institutions in every nation and culture, with the ultimate goal of ending tyranny in our world.[14]

"Freedom" became the banner for human rights. Who could be against freedom? Politicians and advocates could craft their understanding of "freedom" so that it was broad enough to address subjects to their own interests—and the interests of states—which leads to a high degree of politicization of human rights issues.

One of the international human rights principles that has been highly politicized is the right to self-determination, which means the right to freely determine one's political status and pursue economic, social, and cultural development. Although states recognize this principle of self-determination as an international legal right, its application and enforcement have been very uneven and have depended on the interests of the state in question, as well as the interests of other states that support the violating state. States that have issues with respect to promoting self-determination within their borders, and their supporters, have objected to the application of the principle of self-determination and have come up with excuses to justify the non-enforcement and applicability of this principle.

One prominent and illustrative example of this type of politicization concerns China. In response to accusations of its violation of the right to self-determination in Tibet, China argues that Tibet is an integral part of the People's Republic, has been a part of China since the thirteenth century, and should thus be ruled from Beijing. From these claims, China argues that its crackdown on demonstrations by Tibetans is nothing more than an exercise of its right to enforce its laws against internal dissidents, and to protect its territorial sovereignty.[15]

Tibetans, however, disagree and argue that the region of the Himalayas has been an independent region for many centuries, including the period from 1912, when Tibet declared itself independent, to 1951, when it was invaded by China. China's conduct towards Tibet is supported by countries such as Russia, Sudan, and Sri Lanka that have their own internal separatist issues. Their interest in not criticizing China reflects their own desire to be impervious to outside interference in what they consider "internal affairs."

The politicization of human rights is also evident in the general trade-off between human rights and economics. As China is a major economic power in its own right that also holds a significant amount of Western debt, criticism has been muted. For instance, many countries that regularly criticized China prior to the ongoing global economic and financial crisis are now very reluctant to criticize China's human rights record.

Chinese politicians and journalists have chastised the US State Department for issuing its country reports on human rights practices in more than 190 countries while ignoring the conditions in its own country. Among the many US human rights issues that China and Russia have singled out for extra attention are issues related to the poor US economy and the lack of basic social welfare guaranteed in their own countries and elsewhere.[16]

Accountability of non-state actors

The establishment of UN human rights institutions was ground-breaking in the sense that it recognized a new subject of international law—private individuals—and attempted to hold them responsible.[17] But this recognition was limited largely to individuals as the holders of *rights*, with states still considered the principal, if not exclusive, holder of *duties*. This orientation has been reconsidered in recent years, to the extent that there is an increasing realization that non-state actors, groups, and organizations can also be held responsible for violating international human rights standards. Chris Jochnick explains:

> The narrow focus of human rights law on state responsibility is not only out of step with current power relations, but also tends to obscure them. The exclusive concern with national governments not only distorts the reality of the growing weakness of national-level authority, but also shields other actors from greater responsibility.[18]

As indicated earlier, NGOs are increasingly asserting that human rights standards should be applied to a wider range of actors than traditionally realized, including transnational corporations and other intergovernmental organizations as well.[19] For instance, obstacles still exist to holding the UN, as a collective, responsible for human rights violations. The UN is not a party to any human rights instruments and, indeed, some treaties specify in these provisions that only states may be parties to the instrument, thereby foreclosing participation in these regimes by collective intergovernmental organization. Even though the UN Charter holds that human rights must be promoted, no state can hold the UN itself responsible in the International Court of Justice (ICJ) for a failure to do so.

Furthermore, the ability to hold the UN accountable to international standards is complicated by the practice of granting privileges and immunities to actors within UN organizations.[20] In Article 105, the UN Charter recognizes that the organization "shall enjoy in the territory of each of its Members such privileges and immunities as are necessary for the fulfillment of its purposes." The exact nature of the privileges is elaborated through separately negotiated, state-specific agreements.[21]

An argument for holding the UN accountable under international human rights standards draws upon the notion of "functional necessity." This line of reasoning acknowledges that because an international organization is "obliged to pursue and try to realize its own purpose"[22] it may exercise the powers implied in its purposes.[23]

The United Nations and members of the UN system are bound by international human rights norms when it is acting as a state.[24] The reasoning here is that "states should not be allowed to escape their human rights obligations by forming an international organization to do their dirty work."[25] The UN enjoys many of the benefits given to states, such as certain privileges and immunities. As the ICJ noted in the seminal *Reparations Case*, the UN has legal personality based on the notion of functional necessity. In short, the UN is "exercising and enjoying functions and rights which can only be explained on the basis of the possession of a large measure of international personality and the capacity to operate upon an international plane." The "legal personality" of the UN permits it, like states, to conclude treaties, to make claims on behalf of its agents, and to engage in activities for the fulfillment of its purposes.[26]

This approach dilutes the distinction between states and international organizations, and emphasizes the role and capacity exercised by an organization by characterizing it as more than what its official status claims to be. Article 30 of the UDHR and Article 5 of the ICCPR recognize that "any State, group or person" may not derogate from the rights and freedoms enumerated in each instrument. This allows leeway for holding a collective like the UN accountable. At a minimum, the argument can be made that because the UN is bound by customary international law, it must follow those international human rights standards that have reached customary international law status.[27] As explained in greater depth in other chapters in this volume, the actors involved in peacebuilding have assumed human rights responsibilities in their role as "both state and state builder."[28] As a state substitute they are obligated to "respect and ensure" human rights,[29] and as a state builder they are tasked with laying the foundation for a future state that will both respect and protect human rights.

Human security

The current human rights framework can be envisioned as consisting of legally binding obligations and mechanisms that hold states accountable for individual rights violations. Treaty ratification thus triggers a process according to which state responsibility is engaged. With only a nod to the successes of human rights advocates, some academics have enlisted "human security" to take the place of human rights.[30] This new concept, whose contours are contested, remains untethered to a system of state accountability and rights mechanisms of enforcement.[31]

According to this line of thinking, the human subjects of security can only be understood as a collective, a "network of responsibility and care in determining people's everyday experiences of security and insecurity."[32] One of the concept's leading proponents emphasizes "the duty to care" of the "responsibility holder." Fiona Robinson uses the term "beings in relation," which she acknowledges is close to Carol Gould's "individuals-in-relation."[33] Robinson's formulation, unlike Gould's, "focuses primarily upon affective relations of responsibility and care that may include, but by no means are limited to, relations among family members and friends rather than those existing among members of social groups, such as nations and ethnic or religious groups."[34]

The appeal of this reorientation holds true for advocates of the concept of human security. According to the Human Security Centre, "While national security focuses on the defense of the State from external attack, human security is about protecting individuals and communities from any form of political violence . . . human security and national security should be—and are—mutually reinforcing."[35] The new concept of security "equates security with people rather than territories."[36] In doing so, human security addresses one of the key criticisms of human rights supporters—namely, that human rights are inconsistent with national security.

Conclusion

Proponents of global governance acknowledge many of the previous concerns. After all, they have generated the global governance mantra "tear down state-centrism!" The ultimate goal of global governance is to change international relations by modifying the structural context and the importance of strategic interactions. The United Nations and its system of organizations has clearly been an essential element in moving beyond the confines of state borders and rendering human rights an international issue and responsibility.

Additional reading

1. Julie Mertus, *The United Nations and Human Rights*, 2nd edition (London: Routledge, 2009).
2. Philip Alston and James Crawford, eds., *The Future of UN Human Rights Treaty Monitoring* (Cambridge: Cambridge University Press, 2000).
3. Tim Dunne and Nicholas J. Wheeler, eds., *Human Rights in Global Politics* (Cambridge: Cambridge University Press, 1999).
4. Office of the High Commissioner for Human Rights, http://www.ohchr.org/EN/Pages/WelcomePage.aspx.
5. Burns H. Weston and Stephen Marks, *The Future of International Human Rights* (New York: Transnational Publishers, Inc., 1999).

Notes

1 Jennifer Jackson Preece, *National Minorities and the European Nation-State System* (New York: Oxford University Press, 1998).
2 Julie A. Mertus, *Kosovo: How Myths and Truths Started a War* (Berkeley, CA: University of California Press, 1999).
3 Michael Haas, *International Human Rights: A Comprehensive Introduction* (London: Routledge, 2008).
4 James Cotton, "Against the Grain: The East Timor Intervention," *Survival* 43 (2001): 139.
5 Fredrick Megret and Florian Hoffmann, "The UN as a Human Rights Violator? Some Reflections on the United Nations Changing Human Rights Responsibilities," *Human Rights Quarterly* 25, no. 2 (2003): 314–342.

6 Ruth E. Gordon, "Some Legal Problems with Trusteeship," *Cornell International Law Journal* 28 (1995): 301.

7 Elizabeth Abraham, "The Sins of the Savior: Holding the United Nations Accountable to International Human Rights Standards for Executive Order Detentions in Its Mission in Kosovo," *American University Law Review* 52, no. 5 (2003): 1291–1337; Fredrick Rawski, "To Waive or Not to Waive: Immunity and Accountability in UN Peacekeeping Operations," *Connecticut Journal of International Law* 18 (2002): 103, 125; David Marshall and Shelley Inglis, "The Disempowerment of Human Rights-Based Justice in the United Nations Mission in Kosovo," *Harvard Human Rights Journal* 16 (2003): 95; and Ralph Wilde, "Accountability and International Actors in Bosnia and Herzegovina, Kosovo and East Timor," *International Law Students Association Journal of International and Comparative Law* 18 (2001): 455.

8 Morten Kjaerum, "The UN Reform Process in an Implementation Perspective," in *Human Rights in Turmoil: Facing Threats, Consolidating Achievements*, S. Lagoutte, H.-O. Sano, and P. Scharff Smith (Leiden: Martinus Nijhoff Publishers, 2007): 7–23.

9 Bertrand G. Ramcharan, *Human Rights Council* (London: Routledge, 2011).

10 Beth Simmons, *Mobilizing for Human Rights: International Law in Domestic Politics* (Cambridge: Cambridge University Press, 2009), 302–303.

11 Thomas G. Weiss and Ramesh Thakur, *Global Governance and the UN: An Unfinished Journey* (Bloomington: Indiana University Press, 2010).

12 Catherine Shanahan Renshaw, "National Human Rights Institutions and Civil Society Organizations: New Dynamics of Engagement at Domestic, Regional, and International Levels," *Global Governance* 18, no. 3 (2012): 299–316.

13 Sonia Cardenas, "Emerging Global Actors: The United Nations and National Human Rights Institutions," *Global Governance* 9, no. 1 (2003): 23–42.

14 George W. Bush, "Second Inaugural Address" (Washington, DC, 20 January 2005).

15 Mapuche Foundation, "Self-determination," 19 July 2006, www.mapuche.nl/english/self determination060717.html.

16 Citations here and above from *China Daily*, "Full Text: US Human Rights Record in 2009," http://www.chinadaily.com.cn/china/2010-03/12/content_9582821.htm. The article specifically states: "In the USA, there are 12.8 million unemployed, 40 million people live without health insurance and 14.5 percent of families face food shortages. The standard of living for the indigenous population of the country is very low and there are signs of economic segregation. Among the developed countries of the world, the USA has one of the weakest systems to protect workers' rights to organize and bargain collectively. Over the past decade, the USA has failed to ratify any conventions of the International Labour Organization (ILO)."

17 Louis Sohn, "The New International Law: Protection of the Rights of Individuals Rather than States," *American University Law Review* 32, no. 1 (1982): 1–64.

18 Chris Jochnick, "Confronting the Impunity of Non-State Actors: New Fields for the Promotion of Human Rights," *Human Rights Quarterly* 21, no. 1 (1999): 56–79.

19 Steve Coll, *Private Empire: ExxonMobil and American Power* (New York: Penguin Press 2012).

20 Convention on the Privileges and Immunities of the United Nations, art. 3, sec. 9, Feb. 13, 1946, § 2, 21 U.S.T. 1418, 1422, 1 UNT.S. 15, 20; UN Charter art. 105(1) (requiring member states to recognize UN privileges and immunities).

21 UNMIK Regulation 2000/47, On the Status, Privileges and Immunities of KFOR and UNMIK and their Personnel in Kosovo (18 August 2000), http://www.unmikonline.org/regulations/2000/reg47-00.htm.

22 Zenon Stavrinides, "Human Rights Obligations under the UN Charter," *International Journal of Human Rights* 3, no. 2 (1999): 40.

23 Manuel Rama-Montaldo, "International Legal Personality and Implied Powers of International Organizations," *British Yearbook of International Law* 111 (1971): 147–149.

24 Megret and Hoffmann, "The UN as a Human Rights Violator?," 314–342. See also G. T. Mitoma, "Civil Society and International Human Rights: The Commission to Study the Organization of Peace and the Origins of the UN Human Rights Regime," *Human Rights Quarterly* 30, no. 3 (2008): 607–630.

25 August Reinsch, "Securing the Accountability of International Organizations," *Global Governance* 7, no. 1 (2001): 137–138.

26 Reparation for Injuries Suffered in the Service of the United Nations, 1949 I.C.J. 174, 179 (April 11), 179.

27 Megret and Hoffmann, "The UN as a Human Rights Violator?," 317.

28 James Cotton, "Against the Grain: the East Timor Intervention," *Survival: Global Politics and Strategy* 43 (2001): 139.

29 Vienna Declaration, pt. 1, para. 2.3.th.

30 While some scholars focus on the security aspect of this debate, others prefer to concentrate on additional aspects of collective security. See, for example, Truong Thahn-Dam, Saskia Wieringa and Amritta Chhachhi, *Engendering Human Security* (New York: Zed Books, 2008).

31 Verena Fritz and Alina Rocha Menocal, "Developmental States in the New Millennium: Concepts and Challenges for a New Aid Agenda," *Development Policy Review* 25, no. 5 (2007): 531–552.

32 Fiona Robinson, *The Ethics of Care: A Feminist Approach to Human Security* (Philadelphia, PA: Temple University Press, 2011), 10.

33 Carol Gould, *Globalizing Democracy and Human Rights* (Cambridge: Cambridge University Press, 2004).

34 Robinson, *The Ethics of Care*, 10, fn. 1.

35 The Human Security Centre, "What Is Human Security?," *The Human Security Report 2005, War and Peace in the 21st Century* (New York: Oxford University Press, 2005).

36 United Nations Development Programme, *Human Development Report 1994* (New York: Oxford University Press, 1994).

CONTENTS

The Pursuit of International Justice

Richard J. Goldstone

In the past two decades, the pursuit of international justice has reinvigorated international humanitarian law (or the law of war, as it used to be called).[1] The prosecution and threatened prosecution of war criminals has now become the subject of daily news reports. It is this pursuit that forms the thrust of this chapter.

The origins of international humanitarian law are to be found in some early battlefield rules and limitations placed upon the manner in which armies were allowed to behave, especially toward those of the enemy who were injured or captured. These laws were founded in religion and chivalry. They were based also on reciprocity—if you treat my soldiers in a humane manner I will reciprocate and treat yours similarly. Such humane treatment has unfortunately been the exception rather the rule and the more common approach was that in war there was no legal limit to the pursuit of victory. In the words of Thucydides in the fifth century BC, "to a king or commonwealth, nothing is unjust which is useful."[2] The thrust of this chapter is not the history of international humanitarian law. It is rather to examine and consider the major issues relating to the present-day pursuit of international justice.

This chapter traces the history of modern international humanitarian law, beginning with the 1945 Nuremberg Trial of the major Nazi war criminals. It considers the courts that were established in the last decade of the twentieth century—namely, the two United Nations ad hoc tribunals for the former Yugoslavia and for Rwanda, the various hybrid or mixed tribunals, and the International Criminal Court (ICC). It describes the major current debates around these tribunals and concludes with a brief consideration of likely future developments.

The origins

As World War II drew to a close, it was famously agreed by the victorious nations (France, the Soviet Union, the United Kingdom, and the United States) that the rule of law should be applied at the international level of criminal justice. It was agreed that the Nazi leaders should not be summarily executed but afforded the benefit of a fair trial.

The Nuremberg Trial had a deep influence on both lawyers and politicians of the time and it was widely anticipated that a permanent international criminal court would be established to prosecute the most serious war crimes. One finds reference to such a court in Article 6 of the Genocide Convention of 1948, where it is provided that genocide could be prosecuted "by such international penal tribunal as may have jurisdiction with respect to those contracting parties which shall have accepted its jurisdiction."[3] It was thought that such an international court would be established by treaty. That did not happen, and the endeavor foundered on the sea of the Cold War and was not to be revived for almost half a century.

Modern international criminal courts

It took a European catastrophe, the Balkan war of the early 1990s, to move the United Nations Security Council in 1993 to set up the first ever truly international criminal tribunal. It had not done so in light of even more egregious war crimes committed not too long before in Cambodia and Iraq. It was the politics and the political will of the most powerful Western nations that determined that something had to be done in the face of the war crimes being committed in pursuance of a policy of ethnic cleansing in Central Europe. That "something," was a unanimous 1993 Resolution 827 by the Security Council to set up the International Criminal Tribunal for the former Yugoslavia (ICTY). This development had become politically possible after 1989 with the disintegration of the Soviet Union and the end of the Cold War. The terrible genocide perpetrated in Rwanda in the middle of 1994 led to Security Council Resolution 955 that established the International Criminal Tribunal for Rwanda (ICTR). These two tribunals are often referred to as "the ad hoc tribunals."

In establishing both tribunals, the Security Council relied upon its peremptory powers under Articles 39–42 of Chapter VII of the UN Charter. It is there that one finds the only authority vested in the Security Council to pass resolutions binding on all member states. Article 39 of the Charter provides that the Security Council may determine that a situation constitutes a threat to the peace, breach of the peace, or act of aggression. Having made such a determination, the Council may make recommendations, or decide what measures shall be taken in accordance with Article 41 and 42, to maintain or restore international peace and security. Under Article 41 it may decide that measures "not involving the use of armed force are to be employed to give effect to its decision." Such measures may include "complete or partial interruption of economic

relations and of rail, sea, air, postal, telegraphic, radio, and other means of communication, and the severance of diplomatic relations." If those measures are or prove to be
inadequate, under Article 42 the Security Council may take "such action by air, sea, or
land forces as may be necessary to maintain or restore international peace and security.
Such actions may include demonstrations, blockade, and other operations by air, sea,
or land forces of Members of the United Nations." It will immediately become apparent
that those provisions of the Charter are silent on the establishment of a criminal tribunal.
The Council held, however, that the establishment of a criminal court as a peacekeeping tool was impliedly included in the powers conferred upon it by the provisions
of Article 41, i.e. a measure not involving the use of force. It is significant that the power
to establish the two tribunals depended upon the Council making the connection
between justice and peace.

The two ad hoc tribunals were sufficiently successful to encourage the establishment
of the so-called hybrid or mixed tribunals. These are criminal courts establishment by
agreement between a national government and the United Nations. This method led to
the establishment of criminal courts in Sierra Leone, East Timor, Kosovo, and Lebanon.
At the same time efforts were being made to establish a permanent international criminal
court. The statute for such a court was agreed by 120 nations at a diplomatic conference
held in Rome in the middle of 1998.[4] The ICC began its operations on 1 July 2002.
Over 120 nations have ratified the Rome Statute. They comprise the supervising body
of the ICC, called the Assembly of States Parties (ASP). With the ad hoc tribunals and
hybrid or mixed tribunals having completed their work or soon to complete it, the ICC
will in the coming few years become the only international criminal court in the global
community.

The ad hoc tribunals, as sub-organs of the Security Council, were given primacy and
could determine which cases they would investigate. National jurisdictions are obliged
to defer to decisions made in this regard by the ad hoc tribunals. In the first trial before
the ICTY, that of Dusan Tadic, the defendant had been arrested and indicted by a court
in Germany. When the ICTY decided that he should be tried before it in The Hague,
the German authorities, somewhat unhappily, accepted that position and Tadic was
transferred to the ICTY for trial. The ICC works on the converse principle that it is a
court of last and not first resort. The philosophy underlying this approach is that war
criminals should preferably be investigated and tried by the courts of their own nations.
Only if such courts are unable or unwilling to do so will the ICC have jurisdiction. Part
of the duty of the ICC Prosecutor is to assist and enable national courts to act against
war criminals physically within their areas of jurisdiction.

Situations may come before the ICC in three ways. They may be referred by the
government of a nation that has ratified the Rome Statute;[5] by the Security Council;[6]
or they may be investigated by the Prosecutor relying on his own powers.[7] The exercise
of the last-mentioned power is subject to the approval of a pre-trial chamber of the Court.

The politics of international criminal courts

The tribunals of the 1990s owed their very existence to political decisions reached by
the United Nations. In other words, those tribunals were established not solely with

regard to the seriousness of the crimes committed, but also for political reasons. Other humanitarian crises that escaped scrutiny under the system of ad hoc tribunals were overlooked not necessarily because the atrocities were less heinous, but because of the crass political realities of international relations. The ICC operates on a fundamentally different basis—prosecution is not contingent on an extraordinary moment of political will by the Security Council. That said, however, the reality is that major powerful nations have failed to ratify the Rome Statute and their nationals are not subject to its jurisdiction unless they commit a war crime in a country that has ratified the Statute. In particular, the United States, China, Russia, and India remain outside the Rome Statute. The first three, as permanent members of the Security Council, are also able to veto the reference of a situation to the ICC by the Council. This effectively places nations that have not ratified the Rome Statute and receive protection from a permanent member of the UN beyond the jurisdiction of the ICC. In this way Syria has been protected by Russia, Sri Lanka by China, and Israel by the United States. That this is a defect in the ICC system cannot be denied. The only solution is to continue to pressure all governments to ratify the Rome Statute.

We should also take notice of complaints coming from many African quarters at the fact that the seven situations presently before the ICC are all African. The African Union and a number of African political leaders have caviled at this and make allegations to the effect that the ICC is an instrument created by Western nations to judge Africans. The criticism is based more upon perception than fact. It is rather unfair if one takes into account that of the seven situations only two have resulted from the Prosecutor exercising his own powers (Kenya and the Ivory Coast). Of the remaining five, three were referred by the African governments themselves (Uganda, Democratic Republic of the Congo, and the Central African Republic) and two by the Security Council (Sudan and Libya). This notwithstanding, the perception cannot be wished away and the Court will have increased credibility in Africa when situations from other continents come before the ICC. The situation might also be alleviated by the fact that since July 2012 the Chief Prosecutor, Fatou Bensouda, is an African and former Minister of Justice of Gambia.

This chapter now discusses the successes and failures of these international criminal courts and tribunals, the major issues that are currently being debated, and finally assesses the prospects of the ICC.

Success and failure

What are the major successes of international criminal courts? When the first international criminal courts were established many questioned their ability to hold fair trials. Doubts were founded on the potential problems that might emerge from having judges, prosecutors, defense lawyers, and investigators coming from diverse and disparate legal systems. Would they be able to work together and find a common legal language? This was a serious concern to me in 1994 as effectively the first Chief Prosecutor of the ICTY. The Office of the Prosecutor was a United Nations office and accordingly was justifiably required to reflect both global geographic and gender balance. It was our experience that the different legal cultures have more in common with each other than differences. All of them have at their core the need to seek the truth and to convict defendants on appropriately gathered and rigorously tested evidence. In the result the ICTY and the international criminal courts that followed have by and large held fair trials. In no small measure, this is to the credit of the judges and prosecutors who recognized and acted upon their responsibility to ensure the fairness of the proceedings. The conduct of trials before these courts has certainly not been as efficient as it might have been, and lessons have been learned and applied. In the end there have been many convictions and acquittals, and the global community no longer questions the ability of these courts and tribunals to hold fair trials. This is a signal of success and one that is too frequently left out of account in the debates on international criminal justice.

Another important success of international criminal courts is the way in which they have substantially advanced and developed international humanitarian law. In my opinion, the most important single area of advance is that in relation to gender crimes, and especially systematic mass rape as a war crime. Prior to the establishment of these courts international humanitarian law all but ignored rape as a war crime. In consequence of imaginative lawyering by some of the judges, prosecutors, and with important contributions from academic and practicing lawyers, judgments were handed down by the ad hoc tribunals that recognized the importance of gender-related war crimes. The high water mark was the holding by the ICTR in the Akayesu case that rape can constitute a form of genocide.[8] The legacy of this work by the ad hoc tribunals is to be found in the holistic and broad definitions of gender-related crimes in the Rome Statute that establishes the ICC.[9] Other important areas of international humanitarian law that have been advanced include decisions on the legality of the ad hoc tribunals,[10] defining culpability under command responsibility,[11] extending command responsibility to civilian enterprises,[12] holding that an individual can be personally responsible for the commission of genocide,[13] and that members of the media can be held responsible for genocide.[14] There can be no doubt that the work of the ICC will continue along these lines. Its first conviction was for the recruitment of child soldiers and has focused international attention upon a neglected and egregious war crime.[15]

Of course, that over 120 nations have ratified the Rome Statute is a success well beyond the anticipation of the most ardent supporters of the ICC. Indeed, the Rome Statute required 60 ratifications before it became operative. In 1998, it was anticipated that it might take a decade or more to reach that number. In the result it took less than four years and the number has doubled since then. As already indicated, leading powerful and populous nations have not ratified the Rome Statute and this remains a major problem for the Court.

The legitimacy of the ICC also depends on the limits of its scope. Only the most serious international crimes fall within the jurisdiction of the ICC. The crimes are genocide, crimes against humanity, war crimes, and aggression. However, in the absence of agreement at Rome on a definition of "aggression," the inclusion of this crime was held in abeyance for nine years after the inception of the jurisdiction of the ICC. Only crimes committed after 1 July 2002 fall within the jurisdiction of the Court. In the case of nations ratifying the Rome Treaty after the date the Court became operative, the Treaty becomes effective with regard to them only prospectively, i.e. from the date of such ratification.

The crime of aggression was taken up at the first ICC Review Conference, held in the middle of 2010 in Kampala, Uganda. The members of the ASP agreed by consensus on a definition of the crime. An "act of aggression" is committed by military action by a state against the territory of another state or an attack by the armed forces of a state on the land, sea, or air forces of another state. The crime of aggression is defined to include the planning, preparation, or execution by someone who holds control over the political or military action of a state of an act of aggression. By its character, gravity, and scale it must constitute a manifest violation of the Charter of the United Nations. In short, the crime of aggression can only be committed by someone in a leadership position and only if there is a manifest violation of the prohibition on the use of force contained in the Charter of the United Nations. Under Article 52 of the United Nations Charter, legitimate self-defense would not constitute aggression. This crime of aggression will not fall within the jurisdiction of the ICC until 2017 and then only after at least 30 states ratify these provisions. And, even then, individual states will be entitled to opt out of the provisions.

The fact that universal impunity for the commission of serious war crimes has been ended is another success of international justice. The extent to which this acts as a deterrent is difficult to establish and anecdotal evidence is difficult to obtain. Yet the threat of criminal prosecution and being labeled as a war criminal must weigh on the minds of at least some political and military leaders when they determine their military strategies.

The work of the international criminal courts has brought important benefits to the people of the countries that have been the focus of investigation. In particular, fabricated denials of the commission of war crimes have been made more difficult in light of the evidence of many hundreds of witnesses. The ICTY has brought to trial every one of the defendants indicted by it. This is a feat that appeared to be impossible a few short years ago. The major defendants indicted by the ICTR have appeared in Arusha, the seat of the Tribunal. Proof of the true facts and circumstances that resulted in extreme violence and massive war crimes is an important benefit for societies that wish to repair the fractured relationships between formerly antagonistic ethnic or religious groups. It has proven to be beneficial in countries such as Rwanda, Bosnia and Herzegovina, and Sierra Leone, to mention but three obvious situations. No price tag can be placed on those benefits. The real bottom line is that the world must be a better place without impunity for war criminals and in which there is a court that is empowered to bring such war criminals before them and, if found guilty, to appropriately punish them. That many victims demand this acknowledgment and justice and may benefit from it has been demonstrated by their reaction to the work of these courts.

One has to recognize that the deterrent effect of a criminal justice system will always be unpredictable. It is no different in a domestic situation. In any country the crime rate will depend directly on the efficiency of the criminal justice system. The more effective it is, the lower will be the crime rate. The converse is also true—in countries with inefficient or ineffective criminal justice the crime rate will become higher. No matter how efficient the system, some criminals will still anticipate escaping justice and crimes will continue to be perpetrated. And some unbalanced people, sadly, will never be deterred. It is no different in the international community of states. If political and military leaders anticipate being brought before a court and facing possible conviction and punishment, this may deter some of them from committing war crimes. It will not deter them all. But, just as the imperfect deterrence of even the most efficient domestic criminal justice systems does not undermine its purpose or legitimacy, the fact that some war criminals will never be deterred should not blind us to the important reality that some war criminals will be deterred. And the many thousands of innocent civilians who are spared as a result must not be forgotten.

The current debate

What of the criticisms of the international criminal courts? It cannot be denied that international courts are expensive. At their height of operations the ICTY and ICTR together accounted for about 10 percent of the total operating budget of the UN. The question that has to be asked is whether it has been worth it. Criminal prosecutions by their nature are expensive endeavors. If the proceedings are to be fair they cannot be rushed. In particular the defendant has to be given sufficient time to prepare his or her defense, and this includes the unfettered right to receive all the relevant evidence in the possession of the Prosecutor. If justice is to be done and be seen to be done, then there are no financial shortcuts. The alternative to such prosecutions is to continue the effective regime of impunity for egregious war crimes that obtained prior to the establishment of these courts.

Another criticism relates to the punishments that are imposed by these courts. This is a problem without a solution and it must be admitted that there is no punishment that is commensurate with the serious war crimes that these tribunals are prosecuting. The maximum punishment is life imprisonment and that has been reserved by the judges for the leaders who are most responsible for the commission of the offenses. One cannot impose the same sentence for the negligent yet unlawful killing of 1,000 innocent civilians during a battle as for the murder of some tens of thousands of innocent civilians in the execution of planned genocidal acts. This problem has understandably brought grief to many victims and survivors, who feel that some sentences have been too lenient. This problem is exacerbated by the fact that some of the worst war criminals who are convicted by international tribunals serve their prison sentences in prisons that are more "comfortable" than the prisons in their home countries. This is also a problem without a solution. International courts cannot be party to incarceration in prisons that do not meet internationally acceptable prison conditions.

The most difficult criticism to meet is that international justice too frequently works against and not in favor of peace. Clearly in some situations a war crimes investigation and the issuing of indictments and arrest warrants might retard peace negotiations or otherwise endanger policy goals. Tribunals do not operate in a vacuum, and their actions undoubtedly have an impact on the ground. For instance, it has been much debated why the ICTY Prosecutor issued the second indictment against Radovan Karadzic and Ratko Mladic during the week that the Dayton peace talks were being held. The prosecutor was accused by some of using the indictment to ensure that the ICTY was not used as a "bargaining chip" in the negotiations. Similar arguments were raised when the ICTY indicted Slobodan Milosevic during the NATO bombing over Kosovo and at a time when talks were being held with Milosevic aimed at stopping the war. More recently concerns have been expressed with regard to the issuing of arrest warrants by the ICC against Ugandan leaders and against the president of Sudan, Omar Al-Bashir. In the Ugandan case, the principal mediator threatened to resign if such arrest warrants were issued, and in the case of Al-Bashir, the African Union expressed its displeasure at the move and requested the Security Council to suspend the ICC proceedings.

The experiences of all the war crimes courts to date have been such that their work does not appear to have prejudiced the peace or imperiled the lives of people in the countries in which they have operated. The little anecdotal evidence to date points in the opposite direction. It was the agreement reached by the warring parties at Dayton in November 1995 that brought the war in the former Yugoslavia to an end. That meeting could not have taken place if Radovan Karadzic, the Bosnian Serb leader and Commander-in-Chief of the Bosnian Serb Army, had been able to attend it. This was only four months after the Bosnian Serb Army had massacred some 8,000 civilian men and boys at Srebrenica. That was held by both the ICTY and the International Court of Justice to constitute an act of genocide. It would not have been morally or politically possible at that time for the leaders of Bosnia and Herzegovina to attend a meeting with Karadzic. In September 1995 as Prosecutor, I had issued a second indictment against Karadzic and his army chief, Ratko Mladic, based upon events in Srebrenica. That effectively prevented Karadzic from attending the Dayton meeting—he would have been arrested by the United States and transferred to The Hague for trial. He had no option but to accept being represented at Dayton by the president of Serbia, Slobodan Milosevic. In effect the indictment facilitated the Dayton meeting and the end of the war in the former Yugoslavia followed from it. This is a clear illustration of justice assisting peace. While an arrest warrant might have the opposite consequence and make peace negotiations more difficult, that has not happened thus far.

Even though some political leaders who are sought by the ICC remain at large, their capacity to carry out their duties has been curtailed by the issue of arrest warrants. For President Al-Bashir, the outstanding arrest warrant has had serious consequences. There are now more than 120 nations that are obliged to arrest him should he visit their shores. It was for this reason, for example, that President Al-Bashir was not invited to attend the 2010 inauguration of President Zuma in South Africa. The South African Government explained to the Sudanese Ambassador to Pretoria that if their head of state were to visit South Africa, the South African authorities would have no option but to arrest him and transfer him to the The Hague. Malawi more recently followed South Africa's example and refused to have Al-Bashir attend the annual summit of the AU that was being hosted in its capital, Lilongwe. The AU refused to accept that position and the meeting was transferred to the seat of the AU, Addis Ababa, where Al-Bashir attended the meeting. It is also most unfortunate that President Al Bashir has been allowed to visit three African members of the ICC, Chad, Kenya, and Djibouti. Those countries have failed to honor the international obligations they solemnly assumed by ratifying the Rome Statute.

I have attempted to discuss the major benefits and disadvantages of international criminal courts. That there is merit on both sides of the argument cannot be denied. However, in the end the benefits considerably outweigh the disadvantages. The bottom line is that impunity for war criminals is in the process of being universally withdrawn and we are the better for that.

The future

What of the future of the ICC? International criminal justice has developed a strong forward momentum. The number of nations that have ratified the Rome Statute is impressive. At the same time the absence of leading powerful nations is certainly retarding the endeavor. Never has international criminal justice been more in the news and there are daily references in the print and electronic media to it. It was entirely unexpected that the Security Council would refer situations to the ICC.

The progress of international criminal law has undoubtedly furthered the application of the recently developed doctrine called the "Responsibility to Protect." This doctrine was born out of egregious examples of nations failing to intervene in the face of the most serious violations of the human rights of innocent civilians by their own governments. For instance, the world stood by when, in the middle of 1994, over 800,000 innocent children, women, and men were slaughtered in the Rwandan genocide. A military force well within the peacekeeping capabilities of the United Nations could effectively have prevented much of the killing. There are other examples. One thinks, of course, of the killing fields in Cambodia.

In 2001 the International Commission on Intervention and State Sovereignty recommended the recognition by all governments of a "responsibility to protect" their own citizens. If they are unwilling or unable to do so, the responsibility shifts to the international community. This doctrine was endorsed by the 2005 World Summit. The then secretary-general, Kofi Annan, emphasized that in such an event the international community must use a range of measures designed to protect endangered populations, including diplomatic and humanitarian efforts and, only as a last resort, the use of military force.

Of course, politics will play a determinative role in whether or when this doctrine of Responsibility to Protect will be implemented. There was a signal failure in the case of Syria when Russia and China vetoed Security Council resolutions that would have enabled the Council to become seized of the situation there. Those two nations argued that it was not for the Security Council to become involved in the internal affairs of Syria, let alone to bring about regime change.

The first time that the United Nations Security Council took active steps under this doctrine of Responsibility to Protect was in respect of the situation in Libya. On 26 February 2011, the Security Council unanimously adopted Resolution 1973 referring the Libyan situation to the Prosecutor of the ICC. In accordance with the Rome Statute, the Prosecutor has the responsibility for determining whether to proceed with such an investigation. After a preliminary investigation, the Prosecutor determined that there was sufficient evidence to believe that crimes against humanity had been and still were being committed by the regime of Muammar Gaddafi. As he reported to the Security Council at the beginning of May 2011, there was also relevant evidence of the commission of rape, deportation, and forcible transfer that constituted war crimes under the Rome Statute. The investigation that followed was directed at those who appeared to bear the highest responsibility for the commission of those war crimes. Over 10,000 people were reported killed and many more tens of thousands injured.

There are considerable challenges facing the ICC. Perhaps the most serious arises from its complete reliance on governments for its ability to function. The ICC has no powers of its own to execute its arrest warrants or to compel compliance with its orders or requests. It requires the consent of governments to send its investigators into their jurisdictions; it requires the cooperation of governments to have its requests and orders recognized and implemented; and, most important, it requires governmental cooperation to have its arrest warrants executed. When that assistance is withheld its work is completely frustrated. That is illustrated by the failure to have before the Court the leading members of the Sudanese Government against whom arrest warrants have been issued, and especially President Al-Bashir. The same applies to the leaders of the Ugandan Lords Resistance Army. This problem has been compounded by the supine attitude of the Security Council even in respect of the two situations it has referred to the ICC. The willful ignoring of the ICC by the Sudanese Government and the Transitional Government of Libya has not appeared on the radar screen of the Security Council. That is regrettable for the Court and also for the Council itself. After all, it is its peremptory and binding resolutions that are being ignored.

Conclusion

International justice and particularly the ICC have brought about a distinct change in international relations and in some domestic situations. It is now more widely accepted that impunity for war criminals should be withdrawn and that, as a general rule, war crimes should be investigated and prosecuted. That most of the powerful states (and especially China, Russia, and the United States) exempt themselves from this international oversight weakens but certainly does not destroy its potency. Even those countries that support the doctrine, and, in the case of Libya, voted in favor of a Security Council resolution referring the situation in Libya to the ICC, from time to time can be leery. Warnings by political leaders about the commission of war crimes and to the ICC have become almost a daily occurrence.

It is too frequently forgotten that the main beneficiaries of any justice system are the victims, the survivors of egregious criminal conduct. It is for this reason that, unlike its predecessors, the Rome Statute has devoted much attention and conferred many innovative rights on victims. The ICC judges are slowly and carefully working out the details of how to apply those rights from the stage of investigation to the trial and appeal. It is important that those rights do not have a negative impact on the fair trial rights of defendants.

It should have become apparent to readers of this chapter that the pursuit of international justice is still in its early years. It has not yet matured into a settled and universally accepted system. That huge strides have been made cannot be doubted and neither can the tremendous challenges that still face the Court. An international rule of law has also developed in recent years and international criminal justice is very much a part of that enterprise. The potential is there. Much work remains to be done to make it a reality. That work rests not only with the ICC but also with political leaders and, above all, with civil society.

Additional reading

1. Richard J. Goldstone and Adam M. Smith, *International Judicial Institutions* (London: Routledge, 2009).
2. International Criminal Court, www.icc-cpi.int.
3. Coalition for the International Criminal Court, www.iccnow.org.
4. David Scheffer, *All the Missing Souls: A Personal History of the War Crimes Tribunals* (Princeton: Princeton University Press, 2012).
5. William Schabas, *An Introduction to the International Criminal Court* (Cambridge: Cambridge University Press, 2011).
6. Sarah B. Sewall and Carl Kaysen, eds., *The United States and the International Criminal Court: National Security and International Law* (Lanham, MD: Rowman & Littlefield, 2000).

Notes

1 This essay draws on Richard J. Goldstone and Adam. M. Smith, *International Judicial Institutions: The Architecture of International Justice at Home and Abroad* (London: Routledge, 2009), and the "Fifth Maha Chakri Sirindhorn Lecture," delivered by Richard J. Goldstone in Bangkok on 13 June 2011.
2 Henry Wheaton, *International Law* (Cambridge, MA: Harvard University Press, 1836), 18.
3 Convention on the Prevention and Punishment of the Crime of Genocide, U.N.T.S. no. 1021, vol. 78 (1951), art. 6.
4 Rome Statute for the International Criminal Court, UN document A/CONF. 183/9, 17 July 1998.
5 Ibid., art. 13(a).
6 Ibid., art. 13(b).
7 Ibid., art. 13(c).
8 *Prosecutor v Akayesu*, Case No.ICTR-96-4-T.
9 Rome Statute of the International Criminal Court, UN document A/CONF.183/9, 17 July 1998, art. 7 and 8.
10 *Prosecutor v Tadic*, Case No.IT-94-1-AR72.
11 *Prosecutor v Blaskic*, Case No.IT-95-14.
12 *Prosecutor v Musema*, Case No.ICTR-96-13-A.
13 *Prosecutor v Kambanda*, Case No.ICTR-97-23-DP.
14 *Prosecutor v Barayugwiza*, Case No.ICTR-97-19-1.
15 *Prosecutor v Lubanga*, Case No.ICC-01/04.

Humanitarian Intervention and R2P

Simon Chesterman

Which is more important: protecting sovereignty or protecting human rights? That is the stark manner in which some frame the question posed by humanitarian intervention. When a government has turned on its own people, or is unable or unwilling to protect them, should the international community of states merely stand by and watch? An alternative framing of the question is whether one country should be allowed to determine unilaterally that a threat to human rights in another country justifies military action. If that were the case, how would we ensure that such a right of humanitarian intervention is not abused? Between these extremes, the United Nations Security Council has the power to authorize the use of military force. But Article 39 of the UN Charter specifies that the council can only do this in response to a "threat to the peace, breach of the peace, or act of aggression." When can a threat to human rights be said to reach the level of a threat to the peace?

This chapter first sets out the international rules governing the use of force and the attempts—largely unsuccessful—to fit humanitarian intervention into those rules. It then examines the claim that certain cases of alleged humanitarian intervention might best be seen as "exceptions" to the rule. Third, it considers the emergence of the doctrine of Responsibility to Protect (R2P) as an attempt at a new framing of these old questions.[1]

International law

The status of humanitarian intervention in international law is, on the face of it, quite simple. The UN Charter clearly prohibits the use of force. The renunciation of war must be counted among the greatest achievements of international law in the twentieth century; that this was also the bloodiest of centuries is a sober warning as to the limits of law's power to constrain the behavior of states.

The passage in Article 2(4) agreed by states at the San Francisco conference of 1945 was broad in its scope: "All Members shall refrain in their international relations from the threat or use of force against the territorial integrity or political independence of any state, or in any other manner inconsistent with the Purposes of the United Nations." The prohibition was tempered by only two exceptions. First, Article 51 preserved the "inherent right of individual or collective self-defense." Second, the newly established Security Council was granted the power to authorize enforcement actions under Chapter VII. Although this latter species of military action is sometimes considered in the same breath as unilateral humanitarian intervention, council authorization changes the legal questions to which such action gives rise.

Both exceptions provide examples of how legal rights concerning the use of force have tended to expand. Self-defense, for example, has been invoked in ever-wider circumstances to justify military actions such as a pre-emptive strike against a country's nuclear program, and in "response" to a failed assassination attempt in a foreign country. It also provided the initial basis for the extensive US military actions in Afghanistan in late 2001. Security Council-authorized actions have expanded even further, mandating actions in Somalia and Haiti in the 1990s that would never have been contemplated by the founders of the United Nations in 1945. Nevertheless, neither exception encompasses humanitarian intervention, meaning the threat or use of armed force in the absence of a Security Council authorization or an invitation from the recognized government with the object of protecting human rights.

A third possible exception concerns the role of the General Assembly. This dates back to the Korean War and fears that a Soviet veto would block the council from acting. For some months in 1950 the ambassador from what was then the Union of Soviet Socialist Republics (USSR) boycotted the Security Council in protest at the UN's continuing recognition of the recently defeated Kuomintang regime in China. In his absence, three resolutions were passed which in effect authorized the United States to lead a military operation against North Korea under the UN flag. The return of the Soviet delegate precluded any further council involvement. At the initiative of Western states in 1950, the General Assembly adopted Resolution GA Res 377A(V), *Uniting for Peace*, which provided that it would meet to recommend collective measures in situations where the veto prevented the Security Council from fulfilling its primary responsibility for the maintenance of international peace and security. In the case of a breach of the peace or act of aggression, the measures available were said to include the use of armed force.

The legality of the General Assembly doing more than authorize peacekeeping with the consent of parties is dubious, but a resolution was passed recommending that all states lend every assistance to the UN action in Korea. *Uniting for Peace* was used again in relation to the Suez crisis in 1956 and in the Congo in 1960. The procedure has fallen into disuse, however. In particular, it appears not to have been seriously contemplated during the Kosovo crisis—reportedly because of fears that the North Atlantic Treaty Organization (NATO) would have been unable to muster the necessary two-thirds majority support of the member states.

At first glance, then, traditional international law does not allow for humanitarian intervention. There have, however, been many attempts to bring humanitarian intervention within the remit of this body of law. These have tended to follow two strategies: limiting the scope of the prohibition of the use of force, or arguing that a new customary norm has created an additional exception to the prohibition.

As cited above, Charter Article 2(4) prohibits the use of force in very broad language. Nevertheless, it has sometimes been argued that certain uses of force might not contravene this provision. For example, it has been argued that the US invasion of Panama in 1989 was consistent with the UN Charter because "the United States did not intend to, and has not, colonialized [sic], annexed or incorporated Panama."[2] As Oscar Schachter archly observed, this demands an Orwellian construction of the terms "territorial integrity" and "political independence."[3] It also runs counter to various statements by the General Assembly and the International Court of Justice (ICJ) concerning the meaning of nonintervention, as well as the practice of the Security Council, which has condemned and declared illegal the unauthorized use of force even when it is "temporary." This is consistent with the drafting history of the provision, which, the US delegate to the San Francisco conference (among others) emphasized, left "no loopholes."

Is it possible, however, that a new norm might have developed to create a separate right of humanitarian intervention? Customary international law allows for the creation of such norms through the evolution of consistent and widespread state practice when accompanied by the necessary *opinio juris*—the belief that a practice is legally obligatory. Some writers have argued that there is evidence of such state practice and *opinio juris*, typically pointing to the Indian action to stop the slaughter in East Pakistan in 1971, Tanzania's actions against Idi Amin in neighboring Uganda in 1978–79, and Vietnam's intervention in Kampuchea in 1978–79. In none of these cases, however, were humanitarian concerns invoked as a justification for the use of force. Rather, self-defense was the primary justification offered in each case, with humanitarian (and other) justifications being at best secondary considerations.

Such justifications are important, as they may provide evidence of change in the law. As the ICJ has observed:

> The significance for the Court of cases of State conduct *prima facie* inconsistent with the principle of nonintervention lies in the nature of the ground offered as justification. Reliance by a State on a novel right or an unprecedented exception to the principle might, if shared in principle by other States, tend towards a modification of customary international law.[4]

The fact that states continued to rely on traditional justifications—most notably self-defense—undermines arguments that the law has changed.

The international response to each incident is also instructive. In relation to India's action (which led to the creation of Bangladesh), a Soviet veto prevented a US-sponsored resolution calling for a ceasefire and the immediate withdrawal of armed forces. Tanzania's actions were broadly tolerated and the new regime in Kampala was swiftly recognized, but states that voiced support for the action typically confined their comments to the question of self-defense. Vietnam's successful ouster of the murderous regime of Pol Pot, by contrast, was met with positive hostility. France's representative, for example, stated that

> [t]he notion that because a régime is detestable foreign intervention, is justified and forcible overthrow is legitimate is extremely dangerous. That could ultimately jeopardize the very maintenance of international law and order and make the continued existence of various régimes dependent on the judgment of their neighbors.[5]

Similar statements were made by the United Kingdom and Portugal, among others. Once again, only a Soviet veto prevented a resolution calling upon the foreign troops to withdraw; Pol Pot's delegate continued to be recognized as the legitimate representative of Kampuchea (later Cambodia) at the United Nations until as late as 1990. Even if one includes these three "best cases" as evidence of state practice, the absence of accompanying *opinio juris* fatally undermines claims that they marked a change in the law.

Later examples of allegedly humanitarian intervention without explicit Security Council authorization, such as the no-fly zones in protection of the Kurds in northern Iraq from 1991 and NATO's intervention in Kosovo in 1999, raise slightly different questions. Acting states have often claimed that their actions have been "in support of" Security Council resolutions, though in each case it is clear that the council did not decide to authorize the use of force. Indeed, it is ironic that states began to claim the need to act when the Security Council faltered in precisely the same decade that its activities expanded so greatly. At a time when there was a far stronger argument that paralysis of the UN system demanded self-help, the ICJ considered and rejected arguments that "present defects in international organization" could justify an independent right of intervention.[6]

Interestingly, despite the efforts by some legal scholars to argue for the existence of a right of humanitarian intervention, states themselves have continued to prove very reluctant to embrace such a right—even in defense of their own actions. This was particularly true in the case of NATO's intervention in Kosovo. Such reluctance appears to have stemmed in part from the dubiousness of such a legal argument, but also from the knowledge that if any right were embraced it might well be used by other states in other situations.

Unusually among its member states, in October 1998 Germany referred to NATO's threats against the Federal Republic of Yugoslavia as an instance of "humanitarian intervention." The Bundestag affirmed its support for the Western Alliance—provided that it was made clear that this was not a precedent for further action. This desire to avoid setting a precedent was reflected in statements by NATO officials. US secretary of state Madeleine Albright later stressed that the air strikes were a "unique situation *sui generis* in the region of the Balkans," concluding that it was important "not to overdraw the various lessons that come out of it."[7] UK prime minister Tony Blair, who had earlier suggested that such interventions might become more routine, subsequently retreated from this position, emphasizing the exceptional nature of the air campaign. This was consistent with the more sophisticated UK statements on the legal issues.

This trend continued in the proceedings brought by the Federal Republic of Yugoslavia against ten NATO members before the International Court of Justice. In hearings on provisional measures, only Belgium presented an elaborate legal justification for the action, relying variously on Security Council resolutions, a doctrine of humanitarian intervention (as compatible with Article 2(4) of the UN Charter or based on historical precedent), and the argument of necessity. The United States, by contrast, emphasized the importance of Security Council resolutions, and, together with four other delegations (Germany, the Netherlands, Spain, and the United Kingdom), made reference to the existence of a "humanitarian catastrophe." Four delegations did not offer any clear legal justification (Canada, France, Italy, and Portugal). The phrase "humanitarian catastrophe" recalled the doctrine of humanitarian intervention, but some care appears to have been taken to avoid invoking the doctrine by name. The formulation was first used by the United Kingdom as one of a number of justifications for the no-fly zones over Iraq, but no legal pedigree had been established beyond this. The court ultimately ruled against Yugoslavia for technical reasons concerning its jurisdiction, never discussing the merits of the case.

Such reticence to embrace a clear legal position was repeated in two major commissions that investigated the question of humanitarian intervention. The Kosovo Commission, headed by Richard Goldstone, concluded somewhat confusingly (from an international legal perspective) that NATO's Kosovo intervention was "illegal but legitimate."[8] The International Commission on Intervention and State Sovereignty (ICISS), chaired by Gareth Evans and Mohamed Sahnoun, acknowledged that, as a matter of "political reality," it would be impossible to find consensus around any set of proposals for military intervention that acknowledged the validity of any intervention not authorized by the Security Council or the General Assembly:

> But that may still leave circumstances when the Security Council fails to discharge what this Commission would regard as its responsibility to protect, in a conscience-shocking situation crying out for action. It is a real question in these circumstances where lies the most harm: in the damage to international order if the Security Council is bypassed or in the damage to that order if human beings are slaughtered while the Security Council stands by.[9]

Key elements of the ICISS report *The Responsibility to Protect* were adopted by the UN World Summit in a 2005 resolution of the General Assembly, which acknowledged that a state's unwillingness or inability to protect its own population from genocide, war crimes, ethnic cleansing, or crimes against humanity may give rise to an international "responsibility to protect." This was limited to peaceful means, however, except in extreme circumstances where the provisions of Chapter VII of the UN Charter may be invoked.[10] The report and the UN resolution were carefully silent about what happens if the council does *not* agree.

What do international lawyers make of all this? It seems fairly clear that there is no positive right of humanitarian intervention without authorization by the Security Council. Nor, however, does it appear that a coherent principle is emerging to create such a right. Rather, the arguments as presented tend to focus on the non-application of international law to particular incidents. The next section will explore the implications of such an approach to international law, and where it might lead.

An exception to the rule?

James Rubin provides a graphic illustration of the debates between NATO capitals on the question of the legality of the Kosovo intervention:

> There was a series of strained telephone calls between [US secretary of state Madeleine] Albright and [UK foreign secretary Robin] Cook, in which he cited problems "with our lawyers" over using force in the absence of UN endorsement. "Get new lawyers," she suggested. But with a push from Prime Minister Tony Blair, the British finally agreed that UN Security Council approval was not legally required.[11]

Such equivocation about the role of international law in decision-making processes is hardly new; the history of international law has often been the struggle to raise law above the status of being merely one foreign policy justification among others. As indicated earlier, however, most of the acting states appear to have taken some care to present the Kosovo intervention as an exception rather than a rule.

Various writers have attempted to explain the apparent inconsistency by reference to national legal systems. Ian Brownlie, for example, likened this approach to the manner in which some legal systems deal with the question of euthanasia:

> [I]n such a case the possibility of abuse is recognized by the legal policy (that the activity is classified as unlawful) but . . . in very clear cases the law allows mitigation. The father who smothers his severely abnormal child after several years of devoted attention may not be sent to prison, but he is not immune from prosecution and punishment. In international relations a difficulty arises in that "a discretion not to prosecute" is exercisable by States collectively and by organs of the United Nations, and in the context of *practice* of States, mitigation and acceptance in principle are not always easy to distinguish. However, the euthanasia parallel is useful since it indicates that moderation is allowed for in social systems even when the principle remains firm. Moderation in application does not display a legislative intent to cancel the principle so applied.[12]

Obviously, as the demand for any such violation of an established norm increases, so the need for legal regulation of the "exception" becomes more important. This seems to be occurring in the case of euthanasia, as medical advances have increased the discretion of doctors in making end-of-life decisions. In many jurisdictions, continued reliance on the possibility of a homicide charge is now seen as an inadequate legal response to the ethical challenges posed by euthanasia. In relation to humanitarian intervention, however, such demand remains low and it is widely recognized that legal regulation of any "exception" is unlikely in the short term.

For this reason, an alternative analogy is sometimes used: that of a person acting to prevent domestic violence in circumstances where the police are unwilling or unable to act. The analogy is appealing as it appears to capture the moral dilemma facing an intervener, but is of limited value as such acts are typically regulated by reference to the existing authority structures. An individual in most legal systems may defend another person against attack, and in certain circumstances may exercise a limited power of arrest. In the context of humanitarian intervention, this analogy merely begs the question of its legality.

The better view, then, appears to be that humanitarian intervention is illegal but that the international community may, on a case-by-case basis, tolerate the wrong. In such a situation, claims that an intervention was "humanitarian" should be seen not as a legal justification but as a plea in mitigation. Such an approach has the merits of a basis in international law. In the Corfu Channel case, the United Kingdom claimed that an intervention in Albanian territorial waters was justified on the basis that nobody else was prepared to deal with the threat of mines planted in an international strait during World War II. The ICJ rejected this argument in unequivocal terms, but held that a declaration of illegality was itself a sufficient remedy for the wrong.

Similarly, after Israel abducted Adolf Eichmann from Argentina to face criminal charges for his role in the Nazi Holocaust, Argentina lodged a complaint with the Security Council, which passed a resolution stating that the sovereignty of Argentina had been infringed and requesting Israel to make "appropriate reparation." Nevertheless, "mindful" of the concern that Eichmann be brought to justice, in resolution 138 (1960) the Security Council clearly implied that "appropriate reparation" would not involve his physical return to Argentina. The governments of Israel and Argentina subsequently issued a joint communiqué resolving to "view as settled the incident which was caused in the wake of the action of citizens of Israel which violated the basic rights of the State of Argentina."[13]

This is also broadly consistent with current state practice. During the Kosovo intervention, some suggested that the action threatened the stability of the international order—in particular the relevance of the Security Council as the Charter body with primary responsibility for international peace and security. In fact, the Security Council became integral to resolution of the dispute (despite the bombing of the embassy of one permanent member by another). In Resolution 1244 (1999) and acting under Chapter VII, the Council welcomed Yugoslavia's acceptance of the principles set out in the 6 May 1999 meeting of G8 Foreign Ministers and authorized member states and "relevant international organizations" (in other words NATO) to establish an international security presence in Kosovo. The resolution was passed within hours of the suspension of bombing, and its preamble contained a half-hearted endorsement of the role of the

Security Council: "*Bearing in mind* the purposes and principles of the Charter of the United Nations, and the primary responsibility of the Security Council for the maintenance of international peace and security." More importantly, the resolution reaffirmed the commitment "of all Member States to the sovereignty and territorial integrity of the Federal Republic of Yugoslavia" even as it called for "substantial autonomy" for Kosovo. The tension between these provisions left the province in a legal limbo, and continues to complicate the independence it declared in early 2008.

Later in 1999, military action in East Timor affirmed more clearly the continued role of the Security Council, with authorization being a condition precedent for the Australian-led INTERFET action. This authorization, in turn, depended on Indonesia's consent to the operation. Though it was presented at the time as evidence that the international community was prepared to engage in Kosovo-style interventions outside Europe, the political and legal conditions in which the intervention took place were utterly different. The view that they were comparable reflected the troubling assumption that, when facing a humanitarian crisis with a military dimension, there is a choice between doing something and doing nothing, and that "something" means the application of military force. This narrow view was challenged by then UN secretary-general Kofi Annan, who has stressed that "it is important to define intervention as broadly as possible, to include actions along a wide continuum from the most pacific to the most coercive."[14] Similarly, the International Commission on Intervention and State Sovereignty sought to turn this policy question on its head. Rather than examining at length the right to intervene, it focused on the responsibility of states to protect vulnerable populations at risk from civil wars, insurgencies, state repression, and state collapse.[15]

R2P

Implicit in many arguments for a right of humanitarian intervention is the suggestion that international law currently prevents interventions that should take place. This is simply not true. Interventions do not take place because states choose not to undertake them. On the contrary, states have frequently intervened for a great many reasons, some of them more humanitarian than others. For those who would seek to establish a law or a general ethical principle to govern humanitarian intervention, a central question must be whether it could work in practice. Do any of the incidents commonly marshaled as examples of humanitarian intervention provide a model that should be followed in future? Should Kosovo, for example, be a model for future negotiations with brutal regimes? If so, why were the terms presented to Serbia at Rambouillet more onerous than those offered after a 78-day bombing campaign?

That said, on closer analysis it becomes clear that the real problem confronting human rights today is not how to legitimize questionable actions such as the Kosovo intervention, but how to respond to situations like Rwanda—where genocide took place and no action was taken at all. Put differently, the problem is not the legitimacy of humanitarian intervention, but the overwhelming prevalence of inhumanitarian nonintervention. Addressing that problem requires mobilizing the political will of member states as much as it does the creation of new legal rules. In this context, the ICISS rhetorical shift—

from a *right* of intervention to the *responsibility* to protect—may mark the most significant advance in this contested area of international relations.

The move from right to responsibility is more than wordplay. In particular, shifting the debate away from a simple question of the legality of humanitarian intervention, in the strict sense of the word, serves two distinct policy goals. First, the legal debate is sterile. It is unlikely that a clear and workable set of criteria could be adopted on a right of humanitarian intervention. Any criteria general enough to achieve agreement would be unlikely to satisfy any actual examples of allegedly humanitarian intervention. Indeed, it is clear from the statements of NATO leaders during and after the Kosovo campaign that they did not want the air strikes to be regarded as a model for dealing with future humanitarian crises. The alternative—a select group of states (Western liberal democracies, for example) agreeing on criteria amongst themselves—would be seen as a vote of no confidence in the United Nations and a challenge to the very idea of an international rule of law. Such problems echo the troubled history of just war theory: in particular, concerns that the criteria for military action were arbitrary and that the power to act was limited to the privileged few.

More importantly, however, the focus on a responsibility to protect highlights the true problem at the heart of this ongoing debate. The problem is not that states are champing at the bit to intervene in support of human rights around the globe, prevented only by an intransigent Security Council and the absence of clear criteria to intervene without its authority. Rather, the problem is the absence of the will to act at all.

Responsibility to protect, as a result, has achieved considerable traction in a short time. Nevertheless, the recent case of Libya suggests the wariness of the Security Council in embracing R2P—even in what one might regard as a perfect case for its application. State leaders are usually more circumspect in the threats they make against their population than was Muammar el-Qaddafi; impending massacres are rarely so easy to foresee. Combined with the support of African states and the Arab League for intervention, most states on the council were unwilling to allow atrocities to occur— and others unwilling to be seen as the impediment to action.

Even then, Security Council Resolution 1973 (2011), which authorized the use of all necessary measures to protect civilians, was vague about what might happen next. As in many previous cases, the commitment of leaders to confining their countries' involvement to air strikes alone and for a limited duration was transparently a political rather than military decision. The commencement of military action, as in many previous cases, swiftly showed that air strikes alone were unlikely to be effective. The potential tragedy of Benghazi soon devolved into farce as the Libyan rebels were revealed to be a disorganized rabble.[16]

Do something, do *anything*, is not a military strategy. The outcome for Libya remains uncertain, while hand-wringing continues as Syria implodes. How these conflicts play out will have consequences that reach far beyond the countries themselves. The doctrine of the responsibility to protect may have made it harder to say "no," but what happens next will clearly affect the likelihood of whether future leaders will say "yes."

Conclusion

In the aftermath of the 9/11 terrorist attacks on New York and Washington, DC, the United States swiftly sought and received the Security Council's endorsement of its position in Resolution 1368 that this was an attack on the United States and that action taken in self-defense against "those responsible for aiding, supporting or harboring the perpetrators, organizers and sponsors of these acts" was justified. Self-defense does not require any form of authorization (though measures taken should be "immediately reported" to the Council), but the fact that the United Nations was involved so quickly in a crisis was widely seen as a welcome counterpoint to the unilateralist impulses of the George W. Bush Administration.

Nevertheless, the decision to seek Security Council approval also reflected a troubling trend through the 1990s. Military action under its auspices has taken place only when circumstances coincided with the national interests of a state that was prepared to act, with the Council in danger of becoming what Richard Falk has described as a "law-laundering service."[17] Such an approach downgrades the importance of authorization to the point where it may be seen as a policy justification rather than a matter of legal significance. A consequence of this approach is that when authorization is not forthcoming a state or group of states will feel less restrained from acting unilaterally. This represents a fundamental challenge to the international order established at the conclusion of World War II, in which the interests of the powerful would be balanced through the exercise (real or threatened) of the veto.

In the context of humanitarian intervention, many appeared to hope that such a departure from "traditional" conceptions of sovereignty and international law would privilege ethics over states' rights. In fact, as we have seen, humanitarian intervention has long had a troubled relationship with the question of national interest. Most attempts by scholars to formulate a doctrine of humanitarian intervention require that an acting state be disinterested or "relatively disinterested." By contrast, in one of the few articulations of such a doctrine by a political leader, then UK prime minister Blair proposed his own criteria, one of which was whether "we" had national interests involved.[18]

The war on terror reduced the probability of "humanitarian" interventions in the short term, but raised the troubling prospect of more extensive military adventures being undertaken without clear legal justification. President George W. Bush's 2002 State of the Union speech, in particular, in which he referred to an "axis of evil," suggested a preparedness to use ethical arguments (and absolute ethical statements) as a substitute for legal—or, it might be argued, rational—justification. The 2003 Iraq war is often invoked as an example of the pernicious consequences that might follow.

All such developments should be treated with great caution. A right of humanitarian intervention depends on one's acceptance that humanitarian ends justify military means. As the history of this doctrine shows, the ends are never so clear and the means are rarely so closely bound to them. In such a situation where there is no ideal, where Kosovo presents the imperfect model (and lingers today as a testament to NATO's imperfect victory), it may be better to hold that humanitarian intervention without Security Council authorization remains both illegal and morally suspect, but that arguments can be made on a case-by-case basis that, in an imperfect world, international order may yet survive the wrong.

When the Security Council *does* provide a clear authorization for the use of force—or an ambiguous one, as it did in the case of Libya—this simplifies the legal issues. Yet diplomatic agreement to adopt a resolution does not always come with a coherent political or military strategy. In this context, the responsibility to protect has certainly made it harder for states to stand by silently when confronted by a humanitarian crisis. It has not simplified the question of what they should do.

Additional reading

1. Gareth Evans, *The Responsibility to Protect: Ending Mass Atrocity Crimes Once and for All* (Washington, DC: Brookings Institution, 2008).
2. J. L. Holzgrefe and Robert O. Keohane, eds., *Humanitarian Intervention: Ethical, Legal and Political Dilemmas* (Cambridge: Cambridge University Press, 2003).
3. Anne Orford, *International Authority and the Responsibility to Protect* (Cambridge: Cambridge University Press, 2011).
4. Thomas G. Weiss, *Humanitarian Intervention: Ideas in Action*, 2nd edition (Cambridge: Polity Press, 2012).

Notes

1 This chapter draws upon ideas explored at greater length in Simon Chesterman, *Just War or Just Peace? Humanitarian Intervention and International* (Oxford: Oxford University Press, 2001), and Simon Chesterman, "Violence in the Name of Human Rights," in *The Cambridge Companion to Human Rights Law*, eds. Conor Gearty and Costas Douzinas (Cambridge: Cambridge University Press, 2012).
2 Anthony D'Amato, "The Invasion of Panama Was a Lawful Response to Tyranny," *American Journal of International Law* 84 (1990): 520.
3 Oscar Schachter, "The Legality of Pro-Democratic Invasion," *American Journal of International Law* 78 (1984): 649.
4 *Case Concerning the Military and Paramilitary Activities in and Against Nicaragua (Nicaragua v. United States of America)*, International Court of Justice, 27 June 1986, ICJ Rep, http://www.icj-cij.org, 109.
5 S/PV.2109 (1979), para. 36 (France).
6 *Corfu Channel (United Kingdom v. Albania) (Merits)*, 1949, ICJ Rep 4, http://www.icj-cij.org, 35.
7 Madeleine Albright, Press Conference with Russian Foreign Minister Igor Ivanov, Singapore, 26 July 1999.
8 Independent International Commission on Kosovo, *The Kosovo Report* (Oxford: Oxford University Press, 2000), 4.
9 International Commission on Intervention and State Sovereignty, *The Responsibility to Protect* (Ottawa: International Development Research Centre, December 2001), http://www.responsibilitytoprotect.org, 54–55.
10 2005 World Summit Outcome Document, UN Doc A/RES/60/1 (16 September 2005), http://www.un.org/summit2005, paras. 138–139.
11 James Rubin, "Countdown to a Very Personal War," *Financial Times*, 30 September 2000.

12 Ian Brownlie, "Thoughts on Kind-Hearted Gunmen," in *Humanitarian Intervention and the United Nations*, ed. Richard B. Lillich (Charlottesville: University Press of Virginia, 1973), 146 (emphasis in original).

13 Joint Communiqué of the Governments of Israel and Argentina, 3 August 1960, reprinted in 36 ILR 59.

14 Kofi A. Annan, Address to the General Assembly, UN Press Release SG/SM/7136, New York, 20 September 1999, http://www.un.org/news/Press/docs/1999/19990920.sgsm7136.html.

15 International Commission on Intervention and State Sovereignty, *The Responsibility to Protect* (Ottawa: International Development Research Centre, 2001).

16 See further Simon Chesterman, "Leading from Behind: The Responsibility to Protect, the Obama Doctrine, and Humanitarian Intervention after Libya," *Ethics and International Affairs* 25 (2011): 279.

17 Richard A. Falk, "The United Nations and the Rule of Law," *Transnational Law and Contemporary Problems* 4 (1994): 628.

18 Michael Evans, "Conflict Opens 'Way to New International Community': Blair's Mission," *The Times*, 23 April 1999. The five criteria were: Are we sure of our case? Have we exhausted all diplomatic options? Are there military options we can sensibly and prudently undertake? Are we prepared for the long term? And do we have national interests involved?

CONTENTS

Crisis and Humanitarian Containment

Fabrice Weissman

From international nongovernmental organizations (NGOs) to UN agencies, donors to observers of the humanitarian scene, opinion is unanimous: "humanitarian space is shrinking."[1] Trapped in the midst of military–humanitarian confusion and postcolonial state hostility, aid agencies are said to face more difficulties than ever to assist victims of conflicts and natural disasters.[2]

Yet this pessimistic observation seems contradicted by the significant rise in the number of public and private actors delivering assistance across the globe in the name of humanitarian principles.[3] Within the past 20 years, international funding for humanitarian aid has increased tenfold, reaching $14bn in 2011 compared to $800m in 1988. Moreover, since the demise of the twentieth century's totalitarian systems, few regimes or political movements openly reject humanitarian law and ethics. Even theologians close to al-Qaeda recognize the merits of "genuine" humanitarian action.[4] Indignation at the suffering of distant others and the promotion of altruism in the name of humanity now feature as standard legitimating discourses in national and international political arenas.

Universal humanitarian language goes hand in hand with controversies on its use and meaning. In particular, there is no consensus about the freedom of action that a foreign humanitarian organization can claim "in the name of universal medical ethics and the right to humanitarian assistance"—to use the terms in the charter of Médecins Sans Frontières (MSF). There is, however, a space for negotiation, power relationships, and interests. In practice, humanitarian organizations' room for maneuver results from constant deal-making with local authorities and state powers. Humanitarians' freedom of action depends, in large part, on the diplomatic and political support at their disposal, and thus on the potential benefits they can provide to those who wield power.

Therefore, the political manipulation of humanitarians is not a shift away from their original courses or the reason for their recent difficulties but the primary condition of their action. The main challenge for aid agencies is not to preserve a space free of all political manipulation but to negotiate compromises reflecting the best balance possible between their interests and those of political powers. This brings us to the heart of the matter: What is an acceptable compromise for a humanitarian actor? What is a decent policy of humanitarian assistance? Drawing on my field and analytical experience, I explore this problématique, starting with an overview of actors and interests before describing how, since the end of the Cold War, aid agencies have sought to position themselves in the dilemmas arising from their inevitable engagement in global and local political arenas.[5]

The political–humanitarian arena

The arena for contemporary humanitarian action can best be understood by parsing the actors as well as probing the material and symbolic stakes involved.

Actors

The power relationships relief agencies are engaged in involve a very large number of players—from the narrowly local to the broadly global. In armed conflicts, humanitarian organizations must first reach an understanding with the local armed forces: from the defense ministry in the capital to the young soldier controlling a checkpoint on a provincial road; from an exiled rebel leader to field commanders in the bush; from gang leaders who control a territory to bandits who control none. Humanitarian actors must also come to terms with the various civil authorities—interior, health, agriculture, water, labor, immigration, and customs ministries and their province, district, and village representatives, as well as governors, prefects, mayors, village and family heads, religious leaders, influential businessmen, refugee camps or slums representatives, political parties, local NGOs, unions, and activist groups. These parties are usually involved in emergency operations as part of national response programs or solidarity networks. They play a decisive role in the success or failure of humanitarian actors. But their perception of the resources and risks that a foreign humanitarian organization brings differs depending on whether they oppose or support the authorities in power, represent one ministry versus another, give orders or carry them out, represent the local community or the central authorities.

Aid agencies also have to negotiate their space with the other international actors. In addition to UN political and military missions and outside military forces occupying an area or providing military support to one of the parties to the conflict (e.g. Afghanistan, Iraq, Somalia, Libya, and Syria), they have to deal with donor representatives, UN agencies, and NGOs—actors between whom disagreements can be profound and competition fierce.

What humanitarian actors can offer the political and military forces in these countless negotiations are the material and symbolic assets they bring to the political arena. Their assets are threefold: the goods and services that they deliver to the population; the economic resources that they inject into the local economy; and the publicity that they can generate for the forces involved.

Material stakes

Public health technologies deployed by humanitarian actors are invaluable to governments or armed groups willing to mobilize, displace, encamp, or detain civilians.[6] The prime example is refugee camps, where humanitarian organizations usually play a dual role. On one hand, they are unwillingly supporting mechanisms designed to control and keep at bay populations considered undesirable by governments.[7] On the other hand, they indirectly help strengthen political and military groups that frequently reconstitute themselves within camps—for example the genocide leaders who took control of a number of Rwandan refugee camps in Zaire between 1994 and 1996.[8] Camps for internally displaced persons (IDPs) are no exception, as illustrated by the transformation of many Darfur camps into bastions of opposition to the Khartoum regime.[9] Conversely, between 2006 and 2009, the Sri Lankan government proved remarkably skillful at using humanitarian organizations to serve its policy of internment and surveillance vis-à-vis populations evacuated from rebel-held areas—a policy aimed at suppressing any attempt at independent political reorganization among IDPs.[10]

Outside of camps, the public services provided by humanitarian organizations in health care, food, housing, and water are key resources for any rebel movement, government, or occupying army seeking to administer a territory and meet the population's social expectations. Aid projects conducted by the international forces in Afghanistan with the help of some humanitarian organizations have certainly not had the expected "stabilizing" effect.[11] In the 1980s, however, guerrilla movements like the Eritrean and Tigrean People's Liberation Fronts successfully incorporated humanitarian aid into selective redistribution policies, allowing them to control and mobilize a significant portion of the population.[12]

Humanitarian action can also be of economic value to authorities. In addition to the varying amounts of humanitarian resources captured via levies, diversion, theft, and looting, aid agencies inject significant economic resources in the form of salaries, rentals, service contracts, and local purchases. Such expenditures have a ripple effect on the local economy from which the authorities are usually the first to benefit, thanks to their stranglehold on the most profitable markets (e.g. land, house, office, and warehouse rentals, transportation and private security services).[13] Competition to capture this income is one of the main sources of insecurity for aid staff in Somalia (where the majority of security incidents are related to the negotiation of employment and service contracts), the Democratic Republic of Congo (DRC), and many other countries.

Symbolic stakes

NGOs and UN agencies are a favorite information source for journalists. They engage directly in the public debate, using the media to alert public opinion and mobilize financial and political resources. In so doing, they help portray crisis situations and push them onto the media and diplomatic agenda. They contribute to building an international public space, where the conduct of political actors—both within and beyond their borders—is submitted to public scrutiny.

In describing the world, humanitarian organizations usually employ a standard narrative whose ideal type is the "humanitarian crisis."[14] Designed to mobilize public opinion through emotion, it describes situations of violence as a morality play centered on the suffering of victims. According to Luc Boltanski, two narratives are generally used to render the spectacle of pain morally and psychologically tolerable.[15] One appeals to public opinion's pity (topic of sentiment), the other to its indignation and anger (topic of denunciation).

The topic of sentiment superimposes onto the spectacle of suffering the image of humanitarians in action (a nurse at the bedside of a malnourished child, logisticians organizing food distributions in the midst of a destitute throng, a doctor dressing the wounds of an injured man). Extolling the gratitude of the victim toward his benefactor, this representation directs the viewer's sympathy to the humanitarian actor, erasing any consideration about the source of the disaster, which is blamed on some impersonal cause (the madness of war thus relegated to the ranks of natural disaster). By narrowing the drama to the humanitarian–victim pair, politics is elided. French TV coverage of the July 1994 exodus of nearly two million Rwandan Hutu refugees—among which were many genocide perpetrators—to eastern Zaire was a perfect example of this narrative's power to conceal. It portrayed people who had participated in the genocide as victims, just like the refugees, and governments that had refused an intervention to stop the extermination as saviors. The spectacle of foreign armies and NGOs coming to the rescue of cholera victims as an epidemic ravaged the refugee camps effectively erased the world's passive consent to the earlier annihilation of the Tutsi.

The topic of denunciation gives us two additional figures: the persecutor and the savior. The spectacle of suffering is thus used to stir up the indignation and anger of the spectators, who are mobilized to urge potential saviors (powerful countries and multilateral organizations) to track down, neutralize, and punish the persecutor. As Boltanski points out, this narrative inevitably relies on a more or less explicit theory of power. The latter is essential to attribute blame through causal chains linking the fate of the victim to the action of a persecutor and the lack of action by a savior. Exploiting the register of anger, and thus violence, this narrative lends itself particularly well to war propaganda. It is, in fact, frequently employed by humanitarian organizations demanding international military intervention to protect civilians—for example by the United Nations or Western governments using the spin of "humanitarian war" to justify the use of force, as did NATO in Kosovo, Afghanistan, and Libya.

By reducing crisis situations to a morality play with a cast of two to four (the victim, the persecutor, the humanitarian, and the savior), the "humanitarian crisis" paradigm makes it possible to both obscure the political (topic of sentiment) and exalt it in its most extreme form—that is, moral war (topic of denunciation). In both these cases, humanitarian actors have a dual role: they are both the mediator, allowing the spectators to feel affected by someone else's suffering, and the experts, attesting to someone's status as victim, persecutor or savior. When confronted with competing victim demands, or denials by persecutors, the humanitarian actor offers an opinion generally considered to be independent and informed. Legitimacy is based on his assumed disinterestedness and impartiality, as well as on the special expertise that allows him to discriminate between "true" and "false" victims, or to assess their "degree of victimization."[16] By counting the dead and the sick, by quantifying the severity of the privation ("dearth," "food crisis," or "famine"), by documenting the psychological or physical trauma, or by characterizing any collective or individual violence (using categories such as "massacres," "ethnic cleansing," and "genocide," or "sexual violence," "torture," and "war wounds"), humanitarians help to objectify the suffering and validate victim, persecutor, or savior status internationally.

Yet, naming the persecutor amounts nowadays to naming the enemy that may need quelling militarily—in accordance with the doctrine of the "responsibility to protect"— or at the very least brought before the International Criminal Court (ICC). Naming the victim means designating the people entitled to unconditional support, no matter what their political trajectory or orientation. The implications of being assigned victim, persecutor, or savior status in the international public space explain the intensity of the controversy that inevitably surrounds humanitarian discourses and assessments.[17]

In these battles over who gets qualified as what, a humanitarian actor may maintain a cooperative, complicit, instrumental, or confrontational relationship with states and political forces looking to disqualify their enemy and claim the moral high ground. They are "cooperative" when humanitarian organizations like Oxfam, for example, commit themselves to help the UN Security Council, and the ICC authenticates victims to protect and persecutors to accuse.[18] They are "complicit" when NATO justifies the Kosovo war using surveys conducted by humanitarian organizations—largely favorable to the intervention—describing the terror and deportation tactics employed by Serb nationalists. They are "instrumental" when armed groups like the Liberation Tigers of Tamil Eelam deliberately expose the population to government fire in the hope that humanitarian actors—pointing to the number of civilian victims—mobilize the media and influential foreign governments to force the Sri Lankan government to give up its offensive. And they are "confrontational" when powers deny causing the suffering the humanitarian organizations blame them for (like the Sri Lankan government) or accuse them of having failed to prevent (like the French government in Rwanda).

The controversial role of humanitarian actors

Though these countless political transactions are the daily bill-of-fare for aid practitioners, they are generally masked by the legal and moral rhetoric of humanitarian discourse. Such interactions are, however, the subject of an abundant institutional and academic literature, focusing primarily on the "perverse effects" of aid. A few isolated essays in the 1980s[19] were followed, in the 1990s, by a wealth of critical studies.[20] The brutal force used by UN troops to deliver relief supplies in Somalia (1992–93), the impotence of aid actors in the face of extermination policies in Rwanda and the Great Lakes (1993–98), the appropriation of humanitarian aid by perpetrators of the Rwandan genocide in Zaire (1994–96), or armed factions in Liberia and Sierra Leone (1990–1997), UN and NGO participation in forced population transfers in the former Yugoslavia (1991–95), and the containment policies of Western governments in the Balkans and Central Africa, where the topic of humanitarian sentiment was used to justify limited engagement to the public; all of these events raise a multiplicity of questions about the roles and responsibilities of humanitarians in armed conflicts, and about what constitutes a fair humanitarian compromise with political powers.

In this regard, at least two conceptions crystallized in the early twenty-first century. The first (sometimes called "new humanitarianisms")[21] asserts that the only acceptable compromise for humanitarian actors is to join the struggle for human rights. In addition to relief work, humanitarians must pressure and help the UN and liberal democracies to neutralize and punish war criminals and build liberal peace for war-torn societies. The second, which for lack of a better term is called "autonomous humanitarianism," argues for the legitimacy of action whose sole aim is to save lives here and now, provided aid operations do not cross the blurry—but very real—line beyond which assistance for victims imperceptibly turns into support for their tormentors. These two concepts constitute the driving forces behind broad currents of thought present to a varying degree within all aid institutions.

The new humanitarianisms: gambling on liberal peace

By the end of the 1990s, the so-called new humanitarianism was subscribed to by the vast majority of officials from NGOs, UN agencies, donors, networks of experts, and academics. This label relied upon a radical critique of aid policies whose sole aim is to save lives. As Michael Barnett and Jack Snyder argue, such assistance programs did not just save lives, "they fueled conflict and repression."[22] On the one hand, material resources brought by humanitarian actors feed the war economy of governments and rebel groups; on the other hand, the topic of sentiment used in the humanitarian narrative by the media masks the political origin of crises and allows "outside states to appear to be doing something about a crisis without having to intervene in more effective ways." In other words, aid staff can prolong suffering although they are supposed to help populations in danger. That is why humanitarian organizations cannot simply treat the symptoms of crises, but must also tackle their "root causes"—or at least pressure Western governments and multilateral institutions to do so.

According to the new humanitarians, the root causes of the 1990s crises were first to be found in the emergence of "new wars."[23] Subscribing to Mary Kaldor's views, most aid officials considered post-Cold War armed conflicts as more absurd and brutal than ever. They were said to be solely motivated by ethnic bigotry and greed, predominantly financed by illegal trade and predation, and killed more civilians than combatants.[24] Hegemonic in the aid world, this view of war as a generalized crime scene led NGOs and UN agencies to advocate a police and judicial approach to conflicts. Through the notion of "protection," the humanitarian agenda thus embraced the fight against impunity, the creation of the International Criminal Court, and support for the responsibility to protect doctrine, enjoining members of the international community of states to use any means, including the use of military force under a modified just war doctrine, to stop serious violations of international law in states declared failing or criminal.

This punitive paradigm was complemented by a revolutionary one, according to which armed conflicts were also the symptom of dysfunctional societies, incapable of self-regulation. Hence, "tackling the root causes of humanitarian crises" meant profound transformation of institutions, behavior, and mind-sets in order to foster the respect for human rights and economic development in dysfunctional societies. [25]

As Mark Duffield points out, this enlargement of the humanitarian agenda to punitive and revolutionary ambitions coincided, in the late 1990s, with a redefinition of the security concerns of liberal states. After the fall of the Berlin Wall, conflicts and instability on the peripheries of the North were considered fertile ground for the proliferation of global threats (migration, refugee influx, pandemics, transnational crime, terrorism, impediments to international trade). The transformation of war-torn societies into stable, representative states became the goal of more ambitious development policies, advocated at the turn of the twenty-first century by the World Bank, the Organisation for Economic Co-operation and Development (OECD), the European Union, and many foreign aid ministries such as Britain's Department for International Development (DfID) or the US Agency for International Development (USAID).[26] NGOs were seen as a preferred instrument for this "transformational diplomacy,"[27] especially as mediators with crisis-riddled societies being asked to adopt—via participatory methods—the market democracy model. Like Claire Short, the British Minister for International Development from 1997 to 2003, donors encouraged humanitarian organizations to "work with states and international organizations that are seeking to establish a democratic, law-abiding, rights-observing, market-oriented, economically rational state that provides improved conditions for all of its citizens."[28]

It thus became difficult for NGOs to "separate their own development and humanitarian activities from the pervasive logic of the North's new security regime."[29] The growth of new humanitarianisms was accompanied by a proliferation of armed international interventions. Military operations officially aimed at protecting civilians in Kosovo (1999), East Timor (1999), and Sierra Leone (2000) were followed by the invasions of Afghanistan (2001) and Iraq (2003). UN peace operations also grew, as their mandates became ever broader, including monitoring ceasefires, distributing humanitarian aid, disarming and reintegrating former combatants, repatriating IDPs and refugees, holding elections, reforming armies and national police forces, restructuring judicial institutions and public services, developing market economies, promoting good governance, and defending human and women's rights, among other things.

With the exception of Iraq, where European and American NGOs were divided about the legitimacy to go to war, the vast majority of humanitarian organizations aligned themselves with international forces and participated in peacebuilding policies steered from New York or Washington—in Kosovo, East Timor, Sierra Leone, Afghanistan, the DRC, Sudan, and elsewhere. While the abundance of institutional funding was certainly an inducement, humanitarians also believed they were contributing to the "only truly humanitarian objective—hastening the end of a war" and "replacing a murderous regime with a civilized government as quickly as possible," in the words of former humanitarian volunteer Michael Barry, at the height of the new humanitarianism, when the Taliban fell in Afghanistan in 2001.[30]

Aside from the International Committee of the Red Cross (ICRC) and a handful of NGOs, at the turn of the twenty-first century humanitarian organizations had solidified an alliance with the liberal democracies and the UN based on common goals: neutralizing and punishing war criminals as well as establishing a liberal peace in dysfunctional societies torn apart by "new wars." That alliance appeared to be the only possible response to the dilemmas posed by humanitarian action's inescapable involvement in the murky waters of national and international politics. This privileged partnership was not without its tensions, however. Humanitarian organizations alternately reproached the Western governments for neglecting them when allocating funding, failing to devote enough military resources to peacebuilding,[31] or refusing to get involved in countries where their national interests were not directly at stake.[32]

Autonomous humanitarianism or the policy of survival

Though widely supportive of the new humanitarianism during the Cold War,[33] Médecins Sans Frontières was among the organizations that began to distance itself from it in the mid-1990s. Seeing conflicts as the continuation of politics by other means, rather than as a generalized crime or dysfunction, senior MSF leaders considered the project of transforming war-torn societies in the image of market democracies as a sort of revolutionary messianism.[34] Not only was the latter rooted in a colonial belief in the West's "civilizing mission," it also reflected a hubristic confidence in all-powerful human control over society—"the shared faith and universal illusion of modern societies," in the words of Raymond Aron, who saw it as the source of the "excessive ambitions from which totalitarian regimes emerge."[35] The limited success of UN peace operations and the Afghanistan and Iraq invasions in achieving their objectives at least showed that the liberal peace project was riskier and more costly—in terms of human lives—than their supporters acknowledged.[36]

The new humanitarianism's infatuation with criminal justice and humanitarian interventions was also criticized. As one MSF representative commented, "a faction head in Congo, or an American officer in Afghanistan, indeed all those who might have a concern, founded or not, that they may one day have to account for their actions in front of a court, will see in the provision of the ICC a powerful incentive to remove any humanitarian presence."[37] The ICC Prosecutor and the NGOs supporting his action called explicitly for humanitarian organizations to provide information to help him determine the appropriateness of launching an investigation and preparing the cases.[38]

Coupled with this controversy was a fierce criticism of the intrinsic virtues of the international criminal justice system,[39] as well as of the responsibility to protect.[40] Empirical data about foreign interventions conducted in Kosovo, Sierra Leone, Timor, and Libya showed that deploying armed forces and protecting civilians were two different things. Offering military protection is an act of war in its own right, which means engaging in hostilities without any certainty of success or of avoiding a bloodbath for civilian populations. No technical or legal riposte to the violence of war can ensure that populations who are supposed to be helped will actually be protected and assisted. The calling for the military protection of a population signals the desire for a "just war" and the advent through violence of a new political order: an undertaking that always has uncertain outcomes and which inevitably creates victims among the people it is trying to save.

Under these conditions, proponents of autonomous humanitarianism demand the legitimacy of impartial relief action whose goal, limited in appearance, is not to police or resolve conflicts but to make sure they cost the fewest human lives possible.[41] In support of this policy of survival, they reaffirm a commitment to neutrality, which is understood as a refusal to take part in hostilities or to pronounce judgment on the legitimacy of the objectives pursued by the belligerents (including those intervening on behalf of the responsibility to protect doctrine). In accordance with classical humanitarian tradition, autonomous humanitarianism believes this is a necessary condition to asserting a position as a third party to the conflict, and to being tolerated by all the existing forces.

Proponents acknowledge, however, that their approach has limits. There is always a risk of "rotten compromise," in which the material and symbolic resources that aid actors bring to the political arena are used against the population whom they are intended to help. This is why humanitarian workers must demand a minimum freedom of action and assessment (the freedom to move about and communicate with the population, and to plan and monitor their operations), to ensure that their action is not completely diverted from its objective. If they are unable to keep the diversion within acceptable limits by mobilizing a variety of political support—from the most local to the most global sources—they must abstain.

This is what happened in October 1998, for instance, when MSF decided to withdraw from North Korea—then in the grips of a severe famine—citing "the impossibility of assessing needs with complete independence and controlling the proper distribution of food."[42] It lambasted donors, accusing them of approving the diversions as part of a strategy to stabilize North Korea rather than "supporting the humanitarian organizations in their efforts to gain real access to the victims." And that was not the only confrontation with power. By 1985 MSF had already been expelled from Ethiopia for protesting against the use of food relief operations in a particularly murderous strategy of forced population transfer. In April 1997, the organization suspended its activities in eastern Zaire, denouncing the use of humanitarian actors by the army of the new Rwandan regime and its Congolese allies as bait to localize, and then massacre, fleeing groups of refugees. In each of these three situations, MSF felt that without a significant change in aid practices and the political framework in which they were implemented, abstaining was preferable to action.

The organization's position during the Rwandan genocide reflected a noticeably different logic. In June 1994, MSF made the unusual decision to call for international military intervention against the perpetrators of "the planned, methodical extermination of a community." In this case, it was not a matter of condemning the use of aid against its intended beneficiaries, but of pointing out that humanitarian workers were virtually powerless to save lives, so broad and systematic was the killing. The severity of the exterminatory practices justified setting humanitarian logic aside and taking a chance on war. Yet foreign powers refused, using the presence of international organizations to assuage public opinion while denying that the massacres were genocide. MSF's 1994 call to arms is seen as an exception, justified by the extreme severity of the violence and its minimization in the public sphere. It underlines the fact that, for the organization, saving lives is not just a matter of material assistance but sometimes requires exposing or qualifying serious violence and getting it onto the international agenda.

In fact, while autonomous humanitarianism is critical of the new humanitarianism's punitive and revolutionary aspirations, it agrees that publicly exposing government and rebel group conduct is essential to establishing a balance of power with the authorities, without which it is generally impossible to deploy effective relief operations and contain the violence of war. The fact that the brutality of the Chechen (1991–2003) and Algerian (1992–2002) conflicts never became international political issues is partly to blame for the intense violence against non-combatants and the marginality, even absence, of relief operations, commented MSF in 2003.[43]

Yet deciding the circumstances in which action becomes complicit prompts heated debate. Such discussions revolve around one central question: To whom are humanitarian actors most useful—the victims, or their persecutors? Are humanitarian relief workers in the right place helping the right people, and are they doing what the standards of their profession demand? Why do the authorities tolerate their presence? What are they getting out of it? Which national and international sources of support are humanitarian actors likely to mobilize when they engage in the public space? These are the kinds of questions guiding the decision to continue, confront, or withdraw.

Conclusion

The "shrinking space" discourse reflects in reality the failure of new humanitarianism— not just to achieve its goal of liberal peacebuilding, but even to save lives. This double setback is helping restore some degree of popularity to autonomous humanitarianism within the aid community. It would be a mistake, however, to imagine that the latter is based on the search for a space safe from all political influence. On the contrary, autonomous humanitarian actors accept themselves as full-fledged political actors whose specific agenda is not to govern or to police societies, but to ensure the survival of the greatest number of people through war times and disasters. As such, they need to alternately engage in cooperative and confrontational relationships with states, international organizations, and non-state players, bearing in mind the risks of "rotten compromise."[44]

With the liberal democracies and the United Nations—upon whom they relied during the last 50 years—going to war, humanitarian actors are now being forced to diversify their diplomatic and political support. One of their main current challenges is to distance themselves equally from the liberal imperialism of their societies of origin and the sovereign despotism of many of the countries in which they intervene.

Additional reading

1. Michael Barnett and Thomas G. Weiss, eds., *Humanitarianism in Question: Politics, Power, Ethics* (Ithaca: Cornell University Press, 2008).
2. Mark Duffield, *Global Governance and the New Wars: The Merging of Development and Security* (London: Zed Books, 2001).
3. Michel Feher, ed., *Nongovernmental Politics* (New York: Zone Books, 2007).
4. Claire Magone, Michaël Neuman, and Fabrice Weissman, eds., *Humanitarian Negotiations Revealed: The MSF Experience* (London: Hurst & Co, 2011).
5. Fiona Terry, *Condemned to Repeat? The Paradox of Humanitarian Action* (Ithaca: Cornell University Press, 2002).
6. Thomas G. Weiss, *Humanitarian Business* (Cambridge: Polity Press, 2013).

Notes

1 See, for example, Bernie Doyle, Raouf Mazou, and Vicky Tennant, *Safeguarding Humanitarian Space: A Review of Key Challenges for UNHCR* (Geneva: UNHCR Policy Development and Evaluation Service, 2010) and OCHA, "Analysis: Humanitarian Action Under Siege," IRIN (1 August 2009), http://www.irinnews.org/report.aspx?reportid=85752.

2 On the crisis of confidence of humanitarian actors, see Michael Barnett and Thomas G. Weiss, "Humanitarianism: A Brief History of the Present," in *Humanitarianism in Question: Politics, Power, Ethics*, eds. Michael Barnett and Thomas G. Weiss (Ithaca: Cornell University Press, 2008), 1–48.

3 Don Hubert and Cynthia Brassard-Boudreau, "Shrinking Humanitarian Space? Trends and Prospects on Security and Access," *Journal of Humanitarian Assistance*, 24 November 2010, http://sites.tufts.edu/jha/archives/863.

4 Abū Muhammad al-Maqdisī, *Waqafat me'a themerat al-jihad (An Appraisal of the Fruits of Jihad)*, Rabi' Al-Thani 1425 AH (July 2004, Qefqefa prison), cited in Fred Burton and Scott Stewart, "Jihadist Ideology and the Targeting of Humanitarian Aid Workers," *STRATFOR Global Intelligence* (22 October 2008), http://www.stratfor.com/weekly/20081022_jihadist_ideology_and_targeting_humanitarian_aid_workers.

5 Dorothea Hilhorst and Bram J. Jansen, "Humanitarian Space as Arena: A Perspective on the Everyday Politics of Aid," *Development and Change* 41, no. 6 (2010): 1117–1139.

6 François Jean, "Aide humanitaire et économie de guerre," in *Economie des Guerres Civiles*, eds. François Jean and Jean-Christophe Rufin (Paris: Hachette Littérature, 1996), 543–589.

7 Michel Agier, *Managing the Undesirables: Refugee Camps and Humanitarian Government* (Malden: Polity Press, 2011).

8 Fiona Terry, *Condemned to Repeat? The Paradox of Humanitarian Action* (Ithaca: Cornell University Press, 2002), 155–215.

9 Clea Kahn, *Conflict, Arms, and Militarization: The Dynamics of Darfur's IDP Camps* (Geneva: Small Arms Survey, 2008).

10 Claire Magone, Michaël Neuman, and Fabrice Weissman, *Humanitarian Negotiations Revealed: The MSF Experience* (London: Hurst & Co, 2011), 23–49.

11 Geert Gompelman, *Winning Hearts and Minds? Examining the Relationship between Aid and Security in Afghanistan's Faryab Province* (Boston: Feinstein International Center, Tufts University, 2011).

12 Mark Duffield and John Prendergast, *Without Troops & Tanks: The Emergency Relief Desk and the Cross Border Operation into Eritrea and Tigray* (Lawrenceville, NJ: Red Sea Press, 1994).

13 Karen Büscher and Koen Vlassenroot, "Humanitarian Presence and Urban Development: New Opportunities and Contrasts in Goma, DRC," *Disasters* 34, Supplement s2 (2010): 256–273.

14 René Backmann and Rony Brauman, *Les Médias et l'humanitaire* (Paris: Victoires, 1998).

15 Luc Boltanski, *Distant Suffering: Morality, Media and Politics* (Cambridge: Cambridge University Press, 1999).

16 Sandrine Lefranc and Lilian Mathieu, eds., *Mobilisations des victimes* (Rennes: Presses Universitaires de Rennes, 2009).

17 Marc Le Pape, Johanna Siméant, and Claudine Vidal, eds., *Crises extrêmes: Face aux Massacres, aux guerres civiles et aux génocides* (Paris: Editions La Découverte, 2006).

18 Oxfam, *Note on the International Criminal Court* (Oxford: Oxfam International Policy Compendium, 2007), and Oxfam, *Protection of Civilians in 2010: Facts, Figures, and the UN Security Council's Response* (Oxford: Briefing Paper, 2010).

19 William Shawcross, *The Quality of Mercy: Cambodia, Holocaust and Modern Conscience* (New York: Simon & Schuster, 1984); François Jean, *Éthiopie, du bon usage de la famine* (Paris: Médecins Sans Frontières, 1986); and Jean-Christophe Rufin, *Le Piège: Quand l'Aide humanitaire remplace la guerre* (Paris: Jean-Claude Lattes, 1986).

20 Among the most influential academic works are David Keen, *The Benefits of Famine: A Political Economy of Famine and Relief in Southwestern Sudan, 1983–1989* (Princeton: Princeton University Press, 1994); Mary B. Anderson, *Do No Harm: How Aid Can Support Peace—Or War* (Boulder: Lynne Rienner, 1999); and Terry, *Condemned to Repeat*.

21 Fiona Fox, "New Humanitarianism: Does It Provide a Moral Banner for the 21st Century?," *Disasters* 25, no. 4 (2001): 275–289.

22 Michael Barnett and Jack Snyder, "The Grand Strategies of Humanitarianism," in *Humanitarianism in Question*, eds. Barnett and Weiss, 148.

23 Mary Kaldor, *New and Old Wars* (Stanford, CA: Stanford University Press, 1999).

24 Roland Marchal and Christine Messiant, "Les Guerres civiles à l'ère de la globalisation: Nouvelles Réalités et nouveaux paradigmes," *Critique Internationale* 18 (2003): 91–112.

25 Mark Duffield, *Global Governance and the New Wars: The Merging of Development and Security* (London: Zed Books, 2001), 22–43.

26 Ibid.

27 In the words of former US Secretary of State Condoleezza Rice, "Transformational Diplomacy," *Comments Delivered at Georgetown University*, 18 January 2006, http://merln.ndu.edu/archivepdf/nss/state/59306.pdf.

28 Cited in Barnett and Snyder, "The Grand Strategies," 151.

29 Duffield, *Global Governance*, 16.

30 Michael Barry, "L'Humanitaire n'est jamais neutre," *Libération*, 6 November 2001.

31 In Afghanistan, for example, NGOs have called for strengthening NATO troops "so that democracy can flourish" (International Council of Voluntary Agencies, "Afghanistan: A Call for Security," 17 June 2003), then for a redirection of foreign funding to them because there are "links between development and security," and by their activities they contribute to "stability in the country" (International Council of Voluntary Agencies Report, "Falling Short: Aid Effectiveness in Afghanistan," 28 March 2008).

32 Oxfam, *Protection of Civilians*, 28.

33 Magone, Neuman, and Weissman, *Humanitarian Negotiations Revealed*, 233–262.

34 Rony Brauman, "Les Nouveaux Lénines de l'humanitaire," *Alternatives Internationales*, June 2011, http://www.alternatives-internationales.fr/les-nouveaux-lenines-de-l-humanitaire_fr_art_1095_54590.html.

35 Raymond Aron, *Essai sur les libertés* (Paris: Hachette, Pluriel, 1998), 41–42 and 213–214.

36 Jean-Hervé Bradol, "The Sacrificial International Order and Humanitarian Action," in *In the Shadow of Just Wars: Humanitarian Action, Violence, and Politics*, ed. Fabrice Weissman (London: Hurst & Co, 2004), 1–22.

37 Éric Dachy, "Justice and Humanitarian Action: A Conflict of Interest," in *In the Shadow of Just Wars*, ed. Weissman, 318.

38 International Coalition for the ICC, "The Role of NGOs," http://www.iccnow.org/?mod=roleofngos.

39 Fabrice Weissman, "Humanitarian Aid and the International Criminal Court: Grounds for Divorce," *Making Sense of Sudan*, http://africanarguments.org/2009/07/20/humanitarian-aid-and-the-international-criminal-court-grounds-for-divorce-1/, July 2009.

40 Fabrice Weissman, "Not in Our Name: Why Médecins Sans Frontières Does Not Support the 'Responsibility to Protect,'" *Criminal Justice Ethics* 29, no. 2 (2010): 194–207.

41 "Autonomous humanitarianism" is not common parlance in the aid world, but rather the way that we have chosen to designate a general notion of humanitarian action that contrasts with the "new humanitarianism," and which has been championed by most Médecins Sans Frontières leaders since the 1990s, along with a few analysts such as David Rieff, *A Bed for the Night: Humanitarianism in Crisis* (New York: Simon & Schuster, 2002).

42 Philippe Biberson, "L'Aide humanitaire paralysée," *Le Figaro*, 14 October 1998.

43 Bradol, "The Sacrificial International Order," 29.

44 Michel Feher, ed., *Nongovernmental Politics* (New York: Zone Books, 2007).

Post-conflict Peacebuilding

Rob Jenkins

Post-conflict peacebuilding, at its core, is about preventing the recurrence of widespread and systematic violence. It is, in that sense, a subset of the conflict-prevention sector within the wider security field. How exactly to build peace, which actors should be most centrally involved, and the most appropriate timeframe for ensuring durable results are among the many hotly debated questions associated with the theory and practice of peacebuilding.

Before addressing these issues, however, a number of conceptual ambiguities need clarifying, which is where this chapter begins. The remainder of the chapter undertakes three analytical tasks. First, it traces the evolution of the idea of peacebuilding and the real-world environment in which it takes place, paying special attention to the relationship between the two. Second, the chapter outlines several key debates concerning the practice of peacebuilding, arguing that many of the most contentious issues have persisted over time. Third, the chapter highlights emerging challenges arising from the changing international context in which the rebuilding of war-torn states must increasingly be pursued.

Clearing the conceptual ground

In theory, peacebuilding can refer to measures taken before the initial outbreak of violence, rather than just those designed to prevent its recurrence—hence the "post-conflict" qualifier in the title of this chapter. In practice, however, it has been focused on rebuilding after war. Thus, in both academic and practitioner discourse, the label almost always refers to post-conflict peacebuilding.

Associating peacebuilding—explicitly or implicitly—with post-conflict activity does not, however, specify the point in the post-conflict period when peacebuilding begins. Is it after a *de facto* cessation of hostilities? Or following the signing of a comprehensive peace agreement? Or after the departure of peacekeepers? A 2008 review of gaps in the international community's approach to rebuilding failed states acknowledged a continued lack of clarity as to the period covered by post-conflict peacebuilding: "The term . . . is used in two ways—either to refer to the entire post-conflict exercise, or to refer to the post-peacekeeping phase." The report recommended that this ambiguity be overcome by using the term "early recovery" and "late recovery" to refer to different phases of the post-conflict period—a convention that has been adopted unevenly at best.[1]

Peacebuilding, moreover, may refer to the consolidation of peace following conflict between or within countries, though as a practical matter the term is used mainly with respect to civil war. The difference has substantive implications. Priority actions following an internal conflict often differ from those arising in the aftermath of an interstate war. When a country's institutions of governance have failed to accommodate political divisions, particularly when these reflect ethnic or religious differences, the perceived need to overhaul the state is generally stronger than in countries that have suffered casualties and physical damage at the hands of a rival state.

Peacebuilding is also a term that may or may not assume the involvement of external actors in the process of reconstruction. Thus, *international* peacebuilding is technically a subset of a larger phenomenon. In practice, it tends to imply considerable engagement by foreign governments, multilateral institutions, and international nongovernmental organizations (INGOs), though the roles they can legitimately play are almost always a matter of contention. Michael Barnett and coauthors argue that peacebuilding is "generically understood as *external* interventions that are intended to reduce the risk that a state will erupt into or return to war."[2]

Finally, it is important to distinguish peacebuilding from various cognate concepts. It is related to but distinct from peacekeeping, a term far better known to the public, but one which, like peacebuilding, does not appear in the UN Charter. Peacekeeping, invented in the late 1940s and early 1950s, was justified as an implied power deriving from the Security Council's Chapter VII mandate to address threats to international peace and security. While peacekeeping traditionally centered on monitoring ceasefires and disarming and demobilizing combatants, peacebuilding ranges well beyond narrowly defined security issues to encompass matters of economic development and institution building. Indeed, it was when peace agreements began to become far more complex, necessitating the emergence of so-called "multidimensional peacekeeping operations," that a more specified field of endeavor, known as peacebuilding, entered the official discourse.

Peacebuilding can also be distinguished from state building, though in some quarters the terms are used interchangeably. A 2008 paper commissioned by the Organisation for Economic Co-operation and Development (OECD) declared that "state building is not peacebuilding." It conceded, however, that "state building is likely to be a central element of [efforts] . . . to institutionalise peace."[3] Restoring state authority and creating effective bureaucracies are seen as necessary but not sufficient preconditions for lasting peace. However, one could also argue that state building is a task beyond peacebuilding. Benjamin Reilly, for instance, claims that over the past 20 years "the focus of most UN missions has shifted from one of *pure* peacebuilding to one of state rebuilding."[4]

Peacebuilding is also distinct from the idea of "human security." Both attempt to transcend divisions separating the development and security fields. In fact, John Cockell defines peacebuilding as "a sustained process of preventing internal threats to human security from causing protracted, violent conflict."[5] Human security, which rose to popularity when it featured in the 1994 *Human Development Report*,[6] represents two conceptual shifts. The first concerns the unit of analysis—away from the vulnerability of nations and governments and toward the protection of individuals and social groups. The second concerns the nature of the threats faced—not just protection from organized armed aggression, but also reduced exposure to famine and pollution, as well as to such actors as drug traffickers and business oligopolies. The process of peacebuilding may, but need not, adopt these new perspectives.

Conceptual and institutional development

The first definitive statement on peacebuilding was UN Secretary-General Boutros Boutros-Ghali's 1992 *An Agenda for Peace*, which referred to "post-conflict peacebuilding" as "action to identify and support structures which will tend to strengthen and solidify peace in order to avoid a relapse into conflict."[7] The precise types of action might vary from case to case, but the repertoire would include reforming security services to place them under civilian control; disarming, demobilizing, and reintegrating soldiers; restoring basic services; and ensuring justice for victims of human rights abuses.

It was no accident that the international community of states became preoccupied with rebuilding post-war states around this time. The end of the Cold War had precipitated conflict in parts of the former Soviet Union (such as Azerbaijan), as well as the disintegration of several one-time Soviet client states (such as Ethiopia). The United Nations also appeared ready to act in a more robust and unified way in places of long-standing strife, such as Cambodia and Namibia. The time for a doctrine, however vaguely stated, had arrived.

Over the subsequent decade, the idea of peacebuilding continued to evolve alongside efforts to reconstruct post-conflict countries. The influence between theory and practice was mutual. Among the real-world cases that crucially affected the progressive elaboration of peacebuilding doctrine was the international community's 1994 failure to prevent genocide in Rwanda. While the Rwandan tragedy is sometimes portrayed as a failure of peacekeeping, or an act of political cowardice, it also represented a failure of the many international actors working to enhance local capacities for managing conflict. Rwanda's genocide was a recrudescence, in more extreme form, of ethnic bloodletting that had erupted periodically since the country became independent. Clearly, the rebuilding that had taken place following each episode had been insufficiently attentive to the root causes of violent conflict. The Rwandan case underlined the need for long-term peacebuilding.

It was partly in response to Rwanda—as well as to the huge challenges facing the UN as the Bosnian conflict wound down—that Boutros-Ghali's definition of peacebuilding was refined in the 1995 "Supplement" to *An Agenda for Peace*. The updated version stressed that the development of national institutions and the capacity to operate them impartially were necessary if peace was to withstand the disruptions that arise in the life of any society.[8] Its central premise was also taken up by scholars such as Michael Doyle and Nicholas Sambanis, whose seminal 2000 article stated that, "[i]n plural societies, conflicts are inevitable. The aim of peacebuilding is to foster social, economic, and political institutions and attitudes that will prevent these conflicts from turning violent."[9]

By this time, it was widely accepted that peacebuilding was less about post-war "reconstruction" and more about longer-term measures to construct the social, economic, and political foundations of lasting peace. Practitioners increasingly moved beyond immediate technical problems, such as a lack of physical, administrative, or economic infrastructure, to a more political approach of engaging with parties to conflict and addressing grievances such as developmental imbalances or political exclusion. This was reflected in a report produced in 2000 by a panel of experts tasked by Secretary-General Kofi Annan with assessing the performance of UN peace operations. What came to be known as the "Brahimi Report" (named for panel chair Lakhdar Brahimi, former foreign minister of Algeria and UN troubleshooter) defined peacebuilding as "activities undertaken on the far side of conflict to reassemble the foundations of peace and provide the tools for building on those foundations something that is more than just the absence of war."[10]

Barnett and coauthors argue that the term peacebuilding took root among official agencies during the 1990s and early 2000s because it represented the kind of seemingly neutral concept around which the appearance of consensus could be built. Indeed, in the two decades since *An Agenda for Peace* endorsed the idea of peacebuilding, its definition has been modified to suit changing circumstances as well as the bureaucratic imperatives and political interests of a variety of actors, including UN agencies, bilateral aid programs, nongovernmental organizations, and former warring parties themselves. As they put it, "[t]he willingness of so many diverse constituencies with divergent and sometimes conflicting interests to rally around peacebuilding also suggests that one of the concept's talents is to camouflage divisions over how to handle the postconflict challenge."[11] Others argue that "[i]n the UN context, the term peacebuilding clearly won the competition against the terms 'state-building' and 'nation-building,' which many regard as less politically acceptable because they convey greater intrusiveness and a broader political mandate."[12] They claim that some members of the High-level Panel on Threats, Challenges and Change (HLP) "would have preferred the term 'state-building' . . . [but] ended up favoring the term 'peacebuilding' for the very reason that it was more acceptable politically."[13]

It was, in fact, the desire to address the fragmented institutional environment for undertaking peacebuilding that led the HLP to recommend the creation of a new UN "peacebuilding architecture." The panel's recommendations were then repackaged and elaborated upon in Annan's 2005 manifesto for UN reform, *In Larger Freedom*. It argued that a Peacebuilding Commission, supported by a small administrative entity, was necessary to fill "a gaping hole in the United Nations institutional machinery: no part of the United Nations system effectively addresses the challenge of helping countries with the transition from war to lasting peace."[14]

The *Outcome Document* of the 2005 World Summit in New York endorsed creating the Peacebuilding Commission (PBC), more or less along the lines outlined in *In Larger Freedom*, but without a mandate to engage in "early warning" activities. "Pre-conflict" peacebuilding would be placed beyond the new commission's mandate. Three months later, in December 2005, Security Council Resolution 1645 and General Assembly

Resolution 60/180, which were identically worded, were passed. The PBC would be an intergovernmental body consisting of 31 member states, which would serve two-year terms, and be drawn from five functional and organizational constituencies: seven members from the Security Council (including all five of the council's permanent members); seven from the General Assembly; seven from the Economic and Social Council (ECOSOC); five from among the top ten contributors of troops to UN peace operations; and five from the top ten financial contributors to UN peace operations.

The PBC held its inaugural meeting in June 2006 and was expected to have its greatest impact in its various country-specific configurations, through which it deliberates on individual post-conflict countries placed on its agenda. There are several routes through which a country can find itself on the PBC's agenda, but in practice it requires the consent of the country concerned, PBC members, and the Security Council. All 31 PBC members are permitted to participate in all CSCs (country-specific configurations). Other member states are invited to join in CSC deliberations—states that PBC members consider likely to enhance the proceedings, because of their recent experience recovering from conflict or close ties with (including geographic proximity to) the post-conflict country under consideration. CSCs may also include, as deemed necessary, regional and sub-regional bodies and international financial institutions. A standing invitation to CSC meetings is extended to the senior representative of the UN field presence in the country concerned. Improving coordination is the PBC's primary function.

The PBC is supported administratively by a small Peacebuilding Support Office (PBSO), located organizationally within the Executive Office of the Secretary-General. The PBSO's creation was formally authorized by the same December 2005 resolutions that established the PBC. It is headed by an assistant secretary-general for peacebuilding support. The PBSO does not have an operational mandate, meaning that it does not normally have field staff and does not manage or implement programs as part of UN missions. Instead, the PBSO, in addition to servicing the intergovernmental process, is supposed to serve as the UN's repository of best practice in the area of post-conflict peacebuilding. It was expected to perform this function by organizing consultations and facilitating the systematic exchange of insights and information between policy analysts and program implementers within and beyond the UN system.

The PBC's founding resolutions also created a standing Peacebuilding Fund (PBF). The fund is based on voluntary contributions. The fund's establishment was motivated by a desire to prevent disruptions in funding that typically occur when a country moves beyond the humanitarian-response stage, but has not yet consolidated state authority sufficiently to allow large volumes of donor funding to reach the places, people, and institutions that need it. Of particular concern were the often slow and cumbersome procedures required to establish and operate country-level multi-donor trust funds, which tend to be managed by either the World Bank or the UNDP on behalf of contributing donors. The PBF was therefore expected to respond to changing conditions on the ground; to fill "critical peacebuilding gaps"; to disburse funds quickly; and to prioritize catalytic interventions—those that can kickstart dormant processes and attract longer-term donor support. A target of $250 million was specified for this standing fund.

The three institutional components of the "new peacebuilding architecture"—the PBC, the PBSO, and the PBF—were conceived as a package and ostensibly dedicated to a common endeavor. In practical terms, however, to label them a new "architecture" for peacebuilding—implying the existence of a functional system—is a bit of a stretch. The architectural metaphor implies a definite plan, based on sound structural engineering, whereas the foundation on which the UN's new peacebuilding architecture (PBA) has been constructed is fundamentally unstable. While the PBA is new, it rests atop an existing, at times precarious, substratum of organizations and a history of partially implemented institutional reforms. The PBA is just one element in a much larger organizational universe. Its creators' insistence that it would be the new peacebuilding architecture, rather than an additional piece to an existing and perpetually in flux peacebuilding landscape, was meant to signal a definitive break with the fragmented approach of the past. Yet, the precise mandate of each of the PBA's institutional components and the division of responsibility among them have been sources of continuous disagreement.

Current debates

Despite the creation of a new UN peacebuilding architecture, current controversies in the field of peacebuilding are in many respects the same as those that have dominated discussions since the 1992 appearance of *An Agenda for Peace*. A perennial concern is the appropriate role for international actors—both formal multilateral bodies and the network of nongovernmental organizations that provide a great deal of the support on which effective reconstruction relies. Governments of post-conflict countries frequently complain that external actors are driven by their own agendas. States with a foreign policy interest in the country or region concerned, it is argued, are focused on enhancing their strategic position. As the world's pre-eminent military and economic power, the United States often typifies this syndrome, but the British, French, and other governments are seen as pursuing similar methods. Even relatively well-intentioned donor governments are regarded as prioritizing the issues on which they have developed particular capacities. If, for instance, a Nordic donor has developed a rapid-reaction capacity to assist in the development of truth and reconciliation processes, its aid agencies will press hard for seeing its resources put to that use, regardless of whether this is a priority for domestic actors on the ground.

That external actors are a welcome, often necessary, complement to domestic efforts at rebuilding peace in the aftermath of war is not at issue. But there is a general sense among senior government officials in conflict-torn countries that external assistance is less geared than it should be to building up "national capacities" to undertake such crucial tasks as operating public expenditure management systems and delivering public services. While training and "capacity-building" programs abound, often they are instituted too late or target the wrong staff.

Complaints of donor-driven agendas in the peace-consolidation process parallel charges found in the wider development assistance field. The need to promote "national ownership" of peacebuilding strategies is a constant point of debate among practitioners at almost every level of international engagement. One aspect of debates over national ownership concerns the role of local and national NGOs (and INGOs). Absent a capable state apparatus, NGOs often undertake functions customarily performed by government agencies. In many countries, without prodding and logistical support from NGOs, crucial peacebuilding activities, such as opening and operating schools for former child soldiers, would not have taken place.

A related debate concerns the extent to which peacebuilding should embrace a wide-reaching agenda or be relatively compact. Which direction a given country case goes can depend in part on the extent of physical, social, and institutional devastation wrought by the war. This, in turn, may reflect the conflict's duration, the diversity of actors involved, whether access to natural resources was a motive or means (or both) for prosecuting the war. Another crucial determinant of the breadth of the peacebuilding agenda is the character of the post-conflict country's external relations—with its immediate neighbors, its military allies, its donors, and its former colonial powers, among others. Perhaps the most influential factor is the degree to which—in that particular case, at that particular moment—the international community regards state rebuilding as essential.

Whether or not one's definition of peacebuilding incorporates state building is, as noted earlier, a major fault-line running through the peacebuilding field. Roland Paris and Tim Sisk argue that "[s]tatebuilding—the construction of legitimate, effective governmental institutions—is a crucial element in any larger effort to create the conditions for a durable peace." In the absence of such institutions, "postconflict societies are much less likely to escape the dual 'traps' of violence and poverty."[15] Unfortunately, the meaning of state building is just as contested as the meaning of peacebuilding. A minimalist conception of the state includes recognition by other states, an ability to exercise control over a given territory, and a monopoly over the legitimate use of force. A maximalist position, on the other hand, can encompass a much more ambitious set of objectives. Ashraf Ghani and Clare Lockhart identify ten functions associated with statehood, and therefore the state-building project.[16] These include a willingness and ability to manage public funds, to act as stewards of national culture and natural resources, to invest in citizens (and indeed to define the rights and obligations of citizenship itself), and to encourage the development of markets. Most conceptions of statehood fall somewhere between these extremes.

The rise of peacebuilding as a concept during the past two decades partly reflected "the international community's embrace of what Linz and Stepan labeled the 'democratic Zeitgeist' of the post-cold war era."[17] During the 1990s, the democratic peace thesis was effectively extended from the international to the intra-national plane. It was Boutros-Ghali himself who stated that democratic governments, because of their superior claims to legitimacy, "were less likely to have domestic conflicts," in addition to being less inclined toward interstate war.

There has been considerable criticism of the "liberal peacebuilding agenda," which is based on the premise that sustainable peacebuilding requires, and therefore should prioritize, the creation of democratic states and market-based economies. One concern has been the degree to which the liberal agenda is externally imposed, the hasty manner in which it may be pursued, or the emphasis on private sector development that, in practice, often underlies its implementation. Another line of complaint stresses that building sustainable peace requires more attention to state consolidation than to the type of state being consolidated. The preoccupation of Western aid donors and INGOs with human rights is sometimes seen as counterproductive, for instance. For fledgling states emerging from prolonged conflicts, the urgent need is to pacify groups that threaten the state's capacity to penetrate society, to control its borders, and to secure a monopoly over the use of force—a process which, historically, European states accomplished with scant regard for human rights.[18]

A variant of this critique is Paris' account of peacebuilding, *At War's End*,[19] which concludes that the international community has been excessively concerned with rushing toward political and economic liberalization. Paris is in good company, his views chiming with those of authors such as Benjamin Reilly, who argues that hasty elections produce poor outcomes.[20] Cambodia is often held up as an example not to be emulated. One study found that hasty early decisions on the structure of democratic institutions in Cambodia had long-lasting political effects.[21] But Paris is not without his detractors. Charles Call and Elizabeth Cousens contend that Paris uses an unreasonably "ambitious standard" for "success,"[22] classifying Namibia and Mozambique as the only successful cases in his sample. A more fundamental shortcoming is that economic and political liberalization were less intensive or extensive than Paris claims. No systematic cross-national evidence is supplied to justify the classification of post-conflict economic recovery programs as extremely "market-oriented." In fact, the legacy of conflict in some countries meant that there was little or no state to scale back. This naturally reoriented donors toward building state capacity, implying a *de facto* increase in size of government. It is also doubtful whether, in the cases Paris analyses, policy and institutional reforms were implemented as thoroughly as his conclusions assume.

Key criticisms and emerging issues

As the long-standing and potentially irresolvable debates outlined thus far indicate, the international community's approach to post-conflict peacebuilding has been the subject of persistent criticism, for both its conceptual inconsistencies and severe shortcomings in implementation. However, the fallout from these criticisms, and the nature of the responses by international actors, is increasingly being shaped by trends of far-reaching significance. Three of these are discussed here.

The first is the enhanced influence of so-called emerging powers. This goes beyond China, whose veto at the Security Council has long made it an established power. Countries such as India, Mexico, Turkey, South Africa, Indonesia, Nigeria, Brazil, South Korea, and others are attempting to play a more active role in global governance. This has included greater attention to issues of peacebuilding.[23] Many of these countries are now providers of foreign aid—or, rather, as they tend to classify it, "South–South Development Cooperation." When applied in post-conflict contexts, such assistance can influence the way in which fledgling national authorities go about the process of rebuilding their economies and political institutions. The effects can be both substantive and strategic. Countries such as India often emphasize the provision of infrastructure geared toward extractive industries—ports, long-distance highways, and so forth—and this can have a major impact on a post-conflict country's economic trajectory.

Strategically, the existence of foreign-assistance providers beyond the usual group of largely Western donor governments (and multilateral institutions) can provide national authorities in post-conflict countries additional negotiating leverage with their external partners. So-called "non-traditional" aid donors—such as Turkey or Brazil—are far less concerned with promoting particular varieties of state–society relations. They tend not to prioritize the promotion of social equality, or institutional mechanisms to ensure the promotion and protection of human rights. Unlike traditional donor countries, South Korea and other new providers of development assistance are likely to be more transparent in demanding that any aid they provide be linked to preferential access to trade and investment opportunities.

A second emerging trend is the increasing questioning of the "aid effectiveness" agenda—particularly its emphasis on "national ownership" and the need for all external activities to be routed through government bodies as a way of building state capacity. Efforts by donors and other external actors to bypass states in the interests of operational efficiency can be self-defeating. This is true particularly with respect to public finance systems.[24] Yet, while granting that a mismatch often exists between what external actors are willing or able to offer by way of programmatic assistance and what national authorities on the ground say they need, many international actors regard some calls for "national ownership" of peacebuilding processes as an attempt by ruling elites to corner an undue proportion of external resources.

If foreign assistance disproportionately benefits one political party, or a particular set of ethnic groups, or certain regions, then it may prove counterproductive, potentially even fueling future conflict. Hence, some UN officials engaged in post-conflict reconstruction have insisted that national ownership cannot be an excuse for the central government monopolizing decision-making over the distribution of resources, whether financial or technical. For ownership to be genuinely "national," according to this view, it must incorporate the views of civil society, including organizations representing marginalized constituencies. National ownership must also be extended to the grassroots, ensuring buy-in to peacebuilding strategies from among local government actors, opposition parties, and residents of regions cut off from the national mainstream.

Another voice that has called into question the excessive focus on the state is former World Bank economist Paul Collier. After making important contributions to debates concerning the causes of civil war, Collier has more recently addressed the related but distinct question of what rekindles conflict. The answer, he has argued, is misaligned incentives—particularly with respect to the relative payoffs from various violent and non-violent options available to the (mainly young) men that fuel organized violence. Collier argued that "[b]roadly based economic development is the only true exit strategy . . . Its pillars are jobs and basic services."[25] But Collier took issue with that part of the "aid effectiveness" agenda that stressed the government as the primary channel for pursuing these key peacebuilding objectives. In late 2008, in the context of rising rebel violence in the Democratic Republic of Congo (DRC), Collier argued against what he portrayed as donor agencies' overly literal commitment to the Paris Declaration aspiration to work through national states (and treasuries) when possible. In places like DRC, he maintained, the state is too privatized—that is, easily used by influential actors for private gain—to generate tangible peace dividends rapidly. Because services and jobs were needed right away, Collier argued, all channels had to be mobilized to their fullest extent, which meant donors "bypassing the state" by directly funding NGOs, the private sector, and local councils—a practice directly antithetical to the aid effectiveness/"national ownership" discourse.

A third trend that may well shape the future of international peacebuilding has been concern as to whether the UN's "new peacebuilding architecture," which is by now seven years old, will ever be up to the tasks assigned to it. The PBC was endowed with a number of birth defects. As the *Economist* once put it: "As first conceived, [the PBC] would have had enforcement powers and tried to pre-empt state failure, not just cure it. But many governments, jealously guarding the cloak of statehood, lobbied to keep the commission weak."[26] The PBC's weakness was not surprising. It was a child of its time: it was born in the still-bitter aftermath of the 2003 US-led invasion of Iraq, which occurred without Security Council authorization. Lacking direct control over the humanitarian and development agencies concerned, the PBC and PBSO have been unable to "coordinate" the efforts of the United Nations and other actors working in post-conflict countries.[27] The PBC's chief contribution during its first half-decade may have been as a new venue—one possibly more advantageous to Southern states—for enacting these underlying rivalries.

When it comes to its engagement in country-specific situations, the PBC has done little to relieve the burden on the Security Council, which is barely able to cope with the weight of "matters" of which it is "seized." As of this writing, almost seven years after the resolutions that created the PBC were enacted, the PBC has had just six cases on its agenda: Burundi, the Central African Republic, Guinea, Guinea-Bissau, Liberia, and Sierra Leone.

Following a very unpromising start, the PBC and PBSO made some attempts at institutional revival. They have both sought to breathe life into some of the thematic peacebuilding issues that were included in their original mandates. The PBSO, for instance, worked during 2010 to build consensus across the UN system on the need for a concerted effort to increase women's participation in peacebuilding. This included pressuring UN entities to devote 15 percent of their peacebuilding expenditures to projects that have women as their primary beneficiaries or that focus on promoting gender equality. But the PBSO has subsequently shown itself unable to continue driving this agenda effectively—for instance, to use its strategic position within the Executive Office of the Secretary-General to expose inaction by other UN entities. Instead, it has expended great effort attempting to "coordinate" UN deliberations over how peace and security issues might be incorporated into whatever replaces the Millennium Development Goals once they expire in 2015.

An analysis of the PBA's institutional components during its first five years reveals actors operating very much as some scholars of international relations have theorized. The PBC has been sidelined into almost complete irrelevance by the Security Council's five permanent members, who dislike the idea of having their decisions second-guessed by a generally ill-informed 31-member body that includes many states with almost no ability to contribute to the global public goods on which lasting peace at least partly relies. As for the PBSO, its bureaucrats have, as expected, sought a degree of autonomy from member states, their nominal "principals," through the selective acquisition of organizational roles within and beyond the UN system. They have done so using the familiar arsenal at their disposal—control over information, agenda-setting advantages conferred by "expertise," and the *de facto* authority derived by the relative staying power of UN bureaucrats compared to the ever-rotating cast of diplomatic actors found in member state missions.

Conclusion

The meaning of peacebuilding will continue to be the subject of contention for as long as priorities for establishing lasting peace are a source of disagreement. Little international consensus is likely anytime soon about key questions: whether to emphasize the provision of justice over the restoration of order; whether to invest in state capacity or expand the range of actors engaged in service provision; whether to accelerate social equality or work to restore traditional structures underlying community life. How to rebuild states after conflict depends on one's view of the proper role of the state in promoting social and economic change, a topic of constant disagreement even in countries that have not recently been plunged into violent civil conflict.

The institutional mechanisms for improving the international community's response to failing states have improved considerably since the end of the Cold War. But they are still incapable of providing a sufficiently rapid response; nor do they ensure the financial support necessary to quickly restore people's faith in the rule of law. This is partly a reflection of political paralysis, but also stems from the skewed incentives facing officials working in donor governments and international organizations—most of whom are rewarded on the basis of their ability to avoid giving offense to local political actors rather than their capacity to deliver security to ordinary people.

While the engagement of a new set of "emerging powers" into global security governance—including peacebuilding—raises the prospect of additional resources, it also promises to increase the cacophony that has made coordination of peacebuilding efforts so difficult. As demands for greater attention to the human rights dimensions of sustainable peace collide with a tendency toward less ambitious approaches—what the World Bank's *World Development Report 2011* called "inclusive enough" peacebuilding—further rounds of disagreement are likely.

Additional reading

1. Rob Jenkins, *Peacebuilding: From Concept to Commission* (London: Routledge, 2013).
2. Simon Chesterman, *You the People: The United Nations, Transitional Administrations and State-Building* (Oxford: Oxford University Press, 2004).
3. Graciana del Castillo, *Rebuilding War-Torn States: The Challenge of Post-Conflict Economic Reconstruction* (New York: Oxford University Press, 2008).
4. Michael W. Doyle and Nicholas Sambanis, *Making War and Building Peace: United Nations Peace Operations* (Princeton: Princeton University Press, 2006).
5. Edward Newman, Roland Paris, and Oliver Richmond, eds., *New Perspectives on Liberal Peacebuilding* (New York: United Nations University Press, 2009).

Notes

1 Bruce Jones, Richard Gowen, and Jake Sherman, *Building on Brahimi: Peacekeeping in an Era of Strategic Uncertainty* (New York: NYU Center on International Cooperation, 2009), 26.
2 Michael Barnett, Hunjoon Kim, Madalene O'Donnell, and Laura Sitea, "Peacebuilding: What Is in a Name?," *Global Governance* 13, no. 1 (2007): 37 (emphasis added).

3 OECD, "Concepts and Dilemmas of State Building in Fragile Situations: From Fragility to Resilience," *Journal on Development* 9, no. 3 (2008): 13.

4 Benjamin Reilly, "Elections in Post-Conflict Societies," in *The UN Role in Promoting Democracy: Between Ideas and Reality*, eds. Edward Newman and Roland Rich (New York: United Nations University Press, 2006), 113.

5 John G. Cockell, "Conceptualising Peacebuilding: Human Security and Sustainable Peace," in *Regeneration of War-Torn Societies*, ed. Michael Pugh (New York: Palgrave Macmillan, 2000), 15–34.

6 A detailed history of this term is found in S. Neil MacFarlane and Yuen Foong-Khong, *Human Security and the UN: A Critical History* (Bloomington: Indiana University Press, 2006).

7 Boutros Boutros-Ghali, *An Agenda for Peace*, General Assembly and Security Council document A/47/277–S/241111, 17 June 1992, Section 21.

8 Boutros Boutros-Ghali, "Supplement to an 'Agenda for Peace,'" General Assembly and Security Council document A/50/60–S/1995/1, 3 January 1995.

9 Michael Doyle and Nicholas Sambanis, "International Peacebuilding: A Theoretical and Quantitative Analysis," *American Political Science Review* 94, no. 4 (2000): 779.

10 A/55/305, 3.

11 Barnett et al., "What Is in a Name?," 35–58.

12 Thorsten Benner, Andrea Binder, and Philipp Rotmann, "Learning to Build Peace? United Nations Peacebuilding and Organizational Learning: Developing a Research Framework," Research Paper Series No. 7 (Berlin: Global Public Policy Institute, 2007), 13.

13 Ibid., 13.

14 *In Larger Freedom: Towards Development, Security and Human Rights for All—Report from the Secretary-General*, General Assembly document A/59/2005, 21 March 2005.

15 Roland Paris and Timothy D. Sisk, *Managing Contradictions: The Inherent Dilemmas of Postwar Statebuilding* (New York: International Peace Academy, 2007), 1.

16 Ashraf Ghani and Clare Lockhart, *Fixing Failed States: A Framework for Rebuilding a Fractured World* (New York: Oxford University Press, 2008).

17 Lisa A. Hall MacLeod, *Constructing Peace: Lessons from UN Peacebuilding Operations in El Salvador and Cambodia* (Lanham, MD: Lexington Books, 2006), 74.

18 Youssef Cohen, Brian R. Brown, and A. F. K. Organski, "The Paradoxical Nature of State-Making: The Violent Creation of Order," *American Political Science Review* 75, no. 4 (1981): 901–910.

19 Roland Paris, *At War's End: Building Peace after Civil Conflict* (New York: Cambridge University Press, 2004).

20 Reilly, "Elections in Post-Conflict Societies."

21 Sorpong Peou, "The UN's Modest Impact on Cambodia's Democracy," in *The UN Role in Promoting Democracy: Between Ideas and Reality*, eds. Edward Newman and Roland Rich (New York: United Nations University Press, 2006).

22 Charles Call and Elizabeth Cousens, "Ending Wars and Building Peace," *International Studies Perspectives* 9 (2008): 5.

23 Saferworld, *Rising Powers and Conflict: Addressing Conflict and Violence from 2015* (London, November 2012).

24 Michael Carnahan and Clare Lockhart, "Peace-Building and Public Finance," in *Building States to Build Peace*, eds. Charles T. Call and Vanessa Wyeth (Colorado: Lynne Rienner, 2008).

25 Paul Collier, "Naive Faith in the Ballot Box," *Guardian*, 3 November 2008.

26 *Economist*, "Failed States: Where Life Is Cheap and Talk Is Loose," 17 March 2011.

27 See, for example, Dan Smith, *Towards a Framework for Peacebuilding: Getting Their Act Together: Overview Report of the Joint Utstein Study of Peacebuilding* (Oslo: Royal Norwegian Ministry of Foreign Affairs, 2004), http://www.regjeringen.no/upload/kilde/ud/rap/2000/0265/ddd/pdfv/210673-rapp104.pdf.

Human Security as a Global Public Good

Fen Osler Hampson and Mark Raymond

In the second decade of the twenty-first century, there has been renewed focus on human security. It is driven by developments surrounding the Arab Spring, especially events in Libya and Syria that have underscored the continuing importance of the responsibility to protect doctrine when dictators turn their guns against their own people. But as the forces of globalization transform the world, some also argue that income inequalities between the world's richest and poorest countries are widening as trade and investment flows intensify between those countries that can compete in the global economy and those in the South that cannot. This point is convincingly argued in the World Bank's 2007 *Global Economic Prospects* report, which points out that although globalization will contribute to rapid growth in average incomes over the next 25 years, it is also being accompanied by growing income inequality and potentially severe environmental pressures. As a result, the probability of civil unrest in a number of poor and middle-income countries is also rising.[1]

The concept of human security remains a central element of the discourse in international relations. This discourse also points to a new paradigm which asserts that the provision of human security (defined in terms of the protection of basic human liberties, certain key political and civil rights, and basic standards of equity and social justice) should be viewed as not just national but also global public goods. In this paradigm, human security should reach across borders to all peoples regardless of their ethnic or national origins, socio-economic status, religious creed, or political persuasion.

However, it is also recognized that human security is an underprovided public good. Many states are their citizens' own worst enemy and deliberately threaten their lives and rights. Other states suffer incapacities of various kinds (e.g. administrative, fiscal, governance related) and are wracked by conflict, which limits their ability to provide for the basic needs and human security of their citizens. To the extent that human security in its various dimensions (discussed at greater length below) is enjoyed as a public good, it is one that bears the hallmark of a club good, that is to say its benefits are confined in large measure to citizens in rich democracies; some people in poor countries are also secure, but they are a distinct minority.

This chapter explores some of the arguments advanced to explain the human security "deficit" in contemporary international relations. We argue that this deficit is best explained by disaggregating the concept of human security to distinguish three public goods that contribute to the realization of human security: equity, intervention for the purposes of humanitarian protection, and peacebuilding. Doing so provides insight into the reasons that these goods are often undersupplied and demonstrates, further, that they may be most susceptible to provision by different combinations of actors and institutions. Accordingly, we conclude by advocating a portfolio diversification approach to the provision of global public goods related to human security.

Different conceptions of human security

Despite significant research and interest in human security over the past two decades, there is no real consensus on what can or should constitute the focus of what is still loosely termed "human security studies."[2] There remains considerable methodological, definitional, and conceptual disquiet about the real meaning of human security, and about the implications of the human security paradigm for the study and practice of international relations. This reality should come as no surprise, given the nature of the academic enterprise and the different disciplinary and methodological backgrounds informing the work of scholars engaged in human security research. Even so, the evident inability of scholars to advance beyond theoretical debates over definitions toward practical policy recommendations understandably frustrates practitioners in the policy community.

There are arguably three distinct conceptions of human security that shape current debates, which are distinguishable according to their understanding of the nature of the threat. One view emphasizes direct physical harm to vulnerable populations, often but not always committed by states or their agents. It informs international efforts to prevent and respond to genocide and war crimes, and to abolish weapons that are especially harmful to civilians and non-combatants.[3] It lies at the heart of humanitarian interventions directed at improving the basic living conditions of refugees, and anyone uprooted by conflict from their homes and communities. On those rare occasions when military force has been used ostensibly to avert genocide or ethnic cleansing, it has also been justified usually on rather specific humanitarian grounds such as the need to restore basic human rights and dignity. Another group takes a slightly more expansive view, including systematic violations of the fundamental liberal package of basic individual rights to "life, liberty, and the pursuit of happiness," and positing an obligation on the part of the international community to protect and promote these rights.[4]

These two views stand in sharp contrast to a broader view, which suggests that human security should be widely construed to include economic, environmental, social, and other forms of harm to the overall livelihood and wellbeing of individuals. There is a strong social justice component in this broader conception of human security, as well as a wider consideration of threats (real and potential) to the survival and health of individuals. According to this third and considerably more controversial view, the state of the global economy, the forces of globalization, and the health of the environment (including the world's atmosphere and oceans) are all legitimate subjects of concern in terms of how they affect the "security" of the individual.[5]

The "broadeners" have attracted sharp criticism. Yuen Foong-Khong warns that making everything a priority renders nothing a priority—raising false hopes in the policy realm and obscuring real trade-offs between rival human security objectives.[6] Similarly, Andrew Mack makes the sound methodological point that overly broad definitions of human security can block investigation of the very phenomena that need to be understood.[7]

Examining the relationship between poverty and violence, for example, requires us to treat them as separate variables. A definition that conflates dependent and independent variables will confound analysis of causal connections between them. However, as a practical matter many human security initiatives, such as the international campaign to ban trafficking in small and light weapons, fall between the narrower and the broader definitions. Accordingly, these views should not be understood as mutually exclusive; rather, they are best thought of in terms of concentric circles. Nevertheless, as is illustrated below, the choice of conceptual emphasis is consequential in that it leads to concern with different underprovided global public goods related to human security— and thus also to different policy approaches for providing them.

Public goods and human security

Underlying much of the human security literature is a common belief that human security is critical to international security. To the extent that this is true, human security is not simply a private good with benefits accruing to specific individuals; rather, it may also have widely enjoyed positive spinoffs. However, many regions experience chronic shortages of human security. This reality raises the question, who secures it when basic rights are threatened and citizens are subjected to further privations in their daily lives? And like all so-called public goods, the real question is who provides it and at what cost? And like such goods, resolving collective-action problems are inherent to their provision.

In traditional liberal democratic theories of the state, property rights, and the safety and security of citizens are public goods that are provided by nonmarket mechanisms, typically the state. For example, the ultimate responsibility for maintaining law and order in domestic civil society rests with the state that provides this public good. Early liberal theorists like Thomas Hobbes recognized that allowing private citizens to look after their own security was a recipe for social and political anarchy. Hendrik Spruyt has argued convincingly that the comparatively greater ability of the sovereign state to guarantee property rights, relative to its synchronic competitors, helps explain the historical emergence of a homogeneous system of states.[8] The state and the provision of public goods are thus closely linked in theory and in practice. The large body of law that has developed, for example, in the area of contracts constitutes a kind of public good.[9]

The legal rules and instruments of contract law not only guarantee reciprocity, but also permit private transactions to take place in an orderly and businesslike manner. As noted by Inge Kaul, Isabelle Grunberg, and Marc Stern, "Public goods are recognized as having benefits that cannot easily be confined to a single 'buyer' (or set of 'buyers'). Yet, once they are provided, many can enjoy them for free. Street names for example. A clear environment is another. Without a mechanism for collective action, these goods can be underproduced."[10]

Public goods can be broken into two main categories: so-called pure public goods and joint goods. Pure public goods are characterized by jointness and non-excludability.[11] Their benefits are consumed by all members of a community as soon as any one member produces them and consumption does not reduce the quantity or quality of available supply. Relevant examples of the polar case of pure public goods are hard to find; but one such example is knowledge, a public intermediate input into the production function of all firms.

Joint or "club" goods are characterized by their jointness and excludability characteristics. Since the benefits from club goods are excludable, often through the price mechanism, they can be provided through the private sector (e.g. cable and pay television, movie theaters, recreational facilities). Club goods, by definition, can be extended or provided to somebody else without raising marginal costs. When jointness extends to the international level but benefits remain excludable, the optimal club size is international.[12]

"Sustainable human development" proponents of human security argue that most current international economic governance arrangements and abstract arguments about why such institutions are needed—whether they take the form of formal international regimes or some other institutional form—lack mechanisms and instruments that address the serious distributional inequities that arise from the operations of the global markets and the forces of globalization. These inequities ultimately have an adverse impact on human welfare and human security at the local level.

The sustainable human development school thus argues that equity should be considered as a global public good and that equity and social justice must play a key role in international order.[13] The approach thus has an explicit normative agenda. Although some attention has been given over the years to income differences between the rich, developed market economies and the poor, less developed countries, these advocates argue that many of these efforts have been largely ineffective.

The core problem is that the normal operation of the global economy perpetuates highly unequal income distribution, despite ameliorative mechanisms. The question, then, is how to more effectively meet the needs and rights of the disadvantaged. According to Amartya Sen, new concepts of distributive justice will only be widely adopted when "national particularism"—where distributive justice is conceived exclusively in national terms and within a national policy context—gives way to more plural affiliations involving direct "*interpersonal* sympathies and solidarities across borders." Such affiliations must have "a cogency that can substantially transcend national particularism of the estranged polities" such that fairness and distribution are seen in more global but nonetheless interpersonal terms.[14] As Sen further notes, "The freedom-efficiency of the market mechanism, on the one hand, and the seriousness of freedom-inequality problems, on the other hand, are worth considering *simultaneously*. The equity problems have to be addressed, especially in dealing with serious deprivations and poverty."[15]

The value in a public goods approach to explaining the equity deficit is its focus on the sources of undersupply—in this case, of equity—rather than on the sources of demand. The question, from this perspective, is the extent to which equity at the international level is characterized by jointness of supply and non-excludability. It is clear that equity is generally excludable—i.e. that it can be provided to some without the benefits accruing to all. The provision of redistribution can be done on a very granular basis, for example through development grants and charitable giving directed to particular villages or even particular families. While addressing the undersupply of equity may well generate positive social externalities such as reductions in violence (making the benefits of equity partially non-excludable), these too will tend to remain relatively localized in accordance with the patterns of direct redistribution.

The situation with respect to jointness of supply is more complex. To the extent that increased equity produces positive externalities such as peace and a reduction in levels of violence, these are likely to be enjoyed on a joint basis at least in the affected geographic area. If equity is understood in terms of reducing the differential between the highest and lowest quintiles in the global distribution of annual income, then it may also be a joint good in the sense that a reduction in the income differential between France and Indonesia does not preclude a reduction in income differential between Zimbabwe and South Korea. However, understanding equity in this manner requires accepting that citizens in advanced industrial economies would be receiving more of this particular good (making them better off in this sense) as their incomes declined as a result of global redistribution of resources. It is unlikely that such a view will be politically tenable in the short term. Increasing equity ultimately entails distribution either of current resource stocks or future resource flows in favor of the disadvantaged. Thus, global equity is best described, at least under currently prevailing social rules and institutions (sovereign states, free markets, and individual property rights) as blending characteristics of club goods and private goods.

Whereas sustainable development proponents of human security tend to focus on distributional "failures" in the international system to explain why human security is an underprovided public good (at least in terms of its equity and social justice components), analysts who see human security primarily in relation to physical safety and basic civil rights argue that the key failures are primarily *political* as opposed to economic or market based.

In the physical safety and basic rights conceptions of human security, the principal threats to international peace and security come instead "from below"—in the denial of human security to the citizens in one or more states as a result of civil conflict and strife, and/or from transnational economic forces which have marginalized certain groups in the world economy. Thus, in the human security paradigm the problem of international order is redefined and shifted downwards from the systemic (i.e. international) to the sub-systemic (i.e. intrastate) level.

This argument rests on the fact that the nature of international conflict in the twentieth century fundamentally changed. Most of the wars since the second half of the twentieth century have been wars within states, and the result of ethnic, religious, or horizontal inequalities (i.e. the inequitable distribution of wealth and income among different groups within society).[16] These conflicts are fought not by regular armies but between militias, armed civilians, guerrillas, and ethnic groups. These groups arm themselves through the large international market for small arms.

This particular view of human security stresses the rule of law and liberal norms as key ingredients in the establishment of a "just" political order both domestically and internationally. Accordingly, it has its own unique view of the kinds of intervention strategies that may be required to contribute to a peaceful political order. In contrast to realism—which sees a role for force and the balance of power in the management of communal or ethnic conflict—humanitarian and rights/rule of law approaches to human security see the challenges of peacebuilding and third party involvement largely in terms of the creation of participatory governance structures, the development of new social norms, and the establishment of the rule of law and democracy. Thus, in arguing that "failed" or "failing" states are the principal source of mayhem in contemporary international politics, these human security advocates also look to a very different set of institutional responses and mechanisms for addressing these kinds of "political" failures.

Unlike Immanuel Kant, who was essentially noninterventionist when it came to promoting democracy and human rights in those states where such institutions were lacking, the human security paradigm is much more inclined to be proactive and to favor interventionist approaches to defend and secure human rights, broader human security needs, and democracy. Even so, there is considerable disquiet among participants in these debates about when intervention is desirable or the conditions under which force and other instruments of intervention should be used.[17] In the human security view of international politics, however, most of these reservations disappear; intervention, including the use of force, is sanctioned because human security is privileged over international order as a basic public good. In contrast to the focus on equity as a global public good that stems from the sustainable development view of human security, narrower political conceptions of human security focus instead on public goods such as humanitarian protection and intervention as well as state-building measures that seek to instill and internalize cultures of human rights.

To what extent can humanitarian interventions and peacebuilding efforts be accurately understood as pure or impure public goods? As with equity, humanitarian intervention is in most respects excludable. This is true at the strategic level, as evidenced by the selective nature of such efforts. The international community of states can, and does, opt not to intervene in many humanitarian emergencies. It is also true at the tactical level, where rules of engagement can restrict the kinds of operations that are conducted and thus determine which civilians enjoy the protection of the intervention force and which do not. An intervention in one case does not preclude an intervention in another, especially if time horizons are relaxed to permit the possibility of significant additional investment in relevant military and other humanitarian capacities. Relative to the overall size of the global economy, such investments are not out of reach, especially if present military spending were diverted. The possibility of exclusion and joint (in principle) nature of supply suggest that humanitarian intervention is a club good. The key question is whether club members with the capacity to pay can be induced to do so; that is, the problem is one of political will, and the solution may rest on the availability of selective incentives of sufficient value to states (or potentially other actors) with the means to pursue them.

Peacebuilding efforts that focus on establishing and consolidating respect for human rights are non-excludable in particular state-level contexts. Short of situations of institutionalized discrimination, such as apartheid, that are clearly incompatible with modern understandings of human rights, it is difficult to imagine potential cases where rights would be understood and applied in a systematically unequal fashion. It is even more difficult to imagine a case in which such a situation is an intended outcome of a peacebuilding effort. To the extent that human rights cultures have been established above the state level, in regional human rights courts or the International Criminal Court (ICC), they are non-excludable in the sense of providing equal protection. However, legal regimes are typically excludable in the sense of applying to particular geographic jurisdictions. The genocide convention, various major human rights treaties and declarations, and the ICC arguably provide at least a thin layer of genuinely universal protection, but human rights still remain enforceable in practice primarily via domestic courts. The ICC was similarly designed according to the principle of complementarity, as well as with Security Council oversight.[18] The major consequence of these significant vestiges of sovereignty is that enjoyment of the human security public good of human rights remains patchwork in practice and is likely to do so for the foreseeable future.

If the public good is defined in terms not of the rights culture itself but rather of measures and programs to foster and maintain such cultures, these programs are likely to remain excludable sheerly for practical reasons—training workshops and other related activities can only involve finite numbers of participants. Modern information and communications technologies, including streaming video, may potentially relax this constraint; but it is unclear that online education of this kind is fully as effective as in-person instruction. This may be especially true of attempts to create emotional capacities such as tolerance and empathy that are critical to functional rights cultures. Thus, peacebuilding efforts and the rights cultures they create are at best club goods, though perhaps with relatively low costs of provision in contrast with equity and humanitarian intervention.

The situation with respect to jointness of supply is also more tractable regarding efforts to strengthen respect for human rights, mainly because the adoption of such beliefs and accompanying institutions in one political community does not diminish the stock of beliefs and institutions available to other communities. In fact, there are likely opportunities to leverage socialization mechanisms involving both back-patting and social opprobrium, and other means of social influence.[19] Thus, the adoption of such beliefs may encourage further adoption, under the right conditions, leading to virtuous cycles.

Conclusion: providing for human security

If human security in all of its various dimensions is an underprovided public good, which international institutions, mechanisms, and actors are best equipped to provide it and to help address the different kinds of political and market failures that are experienced at both the national and international levels? Among proponents of human security, there is considerable disquiet about the ability of formal international organizations—the United Nations, in particular—to provide for human security in its various dimensions. They argue that international organizations and formal, intergovernmental institutions are unable to provide for human security for a variety of reasons. First, they are paralyzed or hamstrung by conflicts of interest among their most powerful (typically state) members. Second, many suffer from the corrosive "logic" of collective action, to which there are no effective or readily available institutional remedies. Third, financial and other resourcing problems have effectively thwarted or hindered the ability of these organizations to provide public goods in the realm of human security. Fourth, formal institutional and organizational mandates cannot readily be modified or changed to address the human security agenda and provide for this public good.

Despite these shortcomings, formal international organizations still have a role to play in global public good provision. Their legitimacy endows them with the capacity to identify and praise good behavior from other actors, thus encouraging public good provisions. They can also assist in coordinating the efforts of various national governments and private groups, reducing the chance of duplication. Further, their roles in directly providing global public goods could often be enhanced by the provision of additional resources.

Global public goods can also be provided by groups of states, of varying size. This model of provision is referred to either as "middle-power multilateralism" or as "minilateralism." Such ad hoc coalitions are often more able to act quickly and may be more effective in marshaling the needed capacity since powerful states can more easily be assured the resources they provide will be effectively employed in a manner consistent with their values and interests. States can also cooperate more easily with other states they have previously learned to trust.[20]

Others argue on balance that it is preferable that human security be provided on a voluntary basis and through the voluntary sector. They believe this is most efficient, and that it lends greater accountability and legitimacy to decision-making. To the extent that sovereignty stands in the way of the delivery of these public goods, nongovernmental organizations working with their counterparts in other societies are best able to circumvent and work around state actors.

Current patterns of provision of the three human security-related public goods identified in this chapter (equity, intervention, and peacebuilding) vary in ways that reflect both the different characteristics of these goods and related norms and rules that apply to their provision. Attempts to supply global equity involve states, but both voluntary and private sectors as well as formal international organizations play key roles in actual resource provision efforts. To the extent that substantially increasing equity requires successful promotion of the view that the advantaged have ethical obligations to trade resources for equity, developed states also have a key role to play in fostering normative change. In contrast, humanitarian intervention is typically provided via a combination of formal international organizations and state-based coalitions of the willing.[21] This reflects both the need to balance capacity and legitimacy, as well as the desire on the part of states to retain their monopoly on the legitimate use of force. Finally, peacebuilding efforts aimed at strengthening human rights cultures involve a broad range of actors, from the voluntary sector, individual governments, and formal international organizations. This diversity reflects the lower provision costs of this public good compared to the other two and the strong reputational benefits accruing from being seen to engage in what is broadly understood as pro-social behavior.

Given that all three goods resemble club goods (albeit to varying degrees), the key to addressing undersupply is providing selective incentives to actors with relevant capacity. Doing so requires a realization that, while states remain vital players, they are not the only relevant potential club members—at least for the provision of equity and for peacebuilding. Further, encouraging greater provision of these goods is made significantly easier by the insight that the incentives provided to suppliers need not always be costly. Charitable giving and peacebuilding both demonstrate that social recognition and conformity with recognized group norms often provide motivation. Michael Barnett has recently argued that donors are often motivated by intangible payoffs from giving.[22]

Even so, there is perhaps no single mode of delivery and no "preferred" path in the provision of human security. Rather, a diversified approach to human security in which states and non-state actors provide public goods to promote human security may ultimately be best suited to meeting the multidimensional aspects of human security itself.

Additional reading

1. Fen Osler Hampson et al., *Madness in the Multitude: Human Security and World Disorder* (Oxford: Oxford University Press, 2002).
2. Michael Barnett, *Empire of Humanity: A History of Humanitarianism* (Ithaca: Cornell University Press, 2011).
3. Shannon D. Beebe and Mary H. Kaldor, *The Ultimate Weapon Is No Weapon: Human Security and the New Rules of War* (New York: Public Affairs, 2010).
4. International Commission on Intervention and State Sovereignty, *The Responsibility to Protect* (Ottawa: International Development Research Centre, 2001).
5. Mary Kaldor, *Human Security* (Cambridge: Polity Press, 2007).

Notes

1 Frances Stewart and Graham Brown, "Motivations for Conflict: Groups and Individuals," in *Leashing the Dogs of War: Conflict Management in a Divided World*, eds. Chester A. Crocker, Fen Osler Hampson, and Pamela Aall (Washington, DC: United States Institute of Peace, 2007), 197–219; and Geoffrey Gertz and Lawrence Chandy, *Two Trends in Global Poverty* (Washington, DC: Brookings Institution, 2011).

2 Mary Kaldor, *Human Security* (Cambridge: Polity Press, 2007); Derek S. Reveron and Kathleen A. Mahoney Norris, *Human Security in a Borderless World* (Boulder: Westview Press, 2011); Richard A. Matthew, Jon Barnett, Bryan McDonald, and Karen L. O'Brien, eds., *Global Environmental Change and Human Security* (Cambridge, MA: MIT Press, 2009); George Kent, *Freedom from Want: The Human Right to Adequate Food* (Washington, DC: Georgetown University Press, 2005); and Osler Hampson et al., *Madness in the Multitude: Human Security and World Disorder* (Toronto: Oxford University Press, 2002).

3 Kaldor, *Human Security*; Shannon D. Beebe and Mary H. Kaldor, *The Ultimate Weapon Is No Weapon: Human Security and the New Rules of War* (New York: Public Affairs, 2010); Samantha Power, *A Problem from Hell: America and the Age of Genocide* (New York: Harper Perennial, 2003); Boutros Boutros-Ghali, *An Agenda for Peace: Preventive Diplomacy,*

Peacemaking and Peacekeeping (New York: United Nations, 1995); and Jonathan Moore, *The United Nations and Complex Emergencies: Rehabilitation in Third World Transitions* (Geneva: United Nations Research Institute for Social Development, 1996).

4 Richard Pierre Claude and Burns H. Weston, *Human Rights in World Community: Issues and Action*, 3rd edition (Philadelphia: University of Pennsylvania Press, 2006); Johannes Morsink, *The Universal Declaration of Human Rights: Origins, Drafting and Intent* (University Park: University of Pennsylvania Press, 1998); Paul G. Lauren, *The Evolution of Human International Rights: Visions Seen* (University Park: University of Pennsylvania Press, 1998); and Philip Alston, ed., *The United Nations and Human Rights: A Critical Appraisal* (Oxford: Oxford University Press, 1992).

5 Paul Battersby and Joseph M. Siracusa, *Globalization and Human Security* (Lanham, MD: Rowman & Littlefield, 2009); H. Richard Friman and Simon Reich, eds., *Human Trafficking, Human Security, and the Balkans* (Pittsburgh: University of Pittsburgh Press, 2007); Kent, *Freedom from Want*; Matthew et al., eds., *Global Environmental Change and Human Security*; United Nations, *The Copenhagen Declaration and Programme of Action* (New York: Oxford University Press, 1995); United Nations Development Programme, *Human Development Report 1994* (New York: Oxford University Press, 1994); United Nations Development Programme, *Human Development Report 1997* (New York: Oxford University Press, 1997); and Jorge Nef, *Human Security and Mutual Vulnerability: An Exploration into the Global Political Economy of Development and Underdevelopment* (Ottawa: International Development Research Centre, 1999).

6 Yuen Foong-Khong, "Human Security: A Shotgun Approach to Alleviating Human Misery?," *Global Governance* 7, no. 3 (2001): 231–236.

7 Andrew Mack, *Human Security Report 2005: War and Peace in the 21st Century* (New York: Oxford University Press, 2005).

8 Hendrik Spruyt, *The Sovereign State and Its Competitors* (Princeton: Princeton University Press, 1994).

9 Mancur Olson, *The Logic of Collective Action: Public Goods and the Theory of Groups*, 2nd edition (Cambridge, MA: Harvard University Press, 1971).

10 Inge Kaul, Isabelle Grunberg, and Marc A. Stern, "Defining Global Public Goods," in *Global Public Goods: International Cooperation in the 21st Century*, eds. Inge Kaul, Isabelle Grunberg, and Marc A. Stern (New York: Oxford University Press, 1999), 2–19.

11 Duncan Snidal, "Public Goods, Property Rights, and Political Organizations," *International Studies Quarterly* 23, no. 4 (1979): 532–566.

12 Robert O. Keohane, *After Hegemony: Cooperation and Discord in the World Political Economy* (Princeton: Princeton University Press, 1984); and Barbara Koremenos, Charles Lipson, and Duncan Snidal, "The Rational Design of International Institutions," *International Organization* 55, no. 4 (2001): 761–799.

13 Mohan J. Rao, "Equity in a Global Public Goods Framework," in *Global Public Goods*, eds. Kaul, Grunberg and Stern, 28–87.

14 Amartya Sen, "Global Justice and Beyond," in *Global Public Goods*, eds. Kaul, Grunberg and Stern, 120.

15 Amartya Sen, *Development as Freedom* (New York: Alfred A. Knopf, 2000), 119.

16 International Commission on Intervention and State Sovereignty, *The Responsibility to Protect* (Ottawa: International Development Research Centre, 2001); Margareta Sollenberg, Peter Wallensteen, and Andrés Jato, "Major Armed Conflicts," in *SIPRI Yearbook 1999: Armaments, Disarmament, and International Security* (Oxford: Oxford University Press), 15–33; and Mack, *Human Security Report 2005*.

17 Kaldor, *Human Security*; Beebe and Kaldor, *The Ultimate Weapon Is No Weapon*; and Power, *A Problem from Hell*.

18 Jo Stigen, *The Relationship between the International Criminal Court and National Jurisdictions: The Principle of Complementarity* (Leiden: Martinus Nijhoff, 2008).

19 Alistair Iain Johnston, "Treating International Institutions as Social Environments," *International Studies Quarterly* 45, no. 4 (2001): 487–515; Margaret E. Keck and Kathryn Sikkink, *Activists Beyond Borders: Advocacy Networks in International Politics* (Ithaca: Cornell University Press, 1998); and Martha Finnemore and Kathryn Sikkink, "International Norm Dynamics and Political Change," *International Organization* 52, no. 4 (1998): 887–917.

20 On multilateralism, see John Gerard Ruggie, "Multilateralism: The Anatomy of an Institution," *International Organization* 46, no. 3 (1992): 561–598. On minilateralism, see Fen Osler Hampson and Paul Heinbecker, "The 'New' Multilateralism of the Twenty-First Century," *Global Governance* 17, no. 3 (2011): 299–310.

21 Ibid.

22 Michael Barnett, *Empire of Humanity: A History of Humanitarianism* (Ithaca: Cornell University Press, 2011).

INTRODUCTION

The final part of this book turns to manifestations of international organization and global governance in what we have termed the "economic and social world." For us this terrain is extensive and seemingly boundless; the scale of the forms of institutionalization, actors, and sources of authority ensures that we could not hope to cover their full range. What we have assembled, however, are 11 chapters that individually and collectively offer an incisive and extensive examination of global economic and social governance as it is manifest today.

The chapters that follow cover all of the "big issues"—finance, trade, development, environment, poverty, hunger, health, and migration and refugees—the principal intergovernmental institutions—International Monetary Fund, World Trade Organization, World Bank, Global Environment Facility, UN development system, Food and Agriculture Organization, and World Health Organization, to name the most familiar—involved in each area and the host of non-state actors that also play a role therein.

The chapters in this part of the book are arranged to flow from substantive areas of institutionalization—in finance, trade, development, environment, and regional development—to pressing issues—environment, poverty, hunger, health, and migration and refugees. This arrangement is convenient and allows readers to select chapters as they see fit or as their interest takes them. Introductory classes on international organization and global governance, for example, would most likely turn to the most prominent issues in the global economy and their respective institutions exploring "Global financial governance" (Bessma Momani, Chapter 40), "Global trade governance" (Bernard Hoekman, Chapter 41), "Global development governance" (Katherine Marshall, Chapter 42), and "Global environmental governance" (Elizabeth R. DeSombre, Chapter 43).

Thereafter, generalist, specialist, and advanced readers might consider surveying more specific areas. "Climate change" (Matthew J. Hoffmann, Chapter 45) and "Sustainable development" (Roger A. Coate, Chapter 46) combine to flesh out more fully global environmental governance. "The regional development banks and global governance" (Jonathan R. Strand, Chapter 44) and "Poverty reduction" (David Hulme and Oliver Turner, Chapter 47) add further color to the global governance of development. "Food and hunger" (Jennifer Clapp, Chapter 48), "Global health governance" (Sophie Harman, Chapter 49), and "Refugees and migration" (Khalid Koser, Chapter 50) provide further insight into the precarity of the human condition and global efforts seeking its attenuation.

▌Governing the economic and social world: chapter synopses

Bessma Momani begins this final part of the book with an exploration, Chapter 40, of the changing role of the International Monetary Fund (IMF) as the center-point of "Global financial governance." She notes how the IMF's role has been transformed over its 70-year existence from macro-economic assistant and exchange-rate stabilizer to global financial governor. She also details the effects of this transformation on changing the economic complexion of borrowing and lending states alike—with the economies of the latter often being much more congruous with global economic orthodoxy than the former because of IMF intervention. Momani also spells out the pressing need for reform of the Fund and the global financial system to reflect changing economic geography and perceptions of national economic management.

Bernard Hoekman continues to fill in the story of the triumvirate at the heart of global economic governance with his exploration, in Chapter 41, of the World Trade Organization (WTO) as the centerpiece of "Global trade governance." He details the evolution of the multilateral trading system from General Agreement on Tariffs and Trade (GATT) to the creation of the WTO; he explores the key features of the WTO; he examines the principal debates in—and in so doing reveals a measure of the thorny nature of—global trade governance; and also he identifies the issues that are at the heart of the contestation over the current round of multilateral trade negotiations, the Doha round.

Global financial and trade governance, while arenas populated by a range of actors, are most easily identified with a core institution—the IMF and WTO, respectively. "Global development governance" also has a comparable core institution—the World Bank—but it is also an arena that is much more heavily populated and has a range of other central actors, including but not limited to the UN Development Programme and system, the Organisation for Economic Co-operation and Development (OECD), regional development banks, major national aid agencies such as USAID and the UK's Department for International Development (DfID), and such large nongovernmental organizations as BRAC and Oxfam. In Chapter 42, Katherine Marshall leads readers through this densely populated realm of "Global development governance," exploring, among other things, the features and functions of key institutions, highlighting pressing issues, setting global development efforts in their appropriate historical context, and examining the tensions underpinning efforts to renew global development "promises" after the expiry of the Millennium Development Goals (MDGs).

In Chapter 43 Elizabeth R. DeSombre confronts an equally diverse constellation of actors in her exploration of "Global environmental governance." She begins with an examination of the history of global environmental governance, locating its emergence in conservation agreements and global ad hoc conferences beginning with the Stockholm gathering in 1972. She then considers the principal institutions at the heart of the contemporary global governance of the human environment that we actually have, before looking at the role of non-state actors, key debates, and emerging issues.

Jonathan R. Strand completes the book's exploration of the major intergovernmental aspects of global economic and social governance with an examination, in Chapter 44, of "The regional development banks and global governance." They are often miscast as mini-World Banks, and Strand shows the diverse histories, roles, and operating principles that these relatively hidden but nonetheless crucial intergovernmental actors play in shaping development outside of the Western European and North American core. Among his many insights, Strand shows the utility of comparing and contrasting the different approaches to development that each of the regional development banks has, as well as situating and contrasting them in relationship to the major sub-regional development banks.

The remaining chapters in the book track global governance as it is manifest in distinct policy areas. In Chapters 45 and 46 Matthew J. Hoffmann and Roger A. Coate add further color to global environmental governance. Hoffmann deals specifically with "Climate change," setting out the urgency of the problem, detailing the almost comic (as well as tragic) fashion with which it has been dealt at the global level while also pointing out more hopeful initiatives and setting out the key debates and future scenarios. Coate's task is different. He explores the coming together of two distinct ideas—one about the environment and the second about development—to become the foundation upon which all human industry and activity ought to take place, "Sustainable development." Like Hoffmann, Coate details the role of various institutions in coming together to create and nourish a distinct concept; he also concentrates on the political underpinnings of past and current debates and speculates about the future.

In Chapters 47 and 48, David Hulme and Oliver Turner examine "Poverty reduction" and Jennifer Clapp "Food and hunger" to help reveal still more dimensions of the global governance of development. Both chapters deal with destitution, and both have as a central concern the need to redouble efforts to address entrenched and enduring precarity. Hulme and Turner explore the problem of global poverty, examining historical efforts targeted at its reduction—including such laudable but problematic global initiatives as the MDGs—along with where and why it persists, and debates about how it might be reduced and who is involved in governance initiatives designed to bring about its alleviation. Likewise, Clapp maps out the extent of the global food problem, illustrating how food insecurity persists and is growing for sections of the world's population. She covers, among other things, the role of financialization in the production of greater precarity, the reforms that have been put in place but also those areas wherein action is urgently required, and what the future of alleviating global hunger holds.

In Chapters 49 and 50, Sophie Harman examines "Global health governance" and Khalid Koser "Refugees and migration." These final two contributors further consider issues of precarity and efforts to mitigate their most egregious manifestations. Harman argues that efforts to address pressing health concerns have been in place since the very beginning of the modern system of international organization and global governance. While this ensures a jumpstart of sorts for public health at the global level, problems persist that undermine the capacity of the existing apparatus to eliminate human ill health at a time when the knowledge and resources exist but when the international community of states has been unable or unwilling to apply that knowledge and those resources appropriately. Finally, Koser explores the existing institutional architecture for dealing with the insecurities arising from both the pull of economic migration and the push of war and violence that result in forced migration. He sets out key debates and emerging issues that have a heavy bearing on migrants and refugees (including the looming challenges posed by climate change), and considers the prospects for a more formal union between the refugee and migration regimes.

Where to now?

What the chapters in this section, as well as in the volume as a whole, show is the multiple actors, institutions, and mechanisms at work in contemporary global governance. We have also seen how problematic aspects of contemporary global governance are, as well as identified those areas that represent genuine achievements in making the world a more peaceable place. The most visible aspects of this picture are international organizations, and precisely their visibility draws attention and the lion's share of criticism. Yet, what we have also seen is that a host of other actors are part of the problem as well as of the possible solution.

CONTENTS

Global Financial Governance

Bessma Momani

At the start of its nearly 70-year history, the International Monetary Fund's (IMF) role was one of observer and dutiful functionary in the international economic system. However, with the onset of the world debt crisis, the fall of the Soviet Union, and the European financial crisis, the IMF's role as crisis manager has deepened. Moreover, as the world has continued to experience economic and political crises, the IMF has further institutionalized its power and influence in governing the global economy. It is during this period of turmoil and transition that the IMF emerged as an institution tasked with striking the delicate balance between financing and adjustment, and as a provider of economic policy norms. Originally designed as an institution whose primary goal was to help stabilize the system of exchange rates and international payments in the industrialized countries of the post-World War II order, the IMF evolved into an organizational body charged with the difficult task of global governance.

Indeed, particularly in the aftermath of the 2008 global financial crisis, which witnessed the collapse of financial institutions, prolonged downturns in world markets, and the massive and often unpopular bailouts of banks and companies by national governments, the deepening institutionalization of the Fund has manifested itself in the IMF's movement from international organization (the IMF as a lender of last resort) to global financial governor (the IMF as an organization capable of governing the world economy), given the need to coordinate global economic reform not only to ensure the stabilization of currency markets but also to bring about enhanced worldwide macro-economic growth. This new period in the history of the Fund will most likely come to be viewed as one in which it has responded to great criticism and performed its most pivotal role as a norm-setting crisis manager. The direction the G20 chooses to set for the Fund will lay the groundwork for the institution's relevance within the global financial architecture in the coming decades.

The chapter begins with an overview of the history of the IMF. It then moves on to an in-depth discussion of current debates regarding the organization's expanding global role before considering the key criticisms and challenges it faces today, as well as stakeholders' attempts to push reforms that will improve its legitimacy. The chapter concludes that without continued reforms the IMF will struggle to fulfill its mandate, to the detriment of global economic growth and financial stability.

IMF: from Bretton Woods to crisis manager

This section provides an overview of the history of the IMF, a breakdown of its basic governing structure, and, finally, the organization's evolution from its founding as a post-war institution to its current and often controversial role as global financial crisis manager.

In response to the Great Depression of the 1930s and the calamities of World War II, the international community devised the International Monetary Fund and the World Bank at the 1944 Bretton Woods Conference in New Hampshire. Bretton Woods arose from the need to create a system of monetary exchange and financial relations that would prevent crises like those that had rocked the industrialized world in the post-World War I period from happening again. In this new system of fixed exchange rates, world currencies were adjusted to match—or become "pegged to"—the value of gold to protect against market fluctuations. The IMF was imbued with the power to intervene in economic policy when a country could not maintain its balance of payments.

The highest-ranking body in the IMF is its Board of Governors. It is comprised of one governor (typically the head of a central bank or a finance minister) and one alternative governor from each member country. The Board of Governors controls the admittance of new members into the IMF and the withdrawal of existing members. It is this body that retains the right to amend the IMF's Articles of Agreement and By-Laws, as well as the right to approve quota increases and allocations of Special Drawing Rights (see below). The Board of Governors is advised by the institution's Development Committee and the International Monetary Financial Committee.

With its 24 members, the IMF's Executive Board is responsible for the day-to-day workings of the Fund, for example overseeing existing policy relevant to global economic issues. The Executive Board represents all 188 member states, most of which are grouped into constituencies of four or more. Larger states, in particular China and the United States, have their own seats on the Executive Board. Executive Board decisions are made by consensus but there are times when formal votes are taken, after which a report summary of the decision is issued.

The IMF operates on a quota system, which is key to the management of the Fund's financial resources. Member countries are each assigned a quota determined by their relative position in the world economy—that is, countries that join the IMF are assigned a quota in the same range as the existing members with similar economic traits (i.e. size). This quota, in turn, determines a member country's maximum financial commitment to the IMF and its access to IMF funds. Quotas are denominated—or expressed in—Special Drawing Rights (SDR), the IMF's unit of account through which a country may obtain currency via the voluntary exchange of SDR between members, or an IMF designation through which member states with strong external positions are directed to purchase SDRs from those with weaker positions. IMF quotas are an important factor in determining a member state's voting power in IMF decisions, with votes being made up of basic votes plus an additional vote for each SDR 100,000 of quota that each member possesses.

The IMF quota formula used to assess a member's position comprises the following criteria: a weighted average of that country's gross domestic product (50 percent),[1] degree of openness (30 percent), its economic variability (15 percent), and its international reserves (5 percent). Currently—with its quota of SDR 4.1bn (about $64bn)—the United States remains the IMF's largest member, while the smallest, with a current quota of SDR 1.8 million (about $2.7m), is Tuvalu.

With 44 countries present at Bretton Woods, the decision to establish the IMF and World Bank was an achievement of functionalist cooperation. In particular, the IMF, as designed by British economist John Maynard Keynes and American economist Harry Dexter White was crafted to ensure the conditions necessary for stability and growth in the global economy, which, according to Keynes, would help foster a more peaceful and prosperous world. However, the two organizations were relatively feeble, ineffective, and ceremonial. The World Bank, with its mandate to provide loans to countries for development projects, was the busier sister organization, assisting in the rebuilding of war-torn Europe.

Things changed for the IMF in the late 1950s with the return to the free exchange of local and foreign currencies in Western Europe (an exchange otherwise known as current account convertibility), and in the 1960s as the IMF responded to fluctuations in global commodity prices with short-term loans for IMF members from the industrialized world. In 1971, when US president Richard Nixon announced the abandonment of the gold standard—the monetary standard established by Bretton Woods through which world currencies could be exchanged for the fixed rate of gold—it seemed as though the collapse of the Bretton Woods system would damage the very heart of the IMF's organizational strength. Yet, Nixon's announcement had the unintended consequence of creating a new role for the IMF that strengthened its involvement in the global economy. Coupled with an energy crisis in the early 1970s and rising commodity prices, the end of the gold standard turned the IMF's attention away from assisting industrialized developed states toward short-term lending to developing countries, thus taking on a role that its architects never imagined. By the late 1970s, the IMF had not lent to an industrialized country in over 30 years. In addition, the increasing globalization of capital during this time pushed the IMF to shift from managing small balance-of-payment crises to large and expectations-dependent capital account driven crises.

With the threat of the bankruptcy of Mexico in 1982, the world's attention shifted to assisting developing countries out of what seemed a perpetual debt crisis. Here, the IMF relished its newfound purpose of providing structural reform advice to developing countries that were influenced by the neoliberal ideas that filled its hallways. With rescue packages and Fund staff trying to protect crisis-prone countries from gyrations in the global economy, the IMF, and to a lesser extent the World Bank, were labeled as promoters of the "Washington Consensus" (1989), a set of ten policy reforms designed to fix the ailing economies in the developing world (see Table 40.1). These policies were no doubt influenced by neoliberal ideas about the value of markets, criticism of statist

Table 40.1 The ten policies of the Washington Consensus

Policy	Content
Fiscal discipline	Strict criteria should be implemented to avoid large budget deficits relative to GDP
Reordering public expenditure priorities	Moving away from subsidies and government administration towards neglected fields that promise high economic returns
Tax reform	Broadening the tax base and cutting marginal tax rates
Liberalizing interest rates	Allowing interest rates to be determined by the market
Ensuring competitive exchange rates	Allowing interest rates to induce economic growth
Trade liberalization	Including the elimination of trade protectionism and the encouragement of low tariffs
Liberalization of inward foreign direct investment (FDI)	Via the reduction of FDI barriers
Privatization	Including the privatization of state enterprises
Deregulation	Elimination of regulations that restrict the entry of new firms or those that impede financial competition, with exceptions in the areas of safety, environment, and finance
Property rights	Enhanced legal security for property rights and a reduced role of the state in such matters

policies adopted by developing countries in their striving for populism, and the positive view of individual entrepreneurship and liberties.

The IMF gradually moved from being a lender of last resort to playing a pivotal role as a global crisis manager. In the mid-1980s, the IMF played a key role in promoting policy coordination among developed countries' currencies and exchange rate systems as it became increasingly clear that the information gaps in the globalized economic system created inherited vulnerabilities. The *Plaza Accord* (1985), the *Louvre Accord* (1987), and the *Brady Plan* (1989) were key moments of international negotiation that depended upon IMF intervention. This trend continued as the fall of the Soviet Union in 1991 ushered in new members to the liberal global economy. Here, the IMF found its greatest role yet: re-engineering the socialist countries into liberal market-based economies. During this time, as tectonic shifts in the global economy solidified, the Fund embraced its influence as a provider of global ideas in times of crisis.

Financial crises continued to rock the international economy throughout the 1990s and 2000s. The interconnected nature of the global economy produced financial attacks in many Asian countries that spread to Russia, Brazil, Argentina, and Turkey. Of these, the 1997–98 Asian Financial Crisis—in which shortages of foreign exchange, falling currency values, and waning investor confidence in countries such as Thailand, Indonesia, and South Korea threatened to spread to economies the world over—played the greatest role in stoking international fears of worldwide economic meltdown, and underscored the need for a new approach to global financial management. The IMF responded with financial resources and its now infamous and often detested economic advice, or "conditionality." The painful adjustment caused by IMF conditionality came under the scrutiny of many of its members' governments. In particular, the IMF and the World Bank were increasingly criticized for their continued involvement in heavily indebted poor countries (HIPCs), and their repeated recycling of debt in these countries. As nongovernmental organizations (NGOs) and civil society organizations stepped up global campaigns in the capitals of advanced industrial countries in the mid-2000s regarding debt recycling and their low chance of debt repayment, the global effort toward debt forgiveness mounted for HIPCs.

Criticism of the IMF also came from emerging market economies. They had been subjected to IMF conditionality in past decades and now called for reform. Emerging market economies were emboldened in the 2000s as the global economic wealth shifted from the "West to the rest." The call for internal governance changes to reflect this shift in global economic wealth persisted, and soon the IMF found itself in an existential crisis: the developed economies, which had most of the decision-making power in the IMF, were increasingly cash-strapped and incapable of increasing IMF liquidity. At the same time, capital-surplus countries of the predominantly emerging market economies, especially in Asia, were distancing themselves from the IMF and self-insuring against speculative currency attacks (increased market volatility caused by the sudden acquisition of currency by previously inactive investors) by swelling their own currency reserves.

This global imbalance of savings was now coupled with the loss of IMF legitimacy in the eyes of emerging market economies and with the attempts by developed economies to preserve their remaining power in global economic governance. Indeed, it was during this same period of IMF decline that dynamic emerging economies began to consider regional alternatives to the Fund. The IMF, caught in the middle of these sweeping forces and self-interested state actors, was deemed by influential actors as irrelevant. At one point in the mid-2000s, there were even fears that the interest earned on IMF lending would no longer cover the Fund's operational costs. Its irrelevancy was further compounded by many countries' abilities to bypass the IMF and raise funds on capital markets without having to comply with the detested IMF conditionality. Financial policies and reform efforts previously funded by the IMF, such as emergency financing to correct trade imbalances or to meet loan commitments, could now be funded by a country's ability to attract global investment, thus eliminating the need to borrow from the IMF and undermining its role in global financial management. This crisis of confidence in the IMF was, however, short lived.

The international financial crisis that began in 2007–08 re-energized the IMF as the provider of ideas, policy coordination, surveillance, and catalytic financing. Moreover, the newly established G20 reaffirmed the central place of the IMF in governing the global economy. Originally gathered in 1999 as a meeting of finance ministers from the world's most powerful states (i.e. United States, China, and Germany), the G20 was convened in Washington as a leader's summit during the onset of the 2008 financial crisis by President George W. Bush, and today continues its work of coordinating global regulatory reform and economic stimulus. The G20 recognized the need for improved global economic surveillance, and it reinvigorated the IMF with an expanded mandate, new resources, and, most importantly, a renewed governance reform agenda. The Fund was now asked to facilitate and support the coordination of the macro-economic policies of the world's pre-eminent economies, and the accountability of these countries to agreed-upon norms and policy commitments. Further, the Fund extended its surveillance role in developed countries, in assistance with the newly empowered Financial Stability Board via its Financial Sector Assessment Program.

The institutionalization of the IMF emboldened it to monitor the pulse of the global economic system. Its once backseat role in observing the workings of the global economy has developed into that of a rule-making and norm-setting crisis manager entrusted with promoting economic growth, foreseeing global economic instability, and being a first responder to global economic crises.

Current debates

With great power, however, comes great responsibility, and the IMF is currently grappling with a number of issues that are of great debate both inside and outside the Fund. Not an easy task, the IMF must balance the needs and realities of member states, the best practices found in the economic discipline, and the hard global economic realities that challenge global economic stability. At the forefront of current debates facing the IMF are issues of capital account liberalization and flows; surveillance and crisis prevention; and transparency and its relationship with civil society. This section reviews each of these debates.

To begin, capital liberalization—the process whereby government regulation on inflows and outflows of capital is relaxed or eliminated in order to stimulate economic growth—has become an increasingly prevalent phenomenon in the globalized market economy. With the Fund at the helm of the global norm-setting system, states were advised to liberalize the entry and exit of capital to spur savings, promote investment, and diversify economic growth. Yet, the question remains: How would this powerful force of capital flows be governed given its inherent lack of regulation and governance? As Rawi Abdelal argues, a tension existed, first, between American views of ad hoc globalization that preferred to see private markets and actors shaping the future course of financialization (White's legacy) and, second, the European view of entrusting the IMF and other international organizations with managing the influx of capital in globalized financial systems (Keynes' legacy).[2]

For analysts and policy-makers alike, the global financial system became more complex and difficult to navigate. Nonetheless, despite the rising influence of private market actors, the IMF remained the locus of debate on the worthiness of capital controls, and, more importantly, on mapping the ebbs and flows of capital. With each subsequent financial and economic crisis, the IMF increasingly became the central node of managing capital flows and of providing solutions to the debilitating effects of "hot money" (capital that is transferred regularly between financial institutions by investors seeking to maximize interest from short-term gains) and financial contagion (the transition of financial shocks and crises from one economy to another). With the rise of global imbalances, the Fund was also tasked with the formidable challenge of coordinating macro-economic and exchange-rate policy between the world's systemically important economies in an attempt to unwind potentially destabilizing imbalances.[3] Its failure to do so is still being felt today.

In short, the growth in Fund access to data on capital flows and to policy-makers and market actors has increased its role in governing capital flows. Ironically, however, the pressure to liberalize capital came in part from the IMF itself: in its loan conditionality with developing countries and emerging market economies, and, to a lesser extent, from the dominant neoliberal economic discipline and its emphasis on free markets and trade liberalization. As the economic crises of the late 1990s and 2000s continued to cripple countries that were experiencing rapid capital outflows and countries experiencing massive capital inflows of "hot money," the IMF attempted to take a middle road approach. Nevertheless, there is a feeling that the IMF still prefers to endorse the concept of capital liberalization, even for countries where such measures may not be appropriate, and that it only grudgingly accepts government attempts to regulate capital flows if the latter can withstand IMF pressure.[4]

Surveillance and crisis prevention are frequently viewed as the issue areas that are the cornerstone of IMF work. All IMF members are obliged to meet the terms of the Fund's Articles of Agreement, which require IMF staff surveillance annually and periodically in the interest of preventing crises, limiting crisis spillover, and advising corrective measures to promote global economic growth and financial stability. The Fund conducts consultations with all IMF members and, with their consent, releases bilateral surveillance reports to the public. Moreover, it composes regional surveillance reports, called *Regional Outlooks*, which are meant to provide an integrated snapshot of regional economic dynamics. Lastly, the IMF produces a global report called the *World Outlook*, which attempts to assess the opportunities and challenges of the global economy. For the IMF, the work of surveillance and crisis prevention is tremendous and not without difficulty. Yet, despite the abundance of information that IMF staff have at their disposal, the Fund has effectively failed to predict and warn of looming crises. In some cases, small warning bells of trouble had rung, but these failed to alert economic systems in time to cope with the often-drastic change of events. Again, in failing to predict imminent crisis through its surveillance mechanisms, the very legitimacy of one of the key roles of the IMF is undermined.

The IMF surveillance function and its role in global financial governance have also been confined by political capture. The challenge, historically, has been that powerful countries—namely, advanced industrial economies—have often ignored IMF surveillance advice, while weaker, indebted countries that requested funding were mandated to adjust their policies to suit IMF conditions. Powerful IMF members also remain the primary benefactors of the organization, given their contribution of the largest share of financial deposits to the Fund. Moreover, these members provide the largest national contingency of IMF staff and the strongest ideological support for IMF paradigms. Most importantly, they hold the greatest decision-making weight on the Executive Board. Nonetheless, the entrenchment of these powerful IMF players has recently been put to the test, and not all may emerge unscathed.

With the onset of the international financial crisis in 2008, it became clear that the advanced industrial economies were not nearly as stable as previously thought. Similarly, it became apparent that financial markets were subject to market failures to an extent not previously believed. More importantly, core industrial states' policies had enormous ramifications on other economies such that contagion became a reality of globalized banking and financial markets. Advanced economies were now seen as "systemically important" countries that could potentially undermine the global economy, and therefore, despite not being traditional IMF borrowers, many argued that these economies should not escape IMF oversight. To address these concerns, the G20 strengthened the IMF surveillance mechanism by requiring all IMF members to complete Financial Sector Assessment Programs (FSAPs) supervised by the IMF. The G20 also created the Financial Stability Board (FSB) to coordinate with IMF advice on weaknesses in the financial, banking, and economic system. While strengthening IMF surveillance has been a process in the making, the 2008 financial crisis cemented the necessity of having the Fund, working in coordination with other multilateral organizations, by ensuring a universal and systemic approach to governing the flow of capital, banking systems, and exchange-rate policies.

Finally, the IMF is grappling with determining how deeply it should go in its relations with member states. While the IMF is accountable to state governments, it must also be sensitive to the fact that state governments ought to be accountable to their people. Although such accusations seem outdated and exaggerated, the Fund has been repeatedly criticized for dealing with corrupt and undemocratic governments. Indeed, many of the IMF's borrowing clients were also autocratic regimes, especially from the 1970s to the 1990s. The Fund soon realized that member governments that failed to implement IMF policies were also unable to implement IMF programs for lack of country ownership. This meant many of these members were in perpetual IMF loan rescheduling cycles and remained heavily indebted. As more countries within the global community, influenced by NGOs and civil societies, realized that debt relief for its poorest members could be an opportunity to call for political accountability, the IMF entered the uncharted waters of calling for good global governance and applying its own advice to internal good governance and corporate best practices.[5]

Moreover, IMF calls for transparency in member states pushed civil society to similarly call for Fund transparency in its dealings with member states. The IMF has responded positively by opening its doors to civil society organizations at its annual meetings, in its support for the Independent Evaluation Office (an internal, independent IMF watchdog), and in its regular consultation with civil society in member countries on its relationship with member states. While some critics argue that this is window dressing at best, at the very least it can be said that the IMF is changing its access to information policies and its rhetoric on the role of civil society in order to enhance its accountability measures, and arguably its interactions with borrowing states have expanded to include a variety of new actors or new working relationships with them. These include parliamentarians, NGOs, media, academics, think tanks, and labor organizations.[6]

Key criticisms and emerging issues

This section provides detailed discussion of the key criticisms and emerging issues currently facing the IMF, all of which involve the central problems with which the Fund must contend in its efforts toward effective global financial governance: first, how to reform the IMF in order to keep pace with the changing realities of the global economic system and, second, how the Fund should contend with the proliferation of actors and sites of authority that have emerged on the global scene.

As global economic power has become diffused and as it has shifted from the industrialized, developed, Group of 7[7] toward the emerging market economies—including Brazil, Russia, India, and China (the BRICs) and the new expanded membership of the G20—the question of how to reform the IMF such that it better reflects this shift in global economic power is a key concern of IMF stakeholders. This question of reform raises another tension evident in the IMF itself—namely, that even as the organization's authoritative power as a key knowledge actor increases in the realm of global economic governance, it is also generating ideas on policies that are no longer under the complete control of powerful members states. The policy outcomes of an increasingly autonomous and emboldened IMF vis-à-vis a diffused political and economic system of power remains to be seen, and merits greater academic attention and study.

One key criticism faced by the IMF concerns its close relationship with certain member states, despite more recent attempts at accountability and transparency. Shortly after its inception, the G20 encouraged the IMF to meet the short-term liquidity needs of the emerging market economies with a fast disbursing credit line that had no conditionality attached. In response, the Fund created a new Flexible Credit Line (FCL) and the new Precautionary Credit Line (PCL) to provide timely and uncapped access to IMF resources to countries that had been preapproved for financing. Much like when countries affected by the 1997 Asian crisis resorted to using contacts in the US Treasury Department to pressure the IMF to expedite its loan process, it has been pointed out that the countries seeking FCL arrangement were, notably, US geopolitical allies.

Moreover, while the Fund should be commended for reacting quickly to the 2008 international financial crisis with the FCL and PCL, the question remains as to whether the IMF has learned from its past failures. Specifically, throughout the Asian crisis, the IMF failed to instill confidence in Asian economies and precipitated the crisis further via its strict conditionality requirements. Indeed, many Asian countries have asked the Fund to acknowledge its past failure in Asia as an important confidence-building measure toward IMF reform. This apology was never formally made, although assessing the needs of Asian countries and renewing their good faith in the IMF should be a top priority given the Fund's mandate of global financial governance. As it stands, however, the question of whether the damage done is so deep that only a regional fund will serve to allay the fears and meet the needs of the Asian countries—for example the Chiang Mai initiative—remains an open one.

In addition to the new credit lines, the IMF was also tasked with coordinating the newly transformed FSB. By drawing on its universal membership, the IMF assisted the FSB, helping it to expand its limited membership base to include the G20. Unlike the IMF, the FSB lacks an organizational structure and a sizeable support staff. However, the FSB's interaction with senior policy-makers and regulatory supervisors serves as part of a useful feedback loop into IMF surveillance exercises, including the above-mentioned World Economic and Regional Economic Outlooks reports, and bilateral Article IV Consultations. Nonetheless, noting the parallels between FSB and IMF functions, the G20 has asked both organizations to promote added cooperation and inter-organizational communication. The FSB and the IMF could then, for example, work to develop early warning exercises against financial systemic risk and develop a regulatory standard that would keep financial institutions, including hedge funds, in check. We now turn to an in-depth discussion of the IMF's renewed and expanding mandates.

Perhaps the greatest endorsement of a further institutionalization of the IMF mandate occurred when the G20 entrusted the IMF with the role of determining whether sound macro-economic and sustainable policies were being followed by its members, and "naming and shaming" those who failed to implement such standards in order to achieve compliance. Expanding on the IMF's traditional surveillance function, the G20 proposed a document entitled *Framework for Strong, Sustainable, and Balanced Growth*. This loose agreement gave the IMF an added hand in independently intervening in countries that put the international economic system at risk by mismanaging their economic policies. To operationalize the Framework, the G20 created the Mutual Assessment Process (MAP)—an innovative part peer-review, part multilateral surveillance governance mechanism. IMF staff were tasked with supporting the MAP to help deepen global macro-economic policy coordination. This process is designed to bypass the IMF's Executive Board in order to prevent an added layer of politicization of the staff's research and recommendations, and represents a significant increase in the IMF's independence and authority.

Following this move for G20 cooperation on shared policy objectives and medium-term policy frameworks, G20 leaders also allowed IMF staff to, in effect, assess countries' progress against an agreed-upon set of "indicative guidelines."[8] Moreover, G20 members must now submit themselves to the IMF–World Bank FSAP, a move that expands existing FSAP purview to encompass all of the G20, notably the United States, which prior to the international financial crisis had not accepted FSAP reviews.

Given the Fund's renewed mandates, the international community is trusting that the IMF will play its intended role as a "ruthless truth-teller," in the words of IMF co-creator John Maynard Keynes. But this arrangement is problematic to say the least. For example, while in April 2011 G20 and IMF staff agreed to policy targets that members could strive for and that the IMF could assess and monitor, these remained shielded from the public and market actors such that there was no external monitoring of the process. Thus, the politicization of the IMF remains a real issue.[9]

The second means of reinvigorating the IMF came with a series of decisions beginning in 2009 to drastically increase the Fund's lending capacity. The first of these was a one-time allotment of SDR 250bn—by far the largest ever such allotment—designed to boost global liquidity at a time of severe malfunctioning in global money markets. The G20 and other prominent economies also moved to bolster the Fund's short-term lending capacity by agreeing to an expanded New Agreement to Borrow (NAB). This decision effectively tripled the Fund's lending capacity to well over SDR 500bn. Finally, in April 2012 the G20 (with the exception of Canada and the US) announced its commitment to add an additional SDR 277bn to the Fund's capital structure. It is important to note, however, that throughout this process of increased IMF lending capacity, the rising powers, symbolized by the BRICs, have been reticent about providing funds directly into the IMF coffers without first receiving guarantees of meaningful voice and governance reforms.

Given that among the G20 consensus has been to keep IMF quotas as a reflection of contribution to the world economy, the case remained that rising economic powers were still highly underrepresented in quota strength and, therefore, in political strength at the IMF. IMF governance reform therefore involved reallocating quotas to give rising powers more decision-making power by reconfiguring the Executive Board. Voice and governance reforms began in 2008 with the decision to implement quota increases for 54 emerging economies, as well as reforms aimed at improving the participation of low-income countries in the Fund's decision-making process. However, unsatisfied by these modest gains, the BRIC nations were quick to assert their newfound influence in the IMF by demanding that any further expansion of IMF resources be tied to additional governance reform. For example, China's assistant finance minister, Zhu Guangyao, recommended rebalancing the IMF by transferring voting weight from the developed countries (which had 57 percent of voting rights at the IMF and 56 percent of voting rights at the World Bank) to the developing countries (which had 43 percent and 44 percent of voting rights at the IMF and World Bank, respectively). China and the remaining BRICs also proposed that the IMF transfer 7 percent of traditional powers' quota share to the rising powers. In response, the G20 offered a shift of 6 percent of quotas from overrepresented countries to underrepresented countries—in effect setting in motion a movement of quotas from the European countries to the emerging economies.

Representation, however, remains a deep-seated problem for the Fund, and the IMF Executive Board is antiquated, to say the least. This board's outdated composition and overly broad scope of activities have garnered criticism from many stakeholders. In particular, pointing to the overrepresentation of European states on the Board (8 seats out of 24), proponents of Executive Board reform have suggested eliminating appointed seats reserved for the largest contributors, thus making room for non-European countries. Some have pointed out that on legitimacy grounds, for example, it is undemocratic to have the BRICs, as members of the IMF, contribute significant funds to the IMF without having a corresponding share of decision-making power. Similarly, if the April 2012 commitment is approved, the absence of Canada and the US from the agreement will result in a significant departure from standard practice, with funding liabilities no longer being tied to quotas and voting rights. The new dynamic created by this shift in IMF governance warrants future research. Nevertheless, reforming the IMF Executive Board and the underlying quota system would improve IMF legitimacy and ultimately global financial governance.

Conclusion

In the aftermath of the worst global economic downturn since the Great Depression, the IMF has suddenly been reborn, or at least rejuvenated, and restored to its previous position as the crown jewel in the international financial architecture. Moving forward, the health of the international monetary system and the global economy will be tied to the effectiveness of the public goods provision provided by the G20—namely, the promotion of enhanced public goods, including environmental protection, technological development, and international security. Effectiveness will, in turn, be tied to the legitimacy of the institution that the G20 relies most heavily on to generate good governance in dealing with crisis and promoting macro-economic stability—the IMF.

This chapter has reviewed the key historical and contemporary challenges faced by the IMF. The institution's legitimacy has ebbed and flowed as it has dealt with persistent critiques of its policy prescriptions, ideological leanings, and internal governance practices—critiques that today are being made by an ever-broader constituency of stakeholders. The Fund has finally begun to accept and address many of these critiques and has made efforts to reform itself. However, much remains to be done. Sustained reform is a necessity, and if history is any guide the IMF will continue to institutionalize its role in governing the global economic system.

At the same time as the IMF's authoritative power increases, and as it becomes a key knowledge actor in global economic governance, many IMF ideas on policies can no longer be controlled by powerful members states. The recent empowerment of IMF staff through the G20 MAP—a framework through which G20 members collectively seek to identify, evaluate, and craft policy so that shared objectives for economic governance can be implemented—is an important example. The policy and political outcomes of an increasingly autonomous IMF and a diffused and more complex global system of power remain to be seen and merit greater academic study. This chapter has attempted a preliminary start to such a project.

Additional reading

1. James R. Vreeland, *The International Monetary Fund: Politics of Conditional Lending* (New York: Routledge, 2007).
2. James M. Boughton and Dominico Lombardi, eds., *Finance, Development, and the IMF* (London: Oxford University Press, 2009).
3. Mark Copelovitch, *The International Monetary Fund in the Global Economy: Banks, Bonds, and Bailouts* (Cambridge: Cambridge University Press, 2010).
4. Susan Park and Antje Vetterlein, eds., *Owning Development: Creating Global Policy Norms in the IMF and the World Bank* (Cambridge: Cambridge University Press, 2010).
5. Reuben Lamdany and Leonardo Maritnez-Diaz, *Studies of IMF Governance: A Compendium* (Washington, DC: International Monetary Fund, 2009).
6. Ngaire Woods, *The Globalizers: The IMF, World Banks and Their Borrowers* (Ithaca: Cornell University Press, 2006).

Notes

1   With GDP itself measured as a blend of a member country's market exchange rates (60 percent) and its purchasing power parity exchange rates (40 percent), defined as exchange rates that take into account the prices of goods in each country's economy in order to obtain prices unaffected by financial market fluctuations.
2   Rawi Abdelal, *Capital Rules: The Construction of Global Finance* (Boston: Harvard University Press, 2007).
3   Mark Copelovitch, *The International Monetary Fund in the Global Economy: Banks, Bonds and Bailouts* (Cambridge: Cambridge University Press, 2010).
4   Pardee Center, *Regulating Global Capital Flows for Long-run Development* (Boston: Boston University Press, 2012).
5   Ngaire Woods, "Making the IMF and the World Bank More Accountable," *International Affairs* 77, no. 1 (2001): 83–100.

6 Jan Aart Scholte, *Building Global Democracy? Civil Society and Accountable Global Governance* (Cambridge: Cambridge University Press, 2011).

7 Or G7, comprised of finance ministers from the powerful industrialized nations of the United States, Japan, Germany, Britain, France, Canada, and Italy.

8 International Monetary Fund, *Review of the Fund's Involvement in the G20 Mutual Assessment Process* (Washington, DC: International Monetary Fund, 2011).

9 Domenico Lombardi, "Washington Roundtable on the Global Economic Agenda," (Washington, DC: Brookings Institution Press, 2009), http://www.brookings.edu/~/media/research/files/papers/2009/10/global%20economy%20lombardi/10_global_economy_lombardi.pdf.

Global Trade Governance

Bernard Hoekman

The 1995 establishment of the World Trade Organization (WTO) was the capstone of a gradual process of global trade liberalization that started after World War II. Average tariffs for many countries in 1950 were in the 20–30 percent range, complemented by a wide variety of non-tariff barriers (NTBs). As of 2010, the average level of import protection had dropped to the 5–10 percent range in most countries, reflecting a process of economic liberalization that started in the 1980s. In conjunction with technological changes that greatly reduced trade costs—telecommunications, the Internet, container-ization, and other improvements in logistics—these reforms led to a boom in world trade. The value of global trade in goods and services passed the US$20 trillion mark in 2011, or 59 percent of global GDP, up from 39 percent of GDP in 1990.

The global trade regime played an important role in supporting globalization by providing a framework for countries to exchange trade policy commitments and establishing a mechanism through which such commitments could be enforced. The trade regime has proved to be quite effective in sustaining cooperation between members. The scope and coverage of policy disciplines expanded steadily from the creation of the GATT in 1947, as did the membership. The dispute settlement mechanism has been particularly noteworthy: over 450 disputes have been adjudicated since the establishment of the WTO in 1995, most of which resulted in the losing party bringing its measures into compliance. The regime proved resilient during the 2008 financial crisis—there was only limited recourse to the type of protectionist policies that characterized the interwar period and the global recession of the late 1970s/early 1980s. Some 30 countries have acceded to the WTO since 1995—including China and Russia.

Most observers agree that the transparency and dispute settlement dimensions have worked rather well. However, following the successful conclusion of the Uruguay Round in 1994, Members proved unable to bring the Doha Development Round, launched in 2001, to closure. Efforts to include disciplines on investment and competition policies failed. The WTO also came to be subject to criticism by a variety of civil society groups, as well as developing country member governments. Concerns were raised about the unbalanced nature of the Uruguay Round, which extended the trade regime into new areas such as intellectual property protection, including for medicines. Ministerial meetings of the WTO in Seattle (1999) and Cancun (2003) were accompanied by large demonstrations against the organization.[1] But business—a core constituency—also became less enamored with the WTO in the 2000s as it became clear that issues of concern to them could not be addressed. This helps explain why many governments increasingly pursued bilateral and regional trade agreements in the 2000s. Over 500 such agreements have been notified to the WTO, raising obvious questions regarding its efficacy and relevance.

This chapter starts with a brief summary of major milestones and features of the institutional framework governing global trade. It then discusses some of the key debates on the governance of the multilateral trade regime, and major challenges and emerging issues that confront the WTO.

History and development of the trading system

The genesis of the multilateral trading system was the interwar experience of beggar-thy-neighbor protectionism and capital controls put in place by governments as they sought to stimulate domestic economic activity and employment. Following the adoption of the so-called Smoot–Hawley Tariff Act, which raised average US tariffs from 38 to 52 percent, US trading partners imposed retaliatory trade restrictions. A domino effect resulted: as trade flows were diverted to other markets, protectionist measures were taken there, and further retaliation ensued. Even before World War II was over, political leaders sought to establish international institutions to reduce the probability of a repeat performance. New international organizations were created with a mandate to help manage international relations and monetary and exchange-rate policies (the UN and the IMF), and to assist in financing reconstruction and promoting economic development (the World Bank). An international organization was also envisaged to manage trade relations, the International Trade Organization (ITO). Greater trade was expected to support an increase in real incomes, and nondiscriminatory access to markets was expected to reduce the scope for political conflicts or trade disputes spilling over into other domains.[2]

The ITO Charter, negotiated immediately after the war, regulated trade in goods and commodity agreements, as well as subjects such as employment policy and restrictive business practices. In parallel to the ITO negotiations, a group of 23 countries—12 developed and 11 developing—pursued negotiations on a General Agreement on Tariffs and Trade (GATT) and an associated set of tariff reduction commitments. The GATT entered into force on 1 January 1948, on a provisional basis, pending the conclusion and the entry into force of the ITO Charter. However, the ITO never was established as a result of the unwillingness of the US Congress to ratify the Charter. Thus, the only result of the trade negotiations was the GATT, which applied on a "provisional" basis

Table 41.1 From GATT to WTO: some key events

Date	Event
1947	Tariff negotiations between 23 founding parties to the GATT concluded.
1948	GATT provisionally enters into force on 1 January 1948, pending ratification of the Havana Charter establishing an ITO.
1950	China withdraws from GATT. The US Administration abandons efforts to seek Congressional ratification of the ITO.
1960–61	Dillon Round of tariff negotiations.
1962	Long Term Arrangement on Cotton Textiles agreed, permitting quota restrictions on exports of cotton textiles agreed as an exception to GATT rules.
1964–67	The Kennedy Round.
1965	Part IV (on Trade and Development) is added to the GATT, establishing new guidelines for trade policies of—and towards—developing countries.
1973–79	The Tokyo Round results in a set of "codes of conduct" on a variety of trade policy areas that countries could decide to sign on a voluntary basis.
1986	The Uruguay Round is launched in Punta del Este, Uruguay.
1993	Three years after the scheduled end of negotiations, the Uruguay Round is concluded on the basis of a "single undertaking" including new rules on services and intellectual property, and agreement to create a World Trade Organization.
1995	The WTO enters into force on 1 January with 128 founding members.
1997	40 governments agree to eliminate tariffs on computer and telecommunication products on a most-favored nation (MFN) basis (the Information Technology Agreement).
1999	Ministerial meeting in Seattle collapses amid large-scale demonstrations and fails to launch a new "Millennium" round.
2001	The Doha Development Agenda round of negotiations is launched in Qatar.
2003	The "mid-term" Ministerial review meeting in Cancun fails to agree to start negotiations on investment and competition policies and ends in disarray.
2006	The Doha Round is declared to be in a state of suspension.
2008	After a concerted effort to overcome the stalemate, Doha talks break down again.
2013	Efforts continue to salvage some of the agreements negotiated in the Doha Round. The number of WTO members reaches 159. The number of preferential trade agreements notified to the WTO passes 500.

Note: Updated from Bernard Hoekman and Michel Kostecki, *The Political Economy of the World Trading System*, 3rd edition (Oxford: Oxford University Press, 2009).

for over 40 years until it became part of the WTO in 1995. While formally never more than a treaty, the GATT gradually evolved into an international institution. Over time more countries acceded to the GATT, and the coverage of the treaty was expanded and modified. Some major milestones are noted in Table 41.1.

The Contracting Parties to the GATT conducted eight rounds of multilateral negotiations between 1947 and 1993. Up to the Kennedy Round, negotiators were essentially preoccupied with the reduction of tariff barriers. Starting in the mid-1960s, recurring negotiating rounds expanded the scope of the GATT to cover NTBs, such as antidumping measures, quantitative restrictions, and product standards. An Agreement on Technical Barriers to Trade was negotiated in the Tokyo Round (1979), followed by agreements on sanitary and phytosanitary measures, intellectual property rights, and measures affecting trade in services in the Uruguay Round (1993). The result has been a gradual extension of the trading system to cover a number of domestic policies that affected the conditions of competition prevailing on markets and that could impede "market access" abroad, even if the measures concerned did not necessarily aim at discriminating against foreign industries.

The evolution of the GATT/WTO is the result of political bargaining, with the terms of the bargain at any point in time (and changes over time) influenced by both governmental and nongovernmental actors. Initially largely a tariff agreement, as average tariffs fell over time, and attention shifted to non-tariff policies affecting trade, the set of interest groups/stakeholders expanded. Thus, the extension of the WTO to include agreements on services and intellectual property rights reflected the interests of industry groups in Organisation for Economic Co-operation and Development (OECD) nations—telecom providers, banks, pharmaceutical firms—to improve access to foreign markets for their products. The interest that these groups had in negotiating new disciplines allowed developing and other countries to demand a quid pro quo in areas that were important to them, including trade in agricultural products and textiles and clothing. These were sectors with above average levels of protection in many OECD countries because in the 1960s and 1970s they were to a large extent removed from the ambit of GATT rules and disciplines—reflecting not just the political power of the workers and farmers employed in these sectors in the industrial countries but also the negotiating strategies that were pursued by developing countries during that period. Rather than engage in reciprocal exchanges of liberalization commitments, developing countries as a group demanded special and differential treatment and less than full reciprocity. As a result, OECD countries had little incentive to remove high trade barriers in sectors of export interest to developing nations.[3]

For much of the GATT period (1947–94), the United States acted as a hegemon, with limited concern for free-riding or non-cooperative behavior by developing countries—which were mostly small players in the trading system. The focus of rule-making and negotiations revolved primarily around OECD nations, in particular the "Quad"—Canada, the European Community (EC), Japan, and the US. This began to change in the late 1980s as a result of the growing economic significance of a number of developing countries in Asia and Latin America. An important development was the emergence of US unilateralism in the 1980s, as reflected in provisions such as Section 301 of the 1974/1988 US Trade Act, which required the US Trade Representative (USTR) to identify and potentially retaliate against countries that maintained policies that were detrimental to US exports, which was defined to include inadequate protection of intellectual property rights. While such exploitation of differences in size ("market power") is an important feature of the operation of the trading system, the rapid increase in the national products of emerging market economies—most notably China—since the mid-1980s means that there are today more players in the WTO who can and will block efforts to push the system into a direction that they do not support. An illustration is the failure of EU and US efforts to obtain agreement to launch talks on WTO disciplines for investment, procurement, and competition policies.

Key features of the WTO

The WTO has five major functions: to facilitate the implementation, administration, and operation of the Agreement; to provide a forum for negotiations; to administer the Dispute Settlement Understanding; to administer the Trade Policy Review Mechanism; and to cooperate with the IMF and World Bank Group to achieve greater coherence in global economic policy-making.

Decision-making in the WTO operates by consensus. Voting is technically possible but in practice does not occur. Consensus implies that any motion or decision can be blocked if any member objects. While in principle this ensures that no country can be steamrollered into accepting decisions or agreements it objects to—giving it leverage to seek either concessions to agree to a matter or to refuse to consent to a change in the rules of the game—in practice the largest players carry more weight than do small ones. One way small countries seek to increase their weight in decision-making is through coalitions. Examples include the G20, an alliance that includes Brazil, China, and India, and the G11, a group of developing countries that were active in the nonagricultural market access talks in the Doha Round.[4]

In negotiations the analogue to consensus is the single undertaking: "nothing is agreed until everything is agreed," that is, the results of a multilateral round are treated as a package deal. Note both the consensus principle and the single undertaking are practices, not formal rules. The consensus practice has a long history in the GATT/WTO, whereas the single undertaking is a practice that was first employed successfully in the Uruguay Round and was central to the creation of the WTO (that is, the WTO was a package deal, take it all or leave it).

The nondiscrimination principle—what in trade parlance is called most-favored nation (MFN)—requires that any concession or commitment be accorded to all members. WTO members may not grant a subset of countries with which they have negotiated concessions better treatment than countries that have not offered such concessions. The only exception is if members conclude free trade agreements with each other or negotiate a so-called plurilateral agreement. Under such an agreement, a subset of WTO members can agree to specific disciplines that apply only to them, and need not apply the associated benefits to non-signatories. However, a plurilateral agreement can only be appended to the WTO on the basis of consensus (and unanimity if there is recourse to voting). Thus, the plurilateral option offers a mechanism for groups of WTO members to agree to rules in a policy area that is not covered by the WTO or goes beyond existing disciplines as long as the membership as a whole perceives this is not detrimental to their interests. Plurilaterals are not without contention. Their use during the Tokyo Round was one of the reasons why the single undertaking was pursued in the Uruguay Round, as many countries were of the view that the Tokyo Round plurilateral agreements had led to excessive fragmentation of the trading system.

The management of the WTO is collective. The WTO is governed by a Ministerial Conference of all members that is scheduled to meet, but has not always, at least once every two years. Between such meetings the WTO is managed by a General Council at the level of officials. This meets about 12 times a year, with WTO members usually represented by heads of delegations based in Geneva. The General Council turns itself, as needed, into a body to adjudicate trade disputes (the Dispute Settlement Body) and to review trade policies of the member countries (the Trade Policy Review Body). Three subsidiary councils operate under the guidance of the General Council: the Council for Trade in Goods; the Council for Trade in Services; and the Council for Trade Related Aspects of Intellectual Property Rights. Separate committees, working parties, and subcommittees deal with specific subject areas covered by multilateral agreements.

All councils, committees, and so forth, as well as all negotiating groups, are chaired by a WTO member representative. The only exception is the Trade Negotiations Committee, the body that oversees multilateral trade talks, which is chaired by the director-general. The latter does not have a defined role in the agreement establishing the WTO. This was left to the Ministerial Conference to determine, which to date it has not done.

The main actors in day-to-day activities of the WTO are the officials that are affiliated with the delegations of members. The member-driven and network nature of the organization puts a considerable strain on the delegations in Geneva and officials in capitals. There are thousands of meetings in the WTO every year. This level of activity makes it very difficult, if not impossible, for citizens of members to keep track of what is happening. At the time of writing there are 159 members. Few, if any, members participate in all meetings and activities, but all committees are open to all members. WTO practice is for members to organize in informal small groups to develop proposals that may subsequently be put forward to the broader membership, either formally through existing bodies and committees or informally to other members/groups. In WTO-speak this process is described as the "concentric circles" approach to agenda setting.

The Secretariat provides technical and logistical support when requested by committees or councils. It has very little formal power of initiative. It is prohibited from identifying potential violations of WTO rules by members and may not interpret WTO law or pass judgment on the conformity of a member's policy. These are matters that are the sole prerogative of members. Similarly, dispute settlement panels are staffed by members of WTO delegations or outside experts drawn from a roster that has been pre-approved by the membership, not the Secretariat.

Dispute settlement in the WTO aims at maintaining the balance of negotiated concessions. If a member is found to have violated a commitment, the remedy is *prospective*: the offending member is simply called upon to bring its measures into compliance. How this should be done is left to the member to determine. If a member does not comply with the ruling of the dispute settlement bodies, retaliation may be authorized in an amount equal in effect to the action taken by the country that violated a commitment. This introduces a significant asymmetry in that small countries that cannot affect their terms of trade cannot exercise much pressure through retaliation against large countries that continue to violate their commitments.

Current debates

The one-member, one-vote, consensus-driven modus operandi of the WTO, combined with a binding dispute settlement mechanism that works well, helps explain why it is difficult to amend the WTO or to conclude multilateral trade talks on a timely basis. There has been much discussion of the reasons for the inability of WTO members to conclude the Doha Round.[5] The failure of the Doha negotiations is a major negative for the WTO as an institution as it is the first multilateral round to have been held under its auspices. Not surprisingly, current debates on the WTO often focus on the reasons for—and implications of—the difficulty of "getting to yes." There are many strands of argument and analysis. Is it because of the governance of the WTO—the consensus rule? Is it a consequence of the negotiating modalities that are employed—such as the single undertaking? Or is the deadlock and disagreement more a function of the (rapid) shifts in relative economic fortunes—the "rise of the rest" and in particular the explosive growth in the share of world trade that has been realized by China? Or, related, that the membership has been expanding rapidly—standing at 159 today compared to "only" 128 in 1995—and that the resulting heterogeneity in interests, commitments, and capacities across members is making agreement difficult to obtain?

Some proposals to address the failure to conclude a Doha deal have centered on the single undertaking practice and consensus-based decision-making. One of the premises of the single undertaking approach in multilateral trade negotiations is that it ensures that all participants will obtain a net benefit from an overall deal. By allowing for issue linkages and requiring a package deal, countries can make trade-offs across issues and increase the overall gains from cooperation. However, the approach also creates potential "hold-up" problems and can have the effect of inducing negotiators to devote (too) much time to seeking exceptions and exemptions. This has led to proposals that WTO members shift towards "variable geometry" and approaches that permit a subset of the membership to move forward on an issue, while allowing others to abstain. Two types of approaches have been suggested, with some advocating that agreements apply only to signatories (as in the case of plurilateral agreements) and others arguing that any agreements between a smaller group of WTO members should abide by the MFN principle, implying that any such deals would need to be so-called critical mass agreements (i.e. that a sufficiently large number of countries participate so as to address potential concerns about free-riding by non-participants).[6]

While agreements among a subset of the membership would allow countries to move forward on issues that are not yet the subject of WTO rules, it is not clear that pursuit of either of these options would make much of a difference in addressing the problems that have helped to hold up a Doha Round agreement. The lack of progress in the Doha Round reflects the assessment of major players that what has emerged on the table is not of sufficient interest to them—it is not that a small group of small countries are holding up a deal. Trade agreements are self-enforcing treaties: if the large players do not see it in their interest to make a deal, they will not—whether the proposed deal involves just a small number of countries or all of the WTO membership. Any outcome, even if endorsed by a majority, will not be implemented if one or more large countries find it unacceptable. Because the WTO is an incomplete contract, governments have a revealed preference for maintaining tight control over the functioning of the organization. There are good reasons why there seems to be a "consensus on consensus." Indeed, economic analysis suggests that the effects of moving away from the status quo on the incentives to cooperate may be perverse—reducing the willingness to agree to rules and to make commitments.[7]

Another likely factor is the increasing complexity of the policy agenda that confronts countries.[8] As tariffs have come down in recent decades, the policies that create negative pecuniary spillovers for trading partners are increasingly "behind-the-border" and regulatory in nature. Agreeing on ways to reduce the market segmenting effects of policies that are aimed at achieving social objectives or addressing market failures is inherently a more complex endeavor than negotiating down tariffs or agreeing to abstain from using quantitative restrictions. Related to this are arguments that some of the policy areas that are critical for international business are not on the WTO table, and that the very slowness of the processes used in the WTO makes the negotiations (and the organization) less relevant. In the span of the decade following the launch of the Doha Round, for example, technologies have changed dramatically, the use of mobile telephone networks and mobile broadband has exploded, giving rise to a host of new policy issues that are not on the table—for example relating to data security and privacy of cross-border flows of information and data.

Another subject of debate concerns the implications of the difficulty that states are having to agree to expand the WTO rule book and deepen their commitments to open domestic markets to foreign competition (that is, to reduce the extent of discrimination against foreign products). A specific focus of debate in this connection is the outside option that is now being pursued by virtually every country in the world—preferential trade agreements (PTAs). There is a long-standing debate among political scientists and economists whether PTAs are good or bad for the trading system—building blocks or stumbling blocks.[9] Much of the relevant literature tends to focus on agreements liberalizing trade in goods, but the practice in the last decade has been for PTAs to deal with the very issues that have proven to be controversial in the WTO. In practice PTAs are often mechanisms for subsets of countries to move forward in liberalizing access to markets for goods, services, and investment (FDI) and to agree on rules of the game for policies that are not subject to WTO disciplines. Fears of large-scale trade diversion and discrimination against non-members of PTAs have not materialized—in large part because countries often have implemented trade reforms on a nondiscriminatory basis as well. But the proliferation of PTAs generates significant transactions costs for businesses as provisions differ across agreements. So far the largest trading nations/blocs (EU, US, China) have yet to negotiate PTAs between themselves.

Yet another area of vigorous debate concerns the appropriate approach in the WTO to economic development. Historically, differences in size and power were addressed through "special and differential treatment" (SDT) of developing countries.[10] This involved agreement that developing countries were not expected to reciprocate fully in trade negotiations and a promise by rich countries to provide preferential access to their markets. As a result, developing countries have greater legal latitude to use trade policies (sometimes called policy space). An example is the rule banning use of export subsidies, from which the poorest countries were exempted. A major motivation for SDT was a perception that trade policy can be a useful instrument to promote industrial development by sheltering nascent ("infant") industries from international competition. Technical and managerial changes have greatly increased the importance of international production chains and created opportunities for firms in low-income countries to specialize in a specific part of a supply chain. These developments have greatly reduced the effectiveness of border protection as an instrument of industrial policy because firms need to be able to import materials that they process into what they export. This has led to greater emphasis on other instruments to assist developing countries, including "aid for trade"— development assistance that is targeted towards enhancing trade capacity. The design and impact of trade-related development assistance in low-income nations is a subject of active debate.[11]

Key challenges and emerging issues

The economic theory of trade agreements is premised on the notion that the motivation for governments to negotiate trade agreements is to improve access to export markets. The objective is to "level the playing field" for foreign firms. Numerous policies can affect access to markets, not just tariffs and quotas that are applied at the border. A major challenge confronting the WTO looking forward is what to include and what not; what should remain sovereign and what should become subject to common disciplines. The WTO has established a good track record when it comes to providing a framework for disciplines on border measures, but has done less to deal with other policies that may also negatively affect foreign firms. Examples include climate change-motivated policies, subsidies of varying types, and the market segmenting effects of regulatory regimes more generally. Increasingly this is an agenda that involves services activities. In most countries upwards of 60 percent of gross domestic product (GDP) is generated in services sectors, where competition/contestability is often affected by regulation that may have disproportionate effects on foreign providers. This confronts policy-makers and polities with the challenge of how best to proceed in ensuring that markets are contestable, while attaining social and economic regulatory objectives.

The lack of progress in the Doha Development Agenda raises the question of whether the political economy dynamics that generated large-scale merchandise trade liberalization carry over to the "new(er)" agenda of "behind-the-border" pro-competitive regulatory reforms. In the 1980s and 1990s domestic policy reform was primarily a function of autonomous decisions by developing country governments, reflecting domestic political economy forces. Multilateral trade negations were primarily used as a vehicle to lock in national trade reforms. It is not clear when it comes to services sectors and regulatory areas whether a similar dynamic will prevail. The mechanics of trade negotiations—a process of bargaining on quid pro quo "concessions"—is not necessarily effective in driving domestic reforms that improve national welfare. Indeed, the mercantilist nature of such efforts may create perverse incentives by inducing governments to make what would be welfare-enhancing policy changes conditional on actions by trading partners. Even if these eventually can be agreed, the history of the Doha Round illustrates that such an approach will take much time and thus can give rise to potentially large opportunity costs of delay. More fundamentally, a process of negotiating regulatory reforms may never be successful or appropriate given the large differences in country circumstances and social preferences that exist.

Given the complexity of many of the regulatory issues that are the subject of discussion in trade agreements, a greater effort is needed to build an understanding at the national level of the effects of prevailing policies and the likely impacts of alternative proposed reforms. Many such reforms do not require—and should therefore not be made conditional on—actions by other governments (trading partners). This does not mean that there are no gains from multilateral agreements on the rules of the game or that negotiations cannot be used as a mechanism to improve access to foreign markets. Nor does it imply that international cooperation cannot help countries identify beneficial reforms. International cooperation can be a mechanism to harness the potential for greater services in trade and investment to support more inclusive growth. But it appears that this requires a shift away from a focus on reciprocal negotiations and towards a process that centers attention much more on the potential gains from *unilateral* (autonomous) action by governments.

Different approaches can be envisaged in pursuing cooperation between states on policies that negatively affect foreign firms. Binding international law—the standard modus operandi of the WTO—is one option. Others include "soft law" forms of bilateral or multilateral cooperation and delegation to independent entities that are given a transparency and analysis mandate—for example tasked with assessing whether and how large any negative spillovers are. In many cases there will be a significant degree of uncertainty as to what the *net* effects of policies are, taking into account the *overall* impact of the relevant policy measures that have a bearing on firm-level competitiveness. A key precondition for agreement on binding international rules is a shared recognition that the negative spillovers associated with a policy (set of policies) are significant and that a specific set of binding disciplines will result in greater efficiency (lower costs). At present there is no such recognition when it comes to important policy areas that are argued to generate negative competitiveness spillovers. This suggests that countries need to work towards putting in place the preconditions for stronger forms of international cooperation—by improving the transparency of applied policies; supporting independent analysis of the effects of policies; and establishing mechanisms through which governments can consult and exchange information.

The importance of policy coherence has already been noted. Much of the literature on policy coherence in the WTO context has focused on the extent to which the activities of other international organizations (IOs) promote the objectives of the WTO and allow countries to exploit the policy space that is provided by WTO rules. Other dimensions of policy coherence are likely to become increasingly prominent looking forward. An example is the consistency of the macro-economic policies pursued by countries with their trade policy commitments. A perennial issue in this regard—going back to well before the creation of the WTO—is concern regarding the potential for manipulation of exchange rates to affect trade competitiveness and undermine negotiated market access commitments. Another example concerns climate change-related policies and their direct and indirect impact on trade policies and trade and investment flows.

A final challenge to the trading system that must be mentioned is the proliferation of PTAs. As mentioned, over 500 PTAs have been notified to the WTO. The implication is that the trading system is increasingly fragmented—the famous spaghetti bowl analogy.[12] While PTAs are a challenge for the WTO, they are also an opportunity as they indicate that governments are willing to make binding commitments on trade matters, even if they are not able or willing to make progress in the WTO. The proliferation of PTAs offers the WTO membership as a whole an opportunity to learn from the many experiments and approaches that are being pursued. PTAs are in some sense laboratories. Over time the best of what is pursued in specific PTAs may be transferable to the WTO. A precondition for such learning is transparency: WTO members need to have information on what is being done in the PTA context, suggesting an important role for the WTO is to provide this information through monitoring and facilitation of regular discussion of the experiences of different PTAs.

Conclusion

The WTO, and the GATT as its predecessor, is in many ways a unique international organization. It has played an important role in supporting global economic growth and poverty reduction by creating a framework of rules of the game for trade policies. Since its creation in 1995 the WTO membership has confronted major difficulties in agreeing on where the institution should go. Many developing countries want to see the rules and processes adapted to better support development objectives. Many high-income countries are of the view that the emerging market countries need to do more to open their markets. The disagreements among the membership are leading to ever more regional trade agreements and splintering of the trade regime.

Additional reading

1. Bernard M. Hoekman, Aaditya Mattoo, and Philip English, eds., *Development, Trade and the WTO: A Handbook* (Washington, DC: World Bank, 2002).
2. Rorden Wilkinson, *The WTO: Crisis and the Governance of Global Trade* (London: Routledge, 2006).
3. Paul Blustein, *Misadventures of the Most Favored Nations: Clashing Egos, Inflated Ambitions, and the Great Shambles of the World Trade System* (New York: Perseus-Public Affairs, 2009).
4. ICTSD, *The Future and the WTO: Confronting the Challenges. A Collection of Short Essays* (Geneva, 2012).
5. Douglas A. Irwin, Petros C. Mavroidis, and Alan O. Sykes, *The Genesis of the GATT* (Cambridge: Cambridge University Press, 2008).
6. Debra P. Steger, ed., *Redesigning the World Trade Organization for the Twenty-First Century* (Waterloo, Ont.: Wilfred Laurier University Press, 2010).

Notes

1 Joseph Stiglitz, "Two Principles for the Next Round, or, How to Bring Developing Countries in from the Cold," *The World Economy* 23 (2000): 437–454; John S. Odell, "Growing Power Meets Frustration in the Doha Round's First Four Years," in *Developing Countries and Global Trade Negotiations*, eds. Larry Crump and S. Javed Maswood (London: Routledge, 2007); J. Michael Finger and Philip Schuler, "Implementation of Uruguay Round Commitments: The Development Challenge," *The World Economy* 23 (2000): 511–525; Amrita Narlikar and Rorden Wilkinson, "Collapse at the WTO: A Cancun Post-mortem," *Third World Quarterly* 25, no. 3 (2004): 447–460.
2 Bernard Hoekman and Michel Kostecki, *The Political Economy of the World Trading System*, 3rd edition (Oxford: Oxford University Press, 2009).
3 Robert E. Hudec, *Developing Countries in the GATT Legal System* (London: Trade Policy Research Centre, 1987).

4 Amrita Narlikar and Diana Tussie, "The G20 at the Cancun Ministerial: Developing Countries and Their Evolving Coalition in the WTO," *The World Economy* 27, no. 7 (2004): 947–966.

5 Kent Jones, *The Doha Blues: Institutional Crisis and Reform in the WTO* (Oxford: Oxford University Press, 2010).

6 Robert Wolfe, "The WTO Single Undertaking as Negotiating Technique and Constitutive Metaphor," *Journal of International Economic Law* 12, no. 4 (2009): 835–858; Peter Gallagher and Andrew Stoler, "Critical Mass as an Alternative Framework for Multilateral Trade Negotiations," *Global Governance* 15, no. 3 (2009): 375–392.

7 Bernard Hoekman, "WTO Reform: A Synthesis and Assessment of Recent Proposals," in *The Oxford Handbook on the WTO*, eds. Amrita Narlikar, Martin Daunton, and Robert Stern (Oxford: Oxford University Press, 2012).

8 Hoekman and Kostecki, *The Political Economy*.

9 Jagdish Bhagwati, "Regionalism and Multilateralism: An Overview," in *New Dimensions in Regional Integration*, eds. Jaime De Melo and Arvind Panagariya (Cambridge: Cambridge University Press, 1993).

10 Hudec, *Developing Countries in the GATT Legal System*; Hoekman and Kostecki, *The Political Economy*, ch. 12.

11 Bernard Hoekman, "Operationalizing the Concept of Policy Space in the WTO: Beyond Special and Differential Treatment," *Journal of International Economic Law* 8, no. 2 (2005): 405–424; Dani Rodrik, "Industrial Policy for the Twenty-First Century," CEPR Discussion Paper 4767 (2004); Faizel Ismail, *Mainstreaming Development into the WTO: Developing Countries in the Doha Round* (Jaipur: Consumer Unity & Trust Society, 2007); and Dominique Njinkeu and Hugo Cameron, eds., *Aid for Trade and Development* (Cambridge: Cambridge University Press, 2008).

12 Jagdish Bhagwati, *The World Trading System at Risk* (Princeton: Princeton University Press, 1991).

Global Development Governance

Katherine Marshall

Stunning changes since 'the end of World War II have reshaped world economies, societies, politics, religions, and cultures. Among the transformations are vast demographic changes—the world population increased from 2.3 to 7 billion people who are ever more mobile, with the majority now living in cities, instead of rural areas as through most of human history. The miracle of the Internet and other technological changes have transformed communications of all kinds. Geopolitics has shifted fundamentally, as have the patterns of war that so dominated the first part of the twentieth century. A bipolar divided world of tense standoffs has made way for a complex and shifting situation of alliances and ideological colors where conflicts are nasty and often long but generally more confined and on the decline. Among the most remarkable transformations is the change from a world that was often seen as irretrievably divided into three: the wealthy capitalist world, the Communist/socialist world, and the large majority "underdeveloped" world.

Today the map looks far different and though many cling to notions of rich and poor, North and South, the reality is far more complex, a configuration of nations and communities that fit uncomfortably with inherited categories and divides. Perhaps most important, the core vision of the 1948 Universal Declaration of Human Rights has truly taken hold: that all people are truly born equal, entitled to a decent life and opportunities. True and full equality remains largely an ideal, but various notions of equity, meaning fairness and balance, today provide the ethical foundation for international relations, at least as an aspiration and principle. Poverty, long seen as inevitable, today is a scourge to be conquered, and because ending poverty is not only just but attainable, it is increasingly seen as a common responsibility. Yet the new world faces remarkable challenges, not least looming climate change, sharp inequalities, financial fragility, and a new global reality where tensions erupt in an instant, spreading across the world with stunning speed.

This chapter explores this history and its related contemporary challenges through the lens of the global architecture of international development. It begins by sketching the history and ideas that have given rise to the complex array of institutions, multilateral and national, public and private, that work to end poverty and advance social justice. Then it describes the workings of this "system" of institutions, and efforts that have arisen to govern it. The chapter continues by looking more broadly to the actors involved in development, beyond the formal, governmental institutions involved, and how their interventions shape and are shaped by the evolving systems that have emerged to govern them at a global level. Then it looks to the global challenges and forces that are reshaping the international development world, calling into question both underlying assumptions and institutions. The conclusion returns to the fundamental challenge that development represents, and whether and how the ideal of global governance can aptly be ascribed to either the ends involved or the means in place to meet it.

Development ideas and challenges

The turning of the millennium in 2000 was the occasion for worldwide soul-searching about the past and a goal to revive and raise aspirations for the future. Within the community of nations that was born between 1944 and 1946, the culmination was the September 2000 Millennium Summit at the United Nations. Development and peace, intertwined, were at the center of reflection and action. There was much to applaud but also a great deal to bemoan. Many nations that were barely a gleam in the eye of patriots in 1945 were thriving and great strides could be claimed in fighting hunger, disease, and ignorance. But wars and misery persisted, albeit often in new forms. Not only did they represent harsh realities of human suffering; with new technologies they were instantly visible and a source of acute shame or blame. Ambitious development initiatives showed mixed results.

The Millennium Declaration and the Millennium Development Goals (MDGs) that were hammered out after the summit as a guide and incentive for action were a reaffirmation of the United Nations' vision of a peaceful, prosperous, and more just world. They reflected the underlying goal of a global social compact and encompassed a commitment to new and bolder forms of partnership. The MDGs also reflected a sense that focus was critical to success in any strategy, so that the goals were refined to the finite number of eight, and deadlines and measurable ends, seen as vital to accountability, were included, with 2015 set as the principle deadline for results. The MDGs also emphasized human development, and focused more on the development of human capabilities through education and health and on quality of life than on economic prosperity. The Millennium Declaration, in its bold reaffirmation of a right to development, linked peace and human development in far more explicit ways than had predecessor documents.

The Millennium Declaration and the annual progress reviews that look to the 2015 deadline for meeting goals reflect a sea-change in thinking and action about development. As World War II ended, notions of development were quite embryonic, both as to the

---

BOX 42.1 REAFFIRMING A GLOBAL VISION FOR DEVELOPMENT IN 2000

The Millennium Declaration (signed by 189 heads of state)

We will spare no effort to free our fellow men, women and children from the abject and dehumanizing conditions of extreme poverty, to which more than a billion of them are currently subjected. We are committed to making the right to development a reality for everyone and to freeing the entire human race from want.

. . . We resolve therefore to create an environment—at the national and global levels alike—which is conducive to development and to the elimination of poverty.

The Millennium Development Goals

1. Eradicate extreme poverty and hunger
2. Achieve universal primary education
3. Promote gender equality and empower women
4. Reduce child mortality
5. Improve maternal health
6. Combat HIV/AIDS, malaria and other diseases
7. Ensure environmental sustainability
8. Develop a global partnership for development

---

end goals and what it would take to get there. The notion that the world was divided into haves and have-nots was generally, if implicitly, accepted. Few truly envisioned what was after all embedded in the lofty documents that launched the United Nations: a world, if not equal, at least equitable and fair, where every human being would have opportunities to thrive. Poverty was still seen as an inevitable if regrettable condition.

Box 42.2 gives an idea of the mosaic of development today and provides a grounding for optimism in what has been achieved in the way of development. Vast changes in the nature of poverty but also in the way it is perceived reflect in part the deliberate efforts of the community of nations, pressured by ideals but also by a process of shaming and competition. Development, in short, has been the result not only of economic and social forces but of an array of institutions and programs, transnational and national, public and private, which aimed deliberately at such a global transformation.

In the decades after 1945, development took form first as an idea and an ideal, then as a set of institutions, practices, projects, and programs. South Korea and Singapore were transformed from seemingly hopeless societies into thriving nations. China, India, and Brazil defied the pessimists who bemoaned their intractable problems. Development plans, in the sense of deliberate strategies and programs, proliferated. Some succeeded, some failed spectacularly. Thinking about what drove change and how it could be influenced through policy and investment changed radically, from simplistic recipes centered

BOX 42.2 IMAGES OF GLOBAL DEVELOPMENT, MAPPING POVERTY IN 2011

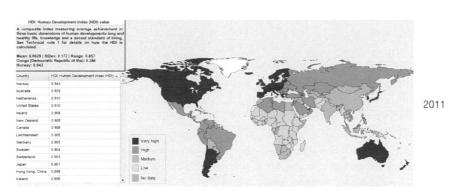

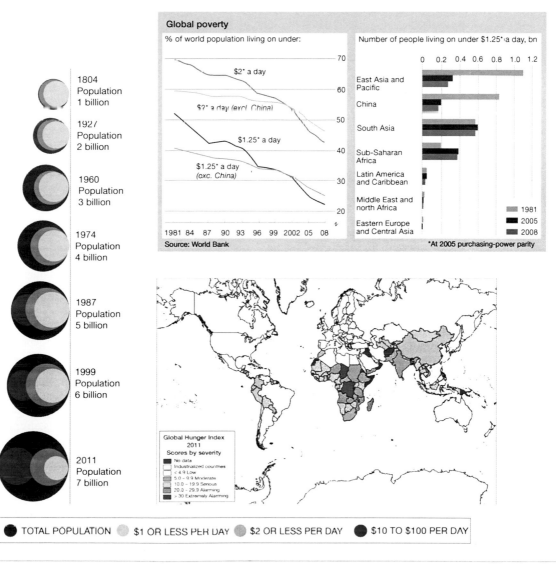

on capital investment to a healthy respect for the complexity of social and economic change and the instruments that could bring it about. The scope of what was considered development expanded. In the early years, health and education were not directly associated with development but came to be seen as central. The idea that women deserved special focus was scoffed at for a time, but integrating women into mainstream development strategies also came to be seen as vital for successful social transformation. Science and technology as well as ports, power, and roads became part of the development venture. And growing awareness of the actual and potential impact of climate change and environmental degradation changed both language and approaches.[1]

By 2013, the notion of development had become so broad that it encompassed virtually every dimension of social and economic life. A multitude of institutions are involved in development today; indeed, few global institutions are not part of the venture when it is broadly defined. Trade and investment were long seen as the central planks that would ensure growth and progress. Today the digital divide and technology, micro-finance, nutrition, legal systems, and scientific research are all part of the development venture. The same applies for academic and professional disciplines.

Initially largely a matter for economists and diplomats, today virtually every discipline, from engineering and anthropology to psychology and medicine, is involved. And, increasingly in the era of the Internet, debates about what works and what does not, who is responsible, and the ethics of action have broadened and raged. From an enterprise where strategies were concocted in (literally) smoke-filled rooms by white men, development today is a topic where citizens and leaders in every corner of the world are involved. Few governments do not accept at a level of principle that they, individually and as part of the United Nations, have a responsibility to advance global development or at least to fight abject poverty through foreign aid and appropriate policies. Global social movements, for example the Jubilee Debt Campaign and Make Poverty History, have transformed development from technocratic, poorly understood territory into a complex array of global campaigns and continuing exchange and action.

In sketching this complex history, six key challenges-cum-changes stand out. The first affects the complex motivations for foreign aid for development. In the early years support by richer countries for international development was quite baldly justified by a blend of interests and charity. Interests involved a recipient's fit with the donor's diplomatic, strategic, and commercial interests. Especially where humanitarian emergencies were involved, compassion and charity were also evoked, building on ancient religious traditions of charity and nineteenth century traditions of social welfare. Today notions of human rights and the "right to development" (embedded, however hazily, in human rights) are a central justification, though interests, charity, and fear play their parts also.[2]

Most early development programs were the domain of "experts," mostly coming from abroad. "Technical assistance" was provided by well-paid professionals from wealthier countries, who compensated for human capacity shortages and called many shots. Gradually, however, the folly of designing programs without hearing and heeding the voices of those who were to benefit became apparent and "consultation" emerged as a norm. This progressed to "participation" and then to "empowerment," a contemporary development norm. More fundamentally the essential right of a country to manage its own destiny is reflected in the core objective of "country ownership." While the essential meaning of ownership and empowerment is subject to plenty of debate, the shifting vocabulary reflects, here, as it does for charity versus rights, a vital change in the understanding of the ethics of development work as well as its practice.

Much early development work assumed rather simplistically that either market forces or (in countries where Communist influence prevailed) economic planning and direction would transform societies, propelling modernization through growth. Reality soon intervened, as did academic research and the wise insights of leaders and thinkers like Julius Nyerere, Luis Ignacio Lula da Silva, Amartya Sen, Sadako, Robert McNamara, James D. Wolfensohn, and many others. Far more than investment and free trade were needed. The sticky poverty that kept the poorest in societies from benefiting from progress drew attention to the complexities of poverty, which involved culture, religion, psychology, and above all institutions. Development became an increasingly multi-disciplinary, multi-sectoral venture. The essential notion of human capabilities—developing human capital through education, health, and opportunity, moved from the periphery to the center.

Understandings about the respective roles of public and private sectors, and of the civil society organizations that have exploded in complex mosaics in recent decades, have changed radically. The proper role of the state remains an issue for debate, both globally and in many countries, but simplistic notions that governments could "pick winners" and steer progress in specific directions have been shattered by the growing dominance of private enterprise in resource flows and by the witness of dynamic market-led progress in many settings, which have so often astounded both policy gurus and politicians who thought they were in control. The growing role of private actors has focused sharp attention on financial sectors, on trade reform, and above all on proper regulation and the perils of predatory corruption. Social entrepreneurship, galvanizing the energies of often small-scale actors to bring transformation, and microfinance, small-scale lending that can unleash the potential energies of poor people, especially women, and draw on their own resources to bring change, today are essential parts of what is understood to bring development. As civil society organizations have multiplied, transparency and citizen engagement have taken on far greater importance. *Why Nations Fail*, a sweeping and thought-provoking analysis by Daron Acemoglu and James Robinson published in 2012, draws the central lesson that it is inclusive institutions that matter most.[3] Strong institutions that go beyond the interests of elites are what make for development success.

Monitoring and evaluation entered the vocabulary fairly early on because public financial resources were involved, but the importance of accountability and working to achieve specific results now has an unshakable grip on development thinking. Measuring and setting targets has reached the level of an art. One driver has been growing awareness of the reality of corruption and massive losses of development resources to illicit private gain (that is, corruption in its many forms) in some countries. Transparency (to shed light on decision-making and actual spending) and anti-corruption strategies as a part of good governance are indispensable aspects of development thinking and action today.

Finally, states that are, for various reasons, fragile (poorly governed, facing insurmountable development challenges, or riven by conflict) need different, tailored treatment. This group of some 35 countries is often most in need of external support yet defies traditional development approaches, because leadership and institutions are so weak. At an international gathering in Busan in late 2011, a "New Deal" was announced for this group of countries. Similar appreciations apply for the poorest communities, even those located in affluent societies and countries. A set of new approaches, institutions, and financing mechanisms are emerging to deal with the stubborn cases at the bottom of the socio-economic ladder.[4]

Development institutions

The institutions involved in international development and humanitarian work have increased, in quite stunning ways, in number and complexity since the late 1940s. They include today an elaborate set of formal development institutions and a host of other institutions that, with varying degrees of formality, are involved in the development enterprise (here termed development actors). Given the proliferation of institutions and programs, a variety of institutions and mechanisms have emerged to coordinate and guide the "system" of institutions. However, while the terms "development architecture," "international system," and "international community" are fairly commonly used, the institutional array has in practice evolved organically, without a grand design or strategy, and this historical reality is clearly reflected in the realities of institutions at work. This section focuses on the formal institutions and on the relationships among them and between development institutions and the governments of the countries where development work takes place.

Taken chronologically, the first development institution that emerged, while World War II was still raging and the post-war United Nations was still on the drawing board, was the International Bank for Reconstruction and Development, or the World Bank, born in 1944 at the Bretton Woods Conference in New Hampshire. Its name reflects the reality that development was almost an afterthought: the focus at the time was on the International Monetary Fund (IMF), responding to the understanding that hammering out some kind of order in global financial systems to avoid the crises that had dogged the interwar period was the priority (Bretton Woods was primarily about the IMF), and on post-war reconstruction. The World Bank succeeded and worked alongside the United Nations Relief and Rehabilitation Agency (UNRRA), founded in 1943, with a similar concern and focus on what would come after the war ended. Like the IMF and the World Bank, it was essentially an American institution in its early years. The World Bank began operating in 1946, with the first development loans in 1948 (to India and Chile); the US Marshall Plan essentially displaced both the World Bank and UNRRA in their post-war relief and rehabilitation work, and the focus shifted towards development. Reflecting the then understanding that development was primarily about capital (and trade—giving rise to a parallel set of institutions), a series of multilateral development banks and institutions followed suit, the first being the Inter-American Development Bank (IDB) in 1959.

Today there are some 20 such institutions, operating at global and regional levels, with varying sources of capital and differing systems of governance. The World Bank plays a special (if contested) role as a leader in the development field because of its long history of engagement, its large commitment to intellectual leadership, for example through the annual World Development reports, and, perhaps most of all, its capacity to mobilize financial resources, both through borrowing on private markets and through capital shares and gifts from wealthier nations.

The United Nations includes a wide range of core and specialized agencies that have taken on important roles in development, and these also took shape, and multiplied, over time. Today the lead institution within the United Nations system is the United Nations Development Programme (UNDP), which is looked to as both intellectual leader and coordinator. It was created in 1965, merging the United Nations Expanded Programme of Technical Assistance, created in 1949, and the United Nations Special Fund, established in 1958. At a more formal level both the United Nations General Assembly and the Economic and Social Council (ECOSOC) are frequently involved in development issues. The United Nations Children's Fund (UNICEF), the Food and Agriculture Organization (FAO), the United Nations Population Fund (UNFPA), and virtually all the other specialized UN agencies are directly and actively involved in development work.

Looking at the regional level, the most active and significant institution is the European Union (EU). Its development focus and mandate date from the 1957 Treaty of Rome and its activities have expanded over the years. At first confined to territories (colonies as well as states that had become independent) linked directly to European Community members, today the EU is one of the largest sources of development assistance. The Islamic Development Bank, active in many of the 56 member nations of the Organisation of the Islamic Conference, is an increasingly significant player.

Finally, many countries have established bilateral development programs. Their number has increased rapidly, from five or six in the mid-1940s to at least 56 today (and the number is ever increasing).[5] Among the best known are the American Agency for International Development (USAID) and the UK's Department for International Development (DfID). Most bilateral programs had multiple rationales and origins, ranging from humanitarian objectives (responding to disasters) to commercial interests. Bilateral concerns tend to figure prominently in many bilateral aid programs. Bilateral aid takes many and increasingly complex forms. In the United States, for example, at least 26 federal government departments are involved in international development assistance in various ways, and state governments also have a variety of programs. Programs vary from explicit trade promotion to programs like the Peace Corps and university support for training and research.

The bilateral aid system (if it can properly be so termed) has an institutional support mechanism, the Development Assistance Committee (DAC) of the Organisation for Economic Co-operation and Development (OECD). Created in 1960, it is considered "the venue and voice of the world's major bilateral donors." Among its products are statistics on official development assistance (ODA).[6] DAC has broadened the scope of its work over the years, and increasingly has sought to include newer development players. It is the leader in the recent efforts to harmonize aid and establish norms for development work, and was the convenor of the 2011 Busan Conference in Korea.[7]

Development actors

In the early decades of international development work, public agencies clearly led the way, and the prevailing assumption was that governments were the leaders both of development processes in poorer countries and in providing and orchestrating development assistance. This has changed radically. Both in terms of the number of actors and in overall aid flows, what prevails today is a far more diverse picture. Among the most significant changes are the sharp increase in volume and proportion of financial flows to developing countries coming from private sector actors and the active role of a wide range of civil society entities. Also significant (this dating back further) are private philanthropists and foundations (notable among them the Ford and Rockefeller Foundations, with the Bill and Melinda Gates Foundation today dwarfing the growing array of foundations, large and small). Finally the role of academic institutions and media, as shapers of ideas and a source of expertise, has grown in importance. Many universities have actively developed training programs targeted at development leaders —Harvard University, Columbia, Georgetown, London School of Economics, the University of Manchester, Singapore's Lee Kuan Yew program, CERDI (Center for Studies and Research on Development at the University of Auvergne) and the Dutch Institute of Social Studies are just a few examples, and many more have large research programs. Media focus on development is less sharply defined but again there is an array of exchanges and special training programs.

From the earliest days of development the private sector was seen as the principle driver for investment and thus progress. In the 1950s, the International Finance Corporation (IFC) was established within the World Bank Group so that riskier investments and joint ventures could be encouraged, and since then a variety of investment guarantee mechanisms have also emerged to encourage investment. Governments have developed mechanisms to encourage their companies to invest and operate overseas, and private companies have increasingly looked to emerging economies. This aggregation of efforts, public and private, has borne fruit and, worldwide, private aid flows have increased dramatically, dwarfing official development assistance, and obviously making important contributions to development, for example in water supply and industry. In the US funding from private aid actors—including foundations, corporations, NGOs, universities, and religious organizations—exceeded US government assistance in 2007: US$33.4bn compared with US$21.8bn.

The creative energies of the wide range of private actors are now seen as a motor not only for investment but also for innovation. Large transnational companies are clearly major investors, in infrastructure and mining, for example, but there is growing interest in social entrepreneurs who may operate at a smaller scale and in mechanisms like the "patient capital" that the Acumen Fund promotes. Microfinance and support for small and medium-sized enterprises has been a popular avenue for development. The increasing understanding of the potential of even very poor people to act when given the resources, coupled with growing appreciation of their market power as the "bottom of the pyramid," has prompted growing interest in a host of new mechanisms to mobilize and channel private capital and energies towards development ends.

All is not easy where the private sector is concerned. Microfinance has real potential downsides if it is seen as a silver bullet and if insufficient attention is paid to solid institutional and financial practices. A rash of suicides in India and other events have brought a welcome sobriety to the enthusiasm that prevailed in microfinance circles, but unleashing the energies of poor people is a vital insight and important mechanisms have emerged as a result. Likewise, the potential for large transnational companies to spur development and create jobs is enormous, but these global giants dwarf the capacities of many poor country governments to regulate and their motives are rarely altruistic and centered on development and poverty alleviation (with the exception of growing corporate social responsibility programs). A live issue for development actors is the nature of partnerships involving private companies and other actors: how to ensure effective regulatory measures that do not stifle innovation and investment, how to benefit from the undoubted skills and verve of the private actors? Creating a positive investment climate at the policy, legal, and practical level has emerged as a central development concern, including removing barriers to investment and correcting obvious market distortions. Issues like large-scale land purchases in Africa and aggressive natural resource protection programs are live issues on the agenda, though who can and should act to check excesses and channel energies in positive directions is far from clear.

"Global civil society" is one of the more contested terms used today because it involves so many different kinds of institutions, but this loosely defined group has taken an increasingly important place among development actors. The field includes many ancient actors, notably churches, missions, temples, and the like that have for centuries run schools and clinics and engaged in small-scale development projects at community level. In the period after World War II organizations like CARE, Oxfam, Catholic Relief Services (CRS), and several Jewish organizations emerged with essentially humanitarian, relief objectives. Over time their numbers multiplied and their mandates shifted from short-term relief towards longer-term development.

Today there are many thousand transnational organizations (most commonly termed nongovernmental organizations, or NGOs) that operate in every sector and virtually every country worldwide. Some, like World Vision and CARE, are enormous organizations, often with a franchise-type organization that gives increasing weight to country-based affiliates. Islamic Relief, a transnational entity that emerged in response to droughts and state collapse in the Horn of Africa, is an example of an array of newer entities in the development field, and it now operates (from a base in Birmingham, UK) with a growing number of national affiliates. These organizations are commonly engaged both in advocacy, for policies and development assistance, and in operations, especially at the community level. Many work in close partnership with bilateral aid programs as well as with parts of the United Nations. With the proliferation of civil society organizations, coordinating and support bodies, for example Interaction in the United States, and Civicus globally, have emerged as a voice and practical network for support.

Nonetheless much attention is drawn today to the question of how civil society is represented in development circles. A common complaint is that "if you are not at the table, you end up on the menu." Which tables, however, and which representatives? Which voice? The broad realm of civil society took on a far more visible presence during the 1980s and 1990s. The earliest protests and demands for action centered on environmental issues and the norms that international development institutions followed in making investments, but these specific concerns broadened, and for a time what one actor termed a "swarm" of NGOs came close to paralyzing development operations in some sectors. The era of sharp protests and conflicts culminated in the late 1990s in violent demonstrations in Seattle in 1999, during meetings of the World Trade Organization (WTO), and Genoa, during the 2001 meetings of the G8, but virtually every large development gathering at the time involved hordes of security forces and chain link fences that separated "delegates" from civil society actors eager to make their voices known.

It was largely the terrorist attacks and especially 11 September 2001 that changed the picture; new security concerns took precedence and the energies of what had always been a highly diverse grouping of protesters turned towards more decentralized targets and forms of action. The result of the years of tension, however, was significant, indeed transformative, for the world of development. One of the lasting changes was the opening up of both the operations of development institutions (transparency), with far more information available today than several decades ago, and a raft of new accountability mechanisms and a continuing emphasis on results. The Inspection Panels created for both the World Bank and the regional banks, where those who argue that development actions have brought them harm have the right to appeal, are examples. The Jubilee Debt Campaign that called on ancient Biblical ideas of a periodic "jubilee" of debt forgiveness, was instrumental in changing long-set policies on debt, taking the year 2000 as an inspiration. Large public mobilizations, for example in Gleneagles, UK, in 2005, come under the loose banner of the appeal to "make poverty history," and they engage both civic groups and celebrities like Bono and Angelina Jolie in making development a public moral call and cause. Civil society actors are a clear and active presence in most policy forums today.

Large transnational foundations like the Rockefeller and Ford Foundations have long played dynamic roles in development work. Above all, their independence from both domestic and international politics and their fungible resources have allowed them to support innovation and to intervene in areas like human rights where political leaders feared to tread. The enormous resources of the Bill and Melinda Gates Foundation today have directed new admiration and hope, as well as some fears, to the power of this group of institutions and actors. A host of smaller foundations and private philanthropists (institutional and individual) also play important roles in the development field, though often they come under the radar of both attention and resource counting. Again, they can support important innovations and ensure that support goes to the communities where people are in need. The drawback is that with increasing awareness that strategic focus is a vital element for success the proliferation of individual, often uncoordinated efforts is a matter for concern. This applies, for example, to the millions who visit poor countries with church mission groups.

There is increasing attention to a long-neglected source of development finance and development innovation: remittances from people living overseas. This vast set of actors was long ignored despite its fairly obvious relevance for development, in part because it is not easy to measure and to track, much less to direct. But the energy and resources of both diaspora communities and the remittances they send home are an important resource. The World Bank estimates that recorded flows reached US$325bn in 2010, up from US$307bn in 2009.

Falling in all categories are those loosely termed "new actors." What is significant here is that they are so varied and the picture is so dynamic. Although China has been engaged in development support for decades, the sharp increase in its profile in recent years and the fact that the government was rarely part of the formal development "clubs" means that it is sometimes seen as a "new" actor. More apt are the BRICS (Brazil, Russia, India, China, South Africa) and Indonesia, which indeed are finding new voice and taking on new roles in the development world, both transmitting ideas and also in finance. The rich countries of the Arab world are witnessing an explosion of bilateral programs as well as many new private foundations. "South–South" cooperation has long been an important idea, deflating the notion that all technical expertise and support flows from the "rich West" to the "poor South," but in the complex geopolitical configurations of today such unexpected partnerships are taking on greater prominence. An illustration among many is advice flowing between Malaysia and South Africa (in both directions) on land reform, development of smallholder agriculture in relation to large farm sectors, and mechanisms to encourage and empower minority business.

Development governance?

The development world today sometimes seems like something from the *Sorcerer's Apprentice*, with an ever multiplying number of institutions at work, amidst an ever louder concern for strategic focus, accountability, and consistent, higher-quality effort in order to achieve development results. Is this development system a system? Is it in any manner governed? And indeed, is it governable?

What emerges clearly from the earlier discussion is that today's array of institutions involved in international development in no way constitutes a planned, organized, rational system. The institutions have emerged as a product of many forces of history. More significant, against the insight that international development today in effect is intertwined with virtually every dimension of international social, political, economic, and cultural affairs, every discipline, and all countries of the world, the lack of coherence is hardly surprising. That said, international development is set within broad global objectives, most prominently those set out in the MDGs, but also in the international humanitarian system, with its norms and coordinating mechanisms, and the covenants and implementation mechanisms that support international human rights.

The most purposeful mechanisms that have emerged with the objective of supporting a more coherent approach to global development fall within the United Nations system, including the international financial institutions (the so-called IFIs) and the multilateral development banks. The most visible and significant efforts to address well-known weaknesses of international development governance are the series of aid harmonization initiatives, starting with the OECD Development Assistance Committee (DAC) meeting in Rome in 2003, followed by a succession of efforts to build on that consensus in Paris in 2005, Accra in 2008, and Busan in 2011. Not all development actors (by any measure) are part of these efforts, and not all issues are addressed, but they constitute a purposeful effort to bring more coherence into what is recognized as an imperfect system. This succession of meetings and related events addressed long-standing issues of harmonizing aid practices, considering appropriate mechanisms for conditionality, procurement, tied aid, and other issues. Meanwhile efforts were made to align foreign aid with national public investment programs, often through budget support, and to promote important learning, for example about the benefits of educating girls and the need for far more active policies and investment in agriculture. One important outcome of the December 2011 Busan meeting was an aid transparency initiative, aimed at improving the quality and timeliness of information about development programs.[8]

Another was more explicit recognition of the need for a special set of measures, including more flexible financing mechanisms, to address the needs of fragile states.

The governance of development is also a leading topic for the United Nations, and especially the General Assembly. Almost from its inception the General Assembly has been a forum where the practical and ethical concerns of global inequality and development are on the agenda. Issues like HIV and AIDS, gender justice, food security, and maternal mortality have been the subject of countless international conferences and feature regularly on the General Assembly (GA) agenda as well as ECOSOC and other UN bodies. Since 2000, a series of special conferences (notably the 2002 Monterey Conference on Financing for Development) and regular GA meetings have worked to make the principles of accountability enshrined in the MDGs a living reality.

Other important global forums where development priorities and issues are sometimes at the center are the array of Gs—that is, the G7 (the group of the wealthiest nations), G8, G7+ (fragile states forum), G77, G24, and, most significant in the present era, the G20. The latter includes countries that represent some 80 percent of the world's population and, when economic crises do not drive them from the center of the agenda, takes up development priorities. A new grouping is titled the G7+, consisting of fragile states led by Afghanistan and Timor Leste, that is behind the Busan "New Deal" initiative.

There are other significant mechanisms, some of them formal, but others informal. Among the latter is the Paris Club, an informal mechanism run by the French Treasury that has led the processes underlying bilateral debt negotiations. The London Club, now largely in abeyance, was a similar mechanism directed towards commercial bank debt.

And regional fora, for example the Southern African Development Community (SADC), ASEAN (Association of Southeast Asian Nations), and the African Union, play increasingly significant roles in development advocacy and, less often, leadership and coordination of specific development programs. Where they are most significant is where post-conflict abuts with development, as they play roles in the broader effort to resolve the barriers that block development (security issues, financial arrears, or investment disputes, for example) and mobilizing resources.

The most important, pragmatically grounded development governance in practice takes place at the country level. There are time-honored mechanisms, some now largely in abeyance, which include the Aid Consortia for India, Pakistan, and Bangladesh. The World Bank and the UNDP have led many country aid coordination mechanisms, though these are increasingly giving way to country-led mechanisms.

The multilateral banks, and especially the World Bank, play critical roles in the many situations where resource mobilization is urgent and essential for progress. This applies often in post-conflict or post-disaster situations. Thus, in the new focus on fragile states (the New Deal is part of this global focus), mobilizing extraordinary resources is an essential element. Meetings termed, for example, the "Friends of X country" are organized to seek consensus on the strategic framework for assistance, priorities, and modalities.

The formal coordinating bodies and mechanisms focus on a wide range of development issues, though the level of aid flows is a common issue. With the financial pinch in many wealthier countries, continuing bilateral and multilateral aid flows are always in question, and the long-standing concern that flows are erratic and unpredictable, making the job of development managers especially difficult, is always there, notwithstanding the very general, unrealized pledge that wealthier countries will devote 0.7 percent of their gross national income to development assistance.

A central question in 2013 is what comes after the 2015 deadline for achievement of the MDGs. Will the current, only partially achieved, MDGs be rolled over? Will new targets be added? Will the effort essentially wither as global attention shifts to new priorities?

The discussion is already underway. The UN Secretary-General has appointed a 27-person group to lead the discussion of development, or sustainable development goals, that will come after 2015, and to ensure wide consultations in the process. It is too early to predict the outcome. What is certain is that the year 2015 will provide an opportunity to take stock of the development challenge in light of twenty-first century objectives that include old priorities, notably human rights and peace, gender justice, and the true elimination of abject poverty. New realities also need to be reflected, including the "flattening" and broadening of development actors, the voices of the largely voiceless, fighting corruption with greater passion and effectiveness, and ensuring a true commitment to the rule of law and opportunity for all. The rapprochement, if not the merging, of climate change and development agendas appears to be a new reality. The ideals for new, balanced partnerships built on mutual respect and a philosophy of development grounded in rights, not charity, are likely to take on greater prominence, especially where the poorest, most fragile nations and communities are concerned.

Conclusion

The challenges to the global governance of development touch the most fundamental challenges for global governance overall. That is because development can no longer be seen as a segmented effort through which richer countries "help" poorer countries. Rather, it presents the far broader challenge of how the international community of states in 2013 sees the ideal society and economy that human rights are really about. What are responsibilities? Proper means? Measures of success? Accountability? Appropriate conditionality? It is telling that in discussions about the paradigm for development the idealistic vision of a small country, the Kingdom of Bhutan, has captured not only imaginations but also academic and political attention. The reason is that Bhutan articulates its development framework as a search for "Gross National Happiness." Development is about where we should be going as well as how we get there.

The international development system today is not a system that can be readily defined, and far less can it be governed in its entirety. It is far too complex and dynamic, with a vast number of often very independent actors. There are many mechanisms that aim to increase the coherence of the system and also ensure far more accountability, an important priority given that unequal power is the essence of the development challenge. Some, like the OECD/DAC initiatives to assure greater aid harmonization, are yielding encouraging results. Country-led coordination mechanisms show increasing rigor and impact. There is much wisdom that has emerged from six decades of experience with purposeful development efforts, and important success stories to underscore the conviction that ending poverty is indeed a possible dream. Norms and standards for development work, ways to measure achievements, and innovative ideas that integrate, for example, environmental concerns with social policies are all clearer now than ever before.

Nonetheless, stepping back from the specifics of aid harmonization, accountability measures, and UN assessments of progress or lack thereof towards the MDGs, it is clear that the systems are changing rapidly, reflecting the major forces of change that are transforming the geopolitical landscape. The systems in place, such as they are, largely reflect the political and economic realities of past decades. They are, for example, predicated on a system of "donors" and "recipients," of public aid flows to support development projects designed to address identified needs, and centered in the countries that held power after World War II. They assume a world divided into two or three categories of countries. Many of the institutions have adapted to changing realities in important ways. They have opened up their tightly held documentation and data to public scrutiny, and more of the "clubs" are including new actors. Civil society, long exiled from the tables where policies were made, is welcome in many places. Women are part of the discussion. Corruption is openly, even constantly, discussed, with action programs to address it. Climate change is seen as an integral part of the development agenda.

Yet, in many ways the formal institutional structures still reflect the power and social realities of a bygone era, and the shape of new structures is only slowly emerging. It is obvious, nonetheless, that future mechanisms will be far more complex and will move and change faster than those slowly shaped by consensus in past processes. They will involve far more actors, will be messier, and, if anything, will be harder to govern and harder to assess. That is the reality of global development governance today.

Additional reading

1. Katherine Marshall, *The World Bank: From Reconstruction to Development to Equity* (London: Routledge, 2008).
2. Rorden Wilkinson and David Hulme, eds., *The Millennium Development Goals and Beyond: Global Development after 2015* (London: Routledge, 2012).
3. Stephen Browne, *United Nations Development Programme and System* (London: Routledge, 2011).
4. Daron Acemoglu and James Robinson, *Why Nations Fail: The Origins of Power, Prosperity, and Poverty* (London: Profile Books, 2012).
5. Robert Calderisi, *Healing the Nations: The Catholic Church and World Development* (New Haven, CT: Yale University Press, 2013).
6. Paul Collier, *The Bottom Billion: Why the Poorest Countries Are Failing and What Can Be Done about It* (Oxford: Oxford University Press, 2008).
7. William Easterly, *The White Man's Burden: Why the West's Efforts to Aid the Rest Have Done So Much Ill and So Little Good* (London: Penguin Books, 2007).

Notes

1   Katherine Marshall, *The World Bank: From Reconstruction to Development to Equity* (London: Routledge, 2008), provides a fuller history.

2   Katherine Marshall, "Climbing up to the Light," *Reflections: A Magazine of Theological and Ethical Inquiry* 97, no. 2 (2010): 5–7.

3   Daron Acemoglu and James Robinson, *Why Nations Fail: The Origins of Power, Prosperity, and Poverty* (London: Profile Books, 2012).

4   Among others, the work of British economist Paul Collier has helped to bring about a paradigm shift, with a new focus on what he termed "the Bottom Billion."

5   The World Bank, "Aid Architecture: An Overview of the Main Trends in Official Development Assistance Flows," February 2007, http://www.worldbank.org/ida/papers/IDA15_Replenishment/Aidarchitecture.pdf.

6   For a history, see OECD, "DAC in Dates: The History of the OECD's Development Assistance Committee," http://www.oecd.org/dac/1896808.pdf.

7   For a detailed and perceptive analysis of the Busan process and outcome, see J. Brian Atwood, "Creating a Global Partnership for Effective Development Cooperation" (Center for Global Development, October 2012), http://www.cgdev.org/files/1426543_file_Atwood_Busan_FINAL.pdf.

8   Aid Transparency Initiative, http://www.aidtransparency.net.

Global Environmental Governance

Elizabeth R. DeSombre

Environmental issues require global governance. Even the most local-seeming actions (driving a car, generating electricity) have environmental effects that cross international boundaries. These problems cannot be addressed successfully without some level of international coordination. The common-pool resource nature of environmental problems (meaning that people often cannot be excluded from engaging in resource use or pollution generation, and that accessing a resource by one reduces its usefulness for others) suggests that action is unlikely to be able to prevent or reduce environmental degradation unless undertaken collectively.

The governance of issues relating to the global environment is multifaceted and decentralized. Although the United Nations plays a major role in many of the institutions that address environmental issues it is less of a central coordinating institution than a facilitator. Instead, global and regional environmental issues have been taken up primarily by issue-focused environmental institutions created to address these issues individually as they arose. While such an approach has led to a proliferation of institutions (and the associated danger of convention fatigue) with the possibility of duplication of effort or even contradiction across intersecting institutions, it has also allowed for reasonably nimble institutions that can focus on environmental issues as they emerge.

This process has also involved important action by non-state actors and cooperation involving voluntary efforts, certification, and other forms of governance. These approaches have become more important over time as traditional intergovernmental and regulatory efforts have encountered difficulty. In addition a call for increasing centralization of governance, whether practical or not, has accompanied increasing levels of coordination among institutions with related mandates. What currently exists is a cacophony of coordinated (and sometimes uncoordinated) governance strategies that make incremental progress in addressing environmental problems as they arise.

This chapter begins by exploring the history of the development of global environmental governance, beginning with early conservation agreements and global conferences to address international approaches to environmental governance. It then gives an overview of the current institutional structure of governance by environmental issue area (including the UN's general environmental governance processes). It concludes with the increasing role of non-state actors and informal processes to address global environmental issues, and efforts to coordinate across the many and overlapping institutional structures that exist.

History and development

International efforts to address environmental issues date back centuries. These measures often began as ad hoc efforts to deal with problems that required international action; these efforts became increasingly institutionalized. The earliest issues were over resource conservation and access. The 1911 Fur Seals Convention restricted catches of seals, and an International Fisheries Commission was created in 1923 to oversee halibut stocks.

Over time there has been an evolution in the issues about which international cooperative efforts have been undertaken, moving from sustainable harvesting of fish and marine mammal resources through ocean and air pollution, to broader conservation of species and ecosystems for reasons beyond sustainable use, to issues of movement and disposal of toxic substances. The focus of intergovernmental agreements, still the most common approach, has shifted over time, in process as well as substance, with special consideration and increased decision-making power accruing to developing countries. More recent approaches have moved past binding intergovernmental institutions to involve pledges of collective voluntary action (from businesses or states) and other strategies like certification and provision of information.

Conference diplomacy

Global conferences have played a prominent role within intergovernmental approaches to environmental governance. A set convened by the UN at ten-year intervals has focused international attention on global environmental issues. The first of these was the United Nations Conference on the Human Environment held in Stockholm in June 1972. The primary output of this event was the Declaration of the United Nations Conference on the Human Environment and an Action Plan for the Human Environment, along with a set of resolutions, the most important of which recommended the creation of structures within the world organization to bring environmental issues more formally and continually under the UN's mandate.[1]

This later recommendation was taken up by the General Assembly, which created the United Nations Environment Programme (UNEP) as a direct response to the conference recommendations. Other international agreements protecting endangered species and cultural heritage, as well as addressing marine pollution and acid rain, can trace their roots to this international gathering. A special open session of the UN Governing Council ten years later suggested that the implementation of the goals enumerated at Stockholm was mixed.

Twenty years after the gathering at Stockholm the United Nations again organized a major international environmental conference. The United Nations Conference on Environment and Development (also called the Earth Summit), held in Rio de Janeiro, Brazil, in June 1992, was, at the time, the largest gathering of world leaders. The UN Framework Convention on Climate Change (UNFCCC) and the Convention on Biological Diversity were negotiated in time to be signed at the conference. States also negotiated two other non-binding statements. The Rio Declaration on Environment and Development included support for the polluter-pays principle and reiterated support for states in the exercise of sovereignty over their natural resources; and Agenda 21, an action plan.[2]

The ten-year tradition continued with the World Summit on Sustainable Development held in Johannesburg, South Africa, in 2002, and a conference called Rio+20, held again in 2012 in Brazil. The 2002 conference asked states for voluntary (and often vague) commitments to improve water and sanitation, energy, health, environment, and biodiversity. It also focused on business, with a set of public–private partnerships called "Type II agreements" reached to advance conference goals.[3] The 2012 conference was a three-day event that did not result in any major new commitments or initiatives, although many states made individual pledges about environmental behavior and side agreements were concluded between individual corporations and governments

Opinions differ on the usefulness of these conferences. At minimum, the 1972 and 1992 conferences appear to have attracted public attention and focused governmental and intergovernmental action. The timing peg for negotiating the 1992 treaties may have pushed states toward agreement, and the principles elaborated in the Stockholm and Rio declarations and action plans have been taken up across different governance levels since then. But at their worst these events may detract attention from other, more serious, efforts at governance, and even provide public cover for inaction, with public statements from high-ranking officials garnering more attention than the lack of action that follows.

Agreements and institutions

The most notable feature of global environmental governance is simply how many different institutions there are. Much intergovernmental environmental cooperation involves the negotiation of individual issue-specific agreements, and institutions are created to oversee the implementation of these agreements. The institutions then contribute to further evolution of the agreements; experience with implementation and the knowledge created by scientific bodies then lead to the negotiation of deeper obligations. When a new environmental problem emerges, the first step to addressing it involves the negotiation of a new agreement and creation of a different institution to oversee that process, rather than working within existing organizations. The most important of these institutions are discussed by issue area next.

Ocean resources

The earliest efforts at international cooperation were about resources harvested from, or migrating through, the unowned spaces of the oceans. Initial cooperative efforts were undertaken by those who relied on the resources in question, to ensure that these resources were not overharvested. The most numerous of these are fisheries institutions—Regional Fisheries Management Organizations (RFMOs)—regulating by species, by region, or a combination of the two. Other organizations, most notably the International Whaling Commission, oversee marine mammal harvesting, using similar processes.

There are approximately 19 RFMOs with a regulatory function. Most have a scientific commission, charged with making recommendations on what a sustainable catch limit for the stocks in question would be, and a fishery commission, composed of member state representatives, that makes the regulations. Frequently these decisions can be made without unanimous voting. But because states would be reluctant to join international organizations in which they could be subject to rules they had not agreed to, RFMOs that operate in this manner generally allow states to opt out of such regulations as long as they do so within a specified time and process.[4]

Fisheries are extremely difficult to manage. Non-participation in fisheries regulation is easy; some states do not join or ship owners can change registration to flag their vessels in states that are not members of the relevant RFMOs, which renders them not technically bound to uphold the rules. And non-compliance with obligations that ship owners are subject to is a serious problem in some regions. Some RFMOs, like the Commission for the Conservation of Antarctic Marine Living Resources and some of the tuna commissions, have nevertheless done a reasonably good job at managing the fish stocks they control. But a broader problem emerges from the regional and multi-institution approach of the RFMOs: catch limits set individually by institutions when the overall capacity of the global fishing fleet is not managed in any way lead successful management in one area to increase pressure elsewhere, as ships facing fishing restrictions move to new areas or species, demonstrating one of the problems with a diffuse institutional structure.[5]

Ocean pollution

Other early ocean agreements focused on pollution. The International Maritime Organization (IMO) oversees many of them, although some were negotiated separately and brought under the IMO umbrella while others remain separate. The IMO focuses on issues of shipping more broadly, and so also addresses non-environmental issues. It was created (originally named the Intergovernmental Maritime Consultative Organization) in 1948, as a UN organization.

The primary environmental rules the IMO oversees are negotiated in separate treaties. The most important of these is the International Convention for the Prevention of Pollution from Ships (known as MARPOL), negotiated originally in 1973 and modified in 1978. MARPOL's original focus and early success were preventing oil pollution, first from intentional operational discharges and then also with rules that made oil discharges from accidents less likely. The primary innovation of this process was the imposition of equipment standards; all new ships had to be built (and old ones sometimes retrofitted) in ways that made intentional oil pollution nearly impossible and discharges from accidents less likely.[6]

Another major agreement the IMO oversees (but was not responsible for negotiating) is the 1972 Convention on the Prevention of Marine Pollution by the Dumping of Wastes and Other Matter, called for at the Stockholm conference. This agreement initially prohibited states from dumping any materials into the ocean listed on the negotiated blacklist; an IMO-led renegotiation (via protocol) in 1996 instead prohibited the dumping of all materials except those listed on an annex that were demonstrated not to cause harm.[7] Other efforts to protect the oceans from pollutions from such things as ballast water and fouling systems are also overseen by the IMO.

Species and biodiversity protection

Over time concern for certain species for reasons other than conserving them for future resource use emerged, and a set of institutions were created to protect species in different ways. This distinction is not a bright line—even within these newer institutions some states participate with a conservation (i.e. sustainable use) perspective and others with preservation goals, and the language of the governing agreements usually reflects these multiple approaches.

The first such agreement, the 1973 Convention on International Trade in Endangered Species of Fauna and Flora (CITES), restricts trade in endangered species. The agreement lists species in three appendices, providing different levels of protection. Those with the highest level of protection cannot be traded at all unless the trade is specifically designed to improve conservation, while others can be traded but require permits that justify the trade as not harming overall conservation status. A Conference of the Parties meets every two years to make decisions. Adding a species to, or removing it from, an appendix requires a two-thirds majority vote, with states able to lodge objections to decisions they oppose and thus not be bound by those rules. States also are required to create scientific authorities and national management authorities to oversee the permit process and ensure that trade in listed species is conducted in accordance with the agreement's provisions.

CITES is extremely difficult to implement because of the number of sub-state actors whose behavior needs to be monitored, the porosity of national borders, the high profits that can be earned from contravening its requirements, and the tens of thousands of species covered. Implementation is self-reported and (as with other international agreements) mandated reports are often late or absent.[8] CITES has nevertheless had some high-profile successes, including protection of some African elephant populations once the species was listed on Appendix I, and some wild cats.

The Convention for the Conservation of Migratory Species (CMS) protects species that move internationally through migration. It also creates appendices with varying levels of protection in a manner similar to the process in CITES, and calls for the negotiation of specific conservation agreements among range states of any threatened species. These range states do not need to be members of the parent treaty in order to participate in the negotiated agreements. There are currently six binding agreements, along with a number in negotiation. There are also non-binding memoranda of understanding (MOUs) that acknowledge the threatened status of species they cover and create generally short-term cooperative processes for coordination and research. These agreements can be negotiated more quickly than binding agreements and do not require ratification; they thus can work more efficiently than some formal agreements.[9]

The biggest change from general focus on species protection to a broader concept of conservation came from the 1992 agreement signed at the United Nations Convention on Biological Diversity (CBD). Its goal is to protect the diversity of species, genetic material, and ecosystems, and allow for the sustainable use and equitable sharing of the benefits of biodiversity. States are required to study and report on the condition of, and threats to, biodiversity within their borders. A more substantive protocol creates a process that requires "advanced informed agreement" before states trade in living modified organisms and allows states to prohibit such trade. This process also creates a clearinghouse for information on these organisms.[10]

The CBD was not the first to tackle protection of ecosystems and natural areas. The Convention on Wetlands of International Importance Especially as Waterfowl Habitat (known as the Ramsar Convention) was one of the first agreements to protect an ecosystem. In this case it did both for the protection of migratory bird species that rely on wetlands and because of an early acknowledgment when the agreement was negotiated in 1971 of the importance of wetlands in their own right. States are required to designate and protect at least one wetland within their borders, although most protect many more.[11]

A similar agreement is the Convention Concerning the Protection of World Cultural and Natural Heritage. It operates by state commitments to protect certain sites of importance designated within their borders, although a World Heritage Committee composed of 21 member states elected for six-year terms makes decisions on whether these sites are worthy of recognition under the convention.

Following a slightly different model is the 1994 Convention to Combat Desertification in Those Countries Experiencing Drought and/or Desertification, Particularly in Africa (UNCCD). This agreement focuses on preventing or responding to land degradation; its primary processes involve knowledge and technology transfer to build capacity in affected states; and a funding mechanism was recently added.

Air and atmospheric pollution

The first major international air pollution agreement was the Convention on Long-Range Transboundary Air Pollution, negotiated primarily among Western and Eastern European states (with the participation of the United States and Canada) in a Cold War context in 1979. This agreement requires, through protocols, the reduction of emissions that cause acid rain and other types of air pollution. It has been innovative; over time it has required different approaches to reductions, taking into consideration the sources and effects of the pollutants, and eventually coming to focus on the interaction among pollutants. Its scientific monitoring processes, including those to require self-study among member states, can be credited for some of the willingness by states to participate, as they came to realize that they were more affected by these pollutants than they realized.[12]

Among the most successful environmental governance processes is the one to protect the ozone layer and thus shield the earth from excess UV radiation. This governance process was led by scientific discovery and hypothesis. Long before there was any evidence of damage to the ozone layer, research had determined that certain chemicals (primarily CFCs and halons) were capable of destroying ozone in the presence of sunlight; these substances were stable and long lived and thus could, in principle, make it to the stratosphere. Under an initial treaty states pledged to protect the ozone layer, to report on behavior, and to collaborate scientifically, but it was not until the negotiation of the Montreal Protocol on Substances that Deplete the Ozone Layer (1987) that states agreed to restrict their use of ozone depleting substances. They agreed to freeze and then reduce consumption of five specified ozone depleting substances. Over time, and as scientific research demonstrated the magnitude of the problem, the reductions were deepened to complete phase-out, the timeline for these reductions compressed, and new substances restricted. The actions taken have dramatically slowed—and are starting to contribute to a turnaround in—the depletion of the ozone layer.[13]

Also important in this process was the special consideration given to developing countries. They were granted a time lag before any negotiated restrictions applied to them, and a funding mechanism to meet the "incremental costs" of the treaty's obligations. This Montreal Protocol Multilateral Fund included equal representation from developed and developing countries on its decision-making body, and decisions required a two-thirds majority vote, which needed to include a majority from each of the two groupings. These concessions came about in part because of strong negotiation power on the part of developing states, without whom the agreement would have failed. And they created an important precedent: most agreements since then have included special consideration for developing countries, and many have included funding mechanisms, and double-majority voting rules.

Perhaps the hardest global environmental issue to address has been climate change; the increases in global average temperatures brings numerous possible global impacts which are many and varied. The institutional structure within which regulatory efforts are situated comes from the UNFCCC, signed in Rio in 1992. States agreed in principle to prevent dangerous human interference in the climate system, but it was not until the 1997 Kyoto Protocol that developed states committed to specific emissions reductions, to be achieved by 2012. Although the Protocol motivated action and some states met their targets, others did not; some (such as Canada) decided partway through the commitment period not to pursue them, and the United States refused to ratify the agreement and was thus not bound by its obligations. Efforts to negotiate a second set of binding emissions targets were not immediately successful, and states and international conferences have focused more recently on voluntary commitments and non-state action.[14]

Even before the regulatory structure was negotiated governments and existing intergovernmental organizations in 1988 created the Intergovernmental Panel on Climate Change (IPCC)—a collaborative scientific undertaking under the auspices of the World Meteorological Organization and UNEP to assess the state of global scientific understanding about climate change. States appoint scientific experts to serve but they do so as individuals, rather than as state representatives, and information presented is subject to rigorous peer review. The organization issued its first report in 1990 and has issued multi-volume reports at regular intervals since. This information is frequently used as the basis of regulatory discussions. Over time it has demonstrated increasing confidence in human effects on the global climate system and has predicted increasingly severe impacts. Its efforts were recognized with the 2007 Nobel Peace Prize, shared with former US Vice-President Al Gore.

Toxic materials

The movement of hazardous materials across borders accounts for another set of environmental governance structures.[15] One way hazards travel internationally is when sent from one place to another for disposal. An increasingly stringent regulatory environment in developed countries made it expensive and difficult to dispose of hazardous materials in these locations. Developing countries often had laxer rules or less oversight of existing disposal processes and so companies from industrialized countries often paid to send their hazardous waste there.

On the face of it, these interactions are voluntary. In practice, states with high poverty levels frequently do not have the ability to control what crosses their borders or the capacity to know what all their sub-state actors are doing. In this context, the Basel Convention on the Transboundary Movement of Hazardous Wastes and Their Disposal was negotiated in 1989. Although this agreement did not, initially, go as far as many developing states wanted, it did create a process by which states must be notified before hazardous waste is shipped to them, and enumerates their right to refuse such shipments either individually or categorically.

Most important since its creation is the negotiation of a protocol that would ban the export of hazardous waste from a list of developed states to developing states. Although the amendment was negotiated in 1995, it requires ratification by three-quarters of the member states to become legally binding; the ratification level has remain stalled at just short of that number for years.

Other sets of governance structures address additional ways that toxic materials may move internationally. One such process concerns chemicals and pesticides in international trade. Substances that have been deemed to be too toxic to use, or dispose of, in one state may be sold to another without its knowledge of these decisions. This issue was initially addressed through a non-binding "prior informed consent" procedure created by chemical manufacturers, states, and intergovernmental organizations. States and businesses were less reluctant to take on these rules when they knew they could not be legally enforced. There was nevertheless pressure to make these provisions binding, which led to the 1998 negotiation of the Rotterdam Convention for the Prior Informed Consent Procedure for Certain Hazardous Chemicals and Pesticides in International Trade.

This process essentially formalized the previous non-binding procedure. The secretariat maintains a list of chemicals and pesticides whose use has been restricted by two states in different regions. If a chemical appears on this list, all states must indicate whether they refuse to accept any shipments of this substance, generally are willing to accept shipments, or agree to accept shipments under certain circumstances. States may only export a listed chemical if they have received prior informed consent from the state to which they are sending it, and must abide by any conditions (including a complete refusal) indicated by receiving states.

A different mechanism addresses persistent organic pollutants (POPs), a type of bio-accumulating pollution (frequently pesticides or by-products of industrial pollutants) that can cause cancer and other health problems. They move in the air or food chain. The regulatory process for addressing them was created by the Stockholm Convention on Persistent Organic Pollutants (2001). Under this agreement a negotiated set of pollutants are listed in annexes depending on whether their use and production is scheduled to be eliminated or not. Trade in these substances is prohibited except for reasons of "environmentally sound disposal" or in the case of exemptions states are allowed to register. The most controversial of controlled substances is the pesticide DDT, which is environmentally problematic but considered important for malaria protection in parts of the developing world. Many states have registered exemptions for this substance for this reason.

The United Nations

Other than the single-purpose institutions created to address specific environmental concerns, there are some overarching institutional structures for global environmental governance. Of these, the most important is the United Nations. The UN has a number of subsidiary agencies and programs with roles in global environmental governance. The most important of these is UNEP, created in the wake of the Stockholm Conference.

It can be difficult to describe precisely what UNEP does because it plays so many different roles in environmental governance.[16] It has convened and run the negotiation of major international environmental agreements, provided secretariat functions to a number of the institutions created to oversee these agreements, coordinated monitoring and scientific research, and worked to build the capacity of states (and other non-state entities) to protect the environment.

One of the most notable roles of UNEP has been in the creation of the 1974 Regional Seas Programme; it plays multiple roles in this program. Overall, there are 18 regional seas currently protected through this process, although only six are directly managed by UNEP. States surrounding regional seas create action plans on how to study and protect a given sea. The first and highest-profile of these agreements was the Mediterranean Action Plan, created in 1975. Political cooperation has been impressive (including in seas that include states openly antagonistic to each other); scientific cooperation and environmental improvement have been more mixed.

Structurally, UNEP is a program rather than an agency, which limits its independence in the UN hierarchy. It was conceived as a way to bring together and organize the existing environmental capacities within the UN organization as a whole. It operates with a 58-member Governing Council in which states serve staggered four-year terms, elected to ensure regional representation. Its headquarters are located in Nairobi, Kenya, making it the first major UN entity to be based in a developing country. Although the UN was lauded for this decision, in practical terms the Nairobi location has added to the difficulties of attracting and retaining staff, and has made it difficult and costly to arrange travel to or from headquarters.

An important global institution that intersects with the United Nations but is not strictly under its control is the Global Environment Facility (GEF), the primary standing mechanism for funding relating to the global environment. It was created as a collaboration between the World Bank, UNEP, and other development organizations.

The pilot GEF program began in 1990. Unlike other global funding mechanisms, the idea behind the GEF was that funding would primarily be given out as grants, rather than loans, so that supported projects would not have to be revenue generating. Since the pilot phase the GEF's process has been modified to increase the participation of affected communities in decision-making, increase accountability, to expand the number of countries represented in the primary decision-making processes, and to expand the list of issues for which GEF funding is available.

Currently the GEF operates with a 32-member council, with half the membership from developed countries and half from developing countries. It meets twice a year and decisions require a two-thirds majority vote that must constitute a majority of each of the two constituent groups. Funding is contributed by donors in four-year "replenishment" cycles. The GEF currently serves as the official funding mechanism for four treaties: the CBD, the UNFCCC, the UNCCD, and the Stockholm Convention. It also provides funding for other projects relating to global or transboundary environmental protection.

Non-state approaches

Although the history of global environmental governance is focused on state-level binding obligations, the role of non-state actors—always important—has been increasing. Scientists and scientific organizations (such as the IPCC) have built international consensus on the nature and severity of environmental problems. Citizen groups have persuaded states to take domestic action, which on issues with international causes and consequences has led to pressure for global action. And business and industry have been implicated in both causing, and finding solutions for, environmental problems.

These roles have deepened, and grown more nuanced, over time. The number of environmental organizations, both domestic and international, has grown dramatically in the last half-century, and the focus and reach of these organizations have expanded as well. One of the most notable areas of expansion has been the growth of organizations of indigenous people and other groups in developing countries. The role of advocates has gone far beyond the traditional model of simply encouraging state action. Activists frequently work around the state to accomplish international goals. They attend international negotiations and meetings and may be recognized to speak. And, in contexts in which state or intergovernmental action is inadequate, they may work directly across borders to change the behavior of people or states elsewhere, or may themselves provide funding to implement conservation goals without a broader regulatory context.[17] Activists (as well as businesses and scientists) are also often directly involved in the informal governance processes discussed below.

Current debates and emerging issues

Those examining or participating in global environmental governance have recently focused on several broad questions. The first, within the context of intergovernmental organizations, is the question of centralized versus multiple institutions. The current structure of many institutions was never an intentional design; it simply is what emerged piecemeal as governance structures were created to address environmental problems as they, and the will to address them, emerged. Persistent calls have nonetheless been voiced for the centralization of environmental governance, creating something like a global environmental organization that could oversee the negotiation and implementation of international environmental agreements and action. Related efforts make the same argument on a smaller scale and within specific issue areas (such as observing the need for a global fisheries organization).

There are some advantages to the multi-institution approach. For instance, structures can be created specific to the issue being addressed, and those states that are concerned about an issue or willing to move forward on regulation can do so without needing the agreement of others who may not be interested in participating. It creates other difficulties, though.

Separately negotiated agreements and the organizations to oversee them can occasionally work at cross-purposes when their mandates overlap. For instance, some of the substitutes for ozone depleting substances approved for use by the Montreal Protocol governance process turned out to be strong greenhouses gases, thereby contributing to climate change; the institutional structures charged with protecting the ozone layer had no specific mandate to take climate change concerns into consideration when making their rules. Similarly, restrictions by one RFMO to decrease fishing levels often result in fishing vessels moving to the regulatory area of a different RFMO and increasing pressure on the stock it is attempting to protect. Other arguments in favor of the creation of more centralized forms of global environmental governance suggest that such institutions would have the ability to act as a counterweight to centralized organizations on other issue areas, such as trade or development.

Yet institutionally, while it might have been possible to create a centralized organization at the time that global environmental institutions were first emerging (and it might have been possible for UNEP, had it been given a different institutional structure, to be that organization), it is much more difficult to create one in a context of multiple existing organizations. Moreover, it is possible that a global environment organization might magnify the difficulties of environmental cooperation, holding action on one issue hostage to controversy over a different issue. And what some decry as "forum shopping" among institutions also allows environmentally concerned actors to make progress in (for example) protecting dolphins or whales in one institution (CITES), while a different institution (the International Whaling Commission) might be reluctant or unable to do so.

Without consensus over the usefulness or practicality of centralization, cooperation across related organizations has become increasingly common. The five RFMOs addressing tuna fishing in different regions have begun to meet collectively on a regular basis. The problem of substitutes for ozone depleting substances that increased greenhouse gas emissions was addressed through discussion between the two institutions and the willingness of the ozone protection institutions to take issues other than ozone depletion into consideration when determining acceptable action. The decision-making bodies and secretariats for the three major toxics treaties also regularly consult.

A second important area of discussion is the role of formal versus informal governance structures. In some ways, informal governance—non-binding measures, activity by non-state actors—has always been a part of global environmental governance, every time states sign a memorandum of understanding or negotiate scientific cooperation. But the topic has become especially compelling in light of the recent failures of formal efforts at governance on a number of issues, most notably climate change. Instead, those pursuing climate governance have worked on encouraging a large number of creative sub-state, or voluntary, actions.[18] Certification, in which some approaches are deemed to be less environmentally problematic (frequently by a nongovernmental entity) and the information from which is used by others to make purchasing decisions, can change behavior without rules.[19]

Whether making a virtue of necessity, or genuinely believing that non-binding obligations create flexibility advantages, environmental advocates have argued in favor of action to address global environmental problems that are based less on legally binding state-based commitments than on a voluntary commitment of information provision. Evidence abounds of the advantages of non-binding obligations. States or other actors may be reluctant to agree to legal obligations they are not certain to be able to achieve, but willing to create goals or try experiments if the cost of failure is not non-compliance.[20]

Conclusion

Global environmental problems are complex and multifaceted, as are the institutional processes that provide governance on these issues. A large number of single-issue agreements create institutional processes to oversee state cooperation to address diffuse and difficult issues. As scientific information and public pressure increases the need to address these problems, states have undertaken or mandated impressive changes in central behaviors that have decreased environmental harm worldwide from what it would otherwise have been.

As environmental problems grow more complex and more connected to broader aspects of human behavior—and especially as some states, such as the United States, have become more reluctant to participate in intergovernmental cooperation—the focus has shifted to the role of non-state actors and informal forms of governance. In instances such as these, states, businesses seeking market advantages, or concerned individuals, among others, have been able to move forward when state-based cooperative outcomes are lacking, or because they see advantages in these approaches more generally.

Additional reading

1. Elizabeth R. DeSombre, *Global Environmental Institutions* (New York: Routledge, 2006).
2. Steinar Andresen, Elin Lerum Boasson, and Geir Hønneland, *International Environmental Agreements: An Introduction* (New York: Routledge, 2012).
3. Frank Biermann and Philipp Pattberg, *Global Environmental Governance Reconsidered* (Cambridge, MA: MIT Press, 2012).
4. Pamela S. Chasek and Lynn M. Wagner, eds., *The Roads From Rio* (New York: Routledge, 2012).
5. IISD, "Linkages: News, Information, and Analysis on International Environment and Sustainable Development Negotiations and Policy Making," http://www.iisd.ca/.

6. Mostafa Tolba and Iwona Rummel-Bulska, *Global Environmental Diplomacy: Negotiating Environmental Agreements for the World, 1973–1992* (Cambridge, MA: MIT Press, 1998).

Notes

1 Wade Rowland, *The Plot to Save the World: The Life and Times of the Stockholm Conference on the Human Environment* (Toronto: Clarke, Irwin & Company Ltd., 1973).

2 Michael Grubb, Kay Thompson, and Francis Sullivan, *The Earth Summit Agreements: A Guide and Assessment* (London: Earthscan Publications, 1993).

3 Pablo Gutman, "What Did WSSD Accomplish? An NGO Perspective," *Environment* 45, no. 2 (2003): 20–26.

4 Howard S. Schiffman, *Marine Conservation Agreements: The Law and Policy of Reservations and Vetoes* (Leiden: Martinus Nijhoff, 2008).

5 J. Samuel Barkin and Elizabeth R. DeSombre, *Saving Global Fisheries: Reducing Fishing Capacity to Promote Sustainability* (Cambridge, MA: MIT Press, 2013).

6 Ronald B. Mitchell, *Intentional Oil Pollution at Sea* (Cambridge, MA: MIT Press, 1994).

7 IMO, "London Convention and Protocol," http://www.imo.org/OurWork/Environment/SpecialProgrammesAndInitiatives/Pages/London-Convention-and-Protocol.aspx, 2012.

8 Edith Brown Weiss, "The Five International Treaties: A Living History," in *Engaging Countries*, eds. Edith Brown Weiss and Harold Jacobson (Cambridge, MA: MIT Press, 1998).

9 Richard Caddell, "International Law and the Protection of Migratory Wildlife: An Appraisal of Twenty-Five Years of the Bonn Convention," *Colorado Journal of International Law and Policy* 16 (2005): 113–156.

10 Philippe Le Prestre, ed., *Governing Global Biodiversity* (Aldershot: Ashgate, 2003).

11 John Lanchbery, "Ramsar Convention," in *Encyclopedia of Global Change*, Vol. 2, ed. Andrew S. Goudie (Oxford: Oxford University Press, 2002), 289–290.

12 Henrik Selin and Stacy D. VanDeveer, "Mapping Institutional Linkages in European Air Pollution Politics," *Global Environmental Politics* 3, no. 3 (August 2003): 14–46.

13 Edward A. Parson, *Protecting the Ozone Layer: Science and Strategy* (Oxford: Oxford University Press, 2003).

14 Matthew J. Hoffmann, *Climate Governance at the Crossroads* (Oxford: Oxford University Press, 2011).

15 Henrik Selin, *Global Governance of Hazardous Chemicals* (Cambridge, MA: MIT Press, 2010).

16 Maria Ivanova, "UNEP in Global Environmental Governance: Design, Leadership, Location," *Global Environmental Politics* 8, no. 1 (2010): 30–59.

17 Paul Wapner, *Environmental Activism and World Civic Politics* (Albany: SUNY Press, 1996).

18 Hoffmann, *Climate Governance*.

19 Lars H. Gulbrandsen, *Transnational Environmental Governance* (Cheltenham: Edward Elgar, 2010).

20 David Victor, "'Learning by Doing' in the Nonbinding International Regime to Manage Trade in Hazardous Chemicals and Pesticides," in *The Implementation and Effectiveness of International Environmental Commitments*, eds. David G. Victor, Kal Raustiala, and Eugene B. Skolnikoff (Cambridge, MA: MIT Press, 1998), 221–281.

The Regional Development Banks and Global Governance

Jonathan R. Strand

Even casual observers of world politics recognize the significance of the International Monetary Fund (IMF) and World Bank as major players in global economic governance. These two organizations make headlines daily and are often cast as heroes or villains in analyses of their roles in governing the global political economy. Along with the World Trade Organization, the IMF and World Bank are among the most studied formal organizations. However, to understand global economic governance more completely it is necessary to move beyond this triad to include other formal institutions that play essential roles in governing the global economy.

This chapter examines the place of regional development banks (RDBs) in global economic governance. RDBs are multilateral development banks that engage in lending and other activities designed to foster economic growth in developing countries. Like the World Bank, RDBs provide various types of loans as well as policy advice to member governments. RDBs should not, however, be viewed as miniature versions of the World Bank. While the RDBs occupy much of the same global governance terrain as the World Bank, they differ from the World Bank in important ways and have their own organizational cultures and historical contexts. These differences often highlight critical doctrinal disputes between governments as well as the unfolding of new norms and forms of institutionalization.

There are four major RDBs and several others that operate at a sub-regional level. The major RDBs are the African Development Bank (AfDB), Asian Development Bank (ADB), Inter-American Development Bank (IDB), and the European Bank for Reconstruction and Development (EBRD). The first three of these RDBs were created during the Cold War, while the EBRD was created at the end of the Cold War. Sub-regional Development Banks (SDBs) have more narrow scopes of operation than the larger RDBs. The most important SDBs are the Caribbean Development Bank (CDB), the Central American Bank for Economic Integration (CABEI), the East African Development Bank (EADB), and the West African Development Bank (BOAD). These four SDBs have limited geographic range and notably the United States is not a member of any SDB. The RDBs and SDBs operate at the regional and sub-regional levels, but because of the roles they play in world politics in general and development policy in particular they should be viewed as pieces of global economic governance. For instance, RDBs and SDBs have been involved in political debates about development economics and have responded to changing global norms such as the incorporation of "good governance" in lending policies. This chapter concentrates attention on the RDBs but also includes some coverage of the SDBs.

The chapter unfolds as follows. The next section provides a brief history of the RDBs and SDBs. Thereafter, the chapter examines the question: who controls these institutions? It then turns to a discussion of the three main activities of the RDBs: project lending, policy-based lending, and policy advice. This section highlights how the RDBs are often focal points for discord between powerful states as well as pressures from civil society organizations. This last substantive section explores how RDBs and SDBs have responded to changing norms regarding the accountability of borrowers. The conclusion reflects on the future of the RDBs and SDBs in light of changes to ideas and material power in the world political economy.

RDBs in historical context

Developing countries have many sources of capital available to them, including private capital markets, bilateral aid, and aid offered through multilateral institutions. After World War II many developing economies could not qualify for loans from private capital markets because of concerns about their ability to repay them. Bilateral foreign aid was also (and remains) problematic as it was often seen as politically motivated since donor governments have control over the disbursement and use of such capital; whereas multilateral aid was (and again continues to be) viewed by many as less political since capital from multiple donors is pooled together and individual donors have less first-hand oversight of how the aid is distributed.

The World Bank is the foremost multilateral development institution and given its size and expertise the need for regional development institutions might be called into question. The World Bank was created, in part, to promote economic development. From the perspective of the twenty-first century, an observer might ask, why create smaller regional banks? Would it not be better to spend the money by increasing the size and scope of the World Bank? To understand why RDBs and SDBs were created, the historical context of each institution needs to be explored.

The creation of international organizations was not methodical and the ideational linkage of the RDBs and SDBs to the World Bank was less continuous than it appears to us today. Early in its history the World Bank failed to approve most loan applications from poorer countries because of concerns about the creditworthiness of the borrowers. It was also the case that the primary focus of the World Bank during its early years was on reconstruction of Europe. Indeed, World Bank lending to the poorest borrowers was meager until the creation of a "soft loan" window, the International Development Association (IDA), in 1960. In other words, the World Bank was not satisfying all of the demand for multilateral development assistance and this in part accounts for the formation of RDBs.

In addition to the practical need for capital, the Cold War context was important in the creation of the RDBs. The United States, which was instrumental in creating the World Bank and IMF, sought other institutionalized means to promote US foreign policy and American views on what pathways countries should follow—that is, that they should be market oriented rather than socialist—to achieve development. For instance, American foreign policy-makers were concerned that Soviet influence in the Western Hemisphere could increase and the IDB was viewed as one vehicle to promote US goals and support American allies. The IDB was the first of the RDBs to be created, starting operations in 1959.

The interests of middle-income and lower-income countries also were vital in the creation of the RDBs. Immediately after its creation the World Bank concentrated on reconstruction projects in Western Europe, before turning its attention to newly independent—that is, the decolonized—countries. Some non-Western independent countries were concerned that the World Bank would not pay enough attention to their needs. Smaller, regionally focused multilateral institutions were viewed as more amenable to regional and individual country interests. In short, a lot of the interest in creating the IDB and ADB came from middle-income countries. Also, in the case of the ADB, Japan—which had joined the IMF and World Bank in 1952—was emerging from a period of formal US occupation which ended in 1951 and was keen to have opportunities to positively (re-)engage regional countries, many of which suffered immensely during Japan's decades of occupation and imperialism.

The ADB began operations in 1966 and made its first loans in 1968. Early lending by the ADB was influenced by American military concerns in Southeast Asia and Japan's efforts to rebuild its economy. Throughout the ADB's history, Japan has played a particularly significant role in the management of the bank as well as the ideas under-pinning the ADB's views on economic development.[1]

The Cold War context proved to be quite different in the creation of the other two RDBs. The AfDB was shaped by a political movement which sought to increase solidarity and cooperation among sub-Saharan African countries.[2] The United States and other developed countries were not as instrumental in the AfDB's formation. Several members had been unable to qualify for World Bank and private banking loans and therefore looked to the AfDB for assistance. When it began operations, the AfDB was expected to be a development bank controlled by African governments. The agreement creating the AfDB was finalized in 1963 and the bank opened its doors in 1964.

A difficulty for the AfDB was that it was undercapitalized at the outset since it excluded wealthy, non-regional governments. Eventually regional member governments forwent some control over the AfDB in order to receive contributions from wealthy countries. Today the AfDB has 78 member governments, including 24 from outside the region. For most of its history the AfDB was based in Abidjan, Côte d'Ivoire, but because of domestic political instability the bank moved to Tunisia, albeit recently there has been an effort to return to its original headquarters.

The EBRD was created in 1991 at the end of the Cold War with a mandate to assist economies in Central and Eastern Europe in transitioning to a market-oriented system. Unlike the negotiations to create other RDBs, there was a lot of consensus on the need for a new development organization. The EBRD's relative newness as an organization with a different historical context than the other three RDBs helps explain why the EBRD engages in a great deal more political activity than other RDBs.[3] The EBRD is often thought of as a political bank not only because it has an obligation to build political institutions but also because there has often been a political divide between the United States and the UK, on one hand, and France and other continental European governments, on the other hand.[4] Today the EBRD has over 60 governments and two other European agencies as members.

Like the RDBs, SDBs have distinct histories and need to be understood against the backdrop of the stakeholders that created and control them. Of the SDBs, the CDB is perhaps the most widely studied. In 1970 the CDB began operations with a mandate to engage in lending and other assistance to promote economic growth in the Caribbean. Its membership includes most countries with water access to the Caribbean, except for the United States and Cuba. There are also five member countries from outside of the region: Canada, China, Germany, Italy, and the UK. While the United States is not a member, it was involved in the creation of the bank and contributes capital to special funds and projects. China joined the CDB in 1998, and soon after those Caribbean governments that had previously recognized the Republic of China (Taiwan) as the legitimate sovereign changed their recognition to Beijing. China subsequently created a fund for special projects and contributes to the regular CDB lending window.

Founded by four Central American governments in 1960, CABEI has 13 members and began operations in 1961. CABEI has concentrated on projects that enhance investment opportunities, "giving precedence to the export, basic services (infrastructure, electricity, communications), and agricultural sectors."[5] The bank is based in Tegucigalpa, Honduras, and primarily promotes projects in Belize, Guatemala, Panama, Dominican Republic, El Salvador, Honduras, Nicaragua, and Costa Rica. In addition to these eight members, there are five members from outside the region that contribute to the bank. The only members from outside the Western Hemisphere are Spain and the Republic of China (Taiwan). In addition to loans, CABEI engages in efforts designed to promote educational programs and environmental projects with a focus on biodiversity.

The EADB was originally created in the late 1960s but was dissolved in 1977 because of the failure of the East African Cooperation (EAC) Treaty. In 1980, the EADB was relaunched with its own charter separate from the EAC Treaty. The EADB has four members (Kenya, Rwanda, Tanzania, and Uganda) and several associated members, which include other global institutions such as the AfDB. In recent years, the largest share of loans issued by the EADB has been for construction and real estate development. The bank also funds loans to borrowers who operate microfinance programs. While the governments of Kenya, Tanzania, Rwanda, and Uganda are in control of the operations of the bank, the EADB also has private sector shareholders, such as Barclays Bank.

In 1973, BOAD was established by eight governments as an organ of the West African Monetary Union. The bank began operations in 1976 and in recent years has focused on poverty reduction, facilitating private investment, and promoting deeper economic integration in West Africa. BOAD is largely controlled by member governments but it also includes among its membership the Export and Import Bank of India.

These smaller institutions have very specialized missions and, while they do not lend as much capital as the larger RDBs, they have engaged in important development projects. SDBs have mobilized capital and served as agents of regional integration. And while they are less conspicuous than the RDBs, the relatively small size of the SDBs can make them better equipped to grapple with local problems. Together, RDBs and SDBs are significant parts of global economic governance. They were not created to supplement or complement the World Bank but, rather, were created by governments in specific historical contexts for particular political purposes. Thus while it may be tempting to view the RDBs as "mini" World Banks, doing so clouds their significantly different origins.

Inside out: internal governance

RDBs and SDBs were created by governments to engage in lending and other activities designed to promote economic development. As formal intergovernmental organizations, their members agree to adhere to each organization's foundational treaty. These treaties provide guidance regarding how the banks will be organized, how they will make decisions, and their substantive mandates. The rules used for internal governance can influence the lending and other activities of the banks. In addition to the role played by member governments, these institutions comprise large and distinct bureaucracies which also shape the way they operate. The literature on the RDBs and SDBs—as well as other IOs—often debates whether governments or bureaucrats matter more in understanding the behavior of IOs. Some scholars emphasize the power bestowed on governments and the rules used to make decisions. In the context of the RDBs this often leads to analyses of voting rules to determine which governments have more power. Other scholars point out that bureaucracies have their own vested interests and can at times undermine the intent of decisions made by governments. Most studies agree that within IOs there is a complex interplay of power, ideas, and rules that require a nuanced approach to recognize the actors and forces that matter.

At first glance, it seems these IOs are controlled by member governments since members are "shareholders" and are assigned voting rights. RDBs have complex voting rules which include weighted voting and selective representation. Weighted voting systems are fairly common in domestic and international settings and usually rationalized as necessary in instances where some voters have an empirical claim to more votes than others. The RDBs use weighted voting to apportion influence on the assumption the governments which contribute more money should have more influence over decisions. Consider, for instance, that in the ADB New Zealand holds 202,510 votes (1.53 percent), while Japan and the United States each have 1,696,120 votes (12.82 percent) and Samoa holds only 39,838 (0.3 percent). Japan and the United States have always held the most votes in the ADB and today have more than twice as many votes than the next largest member, China (5.47 percent). Not surprisingly, weighted voting is often criticized since most of the votes in the RDBs are held by the wealthiest members and there is concern that the members that borrow money have little voice over the terms. Weighting votes based on the size of a country's contributions can give the perception that the RDBs are controlled much like private corporations, where the largest shareholders have the most votes. To surmount this view, most RDBs assign some votes without regard to contributions. Referred to as "basic votes," they are used by all the RDBs except the EBRD. In the ADB, basic votes are assigned to all members as an equal share of 20 percent of total votes. The IDB and AfDB assign a set number of votes to each member: 135 for the IDB and 625 for the AfDB.

The weighted voting systems of the RDBs are more complicated than those of the IMF and World Bank. Three of the RDBs make an effort to maintain a regional flavor in the allocation of votes. In the IDB, one rule mandates at least half of all votes must be held by regional borrowing members. Another IDB rule provides a "basement" limit on the votes held by the two regional lending members: the United States and Canada. These two rules leave only approximately 16 percent of the votes to be allocated to lending non-regional members like Italy, Japan, and Norway. When China joined the IDB in 2009, it meant the relative share of votes held by other non-regional members declined.

A more extreme rule, once used by the AfDB, barred wealthy countries from joining and holding votes, though they could contribute money to special funds. In an effort to obtain more capital, in the early 1980s the AfDB began to allow wealthy countries to become full members but it also put in place a rule limiting the percentage of votes held by non-regional countries.

In the ADB, at least 60 percent of all votes must be allocated to regional members. While the EBRD does not use the regional/non-regional dichotomy, there is a complex nesting of European agencies. The EBRD does not just comprise national governments as members. The European Investment Bank and the European Union are also members of the EBRD and they have more votes than some member states. As such, the voting systems of the RDBs deviate in significant ways from, and are more multifaceted than, the World Bank's.

Weighted voting, while the most obvious aspect of internal governance, is not the only factor determining which members have the most influence. All members have a seat on a general voting body but there is a smaller, more important voting body in each RDB. These smaller executive boards make more of the major decisions and carry out daily business, while the large bodies meet only once or twice a year. On the executive boards there are some governments with individual seats, but most are aggregated into voting groups and each group selects a representative. The IDB has only two individual seats, held by Canada and the United States, while the remaining 46 members are aggregated into 12 voting groups. This form of selective representation makes meetings of the executive boards more manageable but also results in the majority of members not directly representing themselves.

The complex, formal elements of internal governance and associated emphasis on the representation of governments can lead to conclusions about the exercise of power within an RDB. In terms of influence, wealthier countries that contribute the bulk of resources have more influence. Borrowing governments have only a handful of votes and are usually not guaranteed seats on the executive boards. This has been described as a polarization of members into wealthy "rule-makers" and poorer "rule-takers," with the former rarely required to live by the rules they make. Such state-centric claims are not without foundation, but there are other influential stakeholders within RDBs that at times are more important than member governments.

As noted above, RDBs are large bureaucracies comprised of leadership and rank-and-file staff, all of whom exert a degree of influence. Even if governments vote to implement a policy, it is left to the bureaucracies to operationalize and interpret the policy. In this activity there are opportunities for staff members and the structure of the bureaucracy itself to have an impact on policy-making. Most of the high-ranking staff members hired by the RDBs have very similar training. For instance, the RDBs hire economists with fairly narrow training from universities emphasizing neoclassical economic ideas. The RDB with the largest number of staff is the ADB, with about 3,000. Most of the ADB's staffers are from the Philippines, but only a few of them hold high-level posts. There are about 150 employees from Japan, including several of the key leadership positions. In fact the president of the ADB has always been a citizen of Japan with a close affiliation to Japan's Ministry of Finance. There are also about 150 Americans working at the bank and at least one of the four vice-presidents has been an American.

Headquartered in Washington, DC, the IDB has around 2,000 employees. Given its physical proximity to the United States Treasury Department, the IDB has long been viewed as dominated by US foreign policy interests. Most of the IDB's employees are based in Washington, DC; and while the head of the IDB has always been from a developing country, at least one other key position has always been held by an American. The AfDB's leadership is primarily drawn from developing countries, and of its 2,000 staff members almost all are from developing countries. The RDB with the least emphasis on the nationality of leadership and staff is the EBRD.

Consideration of the national origin of staff members only goes so far in defining the internal culture of the RDBs. Nevertheless, the norms that have developed regarding leadership positions influence the policies and ideas pursued by the banks. For instance, in the ADB the number of Japanese staffers and Japan's monopoly on the presidency give the appearance of conspicuous Japanese influence. Early on in the bank's history, however, the United States often had more influence over key policies.[6] But this relationship changed in the late 1970s and early 1980s as Japan sought a more assertive role. More recently, Japan and the United States have openly differed over the lending goals of the ADB.

One shortcoming of the norms of national origin—that is, a person from X country would normally be expected to hold Y post—is that the best person may not be selected for key leadership positions. Put differently, it is instructive to ask, "Is the president of the ADB a Japanese citizen because s/he is the most qualified person for the position or because Japan has more influence over the selection of the president?" This critical question can be asked of the other key leadership positions. Additionally, there is a tendency within the RDBs for policy inertia generated by an institutional path dependency. The RDBs, like other organizations, change slowly and can be insular from shifting norms and alterations in material power relations.[7] In sum, the organizational cultures of the RDBs as well as internal governance place special emphasis on the role of regional members, but the RDBs remain grounded in economic ideas stemming from the prevailing neoliberal paradigm. Within the RDBs, the governments with the greatest influence are also those with primacy in other forums of global economic governance (e.g. ASEAN+3, G20, EU).

Discord over ideas and lending activities

The RDBs engage in three main activities. First, from the outset they were designed to promote economic development through project lending. To this end, the RDBs receive capital contributions from all members and pool these resources for lending purposes. These contributions can be either paid-in capital where the funds are placed under the control of an RDB or merely commitments by members to provide capital if needed to guarantee loans. The majority of capital committed to the RDBs is in this latter form of "callable capital." Project loans are the most common type of lending activity undertaken by the RDBs. As the name implies, these loans are designed to fund specific projects. For example, in 2012 the IDB began the preliminary research, including an assessment of the environmental impact, of a loan that would help fund a private corporation's efforts to build a wind farm in Costa Rica.[8] Over the years, the RDBs have developed themes to guide project lending. Many of the projects are a result of private sector firms identifying a need and convincing a developing country and other stakeholders to facilitate RDB funding.

The second mission of the RDBs is to provide capital to help governments facing financial crises, such as during the Latin American debt crisis of the 1980s. Policy-oriented lending is often controversial since borrowing governments are required to change public policies, and often the effects of policy changes are not proportional on all domestic sectors and populations. Usually associated with IMF lending, the RDBs have taken part in this type of conditional lending. Loans made for such purposes are designed to assist governments facing budgetary or other emergencies. Policy lending requires the borrowing government to commit to economic reforms such as increasing economic openness, reducing budget deficits, and privatizing state-owned enterprises.

In addition to high-profile lending activities, the RDBs have a third mandate to provide members policy advice. Policy advice often goes hand in hand with lending programs, especially for crisis lending. The RDBs undertake regular evaluations of members' economies, and such surveillance activities can influence the views of private investors and other IOs.

These three activities are not unconnected from one another, and as received wisdom regarding governance and development has changed over the past 50 years, discord among stakeholders has occurred. Recall that the bureaucracies of the RDBs are subject to the influence of member governments but member governments rely on the staff to implement policies. During crises, or moments when discord occurs between powerful members, the organizational culture of an RDB can have an impact upon the outcome of disagreements. There have been high-profile disputes about the mandates of the RDBs in response to changes in ideas about economic development policies and the rising influence of emerging markets.

Two areas in particular have resulted in major debates within the RDBs. The first area is the introduction of—and adoption by—IOs of new ideas about accountability and "good governance." The RDBs followed the World Bank's lead in defining good governance and developing their own accountability mechanisms. The second area is more theoretically driven and involves debate about the development mandates of the RDBs. In particular, there have been disagreements between major stakeholders about the proper role of the state in development policies. These are fundamentally conflicts over ideas and these ideational clashes are concomitant with changes to relative material power of stakeholders as they try to influence key concepts underpinning the lending policies of the RDBs.

The RDBs emulated the World Bank and have set standards for "good governance." Good governance is often defined with reference to transparency, accountability, and adherence to rules.[9] Since the late 1990s, each RDB has formulated procedures associated with good governance and has established independent evaluation offices. These new agencies have varying degrees of independence and responsibilities but in general they take stock of the impacts of RDB lending and allow groups adversely affected to file complaints. Good governance and evaluation offices are viewed by some skeptics as merely window dressing exercises that result in little tangible change to RDB activities because the "independent" agencies are not completely free from the influence of the bureaucracies and, more importantly, these agencies do not possess the ability to dictate changes to RDB policies and procedures.

In addition to the adoption of good governance and creation of independent evaluation agencies, the RDBs have been institutional battlefields for debates about development policies. For example, Japan and other East Asian governments have attempted to have their post-World War II development experiences accepted by the World Bank and the RDBs as suitable options for developing countries to emulate. Japan and other East Asian economies pursued state-centric economic growth strategies labeled "export-led growth," the "development state model," or the "East Asian development model." Regardless of the name, the set of policies associated with it do not fit neatly into neoliberal economic orthodoxy. The United States and the World Bank have both resisted efforts to have such state-centric views of development accepted as alternatives to market-oriented politics such as economic openness. Japan was successful in getting the World Bank to explore the development experiences of Asian economies but was not able to have these illiberal policies systematically incorporated into World Bank practices.[10] Perhaps not surprisingly, given its influence within the ADB, Japan was more successful in obtaining support for its ideas about East Asian development within the ADB.[11] ADB studies on the "East Asian Miracle" concluded that government intervention in the economy can stimulate development and can be considered a challenge to the neoliberal orthodoxy associated with development lending. The East Asian Financial Crisis of 1997–99, however, undermined the credibility of the "miracle" and there was little change to the tenets of ADB lending.

More recently, there has been disagreement between the United States and Japan on the ADB's strategic plan. In the ADB's *Strategy 2020* report, the bank outlined its vision for changing its lending doctrine.[12] With the support of Japan's Ministry of Finance, *Strategy 2020* established new goals such as promoting regional institution building, advocating sustainable development, and greater private sector involvement in lending. *Strategy 2020* also delineated several core values such as "adherence to the highest professional and ethical standards . . . outstanding leadership and service . . . commitment to partnerships with members of the international community . . . [and] accountability and focus on results by defining clear objectives."[13]

Strategy 2020 has been controversial and when it was introduced it was not supported by the United States. In addition to US resistance, civil society organizations were also critical. One NGO, for example, asserted *Strategy 2020* had a clear "corporate bias."[14] In addition, there was political disagreement over the direction of the bank, with Japan and other regional members seeking "to strike out in new directions and help weld Asia together physically and in terms of policies," while the United States and some European members wanted the ADB "to stick to policies designed to reduce poverty and increase social well being."[15] One European representative voiced skepticism about the new vision for the ADB, stating it "must remain firmly anchored to its vision of an Asia and Pacific region free from poverty . . . All other strategic objectives must be pursued in ways that contribute to this goal."[16] In an unusually public display of discord, when *Strategy 2020* came up for approval the Unites States voted against it.[17] Some borrowing members were also concerned about the shift away from traditional projects aimed at poverty reduction. Despite US resistance to *Strategy 2020*, an ADB senior staff member claimed there was no real impact on bank operations, with the implication that American opposition had only a nominal impact.[18]

Another example of discord between major shareholders regarding the mandate, vision, and character of an RDB is the recent disagreement about expanding the EBRD to North Africa. In response to the Arab Spring, the US and some European EBRD members proffered the idea of EBRD membership being extended to countries in North Africa and the Middle East. Overall there has been a lot of support for the general idea of expanded lending to the region, but the degree to which the bank extends its operations to North Africa has been a matter of debate.[19] The crux of the debate is over whether to offer full membership or merely to extend lending operations to countries in North Africa and the Middle East. In 2011 Jordan and Tunisia became members, although it remains unclear to what extent the EBRD's political mandate will be applied to these new members and other potential members.

What we see, then, is that RDBs are at the confluence of battles over ideas among powerful actors in global governance. The RDBs do not merely reflect the doctrines on development pursued by the World Bank because they have different organizational and historical contexts as well as allowing for a greater role for regional members. The RDBs are vital instruments of global economic governance and for students of IO provide additional examples of institutional design. Moreover, it is very likely that as China, India, and other economic actors rise in importance they will seek to influence the RDBs with their own ideas about governance and development.

Conclusion

The RDBs have formal rules which determine how decisions are made on loans and important policy matters. The role of the bureaucracies, including the leadership staffs as well as the foundational ideas about development, also explains which players have power in specific contexts. In other words, observers should not point to one aspect of RDB governance and behavior, such as their weighted voting systems or nationalities of leadership, in order to understand their role. The RDBs, as organizations, exist in an environment where they are subject to material pressures and ideational conflicts from global society as well as from within their own structures.

Often overlooked in studies of global governance, the RDBs and SDBs provide important lessons in how economic ideas are operationalized into development practice. Moreover, lending does not occur divorced from politics, and these IOs are at the center of great debates about development. While the RDBs and SDBs have regional flavors, they are still subject to the influence of great powers and the ideas behind pro-globalization neoliberal economic policies. With the rising status in the world economy of emerging markets, such as China, Brazil, and India, questions loom about how the RDBs will adjust to such systemic political change.

Additional reading

1. Jonathan R. Strand, *Regional Development Banks: Lending with a Regional Flavor* (London: Routledge, 2014).
2. Sarah Babb, *Behind the Development Banks: Washington Politics, World Poverty, and the Wealth of Nations* (Chicago and London: University of Chicago Press, 2009).
3. Roy Culpeper, *Titans or Behemoths?* (Boulder: Lynne Rienner, 1997).
4. Tamar L. Gutner, *Banking on the Environment* (Cambridge, MA: MIT Press, 2002).

Notes

1 Gerald Chan, "Japan and the World Bank: From Burden-Sharing to Power-Sharing," *Japanese Studies Bulletin* 12, no. 3: (1992): 2–18; Ryokichi Hirono "Japan's Leadership Role in the Multilateral Development Institutions," in *Yen for Development: Japanese Foreign Aid and the Politics of Burden-Sharing*, ed. Shafiqul Islam (New York: Council on Foreign Relations Press 1991); Dick Wilson, *A Bank for Half the World: The Story of the Asian Development Bank, 1966–1986* (Manila: ADB, 1987).

2 Karen A. Mingst, *Politics and the African Development Bank* (Lexington: University of Kentucky Press 1990); Christopher L. Shaw, "*Par Inter Paribus*: The Nature of Power in Cooperation. Lessons (for the United States) from the African Development Bank," *African Affairs* 90, no. 361 (1991): 537–558.

3 European Bank for Reconstruction and Development, *Political Aspects of the Mandate of the EBRD* (London: EBRD, 1993).

4 Steven Weber, "Origins of the European Bank for Reconstruction and Development," *International Organization* 48, no. 1 (1994): 1–38.

5 Daniel Titelman, "Subregional Financial Cooperation: The Experiences of Latin America and the Caribbean," in *Regional Financial Cooperation*, ed. Jose Antonio Ocampo (Baltimore, MD: Brookings Institution Press and United National Economic Commission for Latin America and the Caribbean, 2006), 208.

6 Dennis T. Yasutomo, *The New Multilateralism in Japan's Foreign Policy* (New York: St. Martin's Press, 1995), 83.

7   John W. Head, *The Future of the Global Economic Organizations: An Evaluation of Criticisms Leveled at the IMF, the Multilateral Development Banks, and the WTO* (Ardsley, NY: Transnational Publishers Inc., 2005), 115.

8   Inter-American Development Bank, *CR-L1060 Chiripa Wind Power Project, Costa Rica: Draft Environmental and Social Strategy (ESS)*, 11 December 2012, http://www.iadb.org/en/projects/project-description-title,1303.html?id=CR-L1060.

9   Thomas G. Weiss, "Governance, Good Governance, and Global Governance: Conceptual and Actual Challenges," *Third World Quarterly* 21, no. 5 (2000): 795–814.

10 World Bank, *The East Asian Miracle* (New York: Oxford University Press 1993); Robert Wade, "Japan the World Bank, and the Art of Paradigm Maintenance: The East Asian Miracle in Political Perspective," *New Left Review* 217 (1996): 3–37.

11 Asian Development Bank, *Emerging Asia* (Manila: ADB, 1997).

12 Asian Development Bank, *Strategy 2020: The Long-Term Strategic Framework of the Asian Development Bank, 2008–2020* (Manila: ADB, 2008).

13 Ibid., 22.

14 Bank Information Center, "ADB's 2020 Strategy Confirms Corporate Bias," 11 April 2008, http://www.forum-adb.org/BACKUP/pdf/PDF-LTSF/LTSF%20PR-final.pdf.

15 *Business Times Singapore*, "ADB Divided over Future Direction: Asian Members Want New Course, Advanced Nations Remain Traditional," 8 May 2006.

16 *Wall Street Journal*, "Friction over ADB's Role: East Asian Members Use Lender to Foster Financial Integration," 8 May 2006.

17 *Financial Times*, "US Shoots Down ADB's Strategic Plan," 9 April 2008.

18 *International Herald Tribune*, "U.S. and Asia Development Bank Split over Lending Policies," 25 April 2008.

19 Phil Thornton and Taimur Ahmad, "Divisions Emerge over EBRD Expansion Plan," *Emerging Markets*, 19 May 2011, http://www.emergingmarkets.org/Article/2830855/Divisions-emerge-over-EBRD-expansion-plan.html.

CHAPTER 45

Climate Change

Matthew J. Hoffmann

CONTENTS

Climate change may be *the* governance challenge of our time and may remain so for the next century. Climate change is truly global in multiple senses—the climate system is a global one; and the energy and economic systems that are causing the problems are global. Yet, in important ways, climate change is a profoundly local problem—the anthropogenic greenhouse gas emissions at the heart of the problem are produced everywhere, and the effects of climate change will be felt differently in different locales. The governance task is thus enormous. The latest climate science tells us that we are already on track for significant planetary warming and that to hold this warming to two degrees centigrade (a level that *may* allow us to avoid some of the most dire ramifications of climate change) global emissions of greenhouse gases must peak in the next decade and fall off from there rapidly, moving the world towards decarbonization by the end of the century. Governing this problem means finding ways to mitigate it (move relatively rapidly to a decarbonized world) and adapt to it (deal with the ramifications of warming that we are almost certainly already locked into).

Governing climate change thus is unlike any global governance challenge that we have faced previously because of how pervasive the causes and effects of climate change are and how deeply embedded fossil fuels are in the global economy and energy systems. Global climate governance, to be effective, needs to put the world on a path of massive transformation. In many ways, then, climate change has become the keystone issue in global environmental politics. It is directly connected to many other issues, like deforestation, biodiversity loss, and desertification, as a cause or consequence, and it is impossible to conceive of pursuing the agenda of sustainable development, like the world attempted in the Rio+20 meetings in 2012, without also addressing climate change.

This chapter chronicles the global response to climate change, and how the global governance of this issue emerged and evolved. The next section briefly outlines the scope of the problem, in terms of both its causes and effects. The chapter then discusses the

BOX 45.1 ORIENTING TERMS AND DYNAMICS

Greenhouse effect

Ironically, the greenhouse effect is actually something that allows us to live on Earth. The atmosphere acts as a greenhouse, holding in solar radiation that would otherwise reflect off the Earth and be sent into space. Without this greenhouse effect, the planet would be too cold to support life as we know it.

Greenhouse gases

There are a number of gases that produce the greenhouse effect—gases that trap solar radiation and keep the planet warm. These are both naturally occurring and human made (and some are both): water vapor, carbon dioxide, methane, nitrous oxide, and hydrofluorocarbons. Of the anthropogenic gases, carbon dioxide is by far the most prevalent, though some other gases, like methane, have larger warming effects. The gases have different sources as well. Carbon dioxide, for instance, results from the combustion of fossil fuels (coal, gasoline, oil). Methane, on the other hand, is produced by the decay of organic matter (landfills produce a lot of methane).

Global warming (anthropogenic)

Since the industrial revolution, concentrations of human-produced greenhouse gases, especially carbon dioxide, have increased dramatically compared to natural baseline concentrations of these gases. Because most of the world's energy and economic systems are tied closely to the burning of fossil fuels (for energy production, transportation, agriculture, and industrial processes), we have caused large increases in the amount of greenhouse gases in the atmosphere. This increasing concentration of greenhouse gases leads to enhanced warming—more solar radiation is trapped in the atmosphere instead of being radiated out into space. Climate scientists tell us that the Earth is already warming and that we could expect to see global average temperatures increase anywhere from two to six degrees centigrade in the course of this century.

Climate change

This is the broad term for the ramifications of global warming. Warming of the atmosphere alters the dynamics of the climate. Possible changes include: altered precipitation and drought patterns, changing storm frequencies and strengths, transformed seasons and incidences of extreme heat and even cold. Other impacts from warming include rising sea levels, melting of glaciers and polar ice caps, species migrations/extinctions, altered disease vectors and trajectories.

UN-based multilateral governance of climate change that emerged in the late 1980s and remains a key component of the global response. Multilateral governance is not the sum total of the global response to climate change, however. The discussion of governance therefore also explores emerging transnational governance efforts. The chapter concludes with some of the key debates that currently animate the academic and policy discussions around global climate governance.[1]

Climate change as a problem to be governed[2]

The 2007 report from the Intergovernmental Panel on Climate Change (IPCC), whose writers were awarded the Nobel Peace Prize that year, found consensus in the scientific community that greenhouse gas emissions have significantly increased because of human activity and, further, that the modest temperature increases we have already experienced are "very likely due to the observed increase in anthropogenic greenhouse gas concentrations."[3] For at least the last five years, then, the scientific community has agreed that human activity was behind the observed increases in greenhouse gas concentrations and that we could expect significant warming and other effects because of it. This understanding has not wavered since 2007, and, if anything, the consensus in the scientific community has strengthened and its warnings about climate change have become more serious.

In 2011, the National Research Council in the United States warned that the most up-to-date understanding is that "Projections of future climate change anticipate an additional warming of 2.0 to 11.5°F (1.1 to 6.4°C) over the 21st century, on top of the 1.4°F already observed over the past 100 years."[4] In addition, the International Energy Agency (IEA) estimates that if current trends of increasing energy use are not altered, the world is headed for at least 6°C of warming.[5] The current political consensus is that constraining global temperature increases to 2°C is crucial, but that time is rapidly running out to do so. In 2009 a prominent gathering of climate scientists and policymakers declared what has now become a relatively taken for granted understanding: "If global warming is to be limited to a maximum of two degrees C. above pre-industrial values, global emissions need to peak between 2015 and 2020 and then decline rapidly."[6]

Knowledge about expected warming from current and anticipated concentrations of greenhouse gases is increasingly troubling, even frightening, as the climate science community learns more about the kind of impacts we can expect. The possible impacts of climate change are well known—glaciers melting, sea-level rise, altered storm patterns and severity, altered precipitation patterns, and more—but it appears as though at least some impacts are coming sooner than anticipated in earlier models and with greater magnitude. Already in 2009 there was a warning that "The pace and scale of climate change may now be outstripping even the most sobering predictions of the last report of the Intergovernmental Panel of Climate Change."[7] Since 2009, a steady stream of reports are detailing how climate change has already begun and that the impacts, like the melting arctic ice cap, are coming more quickly than anticipated. The juxtaposition in 2012 of a record-breaking warm winter in North America, bizarre cold snaps and heatwaves in Europe, and "Superstorm Sandy" in November on the US East Coast have added an experiential element to the notion that we are already experiencing significant climate change.

The scientific community has provided a consensual understanding of the problem that has generated a good deal of urgency in many corners of the world. However, scientific consensus on the problem has not generated political consensus and will to take significant global action. There are many reasons, some of which the chapter explores in the next section. At least some of the disconnects between scientific consensus and action, however, are because of uncertainties in climate science. The climate system is enormously complex and there are inherent uncertainties in climate change that we may never unravel entirely. As it stands, there are some key unknowns. There are a number of intervening factors between concentrations of greenhouse gases, temperature increase, and climatic changes like increased severity and frequency of storms, cycles of droughts and floods, and patterns of precipitation, and climate science has yet to figure them all out. In addition, natural variability in the climate can mask and/or exacerbate the effect of anthropogenic greenhouse gas emissions. Finally, even though the warming of the atmosphere is a global phenomenon, the magnitude and geographic extent of the effects of climate change are uncertain—in other words, we do not know how bad it will be, where and when.

The problem, at one level, is thus fairly clear and relatively simple, at least to state. Increasing concentrations of greenhouse gases raise global temperatures. Increased global temperatures lead to a number of serious consequences that could have a severe impact on much of humanity. Heading off these consequences is a matter of emitting fewer greenhouse gases, especially less carbon dioxide, and thus substantially decarbonizing our economies and energy systems. The mechanics of climate change are simple, but governing the global response to this problem is far from simple.

Development and evolution of global climate governance

When climate change was put on the international political agenda in the late 1980s, there was no question as to the mode of governance that would be employed to respond to this problem. Multilateral treaty-making, supervised by the United Nations, was taken for granted and essentially synonymous with climate governance. It was understood that climate change was a global problem, not solvable by the actions of individual states, and that it would require a global solution. This made a great deal of sense from certain perspectives. Climate change is often characterized as a classic public goods problem— a stable climate is non-excludable and non-rivalrous and thus ripe for under-provision. The solution was to be a global treaty that would forge cooperation to address the problem. The story of global climate governance, therefore, has to begin with the multilateral negotiation process. This section of the chapter discusses how these negotiations developed and evolved over time—the foundations, participants, successes, and failures of this governance mechanism. This discussion sets the stage for the subsequent exploration of how in the last decade multilateral governance has been joined by other governance mechanisms, and the implications of this development for the building of an effective global response to climate change.

The climate negotiations saga

The most straightforward way to get a handle on the evolution of the climate regime is to understand some of the key milestones and then elucidate the political dynamics that created them. The story begins in earnest in 1988, a year that saw the World Conference on the Changing Atmosphere in Toronto and the founding of the IPCC. The Toronto Conference was the first to seriously move climate change from the scientific agenda to the policy or political agenda, as scientists and government ministers from a number of countries came together to call for what now looks like drastic action on climate change (20 percent reductions of 1988 emissions by 2005). This was the beginning of serious international *political* consideration of climate change. An event of even greater long-term importance, however, was the founding of the IPCC. The UN General Assembly sought a firm scientific foundation for taking action on climate change and initiated the IPCC to gather and report on the science of climate change (its causes, effects, and possible policy options). Since that time, the periodic IPCC reports (1990, 1997, 2007) have served as a benchmark for the consensus on climate change. It should be noted, however, that IPCC reports are a combination of scientific literature review and political messaging—states have a good deal of say about what goes into the reports. The next report is scheduled for 2014.

In 1990 the IPCC produced its first report on the state of knowledge of climate change, and the United Nations kicked off international negotiations, tasking the Intergovernmental Negotiating Committee (INC) with negotiating a global agreement to respond to climate change. The fruits of the INC labor would be realized in 1992 with the signing of the UN Framework Convention on Climate Change (UNFCCC) at the Earth Summit in Rio. The UNFCCC did not mandate any legally binding reductions of greenhouse gas emissions—this was a bridge too far at this stage of the climate regime given US reluctance to such measures and the bargaining positions of other major states and blocs that will be discussed below. What the UNFCCC did lay out, however, were aspirational goals to take actions that would maintain the stability of the climate and return emissions to 1990 levels, along with strictures for states to report their emissions and to develop means of technology transfer of climate-friendly technology.

Some observers and participants (particularly Europeans) were disappointed that the UNFCCC did not go further and mandate more concrete actions. However, beginning with a framework convention that lays out agreed goals and that is to be followed up by more specific protocols was, by this time, an established mode for successfully responding to a global environmental problem—ozone depletion. As such, the UNFCCC had within it commitments and provisions for continuing the negotiations and moving towards protocols that would take up specific actions. These negotiations have been undertaken annually since the UNFCCC came into force in 1994.

The transition from a broad aspirational climate change response to a treaty that would mandate action began in earnest in 1995 when the United States signaled, for the first time, its willingness to consider binding emissions reductions in a global accord. This opened the way for the negotiations that produced the Kyoto Protocol in 1997 because US reluctance on emissions reductions was the single large obstacle to moving ahead in the climate regime. This landmark treaty was the result of intense bargaining along both

North–North and North–South dimensions that are discussed below; and it remains the most comprehensive climate treaty ever concluded. The breakthrough was an agreement by the North to collectively reduce their greenhouse gas emissions 5 percent below 1990 levels by 2012. In addition, the international community of states agreed to a number of "flexibility" mechanisms that states could use to reach their reduction commitments. These included a global emissions trading system and the Clean Development Mechanism, whereby actors in the global North could pay for projects in the global South and receive the emissions reductions credits that resulted. While almost everyone acknowledged that the Kyoto Protocol, alone, would be insufficient to stave off climate change, it was considered to be a good down-payment, and we now look back fondly and with envy on the halcyon days of the mid-1990s when real progress was made in the climate negotiations.

The signing of the Kyoto Protocol would prove to be the high point of the climate regime, and very quickly it became apparent that bringing the protocol into force would be a challenge and that its prospects for being effective where dim. The US Senate, before the protocol was even signed, pledged to not ratify any agreement that did not include commensurate mandates for large developing countries (which the protocol did not have). This immediately called into question whether the single largest emitter at the time (subsequently overtaken by China) would participate. In addition, because the protocol could only come into force if states representing 55 percent of global emissions were represented, the US withdrawal meant that almost every other Northern state would have to ratify.

In 2001, a difficult situation became almost impossible, as the US withdrew its signature from the Kyoto Protocol under the new president George W. Bush. Even as the rest of the international community moved ahead with negotiations to flesh out the details of ratifying and implementing the Kyoto Protocol, the largest player withdrew. It came into force in 2005 but under a pall. Even though the states that ratified the Kyoto Protocol ultimately reached their goal of a 5 percent reduction from 1990 levels, it is often considered a failure because it was not the global agreement that most deemed necessary.

Since 2007 the politics of negotiating and implementing the Kyoto Protocol have given way to the politics of what to do next. The last five years of UN negotiations have been substantially geared towards negotiating a replacement for the Kyoto Protocol. Most of the hope for these more recent negotiations was concentrated around the 2009 negotiations in Copenhagen. Hopeful signs coming from the United States after the election of President Barack Obama and from China in terms of willingness to consider significant action raised expectations for the Copenhagen negotiations. Yet even with a relatively climate-friendly administration in the United States and Chinese signals that it was ready to consider more stringent action, the international community of states was not able to achieve a legally binding replacement for the Kyoto Protocol. The "Hopenhagen" negotiations began with unrealistic expectations about the possibility of achieving a comprehensive, legally binding agreement to combat global warming. It ended as "Brokenhagen," achieving only a maligned Copenhagen Accord that failed to commit major greenhouse gas emitters to a new binding agreement. Instead, a system of voluntary pledges of emissions reductions along with an unspecified process of reviewing progress on those pledges was agreed to in Copenhagen and reaffirmed in Cancun in 2010.

Today, the international community of states is essentially back where it started in 1992, in regards to the pursuit of a legally binding accord. The 2011 climate negotiations in Durban ended with an agreement to continue pursuing negotiations toward a global treaty, with a target date of 2015 to conclude the next deal. The 2012 negotiations in Doha were conceived by some as a bridge between the global climate governance system dominated by the Kyoto Protocol and the as yet unknown system. The international community reaffirmed the goal of reaching agreement by 2015, but little visible progress towards the next legally binding instrument was made. Reaching the Durban goal of a new treaty by 2015 will depend substantially on whether quick progress is made in the 2013 and 2014 meetings. We thus have witnessed 20 years of multilateral climate governance, with very little concrete action to show for all of the "governing."

Foundations of multilateral climate governance

The story of what has happened in multilateral climate governance in the last two decades is important. However, it is even more important to understand why this governance mechanism unfolded in the way that it did, and especially why it has failed spectacularly to produce an effective response to climate change. This brief discussion examines crucial principles that underpinned the negotiations and the bargaining dynamics of major players.

In 1990 the international community began negotiating over climate change in earnest. The world had in hand the first report of the IPCC, laying out what the scientific community understood about the problem. Countries also had fresh in their minds the recent success of the ozone depletion negotiations—where agreement had just been reached to essentially eliminate ozone depleting chemicals. So while these were new negotiations over a daunting problem, the slate was not blank. Two key principles were already in place that shaped the trajectory of the negotiations in important ways.

The first of these was universal participation, the idea that all states should have a voice and role in the negotiations over a global problem like climate change.[8] The response to climate change would not be formulated in the rarefied air of the UN Security Council or the G7, or among a group of the largest producers of greenhouse gases (as the successful ozone depletion negotiations had begun). On the contrary, over 100 states attended the initial climate negotiations and from the beginning the "global" in global climate change governance referred both to the geographic extent of the problem *and* to the level of political participation. The climate change negotiations began as, and remain to this day, a process encompassing essentially all states. This principle served to enhance the legitimacy of the governance process because it ensured that all states would have a voice in this most pressing of problems. However, it also has made the negotiations unwieldy at times and multiplied the number of competing interests that are represented in the bargaining.

The second foundational principle of multilateral climate governance was the idea of common but differentiated responsibilities. This principle, developed in the course of the ozone depletion negotiations in the 1980s, was a means to navigate thorny

South–North issues that arose in global negotiations over something as significant as climate change, issues that have both economic development and environmental dimensions. This was a compromise principle. On the one hand, Northern states were concerned about the need to have a broad response to climate change given the knowledge that Southern states would, in the near future, be the source of the majority of greenhouse gas emissions. China in fact passed the United States in terms of absolute emissions in the mid-2000s, to become the world's most prolific emitter of greenhouse gases.

The global South, on the other hand, wanted recognition that action on climate change would be expensive and that not all states were in a position to take the same kind of action; and this argument was bolstered by the fact that the historical responsibility for greenhouse gas concentrations lay overwhelmingly with the North. Thus, the negotiations were framed by the notion that everyone has a responsibility to act, but that responsibility differs by development level. Differing interpretations of this principle—what is common, what is differentiated, who should have responsibilities, when, and what kind—have been at the core of some of the toughest debates in the last two decades.

These underlying principles structured the UN-led negotiations in the 1990s and are still felt in the annual negotiations today. They structured what has been an incredibly stable set of bargaining dynamics throughout the evolution of multilateral climate governance. While the negotiating process has gone on for two decades, the basic issues that hold up the negotiations have remained virtually unchanged. The political economy of state-centric, multilateral climate governance looks pretty much the same today as it did when the negotiations began in 1990 for the UNFCCC.[9]

The negotiation fault-lines are evident in North–North, North–South, and South–South dimensions. The North–North debate is perennially engaged by the European Union (EU), which for a number of reasons has been a leader on climate action throughout, and by the United States/Canada/Japan/Russia, which have always taken a more cautious or even obstructionist stance in the multilateral negotiations. The North–South debate tends to be over participation, timing, and resources. While CBDR (common but differentiated responsibilities) is an accepted principle, states in the global North have continued to push especially large developing states to move more quickly and take on commensurate responsibilities to those of the Northern states. States in the global South tend to take the position that their action should be delayed and that any action they take should be compensated. Of course, the global South is not homogeneous, and there are both groups of states at the forefront of progressive action—especially small island nations that face an existential threat from climate change—and groups, like oil producers, that are among the most recalcitrant states in the negotiations.

Thus the political logic of the multilateral negotiations has been stable and the bargaining environment has become one of stalemate. Given its pre-eminent position as an energy consumer and carbon dioxide producer, the United States does not want to incur what would be significant costs to its economy to deal with the problem, especially in the absence of action by major economic competitors like China. Large developing countries that have rapidly grown in terms of energy consumption and carbon dioxide emissions (in absolute if not per capita terms) prioritize development over action on climate change and also argue that a problem historically caused in the North should be dealt with by them first. The United States is reluctant, at best, to take significant action. China, India, Brazil, and other developing states are reluctant, at best, to take significant action. The EU, which has taken significant action, has not been able to convince either side to make significant concessions.

Beyond multilateral climate governance?[10]

This story is familiar to those working in the political economy literature, and the stalemate that developed in the late 1990s and forestalled progress on climate change is in some ways over-determined. Setting aside the scientific uncertainty discussed above, climate change is an unbelievably difficult political problem, with a host of obstacles to the kind of cooperation being sought in the multilateral negotiations towards a binding legal treaty:

- The global economy is almost entirely dependent on the use of fossil fuels (for energy production, transportation, agriculture) and we have yet to come up with full replacements. There are vastly different interests across the diverse states about how to approach transformation in this situation.
- States are very different in both their absolute and per capita emissions along with their historical and current emissions, making it difficult to find common ground on responsibility for addressing climate change. Should China and the United States have similar responsibility because of their roughly equal current emissions or very different responsibilities because US per capita emissions are four to five times as big as China's?
- Most simply, an international agreement on emissions reductions would have to impose short-term concentrated costs (i.e. the treaty would identify who would have to cut) that promised long-term diffuse benefits (i.e. future generations would benefit more from our action on climate change than we will).

From this perspective slow progress in the multilateral governance process is far from surprising. All of these characteristics point toward a difficult, if not insoluble, collective action problem. If the multilateral process was the only governance mechanism available, despair over the global response to climate change might rightly rule the day. After 20 years of negotiations, success in the multilateral climate governance process has become self-referential—agreeing to continue negotiating—a degenerative dynamic in the face of impending climate crisis. Fortunately, the state-centric governance mode of multilateral treaty-making is not equivalent to climate governance and other mechanisms have begun to emerge into the void left by stalemate in the negotiations.

We are witnessing a transition in dominant ideas of what climate governance consists of as received ideas about the appropriate way to define and address climate change, long taken for granted, are changing. From the beginning of the 1990s, the multilateral approach along with the concomitant principles of universal participation and CBDR were conceived of as *the* way to govern climate change. But even given the global dimensions of the problem, universal multilateral negotiations are not necessarily a natural governing approach. In fact, climate change is a problem that has both local and global effects, and causes of the problem are found everywhere. In addition, multilateral treaty-making is very difficult in situations for which the goal is to distribute concentrated costs. Thus, not only is multilateral governance not necessarily the only governance mechanism that could be imagined, it may not even be the best one. The last decade of stalemate has led those interested in responding to climate change both to question the multilateral approach and to imagine different ways of governing climate change. Changing ideas about the mode can have a significant impact on governance outcomes—how we respond to climate change.

Specifically, in the last decade we have been witness to an explosion of transnational climate governance initiatives.[11] Community, local, state, regional, and global initiatives working on different aspects of climate change have emerged and proliferated in the face of stalemate and inactivity in the UN negotiations. These initiatives have been working to develop the technological, institutional, economic, and political capacity to move quickly on climate change. Organizations like the Climate Group[12] are bringing together local governments and corporations to do large-scale pilot projects of climate-friendly technology. Initiatives like the Regional Greenhouse Gas Initiative[13] bring together Northeastern US states in an emissions trading system that is demonstrating how a price can be put on carbon. Networks of municipalities like the C40 group of large cities and the Cities for Climate Protection are demonstrating how local, municipal action on climate change can have an effect beyond the borders of individual cities.

A very different kind of global climate governance may result. It would be decentralized and bottom up as opposed to the top-down centralized UN treaty negotiations. It would be the product of actions by multiple kinds of political actors (local communities, cities, states, corporations, NGOs, and nation-states) instead of being state centric. Where the multilateral governance process is concentrated on negotiating emissions reductions, transnational climate governance initiatives would be focused on multiple kinds of goals like energy efficiency, smart grids, smart transportation systems, renewable energy, carbon markets, cultural change, and many more.

The emergence of transnational climate governance also signals a major transition in how non-state actors participate in global climate governance. NGOs and corporations certainly played a role in the evolution of multilateral climate governance.[14] Their goals, however, were oriented toward the multilateral treaty-making process, attempting to influence state negotiating positions and the treaty outcomes. In the emerging transnational governance processes, non-state actors are, in important ways, governing climate change themselves. They have been seizing the authority to make rules for other actors to follow in responding to climate change, becoming active governors of climate change on their own.

A number of these initiatives are partnerships between corporations, NGOs, and cities around the world. Cities are motivated to explore climate-friendly technologies for the economic benefits they promise, while corporations find cities ideal places to experiment with or pilot new technologies, and NGOs bring the two together. Working in concert makes it possible to demonstrate to cities that climate-friendly technology can work to reduce emissions, enhance transportation and energy delivery systems, and benefit them economically, and to demonstrate to corporations that there will be a demand for their products. The Climate Group's LED (light-emitting diode) lighting project is a key example of this process. Large-scale demonstration projects facilitated by the Climate Group have shown that the technology can be beneficial for cities, and demand is now growing. Lighting accounts for 10 percent of global greenhouse gas emissions. By networking municipal governments and corporations, the Climate Group has been able to facilitate a global pilot program to bring LED street lighting (50–70 percent lower emissions than traditional lighting) to major global cities (e.g. New York, London, Hong Kong, Mumbai, and Calcutta), engaging a dozen corporations that manufacture LED lighting.[15]

Such efforts look very different than climate governance through the negotiation of a legally binding instrument, but they are comparable in that both are processes of authoritative rule-making that is designed to shape or guide the behavior of actors in the global response to climate change. Transnational governance initiatives are smaller and more dispersed, but they are also nimble and innovative, and they may provide a catalyst for the kinds of political action that can break the multilateral stalemate.

Conclusion

This chapter does not have a definitive conclusion because global climate governance is still unfolding in ways that are likely to surprise in the coming decades. The global response to climate change is currently in a period of profound instability. The multilateral process has been crippled by years of stalemate and seems unable to get forward traction, but it is not dead yet. On the contrary, a great virtue of the multilateral process is that it is regularized—states come together annually to keep at the negotiations, searching for a global compromise. The multilateral process provides a focal point that keeps climate change high on the international agenda and serves as a forum for both state-centric and transnational governance mechanisms to continue their work and cross-fertilize. Transnational climate governance, on the other hand, is emerging in a dynamic way that has the potential to move forward on a range of fronts necessary to fully respond to climate change. Yet, the initiatives that make up the transnational response are relatively small scale, so it is not entirely clear how relevant an impact they can or will have moving forward. Global climate governance is no longer understood as a singularly multilateral process, but the new shape of climate governance is still being molded.

This instability in the practices of global climate governance is mirrored in the academic study of climate governance. There are some key questions being investigated that concern the architecture of the multilateral response. These still treat multilateral negotiations as the key governance mechanism, but are examining revisions to the underlying principles (especially universal participation) and the process of making a climate treaty.[16] Similarly, scholars working on the transnational climate governance front have a research agenda that examines its emergence, development, and relevance.[17] The key open question that both parts of the literature should turn to is how these multi-level governance dynamics interact and what conditions will facilitate an effective response coming from the combination of multilateral and transnational mechanisms. When we have those answers, we may have great hope that the global response to climate change is likely to be an effective one.

Additional reading

1. Matthew Hoffmann, *Climate Governance at the Crossroads: Experimenting with a Global Response* (New York: Oxford University Press, 2011).
2. Harriet Bulkeley and Peter Newell, *Governing Climate Change* (London: Routledge, 2010).
3. Mike Hulme, *Why We Disagree about Climate Change: Understanding Controversy, Inaction, and Opportunity* (Cambridge: Cambridge University Press, 2009).
4. Joseph Aldy and Robert Stavins, eds., *Architectures for Agreement: Addressing Global Climate Change in the Post-Kyoto World* (Cambridge: Cambridge University Press, 2007).
5. Stephen Gardiner, *A Perfect Moral Storm: The Ethical Tragedy of Climate Change* (New York: Oxford University Press, 2011).
6. David Victor, *Global Warming Gridlock* (Cambridge: Cambridge University Press, 2011).

Notes

1 This chapter draws on research and text from a number of prior publications, including Matthew Hoffmann, *Ozone Depletion and Climate Change: Constructing a Global Response* (Albany: SUNY Press, 2005); and Matthew Hoffmann, *Climate Governance at the Crossroads: Experimenting with a Global Response* (New York: Oxford University Press, 2011).

2 This section draws on research and text from Matthew Hoffmann, "Global Climate Change," in *Handbook of Global Climate and Environment Policy*, ed. Robert Falkner (Oxford: Wiley Blackwell, forthcoming).

3 Intergovernmental Panel on Climate Change, *Contribution of Working Groups I, II and III to the Fourth Assessment Report of the Intergovernmental Panel on Climate Change* (2007), http://www.ipcc.ch/publications_and_data/ar4/syr/en/contents.html.

4 National Research Council, *Advancing the Science of Climate Change* (2011), http://nas-sites.org/americasclimatechoices/sample-page/panel-reports/87-2/.

5 International Energy Agency, *Tracking Clean Energy Progress, Energy Technology Perspectives 2012* excerpt as IEA input to the Clean Energy Ministerial (2012), http://www.iea.org/media/etp/Tracking_Clean_Energy_Progress.pdf.

6 Ian Allison, Nathan Bindoff, Robert A. Bindschadler et al., *The Copenhagen Diagnosis: Updating the World on the Latest Climate Science* (2009), http://www.copenhagendiagnosis.com/.

7 United Nations Environment Programme, *Climate Change Science Compendium* (2009), http://www.unep.org/Documents.Multilingual/Default.asp?DocumentID=596&ArticleID=6326&l=en.

8 Hoffmann, *Ozone Depletion and Climate Change*.

9 See, for example Susan Sell, "North–South Environmental Bargaining: Ozone, Climate Change, and Biodiversity," *Global Governance* 2, no. 1 (1996): 93–116; David Victor, *Global Warming Gridlock* (Cambridge: Cambridge University Press, 2011); Scott Barrett, *Environment and Statecraft* (Oxford: Oxford University Press, 2003).

10 This section draws on ideas and text from Hoffmann, *Climate Governance*.

11 See, for example, Hoffmann, *Climate Governance*; Harriet Bulkeley and Peter Newell, *Governing Climate Change* (London: Routledge, 2010).

12 http://www.theclimategroup.org.

13 http://www.rggi.org.

14 Michele Betsill and Elisabeth Corell, eds., *NGO Diplomacy: The Influence of Nongovernmental Organizations in International Environmental Negotiations* (Cambridge, MA: MIT Press, 2008).

15 http://www.theclimategroup.org/programs/led.
16 Joseph Aldy and Robert Stavins, eds., *Architectures for Agreement: Addressing Global Climate Change in the Post-Kyoto World* (Cambridge: Cambridge University Press, 2007).
17 Hoffmann, *Climate Governance*; Harriet Bulkeley, Liliana Andonova, Karin Backstrand et al., "Governing Climate Change Transnationally: Assessing the Evidence from a Database of Sixty Initiatives," *Environment and Planning* 30, no. 4 (2012): 591–612.

Sustainable Development

Roger A. Coate

By 2012 and the United Nations Conference on Sustainable Development (Rio+20) in Rio de Janeiro from 20 to 22 June, the concept of sustainable development had come to occupy center stage on the global agenda. This was clearly reflected by UN Secretary-General Ban Ki-moon during his Rio+20 press conference. He declared that he had made sustainable development the "number one priority" for his second term as secretary-general and emphasized that "sustainable development is an idea whose time has come."[1]

What is sustainable development? A nominal definition is needed to begin the discussion. For that purpose, the definition articulated by the World Commission on Environment and Development (the Brundtland Commission) twenty-five years ago will be used because it has more or less stood the test of time:

> Sustainable development is development that meets the needs of the present without compromising the ability of future generations to meet their own needs. It contains within it two concepts: the concept of needs, in particular the essential needs of the world's poor, to which overriding priority should be given; and the idea of limitations imposed by the state of technology and social organization on the environment's ability to meet present and future needs.[2]

Is sustainable development more than a wooly concept? How and why has the international community of states come to focus on it as the organizing principle for global action? Who have been the main players in the evolution of sustainable development? What have been the institutional arenas in which these politics have been played out? Where do we stand now and what are the current debates and prospects for the future?

This chapter explores the evolutionary and dialectical processes by which two originally distinct concepts—development and environment—have become integrated in this one overarching principle. Particular attention is paid to the dynamic interplay of governmental, intergovernmental, and non-state actors. Both the development and environment areas have been distinctive in the extraordinary degree to which civil society actors have been actively engaged. The intent is to focus on the most relevant, benchmark events and actors rather than to try to be all inclusive.

This chapter begins by analyzing the evolution of the UN's work in the development sphere. The discussion turns to the emergence of the concept "ecodevelopment" and sustainability thinking, as well as the concept of "sustainable development" itself. Subsequently, the evolution of international discourse, practice, and institutionalization of sustainable development in the global arena is laid out, beginning with the UN Conference on Environment and Development. Building on this foundation, the subsequent political dynamics of ecodevelopment politics are explored. The chapter then examines current sustainable development discourse and practice, and concludes with a somewhat pessimistic outlook for the future.

The evolution of developmentalism

Most accounts of the history of sustainable development begin with a focus on environment and the nature and process by which environmental consciousness entered onto the global agenda and subsequently became merged with development. Here, the focus will begin with an overview of the nature and role of development as it emerged on the multilateral scene. This is a more logical place to start as it is the predecessor concept. The section then explores how, when, and why environment became infused in global development discourse.

Kenneth Dadzie has provided a helpful framework for understanding the evolution of UN development discourse and practice. He argues that there have been four major phases in dealing with development concerns.[3] Weiss et al. have dubbed these: national state capitalism (1945–62); international affirmative action (1962–81); return to neoliberalism (1981–89); and sustainable development (1989–present).[4] During the earliest years of the United Nations, development was defined mainly in terms of national economic growth. The emphasis was on the reconstruction and development of war-torn societies after World War II and building the national economies of states emerging from colonialism. The dominant strategy was promoting state-capitalism, national economic growth, and national self-reliance through state-centered economic liberalism.

The second phase of the global discourse on development focused heavily on the notion of redressing perceived structural imbalances within the global political economy. The political dynamic was primarily North–South and centered on the call from the global South for a New International Economic Order (NIEO) to deal with such imbalances. The main thrust came during the Sixth Special Session of the General Assembly in 1974, at which the Declaration and Program of Action on the Establishment of a New International Economic Order was adopted. The demands of the declaration were wide-ranging but fell roughly into four broad themes: economic sovereignty, trade, aid, and participation.[5] These concerns were raised repeatedly in various settings during the remainder of the decade.

The year 1981 brought a renewed and invigorated response from an important corner of the North. The Ronald Reagan era in Washington and the Margaret Thatcher period in London brought unyielding pressure to replace the Keynesian model that had dominated much of the post-World War II era with a return to a free-market-capitalist approach. The end of the Cold War provided the political space needed for the United States, the United Kingdom, and other Western governments to largely ignore Third World rhetoric and demands. This new development vision, dubbed the "Washington Consensus,"[6] represented a return to minimal regulation and maximum private entrepreneurship.

All things pass, as did the Reagan and Thatcher years and much of the unbending orthodoxy of neoliberalism. The global debate between those stressing the role of markets and free trade versus those emphasizing public regulation and assistance for both social and economic reasons slowly gave rise to a new synthesis, embodied in the idea of sustainable development.

The emergence of ecodevelopment and sustainability thinking

As early as 1960, the notion of sustainability began creaking its way into UN development discourse. General Assembly Resolution 1701 (XVI) designated the 1960s as the [First] United Nations Development Decade, whose goal was: "to mobilize and to sustain support for the measures required on the part of both developed and developing countries to accelerate progress toward self-sustaining growth of the economy of the individual nations and their social advancement." Yet, at the international governmental level, the sentiment ended there. It would take another decade—the Second UN Development Decade—for ecodevelopment to actually begin the integration process in the global agenda.

However, in various corners of civil society, action was breaking onto the surface and garnering important attention. The notion of the existence of a living envelope surrounding the Earth—the biosphere—began to take hold in scientific circles in the 1920s and 1930s. Along with this concept came the realization that humans possess the capacity to do much damage to this vital life-enabling system. In response to this and other concerns, the first international environmental nongovernmental organization (NGO), the International Union for the Conservation of Nature and Natural Resources (IUCN), was formed in 1948. In 1962, for example, Rachel Carson's *Silent Spring* helped bring public attention to environmental health hazards caused by human actions. In 1968, Paul Ehrlich's *Population Bomb* and Garrett Hardin's classic essay "The Tragedy of the Commons" helped to further galvanize concern over the future of Planet Earth. *Only One Earth* by René Dubos and Barbara Ward came out in 1971, and the Club of Rome added to awareness with the publication in 1972 of *Limits to Growth*.

Other NGOs with an international scope began springing up, such as Friends of the Earth (1969), the International Development Research Centre (IDRC, 1970), the Natural Resources Defense Council (1970), Greenpeace (1971), the International Institute for Environment and Development (IIED, 1971), and Environnement et Développement du Tiers-Monde (ENDA, 1972). World Watch Institute joined the growing chorus in 1975.

The United Nations Educational, Scientific, and Cultural Organization (UNESCO) was the first UN agency to move robustly on the environmental front. In 1965, it launched a ten-year program—the International Hydrological Decade—to promote the study of hydrological resources, including water pollution. The following year, the UNESCO General Conference took note of the possible detrimental impacts of human actions on the living envelope surrounding the Earth and called for an international conference to consider the issue. Then in 1968, UNESCO hosted the International Conference of Experts on the Biosphere. The Food and Agricultural Organization (FAO), the IUCN, the World Health Organization (WHO), and the United Nations co-sponsored the event. One outcome of the conference was the conceptual linking of the human social order with nature and the environment. Building on the concept "biosphere," conferees discussed the concept of ecologically sustainable development.

UNESCO moved forward on several other environmental fronts. It established an interdisciplinary research program—"Man and the Biosphere"—to investigate relations between humans and nature. Significant early UNESCO programs include the International Hydrological Decade and International Oceanographic Commission (IOC). UNESCO headquarters in Paris serves as the host for the NGO International Council of Scientific Unions (ICSU). ICSU, in turn, facilitates a number of international environment-related scientific programs that were established during this early period, including: the International Biological Programme; the International Geosphere–Biosphere Programme (IGBP); and the Scientific Committee on the Problems of the Environment (SCOPE).

In 1968, the UN General Assembly Resolution 2398 (XXIII) called for convening a global conference on the environment, the UN Conference on the Human Environment (UNCHE). It was in the preparatory work for this conference that the first significant merger of environment and development occurred. At the UNCHE Preparatory Committee meeting in Founex, France, the concept of "ecodevelopment" was proposed by the conference's secretary-general, Maurice Strong, in order to move beyond a logjam between participants from the North and global South. Strong suggested that long-term development depended on dealing with shorter-term environmental problems, which appeased negotiators from the North. He further argued that donor countries should provide additional financial resources to countries of the global South in order for them to undertake relatively more expensive environmentally sound development policies. This concept—"additionality"—caught on, and a crucial bargain was struck.

Well over 200 NGOs were engaged in some aspect of the UNCHE process. Some of these, such as the IUCN and ICSU played rather important roles as consultants to Secretary-General Strong. The conference outcome document, the Declaration on the Human Environment, laid out 26 principles for environmental governance and 109 recommendations for action. One of the most significant recommendations coming out of the conference was the creation of the UN Environment Programme (UNEP).

The General Assembly seized on this recommendation and formally created UNEP in 1973. After UNEP was formed, a special liaison mechanism was established, the Environment Liaison Centre International (ELCI), by which NGOs could systematize civil society relations with the UN agency.

The UN Conference on the Human Environment was followed by several other conferences in the 1970s in which development issues were infused in the debate over other issues. These included: the UN Conference on the Law of the Sea (UNCLOS, 1974–81); World Population Conference (1974); World Food Conference (1974); UN World Conference of the International Women's Year (1975); the UN Conference on Human Settlements (Habitat, 1976); the Conference on Desertification (1977); and the World Climate Conference (1979). As one looks at the concept of sustainable development as manifest today, the linkages with these earlier global forums and the debates therein become apparent.

The decade of the 1980s is often referred to as the "lost development decade" because of paltry growth rates in most developing countries. Yet it bore witness to some of the most important ecodevelopment events and activities. As the decade began, the IUCN launched its *World Conservation Strategy* report. It called for a new international development strategy, based on "sustainable development," and discussed the roles of poverty, rapid population growth, social inequities, and international trading systems in environmental degradation. The report of the Independent Commission on International Development Issues (the Brandt Report) was published in 1980, calling for a new political economic relationship between North and South. In 1981 WHO launched the Global Strategy for Health for All by the Year 2000. The following year, UNCLOS adopted the UN Convention on the Law of the Sea. The Second World Population Conference (1984), the Third World Conference on Women (1985), the Vienna Climate Change Conference (1985), and the follow-up adoption of the Montreal Protocol on Substances that Deplete the Ozone Layer (1987) added momentum regarding ecodevelopment. As the decade was drawing to a close, the Intergovernmental Panel on Climate Change (IPCC) was created by the UNEP and the World Meteorological Organization (WMO) "to provide internationally coordinated scientific assessments of the magnitude, timing and potential environmental and socio-economic impact of climate change and realistic response strategies."[7]

The cornerstone, however, was the Brundtland Commission's report, *Our Common Future*. The conceptualizations provided by the report served to cement sustainable development as an integrating concept that would underpin the work of both multilateral institutions and civil society organizations for decades to come. One indication of its breadth of impact was the formation of the Business Council for Sustainable Development, which in 1992 published *Changing Course*, arguing that business indeed does have an interest in sustainable development.

The Earth Summit and beyond

In important ways, the Brundtland Commission laid the foundation for what was to become an even greater benchmark, the UN Conference on Environment and Development (UNCED, or "Earth Summit"), hosted in Rio de Janeiro in 1992. Similar to UNCHE, the preparatory work for UNCED is where the real action was centered, not at the conference itself. The Rio process last for nearly three years, and as UNCED Secretary-General Maurice Strong commented, "the process was the policy."[8] Strong understood well the importance of building a consensus from the ground up and having all critical decisions made before the actual gathering itself.

Yet qualitative and quantitative targets and acceptable limits still eluded negotiators as they rushed to finalize agreement on the conventions, statements of principles, and plan of action. As had been the case 20 years earlier, North–South tensions reflected competing world views. Southern governments tended to view ozone depletion, hazardous waste pollution, and global warming as products of industrialization and over-consumption in the North. Why should they bear the costs of these new Northern priorities? If Northern governments wanted the active partnership of the South in dealing with such problems, then Northern donors should make available additional financial and technical resources. Again, the concept of "additionality" came to the fore.

Resolving the debate over deforestation was particularly difficult. These North–South tensions were brought into particularly sharp focus. Southern governments forcefully resisted any incursion into the principle of sovereignty over natural resources. Tensions also prevailed in drafting the Rio Declaration, which was to guide governments and nongovernmental actors in implementing the many provisions of Agenda 21. The final compromise incorporated many of the most important elements of the development and environment perspectives of both sides. The 27 principles embodied in the Rio Declaration were ones stating that the cost of pollution should be borne at the source and should be reflected in product cost at all stages of production. Agenda 21 comprised over 600 pages and covered a large variety of issues, many of which were quite contentious, including issues related to biodiversity, biotechnology, deforestation, and institutional and procedural issues involving financing, technology transfer, and institutional arrangements for carrying out the elements of the action agenda.

Two legally binding international conventions—on biodiversity, the Convention on Biodiversity, and on climate change, the UN Framework Convention on Climate Change (UNFCCC)—were incorporated as part of the larger Rio process. The final draft documents emerging from the Earth Summit represented "framework conventions." These conventions designated general principles and obligations, but specific timetables and targets were left to be specified at future negotiations over protocols.

A number of these issues remained unresolved at the close of UNCED. Foremost among them was how to generate the financial resources needed to implement the program of action and associated activities. Governance issues were linked to the issue of financing. Who was to decide when and how such resources are to be spent? Southern participants proposed the creation of a new "green fund," which would operate on more egalitarian voting principles. A partial compromise was achieved to enhance the South's participation while retaining for donor states elements of control. Interim financing for Agenda 21 implementation would be provided under the aegis of the World Bank group. The Global Environment Facility (GEF) would be expanded and its rules altered to provide for decision-making by consensus among equally represented groupings of donors and recipients.

One of the most significant outcomes of the Earth Summit was the creation of the UN Commission on Sustainable Development (CSD), under the jurisdiction of the UN

Economic and Social Council (ECOSOC). The CSD was mandated to oversee the implementation of the provisions of Agenda 21 and coordinate the sustainable development activities of the various organizations within the UN system. It was also mandated to strengthen and integrate the role of major societal groups and civil society actors as effective participants in sustainable development decision-making at all levels. The text of Agenda 21 specifically addressed the roles of eight major groups: NGOs, indigenous peoples, local governments, workers, businesses, scientific communities, farmers, and women, children, and youth.

However, the matter of how the CSD was to be empowered to fulfill its mandate effectively was left unspecified. This was especially problematic given its mandated role of being the primary mechanism within the UN system for coordinating sustainable development, especially with regard to UNEP, the World Bank, the Committee of International Development Institutions on the Environment, and other intergovernmental bodies. Despite such shortcomings, the CSD and its counterpart in the UN Secretariat, the Division of Sustainable Development, serve as focal points for coordinating UN implementation activities for sustainable development. In its Multi-year Programme of Work, the CSD systematically reviews progress and makes recommendations for further action on specific clusters of issues.

Following on from UNCED, the decade of the 1990s witnessed an almost unending series of global ad hoc conferences on social and economic matters.[9] These included: the World Conference on Human Rights (1993); the International Conference on Population and Development (ICPD, 1994); the UN Global Conference on Sustainable Development of Small Island Developing States (1994); the World Summit on Social Development (1995); the Fourth World Conference on Women (1995); the Second UN Conference on Human Settlements (1996); and the World Food Summit (1996). In addition, the World Conference on Education for All, the Second World Climate Conference, and the World Summit for Children had all been held in 1990 prior to UNCED. What was clear at each of these gatherings and the preparatory processes that led up to them was that the concept of sustainable development and its evolving meanings were more or less center stage.

In the context of all this, in May 1994 UN Secretary-General Boutros-Ghali presented the General Assembly with his *An Agenda for Development*,[10] a companion volume to his earlier *An Agenda for Peace*. In this new "agenda," he declared development to be a fundamental human right and presented a general framework within which he highlighted the interdependent nature of peace, economy, civil society, democracy, social justice, and environment as indispensble components of the development process. Development increasingly came to be viewed in human, as opposed to exclusively national economic, terms.

In the mid-1990s the UNDP/UNFPA Executive Board decision 94/14 adopted "sustainable human development" as a new mission for technical assistance. Moreover, in its 1993 *Human Development Reports*, the UNDP provided a basic framework for focusing discourse. It suggested that the UN's development work should be based on at least five "new pillars": new concepts of human security, new models of sustainable human development, new partnerships between states and markets, new patterns of national and global governance, and new forms of international cooperation. Each *Human Development Report* has served to elaborate, extend, and clarify specific aspects of the development–human security nexus. Participation and empowerment have been two of the priority themes running throughout these annual reports.

A centerpiece of the UN's sustainable development agenda is the Millennium Development Goals (MDGs) process, targets that were developed in the wake of the Millennium Summit in 2000. UN member states specified eight time-bound goals and associated targets and measurable indicators to be achieved by 2015 for eradicating poverty and promoting sustainable human development and security. Seven of the eight main goals focus on substantive objectives: eradicating extreme poverty and hunger; achieving universal primary education; promoting gender equality and empowering women; reducing infant mortality; improving maternal health; combating HIV/AIDS, malaria and other diseases; and better ensuring environmental sustainability. The eighth MDG—a global partnership for development—deals with creating the capacity to achieve the other seven. Cumulatively, the MDGs can be seen as both mutually reinforcing and intertwined. A UN system-wide strategy has been designed for mobilizing support and monitoring progress toward achieving the MDGs.

The MDG strategy places special emphasis on the situation of landlocked developing countries (LLDCs) and small island developing states (SIDS). These two groups of states increasingly have drawn the special attention of the international community since the early 1990s. SIDS are exceptionally vulnerable to environmental change. The situation confronting SIDS was addressed at the Earth Summit in Rio in 1992 and has been an issue before the CSD since its creation in the aftermath of the summit. The Global Conference on the Sustainable Development of Small Island Developing States was held in Bridgetown, Barbados, 25 April—6 May 1994. The conference adopted the Barbados Programme of Action (BPoA), which set forth specific recommendations and actions for promoting the sustainable development of SIDS.[11] Ten years following the adoption of the BPoA to address the special problems of SIDS, Mauritius hosted a conference to review progress on its implementation in January 2005. The conferees adopted a proactive strategy—the Mauritius Strategy—for implementing the BPoA, stressing the importance of climate change and energy issues and calling for more effective integration of SIDS into the world trading system.

The 1990s had witnessed a significant decline in official development assistance (ODA). At the turn of the twenty-first century, the global political climate provided space for dealing with this issue. At both the Ministerial Conference of the World Trade Organization (WTO) held in Doha, Qatar, in November 2001 and the summit-level UN-sponsored Conference on Financing for Development in Monterrey, Mexico, in March 2002, donor countries conveyed an increased commitment to provide resources. The Monterrey meeting brought together stakeholders representing governments, business, civil society, and international institutions for a formal exchange of views. The "Monterrey Consensus," as that conference's outcome document was called, recognized the need to increase ODA significantly in order to meet the MDGs.[12] The importance here was not an actual commitment and delivery of needed financing, but the growing consensus that such a commitment was necessary to fight poverty.

A decade after the Earth Summit in Rio, the United Nations convened the World Summit on Sustainable Development in Johannesburg in September 2002 in an attempt to reinvigorate sustainable development activities in the wake of deepening poverty and environmental degradation. In this regard, the summit's outcomes are questionable.

However, again "process was the product." The summit reflected a new approach to conferencing and to sustainable development more generally. It represented a dialogue among major stakeholders from governments, civil society, and the private sector. Participants focused primarily on the creation of new partnerships to bring additional resources to bear for sustainable development.

UN member states tried again to reinvigorate the MDG process, by convening the 2005 World Summit. And again, the outcome was marginal. In the ecodevelopment area limited steps were agreed, including: a restated but ambiguous commitment to achieve the MDGs; a commitment by developing countries to adopt national initiatives for achieving the MDGs; an agreement to move toward ensuring long-term debt sustainability through the cancellation of 100 percent of official multilateral and bilateral debt of the heavily indebted poor countries (HIPCs) and increased grant-based development financing; a commitment to move toward innovative sources of development financing; an agreement to create a worldwide early warning system for natural hazards; and, in regard to climate change, a commitment to provide assistance to small island developing states and other highly vulnerable states.

The remainder of the decade witnessed fits, starts, and failures in regard to ecodevelopment, as forward progress basically stagnated on most fronts, such as the annual UNFCCC Conferences of the Parties (CoPs) meetings. In October 2008 UNEP called for a "Global Green New Deal" and launched the Green Economy Initiative (GEI). The GEI represents a medium- to long-term strategy to blunt the force of and turn around global environmental degradation. It incorporates three ongoing key elements: the Green Economy report, the Economics of Ecosystems and Biodiversity (TEEB), and the Green Jobs report. The Green Economy report is designed to provide an overview, analysis, and synthesis of how public policy can be used to help accelerate the transition towards a green economy. The TEEB is a partnership project focusing on the economic value of biodiversity and ecosystem services. The Green Jobs report examines green-related employment trends. The jury, however, is still out with regard to the impact this initiative may have. The 2008 global financial crisis and the subsequent recession —turmoil which, at the time of writing, we are still in—have been major setbacks for making sustainability a priority for states when they face rising unemployment, economic recession, and austerity.

A way forward?

Are the next ten years poised to reverse the lack of progress regarding promoting and moving forward the sustainable development agenda? There are positive signs. As noted, Ban Ki-moon has made sustainable development the top priority for his second administration as secretary-general. He has stressed the need "to invent a model—a new model that offers growth and social inclusion—a model that is more respectful of the planet's finite resources."[13]

Following his election for a second term, Ban Ki-moon laid out his agenda for the coming five years, focusing on three priority goals: accelerating progress on the MDGs; addressing climate change; and forging a consensus around, as well as implementing, a post-2015 sustainable development framework.[14] The latter goal would entail defining "a new generation of sustainable development goals building on the MDGs and outlin[ing] a road map for consideration by member states." He cautioned that in order to achieve sustainable development goals "the most important tool will be energy. Energy is the golden thread."[15]

In this context, the secretary-general launched the "Sustainable Energy for All Initiative" in conjunction with the UN's International Year of Sustainable Energy for All (2012).[16] "Providing sustainable energy for all could be the biggest opportunity of the 21st century," he stated. "Sustainable energy is the golden thread that connects economic growth, social equity, and a climate and environment that enables the world to thrive. This initiative is bringing together governments, the private sector, and civil society in a partnership that's delivering real results."[17] The initiative has three objectives: to provide universal energy access; to double the rate of global energy efficiency improvement; and to double the share of renewable energy in the global energy mix. It focuses on three interrelated objectives to be achieved by 2030: Ensure universal access to modern energy services; double the global rate of improvement in energy efficiency; double the share of renewable energy in the global mix. The secretary-general stressed that sustainable energy lies at the center of achieving sustainable development.[18]

In May 2012, Ban Ki-moon established the Secretary-General's High-level Panel of Eminent Persons on the Post-2015 Development Agenda, tasked with developing ideas for such a post-2015 development agenda.[19] In addition, on 9 August 2012, he launched "The Sustainable Development Solutions Network" (SDSN). This is a special independent global network of research centers, universities, and technical institutions that will work with civil society, private sector, UN, and other international actors to promote sustainable development, directed by the secretary-general's special advisor on MDGs, Jeffrey Sachs.

Forty years after UNCHE and 20 years after UNCED, the government of Brazil hosted the UN Conference on Sustainable Development (UNCSD or Rio+20) on 20–22 June 2012. This was a summit-level meeting with an associated civil society forum, Sustainable Development Dialogues, before the summit on 16–19 June, and a Partnerships Forum that had been requested by the General Assembly on 20–22 June. The conference outcome document, "The Future We Want," summarizes the results.[20] It stressed the dynamic nature of three interdependent dimensions of sustainable development: economic, social, and environmental aspects:

> We recognize that poverty eradication, changing unsustainable and promoting sustainable patterns of consumption and production, and protecting and managing the natural resource base of economic and social development are the overarching objectives of and essential requirements for sustainable development. We also reaffirm the need to achieve sustainable development by: promoting sustained, inclusive and equitable economic growth, creating greater opportunities for all, reducing inequalities, raising basic standards of living; fostering equitable social development and inclusion; and promoting integrated and sustainable management of natural resources and ecosystems that supports inter alia economic, social and human development while facilitating ecosystem conservation, regeneration and restoration and resilience in the face of new and emerging challenges.[21]

Rio+20 launched a process to develop a set of Sustainable Development Goals (SDGs), which should build upon the Millennium Development Goals and converge with the post-2015 development agenda. The conference adopted a general set of guidelines on green economy policies. It also adopted the ten-year programmatic framework on sustainable consumption and production patterns and invited the General Assembly to designate a member state body to take any necessary steps to fully operationalize the framework. It called on the General Assembly to: establish an intergovernmental process to prepare options on a strategy for sustainable development financing; create a high-level political forum for sustainable development; establish an intergovernmental process under the General Assembly to prepare options on a strategy for sustainable development financing; and strengthen the UNEP. Finally, the conference took a number of decisions on various thematic areas, including energy, food security, oceans, and cities.[22]

Persistent controversies and issues

After nearly half a century of ecodevelopment discourse and practice, the dialectic at play is still controversial and conflictual. The global debate continues and the future of sustainable development remains murky. Three prominent individuals' reflections on the process and outcomes of Rio+20 help to understand such dynamic tensions. Gro Brundtland, for example, cautioned that "the Rio+20 declaration does not do enough to set humanity on a sustainable path . . . We can no longer assume that our collective actions will not trigger tipping points, as environmental thresholds are breached, risking irreversible damage to both ecosystems and human communities."[23] Mary Robinson, former president of Ireland and former UN high commissioner for human rights, complained: "This is a 'once in a generation' moment when the world needs vision, commitment and above all, leadership. Sadly, the current document is a failure of leadership."[24] Fernando Cardoso, former president of Brazil, who presided over the 1992 Earth Summit, argued that the Rio+20 declaration was imbalanced, concentrating more on development than environment. He said: "I am concerned that the final declaration does not give the same weight to environmental protection as it does to human development and growth . . . We have to accept that the solutions to poverty and inequality lie in sustainable growth, not growth at all costs."[25]

From another perspective, Brazilian theologian Leonardo Boff has challenged the assumption embedded in the Rio+20 Conference outcome document that there is an equality among the environmental, social, and economic dimensions of sustainable development. "The magic phrase now is green economy, the meaning of which is unclear," he argued. "As long as there is no appreciation of the limits of the planet, it is useless to think of social justice and economic development."[26]

The World Watch Institute, on the other hand, summarized things this way: "This failure to act is the product of many factors. One is simply a lack of vision." The article continued: "[T]he 'international community' is such a collection of unequal entities—with vastly different levels of power and widely diverging interests—that it is challenging in the extreme to find a sufficiently ambitious common denominator." The Institute argued that "Fundamentally, the problem . . . is that governments are highly averse to making meaningful commitments, especially those that challenge established economic structures and corporate interests."[27]

On reflection, the global sustainable development discourse so far in this decade creates the disturbing image of the Titanic and the refrain: "And the band played on."

Conclusion

Sustainable development entails coping with and overcoming a nexus of complex, dynamically interdependent, contradictory, and seemingly overwhelming problems and issues. Some crucial sustainable development issues—climate change and green economy, to name just two—are some of the most highly divisive political issues and are linked inherently to conflicting ideologies and self-interests. While almost all scientific studies validate global warming as a predominant concern for the future of humankind, the concept of "climate change" and the notion of "green economy" remain politically highly contested issues as they pit conflicting ideological belief structures, social values, and self-centered interests against one another.

Perhaps more importantly, persisting tensions, controversies, and trade-offs remain over the relative importance of "development" versus "environment," as well as treating economic, social, and environmental dimensions of sustainable development as deserving equal consideration. The underlying trade-offs have real political impacts and implications. Such considerations provide the context within which the newly established high-level group and the SDG process must operate.

The world's current governance models are simply not adequate to incorporate the diverse interests and make meaningful the necessary contributions of the vast array of different types of stakeholders. The so-called "Arab Spring" and resulting political transformations in Libya, Egypt, Syria, Yemen, and Gaza, as well as the continuing political crises in Afghanistan, Iraq, and Pakistan, clearly indicate this deficiency. Not all interests are equal, and most do not go far beyond individual or group self-interests. Unless new models of governance at all levels can be found and put in place in reasonably quick order, this, as World Watch Institute has suggested, may be "how the world will end: in the face of protracted inaction."[28]

Additional reading

1. Thomas G. Weiss et al., *The United Nations and Changing World Politics*, 7th edition (Boulder: Westview Press, 2013), chs. 9–11.
2. World Commission on Environment and Development, *Our Common Future* (Oxford: Clarendon Press, 1987).
3. Lorraine Elliott, *The Global Politics of the Environment* (New York: New York University Press, 1998).
4. United Nations, *Report of the United Nations Conference on Sustainable Development* (A/CONF. 216/16), 20–22 June 2012.
5. Boutros Boutros-Ghali, *An Agenda for Development* (New York: United Nations, 1995).

Notes

1 United Nations, *Press Conference by Secretary-General Ban Ki-moon on Rio+20* (SG/SM/14336, ENV/DEV/1286), 6 June 2012.

2 World Commission on Environment and Development, *Our Common Future* (Oxford: Clarendon Press, 1987).

3 Kenneth Dadzie, "The UN and the Problem of Economic Development," in *United Nations, Divided World: The UN's Roles in International Relations*, 2nd edition, eds. Adam Roberts and Benedict Kingsbury (Oxford: Clarendon Publishers, 1995), 297–326.

4 Thomas G. Weiss et al., *The United Nations and Changing World Politics*, 7th edition (Boulder: Westview Press, 2013).

5 Robert S. Jordan, "Why an NIEO? The View from the Third World," in *The Emerging International Economic Order: Dynamic Processes, Constraints and Opportunities*, eds. Harold K. Jacobson and Dusam Aidjanski (Beverly Hills, CA: Sage, 1982), 59–80.

6 John Williamson, "The Washington Consensus Revisited," in *Economic and Social Development in the 21st Century*, ed. Louis Emmerij (Baltimore, MD: Johns Hopkins University Press, 1997), 48–61.

7 United Nations, "Protection of Global Climate for Present and Future Generations of Mankind," General Assembly Resolution 43/53, 6 December 1988.

8 Maurice Strong, *Where on Earth Are We Going?* (New York: Norton, 2001).

9 Michael G. Schechter, *United Nations Global Conferences* (London: Routledge, 2005).

10 Boutros Boutros-Ghali, *An Agenda for Development* (New York: United Nations, 1995).

11 United Nations, *Report of the Global Conference on the Sustainable Development of Small Island Developing States* (A/CONF.167/9, part I, Annex I), October 1994.

12 Barry Herman, "Civil Society and the Financing for Development Initiative at the United Nations," in *Civil Society and Global Finance*, eds. Jan Aart Scholte and Albrecht Schnabel (London: Routledge, 2002), 162–177.

13 United Nations, *Press Conference by Secretary-General Ban Ki-moon on Rio+20* (SG/SM/14336, ENV/DEV/1286), 6 June 2012.

14 Ban Ki-moon, *The Secretary-General's Five-Year Action Agenda*, 25 January 2012, http://www.un.org/sg/priorities/index.shtml.

15 United Nations, "Sustainable Development," http://www.un.org/sg/priorities/sustainable_development.shtml; United Nations, "Sustainable Development Goals," http://sustainabledevelopment.un.org/index.php?menu=1300.

16 United Nations, "International Year of Sustainable Energy for All," General Assembly Resolution A/Res/65/151, 20 December 2010.

17 United Nations, "UN Secretary-General Announces New Leadership for Sustainable Energy for All Initiative," http://www.sustainableenergyforall.org/news/item/140-un-secretary-general-announces-new-leadership-for-sustainable-energy-for-all-initiative.

18 United Nations, *Report of the Secretary-General on the Work of the Organization* (General Assembly document A/67/1), 8 August 2012.

19 United Nations, *Secretary-General Assembles High-level Panel on Post-2015 Development Agenda, Appointing 26 Members of Government, Civil Society, Private Sector*, Secretary-General document SG/A/1364, DEV/2949, 31 July 2012.

20 United Nations, *Report of the United Nations Conference on Sustainable Development*, General Assembly document A/CONF. 216/16, New York, 2012.

21 Ibid., para. 4.

22 United Nations Sustainable Development Knowledge Platform, http://sustainabledevelopment.un.org/rio20.html.

23 The Elders, "Rio+20 Is Not the Response We Need to Safeguard People and the Planet," Road Logs RIO+, Rio de Janeiro, 7 July 2012, http://roadlogs.rio20.net/rio20-is-not-the-response-we-need-to-safeguard-people-and-the-planet.

24 Ibid.

25 Ibid.

26 Leonardo Boff, "The Terms of the Present Ecological Debate," Road Logs RIO+, Rio de Janeiro, 7 July 2012, http://roadlogs.rio20.net/the-terms-of-the-present-ecological-debate.

27 World Watch Institute, "The Future We Need: Reflections on Rio+20," Road Logs RIO+, Rio de Janeiro, 7 July 2012, http://roadlogs.rio20.net/the-future-we-need-reflections-on-rio20.

28 Ibid.

Poverty Reduction

David Hulme and Oliver Turner

In today's affluent world approximately one-third of the human population lives in a state of poverty. Around 870 million people—more than the populations of the United States and European Union combined—suffer from chronic hunger and nearly 900 million people have no access to safe drinking water. More than 350,000 women die every year during pregnancy or childbirth. In the 30 minutes it takes to read this chapter, approximately 400 children under the age of five will have died, mostly from readily preventable causes. Every day around the world hundreds of millions of people are denied the opportunity to lead a secure and productive life—but it does not have to be this way. Humanity has developed the technology and accumulated the recourses to satisfy the basic needs of all. Food, education, healthcare services, and others could be provided if our world was organized differently. In short, poverty can be reduced if tackled more efficiently through the structures of global governance.

As this chapter shows, key international organizations along with myriad additional actors have long been involved in the challenge of alleviating global poverty. The United Nations, the World Bank, civil society groups, and even celebrities have been, and remain, variously active in this regard, with mixed degrees of success. At times poverty has been elevated towards the top of the global agenda, attracting focus and investment from heads of state and other political elites. At others it has been relegated so that issues including national security and economic stability have drawn attention and resources away from the world's poor, often with predictably lamentable results. This chapter's cursory examination of how the mechanisms of global governance have approached the issue of world poverty nonetheless aims to demonstrate that resolving the problem will require those mechanisms to function more effectively.

The chapter begins with a brief historical and contemporary overview of how global poverty has been conceived and approached within the international arena, particularly since the mid-twentieth century when the first multilateral institutions capable of providing leadership on the matter were established. It then asks why poverty persists and where in the world it is most pervasive, before exploring the various arguments which have been advanced over time as to how the problem may be solved. The chapter then describes the multitude of actors who make up the vast framework of global governance structures active in attempted poverty alleviation. It ends by exploring potentially critical future issues and developments which are likely to have an impact on world poverty, as well as on efforts to reduce its severity. The chapter concludes with a consideration of how the seemingly unattainable feat of consigning poverty to history may not be as unrealistic as might be believed.

Global poverty: historical and contemporary contexts

The idea that the most basic needs can be provided to all is relatively recent. Throughout history, the majority of humanity has been materially poor, with hunger and food insecurity the norm, life expectancies short, epidemic disease levels and mortality high, and exposure to the elements a daily experience. Between 1 CE and 1000 CE, world per capita growth rates were around zero or even negative for some areas, including Western Europe.[1] Between then and 1820, global life expectancy rose only from 24 to 26 years and per capita income (in 1990 US$) increased from just $453 to $667.[2] From around 1820 things changed dramatically. Average life expectancy rose from 26 years to 66 years and average per capita income increased from $667 to $5,709 by 2000. Advances in the human condition, however, became very unevenly spread and many were left behind.

Importantly for poverty as an issue of global governance, US president Franklin D. Roosevelt's "Four Freedoms" speech of 6 January 1941 identified freedom from want as an international priority. The United Nations was founded in 1945 with the aim of ensuring peace and preventing international warfare, creating economic stability and, more broadly, promoting human betterment. UN agencies such as the Food and Agriculture Organization (FAO), the World Health Organization (WHO) and the International Labour Organization (ILO) led on improvements in global agriculture, health, education, and science, among many other things, with the collective aim of supporting the needs of people as well as states. In 1947 the UN produced the first global consensus on eradicating poverty: the Universal Declaration of Human Rights. The key articles in relation to poverty are 25 and 28:

> Everyone has the right to a standard of living adequate for the health and well-being of his family, including food, clothing, housing and medical care . . . Everyone is entitled to a social and international order in which the rights and freedoms set forth in this Declaration can be fully realised.[3]

These grand ideals, however, did not produce the expected results. Throughout the 1950s development, human rights, and the nascent idea of alleviating poverty were sidelined as Cold War security concerns dominated international meetings. The environment changed briefly in the 1960s with the election of US president John F. Kennedy.[4] Yet, for the most part it was left to academics and social activists to raise public awareness of global poverty and push for corresponding action. The period 1950–73 has been described as a "golden age" for economic growth.[5] Average GDPs per capita in Africa, Asia, and Latin America increased alongside significant improvements in life expectancy and other social indicators. Yet the patterns were complex and prosperity for all did not follow.

During the 1980s US president Ronald Reagan and UK prime minister Margaret Thatcher promoted neoliberal ideas and a shift of intellectual authority for development from the UN to the International Monetary Fund (IMF) and World Bank (often referred to as the Bretton Woods Institutions, or BWIs). The BWIs pursued neoliberal policies which assumed that if the state could be rolled back through deregulation and privatization, and if the market was allowed to determine resource allocations—collectively thought of as "structural adjustment"—rapid economic growth would ensue. This "Washington Consensus," in which free market forces rather than state interference were relied upon as the primary driver of growth and prosperity, dominated development thinking in the 1980s and early 1990s. It is now widely judged to have produced "a lost decade" for Africa and others.

In many ways, 1990 marked a tipping point for ideas about poverty. As the Cold War ended and doubts circulated about structural adjustment, the World Bank chose poverty as its main theme and acknowledged the need for economic reform to be accompanied by social policies. It introduced the "dollar-a-day" headcount and estimated that around 1.1 billion people around the world lived in extreme poverty. The first *Human Development Report* also promoted an alternative to neoliberal economic growth, making the idea of human development accessible to professionals and the media. Key UN conferences were held, including the World Summit for Children in 1990, the Women's Conference in Beijing in 1995 and the Food Summit in 1996. Most importantly, in 1995 117 heads of state and government attended the World Summit on Social Development (WSSD) in Copenhagen. It was there that a form of global consensus was first reached that poverty reduction was the priority goal for development.[6] The aim of eradicating "dollar-a-day" poverty was also approved. These events raised public awareness but foreign aid from rich countries as a share of GDP continued its long-term decline.

In 1998 control of the global poverty agenda returned to the United Nations. Its new secretary-general, Kofi Annan, was keen to prioritize poverty; and in May 1999 he identified "development, including poverty eradication," as a central issue.[7] The ideas that had emerged in Copenhagen were now being institutionalized as development became synonymous with poverty reduction. At the UN Millennium Summit in 2000, eight Millennium Development Goals (MDGs) to be achieved by 2015 were agreed. These commitments ranged from eliminating gender disparities in children's education, to halting the spread of HIV/AIDS, to reducing degradation of the world's biodiversity. The first was a pledge to halve extreme poverty and hunger. Ominously, however, data available at the time confirmed the enormous scale of global poverty. The *World Development Report 2000/2001* explained that

Of the world's 6 billion people, 2.8 billion . . . live on less than $2 a day, and 1.2 billion . . . live on less than $1 a day. In rich countries fewer than 1 child in 100 does not reach its fifth birthday, while in poorer countries as many as a fifth do not. And while in rich countries fewer than 5 percent of all children under five are malnourished, in poor countries as many as 50 percent are.[8]

It was recognized that sub-Saharan Africa experienced the most extreme and multi-dimensional chronic poverty, while South Asia had the largest numbers of poor people. Yet once again dire need was not met with appropriate policy and while the MDGs were being negotiated prospects for a concerted push against global poverty weakened. The World Bank was ambivalent towards the goals and the IMF paid them only lip-service. They were informally approved at the 2002 Financing for Development Summit in Monterrey, Mexico, where the United States and the European Union (EU) pledged additional resources for poverty reduction. Nonetheless, keeping poverty on the inter-national agenda since then has been difficult as national self-interest and other priority issues have dominated. The 2005 meeting of G8 countries in Gleneagles, Scotland, and the UN high-level event of 2008—both led by the United Kingdom—were designed to refocus states towards poverty, but with only marginal effect. Worse, the recent economic crises have put poverty reduction into reverse. The FAO, for example, estimates that an additional 100 million people fell into hunger over 2008 and 2009.[9]

It could be argued that the graduation of global poverty onto the international agenda is evidence of progressive social change on the grandest scale. Alternatively, it could be seen as the world's most successful confidence trick, with rich nations, powerful organizations, and global elites retaining the existing structures of power and resource access while maintaining their legitimacy, and at next to no cost to themselves. Most pertinently, progress towards achieving the MDGs has been mixed at best. The United Nation's 2012 MDG progress report acknowledges that while important gains have been made, such as halving the number of people living on less than $1.25 a day, as well as those without access to safe drinking water, numerous key targets will almost certainly be missed in 2015. These include providing 75 percent of the world's population with basic sanitation, ensuring every child has the opportunity of primary education, and reducing by three-quarters the rate of maternal mortality.[10] For the majority of member states, then, the years since 2000 have been "business as usual" at the UN General Assembly—that is, making grand statements about the eradication of poverty without demonstrating commitment through action.

Why does poverty persist, and where?

In the first instance, we can say that poverty persists because those of us doing well—powerful countries, corporations, political and economic elites, middle-class people in rich and poor countries—simply "don't care" or "don't care enough." We place a low priority on the welfare of the "distant needy," while maintaining, or increasing, our control over resources, technology, and organizational capacities. Second, debates about poverty and development are often unbalanced and likely to favor the better-off. It is they who finance and shape knowledge-creating institutions such as schools, universities, and think tanks that work primarily for their benefit. Third, the institutional framework tasked with addressing global poverty is in many ways unfit for purpose. The UN struggles on but is in need of reform. The General Assembly, for instance, makes big promises but member states do not deliver; and its numerous agencies remain poorly coordinated and broadly ineffectual. The governance structures of the World Bank and IMF are also largely inappropriate and arguably illegitimate, as both are dominated by the United States and Western Europe. At the same time, non-state institutions have made only limited progress. While NGOs (non-profit agencies usually registered as charities) and civil society groups (among others) promote public awareness and concern about global poverty, a coordinated movement demanding its eradication currently seems unlikely to emerge.

Disappointments with overall achievements in global poverty eradication since 2000 do not mean that nothing has been achieved. Besides partial success through the MDGs, debt cancellation has been unprecedented; aid flows have stabilized; the EU has ensured that new members commit to foreign aid; and countries such as Ghana, Rwanda, Mozambique, and Tanzania have improved their capacity to plan and program poverty reduction. Global poverty is now on the international agenda, but it remains a secondary priority in relation to terrorism, energy security, financial stability, and others. The grand promises made by national leaders around the turn of the century have made a small difference, but they have not been honored. Neither have the same leaders been held accountable.

While the contemporary map of global poverty indicates that income poverty is vast in both Africa and South Asia, the analytical focus of global poverty has increasingly shifted towards sub-Saharan Africa. Given the continent's lost decade of the 1980s, followed by economic stagnation and the HIV/AIDS pandemic of the 1990s, this is no surprise. However, if one maps the data for Asia and disaggregates it for Indian states and Chinese provinces—which is not unreasonable given that most of these sub-national units have populations much bigger than those of the average African country—a second poor continent emerges: *sub*-Siberian Asia. This is a virtually contiguous area that stretches across northern India and Nepal to Bangladesh, Burma, and Laos, takes in much of central and western China with Mongolia, includes Central Asia (Kazakhstan, Kyrgyzstan, Uzbekistan, Turkmenistan, and Tajikistan), and completes in Afghanistan and Pakistan.

Proposing the recognition of sub-Siberian Asia is not to argue that Africa does not require special attention, analytically or in terms of assistance. What it does suggest is that the global geography of extreme poverty needs to be understood as "sub-Saharan Africa and sub-Siberian Asia plus some other countries." Assuming that poverty in China and especially India will steadily fall because both of their average growth rates are currently high fails to recognize that these are continental-scale countries. The lights in Bangalaru and Hangzhou may be shining 24/7, but it is hard to find the money to buy a candle in rural Tripura and Guizhou.

Debates over reducing poverty

There is no clear "solution" to the problem of global poverty. Poverty reduction, like its intellectual and policy antecedent rural development, is about trying "to change the functioning of a complex, dynamic system in order to make progress in attaining multiple objectives."[11] Examined here are theories of why mass poverty occurs through the sequence of ideas that have dominated the history of international development, across three historical eras.

The first—modernization theory of the 1950s and 1960s—posited that a lack of development (and associated mass poverty) across third world countries was the result of economic backwardness and traditional social structures. Once these countries "caught up" with the industrialized world—technologically, institutionally, socially—mass affluence would eradicate poverty everywhere. The modernization account was attractive but by the late 1960s there was mounting evidence that it was not delivering on its promises. Neo-Marxists and dependency theorists explained that the third world had been integrated into the world economic system in a way that permitted its exploitation through "unequal development."[12] The poor were kept poor so that the elites of wealthy countries could have high material living standards. This analysis demanded radical actions, including peasant revolution and strategies of autonomous development. These arguments played out well in the academic realm, but most countries that pursued such strategies (such as Sri Lanka in the early 1970s and Nicaragua and Tanzania in the 1970s and 1980s) did not fare well.

As noted earlier, neoliberal ideas became dominant intellectually in the late 1970s and politically by the early 1980s. They posited that countries were poor because of public policies that distorted prices and incentive systems and public institutions that were wasteful and rent-seeking. Once economies were liberalized and opened up to international trade, the theory stated, competition would promote efficiency and a country could pursue its comparative advantages. Economic growth would ensue and with increased demand would follow job creation and prosperity. These "Washington Consensus" policies were pursued with varying degrees of enthusiasm by countries in Africa, Asia, and Latin America. The results were generally poor and often harmful to poor people (especially with the introduction of fees for health and education). A rapid shift in Russia after the Cold War from centralized economic planning to a faith in free market forces was catastrophic for its people. Economic growth and poverty reduction occurred in the 1990s in China and India, but in both cases the state retained a key role.

As the millennium approached, the sweeping policy narratives of the second half of the twentieth century faltered. More pluralist frameworks such as the post-Washington Consensus, which promotes a more context-specific approach to poverty alleviation as well as the inclusion of those most affected by poverty, began to fill the global policy space. These frameworks recognized major roles for the market, the state, and civil society and emphasized a range of goals, including strengthening institutions. Growth, in short, was not enough. There was an increased recognition of the complexity of poverty and the breadth and variety of policies needed to reduce it in different countries and for different groups. Despite attempts by the US Treasury Department to ensure that the World Bank's flagship millennium publication (*World Development Report 2000–2001*) highlighted economic growth and market-led policies, the report produced a framework based on three integrated strategies: opportunity (market-based growth), empowerment (social and political reform), and security (a social safety net to protect people from vulnerability).[13] Thinking since that time has become increasingly nuanced, and social policy in developing countries has moved beyond health and education to include social protection policies, such as cash transfers for the poor and non-contributory old age pensions.[14]

Poverty and global governance: who is involved?

The institutional landscape for tackling global poverty is a vast terrain which lacks clear boundaries and is constituted by a wide range of multilateral, national, sub-national, and local institutions spread across the public sector, private business, and civil society. The multitudinous actors involved often have differing interests and visions of "what should be done," and coalesce into a variety of formal and informal associations and networks. The institutions, associations, and networks involved are not elements of a rationally designed international institutional architecture. In short, no one is "in charge" of global poverty eradication. It is important, nonetheless, to make sense of this architecture, beginning with the most influential multilateral institutions.

As we have seen, the UN's MDGs now constitute the centerpiece of efforts for global poverty reduction. Yet, within the vast UN system, a bewildering array of organizations promotes, analyzes, implements, and monitors global poverty reduction.[15] They include the UNDP, FAO, WHO, ILO, UNESCO, UNAIDS, and many others. Within the wider UN system, the World Bank is arguably the most influential in terms of setting the agenda on global poverty because of its monetary lending and its capacity to shape thinking. It has the largest concentration of development economists in the world, meaning its "analytical machine has more intellectual juice"[16] than other multilaterals and development agencies. In contrast, the IMF's commitment to poverty reduction remains shallow. In 2006 its chief economist for Africa advised that "the MDGs are European social policy. The IMF doesn't do European social policy."[17] The World Trade Organization (WTO) is not formally part of the UN system or a "development" organization and operates principally as a forum in which states negotiate trade deals. It has, however, recently been tasked with helping to reduce global poverty through the declaration of its Doha Round of trade negotiations as a "development round."[18]

Beyond these organizations, states meet in a variety of formal and informal associations which are to varying extents committed to reducing global poverty. For rich countries the key formal grouping is the Organisation for Economic Co-operation and Development (OECD), whose interests in international development and global poverty are articulated through its Development Assistance Committee. The African Union has particular significance because of its potential role in improving governance and policies across the continent and reducing poverty and conflict. The EU struggles to find a common external position but has reached an internal agreement to focus on the MDGs, increase aid, and induct new member states into international development. As a more informal association the G7/8 has focused on the interests of its members, such as trade policy, energy security, and financial stability, though in recent times it has taken a stronger interest in developing countries. The emergence of the G20 in 2009 led to a burst of optimism in development circles, but this new association has shown little commitment to poverty reduction.

Despite the importance of multinational organizations and collectives of states, however, national governments are still recognized as the most important institution for reducing poverty. It is the governments of the poorest which create conditions for economic growth and oversee the delivery of basic services. Rich governments largely determine the volume of international finance allocated for global poverty reduction and have most influence over international institutions. In addition, when sub-national governments such as district councils and municipal authorities function well the conditions for health and education provision and increased productivity, among other things, become available. When they do not work well—which is common in many poor countries—poverty is more likely to persist.

Since the end of the Cold War, non-state actors have become increasingly influential in international affairs, with significance for global poverty. Civil society groups promote the idea of tackling poverty around the world and have been granted formal recognition at the UN. NGOs are now far more numerous and some, such as BRAC, which employs more than 115,000 staff in Bangladesh and has a budget in excess of $700 million per annum, are enormous. Social movements are also gaining increasing prominence, although, as noted earlier, a highly organized anti-poverty movement has not yet emerged. In addition, a new generation of "philanthrocapitalists" use their fortunes to engage in poverty reduction. While Bill Gates is the most highly publicized, this phenomenon is also established in India, China, Africa, and Latin America. Relatedly, a small number of celebrities such as Bob Geldof and Bono have gained considerable influence over global poverty policy. They practice what Andrew Cooper terms "celebrity diplomacy" and at times are treated as virtual heads of state.[19]

The private sector is another important component of poverty reduction efforts. Indirectly it can create jobs for poor people and growth for small economies, and more businesses are now directly active through social responsibility and fair trade programs. Public–private partnerships include the Global Fund for HIV/AIDS, Malaria and TB (Global Fund) and the Global Alliance for Vaccines and Immunisation (GAVI), a partnership involving UNICEF, WHO, the World Bank, and the Gates Foundation. Finally, epistemic communities—"network[s] of professionals with recognized expertise and competence in a particular domain"[20]—are significant. They include orthodox liberal ("Chicago School") economists who, during the 1970s, formed an epistemic community that dominated thinking about international development. Recently, leading interventionist liberal economists such as Ravi Kanbur, Dani Rodrik, and Joseph Stiglitz have challenged orthodox liberal prescriptions, though have found it hard to establish a focused and supported epistemic community.

The future of global poverty

The main prediction underpinning present-day thinking about global poverty is that it will steadily decline. Given humanity's vast material capabilities this assumption does not seem unreasonable. A number of emerging issues, however, may force us to rethink both the processes that cause poverty and the policies we adopt to reduce it.

One issue area is that projections of future global poverty reduction are based on the assumption that relatively high levels of global economic growth, especially in China and India, will continue. This trend may influence poverty in three ways. First, poverty within these countries may be reduced via the domestic impact of economic growth, though most effectively if the benefits are distributed more evenly than at present. Second, the growth of these countries could encourage development elsewhere. Notably, China's demand for natural resources has generated more intensive bilateral relations with, and increased investment in, Africa. These links are also argued to have had negative effects, however, such as providing support for dubious regimes like that of Robert Mugabe in Zimbabwe and Bashir Ahmed in Sudan, and the possibility that Chinese loans and deals for Africa's resources will create a new wave of highly indebted poor countries. Third, China and India may play a greater role in global public policy as both are expanding their foreign aid activities and both have the potential to lead on poverty eradication. Recent experience, however, suggests that this is not likely at the present time. In the UN and G20, for example, the focus of Beijing and New Delhi has been largely upon short-term self-interest; and in the WTO neither has yet assumed a pivotal role despite hype and hand-wringing to the contrary.[21]

Away from Asia, three other issues merit attention. The first is the hope that the economies of at least one of Africa's slumbering giants, Nigeria or South Africa, will grow significantly. Both could help increase material capabilities across the continent, provide an African economic model for emulation, and possibly transform the negative, but gradually improving, image of Africa for investment. In addition, Latin America is becoming a hearth for new poverty reduction and economic growth models and policies. The success of cash transfer programs in Mexico (Oportunidades) and Brazil (Bolsa Familia), for example, has encouraged their export to African and other poor countries. Multilateral and bilateral agencies such as the World Bank and the UK's Department for International Development have been part of this process, but the role of research and higher education capacities in the region has also been key. Also important is the question of whether the United States will use its influence to reform the structures and processes of global governance. Arguably, Washington can achieve long-term advantages by calling for the creation of new or modified global institutions while it remains the world's only superpower. If it delays 20 or 30 years, the relative waning of US power may be more evident and its capacity to foment change may be reduced.

Another key issue area is that of climate change. Despite the protestations of some, a broad scientific consensus now exists that global warming is well underway. The three most significant changes for human populations are likely to be rises in sea levels, changes in temperature and precipitation, and the increased frequency of extreme weather events. Most predicted scenarios indicate that poor people will suffer most, for two main reasons. First, wealthy peoples and countries have more resources to devote to adapting to climate change than do their poorer counterparts. Second, the parts of the world with the highest concentrations of poverty, in sub-Saharan Africa and sub-Siberian Asia, will likely experience a greater share of the negative consequences of climate change than middle to high latitude regions, such as Europe, North America, and Japan. These negative predictions make the question of "what can be done" to prevent radical climate change additionally pressing.

A final key issue area is the changing nature of poverty itself, with two especially pertinent considerations. The first is the urbanization of poverty. Until recently most research, and most policy initiatives, focused on rural poverty. There were good reasons: the numbers and proportions of poor in rural areas were much higher than in urban areas; and economic and social indicators were almost universally lower for rural people. However, today more than half the world's population lives in towns, cities, or megalopolises. Poverty is the issue, and so it must be understood and tackled across the rural–urban continuum, in villages, rural centers, towns, cities, and hyper-cities. Ultimately then, while the World Bank's predictions for extreme global poverty are that it will continue to gradually decline in the medium and long term (once a recovery from the recent fuel, food, and credit crunches has been completed), there are no grounds for complacency. Geopolitically and environmentally we are moving into a different world, and future strategies to address the planet's widespread poverty must evolve.

The second consideration is rising inequality. As Richard Jolly observes, the UN has previously overlooked the significance of inequality when monitoring progress towards the MDGs. Yet even in countries where gains have been made the gap between rich and poor has increased.[22] Since implementing dramatic economic reforms in the late 1970s, for example, Beijing has lifted around 650 million Chinese out of poverty— an astonishing achievement. During that time, however, China has gone from being among the world's most equal societies to among the most unequal. This is important because inequality has negative consequences for all. Indeed, a recent study found that across relatively wealthy societies the populations of those with the highest rates of economic inequality experience more crime, lower educational attainment, and elevated health and social problems, among others.[23] There are tentative signs that the need to address inequality is forming part of a post-2015 global poverty strategy. UNICEF, UNDP, and UNCTAD, as well as concerned groups including Academics Stand Against Poverty, for example, have placed inequality firmly onto their agendas. The UN's 2012 MDG progress report asserts that "inequality remains a concern," though it does little to suggest that it is due to become a priority.[24] As ever, therefore, disparities between rhetoric and action are likely to represent one of the biggest obstacles to tackling global poverty in the future.

Conclusion

This chapter has depicted the world's appalling scale of poverty. The World Bank estimates that 1.377 billion people currently live beneath the US$1.25-a-day extreme poverty line and 2.562 billion people beneath the US$2-a-day line.[25] While this represents relative progress, with the proportion of extreme poor in the developing world down from 52 percent to 25 percent between 1981 and 2005, and the US$2-a-day poor down from 69 percent to 47 percent, the absolute figures are unacceptable in a world with an average GDP per capita of US$24.58 a day. A redistribution of just 0.33 percent (one-third of one percent) of global income to the poorest would eradicate extreme poverty. A redistribution of 1.28 percent would eradicate US$2-a-day poverty. Clearly, the overriding constraint to solving the most serious problems of global poverty is not a lack of resources. What is missing is a lack of will. Perhaps above all else, a meaningful transformation of ideas about poverty is required to establish a new set of norms.

Norms are commonly accepted understandings about "the way the world is," and when international norms change, previously accepted phenomena can become unacceptable. In 1800, for example, most British people thought of slavery as unobjectionable. By 1850, however, it was widely considered unreasonable and immoral. Ideas about slavery had changed and as a norm it came under attack. During the nineteenth century, slavery fell out of favor across Europe and North America; and by the twentieth century it was declared illegal across the world. Similar shifts can be traced over international norms about votes for women, the conduct of war, and racial segregation. During the 1990s a type of global norm emerged around the need to eradicate poverty, culminating in 2000 with the MDGs. There was an international cascade, with most states signing non-binding agreements that the goals would be pursued. However, the internalization of the norm has been weak and commitment to MDG achievement has not been upheld.[26]

Historical evidence indicates that the human condition is improving and that in proportional terms poverty is being reduced. Yet levels remain high and the absolute numbers involved have increased in recent years. Feeling angst has little value; action is required. In the short term, practical moves are required by national leaders and relevant agencies to maintain pressure upon rich governments to honor the MDGs; to encourage developing countries to improve domestic governance; and to lobby for useful reform in the World Bank, IMF, and elsewhere. We can all contribute to, or volunteer for, a development NGO, buy fair trade products, and reduce our carbon footprints. In the longer term, we are required to become part of a process that facilitates a change in international social norms, ensuring recognition among the people of rich and poor countries that extreme poverty is morally unacceptable. Progress may seem slow, but poverty can be eradicated if enough people take the necessary small steps to achieve this aim.

Additional reading

1. David Hulme, *Global Poverty: How Global Governance Is Failing the Poor* (London: Routledge, 2010).
2. Rorden Wilkinson and David Hulme, eds., *The Millennium Development Goals and Beyond: Global Development after 2015* (London: Routledge, 2012).
3. Daron Acemoglu and James Robinson, *Why Nations Fail: The Origins of Power, Prosperity and Poverty* (New York: Crown, 2012).
4. Jennifer Clapp and Rorden Wilkinson, eds., *Global Governance, Poverty and Inequality* (London: Routledge, 2010).
5. Charles Kenny, *Getting Better: Why Global Development Is Succeeding – and How We Can Improve the World Even More* (New York: Basic Books, 2011).
6. Paul Collier, *The Bottom Billion: Why the Poorest Countries Are Failing and What Can Be Done about It* (Oxford: Oxford University Press, 2007).

Notes

1 Angus Maddison, *The World Economy: A Millennial Perspective* (Paris: OECD Publishing, 2001), 28.
2 Ibid., 27–31.
3 United Nations, *Universal Declaration of Human Rights*, art. 25 and 28, http://www.un.org/en/documents/udhr/index.shtml.
4 John Toye and Richard Toye, "From Multilateralism to Modernisation: US Strategy on Trade, Finance and Development in the United Nations, 1945–63," *Forum for Development Studies* 32, no. 1 (2005): 140–144.

5 Maddison, *The World Economy*, 125.

6 UNDP, *Human Development Report 1997* (Oxford: Oxford University Press, 1997), 108.

7 James Traub, *The Best Intentions: Kofi Annan and the UN in the Era of American World Power* (London: Bloomsbury, 2006), 147.

8 World Bank, *World Development Report 2000/2001* (Washington, DC: World Bank, 2001), 3.

9 FAO, *The State of Food Insecurity in the World* (Rome: FAO, 2009), 4.

10 United Nations, *The Millennium Development Goals Report 2012* (New York: United Nations, 2012).

11 Bruce Johnston and William Clark, *Redesigning Rural Development: A Strategic Perspective* (Baltimore: Johns Hopkins University Press, 1982), 26.

12 Neo-Marxists and dependency theorists apply Karl Marx's concepts to international development but in a way that differs from Marx's analysis.

13 See Robert Wade, "US Hegemony and the World Bank: The Fight over People and Ideas," *Review of International Political Economy* 9, no. 2 (2002): 215–243.

14 Armando Barrientos and David Hulme, eds., *Social Protection for the Poor and Poorest: Concepts, Policies and Politics* (London: Palgrave, 2008).

15 Stephen Browne and Thomas G. Weiss, *Making Change Happen: Enhancing the UN's Contributions to Development* (New York: World Federation of United Nations Associations, 2012).

16 Sebastian Mallaby, *The World's Banker: A Story of Failed States, Financial Crises, and the Wealth and Poverty of Nations* (New York: Penguin, 2004), 3.

17 This official prefers not to be named because, officially, the IMF is committed to MDG achievement.

18 Rorden Wilkinson and James Scott, eds., *Trade, Poverty and Development: Getting Beyond the WTO's Doha Deadlock* (London: Routledge, 2013).

19 Andrew Cooper, "Celebrity Diplomacy and the G8: Bono and Bob as Legitimate International Actors," CIGI Working Paper no. 29 (Waterloo: CIGI, 2007).

20 Peter Haas, "Epistemic Communities and International Policy Coordination: Introduction," *International Organization* 46, no. 1 (1992): 1–35.

21 Rorden Wilkinson, "Emerging Powers and the Governance of Global Trade," in *The Handbook of the International Political Economy of Governance*, eds. Anthony Payne and Nicola Phillips (Cheltenham: Edward Elgar, 2014).

22 Richard Jolly, "MDG Targets Are Overlooking Inequality," *Guardian*, 22 September 2012, http://www.guardian.co.uk/global-development/poverty-matters/2011/sep/22/mdg-targets-overlooking-inequality.

23 Richard Wilkinson and Kate Pickett, *The Spirit Level: Why More Equal Societies Almost Always Do Better* (London: Allen Lane, 2009).

24 United Nations, *Millennium Development Goals Report 2012*, 53.

25 Shaohua Chen and Martin Ravallion, "The Developing World Is Poorer Than We Thought, But No Less Successful in the Fight Against Poverty," World Bank Policy Research Working Paper no. 4703 (Washington, DC: World Bank, 2008).

26 David Hulme, *Global Poverty: How Global Governance Is Failing the Poor* (London: Routledge, 2010); Rorden Wilkinson and David Hulme, eds., *The Millennium Development Goals and Beyond: Global Development after 2015* (London: Routledge, 2012).

CONTENTS

Food and Hunger

Jennifer Clapp

In the 2010–12 period, approximately 870 million people in the world were under-nourished, meaning they did not consume enough food to maintain a healthy life. That number represents around 12.5 percent of the world's population. The prevalence of hunger in the developing world in this period was higher, at around 15 percent of the population, or approximately 1 in 7 people. These figures show some improvement from the early 1990s, when there were 1 billion hungry people, representing around 19 percent of the world's population.[1] While these numbers indicate some improvement in the global battle against hunger over the past two decades, they still raise concern and show that much remains to be accomplished to improve world food security. The most recent figures on undernourishment, for example, are based on caloric needs for a sedentary lifestyle, something that we cannot easily assume meets the basic food needs for poor people in developing countries. If we consider that most poor people in developing countries lead a normally active lifestyle, the number of hungry people nearly doubles.[2]

The forces that contribute to hunger are wide-ranging and complex. They include, for example, poverty, high and volatile food prices, nutritional inadequacy of available foods, and agricultural production shortfalls, among others. Our understanding of these forces, and how they contribute to food insecurity, has also evolved over the years. In this context, it is not surprising that the global governance architecture for addressing hunger—the institutions and frameworks that shape the global response to food insecurity—is also highly complex. Governance in this area covers an array of functions that address different aspects of hunger and food insecurity. The institutions and actors involved include international organizations dedicated to a variety of tasks such as food aid, assistance to improve agricultural production, and interventions to improve nutrition, as well as nongovernmental organizations and private actors that take on supportive roles in these areas.

This chapter details the ways in which our evolving understandings of food security have been reflected in the mandates and agendas of the key global institutions that address hunger and food insecurity in the past 75 years. Although our widening understanding of the forces that contribute to food insecurity has enabled responses from different institutional quarters, the global governance of food and hunger has been highly fragmented in practice, characterized by poor coordination of tasks, which limits its ability to address issues that cut across the mandates of organizations or that fall between the cracks. The 2007–08 food crisis, and subsequent period of food price volatility from 2009 to 2012, illustrated this fragmentation, and has signaled a need to improve the global governance of food security. Some reforms have taken place since that time, and have made important steps toward improving coordination. But ongoing fragility in the global food security situation indicates that much work remains to be done.

The chapter begins by mapping the history of global food security governance and shows how changing definitions of food security have influenced the contours of the global governance architecture that addresses hunger. Next it outlines the challenges presented by the 2007–08 food crisis and ongoing food price volatility, illustrating that fragmentation in global food security governance in practice has hindered the global response to economic shocks that exacerbate world hunger. It concludes by discussing some of the recent revisions to the global food security governance framework and their implications.

The evolving landscape of global food security governance

Many definitions of food security have been put forward over the years. The most commonly cited definition is the one first adopted at the 1996 World Food Summit and refined by the Food and Agriculture Organization of the United Nations (FAO) in 2001 to add the word "social": "Food security exists when all people, at all times, have physical, social and economic access to sufficient, safe and nutritious food which meets their dietary needs and food preferences for an active and healthy life."[3] This current conceptualization of food security is the product of an evolution of our understanding of the term. In the 1930s to 1940s, it was widely assumed that food availability, that is, the amount produced, was what mattered most in determining whether people consumed enough food.

Important breakthroughs in the analysis of what determines people's ability to eat a sufficient diet over the last 70–80 years has helped to widen how we view, and address, food insecurity. The understanding of the concept now considers a range of factors, as well as the complex relationship between them.[4] The above definition, for example, brings out four main dimensions of food security that the FAO stressed in recent years as foundational pillars: availability (sufficient food), access (physical, economic, and social access), utilization (safe and nutritious food that meets dietary needs), and stability (at all times).[5] The way the global food security governance architecture has changed and · grown over the years has reflected the evolution in our understanding of food security from one based primarily on availability to one that recognizes a much more complex make-up of various dimensions.

The FAO was established in 1945 and is located in Rome. It was initially focused primarily on the availability pillar of food security, with activities centered on ways to increase food production through the modernization and improvement of agriculture.

Other governance bodies also supported the theme of food production over the years through the promotion of the Green Revolution. This entailed the development and dissemination of high-yielding seed varieties and agricultural input packages in developing countries that were explicitly aimed at bringing about massive increases in food production. As part of this broader Green Revolution initiative, various regional and crop-specific agricultural research centers were established in the 1960s and 1970s, including, for example, the International Rice Research Institute (IRRI) in the Philippines and the International Maize and Wheat Improvement Center (CIMMYT) in Mexico. These research institutes were brought together in 1971 under a coordinating umbrella known as the Consultative Group on International Agricultural Research (CGIAR), overseen by the World Bank. Today there are 18 CGIAR food and agriculture research institutes worldwide.[6]

The access, or distribution, dimension of food security gained more attention globally in the 1950s and 1960s. In this period, a number of key donor countries, including the United States, Canada, and the European Community (EC, later European Union, EU), institutionalized programs for international food aid. Early food aid provided a means by which donor countries could provide assistance to developing countries by giving their own agricultural surpluses that resulted from their own policies to modernize and industrialize their own agricultural sectors in previous decades.[7] Although it drew its fair share of criticism because of its politicized nature and its tendency to be self-serving on the part of donors, food aid was considered a key policy tool in the fight against world hunger in the early days.

In the 1960s, for example, food aid made up around one-quarter of all international development assistance, and the 1963 establishment of the World Food Programme (WFP) provided a multilateral delivery channel for international food aid. The WFP, also located in Rome, initially delivered only a small portion of international food aid alongside the bilateral aid delivered by the major donor countries. Today, the WFP delivers some 75 percent of all food aid. The Food Aid Convention—a treaty among donor countries that pledges amounts of aid and maps out norms for food aid practice—was first agreed in 1967 and has been periodically updated ever since. The latest version of this agreement, agreed in 2012, has been renamed the Food Assistance Convention to take into account a wider array of food-related assistance activities.[8]

By the early 1970s, major global governance initiatives to improve both availability and access to food were in place, as noted above. These initiatives, however, soon appeared to be inadequate in the face of a major food crisis that erupted in the mid-1970s. Food prices increased dramatically between 1973 and 1975, with prices for food staples such as wheat, corn, and soy tripling from their 1971 levels. The result of these rapid price increases was havoc in the global food system. Food stocks reached record lows in 1974. The disruption to global grain markets sparked widespread panic, driving prices up further. The crisis illustrated all too clearly that the global food system was highly fragile and prone to major disruptions that could result in a spike in levels of hunger around the world.[9]

The 1970s food crisis was the product of multiple complex factors, which prompted a rethink of our conceptualization of food security and how to promote it through global cooperation. Although there was a drop in world food production tied to poor weather in 1972–74, and a disruption to food aid deliveries as a result, there were further complex contributors to the crisis. More industrialized agricultural production systems that were promoted by agencies such as the FAO, the World Bank, and the CGIAR were heavily reliant on fossil fuels, and when oil prices spiked in this same period food prices followed suit. There were also major shifts in grain markets at this time, with the Soviet Union buying up massive quantities of grain as prices rose, leaving little for developing countries to receive as aid, and what was left on the market was largely out of their reach due to its higher price.[10]

The food crisis of the 1970s prompted a number of reforms to the institutional framework for global food security governance. Most of these reforms emerged from recommendations made at the 1974 World Food Conference that was convened to address the crisis. The reforms that emerged from this gathering bolstered the pillars of food security that were already supported by the governance framework—production and distribution—and also expanded that framework in a number of ways.

There was an attempt to bolster the availability pillar, especially in the world's poorest countries that were hardest hit by the crisis. The International Fund for Agricultural Development (IFAD) explicitly sought to increase agricultural production and improve rural livelihoods in developing countries through investment in agricultural projects.[11] The incorporation of rural livelihoods into its mandate expands the understanding of food security to include the integration of production and consumption through a livelihood perspective to development. There were also other reforms to the food security governance framework that addressed the access pillar, which included efforts to improve food aid practices among donors. Donors were requested to increase their commitment to food aid, and to follow better practices to target the neediest countries. These requests came about because of widespread criticism in the 1960s and 1970s that donors were channeling most of their food donations to political allies, rather than the world's hungriest people.[12]

The conceptualization of what were important factors for food security was also widened at this time, along with new accompanying food security governance institutions. Three new UN bodies were established that gave weight to the emerging understanding of the significance of the stabilization and utilization pillars of food security. A new intergovernmental body under the FAO, the Committee on World Food Security (CFS), was established in 1974 to serve as a forum for reviewing food security policy which would have an impact on stability. The initial work of the CFS was primarily focused on grain production and the stabilization of grain markets.[13] The UN Standing Committee on Nutrition (SCN) was also established in 1977 to monitor nutritional programs across the UN system to improve utilization.[14] The World Food Council also came out of the World Food Conference; it was set up to serve as a body to coordinate national agriculture ministries on issues of hunger and malnutrition.[15] In 1975 another institution was established, the International Food Policy Research Institute (IFPRI), with an explicit focus on policy research for agricultural development, including economic and nutrition policy. IFPRI joined the CGIAR system in 1980, reflecting a growing recognition of the need to incorporate policy dimensions into agricultural research activities.

The four pillars of food security that are highlighted today were thus supported through various governance initiatives at the international level by the early 1980s. The significance of these different components was solidified with the publication of leading economist Amartya Sen's important research findings in the early 1980s that demonstrated that food supply alone was not sufficient to ensure food security, and that other forces, including well-functioning markets, enabling livelihoods, and public policy, were also important.[16] This work helped to reinforce the broad-based approach to food security, which eventually led to the adoption at the 1996 World Food Summit of the definition of food security noted above.

Throughout the 1980s and 1990s, other actors also began to play an increasingly important role in shaping international food security governance norms and practices. Nongovernmental organizations (NGOs) focused on food security and development took on both operational and advocacy roles as governments increasingly began to rely on these organizations to operationalize their food security policy and programs. Such nongovernmental organizations as CARE and World Vision, for example, took on roles as food aid delivery agencies, while others, such as Oxfam and the World Development Movement, took on advocacy roles around international food policy. At the same time, corporate actors began to take on a greater role in global food security governance through public–private partnerships. The Global Alliance for Improved Nutrition (GAIN), for example, was established in 2002 as a partnership between international organizations, the agrifood industry, and civil society organizations to promote initiatives in the areas of nutrition and food fortification.[17] The WFP also began to make more linkages with private donors and developed partnerships with agrifood and other corporations to support its food assistance work.

The 1980s and 1990s were also a period of low agricultural commodity prices compared to the spikes experienced in the 1970s. In this period, some backtracking and further changes in the multilateral institutional landscape for food security occurred. In 1993, the World Food Council was disbanded on the grounds that it seemed to be superfluous as a separate body, and its activities were absorbed by the FAO and WFP. Renewals to the Food Aid Convention in 1995 and 1999 saw donors reduce their overall commitments to food aid, and levels of food aid delivered fell sharply. The WTO Agreement on Agriculture (AoA) also came into place on 1 January 1995, which included new rules on the international trade in agricultural products for the first time in a multilateral trade agreement. These rules, designed to reduce trade distortions in the sector, had important implications for food security, as will be discussed below.[18]

Although some downsizing of activity took place in this period, progress was made in new directions on the food security front. In 2000 the UN created the post of the UN special rapporteur on the right to food, whose mandate is to promote the realization of the right to food through measures taken at the national, regional, and international levels. The creation of this post recognizes the significance of the need to promote the human right to food, first articulated in the 1948 Universal Declaration of Human Rights, within the UN system. The special rapporteur works with UN agencies, other international organizations, NGOs, and governments in raising awareness of right to food issues and promoting policy changes.[19]

The challenges presented by the 2007–08 food crisis

According to FAO figures, from 1990 to 2006 there had been some steady, albeit slow, progress in reducing the number and proportion of food-insecure people in the world.

But after 2006, the world went from a situation of low agricultural and food commodity prices to one of high and volatile food prices, with enormous consequences for food security. In late 2007 and early 2008, world food prices rose sharply, with prices for key staple crops doubling within months. These rapid price increases occurred under conditions that many characterized as a "perfect storm"—a combination of high energy prices, soaring investment in agricultural commodities and biofuels, drought in some parts of the world, rising demand in rapidly industrializing countries, and a global financial meltdown. The global food crisis put an abrupt halt to progress toward addressing world hunger. The number of hungry people increased slightly and has remained steady in the 2009–12 period. The crisis showed that hunger and food insecurity are highly complex issues that are extremely difficult to address when crises emerge, even with a wide-ranging set of specialized institutions and arrangements focused on ending hunger. The crisis revealed the limits of that governance framework and pointed to the need for further refinements to it.

The 2007–08 crisis and the subsequent volatility on food markets in the 2009–12 period demonstrated the extent to which food security is deeply intertwined with global economic forces. It also showed the extent to which the existing food security governance framework was not empowered to address the complex contributors to the crisis due to institutional fragmentation that results in the separation of governance tasks not only among the food-related institutions, but also with other institutions in the global economy that have relevance for food security.

The food security pillars of access and stability of supply in particular have been affected by turmoil on global food markets. When those markets are disrupted by shifting trade patterns and rising prices, people's ability to access food, and to do so on a regular basis, can become severely compromised. In such situations, it is typically the most vulnerable people in the world's poorest countries—those who spend some 50–80 percent of their income on food—who are affected most profoundly. The linkages between the global economic situation and food security are acknowledged in the governance work on the four pillars, but because of the separation of governance authority in different parts of the system, the existing food governance agencies have little authority to address broader economic arrangements that affect food security.

Broader economic forces impeded food security during the crisis in two important ways. First, the world's poorest countries had become highly vulnerable to the food crisis. In large part this was because global trade and investment patterns over a period of 30–40 years encouraged a growing dependence on food imports. The inclusion of agriculture into global trade rules in the WTO AoA was important because those rules provided little incentive, and in fact were a disincentive, to produce food in developing countries. Developing countries complain that they have been forced to open up their markets to food imports under these rules, but rich countries were allowed to continue to subsidize their own farmers, making it hard for developing country farmers to compete. The AoA was widely recognized as being unfair to developing countries from the start, and the WTO itself even built in an agenda that required that the AoA be revisited in the subsequent round of trade negotiations. Since the launch of the Doha Round of WTO trade negotiations in 2001, a serious overhaul of agricultural trade rules has been on the agenda. For over a decade, however, there has been very little progress, leaving the world stuck with uneven, and many developing countries would say, unfair rules governing agricultural trade.[20]

Also contributing to vulnerability in the world's poorest countries was a marked decline in agricultural investment from World Bank and bilateral donors. During the period of low agricultural commodity prices from the 1980s to early 2000s, there was a steady drop in agricultural investment in developing countries. The share of overseas development assistance targeted at agriculture in the late 1970s was 20 percent. This number fell to just 4 percent in 2005, and is still under 6 percent today.[21] This drop in international assistance was accompanied by a decline in developing countries' own investment in the sector. The decline in investment has meant that agriculture has been largely under-resourced in the world's poorest countries. Under these conditions, developing countries became increasingly vulnerable to market disruptions as their dependence on imported food rose. Meanwhile, new foreign investment since the most recent food crisis has been largely from investors interested in acquiring large tracts of agricultural land. It is unclear whether this kind of investment will be useful for food security because much of the acquired land is being cultivated with biofuel crops or with food crops intended for export to the investor country.[22]

The second major way in which the broader economic context affected food security in the crisis was through volatility of agricultural markets and food prices. When agricultural commodity prices rose sharply and became highly volatile after 2006, the situation became intolerable for the world's poorest countries that had come to rely on food imports because their own agricultural production capacity had been weakened. The food price spikes, as noted above, were affected by many factors in the global economy. Two forces in particular deserve mention as they are not the product of a dramatic drop in food supply, but rather are market-based causes linked to investment booms in the global economy, that are themselves linked to rule changes in the world's richest countries. One of these is speculation by financial investors on commodity futures markets. Investors engage in speculation when they buy into agricultural commodity markets purely for the purpose of making a profit, and they have no real interest in using the products they are buying and selling. Relaxed financial market legislation over the past decade in the US in particular enabled banks and other financial institutions to sell financial products to investors that are based on prices and movements in agricultural commodity markets. The demand for these products has soared since the turn of the century, thereby driving up demand and hence prices for food.[23]

Rising investment in biofuels has also fueled rising and volatile food prices. Biofuels affect food prices by taking food crops such as maize out of food markets and putting them instead into fuel markets. In the US, for example, the largest producer and exporter of maize, some 40 percent of the maize crop went into biofuel production in 2012, leaving less maize on global grain markets. This, in turn, drove up prices for the maize that was available as a food grain. Globally, some 15 percent of maize production is now directed toward the production of ethanol. A recent study of the US National Academy of Sciences estimated that some 20–40 percent of recent food price increases was attributable to the boom in biofuel production.[24] According to another study, increased diversion of maize into biofuel production has added an estimated US$6.6bn to the cost of food imports in developing countries over the past five years.[25]

When the sudden volatility in world markets was overlaid with the vulnerability in the world's poorest countries, it had profound implications for food security. The changes in the global economic landscape affected both the access and stability pillars of food security in important ways. Yet the economic forces that contributed directly to vulnerability and volatility—trade policy, declining agricultural investment, financial speculation in agricultural commodities, and increased diversion of food crops into biofuel production—are ones that the food agencies are not authorized to address in any direct way. Although the global food institutions can recommend policy direction for their member governments on these important issues, it is ultimately governments that have the most control over these broader forces. Under these circumstances, the views of some of the world's most powerful governments tend to prevail, and their interests tend to be to keep the status quo. Food governance institutions do not have the authority to hold these governments to account on economic issues. The global food security governance institutions are instead relegated to providing largely scientific solutions for food production and nutrition, food assistance for distribution, and policy advice, not always adhered to by governments, on stability questions. Moreover, although the various agencies within the food security governance framework are each dedicated to a particular pillar of food security, their coordination with each other when issues cut across those pillars is not particularly strong. Overall, this lack of authority on some issues, and lack of coordination on others, has resulted in a weak response to the crisis.

What future for global food and hunger governance?

The 2007–08 food crisis sparked further reforms in the global food security governance framework. An emergency meeting was held in mid-2008 and the UN established a High-level Task Force on the Food Security Crisis (HLTF) to assess the situation. The HLTF—comprised of representatives from over 20 UN agencies and funds, as well as from the World Bank, International Monetary Fund (IMF), and WTO—produced the Comprehensive Framework for Action (CFA) document in 2008 that aimed to provide a single process for coordination of food crisis response across the UN system.[26] This document provides an analysis of the various dimensions of the food crisis and possible actions that could be taken. A World Summit on Food Security was held in Rome in late 2009 to assess the broader situation, at which the Rome Principles for Sustainable Global Food Security were adopted. These principles outline the guiding norms for addressing food insecurity, and emphasize the need for strategic coordination of action across multiple agencies and levels of governance as well as a comprehensive approach to food security.[27]

One of the recommendations of the HLTF was to reform the UN Committee on World Food Security, one of the UN bodies set up after the 1970s food crisis but which had largely failed to operate as an effective forum for policy coordination. Negotiations on reform of the CFS took place over the course of 2009. The reformed CFS now includes not just governmental inputs into the policy process, but also civil society voices, and a new body, the High-level Panel of Experts (HLPE), was created to provide advice on different aspects of food policy to the CFS.[28] In this context, some of the expert reports have called for bold policy changes, such as: new globally managed food reserves; stepped-up policy reforms such as an overhaul to biofuels regulations in producing countries; more stringent regulation on financial speculation in commodities; and an overhaul of agricultural trade rules. The CFS is currently producing a Global Strategic Framework for food security and nutrition, a document due to be completed in 2012. With these various reforms in place, the CFS now functions much more effectively as a forum for debating these issues, but the body itself still lacks teeth to implement policy changes.

Part of the reason for the weakness of the CFS as a governing body is that it only provides advice, and many of its member governments have vested interests in certain policy frameworks and approaches. Also affecting the ability of the CFS to bring about policy change is the fact that the world's most powerful governments have put their efforts on food security not with the CFS, but with the recently established global economic governance body, the Group of 20 (G20). In 2010 the G20, originally established to address financial and economic issues, began to develop a food security agenda. With its economic focus and membership of the world's most powerful governments, the G20 could have made progress by pressing its members—home to most of the commodity markets where speculation takes place, the largest producers of biofuels, and the source of most international agricultural investment—on key issues related to food security that stem from the global economic forces. But the G20 has thus far failed to recommend regulatory action on these issues.[29]

The main contribution of the G20 to food security has been to undertake an initiative, the Agricultural Market Information System (AMIS). Housed in the FAO, AMIS is a collaborative effort among nine international organizations. The idea behind the initiative is to gather and disseminate more information on physical commodity production and market transactions in the hopes that it would help to reduce market uncertainty, and contribute to better-functioning, less volatile international food markets. Under the AMIS umbrella are two groups—the Global Food Market Information Group and the Rapid Response Forum. The former provides information and analysis of global food markets, and the latter works to improve policy dialogue in situations of high food insecurity with a view to enhancing emergency response. Although AMIS is still in its early days of operation, some analysts have expressed skepticism at its ability to prevent future market disruptions of the type that has caused food price volatility in recent years. There are a number of areas where agricultural information is not available. And it is unclear how AMIS would work with the private sector, particularly the four global grain trading companies (ADM, Bunge, Cargill, and Louise Dreyfus) that control an estimated 75 percent or more of the international cereal trade.[30]

Conclusion

This chapter shows that the key global institutions that address hunger and food insecurity have evolved over time with our changing understanding of what constitutes food security. As our conceptualization of food security has expanded beyond a focus on food availability to also incorporate access, stability, and utilization, the food security governance framework at the international level has responded by adding new institutions and activities aimed at addressing all four of these pillars of food security. While this framework does cover the main components of current thinking on what contributes to enhanced food security, in practice this framework has been fragmented, leading to poor coordination on key issues that cut across the pillars or fall between them.

The fragmentation of the institutional landscape for global food security was highlighted in the aftermath of the 2007–08 food crisis and ongoing episodes of food price volatility. The recent food crisis and turmoil on global food markets has illustrated the tight linkages between broader forces in the global economy and food security. Economic problems such as unbalanced trade rules and declining agricultural investment in developing countries have contributed to vulnerability to food crises in the world's poorest countries. On top of this vulnerability has been ongoing volatility, spurred in large part by speculative financial investments in agricultural commodities and the biofuel boom.

Addressing these contributors to food insecurity requires a broad and comprehensive approach not only across the different food agencies that tackle specific pillars of food security, but also between the food agencies and broader economic governance frameworks that address trade, investment, and finance. The need for a more comprehensive and coordinated approach to food security at the global level is well understood among analysts and policy-makers. Bringing about that change, however, has been difficult in practice because of competing agendas of different bodies, such as the differences between the G20's food security agenda and that of the CFS.

Recent reforms to the broader food security framework, including the creation of the HLTF, the reforms to the CFS, and new initiatives such as AMIS, show movement in the right direction. However, much work remains to make the global food security framework more comprehensive and effective. Achieving such a goal would require deeper structural reforms, particularly those that tackle the broader economic forces affecting food security. For such reforms to happen, a broader consensus across all countries on how to best restructure the global economy in ways that support, rather than hinder, food security will need to be forged.

Additional reading

1. Jennifer Clapp, *Food* (Cambridge: Polity Press, 2012).
2. Christopher Barrett, "Measuring Food Insecurity," *Science* 327 (2010): 825–828.
3. Jean Drèze and Amartya Sen, *Hunger and Public Action* (Oxford: Oxford University Press, 1989).
4. Bryan McDonald, *Food Security* (Cambridge: Polity Press, 2010).
5. John Shaw, *World Food Security: A History since 1945* (London: Palgrave Macmillan, 2007).

Notes

1 FAO, *The State of Food Insecurity in the World 2012* (Rome: FAO, 2012), 8.
2 Ibid., Annex 2, 55.

3 See FAO, *Trade Reforms and Food Security* (Rome: FAO, 2003), http://www.fao.org/docrep/ 005/y4671e/y4671e06.htm; FAO, *State of Food Insecurity in the World 2001* (Rome: FAO, 2001), http://www.fao.org/docrep/003/y1500e/y1500e00.htm.

4 See Christopher Barrett, "Measuring Food Insecurity," *Science* 327 (2010), 825–828.

5 See FAO, *An Introduction to the Basic Concepts of Food Security*, http://www.fao.org/ docrep/013/al936e/al936e00.pdf.

6 See CGIAR, http://www.cgiar.org/who-we-are/history-of-cgiar.

7 See Jennifer Clapp, *Hunger in the Balance: The New Politics of International Food Aid* (Ithaca: Cornell University Press, 2012).

8 Edward Clay, *Trade Policy Options for Enhancing Food Aid Effectiveness* (Geneva: ICTSD and FAO, 2012).

9 On the 1970s food crisis, see Emma Rothschild, "Food Politics," *Foreign Affairs* 54, no. 2 (1976): 285–307.

10 Jennifer Clapp, *Food* (Cambridge: Polity, 2012).

11 See IFAD, http://www.ifad.org.

12 John Shaw, *The UN World Food Programme and the Development of Food Aid* (London: Palgrave, 2001).

13 Committee on World Food Security, *Coming to Terms with Terminology*, CFS 2012/39/4, 2012.

14 Richard Longhurst, "Global Leadership for Nutrition: The UN's Standing Committee on Nutrition (SCN) and Its Contributions" (Sussex: IDS), Discussion paper 2010 (390), http://www.ids.ac.uk/files/dmfile/dp390.pdf.

15 Shaw, *The UN World Food Programme*, 81–82.

16 Amartya Sen, *Poverty and Famines* (Oxford: Oxford University Press, 1981). See also Jean Drèze and Amartya Sen, *Hunger and Public Action* (Oxford: Oxford University Press, 1989).

17 Christopher Kaan and Andrea Liese, "Public Private Partnerships in Global Food Governance: Business Engagement and Legitimacy in the Global Fight against Hunger and Malnutrition," *Agriculture and Human Values* 28 (2011): 385–399.

18 See Jennifer Clapp, "WTO Agriculture Negotiations: Implications for the Global South," *Third World Quarterly* 27, no. 4 (2006): 563–577.

19 Olivier De Schutter, "Reshaping Global Governance: The Case of the Right to Food," *Global Policy* 3, no. 4 (2012): 480–483.

20 Olivier De Schutter, "The World Trade Organization and the Post-Global Food Crisis Agenda: Putting Food Security First in the International Trade System," Activity Report of the UN Special Rapporteur on the Right to Food (2011); Jennifer Clapp, "Food Security and the WTO," in *Trade, Poverty, Development: Getting beyond the Doha Deadlock*, eds. Rorden Wilkinson and James Scott (London: Routledge, 2012), 57–71.

21 Ibid., 162.

22 Olivier De Schutter, "How Not to Think of Land-grabbing: Three Critiques of Large-scale Investments in Farmland," *Journal of Peasant Studies* 38, no. 2 (2011): 249–279.

23 Jayati Ghosh, "The Unnatural Coupling: Food and Global Finance," *Journal of Agrarian Change* 10, no. 1 (2010): 72–86; Jennifer Clapp and Eric Helleiner, "Troubled Futures? The Global Food Crisis and the Politics of Agricultural Derivatives Regulation," *Review of International Political Economy* 19, no. 2 (2012): 181–207.

24 Cited in Tim Wise, *The Cost to Developing Countries of US Corn Ethanol Expansion*, Global Development and Environment Institute Working Paper 12–2 (2012), 2.

25 Wise, *The Cost to Developing Countries*, 2.

26 UNHLTF, *Elements of a Comprehensive Framework for Action* (New York: United Nations, 2008).

27 World Summit on Food Security, *Declaration of the World Summit on Food Security*, (Rome: FAO, 2009), http://www.fao.org/fileadmin/templates/wsfs/Summit/Docs/Final_Declaration/ WSFS09_Declaration.pdf.

28 Nora McKeon, *Global Governance for World Food Security* (Berlin: Heinrich-Boll-Stiftung, 2011); Institute for Agriculture and Trade Policy, *Resolving the Food Crisis: Assessing Global Policy Reforms Since 2007* (2012), http://www.ase.tufts.edu/gdae/Pubs/rp/ResolvingFood Crisis.pdf.

29 Jennifer Clapp and Sophia Murphy, "The G20 and Food Security: A Mismatch in Global Governance?," *Global Policy* 4, no. 2 (2013): 129–138.

30 Sophia Murphy, David Burch, and Jennifer Clapp, *Cereal Secrets* (Oxford: Oxfam UK, 2012), http://www.oxfam.org/sites/www.oxfam.org/files/rr-cereal-secrets-grain-traders-agriculture-30082012-en.pdf.

Global Health Governance

Sophie Harman

From the first International Sanitary Conference in 1851 to the formation of partnerships such as the GAVI Alliance (previously the Global Alliance for Vaccines and Immunisation) global health has set the model for many forms of global governance. Health—commonly defined as the state of physical and mental wellbeing—goes to the heart of questions of justice, equality, and liberty. The health of a population, community, or individual is a key indicator of wellbeing, wealth, and security. How health is provided or understood, as the responsibility either of the individual to take care of their minds and bodies or of the state to manage the structural determinants of ill health and redistribute wealth in a way to allow individuals to do so, has been at the crux of contemporary political debate on welfare provision and personal liberty for centuries. Health concerns have the ability to prevent the trade of goods, shut down airports, exacerbate poverty, engender fear, and destabilize armies. Yet health is often labeled as a soft topic in international politics and a side issue to security and economic concerns.

The purpose of this chapter is twofold: to provide an introduction to what global health governance is, the mechanisms of governing, and the core debates and issues therein; and in so doing, to situate health at the center of questions of global governance and international organization. The chapter begins by providing a brief sketch of the emergence of global health governance from the golden age of the 1800s to the contemporary era of new partnerships and pandemics. It then explores some of the key debates in global health governance over horizontal and vertical interventions, the securitization of health, treatment access, and international health law. Next the chapter reviews some of the current criticisms and emerging issues in global health governance with regard to leadership, the role of science and technology, and accountability in partnerships and new models of philanthropy. The chapter concludes with some comments about the future of global health governance.

The development of global health governance

Global health governance has undergone several phases of development and change. The first phase began in the "golden age" of biomedical discovery of the 1800s that not only set the framework for scientific breakthrough but laid the foundations for the institutions of global health. This phase ended with the consolidation of institutions such as the League of Nations Health Organisation and Office International d'Hygiène Publique (OIHP) into the World Health Organization (WHO) in the aftermath of World War II. The second phase, understood broadly as between the 1970s and 1990s, saw the eradication of one disease (smallpox) and the devastating impact of another (HIV/AIDS), and the emergence of a neoliberal paradigm in how global health policy was understood and practiced. The final phase has been the development of global health in the contemporary era, with the rise of partnerships, new forms of philanthropy, and multiple stakeholders and ideas involved in global health.

Notable about these periods of change is the shift from international health to global health governance. International health governance often refers to state-based interaction and intergovernmental institutions that were established in two phases. Accelerated economic, social, and political globalization from the second phase onwards increased the globality and supranational nature of decision-making in new and old institutions, and opened up space for the presence of private actors and partnerships in global health. Globality in decision-making and the plethora of state and non-state-based actors thus generated a shift from international to *global* health governance in the third phase. These periods are discussed next.

Phase 1: 1850s–1950s, the institutional foundations of global health

The "golden age" of global health primarily refers to the mid-1800s and the discovery of x-rays, the stethoscope, and, crucially, the finding that disease is caused by microbes (germs). Scientists such as Robert Koch and Louis Pasteur and their scientific breakthrough of germ theory made them celebrities in this era. However, this age was also notable because of the institutions formed to prevent the global spread of germs across trade routes and migratory patterns, and to promote hygiene across populations. Efforts to standardize and regulate global systems to monitor and control the spread of germs came into being through the creation of the International Sanitary Regulations in 1903 and the OIHP in 1907.

During the same period, private philanthropy took great interest in funding medical research and treatment; for example, the American oil philanthropist John D. Rockefeller established the Rockefeller Institute for Medical Research in 1901 and the Rockefeller University Hospital in 1910. The International Sanitary Regulations and the OIHP provided the basis for the League of Nations Health Organisation of 1920, designed to address post-war health concerns such as influenza and typhus, and funded by a combination of state commitments and private philanthropy. The Health Organisation was to reflect the need to establish peace through healthy populations and to provide an arena in which to coordinate and monitor new threats or issues pertinent to the health of the world's population. As with the League, the progress of the Health Organisation in its initial stages was limited by the onset of World War II; however, the need to link health and peace was an idea that remained central to questions of global coordination.[1]

Four clear implications for global health resulted from the institution building beginning at the end of World War II with the formation of the United Nations and the Bretton Woods Institutions (the World Bank and the International Monetary Fund, as well as the still-born International Trade Organization). The first was that health was going to be addressed by a broad array of UN organizations, including the United Nations Children's Fund (UNICEF, for child famine and disease), United Nations Population Fund (UNFPA, for reproductive health), and the United Nations Development Programme (UNDP, for the right to health, for tuberculosis, and HIV/AIDS). The second was that health was to be intrinsically linked to development, economic reform, and post-war infrastructure building and thus covered by the mandate of financial institutions such as the World Bank. Third, a standalone institution was required to prevent the spread of disease and promote better health around the world; hence in 1948 the WHO was established as *the* global health institution.

The WHO built upon and drew together existing International Sanitary Regulations, the OIHP, and the remnants of the League of Nations Health Organisation to become the lead UN and international body to promote health for all, monitor threats to the health of the world's population, and offer advice, guidelines, and recommendations to states on health matters. Underpinning the formation of the WHO were two prominent ideas: that health is a global public good—it is non-rivalrous in consumption and non-excludable, or in other words everyone should have access to it and one person's consumption should not prevent another's; and that health is a human right.[2]

The WHO has a decentralized structure, operating from its Geneva headquarters and six regional offices. The annual World Health Assembly (WHA), made up of states, sets the agenda and approves the budget of the organization, and the secretariat, headed by the director-general, is responsible for the day-to-day operations of the institution in collaboration with the regional and country offices. The WHO is responsible for leadership, coordination and partnership, research agendas and knowledge dissemination, standard setting, institutional support, and monitoring and evaluation of its own and state practice. The WHO has established two key sources of international law: the International Health Regulations (based on the International Sanitary Regulations) that bind all states to monitor and report disease outbreaks with mixed results; and the Framework Convention on Tobacco Control (FCTC) that has seen a revolution in tobacco labeling, advertising, and public smoking.[3] Member state obligatory contributions only make up a small proportion of the WHO's budget (28 percent), with the remaining funds from voluntary contributions.[4] On the one hand, this funding formula has made the WHO a much more flexible and autonomous institution and less beholden to member states. On the other hand, it has resulted in periodic funding shortfalls and a loss of autonomy, as discussed below.

Phase 2: 1970s–1990s, disease eradication and emergence and the rise of neoliberalism

The late 1970s saw two highlights for the WHO and global public health. The first was the eradication of smallpox by 1980, the only disease ever to be eradicated. The second was the adoption of the Alma Ata Declaration of 1978 that reaffirmed the WHO's and its member states' commitments to health for all. However, this commitment to health for all and the notion of health as a public good was to be challenged by the increasingly market-based approaches to health policy, commonly labeled neoliberalism, adopted in the 1980s.

Definitions of neoliberalism are well rehearsed, but for the purposes of health they refer to opening up health delivery to competition in provision, the privatization of aspects of public health, reduced government provision and regulation, and the adoption of a market for deciding who provides a range of healthcare needs, who pays for them, and how. The stated, but contested, benefits of neoliberal policies are increased expertise, efficiency, and plurality of choice in the health system. Neoliberal reform of health systems was a key component of a number of structural adjustment loans of the IMF and World Bank to developing countries in the 1980s and early 1990s. Reforms of this type were also evident in the increased privatization of the National Health Service (NHS) in the UK and remain at the heart of debates over socialized and publicly provided health care in European and North American politics.

The impact of neoliberal reforms in developing countries was particularly acute: cuts to public financing of health systems were often not met by an influx of private investment or fully adopted. The result was health systems, for example hospitals, health professionals, and drug provision, which were underfunded. There was little money for public health campaigns, and the cost of health care was put onto the individual through payment of user fees.[5] At the same time these policies were being pursued an unknown disease was killing gay men, intravenous drug users, and hemophiliacs in the United States and Europe.[6] Formally identified as Acquired Immune Deficiency Syndrome (AIDS), caused by the Human Immunodeficiency Virus (HIV), in 1981, this disease was to go on to kill 30 million people, infect 60 million, and orphan 16 million children by 2011.[7]

The simultaneous rise of HIV/AIDS and neoliberal approaches to governing global health is particularly pertinent for understanding global health. Both confronted what constituted public health privately provided, both happened at a time of rapid economic change, and both placed strains on existing health systems, particularly in developing countries. It is important to note that neoliberal approaches to health challenged the provision of treatment and funding for a range of other health issues, such as tuberculosis, malaria, maternal health, and neglected tropical disease. However, what is specific—or, for some, "exceptional"—about HIV/AIDS is the stigma surrounding it, the silence and ignorance of political leaders, misinformation about how self-protection can be enacted, the gendered dimensions of how people are infected and affected, and the link between the disease and poverty and inequality.[8] What is notable about HIV/AIDS is the widespread transnational activism it generated from highly organized gay community groups caring for and educating people about the spread of HIV, to young children such as Nkosi Johnson in South Africa advocating for the government of Thabo Mbeki to provide treatment for people living with HIV/AIDS. Such activism, institutional leadership, and guilt of state denial saw the creation of the first standalone UN agency for a specific health issue—the Joint United Nations Programme on HIV/AIDS (UNAIDS)—and the rise of partnerships and multiple actors wanting to address the disease.

Phase 3: 2000s, partnerships, goals, innovation, and pandemic flu

The new century was to be the era of unprecedented global health financing and partnership building. The millennium began with the launching of the eight Millennium Development Goals (MDGs), three of which were directly related to health: Goal 4—Child Health; Goal 5—Maternal Health; and Goal 6—Combat HIV/AIDS and other diseases. The purpose of the goals is to provide measurable markers for progress in combating poverty and generating global political will and support for key areas. The sixth goal in particular generated an upsurge in public–private partnerships with the aim of developing new drugs and vaccines, low-cost treatment, and access to treatment and new models of prevention. Partnerships such as the International AIDS Vaccine Initiative (IAVI) were reinvigorated, and the GAVI Alliance and UNITAID were created to, respectively, provide investment in vaccine research and reduce the market price of treatment for AIDS, tuberculosis, and malaria. Celebrities acted as advocates for health concerns and endorsed product development partnerships to benefit health campaigns. The G8/G20 prioritized health in communiqués and summits.[9] The culmination of the trend towards partnership, celebrity endorsement, G8 interest, and the prioritization of goal-oriented strategy was the creation of the Global Fund to fight AIDS, Tuberculosis and Malaria (hereafter the Global Fund) in 2002.

The Global Fund is one of the first institutions of global health governance to have a board made up of both states and non-state representatives from civil society, campaign groups, and the private sector with equal voting power. The purpose of the Global Fund is to provide funding for countries to address AIDS, tuberculosis, and malaria. It is based in Geneva and has no in-country presence, preferring to work with partners in-country. Since its creation it has positioned itself as one of the key providers of anti-retroviral treatment for people living with HIV (alongside the US government's President's Emergency Plan for AIDS Relief—PEPFAR—project), and is seen as a model of partnership and funding that could be replicated in other areas of governance such as the environment.

As pertinent as the establishment of the Global Fund was to health during this time was the creation in 2000 of the Bill and Melinda Gates Foundation and its Global Health Program. The Gates Foundation is the biggest source of private wealth for global health, with an annual budget exceeding that of the WHO.[10] The Gates Foundation is financed by the private wealth of the Gates family and donations from investors such as Warren Buffet. A key focus is on innovation, principally scientific and technology-based solutions to some of the world's biggest health problems. Hence, it has invested substantially in polio eradication and the development of vaccines to combat HIV, guinea worm, and malaria. The foundation gives money to new partnerships such as the Global Fund and GAVI, and also old institutions such as the World Bank.[11] Representatives of the foundation attend the WHA and both Bill and Melinda Gates have a large media presence in shaping debates on global health through social media, TED talks, and newspaper opinion pieces.

The governance of global health in 2000 also became defined by a security agenda in which health issues were framed as security threats or risks to the global population. A particular area in which this played out was in response to the two pandemic flu outbreaks: H1N1 "Swine Flu" in 2009 and H5N1 "Bird Flu" in 2003.[12] For many this was particularly the case with H5N1, which generated the stockpiling of the drug

Tamiflu, raised concerns (but not restrictions) about the relationship between travel and contraction and the spread of the disease, and stoked fear among the global population. Fear in particular served as a tool to generate public interest toward an array of health concerns as well as public finance and political attention towards different health issues.

The 2000s was an era marked by rapid institutionalization and the targeted funding of particular health concerns. One result has been an increased role for the private sector in which public actors accommodated private ways of addressing policy and new forms of governance based on civil society inclusion in institutionalized forms of decision-making and goal-oriented strategies. This period has also marked a return to old ways of governing health, through scientific research, celebrity, and private philanthropy. However, the majority of efforts during this period have concentrated on a narrow number of health issues, such as infectious disease and pandemic flu. Less attention has been paid to non-communicable diseases in developing countries, or issues such as maternal health that were supposed to be prioritized at the beginning of the millennium. Hence the new structures of governance have not addressed *global* health but specific diseases in developing countries.

Current debates

The history and structures of global health governance suggest a picture of collaboration, adoption, adaptation, and inclusion of multiple different actors from the private and public sector operating at both the global and local level. In fact, many observers view the unusual mix of actors and types of operations as innovations that help to shed light on global governance more generally. However, with such a mix comes a set of challenges and debates over what issues should be prioritized, how, and by whom. For instance, crucial to the debate over vertical and horizontal forms of policy-making and aid intervention is the assertion that big infectious diseases such as HIV/AIDS and malaria and non-communicable diseases such as breast cancer receive unprecedented global attention and financial support to tackle them.

The result of vertical interventions that tackle specific diseases is, on the one hand, positive, because it heightens global awareness of the issue, galvanizes political support and generates money to support endeavors to address it, and shows what coordinated mass action can do to address health concerns. Critics of such vertical interventions suggest that they are effective and worthwhile, but not if they detract from wider health spending; particularly on areas lacking in investment, such as health systems. For many high-profile opinion formers in global health, such as the medical journal *The Lancet*,[13] vertical spending has somewhat distorted the global health agenda and led to neglect in health systems. The perverse result is that the targets of vertical interventions cannot be met as they rest on the horizontal aspects of health systems such as well-staffed and equipped hospitals. The nub of this argument is that horizontal interventions are costly, long term, and often beyond the remit of health specialists. Vertical interventions, by contrast, show results and are an easier sell in getting governments and their tax-paying citizens behind an issue.

A common explanation as to why vertical interventions such as HIV/AIDS have attracted so much attention is that the disease was framed as an issue of international security by the United Nations Security Council.[14] HIV/AIDS became seen as exceptional and warranting extraordinary measures by playing on people's fears and highlighting the threat of the disease on armies and thus state security;[15] the health of people living in developing countries and thus development outcomes; the threat of risk perception and individual security; and the movement of people and international security. For some, the framing of HIV/AIDS as a security threat was a deliberate ploy to get money and attention to address the disease and less about the promotion of public health.[16] To an extent this has worked.

However, "securitizing" a disease, those suffering from it, and the people, such as orphans or vulnerable children, affected by it can also be seen as problematic when thinking about how to secure these people, and the manipulation and control of people's bodies this may entail.[17] Seeing people living with HIV/AIDS as a threat to a population's security may lead to quarantine, exclusion, and, most commonly, embed problems of stigma that are so endemic to the spread of the disease.[18] Moreover, seeing individuals as security threats can directly impact on the rights of those individuals as citizens of particular states and wider claims to human rights. The fact that the majority of people living with HIV/AIDS are women has specific connotations for gender norms and women's rights. Hence, at the heart of the securitization debate is the tension between framing health issues in certain ways to generate greater political attention and money to address the issue, and safeguarding the human rights of individuals.

Access to treatment remains a key contention in debates over global health. The different pricing of drugs in developed and developing countries, patent laws, procurement practices, drug trials, and drug licensing practices are all subject to public health scrutiny and commercial interests. Drug companies play a key function within global health governance: they provide the upfront costs for research and development into treatment and the most advanced ways of managing pain, preventing death, and prolonging life. Hence, preventing illness and treating the sick in many ways depends on these companies. However, with such dependency comes influence. Drug companies are influential not only in providing a core need within global health, but in setting the parameters in which that need is accessed. A core example of this is the case of the amendment to the World Trade Organization's (WTO) Agreement on Trade Related Aspects of Intellectual Property Rights (TRIPs). The amendment to the TRIPs agreement was born out of a contention over parallel licensing—the right to produce copies of, or, for some, counterfeit, products—of access to anti-retroviral drugs to prolong the lives of people living with HIV/AIDS in South Africa.

The original TRIPs agreement was introduced to protect intellectual property rights (IPRs) globally whilst allowing some gray areas for competition. However, for many this agreement was seen to favor the holders of IPR to the detriment of those needing access to them, or, in other words, the drugs companies rather than those in need of the drugs.[19] This contention came to a head in 1998 when 39 pharmaceutical companies in collaboration with the US government launched a case against the South African Medicines Act, arguing it acted in contravention of South Africa's WTO commitments. In what has generally been seen as a triumph of health over trade, the case was eventually withdrawn. This was in part the result of a sustained public health campaign and arguments put forward by transnational advocacy groups such as the Treatment Action Campaign, but was also in part the consequence of the unfair advantage 39 companies were seen as having from the government subsidies they received to invest in research and development. The contention was thus not only about in whose interests these companies act, but also about how public funding can turn to private gain.

Tensions over public funding for private gain have also played out in other aspects of global health such as virus sharing. As part of the WHO's Global Outbreak Alert and Response Network (GOARN), the Global Influenza Surveillance and Response System requires states to share virus samples and information. However, in 2007 Indonesia refused to share its samples of the H5N1 virus, thus breaking a key convention and norm of global health governance. The rationale of the Indonesian government was that the samples that it publicly collected and would publicly share would then be passed on by the WHO to private pharmaceutical companies to develop a vaccine or treatment that would be sold back to Indonesia at a price it could not afford.[20]

The Indonesia case generated several issues that remain contentious for global health governance. The first is with regard to who owns or has sovereignty over viruses. This has implications for both how viruses are shared and who reaps the benefits of such sharing, as well as who takes responsibility for a virus should it be owned by a specific state or political entity. For example, should a pandemic outbreak happen in country X, is it then liable for the impact the virus has on country Y? And if so, what form should such liability take? The second contention points to the problem over public goods for private gain and the extent to which states fulfill specific functions for the private rather than the public sector without recompense in lower drug prices and the provision of the public good of health. The final contention is over the problem of cooperation—that is, how to make states cooperate in the global public good of health when their sovereignty is challenged by international institutions and global norms of virus sharing.

For solutions to these many problems, people look to the WHO for guidance, recommendations, and potential solutions. However, the WHO has often been found wanting in many ways, thereby adding fuel to protracted discussions over its reform. The arguments for WHO reform are as follows. First, the organization lacks the resources to fully fulfill its core functions, and the way it is funded—where states contribute a core amount and then offer additional funds for specific health topics—limits its ability to plan operations, establish priorities independently, and undertake key initiatives. Second, the WHO is too decentralized to take a clear leadership role for the globality of health. Its decentralized structures make the WHO flexible in responding to local concerns but also hard to govern in a coherent manner, confusing budgeting and planning further. Third, WHO is active in a crowded terrain comprising multiple different actors and partnerships, all of which have to compete for contributions. For some the WHO has been at the forefront of partnerships, whereas for others it has failed to adapt to the changes in who governs global health and the nature of how global health policy is financed. Finally, the WHO is only one site of policy knowledge, advice, and expertise. While the WHO maintains its advisory role to states on virus outbreaks, pre-qualifications of drugs, and multiple aspects of health policy, its legitimacy for doing so is being tried by cases such as the Indonesian incident and the growth of alternative sources of knowledge funded by partnerships and private philanthropy.

Compounding matters are debates and rumors about redundancies at the WHO,[21] with questions about its relevance breeding low staff morale and inertia, which combine to limit the organization's ability to maintain and highlight its relevance. These debates are widespread within the WHO, in academic blogs on global health, in research, and among other institutions that partner with the WHO in its operations.[22] However, there is much to suggest that such a debate may be constant and ongoing. For many of the central institutions of global governance, a credible alternative to the WHO does not exist; and little consensus exists on how it ought to be reformed.

Emerging issues

A key issue to emerge from contemporary debates in global health is leadership, or the lack thereof. The multitude of actors involved in global health in recent decades has led to a problem of direction and competing interests fighting over finance. A multiplicity of actors bring a plurality of ideas but also dilute claims to the public nature of global health. Leadership from civil society campaigners and key institutions has generated support and investment in a range of health issues from HIV/AIDS to breast cancer and Parkinson's disease. Sites of leadership can be found in the directors of intergovernmental agencies, advocates of specific health issues, celebrities, philanthropists, and some government leaders. Effective leadership has drawn on all of these elements to generate support over a specific issue. However, transnational advocacy health campaigns currently have little exposure in the global media, heads of new and old institutions are leaving after short periods of time, and there is little direction as to what should be prioritized and how, or how we should think about global health and the role of its global governance.

Questions about how global health should be addressed relate to tensions between the provision of public health that is based on socialized systems of health care, market forms of delivery, a mix between the public and the private, and ideas that health should not be public but would be more effectively delivered as a private good. The problem of leadership is not necessarily to overcome the challenges between public and private ideas of global health and what should be prioritized and how, but rather how to provide guidance and direction that generate support from global health policy-makers, practitioners, and advocates. In the current arrangements of global health governance, such leadership is lacking and is badly needed.

It could be argued that strong leadership from a particular institution or individual is not necessary or wanted given that the future of global health governance appears to lie in partnerships. However, the degree to which such partnerships are effective and equitable for all partners, including the least powerful, is somewhat hazy. The partnerships that emerged in the 2000s are coming into question, with corruption allegations in the Global Fund leading to a shortfall in finance and a suspension, until 2014, of new rounds of funding.[23] Despite progress in aspects of immunization and claims that we are nearing the eradication of polio, partnerships are yet to deliver the large breakthroughs in the promised scientific research and innovations. Moreover, many partnerships are seen as subject to the interests of major donors, and their interests in global health embed market-based ways of thinking about and delivering health. For some this is particularly the case with the investment of the Bill and Melinda Gates Foundation in GAVI.[24] Thus, partnership can be less about plurality of policy ideas and options and deliberative decision-making, and more about forms of decision-making that favor the interests of the larger donor and market forms of delivery.

The final emerging issue pertinent to global health governance is in many ways an old one: the rise of technocratic solutions to health problems, and the progress of science over politics. A review of high-profile health journals, conferences such as the International AIDS Conference, and the World Health Assembly press releases suggests that the future of global health lies in science and innovation. However, a singular reliance on science can limit discussions and throw up problems of personal responsibility, state provision, and private profit. It can also constrain the space for politics and ideas of who gets access to such scientific innovations, how, and who pays for them. Science is a vital part of the provision of global health that has prolonged life, alleviated suffering, and revealed the potential of humanity. However, an emphasis on science without arenas of political contestation and discussion will see a replay of questions of equity, property rights, public goods, and who owns innovation evident in the TRIPs debate, HIV/AIDS campaigns, and problems of virus sharing. A key emerging issue within global health governance is thus the space for politics in increasingly technocratic forms of governing.

Conclusion

The emerging issues of leadership, partnership, and the technocratic turn of global health governance all point to questions over the purpose and limits of global health governance. As this chapter has shown, the initial intent of institutions of global health was to regulate and prevent the spread of disease and to promote peace through the provision of the highest attainable access to physical and mental wellbeing. Intertwined with global health governance have been efforts for scientific discoveries to solve health concerns and questions over how health should be provided, by whom, and the role of the private and public sector therein. These questions are as pertinent today as they were in the nineteenth century as various actors come together to challenge the notion of public health and whose interests the institutions and processes of global health governance serve. Politics remains at the heart of global health governance, yet increased technocratic agendas for global governance more broadly shrink formal spaces for political contestation to the detriment of future collaboration and the promotion of global *public* health. Politics, not just scientific discovery, thus remains the key challenge ahead for global health governance.

Additional reading

1. Sophie Harman, *Global Health Governance* (London: Routledge, 2012).
2. Sara Davies, *Global Politics of Health* (Cambridge: Polity Press, 2010).
3. David Fidler, *International Law and Infectious Diseases* (Oxford: Clarendon Press, 1999).
4. David Fidler and Lawrence Gostin, *Biosecurity in the Global Age: Biological Weapons, Public Health and the Rule of Law* (Palo Alto, CA: Stanford University Press, 2008).
5. Adrian Kay and Owain David Williams, eds., *Global Health Governance: Crisis, Institutions, and Political Economy* (Basingstoke: Palgrave Macmillan, 2009).
6. Kelley Lee, Kent Buse, and Suzanne Fustukian, eds., *Health Policy in a Globalising World* (Cambridge: Cambridge University Press, 2002).

Notes

1 Sophie Harman, *Global Health Governance* (London: Routledge, 2012).

2 David Woodward and Richard Smith, "Global Public Goods and Health: Concepts and Issues," in *Global Public Goods for Health: Health Economics and Public Health Perspectives*, eds. Richard Smith, Robert Beaglehole, David Woodward, and Nick Drager (Oxford: Oxford University Press, 2003), 3–29; United Nations General Assembly, *The Right to Health: Note by the Secretary General* (General Assembly document A/63/263), 2008.

3 WHO, *International Health Regulations 2005*, http://www.who.int/ihr/en; and WHO, *Framework Convention on Tobacco Control* (2012), http://www.who.int/fctc/en/.

4 WHO, *Working for Health: An Introduction to the World Health Organization* (2012), http://www.who.int/about/brochure_en.pdf.

5 Harman, *Global Health Governance*.

6 For detailed accounts of the emergence of HIV/AIDS in Europe and the United States, see Randy Shilts, *And the Band Played On* (New York: St. Martin's Griffin, 1988); Virginia Berridge, *AIDS in the UK: The Making of Policy, 1981–1994*, 2nd edition (Oxford: Oxford University Press, 2002).

7 WHO, *Global Health Observatory: HIV/AIDS* (2012), http://www.who.int/gho/hiv/en/index.html; and AVERT, *AIDS Orphans* (2011), http://www.avert.org/aids-orphans.htm #contentTable0.

8 Franklyn Lisk, *Global Institutions and the HIV/AIDS Epidemic: Responding to an International Crisis* (Abingdon: Routledge, 2009); Fantu Cheru, "Debt, Adjustment and the Politics of Effective Response to HIV/AIDS in Africa," *Third World Quarterly* 23, no. 2 (2002): 299–312; Tony Barnett, "HIV/AIDS and Development Concern Us All," *Journal of International Development* 16 (2004): 943–949; Maria deBruyn, "Women and AIDS in Developing Countries," *Social Science and Medicine* 34, no. 3 (1992): 249–262.

9 John J. Kirton and Jenevieve Mannell, "The G8 and Global Health Governance," in *Governing Global Health: Challenge, Response, Innovation*, eds. Andrew F. Cooper, John J. Kirton, and Ted Schrecker (Aldershot: Ashgate, 2007), 115–146.

10 Harman, *Global Health Governance*.

11 Sophie Harman, *The World Bank and HIV/AIDS: Setting a Global Agenda* (Abingdon: Routledge, 2010), 114.

12 Stefan Elbe, *Security and Global Health* (Cambridge: Polity Press, 2010); and Stefan Elbe, "Pandemics on the Radar Screen: Health Security, Infectious Disease, and the Medicalisation of Insecurity," *Political Studies* 59, no. 4 (2011): 848–866.

13 Phyllida Travis, Sara Bennett, Andy Haines et al., "Overcoming Health-Systems Constraints to Achieve the MDGs," *The Lancet* 364 (2005): 900–906.

14 United Nations Security Council Resolution 1308, 17 July 2000; Colin McInnes, "HIV/AIDS and Security," *International Affairs* 82, no. 2 (2006): 315–326.

15 Peter W. Singer, "AIDS and International Security," *Survival* 44, no. 2 (2001): 145–158.

16 Colin McInnes and Kelley Lee, "Health, Security and Foreign Policy," *Review of International Studies* 32, no. 1 (2006): 5–23; Colin McInnes and Simon Rushton, "HIV, AIDS, and Security: Where Are We Now?," *International Affairs* 86 (2010): 225–245.

17 Stefan Elbe, "Should HIV/AIDS Be Securitized? The Ethical Dilemmas of Linking HIV/AIDS and Security," *International Studies Quarterly* 50 (2006): 121–146.

18 Elbe, "Should HIV/AIDS Be Securitized?" Recent incidents of quarantining people with HIV/AIDS can be seen in Cuba and the Philippines.

19 Carlos Correa, "Health and Intellectual Property Rights," *Bulletin of the World Health Organization* 79, no. 5 (2001): 381; Caroline Thomas, "Trade Policy and the Politics of Access to Drugs," *Third World Quarterly* 23, no. 2 (2002): 251–264.

20 Adam Kamradt-Scott and Kelley Lee, "The 2011 Pandemic Influenza Preparedness Framework: Global Health Secured or Missed Opportunity?," *Political Studies* 59, no. 4 (2011): 831–847. For further debates on this issue, see "Tackling Pandemics as a Governance Challenge," *Global Health Governance* Special Issue 11, no. 2 (2010).

21 Simon Bradley, "WHO Faces Multi-Million Franc Lawsuits over Jobs" (2011), http://www.swissinfo.ch/eng/business/WHO_faces_multi-million_franc_lawsuits_over_jobs.html?cid=31503712. Journalists for Associated Press have also informally reported Geneva radio adverts advertising legal representation for WHO employees.

22 For debates about WHO reform, see Global Health Watch, "WHO Reform 2010–12," (2011), http://www.ghwatch.org/node/523#focus.

23 Peter Moszynski, "Global Fund Suspends New Projects until 2014 Because of Lack of Funding," *British Medical Journal* 343 (2011): d7755.

24 David McCoy, Gayatri Kembhavi, Jinesh Patel, and Akish Luintel, "The Bill and Melinda Gates Foundation's Grant-Making Programme for Global Health," *The Lancet* 373, no. 9675 (2009): 1645–1653.

Refugees and Migration

Khalid Koser

In legal, normative, and institutional terms, refugees and international migrants comprise quite distinct categories. There is a widely ratified international convention on refugees that defines clearly who refugees are, provides a legal and normative framework for protecting and assisting them, and that forms the basis of the mandate for a specific United Nations agency devoted to refugees. In contrast there is no UN migration organization; rather, there is a network of intergovernmental organizations within and outside the world organization that focus on specific aspects of international migration. Similarly, the legal and normative framework pertaining to international migrants cannot be found in a single document, but is derived from customary law, a variety of binding global and regional legal instruments, non-binding agreements, and policy understandings reached by states at the global and regional level.

At a sociological level, it has been argued that the distinction between refugees and migrants is not as clear as implied by the separation of the regimes that govern them. Focusing on individual decision-making, for example, reveals that most refugees and migrants move because of mixed motivations that combine political, economic, and social reasons.[1] The categories of "refugee" and "migrants" are themselves also diverse, and cover a wide range of people, some of whose circumstances may be closer to those of people in the alternative category, for example the victims of human trafficking are defined as a type of migrant but certainly require specific assistance and protection.[2] The prospect of displacement across international borders as a result of the effects of climate change will further blur the traditional distinctions between migrants and refugees. Growing interaction can also be observed at the institutional level, with the evolution of a range of dialogue processes between agencies variously responsible for migration and refugees, as well as operational partnerships, for example during the recent Libyan crisis.

This tension between divergent legal, normative, and institutional frameworks and convergent practical realities is a theme that runs through this chapter. It starts by explaining the history and development of the three types of frameworks for refugees and migration. The chapter then analyzes current debates pertaining to the refugee and migration regimes. The final substantive section turns to emerging issues, with a particular focus on climate change, before briefly concluding by considering prospects for a more formal union between the refugee and migration regimes.

History and development of the refugee and international migration regimes

Given the separation of the regimes governing refugees and international migrants, this section considers each in turn, describing the legal, normative, and institutional frameworks pertaining to refugees and international migrants, and how they have evolved over time.

Refugees

By the end of 2011 there were an estimated 15.2 million refugees worldwide.[3] This total included 4.8 million Palestinian refugees, who, as explained below, are registered by a different international organization than other refugees. Pakistan was host to the largest number of non-Palestinian refugees, about 1.7 million, almost all of whom were Afghans; and Afghanistan was the top origin country for refugees, accounting for almost one in four of the world's refugees besides the Palestinians.

An international regime to define and provide legal protection for refugees started to emerge only after the World War I. In 1921 the League of Nations created the Office of the High Commissioner for Refugees; an office with a limited geographical scope that has been characterized as neither effective nor enduring.[4] In response to massive displacement during World War II, the Allied Powers established the intergovernmental United Nations Relief and Rehabilitation Agency (UNRRA) in 1943, with a narrow mandate to oversee the repatriation of people displaced in Europe. The UNRRA was abolished in 1947 and the International Refugee Organization (IRO) created in its place, with a more comprehensive mandate but also focused exclusively on resolving the displacement arising from the war.[5] In parallel a separate UN agency was established in 1948 to provide relief and works programs for Palestinian refugees; and the UN Relief and Works Agency (UNRWA) began operations in 1950.

In part because of the emergence of new refugee flows, as a result of the partition of India in 1947 but also arising from events in Korea and China, consensus grew that a new UN refugee agency was required, culminating in the creation of the Office of the UN High Commissioner for Refugees (UNHCR) in 1951. When he was appointed the first UN high commissioner, Gerrit Jan van Heuven Goedhart received a mandate that was expected to last for only three years and controlled virtually no funds.[6] The current high commissioner, Antonio Guterres, leads an agency with 7,500 staff present in over 120 countries and an annual budget of about $3.5 billion. It is arguably the leading humanitarian organization in the world.

The 1951 UN Convention relating to the Status of Refugees provides the legal foundation and basic statute for UNHCR's work. It defines a refugee as someone who, "'owing to a well-founded fear of being persecuted for reasons of race, religion, nationality, membership of a particular social group or political opinion, is outside the country of his nationality, and is unable to, or owing to such fear, is unwilling to avail himself of the protection of that country."[7] It is worth noting that this definition focuses only on people who have been displaced across borders, and does not therefore include an estimated 28 million internally displaced persons (IDPs) around the world today.

The original definition covered only those who were displaced as a result of "events occurring before 1 January 1951," and thus focused mainly on Europe. This time constraint—and by extension geographical limitation—was removed, along with other changes to bring the unlimited and universal UNHCR statute into line with the 1951 Convention, by the 1967 Protocol relating to the Status of Refugees. In 2011 there were 142 states parties to both the Convention and Protocol.

Besides the legal definition of a refugee, the 1951 Convention also elaborates a normative framework, by identifying a number of specific obligations upon states parties. Foremost is the principle of *non-refoulement*, which prescribes that a refugee cannot be returned to any country where he or she would be at risk of persecution. Other important principles included the prescription of freedom from penalties for illegal entry; and a series of social, economic, and political rights, including employment, education, freedom to practice religion, access to courts and legal assistance, and the freedom of movement.

In addition to protecting and assisting refugees, the UNHCR mandate also extends to identifying durable solutions for them, of which there are three. Voluntary repatriation describes the return to their country of origin of refugees, once it is safe to do so—in 2011 around half a million refugees went home. Local integration describes the permanent settlement of refugees in their country of asylum. This is hard to measure, but it is estimated that over the last decade about 900,000 refugees have been given citizenship in the country where they sought asylum—two-thirds of them in the United States. Resettlement describes a process whereby refugees are moved from their country of asylum for permanent resettlement in another country. The most significant countries of resettlement worldwide are the United States, Canada, and Australia. In 2011 about 80,000 refugees were resettled worldwide.[8]

International migration

There were an estimated 214 million international migrants in the world in 2008, representing an increase of almost 40 million in the first decade of the twenty-first century, over double the number of international migrants in 1980. This figure does not include irregular migrants, currently estimated to number between 20 and 30 million.[9]

In contrast to refugees, there is no single document consolidating the legal and normative framework on migration. International migrants have rights under two sets of international instruments. The first are the core human rights treaties currently in force, namely the International Covenant on Civil and Political Rights (ICCPR), the International Covenant on Economic, Social and Cultural Rights (ICESCR), the Convention Against Torture (CAT), the Convention on the Elimination of All Forms of Racial Discrimination (CERD), the Convention on the Elimination of All Forms of Discrimination Against Women (CEDAW), the Convention on the Rights of the Child (CRC), and the Convention on the Rights of Persons with Disabilities (CRPD).

The second instrument is the UN Convention on the Protection of the Rights of All Migrant Workers and Members of Their Families, adopted by the UN General Assembly in 1990. This convention is intended to reinforce the international legal framework concerning the human rights of migrant workers by adopting a comprehensive instrument applicable to the whole migration process and regulating the legal status of migrant workers and their families. It protects the basic rights of all migrant workers and their families and grants regular migrants a number of additional rights on the basis of equality with nationals. It has not been widely ratified, and certainly not when compared with the 1951 Refugee Convention. There are currently 46 States Parties, none of which is a major destination country for migrants.

Nevertheless, the convention has recently received further endorsement within the UN system; in December 2010 the UN Committee on Migrant Workers approved formal jurisprudence that elaborates the rights of migrant domestic workers on the basis of an interpretation of the 1990 Convention. At a conference to mark the 20th anniversary of the Convention on Migrant Workers, the UN Office of the High Commissioner for Human Rights (OHCHR) called for those states that have not yet done so to ratify the convention. The Global Migration Group—an inter-agency conglomerate of UN and international organizations—also called for its ratification and implementation during the 2011 one-day Informal Thematic Debate on International Migration and Development convened by the General Assembly at its 65th session.

Migrant workers are also provided rights under international labor law, which includes two specific International Labour Organization (ILO) conventions, 97 and 143, concerned with the protection of migrant workers. The trafficking and smuggling protocols supplementing the UN Convention against Transnational Organized Crime also make reference to protecting the human rights of trafficked victims and smuggled migrants. ILO labor standards have also had a significant impact, especially on domestic law in ILO member states. Migrants' rights are also protected under regional treaties (e.g. under the European Court of Human Rights and the Inter-American Court of Human Rights). In addition, national courts are increasingly applying international human rights law and case law and advisory opinions from regional treaties to cases that come before them.

Also in contrast to refugees, there is no single UN agency responsible for safeguarding the legal and normative framework on international migration. Instead responsibility is divided across a whole range of institutions and organizations at the international, regional, and national levels. The ILO, founded in 1919, is the only UN organization with a constitutional mandate that applies to migration, but it is focused only on migrant workers, and specifically on their employment rights. The protection of migrant workers is also a significant focus for regional organizations and regional consultative processes on international migration around the world. They are addressed through provisions in numerous bilateral labor agreements between sets of states (although these provisions are not always effectively implemented). At the national level, numerous government agencies are dedicated to promoting the legal rights of migrants and protecting them in the workplace. Civil society organizations are also very active in this arena.

The most prominent international agency working on international migration is the International Organization for Migration (IOM), which is outside the UN system and does not have a specific mandate for migrant protection. Nonetheless, its guiding principle is to promote humane migration, and it supports numerous projects aimed at protecting the rights of migrant workers around the world. IOM was founded in 1951 as the Provisional Intergovernmental Committee for the Movement of Migrants from Europe (PICMME) and has gone through a series of name changes: PICMME to the Intergovernmental Committee for European Migration (ICEM) in 1952; the Intergovernmental Committee for Migration (ICM) in 1980; and the International Organization for Migration in 1989. Over this time period the agency has evolved from a small members' organization for migrant receiving states to a global agency with 146 member and 13 observer states. It has also evolved from a largely technical and service-oriented agency to a more holistic migration agency.

Current debates

There are numerous policy debates concerning refugees and migration. UNHCR is developing a policy on urban refugees, who may now outnumber refugees in camps; and is concerned with finding new durable solutions for refugees in protracted refugee situations; and it remains conflicted about its role in protecting and assisting IDPs. IOM is currently focusing significant attention on migrants in transit countries; migrants caught up in conflicts and political crises; and on so-called "mixed migration," which it describes as "complex population movement including refugees, asylum seekers, economic migrants and other migrants." While cognizant of these policy issues, this section focuses on current debates concerning the global governance of refugees and international migration.

Refugees

Probably the most significant debate with direct implications for the refugee regime concerns the relevance to contemporary realities of a legal definition written in a specific geographical and historical context over 60 years ago. As explained above, the time limitation and implied geographical scope included in the original definition was removed by the 1967 Protocol. Still, it is often argued that the definition risks excluding contemporary refugees, for example who are fleeing situations of ethnic violence, or escaping the threat of gender-based persecution or persecution on the basis of sexual orientation. The 1951 Convention definition also does not include persecution by non-state actors as the basis for a claim.

Most commentators agree that it is unlikely that the 1951 Convention definition of a refugee would be opened to renegotiation. Certainly a new convention or protocol would be unlikely to gain the near-universal ratification currently enjoyed if it included a more generous and inclusive definition of a refugee. Three broad responses have therefore developed to bring refugee status determination into line with current realities.

First, there have emerged several regional instruments pertaining to the assistance and protection of refugees that adapt the legal definition to the regional context.

The Organization of African Unity (OAU) Convention Governing the Specific Aspects of Refugee Problems in Africa, adopted in 1969, for example, added to the definition that a refugee is "Any person compelled to leave his or her country owing to external aggression, occupation, foreign domination or events seriously disturbing public order in either part or the whole of his country of origin or nationality."[10] In 1984, the Organization for American States (OAS) adopted the Cartagena Declaration, which determined that the definition of a refugee also includes "Persons who have fled their countries because their lives, safety or freedom have been threatened by generalized violence, foreign aggression, internal conflicts, massive violation of human rights or other circumstances which have seriously disturbed public order."[11] In Europe, the 1950 European Convention on Human Rights has led to the adoption in the European Union (EU) of provisions on "subsidiary" or "complementary" protection for displaced people who do not fall within the legal definition of a refugee but are still recognized as in need of protection. These provisions were widely adopted in response to displacement from the Bosnian and Kosovo crises during the mid-1990s.

Second, there are significant regional variations in the way that refugee status is determined. In general in most industrialized countries, refugee status is granted on the basis of an individual assessment. Thus, the cases of claimants are assessed against the criteria of the 1951 UN Convention, and any other criteria defined in national laws or policies. In contrast, in many emerging or developing countries, and especially in the poorest, refugee status is mainly granted on a *prima facie* basis, in particular where large numbers of people cross a border from a conflict zone and the host state lacks the capacity to undertake individual determinations. It has been estimated that at least two-thirds of the world's refugees have not been subject to individual refugee status determination.[12] The relatively small numbers of these refugees who are subsequently resettled in more developed countries are subject to an individual screening process.

Third, in reality most states that do rely on individual assessments increasingly apply a wider interpretation of the criteria than those determined in the 1951 Convention, although they are not required to in law. Thus, in some countries someone fleeing persecution as a homosexual may be recognized as a refugee, and in others not; and, furthermore, the way that individual states interpret the criteria varies over time.

International migration

Turning to international migration, perhaps the principal debate as regards the legal and normative framework is how to implement it. Certainly the framework for protecting the rights of migrant workers is far from perfect, and the institutional infrastructure for its implementation has definite weaknesses. It is generally agreed, however, that a sufficient legal framework exists to protect the rights of most migrant workers and sufficiently robust institutional responsibility. Nevertheless, many migrant workers continue to experience violence, abuse, exploitation, and discrimination.

One problem relates to the ratification of existing instruments. There is a particularly vigorous debate surrounding the UN Convention on the Protection of the Rights of All Migrant Workers and Members of Their Families. Some of the main reasons provided for non-ratification, especially by major migrant destination countries, include the convention's breadth and complexity, the technical and financial obligations it places on states that have ratified, the view that it contradicts or adds no value to existing national migration legislation, concerns that it provides migrants—and especially those with irregular status—rights that are not found in other human rights treaties, and claims that it generally disallows for differentiation between regular and irregular migrants.

Significant problems persist in making the rights guaranteed in the convention a reality, even for those states that are party to it, arising at times from a lack of political will but also from a lack of capacity and resources. Neither is there a sufficient infrastructure for monitoring or enforcing state compliance. To help fill this gap it has been suggested that capacity building is especially required among civil society to increase its effectiveness in lobbying for the rights of migrants and migrant workers, monitoring and reporting on conditions for migrant workers, and providing migrant workers with services. Effective practice also stresses empowering migrants by providing them with information about their rights in the labor market, giving them the identification and rights needed to access banks and other institutions abroad, and developing incentives to encourage migrants to report the worst abuses of their rights.

For those states that are not yet party to the convention, the emphasis has been on trying to ensure that domestic law and regulations conform to international human rights standards. It has been suggested that one way to facilitate this is to articulate the dispersed legal and normative framework in a single compilation of all treaty provisions and other norms that are relevant to international migration and the human rights of migrants.[13]

A second current debate starts with the observation that in contrast to many other cross-border issues of our time—e.g. trade, finance, and the environment—international migration lacks a coherent institutional framework at the global level. The case for a more integrated international institutional arrangement rests on five main arguments.[14] First, contemporary international migration is now occurring at unprecedented levels and has a truly global reach. Second, the forces that drive international migration are powerful, and national migration policies alone can no longer effectively manage or control migration. Third, there are growing numbers of migrants around the world who are vulnerable and exploited, and insufficiently protected by either states or international institutions. Fourth, as discussed below, the effects of climate change on migration are likely to present new management and protection challenges. Finally, momentum for change is slowly developing—for instance, there has been greater collaboration between global institutions with an interest in international migration in recent years.

Convincing though these arguments may be, the obstacles to better global international migration governance should not be underestimated. In particular, the reluctance of most states to yield national control over international migration is understandable. Sovereign states have the right to determine who enters and remains on their territory, and international migration can also have an impact on other essential aspects of state sovereignty, including economic competitiveness, national and public security, and social cohesion. States are likely to remain the principal actors in migration governance.

Emerging issues

The highest-profile emerging issue, with implications both for the refugee and international migration regimes, concerns the prospects of climate change displacing people from their homes. There is very little consensus about even some of most of the basic questions. The nature of the relationship between climate change and migration remains unclear. There are likely to be direct effects, for example where natural disasters destroy homes, or rising sea levels make coastal areas uninhabitable; and there are also likely to be indirect effects, for example where increased global warming and drought disrupt agricultural production, or competition over natural resources is intensified, potentially resulting in conflict. Estimates of the number of people likely to be displaced vary widely, as do the time horizons.[15] There also is no consensus about where those affected will move. Most experts think that the majority of displacement as a result of the effects of climate change will be internal, but the prospects of significant cross-border movements cannot be discounted.[16]

People moving inside their own country as a result of the effects of climate change would fall within the definition of IDPs as described in the "1998 Guiding Principles on Internal Displacement," although it is important to note significant gaps in IDP protection.[17] But there are important gaps in the legal and normative framework as regards people who cross an international border. These people would not qualify as refugees under the 1951 Convention definition, but neither would they be economic migrants. Thus, their status remains unclear in international law. The same is the case for people who may have to leave low-lying island states that become uninhabitable as a result of the effects of rising sea levels. They would be in a legal limbo as neither migrants nor refugees. It is also unclear whether they would be legally defined as stateless, as under international law statelessness means to be without nationality, not without state.

Proposals to fill legal gaps are currently being discussed at a variety of levels. The prospects for a new international treaty or a protocol to the 1951 Refugee Convention are slim, as indicated earlier, and also have significant shortcomings. Obstacles include: resistance by UNHCR and its governing member states; the length of time it takes to negotiate international conventions in the field of human rights; and the reality that many states would refuse to ratify a protocol or new convention. These legal and political obstacles are compounded by a lack of clear empirical evidence on the numbers of people expected to be displaced across borders by the effects of environmental change, the time horizon involved, and the extent to which this is likely to be a regional or truly global issue.

Instead, efforts at the multilateral level are focusing on the development and consolidation of normative principles that can inform regional or national laws and policies on environmental migration. One example is the Nansen Principles. These principles were developed at a conference co-hosted by the Government of Norway and UNHCR in Oslo in June 2011; and they were adopted by over 200 delegates, including representatives of UN and civil society organizations. They recommend building on existing norms in international law, and identify the responsibility of local, national, and international actors. The direct analogy for developing normative principles to fill protection gaps is the evolution of the "Guiding Principles on Internal Displacement."

These comprise a non-binding expert document that has been used to lobby for national legislation on internal displacement in about 30 countries and in several places at the regional level.[18]

A range of proposals is also being considered at the level of national policy in various countries. One is to develop a new humanitarian category for environmental migrants. This is what was proposed in a bill introduced to parliament by the Australian Greens in 2007, which calls for a "climate refugee" visa category for people fleeing

> a disaster that results from both incremental and rapid ecological and climatic change and disruption, that includes sea level rise, coastal erosion, desertification, collapsing ecosystems, fresh water contamination, more frequent occurrence of extreme weather events such as cyclones, tornados, flooding and drought, and that means inhabitants are unable to lead safe or sustainable lives in their immediate environment.[19]

The debate that followed in the Australian Senate was, however, largely critical of the proposed bill, and a particular concern was that by becoming the first country to develop a specific visa category for environmental migrants Australia might become a magnet for environmental migrants from around the world.

A second model is to amend existing legislation to provide temporary protection or refugee-like protection. In the United States, Temporary Protected Status (TPS) was introduced as part of the 1990 Immigration Act to provide at least limited protection to people who are fleeing, or reluctant to return to, potentially dangerous situations in their home country. Between 1995 and 1999 the status was extended to people from Montserrat following volcanic eruptions there, and more recently to Haitians following the 2010 earthquake. Some analysts have suggested that the EU Temporary Protection Directive of 2001 may be interpreted to apply to mass influxes of people from natural disasters.[20] Within the EU, Sweden and Finland have both amended their asylum and human rights laws to incorporate some element of "environmental migration." The 2005 Swedish Aliens Act provides for the possibility to provide subsidiary protection on environmental grounds; while the Finnish Aliens Act of 2004 explicitly acknowledges that unusual environmental circumstances can produce mass influxes of migrants who require temporary protection.

None of these examples of national policies and legislation is comprehensive. An important reservation in the United States is that TPS can only apply to people already resident in the country at the time of the natural disaster, and not to people fleeing the event. Invoking the EU Temporary Protection Directive would require agreement by a majority of member states, which most commentators deem unlikely; and the focus of the directive on "mass influxes" would probably not cover most migrants from environmental change effects who will actually arrive in Europe, as they are likely to be moving over a period of time because of slow onset events such as desertification in the Middle East and North Africa. Neither of the relevant provisions in Sweden or Finland has ever been tested, and there are reservations about how they would function in practice—for example, it is unclear whether the protection envisaged is temporary or permanent.

A third model is to use existing labor migration programs to extend migration opportunities to people vulnerable to or affected by environmental change. There is some debate about whether the New Zealand Pacific Access Category visa may evolve into a migration policy for environmental migration, although that is not its intention. It is conceived as a traditional labor migration program rather than an instrument for humanitarian protection.[21] Thus, for example, it is based on a ballot system, stipulates age restrictions for applicants, who must have a job offer in New Zealand, a minimum income requirement, and a reasonable level of English. This is an important caveat as the scheme does not necessarily target those most vulnerable to or adversely affected by environmental change. Furthermore, the scheme targets a limited number of countries only, and thus represents a limited response to environmental migration. Nevertheless, the scheme does target Pacific Islands at risk, including Tuvalu, Kiribati, and Tonga, and arguably provides a basis for admitting people at risk from these islands. For example, the small quota could be extended, or the ballot system and criteria for selecting candidates revised, or the target countries increased, without significant legislative changes.

Conclusion

Environmental migration is a good example of a new migration reality that will challenge the traditional legal, normative, and institutional distinctions that separate the regimes on refugees and international migration. Various proposals have been made for consolidating these regimes, for example by creating a new World Migration Organization with responsibility for both refugees and international migrants; designating a lead agency from among existing agencies; and bringing IOM into the UN system.[22] There are significant political, technical, and financial obstacles to all these proposals, and their implementation seems unlikely in the foreseeable future. Instead, cooperation on the global governance for refugees and migration is likely to continue on an ad hoc and needs-defined basis, and to take the form of informal partnerships and dialogues.

Additional reading

1. Alexander Betts, ed., *Global Migration Governance* (Oxford: Oxford University Press, 2011).
2. Alexander Betts, Gil Loescher, and James Milner, *UNHCR: The Politics and Practice of Refugee Protection*, 2nd edition (London: Routledge, 2012).
3. Khalid Koser, ed., "Special Issue on International Migration and Global Governance," *Global Governance* 16, no. 3 (2010).
4. Khalid Koser and Susan Martin, eds, *The Migration–Displacement Nexus: Patterns, Processes, and Policies* (Oxford: Berghahn, 2011).
5. Etienne Piguet, Antoine Pecoud, and Paul Guchteneire, eds., *Migration and Climate Change* (Cambridge: Cambridge University Press, 2011).

Notes

1 Anthony Richmond, "Reactive Migration: Sociological Perspectives on Refugee Movements," *Journal of Refugee Studies* 6, no. 1 (1993): 7–24.

2 Susan Martin and Amber Calloway, "Internal Displacement and Internal Trafficking: Developing a New Framework for Protection," in *The Migration–Displacement Nexus: Patterns, Processes, and Policies*, eds. Khalid Koser and Susan Martin (Oxford: Berghahn, 2011), 216–238.

3 United Nations High Commissioner for Refugees, *Global Trends 2011* (Geneva: UNHCR, 2012).

4 Alexander Betts, Gil Loescher, and James Milner, *UNHCR: The Politics and Practice of Refugee Protection*, 2nd edition (London: Routledge, 2012).

5 Claudena Skran, *Refugees in Inter-war Europe: The Emergence of a Regime* (Oxford: Oxford University Press, 1995).

6 Gil Loescher, *The UNHCR and World Politics: A Perilous Path* (Oxford: Oxford University Press, 2001).

7 UNHCR, *Convention Relating to the Status of Refugees*, Chapter I, Article I (1951), http://www.unhcr.org/3b66c2aa10.html.

8 United Nations High Commissioner for Refugees, *Global Trends 2011* (Geneva: UNHCR, 2012).

9 International Organization for Migration, *World Migration Report 2011* (Geneva: IOM, 2012).

10 UNHCR, Refugee Act (1989), http://www.unhcr.org/refworld/docid/3ae6b4f28.html.

11 UNHCR, Cartagena Declaration on Refugees, Colloquium on the International Protection of Refugees in Central America, Mexico and Panama (1984), http://www.unhcr.org/refworld/docid/3ae6b36ec.html.

12 Matthew Albert, "Prima Facie Determination of Refugee Status: An Overview and Its Legal Foundation," Refugee Studies Centre Working Paper Series no. 55 (Oxford: Refugee Studies Centre, 2010).

13 Global Commission on International Migration, *Migration in an Interconnected World: Final Report of the Global Commission on International Migration* (Geneva: GCIM, 2005).

14 Khalid Koser, "Introduction: International Migration and Global Governance," *Global Governance* 16, no. 3 (2010): 301–316.

15 Oliver Brown, "Migration and Climate Change," Migration Research Series no. 31 (Geneva: IOM, 2008).

16 Susan Martin, "Climate Change, Migration, and Governance," *Global Governance* 16, no. 3 (2010): 397–414.

17 Khalid Koser, "Gaps in IDP Protection," in *Migration and Climate Change*, eds. Etienne Piguet, Antoine Pecoud, and Paul Guchteneire (Cambridge: Cambridge University Press, 2011), 289–305.

18 Thomas G. Weiss and David Korn, *Internal Displacement: Conceptualization and Its Consequences* (London: Routledge, 2006).

19 The Parliament of the Commonwealth of Australia, *A Bill for an Act to Recognise Refugees of Climate Change Induced Environmental Disasters, and for Related Purposes* (2007), www.comlaw.gov.au/Details/C2007B00149.

20 William Somerville, *Environmental Migration* (Washington, DC: Migration Policy Institute, 2011).

21 Jane McAdam, "Environmental Migration Governance," University of New South Wales Faculty of Law Research Series, Paper 1 (Sydney: University of New South Wales, 2009).

22 Kathleen Newland, "Global Governance of International Migration: A Fragile Evolution," *Global Governance* 16, no. 3 (2010): 331–344.

INDEX

Note: Page numbers in italic type refer to tables

Goedhart, G.J. van. H. (High Commissioner, UN) 669
Going for Growth (OECD) 176–7
Goldman Sachs 266, 271, 288, 299
Goldstein, J. 27, 31
Goldstone, R. 413, 477–87, 492
Gordenker, L. 205–6, 209–22
Gore, A. (Vice-President, USA) 587
Gould, C. 473
Goulding, M. 423
Gourevitch, P. 353
governance: environment 535–6, 580–92; global financial 535–6, 539–51; trade 535–6, 552–63
Gramsci, A. 6, 154, 163–4, 293, 330–1, 379
Great Depression 211, 296, 358, 540, 549
Great Illusion, The (Angell) 109
Greater East Asia Co-Prosperity Sphere (Japan) 195
Greece 11, 127, 346, 402, 431
Green Economy Initiative (GEI) 626–9
Green Revolution 307, 374–6, 379, 646
greenhouse gases (GHGs) 4, 69–70, 590, 605–12, 615
Greenpeace (1971) 66, 77, 621
Gregoratti, C. 305, 309–21
Griffiths, M. 100
Gromyko, A. 444
gross domestic product (GDP) 62, 98, 175, 288, 560, 634, 641
Grotius, H. 90, 144–7
Group 7 (G7) 63, 274, 298, 405, 576, 611, 638
Group 8 (G8) 267–70, 322–4, 573, 576, 635, 638, 660
Group 20 (G20) 198–9, 266–9, 273–4, 322–4, 546–50, 638–40, 652–3
Group 77 (G77) 8, 66, 207, 229–34, 268, 280–1, 576
growth 209, 274, 541, 569, 620, 628; economic 265, 268–9, 539–40, 596, 627, 634, 637–9; global 272; market 353
Grunberg, I.: Stern, M. and Kaul, I. 527
Grundrisse (Foundations of the Critique of Political Economy) (Marx) 171
Guidelines on Cooperating between the United Nations and the Business Sector 311
Guiding Principles on Internal Displacement (1998) 675
Guilhot, N. 375
Guinea-Bissau 435, 521
Gulf Co-operation Council (GCC) 436
Gulf War (1990–1) 300
Gurría, A. (Director-General, OECD) 176–7

Guterres, A. (High Commissioner, UN) 669
Gvosdev, N. 272

Haas, P. 148
Haass, R.N. 367
Hague Conference (1899, 1907) 40–1, 224
Hague Convention (1907) 392
Haiti 424, 489; earthquake aid (2010) 316
Hall, R. 87, 90, 144–56; and Biersteker, T. 76
Hammarskjöld, D. (Secretary-General, UN) 418
Hampson, F.: and Raymond, M. 414, 524–34
Hansenne, M. (Director-General, ILO) 343, 346
Hardin, G. 620
Harman, S. 537, 656–67
Haslam, P. 154
Haufler, V.: Porter, T. and Cutler, C. 76, 151
Havana Summit (1979) 283
Hawkins, D.: and Jacoby, W. 138
Haworth, N.: and Hughes, S. 305–6, 335–48
health 261, 325, 383, 535–7, 625, 637–9, 660–4; crisis 365; global 370, 622; governance 537, 656–67; law 656
heavily indebted poor country (HIPC) 543, 626
Hegel, G.W.F. 152, 161
hegemonic stability 94–7, 293
Hegemonic Stability Theory (HST) 147, 193
hegemony 181, 187–8, 195–6, 286–7, 331, 345, 379; counter- 298; global 60–1, 99; liberal 99; policy 342; power 66, 121, 181, 265, 295
Heiligendamm Process 269–70
Heine, J. (Ambassador) 272
Held, D. 13, 21–2, 60–72
Helleiner, E.: and Clapp, J. 10
Helsinki Final Act: Conference on Security and Co-operation in Europe (1975) 37, 41
Helsinki Watch 377
Hemmer, C.: and Katzenstein, P. 195
Henkin, L. 43
Heritage Foundation 367
Herz, M. 205–6, 236–50
heteronormativity 180–3, 186–7
Hettne, B. 240
Higgins, R. 37
High-level Task Force on the Food Security Crisis (HLTF) 651–3
Hindu nationalism 164
Hiroshima bombing (1945) 444
history 157, 161–2, 167; change, 157–9; world 174–5

GLOBAL INSTITUTIONS SERIES FROM ROUTLEDGE

Edited by **Thomas G. Weiss** and **Rorden Wilkinson**

The Global Institutions Series is edited by Thomas G. Weiss (The CUNY Graduate Center, New York, USA) and Rorden Wilkinson (University of Manchester, UK) and designed to provide readers with comprehensive, accessible, and informative guides to the history, structure, and activities of key international organizations as well as books that deal with topics of key importance in contemporary global governance. Every volume stands on its own as a thorough and insightful treatment of a particular topic, but the series as a whole contributes to a coherent and complementary portrait of the phenomenon of global institutions at the dawn of the millennium.

Books are written by recognized experts, conform to a similar structure, and cover a range of themes and debates common to the series. These areas of shared concern include the general purpose and rationale for organizations, developments over time, membership, structure, decision-making procedures, and key functions. Moreover, current debates are placed in historical perspective alongside informed analysis and critique. Each book also contains an annotated bibliography and guide to electronic information as well as any annexes appropriate to the subject matter at hand.

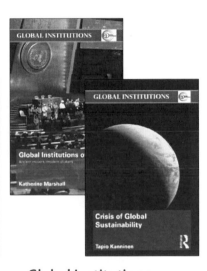

Integrating Africa:
Decolonization's Legacies, Sovereignty and the African Union
By **Martin Welz**

Transformations in Trade Politics:
Participatory Trade Politics in West Africa
By **Silke Trommer**

The Council of Europe:
Structure, History and Issues in European Politics
By **Martyn Bond**

Rules, Politics, and the International Criminal Court:
Committing to the Court
By **Yvonne Dutton**

Global Institutions of Religion:
Ancient Movers, Modern Shakers
By **Katherine Marshall**

Crisis of Global Sustainability
By **Tapio Kanninen**

To browse more titles in the series, please go to **www.routledge.com/books/series/GI**

Routledge
Taylor & Francis Group

Routledge... think about it
www.routledge.com/books/series/GI